The Little Red Book

2015

Passenger Transport Directory

Editor: Ian Barlex
Design: Debbie Walker

D1327655

From the publishers of

BUSES

www.busesmag.com

LIST OF ABBREVIATIONS

ACCT = ... Accountant

ADMIN = ... Administrative

ASST = ... Assistant

CEO = ... Chief Executive Officer

CH = ... Chief

CHMN = ... Chairman

CO = ... Company

COMM MAN = ... Commercial Manager

CONT = ... Controller

DEP = ... Deputy

DIR = ... Director

ENG = ... Engineer

EXEC = ... Executive

FIN = ... Financial

GEN MAN = ... General Manager

H&S = ... Health & Safety

HR = ... Human Relations

INSP = ... Inspector

JNT = ... Joint

MAN = ... Manager

MAN DIR = ... Managing Director

MKTG = ... Marketing

OFF = ... Officer

OP = ... Operating

OPS = ... Operations

PLAN = ... Planning

PRES = ... President

PRIN = ... Principal

PROP = ... Proprietor(s)

PTNRS = ... Partner(s)

REG OFF = ... Registered Office

SEC = ... Secretary

SUPT = ... Superintendent

SVCE = ... Service

TRAF MAN = ... Traffic Manager

TRAF SUPT = ... Traffic Superintendent

TRAN MAN = ... Transport Manager

ACKNOWLEDGEMENTS

I would like to acknowledge the help and support of the team at Key Publishing – especially Debbie Walker, who designs this book, Sue Lloyd, who is Project Manager, and Sam Clark, who handles the advertising – for their hard work and support in producing this edition. Successful production of a publication of this nature can only be a team effort.

I must also thank the large number of readers and contributors who have taken the trouble to get in touch to highlight changes and amendments through the year; if you notice something that needs changing, please do not hesitate to contact me via the Stamford office.

And of course, many thanks to all of our advertisers for their support, without which this directory would be difficult to sustain. Please give them your support and tell them you saw their advertisement in LRB.

HOW LRB ENTRIES ARE COMPILED

As always, our principal source of data has been the thousands of e-mails and web questionnaires we have sent out to operators, manufacturers, suppliers and other organisations. Every year we make significant changes to the circulation list to try to reflect the many changes that have been happening, to omit ceased businesses, add new ones, etc. Where we have not received responses, we have tried to use other publicly available sources to ensure the entries are as accurate as possible.

New entrants to the bus and coach market need not wait for LRB to make contact. If you are active in the industry, and would like to appear in the next edition of LRB (free of charge), please write to the editor of LRB at Key Publishing Ltd, PO Box 100, Stamford, Lincolnshire PE9 1XP, requesting to hear from us for the next edition.

LRB is used by a substantial number of bus and coach operators, as well as by national and local government, trade organisations, tendering authorities, group travel organisers, hotels and leisure attractions.

CONTENTS

INDEX TO ADVERTISERS

KEY TO SYMBOLS IN SECTIONS 4 AND 5

♿	Vehicle suitable for disabled
	Seat belt-fitted Vehicle
R24	24 hour recovery service
T	Toilet-drop facilities available
	Coach(es) with galley facilities
	Replacement vehicle available
R	Recovery service available
❄	Air-conditioned vehicle(s)
	Vintage Coach(es) available
	Open top vehicle(s)
	Coaches with toilet facilities
	Hybrid Buses
	Gas Buses

The Little Red Book

2015

Passenger Transport Directory

77th Annual Edition

Britain's longest established passenger transport directory

Editor: Ian Barlex
Design: Deborah Walker
Advertising: Sam Clark

Managing Director: Adrian Cox
Commercial Director: Ann Saundry

ISBN: 978 0 9462 1939 1

© Key Publishing Ltd 2014

www.keypublishing.com

Published by Key Publishing Ltd
PO Box 100, Stamford, Lincolnshire PE9 1XP
Tel: +44(0) 1780 755 131
Fax: +44(0) 1780 757261

Printed in England by Berforts Information Press Ltd,
Southfield Road, Eynsham, Oxford, OX29 4JB

FSC
Mixed Sources
Product group from well-managed
forests and other controlled sources

Cert no. SW-COC-004238
www.fsc.org
©1996 Forest Stewardship Council

RETURNING FOR 2015!

SAVE THE DATE

BUSES™
2015 FESTIVAL

THE HERITAGE MOTOR CENTRE, GAYDON, WARWICKSHIRE

AUGUST

10am-5pm, SUNDAY

23

766/1

For more information, visit
www.busesfestival.com

I welcome you to the 2015 edition of the *Little Red Book*, now in its 77th year as the leading industry directory.

The past year has once again seen a staggering volume of change throughout the industry, with some new names, and the sad loss of a number of long established ones. It has given me no pleasure at all to have to record that some 30 operators have ceased since the last book, for a variety of reasons, but, as ever, the entrepreneurial spirit lives on, and we have been able to occupy the space with new entries. We have worked hard to completely revise the book to reflect these many developments, including mergers and acquisitions; company closures; new operators; and of course, fleet changes. Once again, the commercial process continues onwards.

We have again been pleased to add new trade suppliers, and to welcome new advertisers from among their number. Please support our advertisers and let them know you read about their services here. As I have said before, it is inevitable that a book of this nature requires updating within hours of its appearance, and in addition to the Stop Press that appears on page 80 this year, we will continue with the popular monthly updates in our sister Buses magazine. If something changes in relation to your entry, please do not wait for us to find out (or not!) for ourselves; feel free to get in touch at the earliest opportunity, and we will include the amendment in an update as well as ensuring next year's book is correct.

Section 1 features the traditional comprehensive trade supplier directory as ever; we try to keep up with the increasing number of overseas vehicle suppliers and their local distributors and agents, but will provide further information in the monthly updates as necessary. There have again been changes involving the major operating groups during the last year, including both acquisitions and disposals; these are included in Section 4. The tram systems and bus rapid transit schemes continue to appear as section 5; the Luton to Dunstable busway is now operating, and the Manchester tram system has seen the opening of the East Manchester and Rochdale lines since we last went to press.

It is worth emphasising again that fleet details change virtually daily, and what we present here can only ever be a snapshot. While I have striven hard to present an accurate picture at the time of going to press, the comprehensive "Fleet News" pages of our sister magazine Buses are recommended. For those who want even greater detail, membership of one or more of the Societies featured in Section 3 of this book will enable you to follow developments extremely closely. The PSV Circle provides nationwide coverage of fleet developments, including the Republic of Ireland; the London Omnibus Traction Society covers London fleets in great detail; while area based organisations such as the M&D and East Kent Bus Club and the Southdown Enthusiasts' Club provide a similar level of detail for their respective areas. They are all recommended for their diligence and accuracy.

We are, again, extremely grateful to the large number of suppliers, authorities, organisations and operators who have taken the trouble to update and return their entries to us. This year, we again adopted the electronic approach, sending e-mails to operators, organisations and authorities, and offering the trade suppliers the opportunity to update their entries via a web page. We have once again been gratified by the significant response that has been forthcoming from all sectors.

As I write this, the results of the Scottish Independence vote are recently in; a case of no change but significant change, one feels. Transport will no doubt be an area which sees more change with the increasing pace of devolution. In the meantime, the industry demonstrated north of the border, with the Glasgow Commonwealth Games, its ability to rise to the challenge of major events; and is about to repeat the effort with the Ryder Cup.

Technological developments continue to be to the fore, and it is reasonable to expect that fleet developments will require us to introduce more new symbols to represent new classes of vehicle before long; although the time gets ever closer when the low-floor symbol will be obsolete, this being a requirement for all vehicles as the DDA legislation is phased in.

I hope readers find the new book a helpful tool during the coming year, and, as ever, we remain entirely open to comments and suggestions, whether they relate to format, content or accuracy.

Ian Barlex, Editor

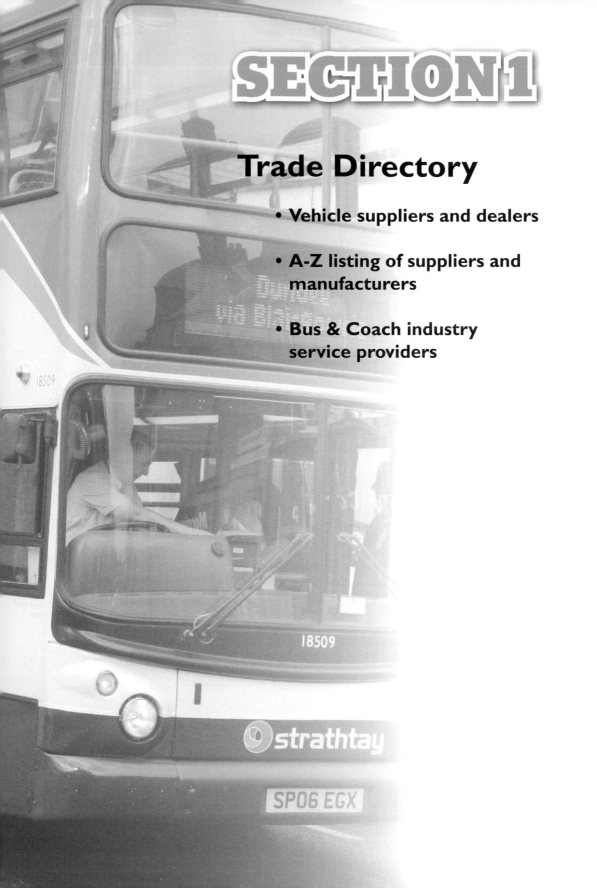

SECTION 1

Trade Directory

- **Vehicle suppliers and dealers**

- **A-Z listing of suppliers and manufacturers**

- **Bus & Coach industry service providers**

Vehicle Suppliers and Dealers

Manufacturers and suppliers of full-size bus and coach chassis and integrals, bus rapid transit vehicles and light rail vehicles

ALEXANDER DENNIS LTD
91 Glasgow Road, Falkirk, FK1 4JB,
United Kingdom
Tel: +44 (0)1324 621 672
Fax: +44 (0)1324 632 469
Email: enquiries@alexander-dennis.com
Web site: www.alexander-dennis.com
Models: Hybrid Midibus and Single-Deck Bus;
Rear-Engined Low-Floor Midibus and Single-Deck
Bus; Hybrid Double-Deck Bus; Rear-Engined Low-
Floor Double-Deck Bus (Two- or Three-Axle).

ARRIVA BUS & COACH
Lodge Garage, Whitehall Road, Gomersal,
Cleckheaton, West Yorkshire, BD19 4BJ,
United Kingdom
Tel: +44 (0)1274 681 144
Email: busandcoachsales@arriva.co.uk
Web site: www.arrivabusandcoach.co.uk

AUTOSAN
ul.Lipinskiego 109, 38-500 Sanok, Poland
Tel: +48 13 465 01 26
Fax: +48 13 465 04 00
Web site: www.autosan.pl
Models: High-Floor School Bus, Single-Deck Bus,
Single-Deck Coach

AYATS
Paratge Can Call, km.1 - 17401, Arbucies, Spain
Tel: +34 972 86 00 29
Fax: +34 972 86 11 14
Web site: www.carroceriasayats.com
UK Supplier Omega Coach Sales
Milton Keynes, United Kingdom
Models: Rear-Engined Integral Single and
Double-Deck Coach Range - up to 15m

BMC UK
UK Supplier Pelican Bus & Coach Sales
Altofts Lane, Wakefield Europort, Castleford,
West Yorkshire, WF105UB, United Kingdom
Tel: +44 (0)1924 227 777
Email: info@bmc-uk.net
Web site: www.bmc-uk.net
Models: Integral Front-Engined School Bus,
Integral Front-Engined Midicoach, Integral Rear-
Engined 11m Low-Floor Single-Deck Bus.

IRIZAR UK LTD
Portland House, Claylands Avenue, Worksop,
S81 7BQ, United Kingdom
Tel: +44 (0)1909 500 514
Email: sales@irizar.co.uk
Web site: www.irizar.co.uk
Models: Integral Luxury Coaches and Bodywork
on Scania Coaches.

IVECO
Iveco Ford Truck Ltd, Iveco Ford House,
Station Road, Watford, WD1 1SR,
United Kingdom
Tel: +44 (0)1923 246 400
Fax: +44 (0)1923 240 574
Models: Midibus, Low-Floor Midibus, Minibuses,
Guided Bus System, Low-Floor Rear-Engined
Single-Deck Bus, Rear-Engined Single-Deck Coach.

KING LONG UK LTD
Three Spires Industrial Estate, Ibstock Road,
Coventry, CV6 6JR, United Kingdom
Tel: +44 (0)2476 363 004
Fax: +44 (0)2476 365 835
Email: sales@kinglonguk.com
Web site: www.kinglonguk.com
Models: 8m, 9m, 12m and 13m Single-Deck
Coach; 9m and 12m Low Floor Single-Deck City
Bus; 13m Low Floor Single-Deck School Bus.

MAN
UK Supplier MAN Bus & Coach
Frankland Road, Blagrove, Swindon, SN5 8YU,
United Kingdom
Tel: +44 (0)1793 448 000
Email: bus.sales@man.co.uk
Web site: www.manbusandcoach.co.uk
Ireland Supplier Brian Noone Ltd
Straffan Road, Maynooth, Co Kildare,
Republic of Ireland
Tel: +353 1 628 6311
Email: reception@noone.ie
Web site: www.noone.ie
Models: Single-Deck Low-Floor Midibus, Single-
Deck Low-Floor Diesel and CNG powered
City Bus, Single-Deck School Bus, Rear-Engined
Double-Deck and Single-Deck Coach.

MERCEDES-BENZ
UK Supplier Evobus (UK) Ltd
Cross Point Business Park, Ashcroft Way,
Coventry, CV2 2TU, United Kingdom
Tel: +44 (0)2476 626 000
Fax: +44 (0)2476 626 006
Email: reception.uk@evobus.com
Web site: www.evobus.com
Models: Rear-Engined Coach, Rear-Engined
Integral Low-Floor Single-Deck Bus, Rear-Engined
Integral Low-Floor Single-Deck Articulated Bus

MOSELEY (PCV) LTD
Elmsall Way, Dale Lane, South Elmsall, Pontefract,
West Yorkshire, WF9 2XS, United Kingdom
Tel: +44 (0)1977 609 000
Fax: +44 (0)1977 609 900
Email: enquiries@moseleycoachsales.co.uk
Web site: www.moseleycoachsales.co.uk

MOSELEY DISTRIBUTORS LTD
Rydenmains, Condorrat Road, Glenmavis, Airdrie,
ML6 0PP, United Kingdom
Tel: +44 (0)1236 750 501
Fax: +44 (0)1236 750 504
Email: enquiries@moseleydistributors.co.uk
Web site: www.moseleydistributors.co.uk

MOSELEY IN THE SOUTH
Summerfield Avenue, Chelston Business Park,
Wellington, TA21 9JF, United Kingdom
Tel: +44 (0)1823 653 000
Fax: +44 (0)1823 663 502
Email: sales@moseleycoachsales.co.uk
Web site: www.moseleycoachsales.co.uk
Models: Futura Single-Deck Luxury Coach;
Synergy Double-Deck Coach

NEOPLAN
UK Supplier MAN Bus & Coach
Frankland Road, Blagrove, Swindon, SN5 8YU,
United Kingdom
Tel: +44 (0)1793 448 000
Email: coach.sales@man.co.uk
Web site: www.manbusandcoach.co.uk
Models: Single-Deck And Double-Deck Rear-
Engine Integral Coaches.

OPTARE PLC
Hurricane Way South, Sherburn In Elmet, Leeds,
LS25 6PT, United Kingdom
Tel: +44 (0)8434 873 200
Fax: +44 (0)8434 873 201
Email: info@optare.com
Web site: www.optare.com
Models: Optare Tempo SR - Rear-Engined
Integral Low-Floor Single-Deck City Bus. Optare
Versa, Optare MetroCity, Optare Solo SR, Optare
Solo EV - Rear-Engined Integral Low-Floor Single-
Deck Midibuses.

PLAXTON (ALEXANDER DENNIS T/A)
Plaxton Park, Cayton Low Road, Eastfield,
Scarborough, North Yorkshire, YO11 3BY,
United Kingdom
Tel: +44 (0)1723 581 500
Email: sales@plaxtonlimited.co.uk

Web site: www.plaxtonlimited.co.uk
Models: Coaches, Buses, Midicoach And Midibus
Bodies. (Part Of Alexander Dennis)

SCANIA (GB) LTD
Delaware Drive, Tongwell, Milton Keynes,
MK15 8HB, United Kingdom
Tel: +44 (0)1908 210 210
Fax: +44 (0)1908 215040
Web site: www.scania.co.uk
Models: Rear-Engined Low-Floor Single-
Deck And Double-Deck Bus Chassis, Integral
Low-Floor Single-Deck Bus, Integral Low-Floor
Double-Deck Bus, Rear-Engined Coach.

SETRA
New Setra vehicles are no longer available for the
UK market. Enquiries: Evobus (UK) Ltd.

TEMSA EUROPE
UK Supplier Arriva Bus & Coach
Lodge Garage, Whitehall Road, Gomersal,
Cleckheaton, West Yorkshire, BD19 4BJ,
United Kingdom
Tel: +44 (0)1274 681 144
Email: info@temsa.com
Web site: www.temsa.com

VAN HOOL
Bernard Van Hoolstraat 58, Lier-Koningshooikt,
Belgium
Tel: +32 3 420 20 20
Email: info@vanhool.be
Web site: www.vanhool.be
Models: Integral Double-Deck and Single-Deck
Coaches.

VDL BOVA
Web site: www.vdlbova.nl
UK Supplier Moseley (PCV) Ltd
Elmsall Way, Dale Lane, South Elmsall, Pontefract,
West Yorkshire, WF9 2XS, United Kingdom
Tel: +44 (0)1977 609 000
Fax: +44 (0)1977 609 900
Email: enquiries@moseleycoachsales.co.uk
Web site: www.moseleycoachsales.co.uk
Moseley in the South Ltd
Summerfield Avenue, Chelston Business Park,
Wellington, TA21 9JF, United Kingdom
Tel: +44 (0)1823 653 000
Fax: +44 (0)1823 663 502
Email: sales@moseleycoachsales.co.uk
Web site: www.moseleycoachsales.co.uk
Models: Futura Single-Deck Luxury Coach;
Synergy Double-Deck Coach.

VDL BUS INTERNATIONAL
UK Supplier Arriva Bus & Coach
Lodge Garage, Whitehall Road, Gomersal,
Cleckheaton, West Yorkshire, BD19 4BJ,
United Kingdom
Tel: +44 (0)1274 681 144
Email: busandcoachsales@arriva.co.uk
Web site: www.arrivabusandcoach.co.uk
Models: Rear-Engined Low-Floor Single-Deck
Bus, Rear-Engined Low-Floor Double-Deck Bus,
Rear-Engined Coach, Rear-Engined Three-Axle
Single- Or Double-Deck Coach.

VOLVO BUS
Wedgnock Lane, Warwick, CV34 5YA,
United Kingdom
Tel: +44 (0)1926 401 777
Email: info.buses.uk@volvo.com
Web site: www.volvobuses.com
Volvo Bus & Coach Sales Centre
Siskin Parkway East, Middlemarch Business Park,
Coventry, CV3 4PE, United Kingdom
Tel: +44 (0)2476 210 250
Fax: +44 (0)2476 210 258
Email: info.buses.uk@volvo.com
Web site: www.volvobuses.com

Models: Rear-Engined Low-Floor Single-Deck Bus and Hybrid Single-Deck Bus, Rear-Engined Coach, Rear-Engined Integral Coach, Rear-Engined Low-Floor Double-Deck Bus and Hybird Double-Deck Bus.

WRIGHTBUS LTD
Galgorm Industrial Estate, Fenaghy Road, Ballymena, BT42 1PY, Northern Ireland
Tel: 028 2564 1212
Fax: 028 2564 9703
Email: info@wright-bus.com
Web site: www.wright-bus.com
Models: Double-Deck Low-Floor Bus & Bus Bodies, FTR advanced bus rapid transit vehicle, Single-Deck Low-Floor Bus Bodies, Single-Deck Low-Floor Midibus and Hybrid Midibus.

YUTONG
UK Supplier Pelican Bus & Coach Sales Altofts Lane, Wakefield Europort, Castleford, West Yorkshire, WF10 5UB, United Kingdom
Tel: +44 (0)1924 227 722
Email: sales@pelican-eng.co.uk
Web site: www.pelicanyutong.co.uk
Models: TC12 Touring Coach.

BODYBUILDERS (9m AND OVER)

ALEXANDER DENNIS LTD
91 Glasgow Road, Falkirk, FK1 4JB, United Kingdom
Tel: +44 (0)1324 621 672
Fax: +44 (0)1324 632 469
Email: enquiries@alexander-dennis.com
Web site: www.alexander-dennis.com

ARRIVA BUS AND COACH LTD
UK Supplier Arriva Bus & Coach Lodge Garage, Whitehall Road, Gomersal, Cleckheaton, BD19 4BJ, United Kingdom
Tel: +44 (0)1274 681 144
Email: busandcoachsales@arriva.co.uk
Web site: www.arrivabusandcoach.co.uk

BEULAS
UK Supplier Base Ltd
Clydesdale Place, Moss Side Industrial Estate, Leyland, PR26 7QS, United Kingdom
Tel: +44 (0)1772 425 355
Web site: www.basecoachsales.com

CAETANO (UK) LTD
Mill Lane, Heather, Coalville, LE67 2QE, United Kingdom
Tel: +44 (0)1530 263 333
Email: office@caetano.co.uk
Web site: www.caetano.co.uk
Models: Single-Deck Coach

EXPRESS COACH REPAIRS LTD
Outgang Lane, Pickering, YO18 7EL, United Kingdom
Tel: +44 (0)1751 475 215
Email: expresscoachrepairs@hotmail.co.uk

FAST EUROPE NV
Hellegatstraat 10, 2590 Berlaar (Lier), Belgium
Tel: +32 (0)16 388 183
Email: info@fast-europe.eu
Web site: www.fast-conceptcar.com
UK Supplier Moseley (PCV) Ltd
Elmsall Way, Dale Lane, South Elmsall, Pontefract, WF9 2XS, United Kingdom
Tel: +44 (0)1977 609 000
Fax: +44 (0)1977 609900
Email: sales@moseleycoachsales.co.uk
Web site: www.moseleycoachsales.co.uk

IRIZAR UK LTD
Portland House, Claylands Avenue, Worksop, S81 7BQ, United Kingdom
Tel: +44 (0)1909 500 514
Email: sales@irizar.co.uk
Web site: www.irizar.co.uk

KING LONG UK LTD
Three Spires Industrial Estate, Ibstock Road, Coventry, CV6 6JR, United Kingdom
Tel: +44 (0)2476 363 004
Fax: +44 (0)2476 365 835
Email: sales@kinglonguk.com
Web site: www.kinglonguk.com

LAWTON SERVICES LTD
Knutsford Road, Church Lawton, Stoke-On-Trent, ST7 3DN, United Kingdom
Tel: +44 (0)1270 882 056
Fax: +44 (0)1270 883 014
Email: info@lawtonservices.co.uk
Web site: www.lawtonservices.co.uk

LEICESTER CARRIAGE BUILDERS
Marlow Road, Leicester, LE3 2BQ, United Kingdom
Tel: +44 (0)116 282 4270
Fax: +44 (0)116 263 0554
Email: enquiries@leicestercarriagebuilders.coop
Web site: www.leicestercarriagebuilders.coop

MARCOPOLO SA
UK Supplier Base Ltd
Clydesdale Place, Moss Side Industrial Estate, Leyland, PR26 7QS, United Kingdom
Tel: +44 (0)1772 425 355
Web site: www.basecoachsales.com

MCV BUS AND COACH LTD
Sterling Place, Elean Business Park, Sutton, Ely, CB6 2QE, United Kingdom
Tel: +44 (0)1353 773 000
Fax: +44 (0)1353 773 001
Email: sales@mcv-uk.com
Web site: www.mcv-uk.com

MOSELEY (PCV) LTD
Elmsall Way, Dale Lane, South Elmsall, Pontefract, West Yorkshire, WF9 2XS, United Kingdom
Tel: +44 (0)1977 609 000
Fax: +44 (0)1977 609 900
Email: enquiries@moseleycoachsales.co.uk
Web site: www.moseleycoachsales.co.uk

NEOPLAN
UK Supplier MAN Bus & Coach
Frankland Road, Blagrove, Swindon, SN5 8YU, United Kingdom
Tel: +44 (0)1793 448 000
Email: coach.sales@man.co.uk
Web site: www.manbusandcoach.co.uk

OPTARE PLC
Hurricane Way South, Sherburn In Elmet, Leeds, LS25 6PT, United Kingdom
Tel: +44 (0)8434 873 200
Fax: +44 (0)8434 873 201
Email: info@optare.com
Web site: www.optare.com

PLAXTON (ALEXANDER DENNIS T/A)
Plaxton Park, Cayton Low Road, Eastfield, Scarborough, North Yorkshire, YO11 3BY, United Kingdom
Tel: +44 (0)1723 581 500
Email: sales@plaxtonlimited.co.uk
Web site: www.plaxtonlimited.co.uk

SUNSUNDEGUI
UK Importer Volvo Bus & Coach Sales Centre Siskin Parkway East, Middlemarch Business Park, Coventry, CV3 4PE, United Kingdom
Tel: +44 (0)2476 210 250
Fax: +44 (0)2476 210 258
Email: info.buses.uk@volvo.com
Web site: www.volvobuses.com
UK Service Tramontana
Chapelknowe Road, Carfin, Motherwell, ML1 5LE, United Kingdom
Tel: +44 (0)1698 861 790
Email: info@tramontanacoach.co.uk
Web site: www.tramontanacoach.co.uk

UNVI BUS & COACH
Poulton Street, Kirkham, Preston, Lancashire,

PR4 2AA, United Kingdom
Tel: 0800 112 3652
Email: dmckinless@unvibusandcoach.co.uk
Web site: www.unvibusandcoach.co.uk
Models: Single-Deck Coach, Midicoach, Minicoach

VAN HOOL
Bernard Van Hoolstraat 58, Lier-Koningshooikt, Belgium
Tel: +32 3 420 20 20
Email: info@vanhool.be
Web site: www.vanhool.be

VDL BERKHOF
UK Supplier Arriva Bus & Coach
Lodge Garage, Whitehall Road, Gomersal, Cleckheaton, BD19 4BJ, United Kingdom
Tel: +44 (0)1274 681 144
Email: busandcoachsales@arriva.co.uk
Web site: www.arrivabusandcoach.co.uk

VDL JONCKHEERE
UK Importer Volvo Bus & Coach Sales Centre Siskin Parkway East, Middlemarch Business Park, Coventry, CV3 4PE, United Kingdom
Tel: +44 (0)2476 210 250
Fax: +44 (0)2476 210 258
Email: info.buses.uk@volvo.com
Web site: www.volvobuses.com
UK Service Tramontana
Chapelknowe Road, Carfin, Motherwell, ML1 5LE, United Kingdom
Tel: +44 (0)1698 861 790
Email: info@tramontanacoach.co.uk
Web site: www.tramontanacoach.co.uk

VOLVO BUS
Wednock Lane, Warwick, CV34 5YA, United Kingdom
Tel: +44 (0)1926 401 777
Email: info.buses.uk@volvo.com
Web site: www.volvobuses.com
Volvo Bus & Coach Sales Centre
Siskin Parkway East, Middlemarch Business Park, Coventry, CV3 4PE, United Kingdom
Tel: +44 (0)2476 210 250
Fax: +44 (0)2476 210 258
Email: info.buses.uk@volvo.com
Web site: www.volvobuses.com

WRIGHTBUS LTD
Galgorm Industrial Estate, Fenaghy Road, Ballymena, BT42 1PY, Northern Ireland
Tel: 028 2564 1212   **Fax:** 028 2564 9703
Email: info@wright-bus.com
Web site: www.wright-bus.com

BODYBUILDERS (SMALL VEHICLES)

ADVANCED MINIBUS LTD
Upper Mantle Close, Clay Cross, S45 9NU, United Kingdom
Tel: +44 (0)1246 250 022
Email: info@minibus.co.uk
Web site: www.minibus.co.uk

ALEXANDER DENNIS LTD
91 Glasgow Road, Falkirk, FK1 4JB, United Kingdom
Tel: +44 (0)1324 621 672
Fax: +44 (0)1324 632 469
Email: enquiries@alexander-dennis.com
Web site: www.alexander-dennis.com

ALTAS COMMERCIAL VEHICLES
16B Kiemeliu Street, Maisiagala, LT-14025, Lithuania
Tel: +370 5 240 4000
Fax: +370 5 240 4111
Email: info@altas-auto.lt
Web site: www.altas-auto.lt
UK Distributor Auto Service (Pontypool) Ltd Rockhill Road, Pontypool, Gwent, NP4 8AN, United Kingdom
Tel: +44 (0)1495 757 111

Web site: www.minibussales.biz
Models: 7 to 23 seat minibuses based on Iveco, Mercedes and Volkswagen chassis.

AVID VEHICLES LTD
Unit 8, Arcot Court, Nelson Industrial Estate, Cramlington, Northumberland, NE23 1BB, United Kingdom
Tel: +44 (0)1670 707 040
Email: info@avidvehicles.com
Web site: www.avidvehicles.com

BLUEBIRD VEHICLES LTD
Business acquired by Mellor Coachcraft (Woodall Nicholson Group) - see below.

COURTSIDE CONVERSIONS LTD
1 Woodward Road, Howden Industrial Estate, Tiverton, Devon, EX16 5HW, United Kingdom
Tel: +44 (0)1884 256 048
Fax: +44 (0)1884 256 087
Web site: www.courtsideconversions.co.uk

CVI (COMMERCIAL VEHICLE INNOVATION)
Moorfoot View, Bilston, Edinburgh, EH25 9SL, United Kingdom
Tel: +44 (0)131 603 4582
Web site: www.john-clark.co.uk

EVM LTD
Comagh Business Park, Kilbeggan, Co Westmeath, Republic of Ireland
Tel: +353 5793 32699
Fax: +353 5793 32691
Email: martin.browne@evm.ie
Web site: www.evm.ie
EVM specialises in building Mercedes Benz Sprinter Minibus's from 8 Seats to 22 Seats. We have new Minibuses for sale on our website at all times. EVM's strengths lie in its close working relationship with Mercedes Benz. We only build on Sprinter Chassis and all our vehicles are fully backed by the strongest aftersales Dealer networks in the world i.e. Mercedes Benz. All our vehicles are covered by a 3 year bumper to bumper, unlimited mileage Chassis warranty. All this combines to give you the customer peace of mind that your investment as supported by EVM and Mercedes Benz.

EVM UK
Units 1-3, Wellingham Way, Crawley Road, Faygate, Horsham, West Sussex, RH12 4SE, United Kingdom
Tel: +44 (0)845 520 5160
Fax: +44 (0)845 520 5161
Web site: www.evm.ie

EXCEL CONVERSIONS LTD
Excel House, Durham Lane, Armthorpe, Doncaster, DN3 3FE, United Kingdom
Tel: +44 (0)1302 835 388
Email: sales@excelconversions.co.uk
Web site: www.excelconversions.co.uk

EXPRESS COACH REPAIRS LTD
Outgang Lane, Pickering, YO18 7EL, United Kingdom
Tel: +44 (0)1751 475 215
Email: expresscoachrepairs@hotmail.co.uk

FERQUI
Poligono Industrial la Barreda, Parcela 16, 33180 Norena, Asturias, Spain
Tel: +34 985 740 420
Fax: +34 985 742 869
Web site: www.ferqui.com
UK Distributor Connaught PSV
Unit 12, Frontier Works, King Edward Road, Thorne, Doncaster, DN8 4HU, United Kingdom
Tel: +44 (0)1405 814 064
Email: info@connaughtpsv.co.uk
Web site: www.connaughtpsv.co.uk
Soroco minicoach and Toro midicoach based on Mercedes chassis

GM COACHWORK LTD
Teign Valley, Trusham, Newton Abbot, Devon, TQ13 0NX, United Kingdom
Tel: 0845 850 1860
Web site: www.gmcoachwork.co.uk

INDCAR SA
Poligono Industrial Torres Pujals, E-17401 Arbucies (Girona), Spain
Tel: +34 972 860165
Fax: +34 972 860 054
Email: indcar@indcar.es
Web site: www.indcar.es
UK Supplier Base Ltd
Clydesdale Place, Moss Side Industrial Estate, Leyland, PR26 7QS, United Kingdom
Tel: +44 (0)1772 425 355
Web site: www.basecoachsales.com

IRIZAR UK LTD
Portland House, Claylands Avenue, Worksop, S81 7BQ, United Kingdom
Tel: +44 (0)1909 500 514
Email: sales@irizar.co.uk
Web site: www.irizar.co.uk

IRMAOS MOTA
Vila Nova de Gaia, Portugal
Web site: www.irmaosmota.pt
UK & Ireland Distributor Brian Noone
Straffan Road, Maynooth, Co Kildare, Republic of Ireland
Tel: +353 1 628 6311
Fax: +353 1 628 5404
Email: reception@noone.ie
Web site: www.noone.ie
UK Agent Minis to Midis Ltd
135 Nutwell Lane, 135 Nutwell Lane, Doncaster, DN3 3JR, United Kingdom
Tel: +44 (0)1302 833 203
Fax: +44 (0)1302 831 756
Email: sales@ministomidis.com
Web site: www.ministomidis.com
Models: Turas range of Mercedes Sprinter and Vario based mini and midicoaches

LAWTON SERVICES LTD
Knutsford Road, Church Lawton, Stoke-On-Trent, ST7 3DN, United Kingdom
Tel: +44 (0)1270 882 056
Fax: +44 (0)1270 883 014
Email: info@lawtonservices.co.uk
Web site: www.lawtonservices.co.uk

LEICESTER CARRIAGE BUILDERS
Marlow Road, Leicester, LE3 2BQ, United Kingdom
Tel: +44 (0)116 282 4270
Fax: +44 (0)116 263 0554
Email: enquiries@leicestercarriagebuilders.coop
Web site: www.leicestercarriagebuilders.coop

MELLOR COACHCRAFT
Miall Street, Rochdale, OL11 1HY, United Kingdom
Tel: +44 (0)1706 860 610
Fax: +44 (0)1706 860 402
Email: mcsales@woodall-nicholson.co.uk
Web site: www.mellor-coachcraft.co.uk

MINIBUS OPTIONS
Bingswood Industrial Estate, Whaley Bridge, High Peak, SK23 7LY, United Kingdom
Tel: +44 (0)1663 735 355
Email: info@minibusoptions.co.uk
Web site: www.minibusoptions.co.uk

MOSELEY (PCV) LTD
Elmsall Way, Dale Lane, South Elmsall, Pontefract, West Yorkshire, WF9 2XS, United Kingdom
Tel: +44 (0)1977 609 000
Fax: +44 (0)1977 609 900
Email: enquiries@moseleycoachsales.co.uk
Web site: www.moseleycoachsales.co.uk

OPTARE PLC
Hurricane Way South, Sherburn In Elmet, Leeds, LS25 6PT, United Kingdom
Tel: +44 (0)8434 873 200
Fax: +44 (0)8434 873 201
Email: info@optare.com
Web site: www.optare.com

PARAMOUNT CONVERSIONS
Unit 10, Cloncollig Commercial Park, Tullamore, County Offaly, Republic of Ireland
Tel: +353 57 932 0170
Fax: +353 57 932 0173
Email: info@paramountconversions.ie
Web site: www.paramountconversions.ie
UK Distributor Minis to Midis Ltd
135 Nutwell Lane, 135 Nutwell Lane, Doncaster, DN3 3JR, United Kingdom
Tel: +44 (0)1302 833 203
Email: sales@ministomidis.com
Web site: www.ministomidis.com
UK Service Agent GB Fleet Maintenance
Geddings Road, Hoddesdon, Hertfordshire, EN11 0NT, United Kingdom
Tel: +44 (0)1992 467 984
Email: sales@gbfleetmaintenance.co.uk
Web site: www.gbfleetmaintenance.co.uk

PVS MANUFACTURING LTD
40 Killycanavan Road, Ardboe, Dungannon, BT71 5BP, Northern Ireland
Tel: +44 (0)28 8673 6969
Fax: +44 (0)28 8673 7178
Email: mail@pvsltd.com
Web site: www.conversionspecialists.com

SITCAR
Via Copernico, n.41, 41043 Formigine (MO), Italy
Tel: +39 059 577 0911   **Fax:** +39 059 573 361
Email: info@sitcar.it
Web site: www.sitcar.it
UK Supplier Moseley (PCV) Ltd
Elmsall Way, Dale Lane, South Elmsall, Pontefract, WF9 2XS, United Kingdom
Tel: +44 (0)1977 609 000
Fax: +44 (0)1977 609 900
Email: sales@moseleycoachsales.co.uk
Web site: www.moseleycoachsales.co.uk

STANFORD COACH WORKS
Mobility House, Stanhope Industrial Park, Wharf Road, Stanford-Le-Hope, SS17 0EH, UK
Tel: +44 (0)1375 676 088
Fax: +44 (0)1375 677 999
Email: sales@stanfordcoachworks.co.uk
Web site: www.stanfordcoachworks.co.uk

SWANSEA COACH WORKS LTD
Fabian Way, Swansea, SA1 8QY, United Kingdom
Tel: +44 (0)1792 650 258
Email: swanseacoachworks@btinternet.com
Web site: www.sprinter-conversions.co.uk

UNVI BUS & COACH
Poulton Street, Kirkham, Preston, Lancashire, PR4 2AA, United Kingdom
Tel: 0800 112 3652
Email: dmckinless@unvibusandcoach.co.uk
Web site: www.unvibusandcoach.co.uk

WILKER GROUP
Frederick Street, Clara, Co Offaly, Republic of Ireland
Tel: +353 5793 31252
Fax: +353 5793 31319
Email: info@wilkergroup.com
Web site: www.wilkergroup.com
UK Subsidiary
Units 1 & 2, Millbuck Park, Millbuck Way, Springvale Industrial Estate, Sandbach, CW11 3HT, United Kingdom
Tel: +44 (0)1270 765 999
Fax: +44 (0)1270 765 007
Email: info@wilkergroup.com
Models: Low-Floor Mini- And Midibuses, Mini- And Midicoaches

BUS RAPID TRANSIT VEHICLES

IVECO
Iveco Ford Truck Ltd, Iveco Ford House,
Station Road, Watford, WD1 1SR,
United Kingdom
Tel: +44 (0)1923 246 400
Fax: +44 (0)1923 240 574

MINITRAM SYSTEMS
Tdi (Europe) Ltd, Clifford Mill, Clifford Chambers,
Stratford Upon Avon, CV37 8HW,
United Kingdom
Contact: Martin Pemberton
Tel: +44 (0)1789 205 011
Fax: +44 (0)1789 133 119
Email: martin.p@tdi.uk.com
Web site: www.tdi.uk.com
Models: Rubber Tyre-Guided/Unguided/Rail
7.8M Vehicle

VOLVO BUS
Wedgnock Lane, Warwick, CV34 5YA,
United Kingdom
Tel: +44 (0)1926 401 777
Email: info.buses.uk@volvo.com
Web site: www.volvobuses.com
Volvo Bus & Coach Sales Centre
Siskin Parkway East, Middlemarch Business Park,
Coventry, CV3 4PE, United Kingdom
Tel: +44 (0)2476 210 250
Fax: +44 (0)2476 210 258
Email: info.buses.uk@volvo.com
Web site: www.volvobuses.com

WRIGHTBUS LTD
Galgorm Industrial Estate, Fenaghy Road,
Ballymena, BT42 1PY, Northern Ireland
Tel: 028 2564 1212
Fax: 028 2564 9703
Email: info@wright-bus.com
Web site: www.wright-bus.com

CHASSIS AND INTEGRAL VEHICLES (FULL-SIZE 8M AND OVER)

ARRIVA BUS AND COACH LTD
UK Supplier Arriva Bus & Coach
Lodge Garage, Whitehall Road, Gomersal,
Cleckheaton, BD19 4BJ, United Kingdom
Tel: +44 (0)1274 681 144
Email: busandcoachsales@arriva.co.uk
Web site: www.arrivabusandcoach.co.uk

CHASSIS AND INTEGRAL VEHICLES (UNDER 9M)

ALEXANDER DENNIS LTD
91 Glasgow Road, Falkirk, FK1 4JB,
United Kingdom
Tel: +44 (0)1324 621 672
Fax: +44 (0)1324 632 469
Email: enquiries@alexander-dennis.com
Web site: www.alexander-dennis.com

AVID VEHICLES LTD
Unit 8, Arcot Court, Nelson Industrial Estate,
Cramlington, Northumberland, NE23 1BB,
United Kingdom
Tel: +44 (0)1670 707 040
Email: info@avidvehicles.com
Web site: www.avidvehicles.com

BLUEBIRD VEHICLES LTD
Business acquired by Mellor Coachcraft (Woodall
Nicholson Group) - see below.

BRADSHAW ELECTRIC VEHICLES
New Lane, Stibbington, Peterborough, PE8 6LW,
United Kingdom
Tel: +44 (0)1780 782 621
Email: sales@bradshawelectricvehicles.co.uk
Web site: www.bradshawelectricvehicles.co.uk
Models: Electric Minibus/Taxi

FORD MOTOR COMPANY
Eagle Way, Brentwood, CM13 3BW,
United Kingdom
Tel: +44 (0)8458 411 111
Web site: www.ford.co.uk
Models: Transit, Complete Minibus Or Chassis-
Cowl.

IRIZAR UK LTD
Portland House, Claylands Avenue, Worksop,
S81 7BQ, United Kingdom
Tel: +44 (0)1909 500 514
Email: sales@irizar.co.uk
Web site: www.irizar.co.uk

IVECO
Iveco Ford Truck Ltd, Iveco Ford House,
Station Road, Watford, WD1 1SR,
United Kingdom
Tel: +44 (0)1923 246 400
Fax: +44 (0)1923 240 574

KING LONG UK LTD
Three Spires Industrial Estate, Ibstock Road,
Coventry, CV6 6JR, United Kingdom
Tel: +44 (0)2476 363 004
Fax: +44 (0)2476 365 835
Email: sales@kinglonguk.com
Web site: www.kinglonguk.com

LEICESTER CARRIAGE BUILDERS
Marlow Road, Leicester, LE3 2BQ,
United Kingdom
Tel: +44 (0)116 282 4270
Fax: +44 (0)116 263 0554
Email: enquiries@leicestercarriagebuilders.coop
Web site: www.leicestercarriagebuilders.coop

MERCEDES-BENZ
UK Supplier Evobus (UK) Ltd
Cross Point Business Park, Ashcroft Way,
Coventry, CV2 2TU, United Kingdom
Tel: +44 (0)2476 626 000
Fax: +44 (0)2476 626 006
Email: reception.uk@evobus.com
Web site: www.evobus.com

MINITRAM SYSTEMS
Tdi (Europe) Ltd, Clifford Mill, Clifford Chambers,
Stratford Upon Avon, CV37 8HW,
United Kingdom
Contact: Martin Pemberton
Tel: +44 (0)1789 205 011
Fax: +44 (0)1789 133 119
Email: martin.p@tdi.uk.com
Web site: www.tdi.uk.com

MISTRAL BUS & COACH PLC
Booths Hall, Booths Park, Chelford Road,
Knutsford, Cheshire, WA16 8GS, United Kingdom
Tel: +44 (0)1565 621 881
Email: sales@mistral-bus.com
Web site: www.mistral-bus.com

MOSELEY (PCV) LTD
Elmsall Way, Dale Lane, South Elmsall, Pontefract,
West Yorkshire, WF9 2XS, United Kingdom
Tel: +44 (0)1977 609 000
Fax: +44 (0)1977 609 900
Email: enquiries@moseleycoachsales.co.uk
Web site: www.moseleycoachsales.co.uk

OPTARE PLC
Hurricane Way South, Sherburn In Elmet, Leeds,
LS25 6PT, United Kingdom
Tel: +44 (0)8434 873 200
Fax: +44 (0)8434 873 201
Email: info@optare.com
Web site: www.optare.com

PLAXTON (ALEXANDER DENNIS T/A)
Plaxton Park, Cayton Low Road, Eastfield,
Scarborough, North Yorkshire, YO11 3BY,
United Kingdom
Tel: +44 (0)1723 581 500
Email: sales@plaxtonlimited.co.uk
Web site: www.plaxtonlimited.co.uk

Models: Coaches, Buses, Midicoach And Midibus
Bodies. (Part Of Alexander Dennis)

RENAULT UK LTD
Rivers Office Park, Denham Way, Rickmansworth,
WD3 9YS, United Kingdom
Tel: +44 (0)844 335 0000
Web site: www.renault.co.uk
Models: Complete Minibus Or Chassis-Cowl;
Electric Vehicle.

TOYOTA (GB) PLC
PO Box 814, Portsmouth, PO6 9AY,
United Kingdom
Tel: +44 (0)344 701 6202
Web site: www.toyota.co.uk
UK Supplier Minis to Midis Ltd
135 Nutwell Lane, Doncaster, DN3 3JR,
United Kingdom
Tel: 01302 833203
Fax: 01302 831756
Email: sales@ministomidis.com
Web site: www.ministomidis.com
Models: Optimo Midicoach, Chassis Cowl

VAUXHALL MOTORS LTD
Griffin House, Osborne Road, Luton, LU1 3YT,
United Kingdom
Tel: 0800 026 0034
Email:
vauxhall.customerassistance@vauxhall.co.uk
Web site: www.vauxhall.co.uk
Models: Complete Minibus Or Chassis-Cowl.

VOLKSWAGEN COMMERCIAL VEHICLES
Yeomans Drive, Blakelands, Milton Keynes,
MK14 5AN, United Kingdom
Tel: 0800 717 131
Web site: www.volkswagen-vans.co.uk
Models: Complete minibus or chassis-cowl.

DEALER

ALEXANDER DENNIS LTD
91 Glasgow Road, Falkirk, FK1 4JB,
United Kingdom
Tel: +44 (0)1324 621 672
Fax: +44 (0)1324 632 469
Email: enquiries@alexander-dennis.com
Web site: www.alexander-dennis.com

ALLIED MOBILITY
230 Balmore Road, Glasgow, G22 6LJ,
United Kingdom
Tel: +44 (0)141 336 1618
Email: info@alliedmobility.com
Web site: www.alliedmobility.com

ARRIVA BUS & COACH
Lodge Garage, Whitehall Road, Gomersal,
Cleckheaton, West Yorkshire, BD19 4BJ,
United Kingdom
Tel: +44 (0)1274 681 144
Email: busandcoachsales@arriva.co.uk
Web site: www.arrivabusandcoach.co.uk

BASE LTD
Clydesdale Place, Moss Side Industrial Estate,
Leyland, PR26 7QS, United Kingdom
Tel: +44 (0)1772 425 355
Web site: www.basecoachsales.com

BLYTHSWOOD MOTORS LTD
Westway, Porterfield Road, Renfrew, PA4 8DJ,
United Kingdom
Tel: +44 (0)141 889 9730
Fax: +44 (0)141 889 8830
Email: blythswoodmotors@aol.com
Web site: www.blythswoodmotors.co.uk

BOB VALE COACH SALES LTD
Eastfield House, Amesbury Road, Thruxton,
Andover, Hampshire, SP11 8ED, United Kingdom
Tel: +44 (0)1264 773 000
Fax: +44 (0)1264 774 833
Web site: www.bobvalecoachsales.com

BRISTOL BUS & COACH SALES
6/7 Freestone Road, St Philips, Bristol,
BS2 0QN, United Kingdom
Tel: +44 (0)117 971 0251
Fax: +44 (0)117 972 3121
Web site: www.bristolbusandcoach.co.uk

BRITISH BUS SALES (MIKE NASH)
PO Box 534, Dorking, Surrey,
RH5 5XB, United Kingdom
Tel: +44 (0)7836 656 692
Email: web@britishbussales.com
Web site: www.britishbussales.com
Vintage and older vehicles a speciality. Open-top
buses, Routemaster's, Leyland's, Bristol's, Volvo's,
AEC's etc. Buses and coaches sourced to order.

CAETANO (UK) LTD
Mill Lane, Heather, Coalville,
LE67 2QE, United Kingdom
Tel: +44 (0)1530 263 333
Email: office@caetano.co.uk
Web site: www.caetano.co.uk

CONNAUGHT PSV
Unit 12, Frontier Works, King Edward Road,
Thorne, Doncaster, DN8 4HU, United Kingdom
Tel: +44 (0)1405 814 064
Email: info@connaughtpsv.co.uk
Web site: www.connaughtpsv.co.uk

DAWSONGROUP PLC
Delaware Drive, Tongwell, Milton Keynes,
MK15 8JH, United Kingdom
Tel: +44 (0)1908 218 111
Fax: +44 (0)1908 218 444
Email: contactus@dawsongroup.co.uk
Web site: www.dawsongroup.co.uk

ENSIGN BUS CO LTD
Juliette Close, Purfleet Industrial Park, Purfleet,
RM15 4YF, United Kingdom
Tel: +44 (0)1708 865 656
Fax: +44 (0)1708 864 340
Email: sales@ensignbus.com
Web site: www.ensignbus.com

EVOBUS (UK) LTD
Cross Point Business Park, Ashcroft Way,
Coventry, CV2 2TU, United Kingdom
Tel: +44 (0)2476 626 000
Fax: +44 (0)2476 626 006
Email: reception.uk@evobus.com
Web site: www.evobus.com

DAVID FISHWICK VEHICLE SALES
North Valley, Byron Road, Colne, Lancashire,
BB8 0BQ, United Kingdom
Tel: +44 (0)1282 867 772
Email: matthew@davidfishwick.net
Web site: www.davidfishwick.com

FLEET AUCTION GROUP
Brindley Road, Stephenson Industrial Estate,
Coalville, Leicestershire, LE67 3HG,
United Kingdom
Tel: +44 (0)1530 833 535
Fax: +44 (0)1530 813 425
Email: info@fleetauctiongroup.com
Web site: www.fleetauctiongroup.com

FURROWS COMMERCIAL VEHICLES
Haybridge Road, Hadley, Telford, Shropshire,
TF1 2FF, United Kingdom
Tel: +44 (0)1952 641 433
Web site: www.furrows.co.uk

GM COACHWORK LTD
Teign Valley, Trusham, Newton Abbot, Devon,
TQ13 0NX, United Kingdom
Tel: 0845 850 1860
Web site: www.gmcoachwork.co.uk

IAN GORDON COMMERCIALS
Schawkirk Garage, Stair, Ayrshire, KA5 5JA,
United Kingdom
Tel: +44 (0)1292 591 764

Fax: +44 (0)1292 591 484
Email: mail@iangordoncommercials.com
Web site: www.iangordoncommercials.com

THOMAS HARDIE COMMERCIALS LTD
Newstet Road, Knowsley Industrial Park,
Liverpool, L33 7TJ, United Kingdom
Tel: +44 (0)151 549 3000
Email: info@thardie.co.uk
Web site: www.thardie.co.uk

HEATONS MOTOR CO
53 Bickershaw Lane, Abram, Wigan, WN2 5PL,
United Kingdom
Tel: +44 (0)1942 864 222
Email: info@heatonsmotorco.co.uk
Web site: www.heatonsmotorco.co.uk

**JOHN HILL COACH SALES
& SERVICES LTD**
11 Wilton Road, Melton Mowbray, Leicestershire,
LE13 0UN, United Kingdom
Tel: +44 (0)1664 568 402
Email: john@hillscoachsales.com
Web site: www.hillscoachsales.com

IRISH COMMERCIALS (SALES)
Naas, Co Kildare, Republic of Ireland
Tel: +353 45 879881
Email: info@irishcomms.ie
Web site: www.irishcomms.ie

IRIZAR UK LTD
Portland House, Claylands Avenue, Worksop,
S81 7BQ, United Kingdom
Tel: +44 (0)1909 500 514
Email: sales@irizar.co.uk
Web site: www.irizar.co.uk

KING LONG UK LTD
Three Spires Industrial Estate, Ibstock Road,
Coventry, CV6 6JR, United Kingdom
Tel: +44 (0)2476 363 004
Fax: +44 (0)2476 365 835
Email: sales@kinglonguk.com
Web site: www.kinglonguk.com

LEINSTER VEHICLE DISTRIBUTORS LTD
Bridge Garage, Urlingford, Co Kilkenny,
Republic of Ireland
Tel: +353 56 88 31899
Email: sales@lvd.ie
Web site: www.lvd.ie

THE LONDON BUS EXPORT CO
PO Box 12, Chepstow, NP16 5UZ,
United Kingdom
Tel: +44 (0)1291 689 741
Fax: +44 (0)1291 689 361
Email: lonbusco@globalnet.co.uk
Web site: www.bus.uk.com

LOUGHSHORE AUTOS LTD
40 Killycanavan Road, Ardboe, Dungannon,
BT71 5BP, Northern Ireland
Tel: +44 (0)28 8673 7325
Fax: +44 (0)28 8673 5882
Email: mail@loughshoreautosltd.com
Web site: www.loughshoreautosltd.com

MAS SPECIAL ENGINEERING LTD
Houghton Road, North Anston, S25 4JJ,
United Kingdom
Tel: +44 (0)1909 550 480
Fax: +44 (0)1909 550 486

NIGEL MCCREE COACH SALES
Loughborough, Leicestershire, LE12 9NE,
United Kingdom
Tel: +44 (0)1509 502 695
Email: nigel@nigelmccree.com
Web site: www.nigelmccree.com

MINIS TO MIDIS LTD
135 Nutwell Lane, Doncaster, DN3 3JR,
United Kingdom
Tel: +44 (0)1302 833 203

Fax: +44 (0)1302 831 756
Email: sales@ministomidis.com
Web site: www.ministomidis.com

MISTRAL BUS & COACH PLC
Booths Hall, Booths Park, Chelford Road,
Knutsford, Cheshire, WA16 8GS, United Kingdom
Tel: +44 (0)1565 621 881
Email: sales@mistral-bus.com
Web site: www.mistral-bus.com

MOSELEY (PCV) LTD
Elmsall Way, Dale Lane, South Elmsall, Pontefract,
West Yorkshire, WF9 2XS, United Kingdom
Tel: +44 (0)1977 609 000
Fax: +44 (0)1977 609 900
Email: enquiries@moseleycoachsales.co.uk
Web site: www.moseleycoachsales.co.uk

MOSELEY DISTRIBUTORS LTD
Rydenmains, Condorrat Road, Glenmavis, Airdrie,
ML6 0PP, United Kingdom
Tel: +44 (0)1236 750 501
Fax: +44 (0)1236 750 504
Email: enquiries@moseleydistributors.co.uk
Web site: www.moseleydistributors.co.uk

MOSELEY IN THE SOUTH LTD
Summerfield Avenue, Chelston Business Park,
Wellington, TA21 9JF, United Kingdom
Tel: +44 (0)1823 653 000
Fax: +44 (0)1823 663 502
Email: sales@moseleycoachsales.co.uk
Web site: www.moseleycoachsales.co.uk

NEXT BUS LTD
The Coach Yard, Vincients Road,
Bumpers Farm Industrial Estate, Chippenham,
Wiltshire, SN14 6QA, United Kingdom
Tel: +44 (0)1249 462 462
Fax: +44 (0)1249 448 844
Email: sales@next-bus.co.uk
Web site: www.next-bus.co.uk

BRIAN NOONE
Straffan Road, Maynooth, Co Kildare,
Republic of Ireland
Tel: +353 1 628 6311
Email: reception@noone.ie
Web site: www.noone.ie

OPTARE PLC
Hurricane Way South, Sherburn In Elmet, Leeds,
LS25 6PT, United Kingdom
Tel: +44 (0)8434 873 200
Fax: +44 (0)8434 873 201
Email: info@optare.com
Web site: www.optare.com

PEMBRIDGE VEHICLE MANAGEMENT
Pembridge House, Park Business Centre,
Plough Road, Goytre, Penperlleni, Usk,
Monmouthshire, NP4 0AL, United Kingdom
Tel: +44 (0)1633 485 858
Fax: +44 (0)1495 785 591
Email: sales@minibussales.co.uk
Web site: www.minibussales.co.uk

H W PICKRELL
Holt Place, Gardiners Lane North, Crays Hill,
Billericay, CM11 2XE, United Kingdom
Tel: +44 (0)1268 521 033
Fax: +44 (0)1268 284 951
Email: sales@hwpickrell.co.uk
Web site: www.hwpickrell.co.uk
Supplier of new and used wheelchair accessible
vehicles

**PLAXTON COACH SALES CENTRE
(ALEXANDER DENNIS T/A)**
Ryton Road, Anston, Sheffield, S25 4DL,
United Kingdom
Tel: +44 (0)1909 551 166
Email: coachsales@plaxtonlimited.co.uk
Web site: www.plaxtoncoachsales.co.uk

PROCTERS COACH & BUS SALES
Tutin Road, Leeming Bar Industrial Estate,
Northallerton, DL7 9UJ, United Kingdom
Tel: +44 (0)1677 425 203
Fax: +44 (0)1677 426 550
Email: sales@procterscoachandbussales.com
Web site: www.procterscoachandbussales.com

SOUTHDOWN PSV LTD
Silverwood, Snow Hill, Copthorne, West Sussex,
RH10 3EN, United Kingdom
Tel: +44 (0)1342 711 840
Fax: +44 (0)1342 719 617
Email: bussales@southdownpsv.co.uk
Web site: www.southdownpsv.co.uk

STAFFORD BUS CENTRE
Unit 27, Moorfields Industrial Estate, Cotes Heath,
ST21 6QY, United Kingdom
Tel: +44 (0)1782 791 774
Fax: +44 (0)1782 791 721
Email: info@staffordbuscentre.com
Web site: www.staffordbuscentre.com

STEPHENSONS OF ESSEX
Riverside Industrial Estate, South Street, Rochford,
SS4 1BS, United Kingdom
Tel: +44 (0)1702 541 511
Fax: +44 (0)1702 549 461
Email: sales@stephensonsofessex.com
Web site: www.stephensonsofessex.com

TAYLOR COACH SALES
102 Beck Road, Isleham, Ely, CB7 5QP,
United Kingdom
Tel: +44 (0)1638 780 010
Fax: +44 (0)1638 780 011
Email: taylorcoach@live.co.uk
Web site: www.taylorcoachsales.co.uk

TOYOTA (GB) PLC
PO Box 814, Portsmouth, PO6 9AY,
United Kingdom
Tel: +44 (0)344 701 6202
Web site: www.toyota.co.uk
UK Supplier Minis to Midis Ltd
135 Nutwell Lane, Doncaster, DN3 3JR,
United Kingdom
Tel: 01302 833203
Fax: 01302 831756
Email: sales@ministomidis.com
Web site: www.ministomidis.com

TRAMONTANA COACH DISTRIBUTORS
Chapelknowe Road, Carfin, Motherwell, ML1 5LE,
United Kingdom
Tel: 01698 861790
Fax: 01698 860778
Email: wdt90@hotmail.co.uk
Web site: www.tramontanacoach.co.uk

UK BUS DISMANTLERS LTD
Streamhall Garage Estate, Linton Trading Estate,
Bromyard, Herefordshire, HR7 4QT,
United Kingdom
Tel: +44 (0)1885 488 448
Fax: +44 (0)1885 482 127
Web site: www.ukbusdismantlers.co.uk

USED COACH SALES LTD
60 The Old Quays, Knutsford Road, Warrington,
WA4 1JP, United Kingdom
Tel: +44 (0)1925 210 202
Web site: www.usedcoachsales.co.uk

VENTURA BUS + COACH SALES
Hobbs Industrial Estate, New Chapel, Lingfield,
RH7 6HN, United Kingdom
Tel: +44 (0)1342 835 206
Fax: +44 (0)1342 835 813
Email: contactus@venturasales.co.uk
Web site: www.venturasales.co.uk

VOLVO BUS & COACH SALES CENTRE
Siskin Parkway East, Middlemarch Business Park,
Coventry, CV3 4PE, United Kingdom
Tel: +44 (0)2476 210 250
Fax: +44 (0)2476 210 258
Email: info.buses.uk@volvo.com
Web site: www.volvobuses.com
Range: New & Pre-Owned Buses And Coaches.

WACTON COACH SALES & SERVICES
Steamhall Garage, Linton Trading Estate,
Bromyard, Herefordshire, HR7 4QL,
United Kingdom
Tel: +44 (0)1885 482 782

WEALDEN PSV LTD
The Bus Garage, 64 Whetsted Road,
Five Oak Green, Tonbridge, Kent, TN12 6RT,
United Kingdom
Tel: +44 (0)1892 833 830
Fax: +44 (0)1892 836 977
Email: sales@wealdenpsv.co.uk
Web site: www.wealdenpsv.co.uk

BEN WEAVER COMMERCIAL VEHICLE SALES
Gower Street, Sheffield, S4 7JW, United Kingdom
Tel: +44 (0)1142 757 076
Fax: +44 (0)1142 756 120
Email: info@usedcommercialvehiclesales.co.uk
Web site:
www.usedcommercialvehiclesales.co.uk

TREVOR WIGLEY & SONS BUS LTD
Boulder Bridge Lane, Carlton, Barnsley, S71 3HJ,
United Kingdom
Tel: +44 (0)1226 713 636
Fax: +44 (0)1226 700 199
Email: wigleys@btconnect.com
Web site: www.twigley.com
Passenger Vehicle Dismantling/Spares

DREW WILSON COACH SALES
Castlehill Yard, Airdrie Road, Carluke, Lanarkshire,
ML8 5EP, United Kingdom
Tel: +44 (0)141 248 5524
Email: enquiries@drewwilson.co.uk
Web site: www.drewwilson.co.uk

YORKSHIRE BUS & COACH SALES
254A West Ella Road, West Ella, Hull, HU10 7SF,
United Kingdom
Tel: +44 (0)1482 653 302
Fax: +44 (0)1482 653 302
Email: craig.porteous@virgin.net

ALSTOM TRANSPORT SA
48 rue Albert Dhalenne,
F-93482 Saint-Ouen Cedex, France
Tel: +33 1 41 66 90 00
Fax: +33 1 41 66 96 66
Web site: www.alstom.com
Models: Rail Vehicles Including Light Rail
Vehicles, Traction Equipment, Infrastructure And
Maintenance Services.

BOMBARDIER TRANSPORTATION
European Headquarters
Schoneberger Ufer 1, 10785 Berlin, Germany
Tel: +49 30 986 07 0
Fax: +49 30 986 07 2000
Web site: www.bombardier.com

BOMBARDIER TRANSPORTATION METROS
Litchurch Lane, Derby, DE24 8AD,
United Kingdom
Tel: +44 (0)1332 344 666
Fax: +44 (0)1332 266 271
Web site: www.bombardier.com/en/
transportation
Models: Light Rail Vehicles, Trams, Guided Or
Unguided Bi-Mode Rubber Tyred Electric Vehicle.

COACH GLAZING SERVICES
Unit 2, Washingford Row, Milltown, Dungannon,
Co. Tyrone, BT71 7BG, Northern Ireland
Contact: Stephen Ferguson,
National Sales Manager
Tel: 0800 954 1934 (NI)/1 800 937 440 (Eire)
Email: info@coachglazingservices.com

MINITRAM SYSTEMS
Tdi (Europe) Ltd, Clifford Mill, Clifford Chambers,
Stratford Upon Avon, CV37 8HW,
United Kingdom
Contact: Martin Pemberton
Tel: +44 (0)1789 205 011
Fax: +44 (0)1789 133 119
Email: martin.p@tdi.uk.com
Web site: www.tdi.uk.com
Models: Rubber Tyre-Guided/Unguided/
Rail 7.8M Vehicle

PARRY PEOPLE MOVERS LTD
Overend Road, Cradley Heath, West Midlands,
B64 7DD, United Kingdom
Tel: +44 (0)1384 569 553
Fax: +44 (0)1384 637 753
Email: info@parrypeoplemovers.com
Web site: www.parrypeoplemovers.com
Models: Ultra Light Rail Vehicles And Trams

TRAM POWER LTD
48 Watling Street, Preston, Lancashire, PR2 8BP,
United Kingdom
Tel: +44 (0)1772 713 900
Email: info@trampower.co.uk
Web site: www.trampower.co.uk
Models: Articulated Lightweight Low-Cost Tram

A-Z LISTING OF BUS, COACH & TRAM SUPPLIERS

LIST OF CATEGORIES

- Air Conditioning/Ventilation
- Audio/Video Systems
- Badges - Drivers/ Conductors
- Batteries
- Bicycle Carriers
- Body Repairs and Refurbishing
- Brakes and Brake Linings
- Cash Handling Equipment
- Chassis Lubricating Systems
- Clutches
- Commentary Systems
- Cooling Systems
- Destination Indicator Equipment
- Door Operating Gear
- Drinks Dispensing Equipment
- Driving Axles and Gears
- Electrical Equipment
- Electronic Control
- Emission Control Devices
- Engine Oil Drain Valves
- Engineering
- Engines
- Exhaust Systems
- Fans and Drive Belts
- Fare Boxes
- Fire Extinguishers
- First Aid Equipment
- Floor Coverings
- Fuel Management and Lubricants
- Garage Equipment
- Gearboxes
- Hand Driers (Coach Mounted)
- Handrails
- Headrest Covers and Curtains
- Heating and Ventilation Systems
- Hub Odometers
- Hybrid Drive Systems
- In-Coach Catering Equipment

- Labels, Nameplates and Decals
- Lifting Equipment
- Lighting and Lighting Design
- Mirrors / Mirror Arms
- Oil Management Systems
- Painting and Signwriting
- Parts Suppliers
- Passenger Information Displays
- Pneumatic Valves/ Cylinders
- Rapid Transit/ Priority Equipment
- Repairs/ Refurbishment
- Retarders and Speed Control Equipment
- Reversing Safety Systems
- Roller Blinds - Passenger and Driver
- Roof Lining Fabrics
- Seat Belts/ Restraint Systems
- Seats, Seat Cushions and Seat Frames
- Shelters/ Street Furniture
- Shock Absorbers and Suspension
- Steering
- Surveillance
- Suspension
- Tachograph Calibrators
- Tachograph Chart Analysis Service
- Tachographs
- Tickets, Ticket Machines and Ticket Systems
- Timetable Display Frames
- Toilet Equipment
- Transmission Overhaul
- Tree Guards
- Tyres
- Uniforms
- Upholstery
- Vacuum Systems
- Vehicle Washing
- Wheeltrims and Covers
- Window Film Protection / Vinyl Bodywrapping
- Windows, Windscreens and Wiper Motors

INDUSTRY SERVICE PROVIDERS

- Accident Investigation
- Accountancy and Audit
- Artwork
- Breakdown and Recovery Services
- Cleaning Services
- Coach Driver Agency
- Coach Hire Brokers/ Vehicle Rental
- Coach Interchange / Parking Facilities
- Computer Systems / Software
- Consultants and Advisory Services
- Driver Training
- Drug and Alcohol Testing
- Exhibition Organisers
- Ferry Operators
- Finance and Leasing
- Graphic Design
- Health & Safety
- Insurance
- Legal and Operations Advisers
- Livery and Graphic Design
- Maps for the Bus Industry
- Marketing Services
- Mechanical Investigation
- On-bus Advertising
- Passenger Representation
- Printing and Publishing
- Promotional Material
- Publications / Books
- Quality Management Systems
- Recruitment
- Reference Books
- Timetable Production
- Tour Wholesalers
- Training and Marketing Services
- Vehicle Certification
- Web Design

AIR CONDITIONING

AIRCONCO LTD
Unit B1, Axis Point, Hareshill Business Park,
Hilltop Road, Heywood, Lancashire, OL10 2RQ,
United Kingdom
Tel: +44 (0)845 402 4014
Fax: +44 (0)845 402 4041
Email: mail@airconcoltd.com
Web site: www.airconco.ltd.uk

AMA AIR CONDITIONING
Unit 19, Spring Mill Industrial Estate, Avening Road,
Nailsworth, GL6 0BH, United Kingdom
Tel: +44 (0)1453 832 884
Fax: +44 (0)1453 832 040
Email: info@ama.ac
Web site: www.ama-airconditioning.co.uk

ARRIVA BUS & COACH
Lodge Garage, Whitehall Road, Gomersal,
Cleckheaton, West Yorkshire, BD19 4BJ,
United Kingdom
Tel: +44 (0)1274 681 144
Email: busandcoachparts@arriva.co.uk
Web site: www.arrivabusandcoach.co.uk

BRT BEARINGS LTD
21-24 Regal Road, Wisbech, Cambridgeshire,
PE13 2RQ, United Kingdom
Tel: +44 (0)1945 464 097
Fax: +44 (0)1945 464 523
Email: brt.sales@brt-bearings.com
Web site: www.brt-bearings.com

CARLYLE BUS & COACH LTD
Carlyle Business Park, Great Bridge Street,
Swan Village, West Bromwich, B70 0X4,
United Kingdom
Tel: 0121 524 1200   **Fax:** 0121 524 1201
Email: westbromwichsales@carlyleplc.co.uk
Web site: www.carlylebusandcoach.com

CARRIER AIR CONDITIONING UK
United Technologies House, Guildford Road,
Leatherhead, Surrey, KT22 9UT, United Kingdom
Tel: +44 (0)870 600 1133
Fax: +44 (0)1372 220 221
Web site: www.carrieraircon.co.uk

CLAYTON HEATERS LTD
Fletchworth Gate Industrial Estate, Coventry,
West Midlands, CV5 6SP, United Kingdom
Tel: +44 (0)2476 691 916
Email: admin@claytoncc.co.uk
Web site: www.claytoncc.co.uk

DIRECT PARTS LTD
Unit 1, Churnet Court,
Churnetside Business Park, Harrison Way,
Cheddleton, ST13 7EF, United Kingdom
Tel: +44 (0)1538 361 777
Fax: +44 (0)1538 369 100
Email: sales@direct-group.co.uk
Web site: www.direct-group.co.uk

EBERSPACHER (UK) LTD
Headlands Business Park, Salisbury Road,
Ringwood, BH24 3PB, United Kingdom
Tel: +44 (0)1425 480 151
Fax: +44 (0)1425 480 152
Email: enquiries@eberspacher.com
Web site: www.eberspacher.com

EVM LTD
Comagh Business Park, Kilbeggan, Co Westmeath,
Republic of Ireland
Tel: +353 5793 32699
Fax: +353 5793 32691
Email: martin.browne@evm.ie
Web site: www.evm.ie

GRAYSON THERMAL SYSTEMS
Wharfdale House, 257 Wharfdale Road, Tyseley,
Birmingham, B11 2DP, United Kingdom
Tel: +44 (0)121 700 5600
Fax: +44 (0)121 700 5601
Email: cs@graysonts.com
Web site: www.graysonts.com

HISPACOLD
UK Agent
Clayton Heaters - see above, United Kingdom
Web site: www.hispacold.es

M A C LTD
34a Waterroyd Lane, Mirfield, West Yorkshire,
WF14 9SG, United Kingdom
Tel: +44 (0)1924 491 252
Fax: +44 (0)1924 480 170
Email: info@mac-aircon.com
Web site: www.mac-aircon.com

OMNI-TECH ELECTRONICS
Unit 9, Prospect House, Ireland Industrial Estate,
Staveley, Chesterfield, Derbyshire, S43 3QE,
United Kingdom
Tel: +44 (0)1246 474 332
Fax: +44 (0)1246 529 010
Email: help@omni-techelectronics.co.uk
Web site: www.buselectronics.co.uk

OPTARE PARTS DIVISION
Hurricane Way South, Sherburn In Elmet, Leeds,
LS25 6PT, United Kingdom
Tel: +44 (0)871 230 1324
Email: parts@optare.com
Web site: www.optare.com

OPTARE PRODUCT SUPPORT
London
Unit 9, Eurocourt, Olivers Close, West Thurrock,
RM20 3EE, United Kingdom
Tel: +44 (0)1708 896 860
Fax: +44 (0)1708 869 920
Email: london.service@optare.com
Manchester
Trafford Park, Manchester, M17 1HG,
United Kingdom
Tel: +44 (0)161 872 7772
Email: manchester.service@optare.com
Rotherham
Denby Way, Hellaby, Rotherham, S66 8HR,
United Kingdom
Tel: +44 (0)1709 535 101
Fax: +44 (0)1709 739 680
Email: rotherham.service@optare.com

PACET MANUFACTURING LTD
Wyebridge House, Cores End Road, Bourne End,
Buckinghamshire, SL8 5HH, United Kingdom
Tel: +44 (0)1628 526 754
Fax: +44 (0)1628 810 080
Email: sales@pacet.co.uk
Web site: www.pacet.co.uk

PLAXTON SERVICE
Ryton Road, Anston, Sheffield, S25 4DL,
United Kingdom
Tel: +44 (0)1909 551 155
Fax: +44 (0)1909 550 050
Email: service@plaxtonlimited.co.uk
Web site: www.plaxtonaftercare.co.uk

PREMIER COMPONENTS UK LTD
Unit 701, Long Marston Storage, Campden Road,
Long Marston, Stratford-upon-Avon,
Warwickshire, CV37 8QR, United Kingdom
Tel: +44 (0)1789 721 010
Fax: +44 (0)1789 722 429
Web site: www.premiercore.com

SCANIA (GB) LTD
Delaware Drive, Tongwell, Milton Keynes,
MK15 8HB, United Kingdom
Tel: +44 (0)1908 210 210
Fax: +44 (0)1908 215040
Web site: www.scania.co.uk

WEBASTO THERMO & COMFORT UK LTD
Webasto House, White Rose Way,
Doncaster Carr, South Yorkshire, DN4 5JH,
United Kingdom
Tel: +44 (0)1302 322 232
Web site: www.webasto.com/gb

AUDIO/VIDEO SYSTEMS

AUTOSOUND LTD
4 Lister Street, Dudley Hill, Bradford, BD4 9PQ,
United Kingdom
Tel: +44 (0)1274 688 990
Fax: +44 (0)1274 651 318
Web site: www.autosound.co.uk

AVT SYSTEMS LTD
Unit 3 & 4, Tything Road East, Alcester,
Warwickshire, B49 6ES, United Kingdom
Tel: +44 (0)1789 400 357
Fax: +44 (0)1789 400 359
Email: enquiries@avtsystems.co.uk
Web site: www.avtsystems.co.uk

EVM LTD
Comagh Business Park, Kilbeggan, Co Westmeath,
Republic of Ireland
Tel: +353 5793 32699
Fax: +353 5793 32691
Email: martin.browne@evm.ie
Web site: www.evm.ie

EXPRESS COACH REPAIRS LTD
Outgang Lane, Pickering, YO18 7EL,
United Kingdom
Tel: +44 (0)1751 475 215
Email: expresscoachrepairs@hotmail.co.uk

INIT INNOVATIONS IN TRANSPORTATION LTD
Price House, 37 Stoney Street, The Lace Market,
Nottingham, NG1 1LS, United Kingdom
Tel: +44 (0)870 890 4648
Email: sales@init.co.uk
Web site: www.init.co.uk

KCP CAR & COMMERCIAL LTD
Unit 15, Hillside Road, Kempson Way,
Bury St Edmunds, Suffolk, IP32 7EA,
United Kingdom
Tel: +44 (0)1284 750 777
Fax: +44 (0)1284 750 773
Email: kcponline@yahoo.co.uk
Web site: kcpcarandcommercial.co.uk

LAWTON SERVICES LTD
Knutsford Road, Church Lawton, Stoke-On-Trent,
ST7 3DN, United Kingdom
Tel: +44 (0)1270 882 056
Fax: +44 (0)1270 883 014
Email: info@lawtonservices.co.uk
Web site: www.lawtonservices.co.uk

NIMBUS JOURNEY INFORMATION LTD
Suite F4 and F5, Worth Corner, Turners Hill Road,
Crawley, West Sussex, RH10 7SL, United Kingdom
Tel: +44 (0)1293 887 308
Email: sales@nimbusjourneyinfo.co.uk
Web site: www.nimbusjourneyinfo.co.uk

OPTARE PARTS DIVISION
Hurricane Way South, Sherburn In Elmet, Leeds,
LS25 6PT, United Kingdom
Tel: +44 (0)871 230 1324
Email: parts@optare.com
Web site: www.optare.com

PLAXTON SERVICE
Ryton Road, Anston, Sheffield, S25 4DL,
United Kingdom
Tel: +44 (0)1909 551 155
Fax: +44 (0)1909 550 050
Email: service@plaxtonlimited.co.uk
Web site: www.plaxtonaftercare.co.uk

PSV PRODUCTS
60 The Old Quays, Warrington, Cheshire,
WA4 1JP, United Kingdom
Tel: +44 (0)1925 210 220
Email: info@psvproducts.com
Web site: www.psvproducts.com

BADGES - DRIVERS/CONDUCTORS

GSM GRAPHIC ARTS LTD
Castlegarth Works, Thirsk, YO7 1PS,
United Kingdom
Tel: +44 (0)1845 522 184
Fax: +44 (0)1845 522 206
Web site: www.gsmgraphicarts.co.uk

MARK TERRILL PSV BADGES
5 De Grey Close, Lewes, BN7 2JR,
United Kingdom
Tel: +44 (0)1273 474816
Email: mark.terrill2010@gmail.com

BATTERIES

ARRIVA BUS & COACH
Lodge Garage, Whitehall Road, Gomersal,
Cleckheaton, West Yorkshire, BD19 4BJ,
United Kingdom
Tel: +44 (0)1274 681 144
Email: busandcoachparts@arriva.co.uk
Web site: www.arrivabusandcoach.co.uk

BANNER BATTERIES GB LTD
Units 5-8, Canal View Business Park,
Wheelhouse Road, Rugeley, Staffordshire,
WS15 1UY, United Kingdom
Tel: +44 (0)1889 571 100
Fax: +44 (0)1889 577 342
Email: office.bgb@bannerbatteries.com
Web site: www.bannerbatteries.com

CARLYLE BUS & COACH LTD
Carlyle Business Park, Great Bridge Street,
Swan Village, West Bromwich, B70 0X4,
United Kingdom
Tel: 0121 524 1200
Fax: 0121 524 1201
Email: westbromwichsales@carlyleplc.co.uk
Web site: www.carlylebusandcoach.com

CUMMINS UK
40-44 Rutherford Drive, Park Farm South,
Wellingborough, NN8 6AN, United Kingdom
Tel: +44 (0)1933 334 200
Fax: +44 (0)1933 334 198
Email: cduksales@cummins.com
Web site: www.cummins.com

EXPRESS COACH REPAIRS LTD
Outgang Lane, Pickering, YO18 7EL,
United Kingdom
Tel: +44 (0)1751 475 215
Email: expresscoachrepairs@hotmail.co.uk

THOMAS HARDIE COMMERCIALS LTD
Newstet Road, Knowsley Industrial Park,
Liverpool, L33 7TJ, United Kingdom
Tel: +44 (0)151 549 3000
Email: info@thardie.co.uk
Web site: www.thardie.co.uk

JOHNSON CONTROLS BATTERIES LTD
3rd Floor, Aston House, 62-68 Oak End Way,
Gerrards Cross, Buckinghamshire, SL9 8BR,
United Kingdom
Tel: +44 (0)1753 480 610
Fax: +44 (0)1753 480 611
Email: vb-uk-enquiries@jci.com
Web site: www.varta-automotive.com

KCP CAR & COMMERCIAL LTD
Unit 15, Hillside Road, Kempson Way,
Bury St Edmunds, Suffolk, IP32 7EA,
United Kingdom
Tel: +44 (0)1284 750 777
Fax: +44 (0)1284 750 773

Email: kcponline@yahoo.co.uk
Web site: kcpcarandcommercial.co.uk

MAS SPECIAL ENGINEERING LTD
Houghton Road, North Anston, S25 4JJ,
United Kingdom
Tel: +44 (0)1909 550 480
Fax: +44 (0)1909 550 486

OPTARE PARTS DIVISION
Hurricane Way South, Sherburn In Elmet, Leeds,
LS25 6PT, United Kingdom
Tel: +44 (0)871 230 1324
Email: parts@optare.com
Web site: www.optare.com

OPTARE PRODUCT SUPPORT
London
Unit 9, Eurocourt, Olivers Close, West Thurrock,
RM20 3EE, United Kingdom
Tel: +44 (0)1708 896 860
Fax: +44 (0)1708 869 920
Email: london.service@optare.com
Manchester
Trafford Park, Manchester, M17 1HG,
United Kingdom
Tel: +44 (0)161 872 7772
Email: manchester.service@optare.com
Rotherham
Denby Way, Hellaby, Rotherham, S66 8HR,
United Kingdom
Tel: +44 (0)1709 535 101
Fax: +44 (0)1709 739 680
Email: rotherham.service@optare.com

BICYCLE CARRIERS

PLAXTON SERVICE
Ryton Road, Anston, Sheffield, S25 4DL,
United Kingdom
Tel: +44 (0)1909 551 155
Fax: +44 (0)1909 550 050
Email: service@plaxtonlimited.co.uk
Web site: www.plaxtonaftercare.co.uk

BODY REPAIRS AND REFURBISHING

AK CARPETS LTD
Unit 4, Robinson Court, Brockholes Way,
Claughton on Brock, Lancashire, PR 0PZ,
United Kingdom
Tel: +44 (0)1995 643 033
Fax: +44 (0)1995 643 231
Email: info@akcarpets.com
Web site: www.akcarpets.com

ARRIVA BUS & COACH
Lodge Garage, Whitehall Road, Gomersal,
Cleckheaton, West Yorkshire, BD19 4BJ,
United Kingdom

COMBINING ADVANCED TECHNOLOGY
WITH SUPERIOR PERFORMANCE,
FOR MAXIMUM COST EFFICIENCY

It all starts with **VARTA**

Tel: +44 (0)1274 681 144
Email: busandcoachparts@arriva.co.uk
Web site: www.arrivabusandcoach.co.uk

BULWARK BUS & COACH ENGINEERING LTD
Unit 5, Bulwark Business Park, Bulwark,
Chepstow, NP16 6QZ, United Kingdom
Tel: +44 (0)1291 622 326
Fax: +44 (0)1291 622 726
Email: bulwarkbusandcoach@tiscali.co.uk
Web site: www.bulwarkbusandcoach.co.uk

CARLYLE BUS & COACH LTD
Carlyle Business Park, Great Bridge Street,
Swan Village, West Bromwich, B70 0X4,
United Kingdom
Tel: 0121 524 1200
Fax: 0121 524 1201
Email: westbromwichsales@carlyleplc.co.uk
Web site: www.carlylebusandcoach.com

CHANNEL COMMERCIALS PLC
Unit 6, Cobbs Wood Industrial Estate,
Brunswick Road, Ashford, TN23 1EH,
United Kingdom
Tel: 0844 247 7742
Fax: +44 (0)1233 636 322
Web site: www.channelcommercials.co.uk

EASTGATE COACH TRIMMERS
3 Thornton Road Industrial Estate, Pickering,
YO18 7HZ, United Kingdom
Tel: +44 (0)1751 472 229
Email: info@eastgate-coachtrimmers.co.uk
Web site: eastgate-coachtrimmers.co.uk

EVM LTD
Comagh Business Park, Kilbeggan, Co Westmeath,
Republic of Ireland
Tel: +353 5793 32699
Fax: +353 5793 32691
Email: martin.browne@evm.ie
Web site: www.evm.ie

EXPRESS COACH REPAIRS LTD
Outgang Lane, Pickering, YO18 7EL,
United Kingdom
Tel: +44 (0)1751 475 215
Email: expresscoachrepairs@hotmail.co.uk

FERRYMILL MOTORS
Campsie Road, Torrance, Glasgow, G64 4NP,
United Kingdom
Tel: +44 (0)1360 620 544
Fax: +44 (0)1360 620 990
Email: info@ferrymillmotors.co.uk
Web site: www.ferrymillmotors.co.uk

FULL CIRCLE ENTERPRISES LTD
Heath Road, Banham, Norfolk, NR16 2HS,
United Kingdom
Tel: +44 (0)1953 887 951
Fax: +44 (0)1953 888 985
Email: info@fullcircleenterprises.co.uk
Web site: www.fullcircleenterprises.co.uk

HANTS & DORSET TRIM LTD
Unit 4E, Barton Park, Chickenhall Lane, Eastleigh,
Hampshire, SO0 6RR, United Kingdom
Tel: +44 (0)2380 644 200
Fax: +44 (0)2380 647 802
Email: enquiries@hdtrim.co.uk
Web site: www.hantsanddorsettrim.co.uk

HAPPICH UK LTD
Unit 26, Webb Ellis Industrial Estate, Wood Street,
Rugby, Warwickshire, CV21 2NP, United Kingdom
Tel: +44 (0)1788 50703
Fax: +44 (0)1788 44972
Email: info@happich.co.uk
Web site: www.happich.de

THOMAS HARDIE COMMERCIALS LTD
Newstet Road, Knowsley Industrial Park,
Liverpool, L33 7TJ, United Kingdom

Tel: +44 (0)151 549 3000
Email: info@thardie.co.uk
Web site: www.thardie.co.uk

INVERTEC LTD
Whelford Road, Fairford, GL7 4DT,
United Kingdom
Tel: +44 (0)1285 713 550
Fax: +44 (0)1285 713 548
Email: info@invertec.co.uk
Web site: www.invertec.co.uk

**LAWMAN COMMERCIAL
SERVICES LTD**
31 Merrylees Industrial Estate, Leeside, Desford,
Leicestershire, LE9 9FS, United Kingdom
Tel: +44 (0)1530 231 235
Email: sales@lawmancommercials.com
Web site: www.lawmancommercials.net

LAWTON SERVICES LTD
Knutsford Road, Church Lawton, Stoke-On-Trent,
ST7 3DN, United Kingdom
Tel: +44 (0)1270 882 056
Fax: +44 (0)1270 883 014
Email: info@lawtonservices.co.uk
Web site: www.lawtonservices.co.uk

LEICESTER CARRIAGE BUILDERS
Marlow Road, Leicester, LE3 2BQ,
United Kingdom
Tel: +44 (0)116 282 4270
Fax: +44 (0)116 263 0554
Email: enquiries@leicestercarriagebuilders.coop
Web site: www.leicestercarriagebuilders.coop

LONDON BUS & TRUCK LTD
Units 1-4, Northfleet Industrial Estate,
Lower Road, Northfleet, Kent, DA11 9SN,
United Kingdom
Tel: +44 (0)1474 361 199
Email: enquiries@londonbusandtruck.co.uk
Web site: www.londonbusandtruck.co.uk

MARTYN INDUSTRIALS LTD
5 Brunel Way, Durranhill Industrial Park, Harraby,
Carlisle, CA1 3NQ, United Kingdom
Tel: +44 (0)1228 544 000
Email: enquiries@martyn-industrials.co.uk
Web site: www.martyn-industrials.com

MAS SPECIAL ENGINEERING LTD
Houghton Road, North Anston, S25 4JJ,
United Kingdom
Tel: +44 (0)1909 550 480
Fax: +44 (0)1909 550 486

MCV BUS AND COACH LTD
Sterling Place, Elean Business Park, Sutton, Ely,
CB6 2QE, United Kingdom
Tel: +44 (0)1353 773 000
Fax: +44 (0)1353 773 001
Email: sales@mcv-uk.com
Web site: www.mcv-uk.com

MELLOR COACHCRAFT
Miall Street, Rochdale, OL11 1HY,
United Kingdom
Tel: +44 (0)1706 860 610
Fax: +44 (0)1706 860 402
Email: mcsales@woodall-nicholson.co.uk
Web site: www.mellor-coachcraft.co.uk

MOSELEY (PCV) LTD
Elmsall Way, Dale Lane, South Elmsall, Pontefract,
West Yorkshire, WF9 2XS, United Kingdom
Tel: +44 (0)1977 609 000
Fax: +44 (0)1977 609 900
Email: enquiries@moseleycoachsales.co.uk
Web site: www.moseleycoachsales.co.uk

MOSELEY DISTRIBUTORS LTD
Rydenmains, Condorrat Road, Glenmavis, Airdrie,
ML6 0PP, United Kingdom

Tel: +44 (0)1236 750 501
Fax: +44 (0)1236 750 504
Email: enquiries@moseleydistributors.co.uk
Web site: www.moseleydistributors.co.uk

N & M FIBREGLASS LTD
Units 1, 2 & 4 The Barns, Hewell Lane,
Tardebigge, Bromsgrove, Worcestershire, B60 1LP,
United Kingdom
Tel: +44 (0)1527 870 282
Fax: +44 (0)1527 576 269
Email: sales@nandmfibreglass.co.uk
Web site: www.nandmfibreglass.co.uk

OPTARE PARTS DIVISION
Hurricane Way South, Sherburn In Elmet, Leeds,
LS25 6PT, United Kingdom
Tel: +44 (0)871 230 1324
Email: parts@optare.com
Web site: www.optare.com

OPTARE PRODUCT SUPPORT
London
Unit 9, Eurocourt, Olivers Close, West Thurrock,
RM20 3EE, United Kingdom
Tel: +44 (0)1708 896 860
Fax: +44 (0)1708 869 920
Email: london.service@optare.com
Manchester
Trafford Park, Manchester, M17 1HG,
United Kingdom
Tel: +44 (0)161 872 7772
Email: manchester.service@optare.com
Rotherham
Denby Way, Hellaby, Rotherham, S66 8HR,
United Kingdom
Tel: +44 (0)1709 535 101
Fax: +44 (0)1709 739 680
Email: rotherham.service@optare.com

PLAXTON SERVICE
Ryton Road, Anston, Sheffield, S25 4DL,
United Kingdom
Tel: +44 (0)1909 551 155
Fax: +44 (0)1909 550 050
Email: service@plaxtonlimited.co.uk
Web site: www.plaxtonaftercare.co.uk

RH BODYWORKS
A140 Norwich-Ipswich Road, Brome, Eye, Suffolk,
IP23 8AW, United Kingdom
Tel: +44 (0)1379 870 666
Fax: +44 (0)1379 871 140
Email: enquiries@rhbodyworks.co.uk
Web site: www.rhbodyworks.co.uk

THORNTON BROTHERS LTD
North Seaton Industrial Estate, Ashington,
Northumberland, NE63 0YB, United Kingdom
Tel: +44 (0)1670 854 500
Fax: +44 (0)1670 854 015
Email: info@thornton-t180.co.uk
Web site: www.thornton-t180.co.uk

TRUCKALIGN CO LTD
VIP Group, VIP Industrial Park,
Anchor & Hope Lane, London, SE7 7RY,
United Kingdom
Tel: +44 (0)20 8858 3781
Fax: +44 (0)20 8858 5663
Email: admin@vipgroupltd.co.uk
Web site: www.vipgroup.co.uk

TTS UK
Total Tool Solutions Ltd, Newhaven Business Park,
Lowergate, Milnsbridge, Huddersfield, HD3 4HS,
United Kingdom
Tel: +44 (0)1484 642 211
Fax: +44 (0)1484 461 002
Email: sales@ttsuk.com
Web site: www.ttsuk.com

VOLVO BUS AND COACH CENTRE
Parts Sales & Body Repair/Refurbishment
Specialists - Byron Street Extension,
Loughborough, LE11 5HE, United Kingdom
Tel: +44 (0)1509 217 700
Fax: +44 (0)1509 238 770
Email: dporter@volvocoachsales.co.uk
Web site: www.volvobuses.com

WILKINSONS VEHICLE SOLUTIONS
Lancaster Road, Carnaby Industrial Estate,
Bridlington, East Yorkshire, YO15 3QY,
United Kingdom
Tel: +44 (0)1262 603 307
Fax: +44 (0)1262 608 208
Email: info@wilkinsonsvs.co.uk
Web site: www.wilkinsonsvehiclesolutions.co.uk

BRAKES AND BRAKE LININGS

ARRIVA BUS & COACH
Lodge Garage, Whitehall Road, Gomersal,
Cleckheaton, West Yorkshire, BD19 4BJ,
United Kingdom
Tel: +44 (0)1274 681 144
Email: busandcoachparts@arriva.co.uk
Web site: www.arrivabusandcoach.co.uk

ARVIN MERITOR
Park Lane, Great Alne, Alcester, Warwickshire,
B49 6HS, United Kingdom
Tel: +44 (0)1789 768 270
Web site: www.meritor.com

CAPARO AP BRAKING LTD
Brake House, Tachbrook Road, Leamington Spa,
CV31 3SF, United Kingdom
Tel: +44 (0)1926 473 737
Email: sales.enquiries@caparoapbraking.com
Web site: www.caparoapbraking.com

CRESCENT FACILITIES LTD
72 Willow Crescent, Chapeltown, Sheffield,
S35 1QS, United Kingdom
Tel: +44 (0)114 245 1050
Email: cfl.chris@btinternet.com

DIRECT PARTS LTD
Unit 1, Churnet Court,
Churnetside Business Park, Harrison Way,
Cheddleton, ST13 7EF, United Kingdom
Tel: +44 (0)1538 361 777
Fax: +44 (0)1538 369 100
Email: sales@direct-group.co.uk
Web site: www.direct-group.co.uk

IMEXPART LTD
Links 31, Willowbridge Way, Whitwood,
Castleford, WF10 5NP, United Kingdom
Tel: +44 (0)1977 553 936
Email: sales@imexpart.com
Web site: www.imexpart.com

IMPERIAL ENGINEERING
Delamare Road, Cheshunt, Hertfordshire,
EN8 9UD, United Kingdom
Tel: +44 (0)1992 634 255
Fax: +44 (0)1992 630 506
Email: orders@imperialengineering.co.uk
Web site: www.imperialengineering.co.uk

KCP CAR & COMMERCIAL LTD
Unit 15, Hillside Road, Kempson Way,
Bury St Edmunds, Suffolk, IP32 7EA,
United Kingdom
Tel: +44 (0)1284 750 777
Fax: +44 (0)1284 750 773
Email: kcponline@yahoo.co.uk
Web site: kcpcarandcommercial.co.uk

**KNORR-BREMSE SYSTEMS FOR
COMMERCIAL VEHICLES LTD**
Century House, Folly Brook Road,
Emerald Park East, Emersons Green, Bristol,
BS16 7FE, United Kingdom
Tel: +44 (0)117 984 6100
Email: uksales@knorr-bremse.co.uk
Web site: www.knorr-bremse.co.uk

NUTEXA FRICTIONS LTD
New Hall Lane, Hoylake, Wirral, CH47 4BP,
United Kingdom
Tel: +44 (0)151 632 5903
Fax: +44 (0)151 632 5908
Email: sales@nutexafrictions.co.uk
Web site: www.nutexafrictions.co.uk

OMNI-TECH ELECTRONICS
Unit 9, Prospect House, Ireland Industrial Estate,
Staveley, Chesterfield, Derbyshire, S43 3QE,
United Kingdom
Tel: +44 (0)1246 474 332
Fax: +44 (0)1246 529 010
Email: help@omni-techelectronics.co.uk
Web site: www.buselectronics.co.uk

OPTARE PARTS DIVISION
Hurricane Way South, Sherburn In Elmet, Leeds,
LS25 6PT, United Kingdom
Tel: +44 (0)871 230 1324
Email: parts@optare.com
Web site: www.optare.com

OPTARE PRODUCT SUPPORT
London
Unit 9, Eurocourt, Olivers Close, West Thurrock,
RM20 3EE, United Kingdom
Tel: +44 (0)1708 896 860
Fax: +44 (0)1708 869 920
Email: london.service@optare.com
Manchester
Trafford Park, Manchester, M17 1HG,
United Kingdom
Tel: +44 (0)161 872 7772
Email: manchester.service@optare.com
Rotherham
Denby Way, Hellaby, Rotherham, S66 8HR,
United Kingdom
Tel: +44 (0)1709 535 101
Fax: +44 (0)1709 739 680
Email: rotherham.service@optare.com

PARTLINE LTD
Dockfield Road, Shipley, BD17 7AZ,
United Kingdom
Tel: +44 (0)1274 531 531
Fax: +44 (0)1274 531 088
Email: sales@partline.co.uk
Web site: www.partline.co.uk

PLAXTON SERVICE
Ryton Road, Anston, Sheffield, S25 4DL,
United Kingdom
Tel: +44 (0)1909 551 155
Fax: +44 (0)1909 550 050
Email: service@plaxtonlimited.co.uk
Web site: www.plaxtonaftercare.co.uk

PREMIER COMPONENTS UK LTD
Unit 701, Long Marston Storage, Campden Road,
Long Marston, Stratford-upon-Avon,
Warwickshire, CV37 8QR, United Kingdom
Tel: +44 (0)1789 721 010
Fax: +44 (0)1789 722 429
Web site: www.premiercore.com

ROADLINK INTERNATIONAL LTD
Strawberry Lane, Willenhall, West Midlands,
WV13 3RL, United Kingdom
Tel: +44 (0)1902 636 206
Fax: +44 (0)1902 631 515
Email: sales@roadlink-international.co.uk
Web site: www.roadlink-international.co.uk

TMD FRICTION UK LTD
PO Box 18, Hunsworth Lane, Cleckheaton,
West Yorkshire, BD19 3UJ, United Kingdom
Tel: +44 (0)1274 854 000
Fax: +44 (0)1274 854 001
Email: info@tmdfriction.com
Web site: www.tmdfriction.com

TTS UK
Total Tool Solutions Ltd, Newhaven Business Park,
Lowergate, Milnsbridge, Huddersfield, HD3 4HS,
United Kingdom
Tel: +44 (0)1484 642 211
Fax: +44 (0)1484 461 002
Email: sales@ttsuk.com
Web site: www.ttsuk.com

WABCO AUTOMOTIVE UK LTD
Unit A1, Grange Valley Road, Batley,
West Yorkshire, WF17 6GH, United Kingdom
Tel: +44 (0)1924 595 400
Email: info.uk@wabco-auto.com
Web site: www.wabco-auto.com

CASH HANDLING EQUIPMENT

CUMMINS-ALLISON LTD
William H Klotz House, Colonnade Point,
Central Boulevard, Prologis Park, Coventry,
CV6 4BU, United Kingdom
Tel: +44 (0)24 7633 9810
Email: sales@cummins-allison.co.uk
Web site: www.cumminsallison.com

ETMSS LTD
Ground Floor Austin House, 43 Poole Road,
Westbourne, Bournemouth, Dorset, BH4 9DN,
United Kingdom
Contact: David Price, Sales Director
Tel: +44 (0)844 800 9299
Email: info@etmss.com
Web site: www.etmss.com
Coin dispensers, cash scoops & trays, vaults, ticket
bins, ticket roll holders, hand-held ticket punches.

JOHN GROVES TICKET SYSTEMS
Unit 10, North Circular Business Centre,
400 NCR, London, NW10 0JG, United Kingdom
Tel: +44(0)208 452 6512
Fax: 020 8830 1223
Email: sales@jgts.co.uk
Web site: www.jgts.co.uk

QUICK CHANGE (UK)
Yew Tree Cottage, Newcastle, Monmouthshire,

NP25 5NT, United Kingdom
Tel: +44 (0)1600 750 650
Email: ttservices@tiscali.co.uk
Web site: www.ticket-machines.co.uk

SCAN COIN LTD
Dutch House, 110 Broadway, Salford Quays,
M50 2UW, United Kingdom
Tel: +44 (0)845 388 1102
Fax: +44 (0)161 873 0501
Email: sales@scancoin.co.uk
Web site: www.scancoin.co.uk

MARK TERRILL TICKET MACHINERY
5 De Grey Close, Lewes, BN7 2JR,
United Kingdom
Tel: +44 (0)1273 474816
Email: mark.terrill2010@gmail.com

THOMAS AUTOMATICS
Unit 18, Meadow Lane Industrial Estate,
Loughborough, LE11 1JP, United Kingdom
Tel: +44 (0)1509 225 690
Email: sales@thomasa.co.uk
Web site: www.thomasa.co.uk

TICKETER
Chilton House, Charnham Lane, Hungerford,
Berkshire, RG10 0EY, United Kingdom
Tel: +44 (0)20 3195 8800
Email: support@ticketer.co.uk
Web site: www.ticketer.org.uk

TRANSPORT TICKET SERVICES LTD
Yew Tree Cottage, Newcastle, Monmouth,
NP25 5NT, United Kingdom
Tel: +44 (0)1600 750 650
Email: ttservices@tiscali.co.uk
Web site: www.ticket-machines.co.uk

CHASSIS LUBRICATING SYSTEMS

ARRIVA BUS & COACH
Lodge Garage, Whitehall Road, Gomersal,
Cleckheaton, West Yorkshire, BD19 4BJ,
United Kingdom
Tel: +44 (0)1274 681 144
Email: busandcoachparts@arriva.co.uk
Web site: www.arrivabusandcoach.co.uk

GROENEVELD UK LTD
The Greentec Centre, Gelders Hall Road,
Shepshed, Leicestershire, LE12 9NH,
United Kingdom
Tel: +44 (0)1509 600 033
Fax: +44 (0)1509 602 000
Email: info-uk@groeneveld-group.com
Web site: www.groeneveld-group.com

PLAXTON SERVICE
Ryton Road, Anston, Sheffield, S25 4DL,
United Kingdom
Tel: +44 (0)1909 551 155
Fax: +44 (0)1909 550 050
Email: service@plaxtonlimited.co.uk
Web site: www.plaxtonaftercare.co.uk

CLUTCHES

ARRIVA BUS & COACH
Lodge Garage, Whitehall Road, Gomersal,
Cleckheaton, West Yorkshire, BD19 4BJ,
United Kingdom
Tel: +44 (0)1274 681 144
Email: busandcoachparts@arriva.co.uk
Web site: www.arrivabusandcoach.co.uk

CAPARO AP BRAKING LTD
Brake House, Tachbrook Road, Leamington Spa,
CV31 3SF, United Kingdom
Tel: +44 (0)1926 473 737
Email: sales.enquiries@caparoapbraking.com
Web site: www.caparoapbraking.com

COACH-AID LTD
Greyfriars Workshop, Greyfriars Way, Stafford,
Staffordshire, ST16 2SH, United Kingdom

Tel: +44 (0)1785 222 666
Email: workshop@coach-aid.com
Web site: www.coach-aid.com

IMEXPART LTD
Links 31, Willowbridge Way, Whitwood,
Castleford, WF10 5NP, United Kingdom
Tel: +44 (0)1977 553 936
Email: sales@imexpart.com
Web site: www.imexpart.com

KCP CAR & COMMERCIAL LTD
Unit 15, Hillside Road, Kempson Way,
Bury St Edmunds, Suffolk, IP32 7EA,
United Kingdom
Tel: +44 (0)1284 750 777
Fax: +44 (0)1284 750 773
Email: kcponline@yahoo.co.uk
Web site: kcpcarandcommercial.co.uk

NUTEXA FRICTIONS LTD
New Hall Lane, Hoylake, Wirral, CH47 4BP,
United Kingdom
Tel: +44 (0)151 632 5903
Fax: +44 (0)151 632 5908
Email: sales@nutexafrictions.co.uk
Web site: www.nutexafrictions.co.uk

OPTARE PARTS DIVISION
Hurricane Way South, Sherburn In Elmet, Leeds,
LS25 6PT, United Kingdom
Tel: +44 (0)871 230 1324
Email: parts@optare.com
Web site: www.optare.com

OPTARE PRODUCT SUPPORT
London
Unit 9, Eurocourt, Olivers Close, West Thurrock,
RM20 3EE, United Kingdom
Tel: +44 (0)1708 896 860
Fax: +44 (0)1708 869 920
Email: london.service@optare.com
Manchester
Trafford Park, Manchester, M17 1HG,
United Kingdom
Tel: +44 (0)161 872 7772
Email: manchester.service@optare.com
Rotherham
Denby Way, Hellaby, Rotherham, S66 8HR,
United Kingdom
Tel: +44 (0)1709 535 101
Fax: +44 (0)1709 739 680
Email: rotherham.service@optare.com

PARTLINE LTD
Dockfield Road, Shipley, BD17 7AZ,
United Kingdom
Tel: +44 (0)1274 531 531
Fax: +44 (0)1274 531 088
Email: sales@partline.co.uk
Web site: www.partline.co.uk

PLAXTON SERVICE
Ryton Road, Anston, Sheffield, S25 4DL,
United Kingdom
Tel: +44 (0)1909 551 155
Fax: +44 (0)1909 550 050
Email: service@plaxtonlimited.co.uk
Web site: www.plaxtonaftercare.co.uk

SHAWSON SUPPLY LTD
12 Station Road, Saintfield, County Down,
BT24 7DU, Northern Ireland
Tel: +44 (0)28 9751 0994
Email: info@shawsonsupply.co.uk
Web site: www.shawsonsupply.co.uk

COMMENTARY SYSTEMS

V6E LTD
Severnside Trading Estate, St Andrews Road,
Avonmouth, Bristol, BS11 9EB, United Kingdom
Tel: +44 (0)1454 880 100
Email: info@v6e.co.uk
Web site: www.v6e.co.uk

COOLING SYSTEMS

ARRIVA BUS & COACH
Lodge Garage, Whitehall Road, Gomersal,
Cleckheaton, West Yorkshire, BD19 4BJ,
United Kingdom
Tel: +44 (0)1274 681 144
Email: busandcoachparts@arriva.co.uk
Web site: www.arrivabusandcoach.co.uk

CARLYLE BUS & COACH LTD
Carlyle Business Park, Great Bridge Street,
Swan Village, West Bromwich, B70 0X4,
United Kingdom
Tel: 0121 524 1200
Fax: 0121 524 1201
Email: westbromwichsales@carlyleplc.co.uk
Web site: www.carlylebusandcoach.com

CLAYTON HEATERS LTD
Fletchworth Gate Industrial Estate, Coventry,
West Midlands, CV5 6SP, United Kingdom
Tel: +44 (0)2476 691 916
Email: admin@claytoncc.co.uk
Web site: www.claytoncc.co.uk

DIRECT PARTS LTD
Unit 1, Churnet Court,
Churnetside Business Park, Harrison Way,
Cheddleton, ST13 7EF, United Kingdom
Tel: +44 (0)1538 361 777
Fax: +44 (0)1538 369 100
Email: sales@direct-group.co.uk
Web site: www.direct-group.co.uk

GRAYSON THERMAL SYSTEMS
Wharfdale House, 257 Wharfdale Road, Tyseley,
Birmingham, B11 2DP, United Kingdom
Tel: +44 (0)121 700 5600
Fax: +44 (0)121 700 5601
Email: cs@graysonts.com
Web site: www.graysonts.com

KCP CAR & COMMERCIAL LTD
Unit 15, Hillside Road, Kempson Way,
Bury St Edmunds, Suffolk, IP32 7EA,
United Kingdom
Tel: +44 (0)1284 750 777
Fax: +44 (0)1284 750 773
Email: kcponline@yahoo.co.uk
Web site: kcpcarandcommercial.co.uk

OPTARE PRODUCT SUPPORT
London
Unit 9, Eurocourt, Olivers Close, West Thurrock,
RM20 3EE, United Kingdom
Tel: +44 (0)1708 896 860
Fax: +44 (0)1708 869 920
Email: london.service@optare.com
Manchester
Trafford Park, Manchester, M17 1HG,
United Kingdom
Tel: +44 (0)161 872 7772
Email: manchester.service@optare.com
Rotherham
Denby Way, Hellaby, Rotherham, S66 8HR,
United Kingdom
Tel: +44 (0)1709 535 101
Fax: +44 (0)1709 739 680
Email: rotherham.service@optare.com

PACET MANUFACTURING LTD
Wyebridge House, Cores End Road, Bourne End,
Buckinghamshire, SL8 5HH, United Kingdom
Tel: +44 (0)1628 526 754
Fax: +44 (0)1628 810 080
Email: sales@pacet.co.uk
Web site: www.pacet.co.uk

PARTLINE LTD
Dockfield Road, Shipley, BD17 7AZ,
United Kingdom
Tel: +44 (0)1274 531 531
Fax: +44 (0)1274 531 088
Email: sales@partline.co.uk
Web site: www.partline.co.uk

PLAXTON SERVICE
Ryton Road, Anston, Sheffield, S25 4DL,
United Kingdom
Tel: +44 (0)1909 551 155
Fax: +44 (0)1909 550 050
Email: service@plaxtonlimited.co.uk
Web site: www.plaxtonaftercare.co.uk

SILFLEX LTD
Coed Cae Lane, Pontyclun, South Wales,
CF72 9HJ, United Kingdom
Tel: +44 (0)1443 238 464
Fax: +44 (0)1443 237 781
Email: hosesolutions@silflex.com
Web site: www.silflex.com

DESTINATION INDICATOR EQUIPMENT

ARRIVA BUS & COACH
Lodge Garage, Whitehall Road, Gomersal,
Cleckheaton, West Yorkshire, BD19 4BJ,
United Kingdom
Tel: +44 (0)1274 681 144
Email: busandcoachparts@arriva.co.uk
Web site: www.arrivabusandcoach.co.uk

HANOVER DISPLAYS LTD
Southerham House, Southerham Lane, Lewes,
BN8 6JN, United Kingdom
Tel: +44 (0)1273 477 528
Email: sales@hanoverdisplays.com
Web site: www.hanoverdisplays.com

INDICATORS INTERNATIONAL LTD
41 Aughrim Road, Magherafelt, BT45 6JX,
Northern Ireland
Tel: +44 (0)28 7963 2591
Fax: +44 (0)28 7963 3927
Email: info@indicators-int.com
Web site: www.indicators-int.com

INVERTEC LTD
Whelford Road, Fairford, GL7 4DT,
United Kingdom
Tel: +44 (0)1285 713 550
Fax: +44 (0)1285 713 548
Email: info@invertec.co.uk
Web site: www.invertec.co.uk

MCKENNA BROTHERS LTD
McKenna House, Jubilee Road, Middleton,
Manchester, M24 2LX, United Kingdom
Tel: +44 (0)161 655 3244
Fax: +44 (0)161 655 3059
Email: info@mckennabrothers.co.uk
Web site: www.mckennabrothers.co.uk

OMNI-TECH ELECTRONICS
Unit 9, Prospect House, Ireland Industrial Estate,
Staveley, Chesterfield, Derbyshire, S43 3QE,
United Kingdom
Tel: +44 (0)1246 474 332
Fax: +44 (0)1246 529 010
Email: help@omni-techelectronics.co.uk
Web site: www.buselectronics.co.uk

PLAXTON SERVICE
Ryton Road, Anston, Sheffield, S25 4DL,
United Kingdom
Tel: +44 (0)1909 551 155
Fax: +44 (0)1909 550 050
Email: service@plaxtonlimited.co.uk
Web site: www.plaxtonaftercare.co.uk

DOOR OPERATING GEAR

AIR DOOR SERVICES
The Pavilions, Holly Lane Industrial Estate,
Atherstone, CV9 2QZ, United Kingdom
Tel: +44 (0)1827 711 660
Email: airdoorservices@aol.com

ARRIVA BUS & COACH
Lodge Garage, Whitehall Road, Gomersal,
Cleckheaton, West Yorkshire, BD19 4BJ,

United Kingdom
Tel: +44 (0)1274 681 144
Email: busandcoachparts@arriva.co.uk
Web site: www.arrivabusandcoach.co.uk

CARLYLE BUS & COACH LTD
Carlyle Business Park, Great Bridge Street,
Swan Village, West Bromwich, B70 0X4,
United Kingdom
Tel: 0121 524 1200
Fax: 0121 524 1201
Email: westbromwichsales@carlyleplc.co.uk
Web site: www.carlylebusandcoach.com

CARWOOD BDS LTD
Unit D, Gillett Street, Hull, HU3 4JF,
United Kingdom
Tel: +44 (0)1482 212 400
Fax: +44 (0)1482 900 020
Email: enquiries@carwoodbds.com
Web site: www.carwoodbds.com

EXPRESS COACH REPAIRS LTD
Outgang Lane, Pickering, YO18 7EL,
United Kingdom
Tel: +44 (0)1751 475 215
Email: expresscoachrepairs@hotmail.co.uk

KARIVE LTD
PO Box 205, Southam, Warwickshire, CV47 0ZL,
United Kingdom
Tel: +44 (0)3333 446 700
Fax: +44 (0)3333 446 701
Email: info@karive.co.uk
Web site: www.karive.co.uk
Karive is the BCE.Srl agent for the UK and Ireland
in addition to assisting with the specification of
new doors from Italy direct to bodybuilders,
Karive also stocks a full range of spare parts for
both current and previous door designs.

KCP CAR & COMMERCIAL LTD
Unit 15, Hillside Road, Kempson Way,
Bury St Edmunds, Suffolk, IP32 7EA,
United Kingdom
Tel: +44 (0)1284 750 777
Fax: +44 (0)1284 750 773
Email: kcponline@yahoo.co.uk
Web site: kcpcarandcommercial.co.uk

**KNORR-BREMSE SYSTEMS FOR
COMMERCIAL VEHICLES LTD**
Century House, Folly Brook Road,
Emerald Park East, Emersons Green, Bristol,
BS16 7FE, United Kingdom
Tel: +44 (0)117 984 6100
Email: uksales@knorr-bremse.co.uk
Web site: www.knorr-bremse.co.uk

LAWTON SERVICES LTD
Knutsford Road, Church Lawton, Stoke-On-Trent,
ST7 3DN, United Kingdom
Tel: +44 (0)1270 882 056
Fax: +44 (0)1270 883 014
Email: info@lawtonservices.co.uk
Web site: www.lawtonservices.co.uk

OMNI-TECH ELECTRONICS
Unit 9, Prospect House, Ireland Industrial Estate,
Staveley, Chesterfield, Derbyshire, S43 3QE,
United Kingdom
Tel: +44 (0)1246 474 332
Fax: +44 (0)1246 529 010
Email: help@omni-techelectronics.co.uk
Web site: www.buselectronics.co.uk

OPTARE PARTS DIVISION
Hurricane Way South, Sherburn In Elmet, Leeds,
LS25 6PT, United Kingdom
Tel: +44 (0)871 230 1324
Email: parts@optare.com
Web site: www.optare.com

OPTARE PRODUCT SUPPORT
London
Unit 9, Eurocourt, Olivers Close, West Thurrock,

RM20 3EE, United Kingdom
Tel: +44 (0)1708 896 860
Fax: +44 (0)1708 869 920
Email: london.service@optare.com
Manchester
Trafford Park, Manchester, M17 1HG,
United Kingdom
Tel: +44 (0)161 872 7772
Email: manchester.service@optare.com
Rotherham
Denby Way, Hellaby, Rotherham, S66 8HR,
United Kingdom
Tel: +44 (0)1709 535 101
Fax: +44 (0)1709 739 680
Email: rotherham.service@optare.com

PARTLINE LTD
Dockfield Road, Shipley, BD17 7AZ,
United Kingdom
Tel: +44 (0)1274 531 531
Fax: +44 (0)1274 531 088
Email: sales@partline.co.uk
Web site: www.partline.co.uk

PERCY LANE PRODUCTS LTD
Lichfield Road, Tamworth, B79 7TL,
United Kingdom
Tel: +44 (0)1827 63821
Fax: +44 (0)1827 310 159
Web site: www.percylane.com

PLAXTON PARTS
Ryton Road, Anston, Sheffield, S25 4DL,
United Kingdom
Tel: +44 (0)844 822 6224
Fax: +44 (0)1909 550 050
Email: parts@plaxtonlimited.co.uk
Web site: www.plaxtonaftercare.co.uk

PLAXTON SERVICE
Ryton Road, Anston, Sheffield, S25 4DL,
United Kingdom
Tel: +44 (0)1909 551 155
Fax: +44 (0)1909 550 050
Email: service@plaxtonlimited.co.uk
Web site: www.plaxtonaftercare.co.uk

PNEUMAX LTD
110 Vista Park, Mauretania Road, Nursling,
Southampton, SO16 0YS, United Kingdom
Tel: +44 (0)2380 740 412
Fax: +44 (0)2380 739 340
Email: sales@pneumax.co.uk
Web site: www.pneumax.co.uk

PSV TRANSPORT SYSTEMS LTD
21 Impresa Park, Pindar Road, Hoddesdon,
Hertfordshire, EN11 0DL, United Kingdom
Tel: +44 (0)1992 479 950
Fax: +44 (0)1992 471 676
Email: sales@psv-transport-systems.co.uk
Web site: www.psv-transport-systems.co.uk

**TRANSPORT DOOR
SOLUTIONS LTD**
43 Broton Drive, Halstead, Essex, CO9 1HB,
United Kingdom
Tel: +44 (0)1787 473 000
Fax: +44 (0)1787 477 040
Email: sales@transportdoorsolutions.co.uk
Web site: www.transportdoorsolutions.co.uk

VAPOR RICON EUROPE LTD
Meadow Lane, Loughborough, Leicestershire,
LE11 1HS, United Kingdom
Tel: +44 (0)1509 635 924
Fax: +44 (0)1509 261 939
Email: ricon@wabtec.com
Web site: www.ricon.eu

WABCO AUTOMOTIVE UK LTD
Unit A1, Grange Valley Road, Batley,
West Yorkshire, WF17 6GH, United Kingdom
Tel: +44 (0)1924 595 400
Email: info.uk@wabco-auto.com
Web site: www.wabco-auto.com

DRINKS DISPENSING EQUIPMENT

ARRIVA BUS & COACH
Lodge Garage, Whitehall Road, Gomersal,
Cleckheaton, West Yorkshire, BD19 4BJ,
United Kingdom
Tel: +44 (0)1274 681 144
Email: busandcoachparts@arriva.co.uk
Web site: www.arrivabusandcoach.co.uk

BRADTECH LTD
Unit 3, Ladford Covert, Seighford, Stafford,
ST18 9QL, United Kingdom
Tel: +44 (0)1785 282 800
Fax: +44 (0)1785 282 558
Email: sales@bradtech.ltd.uk
Web site: www.bradtech.ltd.uk

DRINKMASTER LTD
Plymouth Road, Liskeard, Cornwall, PL14 3PG,
United Kingdom
Tel: +44 (0)1579 342 082
Web site: www.drinkmaster.co.uk

ELSAN LTD
Bellbrook Park, Uckfield, East Sussex, TN22 1QF,
United Kingdom
Tel: +44 (0)1825 748 200
Fax: +44 (0)1825 761 212
Email: sales@elsan.co.uk
Web site: www.elsan.co.uk

EXPRESS COACH REPAIRS LTD
Outgang Lane, Pickering, YO18 7EL,
United Kingdom
Tel: +44 (0)1751 475 215
Email: expresscoachrepairs@hotmail.co.uk

LAWTON SERVICES LTD
Knutsford Road, Church Lawton, Stoke-On-Trent,
ST7 3DN, United Kingdom
Tel: +44 (0)1270 882 056
Fax: +44 (0)1270 883 014
Email: info@lawtonservices.co.uk
Web site: www.lawtonservices.co.uk

PLAXTON PARTS
Ryton Road, Anston, Sheffield, S25 4DL,
United Kingdom
Tel: +44 (0)844 822 6224
Fax: +44 (0)1909 550 050
Email: parts@plaxtonlimited.co.uk
Web site: www.plaxtonaftercare.co.uk

PLAXTON SERVICE
Ryton Road, Anston, Sheffield, S25 4DL,
United Kingdom
Tel: +44 (0)1909 551 155
Fax: +44 (0)1909 550 050
Email: service@plaxtonlimited.co.uk
Web site: www.plaxtonaftercare.co.uk

PSV PRODUCTS
60 The Old Quays, Warrington, Cheshire,
WA4 1JP, United Kingdom
Tel: +44 (0)1925 210 220
Email: info@psvproducts.com
Web site: www.psvproducts.com

SHADES TECHNICS LTD
Units E3 & E4, RD Park, Stephenson Close,
Hoddesdon, Hertfordshire, EN11 0BW,
United Kingdom
Tel: +44 (0)1992 476 830
Email: info@shades-technics.com
Web site: www.shades-technics.com

**TRAMONTANA COACH
DISTRIBUTORS**
Chapelknowe Road, Carfin, Motherwell, ML1 5LE,
United Kingdom
Tel: 01698 861790
Fax: 01698 860778
Email: wdt90@hotmail.co.uk
Web site: www.tramontanacoach.co.uk

DRIVING AXLES AND GEARS

ALBION AUTOMOTIVE LTD
1187 South Street, Scotstoun, Glasgow, G14 0DT,
United Kingdom
Tel: +44 (0)141 434 2400
Fax: +44 (0)141 959 6362
Email: aameurope@aam.com
Web site: www.aam.com

ARRIVA BUS & COACH
Lodge Garage, Whitehall Road, Gomersal,
Cleckheaton, West Yorkshire, BD19 4BJ,
United Kingdom
Tel: +44 (0)1274 681 144
Email: busandcoachparts@arriva.co.uk
Web site: www.arrivabusandcoach.co.uk

ARVIN MERITOR
Park Lane, Great Alne, Alcester, Warwickshire,
B49 6HS, United Kingdom
Tel: +44 (0)1789 768 270
Web site: www.meritor.com

DIRECT PARTS LTD
Unit 1, Churnet Court,
Churnetside Business Park, Harrison Way,
Cheddleton, ST13 7EF, United Kingdom
Tel: +44 (0)1538 361 777
Fax: +44 (0)1538 369 100
Email: sales@direct-group.co.uk
Web site: www.direct-group.co.uk

HL SMITH TRANSMISSIONS LTD
Enterprise Business Park, Cross Road, Albrighton,
Wolverhampton, WV7 3BJ, United Kingdom
Tel: +44 (0)1902 373 011
Fax: +44 (0)1902 373 608
Web site: www.hlsmith.co.uk

KCP CAR & COMMERCIAL LTD
Unit 15, Hillside Road, Kempson Way,
Bury St Edmunds, Suffolk, IP32 7EA, UK
Tel: +44 (0)1284 750 777
Fax: +44 (0)1284 750 773
Email: kcponline@yahoo.co.uk
Web site: kcpcarandcommercial.co.uk

LH GROUP SERVICES LTD
Graycar Business Park, Barton Under Needwood,
Burton-On-Trent, DE13 8EN, United Kingdom
Tel: +44 (0)1283 722 600
Email: enquiries@lh-group.co.uk
Web site: www.lh-group.co.uk

MITCHELL POWERSYSTEMS
Mitchell Diesel Ltd, Fulwood Road South,
Sutton-In-Ashfield, Nottinghamshire, NG17 2JZ,
United Kingdom
Tel: +44 (0)1623 550 550
Fax: +44 (0)1623 443 041
Email: sales@mitchells.co.uk
Web site: www.mitchells.co.uk

NEXT BUS LTD
The Coach Yard, Vincients Road,
Bumpers Farm Industrial Estate, Chippenham,
Wiltshire, SN14 6QA, United Kingdom
Tel: +44 (0)1249 462 462
Fax: +44 (0)1249 448 844
Email: sales@next-bus.co.uk
Web site: www.next-bus.co.uk

OPTARE PARTS DIVISION
Hurricane Way South, Sherburn In Elmet, Leeds,
LS25 6PT, United Kingdom
Tel: +44 (0)871 230 1324
Email: parts@optare.com
Web site: www.optare.com

PARTLINE LTD
Dockfield Road, Shipley, BD17 7AZ,
United Kingdom
Tel: +44 (0)1274 531 531
Fax: +44 (0)1274 531 088
Email: sales@partline.co.uk
Web site: www.partline.co.uk

PLAXTON SERVICE
Ryton Road, Anston, Sheffield, S25 4DL,
United Kingdom
Tel: +44 (0)1909 551 155
Fax: +44 (0)1909 550 050
Email: service@plaxtonlimited.co.uk
Web site: www.plaxtonaftercare.co.uk

TTS UK
Total Tool Solutions Ltd, Newhaven Business Park,
Lowergate, Milnsbridge, Huddersfield, HD3 4HS,
United Kingdom
Tel: +44 (0)1484 642 211
Fax: +44 (0)1484 461 002
Email: sales@ttsuk.com
Web site: www.ttsuk.com

ZF POWERTRAIN
Stringes Close, Willenhall, WV13 1LE,
United Kingdom
Tel: +44 (0)1902 366 000
Email: sales@powertrain.co.uk
Web site: www.zfpowertrain.co.uk

ELECTRICAL EQUIPMENT

ARRIVA BUS & COACH
Lodge Garage, Whitehall Road, Gomersal,
Cleckheaton, West Yorkshire, BD19 4BJ,
United Kingdom
Tel: +44 (0)1274 681 144
Email: busandcoachparts@arriva.co.uk
Web site: www.arrivabusandcoach.co.uk

AUTOSOUND LTD
4 Lister Street, Dudley Hill, Bradford, BD4 9PQ,
United Kingdom
Tel: +44 (0)1274 688 990
Fax: +44 (0)1274 651 318
Web site: www.autosound.co.uk

AVT SYSTEMS LTD
Unit 3 & 4, Tything Road East, Alcester,
Warwickshire, B49 6ES, United Kingdom
Tel: +44 (0)1789 400 357
Fax: +44 (0)1789 400 359
Email: enquiries@avtsystems.co.uk
Web site: www.avtsystems.co.uk

BRADTECH LTD
Unit 3, Ladford Covert, Seighford, Stafford,
ST18 9QL, United Kingdom
Tel: +44 (0)1785 282 800
Fax: +44 (0)1785 282 558
Email: sales@bradtech.ltd.uk
Web site: www.bradtech.ltd.uk

BUS ELECTRICAL
United Kingdom
Tel: +44 (0)1254 701 242
Email: enquiries@buselectrical.com
Web site: www.buselectrical.com

CAREYBROOK LTD
PO Box 205, Southam, Warwickshire, CV47 0ZL,
United Kingdom
Contact: John Turner, Director
Tel: +44 (0)3333 446 900
Fax: +44 (0)3333 446 901
Email: info@careybrook.co.uk
Web site: www.careybrook.co.uk
Careybrook offers the full range of Calix engine
heaters together with battery chargers and
cabling.

CARLYLE BUS & COACH LTD
Carlyle Business Park, Great Bridge Street,
Swan Village, West Bromwich, B70 0X4,
United Kingdom
Tel: 0121 524 1200
Fax: 0121 524 1201
Email: westbromwichsales@carlyleplc.co.uk
Web site: www.carlylebusandcoach.com

PAUL CLARK SERVICES LTD
Unit 8, Kemrey Trade Centre, Aspen Close,
Swindon, Wiltshire, SN2 8AJ, United Kingdom

Tel: +44 (0)8456 060 474
Email: info@paulclarkservices.co.uk
Web site: www.paulclarkservices.co.uk

CRESCENT FACILITIES LTD
72 Willow Crescent, Chapeltown, Sheffield,
S35 1QS, United Kingdom
Tel: +44 (0)114 245 1050
Email: cfl.chris@btinternet.com

DIRECT PARTS LTD
Unit 1, Churnet Court,
Churnetside Business Park, Harrison Way,
Cheddleton, ST13 7EF, United Kingdom
Tel: +44 (0)1538 361 777
Fax: +44 (0)1538 369 100
Email: sales@direct-group.co.uk
Web site: www.direct-group.co.uk

EXPRESS COACH REPAIRS LTD
Outgang Lane, Pickering, YO18 7EL,
United Kingdom
Tel: +44 (0)1751 475 215
Email: expresscoachrepairs@hotmail.co.uk

INTELLITEC MV LTD
Unit 9, Woodway Court, Thursby Road,
Bromborough, Wirral, CH62 3PR,
United Kingdom
Tel: +44 (0)151 482 8971
Fax: +44 (0)151 482 8977
Email: ps@intellitecmv.com
Web site: www.intellitecmv.com

INVERTEC LTD
Whelford Road, Fairford, GL7 4DT,
United Kingdom
Tel: +44 (0)1285 713 550
Fax: +44 (0)1285 713 548
Email: info@invertec.co.uk
Web site: www.invertec.co.uk

KCP CAR & COMMERCIAL LTD
Unit 15, Hillside Road, Kempson Way,
Bury St Edmunds, Suffolk, IP32 7EA,
United Kingdom
Tel: +44 (0)1284 750 777
Fax: +44 (0)1284 750 773
Email: kcponline@yahoo.co.uk
Web site: kcpcarandcommercial.co.uk

LONDON BUS & TRUCK LTD
Units 1-4, Northfleet Industrial Estate,
Lower Road, Northfleet, Kent, DA11 9SN,
United Kingdom
Tel: +44 (0)1474 361 199
Email: enquiries@londonbusandtruck.co.uk
Web site: www.londonbusandtruck.co.uk

OPTARE PARTS DIVISION
Hurricane Way South, Sherburn In Elmet, Leeds,
LS25 6PT, United Kingdom
Tel: +44 (0)871 230 1324
Email: parts@optare.com
Web site: www.optare.com

PARTLINE LTD
Dockfield Road, Shipley, BD17 7AZ,
United Kingdom
Tel: +44 (0)1274 531 531
Fax: +44 (0)1274 531 088
Email: sales@partline.co.uk
Web site: www.partline.co.uk

PLAXTON PARTS
Ryton Road, Anston, Sheffield, S25 4DL,
United Kingdom
Tel: +44 (0)844 822 6224
Fax: +44 (0)1909 550 050
Email: parts@plaxtonlimited.co.uk
Web site: www.plaxtonaftercare.co.uk

PLAXTON SERVICE
Ryton Road, Anston, Sheffield, S25 4DL,
United Kingdom
Tel: +44 (0)1909 551 155
Fax: +44 (0)1909 550 050
Email: service@plaxtonlimited.co.uk
Web site: www.plaxtonaftercare.co.uk

PNEUMAX LTD
110 Vista Park, Mauretania Road, Nursling,
Southampton, SO16 0YS, United Kingdom
Tel: +44 (0)2380 740 412
Fax: +44 (0)2380 739 340
Email: sales@pneumax.co.uk
Web site: www.pneumax.co.uk

PREMIER COMPONENTS UK LTD
Unit 701, Long Marston Storage, Campden Road,
Long Marston, Stratford-upon-Avon,
Warwickshire, CV37 8QR, United Kingdom
Tel: +44 (0)1789 721 010
Fax: +44 (0)1789 722 429
Web site: www.premiercore.com

PRESTOLITE ELECTRIC
Unit 48, The Metropolitan Park, 12-
16 Bristol Road, Greenford, Middlesex, UB6 8UP,
United Kingdom
Contact: Steve Trulock
Tel: +44 (0)20 8231 1137
Fax: +44 (0)20 8575 9575
Email: eu_info@prestolite.com
Web site: www.prestolite.com
Alternators and starter motors

PSV TRANSPORT SYSTEMS LTD
21 Impresa Park, Pindar Road, Hoddesdon,
Hertfordshire, EN11 0DL, United Kingdom
Tel: +44 (0)1992 479 950
Fax: +44 (0)1992 471 676
Email: sales@psv-transport-systems.co.uk
Web site: www.psv-transport-systems.co.uk

ELECTRONIC CONTROL

ACTIA UK LTD
Unit 81, Mochdre Industrial Estate, Newtown,
SY16 4LE, United Kingdom
Tel: +44 (0)1686 611 150
Fax: +44 (0)1686 621 068
Email: mail@actia.co.uk
Web site: www.actia.co.uk

ARRIVA BUS & COACH
Lodge Garage, Whitehall Road, Gomersal,
Cleckheaton, West Yorkshire, BD19 4BJ,
United Kingdom
Tel: +44 (0)1274 681 144
Email: busandcoachparts@arriva.co.uk
Web site: www.arrivabusandcoach.co.uk

CRESCENT FACILITIES LTD
72 Willow Crescent, Chapeltown, Sheffield,
S35 1QS, United Kingdom

Tel: +44 (0)114 245 1050
Email: cfl.chris@btinternet.com

INTELLITEC MV LTD
Unit 9, Woodway Court, Thursby Road,
Bromborough, Wirral, CH62 3PR, UK
Tel: +44 (0)151 482 8971
Fax: +44 (0)151 482 8977
Email: ps@intellitecmv.com
Web site: www.intellitecmv.com

KCP CAR & COMMERCIAL LTD
Unit 15, Hillside Road, Kempson Way,
Bury St Edmunds, Suffolk, IP32 7EA,
United Kingdom
Tel: +44 (0)1284 750 777
Fax: +44 (0)1284 750 773
Email: kcponline@yahoo.co.uk
Web site: kcpcarandcommercial.co.uk

**KNORR-BREMSE SYSTEMS FOR
COMMERCIAL VEHICLES LTD**
Century House, Folly Brook Road,
Emerald Park East, Emersons Green, Bristol,
BS16 7FE, United Kingdom
Tel: +44 (0)117 984 6100
Email: uksales@knorr-bremse.co.uk
Web site: www.knorr-bremse.co.uk

OMNI-TECH ELECTRONICS
Unit 9, Prospect House, Ireland Industrial Estate,
Staveley, Chesterfield, Derbyshire, S43 3QE,
United Kingdom
Tel: +44 (0)1246 474 332
Fax: +44 (0)1246 529 010
Email: help@omni-techelectronics.co.uk
Web site: www.buselectronics.co.uk

OPTARE PARTS DIVISION
Hurricane Way South, Sherburn In Elmet, Leeds,
LS25 6PT, United Kingdom
Tel: +44 (0)871 230 1324
Email: parts@optare.com
Web site: www.optare.com

PLAXTON PARTS
Ryton Road, Anston, Sheffield, S25 4DL,
United Kingdom
Tel: +44 (0)844 822 6224
Fax: +44 (0)1909 550 050
Email: parts@plaxtonlimited.co.uk
Web site: www.plaxtonaftercare.co.uk

PLAXTON SERVICE
Ryton Road, Anston, Sheffield, S25 4DL,
United Kingdom
Tel: +44 (0)1909 551 155
Fax: +44 (0)1909 550 050
Email: service@plaxtonlimited.co.uk
Web site: www.plaxtonaftercare.co.uk

PSV TRANSPORT SYSTEMS LTD
21 Impresa Park, Pindar Road, Hoddesdon,
Hertfordshire, EN11 0DL, United Kingdom
Tel: +44 (0)1992 479 950
Fax: +44 (0)1992 471 676
Email: sales@psv-transport-systems.co.uk
Web site: www.psv-transport-systems.co.uk

WABCO AUTOMOTIVE UK LTD
Unit A1, Grange Valley Road, Batley,
West Yorkshire, WF17 6GH, United Kingdom
Tel: +44 (0)1924 595 400
Email: info.uk@wabco-auto.com
Web site: www.wabco-auto.com

EMISSION CONTROL DEVICES

ARRIVA BUS & COACH
Lodge Garage, Whitehall Road, Gomersal,
Cleckheaton, West Yorkshire, BD19 4BJ,
United Kingdom
Tel: +44 (0)1274 681 144
Email: busandcoachparts@arriva.co.uk
Web site: www.arrivabusandcoach.co.uk

CUMMINS UK
40-44 Rutherford Drive, Park Farm South,
Wellingborough, NN8 6AN, United Kingdom
Tel: +44 (0)1933 334 200
Fax: +44 (0)1933 334 198
Email: cduksales@cummins.com
Web site: www.cummins.com

DINEX EXHAUSTS LTD
14 Chesford Grange, Woolston, Warrington,
WA1 4RE, United Kingdom
Tel: +44 (0)1925 849 849
Fax: +44 (0)1925 849 850
Email: dinex@dinex.co.uk
Web site: www.dinex.dk

EMISSION CONTROL LTD
Global Works, 1/6 Crescent Mews, London,
N22 7GG, United Kingdom
Tel: +44 (0)208 888 4982
Fax: +44 (0)20 8881 1353
Email: info@emissioncontroluk.com
Web site: www.emissioncontroluk.com

GB FLEET MAINTENANCE
Geddings Road, Geddings Road, Hoddesdon,
Hertfordshire, EN11 0NT, United Kingdom
Tel: + 44 (0)1992 467 984
Email: sales@gbfleetmaintenance.co.uk
Web site: www.gbfleetmaintenance.co.uk

KCP CAR & COMMERCIAL LTD
Unit 15, Hillside Road, Kempson Way,
Bury St Edmunds, Suffolk, IP32 7EA,
United Kingdom
Tel: +44 (0)1284 750 777
Fax: +44 (0)1284 750 773
Email: kcponline@yahoo.co.uk
Web site: kcpcarandcommercial.co.uk

OPTARE PARTS DIVISION
Hurricane Way South, Sherburn In Elmet, Leeds,
LS25 6PT, United Kingdom
Tel: +44 (0)871 230 1324
Email: parts@optare.com
Web site: www.optare.com

PLAXTON SERVICE
Ryton Road, Anston, Sheffield, S25 4DL,
United Kingdom
Tel: +44 (0)1909 551 155
Fax: +44 (0)1909 550 050
Email: service@plaxtonlimited.co.uk
Web site: www.plaxtonaftercare.co.uk

ENGINE OIL DRAIN VALVES

ARRIVA BUS & COACH
Lodge Garage, Whitehall Road, Gomersal,
Cleckheaton, West Yorkshire, BD19 4BJ,
United Kingdom
Tel: +44 (0)1274 681 144
Email: busandcoachparts@arriva.co.uk
Web site: www.arrivabusandcoach.co.uk

**FUMOTO ENGINEERING OF
EUROPE LTD**
Normandy House, 35 Glategny Esplanade,
St Peter Port, Guernsey, GY1 2BP,
United Kingdom
Tel: +44 (0)1481 716 987
Fax: +44 (0)1481 700 374
Email: info@fumoto-valve.com
Web site: www.tankcontainers.co.uk

PARTLINE LTD
Dockfield Road, Shipley, BD17 7AZ,
United Kingdom
Tel: +44 (0)1274 531 531
Fax: +44 (0)1274 531 088
Email: sales@partline.co.uk
Web site: www.partline.co.uk

ENGINEERING

ARRIVA BUS & COACH
Lodge Garage, Whitehall Road, Gomersal,

Cleckheaton, West Yorkshire, BD19 4BJ,
United Kingdom
Tel: +44 (0)1274 681 144
Email: busandcoachparts@arriva.co.uk
Web site: www.arrivabusandcoach.co.uk

BRITCOM INTERNATIONAL LTD
York Road, Market Weighton, East Yorkshire,
YO43 3QX, United Kingdom
Tel: +44 (0)1430 871 010
Fax: +44 (0)1430 872 492
Email: sales@britcom.co.uk
Web site: www.britcom.co.uk

BULWARK BUS & COACH ENGINEERING LTD
Unit 5, Bulwark Business Park, Bulwark,
Chepstow, NP16 6QZ, United Kingdom
Tel: +44 (0)1291 622 326
Fax: +44 (0)1291 622 726
Email: bulwarkbusandcoach@tiscali.co.uk
Web site: www.bulwarkbusandcoach.co.uk

PAUL CLARK SERVICES LTD
Unit 8, Kemrey Trade Centre, Aspen Close,
Swindon, Wiltshire, SN2 8AJ, United Kingdom **Tel:**
+44 (0)8456 060 474
Email: info@paulclarkservices.co.uk
Web site: www.paulclarkservices.co.uk

COACH-AID LTD
Greyfriars Workshop, Greyfriars Way, Stafford,
Staffordshire, ST16 2SH, United Kingdom
Tel: +44 (0)1785 222 666
Email: workshop@coach-aid.com
Web site: www.coach-aid.com

CUMMINS UK
40-44 Rutherford Drive, Park Farm South,
Wellingborough, NN8 6AN, United Kingdom
Tel: +44 (0)1933 334 200
Fax: +44 (0)1933 334 198
Email: cduksales@cummins.com
Web site: www.cummins.com

DIRECT PARTS LTD
Unit 1, Churnet Court,
Churnetside Business Park, Harrison Way,
Cheddleton, ST13 7EF, United Kingdom
Tel: +44 (0)1538 361 777
Fax: +44 (0)1538 369 100
Email: sales@direct-group.co.uk
Web site: www.direct-group.co.uk

FREIGHT TRANSPORT ASSOCIATION
Hermes House, St John's Road, Tunbridge Wells,
TN9 9UZ, United Kingdom
Tel: +44 (0)1892 526 171
Fax: +44 (0)1892 534 989
Web site: www.fta.co.uk

THOMAS HARDIE COMMERCIALS LTD
Newstet Road, Knowsley Industrial Park,
Liverpool, L33 7TJ, United Kingdom

Tel: +44 (0)151 549 3000
Email: info@thardie.co.uk
Web site: www.thardie.co.uk

IMPERIAL ENGINEERING
Delamare Road, Cheshunt, Hertfordshire,
EN8 9UD, United Kingdom
Tel: +44 (0)1992 634 255
Fax: +44 (0)1992 630 506
Email: orders@imperialengineering.co.uk
Web site: www.imperialengineering.co.uk

KCP CAR & COMMERCIAL LTD
Unit 15, Hillside Road, Kempson Way,
Bury St Edmunds, Suffolk, IP32 7EA,
United Kingdom
Tel: +44 (0)1284 750 777
Fax: +44 (0)1284 750 773
Email: kcponline@yahoo.co.uk
Web site: kcpcarandcommercial.co.uk

LH GROUP SERVICES LTD
Graycar Business Park, Barton Under Needwood,
Burton-On-Trent, DE13 8EN, United Kingdom
Tel: +44 (0)1283 722 600
Email: enquiries@lh-group.co.uk
Web site: www.lh-group.co.uk

LONDON BUS & TRUCK LTD
Units 1-4, Northfleet Industrial Estate,
Lower Road, Northfleet, Kent, DA11 9SN,
United Kingdom
Tel: +44 (0)1474 361 199
Email: enquiries@londonbusandtruck.co.uk
Web site: www.londonbusandtruck.co.uk

MARSHALLS COACHES LLP
Firbank Way, Leighton Buzzard, Bedfordshire,
LU7 3YP, United Kingdom
Tel: +44 (0)1525 376 077
Email: info@marshalls-coaches.co.uk
Web site: www.marshalls-coaches.co.uk

MAS SPECIAL ENGINEERING LTD
Houghton Road, North Anston, S25 4JJ,
United Kingdom
Tel: +44 (0)1909 550 480
Fax: +44 (0)1909 550 486

MITCHELL POWERSYSTEMS
Mitchell Diesel Ltd, Fulwood Road South,
Sutton-In-Ashfield, Nottinghamshire, NG17 2JZ,
United Kingdom
Tel: +44 (0)1623 550 550
Fax: +44 (0)1623 443 041
Email: sales@mitchells.co.uk
Web site: www.mitchells.co.uk

OPTARE PARTS DIVISION
Hurricane Way South, Sherburn In Elmet, Leeds,
LS25 6PT, United Kingdom
Tel: +44 (0)871 230 1324
Email: parts@optare.com
Web site: www.optare.com

OPTARE PRODUCT SUPPORT
London
Unit 9, Eurocourt, Olivers Close, West Thurrock,
RM20 3EE, United Kingdom
Tel: +44 (0)1708 896 860
Fax: +44 (0)1708 869 920
Email: london.service@optare.com
Manchester
Trafford Park, Manchester, M17 1HG,
United Kingdom
Tel: +44 (0)161 872 7772
Email: manchester.service@optare.com
Rotherham
Denby Way, Hellaby, Rotherham, S66 8HR,
United Kingdom
Tel: +44 (0)1709 535 101
Fax: +44 (0)1709 739 680
Email: rotherham.service@optare.com

PLAXTON SERVICE
Ryton Road, Anston, Sheffield, S25 4DL,
United Kingdom
Tel: +44 (0)1909 551 155
Fax: +44 (0)1909 550 050
Email: service@plaxtonlimited.co.uk
Web site: www.plaxtonaftercare.co.uk

PNEUMAX LTD
110 Vista Park, Mauretania Road, Nursling,
Southampton, SO16 0YS, United Kingdom
Tel: +44 (0)2380 740 412
Fax: +44 (0)2380 739 340
Email: sales@pneumax.co.uk
Web site: www.pneumax.co.uk

QUEENSBRIDGE (PSV) LTD
Milner Way, Longlands Industrial Estate, Ossett,
WF5 9JE, United Kingdom
Tel: +44 (0)1924 281 871
Fax: +44 (0)1924 281 807
Email: enquiries@queensbridgeltd.co.uk
Web site: www.queensbridgeltd.co.uk

RSH SERVICES
Southedge Works, Hipperholme, Halifax, HX3 8EF,
United Kingdom
Tel: +44 (0)1422 202 840
Fax: +44 (0)1422 206 070

TDI (EUROPE) LTD
Clifford Mill, Clifford Chambers,
Stratford Upon Avon, CV37 8HW,
United Kingdom
Tel: +44 (0)1789 205 011
Email: martin.p@tdi.uk.com
Web site: www.tdi.uk.com

TTS UK
Total Tool Solutions Ltd, Newhaven Business Park,
Lowergate, Milnsbridge, Huddersfield, HD3 4HS,
United Kingdom
Tel: +44 (0)1484 642 211
Fax: +44 (0)1484 461 002
Email: sales@ttsuk.com
Web site: www.ttsuk.com

ENGINES

ARRIVA BUS & COACH
Lodge Garage, Whitehall Road, Gomersal,
Cleckheaton, West Yorkshire, BD19 4BJ,
United Kingdom
Tel: +44 (0)1274 681 144
Email: busandcoachparts@arriva.co.uk
Web site: www.arrivabusandcoach.co.uk

PAUL CLARK SERVICES LTD
Unit 8, Kemrey Trade Centre, Aspen Close,
Swindon, Wiltshire, SN2 8AJ, United Kingdom
Tel: +44 (0)8456 060 474
Email: info@paulclarkservices.co.uk
Web site: www.paulclarkservices.co.uk

CREWE ENGINES
Warmingham Road, Crewe, CW1 4PQ,
United Kingdom
Tel: +44 (0)1270 526 333

Fax: +44 (0)1270 526 433
Email: sales@creweengines.co.uk
Web site: www.creweengines.co.uk

CUMMINS UK
40-44 Rutherford Drive, Park Farm South,
Wellingborough, NN8 6AN, United Kingdom
Tel: +44 (0)1933 334 200
Fax: +44 (0)1933 334 198
Email: cduksales@cummins.com
Web site: www.cummins.com

FUEL THEFT SOLUTIONS LTD
Unit 1, Yew Tree Business Units, Newcastle Road,
Betchton, Sandbach, Cheshire, CW11 4TD,
United Kingdom
Tel: 0845 077 3921
Fax: 0845 077 3922
Email: sales@dieseldye.com
Web site: www.dieseldye.com

IMEXPART LTD
Links 31, Willowbridge Way, Whitwood,
Castleford, WF10 5NP, United Kingdom
Tel: +44 (0)1977 553 936
Email: sales@imexpart.com
Web site: www.imexpart.com

IVECO
Iveco Ford Truck Ltd, Iveco Ford House,
Station Road, Watford, WD1 1SR,
United Kingdom
Tel: +44 (0)1923 246 400
Fax: +44 (0)1923 240 574

KCP CAR & COMMERCIAL LTD
Unit 15, Hillside Road, Kempson Way,
Bury St Edmunds, Suffolk, IP32 7EA,
United Kingdom
Tel: +44 (0)1284 750 777
Fax: +44 (0)1284 750 773
Email: kcponline@yahoo.co.uk
Web site: kcpcarandcommercial.co.uk

LAWMAN COMMERCIAL SERVICES LTD
31 Merrylees Industrial Estate, Leeside, Desford,
Leicestershire, LE9 9FS, United Kingdom
Tel: +44 (0)1530 231 235
Email: sales@lawmancommercials.com
Web site: www.lawmancommercials.net

LH GROUP SERVICES LTD
Graycar Business Park, Barton Under Needwood,
Burton-On-Trent, DE13 8EN, United Kingdom
Tel: +44 (0)1283 722 600
Email: enquiries@lh-group.co.uk
Web site: www.lh-group.co.uk

MAN TRUCK & BUS UK LTD
Frankland Road, Blagrove, Swindon, Wiltshire,
SN5 8YU, United Kingdom
Tel: +44 (0)1793 448 000
Email: bus.sales@man.co.uk
Web site: www.manbusandcoach.co.uk

MITCHELL POWERSYSTEMS
Mitchell Diesel Ltd, Fulwood Road South,
Sutton-In-Ashfield, Nottinghamshire, NG17 2JZ,
United Kingdom
Tel: +44 (0)1623 550 550
Fax: +44 (0)1623 443 041
Email: sales@mitchells.co.uk
Web site: www.mitchells.co.uk

NEXT BUS LTD
The Coach Yard, Vincients Road,
Bumpers Farm Industrial Estate, Chippenham,
Wiltshire, SN14 6QA, United Kingdom
Tel: +44 (0)1249 462 462
Fax: +44 (0)1249 448 844
Email: sales@next-bus.co.uk
Web site: www.next-bus.co.uk

OMNI-TECH ELECTRONICS
Unit 9, Prospect House, Ireland Industrial Estate,
Staveley, Chesterfield, Derbyshire, S43 3QE, UK
Tel: +44 (0)1246 474 332
Fax: +44 (0)1246 529 010
Email: help@omni-techelectronics.co.uk
Web site: www.buselectronics.co.uk

OPTARE PARTS DIVISION
Hurricane Way South, Sherburn In Elmet, Leeds,
LS25 6PT, United Kingdom
Tel: +44 (0)871 230 1324
Email: parts@optare.com
Web site: www.optare.com

OPTARE PRODUCT SUPPORT
London
Unit 9, Eurocourt, Olivers Close, West Thurrock,
RM20 3EE, United Kingdom
Tel: +44 (0)1708 896 860
Fax: +44 (0)1708 869 920
Email: london.service@optare.com
Manchester
Trafford Park, Manchester, M17 1HG,
United Kingdom
Tel: +44 (0)161 872 7772
Email: manchester.service@optare.com
Rotherham
Denby Way, Hellaby, Rotherham, S66 8HR,
United Kingdom
Tel: +44 (0)1709 535 101
Fax: +44 (0)1709 739 680
Email: rotherham.service@optare.com

PARTLINE LTD
Dockfield Road, Shipley, BD17 7AZ, UK
Tel: +44 (0)1274 531 531
Fax: +44 (0)1274 531 088
Email: sales@partline.co.uk
Web site: www.partline.co.uk

PERKINS GROUP LTD
Frank Perkins Way, Peterborough, PE1 5FQ, UK
Tel: +44 (0)1733 583 000
Fax: +44 (0)1733 582 240
Web site: www.perkins.com

PREMIER COMPONENTS UK LTD
Unit 701, Long Marston Storage, Campden Road,
Long Marston, Stratford-upon-Avon,
Warwickshire, CV37 8QR, United Kingdom
Tel: +44 (0)1789 721 010
Fax: +44 (0)1789 722 129
Web site: www.premiercore.com

QUEENSBRIDGE (PSV) LTD
Milner Way, Longlands Industrial Estate, Ossett,
WF5 9JE, United Kingdom
Tel: +44 (0)1924 281 871
Fax: +44 (0)1924 281 807
Email: enquiries@queensbridgeltd.co.uk
Web site: www.queensbridgeltd.co.uk

SHAWSON SUPPLY LTD
12 Station Road, Saintfield, County Down,
BT24 7DU, Northern Ireland
Tel: +44 (0)28 9751 0994
Email: info@shawsonsupply.co.uk
Web site: www.shawsonsupply.co.uk

CRAIG TILSLEY & SON LTD
Moorfield Industrial Estate, Cotes Heath,
Stoke On Trent, ST21 6QY, United Kingdom
Tel: +44 (0)1782 791 524
Fax: +44 (0)1782 791 316
Email: info@craigtilsley.co.uk
Web site: www.craigtilsley.co.uk

TTS UK
Total Tool Solutions Ltd, Newhaven Business Park,
Lowergate, Milnsbridge, Huddersfield, HD3 4HS,
United Kingdom
Tel: +44 (0)1484 642 211
Fax: +44 (0)1484 461 002
Email: sales@ttsuk.com
Web site: www.ttsuk.com

WALSH'S ENGINEERING LTD
Barton Moss Road, Eccles, Manchester, M30 7RL,
United Kingdom
Tel: +44 (0)161 787 7017
Fax: +44 (0)161 787 7038
Email: walshs@gardnerdiesel.co.uk
Web site: www.gardnerdiesel.co.uk

EXHAUST SYSTEMS

ARRIVA BUS & COACH
Lodge Garage, Whitehall Road, Gomersal,
Cleckheaton, West Yorkshire, BD19 4BJ,
United Kingdom
Tel: +44 (0)1274 681 144
Email: busandcoachparts@arriva.co.uk
Web site: www.arrivabusandcoach.co.uk

ARVIN MERITOR
Park Lane, Great Alne, Alcester, Warwickshire,
B49 6HS, United Kingdom
Tel: +44 (0)1789 768 270
Web site: www.meritor.com

CARLYLE BUS & COACH LTD
Carlyle Business Park, Great Bridge Street,
Swan Village, West Bromwich, B70 0X4,
United Kingdom
Tel: 0121 524 1200
Fax: 0121 524 1201
Email: westbromwichsales@carlyleplc.co.uk
Web site: www.carlylebusandcoach.com

CRESCENT FACILITIES LTD
72 Willow Crescent, Chapeltown, Sheffield,
S35 1QS, United Kingdom
Tel: +44 (0)114 245 1050
Email: cfl.chris@btinternet.com

DINEX EXHAUSTS LTD
14 Chesford Grange, Woolston, Warrington,
WA1 4RE, United Kingdom
Tel: +44 (0)1925 849 849
Fax: +44 (0)1925 849 850
Email: dinex@dinex.co.uk
Web site: www.dinex.dk

EMINOX LTD
Miller Road, Corringham Road Industrial Estate,
Gainsborough, DN21 1QB, United Kingdom
Tel: +44 (0)1427 810 088
Fax: +44 (0)1427 810 061
Email: enquiries@eminox.com
Web site: www.eminox.com

GB FLEET MAINTENANCE
Geddings Road, Geddings Road, Hoddesdon,
Hertfordshire, EN11 0NT, United Kingdom
Tel: + 44 (0)1992 467 984
Email: sales@gbfleetmaintenance.co.uk
Web site: www.gbfleetmaintenance.co.uk

GREEN URBAN TECHNOLOGIES
North Lakes Business Park, Skiddaw Workshops,
Flusco, Penrith, Cumbria, CA11 0JG,
United Kingdom
Tel: +44 (0)1768 480 111
Email: info@greenurban.co.uk
Web site: www.greenurban.co.uk

IMEXPART LTD
Links 31, Willowbridge Way, Whitwood,
Castleford, WF10 5NP, United Kingdom
Tel: +44 (0)1977 553 936
Email: sales@imexpart.com
Web site: www.imexpart.com

KCP CAR & COMMERCIAL LTD
Unit 15, Hillside Road, Kempson Way,
Bury St Edmunds, Suffolk, IP32 7EA,
United Kingdom
Tel: +44 (0)1284 750 777
Fax: +44 (0)1284 750 773
Email: kcponline@yahoo.co.uk
Web site: kcpcarandcommercial.co.uk

OPTARE PARTS DIVISION
Hurricane Way South, Sherburn In Elmet, Leeds,
LS25 6PT, United Kingdom
Tel: +44 (0)871 230 1324
Email: parts@optare.com
Web site: www.optare.com

OPTARE PRODUCT SUPPORT
London
Unit 9, Eurocourt, Olivers Close, West Thurrock,
RM20 3EE, United Kingdom
Tel: +44 (0)1708 896 860
Fax: +44 (0)1708 869 920
Email: london.service@optare.com
Manchester
Trafford Park, Manchester, M17 1HG,
United Kingdom
Tel: +44 (0)161 872 7772
Email: manchester.service@optare.com
Rotherham
Denby Way, Hellaby, Rotherham, S66 8HR,
United Kingdom
Tel: +44 (0)1709 535 101
Fax: +44 (0)1709 739 680
Email: rotherham.service@optare.com

PARTLINE LTD
Dockfield Road, Shipley, BD17 7AZ,
United Kingdom
Tel: +44 (0)1274 531 531
Fax: +44 (0)1274 531 088
Email: sales@partline.co.uk
Web site: www.partline.co.uk

TTS UK
Total Tool Solutions Ltd, Newhaven Business Park,
Lowergate, Milnsbridge, Huddersfield, HD3 4HS,
United Kingdom
Tel: +44 (0)1484 642 211
Fax: +44 (0)1484 461 002
Email: sales@ttsuk.com
Web site: www.ttsuk.com

FANS AND DRIVE BELTS

ARRIVA BUS & COACH
Lodge Garage, Whitehall Road, Gomersal,
Cleckheaton, West Yorkshire, BD19 4BJ, UK
Tel: +44 (0)1274 681 144
Email: busandcoachparts@arriva.co.uk
Web site: www.arrivabusandcoach.co.uk

BRT BEARINGS LTD
21-24 Regal Road, Wisbech, Cambridgeshire,
PE13 2RQ, United Kingdom
Tel: +44 (0)1945 464 097
Fax: +44 (0)1945 464 523
Email: brt.sales@brt-bearings.com
Web site: www.brt-bearings.com

CARLYLE BUS & COACH LTD
Carlyle Business Park, Great Bridge Street,
Swan Village, West Bromwich, B70 0X4,
United Kingdom
Tel: 0121 524 1200
Fax: 0121 524 1201
Email: westbromwichsales@carlyleplc.co.uk
Web site: www.carlylebusandcoach.com

CLAYTON HEATERS LTD
Fletchworth Gate Industrial Estate, Coventry,
West Midlands, CV5 6SP, United Kingdom
Tel: +44 (0)2476 691 916
Email: admin@claytoncc.co.uk
Web site: www.claytoncc.co.uk

CRESCENT FACILITIES LTD
72 Willow Crescent, Chapeltown, Sheffield,
S35 1QS, United Kingdom
Tel: +44 (0)114 245 1050
Email: cfl.chris@btinternet.com

CUMMINS UK
40-44 Rutherford Drive, Park Farm South,
Wellingborough, NN8 6AN, United Kingdom
Tel: +44 (0)1933 334 200
Fax: +44 (0)1933 334 198

Email: cduksales@cummins.com
Web site: www.cummins.com

DIRECT PARTS LTD
Unit 1, Churnet Court,
Churnetside Business Park, Harrison Way,
Cheddleton, ST13 7EF, United Kingdom
Tel: +44 (0)1538 361 777
Fax: +44 (0)1538 369 100
Email: sales@direct-group.co.uk
Web site: www.direct-group.co.uk

GRAYSON THERMAL SYSTEMS
Wharfdale House, 257 Wharfdale Road, Tyseley,
Birmingham, B11 2DP, United Kingdom
Tel: +44 (0)121 700 5600
Fax: +44 (0)121 700 5601
Email: cs@graysonts.com
Web site: www.graysonts.com

KCP CAR & COMMERCIAL LTD
Unit 15, Hillside Road, Kempson Way,
Bury St Edmunds, Suffolk, IP32 7EA,
United Kingdom
Tel: +44 (0)1284 750 777
Fax: +44 (0)1284 750 773
Email: kcponline@yahoo.co.uk
Web site: www.kcpcarandcommercial.co.uk

OPTARE PARTS DIVISION
Hurricane Way South, Sherburn In Elmet, Leeds,
LS25 6PT, United Kingdom
Tel: +44 (0)871 230 1324
Email: parts@optare.com
Web site: www.optare.com

PACET MANUFACTURING LTD
Wyebridge House, Cores End Road, Bourne End,
Buckinghamshire, SL8 5HH, United Kingdom
Tel: +44 (0)1628 526 754
Fax: +44 (0)1628 810 080
Email: sales@pacet.co.uk
Web site: www.pacet.co.uk

PARTLINE LTD
Dockfield Road, Shipley, BD17 7AZ,
United Kingdom
Tel: +44 (0)1274 531 531
Fax: +44 (0)1274 531 088
Email: sales@partline.co.uk
Web site: www.partline.co.uk

QUEENSBRIDGE (PSV) LTD
Milner Way, Longlands Industrial Estate, Ossett,
WF5 9JE, United Kingdom
Tel: +44 (0)1924 281 871
Fax: +44 (0)1924 281 807
Email: enquiries@queensbridgeltd.co.uk
Web site: www.queensbridgeltd.co.uk

FARE BOXES

**CUBIC TRANSPORTATION SYSTEMS
LTD**
AFC House, Honeycrock Lane, Salfords, Redhill,
RH1 5LA, United Kingdom
Tel: +44 (0)1737 782 200
Web site: www.cubic.com

ETMSS LTD
Ground Floor Austin House, 43 Poole Road,
Westbourne, Bournemouth, Dorset, BH4 9DN,
United Kingdom
Contact: David Price, Sales Director
Tel: +44 (0)844 800 9299
Email: info@etmss.com
Web site: www.etmss.com
Vaults, cash scoops & trays, ticket bins, ticket roll
holders, hand-held ticket punches, coin dispensers.

JOHN GROVES TICKET SYSTEMS
Unit 10, North Circular Business Centre,
400 NCR, London, NW10 0JG, United Kingdom
Tel: +44(0)208 452 6512
Fax: 020 8830 1223
Email: sales@jgts.co.uk
Web site: www.jgts.co.uk

MARK TERRILL TICKET MACHINERY
5 De Grey Close, Lewes, BN7 2JR,
United Kingdom
Tel: +44 (0)1273 474816
Email: mark.terrill2010@gmail.com

TICKETER
Chilton House, Charnham Lane, Hungerford,
Berkshire, RG10 0EY, United Kingdom
Tel: +44 (0)20 3195 8800
Email: support@ticketer.co.uk
Web site: www.ticketer.org.uk

FIRE EXTINGUISHERS

ARRIVA BUS & COACH
Lodge Garage, Whitehall Road, Gomersal,
Cleckheaton, West Yorkshire, BD19 4BJ,
United Kingdom
Tel: +44 (0)1274 681 144
Email: busandcoachparts@arriva.co.uk
Web site: www.arrivabusandcoach.co.uk

CARLYLE BUS & COACH LTD
Carlyle Business Park, Great Bridge Street,
Swan Village, West Bromwich, B70 0X4,
United Kingdom
Tel: 0121 524 1200
Fax: 0121 524 1201
Email: westbromwichsales@carlyleplc.co.uk
Web site: www.carlylebusandcoach.com

CLAYTON HEATERS LTD
Fletchworth Gate Industrial Estate, Coventry,
West Midlands, CV5 6SP, United Kingdom
Tel: +44 (0)2476 691 916
Email: admin@claytoncc.co.uk
Web site: www.claytoncc.co.uk

EXPRESS COACH REPAIRS LTD
Outgang Lane, Pickering, YO18 7EL,
United Kingdom
Tel: +44 (0)1751 475 215
Email: expresscoachrepairs@hotmail.co.uk

HAPPICH UK LTD
Unit 26, Webb Ellis Industrial Estate, Wood Street,
Rugby, Warwickshire, CV21 2NP,
United Kingdom
Tel: +44 (0)1788 50703
Fax: +44 (0)1788 44972
Email: info@happich.co.uk
Web site: www.happich.de

KCP CAR & COMMERCIAL LTD
Unit 15, Hillside Road, Kempson Way,
Bury St Edmunds, Suffolk, IP32 7EA,
United Kingdom
Tel: +44 (0)1284 750 777
Fax: +44 (0)1284 750 773
Email: kcponline@yahoo.co.uk
Web site: www.kcpcarandcommercial.co.uk

LAWTON SERVICES LTD
Knutsford Road, Church Lawton,
Stoke-On-Trent, ST7 3DN, United Kingdom
Tel: +44 (0)1270 882 056
Fax: +44 (0)1270 883 014
Email: info@lawtonservices.co.uk
Web site: www.lawtonservices.co.uk

PARTLINE LTD
Dockfield Road, Shipley, BD17 7AZ,
United Kingdom
Tel: +44 (0)1274 531 531
Fax: +44 (0)1274 531 088
Email: sales@partline.co.uk
Web site: www.partline.co.uk

PLAXTON PARTS
Ryton Road, Anston, Sheffield, S25 4DL,
United Kingdom
Tel: +44 (0)844 822 6224
Fax: +44 (0)1909 550 050
Email: parts@plaxtonlimited.co.uk
Web site: www.plaxtonaftercare.co.uk

PSV PRODUCTS
60 The Old Quays, Warrington, Cheshire,
WA4 1JP, United Kingdom
Tel: +44 (0)1925 210 220
Email: info@psvproducts.com
Web site: www.psvproducts.com

FIRST AID EQUIPMENT

ARRIVA BUS & COACH
Lodge Garage, Whitehall Road, Gomersal,
Cleckheaton, West Yorkshire, BD19 4BJ,
United Kingdom
Tel: +44 (0)1274 681 144
Email: busandcoachparts@arriva.co.uk
Web site: www.arrivabusandcoach.co.uk

BRADTECH LTD
Unit 3, Ladford Covert, Seighford, Stafford,
ST18 9QL, United Kingdom
Tel: +44 (0)1785 282 800
Fax: +44 (0)1785 282 558
Email: sales@bradtech.ltd.uk
Web site: www.bradtech.ltd.uk

CARLYLE BUS & COACH LTD
Carlyle Business Park, Great Bridge Street,
Swan Village, West Bromwich, B70 0X4,
United Kingdom
Tel: 0121 524 1200
Fax: 0121 524 1201
Email: westbromwichsales@carlyleplc.co.uk
Web site: www.carlylebusandcoach.com

EXPRESS COACH REPAIRS LTD
Outgang Lane, Pickering, YO18 7EL,
United Kingdom
Tel: +44 (0)1751 475 215
Email: expresscoachrepairs@hotmail.co.uk

HAPPICH UK LTD
Unit 26, Webb Ellis Industrial Estate, Wood Street,
Rugby, Warwickshire, CV21 2NP, United Kingdom
Tel: +44 (0)1788 50703
Fax: +44 (0)1788 44972
Email: info@happich.co.uk
Web site: www.happich.de

KCP CAR & COMMERCIAL LTD
Unit 15, Hillside Road, Kempson Way,
Bury St Edmunds, Suffolk, IP32 7EA,
United Kingdom
Tel: +44 (0)1284 750 777
Fax: +44 (0)1284 750 773
Email: kcponline@yahoo.co.uk
Web site: kcpcarandcommercial.co.uk

LAWTON SERVICES LTD
Knutsford Road, Church Lawton, Stoke-On-Trent,
ST7 3DN, United Kingdom
Tel: +44 (0)1270 882 056
Fax: +44 (0)1270 883 014
Email: info@lawtonservices.co.uk
Web site: www.lawtonservices.co.uk

PARMA INDUSTRIES
34-36 Carlton Park Industrial Estate,
Saxmundham, Suffolk, IP17 2NL, United Kingdom
Tel: +44 (0)1728 745 700
Fax: +44 (0)1728 745 718
Email: sales@parmagroup.co.uk
Web site: www.parmagroup.co.uk

PARTLINE LTD
Dockfield Road, Shipley, BD17 7AZ, UK
Tel: +44 (0)1274 531 531
Fax: +44 (0)1274 531 088
Email: sales@partline.co.uk
Web site: www.partline.co.uk

PLAXTON PARTS
Ryton Road, Anston, Sheffield, S25 4DL,
United Kingdom
Tel: +44 (0)844 822 6224
Fax: +44 (0)1909 550 050
Email: parts@plaxtonlimited.co.uk
Web site: www.plaxtonaftercare.co.uk

PSV PRODUCTS
60 The Old Quays, Warrington, Cheshire,
WA4 1JP, United Kingdom
Tel: +44 (0)1925 210 220
Email: info@psvproducts.com
Web site: www.psvproducts.com

FLOOR COVERINGS

AK CARPETS LTD
Unit 4, Robinson Court, Brockholes Way,
Claughton on Brock, Lancashire, PR 0PZ,
United Kingdom
Tel: +44 (0)1995 643 033
Fax: +44 (0)1995 643 231
Email: info@akcarpets.com
Web site: www.akcarpets.com

ALTRO TRANSFLOR
Works Road, Letchworth Garden City, SG6 1NW,
United Kingdom
Tel: +44 (0)1462 480 480
Fax: +44 (0)1462 480 010
Email: enquiries@altro.com
Web site: www.altro.co.uk

ARRIVA BUS & COACH
Lodge Garage, Whitehall Road, Gomersal,
Cleckheaton, West Yorkshire, BD19 4BJ,
United Kingdom
Tel: +44 (0)1274 681 144
Email: busandcoachparts@arriva.co.uk
Web site: www.arrivabusandcoach.co.uk

AUTOMATE WHEEL COVERS LTD
California Mills, Oxford Road, Gomersal,
Cleckheaton, BD19 4HQ, United Kingdom
Tel: +44 (0)1274 862 700
Fax: +44 (0)1274 851 989
Email: sales@wheeltrimshop.com
Web site: www.wheeltrimshop.com

AUTOMOTIVE TEXTILE INDUSTRIES
Unit 15 & 16, Priest Court,
Springfield Business Park, Grantham, NG31 7BG,
United Kingdom
Tel: +44 (0)1476 593 050
Fax: +44 (0)1476 593 607
Email: sales@atindustries.co.uk
Web site: www.atindustries.co.uk

CARLYLE BUS & COACH LTD
Carlyle Business Park, Great Bridge Street,
Swan Village, West Bromwich, B70 0X4,
United Kingdom
Tel: 0121 524 1200
Fax: 0121 524 1201
Email: westbromwichsales@carlyleplc.co.uk
Web site: www.carlylebusandcoach.com

DUOFLEX LTD
Trimmingham House, 2 Shires Road,
Buckingham Road Industrial Estate, Brackley,
Northamptonshire, NN13 7EZ, United Kingdom
Tel: +44 (0)1280 701 366
Fax: +44 (0)1280 704 799
Email: info@duoflex.co.uk
Web site: www.duoflex.co.uk

EXPRESS COACH REPAIRS LTD
Outgang Lane, Pickering, YO18 7EL,
United Kingdom
Tel: +44 (0)1751 475 215
Email: expresscoachrepairs@hotmail.co.uk

LAWTON SERVICES LTD
Knutsford Road, Church Lawton, Stoke-On-Trent,
ST7 3DN, United Kingdom
Tel: +44 (0)1270 882 056
Fax: +44 (0)1270 883 014
Email: info@lawtonservices.co.uk
Web site: www.lawtonservices.co.uk

MARTYN INDUSTRIALS LTD
5 Brunel Way, Durranhill Industrial Park, Harraby,
Carlisle, CA1 3NQ, United Kingdom
Tel: +44 (0)1228 544 000
Email: enquiries@martyn-industrials.co.uk
Web site: www.martyn-industrials.com

PLAXTON PARTS
Ryton Road, Anston, Sheffield, S25 4DL,
United Kingdom
Tel: +44 (0)844 822 6224
Fax: +44 (0)1909 550 050
Email: parts@plaxtonlimited.co.uk
Web site: www.plaxtonaftercare.co.uk

SAFETYTREAD
Bell Plastics Ltd
450 Blandford Road, Poole, Dorset, BH16 5BN,
United Kingdom
Tel: +44 (0)1202 625 596
Fax: +44 (0)1202 625 597
Email: safetytread@bellplastics.co.uk
Web site: www.safety-tread.co.uk

TIFLEX LTD
Tiflex House, Liskeard, Cornwall, PL14 4NB,
United Kingdom
Tel: +44 (0)1579 320 808
Fax: +44 (0)1579 320 802
Web site: www.tiflex.co.uk

FUEL MANAGEMENT AND LUBRICANTS

ALP TANK CONTAINERS
Normandy House, Glategny Esplanade,
St Peter Port, Guernsey, GY 2BP, United Kingdom
Tel: +44 (0)20 7352 2727
Fax: +44 (0)20 7352 3990
Email: info@tankcontainers.co.uk
Web site: www.tankcontainers.co.uk

ARRIVA BUS & COACH
Lodge Garage, Whitehall Road, Gomersal,
Cleckheaton, West Yorkshire, BD19 4BJ,
United Kingdom
Tel: +44 (0)1274 681 144
Email: busandcoachparts@arriva.co.uk
Web site: www.arrivabusandcoach.co.uk

TERENCE BARKER TANKS
Phoenix Road, Haverhill, Suffolk, CB9 7EA,
United Kingdom
Tel: +44 (0)1440 712 905
Fax: +44 (0)1440 715 460
Email: sales@tbtanks.co.uk
Web site: www.terencebarkertanks.co.uk

CUMMINS UK
40-44 Rutherford Drive, Park Farm South,
Wellingborough, NN8 6AN, United Kingdom
Tel: +44 (0)1933 334 200
Fax: +44 (0)1933 334 198
Email: cduksales@cummins.com
Web site: www.cummins.com

ENERGENICS EUROPE LTD
5 Begbroke Science Park, Begbroke Hill,
Woodstock Road, Begbroke, Oxfordshire,
OX5 1PF, United Kingdom
Tel: +44 (0)1865 233 010
Fax: +44 (0)1865 233 024
Email: info@energenics.co.uk
Web site: www.energenics.co.uk

FUEL THEFT SOLUTIONS LTD
Unit 1, Yew Tree Business Units, Newcastle Road,
Betchton, Sandbach, Cheshire, CW11 4TD,
United Kingdom
Tel: 0845 077 3921
Fax: 0845 077 3922
Email: sales@dieseldye.com
Web site: www.dieseldye.com

INTERLUBE SYSTEMS LTD
St Modwen Road, Parkway Industrial Estate,
Plymouth, PL6 8LH, United Kingdom
Tel: +44 (0)1752 676 000
Fax: +44 (0)1752 676 001
Email: info@interlubesystems.co.uk
Web site: www.interlubesystems.co.uk

J MURDOCH WIGHT LTD
Systems House, Pentland Industrial Estate,
Loanhead, Midlothian, EH20 9QH,
United Kingdom
Tel: +44 (0)131 440 3633
Email: enquiries@jmw-systems.co.uk
Web site: www.jmw-systems.co.uk

KCP CAR & COMMERCIAL LTD
Unit 15, Hillside Road, Kempson Way,
Bury St Edmunds, Suffolk, IP32 7EA,
United Kingdom
Tel: +44 (0)1284 750 777
Fax: +44 (0)1284 750 773
Email: kcponline@yahoo.co.uk
Web site: kcpcarandcommercial.co.uk

TOKHEIM UK LTD
Unit 1, Baker Road,
West Pitkerro Industrial Estate, Dundee,
DD5 3RT, United Kingdom
Tel: +44 (0)1382 483 500
Fax: +44 (0)1382 731 835
Web site: www.tokheim.com

TRISCAN SYSTEMS LTD
4 Petre Court, Petre Road, Accrington, Lancashire,
BB5 5HY, United Kingdom
Tel: +44 (0)845 225 3100
Email: info@triscansystems.com
Web site: www.triscansystems.com

GARAGE EQUIPMENT

ARRIVA BUS & COACH
Lodge Garage, Whitehall Road, Gomersal,
Cleckheaton, West Yorkshire, BD19 4BJ,
United Kingdom
Tel: +44 (0)1274 681 144
Email: busandcoachparts@arriva.co.uk
Web site: www.arrivabusandcoach.co.uk

BUTTS OF BAWTRY GARAGE EQUIPMENT
Station Yard, Station Road, Bawtry, Doncaster,
DN10 6QD, United Kingdom
Tel: +44 (0)1302 710 868
Fax: +44 (0)1302 719 481
Email: info@buttsequipment.com
Web site: www.jhmbuttco.com

COMMERCIAL GARAGE EQUIPMENT (MIDLANDS) LTD
19-20 Aintree Road, Keytec 7 Business Park,
Pershore, Worcestershire, WR10 2JN,
United Kingdom
Tel: +44 (0)1386 244 758
Email: sales@commercialgarageequipment.co.uk
Web site: www.commercialgarageequipment.co.uk

DIRECT PARTS LTD
Unit 1, Churnet Court,
Churnetside Business Park, Harrison Way,
Cheddleton, ST13 7EF, United Kingdom
Tel: +44 (0)1538 361 777
Fax: +44 (0)1538 369 100
Email: sales@direct-group.co.uk
Web site: www.direct-group.co.uk

FUEL THEFT SOLUTIONS LTD
Unit 1, Yew Tree Business Units, Newcastle Road,
Betchton, Sandbach, Cheshire, CW11 4TD,
United Kingdom
Tel: 0845 077 3921
Fax: 0845 077 3922
Email: sales@dieseldye.com
Web site: www.dieseldye.com

GEMCO EQUIPMENT LTD
153-156 Bridge Street, Northampton, NN1 1QG,
United Kingdom
Tel: +44 (0)1604 828 500
Email: sales@gemco.co.uk
Web site: www.gemco.co.uk

KCP CAR & COMMERCIAL LTD
Unit 15, Hillside Road, Kempson Way,
Bury St Edmunds, Suffolk, IP32 7EA,
United Kingdom
Tel: +44 (0)1284 750 777
Fax: +44 (0)1284 750 773
Email: kcponline@yahoo.co.uk
Web site: kcpcarandcommercial.co.uk

MAJORLIFT HYDRAULIC EQUIPMENT LTD
Arnold's Field Industrial Estate, Wickwar,
Wotton-Under-Edge, Gloucestershire, GL12 8JD,
United Kingdom
Tel: +44 (0)1454 299 299
Fax: +44 (0)1454 294 003
Email: info@majorlift.com
Web site: www.majorlift.co.uk

SOMERS TOTALKARE LTD
Unit 1, Coombs Wharf, Chancel Way, Halesowen,
West Midlands, B62 8PP, United Kingdom
Tel: +44 (0)121 585 2700
Fax: +44 (0)121 585 2725
Email: sales@stkare.co.uk
Web site: www.stkare.co.uk

STERTIL UK LTD
Unit A, Brackmills Business Park, Caswell Road,
Northampton, NN4 7PW, United Kingdom
Tel: +44 (0)1604 662 049
Fax: +44 (0)1604 662 014
Web site: www.koni.stertil.co.uk

PHIL STOCKFORD GARAGE EQUIPMENT LTD
Unit 7, Badger Way,
North Cheshire Trading Estate, Prenton,
Wirral, L43 3HQ, United Kingdom **Tel:**
+44 (0)151 609 1007
Fax: +44 (0)151 609 1008
Email: info@vehicle-lifts.co.uk
Web site: www.vehicle-lifts.co.uk

TECALEMIT GARAGE EQUIPMENT CO LTD
Eagle Road, Langage Business Park, Plympton,
Plymouth, Devon, PL9 8BN, United Kingdom
Tel: +44 (0)1752 219 111
Fax: +44 (0)1752 219 128
Email: sales@tecalemit.co.uk
Web site: www.tecalemit.co.uk

TTS UK
Total Tool Solutions Ltd, Newhaven Business Park,
Lowergate, Milnsbridge, Huddersfield, HD3 4HS,
United Kingdom
Tel: +44 (0)1484 642 211
Fax: +44 (0)1484 461 002
Email: sales@ttsuk.com
Web site: www.ttsuk.com

V L TEST SYSTEMS LTD
3-4 Middle Slade, Buckingham Industrial Park,
Buckingham, MK18 1WA, United Kingdom
Tel: +44 90)1280 822 488
Fax: +44 (0)1280 822 489
Email: sales@vltestuk.com
Web site: www.vltest.com

VARLEY & GULLIVER LTD
57 Alfred Street, Sparkbrook, Birmingham,
B12 8JR, United Kingdom
Tel: +44 (0)121 773 2441
Fax: +44 (0)121 766 6875
Email: sales@v-and-g.co.uk
Web site: www.v-and-g.co.uk

GEARBOXES

ALLISON TRANSMISSION
Millbrook Proving Ground, Millbrook, Bedford,
MK45 2JQ, United Kingdom
Tel: +44 (0)1525 408 600
Fax: +44 (0)1525 408 610
Web site: www.allisontransmission.com

ARRIVA BUS & COACH
Lodge Garage, Whitehall Road, Gomersal,
Cleckheaton, West Yorkshire, BD19 4BJ,
United Kingdom
Tel: +44 (0)1274 681 144
Email: busandcoachparts@arriva.co.uk
Web site: www.arrivabusandcoach.co.uk

DAVID BROWN VEHICLE TRANSMISSIONS LTD
Park Gear Works, Lockwood, Huddersfield,
HD4 5DD, United Kingdom
Tel: +44 (0)1484 465 500
Fax: +44 (0)1484 465 501
Email: uk@davidbrown.com
Web site: www.davidbrown.com

GARDNER PARTS LTD
Centurion Court, Centurion Way, Leyland,
Lancashire, PR25 3UQ, United Kingdom
Tel: +44 (0)1772 642 460
Fax: +44 (0)1772 621 333
Email: sales@gardnerparts.co.uk
Web site: www.gardnerparts.co.uk

KCP CAR & COMMERCIAL LTD
Unit 15, Hillside Road, Kempson Way,
Bury St Edmunds, Suffolk, IP32 7EA,
United Kingdom
Tel: +44 (0)1284 750 777
Fax: +44 (0)1284 750 773
Email: kcponline@yahoo.co.uk
Web site: kcpcarandcommercial.co.uk

LH GROUP SERVICES LTD
Graycar Business Park, Barton Under Needwood,
Burton-On-Trent, DE13 8EN, United Kingdom
Tel: +44 (0)1283 722 600
Email: enquiries@lh-group.co.uk
Web site: www.lh-group.co.uk

MITCHELL POWERSYSTEMS
Mitchell Diesel Ltd, Fulwood Road South,
Sutton-In-Ashfield, Nottinghamshire, NG17 2JZ,
United Kingdom
Tel: +44 (0)1623 550 550
Fax: +44 (0)1623 443 041
Email: sales@mitchells.co.uk
Web site: www.mitchells.co.uk

NEXT BUS LTD
The Coach Yard, Vincients Road,
Bumpers Farm Industrial Estate, Chippenham,
Wiltshire, SN14 6QA, United Kingdom
Tel: +44 (0)1249 462 462
Fax: +44 (0)1249 448 844
Email: sales@next-bus.co.uk
Web site: www.next-bus.co.uk

OPTARE PARTS DIVISION
Hurricane Way South, Sherburn In Elmet, Leeds,
LS25 6PT, United Kingdom
Tel: +44 (0)871 230 1324
Email: parts@optare.com
Web site: www.optare.com

OPTARE PRODUCT SUPPORT
London
Unit 9, Eurocourt, Olivers Close, West Thurrock,
RM20 3EE, United Kingdom
Tel: +44 (0)1708 896 860
Fax: +44 (0)1708 869 920
Email: london.service@optare.com
Manchester
Trafford Park, Manchester, M17 1HG,
United Kingdom
Tel: +44 (0)161 872 7772
Email: manchester.service@optare.com
Rotherham
Denby Way, Hellaby, Rotherham, S66 8HR,
United Kingdom
Tel: +44 (0)1709 535 101
Fax: +44 (0)1709 739 680
Email: rotherham.service@optare.com

PARTLINE LTD
Dockfield Road, Shipley, BD17 7AZ,
United Kingdom
Tel: +44 (0)1274 531 531
Fax: +44 (0)1274 531 088
Email: sales@partline.co.uk
Web site: www.partline.co.uk

QUEENSBRIDGE (PSV) LTD
Milner Way, Longlands Industrial Estate, Ossett,
WF5 9JE, United Kingdom
Tel: +44 (0)1924 281 871
Fax: +44 (0)1924 281 807
Email: enquiries@queensbridgeltd.co.uk
Web site: www.queensbridgeltd.co.uk

SHAWSON SUPPLY LTD
12 Station Road, Saintfield, County Down,
BT24 7DU, Northern Ireland
Tel: +44 (0)28 9751 0994
Email: info@shawsonsupply.co.uk
Web site: www.shawsonsupply.co.uk

**SHELLEY TRANSMISSION
SERVICES LTD**
Eagle Street, off Bilston Road, Wolverhampton,
WV2 2AQ, United Kingdom
Tel: +44 (0)1902 351 178
Fax: +44 (0)1902 352 545
Email: enquiries@shelleytransmission.co.uk
Web site: www.shelleytransmission.co.uk

HL SMITH TRANSMISSIONS LTD
Enterprise Business Park, Cross Road, Albrighton,
Wolverhampton, WV7 3BJ, United Kingdom
Tel: +44 (0)1902 373 011

Fax: +44 (0)1902 373 608
Web site: www.hlsmith.co.uk

VOITH TURBO LTD
6 Beddington Farm Road, Croydon, CR0 4XB,
United Kingdom
Tel: +44 (0)20 8667 0333
Fax: +44 (0)20 8667 0403
Email: road.uk@voith.com
Web site: www.uk.voithturbo.com

VOITH
Engineered reliability.

Voith Turbo Ltd.

6 Beddington Farm Road,

Croydon, Surrey, CR0 4XB

Phone 0208 667 0333

Fax 0208 667 0403

Road.UK@voith.com

VOR TRANSMISSIONS LTD
Little London House, St Anne's Road, Willenhall,
WV13 1DT, United Kingdom
Tel: +44 (0)1902 604 141
Fax: +44 (0)1902 603 868
Email: sales@vor.co.uk
Web site: www.vor.co.uk

TREVOR WIGLEY & SONS BUS LTD
Boulder Bridge Lane, Carlton, Barnsley, S71 3HJ,
United Kingdom
Tel: +44 (0)1226 713 636
Fax: +44 (0)1226 700 199
Email: wigleys@btconnect.com
Web site: www.twigley.com

ZF POWERTRAIN
Stringes Close, Willenhall, WV13 1LE,
United Kingdom
Tel: +44 (0)1902 366 000
Email: sales@powertrain.co.uk
Web site: www.zfpowertrain.co.uk

HAND DRIERS (COACH MOUNTED)

BRADTECH LTD
Unit 3, Ladford Covert, Seighford, Stafford,
ST18 9QL, United Kingdom
Tel: +44 (0)1785 282 800
Fax: +44 (0)1785 282 558
Email: sales@bradtech.ltd.uk
Web site: www.bradtech.ltd.uk

CARLYLE BUS & COACH LTD
Carlyle Business Park, Great Bridge Street,
Swan Village, West Bromwich, B70 0X4,
United Kingdom
Tel: 0121 524 1200
Fax: 0121 524 1201
Email: westbromwichsales@carlyleplc.co.uk
Web site: www.carlylebusandcoach.com

HAPPICH UK LTD
Unit 26, Webb Ellis Industrial Estate, Wood Street,
Rugby, Warwickshire, CV21 2NP, United Kingdom
Tel: +44 (0)1788 50703
Fax: +44 (0)1788 44972
Email: info@happich.co.uk
Web site: www.happich.de

PLAXTON PARTS
Ryton Road, Anston, Sheffield, S25 4DL,
United Kingdom
Tel: +44 (0)844 822 6224
Fax: +44 (0)1909 550 050
Email: parts@plaxtonlimited.co.uk
Web site: www.plaxtonaftercare.co.uk

PLAXTON SERVICE
Ryton Road, Anston, Sheffield, S25 4DL,
United Kingdom
Tel: +44 (0)1909 551 155
Fax: +44 (0)1909 550 050
Email: service@plaxtonlimited.co.uk
Web site: www.plaxtonaftercare.co.uk

RSH SERVICES
Southedge Works, Hipperholme, Halifax, HX3 8EF,
United Kingdom
Tel: +44 (0)1422 202 840
Fax: +44 (0)1422 206 070

SHADES TECHNICS LTD
Units E3 & E4, RD Park, Stephenson Close,
Hoddesdon, Hertfordshire, EN11 0BW,
United Kingdom
Tel: +44 (0)1992 476 830
Email: info@shades-technics.com
Web site: www.shades-technics.com

UNWIN SAFETY SYSTEMS
Unwin House, The Horseshoe, Coat Road,
Martock, TA12 6EY, United Kingdom
Tel: +44 (0)1935 827 740
Fax: +44 (0)1935 827 760
Email: sales@unwin-safety.co.uk
Web site: www.unwin-safety.com

HANDRAILS

**ABACUS TRANSPORT
PRODUCTS LTD**
Abacus House, Highlode Industrial Estate, Ramsey,
Huntingdon, PE26 2RB, United Kingdom
Tel: +44 (0)1487 710 700
Fax: +44 (0)1487 710 626
Email: sales@abacus-tp.com
Web site: www.abacus-tp.com

ARRIVA BUS & COACH
Lodge Garage, Whitehall Road, Gomersal,
Cleckheaton, West Yorkshire, BD19 4BJ,
United Kingdom
Tel: +44 (0)1274 681 144
Email: busandcoachparts@arriva.co.uk
Web site: www.arrivabusandcoach.co.uk

CARLYLE BUS & COACH LTD
Carlyle Business Park, Great Bridge Street,
Swan Village, West Bromwich, B70 0X4,
United Kingdom
Tel: 0121 524 1200
Fax: 0121 524 1201
Email: westbromwichsales@carlyleplc.co.uk
Web site: www.carlylebusandcoach.com

EXPRESS COACH REPAIRS LTD
Outgang Lane, Pickering, YO18 7EL,
United Kingdom
Tel: +44 (0)1751 475 215
Email: expresscoachrepairs@hotmail.co.uk

LAWTON SERVICES LTD
Knutsford Road, Church Lawton,
Stoke-On-Trent, ST7 3DN, United Kingdom
Tel: +44 (0)1270 882 056
Fax: +44 (0)1270 883 014
Email: info@lawtonservices.co.uk
Web site: www.lawtonservices.co.uk

NEWBY FOUNDRIES LTD
1 Cornwall Road, Smethwick, West Midlands,
B66 2JT, United Kingdom
Tel: +44 (0)121 555 7615
Fax: +44 (0)121 505 3626
Email: sales@newbyfoundries.co.uk
Web site: www.newbyfoundries.co.uk

PARTLINE LTD
Dockfield Road, Shipley, BD17 7AZ,
United Kingdom
Tel: +44 (0)1274 531 531
Fax: +44 (0)1274 531 088
Email: sales@partline.co.uk
Web site: www.partline.co.uk

PLAXTON PARTS
Ryton Road, Anston, Sheffield, S25 4DL,
United Kingdom
Tel: +44 (0)844 822 6224
Fax: +44 (0)1909 550 050
Email: parts@plaxtonlimited.co.uk
Web site: www.plaxtonaftercare.co.uk

PLAXTON SERVICE
Ryton Road, Anston, Sheffield, S25 4DL,
United Kingdom
Tel: +44 (0)1909 551 155
Fax: +44 (0)1909 550 050
Email: service@plaxtonlimited.co.uk
Web site: www.plaxtonaftercare.co.uk

HEADREST COVERS AND CURTAINS

ABACUS TRANSPORT PRODUCTS LTD
Abacus House, Highlode Industrial Estate, Ramsey,
Huntingdon, PE26 2RB, United Kingdom
Tel: +44 (0)1487 710 700
Fax: +44 (0)1487 710 626
Email: sales@abacus-tp.com
Web site: www.abacus-tp.com

ARRIVA BUS & COACH
Lodge Garage, Whitehall Road, Gomersal,
Cleckheaton, West Yorkshire, BD19 4BJ,
United Kingdom
Tel: +44 (0)1274 681 144
Email: busandcoachparts@arriva.co.uk
Web site: www.arrivabusandcoach.co.uk

DUOFLEX LTD
Trimmingham House, 2 Shires Road,
Buckingham Road Industrial Estate, Brackley,
Northamptonshire, NN13 7EZ, United Kingdom
Tel: +44 (0)1280 701 366
Fax: +44 (0)1280 704 799
Email: info@duoflex.co.uk
Web site: www.duoflex.co.uk

EXPRESS COACH REPAIRS LTD
Outgang Lane, Pickering, YO18 7EL,
United Kingdom
Tel: +44 (0)1751 475 215
Email: expresscoachrepairs@hotmail.co.uk

LAWTON SERVICES LTD
Knutsford Road, Church Lawton, Stoke-On-Trent,
ST7 3DN, United Kingdom
Tel: +44 (0)1270 882 056
Fax: +44 (0)1270 883 014
Email: info@lawtonservices.co.uk
Web site: www.lawtonservices.co.uk

LEISUREWEAR DIRECT LTD
4a South Street North, New Whittington,
Chesterfield, S43 2AB, United Kingdom
Tel: +44 (0)1246 454 447
Fax: +44 (0)870 755 9842
Email: sales@leisureweardirect.com
Web site: www.leisureweardirect.com

ORVEC INTERNATIONAL LTD
Malmo Road, Sutton Fields, Hull, HU7 0YF,
United Kingdom
Tel: +44 (0)1482 625 333
Fax: +44 (0)1482 625 355
Email: service@orvec.com
Web site: www.orvec.com

PLAXTON PARTS
Ryton Road, Anston, Sheffield, S25 4DL, UK
Tel: +44 (0)844 822 6224
Fax: +44 (0)1909 550 050
Email: parts@plaxtonlimited.co.uk
Web site: www.plaxtonaftercare.co.uk

HEATING AND VENTILATION SYSTEMS

AIRCONCO LTD
Unit B1, Axis Point, Hareshill Business Park,
Hilltop Road, Heywood, Lancashire, OL10 2RQ,
United Kingdom
Tel: +44 (0)845 402 4014
Fax: +44 (0)845 402 4041
Email: mail@airconcoltd.com
Web site: www.airconco.ltd.uk

ARRIVA BUS & COACH
Lodge Garage, Whitehall Road, Gomersal,
Cleckheaton, West Yorkshire, BD19 4BJ,
United Kingdom
Tel: +44 (0)1274 681 144
Email: busandcoachparts@arriva.co.uk
Web site: www.arrivabusandcoach.co.uk

CAREYBROOK LTD
PO Box 205, Southam, Warwickshire, CV47 0ZL,
United Kingdom
Contact: John Turner, Director
Tel: +44 (0)3333 446 900
Fax: +44 (0)3333 446 901
Email: info@careybrook.co.uk
Web site: www.careybrook.co.uk
Careybrook offers limited spares for the old
"Purmo" and "UWE" heater products.

CARLYLE BUS & COACH LTD
Carlyle Business Park, Great Bridge Street,
Swan Village, West Bromwich, B70 0X4,
United Kingdom
Tel: 0121 524 1200
Fax: 0121 524 1201
Email: westbromwichsales@carlyleplc.co.uk
Web site: www.carlylebusandcoach.com

CLAYTON HEATERS LTD
Fletchworth Gate Industrial Estate, Coventry,
West Midlands, CV5 6SP, United Kingdom
Tel: +44 (0)2476 691 916
Email: admin@claytoncc.co.uk
Web site: www.claytoncc.co.uk

EBERSPACHER (UK) LTD
Headlands Business Park, Salisbury Road,
Ringwood, BH24 3PB, United Kingdom
Tel: +44 (0)1425 480 151
Fax: +44 (0)1425 480 152
Email: enquiries@eberspacher.com
Web site: www.eberspacher.com

GRAYSON THERMAL SYSTEMS
Wharfdale House, 257 Wharfdale Road, Tyseley,
Birmingham, B11 2DP, United Kingdom
Tel: +44 (0)121 700 5600
Fax: +44 (0)121 700 5601
Email: cs@graysonts.com
Web site: www.graysonts.com

HAPPICH UK LTD
Unit 26, Webb Ellis Industrial Estate, Wood Street,
Rugby, Warwickshire, CV21 2NP, United Kingdom
Tel: +44 (0)1788 50703
Fax: +44 (0)1788 44972
Email: info@happich.co.uk
Web site: www.happich.de

OMNI-TECH ELECTRONICS
Unit 9, Prospect House, Ireland Industrial Estate,
Staveley, Chesterfield, Derbyshire, S43 3QE,
United Kingdom
Tel: +44 (0)1246 474 332
Fax: +44 (0)1246 529 010
Email: help@omni-techelectronics.co.uk
Web site: www.buselectronics.co.uk

OPTARE PARTS DIVISION
Hurricane Way South, Sherburn In Elmet, Leeds,
LS25 6PT, United Kingdom
Tel: +44 (0)871 230 1324
Email: parts@optare.com
Web site: www.optare.com

PACET MANUFACTURING LTD
Wyebridge House, Cores End Road, Bourne End,
Buckinghamshire, SL8 5HH, United Kingdom
Tel: +44 (0)1628 526 754
Fax: +44 (0)1628 810 080
Email: sales@pacet.co.uk
Web site: www.pacet.co.uk

PIONEER WESTON
206 Cavendish Place, Birchwood Park, Warrington,
Cheshire, WA3 6WU, United Kingdom
Tel: +44 (0)1925 853 000
Fax: +44 (0)1925 853 030
Email: info@pwi-ltd.com
Web site: www.eriks.co.uk

PLAXTON PARTS
Ryton Road, Anston, Sheffield, S25 4DL,
United Kingdom
Tel: +44 (0)844 822 6224
Fax: +44 (0)1909 550 050
Email: parts@plaxtonlimited.co.uk
Web site: www.plaxtonaftercare.co.uk

PLAXTON SERVICE
Ryton Road, Anston, Sheffield, S25 4DL,
United Kingdom
Tel: +44 (0)1909 551 155
Fax: +44 (0)1909 550 050
Email: service@plaxtonlimited.co.uk
Web site: www.plaxtonaftercare.co.uk

SHADES TECHNICS LTD
Units E3 & E4, RD Park, Stephenson Close,
Hoddesdon, Hertfordshire, EN11 0BW,
United Kingdom
Tel: +44 (0)1992 476 830
Email: info@shades-technics.com
Web site: www.shades-technics.com

**WEBASTO THERMO
& COMFORT UK LTD**
Webasto House, White Rose Way,
Doncaster Carr, South Yorkshire, DN4 5JH,
United Kingdom
Tel: +44 (0)1302 322 232
Web site: www.webasto.com/gb

HUB ODOMETERS

ARRIVA BUS & COACH
Lodge Garage, Whitehall Road, Gomersal,
Cleckheaton, West Yorkshire, BD19 4BJ,
United Kingdom
Tel: +44 (0)1274 681 144
Email: busandcoachparts@arriva.co.uk
Web site: www.arrivabusandcoach.co.uk

**FUMOTO ENGINEERING
OF EUROPE LTD**
Normandy House, 35 Glategny Esplanade,
St Peter Port, Guernsey, GY1 2BP,
United Kingdom
Tel: +44 (0)1481 716 987
Fax: +44 (0)1481 700 374
Email: info@fumoto-valve.com
Web site: www.tankcontainers.com

KCP CAR & COMMERCIAL LTD
Unit 15, Hillside Road, Kempson Way,
Bury St Edmunds, Suffolk, IP32 7EA,
United Kingdom
Tel: +44 (0)1284 750 777
Fax: +44 (0)1284 750 773
Email: kcponline@yahoo.co.uk
Web site: www.kcpcarandcommercial.co.uk

PARTLINE LTD
Dockfield Road, Shipley, BD17 7AZ,
United Kingdom
Tel: +44 (0)1274 531 531
Fax: +44 (0)1274 531 088
Email: sales@partline.co.uk
Web site: www.partline.co.uk

ROADLINK INTERNATIONAL LTD
Strawberry Lane, Willenhall, West Midlands,

WV13 3RL, United Kingdom
Tel: +44 (0)1902 636 206
Fax: +44 (0)1902 631 515
Email: sales@roadlink-international.co.uk
Web site: www.roadlink-international.co.uk

HYBRID DRIVE SYSTEMS

BAE SYSTEMS
Marconi Way, Rochester, Kent, ME1 2XX,
United Kingdom
Tel: +44 (0)1634 204 578
Web site: www.hybridrive.co.uk

GKN HYBRID POWER LTD
Station Road, Grove, Wantage, Oxfordshire,
OX12 0DQ, United Kingdom
Tel: +44 (0)1235 777 700
Fax: +44 (0)1235 777 960
Web site: www.gkn.com

GRAYSON THERMAL SYSTEMS
Wharfdale House, 257 Wharfdale Road, Tyseley,
Birmingham, B11 2DP, United Kingdom
Tel: +44 (0)121 700 5600
Fax: +44 (0)121 700 5601
Email: cs@graysonts.com
Web site: www.graysonts.com

VANTAGE POWER LTD
Unit 7, Greenford Park, Ockham Drive,
Greenford, Middlesex, UB6 0FD, United Kingdom
Tel: +44 (0)20 8813 0850
Email: sales@vantage-power.com
Web site: www.vantage-power.com

IN-COACH CATERING EQUIPMENT

BRADTECH LTD
Unit 3, Ladford Covert, Seighford, Stafford,
ST18 9QL, United Kingdom
Tel: +44 (0)1785 282 800
Fax: +44 (0)1785 282 558
Email: sales@bradtech.ltd.uk
Web site: www.bradtech.ltd.uk

EXPRESS COACH REPAIRS LTD
Outgang Lane, Pickering, YO18 7EL,
United Kingdom
Tel: +44 (0)1751 475 215
Email: expresscoachrepairs@hotmail.co.uk

PLAXTON PARTS
Ryton Road, Anston, Sheffield, S25 4DL,
United Kingdom
Tel: +44 (0)844 822 6224
Fax: +44 (0)1909 550 050
Email: parts@plaxtonlimited.co.uk
Web site: www.plaxtonaftercare.co.uk

PLAXTON SERVICE
Ryton Road, Anston, Sheffield, S25 4DL,
United Kingdom
Tel: +44 (0)1909 551 155
Fax: +44 (0)1909 550 050
Email: service@plaxtonlimited.co.uk
Web site: www.plaxtonaftercare.co.uk

PSV PRODUCTS
60 The Old Quays, Warrington, Cheshire,
WA4 1JP, United Kingdom
Tel: +44 (0)1925 210 220
Email: info@psvproducts.com
Web site: www.psvproducts.com

SHADES TECHNICS LTD
Units E3 & E4, RD Park, Stephenson Close,
Hoddesdon, Hertfordshire, EN11 0BV,
United Kingdom
Tel: +44 (0)1992 476 830
Email: info@shades-technics.com
Web site: www.shades-technics.com

TRAMONTANA COACH DISTRIBUTORS
Chapelknowe Road, Carfin, Motherwell, ML1 5LE,
United Kingdom

Tel: 01698 861790
Fax: 01698 860778
Email: wdt90@hotmail.co.uk
Web site: www.tramontanacoach.co.uk

LABELS, NAMEPLATES AND DECALS

ARRIVA BUS & COACH
Lodge Garage, Whitehall Road, Gomersal,
Cleckheaton, West Yorkshire, BD19 4BJ,
United Kingdom
Tel: +44 (0)1274 681 144
Email: busandcoachparts@arriva.co.uk
Web site: www.arrivabusandcoach.co.uk

FUEL THEFT SOLUTIONS LTD
Unit 1, Yew Tree Business Units, Newcastle Road,
Betchton, Sandbach, Cheshire, CW11 4TD,
United Kingdom
Tel: 0845 077 3921
Fax: 0845 077 3922
Email: sales@dieseldye.com
Web site: www.dieseldye.com

GRAPHIC EVOLUTION LTD
Ad House, East Parade, Harrogate,
North Yorkshire, HG1 5LT, United Kingdom
Tel: +44 (0)1423 706 680
Fax: +44 (0)1423 502 522
Email: info@graphic-evolution.co.uk
Web site: www.graphic-evolution.co.uk

MCKENNA BROTHERS LTD
McKenna House, Jubilee Road, Middleton,
Manchester, M24 2LX, United Kingdom
Tel: +44 (0)161 655 3244
Fax: +44 (0)161 655 3059
Email: info@mckennabrothers.co.uk
Web site: www.mckennabrothers.co.uk

PLAXTON PARTS
Ryton Road, Anston, Sheffield, S25 4DL,
United Kingdom
Tel: +44 (0)844 822 6224
Fax: +44 (0)1909 550 050
Email: parts@plaxtonlimited.co.uk
Web site: www.plaxtonaftercare.co.uk

LIFTING EQUIPMENT

AUTOLIFT LTD
Swallow House, Shilton Industrial Estate, Shilton,
Coventry, CV7 9JY, United Kingdom
Tel: +44 (0)2476 613 223
Fax: +44 (0)2476 619 323
Email: info@autolift.co.uk
Web site: www.autolift.co.uk

LIFTS/RAMPS (PASSENGER)

ARRIVA BUS & COACH
Lodge Garage, Whitehall Road, Gomersal,
Cleckheaton, West Yorkshire, BD19 4BJ,
United Kingdom
Tel: +44 (0)1274 681 144
Email: busandcoachparts@arriva.co.uk
Web site: www.arrivabusandcoach.co.uk

AVS STEPS LTD
Unit 1, Excel Business Park, Church Lane, Wem,
Shropshire, SY45HS, United Kingdom
Tel: +44 (0)1939 235 900
Email: sales@avssteps.co.uk
Web site: www.avssteps.co.uk

COMMERCIAL GARAGE EQUIPMENT (MIDLANDS) LTD
19-20 Aintree Road, Keytec 7 Business Park,
Pershore, Worcestershire, WR10 2JN,
United Kingdom
Tel: +44 (0)1386 244 758
Email: sales@commercialgarageequipment.co.uk
Web site:
www.commercialgarageequipment.co.uk

COMPAK RAMPS CO LTD
VIP Group, VIP Industrial Park,

Anchor & Hope Lane, London, SE7 7RY,
United Kingdom
Tel: +44 (0)20 8858 3781
Fax: +44 (0)20 8858 5663
Email: tony.rodwell@dsl.pipex.com
Web site: www.vipgroup.co.uk

DIRECT PARTS LTD
Unit 1, Churnet Court,
Churnetside Business Park, Harrison Way,
Cheddleton, ST13 7EF, United Kingdom
Tel: +44 (0)1538 361 777
Fax: +44 (0)1538 369 100
Email: sales@direct-group.co.uk
Web site: www.direct-group.co.uk

EXPRESS COACH REPAIRS LTD
Outgang Lane, Pickering, YO18 7EL,
United Kingdom
Tel: +44 (0)1751 475 215
Email: expresscoachrepairs@hotmail.co.uk

HIDRAL S.L
Titanio 5 y 7, 28850 Torrejon de Ardoz,
Madrid, Spain
Tel: +34 91 677 0095
Fax: +34 91 677 1250
Email: info@hidralglobal.com
Web site: www.hidralglobal.com

PASSENGER LIFT SERVICES
Unit 2 Summit Crescent, Smethwick,
West Midlands, B66 1BT, United Kingdom
Tel: +44 (0)121 552 0660
Fax: +44 (0)121 552 0200
Email: enquiries@pls-access.co.uk
Web site: www.passengerliftservices.co.uk

PLAXTON PARTS
Ryton Road, Anston, Sheffield, S25 4DL,
United Kingdom
Tel: +44 (0)844 822 6224
Fax: +44 (0)1909 550 050
Email: parts@plaxtonlimited.co.uk
Web site: www.plaxtonaftercare.co.uk

PLAXTON SERVICE
Ryton Road, Anston, Sheffield, S25 4DL,
United Kingdom
Tel: +44 (0)1909 551 155
Fax: +44 (0)1909 550 050
Email: service@plaxtonlimited.co.uk
Web site: www.plaxtonaftercare.co.uk

PNEUMAX LTD
110 Vista Park, Mauretania Road, Nursling,
Southampton, SO16 0YS, United Kingdom
Tel: +44 (0)2380 740 412
Fax: +44 (0)2380 739 340
Email: sales@pneumax.co.uk
Web site: www.pneumax.co.uk

PSV TRANSPORT SYSTEMS LTD
21 Impresa Park, Pindar Road, Hoddesdon,
Hertfordshire, EN11 0DL, United Kingdom
Tel: +44 (0)1992 479 950
Fax: +44 (0)1992 471 676
Email: sales@psv-transport-systems.co.uk
Web site: www.psv-transport-systems.co.uk

RATCLIFF PALFINGER
Bessemer Road, Welwyn Garden City,
Hertfordshire, AL7 1ET, United Kingdom
Tel: +44 (0)1707 325 571
Fax: +44 (0)1707 327 752
Email: info@ratcliffpalfinger.co.uk
Web site: www.ratcliffpalfinger.co.uk

RICON UK LTD
Meadow Lane, Loughborough, Leicestershire,
LE11 1HS, United Kingdom
Tel: +44 (0)1509 635 920
Fax: +44 (0)1509 261 939
Email: riconuk@wabtec.com
Web site: www.ricon.eu

TRUCKALIGN CO LTD
VIP Group, VIP Industrial Park,
Anchor & Hope Lane, London, SE7 7RY,
United Kingdom
Tel: +44 (0)20 8858 3781
Fax: +44 (0)20 8858 5663
Email: admin@vipgroupltd.co.uk
Web site: www.vipgroup.co.uk

VAPOR RICON EUROPE LTD
Meadow Lane, Loughborough, Leicestershire,
LE11 1HS, United Kingdom
Tel: +44 (0)1509 635 924
Fax: +44 (0)1509 261 939
Email: ricon@wabtec.com
Web site: www.ricon.eu

LIGHTING AND LIGHTING DESIGN

ARRIVA BUS & COACH
Lodge Garage, Whitehall Road, Gomersal,
Cleckheaton, West Yorkshire, BD19 4BJ,
United Kingdom
Tel: +44 (0)1274 681 144
Email: busandcoachparts@arriva.co.uk
Web site: www.arrivabusandcoach.co.uk

AUTOSOUND LTD
4 Lister Street, Dudley Hill, Bradford, BD4 9PQ,
United Kingdom
Tel: +44 (0)1274 688 990
Fax: +44 (0)1274 651 318
Web site: www.autosound.co.uk

BLACKPOOL COACH SERVICES
Burton Road, Blackpool, Lancashire, FY4 4NW,
United Kingdom
Tel: +44 (0)1253 698 686
Web site: www.blackpoolcoachservices.co.uk

BRITAX PMG LTD
Bressingby Industrial Estate, Bridlington,
East Yorkshire, YO16 4SJ, United Kingdom
Tel: +44 (0)1262 670 161
Fax: +44 (0)1262 605 666
Web site: www.britax-pmg.com

CARLYLE BUS & COACH LTD
Carlyle Business Park, Great Bridge Street,
Swan Village, West Bromwich, B70 0X4,
United Kingdom
Tel: 0121 524 1200
Fax: 0121 524 1201
Email: westbromwichsales@carlyleplc.co.uk
Web site: www.carlylebusandcoach.com

EXPRESS COACH REPAIRS LTD
Outgang Lane, Pickering, YO18 7EL,
United Kingdom
Tel: +44 (0)1751 475 215
Email: expresscoachrepairs@hotmail.co.uk

HAPPICH UK LTD
Unit 26, Webb Ellis Industrial Estate, Wood Street,
Rugby, Warwickshire, CV21 2NP, United Kingdom
Tel: +44 (0)1788 50703
Fax: +44 (0)1788 44972
Email: info@happich.co.uk
Web site: www.happich.de

INVERTEC LTD
Whelford Road, Fairford, GL7 4DT,
United Kingdom
Tel: +44 (0)1285 713 550
Fax: +44 (0)1285 713 548
Email: info@invertec.co.uk
Web site: www.invertec.co.uk

KCP CAR & COMMERCIAL LTD
Unit 15, Hillside Road, Kempson Way,
Bury St Edmunds, Suffolk, IP32 7EA,
United Kingdom
Tel: +44 (0)1284 750 777
Fax: +44 (0)1284 750 773
Email: kcponline@yahoo.co.uk
Web site: kcpcarandcommercial.co.uk

OMNI-TECH ELECTRONICS
Unit 9, Prospect House, Ireland Industrial Estate,
Staveley, Chesterfield, Derbyshire, S43 3QE,
United Kingdom
Tel: +44 (0)1246 474 332
Fax: +44 (0)1246 529 010
Email: help@omni-techelectronics.co.uk
Web site: www.buselectronics.co.uk

OPTARE PARTS DIVISION
Hurricane Way South, Sherburn In Elmet, Leeds,
LS25 6PT, United Kingdom
Tel: +44 (0)871 230 1324
Email: parts@optare.com
Web site: www.optare.com

PARTLINE LTD
Dockfield Road, Shipley, BD17 7AZ,
United Kingdom
Tel: +44 (0)1274 531 531
Fax: +44 (0)1274 531 088
Email: sales@partline.co.uk
Web site: www.partline.co.uk

PLAXTON PARTS
Ryton Road, Anston, Sheffield, S25 4DL,
United Kingdom
Tel: +44 (0)844 822 6224
Fax: +44 (0)1909 550 050
Email: parts@plaxtonlimited.co.uk
Web site: www.plaxtonaftercare.co.uk

PLAXTON SERVICE
Ryton Road, Anston, Sheffield, S25 4DL,
United Kingdom
Tel: +44 (0)1909 551 155
Fax: +44 (0)1909 550 050
Email: service@plaxtonlimited.co.uk
Web site: www.plaxtonaftercare.co.uk

PSV TRANSPORT SYSTEMS LTD
21 Impresa Park, Pindar Road, Hoddesdon,
Hertfordshire, EN11 0DL, United Kingdom
Tel: +44 (0)1992 479 950
Fax: +44 (0)1992 471 676
Email: sales@psv-transport-systems.co.uk
Web site: www.psv-transport-systems.co.uk

RESCROFT LTD
20 Oxleasow Road, East Moons Moat, Redditch,
B98 0RE, United Kingdom
Tel: +44 (0)1527 521 300
Fax: +44 (0)1527 521 301
Email: sales@rescroft.com
Web site: www.rescroft.com

MIRRORS/MIRROR ARMS

ASHTREE VISION & SAFETY
Ashtree Works, Brownroyd Street, Bradford,
BD8 9AF, United Kingdom
Tel: +44 (0)1274 546 732
Fax: +44 (0)1274 548 525
Email: sales@avsuk.co
Web site: www.avsuk.co

CARLYLE BUS & COACH LTD
Carlyle Business Park, Great Bridge Street,
Swan Village, West Bromwich, B70 0X4,
United Kingdom
Tel: 0121 524 1200
Fax: 0121 524 1201
Email: westbromwichsales@carlyleplc.co.uk
Web site: www.carlylebusandcoach.com

EXPRESS COACH REPAIRS LTD
Outgang Lane, Pickering, YO18 7EL,
United Kingdom
Tel: +44 (0)1751 475 215
Email: expresscoachrepairs@hotmail.co.uk

KCP CAR & COMMERCIAL LTD
Unit 15, Hillside Road, Kempson Way,
Bury St Edmunds, Suffolk, IP32 7EA,
United Kingdom
Tel: +44 (0)1284 750 777

Fax: +44 (0)1284 750 773
Email: kcponline@yahoo.co.uk
Web site: kcpcarandcommercial.co.uk

LAWTON SERVICES LTD
Knutsford Road, Church Lawton, Stoke-On-Trent,
ST7 3DN, United Kingdom
Tel: +44 (0)1270 882 056
Fax: +44 (0)1270 883 014
Email: info@lawtonservices.co.uk
Web site: www.lawtonservices.co.uk

PARMA INDUSTRIES
34-36 Carlton Park Industrial Estate,
Saxmundham, Suffolk, IP17 2NL, United Kingdom
Tel: +44 (0)1728 745 700
Fax: +44 (0)1728 745 718
Email: sales@parmagroup.co.uk
Web site: www.parmagroup.co.uk

PARTLINE LTD
Dockfield Road, Shipley, BD17 7AZ,
United Kingdom
Tel: +44 (0)1274 531 531
Fax: +44 (0)1274 531 088
Email: sales@partline.co.uk
Web site: www.partline.co.uk

PLAXTON PARTS
Ryton Road, Anston, Sheffield, S25 4DL,
United Kingdom
Tel: +44 (0)844 822 6224
Fax: +44 (0)1909 550 050
Email: parts@plaxtonlimited.co.uk
Web site: www.plaxtonaftercare.co.uk

OIL MANAGEMENT SYSTEMS

ALP TANK CONTAINERS
Normandy House, Glategny Esplanade,
St Peter Port, Guernsey, GY 2BP, United Kingdom
Tel: +44 (0)20 7352 2727
Fax: +44 (0)20 7352 3990
Email: info@tankcontainers.co.uk
Web site: www.tankcontainers.co.uk

ARRIVA BUS & COACH
Lodge Garage, Whitehall Road, Gomersal,
Cleckheaton, West Yorkshire, BD19 4BJ,
United Kingdom
Tel: +44 (0)1274 681 144
Email: busandcoachparts@arriva.co.uk
Web site: www.arrivabusandcoach.co.uk

TERENCE BARKER TANKS
Phoenix Road, Haverhill, Suffolk, CB9 7EA,
United Kingdom **Tel:** +44 (0)1440 712 905
Fax: +44 (0)1440 715 460
Email: sales@tbtanks.co.uk
Web site: www.terencebarkertanks.co.uk

FUEL THEFT SOLUTIONS LTD
Unit 1, Yew Tree Business Units, Newcastle Road,
Betchton, Sandbach, Cheshire, CW11 4TD,
United Kingdom
Tel: 0845 077 3921
Fax: 0845 077 3922
Email: sales@dieseldye.com
Web site: www.dieseldye.com

GROENEVELD UK LTD
The Greentec Centre, Gelders Hall Road,
Shepshed, Leicestershire, LE12 9NH, UK
Tel: +44 (0)1509 600 033
Fax: +44 (0)1509 602 000
Email: info-uk@groeneveld-group.com
Web site: www.groeneveld-group.com

INTERLUBE SYSTEMS LTD
St Modwen Road, Parkway Industrial Estate,
Plymouth, PL6 8LH, United Kingdom
Tel: +44 (0)1752 676 000
Fax: +44 (0)1752 676 001
Email: info@interlubesystems.co.uk
Web site: www.interlubesystems.co.uk

KCP CAR & COMMERCIAL LTD
Unit 15, Hillside Road, Kempson Way,
Bury St Edmunds, Suffolk, IP32 7EA,
United Kingdom
Tel: +44 (0)1284 750 777
Fax: +44 (0)1284 750 773
Email: kcponline@yahoo.co.uk
Web site: kcpcarandcommercial.co.uk

MARTYN INDUSTRIALS LTD
5 Brunel Way, Durranhill Industrial Park, Harraby,
Carlisle, CA1 3NQ, United Kingdom
Tel: +44 (0)1228 544 000
Email: enquiries@martyn-industrials.co.uk
Web site: www.martyn-industrials.com

STERTIL UK LTD
Unit A, Brackmills Business Park, Caswell Road,
Northampton, NN4 7PW, United Kingdom
Tel: +44 (0)1604 662 049
Fax: +44 (0)1604 662 014
Web site: www.koni.stertil.co.uk

PAINTING AND SIGNWRITING

ARRIVA BUS & COACH
Lodge Garage, Whitehall Road, Gomersal,
Cleckheaton, West Yorkshire, BD19 4BJ,
United Kingdom
Tel: +44 (0)1274 681 144
Email: busandcoachparts@arriva.co.uk
Web site: www.arrivabusandcoach.co.uk

BLACKPOOL COACH SERVICES
Burton Road, Blackpool, Lancashire, FY1 1NW,
United Kingdom
Tel: +44 (0)1253 698 686
Web site: www.blackpoolcoachservices.co.uk

**BULWARK BUS & COACH
ENGINEERING LTD**
Unit 5, Bulwark Business Park, Bulwark,
Chepstow, NP16 6QZ, United Kingdom
Tel: +44 (0)1291 622 326
Fax: +44 (0)1291 622 726
Email: bulwarkbusandcoach@tiscali.co.uk
Web site: www.bulwarkbusandcoach.co.uk

CHANNEL COMMERCIALS PLC
Unit 6, Cobbs Wood Industrial Estate,
Brunswick Road, Ashford, TN23 1EH,
United Kingdom
Tel: 0844 247 7742
Fax: +44 (0)1233 636 322
Web site: www.channelcommercials.co.uk

EXPRESS COACH REPAIRS LTD
Outgang Lane, Pickering, YO18 7EL,
United Kingdom
Tel: +44 (0)1751 475 215
Email: expresscoachrepairs@hotmail.co.uk

HANTS & DORSET TRIM LTD
Unit 4E, Barton Park, Chickenhall Lane, Eastleigh,
Hampshire, SO0 6RR, United Kingdom
Tel: +44 (0)2380 644 200
Fax: +44 (0)2380 647 802
Email: enquiries@hdtrim.co.uk
Web site: www.hantsanddorsettrim.co.uk

IGP SOLUTIONS
16 Hillbottom Road, High Wycombe, HP12 4HJ,
United Kingdom
Tel: +44 (0)1494 533 131
Fax: +44 (0)1494 462 675
Email: sales@igpsolutions.com
Web site: www.igpsolutions.com

LAWTON SERVICES LTD
Knutsford Road, Church Lawton, Stoke-On-Trent,
ST7 3DN, United Kingdom
Tel: +44 (0)1270 882 056
Fax: +44 (0)1270 883 014
Email: info@lawtonservices.co.uk
Web site: www.lawtonservices.co.uk

LONDON BUS & TRUCK LTD
Units 1-4, Northfleet Industrial Estate,
Lower Road, Northfleet, Kent, DA11 9SN,
United Kingdom
Tel: +44 (0)1474 361 199
Email: enquiries@londonbusandtruck.co.uk
Web site: www.londonbusandtruck.co.uk

OPTARE PRODUCT SUPPORT
London
Unit 9, Eurocourt, Olivers Close, West Thurrock,
RM20 3EE, United Kingdom
Tel: +44 (0)1708 896 860
Fax: +44 (0)1708 869 920
Email: london.service@optare.com
Manchester
Trafford Park, Manchester, M17 1HG,
United Kingdom
Tel: +44 (0)161 872 7772
Email: manchester.service@optare.com
Rotherham
Denby Way, Hellaby, Rotherham, S66 8HR,
United Kingdom
Tel: +44 (0)1709 535 101
Fax: +44 (0)1709 739 680
Email: rotherham.service@optare.com

RH BODYWORKS
A140 Norwich-Ipswich Road, Brome, Eye, Suffolk,
IP23 8AW, United Kingdom
Tel: +44 (0)1379 870 666
Fax: +44 (0)1379 871 140
Email: enquiries@rhbodyworks.co.uk
Web site: www.rhbodyworks.co.uk

S & G COACHWORKS LTD
Mansfield Woodhouse, Nottinghamshire,
NG19 7FE, United Kingdom
Tel: +44 (0)1623 627 653
Email: sandgcoachworks@aol.co.uk
Web site: www.sandgcoachworks.co.uk

VOLVO BUS AND COACH CENTRE
Parts Sales & Body Repair/Refurbishment
Specialists - Byron Street Extension,
Loughborough, LE11 5HE, United Kingdom
Tel: +44 (0)1509 217 700
Fax: +44 (0)1509 238 770
Email: dporter@volvocoachsales.co.uk
Web site: www.volvobuses.com

PARTS SUPPLIERS

ABACUS TRANSPORT PRODUCTS LTD
Abacus House, Highlode Industrial Estate, Ramsey,
Huntingdon, PE26 2RB, United Kingdom
Tel: +44 (0)1487 710 700
Fax: +44 (0)1487 710 626
Email: sales@abacus-tp.com
Web site: www.abacus-tp.com

AIR DOOR SERVICES
The Pavilions, Holly Lane Industrial Estate,
Atherstone, CV9 2QZ, United Kingdom
Tel: +44 (0)1827 711 660
Email: airdoorservices@aol.com

ARRIVA BUS & COACH
Lodge Garage, Whitehall Road, Gomersal,
Cleckheaton, West Yorkshire, BD19 4BJ, UK
Tel: +44 (0)1274 681 144
Email: busandcoachparts@arriva.co.uk
Web site: www.arrivabusandcoach.co.uk

ASHTREE VISION & SAFETY
Ashtree Works, Brownroyd Street, Bradford,
BD8 9AF, United Kingdom
Tel: +44 (0)1274 546 732
Fax: +44 (0)1274 548 525
Email: sales@avsuk.co
Web site: www.avsuk.co

M BARNWELL SERVICES LTD
Reginald Road, Smethwick, B67 5AS,
United Kingdom
Tel: +44 (0)121 429 8011

Fax: +44 (0)121 434 3016
Email: sales@barnwell.co.uk
Web site: www.barnwell.co.uk

BHI UK
The Bus Depot, 1 Sky Lane, Haddington, Lincoln,
LN5 9FE, United Kingdom
Tel: +44 (0)1522 689 911
Fax: +44 (0)1522 689 922
Email: info@bhiuk.com
Web site: www.bhiuk.com
Handrail padding

BRITISH BUS SALES (MIKE NASH)
PO Box 534, Dorking, Surrey, RH5 5XB,
United Kingdom
Tel: +44 (0)7836 656 692
Email: web@britishbussales.com
Web site: www.britishbussales.com
New and used parts for older vehicles. Useful
contacts for most things in the bus industry.

BRT BEARINGS LTD
21-24 Regal Road, Wisbech, Cambridgeshire,
PE13 2RQ, United Kingdom
Tel: +44 (0)1945 464 097
Fax: +44 (0)1945 464 523
Email: brt.sales@brt-bearings.com
Web site: www.brt-bearings.com

CARLYLE BUS & COACH LTD
Carlyle Business Park, Great Bridge Street,
Swan Village, West Bromwich, B70 0X4,
United Kingdom
Tel: 0121 524 1200
Fax: 0121 524 1201
Email: westbromwichsales@carlyleplc.co.uk
Web site: www.carlylebusandcoach.com

CLAYTON HEATERS LTD
Fletchworth Gate Industrial Estate, Coventry,
West Midlands, CV5 6SP, United Kingdom
Tel: +44 (0)2476 691 916
Email: admin@claytoncc.co.uk
Web site: www.claytoncc.co.uk

COACH-AID LTD
Greyfriars Workshop, Greyfriars Way, Stafford,
Staffordshire, ST16 2SH, United Kingdom
Tel: +44 (0)1785 222 666
Email: workshop@coach-aid.com
Web site: www.coach-aid.com

CRESCENT FACILITIES LTD
72 Willow Crescent, Chapeltown, Sheffield,
S35 1QS, United Kingdom
Tel: +44 (0)114 245 1050
Email: cfl.chris@btinternet.com

CREWE ENGINES
Warmingham Road, Crewe, CW1 4PQ,
United Kingdom
Tel: +44 (0)1270 526 333
Fax: +44 (0)1270 526 433
Email: sales@creweengines.co.uk
Web site: www.creweengines.co.uk

CUMMINS UK
40-44 Rutherford Drive, Park Farm South,
Wellingborough, NN8 6AN, United Kingdom
Tel: +44 (0)1933 334 200
Fax: +44 (0)1933 334 198
Email: cduksales@cummins.com
Web site: www.cummins.com

DINEX EXHAUSTS LTD
14 Chesford Grange, Woolston, Warrington,
WA1 4RE, United Kingdom
Tel: +44 (0)1925 849 849
Fax: +44 (0)1925 849 850
Email: dinex@dinex.co.uk
Web site: www.dinex.dk

DIRECT PARTS LTD
Unit 1, Churnet Court,
Churnetside Business Park, Harrison Way,
Cheddleton, ST13 7EF, United Kingdom

Tel: +44 (0)1538 361 777
Fax: +44 (0)1538 369 100
Email: sales@direct-group.co.uk
Web site: www.direct-group.co.uk

ERENTEK LTD
Malt Kiln Lane, Waddington, Lincoln, LN5 9RT,
United Kingdom
Tel: +44 (0)1522 720 065
Fax: +44 (0)1522 729 155
Email: sales@erentek.co.uk
Web site: www.erentek.co.uk

EXPRESS COACH REPAIRS LTD
Outgang Lane, Pickering, YO18 7EL,
United Kingdom
Tel: +44 (0)1751 475 215
Email: expresscoachrepairs@hotmail.co.uk

GARDNER PARTS LTD
Centurion Court, Centurion Way, Leyland,
Lancashire, PR25 3UQ, United Kingdom
Tel: +44 (0)1772 642 460
Fax: +44 (0)1772 621 333
Email: sales@gardnerparts.co.uk
Web site: www.gardnerparts.co.uk

GB FLEET MAINTENANCE
Geddings Road, Geddings Road, Hoddesdon,
Hertfordshire, EN11 0NT, United Kingdom
Tel: + 44 (0)1992 467 984
Email: sales@gbfleetmaintenance.co.uk
Web site: www.gbfleetmaintenance.co.uk
Service repair agent for Noone Turas, Paramount
Conversions, Unvi and Van Hool

GRAYSON THERMAL SYSTEMS
Wharfdale House, 257 Wharfdale Road, Tyseley,
Birmingham, B11 2DP, United Kingdom
Tel: +44 (0)121 700 5600
Fax: +44 (0)121 700 5601
Email: cs@graysonts.com
Web site: www.graysonts.com

HAPPICH UK LTD
Unit 26, Webb Ellis Industrial Estate, Wood Street,
Rugby, Warwickshire, CV21 2NP, United Kingdom
Tel: +44 (0)1788 50703
Fax: +44 (0)1788 44972
Email: info@happich.co.uk
Web site: www.happich.de

THOMAS HARDIE COMMERCIALS LTD
Newstet Road, Knowsley Industrial Park,
Liverpool, L33 7TJ, United Kingdom
Tel: +44 (0)151 549 3000
Email: info@thardie.co.uk
Web site: www.thardie.co.uk

IMEXPART LTD
Links 31, Willowbridge Way, Whitwood,
Castleford, WF10 5NP, United Kingdom
Tel: +44 (0)1977 553 936
Email: sales@imexpart.com
Web site: www.imexpart.com

IMPERIAL ENGINEERING
Delamare Road, Cheshunt, Hertfordshire,
EN8 9UD, United Kingdom
Tel: +44 (0)1992 634 255
Fax: +44 (0)1992 630 506
Email: orders@imperialengineering.co.uk
Web site: www.imperialengineering.co.uk

JOHN JORDAN LTD
UK and Ireland supplier
Unit 3, Toll Bar Estate, Sedbergh, Cumbria,
LA10 5HA, United Kingdom
Tel: +44 (0)1539 621 884
Email: info@roofbox.co.uk
Web site: www.autosock.co.uk
AutoSock tyre socks give buses and coaches
extraordinary grip on snow and ice. Quick and
easy to fit, small to store.
Maggi's snow chains for coaches are a bigger
version of their car chains - and as quick and
easy to fit.

KCP CAR & COMMERCIAL LTD
Unit 15, Hillside Road, Kempson Way,
Bury St Edmunds, Suffolk, IP32 7EA,
United Kingdom
Tel: +44 (0)1284 750 777
Fax: +44 (0)1284 750 773
Email: kcponline@yahoo.co.uk
Web site: kcpcarandcommercial.co.uk

**KNORR-BREMSE SYSTEMS FOR
COMMERCIAL VEHICLES LTD**
Century House, Folly Brook Road,
Emerald Park East, Emersons Green, Bristol,
BS16 7FE, United Kingdom
Tel: +44 (0)117 984 6100
Email: uksales@knorr-bremse.co.uk
Web site: www.knorr-bremse.co.uk

**LAWMAN COMMERCIAL
SERVICES LTD**
31 Merrylees Industrial Estate, Leeside, Desford,
Leicestershire, LE9 9FS, United Kingdom
Tel: +44 (0)1530 231 235
Email: sales@lawmancommercials.com
Web site: www.lawmancommercials.net

LAWTON SERVICES LTD
Knutsford Road, Church Lawton, Stoke-On-Trent,
ST7 3DN, United Kingdom
Tel: +44 (0)1270 882 056
Fax: +44 (0)1270 883 014
Email: info@lawtonservices.co.uk
Web site: www.lawtonservices.co.uk

LH GROUP SERVICES LTD
Graycar Business Park, Barton Under Needwood,
Burton-On-Trent, DE13 8EN,
United Kingdom
Tel: +44 (0)1283 722 600
Email: enquiries@lh-group.co.uk
Web site: www.lh-group.co.uk

MITCHELL POWERSYSTEMS
Mitchell Diesel Ltd, Fulwood Road South,
Sutton-In-Ashfield, Nottinghamshire, NG17 2JZ,
United Kingdom
Tel: +44 (0)1623 550 550
Fax: +44 (0)1623 443 041
Email: sales@mitchells.co.uk
Web site: www.mitchells.co.uk

MOCAP LTD
Hortonwood 35, Telford, TF1 7YW,
United Kingdom
Tel: +44 (0)1952 670 247
Fax: +44 (0)1952 670 241
Email: sales@mocap.co.uk
Web site: www.mocap.co.uk

MOSELEY (PCV) LTD
Elmsall Way, Dale Lane, South Elmsall, Pontefract,
West Yorkshire, WF9 2XS, United Kingdom
Tel: +44 (0)1977 609 000
Fax: +44 (0)1977 609 900
Email: enquiries@moseleycoachsales.co.uk
Web site: www.moseleycoachsales.co.uk

MOSELEY DISTRIBUTORS LTD
Rydenmains, Condorrat Road, Glenmavis, Airdrie,
ML6 0PP, United Kingdom
Tel: +44 (0)1236 750 501
Fax: +44 (0)1236 750 504
Email: enquiries@moseleydistributors.co.uk
Web site: www.moseleydistributors.co.uk

OMNI-TECH ELECTRONICS
Unit 9, Prospect House, Ireland Industrial Estate,
Staveley, Chesterfield, Derbyshire, S43 3QE,
United Kingdom
Tel: +44 (0)1246 474 332
Fax: +44 (0)1246 529 010
Email: help@omni-techelectronics.co.uk
Web site: www.buselectronics.co.uk

OPTARE PARTS DIVISION
Hurricane Way South, Sherburn In Elmet, Leeds,
LS25 6PT, United Kingdom
Tel: +44 (0)871 230 1324
Email: parts@optare.com
Web site: www.optare.com

PARTLINE LTD
Dockfield Road, Shipley, BD17 7AZ,
United Kingdom
Tel: +44 (0)1274 531 531
Fax: +44 (0)1274 531 088
Email: sales@partline.co.uk
Web site: www.partline.co.uk

PLAXTON PARTS
Ryton Road, Anston, Sheffield, S25 4DL,
United Kingdom
Tel: +44 (0)844 822 6224
Fax: +44 (0)1909 550 050
Email: parts@plaxtonlimited.co.uk
Web site: www.plaxtonaftercare.co.uk

PNEUMAX LTD
110 Vista Park, Mauretania Road, Nursling,
Southampton, SO16 0YS, United Kingdom
Tel: +44 (0)2380 740 412
Fax: +44 (0)2380 739 340
Email: sales@pneumax.co.uk
Web site: www.pneumax.co.uk

PREMIER COMPONENTS UK LTD
Unit 701, Long Marston Storage, Campden Road,
Long Marston, Stratford-upon-Avon,
Warwickshire, CV37 8QR,
United Kingdom
Tel: +44 (0)1789 721 010
Fax: +44 (0)1789 722 429
Web site: www.premiercore.com

PSV TRANSPORT SYSTEMS LTD
21 Impresa Park, Pindar Road, Hoddesdon,
Hertfordshire, EN11 0DL, United Kingdom
Tel: +44 (0)1992 479 950
Fax: +44 (0)1992 471 676
Email: sales@psv-transport-systems.co.uk
Web site: www.psv-transport-systems.co.uk

Q'STRAINT
Units 72-76 John Wilson Business Park,
Whitstable, Kent, CT5 3QT, United Kingdom
Tel: +44 (0)1227 773 035
Fax: +44 (0)1227 770 035
Email: info@qstraint.co.uk
Web site: www.qstraint.com

QUEENSBRIDGE (PSV) LTD
Milner Way, Longlands Industrial Estate, Ossett,
WF5 9JE, United Kingdom
Tel: +44 (0)1924 281 871
Fax: +44 (0)1924 281 807
Email: enquiries@queensbridgeltd.co.uk
Web site: www.queensbridgeltd.co.uk

ROADLINK INTERNATIONAL LTD
Strawberry Lane, Willenhall, West Midlands,
WV13 3RL, United Kingdom
Tel: +44 (0)1902 636 206
Fax: +44 (0)1902 631 515
Email: sales@roadlink-international.co.uk
Web site: www.roadlink-international.co.uk

ROUTEMASTER BUSES LTD
Unit 3, Gate Farm, Wettenhall Road, Nantwich,
Cheshire, CW5 6AL, United Kingdom
Tel: +44 (0)1270 621 769
Email: info@routemasterbuses.co.uk
Web site: www.routemasterbuses.co.uk

SHADES TECHNICS LTD
Units E3 & E4, RD Park, Stephenson Close,
Hoddesdon, Hertfordshire, EN11 0BW,
United Kingdom
Tel: +44 (0)1992 476 830
Email: info@shades-technics.com
Web site: www.shades-technics.com

SHAWSON SUPPLY LTD
12 Station Road, Saintfield, County Down,
BT24 7DU, Northern Ireland
Tel: +44 (0)28 9751 0994
Email: info@shawsonsupply.co.uk
Web site: www.shawsonsupply.co.uk

TRAMONTANA COACH DISTRIBUTORS
Chapelknowe Road, Carfin, Motherwell, ML1 5LE,
United Kingdom
Tel: 01698 861790
Fax: 01698 860778
Email: wdt90@hotmail.co.uk
Web site: www.tramontanacoach.co.uk

TTS UK
Total Tool Solutions Ltd, Newhaven Business Park,
Lowergate, Milnsbridge, Huddersfield, HD3 4HS,
United Kingdom
Tel: +44 (0)1484 642 211
Fax: +44 (0)1484 461 002
Email: sales@ttsuk.com
Web site: www.ttsuk.com

VOLVO BUS AND COACH CENTRE
Parts Sales & Body Repair/Refurbishment
Specialists - Byron Street Extension,
Loughborough, LE11 5HE, United Kingdom
Tel: +44 (0)1509 217 700
Fax: +44 (0)1509 238 770
Email: dporter@volvocoachsales.co.uk
Web site: www.volvobuses.com

WABCO AUTOMOTIVE UK LTD
Unit A1, Grange Valley Road, Batley,
West Yorkshire, WF17 6GH, United Kingdom
Tel: +44 (0)1924 595 400
Email: info.uk@wabco-auto.com
Web site: www.wabco-auto.com

WACTON COACH SALES & SERVICES
Steamhall Garage, Linton Trading Estate,
Bromyard, Herefordshire, HR7 4QL,
United Kingdom
Tel: +44 (0)1885 482 782

WALSH'S ENGINEERING LTD
Barton Moss Road, Eccles, Manchester, M30 7RL,
United Kingdom
Tel: +44 (0)161 787 7017
Fax: +44 (0)161 787 7038
Email: walshs@gardnerdiesel.co.uk
Web site: www.gardnerdiesel.co.uk

TREVOR WIGLEY & SONS BUS LTD
Boulder Bridge Lane, Carlton, Barnsley, S71 3HJ,
United Kingdom
Tel: +44 (0)1226 713 636
Fax: +44 (0)1226 700 199
Email: wigleys@btconnect.com
Web site: www.twigley.com
Passenger Vehicle Dismantling/Spares

ZF POWERTRAIN
Stringes Close, Willenhall, WV13 1LE,
United Kingdom
Tel: +44 (0)1902 366 000
Email: sales@powertrain.co.uk
Web site: www.zfpowertrain.co.uk

PASSENGER INFORMATION DISPLAYS

ARRIVA BUS & COACH
Lodge Garage, Whitehall Road, Gomersal,
Cleckheaton, West Yorkshire, BD19 4BJ,
United Kingdom
Tel: +44 (0)1274 681 144
Email: busandcoachparts@arriva.co.uk
Web site: www.arrivabusandcoach.co.uk

AUTOSOUND LTD
4 Lister Street, Dudley Hill, Bradford, BD4 9PQ,
United Kingdom
Tel: +44 (0)1274 688 990
Fax: +44 (0)1274 651 318
Web site: www.autosound.co.uk

CYBERLYNE COMMUNICATIONS LTD
Unit 5, Hatfield Way,
South Church Enterprise Park, Bishop Auckland,
Durham, DL14 6XF, United Kingdom
Tel: 01388 773761
Fax: 01388 773778
Email: sales@cyberlyne.co.uk
Web site: www.cyberlyne.co.uk

HANOVER DISPLAYS LTD
Southerham House, Southerham Lane, Lewes,
BN8 6JN, United Kingdom
Tel: +44 (0)1273 477 528
Email: sales@hanoverdisplays.com
Web site: www.hanoverdisplays.com

INIT INNOVATIONS IN TRANSPORTATION LTD
Price House, 37 Stoney Street, The Lace Market,
Nottingham, NG1 1LS, United Kingdom
Tel: +44 (0)870 890 4648
Email: sales@init.co.uk
Web site: www.init.co.uk

J MURDOCH WIGHT LTD
Systems House, Pentland Industrial Estate,
Loanhead, Midlothian, EH20 9QH,
United Kingdom
Tel: +44 (0)131 440 3633
Email: enquiries@jmw-systems.co.uk
Web site: www.jmw-systems.co.uk

JOURNEY PLAN LTD
30 Canmore Street, Dunfermline, KY12 7NT,
United Kingdom
Tel: +44 (0)1383 731 048
Email: support@journeyplan.co.uk
Web site: www.journeyplan.co.uk

MCKENNA BROTHERS LTD
McKenna House, Jubilee Road, Middleton,
Manchester, M24 2LX, United Kingdom
Tel: +44 (0)161 655 3244
Fax: +44 (0)161 655 3059
Email: info@mckennabrothers.co.uk
Web site: www.mckennabrothers.co.uk

NIMBUS JOURNEY INFORMATION LTD
Suite F4 and F5, Worth Corner, Turners Hill Road,
Crawley, West Sussex, RH10 7SL, United Kingdom
Tel: +44 (0)1293 887 308
Email: sales@nimbusjourneyinfo.co.uk
Web site: www.nimbusjourneyinfo.co.uk

SSL SIMULATION SYSTEMS LTD
Unit 12, Market Industrial Estate, Yatton, Bristol,
BS49 4RF, United Kingdom
Tel: +44 (0)1934 838 803
Fax: +44 (0)1934 876 202
Web site: www.simulation-systems.co.uk

PNEUMATIC VALVES/CYLINDERS

IMPERIAL ENGINEERING
Delamare Road, Cheshunt, Hertfordshire,
EN8 9UD, United Kingdom
Tel: +44 (0)1992 634 255
Fax: +44 (0)1992 630 506
Email: orders@imperialengineering.co.uk
Web site: www.imperialengineering.co.uk

KCP CAR & COMMERCIAL LTD
Unit 15, Hillside Road, Kempson Way,
Bury St Edmunds, Suffolk, IP32 7EA,
United Kingdom
Tel: +44 (0)1284 750 777
Fax: +44 (0)1284 750 773
Email: kcponline@yahoo.co.uk
Web site: www.kcpcarandcommercial.co.uk

OPTARE PARTS DIVISION
Hurricane Way South, Sherburn In Elmet, Leeds,
LS25 6PT, United Kingdom
Tel: +44 (0)871 230 1324
Email: parts@optare.com
Web site: www.optare.com

PNEUMAX LTD
110 Vista Park, Mauretania Road, Nursling,
Southampton, SO16 0YS, United Kingdom
Tel: +44 (0)2380 740 412
Fax: +44 (0)2380 739 340
Email: sales@pneumax.co.uk
Web site: www.pneumax.co.uk

RAPID TRANSIT/PRIORITY EQUIPMENT

ALSTOM TRANSPORT SA
48 rue Albert Dhalenne, F-93482 Saint-
Ouen Cedex, France
Tel: +33 1 41 66 90 00
Fax: +33 1 41 66 96 66
Web site: www.alstom.com

PARRY PEOPLE MOVERS LTD
Overend Road, Cradley Heath, West Midlands,
B64 7DD, United Kingdom
Tel: +44 (0)1384 569 553
Fax: +44 (0)1384 637 753
Email: info@parrypeoplemovers.com
Web site: www.parrypeoplemovers.com

SIEMENS MOBILITY, TRAFFIC SOLUTIONS
Sopers Lane, Poole, BH17 7ER, United Kingdom
Tel: +44 (0)1202 782 000
Web site: www.siemens.co.uk

SUSTRACO LTD
8 Ashgrove Road, Redland, Bristol, BS6 6LY, UK
Tel: +44 (0)117 930 0901
Web site: www.ultralightrail.com

REPAIRS/REFURBISHMENT

CARLYLE BUS & COACH LTD
Carlyle Business Park, Great Bridge Street,
Swan Village, West Bromwich, B70 0X4,
United Kingdom
Tel: 0121 524 1200
Fax: 0121 524 1201
Email: westbromwichsales@carlyleplc.co.uk
Web site: www.carlylebusandcoach.com

COACH GLAZING SERVICES
Unit 2, Washingford Row, Milltown, Dungannon,
Co. Tyrone, BT71 7BG, Northern Ireland
Contact: Stephen Ferguson,
National Sales Manager
Tel: 0800 954 1934 (NI)/1 800 937 440 (Eire)
Email: info@coachglazingservices.com

COACH-AID LTD
Greyfriars Workshop, Greyfriars Way, Stafford,
Staffordshire, ST16 2SH, United Kingdom
Tel: +44 (0)1785 222 666
Email: workshop@coach-aid.com
Web site: www.coach-aid.com

FERRYMILL MOTORS
Campsie Road, Torrance, Glasgow, G64 4NP,
United Kingdom
Tel: +44 (0)1360 620 544
Fax: +44 (0)1360 620 990
Email: info@ferrymillmotors.co.uk
Web site: www.ferrymillmotors.co.uk

GRAYSON THERMAL SYSTEMS
Wharfdale House, 257 Wharfdale Road, Tyseley,
Birmingham, B11 2DP, United Kingdom
Tel: +44 (0)121 700 5600
Fax: +44 (0)121 700 5601
Email: cs@graysonts.com
Web site: www.graysonts.com

IGP SOLUTIONS
16 Hillbottom Road, High Wycombe, HP12 4HJ,
United Kingdom
Tel: +44 (0)1494 533 131
Fax: +44 (0)1494 462 675
Email: sales@igpsolutions.com
Web site: www.igpsolutions.com

IMPERIAL ENGINEERING
Delamare Road, Cheshunt, Hertfordshire,
EN8 9UD, United Kingdom
Tel: +44 (0)1992 634 255
Fax: +44 (0)1992 630 506
Email: orders@imperialengineering.co.uk
Web site: www.imperialengineering.co.uk

LAWMAN COMMERCIAL SERVICES LTD
31 Merrylees Industrial Estate, Leeside, Desford,
Leicestershire, LE9 9FS, United Kingdom
Tel: +44 (0)1530 231 235
Email: sales@lawmancommercials.com
Web site: www.lawmancommercials.net

RETARDERS AND SPEED CONTROL SYSTEMS

ARRIVA BUS & COACH
Lodge Garage, Whitehall Road, Gomersal,
Cleckheaton, West Yorkshire, BD19 4BJ,
United Kingdom
Tel: +44 (0)1274 681 144
Email: busandcoachparts@arriva.co.uk
Web site: www.arrivabusandcoach.co.uk

GROENEVELD UK LTD
The Greentec Centre, Gelders Hall Road,
Shepshed, Leicestershire, LE12 9NH,
United Kingdom
Tel: +44 (0)1509 600 033
Fax: +44 (0)1509 602 000
Email: info-uk@groeneveld-group.com
Web site: www.groeneveld-group.com

OMNI-TECH ELECTRONICS
Unit 9, Prospect House, Ireland Industrial Estate,
Staveley, Chesterfield, Derbyshire, S43 3QE,
United Kingdom
Tel: +44 (0)1246 474 332
Fax: +44 (0)1246 529 010
Email: help@omni-techelectronics.co.uk
Web site: www.buselectronics.co.uk

PARTLINE LTD
Dockfield Road, Shipley, BD17 7AZ,
United Kingdom
Tel: +44 (0)1274 531 531
Fax: +44 (0)1274 531 088
Email: sales@partline.co.uk
Web site: www.partline.co.uk

PSV TRANSPORT SYSTEMS LTD
21 Impresa Park, Pindar Road, Hoddesdon,
Hertfordshire, EN11 0DL, United Kingdom
Tel: +44 (0)1992 479 950
Fax: +44 (0)1992 471 676
Email: sales@psv-transport-systems.co.uk
Web site: www.psv-transport-systems.co.uk

TELMA RETARDER
UK Distributor EMR Technology Ltd
9 Brindley Close, Daventry, Northants, NN11 8RP,
United Kingdom
Tel: +44 (0)1327 828 722
Fax: +44 (0)1327 651 188
Email: info@emrtech.co.uk
Web site: www.emrtech.co.uk

VOITH TURBO LTD
6 Beddington Farm Road, Croydon, CR0 4XB,
United Kingdom
Tel: +44 (0)20 8667 0333
Fax: +44 (0)20 8667 0403
Email: road.uk@voith.com
Web site: www.uk.voithturbo.com

WABCO AUTOMOTIVE UK LTD
Unit A1, Grange Valley Road, Batley,
West Yorkshire, WF17 6GH, United Kingdom
Tel: +44 (0)1924 595 400
Email: info.uk@wabco-auto.com
Web site: www.wabco-auto.com

REVERSING SAFETY SYSTEMS

ARRIVA BUS & COACH
Lodge Garage, Whitehall Road, Gomersal,
Cleckheaton, West Yorkshire, BD19 4BJ,
United Kingdom
Tel: +44 (0)1274 681 144
Email: busandcoachparts@arriva.co.uk
Web site: www.arrivabusandcoach.co.uk

ASHTREE VISION & SAFETY
Ashtree Works, Brownroyd Street, Bradford,
BD8 9AF, United Kingdom
Tel: +44 (0)1274 546 732
Fax: +44 (0)1274 548 525
Email: sales@avsuk.co
Web site: www.avsuk.co

AUTOSOUND LTD
4 Lister Street, Dudley Hill, Bradford, BD4 9PQ,
United Kingdom
Tel: +44 (0)1274 688 990
Fax: +44 (0)1274 651 318
Web site: www.autosound.co.uk

AVT SYSTEMS LTD
Unit 3 & 4, Tything Road East, Alcester,
Warwickshire, B49 6ES, United Kingdom
Tel: +44 (0)1789 400 357
Fax: +44 (0)1789 400 359
Email: enquiries@avtsystems.co.uk
Web site: www.avtsystems.co.uk

BRIGADE ELECTRONICS PLC
Brigade House, The Mills, Station Road,
South Darenth, DA4 9BD, United Kingdom
Tel: +44 (0)1322 420 300
Fax: +44 (0)1322 420 343
Email: info@brigade-electronics.co.uk
Web site: www.brigade-electronics.com

CARLYLE BUS & COACH LTD
Carlyle Business Park, Great Bridge Street,
Swan Village, West Bromwich, B70 0X4,
United Kingdom
Tel: 0121 524 1200
Fax: 0121 524 1201
Email: westbromwichsales@carlyleplc.co.uk
Web site: www.carlylebusandcoach.com

CLAN TOOLS & PLANT LTD
Caponacre Industrial Estate, Cumnock, Ayrshire,
KA18 1SH, United Kingdom
Tel: +44 (0)1290 424200
Email: info@clantools.com
Web site: www.clantools.com

CYBERLYNE COMMUNICATIONS LTD
Unit 5, Hatfield Way,
South Church Enterprise Park, Bishop Auckland,
Durham, DL14 6XF, United Kingdom
Tel: 01388 773761
Fax: 01388 773778
Email: sales@cyberlyne.co.uk
Web site: www.cyberlyne.co.uk

EXPRESS COACH REPAIRS LTD
Outgang Lane, Pickering, YO18 7EL,
United Kingdom
Tel: +44 (0)1751 475 215
Email: expresscoachrepairs@hotmail.co.uk

GROENEVELD UK LTD
The Greentec Centre, Gelders Hall Road,
Shepshed, Leicestershire, LE12 9NH,
United Kingdom
Tel: +44 (0)1509 600 033
Fax: +44 (0)1509 602 000
Email: info-uk@groeneveld-group.com
Web site: www.groeneveld-group.com

KCP CAR & COMMERCIAL LTD
Unit 15, Hillside Road, Kempson Way,
Bury St Edmunds, Suffolk, IP32 7EA,
United Kingdom
Tel: +44 (0)1284 750 777
Fax: +44 (0)1284 750 773

Email: kcponline@yahoo.co.uk
Web site: kcpcarandcommercial.co.uk

PARTLINE LTD
Dockfield Road, Shipley, BD17 7AZ,
United Kingdom
Tel: +44 (0)1274 531 531
Fax: +44 (0)1274 531 088
Email: sales@partline.co.uk
Web site: www.partline.co.uk

PLAXTON PARTS
Ryton Road, Anston, Sheffield, S25 4DL,
United Kingdom
Tel: +44 (0)844 822 6224
Fax: +44 (0)1909 550 050
Email: parts@plaxtonlimited.co.uk
Web site: www.plaxtonaftercare.co.uk

PLAXTON SERVICE
Ryton Road, Anston, Sheffield, S25 4DL,
United Kingdom
Tel: +44 (0)1909 551 155
Fax: +44 (0)1909 550 050
Email: service@plaxtonlimited.co.uk
Web site: www.plaxtonaftercare.co.uk

ROLLER BLINDS, PASSENGER AND DRIVER

ARRIVA BUS & COACH
Lodge Garage, Whitehall Road, Gomersal,
Cleckheaton, West Yorkshire, BD19 4BJ,
United Kingdom
Tel: +44 (0)1274 681 144
Email: busandcoachparts@arriva.co.uk
Web site: www.arrivabusandcoach.co.uk

CARLYLE BUS & COACH LTD
Carlyle Business Park, Great Bridge Street,
Swan Village, West Bromwich, B70 0X4,
United Kingdom
Tel: 0121 524 1200
Fax: 0121 524 1201
Email: westbromwichsales@carlyleplc.co.uk
Web site: www.carlylebusandcoach.com

HAPPICH UK LTD
Unit 26, Webb Ellis Industrial Estate, Wood Street,
Rugby, Warwickshire, CV21 2NP, United Kingdom
Tel: +44 (0)1788 50703
Fax: +44 (0)1788 44972
Email: info@happich.co.uk
Web site: www.happich.de

LAWTON SERVICES LTD
Knutsford Road, Church Lawton, Stoke-On-Trent,
ST7 3DN, United Kingdom
Tel: +44 (0)1270 882 056
Fax: +44 (0)1270 883 014
Email: info@lawtonservices.co.uk
Web site: www.lawtonservices.co.uk

PLAXTON PARTS
Ryton Road, Anston, Sheffield, S25 4DL,
United Kingdom
Tel: +44 (0)844 822 6224
Fax: +44 (0)1909 550 050
Email: parts@plaxtonlimited.co.uk
Web site: www.plaxtonaftercare.co.uk

PLAXTON SERVICE
Ryton Road, Anston, Sheffield, S25 4DL,
United Kingdom
Tel: +44 (0)1909 551 155
Fax: +44 (0)1909 550 050
Email: service@plaxtonlimited.co.uk
Web site: www.plaxtonaftercare.co.uk

WIDNEY MANUFACTURING LTD
Plume Street, Aston, Birmingham, B6 7RX,
United Kingdom
Tel: +44 (0)121 327 5500
Fax: +44 (0)121 328 2466
Email: info@widney.co.uk
Web site: www.widney.co.uk

ROOF LINING FABRICS

AK CARPETS LTD
Unit 4, Robinson Court, Brockholes Way,
Claughton on Brock, Lancashire, PR 0PZ,
United Kingdom
Tel: +44 (0)1995 643 033
Fax: +44 (0)1995 643 231
Email: info@akcarpets.com
Web site: www.akcarpets.com

ARDEE COACH TRIM LTD
Artnalivery, Ardee, Co Louth, Republic of Ireland
Tel: +353 41 685 3599
Fax: +353 41 685 7016
Email: info@ardeecoachtrim.com
Web site: www.ardeecoachtrim.com

ARRIVA BUS & COACH
Lodge Garage, Whitehall Road, Gomersal,
Cleckheaton, West Yorkshire, BD19 4BJ,
United Kingdom
Tel: +44 (0)1274 681 144
Email: busandcoachparts@arriva.co.uk
Web site: www.arrivabusandcoach.co.uk

AUTOMATE WHEEL COVERS LTD
California Mills, Oxford Road, Gomersal,
Cleckheaton, BD19 4HQ, United Kingdom
Tel: +44 (0)1274 862 700
Fax: +44 (0)1274 851 989
Email: sales@wheeltrimshop.com
Web site: www.wheeltrimshop.com

AUTOMOTIVE TEXTILE INDUSTRIES
Unit 15 & 16, Priest Court,
Springfield Business Park, Grantham, NG31 7BG,
United Kingdom
Tel: +44 (0)1476 593 050
Fax: +44 (0)1476 593 607
Email: sales@atindustries.co.uk
Web site: www.atindustries.co.uk

DUOFLEX LTD
Trimmingham House, 2 Shires Road,
Buckingham Road Industrial Estate, Brackley,
Northamptonshire, NN13 7F7, United Kingdom
Tel: +44 (0)1280 701 366
Fax: +44 (0)1280 704 799
Email: info@duoflex.co.uk
Web site: www.duoflex.co.uk

EXPRESS COACH REPAIRS LTD
Outgang Lane, Pickering, YO18 7EL,
United Kingdom
Tel: +44 (0)1751 475 215
Email: expresscoachrepairs@hotmail.co.uk

HAPPICH UK LTD
Unit 26, Webb Ellis Industrial Estate, Wood Street,
Rugby, Warwickshire, CV21 2NP, United Kingdom
Tel: +44 (0)1788 50703
Fax: +44 (0)1788 44972
Email: info@happich.co.uk
Web site: www.happich.de

MARTYN INDUSTRIALS LTD
5 Brunel Way, Durranhill Industrial Park, Harraby,
Carlisle, CA1 3NQ, United Kingdom
Tel: +44 (0)1228 544 000
Email: enquiries@martyn-industrials.co.uk
Web site: www.martyn-industrials.com

SEAT BELTS/RESTRAINT SYSTEMS

ABACUS TRANSPORT PRODUCTS LTD
Abacus House, Highlode Industrial Estate, Ramsey,
Huntingdon, PE26 2RB, United Kingdom
Tel: +44 (0)1487 710 700
Fax: +44 (0)1487 710 626
Email: sales@abacus-tp.com
Web site: www.abacus-tp.com

**AMSAFE COMMERCIAL PRODUCTS
LTD**
Unit 16/17, Bookham Industrial Park,
Church Road, Bookham, KT23 3EU,
United Kingdom
Tel: +44 (0)1372 451 272
Fax: +44 (0)1372 451 282
Web site: www.amsafe.com

ARDEE COACH TRIM LTD
Artnalivery, Ardee, Co Louth, Republic of Ireland
Tel: +353 41 685 3599
Fax: +353 41 685 7016
Email: info@ardeecoachtrim.com
Web site: www.ardeecoachtrim.com

ARRIVA BUS & COACH
Lodge Garage, Whitehall Road, Gomersal,
Cleckheaton, West Yorkshire, BD19 4BJ,
United Kingdom
Tel: +44 (0)1274 681 144
Email: busandcoachparts@arriva.co.uk
Web site: www.arrivabusandcoach.co.uk

BHI UK
The Bus Depot, 1 Sky Lane, Haddington, Lincoln,
LN5 9FE, United Kingdom
Tel: +44 (0)1522 689 911
Fax: +44 (0)1522 689 922
Email: info@bhiuk.com
Web site: www.bhiuk.com
Seat belts
Seat belt signs

CARLYLE BUS & COACH LTD
Carlyle Business Park, Great Bridge Street,
Swan Village, West Bromwich, B70 0X4,
United Kingdom
Tel: 0121 524 1200
Fax: 0121 524 1201
Email: westbromwichsales@carlyleplc.co.uk
Web site: www.carlylebusandcoach.com

EXPRESS COACH REPAIRS LTD
Outgang Lane, Pickering, YO18 7EL,
United Kingdom
Tel: +44 (0)1751 475 215
Email: expresscoachrepairs@hotmail.co.uk

KCP CAR & COMMERCIAL LTD
Unit 15, Hillside Road, Kempson Way,
Bury St Edmunds, Suffolk, IP32 7EA, UK
Tel: +44 (0)1284 750 777
Fax: +44 (0)1284 750 773
Email: kcponline@yahoo.co.uk
Web site: kcpcarandcommercial.co.uk

LAWTON SERVICES LTD
Knutsford Road, Church Lawton, Stoke-On-Trent,
ST7 3DN, United Kingdom
Tel: +44 (0)1270 882 056
Fax: +44 (0)1270 883 014
Email: info@lawtonservices.co.uk
Web site: www.lawtonservices.co.uk

PARTLINE LTD
Dockfield Road, Shipley, BD17 7AZ,
United Kingdom
Tel: +44 (0)1274 531 531
Fax: +44 (0)1274 531 088
Email: sales@partline.co.uk
Web site: www.partline.co.uk

PLAXTON PARTS
Ryton Road, Anston, Sheffield, S25 4DL,
United Kingdom
Tel: +44 (0)844 822 6224
Fax: +44 (0)1909 550 050
Email: parts@plaxtonlimited.co.uk
Web site: www.plaxtonaftercare.co.uk

PLAXTON SERVICE
Ryton Road, Anston, Sheffield, S25 4DL,
United Kingdom
Tel: +44 (0)1909 551 155
Fax: +44 (0)1909 550 050
Email: service@plaxtonlimited.co.uk
Web site: www.plaxtonaftercare.co.uk

Q'STRAINT
Units 72-76 John Wilson Business Park,
Whitstable, Kent, CT5 3QT, United Kingdom
Tel: +44 (0)1227 773 035
Fax: +44 (0)1227 770 035
Email: info@qstraint.co.uk
Web site: www.qstraint.com

RESCROFT LTD
20 Oxleasow Road, East Moons Moat, Redditch,
B98 0RE, United Kingdom
Tel: +44 (0)1527 521 300
Fax: +44 (0)1527 521 301
Email: sales@rescroft.com
Web site: www.rescroft.com

SECURON (AMERSHAM) LTD
The Hill, Winchmore Hill, Amersham, HP7 0NZ,
United Kingdom
Tel: +44 (0)1494 434 455
Fax: +44 (0)1494 726 499
Email: spsales@securon.co.uk
Web site: www.securon.co.uk

TEK SEATING LTD
14 Decimus Park, Kingstanding Way,
Tunbridge Wells, Kent, TN2 3GP, United Kingdom
Tel: +44 (0)1892 515 028
Fax: +44 (0)1892 529 751
Email: sales@tekseating.co.uk
Web site: www.tekseating.co.uk

**TRAMONTANA COACH
DISTRIBUTORS**
Chapelknowe Road, Carfin, Motherwell, ML1 5LE,
United Kingdom
Tel: 01698 861790
Fax: 01698 860778
Email: wdt90@hotmail.co.uk
Web site: www.tramontanacoach.co.uk

UNWIN SAFETY SYSTEMS
Unwin House, The Horseshoe, Coat Road,
Martock, TA12 6EY, United Kingdom
Tel: +44 (0)1935 827 740
Fax: +44 (0)1935 827 760
Email: sales@unwin-safety.co.uk
Web site: www.unwin-safety.com

SEATS, SEAT CUSHIONS AND SEAT FRAMES

ABACUS TRANSPORT PRODUCTS LTD
Abacus House, Highlode Industrial Estate, Ramsey,
Huntingdon, PE26 2RB, United Kingdom
Tel: +44 (0)1487 710 700
Fax: +44 (0)1487 710 626
Email: sales@abacus-tp.com
Web site: www.abacus-tp.com

ARDEE COACH TRIM LTD
Artnalivery, Ardee, Co Louth, Republic of Ireland
Tel: +353 41 685 3599
Fax: +353 41 685 7016
Email: info@ardeecoachtrim.com
Web site: www.ardeecoachtrim.com

ARRIVA BUS & COACH
Lodge Garage, Whitehall Road, Gomersal,
Cleckheaton, West Yorkshire, BD19 4BJ, UK
Tel: +44 (0)1274 681 144
Email: busandcoachparts@arriva.co.uk
Web site: www.arrivabusandcoach.co.uk

BERNSTEIN ENGINEERING LTD
United Kingdom
Tel: +44 (0)20 8428 3197
Fax: +44 (0)20 8428 3525
Email: contact@bernsteinengineering.co.uk
Web site: www.bernsteinengineering.co.uk

BHI UK
The Bus Depot, 1 Sky Lane, Haddington, Lincoln,
LN5 9FE, United Kingdom
Tel: +44 (0)1522 689 911
Fax: +44 (0)1522 689 922
Email: info@bhiuk.com
Web site: www.bhiuk.com
Seat spares and trim

CAMIRA (FORMERLY HOLDSWORTH FABRICS LTD)
The Watermill, Wheatley Park, Mirfield,
West Yorkshire, WF1 8HE, United Kingdom
Tel: +44 (0)1924 481 965
Fax: +44 (0)1484 859 061
Email: info@camirafabrics.com
Web site: www.camirafabrics.com

CARLYLE BUS & COACH LTD
Carlyle Business Park, Great Bridge Street,
Swan Village, West Bromwich, B70 0X4, UK
Tel: 0121 524 1200
Fax: 0121 524 1201
Email: westbromwichsales@carlyleplc.co.uk
Web site: www.carlylebusandcoach.com

CHAPMAN DRIVER SEATING
109-138 Northwood Street, Birmingham, B3 1SZ,
United Kingdom
Tel: 0845 838 2305
Fax: 0845 838 2909
Email: sales@chapmandriverseating.com
Web site: www.chapmandriverseating.com

COGENT PASSENGER SEATING LTD
Prydwen Road, Swansea West Industrial Park,
Swansea, SA5 4HN, United Kingdom
Tel: +44 (0)1792 585 444
Fax: +44 (0)1792 588 191
Email: enquiries@cogentseating.co.uk
Web site: www.cogentseating.co.uk

DUOFLEX LTD
Trimmingham House, 2 Shires Road,
Buckingham Road Industrial Estate, Brackley,
Northamptonshire, NN13 7EZ, United Kingdom
Tel: +44 (0)1280 701 366
Fax: +44 (0)1280 704 799
Email: info@duoflex.co.uk
Web site: www.duoflex.co.uk

EXPRESS COACH REPAIRS LTD
Outgang Lane, Pickering, YO18 7EL, UK
Tel: +44 (0)1751 475 215
Email: expresscoachrepairs@hotmail.co.uk

HAPPICH UK LTD
Unit 26, Webb Ellis Industrial Estate, Wood Street,
Rugby, Warwickshire, CV21 2NP, United Kingdom
Tel: +44 (0)1788 50703
Fax: +44 (0)1788 44972
Email: info@happich.co.uk
Web site: www.happich.de

HOLDSWORTH (SEE CAMIRA)
The Watermill, Wheatley Park, Mirfield,
West Yorkshire, WF1 8HE, United Kingdom
Tel: +44 (0)1924 481 965
Fax: +44 (0)1484 859 061
Email: info@camirafabrics.com
Web site: www.camirafabrics.com

KAB SEATING LTD
Round Spinney, Northampton, NN3 8RS, UK
Tel: +44 (0)1604 790 500
Fax: +44 (0)1604 790 155
Email: infouk@cvgrp.com
Web site: www.kabseating.com

LAWTON SERVICES LTD
Knutsford Road, Church Lawton, Stoke-On-Trent,
ST7 3DN, United Kingdom
Tel: +44 (0)1270 882 056
Fax: +44 (0)1270 883 014
Email: info@lawtonservices.co.uk
Web site: www.lawtonservices.co.uk

PHOENIX SEATING LTD
Unit 47, Bay 3, Second Avenue, Pensnett Estate,
Kingswinford, DY6 7UZ, United Kingdom
Tel: +44 (0)1384 296 622
Fax: +44 (0)1384 287 831
Email: sales@phoenixseating.co.uk
Web site: www.phoenixseating.com

PLAXTON PARTS
Ryton Road, Anston, Sheffield, S25 4DL, UK
Tel: +44 (0)844 822 6224
Fax: +44 (0)1909 550 050
Email: parts@plaxtonlimited.co.uk
Web site: www.plaxtonaftercare.co.uk

PLAXTON SERVICE
Ryton Road, Anston, Sheffield, S25 4DL,
United Kingdom
Tel: +44 (0)1909 551 155
Fax: +44 (0)1909 550 050
Email: service@plaxtonlimited.co.uk
Web site: www.plaxtonaftercare.co.uk

RESCROFT LTD
20 Oxleasow Road, East Moons Moat, Redditch,
B98 0RE, United Kingdom
Tel: +44 (0)1527 521 300
Fax: +44 (0)1527 521 301
Email: sales@rescroft.com
Web site: www.rescroft.com

RSH SERVICES
Southedge Works, Hipperholme, Halifax, HX3 8EF,
United Kingdom
Tel: +44 (0)1422 202 840
Fax: +44 (0)1422 206 070

SCANDUS UK
Unit 21, Gainsborough Trading Estate,
Rufford Road, Stourbridge, DY9 7ND,
United Kingdom
Tel: +44 (0)1384 443 409
Fax: +44 (0)1384 442 932
Email: paul.sproule@scandusuk.co.uk
Web site: www.scandus.co.uk

TEK SEATING LTD
14 Decimus Park, Kingstanding Way,
Tunbridge Wells, Kent, TN2 3GP, United Kingdom
Tel: +44 (0)1892 515 028
Fax: +44 (0)1892 529 751
Email: sales@tekseating.co.uk
Web site: www.tekseating.co.uk

WEST COAST TRIM
Unit 4D, Burton Road, Blackpool, FY4 4NW,
United Kingdom
Tel: +44 (0)1253 696 033
Email: info@westcoasttrim.co.uk
Web site: www.westcoasttrim.co.uk

SHELTERS/STREET FURNITURE

BUS SHELTERS LTD
Unit 60, Dyffryn Business Park,
Llantwit Major Road, Llandow, Vale of Glamorgan,
CF71 7PY, United Kingdom
Tel: +44 (0)1446 795 444
Fax: +44 (0)1446 793 344
Email: info@shelters.co.uk
Web site: www.shelters.co.uk

MACEMAIN + AMSTAD
Boyle Road, Willowbrook Industrial Estate, Corby,
NN17 5XU, United Kingdom
Tel: +44 (0)1536 401 331
Fax: +44 (0)1536 401 298
Email: sales@macemainamstad.com
Web site: www.macemainamstad.com

NEWBY FOUNDRIES LTD
1 Cornwall Road, Smethwick, West Midlands,
B66 2JT, United Kingdom
Tel: +44 (0)121 555 7615
Fax: +44 (0)121 505 3626
Email: sales@newbyfoundries.co.uk
Web site: www.newbyfoundries.co.uk

QUEENSBURY SHELTERS
Queensbury House, Fitzherbert Road, Farlington,
Portsmouth, PO6 1SE, United Kingdom
Tel: +44 (0)23 9221 0052
Fax: +44 (0)23 9221 0059
Email: shelters@queensbury.org
Web site: www.queensbury.org

TRUEFORM ENGINEERING LTD
Unit 4, Pasadena Trading Estate, Pasadena Close,
Hayes, UB3 3NQ, United Kingdom
Tel: +44 (0)20 8561 4959
Fax: +44 (0)20 8848 1397
Email: sales@trueform.co.uk
Web site: www.trueform.co.uk

SHOCK ABSORBERS AND SUSPENSION

ARRIVA BUS & COACH
Lodge Garage, Whitehall Road, Gomersal,
Cleckheaton, West Yorkshire, BD19 4BJ,
United Kingdom
Tel: +44 (0)1274 681 144
Email: busandcoachparts@arriva.co.uk
Web site: www.arrivabusandcoach.co.uk

CRESCENT FACILITIES LTD
72 Willow Crescent, Chapeltown, Sheffield,
S35 1QS, United Kingdom
Tel: +44 (0)114 245 1050
Email: cfl.chris@btinternet.com

DIRECT PARTS LTD
Unit 1, Churnet Court,
Churnetside Business Park, Harrison Way,
Cheddleton, ST13 7EF, United Kingdom
Tel: +44 (0)1538 361 777
Fax: +44 (0)1538 369 100
Email: sales@direct-group.co.uk
Web site: www.direct-group.co.uk

ERENTEK LTD
Malt Kiln Lane, Waddington, Lincoln, LN5 9RT,
United Kingdom
Tel: +44 (0)1522 720 065
Fax: +44 (0)1522 729 155
Email: sales@erentek.co.uk
Web site: www.erentek.co.uk

GLIDE RITE PRODUCTS
Mill Lane, Passfield, Liphook, GU30 7RP,
United Kingdom
Tel: +44 (0)1428 751 711
Fax: +44 (0)1428 751 766
Email: info@glide-rite.com
Web site: www.glide-rite.com

IMEXPART LTD
Links 31, Willowbridge Way, Whitwood,
Castleford, WF10 5NP, United Kingdom
Tel: +44 (0)1977 553 936
Email: sales@imexpart.com
Web site: www.imexpart.com

KCP CAR & COMMERCIAL LTD
Unit 15, Hillside Road, Kempson Way,
Bury St Edmunds, Suffolk, IP32 7EA, UK
Tel: +44 (0)1284 750 777
Fax: +44 (0)1284 750 773
Email: kcponline@yahoo.co.uk
Web site: kcpcarandcommercial.co.uk

OPTARE PARTS DIVISION
Hurricane Way South, Sherburn In Elmet, Leeds,
LS25 6PT, United Kingdom
Tel: +44 (0)871 230 1324
Email: parts@optare.com
Web site: www.optare.com

PARTLINE LTD
Dockfield Road, Shipley, BD17 7AZ, UK
Tel: +44 (0)1274 531 531
Fax: +44 (0)1274 531 088
Email: sales@partline.co.uk
Web site: www.partline.co.uk

POLYBUSH
Clywedog Road South, Wrexham Industrial Estate,
Wrexham, LL13 9XS, United Kingdom
Tel: +44 (0)1978 664 316
Fax: +44 (0)1978 661 190
Email: sales@polybush.co.uk
Web site: www.polybush.co.uk

ROADLINK INTERNATIONAL LTD
Strawberry Lane, Willenhall, West Midlands,
WV13 3RL, United Kingdom
Tel: +44 (0)1902 636 206
Fax: +44 (0)1902 631 515
Email: sales@roadlink-international.co.uk
Web site: www.roadlink-international.co.uk

SHAWSON SUPPLY LTD
12 Station Road, Saintfield, County Down,
BT24 7DU, Northern Ireland
Tel: +44 (0)28 9751 0994
Email: info@shawsonsupply.co.uk
Web site: www.shawsonsupply.co.uk

STEERING

ARRIVA BUS & COACH
Lodge Garage, Whitehall Road, Gomersal,
Cleckheaton, West Yorkshire, BD19 4BJ, UK
Tel: +44 (0)1274 681 144
Email: busandcoachparts@arriva.co.uk
Web site: www.arrivabusandcoach.co.uk

CRESCENT FACILITIES LTD
72 Willow Crescent, Chapeltown, Sheffield,
S35 1QS, United Kingdom
Tel: +44 (0)114 245 1050
Email: cfl.chris@btinternet.com

DIRECT PARTS LTD
Unit 1, Churnet Court,
Churnetside Business Park, Harrison Way,
Cheddleton, ST13 7EF, United Kingdom
Tel: +44 (0)1538 361 777
Fax: +44 (0)1538 369 100
Email: sales@direct-group.co.uk
Web site: www.direct-group.co.uk

IMEXPART LTD
Links 31, Willowbridge Way, Whitwood,
Castleford, WF10 5NP, United Kingdom
Tel: +44 (0)1977 553 936
Email: sales@imexpart.com
Web site: www.imexpart.com

IMPERIAL ENGINEERING
Delamare Road, Cheshunt, Hertfordshire,
EN8 9UD, United Kingdom
Tel: +44 (0)1992 634 255
Fax: +44 (0)1992 630 506
Email: orders@imperialengineering.co.uk
Web site: www.imperialengineering.co.uk

KCP CAR & COMMERCIAL LTD
Unit 15, Hillside Road, Kempson Way,
Bury St Edmunds, Suffolk, IP32 7EA, UK
Tel: +44 (0)1284 750 777
Fax: +44 (0)1284 750 773
Email: kcponline@yahoo.co.uk
Web site: kcpcarandcommercial.co.uk

OPTARE PARTS DIVISION
Hurricane Way South, Sherburn In Elmet, Leeds,
LS25 6PT, United Kingdom
Tel: +44 (0)871 230 1324
Email: parts@optare.com
Web site: www.optare.com

OPTARE PRODUCT SUPPORT
London
Unit 9, Eurocourt, Olivers Close, West Thurrock,
RM20 3EE, United Kingdom
Tel: +44 (0)1708 896 860
Fax: +44 (0)1708 869 920
Email: london.service@optare.com
Manchester
Trafford Park, Manchester, M17 1HG,
United Kingdom
Tel: +44 (0)161 872 7772
Email: manchester.service@optare.com
Rotherham
Denby Way, Hellaby, Rotherham, S66 8HR,
United Kingdom
Tel: +44 (0)1709 535 101
Fax: +44 (0)1709 739 680
Email: rotherham.service@optare.com

PARTLINE LTD
Dockfield Road, Shipley, BD17 7AZ,
United Kingdom
Tel: +44 (0)1274 531 531
Fax: +44 (0)1274 531 088
Email: sales@partline.co.uk
Web site: www.partline.co.uk

PREMIER COMPONENTS UK LTD
Unit 701, Long Marston Storage, Campden Road,
Long Marston, Stratford-upon-Avon,
Warwickshire, CV37 8QR, United Kingdom
Tel: +44 (0)1789 721 010
Fax: +44 (0)1789 722 429
Web site: www.premiercore.com

**PSS - STEERING & HYDRAULICS
DIVISION**
Folgate Road, North Walsham, NR28 0AJ,
United Kingdom
Tel: +44 (0)1692 406 017
Fax: +44 (0)1692 406 957
Email: sales@pss.co.uk
Web site: www.pss.co.uk

ROADLINK INTERNATIONAL LTD
Strawberry Lane, Willenhall, West Midlands,
WV13 3RL, United Kingdom
Tel: +44 (0)1902 636 206
Fax: +44 (0)1902 631 515
Email: sales@roadlink-international.co.uk
Web site: www.roadlink-international.co.uk

SHAWSON SUPPLY LTD
12 Station Road, Saintfield, County Down,
BT24 7DU, Northern Ireland
Tel: +44 (0)28 9751 0994
Email: info@shawsonsupply.co.uk
Web site: www.shawsonsupply.co.uk

**SHELLEY TRANSMISSION SERVICES
LTD**
Eagle Street, off Bilston Road, Wolverhampton,
WV2 2AQ, United Kingdom
Tel: +44 (0)1902 351 178
Fax: +44 (0)1902 352 545
Email: enquiries@shelleytransmission.co.uk
Web site: www.shelleytransmission.co.uk

HL SMITH TRANSMISSIONS LTD
Enterprise Business Park, Cross Road, Albrighton,
Wolverhampton, WV7 3BJ, United Kingdom
Tel: +44 (0)1902 373 011
Fax: +44 (0)1902 373 608
Web site: www.hlsmith.co.uk

ZF POWERTRAIN
Stringes Close, Willenhall, WV13 1LE,
United Kingdom
Tel: +44 (0)1902 366 000
Email: sales@powertrain.co.uk
Web site: www.zfpowertrain.co.uk

SURVEILLANCE SYSTEMS

21ST CENTURY TECHNOLOGY PLC
Units 3 & 4, ZK Park, 23 Commerce Way,
Croydon, Surrey, CR0 4ZS, United Kingdom
Tel: +44 (0)844 871 7990
Web site: www.21stplc.com

ACTIV CAMERAS
15 Abingdon Way, Stoke On Trent, ST4 8DX, UK
Tel: +44 (0)1782 644 496
Fax: +44 (0)1782 644 497
Email: mail@activcameras.com
Web site: www.activcameras.com

AUTOSOUND LTD
4 Lister Street, Dudley Hill, Bradford, BD4 9PQ,
United Kingdom
Tel: +44 (0)1274 688 990
Fax: +44 (0)1274 651 318
Web site: www.autosound.co.uk

AVT SYSTEMS LTD
Unit 3 & 4, Tything Road East, Alcester,

Warwickshire, B49 6ES, United Kingdom
Tel: +44 (0)1789 400 357
Fax: +44 (0)1789 400 359
Email: enquiries@avtsystems.co.uk
Web site: www.avtsystems.co.uk

BRIGADE ELECTRONICS PLC
Brigade House, The Mills, Station Road,
South Darenth, DA4 9BD, United Kingdom
Tel: +44 (0)1322 420 300
Fax: +44 (0)1322 420 343
Email: info@brigade-electronics.co.uk
Web site: www.brigade-electronics.com

BUS ELECTRICAL
United Kingdom
Tel: +44 (0)1254 701 242
Email: enquiries@buselectrical.com
Web site: www.buselectrical.com

CLAN TOOLS & PLANT LTD
Caponacre Industrial Estate, Cumnock, Ayrshire,
KA18 1SH, United Kingdom
Tel: +44 (0)1290 424200
Email: info@clantools.com
Web site: www.clantools.com

CYBERLYNE COMMUNICATIONS LTD
Unit 5, Hatfield Way,
South Church Enterprise Park, Bishop Auckland,
Durham, DL14 6XF, United Kingdom
Tel: 01388 773761
Fax: 01388 773778
Email: sales@cyberlyne.co.uk
Web site: www.cyberlyne.co.uk

DIRECT PARTS LTD
Unit 1, Churnet Court,
Churnetside Business Park, Harrison Way,
Cheddleton, ST13 7EF, United Kingdom
Tel: +44 (0)1538 361 777
Fax: +44 (0)1538 369 100
Email: sales@direct-group.co.uk
Web site: www.direct-group.co.uk

FUEL THEFT SOLUTIONS LTD
Unit 1, Yew Tree Business Units, Newcastle Road,
Betchton, Sandbach, Cheshire, CW11 4TD,
United Kingdom
Tel: 0845 077 3921
Fax: 0845 077 3922
Email: sales@dieseldye.com
Web site: www.dieseldye.com

GROENEVELD UK LTD
The Greentec Centre, Gelders Hall Road,
Shepshed, Leicestershire, LE12 9NH,
United Kingdom
Tel: +44 (0)1509 600 033
Fax: +44 (0)1509 602 000
Email: info-uk@groeneveld-group.com
Web site: www.groeneveld-group.com

**KNORR-BREMSE SYSTEMS FOR
COMMERCIAL VEHICLES LTD**
Century House, Folly Brook Road,
Emerald Park East, Emersons Green, Bristol,
BS16 7FE, United Kingdom
Tel: +44 (0)117 984 6100
Email: uksales@knorr-bremse.co.uk
Web site: www.knorr-bremse.co.uk

NIMBUS JOURNEY INFORMATION LTD
Suite F4 and F5, Worth Corner, Turners Hill Road,
Crawley, West Sussex, RH10 7SL,
United Kingdom
Tel: +44 (0)1293 887 308
Email: sales@nimbusjourneyinfo.co.uk
Web site: www.nimbusjourneyinfo.co.uk

PSV PRODUCTS
60 The Old Quays, Warrington, Cheshire,
WA4 1JP, United Kingdom
Tel: +44 (0)1925 210 220
Email: info@psvproducts.com
Web site: www.psvproducts.com

SYNECTICS MOBILE SYSTEMS
2 Wyder Court, Bluebell Way, Millenium City Park,
Preston, PR2 5BW, United Kingdom
Tel: +44 (0)1253 891 222
Fax: +44 (0)1253 891 221
Email: sms.sales@synx.com
Web site: www.synx.com

WABCO AUTOMOTIVE UK LTD
Unit A1, Grange Valley Road, Batley,
West Yorkshire, WF17 6GH, United Kingdom
Tel: +44 (0)1924 595 400
Email: info.uk@wabco-auto.com
Web site: www.wabco-auto.com

SUSPENSION

ARRIVA BUS & COACH
Lodge Garage, Whitehall Road, Gomersal,
Cleckheaton, West Yorkshire, BD19 4BJ,
United Kingdom
Tel: +44 (0)1274 681 144
Email: busandcoachparts@arriva.co.uk
Web site: www.arrivabusandcoach.co.uk

CRESCENT FACILITIES LTD
72 Willow Crescent, Chapeltown, Sheffield,
S35 1QS, United Kingdom
Tel: +44 (0)114 245 1050
Email: cfl.chris@btinternet.com

ERENTEK LTD
Malt Kiln Lane, Waddington, Lincoln, LN5 9RT,
United Kingdom
Tel: +44 (0)1522 720 065
Fax: +44 (0)1522 729 155
Email: sales@erentek.co.uk
Web site: www.erentek.co.uk

IMEXPART LTD
Links 31, Willowbridge Way, Whitwood,
Castleford, WF10 5NP, United Kingdom
Tel: +44 (0)1977 553 936
Email: sales@imexpart.com
Web site: www.imexpart.com

IMPERIAL ENGINEERING
Delamare Road, Cheshunt, Hertfordshire,
FN8 9UD, United Kingdom
Tel: +44 (0)1992 634 255
Fax: +44 (0)1992 630 506
Email: orders@imperialengineering.co.uk
Web site: www.imperialengineering.co.uk

KCP CAR & COMMERCIAL LTD
Unit 15, Hillside Road, Kempson Way,
Bury St Edmunds, Suffolk, IP32 7EA,
United Kingdom
Tel: +44 (0)1284 750 777
Fax: +44 (0)1284 750 773
Email: kcponline@yahoo.co.uk
Web site: kcpcarandcommercial.co.uk

PARTLINE LTD
Dockfield Road, Shipley, BD17 7AZ,
United Kingdom
Tel: +44 (0)1274 531 531
Fax: +44 (0)1274 531 088
Email: sales@partline.co.uk
Web site: www.partline.co.uk

PLAXTON SERVICE
Ryton Road, Anston, Sheffield, S25 4DL,
United Kingdom
Tel: +44 (0)1909 551 155
Fax: +44 (0)1909 550 050
Email: service@plaxtonlimited.co.uk
Web site: www.plaxtonaftercare.co.uk

ROADLINK INTERNATIONAL LTD
Strawberry Lane, Willenhall, West Midlands,
WV13 3RL, United Kingdom
Tel: +44 (0)1902 636 206
Fax: +44 (0)1902 631 515
Email: sales@roadlink-international.co.uk
Web site: www.roadlink-international.co.uk

TACHOGRAPH CALIBRATORS

ARRIVA BUS & COACH
Lodge Garage, Whitehall Road, Gomersal,
Cleckheaton, West Yorkshire, BD19 4BJ, UK
Tel: +44 (0)1274 681 144
Email: busandcoachparts@arriva.co.uk
Web site: www.arrivabusandcoach.co.uk

**CONTINENTAL AUTOMOTIVE
TRADING UK LTD**
36 Gravelly Industrial Park, Birmingham, B24 8TA,
United Kingdom
Tel: +44 (0)121 326 1234
Fax: +44 (0)121 326 1299
Web site: www.vdo.com/uk

MARSHALLS COACHES LLP
Firbank Way, Leighton Buzzard, Bedfordshire,
LU7 3YP, United Kingdom
Tel: +44 (0)1525 376 077
Email: info@marshalls-coaches.co.uk
Web site: www.marshalls-coaches.co.uk

OPTARE PRODUCT SUPPORT
London
Unit 9, Eurocourt, Olivers Close, West Thurrock,
RM20 3EE, United Kingdom
Tel: +44 (0)1708 896 860
Fax: +44 (0)1708 869 920
Email: london.service@optare.com
Manchester
Trafford Park, Manchester, M17 1HG,
United Kingdom
Tel: +44 (0)161 872 7772
Email: manchester.service@optare.com
Rotherham
Denby Way, Hellaby, Rotherham, S66 8HR,
United Kingdom
Tel: +44 (0)1709 535 101
Fax: +44 (0)1709 739 680
Email: rotherham.service@optare.com

PLAXTON SERVICE
Ryton Road, Anston, Sheffield, S25 4DL,
United Kingdom
Tel: +44 (0)1909 551 155
Fax: +44 (0)1909 550 050
Email: service@plaxtonlimited.co.uk
Web site: www.plaxtonaftercare.co.uk

TACHOGRAPH CHART ANALYSIS SERVICE

**CONTINENTAL AUTOMOTIVE
TRADING UK LTD**
Continental Automotive Trading UK Ltd
36 Gravelly Industrial Park, Birmingham, B24 8TA,
United Kingdom
Tel: +44 (0)121 326 1234
Fax: +44 (0)121 326 1299
Web site: www.vdo.com/uk

IBPTS
PSV & Rail Consultants
43 Cage Lane, Felixstowe, Suffolk, IP11 9BJ,
United Kingdom
Contact: Ian Baldry, Chief Transport Consultant
Tel: +44 (0)1394 672 344
Email: enquiries@ibpts.co.uk
Web site: www.ibpts.co.uk

LLOYD MORGAN GROUP
Phoenix House, Hemlock Park, Hyssop Close,
Cannock, Staffordshire, WS11 7GA,
United Kingdom
Tel: +44 (0)1543 897 505
Web site: www.lloydmorgangroup.co.uk

NOVADATA TAB LTD
3 Blackwell Drive, Springwood Industrial Estate,
Braintree, Essex, CM7 2QJ, United Kingdom
Tel: +44 (0)1376 552 999
Fax: +44 (0)1376 550 567
Email: enquiries@novadata.co.uk
Web site: www.novatab.co.uk

**TRANSPORT & TRAINING SERVICES
LTD**
Warrington Business Park North, Long Lane,
Warrington, WA2 8TX, United Kingdom
Tel: +44 (0)1925 243 500
Fax: +44 (0)1925 243 000
Email: admin@ttsgroup.uk.com
Web site: www.transporttrainingservices.com

TACHOGRAPHS

ARRIVA BUS & COACH
Lodge Garage, Whitehall Road, Gomersal,
Cleckheaton, West Yorkshire, BD19 4BJ,
United Kingdom
Tel: +44 (0)1274 681 144
Email: busandcoachparts@arriva.co.uk
Web site: www.arrivabusandcoach.co.uk

**CONTINENTAL AUTOMOTIVE
TRADING UK LTD**
Continental Automotive Trading UK Ltd
36 Gravelly Industrial Park, Birmingham, B24 8TA,
United Kingdom
Tel: +44 (0)121 326 1234
Fax: +44 (0)121 326 1299
Web site: www.vdo.com/uk

THOMAS HARDIE COMMERCIALS LTD
Newstet Road, Knowsley Industrial Park,
Liverpool, L33 7TJ, United Kingdom
Tel: +44 (0)151 549 3000
Email: info@thardie.co.uk
Web site: www.thardie.co.uk

KCP CAR & COMMERCIAL LTD
Unit 15, Hillside Road, Kempson Way,
Bury St Edmunds, Suffolk, IP32 7EA, UK
Tel: +44 (0)1284 750 777
Fax: +44 (0)1284 750 773
Email: kcponline@yahoo.co.uk
Web site: kcpcarandcommercial.co.uk

MARSHALLS COACHES LLP
Firbank Way, Leighton Buzzard, Bedfordshire,
LU7 3YP, United Kingdom
Tel: +44 (0)1525 376 077
Email: info@marshalls-coaches.co.uk
Web site: www.marshalls-coaches.co.uk

NOVADATA TAB LTD
3 Blackwell Drive, Springwood Industrial Estate,
Braintree, Essex, CM7 2QJ, United Kingdom
Tel: +44 (0)1376 552 999
Fax: +44 (0)1376 550 567
Email: enquiries@novadata.co.uk
Web site: www.novatab.co.uk

OPTARE PRODUCT SUPPORT
London
Unit 9, Eurocourt, Olivers Close, West Thurrock,
RM20 3EE, United Kingdom
Tel: +44 (0)1708 896 860
Fax: +44 (0)1708 869 920
Email: london.service@optare.com
Manchester
Trafford Park, Manchester, M17 1HG,
United Kingdom
Tel: +44 (0)161 872 7772
Email: manchester.service@optare.com
Rotherham
Denby Way, Hellaby, Rotherham, S66 8HR,
United Kingdom
Tel: +44 (0)1709 535 101
Fax: +44 (0)1709 739 680
Email: rotherham.service@optare.com

PARTLINE LTD
Dockfield Road, Shipley, BD17 7AZ, UK
Tel: +44 (0)1274 531 531
Fax: +44 (0)1274 531 088
Email: sales@partline.co.uk
Web site: www.partline.co.uk

PLAXTON SERVICE
Ryton Road, Anston, Sheffield, S25 4DL,
United Kingdom
Tel: +44 (0)1909 551 155
Fax: +44 (0)1909 550 050
Email: service@plaxtonlimited.co.uk
Web site: www.plaxtonaftercare.co.uk

**WARD INTERNATIONAL
CONSULTING LTD**
70 Marks Tey Road, Fareham, PO14 3UR, UK
Tel: +44 (0)1329 280 280
Fax: +44 (0)1329 667 901
Email: info@wardint.co.uk
Web site: www.wardint.co.uk

TICKETS, TICKET MACHINES AND TICKET SYSTEMS

ACT - APPLIED CARD TECHNOLOGIES
Langley Gate, Kington Langley, Chippenham,
SN15 5SE, United Kingdom
Tel: +44 (0)1249 751 200
Fax: +44 (0)1249 751 201
Email: info@weareact.com
Web site: www.weareact.com

ALMEX UK
Metric House,
Westmead Industrial Estate Westlea, Swindon,
SN5 7AD, United Kingdom
Tel: +44 (0)1793 647 800
Fax: +44 (0)1793 647 932
Email: info@almex.co.uk
Web site: www.hoeft-wessel.com

ATOS ORIGIN
4 Triton Square, Regent's Place, London,
NW1 3HG, United Kingdom
Tel: +44 (0)20 7830 4444
Fax: +44 (0)20 7830 4445
Web site: www.uk.atos.net

BEMROSEBOOTH PARAGON
Stockholm Road, Sutton Fields, Hull, HU7 0XY,
United Kingdom
Tel: +44 (0)1482 826 343
Email: info@bemrosebooth.com
Web site: www.bemrosebooth.com

CANN PRINT
Commercial Centre, Main Road, Kilmarnock,
KA3 6LX, United Kingdom
Tel: +44 (0)1563 572 440
Fax: +44 (0)1563 544 933
Email: info@cannprint.com
Web site: www.cannprint.com

**CUBIC TRANSPORTATION SYSTEMS
LTD**
AFC House, Honeycrock Lane, Salfords, Redhill,
RH1 5LA, United Kingdom
Tel: +44 (0)1737 782 200
Web site: www.cubic.com

DE LA RUE
De La Rue House, Jays Close, Viables, Basingstoke,
RG22 4BS, United Kingdom
Tel: +44 (0)1256 605 000
Fax: +44 (0)1256 605 256
Web site: www.delarue.com

KEITH EDMONDSON TICKET ROLLS
The Garden House, 46 Tittensor Road, Tittensor,
Stoke-On-Trent, ST12 9HQ,
United Kingdom
Tel: +44 (0)1782 372 305
Email: keith@ticketrolls.co.uk
Web site: www.ticketrolls.co.uk

ETMSS LTD
Ground Floor Austin House, 43 Poole Road,
Westbourne, Bournemouth, Dorset, BH4 9DN,
United Kingdom
Contact: David Price, Sales Director
Tel: +44 (0)844 800 9299
Email: info@etmss.com

Web site: www.etmss.com
Ticket rolls, plain & pre-printed.
Ticket wallets & emergency ticket books.
Smart card travel wallets, plain & pre-printed.

JOHN GROVES TICKET SYSTEMS
Unit 10, North Circular Business Centre,
400 NCR, London, NW10 0JG,
United Kingdom
Tel: +44(0)208 452 6512
Fax: 020 8830 1223
Email: sales@jgts.co.uk
Web site: www.jgts.co.uk

IMAGINET
Greyfriars House, Greyfriars Road, Cardiff,
CF10 3AL, United Kingdom
Tel: +44 (0)29 2057 4500
Fax: +44 (0)29 2057 4501
Email: sales@imaginet.co.uk
Web site: www.imaginet.co.uk

**INIT INNOVATIONS IN
TRANSPORTATION LTD**
Price House, 37 Stoney Street, The Lace Market,
Nottingham, NG1 1LS, United Kingdom
Tel: +44 (0)870 890 4648
Email: sales@init.co.uk
Web site: www.init.co.uk

PAYPOINT PLC
1 The Boulevard, Shire Park, Welwyn Garden City,
AL7 1EL, United Kingdom
Tel: +44 (0)8457 600 633
Email: enquiries@paypoint.co.uk
Web site: www.paypoint.co.uk

SCAN COIN LTD
Dutch House, 110 Broadway, Salford Quays,
M50 2UW, United Kingdom
Tel: +44 (0)845 388 1102
Fax: +44 (0)161 873 0501
Email: sales@scancoin.co.uk
Web site: www.scancoin.co.uk

SCHADES LTD
Brittain Drive, Codnor Gate Business Park, Ripley,
Derbyshire, DE5 3RZ, United Kingdom
Tel: +44 (0)1773 748 721
Email: sales@schades.co.uk
Web site: www.schades.dk

MARK TERRILL TICKET MACHINERY
5 De Grey Close, Lewes, BN7 2JR,
United Kingdom
Tel: +44 (0)1273 474816
Email: mark.terrill2010@gmail.com

TICKETER
Chilton House, Charnham Lane, Hungerford,
Berkshire, RG10 0EY, United Kingdom
Tel: +44 (0)20 3195 8800
Email: support@ticketer.co.uk
Web site: www.ticketer.org.uk

TRANSPORT TICKET SERVICES LTD
Yew Tree Cottage, Newcastle, Monmouth,
NP25 5NT, United Kingdom
Tel: +44 (0)1600 750 650
Email: ttservices@tiscali.co.uk
Web site: www.ticket-machines.co.uk

WAYFARER (PARKEON LTD)
10 Willis Way, Fleets Industrial Estate, Poole,
Dorset, BH15 3SS, United Kingdom
Tel: +44 (0)1202 339 339
Fax: +44 (0)1202 339 369
Email: sales_uk@parkeon.com
Web site: www.wayfarer.co.uk

TIMETABLE DISPLAY FRAMES

M BISSELL DISPLAY LTD
Unit 15, Beechwood Business Park,
Burdock Close, Hawks Green, Cannock,
Staffordshire, WS11 7GB, United Kingdom
Tel: 01543 502115

Fax: 01543 502118
Email: sales@bisselldisplay.com
Web site: www.bisselldisplay.com

TOILET EQUIPMENT

ARRIVA BUS & COACH
Lodge Garage, Whitehall Road, Gomersal,
Cleckheaton, West Yorkshire, BD19 4BJ,
United Kingdom
Tel: +44 (0)1274 681 144
Email: busandcoachparts@arriva.co.uk
Web site: www.arrivabusandcoach.co.uk

BRADTECH LTD
Unit 3, Ladford Covert, Seighford, Stafford,
ST18 9QL, United Kingdom
Tel: +44 (0)1785 282 800
Fax: +44 (0)1785 282 558
Email: sales@bradtech.ltd.uk
Web site: www.bradtech.ltd.uk

CARLYLE BUS & COACH LTD
Carlyle Business Park, Great Bridge Street,
Swan Village, West Bromwich, B70 0X4, UK
Tel: 0121 524 1200
Fax: 0121 524 1201
Email: westbromwichsales@carlyleplc.co.uk
Web site: www.carlylebusandcoach.com

ELSAN LTD
Bellbrook Park, Uckfield, East Sussex, TN22 1QF,
United Kingdom
Tel: +44 (0)1825 748 200
Fax: +44 (0)1825 761 212
Email: sales@elsan.co.uk
Web site: www.elsan.co.uk

EXPRESS COACH REPAIRS LTD
Outgang Lane, Pickering, YO18 7EL,
United Kingdom
Tel: +44 (0)1751 475 215
Email: expresscoachrepairs@hotmail.co.uk

LAWTON SERVICES LTD
Knutsford Road, Church Lawton, Stoke-On-Trent,
ST7 3DN, United Kingdom
Tel: +44 (0)1270 882 056
Fax: +44 (0)1270 883 014
Email: info@lawtonservices.co.uk
Web site: www.lawtonservices.co.uk

PLAXTON SERVICE
Ryton Road, Anston, Sheffield, S25 4DL, UK
Tel: +44 (0)1909 551 155
Fax: +44 (0)1909 550 050
Email: service@plaxtonlimited.co.uk
Web site: www.plaxtonaftercare.co.uk

PSV PRODUCTS
60 The Old Quays, Warrington, Cheshire,
WA4 1JP, United Kingdom
Tel: +44 (0)1925 210 220
Email: info@psvproducts.com
Web site: www.psvproducts.com

RATCLIFF PALFINGER
Bessemer Road, Welwyn Garden City,
Hertfordshire, AL7 1ET, United Kingdom
Tel: +44 (0)1707 325 571
Fax: +44 (0)1707 327 752
Email: info@ratcliffpalfinger.co.uk
Web site: www.ratcliffpalfinger.co.uk

SHADES TECHNICS LTD
Units E3 & E4, RD Park, Stephenson Close,
Hoddesdon, Hertfordshire, EN11 0BW,
United Kingdom
Tel: +44 (0)1992 476 830
Email: info@shades-technics.com
Web site: www.shades-technics.com

**TRAMONTANA COACH
DISTRIBUTORS**
Chapelknowe Road, Carfin, Motherwell, ML1 5LE,
United Kingdom
Tel: 01698 861790

Fax: 01698 860778
Email: wdt90@hotmail.co.uk
Web site: www.tramontanacoach.co.uk

TRANSMISSION OVERHAUL

ARRIVA BUS & COACH
Lodge Garage, Whitehall Road, Gomersal,
Cleckheaton, West Yorkshire, BD19 4BJ,
United Kingdom
Tel: +44 (0)1274 681 144
Email: busandcoachparts@arriva.co.uk
Web site: www.arrivabusandcoach.co.uk

PAUL CLARK SERVICES LTD
Paul Clark Services Ltd
Unit 8, Kemrey Trade Centre, Aspen Close,
Swindon, Wiltshire, SN2 8AJ, United Kingdom
Tel: +44 (0)8456 060 474
Email: info@paulclarkservices.co.uk
Web site: www.paulclarkservices.co.uk

GARDNER PARTS LTD
Centurion Court, Centurion Way, Leyland,
Lancashire, PR25 3UQ, United Kingdom
Tel: +44 (0)1772 642 460
Fax: +44 (0)1772 621 333
Email: sales@gardnerparts.co.uk
Web site: www.gardnerparts.co.uk

LH GROUP SERVICES LTD
Graycar Business Park, Barton Under Needwood,
Burton-On-Trent, DE13 8EN, United Kingdom
Tel: +44 (0)1283 722 600
Email: enquiries@lh-group.co.uk
Web site: www.lh-group.co.uk

MITCHELL POWERSYSTEMS
Mitchell Diesel Ltd, Fulwood Road South,
Sutton-In-Ashfield, Nottinghamshire, NG17 2JZ,
United Kingdom
Tel: +44 (0)1623 550 550
Fax: +44 (0)1623 443 041
Email: sales@mitchells.co.uk
Web site: www.mitchells.co.uk

OPTARE PARTS DIVISION
Hurricane Way South, Sherburn In Elmet, Leeds,
LS25 6PT, United Kingdom
Tel: +44 (0)871 230 1324
Email: parts@optare.com
Web site: www.optare.com

OPTARE PRODUCT SUPPORT
London
Unit 9, Eurocourt, Olivers Close, West Thurrock,
RM20 3EE, United Kingdom
Tel: +44 (0)1708 896 860
Fax: +44 (0)1708 869 920
Email: london.service@optare.com
Manchester
Trafford Park, Manchester, M17 1HG,
United Kingdom
Tel: +44 (0)161 872 7772
Email: manchester.service@optare.com
Rotherham
Denby Way, Hellaby, Rotherham, S66 8HR,
United Kingdom
Tel: +44 (0)1709 535 101
Fax: +44 (0)1709 739 680
Email: rotherham.service@optare.com

PREMIER COMPONENTS UK LTD
Unit 701, Long Marston Storage, Campden Road,
Long Marston, Stratford-upon-Avon,
Warwickshire, CV37 8QR, United Kingdom
Tel: +44 (0)1789 721 010
Fax: +44 (0)1789 722 429
Web site: www.premiercore.com

SHAWSON SUPPLY LTD
12 Station Road, Saintfield, County Down,
BT24 7DU, Northern Ireland
Tel: +44 (0)28 9751 0994
Email: info@shawsonsupply.co.uk
Web site: www.shawsonsupply.co.uk

SHELLEY TRANSMISSION SERVICES LTD
Eagle Street, off Bilston Road, Wolverhampton,
WV2 2AQ, United Kingdom
Tel: +44 (0)1902 351 178
Fax: +44 (0)1902 352 545
Email: enquiries@shelleytransmission.co.uk
Web site: www.shelleytransmission.co.uk

HL SMITH TRANSMISSIONS LTD
Enterprise Business Park, Cross Road, Albrighton,
Wolverhampton, WV7 3BJ, United Kingdom
Tel: +44 (0)1902 373 011
Fax: +44 (0)1902 373 608
Web site: www.hlsmith.co.uk

TTS UK
Total Tool Solutions Ltd, Newhaven Business Park,
Lowergate, Milnsbridge, Huddersfield, HD3 4HS,
United Kingdom
Tel: +44 (0)1484 642 211
Fax: +44 (0)1484 461 002
Email: sales@ttsuk.com
Web site: www.ttsuk.com

VOITH TURBO LTD
6 Beddington Farm Road, Croydon, CR0 4XB,
United Kingdom
Tel: +44 (0)20 8667 0333
Fax: +44 (0)20 8667 0403
Email: road.uk@voith.com
Web site: www.uk.voithturbo.com

VOR TRANSMISSIONS LTD
Little London House, St Anne's Road, Willenhall,
WV13 1DT, United Kingdom
Tel: +44 (0)1902 604 141
Fax: +44 (0)1902 603 868
Email: sales@vor.co.uk
Web site: www.vor.co.uk

ZF ECODRIVE - ECODRIVE TRANSMISSIONS LTD
34-35, Devonshire Road,
Oakhill 61 Industrial Estate, Walkden, Manchester,
M28 3PT, United Kingdom
Tel: +44 (0)1204 701 812
Fax: +44 (0)1204 701 516
Web site: www.ecodrive.co.uk

ZF POWERTRAIN
Stringes Close, Willenhall, WV13 1LE,
United Kingdom
Tel: +44 (0)1902 366 000
Email: sales@powertrain.co.uk
Web site: www.zfpowertrain.co.uk

TREE GUARDS

ARRIVA BUS & COACH
Lodge Garage, Whitehall Road, Gomersal,
Cleckheaton, West Yorkshire, BD19 4BJ,
United Kingdom
Tel: +44 (0)1274 681 144
Email: busandcoachparts@arriva.co.uk
Web site: www.arrivabusandcoach.co.uk

CARLYLE BUS & COACH LTD
Carlyle Business Park, Great Bridge Street,
Swan Village, West Bromwich, B70 0X4, UK
Tel: 0121 524 1200
Fax: 0121 524 1201
Email: westbromwichsales@carlyleplc.co.uk
Web site: www.carlylebusandcoach.com

NEWBY FOUNDRIES LTD
1 Cornwall Road, Smethwick, West Midlands,
B66 2JT, United Kingdom
Tel: +44 (0)121 555 7615
Fax: +44 (0)121 505 3626
Email: sales@newbyfoundries.co.uk
Web site: www.newbyfoundries.co.uk

PLAXTON SERVICE
Ryton Road, Anston, Sheffield, S25 4DL,
United Kingdom

Tel: +44 (0)1909 551 155
Fax: +44 (0)1909 550 050
Email: service@plaxtonlimited.co.uk
Web site: www.plaxtonaftercare.co.uk

TYRES

CONTINENTAL TYRE GROUP LTD
Continental House, 191 High Street, Yiewsley,
West Drayton, Middlesex, UB7 7XW,
United Kingdom
Tel: +44 (0)1895 425 900
Web site: www.conti-online.com

GOODYEAR UK
Tyrefort, 88-98 Wingfoot Way, Erdington,
Birmingham, B24 9HY, United Kingdom
Tel: +44 (0)121 306 6000
Fax: +44 (0)121 306 6310
Email: tyre.techuk@goodyear.com
Web site: www.goodyear.eu/uk

HANKOOK TYRE UK LTD
Fawsley Drive, Heartlands Business Park,
Daventry, Northamptonshire, NN11 8UG,
United Kingdom
Tel: +44 (0)1327 304 100
Fax: +44 (0)1327 304 110
Email: sales@hankooktyresuk.co.uk
Web site: www.hankooktire-eu.com/uk

LAWTON SERVICES LTD
Knutsford Road, Church Lawton, Stoke-On-Trent,
ST7 3DN, United Kingdom
Tel: +44 (0)1270 882 056
Fax: +44 (0)1270 883 014
Email: info@lawtonservices.co.uk
Web site: www.lawtonservices.co.uk

OPTARE PRODUCT SUPPORT
London
Unit 9, Eurocourt, Olivers Close, West Thurrock,
RM20 3EE, United Kingdom
Tel: +44 (0)1708 896 860
Fax: +44 (0)1708 869 920
Email: london.service@optare.com
Manchester
Trafford Park, Manchester, M17 1HG,
United Kingdom
Tel: +44 (0)161 872 7772
Email: manchester.service@optare.com
Rotherham
Denby Way, Hellaby, Rotherham, S66 8HR,
United Kingdom
Tel: +44 (0)1709 535 101
Fax: +44 (0)1709 739 680
Email: rotherham.service@optare.com

SNOWCHAINS EUROPRODUCTS
Bourne Enterprise Centre, Wrotham Road,
Borough Green, Kent, TN15 8DG,
United Kingdom
Tel: +44 (0)1732 884 408
Fax: +44 (0)1732 884 564
Email: sales@snowchains.co.uk
Web site: www.snowchains.co.uk

UNIFORMS

FIRST CORPORATE CLOTHING
Units 2 & 4 Llewellyns Quay, The Docks,
Port Talbot, SA13 1RF, United Kingdom
Tel: +44 (0)1639 899 008
Email: sales@firstcorporateuk.com
Web site: www.firstcorporateuk.com

LEISUREWEAR DIRECT LTD
4a South Street North, New Whittington,
Chesterfield, S43 2AB, United Kingdom
Tel: +44 (0)1246 454 447
Fax: +44 (0)870 755 9842
Email: sales@leisureweardirect.com
Web site: www.leisureweardirect.com

UPHOLSTERY

ABACUS TRANSPORT PRODUCTS LTD
Abacus House, Highlode Industrial Estate, Ramsey, Huntingdon, PE26 2RB, United Kingdom
Tel: +44 (0)1487 710 700
Fax: +44 (0)1487 710 626
Email: sales@abacus-tp.com
Web site: www.abacus-tp.com

ARDEE COACH TRIM LTD
Artnalivery, Ardee, Co Louth, Republic of Ireland
Tel: +353 41 685 3599
Fax: +353 41 685 7016
Email: info@ardeecoachtrim.com
Web site: www.ardeecoachtrim.com

AUTOMOTIVE TEXTILE INDUSTRIES
Unit 15 & 16, Priest Court,
Springfield Business Park, Grantham, NG31 7BG,
United Kingdom
Tel: +44 (0)1476 593 050
Fax: +44 (0)1476 593 607
Email: sales@atindustries.co.uk
Web site: www.atindustries.co.uk

BHI UK
The Bus Depot, 1 Sky Lane, Haddington, Lincoln,
LN5 9FE, United Kingdom
Tel: +44 (0)1522 689 911
Fax: +44 (0)1522 689 922
Email: info@bhiuk.com
Web site: www.bhiuk.com
Moquette supplies

CAMIRA (FORMERLY HOLDSWORTH FABRICS LTD)
The Watermill, Wheatley Park, Mirfield,
West Yorkshire, WF1 8HE, United Kingdom
Tel: +44 (0)1924 481 965
Fax: +44 (0)1484 859 061
Email: info@camirafabrics.com
Web site: www.camirafabrics.com

DUOFLEX LTD
Trimmingham House, 2 Shires Road,
Buckingham Road Industrial Estate, Brackley,
Northamptonshire, NN13 7EZ, United Kingdom
Tel: +44 (0)1280 701 366
Fax: +44 (0)1280 704 799
Email: info@duoflex.co.uk
Web site: www.duoflex.co.uk

EXPRESS COACH REPAIRS LTD
Outgang Lane, Pickering, YO18 7EL, UK
Tel: +44 (0)1751 475 215
Email: expresscoachrepairs@hotmail.co.uk

HOLDSWORTH (SEE CAMIRA)
The Watermill, Wheatley Park, Mirfield,
West Yorkshire, WF1 8HE, United Kingdom
Tel: +44 (0)1924 481 965
Fax: +44 (0)1484 859 061
Email: info@camirafabrics.com
Web site: www.camirafabrics.com

LAWTON SERVICES LTD
Knutsford Road, Church Lawton, Stoke-On-Trent,
ST7 3DN, United Kingdom
Tel: +44 (0)1270 882 056
Fax: +44 (0)1270 883 014
Email: info@lawtonservices.co.uk
Web site: www.lawtonservices.co.uk

MARTYN INDUSTRIALS LTD
5 Brunel Way, Durranhill Industrial Park, Harraby,
Carlisle, CA1 3NQ, United Kingdom
Tel: +44 (0)1228 544 000
Email: enquiries@martyn-industrials.co.uk
Web site: www.martyn-industrials.com

SCOTTISH LEATHER GROUP LTD
Locher House, Kilbarchan Road, Bridge of Weir,
Renfrewshire, PA11 3RN, United Kingdom
Tel: +44 (0)1505 691 730
Web site: www.scottishleathergroup.com

TTS UK
Total Tool Solutions Ltd, Newhaven Business Park,
Lowergate, Milnsbridge, Huddersfield, HD3 4HS,
United Kingdom
Tel: +44 (0)1484 642 211
Fax: +44 (0)1484 461 002
Email: sales@ttsuk.com
Web site: www.ttsuk.com

WEST COAST TRIM
Unit 4D, Burton Road, Blackpool, FY4 4NW,
United Kingdom
Tel: +44 (0)1253 696 033
Email: info@westcoasttrim.co.uk
Web site: www.westcoasttrim.co.uk

WIDNEY MANUFACTURING LTD
Plume Street, Aston, Birmingham, B6 7RX,
United Kingdom
Tel: +44 (0)121 327 5500
Fax: +44 (0)121 328 2466
Email: info@widney.co.uk
Web site: www.widney.co.uk

VACUUM SYSTEMS

JTT EQUIPMENT SERVICES LTD
Unit 6, Belton Lane Industrial Estate, Grantham,
Lincolnshire, NG31 9HN, United Kingdom
Tel: +44 (0)1476 576 704
Fax: +44 (0)1476 576 217
Email:
sales@industrial-cleaning-equipment.co.uk
Web site: www.jffltd.co.uk

RESCROFT LTD
20 Oxleasow Road, East Moons Moat, Redditch,
B98 0RE, United Kingdom
Tel: +44 (0)1527 521 300
Fax: +44 (0)1527 521 301
Email: sales@rescroft.com
Web site: www.rescroft.com

TRAMONTANA COACH DISTRIBUTORS
Chapelknowe Road, Carfin, Motherwell, ML1 5LE,
United Kingdom
Tel: 01698 861790
Fax: 01698 860778
Email: wdt90@hotmail.co.uk
Web site: www.tramontanacoach.co.uk

TTS UK
Total Tool Solutions Ltd, Newhaven Business Park,
Lowergate, Milnsbridge, Huddersfield, HD3 4HS,
United Kingdom
Tel: +44 (0)1484 642 211
Fax: +44 (0)1484 461 002
Email: sales@ttsuk.com
Web site: www.ttsuk.com

VEHICLE WASHING

ARRIVA BUS & COACH
Lodge Garage, Whitehall Road, Gomersal,
Cleckheaton, West Yorkshire, BD19 4BJ,
United Kingdom
Tel: +44 (0)1274 681 144
Email: busandcoachparts@arriva.co.uk
Web site: www.arrivabusandcoach.co.uk

AUTOGLYM PSV
Works Road, Letchworth, Hertfordshire,
SG6 1LU, United Kingdom
Tel: +44 (0)1462 677 766
Email: info@autoglym.com
Web site: www.autoglym.com/psv

EXPRESS COACH REPAIRS LTD
Outgang Lane, Pickering, YO18 7EL,
United Kingdom
Tel: +44 (0)1751 475 215
Email: expresscoachrepairs@hotmail.co.uk

HARRISON HIRE & SALES
12/13 Town Green Lane, Settrington, Malton,
North Yorkshire, YO17 8NR, United Kingdom
Tel: +44 (0)1944 768 441
Fax: +44 (0)1944 768 443
Web site: www.hhands.co.uk

JTT EQUIPMENT SERVICES LTD
Unit 6, Belton Lane Industrial Estate, Grantham,
Lincolnshire, NG31 9HN, United Kingdom
Tel: +44 (0)1476 576 704
Fax: +44 (0)1476 576 217
Email:
sales@industrial-cleaning-equipment.co.uk
Web site: www.jffltd.co.uk

KARCHER (UK) LTD
Karcher House, Beaumont Road, Banbury,
Oxfordshire, OX16 1TB, United Kingdom
Tel: +44 (0)1295 752 000
Email: enquiries@karcher.co.uk
Web site: www.karcher.co.uk

KCP CAR & COMMERCIAL LTD
Unit 15, Hillside Road, Kempson Way,
Bury St Edmunds, Suffolk, IP32 7EA,
United Kingdom
Tel: +44 (0)1284 750 777
Fax: +44 (0)1284 750 773
Email: kcponline@yahoo.co.uk
Web site: kcpcarandcommercial.co.uk

MARSHALLS COACHES LLP
Firbank Way, Leighton Buzzard, Bedfordshire,
LU7 3YP, United Kingdom
Tel: +44 (0)1525 376 077
Email: info@marshalls-coaches.co.uk
Web site: www.marshalls-coaches.co.uk

NATIONWIDE CLEANING & SUPPORT SERVICES LTD
Suite 149, Airport House, Purley Way, Croydon,
CR0 0XZ, United Kingdom
Tel: +44 (0)20 8288 3580
Fax: +44 (0)20 8288 3581

Email: enquiries@nationwidefm.com
Web site: www.nationwidefm.com

SMITH BROS & WEBB LTD
Britannia House, Arden Forest Industrial Estate,
Alcester, Warwickshire, B49 6EX, United Kingdom
Tel: +44 (0)1789 400 096
Email: sales@sbw-wash.com
Web site: www.sbw-wash.com

SOMERS TOTALKARE LTD
Unit 1, Coombs Wharf, Chancel Way, Halesowen,
West Midlands, B62 8PP, United Kingdom
Tel: +44 (0)121 585 2700
Fax: +44 (0)121 585 2725
Email: sales@stkare.co.uk
Web site: www.stkare.co.uk

WILCOMATIC LTD
Unit 5 Commerce Park, 19 Commerce Way,
Croydon, Surrey, CR0 4YL, United Kingdom
Tel: +44 (0)20 8649 5760
Fax: +44 (0)20 8686 9571
Email: info@wilcomatic.co.uk
Web site: www.wilcomatic.co.uk

WHEELTRIMS AND COVERS

ABACUS TRANSPORT PRODUCTS LTD
Abacus House, Highlode Industrial Estate, Ramsey,
Huntingdon, PE26 2RB, United Kingdom
Tel: +44 (0)1487 710 700
Fax: +44 (0)1487 710 626
Email: sales@abacus-tp.com
Web site: www.abacus-tp.com

ALCOA WHEEL PRODUCTS EUROPE
UK Contact Chris Edwards
United Kingdom
Tel: +44 (0)7852 245 641
Web site: www.alcoa.com

ARRIVA BUS & COACH
Lodge Garage, Whitehall Road, Gomersal,
Cleckheaton, West Yorkshire, BD19 4BJ,
United Kingdom
Tel: +44 (0)1274 681 144
Email: busandcoachparts@arriva.co.uk
Web site: www.arrivabusandcoach.co.uk

AUTOMATE WHEEL COVERS LTD
California Mills, Oxford Road, Gomersal,
Cleckheaton, BD19 4HQ, United Kingdom
Tel: +44 (0)1274 862 700
Fax: +44 (0)1274 851 989
Email: sales@wheeltrimshop.com
Web site: www.wheeltrimshop.com

CARLYLE BUS & COACH LTD
Carlyle Business Park, Great Bridge Street,
Swan Village, West Bromwich, B70 0X4, UK
Tel: 0121 524 1200
Fax: 0121 524 1201
Email: westbromwichsales@carlyleplc.co.uk
Web site: www.carlylebusandcoach.com

EXPRESS COACH REPAIRS LTD
Outgang Lane, Pickering, YO18 7EL,
United Kingdom
Tel: +44 (0)1751 475 215
Email: expresscoachrepairs@hotmail.co.uk

HATCHER COMPONENTS LTD
Broadwater Road, Framlingham, Suffolk, IP13 9LL,
United Kingdom
Tel: +44 (0)1728 723 675
Fax: +44 (0)1728 724 475
Email: info@hatchercomp.co.uk
Web site: www.hatchercomp.co.uk

OPTARE PARTS DIVISION
Hurricane Way South, Sherburn In Elmet, Leeds,
LS25 6PT, United Kingdom
Tel: +44 (0)871 230 1324
Email: parts@optare.com
Web site: www.optare.com

PARMA INDUSTRIES
34-36 Carlton Park Industrial Estate,
Saxmundham, Suffolk, IP17 2NL, United Kingdom
Tel: +44 (0)1728 745 700
Fax: +44 (0)1728 745 718
Email: sales@parmagroup.co.uk
Web site: www.parmagroup.co.uk

PLAXTON PARTS
Ryton Road, Anston, Sheffield, S25 4DL,
United Kingdom
Tel: +44 (0)844 822 6224
Fax: +44 (0)1909 550 050
Email: parts@plaxtonlimited.co.uk
Web site: www.plaxtonaftercare.co.uk

WINDOW FILM PROTECTION/ VINYL BODY WRAPPING

COACH GLAZING SERVICES
Unit 2, Washingford Row, Milltown, Dungannon,
Co. Tyrone, BT71 7BG, Northern Ireland
Contact: Stephen Ferguson,
National Sales Manager
Tel: 0800 954 1934 (NI)/1 800 937 440 (Eire)
Email: info@coachglazingservices.com

IGP SOLUTIONS
16 Hillbottom Road, High Wycombe, HP12 4HJ,
United Kingdom
Tel: +44 (0)1494 533 131
Fax: +44 (0)1494 462 675
Email: sales@igpsolutions.com
Web site: www.igpsolutions.com

WINDOWS, WINDSCREENS AND WIPER MOTORS

ARRIVA BUS & COACH
Lodge Garage, Whitehall Road, Gomersal,
Cleckheaton, West Yorkshire, BD19 4BJ,
United Kingdom
Tel: +44 (0)1274 681 144
Email: busandcoachparts@arriva.co.uk
Web site: www.arrivabusandcoach.co.uk

AUTOGLASS SPECIALS
1 Priory Business Park, Cardington Road, Bedford,
MK44 3US, United Kingdom
Tel: +44 (0)800 413 044
Web site: www.autoglassspecials.co.uk

BUS & COACH GLAZING
Stakehill Industrial Estate, Anston, Middleton,
Gtr Manchester, M24 2SJ, United Kingdom
Tel: +44 (0)161 655 0150
Fax: +44 (0)161 643 5417
Email: enquiries@busandcoachglazing.co.uk
Web site: www.busandcoachglazing.co.uk

CARLYLE BUS & COACH LTD
Carlyle Business Park, Great Bridge Street,
Swan Village, West Bromwich, B70 0X4, UK
Tel: 0121 524 1200
Fax: 0121 524 1201
Email: westbromwichsales@carlyleplc.co.uk
Web site: www.carlylebusandcoach.com

COACH GLAZING SERVICES
Unit 2, Washingford Row, Milltown, Dungannon,
Co. Tyrone, BT71 7BG, Northern Ireland
Contact: Stephen Ferguson,
National Sales Manager
Tel: 0800 954 1934 (NI)/1 800 937 440 (Eire)
Email: info@coachglazingservices.com

ESPRIT WINDSCREEN SYSTEMS
Unit 44, Winpenny Road,
Parkhouse East Industrial Estate,
Newcastle Under Lyme, Staffordshire, ST5 7RH,
United Kingdom
Tel: +44 (0)1782 565 811
Fax: +44 (0)1782 565 766
Email: sales@espritws.com
Web site: www.espritws.com

EXPRESS COACH REPAIRS LTD
Outgang Lane, Pickering, YO18 7EL, UK
Tel: +44 (0)1751 475 215
Email: expresscoachrepairs@hotmail.co.uk

B HEPWORTH & CO LTD
4 Merse Road, North Moons Moat, Redditch,
B98 9HL, United Kingdom
Tel: +44 (0)1527 61243
Fax: +44 (0)1527 66836
Email: headoffice@b-hepworth.com
Web site: www.b-hepworth.com

IGP SOLUTIONS
16 Hillbottom Road, High Wycombe, HP12 4HJ,
United Kingdom
Tel: +44 (0)1494 533 131
Fax: +44 (0)1494 462 675
Email: sales@igpsolutions.com
Web site: www.igpsolutions.com

LAWTON SERVICES LTD
Knutsford Road, Church Lawton, Stoke-On-Trent,
ST7 3DN, United Kingdom
Tel: +44 (0)1270 882 056
Fax: +44 (0)1270 883 014
Email: info@lawtonservices.co.uk
Web site: www.lawtonservices.co.uk

OMNI-TECH ELECTRONICS
Unit 9, Prospect House, Ireland Industrial Estate,
Staveley, Chesterfield, Derbyshire, S43 3QE,
United Kingdom
Tel: +44 (0)1246 474 332
Fax: +44 (0)1246 529 010
Email: help@omni-techelectronics.co.uk
Web site: www.buselectronics.co.uk

OPTARE PARTS DIVISION
Hurricane Way South, Sherburn In Elmet, Leeds,
LS25 6PT, United Kingdom
Tel: +44 (0)871 230 1324
Email: parts@optare.com
Web site: www.optare.com

OPTARE PRODUCT SUPPORT
London
Unit 9, Eurocourt, Olivers Close, West Thurrock,
RM20 3EE, United Kingdom
Tel: +44 (0)1708 896 860
Fax: +44 (0)1708 869 920
Email: london.service@optare.com
Manchester
Trafford Park, Manchester, M17 1HG,
United Kingdom
Tel: +44 (0)161 872 7772
Email: manchester.service@optare.com
Rotherham
Denby Way, Hellaby, Rotherham, S66 8HR,
United Kingdom
Tel: +44 (0)1709 535 101
Fax: +44 (0)1709 739 680
Email: rotherham.service@optare.com

PARTLINE LTD
Dockfield Road, Shipley, BD17 7AZ,
United Kingdom
Tel: +44 (0)1274 531 531
Fax: +44 (0)1274 531 088
Email: sales@partline.co.uk
Web site: www.partline.co.uk

PERCY LANE PRODUCTS LTD
Lichfield Road, Tamworth, B79 7TL,
United Kingdom
Tel: +44 (0)1827 63821
Fax: +44 (0)1827 310 159
Web site: www.percylane.com

PLAXTON PARTS
Ryton Road, Anston, Sheffield, S25 4DL, UK
Tel: +44 (0)844 822 6224
Fax: +44 (0)1909 550 050
Email: parts@plaxtonlimited.co.uk
Web site: www.plaxtonaftercare.co.uk

PSV GLASS
Hillbottom Road, High Wycombe, HP12 4HJ,
United Kingdom
Tel: +44 (0)1494 533 131
Fax: +44 (0)1494 462 675
Email: salesoffice@psvglass.co.uk
Web site: www.psvglass.com

PSV TRANSPORT SYSTEMS LTD
21 Impresa Park, Pindar Road, Hoddesdon,
Hertfordshire, EN11 0DL, United Kingdom
Tel: +44 (0)1992 479 950
Fax: +44 (0)1992 471 676

Email: sales@psv-transport-systems.co.uk
Web site: www.psv-transport-systems.co.uk

**TRAMONTANA COACH
DISTRIBUTORS**
Chapelknowe Road, Carfin, Motherwell, ML1 5LE,
United Kingdom
Tel: 01698 861790
Fax: 01698 860778
Email: wdt90@hotmail.co.uk
Web site: www.tramontanacoach.co.uk

TTS UK
Total Tool Solutions Ltd, Newhaven Business Park,
Lowergate, Milnsbridge, Huddersfield, HD3 4HS,
United Kingdom
Tel: +44 (0)1484 642 211
Fax: +44 (0)1484 461 002
Email: sales@ttsuk.com
Web site: www.ttsuk.com

VOLVO BUS AND COACH CENTRE
Parts Sales & Body Repair/Refurbishment
Specialists - Byron Street Extension,
Loughborough, LE11 5HE, United Kingdom
Tel: +44 (0)1509 217 700
Fax: +44 (0)1509 238 770
Email: dporter@volvocoachsales.co.uk
Web site: www.volvobuses.com

WIDNEY MANUFACTURING LTD
Plume Street, Aston, Birmingham, B6 7RX,
United Kingdom
Tel: +44 (0)121 327 5500
Fax: +44 (0)121 328 2466
Email: info@widney.co.uk
Web site: www.widney.co.uk

BUS AND COACH INDUSTRY SERVICE PROVIDERS

ACCIDENT INVESTIGATION

PEAK LEGAL SERVICES
15 Parr Fold Avenue, Worsley, Manchester,
M28 7HD, United Kingdom
Contact: Ben Ford, Manager
Tel: +44 (0)161 799 5560/+44 (0)7748 116 797
Email: peaklegalservices@googlemail.com
Web site: www.peak-legal.co.uk
Witness Statements, Driver Interviews and
Statements. Civil Proceedings Rules compliant.
Locus Reports, Accident Photography and all
investigations.

ACCOUNTANCY AND AUDIT

**BARRONS CHARTERED
ACCOUNTANTS**
Monometer House, Rectory Grove, Leigh On Sea,
SS9 2HN, United Kingdom
Tel: +44 (0)1702 481 910
Email: mail@barrons-bds.com
Web site: www.barrons-bds.com

CHRIS BORLAND & ASSOCIATES LTD
3 Axe View, Axe Road, Drimpton, Beaminster,
Dorset, DT8 3RJ, United Kingdom
Tel: +44 (0)1460 271 680
Email: chris.borland@tiscali.co.uk
Internal Audit & Audit Support Services

PRE METRO OPERATIONS LTD
Regent House, 56 Hagley Road, Stourbridge,
West Midlands, DY8 1QD, United Kingdom
Tel: +44 (0)1384 441 325
Email: info@premetro.co.uk
Web site: www.premetro.co.uk

ARTWORK

BEST IMPRESSIONS
15 Starfield Road, London, W12 9SN, UK
Tel: 020 8740 6443
Fax: 020 8740 9134
Email: talk2us@best-impressions.co.uk
Web site: www.best-impressions.co.uk

EXPRESS COACH REPAIRS LTD
Outgang Lane, Pickering, YO18 7EL,
United Kingdom
Tel: +44 (0)1751 475 215
Email: expresscoachrepairs@hotmail.co.uk

FWT
Aztec House, 397-405 Archway Road, London,
N6 4EY, United Kingdom
Tel: +44 (0)20 8347 3700
Fax: +44 (0)20 8347 3700
Email: paul.treadwell@fwt.co.uk
Web site: www.fwt.co.uk

GRAPHIC EVOLUTION LTD
Ad House, East Parade, Harrogate,
North Yorkshire, HG1 5LT, United Kingdom
Tel: +44 (0)1423 706 680
Fax: +44 (0)1423 502 522
Email: info@graphic-evolution.co.uk
Web site: www.graphic-evolution.co.uk

MCV BUS AND COACH LTD
Sterling Place, Elean Business Park, Sutton, Ely,
CB6 2QE, United Kingdom
Tel: +44 (0)1353 773 000
Fax: +44 (0)1353 773 001
Email: sales@mcv-uk.com
Web site: www.mcv-uk.com

BREAKDOWN AND RECOVERY SERVICES

CHANNEL COMMERCIALS PLC
Unit 6, Cobbs Wood Industrial Estate,
Brunswick Road, Ashford, TN23 1EH,
United Kingdom
Tel: 0844 247 7742
Fax: +44 (0)1233 636 322
Web site: www.channelcommercials.co.uk

COACH-AID LTD
Greyfriars Workshop, Greyfriars Way, Stafford,
Staffordshire, ST16 2SH, United Kingdom
Tel: +44 (0)1785 222 666
Email: workshop@coach-aid.com
Web site: www.coach-aid.com

FERRYMILL MOTORS
Ferrymill Motors
Campsie Road, Torrance, Glasgow, G64 4NP,
United Kingdom
Tel: +44 (0)1360 620 544
Fax: +44 (0)1360 620 990
Email: info@ferrymillmotors.co.uk
Web site: www.ferrymillmotors.co.uk

FULL CIRCLE ENTERPRISES LTD
Heath Road, Banham, Norfolk, NR16 2HS,
United Kingdom
Tel: +44 (0)1953 887 951
Fax: +44 (0)1953 888 985
Email: info@fullcircleenterprises.co.uk
Web site: www.fullcircleenterprises.co.uk

J & K RECOVERY LTD
3 Grovebury Road, Leighton Buzzard,
Bedfordshire, LU7 4SQ, United Kingdom
Tel: 4 (0)1525 851 011/
UK Call Centre: 0800 434 6106
Email: info@jkrecovery.co.uk
Web site: www.jkrecovery.co.uk

**LANTERN RECOVERY SPECIALISTS
PLC**
Lantern House, 39/41 High Street, Potters Bar,
Hertfordshire, EN6 5AJ, United Kingdom
Tel: +44 (0)844 247 6090
Web site: www.lanternrecovery.com

MARSHALLS COACHES LLP
Firbank Way, Leighton Buzzard, Bedfordshire,
LU7 3YP, United Kingdom
Tel: +44 (0)1525 376 077
Email: info@marshalls-coaches.co.uk
Web site: www.marshalls-coaches.co.uk

MAS SPECIAL ENGINEERING LTD
Houghton Road, North Anston, S25 4JJ,
United Kingdom
Tel: +44 (0)1909 550 480
Fax: +44 (0)1909 550 486

OPTARE PRODUCT SUPPORT
London
Unit 9, Eurocourt, Olivers Close, West Thurrock,
RM20 3EE, United Kingdom
Tel: +44 (0)1708 896 860
Fax: +44 (0)1708 869 920
Email: london.service@optare.com
Manchester
Trafford Park, Manchester, M17 1HG,
United Kingdom
Tel: +44 (0)161 872 7772
Email: manchester.service@optare.com
Rotherham
Denby Way, Hellaby, Rotherham, S66 8HR,
United Kingdom
Tel: +44 (0)1709 535 101
Fax: +44 (0)1709 739 680
Email: rotherham.service@optare.com

PLAXTON SERVICE
Ryton Road, Anston, Sheffield, S25 4DL,
United Kingdom
Tel: +44 (0)1909 551 155
Fax: +44 (0)1909 550 050
Email: service@plaxtonlimited.co.uk
Web site: www.plaxtonaftercare.co.uk

TOURMASTER RECOVERY
Alderlands, Peterborough Road, Crowland,
Peterborough, PE6 0AA, United Kingdom
Tel: +44 (0)1733 211 639

TRUCKALIGN CO LTD
VIP Group, VIP Industrial Park,
Anchor & Hope Lane, London, SE7 7RY,
United Kingdom
Tel: +44 (0)20 8858 3781
Fax: +44 (0)20 8858 5663
Email: admin@vipgroupltd.co.uk
Web site: www.vipgroup.co.uk

CLEANING SERVICES

EXPRESS COACH REPAIRS LTD
Outgang Lane, Pickering, YO18 7EL, UK
Tel: +44 (0)1751 475 215
Email: expresscoachrepairs@hotmail.co.uk

JENNYCHEM
Sort Mill Road, Mid Kent Business Park, Snodland,
Kent, ME6 5UA, United Kingdom
Tel: +44 (0)1634 245 666
Fax: +44 (0)1634 245 777
Email: jenny@jennychem.com
Web site: www.jennychem.com

JTT EQUIPMENT SERVICES LTD
Unit 6, Belton Lane Industrial Estate, Grantham,
Lincolnshire, NG31 9HN, United Kingdom
Tel: +44 (0)1476 576 704
Fax: +44 (0)1476 576 217
Email: sales@industrial-cleaning-equipment.
co.uk
Web site: www.jffltd.co.uk

SAMMYS GARAGE
Victoria Coach Station, Arrivals Hall,
3 Eccleston Place, London, SW1W 9NF,
United Kingdom
Tel: +44 (0)20 7730 8867

COACH DRIVER AGENCY

DRIVER HIRE CANTERBURY
12-17 Upper Bridge Street, Canterbury, CT1 2NF,
United Kingdom
Tel: +44 (0)1227 479 529
Fax: +44 (0)1227 479 531
Email: canterbury@driverhire.co.uk
Web site: www.driverhire.co.uk

COACH HIRE BROKERS/VEHICLE RENTAL

COACH DIRECT
2nd Floor, 83 High Street, Rayleigh, Essex, SS6 7EJ,
United Kingdom
Tel: +44 (0)1268 747 388
Fax: +44 (0)1268 741 685
Email: info@coachdirect.co.uk
Web site: www.coachdirect.co.uk

COACH-AID LTD
Greyfriars Workshop, Greyfriars Way, Stafford,
Staffordshire, ST16 2SH, United Kingdom
Tel: +44 (0)1785 222 666
Email: workshop@coach-aid.com
Web site: www.coach-aid.com

COACHFINDER LTD
Woodbank House, 24 Matley Close, Newton,
Hyde, SK14 4UE, United Kingdom
Tel: +44 (0)161 368 7877
Email: enquiries@coachfinder.uk.com
Web site: www.coachfinder.uk.com

DAWSONGROUP PLC
Delaware Drive, Tongwell, Milton Keynes,
MK15 8JH, United Kingdom
Tel: +44 (0)1908 218 111
Fax: +44 (0)1908 218 444
Email: contactus@dawsongroup.co.uk
Web site: www.dawsongroup.co.uk

HAYWARD TRAVEL
2 Murch Crescent, Dinas Powys,
Vale of Glamorgan, CF64 4RF, United Kingdom
Tel: +44 (0)2920 515 551
Fax: +44 (0)2920 515 113
Email: sales@haywardtravel.co.uk
Web site: www.haywardtravel.co.uk

NEXT BUS LTD
The Coach Yard, Vincients Road,
Bumpers Farm Industrial Estate, Chippenham,
Wiltshire, SN14 6QA, United Kingdom
Tel: +44 (0)1249 462 462
Fax: +44 (0)1249 448 844
Email: sales@next-bus.co.uk
Web site: www.next-bus.co.uk

TOURMASTER RECOVERY
Alderlands, Peterborough Road, Crowland,
Peterborough, PE6 0AA, United Kingdom
Tel: +44 (0)1733 211 639

WHEELS/MIDLAND RED COACHES
Postal Office, 23 Broad Street, Brinklow,
Warwickshire, CV23 0LS, United Kingdom
Tel: +44 (0)7733 884 914
Fax: +44 (0)2476 354 900
Email: buses@wheels.co.uk
Web site: www.wheels.co.uk

YORKSHIRE BUS & COACH SALES
254A West Ella Road, West Ella, Hull, HU10 7SF,
United Kingdom
Tel: +44 (0)1482 653 302
Fax: +44 (0)1482 653 302
Email: craig.porteous@virgin.net

COACH INTERCHANGE/PARKING FACILITIES

SAMMYS GARAGE
Victoria Coach Station, Arrivals Hall,
3 Eccleston Place, London, SW1W 9NF,
United Kingdom
Tel: +44 (0)20 7730 8867

VICTORIA COACH STATION LTD
164 Buckingham Palace Road, London,
SW1W 9TP, United Kingdom
Tel: +44 (0)20 7027 2541
Web site: www.tfl.gov.uk

COMPUTER SYSTEMS/SOFTWARE

ALMEX UK
Metric House,
Westmead Industrial Estate Westlea, Swindon,
SN5 7AD, United Kingdom
Tel: +44 (0)1793 647 800
Fax: +44 (0)1793 647 932
Email: info@almex.co.uk
Web site: www.hoeft-wessel.com

AUTOPRO SOFTWARE
1 Kingsmeadow, Norton Cross, Runcorn,
WA7 6PB, United Kingdom
Tel: +44 (0)1928 715 962
Email: sales@autoprouk.com
Web site: www.autoprosoftware.co.uk

CIVICA TRANMAN SOLUTIONS
Thornbury Office Park, Midland Way, Thornbury,
Gloucestershire, BS35 2BS, United Kingdom
Tel: +44 (0)1454 874 002
Email: tranman@civica.co.uk
Web site: www.civica.co.uk/tranman

DISTINCTIVE SYSTEMS LTD
Amy Johnson Way, York, YO30 4XT,
United Kingdom
Tel: 01904 692269
Fax: 01904 690810
Email: sales@distinctive-systems.com
Web site: www.distinctive-systems.com

INIT INNOVATIONS IN TRANSPORTATION LTD
Price House, 37 Stoney Street, The Lace Market,
Nottingham, NG1 1LS, United Kingdom
Tel: +44 (0)870 890 4648
Email: sales@init.co.uk
Web site: www.init.co.uk

MIX TELEMATICS
39-40 Cherry Orchard North, Kembury Park,
Swindon, SN2 8UH, United Kingdom
Tel: +44 (0)1793 500100
Web site: www.mixtelematics.com

NIMBUS JOURNEY INFORMATION LTD
Suite F4 and F5, Worth Corner, Turners Hill Road,
Crawley, West Sussex, RH10 7SL, United Kingdom
Tel: +44 (0)1293 887 308
Email: sales@nimbusjourneyinfo.co.uk
Web site: www.nimbusjourneyinfo.co.uk

OMNIBUS
Hollinwood Business Centre, Albert Street,
Hollinwood, Oldham, Lancashire, OL8 3QL,
United Kingdom
Tel: +44 (0)161 683 3100
Fax: +44 (0)161 683 3102
Web site: www.omnibus-systems.co.uk

QUARTIX LTD
Chapel Offices, Park Street, Newtown, Powys,
SY16 1EE, United Kingdom
Tel: +44 (0)870 013 6663
Email: enquiries@quartix.net
Web site: www.quartix.net

ROEVILLE COMPUTER SYSTEMS
Station House, East Lane, Stainforth, Doncaster,
DN7 5HF, United Kingdom
Tel: +44 (0)1302 841 333
Fax: +44 (0)1302 843 966
Email: sales@roeville.com
Web site: www.roeville.com

TAGTRONICS LTD
5 Anchor Court, Commercial Road, Darwen,
Blackburn, BB3 0DB, United Kingdom
Tel: +44 (0)1254 819 205
Fax: +44 (0)1254 873 238
Email: howcanwehelp@tagtronics.co.uk
Web site: www.tagtronics.co.uk

TRAPEZE GROUP (UK) LTD
The Mill, Staverton, Wiltshire, BA14 6PH,
United Kingdom
Tel: +44 (0)844 561 6771
Fax: +44 (0)1225 784 222
Email: info.uk@trapezegroup.co.uk
Web site: www.trapezegroup.co.uk

TRAVEL INFORMATION SYSTEMS
Suite 3, Grand Union House,
20 Kentish Town Road, London, NW1 9NX,
United Kingdom
Tel: +44 (0)20 7284 8071
Fax: +44 (0)20 7267 1133
Email: enquiries@travelinfosystems.com
Web site: www.travelinfosystems.com

VIX ACIS LTD
168 Cowley Road, Cambridge, CB4 0DL,
United Kingdom
Tel: +44 (0)1223 728 700
Fax: +44 (0)1223 506 311
Email: enquiries@acis.uk.com
Web site: www.vixtechnology.com

CONSULTANTS AND ADVISORY SERVICES

4 FARTHINGS INTERNATIONAL RECRUITMENT
Crieff Court, Teddington, Middlesex, TW11 9DS,
United Kingdom
Tel: +44 (0)20 8977 3500
Email: info@4farthings.co.uk
Web site: www.4farthings.co.uk

AUSTIN ANALYTICS
Crown House, 183 High Street, Bottisham,
Cambridge, CB25 9BB, United Kingdom
Contact: John Austin, Managing Consultant
Tel: +44 (0)1223 813 151
Fax: +44 (0)7005 946854
Email: john@analytics.co.uk
Web site: www.analytics.co.uk

AUTOPRO SOFTWARE
1 Kingsmeadow, Norton Cross, Runcorn,
WA7 6PB, United Kingdom
Tel: +44 (0)1928 715 962
Email: sales@autoprouk.com
Web site: www.autoprosoftware.co.uk

BEST IMPRESSIONS
15 Starfield Road, London, W12 9SN,
United Kingdom
Tel: 020 8740 6443
Fax: 020 8740 9134
Email: talk2us@best-impressions.co.uk
Web site: www.best-impressions.co.uk

BESTCHART LTD
6a Mays Yard, Down Road, Waterlooville,
Hampshire, United Kingdom
Tel: +44 (0)23 9259 7707
Fax: +44 (0)23 9259 1700
Web site: www.bestchart.co.uk

CAPOCO DESIGN
Stone Cross, Chicksgrove, Salisbury, SP3 6NA,
United Kingdom
Tel: +44 (0)1722 716 722
Fax: +44 (0)1722 716 226
Email: design@capoco.co.uk
Web site: www.capoco.co.uk

CAREYBROOK LTD
PO Box 205, Southam, Warwickshire, CV47 0ZL,
United Kingdom
Contact: John Turner, Director
Tel: +44 (0)3333 446 900
Fax: +44 (0)3333 446 901
Email: info@careybrook.co.uk
Web site: www.careybrook.co.uk
Careybrook can offer a range of services on
vehicle specification, workshop layout as well as
general management advice and support.

CHADWELL ASSOCIATES LTD
3 Caledonian Close, Ilford, IG3 9QF,
United Kingdom
Tel: +44 (0)208 590 5697
Email: ib@chadwellassociates.co.uk

CLAYTON HEATERS LTD
Fletchworth Gate Industrial Estate, Coventry,
West Midlands, CV5 6SP, United Kingdom
Tel: +44 (0)2476 691 916
Email: admin@claytoncc.co.uk
Web site: www.claytoncc.co.uk

CRONER (WOLTERS KLUWER UK LTD)
145 London Road, Kingston Upon Thames,
KT2 6SR, United Kingdom
Tel: +44 (0)20 8547 3333
Email: cronerinfo@wolterskluwer.co.uk
Web site: www.cronersolutions.co.uk

DCA DESIGN INTERNATIONAL
19 Church Street, Warwick, CV34 4AB,
United Kingdom
Tel: +44 (0)1926 499 461
Email: info@dca-design.com
Web site: www.dca-design.com/transport

PETER EDWARDS TRANSPORT CONSULTANCY LTD
19 Cardinal Close, Old Rossington, Doncaster,
DN11 0XG, United Kingdom
Tel: +44 (0)7802 541 691
Email: pandcedwards@btinternet.com

ELLIS TRANSPORT SERVICES
61 Bodycoats Road, Chandlers Ford, Hampshire,
SO53 2HA, United Kingdom
Tel: +44 (0)2380 488 566
Email: info@transportstationeryservices.com
Web site: www.transportstationeryservices.com

LEONARD GREEN ASSOCIATES
4 Crawshaw Drive, Reedsholme, Rawtenstall,
Rossendale, Lancashire, BB4 8PR, United Kingdom
Tel: +44 (0)1706 218 539
Email: lgreen22@ntlworld.com

IBPTS
PSV & Rail Consultants IBPTS
43 Cage Lane, Felixstowe, Suffolk, IP11 9BJ,
United Kingdom
Contact: Ian Baldry, Chief Transport Consultant
Tel: +44 (0)1394 672 344
Email: enquiries@ibpts.co.uk
Web site: www.ibpts.co.uk

THOMAS KNOWLES - TRANSPORT CONSULTANT
41 Redhills, Eccleshall, Staffordshire, ST21 6JW,
United Kingdom
Tel: +44 (0)1785 859 414
Fax: +44 (0)1785 859 414
Email: thmsknw@aol.com

MAS SPECIAL ENGINEERING LTD
Houghton Road, North Anston, S25 4JJ,
United Kingdom
Tel: +44 (0)1909 550 480
Fax: +44 (0)1909 550 486

MINIMISE YOUR RISK
11 Chatsworth Park, Telscombe Cliffs, Peacehaven,
East Sussex, BN10 7DZ, United Kingdom
Tel: +44 (0)844 335 1051
Email: info@minimiseyourrisk.co.uk
Web site: www.minimiseyourrisk.co.uk

MOTT MACDONALD
Mott Macdonald House, 8-10 Sydenham Road,
Croydon, CR0 2EE, United Kingdom
Tel: +44 (0)20 8774 2000
Email: marketing@mottmac.com
Web site: www.mottmac.com

PARRY PEOPLE MOVERS LTD
Overend Road, Cradley Heath, West Midlands,
B64 7DD, United Kingdom

Tel: +44 (0)1384 569 553
Fax: +44 (0)1384 637 753
Email: info@parrypeoplemovers.com
Web site: www.parrypeoplemovers.com

PEAK LEGAL SERVICES
15 Parr Fold Avenue, Worsley, Manchester,
M28 7HD, United Kingdom
Contact: Ben Ford, Manager
Tel: +44 (0)161 799 5560/
+44 (0)7748 116 797
Email: peaklegalservices@googlemail.com
Web site: www.peak-legal.co.uk
Detailed Reports and Liability advice.

PEOPLE 1ST
2nd Floor, Armstrong House, 38 Market Square,
Uxbridge, UB8 1LH, United Kingdom
Tel: +44 (0)1895 817 000
Email: info@people1st.co.uk
Web site: www.people1st.co.uk

PJA LTD
Sterling House, 19/23 High Street, Kidlington,
Oxon, OX5 2DH, United Kingdom
Tel: +44 (0)7836 634 414
Email: info@pj-associates.co.uk
Web site: www.pj-associates.co.uk

PRE METRO OPERATIONS LTD
Regent House, 56 Hagley Road, Stourbridge,
West Midlands, DY8 1QD, United Kingdom
Tel: +44 (0)1384 441 325
Email: info@premetro.co.uk
Web site: www.premetro.co.uk

PROFESSIONAL TRANSPORT SERVICES LTD
Training & Management
Consultancy Professional Transport Services
32a Church Road, Walpole St Peter, Wisbech,
Cambridgeshire, PE14 7NS, United Kingdom
Contact: Alan Whittington, Senior Partner
Tel: +44 (0)1945 781 328
Email: enquiries@proftranserv.co.uk
Web site: www.proftranserv.co.uk

SALTIRE COMMUNICATIONS
39 Lilyhill Terrace, Edinburgh, EH8 7DR,
United Kingdom
Tel: +44 (0)131 652 0205
Email: gavin.booth@btconnect.com

SKM COLIN BUCHANAN
New City Court, 20 St Thomas Street, London,
SE1 9RS, United Kingdom
Tel: +44 (0)20 7939 6100
Fax: +44 (0)20 7939 6103
Web site: www.jacobs.com

SPECIALIST TRAINING & CONSULTANCY SERVICES LTD
6 Venture Court, Altham Industrial Estate, Altham,
BB5 5TU, United Kingdom
Tel: +44 (0)1282 687 090
Fax: +44 (0)1282 687 091
Email: enquiries@specialisttraining.co.uk
Web site: www.specialisttraining.co.uk

STEER DAVIES GLEAVE
28-32 Upper Ground, London, SE1 9PD,
United Kingdom
Tel: +44 (0)20 7910 5000
Fax: +44 (0)20 7910 5001
Email: sdginfo@sdgworld.net
Web site: www.steerdaviesgleave.com

SYSTRA
Dukes Court, Duke Street, Woking, GU21 5BH,
United Kingdom
Tel: +44 (0)1483 728 051
Fax: +44 (0)1483 723 899
Email: info@mvaconsultancy.com
Web site: www.systra.co.uk

TAS PARTNERSHIP LTD
Guildhall House, 59-61 Guildhall Street, Preston,

Lancashire, PR1 3NU, United Kingdom
Tel: +44 (0)1772 204 988
Fax: +44 (0)1722 562 070
Web site: www.tas.net

TDI (EUROPE) LTD
Clifford Mill, Clifford Chambers,
Stratford Upon Avon, CV37 8HW, UK
Tel: +44 (0)1789 205 011
Email: martin.p@tdi.uk.com
Web site: www.tdi.uk.com

TRANSPORT & TRAVEL RESEARCH LTD
Garrick Suite, 15 Market Street, Lichfield,
Staffordshire, WS13 6JX, United Kingdom
Tel: +44 (0)1543 416 416
Fax: +44 (0)1543 416 681
Email: enquiries@ttr-ltd.com
Web site: www.ttr-ltd.com

TTS UK
Total Tool Solutions Ltd, Newhaven Business Park,
Lowergate, Milnsbridge, Huddersfield, HD3 4HS,
United Kingdom
Tel: +44 (0)1484 642 211
Fax: +44 (0)1484 461 002
Email: sales@ttsuk.com
Web site: www.ttsuk.com

VCA
No1, The Eastgate Office Centre, Eastgate Road,
Bristol, BS5 6XX, United Kingdom
Tel: +44 (0)300 330 5/97
Fax: +44 (0)300 003 2198
Email: enquiries@vca.gov.uk
Web site: www.dft.gov.uk/vca

WARD INTERNATIONAL CONSULTING LTD
70 Marks Tey Road, Fareham, PO14 3UR,
United Kingdom
Tel: +44 (0)1329 280 280
Fax: +44 (0)1329 667 901
Email: info@wardint.co.uk
Web site: www.wardint.co.uk

DRIVER TRAINING

ASSOCIATION OF TRAINERS
Old Farm, Fairfield, Brookland, Romney Marsh,
Kent, TN29 9SA, United Kingdom
Tel: +44 (0)1797 344 251
Email: julia@asot.org.uk
Web site: www.asot.org.uk

DRIVER & VEHICLE STANDARDS AGENCY (DVSA)
The Ellipse, Padley Road, Swansea, SA1 8AN,
United Kingdom
Tel: +44 (0)300 123 9000
Email: enquiries@vosa.gov.uk
Web site: www.gov.uk

IBPTS
PSV & Rail Consultants IBPTS
43 Cage Lane, Felixstowe, Suffolk, IP11 9BJ,
United Kingdom
Contact: Ian Baldry, Chief Transport Consultant
Tel: +44 (0)1394 672 344
Email: enquiries@ibpts.co.uk
Web site: www.ibpts.co.uk

LLOYD MORGAN GROUP
Lloyd Morgan Group
Phoenix House, Hemlock Park, Hyssop Close,
Cannock, Staffordshire, WS11 7GA,
United Kingdom
Tel: +44 (0)1543 897 505
Web site: www.lloydmorgangroup.co.uk

MINIMISE YOUR RISK
11 Chatsworth Park, Telscombe Cliffs, Peacehaven,
East Sussex, BN10 7DZ, United Kingdom
Tel: +44 (0)844 335 1051
Email: info@minimiseyourrisk.co.uk
Web site: www.minimiseyourrisk.co.uk

NOVADATA TAB LTD
3 Blackwell Drive, Springwood Industrial Estate,
Braintree, Essex, CM7 2QJ, United Kingdom
Tel: +44 (0)1376 552 999
Fax: +44 (0)1376 550 567
Email: enquiries@novatab.co.uk
Web site: www.novatab.co.uk

OMNIBUS TRAINING LTD
Unit 112, Lombard House, 2 Purley Way, Croydon,
CR0 3JP, United Kingdom
Tel: +44 (0)20 3006 7259
Fax: +44 (0)20 8684 7835
Email: info@omnibusltd.com
Web site: www.omnibusltd.com

PEOPLE 1ST
2nd Floor, Armstrong House, 38 Market Square,
Uxbridge, UB8 1LH, United Kingdom
Tel: +44 (0)1895 817 000
Email: info@people1st.co.uk
Web site: www.people1st.co.uk

SPECIALIST TRAINING & CONSULTANCY SERVICES LTD
6 Venture Court, Altham Industrial Estate, Altham,
BB5 5TU, United Kingdom
Tel: +44 (0)1282 687 090
Fax: +44 (0)1282 687 091
Email: enquiries@specialisttraining.co.uk
Web site: www.specialisttraining.co.uk

WHEELS/MIDLAND RED COACHES
Postal Office, 23 Broad Street, Brinklow,
Warwickshire, CV23 0LS, United Kingdom
Tel: +44 (0)7733 884 914
Fax: +44 (0)2476 354 900
Email: buses@wheels.co.uk
Web site: www.wheels.co.uk

DRUG AND ALCOHOL TESTING

ALCOLOCK GB LTD
Wansdyke Business Services Centre,
Midsomer Enterprise Park, Midsomer Norton,
Radstock, BA3 2BB, United Kingdom
Tel: +44 (0)1761 408 159
Fax: +44 (0)1761 361 010
Email: info@alcolockgb.com
Web site: www.alcolockgb.com

EXHIBITION ORGANISERS

EXPO MANAGEMENT LTD
Olympus Avenue, Leamington Spa, CV34 6BF,
United Kingdom
Tel: +44 (0)1926 888 123
Fax: +44 (0)1926 888 004
Email: info@expom.co.uk
Web site: www.expom.co.uk

THE LONDON BUS EXPORT CO
PO Box 12, Chepstow, NP16 5UZ,
United Kingdom
Tel: +44 (0)1291 689 741
Fax: +44 (0)1291 689 361
Email: lonbusco@globalnet.co.uk
Web site: www.bus.uk.com

UK COACH RALLY
21 The Poynings, Richings Park, Iver,
Buckinghamshire, SL0 9DS, United Kingdom
Tel: +44 (0)1753 631 170
Fax: +44 (0)1753 655 980
Email: info@coachdisplays.co.uk
Web site: www.coachdisplays.co.uk

FERRY OPERATORS

BRITTANY FERRIES GROUP TRAVEL
The Brittany Centre, Wharf Road, Portsmouth,
PO2 8RU, United Kingdom
Tel: +44 (0)871 244 1456
Email: reservations@brittany-ferries.com
Web site: www.brittany-ferries.co.uk/grouptravel

CALEDONIAN MACBRAYNE LTD
Head Office, The Ferry Terminal, Gourock,
PA19 1QP, United Kingdom
Tel: +44 (0)1475 650 100
Email: enquiries@calmac.co.uk
Web site: www.calmac.co.uk

CONDOR FERRIES LTD
Condor House, New Harbour Road South,
Hamworthy, Poole, BH15 4AJ, United Kingdom
Tel: 0845 609 1024
Fax: +44 (0)1202 685 184
Email: reservations@condorferries.co.uk
Web site: www.condorferries.co.uk

DFDS SEAWAYS
Scandinavia House, Refinery Road, Parkeston,
CO12 4QG, United Kingdom
Tel: +44 (0)871 522 9933
Web site: www.dfdsseaways.co.uk

EUROTUNNEL GROUP
Ashford Road, Folkestone, CT18 8XX,
United Kingdom
Tel: +44 (0)844 335 3535
Web site: www.eurotunnel.com

IRISH FERRIES LTD
Groups Department, Salt Island, Holyhead,
LL65 1DR, United Kingdom
Tel: +44 (0)8717 300 400
Fax: +44 (0)1407 760 340
Email: groups@irishferries.co.uk
Web site: www.irishferries.com

ISLE OF MAN STEAM PACKET COMPANY
Imperial Buildings, Douglas, IM1 2BY, Isle of Man
Tel: +44 (0)1624 661 661
Fax: +44 (0)1624 645 618
Email: iom.reservations@steam-packet.com
Web site: www.steam-packet.com

NORTHLINK FERRIES
Stromness Ferry Terminal, Ferry Road, Stromness,
Orkney, KW16 3BH, United Kingdom
Tel: 0845 6000 449
Email: info@northlinkferries.co.uk
Web site: www.northlinkferries.co.uk

P&O FERRIES
Channel House, Channel View Road, Dover,
CT17 9TJ, United Kingdom
Tel: +44 (0)8716 641 641
Fax: +44 (0)8707 625 325
Email: groups@poferries.com
Web site: www.poferries.com

PENTLAND FERRIES LTD
Pier Road, St Margaret's Hope, Orkney,
KW17 2SW, United Kingdom
Tel: +44 (0)1856 831 226
Fax: +44 (0)1856 831 697
Email: sales@pentlandferries.co.uk
Web site: www.pentlandferries.co.uk

RED FUNNEL
12 Bugle Street, Southampton, SO14 2JY,
United Kingdom
Tel: +44 (0)23 8024 8500
Fax: +44 (0)23 8024 8501
Email: post@redfunnel.co.uk
Web site: www.redfunnel.co.uk

STENA LINE
United Kingdom
Tel: 08445 764 764
Email: group.travel@stenaline.com
Web site: www.stenaline.co.uk/groups

WIGHTLINK LTD
PO Box 59, Portsmouth, PO1 2XB,
United Kingdom
Tel: +44 (0)23 9285 5260
Web site: www.wightlink.co.uk

FINANCE AND LEASING

DAVIES CORPORATE FINANCE
7 Solway Court, Electra Way,
Crewe Business Park, Crewe, CW1 6LD,
United Kingdom
Tel: 0845 077 9117
Email: enquiries@daviescorporate.co.uk
Web site: www.daviescorporate.co.uk

DAWSONGROUP PLC
Delaware Drive, Tongwell, Milton Keynes,
MK15 8JH, United Kingdom
Tel: +44 (0)1908 218 111
Fax: +44 (0)1908 218 444
Email: contactus@dawsongroup.co.uk
Web site: www.dawsongroup.co.uk

FOREST ASSET FINANCE LTD
Bridge House, 6 Pullman Business Park,
Pullman Way, Ringwood, Hampshire, BH24 1HD,
United Kingdom
Tel: +44 (0)1425 485 685
Fax: +44 (0)1425 473 444
Email: info@forestassetfinance.co.uk
Web site: www.forestassetfinance.co.uk

HUXLEY CORPORATE FINANCE
65A High Street, Tarporley, Cheshire, CW6 0DP,
United Kingdom
Tel: +44 (0)1829 730 062
Fax: +44 (0)1829 730 063
Email: info@huxleycf.co.uk
Web site: www.huxleycf.co.uk

LANDMARK FINANCE LTD
Suite 4, Old Grove House, 13 Vine Street,
Hazel Grove, Stockport, Cheshire, SK7 4JS,
United Kingdom
Tel: +44 (0)161 456 4242
Fax: +44 (0)161 483 3733
Email: sales@landmarkltd.co.uk
Web site: www.landmarkltd.co.uk

LHE FINANCE LTD
21 Headlands Business Park, Salisbury Road,
Ringwood, Hampshire, BH24 3PB,
United Kingdom
Tel: +44 (0)1425 474 070
Email: contactus@dawsongroup.co.uk
Web site: www.lhefinance.co.uk

MCV BUS AND COACH LTD
Sterling Place, Elean Business Park, Sutton, Ely,
CB6 2QE, United Kingdom
Tel: +44 (0)1353 773 000
Fax: +44 (0)1353 773 001
Email: sales@mcv-uk.com
Web site: www.mcv-uk.com

MISTRAL ASSET FINANCE
Lowry House, 17 Marble Street, Manchester,
M2 3AW, United Kingdom
Tel: 0800 038 9933
Email: sales@mistral-finance.com
Web site: www.mistral-finance.com

NORTON FOLGATE CAPITAL GROUP
12th Floor, 30 Crown Place, London, EC2A 4EB,
United Kingdom
Tel: +44 (0)20 7965 4777
Email: help@nortonfolgate.co.uk
Web site: www.nortonfolgate.co.uk

STOKE PARK FINANCE LTD
The Studio, Kirkhill House, Broom Road East,
Newton Mearns, Glasgow, G77 5LL,
United Kingdom
Tel: +44 (0)141 639 1410
Fax: +44 (0)141 639 4785
Email: info@stokeparkfinance.co.uk
Web site: www.stokeparkfinance.co.uk

VOLVO FINANCIAL SERVICES
Wedgnock Lane, Warwick, CV34 5YA,
United Kingdom
Tel: +44 (0)1926 401 203
Fax: +44 (0)1926 410278
Web site: www.vfsco.com

GRAPHIC DESIGN

BEST IMPRESSIONS
15 Starfield Road, London, W12 9SN,
United Kingdom
Tel: 020 8740 6443
Fax: 020 8740 9134
Email: talk2us@best-impressions.co.uk
Web site: www.best-impressions.co.uk

BRITISH BUS PUBLISHING LTD
16 St Margaret's Drive, Telford, TF1 3PH,
United Kingdom
Tel: 01952 255669
Email: bill.potter@btconnect.com
Web site: www.britishbuspublishing.co.uk

EXPRESS COACH REPAIRS LTD
Outgang Lane, Pickering, YO18 7EL,
United Kingdom
Tel: +44 (0)1751 475 215
Email: expresscoachrepairs@hotmail.co.uk

FWT
Aztec House, 397-405 Archway Road, London,
N6 4EY, United Kingdom
Tel: +44 (0)20 8347 3700
Fax: +44 (0)20 8347 3700
Email: paul.treadwell@fwt.co.uk
Web site: www.fwt.co.uk

GRAPHIC EVOLUTION LTD
Ad House, East Parade, Harrogate,
North Yorkshire, HG1 5LT, United Kingdom
Tel: +44 (0)1423 706 680
Fax: +44 (0)1423 502 522
Email: info@graphic-evolution.co.uk
Web site: www.graphic-evolution.co.uk

IGP SOLUTIONS
16 Hillbottom Road, High Wycombe, HP12 4HJ,
United Kingdom
Tel: +44 (0)1494 533 131
Fax: +44 (0)1494 462 675
Email: sales@igpsolutions.com
Web site: www.igpsolutions.com

IMAGINET
Greyfriars House, Greyfriars Road, Cardiff,
CF10 3AL, United Kingdom
Tel: +44 (0)29 2057 4500
Fax: +44 (0)29 2057 4501
Email: sales@imaginet.co.uk
Web site: www.imaginet.co.uk

PLUM DIGITAL PRINT
Suite 1, Cornerstone House, Stafford Park 13,
Telford, Shropshire, TF3 3AZ, United Kingdom
Tel: +44 (0)1952 204 920
Web site: www.plumdigitalprint.com

RH BODYWORKS
A140 Norwich-Ipswich Road, Brome, Eye, Suffolk,
IP23 8AW, United Kingdom
Tel: +44 (0)1379 870 666
Fax: +44 (0)1379 871 140
Email: enquiries@rhbodyworks.co.uk
Web site: www.rhbodyworks.co.uk

HEALTH & SAFETY

GAUNTLET RISK MANAGEMENT (COVENTRY)
11 Little Church Street, Rugby, CV21 3AW,
United Kingdom
Tel: +44 (0)1788 578 948
Web site: www.gauntletgroup.com/coventry

INSURANCE

BELMONT INTERNATIONAL LTD
Becket House, Vestry Road, Otford, Kent,
TN14 5EL, United Kingdom
Tel: +44 (0)1732 744 700
Fax: +44 (0)1732 740 276
Email: belmont@belmontint.com
Web site: www.belmontint.com

ELLIS BATES GROUP
Adam House, Ripon Way, Harrogate, N Yorkshire,
HG1 2AU, United Kingdom
Tel: +44 (0)1423 520 052
Web site: www.ellisbatesgroup.com

GAUNTLET RISK MANAGEMENT (COVENTRY)
11 Little Church Street, Rugby, CV21 3AW,
United Kingdom
Tel: +44 (0)1788 578 948
Web site: www.gauntletgroup.com/coventry

JENKINSON INSURANCE
New Ebury House, South Grove, Rotherham,
S60 2AF, United Kingdom
Tel: +44 (0)1709 821400
Web site: www.jenkinsoninsurance.co.uk

P J HAYMAN & CO LTD
Stansted House, Rowlands Castle, Hampshire,
PO9 6BR, United Kingdom
Tel: +44 (0)845 230 0631
Fax: +44 (0)23 9241 9019
Email: info@pjhayman.com
Web site: www.pjhayman.com

MILES SMITH INSURANCE GROUP
6th Floor, One America Square, 17 Crosswall,
London, EC3N 2LB, United Kingdom
Tel: +44 (0)20 7977 4800
Email: info@milessmith.co.uk
Web site: www.milessmith.co.uk

PEAK LEGAL SERVICES
15 Parr Fold Avenue, Worsley, Manchester,
M28 7HD, United Kingdom
Contact: Ben Ford, Manager
Tel: +44 (0)161 799 5560/+44 (0)7748 116 797
Email: peaklegalservices@googlemail.com
Web site: www.peak-legal.co.uk
Retained Liability investigations.

RIGTON INSURANCE SERVICES LTD
Chevin House, Otley Road, Guiseley, Leeds,
LS20 8BH, United Kingdom
Tel: +44 (0)1943 879 539
Fax: +44 (0)1943 875 529
Email: fleet@rigtoninsurance.co.uk
Web site: www.rigtoninsurance.co.uk

TOWERGATE CHAPMAN STEVENS
Towergate House, 22 Wintersells Road,
Wintersells Business Park, Byfleet, Surrey,
KT14 7LF, United Kingdom
Tel: +44 (0)1932 334 140
Fax: +44 (0)1932 351 238
Email: tcs@towergate.co.uk
Web site: www.towergatechapmanstevens.co.uk

VOLVO FINANCIAL SERVICES
Wedgnock Lane, Warwick, CV34 5YA,
United Kingdom
Tel: +44 (0)1926 401 203
Fax: +44 (0)1926 410278
Web site: www.vfsco.com

WILLIS LTD
51 Lime Street, London, EC3M 7DQ, UK
Tel: +44 (0)20 3124 6000
Fax: +44 (0)20 3124 8223
Web site: www.willis.com

WRIGHTSURE GROUP
799 London Road, West Thurrock, RM20 3LH,
United Kingdom

Tel: +44 (0)1708 865 533
Fax: +44 (0)1708 865 100
Email: info@wrightsure.com
Web site: www.wrightsure.com

LEGAL AND OPERATIONS ADVISERS

BACKHOUSE JONES SOLICITORS
The Printworks, Hey Road, Clitheroe, Lancashire,
BB7 9WD, United Kingdom
Tel: 0845 0575 111
Fax: 0845 0575 112
Email: julia.davies@backhouses.co.uk
Web site: www.backhousejones.co.uk

CHRIS BORLAND & ASSOCIATES LTD
3 Axe View, Axe Road, Drimpton, Beaminster,
Dorset, DT8 3RJ, United Kingdom
Tel: +44 (0)1460 271 680
Email: chris.borland@tiscali.co.uk
Service possibilities identification, Service
Registration, Timetable Construction, Stage and
Fare Construction, Revenue Protection policies

ELLIS TRANSPORT SERVICES
61 Bodycoats Road, Chandlers Ford, Hampshire,
SO53 2HA, United Kingdom
Tel: +44 (0)2380 488 566
Email: info@transportstationeryservices.com
Web site: www.transportstationeryservices.com

FOSTER TACHOGRAPHS
189 Watling Street Road, Fulwood, Preston,
PR2 8AE, United Kingdom
Tel: +44 (0)1772 655 155
Fax: +44 (0)1772 793 739
Email: admin@fostertachographs.co.uk
Web site: www.fostertachographs.co.uk

FREIGHT TRANSPORT ASSOCIATION
Hermes House, St John's Road, Tunbridge Wells,
TN4 9UZ, United Kingdom
Tel: +44 (0)1892 526 171
Fax: +44 (0)1892 534 989
Web site: www.fta.co.uk

IBPTS
PSV & Rail Consultants IBPTS
43 Cage Lane, Felixstowe, Suffolk, IP11 9BJ,
United Kingdom
Contact: Ian Baldry, Chief Transport Consultant
Tel: +44 (0)1394 672 344
Email: enquiries@ibpts.co.uk
Web site: www.ibpts.co.uk

PEAK LEGAL SERVICES
15 Parr Fold Avenue, Worsley, Manchester,
M28 7HD, United Kingdom
Contact: Ben Ford, Manager
Tel: +44 (0)161 799 5560/+44 (0)7748 116 797
Email: peaklegalservices@googlemail.com
Web site: www.peak-legal.co.uk
Retained Liability investigations.

PELLYS RJP SOLICITORS
Sworders Court, North Street, Bishops Stortford,
Hertfordshire, CM23 2TN, United Kingdom
Tel: +44 (0)1279 758 080
Fax: +44 (0)1279 467 565
Email: office@pellys.co.uk
Web site: www.pellys.co.uk

PENNINGTONS SOLICITORS LLP
Abacus House, 33 Gutter Lane, London,
EC2V 8AR, United Kingdom
Tel: +44 (0)20 7457 3000
Fax: +44 (0)20 7457 3240
Email: info@penningtons.co.uk
Web site: www.penningtons.co.uk

PRE METRO OPERATIONS LTD
Regent House, 56 Hagley Road, Stourbridge,
West Midlands, DY8 1QD, United Kingdom
Tel: +44 (0)1384 441 325
Email: info@premetro.co.uk
Web site: www.premetro.co.uk

PROFESSIONAL TRANSPORT SERVICES LTD
Training & Management
Consultancy Professional Transport Services
32a Church Road, Walpole St Peter, Wisbech,
Cambridgeshire, PE14 7NS, United Kingdom
Contact: Alan Whittington, Senior Partner
Tel: +44 (0)1945 781 328
Email: enquiries@proftranserv.co.uk
Web site: www.proftranserv.co.uk

WARD INTERNATIONAL CONSULTING LTD
70 Marks Tey Road, Fareham, PO14 3UR,
United Kingdom
Tel: +44 (0)1329 280 280
Fax: +44 (0)1329 667 901
Email: info@wardint.co.uk
Web site: www.wardint.co.uk

LIVERY AND GRAPHIC DESIGN

BEST IMPRESSIONS
15 Starfield Road, London, W12 9SN,
United Kingdom
Tel: 020 8740 6443
Fax: 020 8740 9134
Email: talk2us@best-impressions.co.uk
Web site: www.best-impressions.co.uk

CHANNEL COMMERCIALS PLC
Unit 6, Cobbs Wood Industrial Estate,
Brunswick Road, Ashford, TN23 1EH, UK
Tel: 0844 247 7742
Fax: +44 (0)1233 636 322
Web site: www.channelcommercials.co.uk

EXPRESS COACH REPAIRS LTD
Outgang Lane, Pickering, YO18 7EL,
United Kingdom
Tel: +44 (0)1751 475 215
Email: expresscoachrepairs@hotmail.co.uk

GRAPHIC EVOLUTION LTD
Ad House, East Parade, Harrogate,
North Yorkshire, HG1 5LT, United Kingdom
Tel: +44 (0)1423 706 680
Fax: +44 (0)1423 502 522
Email: info@graphic-evolution.co.uk
Web site: www.graphic-evolution.co.uk

IGP SOLUTIONS
16 Hillbottom Road, High Wycombe, HP12 4HJ,
United Kingdom
Tel: +44 (0)1494 533 131
Fax: +44 (0)1494 462 675
Email: sales@igpsolutions.com
Web site: www.igpsolutions.com

THE LONDON BUS EXPORT CO
PO Box 12, Chepstow, NP16 5UZ,
United Kingdom
Tel: +44 (0)1291 689 741
Fax: +44 (0)1291 689 361
Email: lonbusco@globalnet.co.uk
Web site: www.bus.uk.com

MCKENNA BROTHERS LTD
McKenna House, Jubilee Road, Middleton,
Manchester, M24 2LX, United Kingdom
Tel: +44 (0)161 655 3244
Fax: +44 (0)161 655 3059
Email: info@mckennabrothers.co.uk
Web site: www.mckennabrothers.co.uk

PB BUS MARKETING LTD
Trafalgar Close, Chandlers Ford, Eastleigh,
Hampshire, SO50 4BW, United Kingdom
Tel: +44 (0)2380 251 358
Fax: +44 (0)2380 267 623
Email: enquiries@pbbusmarketing.co.uk
Web site: www.pbbusmarketing.co.uk

MAPS FOR THE BUS INDUSTRY

BEST IMPRESSIONS
15 Starfield Road, London, W12 9SN, UK

Tel: 020 8740 6443
Fax: 020 8740 9134
Email: talk2us@best-impressions.co.uk
Web site: www.best-impressions.co.uk

FWT
Aztec House, 397-405 Archway Road, London,
N6 4EY, United Kingdom
Tel: +44 (0)20 8347 3700
Fax: +44 (0)20 8347 3700
Email: paul.treadwell@fwt.co.uk
Web site: www.fwt.co.uk

PINDAR SCARBOROUGH LTD
Thornburgh Road, Eastfield, Scarborough,
YO11 3UY, United Kingdom
Tel: +44 (0)1723 581 581
Fax: +44 (0)1723 583 086
Email: pindarestimates@pindar.com
Web site: www.pindar.com

MARKETING SERVICES

BEST IMPRESSIONS
15 Starfield Road, London, W12 9SN, UK
Tel: 020 8740 6443
Fax: 020 8740 9134
Email: talk2us@best-impressions.co.uk
Web site: www.best-impressions.co.uk

HERE TO THERE PUBLISHING LTD
Apartment 4, 38-40 Stonehills,
Welwyn Garden City, Hertfordshire, AL8 6PD,
United Kingdom
Contact: Suzy Scott
Tel: +44 (0)1707 246262
Email: general@heretotherepublishing.com
Web site: www.heretotherepublishing.com

IMAGINET
Greyfriars House, Greyfriars Road, Cardiff,
CF10 3AL, United Kingdom
Tel: +44 (0)29 2057 4500
Fax: +44 (0)29 2057 4501
Email: sales@imaginet.co.uk
Web site: www.imaginet.co.uk

PB BUS MARKETING LTD
Trafalgar Close, Chandlers Ford, Eastleigh,
Hampshire, SO50 4BW, United Kingdom
Tel: +44 (0)2380 251 358
Fax: +44 (0)2380 267 623
Email: enquiries@pbbusmarketing.co.uk
Web site: www.pbbusmarketing.co.uk

MECHANICAL INVESTIGATION

COACH-AID LTD
Greyfriars Workshop, Greyfriars Way, Stafford,
Staffordshire, ST16 2SH, United Kingdom
Tel: +44 (0)1785 222 666
Email: workshop@coach-aid.com
Web site: www.coach-aid.com

ELLIS TRANSPORT SERVICES
61 Bodycoats Road, Chandlers Ford, Hampshire,
SO53 2HA, United Kingdom
Tel: +44 (0)2380 488 566
Email: info@transportstationeryservices.com
Web site: www.transportstationeryservices.com

OPTARE PRODUCT SUPPORT
London
Unit 9, Eurocourt, Olivers Close, West Thurrock,
RM20 3EE, United Kingdom
Tel: +44 (0)1708 896 860
Fax: +44 (0)1708 869 920
Email: london.service@optare.com
Manchester
Trafford Park, Manchester, M17 1HG,
United Kingdom
Tel: +44 (0)161 872 7772
Email: manchester.service@optare.com
Rotherham
Denby Way, Hellaby, Rotherham, S66 8HR,
United Kingdom

Tel: +44 (0)1709 535 101
Fax: +44 (0)1709 739 680
Email: rotherham.service@optare.com

PLAXTON SERVICE

Ryton Road, Anston, Sheffield, S25 4DL,
United Kingdom
Tel: +44 (0)1909 551 155
Fax: +44 (0)1909 550 050
Email: service@plaxtonlimited.co.uk
Web site: www.plaxtonaftercare.co.uk

ON-BUS ADVERTISING

ADVERTA
Evans Business Centre, Hartwith Way, Harrogate,
HG3 2XA, United Kingdom
Tel: +44 (0)8456 430 530
Fax: +44 (0)1423 813 471
Email: sales@adverta.co.uk
Web site: www.adverta.co.uk

CYBERLYNE COMMUNICATIONS LTD
Unit 5, Hatfield Way,
South Church Enterprise Park, Bishop Auckland,
Durham, DL14 6XF, United Kingdom
Tel: 01388 773761
Fax: 01388 773778
Email: sales@cyberlyne.co.uk
Web site: www.cyberlyne.co.uk

NIMBUS JOURNEY INFORMATION LTD
Suite F4 and F5, Worth Corner, Turners Hill Road,
Crawley, West Sussex, RH10 7SL, United Kingdom
Tel: +44 (0)1293 887 308
Email: sales@nimbusjourneyinfo.co.uk
Web site: www.nimbusjourneyinfo.co.uk

PASSENGER REPRESENTATION

BUS USERS UK
Terminal House, Shepperton, Middlesex,
TW17 8AS, United Kingdom
Tel: +44 (0)300 111 0001
Email: enquiries@bususers.org
Web site: www.bususers.org
Bus Users UK is the independent organisation
for bus passengers. It is the nominated body for
complaint appeals for passengers throughout
Great Britain (outside London) and also organises
bus users' surgeries as well as campaigning
on behalf of bus users. It is also an umbrella
organisation to support local bus user groups.

PRINTING AND PUBLISHING

BEMROSEBOOTH PARAGON
Stockholm Road, Sutton Fields, Hull, HU7 0XY,
United Kingdom
Tel: +44 (0)1482 826 343
Email: info@bemrosebooth.com
Web site: www.bemrosebooth.com

BEST IMPRESSIONS
15 Starfield Road, London, W12 9SN,
United Kingdom
Tel: 020 8740 6443
Fax: 020 8740 9134
Email: talk2us@best-impressions.co.uk
Web site: www.best-impressions.co.uk

BRITISH BUS PUBLISHING LTD
16 St Margaret's Drive, Telford, TF1 3PH, UK
Tel: 01952 255669
Email: bill.potter@btconnect.com
Web site: www.britishbuspublishing.co.uk
Quality transport book publishers and retailers.

BUS & COACH PROFESSIONAL
Plum Publishing Ltd
Suite 1, Cornerstone House, Stafford Park 13,
Telford, TF3 3AZ, United Kingdom
Tel: +44 (0)1952 204 920
Email: editor@busandcoach.com
Web site: www.busandcoach.com

FWT
Aztec House, 397-405 Archway Road, London,
N6 4EY, United Kingdom
Tel: +44 (0)20 8347 3700
Fax: +44 (0)20 8347 3700
Email: paul.treadwell@fwt.co.uk
Web site: www.fwt.co.uk

GRAPHIC EVOLUTION LTD
Ad House, East Parade, Harrogate,
North Yorkshire, HG1 5LT, United Kingdom
Tel: +44 (0)1423 706 680
Fax: +44 (0)1423 502 522
Email: info@graphic-evolution.co.uk
Web site: www.graphic-evolution.co.uk

HERE TO THERE PUBLISHING LTD
Apartment 4, 38-40 Stonehills,
Welwyn Garden City, Hertfordshire, AL8 6PD,
United Kingdom
Contact: Suzy Scott
Tel: +44 (0)1707 246262
Email: general@heretotherepublishing.com
Web site: www.heretotherepublishing.com

KEY PUBLISHING LTD
Key Publishing Ltd
Units 1-4, Gwash Way Industrial Estate,
Ryhall Road, Stamford, Lincolnshire, PE9 1XP,
United Kingdom
Tel: +44 (0)1780 755 131
Web site: www.keypublishing.com

PB BUS MARKETING LTD
Trafalgar Close, Chandlers Ford, Eastleigh,
Hampshire, SO50 4BW, United Kingdom
Tel: +44 (0)2380 251 358
Fax: +44 (0)2380 267 623
Email: enquiries@pbbusmarketing.co.uk
Web site: www.pbbusmarketing.co.uk

PINDAR SCARBOROUGH LTD
Thornburgh Road, Eastfield, Scarborough,
YO11 3UY, United Kingdom
Tel: +44 (0)1723 581 581
Fax: +44 (0)1723 583 086
Email: pindarestimates@pindar.com
Web site: www.pindar.com

PLUM DIGITAL PRINT
Suite 1, Cornerstone House, Stafford Park 13,
Telford, Shropshire, TF3 3AZ, United Kingdom
Tel: +44 (0)1952 204 920
Web site: www.plumdigitalprint.com

PROMOTIONAL MATERIAL

BEST IMPRESSIONS
15 Starfield Road, London, W12 9SN,
United Kingdom
Tel: 020 8740 6443
Fax: 020 8740 9134
Email: talk2us@best-impressions.co.uk
Web site: www.best-impressions.co.uk

ETMSS LTD
Ground Floor Austin House, 43 Poole Road,
Westbourne, Bournemouth, Dorset, BH4 9DN,
United Kingdom
Contact: David Price, Sales Director
Tel: +44 (0)844 800 9299
Email: info@etmss.com
Web site: www.etmss.com
Smart card travel wallets, plain & pre-printed,
company branding.
Ticket rolls, pre-printed with promotions/
advertising & company branding.

FWT
Aztec House, 397-405 Archway Road, London,
N6 4EY, United Kingdom
Tel: +44 (0)20 8347 3700
Fax: +44 (0)20 8347 3700
Email: paul.treadwell@fwt.co.uk
Web site: www.fwt.co.uk

GRAPHIC EVOLUTION LTD
Ad House, East Parade, Harrogate,
North Yorkshire, HG1 5LT, United Kingdom
Tel: +44 (0)1423 706 680
Fax: +44 (0)1423 502 522
Email: info@graphic-evolution.co.uk
Web site: www.graphic-evolution.co.uk

HERE TO THERE PUBLISHING LTD
Apartment 4, 38-40 Stonehills,
Welwyn Garden City, Hertfordshire, AL8 6PD,
United Kingdom
Contact: Suzy Scott
Tel: +44 (0)1707 246262
Email: general@heretotherepublishing.com
Web site: www.heretotherepublishing.com

IBPTS
PSV & Rail Consultants IBPTS
43 Cage Lane, Felixstowe, Suffolk, IP11 9BJ,
United Kingdom
Contact: Ian Baldry, Chief Transport Consultant
Tel: +44 (0)1394 672 344
Email: enquiries@ibpts.co.uk
Web site: www.ibpts.co.uk

IMAGINET
Greyfriars House, Greyfriars Road, Cardiff,
CF10 3AL, United Kingdom
Tel: +44 (0)29 2057 4500
Fax: +44 (0)29 2057 4501
Email: sales@imaginet.co.uk
Web site: www.imaginet.co.uk

KEY PUBLISHING LTD
Key Publishing Ltd
Units 1-4, Gwash Way Industrial Estate,
Ryhall Road, Stamford, Lincolnshire, PE9 1XP,
United Kingdom
Tel: +44 (0)1780 755 131
Web site: www.keypublishing.com

MARKET ENGINEERING
43-44 North Bar, Banbury, OX16 0TH,
United Kingdom
Tel: +44 (0)1295 277 050
Email: contact@m-eng.com
Web site: www.m-eng.com

PB BUS MARKETING LTD
Trafalgar Close, Chandlers Ford, Eastleigh,
Hampshire, SO50 4BW, United Kingdom
Tel: +44 (0)2380 251 358
Fax: +44 (0)2380 267 623
Email: enquiries@pbbusmarketing.co.uk
Web site: www.pbbusmarketing.co.uk

PINDAR SCARBOROUGH LTD
Thornburgh Road, Eastfield, Scarborough,
YO11 3UY, United Kingdom
Tel: +44 (0)1723 581 581
Fax: +44 (0)1723 583 086
Email: pindarestimates@pindar.com
Web site: www.pindar.com

PLUM DIGITAL PRINT
Suite 1, Cornerstone House, Stafford Park 13,
Telford, Shropshire, TF3 3AZ, United Kingdom
Tel: +44 (0)1952 204 920
Web site: www.plumdigitalprint.com

PUBLICATIONS/BOOKS

BRITISH BUS PUBLISHING LTD
16 St Margaret's Drive, Telford, TF1 3PH,
United Kingdom
Tel: 01952 255669
Email: bill.potter@btconnect.com
Web site: www.britishbuspublishing.co.uk
Publishers of the Bus Handbook series that
feature the principal bus and coach operators of
Britain and Ireland.

BUS & COACH BUYER
4 Milnyard Square, Bakewell Road,
Orton Southgate, Peterborough, PE2 6GX,
United Kingdom

Tel: +44 (0)1733 362 300
Email: bcbsales@busandcoachbuyer.com
Web site: www.busandcoachbuyer.com

BUS & COACH PROFESSIONAL
Plum Publishing Ltd
Suite 1, Cornerstone House, Stafford Park 13,
Telford, TF3 3AZ, United Kingdom
Tel: +44 (0)1952 204 920
Email: editor@busandcoach.com
Web site: www.busandcoach.com

BUSES
Key Publishing Ltd, PO Box 100, Stamford,
Lincolnshire, PE9 1XQ, United Kingdom
Tel: +44 (0)1780 755 131
Fax: +44 (0)1780 757 261
Email: info@keypublishing.com
Web site: www.busesmag.com

BUSES WORLDWIDE
37 Oyster Lane, Byfleet, Surrey, KT14 7HS,
United Kingdom
Tel: +44 (0)1932 352 351
Email: membership@busesworldwide.org
Web site: www.busesworldwide.org
Buses Worldwide (6 issues a year A4); Maltese
Transport News (4 issues per year A5); British
Buses Abroad (4 issues per year A5).
Recent books include Maltese Buses of
Yesteryear, Sri Lankan Buses, Double Deck
Tours (Niagara) etc.

COACH & BUS WEEK
3 The Office Village, Cygnet Park, Forder Way,
Hampton, Peterborough, PE7 8GX,
United Kingdom
Tel: +44 (0)1733 293 243
Web site: www.coachandbusweek.com

CRONER
(WOLTERS KLUWER UK LTD)
145 London Road, Kingston Upon Thames,
KT2 6SR, United Kingdom
Tel: +44 (0)20 8547 3333
Email: cronerinfo@wolterskluwer.co.uk
Web site: www.cronersolutions.co.uk

HERE TO THERE PUBLISHING LTD
Apartment 4, 38-40 Stonehills,
Welwyn Garden City, Hertfordshire,
AL8 6PD, United Kingdom
Contact: Suzy Scott
Tel: +44 (0)1707 246262
Email: general@heretotherepublishing.com
Web site: www.heretotherepublishing.com

KEY PUBLISHING LTD
Key Publishing Ltd
Units 1-3, Gwash Way Industrial Estate,
Ryhall Road, Stamford, Lincolnshire, PE9 1XP,
United Kingdom
Tel: +44 (0)1780 755 131
Web site: www.keypublishing.com

PASSENGER TRANSPORT
Adelaide Wharf, 21 Whiston Road, London,
E2 8EX, United Kingdom
Tel: +44 (0)20 7749 6909
Email: editorial@passengertransport.co.uk
Web site: www.passengertransport.co.uk

PLUM DIGITAL PRINT
Suite 1, Cornerstone House, Stafford Park 13,
Telford, Shropshire, TF3 3AZ, United Kingdom
Tel: +44 (0)1952 204 920
Web site: www.plumdigitalprint.com

ROUTE ONE
Expo Management Ltd, Unit 4,
Minerva Business Park, Lynch Wood,
Peterborough, PE2 6FT, United Kingdom
Tel: +44 (0)1733 405 730
Email: enquiries@route-one.net
Web site: www.route-one.net

SALTIRE COMMUNICATIONS
39 Lilyhill Terrace, Edinburgh, EH8 7DR,
United Kingdom
Tel: +44 (0)131 652 0205
Email: gavin.booth@btconnect.com

SOCIETY OF OPERATIONS
ENGINEERS
22 Greencoat Place, London, SW1P 1PR,
United Kingdom
Tel: +44 (0)20 7630 1111
Fax: +44(0)207 630 6667
Email: soe@soe.org.uk
Web site: www.soe.org.uk

TRANSPORT STATIONERY SERVICES
61 Bodycoats Road, Chandlers Ford, Hampshire,
SO53 2HA, United Kingdom
Tel: +44 (0)7041 471 008
Fax: +44 (0)7041 471 009
Email: info@transportstationeryservices.com
Web site: www.transportstationeryservices.com

QUALITY MANAGEMENT SYSTEMS

DRIVER & VEHICLE STANDARDS
AGENCY (DVSA)
The Ellipse, Padley Road, Swansea, SA1 8AN,
United Kingdom
Tel: +44 (0)300 123 9000
Email: enquiries@vosa.gov.uk
Web site: www.gov.uk

FREIGHT TRANSPORT ASSOCIATION
Hermes House, St John's Road, Tunbridge Wells,
TN4 9UZ, United Kingdom
Tel: +44 (0)1892 526 171
Fax: +44 (0)1892 534 989
Web site: www.fta.co.uk

IBPTS
PSV & Rail Consultants IBPTS
43 Cage Lane, Felixstowe, Suffolk, IP11 9BJ,
United Kingdom
Contact: Ian Baldry, Chief Transport Consultant
Tel: +44 (0)1394 672 344
Email: enquiries@ibpts.co.uk
Web site: www.ibpts.co.uk

TTS UK
Total Tool Solutions Ltd, Newhaven Business Park,
Lowergate, Milnsbridge, Huddersfield, HD3 4HS,
United Kingdom
Tel: +44 (0)1484 642 211
Fax: +44 (0)1484 461 002
Email: sales@ttsuk.com
Web site: www.ttsuk.com

VCA
No1, The Eastgate Office Centre, Eastgate Road,
Bristol, BS5 6XX, United Kingdom
Tel: +44 (0)300 330 5797
Fax: +44 (0)300 003 2198
Email: enquiries@vca.gov.uk
Web site: www.dft.gov.uk/vca

RECRUITMENT

4 FARTHINGS INTERNATIONAL
RECRUITMENT
Crieff Court, Teddington, Middlesex, TW11 9DS,
United Kingdom
Tel: +44 (0)20 8977 3500
Email: info@4farthings.co.uk
Web site: www.4farthings.co.uk

REFERENCE BOOKS

BRITISH BUS PUBLISHING LTD
16 St Margaret's Drive, Telford, TF1 3PH,
United Kingdom
Tel: 01952 255669
Email: bill.potter@btconnect.com
Web site: www.britishbuspublishing.co.uk
Publishers of the Bus Handbook series that
feature the fleets of the principal bus and coach
operators of Britain and Ireland.

TIMETABLE PRODUCTION

BEST IMPRESSIONS
15 Starfield Road, London, W12 9SN,
United Kingdom
Tel: 020 8740 6443
Fax: 020 8740 9134
Email: talk2us@best-impressions.co.uk
Web site: www.best-impressions.co.uk

FWT
Aztec House, 397-405 Archway Road, London,
N6 4EY, United Kingdom
Tel: +44 (0)20 8347 3700
Fax: +44 (0)20 8347 3700
Email: paul.treadwell@fwt.co.uk
Web site: www.fwt.co.uk

HERE TO THERE PUBLISHING LTD
Apartment 4, 38-40 Stonehills,
Welwyn Garden City, Hertfordshire, AL8 6PD,
United Kingdom
Contact: Suzy Scott
Tel: +44 (0)1707 246262
Email: general@heretotherepublishing.com
Web site: www.heretotherepublishing.com

IBPTS
PSV & Rail Consultants IBPTS
43 Cage Lane, Felixstowe, Suffolk, IP11 9BJ,
United Kingdom
Contact: Ian Baldry, Chief Transport Consultant
Tel: +44 (0)1394 672 344
Email: enquiries@ibpts.co.uk
Web site: www.ibpts.co.uk

PB BUS MARKETING LTD
Trafalgar Close, Chandlers Ford, Eastleigh,
Hampshire, SO50 4BW, United Kingdom
Tel: +44 (0)2380 251 358
Fax: +44 (0)2380 267 623
Email: enquiries@pbbusmarketing.co.uk
Web site: www.pbbusmarketing.co.uk

PINDAR SCARBOROUGH LTD
Thornburgh Road, Eastfield, Scarborough,
YO11 3UY, United Kingdom
Tel: +44 (0)1723 581 581
Fax: +44 (0)1723 583 086
Email: pindarestimates@pindar.com
Web site: www.pindar.com

PLUM DIGITAL PRINT
Suite 1, Cornerstone House, Stafford Park 13,
Telford, Shropshire, TF3 3AZ, United Kingdom
Tel: +44 (0)1952 204 920
Web site: www.plumdigitalprint.com

PROFESSIONAL TRANSPORT
SERVICES LTD
Training & Management
Consultancy Professional Transport Services
32a Church Road, Walpole St Peter, Wisbech,
Cambridgeshire, PE14 7NS, United Kingdom
Contact: Alan Whittington, Senior Partner
Tel: +44 (0)1945 781 328
Email: enquiries@proftranserv.co.uk
Web site: www.proftranserv.co.uk

TRAPEZE GROUP (UK) LTD
The Mill, Staverton, Wiltshire, BA14 6PH,
United Kingdom
Tel: +44 (0)844 561 6771
Fax: +44 (0)1225 784 222
Email: info.uk@trapezegroup.co.uk
Web site: www.trapezegroup.co.uk

TRAVEL INFORMATION SYSTEMS
Suite 3, Grand Union House,
20 Kentish Town Road, London, NW1 9NX,
United Kingdom
Tel: +44 (0)20 7284 8071
Fax: +44 (0)20 7267 1133
Email: enquiries@travelinfosystems.com
Web site: www.travelinfosystems.com

TOUR WHOLESALES

ACTION TOURS LTD
5 Aston Street, Shifnal, Shropshire, TR11 8DW,
United Kingdom
Tel: +44 (0)1952 462 462
Fax: +44(0)1952 462 555
Email: info@actiontours.co.uk
Web site: www.actiontours.co.uk

ALBATROSS TRAVEL
14 New Hythe Lane, Larkfield, Kent, ME20 6AB,
United Kingdom
Tel: +44 (0)1732 879 100
Email: sales@albatrosstravel.com
Web site: www.albatrosstravel.com

CIE TOURS INTERNATIONAL
35 Lower Abbey Street, Dublin 1,
Republic of Ireland
Tel: +44 (0)20 8638 0715
Fax: +353 1 874 5564
Email: info@cietours.ie
Web site: www.cietours.com

GREATDAYS TRAVEL GROUP
Chapel House, Borough Road, Altrincham,
WA15 9RA, United Kingdom
Tel: +44 (0)161 928 3242
Fax: +44 (0)161 928 8226
Email: sales@greatdays.co.uk
Web site: www.greatdays.co.uk

INDEPENDENT COACH TRAVEL
Studios 20/21, Colman's Wharf, 45 Morris Road,
London, E14 6PA, United Kingdom
Tel: +44 (0)20 7538 4627
Fax: +44 (0)20 7538 8239
Email: info@ictsqt.co.uk
Web site: www.coachandgrouptravel.com

TRAINING AND MARKETING SERVICES

ASSOCIATION OF TRAINERS
Old Farm, Fairfield, Brookland, Romney Marsh,
Kent, TN29 9SA, United Kingdom
Tel: +44 (0)1797 344 251
Email: julia@asot.org.uk
Web site: www.asot.org.uk

COACH DIRECT
2nd Floor, 83 High Street, Rayleigh, Essex, SS6 7EJ,
United Kingdom
Tel: +44 (0)1268 747 388
Fax: +44 (0)1268 741 685
Email: info@coachdirect.co.uk
Web site: www.coachdirect.co.uk

IBPTS
PSV & Rail Consultants IBPTS
43 Cage Lane, Felixstowe, Suffolk, IP11 9BJ,
United Kingdom
Contact: Ian Baldry, Chief Transport Consultant
Tel: +44 (0)1394 672 344
Email: enquiries@ibpts.co.uk
Web site: www.ibpts.co.uk

MARKET ENGINEERING
43-44 North Bar, Banbury, OX16 0TH,
United Kingdom
Tel: +44 (0)1295 277 050
Email: contact@m-eng.com
Web site: www.m-eng.com

MINIMISE YOUR RISK
11 Chatsworth Park, Telscombe Cliffs, Peacehaven,
East Sussex, BN10 7DZ, United Kingdom
Tel: +44 (0)844 335 1051
Email: info@minimiseyourrisk.co.uk
Web site: www.minimiseyourrisk.co.uk

OMNIBUS TRAINING LTD
Unit 112, Lombard House, 2 Purley Way, Croydon,
CR0 3JP, United Kingdom
Tel: +44 (0)20 3006 7259
Fax: +44 (0)20 8684 7835
Email: info@omnibusltd.com
Web site: www.omnibusltd.com

PEOPLE 1ST
2nd Floor, Armstrong House, 38 Market Square,
Uxbridge, UB8 1LH, United Kingdom
Tel: +44 (0)1895 817 000
Email: info@people1st.co.uk
Web site: www.people1st.co.uk

PROFESSIONAL TRANSPORT SERVICES LTD
Training & Management
Consultancy Professional Transport Services
32a Church Road, Walpole St Peter, Wisbech,
Cambridgeshire, PE14 7NS, United Kingdom
Contact: Alan Whittington, Senior Partner
Tel: +44 (0)1945 781 328
Email: enquiries@proftranserv.co.uk
Web site: www.proftranserv.co.uk

SOCIETY OF OPERATIONS ENGINEERS
22 Greencoat Place, London, SW1P 1PR,
United Kingdom
Tel: +44 (0)20 7630 1111
Fax: +44(0)207 630 6667
Email: soe@soe.org.uk
Web site: www.soe.org.uk

SPECIALIST TRAINING & CONSULTANCY SERVICES LTD
6 Venture Court, Altham Industrial Estate, Altham,
BB5 5TU, United Kingdom
Tel: +44 (0)1282 687 090
Fax: +44 (0)1282 687 091
Email: enquiries@specialisttraining.co.uk
Web site: www.specialisttraining.co.uk

TRANSPORT & TRAINING SERVICES LTD
Warrington Business Park North, Long Lane,
Warrington, WA2 8TX, United Kingdom
Tel: +44 (0)1925 243 500
Fax: +44 (0)1925 243 000
Email: admin@ttsgroup.uk.com
Web site: www.transporttrainingservices.com

TTS UK
Total Tool Solutions Ltd, Newhaven Business Park,
Lowergate, Milnsbridge, Huddersfield, HD3 4HS,
United Kingdom
Tel: +44 (0)1484 642 211
Fax: +44 (0)1484 461 002
Email: sales@ttsuk.com
Web site: www.ttsuk.com

WHEELS/MIDLAND RED COACHES
Postal Office, 23 Broad Street, Brinklow,
Warwickshire, CV23 0LS, United Kingdom
Tel: +44 (0)7733 884 914
Fax: +44 (0)2476 354 900
Email: buses@wheels.co.uk
Web site: www.wheels.co.uk

VEHICLE CERTIFICATION

PLAXTON SERVICE
Ryton Road, Anston, Sheffield, S25 4DL,
United Kingdom
Tel: +44 (0)1909 551 155
Fax: +44 (0)1909 550 050
Email: service@plaxtonlimited.co.uk
Web site: www.plaxtonaftercare.co.uk

VCA
No1, The Eastgate Office Centre, Eastgate Road,
Bristol, BS5 6XX, United Kingdom
Tel: +44 (0)300 330 5797
Fax: +44 (0)300 003 2198
Email: enquiries@vca.gov.uk
Web site: www.dft.gov.uk/vca

WEB DESIGN

BEST IMPRESSIONS
15 Starfield Road, London, W12 9SN,
United Kingdom
Tel: 020 8740 6443
Fax: 020 8740 9134
Email: talk2us@best-impressions.co.uk
Web site: www.best-impressions.co.uk

IMAGINET
Greyfriars House, Greyfriars Road, Cardiff,
CF10 3AL, United Kingdom
Tel: +44 (0)29 2057 4500
Fax: +44 (0)29 2057 4501
Email: sales@imaginet.co.uk
Web site: www.imaginet.co.uk

PB BUS MARKETING LTD
Trafalgar Close, Chandlers Ford, Eastleigh,
Hampshire, SO50 4BW, United Kingdom
Tel: +44 (0)2380 251 358
Fax: +44 (0)2380 267 623
Email: enquiries@pbbusmarketing.co.uk
Web site: www.pbbusmarketing.co.uk

TRAPEZE GROUP (UK) LTD
The Mill, Staverton, Wiltshire, BA14 6PH,
United Kingdom
Tel: +44 (0)844 561 6771
Fax: +44 (0)1225 784 222
Email: info.uk@trapezegroup.co.uk
Web site: www.trapezegroup.co.uk

NOTES

SECTION 2

Tendering & Regulatory Authorities

- **Tendering and Regulatory Authorities, etc**
- **Combined Authorities**
- **ITAs and PTEs**
- **Transport for London**
- **Scottish Regional Transport Authorities**
- **Transport Coordinating Officers**
- **Traffic Commissioners**
- **Competition and Markets Authority**
- **Department for Transport**

TRANSPORT AUTHORITIES

This section has been amended to reflect the progressive creation of City regions in metropolitan areas (except the West Midlands to date) and the resultant restructuring of Integrated Transport Authorities and Passenger Transport Executives. Some city regions embrace authorities outside the traditional metropolitan area boundaries, but at present these retain many traditional responsibilities in respect of transport, and for this year they have been retained in the latter part of this section of LRB.

Greater Manchester Combined Authority
Transport for Greater Manchester Committee
PO Box 532, Town Hall, Albert Square, Manchester M60 2LA
Tel: 0161 234 3291
E-mail: tfgmc@manchester.gov.uk
Web site: www. transportforgreatermanchestercommittee. gov.uk
Chair: Cllr A Fender
Vice-Chairs: Cllr G Harkin, Cllr M Aldred, Cllr D Dickinson
Clerk: Sir Howard Bernstein

Transport for Greater Manchester
2 Piccadilly Place, Manchester M1 3BG
Tel: 0161 244 1000
Web site: www.tfgm.com
TfGM is responsible to the Transport for Greater Manchester Committee of the Greater Manchester Combined Authority. TfGM is responsible for contracting socially necessary bus services and supporting the local rail service. It also owns the Metrolink light rail system on behalf of the Authority and is responsible for planning for the future of the Metrolink network.

TfGM and the Authority are also committed to developing accessible transport, funding Ring and Ride, a fully accessible door to door transport service for people with mobility difficulties.
TfGM administers the concessionary fares scheme, which allows participants (pensioners, children and people with disabilities) either free or reduced rate travel. TfGM owns and is responsible for the upkeep of bus stations and on-street infrastructure. It also provides information about public transport through telephone information lines, timetables, general publicity and Travelshops.
Chief Executive: Dr Jon Lamonte
Chief Operating Officer: Bob Morris
Finance & Corporate Services Director: Steve Warrener
Information Systems Director: David Hytch
Communications & Customer Services Director: Susan Wildman
Metrolink Director: Peter Cushing
Transport Strategy Director: Dave Newton
Bus & Rail Director: Michael Renshaw

Liverpool City Region Combined Authority

Merseytravel Committee
24 Hatton Garden, Liverpool L3 2AN
Tel: 0151 227 5181
Fax: 0151 330 1234
Web site: www.merseytravel.gov.uk
Chair: Cllr Liam Robinson
Vice Chair: Cllr Marlene Quinn
Clerk: Steve Maddox

Merseytravel
24 Hatton Garden, Liverpool L3 2AN
Tel: 0151 227 5181
Fax: 0151 330 1234
Web site: www.merseytravel.gov.uk
Merseytravel is the Executive body that provides professional, strategic and operational transport advice to Liverpool City Region Combined Authority.
It ensures the availability of public transport in Merseyside, including financial support for the Merseyrail rail network and those bus services not provided for by the private sector.
It also promotes public transport by providing bus stations and infrastructure, comprehensive travel tickets and free travel with minimum restrictions for the elderly and those with mobility difficulties.
Merseytravel also owns and operates the Mersey ferries and Mersey tunnels.
Director General & Chief Executive: David Brown
Director of Resources: Vacant
Director of Integrated Transport Services: Frank Rogers
Director of Corporate Development: Elizabeth Chandler
Network Management: David Blainey
Tel: 0151 330 1344
E-mail: david.blainey@merseytravel.gov.uk

North East Combined Authority
Transport North East Committee
Quadrant, Cobalt Business Park, The Silverlink North, North Tyneside, Newcastle upon Tyne NE27 0BY
Web site: www.northeastca.gov.uk
Chair: Cllr Nick Forbes
Vice Chairs: Cllr Neil Foster, Cllr Frank Lott, Cllr Ian Swithenbank
Clerk: K G Lavery

Nexus
Nexus House, St James Boulevard, Newcastle upon Tyne NE1 4AX
Tel: 0191 203 3333
Fax: 0191 203 3180
E-mail: customerservices@nexus.org.uk

Web site: www.nexus.org.uk
Metro: www.twmetro.co.uk
Director General: Bernard Garner
Deputy Director General & Director of Customer Services: Tobyn Hughes
Director of Finance & Resources: John Fenwick
Director of Rail & Infrastructure: Raymond Johnstone
Nexus operates within the policies of the North East Combined Authority. Nexus owns both the Tyne & Wear Metro system and the Shields Ferry (between North Shields and South Shields). Nexus ensures that bus services not operated commercially are provided where there is evidence of social need; operates a demand-responsive transport system, U-call; and organises the provision of special transport for those who can only use ordinary public transport with difficulty if at all. Nexus administers the Concessionary Travel scheme and provides comprehensive travel information and sales outlets for countywide season tickets in Tyne & Wear, as well as related administrative support for the scheme.
Rolling Stock: 90 light rail cars
Ferries: MFs 'Pride of the Tyne' and 'Shieldsman'

Sheffield City Region Combined Authority

Sheffield City Region Combined Authority Transport Committee
18 Regent Street, Barnsley S70 2PQ
Tel: 01226 772800
Fax: 01226 772899
Web site: www.southyorks.gov.uk
Chairman: Cllr M Jameson
Vice-Chairman: Cllr L Bramall
Clerk & Chief Officer, South Yorkshire Joint Secretariat: S Pick

South Yorkshire Passenger Transport Executive
11 Broad Street West, Sheffield S1 2BQ
Tel: 0114 276 7575
Fax: 0114 275 9908
Web site: www.sypte.co.uk
The Executive is responsible to the Sheffield City Region Combined Authority Transport Committee.
Interim Director General: Ben Still
Deputy Interim Director General & Director of Customer Experience: David Young

West Midlands ITA
Democratic Support, Civic Centre, 2nd Floor, St Peter's Square, Wolverhampton WV1 1RL
Tel: 01902 555046
Web site: www.wmita.org.uk
Chair: Cllr R Lawrence
Vice Chair: Cllr Robert Sleigh

Centro (West Midlands PTE)
Centro House, 16 Summer Lane, Birmingham B19 3SD
Tel: 0121 200 2787
E-mail: customerrelations@centro.org.uk
Web site: www.centro.org.uk
The Executive is responsible to the West Midlands Integrated Transport Authority
Director General: Geoff Inskip
Passenger Services Director: Stephen Rhodes
Strategy & Commissioning Director: Tom Magrath
Corporate Services Director: Steve Chatwin
Finance & Planning Director: James Aspinall
Metro Programme Executive: Paul Griffiths
Head of Marketing and Communications: Conrad Jones
Head of Projects: Stephen Terry-Short

West Yorkshire Combined Authority

West Yorkshire Combined Authority Transport Committee
Wellington House, 40-50 Wellington Street, Leeds LS1 2DE
Tel: 0113 251 7272
Fax: 0113 251 7373
E-mail: enquiries@westyorks-ca.gov.uk
Web site: www.westyorks-ca.gov.uk
Chair: Cllr James Lewis

West Yorkshire Passenger Transport Executive (Metro)
Wellington House, 40-50 Wellington Street, Leeds LS1 2DE
Tel: 0113 245 7676
Fax: 0113 251 7333
E-mail: metroline@westyorks-ca.gov.uk
Web site: www.wymetro.com
WYPTE activities are conducted under the corporate name Metro. Metro is financed and supported by the West Yorkshire Integrated Transport Authority.
Acting Director General: John Henkel
Director of Development: David Hoggarth
Director of Finance: A Hirst

PASSENGER TRANSPORT REGIONAL AUTHORITIES

Transport for London
Windsor House, 42-50 Victoria Street, London SW1H 0TL
Tel: 020 7941 4500
Web Site: www.tfl.gov.uk
Chairman: Boris Johnson
Deputy Chairman: Isabel Dedring
Board Members: Peter Anderson, Sir John Armitt CBE, Sir Brendan Barber, Richard Barnes, Charles Belcher, Roger Burnley, Brian Cooke, Baroness Tanni Grey-Thompson DBE, Angela Knight CBE, Michael Liebreich, Eva Lindholm, Daniel Moylan, Bob Oddy, Keith Williams, Steve Wright.
Transport for London (TfL) took over most of the functions of London Transport from July 2000. It is under the control of the Mayor of London and Greater London Authority. TfL assumed control of London Underground Ltd in 2003.
Commissioner of Transport: Sir Peter Hendy, CBE
Managing Director, Finance: Steve Allen
Managing Director, Surface Transport: Leon Daniels
Managing Director, London Underground and London Rail: Mike Brown
Managing Director, Planning: Michele Dix
Managing Director, Customer Experience, Marketing & Communications: Vernon Everitt
General Counsel: Howard Carter
Chief Executive, Crossrail: Rob Holden

TfL subsidiary companies include:
London Buses
Palestra, 197 Blackfriars Road, London SE1 8NJ
Tel: 020 7222 5600
Director of Buses: Mike Weston
Head of Bus Operations: Ken Davidson
Head of Bus Engineering: Gary Filbey
Head of Contracts: Mark O'Donovan
Head of Network Development: John Barry
Head of Technical Services Group: Simon Reed
Victoria Coach Station Ltd
164 Buckingham Palace Road, London SW1W 9TP.
Tel: 020 7027 2520
Fax: 020 7027 2511
General Manager: Mark Geldard
London River Services Ltd
Tower Pier, Lower Thames Street, London EC3N 4DT
Tel: 020 7941 2400

London Underground Ltd
55 Broadway, London SW1H 0BD
Tel: 020 7222 5600
Managing Director: Mike Brown

TfL: London Bus Service Contractors as at August 2014
Abellio London & Surrey (see London & Middlesex, Surrey)
Arriva London (see London & Middlesex)
Arriva Southern Counties (see Essex, Kent)
Arriva The Shires Ltd (see Bedfordshire, Hertfordshire)
CT Plus Ltd (see London & Middlesex)
Go-Ahead London (Blue Triangle, Docklands, London Central Bus Co, London General Transport Services, Metrobus) (see London & Middlesex)
London Sovereign (see London & Middlesex)
London United Busways Ltd (see London & Middlesex)
Metroline Travel Ltd (see London & Middlesex)
Quality Line (Epsom Coaches Group) (see Surrey)
Stagecoach London (see London & Middlesex)
Sullivan Buses Ltd (see Hertfordshire)
TGM Group Ltd (see London & Middlesex)
Tower Transit Operations Ltd (see London & Middlesex)

SCOTTISH REGIONAL TRANSPORT PARTNERSHIPS

Scottish Regional Transport Partnerships deliver regional transport strategies and delivery plans. In some instances, such as Strathclyde Partnership for Transport, they also directly deliver certain services.

ZetTrans (Shetland Transport Partnership)
Area: Shetland
Shetland Islands Council, Office Headquarters, 6 North Ness Business Park, Lerwick ZE1 0LZ
Tel: 01595 744868
Fax: 01595 744880
E-mail: zettrans@shetland.gov.uk
Web site: www.zettrans.org.uk
Lead Officer: Michael Craigie

HITRANS (Highlands and Islands Transport Partnership)
Area: Highland, Moray, Orkney, Western Isles, most of Argyll & Bute
Second Floor, Rear, 7 Ardross Terrace, Inverness IV3 5NQ
Tel: 01463 719002
E-mail: info@hitrans.org.uk
Web site: www.hitrans.org.uk
Chair: Cllr J Stockan (Orkney Islands Council)
Partnership Director: Ranald Robertson

NESTRANS (North East Scotland Transport Partnership)
Area: City of Aberdeen, Aberdeenshire
Archibald Simpson House, 27-29 King Street, Aberdeen AB24 5AA
Tel: 01224 625524
Fax: 01224 626596
Web site: www.nestrans.org
Chairman: Cllr Peter Argyle
Director: Derick Murray

TACTRAN (Tayside and Central Scotland Transport Partnership)
Area: Angus, City of Dundee, Perth & Kinross, Stirling
Bordeaux House, 31 Kinnoull Street, Perth PH1 5EN
Tel: 01738 475775
Fax: 01738 639705
E-mail: info@tactran.gov.uk
Web site: www.tactran.gov.uk
Chair: Cllr Will Dawson
Partnership Director: Eric Guthrie

SESTRAN (South-East of Scotland Transport Partnership)
Area: Borders, Clackmannanshire, East Lothian, City of Edinburgh, Falkirk, Fife, Midlothian, West Lothian
Claremont House, 130 East Claremont Street, Edinburgh EH7 4LB
Tel: 0131 524 5150
Fax: 0131 524 5151
E-mail: enquiries@sestran.gov.uk
Web site: www.sestran.gov.uk
Chair: Cllr R Imrie
Dir: Alex Macaulay

Strathclyde Partnership for Transport (SPT)
Area: 12 member unitary authorities as marked in the Co-Ordinating Officers listing later in this section
Consort House, 12 West George Street, Glasgow G2 1HN
Tel: 0141 332 6811   **Fax:** 0141 332 3076
E-mail: enquiry@spt.co.uk
Web site: www.spt.co.uk
Chair: Cllr James Coleman
Vice Chairs: Cllr Kaye Harmon, Cllr Dennis McKenna
Chief Executive: Gordon Maclennan
Dep Chief Executive: Valerie Davidson
Asst Chief Executive, Operations: Eric Stewart
Director, Finance & Human Relations: Neil Wylie
Director, Projects: Charles Hoskins
Director, Subway Operations: Brian Bell

SWESTRANS (South West of Scotland Transport Partnership)
Area: Dumfries & Galloway
Militia House, English Street, Dumfries DG1 2HR
Tel: 01387 260103
Fax: 01387 260092
E-mail: swestrans@dumgal.gov.uk
Web site: www.swestrans.org.uk
Chair: Cllr Tom McAughtrie
Vic Chairman: David Bryson
Lead Officer: Harry Thomson

Transport Co-ordinating Officers

Under the Transport Act 1978 the non-Metropolitan Counties were given power to co-ordinate public transport facilities in their areas. From 1 April 1996 Welsh Counties and Scottish Regions were replaced by new single-tier authorities. At the same time and subsequently, certain English Counties have been replaced by new single-tier unitary authorities. The major role is now to secure socially necessary services which are not provided commercially. Where provided, the names of the responsible officers are set out below. The list below also includes District and Metropolitan Borough Councils which are not Local Transport Authorities but who have expressed an interest in being included in the book.

ENGLAND

Bath & North East Somerset Council
Public Transport Team, Floor 2 South, Riverside, Temple Street, Keynsham, Bristol BS31 1LA
Public Transport Team Leader: Andy Strong
Senior Public Transport Officer: Richard Smith
Tel: 01225 394201
Fax: 01225 394335
E-mail: transportation@bathnes.gov.uk
Web site: www.bathnes.gov.uk

Bedford Borough Council
Public Transport Team, Transport Operations Group, Borough Hall, Cauldwell Street, Bedford MK42 9AP
Tel: 01234 718005
Fax: 01234 228720
E-mail: businfo@bedford.gov.uk
Web site: www.bedford.gov.uk

Blackburn with Darwen Borough Council
Transport Team, Room 412, Blackburn Town Hall, King William Street, Blackburn BB1 7DY
Tel: 01245 585003
Fax: 01254 265340
E-mail: transport@blackburn.gov.uk
Web site: www.blackburn.gov.uk

Blackpool Council
Transportation Division, Holman House, Layton Depot, Plymouth Road, Blackpool FY3 7HW
Group Leader for Transport: Joe Hegarty
Tel: 01253 476175
E-mail: joe.hegarty@blackpool.gov.uk
Web site: www.blackpool.gov.uk

Bournemouth Borough Council
Mike Holmes, Director of Planning and Transport Services, Town Hall Annex, St Stephen's Road, Bournemouth BH2 6EA
Tel: 01202 451323
Fax: 01202 451000
E-mail: highways@bournemouth.gov.uk
Web site: www.bournemouth.gov.uk

Bracknell Forest Borough Council
Corporate Services, ITU, Commercial Centre, Old Bracknell Lane West, Bracknell RG12 7QT
ITU Operations Manager: Thelma Padwick
Head of Operations: Damien James
Tel: 01344 355234
Fax: 01334 353235
E-mail: thelma.padwick@bracknell-forest.gov.uk
Web site: www.bracknell-forest.gov.uk

Brighton & Hove City Council
Public Transport Team, Hove Town Hall, Hove BN3 3BQ
Tel: 01273 292480
E-mail: local.transport@brighton-hove.gov.uk
Web site: www.brighton-hove.gov.uk

Bristol City Council
Public Transport Section, Brunel House, St George's Road, Bristol BS1 5UY
Tel: 0117 922 4454
Fax: 0117 922 3539
E-mail: passenger.transport@bristol.gov.uk
Web site: www.bristol.gov.uk

Buckinghamshire County Council
Passenger Transport Team, Transport for Buckinghamshire, 10th Floor, County Hall, Walton Street, Aylesbury HP20 1UY
Tel: 0845 230 2882
E-mail: passtrans@buckscc.gov.uk
Web site: www.buckscc.gov.uk

Cambridgeshire County Council
Mailbox CC1301, Castle Court, Shire Hall, Cambridge CB3 0AP
Head of Passenger Transport Services: J Whelan
Transport & Information Strategy Manager: Jeremy Smith
Tel: 01223 715608
Web site: www.cambridgeshire.gov.uk

Central Bedfordshire Council
Public Transport, Priory House, Monks Walk, Chicksands, Shefford SG17 5TQ
Public Transport Manager: Paul Dodge
Head of Highways and Transport Services: Paul Mason
Tel: 0300 300 8308
E-mail: paul.dodge@centralbedfordshire.gov.uk
Web site: www.centralbedfordshire.gov.uk

Cheshire East Council
Cheshire East Transport, Floor 6, Municipal Buildings, Earle Street, Crewe CW1 2BJ
Tel: 0300 123 5500
Web site: www.cheshireeast.gov.uk

Cheshire West & Chester Council
Integrated Transport Service, Rivacre Business Centre, Mill Lane, Ellesmere Port CH66 3TL
Tel: 01244 973218
Fax: 01244 973200
Web site: www.cheshirewestandchester.gov.uk

Connect Tees Valley
Development & Neighbourhood Services, Technical Services, Stockton-on-Tees Borough Council, PO Box 229, Kingsway House, West Precinct, Billingham TS23 2YL
Public Transport Manager: John Kavanagh
Transport Planning Officer: Ian MacGregor
Tel: 01642 526774/524461
Fax: 01642 526713
E-mail: connect@teesvalleyunlimited.gov.uk
Web site: www.connectteesvalley.co.uk
Connect Tees Valley provides public transport information and support for the five Tees Valley Boroughs of Darlington, Hartlepool, Middlesbrough, Redcar & Cleveland and Stockton-on-Tees.

Cornwall Council
Passenger Transport Unit, County Hall, Truro TR1 3AY
Head of Transportation: Nigel Blackler
Tel: 0300 123 4222
E-mail: ptu@cornwall.gov.uk
Web site: www.cornwall.gov.uk

Cumbria County Council
Integrated Transport Team, The Parkhouse Building, Kingmoor Business Park, Carlisle CA6 4SJ
Tel: 0333 240 6965
Fax: 01228 606755
E-mail: integrated.transport@cumbria.gov.uk
Web site: www.cumbria.gov.uk

Darlington Borough Council
See Connect Tees Valley, above

Derby City Council
Traffic & Transportation, The Council House, Corporation Street, Derby DE1 2FS
Group Manager, North East: David Dowbenko
Group Manager, Sustainable Transport: Tony Gascoigne
Team Leader, Sustainable Transport: Chris Hegarty
Team Leader, Transport Procurement & Operations Team: Linda Ayriss
Tel: 01332 641754
E-mail: dave.dowbenko@derby.gov.uk
Web site: www.derby.gov.uk

Derbyshire County Council
Public Transport Unit, County Hall, Matlock DE4 3AG
Tel: 01629 536745
E-mail: public.transport@derbyshire.gov.uk
Web site: www.derbyshire.gov.uk

Devon County Council
Transport Co-ordination Service, Matford Lane Offices, County Hall, Exeter EX2 4QW
Service Manager: Bruce Thompson
Tel: 01392 383483
Fax: 01392 382904
E-mail: bruce.thompson@devon.gov.uk
Web site: www.devon.gov.uk

Dorset County Council
Passenger Transport, Environmental Directorate, County Hall, Colliton Park, Dorchester DT1 1XJ

Acting Group Manager & Public Transport Manager: David Coates
Fleet Operations Officer: David Besant
Public Transport Team Leader: Terry Spracklen
Business Manager: Jan Stevenson
Tel: 01305 221587
Fax: 01305 225166
E-mail: dorsetpassengertransport@dorsetcc.gov.uk
Web site: www.dorsetforyou.com

Durham County Council
Sustainable Transport Team, County Hall, Durham DH1 5UQ
Tel: 0300 026 8667
Fax: 0191 383 3084
E-mail: sustainabletransport@durham.gov.uk
Web site: www.durham.gov.uk

East Riding of Yorkshire Council
1st Floor, The Offices, Beverley Depot, Annie Reed Road, Beverley HU17 0UP
Passenger Services Manager:
David R Boden
Assistant Passenger Services Manager:
Chris Mottershaw
Tel: 01482 395525
Fax: 01482 395090
E-mail: david.boden@eastriding.gov.uk
Web site: www.eastriding.gov.uk

East Sussex County Council
Passenger Transport, County Hall, St Anne's Crescent, Lewes BN7 1UE
Group Manager (Passenger Transport):
Nick Smith
Tel: 0345 608 0194
E-mail: passenger.transport@eastsussexcc.gov.uk
Web site: www.eastsussex.gov.uk

Essex County Council
Passenger Transport, County Hall, Chelmsford CM1 1QH
Head of Passenger Transport: John Pope
Tel: 0845 603 7631
E-mail: publictransport@essex.gov.uk
Web site: www.essex.gov.uk

Gloucestershire County Council
Integrated Transport Unit, Shire Hall, Gloucester GL1 2TH
Tel: 01452 425628
Fax: 01452 425995
Web site: www.gloucestershire.gov.uk

Halton Borough Council
Neighbourhood Travel Team, Places, Economy & Transport Policy, Rutland House, Runcorn WA7 2GW
Tel: 0151 906 1541
E-mail: ntt@halton.gov.uk
Web site: www.halton.gov.uk

Hampshire County Council
Passenger Transport Group, Economy, Transport & Environment Department, Capital House, 48-52 Andover Road, Winchester SO23 7BH
Tel: 0845 603 5633
E-mail: ptgenquiries@hants.gov.uk
Web site: www.hants.gov.uk

Hartlepool Borough Council
See Connect Tees Valley, above

Herefordshire Council
Public Transport, PO Box 236, Plough Lane, Hereford HR4 0LE
Principal Officers: Alan Lewis, Paul Williamson
Tel: 01432 261518
Fax: 01432 383031
E-mail: public.transport@herefordshire.gov.uk
Web site: www.herefordshire.info

Hertfordshire County Council
The Intalink Partnership, c/o Transport Access & Safety Unit, County Hall, CHN 101, Hertford SG13 8TJ
Tel: 0300 123 4050
E-mail: feedback.ptu@hertscc.gov.uk
Web site: www.intalink.org.uk

Hull City Council
Passenger Transport Services, Kingston House, Bond Street, Hull HU1 3ER
Tel: 01482 300300
E-mail: public.transport@hullcc.gov.uk
Web site: www.hullcc.gov.uk

Isle of Wight Council
Transport Team, Floor 5, County Hall, High Street, Newport PO30 1UD
Public Transport Officer: Martyn Mullins
Tel: 01983 823780
Fax: 01983 823707
E-mail: transport.info@iow.gov.uk
Web site: www.iwight.com

Kent County Council
Transport Integration, Aylesford Highways Depot, St Michael's Close, Aylesford ME20 7TZ
Head of Public Transport: Paul Lawry
Tel: 01622 696117
E-mail: paul.lawry@kent.gov.uk
Web site: www.kent.gov.uk

Lancashire County Council
Bus Services Team, Environment Directorate, County Hall, PO Box 100, Preston PR1 0LD
Principal Transportation Officer,
Local Bus: Ashley Weir
Tel: 01772 534660   **Fax:** 01772 533833
E-mail: lcc.bus.services@lancashire.gov.uk
Web site: www.lancashire.gov.uk

Leicester City Council
Sustainable Transport, New Walk Centre A6, Welford Place, Leicester LE1 6ZG
Team Leader, Sustainable Transport:
John Dowson
Transport Development Officer:
Adele Wearing
Tel: 0116 223 2121
E-mail: transportdevelopment@leicester.gov.uk
Web site: www.leicester.gov.uk

Leicestershire County Council
Sustainable Travel Group, County Hall, Glenfield, Leicester LE3 8RJ
Tel: 0116 305 6270
Fax: 0116 305 7181
E-mail: stg@leics.gov.uk
Web site: www.leics.gov.uk

Lincolnshire County Council
Transportation Group, Communities Directorate, City Hall, Beaumont Fee, Lincoln LN1 1DN
Tel: 01522 782070
Fax: 01522 568735
E-mail: transportation_group@lincolnshire.gov.uk
Web site: www.lincolnshire.gov.uk

Luton Borough Council
Passenger Transport Unit, Central Depot, Kingsway, Luton LU4 8AU
Tel: 01582 547219
Fax: 01582 547351
E-mail: ptu@luton.gov.uk
Web site: www.luton.gov.uk

Medway Council
Integrated Transport Team, Gun Wharf, Dock Road, Chatham ME4 4TR
Tel: 01634 331398
Fax: 01634 331625
E-mail: customer.first@medway.gov.uk
Web site: www.medway.gov.uk

Middlesbrough Council
See Connect Tees Valley, above

Milton Keynes Council
Passenger Transport Group, Environment Directorate, Civic Offices, 1 Saxon Gate East, Milton Keynes MK9 3EJ
Tel: 01908 252542
E-mail: passenger.transport@milton-keynes.gov.uk
Web site: www.milton-keynes.gov.uk

Norfolk County Council
Department of Planning & Transportation, County Hall, Martineau Lane, Norwich NR1 2SG
Head of Passenger Transport: Tracy Jessop
Tel: 01603 223831
Fax: 01603 222144
Web site: www.norfolk.gov.uk

Northamptonshire County Council
Northamptonshire Highways, Riverside House, Riverside Way, Bedford Road, Northampton NN1 5NX
Principal Bus and Rail Development Officer: John Ellerby
Tel: 01604 364344
E-mail: jellerby@mgwsp.co.uk
Web site: www.northamptonshire.gov.uk

Northumberland County Council
County Hall, Morpeth NE61 2EF
Transport Support Manager: Ian Coe
Tel: 01670 533986
Fax: 01670 534774
E-mail: ian.coe@northumberland.gov.uk
Web site: www.northumberland.gov.uk

North Lincolnshire Council
Public & Community Transport Team, Community Services, Hewson House, Station Road, Brigg DN20 8XY
Tel: 01724 297460
E-mail: public.transport@northlincs.gov.uk
Web site: www.northlincs.gov.uk

North East Lincolnshire Council
Transport Team, Cofely, Origin 2, 2 Origin Way, Europarc, Grimsby DN37 9TZ
Tel: 01472 326290
E-mail: transportenquiries@nelincs.gov.uk
Web site: www.nelincs.gov.uk

North Somerset Council
Sustainable Travel and Road Safety Team, Town Hall, Walliscote Grove Road, Weston-super-Mare BS23 1UJ
Tel: 01934 426426
E-mail: sustainable.travel@n-somerset.gov.uk
Web site: www.n-somerset.gov.uk

North Yorkshire County Council
Integrated Passenger Transport, County Hall, Northallerton DL7 8AH
Tel: 0845 872 7374
Fax: 01609 779722
E-mail: passenger.transport@northyorks.gov.uk
Web site: www.northyorks.gov.uk

Nottingham City Council
Public Transport Team, Loxley House, Station Street, Nottingham NG2 3NG
Tel: 0115 876 2700
E-mail: public.transport@nottinghamcity.gov.uk
Web site: www.nottinghamcity.gov.uk

Nottinghamshire County Council
Travel & Transport Services, Environment & Resources Department, Trent Bridge House, Fox Road, West Bridgford, Nottingham NG2 6BJ
Tel: 0300 500 8080
Fax: 0115 977 4353
E-mail: passengertransport.en@nottscc.gov.uk
Web site: www.nottinghamshire.gov.uk

Oxfordshire County Council
Bus Services Team, Environment & Economy,
Speedwell House, Speedwell Street, Oxford
OX1 1NE
Bus Services Manager: Allan Field
Tel: 01865 815700
E-mail: allan.field@oxfordshire.gov.uk
Web site: www.oxfordsshire.gov.uk

Peterborough City Council
Passenger Transport Team, Transport &
Infrastructure Planning, 1st Floor, East Wing,
Stuart House, St John's Street, Peterborough
PE1 5DD
Tel: 01733 747474
Fax: 01733 317499
E-mail: buses@peterborough.gov.uk
Web site: www.peterborough.gov.uk

Plymouth City Council
Sustainable Transport Team, Plymouth Transport
& Highways, Department of Development,
Civic Centre, Armada Way, Plymouth
PL1 2AA
Tel: 01752 668000
Fax: 01752 305593
E-mail: publictransport@plymouth.gov.uk
Web site: www.plymouth.gov.uk

Borough of Poole
Transportation Services, Civic Centre, Poole
BH15 2RU
Tel: 01202 262000
E-mail: transportation@poole.gov.uk
Web site: www.boroughofpoole.com

Portsmouth City Council
Passenger Transport Group, Transport & Street
Management, Guildhall Square, Portsmouth
PO1 2BG
Tel: 023 9282 2251
Web site: www.portsmouth.gov.uk

Reading Borough Council
Civic Centre, Reading RG1 7AE
Tel: 0118 939 0813
Web site: www.reading.gov.uk

Redcar & Cleveland Borough Council
See Connect Tees Valley, above

Rochdale Metropolitan Borough Council
Environmental Management Headquarters,
Green Lane, Heywood OL10 2DY
Principal Officer: Alan Lomax
Tel: 01706 922025
E-mail: alan.lomax@rochdale.gov.uk
Web site: www.rochdale.gov.uk

Rutland County Council
Transport Operations, Catmose, Oakham
LE15 6HP
Group Manager, Transport & Accessibility:
Andrew Harris
Tel: 01572 722577
Fax: 01572 758307
E-mail: aharris@rutland.gcsx.gov.uk
Web site: www.rutland.gov.uk

Shropshire County Council
Development Services, Shirehall, Abbey Foregate,
Shrewsbury SY2 6ND
Tel: 0345 678 9006
E-mail: transport@shropshire.gov.uk
Web site: www.shropshire.gov.uk

Slough Borough Council
Transport Strategy Manager, Town Hall, Bath
Road, Slough SL1 3UQ
Head of Transport: Joe Carter
Transport Strategy Manager: Rub Nawaz
Tel: 01753 475111
E-mail: enquiries@slough.gov.uk
Web site: www.slough.gov.uk

Somerset County Council
Integrated Passenger Transport Unit,
County Hall, The Crescent, Taunton TA1 4DY
Group Manager: Mark Pedlar
Tel: 0845 345 9155   **Fax:** 01823 351356
E-mail: transport@somerset.gov.uk
Web site: www.somerset.gov.uk

Southampton City Council
Passenger Transport Team, Planning &
Sustainability, Floor 1, Castle Way, Southampton
SO14 2PD
Tel: 0800 519 1919
E-mail: public.transport@southampton.gov.uk
Web site: www.southampton.gov.uk

Southend-on-Sea Borough Council
Sustainable Transport Team, Civic Centre,
Victoria Avenue, Southend-on-Sea SS2 6ER
Tel: 01702 215003
E-mail: council@southend.gov.uk
Web site: www.southend.gov.uk

South Gloucestershire Council
Integrated Transport Unit, PO Box 2081, Council
Offices, Castle Street, Thornbury BS35 9BP
Tel: 01454 868004
Fax: 01454 864473
E-mail: itu@southglos.gov.uk
Web site: www.southglos.gov.uk

South Somerset District Council
Spatial Planning, The Council Offices, Brympton
Way, Yeovil, Somerset BA20 2HT
Transport Strategy Officer: Nigel Collins
Tel: 01935 462591
E-mail: nigel.collins@southsomerset.gov.uk
Web site: www.southsomerset.gov.uk

Staffordshire County Council
Development Services Department, Riverway,
Stafford ST16 3TJ
Head of Passenger Transport:
Charles Soutar
Tel: 0300 111 8000   **Fax:** 01785 276621
E-mail: publictransport@staffordshire.gov.uk
Web site: www.staffordshire.gov.uk

Stockton-on-Tees Borough Council
See Connect Tees Valley, above

City of Stoke-on-Trent
Safe & Sustainable Transport Team, Civic Centre,
Glebe Street, Stoke-on-Trent ST4 1HH
Tel: 01782 234234
E-mail: transportation@stoke.gov.uk
Web site: www.stoke.gov.uk

Suffolk County Council
Environment & Transport Department,
Endeavour House, 8 Russell Road, Ipswich
IP1 2BX
Public Transport Manager: Mitchell
Bradshaw
Tel: 01473 265050   **Fax:** 01473 216884
E-mail: mitchell.bradshaw@et.suffolkcc.gov.uk
Web site: www.suffolk.gov.uk

Surrey County Council
Travel & Transport Group, Room 365, County
Hall, Penrhyn Road, Kingston-on-Thames
KT1 2DY
Group Manager, Passenger Transport:
Alan Teer
Tel: 020 8541 9371
Fax: 020 8541 9389
E-mail: passenger.transport@surreycc.gov.uk
Web site: www.surreycc.gov.uk

Swindon Borough Council
Passenger Transport Team, Premier House,
Station Road, Swindon SN1 1TZ
Tel: 01793 466214
E-mail: passengertransport@swindon.gov.uk
Web site: www.swindon.gov.uk

Telford & Wrekin Council
Planning & Transport Department, Granville
House, St Georges Road, Donnington Wood,
Telford TF2 7RA
Tel: 01952 202172
E-mail: publictransport@telford.gov.uk
Web site: www.telford.gov.uk

Thurrock Council
Passenger Transport Unit, Strategic
Transportation, Civic Offices, New Road, Grays,
Essex RM17 6SL
Tel: 01375 413886
Fax: 01375 413891
E-mail: passengertransport@thurrock.gov.uk
Web site: www.thurrock.gov.uk

Torbay Council
Strategic Transportation Group, Roebuck House,
Abbey Road, Torquay TQ2 5TF
Tel: 01803 208823
Fax: 01803 208882
E-mail: transportation@torbay.gov.uk
Web site: www.torbay.gov.uk

Warrington Borough Council
Passenger Transport Unit, Palmyra House,
Palmyra Square North, Warrington WA1 1JN
Tel: 01925 442620
Web site: www.warrington.gov.uk

Warwickshire County Council
Transport Operations, Environment & Economy
Directorate, PO Box 43, Shire Hall, Warwick
CV34 4SX
Tel: 01926 412930   **Fax:** 01926 418041
E-mail:
passengertransport@warwickshire.gov.uk
Web site: www.warwickshire.gov.uk

West Berkshire Council
Transport Services Team, Council Offices,
Market Street, Newbury RG14 5LD
Tel: 01635 503248
Fax: 01635 519979
E-mail: transport@westberks.gov.uk
Web site: www.westberks.gov.uk

West Sussex County Council
Transport Co-ordination Group, Highways and
Transport, County Hall, West Street, Chichester
PO19 1RQ
Group Manager: Mark Miller
Tel: 01243 777589
E-mail: buses@westsussex.gov.uk
Web site: www.westsussex.gov.uk

Wiltshire Council
Passenger Transport Unit, County Hall,
Bythesea Road, Trowbridge BA14 8JN
Head of Service – Passenger Transport:
Ian White
Tel: 01225 713322
Fax: 01225 713317
E-mail: ian.white@wiltshire.gov.uk
Web site: www.wiltshire.gov.uk

Royal Borough of Windsor & Maidenhead
Passenger Transport Team, Highways &
Engineering, Community Services, Town Hall,
St Ives Road, Maidenhead SL6 1RF
Tel: 01628 796666
Fax: 01628 796774
E-mail: customerservice@rbwm.gov.uk
Web site: www.rbwm.gov.uk

Wokingham Borough Council
Corporate Transport Unit, Shute End,
Wokingham RG40 1BN
**Transport Procurement & Operations
Manager:** Mark Allen
Tel: 0118 974 6244
Fax: 0118 974 6259
E-mail: mark.allen@wokingham.gov.uk
Web site: www.wokingham.gov.uk

Tendering & Regulatory Authorities

Worcestershire County Council
Integrated Transport Services, County Hall,
Spetchley Road, Worcester WR5 2NP
Tel: 01905 765765
Fax: 01905 768438
E-mail: worcestershirehub@worcestershire.
gov.uk
Web site: www.worcestershire.gov.uk

City of York Council
Sustainable Transport Service, 9 St Leonard's
Place, York YO1 7ET
Sustainable Transport Manager: Andrew
Bradley
Tel: 01904 551550
Fax: 01904 551340
E-mail: transportplanning@york.gov.uk
Web site: www.york.gov.uk

WALES

Isle of Anglesey County Council
Council Offices, Llangefni, Anglesey
LL77 7TW
Principal Officer – Transportation:
Dewi W Roberts
Tel: 01248 752457
Fax: 01248 757332
E-mail: dwrpl@anglesey.gov.uk
Web site: www.anglesey.gov.uk

Blaenau Gwent County Borough Council
Joint Passenger Transport Unit, Baldwin House,
Victoria Business Park, Ebbw Vale NP23 8ED
Tel: 01495 355444
Fax: 01495 301255
E-mail: technical-services@blaenau-gwent.
gov.uk
Web site: www.blaenau-gwent.gov.uk
The JPTU is responsible for passenger transport
co-ordination for both Blaenau Gwent and
Torfaen CBCs

Bridgend County Borough Council
Passenger Transport Co-ordination Unit,
Communities Directorate, Civic Offices,
Angel Street, Bridgend CF31 4WB
Tel: 01656 642559
Fax: 01656 642859
E-mail: transportation@bridgend.gov.uk
Web site: www.bridgend.gov.uk

Caerphilly County Borough Council
Integrated Transport Unit, Ty Pontllanfraith,
Pontllanfraith, Blackwood NP12 2YW.
Team Leader: Huw Morgan
**Senior Transport Officer (Public
Transport):** Roger Reynolds
Tel: 01495 235223
E-mail: travelinks@caerphilly.gov.uk
Web site: www.caerphilly.gov.uk

Cardiff County Council
Traffic & Transportation Service, County Hall,
Atlantic Wharf, Cardiff CF10 4UW
Tel: 029 2087 2087
E-mail: c2c@cardiff.gov.uk
Web site: www.cardiff.gov.uk

Carmarthenshire County Council
Passenger Transport Unit, Parc Myrddin,
Carmarthen SA31 1HQ
Tel: 01267 234567
E-mail:
publictransport@carmarthenshire.gov.uk
Web site: www.carmarthenshire.gov.uk

Ceredigion County Council
Corporate Passenger Transport Unit (CPTU),
Canolfan Rheidol, Llanbadarn Fawr, Aberystwyth
SY23 3UE
Tel: 01970 633555
Fax: 01970 633559
E-mail: cptu@ceredigion.gov.uk
Web site: www.ceredigion.gov.uk

Conwy County Borough Council
Integrated Transport, Library Building,
Mostyn Street, Llandudno, LL30 2RP
**Section Head, Integrated Transport
(Policy):** Bob Saxby
Tel: 01492 575469
Fax: 01492 575552
E-mail: bwsconwy@conwy.gov.uk
Web site: www.conwy.gov.uk

Denbighshire County Council
Passenger Transport, Caledfryn, Smithfield Road,
Denbigh LL16 3RJ
Section Manager: Peter Daniels
Tel: 01824 706898
Fax: 01824 706970
Web site: www.denbighshire.gov.uk

Flintshire County Council
Transportation Unit, Directorate of Environment
& Regeneration, County Hall, Mold
CH7 6NF
Tel: 01352 704530
Fax: 01352 704540
Web site: www.flintshire.gov.uk

Gwynedd Council
Public Transport Officer, Council Offices,
Shirehall, Caernarfon LL55 1SH.
Tel: 01286 679541
Fax: 01286 673324
E-mail: bwsgwynedd@gwynedd.gov.uk
Web site: www.gwynedd.gov.uk

**Merthyr Tydfil County
Borough Council**
Civic Centre, Castle Street, Merthyr Tydfil
CF47 8AN
Senior Transport Officer: Martin Haworth
Tel: 01685 726256
Fax: 01685 722146
E-mail: transport@merthyr.gov.uk
Web site: www.merthyr.gov.uk

Monmouthshire County Council
Monmouthshire Passenger Transport Unit,
County Hall, Cwmbran NP44 2XH
Tel: 01633 644728
Fax: 01633 644666
E-mail: publictransport@monmouthshire.
gov.uk
Web site: www.monmouthshire.gov.uk

**Neath Port Talbot County
Borough Council**
The Quays, Brunel Way, Baglan Energy Park,
Neath SA11 2GG
Integrated Transport Unit Manager:
Peter Jackson
Passenger Transport Manager:
Brendan Griffiths
Tel: 01639 686658
Fax: 01639 686107
E-mail: passengertransport@npt.gov.uk
Web site: www.npt.gov.uk

Newport City Council
Transport Team, Telford Street Depot,
Newport NP19 0ES
Tel: 01633 656656
Fax: 01633 244721
Web site: www.newport.gov.uk

Pembrokeshire County Council
Transport Unit, Transportation, Housing &
Environment, County Hall, Haverfordwest
SA61 1TP
Transport and Fleet Manager: M Hubert
Tel: 01437 764551
Fax: 01437 775008
E-mail:
public.transport@pembrokeshire.gov.uk
Web site: www.pembrokeshire.gov.uk

Powys County Council
Passenger Transport Unit, County Hall, Spa Road
East, Llandrindod Wells LD1 5LG
Passenger Transport Manager: J Forsey
Tel: 0845 602 7035
E-mail: buses@powys.gov.uk
Web site: www.powys.gov.uk

**Rhondda Cynon Taf County
Borough Council**
Integrated Transport Unit, Sardis House,
Sardis Road, Pontypridd CF37 1DU
Head of Service – Transportation:
Roger Waters
Integrated Transport Unit Manager:
Charlie Nelson
Principal Transport Officers: Gwyneth
Elliott, Caroline Harries, Adrian Morgan
Tel: 01443 425001
E-mail: transportationservices@rctcbc.gov.uk
Web site: www.rctcbc.gov.uk

City & County of Swansea
Passenger Transport Team, Environment
Department, County Hall, Oystermouth Road,
Swansea SA1 3SN
Tel: 01792 636466
E-mail: transportation@swansea.gov.uk
Web site: www.swansea.gov.uk

Torfaen County Borough Council
See Blaenau Gwent

Vale of Glamorgan Council
Passenger Transport Unit, The Dock Offices,
Barry Docks, Barry CF63 4RT
Senior Transportation Officer: C Edwards
Tel: 01446 700111
Fax: 01446 704891
E-mail: cedwards@valeofglamorgan.gov.uk
Web site: www.valeofglamorgan.gov.uk

Wrexham County Borough Council
Transport Co-ordination, Crown Buildings,
Chester Street, Wrexham LL13 8BG
Tel: 01978 292000
Fax: 01978 292106
Web site: www.wrexham.gov.uk

SCOTLAND

Councils whose names are marked with an
asterisk (*) are the 12 member councils of
Strathclyde Partnership for Transport (SPT)
(see above), which is responsible for co-
ordinating public transport services and
infrastructure.

Aberdeen City Council
Mark Yule, Technical Officer, Public Transport
Unit, Business Hub 4, Ground Floor North,
Marischal College, Broad Street, Aberdeen
AB10 1AB
Tel: 01224 523073
Fax: 01224 523764
E-mail: mayule@aberdeencity.gov.uk.
Web site: www.aberdeencity.gov.uk

Aberdeenshire Council
Public Transport Unit, Transportation &
Infrastructure, Woodhill House, Westburn Road,
Aberdeen AB16 5GB
Public Transport Manager:
Richard McKenzie
Tel: 01224 664585
Fax: 01224 662005
E-mail: richard.mckenzie@aberdeenshire.
gov.uk
Web site: www.aberdeenshire.gov.uk

Angus Council
Transport Team, Department of Infrastructure
Services, County Buildings, Market Street, Forfar
DD8 3LG
Tel: 01307 461775

Fax: 01307 475037
E-mail: plntransport@angus.gov.uk
Web site: www.angus.gov.uk

Argyll and Bute Council*
Customer Services, Integrated Transport Section,
Kilmory, Lochgilphead PA31 8RT
Integrated Transport Manager: Janne Leckie
Public Transport Officer: Douglas Blades
Tel: 01546 604193
Fax: 01546 604291
E-mail: public.transport@argyll-bute.gov.uk
Web site: www.argyll-bute.gov.uk
Note that for most public transport matters
the Helensburgh and Lomond area of Argyll
and Bute falls within the remit of Strathclyde
Partnership for Transport

Clackmannanshire Council
Public Transport Officer, Roads, Traffic &
Transportation, Kilncraigs, Greenside Street,
Alloa FK10 1EB
Tel: 01259 450000
E-mail: roads@clacks.gov.uk
Web site: www.clacksweb.org.uk

Dumfries & Galloway Council
Sustainable Travel Team, Planning & Environment
Services, Militia House, English Street, Dumfries
DG1 2HR
Team Leader (Sustainable Travel):
Douglas Kirkpatrick
Tel: 0387 260383
Fax: 01387 260111
E-mail: pe.travel.info@dumgal.gov.uk
Web site: www.dumgal.gov.uk

Dundee City Council
Development Department, Dundee House,
50 North Lindsay Street, Dundee DD1 1QE
Tel: 01382 433125
Fax: 01382 433313
Web site: www.dundeecity.gov.uk

East Ayrshire Council*
Council Offices, Greenholm Street, Kilmarnock
KA1 4DJ
Tel: 01563 576000
Web site: www.east-ayrshire.gov.uk

East Dunbartonshire Council*
Broomhill Industrial Estate, Kilsyth Road,
Kirkintilloch G66 1QF
Tel: 0300 123 4510
E-mail: customerservices@eastdunbarton.
gov.uk
Web site: www.eastdunbarton.gov.uk

East Lothian Council
Transport Services, John Muir House,
Haddington EH41 3HA
Transport Officer: Andrew McLellan
Tel: 01620 827700
Fax: 01620 827715
E-mail: amclellan@eastlothian.gov.uk
Web site: www.eastlothian.gov.uk

East Renfrewshire Council*
Senior Transportation Officer, Council
Headquarters, Eastwood Park,
Rouken Glen Road, Giffnock G46 6UG
Tel: 0141 577 8431
E-mail: local_transport@eastrenfrewshire.
gov.uk
Web site: www.eastrenfrewshire.gov.uk

City of Edinburgh Council
City Development, 1 Cockburn Street,
Edinburgh EH1 1BJ
Public Transport Manager: Max Thomson
Tel: 0131 469 3631
Fax: 0131 469 3635.
E-mail: max.thomson@edinburgh.gov.uk
Web site: www.edinburgh.gov.uk

Falkirk Council
Development Services, Abbotsfold House,
David's Loan, Falkirk FK2 7YZ
Public Transport Co-ordinator: Stephen
Bloomfield
Tel: 01324 504950
Fax: 01324 504914
E-mail: transportplanning@falkirk.gov.uk
Web site: www.falkirk.gov.uk

Fife Council
Head of Transportation, Bankhead Central,
Bankhead Park, Glenrothes KY7 6GH
Tel: 03451 555555
Fax: 01592 583643
E-mail: transportation.services@fife.gov.uk
Web site: www.fifedirect.org.uk

Glasgow City Council*
Land & Environmental Services, Richmond
Exchange, 231 George Street, Glasgow
G1 1RX
Tel: 0141 287 9000
Fax: 0141 287 9059
E-mail: land@glasgow.gov.uk
Web site: www.glasgow.gov.uk

The Highland Council
Public Transport Section, TEC Services,
Glenurquhart Road, Inverness IV3 5NX
Transport Development Officer:
David Summers
Tel: 01463 702660
Fax: 01463 702606
E-mail: public.transport@highland.gov.uk
Web site: www.highland.gov.uk

Inverclyde Council*
Municipal Buildings, Greenock PA15 1LY
Tel: 01475 717171
Fax: 01475 712181
Web site: www.inverclyde.gov.uk

Midlothian Council
Travel Team - Room 9, Dundas Buildings,
62A Polton Street, Bonnyrigg EH19 3YD
Principal Officer – Public Transport:
Karl Vanters
Business Manager – Travel and Fleet:
Trevor Docherty
Public Transport Officer: Ricky Dunbar
School Transport Officer: Debbie Hunter
Tel: 0131 561 5443
Fax: 0131 654 2797
E-mail: ptu@midlothian.gov.uk
Web site: www.midlothian.gov.uk

Moray Council
Public Transport Unit, PO Box 6760,
Elgin IV30 9BX
Public Transport Manager: Peter Findlay
Tel: 0300 123 4565
Fax: 01343 545628
E-mail: transport@moray.gov.uk
Web site: www.moray.gov.uk

North Ayrshire Council*
Roads & Transportation, Perceton House,
Irvine KA11 2AL
Tel: 01294 310000
Fax: 01294 324144
E-mail: headofroads@north-ayrshire.gov.uk
Web site: www.north-ayrshire.gov.uk

North Lanarkshire Council*
Roads, Strategy and Sustainable Transport,
Regeneration & Environmental Services, Fleming
House, 2 Tryst Road, Cumbernauld G67 1JW
Tel: 01698 274260
Web site: www.northlanarkshire.gov.uk

Orkney Islands Council
Transportation Service, Council Offices,
School Place, Kirkwall KW15 1NY
Tel: 01856 873535

E-mail: transport@orkney.gov.uk
Web site: www.orkney.gov.uk

Perth & Kinross Council
Public Transport Unit, The Atrium,
137 Glover Street, Perth PH2 0JB
Tel: 0845 301 1130
Fax: 01738 476510
E-mail: publictransport@pkc.gov.uk
Web site: www.pkc.gov.uk

Renfrewshire Council*
Community Resources, North Building,
Renfrewshire House, Cotton Street, Paisley
PA1 1WB
Tel: 0300 300 0380
Fax: 0141 618 7935
E-mail: pt@renfrewshire.gov.uk
Web site: www.renfrewshire.gov.uk

Scottish Borders Council
Passenger Transport Unit, Council Headquarters,
Newtown St Boswells, Melrose TD6 0SA
Tel: 0300 100 1800
E-mail: transport@scotborders.gov.uk
Web site: www.scotborders.gov.uk

Shetland Islands Council
See ZetTrans – Shetland Transport Partnership
- above
Web site: www.shetland.gov.uk

South Ayrshire Council*
Manager of Roads and Transportation, Burns
House, Burns Statue Square, Ayr KA7 1UT
Tel: 0300 123 0900
Web site: www.south-ayrshire.gov.uk

South Lanarkshire Council*
Council Offices, Almada Street, Hamilton
ML3 0AA
Tel: 0303 123 1015
Web site: www.southlanarkshire.gov.uk

Stirling Council
Council Headquarters, Viewforth, 2 Pitt Place,
Stirling FK8 2ET
Tel: 0845 277 7000
E-mail: transportplanning@stirling.gov.uk
Web site: www.stirling.gov.uk

West Dunbartonshire Council*
Manager of Roads and Transportation, Council
Offices, Garshake Road, Dunbarton, G82 3PU
Tel: 01389 737612
Web site: www.west-dunbarton.gov.uk

Western Isles Council
Western Isles Council (Comhairle nan Eilean
Siar), Sandwick Road, Stornoway, Isle of Lewis
HS1 2BW
Tel: 0845 600 7090
Fax: 01851 705349
E-mail: enquiries@cne-siar.gov.uk
Web site: www.cne-siar.gov.uk

West Lothian Council
Whitehill House, 7 Whitestone Place, Whitehill
Industrial Estate, Bathgate EH48 2HA
Public Transport Manager: Ian Forbes
Tel: 01506 776339
Fax: 01506 775265
E-mail: publictransport@westlothian.gov.uk
Web site: www.westlothian.gov.uk

CHANNEL ISLANDS

States of Jersey
Transport & Technical Services, PO Box 412,
South Hill, St Helier, Jersey JE4 8UY
Public Transport Planner: Craig Miller
Tel: 01534 448306
Fax: 01534 445529
E-mail: c.miller@gov.je
Web site: www.gov.je/buses

Tendering & Regulatory Authorities

Traffic Commissioners

The Traffic Commissioners and their Deputies no longer have personal responsibility for specific Traffic Areas, except in Scotland.
Web site: www.gov.uk
Senior Traffic Commissioner: Mrs Beverley Bell
Traffic Commissioners: Joan Aitken, Sarah Bell, Nick Denton, Nick Jones, Kevin Rooney, Richard Turfitt

TRAFFIC AREA OFFICES

EAST OF ENGLAND
Eastbrook, Shaftesbury Road, Cambridge CB2 8DR
Tel: 0300 123 9000
Fax: 0113 249 8142
Area covered: Buckinghamshire, Cambridgeshire, Essex, Hertfordshire, Leicestershire, Lincolnshire, Norfolk, Northamptonshire, Suffolk, Bedford, Central Bedfordshire, Leicester, Luton, Milton Keynes, Peterborough, Rutland, Southend-on-Sea, Thurrock.

NORTH EAST OF ENGLAND
Hillcrest House, 386 Harehills Lane, Leeds LS9 6NF
Tel: 0300 123 9000
Fax: 0113 249 8142
Area covered: Durham, Northumberland, Nottinghamshire, North Yorkshire, South Yorkshire, Tyne & Wear, West Yorkshire, Darlington, East Riding, Hartlepool, Kingston upon Hull, Middlesbrough, North Lincolnshire, North East Lincolnshire, Nottingham, Redcar & Cleveland, Stockton-on-Tees, York.

NORTH WEST OF ENGLAND
Suite 4, Stone Cross Place, Stone Cross Lane North, Golborne, Warrington WA3 2SH
Tel: 0300 123 9000
Fax: 0113 249 8142
Area covered: Cumbria, Derbyshire, Greater Manchester, Lancashire, Merseyside, Blackburn with Darwen, Blackpool, Cheshire East, Cheshire West & Chester, City of Derby, Halton, Warrington.

SCOTLAND
Level 6, The Stamp Office, 10 Waterloo Place, Edinburgh EH1 3EG
Tel: 0300 123 9000
Fax: 0113 249 8142
Traffic Commissioner: Miss Joan Aitken
Area covered: Scotland

LONDON AND THE SOUTH EAST OF ENGLAND
Ivy House, 3 Ivy Terrace, Eastbourne BN21 4QT
Tel: 0300 123 9000
Fax: 0113 249 8142
Area covered: East Sussex, Greater London, Kent, Surrey, West Sussex, Brighton & Hove, Medway.

WEST MIDLANDS AND WALES
38 George Road, Edgbaston, Birmingham B15 1PL
Tel: 0300 123 9000
Fax: 0113 249 8142
Area covered: Herefordshire, Shropshire, Staffordshire, Warwickshire, West Midlands, Worcestershire, Stoke-on-Trent, Telford & Wrekin, Wales.

WEST OF ENGLAND
Jubilee House, Croydon Street, Bristol BS5 0DA
Tel: 0300 123 9000
Fax: 0113 249 8142
Area covered: Cornwall, Devon, Gloucestershire, Hampshire, Oxfordshire, Somerset, Wiltshire, Bath & North East Somerset, Bournemouth, Bracknell Forest, Bristol, Isle of Wight, North Somerset, Plymouth, Poole, Portsmouth, Reading, Slough, Southampton, South Gloucestershire, Swindon, Torbay, West Berkshire, Windsor & Maidenhead, Wokingham.

Competition and Markets Authority

The Competition and Markets Authority has replaced the Office of Fair Trading (OFT) as the body which plays a leading role in promotes competition and protects consumer interests throughout the UK, ensuring that businesses are fair and competitive. The tools to carry out this work are the powers granted to the CMA under consumer and competition legislation.
Chairman: David Currie
Chief Executive: Alex Chisholm
Address: Victoria House, 37 Southampton Row, London WC1B 4AD
Tel: 020 3738 6000
E-mail: general.enquiries@cma.gsi.gov.uk
Web site: www.gov.uk/government/organisations/competition-and-markets-authority

Department for Transport

Permanent Secretary: Philip Rutnam
Great Minster House, 33 Horseferry Road, London SW1P 4DR
Tel: 0300 330 3000
Web site: www.gov.uk/government/organisations/department-for-transport

Executive Agencies: (include)
Driver and Vehicle Standards Agency (DVSA)
The DVSA was formed by the merger of the Driving Standards Agency (DSA) and the Vehicle and Operator Services Agency (VOSA).
Chief Executive: Alastair Peoples
PO Box 280
Newcastle-upon-Tyne NE99 1FP
Tel: 0300 200 1122
E-mail: customer.services@dsa.gsi.gov.uk
Web site: www.gov.uk/government/organisations/driver-and-vehicle-standards-agency

Driver and Vehicle Licensing Agency (DVLA)

Chief Executive: Oliver Morley

Drivers Customer Services (DCS)
Correspondence Team
DVLA
Swansea SA6 7JL
Tel: 0300 790 6801   **Fax:** 0300 123 0784

Vehicle Customer Services (VCS) Team
DVLA
Swansea SA99 1AR
Tel: 0300 790 6802   **Fax:** 0300 123 0798

Highways Agency (HA)
Chief Executive: Graham Dalton
Tel: 0300 123 5000
E-mail: ha_info@highways.gsi.gov.uk
Web Site: www.highways.gov.uk

Vehicle Certification Agency (VCA)
Chief Executive: Paul Markwick
No1, The Estate Office Centre, Eastgate Road, Bristol BS5 6XX
Tel: 0300 330 5797
Fax: 0300 003 2198
E-mail: enquiries@vca.gov.uk
Web site: www.dft.gov.uk/vca

Advisory Non-Departmental Bodies: (include)

The Disabled Persons Transport Advisory Committee
Web site: www.gov.uk/dptac
Members: Will Bee, Sharon Brennan, Helen Dolphin, Olav Ernstzen, Kirsten Hearn, Heather James, Paulette Lappin, Roger Mackett, David Partington MBE, Andrew Probert, Jessica Uguccioni, Tanvi Vyas.
The Disabled Persons Transport Advisory Committee (DPTAC) is a statutory body established under Section 125 of the Transport Act 1985 to advise the Secretary of State for Transport on matters affecting the transport needs of disabled people.

Rail Accident Investigation Branch
The Wharf, Stores Road, Derby DE21 4BA
Chief Inspector: Carolyn Griffiths
Tel: 01332 253300
Fax: 01332 253301
E-mail: enquiries@raib.gov.uk
Web site: www.raib.gov.uk
RAIB is the independent railway accident investigation organisation for the UK and is listed in LRB because its remit covers street tramways.

NOTES

SECTION 3

Organisations and Societies

- **British Operators Organisations**

- **Institutions**

- **International Associations**

- **Other Organisations**

- **First Aid and Sports Associations**

- **Trade Organisations**

- **Societies**

- **Passenger Transport Museums**

BRITISH OPERATORS' ORGANISATIONS

ALBUM – ASSOCIATION OF LOCAL BUS COMPANY MANAGERS
The Association represents the professional views of the Executive Directors and Senior Managers of those bus companies owned by district council and major independent operators on matters specifically affecting locally-owned bus company management and operations.
Chairman: Ben Colson
Secretary: Thomas W W Knowles, 41 Redhills, Eccleshall, Stafford ST21 6JW
Tel & Fax: 01785 859414
E-mail: Thmsknw@aol.com
Web site: www.album-bus.co.uk

THE COACH TOURISM COUNCIL
PO Box 972A, Thames Ditton, Surrey KT1 9XD
Tel: 0870 850 2839
Fax: 020 8398 8777
E-mail: admin@coachtourismcouncil.co.uk
Web site: www.coachtourismcouncil.com, www.findacoachholiday.com
Chairman: Sean Taggart **Chief Executive:** Christopher Wales **Administration:** Paul Ovington
The CTC's mission is to promote tourism and travel by coach.

COMMUNITY TRANSPORT ASSOCIATION
Highbank, Halton Street, Hyde SK14 2NY
Tel: 0161 351 1475
Fax: 0161 351 7221
Advice Service Tel: 0845 130 6195
E-mail: info@ctauk.org
Web site: www.ctauk.org
Chair of the Board of Trustees: Dr Stephen Hickey **Vice-Chair:** Peter Maggs
The community transport sector is vast. There are over 100,000 minibuses serving over 10 million passengers every year being operated for use by voluntary and community groups, schools, colleges and Local Authorities, or to provide door-to-door transport for people who are unable to use other public transport. This door-to-door transport is not limited to minibuses though; there are very many voluntary car schemes throughout the UK where volunteers will use their own cars to provide transport for individuals. Overcoming social exclusion is at the heart of what community transport has always been about. The CTA is committed to helping its members achieve this objective in their area both in terms of the direct support it can offer such as training, developmental support etc. but also by lobbying on behalf of the movement with government and other important agencies.

CONFEDERATION OF PASSENGER TRANSPORT UK
Drury House, 34-43 Russell Street, London WC2B 5HA
Tel: 020 7240 3131
Fax: 020 7240 6565
E-mail: cpt@cpt-uk.org
Web site: www.cpt-uk.org
The Confederation of Passenger Transport UK (CPT) is the trade association representing the UK's bus and coach operators and the light rail sector. CPT has wide responsibilities ranging from representation on government working parties (national, local, EU); establishing operating codes of practice; advising on legal, technical and mechanical standards; management of the Bonded Coach Holiday Scheme, a government recognised consumer travel protection scheme and Coach Marque, an industry quality standard;

24-hour Crisis Control service for members; organisation of industry events and the first point of contact for the media on transport and other related issues.

OFFICERS AND COUNCIL
President (2014): Chris Owens
Chairman: Ian Morgan
Chief Executive: Simon Posner
Deputy Chief Executive: Peter Gomersall
Manager, Chief Executive's Office: Miss Ling Tang
Director of Finance: Ray Coyne
Director of Communications: Christopher Nice
Operations Director: Stephen Smith
Director of Policy Development: Steven Salmon
Director of Coaching: Steven Barber
Deputy Director, Communications: Pauline Gaunt OBE
Deputy Director, Operations: John Burch
Fixed Track Executive: James Hammett
Coaching Consultant: Mike Morgan
Committee Executive: Graham Sutton
Operations & Tourism Executive: Alf Scrimgour
Operational Technical Executive: Colin Moore

Director of Government Relations, Scotland: George Mair
2 Walker Street, Edinburgh EH3 7LA
Tel: 0131 260 5109
E-mail: georgem@cpt-uk.org

Director of Government Relations, Wales: John Pockett
1 Lewis Terrace, Darren Parc, Pontypridd CF37 2AF
Tel: 07989 586545
E-mail: johnp@cpt-uk.org

Director of Government Relations, EU: Paul White
2 Walker Street, Edinburgh EH3 7LA
Tel: 0131 272 2150
Fax: 0131 272 2152

Regional Managers

East Midlands & Yorkshire: Keith McNally
Tel: 07958 720151
E-mail: keithm@cpt-uk.org
London & South East: Karen Tiley
Drury House, 34-43 Russell Street, London WC2B 5HA
Tel: 020 7240 3131
E-mail: karent@cpt-uk.org
Northern: Steve Noble
Tel: 01661 886223
E-mail: steve.noble@cpt-uk.org
North Western: Susan Mullen
Tel: 07710 833577
E-mail: sue.mullen@cpt-uk.org
Scotland: Jeremy Tinsley
2 Walker Street, Edinburgh EH3 7LA
Tel: 0131 260 5107
E-mail: jeremyt@cpt-uk.org
Wales: Colin Thomas
Tel: 07540 688010
E-mail: colint@cpt-uk.org
West Midlands: Phil Bateman MBE
Tel: 07505 889319
E-mail: philb@cpt-uk,org
South West: John Burch
Tel: 07940 929881
E-mail: johnb@cpt-uk.org

GUILD OF BRITISH COACH OPERATORS LTD
PO Box 5657, Southend on Sea, Essex SS1 3WT
Tel: 08456 126225
Fax: 0870 139 9469

E-mail: admin@coach-tours.co.uk
Web site: www.coach-tours.co.uk
Chairman: John Johnson, Johnsons Coaches
Vice Chairman: Deirdre Brown, Eddie Brown Tours
Treasurer: Ian Luckett, Lucketts Travel
Board Members: Ian Fraser, The Kings Ferry; Richard Grey, Grey's of Ely
Administrator: Richard Delahoy
An association of top quality coach companies dedicated to providing a first class service. Guild members provide luxury coaches throughout Britain, offering comprehensive travel management services. With around 800 coaches, a wide geographical spread and a guaranteed commitment to the highest standards, Guild members can meet *all* your travel needs.

INSTITUTIONS

THE CHARTERED INSTITUTE OF LOGISTICS & TRANSPORT
Logistics & Transport Centre, Earlstrees Court, Earlstrees Road, Corby NN17 4AX
Tel: 01536 740100
Fax: 01536 740101
E-mail: enquiry@ciltuk.org.uk.
Web site: www.ciltuk.org.uk
President: Jim Spittle FCILT
Chairman: Neil Ashworth FCILT
Chief Executive: Steve Agg FCILT
The Chartered Institute of Logistics and Transport (UK) is the professional body for individuals and organisations involved in all disciplines, modes and aspects of logistics and transport.
The Institute's 22,000 members have privileged access to a range of benefits and services, which support them, professionally and personally, throughout their careers and help connect them with world-wide expertise. For further information and to join please contact Membership Services, **Tel:** 01536 740104 or visit the CILT (UK) web site above.

THE INSTITUTE OF THE MOTOR INDUSTRY
Fanshaws, Brickendon, Hertford SG13 8PQ
Tel: 01992 511521
Fax: 01992 511548
E-mail: comms@theimi.org.uk
Web site: www.theimi.org.uk
The Institute of the Motor Industry (IMI) is the professional association for individuals working in the retail motor industry and is the leading awarding body of vocational qualifications in the automotive sector. With some 25,000 members and 45,000 registered students at 350 assessment centres, the IMI is focused on improving professional standards through the recognition, qualification and development of individuals.
Qualifications offered by the Institute include NVQs/SVQs, technical certificates, vehicle sales awards, Quality Assured Awards and Certificate/Diploma in automotive retail management (ARMS).
The IMI governs the industry's Automotive Technician Accreditation (ATA) initiative, which has more than 4500 nationally-accredited technicians since launching in 2005.
OFFICERS AND VICE PRESIDENTS
Patron: HRH Prince Michael of Kent GCVO FIMI
President: Graham Smith OBE FIMI
Chair: Adrian Smith FIMI
Chief Executive Officer: Steve Nash FIMI
Finance & IT Director: Christopher Thomas
Chief Operating Officer: Linda Stansfield FIMI

THE INSTITUTE OF TRANSPORT ADMINISTRATION

The Old Studio, 25 Greenfield Road, Westoning MK45 5JD
Tel: 01525 634940
Fax: 01525 750016
E-mail: info@iota.org.uk
Web site: www.iota.org.uk
Registered Friendly Society: No 53 SA

OFFICERS

President: Wing Cdr Peter Green FInstTA
Deputy President: Alan Whittington FInstTA, FRSA, FIBC
Trustees: Brian Bigwood FInstTA, Christopher Sullivan MInstTA, Geoff Fletcher MInstTA
National Chairman: Martin Price MInstTA
National Treasurer and Chairman, Finance & General Purposes Committee: Clive Aisbitt FInstTA
Chairman Education, Membership & Training Committee: Mike Walker FInstTA
Chairman External Affairs Committee: Peter L Tod FInstTA
Director of the Institute: David J S Dalglish FInstTA, FRSA

THE INSTITUTION OF MECHANICAL ENGINEERS

1 Birdcage Walk, London SW1H 9JJ
Tel: 020 7222 7899
Fax: 020 7222 4557
E-mail: enquiries@imeche.org
Web site: www.imeche.org.uk
President: Group Captain Mark Hunt
Chief Executive: Stephen Tetlow
The Institute was founded in 1847, and incorporates as the Automobile Division the former Institution of Automobile Engineers and as the Railway Division the former Institution of Locomotive Engineers.

SOE

22 Greencoat Place, London SW1P 1PR
Tel: 020 7630 1111
Fax: 020 7630 6677
E-mail: soe@soe.org.uk
Web site: www.soe.org.uk
President: Gerry Fleming IEng CEnv FSOE FIRTE
Chief Executive: Peter Walsh CEng CEnv FSOE FIEAust
The SOE is the umbrella professional body for those working in road transport and plant engineering. The Institute of Road Transport Engineers is a professional sector within the SOE, alongside the Institute of Plant Engineers and the Bureau of Engineer Surveyors.

TRL LTD (TRANSPORT RESEARCH LABORATORY)

Crowthorne House, Nine Mile Ride, Wokingham RG40 3GA
Tel: 01344 773131
Fax: 01344 770356
E-mail: enquiries@trl.co.uk
Web site: www.trl.co.uk
Chairman: Charles Rice
Chief Executive: Rob Wallis
Finance Director: Tim Andrews

INTERNATIONAL ASSOCIATIONS

THE INTERNATIONAL ASSOCIATION OF PUBLIC TRANSPORT (UITP)

Offices: Rue Sainte Marie 6, B-1080, Brussels, Belgium
Tel: 00 32 2 673 6100
Fax: 00 32 2 660 1072
E-mail: info@uitp.org
Web site: www.uitp.org
President: Sir Peter Hendy CBE
Secretary General: Alain Flausch

INTERNATIONAL ROAD TRANSPORT UNION (IRU)

Founded in 1948 in Geneva, the IRU is an international association of national road transport federations which has consultative status in the United Nations. One of its two Transport Councils is concerned with road passenger transport.
General Secretariat: IRU, Centre International, 3 Rue de Varembe, B.P.44, 1211 Geneva 20, Switzerland
Tel: 00 41 22 918 2700
Fax: 00 41 22 918 2741
E-mail: iru@iru.org
Web site: www.iru.org
President: Janusz Lacny
Secretary General: Umberto de Pretto

WORLD ROAD ASSOCIATION (PIARC)

The Association is an international body with headquarters in Paris, administered by an elected President and other office bearers. Members are recruited from governments, local authorities, technical and industrial groups and private individuals whose interests are centred on roads and road traffic. The association is maintained by subscriptions from its members. International congresses are held every four years.

OFFICE BEARERS

President: Oscar de Buen Richkarday (Mexico)
Past President: Anne-Marie Leclerc (Australia)
Vice Presidents: M Henneveld (Japan), T Idossou (Burkina Faso), F Zotter (Austria)
Secretary General: J F Corte (France), PIARC, La Grande Arche, Paroi Nord, Niveau 2, 92055 La Defense Cedex, France
Tel: 00 33 1 47 96 81 21
Fax: 00 33 1 49 00 02 02
E-mail: info@piarc.org

BRITISH NATIONAL COMMITTEE

The British National Committee's role is to ensure adequate representation of British methods and experience on PIARC's international committees and Congresses, to disseminate the findings of those committees and generally look after British interests. The present officers of this committee are:
Patron: Minister for Transport
UK Chairman: Joe Burns
UK Secretary: Justin Ward
119 Britannia Walk, London N1 7JE
Tel: 020 7336 1540
E-mail: justin.ward@ciht.org
Web site: www.piarc.co.uk

OTHER ORGANISATIONS

ASSOCIATION OF TRANSPORT CO-ORDINATING OFFICERS (ATCO)

ATCO – Transport Professionals
ATCO Chair: David Blainey, Merseytravel
Tel: 0151 330 1344
E-mail: david.blainey@merseytravel.gov.uk
Web site: www.atco.org.uk

ATCO Membership Enquiries
Tel: 0844 209 6556
E-mail: info@atco-membership.co.uk
Twitter: @ATCOuk

ATCO (Association of Transport Co-Ordinating Officers) has a wide ranging membership base of transport professionals, including senior staff, directly concerned with strategic policy development and implementation for securing of passenger transport services for a wide range of public

transport authorities. These include shire counties and unitary councils in England, Wales and Scotland, Passenger Transport Executives, TfL, the Isle of Man, the States of Jersey and Northern Ireland. The Association has been running for 38 years.
Through exchanging information and views the Association helps formulate policies and standards and promotes transport initiatives aimed at achieving better passenger transport services for all.
Members give advice to the Department for Transport, Local Government Group, the Welsh Assembly and the Convention of Scottish Local Authorities. ATCO works actively with the Community Transport Association and Passenger Transport Executive Group, Confederation of Passenger Transport, Passenger Focus and Bus Users UK.

BUS USERS UK

Terminal House, Shepperton, Middlesex TW17 8AS
Tel: 01932 232574
Complaints Hotline: 0300 111 0001
E-mail: enquiries@bususers.org
Web site: www.bususers.org
Bus Users UK represents and campaigns on behalf of bus users throughout Britain (excluding London). It is a partner in the Bus Appeals Body, and deals with complaints appeals. It also organises bus users' surgeries under the title of "Your Bus Matters".
Life President: Dr Caroline Cahm MBE PhD
Chair: Tracey Jessop
Vice Chair: Jeff Anderson
Chief Executive: Claire Walters
Deputy Chief Executive: Stephen Morris

Bus User Editor: Gavin Booth
39 Lilyhill Terrace, Edinburgh EH8 7DR
Tel: 0131 523 1306
E-mail: editor@bususers.org

BUS USERS CYMRU

PO Box 1045, Cardiff CF11 1JE
Tel: 029 2022 1370
E-mail: wales@bususers.org
Director: Margaret Everson MBE FCILT
Deputy Director: Barclay Davies

BUS USERS SCOTLAND

Hopetoun Gate, 8b McDonald Road, Edinburgh EH7 4LZ
Tel: 0131 523 1309
E-mail: enquiries@bususers.org
Director: Gavin Booth
Deputy Director: Greig Mackay

BUSK UK LTD

18 Windsor Road, Newport NP19 8NS
Tel: 01633 274944
E-mail: enquiries@busk-uk.co.uk
Web site: www.busk-uk.co.uk
Formerly known for its Belt Up School Kids campaign, BUSK is now known through the European Union as an authority on vehicular safety for children and young people.

CAMPAIGN FOR BETTER TRANSPORT

16 Waterside, 44-48 Wharf Road, London N1 7UX
Tel: 020 7566 6480
Fax: 020 7566 6493
Web site: www.bettertransport.org.uk
E-mail: info@bettertransport.org.uk
The Campaign for Better Transport, formerly Transport 2000, is a campaign and research group that seeks greener, cleaner transport patterns through greater use of public transport, walking and cycling.
President: Michael Palin
Chief Executive: Stephen Joseph OBE

COACH DRIVERS CLUB
Unit 4, Minerva Business Park, Lynch Wood,
Peterborough PE2 6FT
Tel: 01733 405738
Fax: 01733 405745
E-mail:
tracey.harrison@coachdriversclub.com
Web site: www.coachdriversclub.com
Manager: Tony Henthorn **Membership
Executive:** Tracey Harrison
The Coach Drivers Club is a membership
club for coach drivers, coaching and tourism.
It offers accident cover, magazine, yearbook,
members' website, legal advice.

LIGHT RAIL TRANSIT ASSOCIATION
c/o 138 Radnor Avenue, Welling, Kent
DA16 2BY
E-mail: office@lrta.org
Web site: www.lrta.org
Founded in 1937 to advocate and encourage
interest in light rail and modern tramways.
Monthly magazine is Tramways & Urban
Transit. Membership enquiries to:
Membership Secretary: Roger Morris
E-mail: membership@lrta.org
President: Geoff Lusher FCILT
Chairman: Andrew Braddock
Deputy Chairman: Vic Simons
Treasurer: Hans Retallick

LOCAL
GOVERNMENT ASSOCIATION
Local Government House, Smith Square,
London SW1P 3HZ
Tel: 020 7664 3000
Fax: 020 7664 3030
E-mail: info@local.gov.uk
Web site: www.local.gov.uk
The Local Government Association was
formed by the merger of the Association of
County Councils, the Association of District
Councils and the Association of Metropolitan
Authorities in 1997. The LGA has just under
500 members, including all shire district
councils; metropolitan district councils;
county councils; unitary authorities; London
authorities; and Welsh authorities. In addition,
the LGA represents police authorities,
fire authorities and passenger transport
authorities. The LGA provides the national
voice for local communities in England and
Wales; its members represent over 50 million
people, employ more than 2 million staff and
spend over £65 billion on local services.
Amongst the LGA's policy priorities is
integrated transport; local authorities lead the
way in encouraging the use of public transport
and thereby reducing congestion, ill-health and
environmental damage through a programme
of partnerships between local authorities and
other agencies.
President: Lord Richard Best
Chairman: Sir Merrick Cockell
(Conservative, Kensington & Chelsea)
Vice-Chairs: Cllr Marianne Overton, Cllr
Gary Porter CBE, Cllr David Sparks OBE, Cllr
Gerald Vernon-Jackson
Chief Executive: Carolyn Downs

LONDON TRAVELWATCH
Dexter House, 2 Royal Mint Court, London
EC3N 4QN
Tel: 020 3176 2999
E-mail: info@londontravelwatch.org.uk
Web Site: www.londontravelwatch.org.uk
Formerly the London Transport Users
Committee, London TravelWatch is the
independent statutory body set up to
represent the interests of the users of all
transport for which the Greater London
Authority and Transport for London is
responsible for operating, providing, procuring
and licensing. London TravelWatch is also the
Rail Passengers Committee for London.

Chair: Stephen Locke
Chief Executive: Janet Cooke

PASSENGER FOCUS
Fleetbank House, 2-6 Salisbury Square,
London EC4Y 8JX
Tel: 0300 123 0860
Fax: 020 7630 7355
7th Floor, Piccadilly Gate, Store Street,
Manchester M1 2WD
Tel: 0300 123 2140
Fax: 0161 236 1574
E-mail: info@passengerfocus.org.uk
Web site: www.passengerfocus.org.uk
Passenger Focus is the independent passenger
watchdog, set up by the Government to
protect the interests of rail passengers and
bus passengers in England (outside London).
Chairman: Colin Foxall CBE
Board Members: Philip Mendelsohn,
Stephen Locke, Marian Lauder MBE, Bob
Linnard, Isabel Liu, Philip Rowen, Professor
Paul Salveson MBE, Dr Stuart Burgess CBE,
Diane McCrea
Chief Executive: Anthony Smith
Passenger Team Director: David
Sidebottom

PASSENGER TRANSPORT
EXECUTIVE GROUP
Wellington House, 40-50 Wellington Street,
Leeds LS1 2DE
Tel: 0113 251 7204
Fax: 0113 251 7333
E-mail: info@pteg.net
Web site: www.pteg.net
Chair: David Brown
Director, PTEG Support Unit:
Jonathan Bray
PTEG brings together and promotes the
interests of the six Passenger Transport
Executives (PTEs) in England. Bristol &
West of England Partnership, Leicester City
Council, Nottingham City Council, Strathclyde
Partnership for Transport and Transport for
London are associate members.

PEOPLE 1st (incorporating GOSKILLS)
2nd Floor, Armstrong House, 38 Market Square,
Uxbridge UB8 1LH
Tel: 01895 817000
E-mail: info@people1st.co.uk
Web site: www.people1st.co.uk
Managing Director: Simon Tarr
People 1st is the Sector Skills Council for
hospitality, passenger transport, travel and
tourism in the UK.

ROAD OPERATOR SAFETY COUNCIL
(ROSCO)
Osborn House, 20 High Street South, Olney,
Buckinghamshire MK46 5JF
Tel: 01234 714420
E-mail: admin@rosco-uk.org
Web site: www.rosco-uk.org
'ROSCO' has been providing a safe driving
award scheme for UK Bus and Coach
Operators since 1955. Over 100 companies
and 50,000 drivers enter the scheme each
year. Awards are presented to drivers who
avoid any prosecution for Road Traffic Act
offences, and do not have any blameworthy
accidents.
Chairman: Peter J S Shipp
Vice Chairman: John E H Miller
Executive Officer: Gill Edmondson

THE ROYAL SOCIETY FOR THE
PREVENTION OF ACCIDENTS
28 Calthorpe Road, Edgbaston, Birmingham
B15 1RP
Tel: 0121 248 2000
Fax: 0121 248 2001
E-mail: help@rospa.com
Web site: www.rospa.com

RoSPA promotes safety at work and in the
home, at leisure and in schools, on (or near
water) and on the roads, through providing
information, publicity, training and consultancy.
The Society works with central and local
government, the caring services, the police and
public and private sector organisations large
and small. Some work is funded by grant and
sponsorship, but most relies on the support of
the Society's membership.
The Society also produces and supplies a
comprehensive selection of publications
ranging from reference books to low-cost
booklets for mass distribution.
Training Offered: Training courses cover
practical skills and management training
through to professional qualifications in
Health and Safety.
President: Lord McKenzie of Luton
Chief Executive: Tom Mullarkey MBE

TRANSPORT BENEVOLENT FUND
New Loom House, 101 Back Church Lane,
London E1 1LU
Tel: 0300 333 2000
Fax: 0870 831 2882
E-mail: help@tbf.org.uk
Web site: www.tbf.org.uk
TBF is a Registered Charity in England
and Wales (No 1058032) and in Scotland
(SC040013) and was founded in 1923.
Membership is open to most staff engaged
in the public transport industry. Members
pay £1 a week and in return are granted,
at the discretion of the Trustees, cash help,
convalescence, recuperation, a wide range
of complementary medical treatments, legal
advice, and medical equipment in times of
need. Membership covers the employee
and their partner and dependent children.
Subject to age and length of membership, free
membership may be awarded on leaving the
industry. There are payroll deduction facilities
in many companies.
General Manager: John Sheehy
Senior Trustee: Christopher Sullivan
(President)
Patrons: Sir Brian Souter (Stagecoach
Group), Sir Peter Hendy CBE (Transport
for London), Lew Adams OBE (BT Police
Authority), David Martin (Arriva), Simon
Posner (CPT UK), Nigel Stevens (Transdev),
Dean Finch (National Express), Tim O'Toole
CBE (First), David Brown (Go-Ahead Group),
Mark Howarth (Western Greyhound), Mick
Whelan (ASLEF), Manuel Cortes (TSSA), Prof
Richard Parry-Jones (Network Rail), Michael
Roberts (ATOC), Len McCluskey (Unite),
Richard Casling (RATP Dev UK), Jaspal Singh
(Metroline) and Mick Cash (RMT).

TRANSPORT FRIENDLY SOCIETY
3rd Floor, Derbyshire House, St Chad's Street,
London WC1H 8AG
Tel: 020 7833 2616
Fax: 020 7833 4426
E-mail: info@tfs.uk.com
Web site: www.tfs.uk.com
The TFS is a mutual organisation, in being
since 1885, which is run by public transport
workers for the benefit of those working in
the industry, their family, and friends.

SPORTS ASSOCIATIONS

NATIONAL PASSENGER TRANSPORT
SPORTS ASSOCIATION
Correspondence Address: 1 Sutherland
Mansions, Park Lane, Whitchurch, Cardiff
CF14 7BA
President: Ian Davies
Vice President: Geoff Lusher
Chairman: Murray McDonald
Treasurer: Jack McClean

Tel: 029 2065 5431
E-mail: murraymac@ntlworld.com
Web site: www.nptsa.co.uk
The association organises inter-company sporting activities for the bus, coach, light rail and heavy rail industries. Four of the major groups are corporate sponsors, and 15 different sports are covered. Up to date information on the Association and each sporting competition is published on our website. Further information is available from the Chairman, address above.

TRADE ORGANISATIONS AND ASSOCIATIONS

BEAMA LTD
The British Electrotechnical & Allied Manufacturers' Association
Founded 1902, Incorporated 1905.
Offices: Westminster Tower, 3 Albert Embankment, London SE1 7SL
Tel: 020 7793 3000
Fax: 020 7793 3003
E-mail: info@beama.org.uk
Web site: www.beama.org.uk
Objectives: By co-operative action to promote the interests of the industrial, electrical and electronic manufacturing industries of Great Britain.
Chief Executive Officer: Dr Howard Porter

FEDERATION OF ENGINE REMANUFACTURERS LTD
After Market House, 5 Marlin Office Village, 1250 Chester Road, Castle Bromwich, Birmingham B35 7AZ
Tel: 0121 749 4767 **Fax:** 0121 730 2745
E-mail: enquiries@fer.co.uk
Web Site: www.fer.co.uk.

FREIGHT TRANSPORT ASSOCIATION VEHICLE INSPECTION SERVICE
Hermes House, St John's Road, Tunbridge Wells TN4 9UZ
Tel: 01892 526171
Fax: 01892 534989
Web Site: www.fta.co.uk
The Freight Transport Association represents the interests of over 11,000 companies throughout the UK. FTA carries out over 100,000 vehicle inspections each year including many PSVs. The FTA Vehicle Inspection Service supports operators in maintaining their vehicles in a roadworthy condition - both mechanically and legally. Further details are available from Vehicle Inspections, FTA, Tunbridge Wells (01892 526171).
Publications: Freight (monthly journal), FTA Yearbook.
Chief Executive: Theo de Pencier.

LOW CARBON VEHICLE PARTNERSHIP
3 Birdcage Walk, London SW1H 9JJ
Tel: 020 7304 6880 **Fax:** 020 3008 6180
E-mail: secretariat@lowcvp.org.uk
Web site: www.lowcvp.org.uk
The LowCVP is an action and advisory group providing a forum through which partners can work together towards shared goals and take the lead in the transition to a low-carbon future for road transport in the UK.
Chairman: Darran Messem

MIRA LTD
Registered Office: MIRA Ltd, Watling Street, Nuneaton CV10 0TU
Tel: 024 7635 5000
Fax: 024 7635 5355
E-mail: enquiries@mira.co.uk
Web site: www.mira.co.uk
MIRA is an independent product engineering

and technology centre and offers skills in innovation, problem-solving and consultancy.
Chairman: Michael Beasley CBE
Chief Executive Officer: Dr George Gillespie
Chief Commercial & Technical Officer: Dr Geoff Davis
Chief Financial Officer: Tim Nathan
Chief Operating Officer: Declan Allen

SOCIETY OF MOTOR MANUFACTURERS & TRADERS LIMITED (SMMT)
71 Great Peter Street, London SW1P 2BN
Tel: 020 7235 7000
Fax: 020 7235 7112
E-mail: membership@smmt.co.uk
Web site: www.smmt.co.uk
Chief Executive: Michael Hawes

THE VEHICLE BUILDERS & REPAIRERS ASSOCIATION LTD
1 Howley Park Business Village, Pullan Way, Morley, Leeds LS27 0BZ
Tel: 0113 253 8333 **Fax:** 0113 238 0496
E-mail: vbra@vbra.co.uk
Web site: www.vbra.co.uk
The VBRA is the representative organisation for vehicle manufacturers and vehicle/car body repairers. An OFT approved Code of Practice has been drawn up to govern the conduct of members.
Director General: Malcolm Tagg

SOCIETIES

THE ASSOCIATION OF FRIENDS OF THE BRITISH COMMERCIAL VEHICLE MUSEUM TRUST
The Association was formed when The British Commercial Vehicle Museum was opened in 1983. Its aims are to support the full-time staff in matters of publicity, fund raising, maintenance and documentation of exhibits, work in the archives, organising rallies, etc. Facilities for members include a newsletter, free admission to the museum to undertake museum work and socialise with colleagues. New members are always welcome and special rates exist for families, students and senior citizens.
Hon Chairman: H Hatcher
Hon Secretary: A Pritchard
Hon Treasurer: A Pritchard
Members of the Committee: E Simister, D Lewis, J Gardner
Museum Manager: A Buchan
Address: The British Commercial Vehicle Museum, King Street, Leyland, Preston PR25 2LE
Tel: 01772 451011

ASTON MANOR ROAD TRANSPORT MUSEUM
Shenstone Drive, Northgate, Aldridge, Walsall WS9 8TP
Tel: 01922 454761
E-mail: amrtm1@aol.co.uk
Web site: www.amrtm.org
A Company limited by guarantee, registered as a charity.
The museum lost its battle with Birmingham City Council and was forced to leave its historic premises in Aston. It is now located at Aldridge in the West Midlands in premises shared with Volant Passenger Vehicle Solutions, and is again open regularly to the public.
Chairman: Martin Fisher
Vice Chairman: Richard Gray

BRITISH BUS PRESERVATION GROUP
42A Moss Lane, Platt Bridge, Wigan WN2 3TL
E-mail: info@bbpg.co.uk
Web site: www.bbpg.co.uk

The Group's role is to help rescue historic buses and coaches for preservation by providing advice and assistance with the problems that arise, particularly for newcomers to the hobby. We also aim to alert as many people as possible to rare buses and coaches that are in danger of being lost forever in the hope that rescuers can be found for them.
Chairman & Treasurer: Geoff Percy, E-mail: chairman@bbpg.co.uk.
Secretary: Mike Lloyd, E-mail: secretary@bbpg.co.uk.
Membership Secretary: Steve Mortimore, E-mail: members@bbpg.co.uk.
Storage Co-ordinator: Nick Larkin, E-mail: storage@bbpg.co.uk.
Vehicle Co-ordinator: Dr John Willis, E-mail: vehicles@bbpg.co.uk.

BRITISH TROLLEYBUS SOCIETY
Web site: www.britishtrolley.org.uk
Formed as the Reading Transport Society in 1961, the present title was adopted in 1971, having acquired a number of trolleybuses for preservation from all over Britain. In 1969 it founded the Trolleybus Museum at Sandtoft, near Doncaster, where its vehicles are housed and regularly operate on mains power from the overhead wiring. West Yorkshire Transport Circle merged into the Society in January 1991. Currently membership stands at about 320. Members receive the monthly journal Trolleybus containing news and articles from home and abroad. Additionally members can subscribe to Bus Fare and Wheels, monthly magazines for motorbus operation in the Thames Valley and West Yorkshire areas respectively. Monthly meetings are also held in Reading, London and Bradford.
Secretary: A. J. Barton, 2 Josephine Court, Southcote Road, Reading RG30 2DG
Tel: 0118 958 3974
E-mail: secretary@britishtrolley.org.uk

BUSES WORLDWIDE
37, Oyster Lane, Byfleet, Surrey KT14 7HS
Tel: 01932 352351
E-mail: membership@busesworldwide.org
Web site: www.busesworldwide.org
Buses Worldwide is the international society for those interested in buses and coaches beyond their own country.
Chairman: Steve Guess
Vice-Chairman: Brian Grigg
Secretary: Simon Brown
Treasurer and Membership: Stuart Harvey
Editor, Buses Worldwide: Malcolm Chase
Editor, Maltese Transport News: Darren Vickers
Editor, British Buses Abroad: Paul Bateson

CLASSIC BUS HERITAGE TRUST LTD (INCORPORATING THE ROUTEMASTER HERITAGE TRUST)
The Classic Bus Heritage Trust aims to advance preservation of buses and coaches by fostering the interests of the general public. It is a Registered Charity.
Treasurer & Hon Sec: W. Ackroyd, 8 Twining Road, Ventnor, Isle of Wight PO38 1TX

ESSEX BUS ENTHUSIASTS' GROUP
272 Shoebury Road, Southend-on-Sea, Essex SS1 3TT
E-mail: admin@signal-training.com
Web site: www.essexbus.org.uk
EBEG was formed in 1962, under its previous title, Eastern National Enthusiasts' Group. The present title was adopted in 1987 to reflect more fully the activities of the group. EBEG publishes a monthly illustrated magazine 'Essex Bus News', holds regular meetings in South and North Essex, and offers

publications, photo sales, and coach tours. Annual subscription of £21 includes 12 issues of Essex Bus News.
Secretary: Alan Osborne
Membership Secretary/Treasurer: Richard Delahoy

GB BUS GROUP
Membership Enquiries: gbbgsecretary_memsec@yahoo.co.uk
Web site: www.gbbusgroup.co.uk
Chairman: Vacant
Secretary: Hazel Roberts
Treasurer: Frank Gold
The GB Bus Group was formed in 2006 to help attract new enthusiasts to the hobby. It provides a monthly magazine as well as a full range of bus and coach fleet books covering UK and Ireland. The GB Bus Group is a member of the UK Transport Group.

HISTORIC COMMERCIAL VEHICLE SOCIETY
The Society was founded in 1958 and four years later absorbed the Vintage Passenger Vehicle Society and the London Vintage Taxi Club. Its membership of over 4,000 owns more than 6,000 preserved vehicles. Activities include the organisation of rallies, among them the well known London to Brighton and Trans-Pennine runs. The club caters for all commercial vehicles over 20 years old.
OFFICERS
President: Lord Montagu of Beaulieu
Co Sec: David Heasman, "Southern", Hardwick, Aylesbury HP22 4DU
E-mail: hcvs2011@gmail.com
Web site: www.hcvs.co.uk

LEYLAND NATIONAL GROUP
E-mail: chairman@leylandnationalgroup.co.uk
Web site: www.leylandnationalgroup.co.uk
The Leyland National Group was formed in 1997 and has members throughout Great Britain and abroad. Although the group does not own any vehicles itself, some of its members are bus owners. There are more than 100 Leyland Nationals from a variety of operators preserved by group members. However, one does not need to own a bus to join the group, as membership is open to anyone with an interest in Leyland Nationals. The group also caters for those interested in the derivatives of the Leyland National; the Leyland-DAB, Leyland B21 and Leyland National bodied rail vehicles. Members receive a colour illustrated quarterly magazine, exclusive access to the members' only area on the group's website as well as other benefits. Please contact the Membership Secretary for more information about the group, the benefits of membership and to receive a membership application form.
Chairman: Alan Fairbrother
Treasurer: Mike Bellinger
Magazine Editor: Gavin Robinson
Membership Secretary: Andrew Fraulo
E-mail: membership@leylandnationalgroup.co.uk
Web site: www.leylandnationalgroup.co.uk

LINCOLNSHIRE VINTAGE VEHICLE SOCIETY
Road Transport Museum, Whisby Road, North Hykeham, Lincoln LN6 5TR
Tel: 01522 500566/689497
E-mail: info@lvvs.org.uk
Web site: www.lvvs.org.uk
The LVVS was founded in 1959 by local businessmen with the aim of forming a road transport museum. Charitable status was obtained some time ago, and with a capital grant from its local district council, it has now completed the first stage of its new

museum project. Over 60 vehicles dating from the 1920s to the 1980s can be seen in the new exhibition hall with many more in the workshop.
Opening times: November–April Sundays 13.00-16.00. May–October Mon-Fri 12.00-16.00, Sun 10.00-16.00.
Chairman: S Milner
Hon Treasurer: J Child
Secretary: Mrs J Jefford

THE LONDON BUS MUSEUM
Registered Charity: 1053383
Registered Company: 1061762
Cobham Hall, Brooklands Road, Weybridge, Surrey, KT13 0QN
Tel: 01932 837994
E-mail: londonbusmuseum@gmail.com
Web site: www.londonbusmuseum.com
Open daily to the public, the museum houses the world's largest collection of historic working London buses, covering a century of transport from 1870s horse buses to the last pre-low floor types. Admission is shared with Brooklands Museum.
Hon Vice Presidents: Sir Peter Hendy CBE, Leon Daniels
Chairman: Guy Marriott (to 27 September 2014)
Curatorial Director: Vacant
Interim Treasurer: Peter Osborn
Managing Director: Gerry Job
Rolling Stock Director: Roger Stagg
Human Resources Director: Steve Edmonds

LONDON OMNIBUS TRACTION SOCIETY (LOTS)
Unit N305, Westminster Business Square, 1-45 Durham Street, Vauxhall, London SE11 5JH
Web site: www.lots.org.uk
Formed nearly fifty years ago in 1964, LOTS is the largest bus enthusiast society in the United Kingdom.
A colour Illustrated monthly newsletter is sent to all members. This covers all the current operators in the former London Transport area and includes General and Industry News, Route Developments, Vehicle News for the area, subsequent vehicle movements and service vehicle updates. Meetings are held most months in central London featuring guest speakers, slide and film presentations during the year as well as the annual free bus rides from central London using vehicles of London interest.
Regular LOTS publications include fleet allocations and route working publications as well as the popular annual *London Bus and Tram Fleetbook* and the London Bus annual review. A quarterly 64 -page glossy magazine, *the London Bus Magazine* (LBM) has been produced for over 40 years.
Regular sales lists are produced and sent out to all members. An information service is also available to all members to help answer those historical queries.
The Autumn Transport Spectacular (ATS) is held in London every autumn and is one of London's biggest transport sales.
All enquiries should be directed to the above address.

THE M & D AND EAST KENT BUS CLUB
2 Gaiger Close, Chelmsford Essex CM1 6UR
E-mail: mdekbusclub@gmail.com
Web site: www.mdekbusclub.org.uk
This club was formed in 1952 with the object of bringing together all those interested in road passenger transport in an area covering Kent and East Sussex. Facilities for members include an illustrated monthly news booklet ("Invicta"), information service, tours, meetings, vehicle photograph sales and vehicle

preservation. A series of publications is also produced, including illustrated fleet histories.
Hon Chairman: Richard Mellor
Hon Secretary: Lee Crust
Hon Editor: Nicholas King
Hon Treasurer: John Collins
Membership Officer: Alex Fairley
Photographic Officer: Brian Weeden
Sales Officer: Myles Chantler
Tours Officer: David Cobb
Management Committee: Richard Mellor, Lee Crust, John Collins, Nicholas King, Richard Lewis, Myles Chantler, David Jenkins. There are Area Organisers providing local contact points and arranging Club member meetings in Dover, Folkestone, Hastings, North-East Kent, Maidstone and the Medway Towns.

THE NATIONAL TRAMWAY MUSEUM
Crich, Matlock DE4 5DP
Tel: 01773 854321
Fax: 01773 854320
E-mail: enquiry@tramway.co.uk
Web site: www.tramway.co.uk
The Society was founded in 1955 to establish and operate a working tramway museum. The Museum is at Crich Tramway Village, Crich, near Matlock, in Derbyshire, and owns over 70 English, Irish, Scottish, Welsh and overseas tramcars. Members receive a copy of the Society's quarterly journal and can participate in the running of the museum.
Patron: HRH The Duke of Gloucester GCVO
Vice-Presidents: G S Hearse, G B Claydon, D J H Senior
Chairman: C Heaton
Vice-Chairman: J A Blythe
Hon Secretary: I M Dougill
Hon Treasurer: M V Ballinger
Tramway Operations Manager: M D Gurr

NATIONAL TROLLEYBUS ASSOCIATION
2 St John's Close, Claines, Worcester WR3 7PT
Tel: 01449 740876
Web site: www.trolleybus.co.uk/nta
Formed in 1963, and incorporated in 1968 as The Trolleybus Museum Co Ltd. The vehicles and ancillary equipment collected by the NTA since its inception are now owned by the company, which is limited by guarantee and is a registered charity. Members receive Trolleybus Magazine, a printed and illustrated bi-monthly journal documenting all aspects of trolleybus operation past and present throughout the world.
Chairman: M J Russell
Secretary: J H Ward
Treasurer: E M H Humphreys
Membership Secretary: D Lawrence
Enquiries: tmbmembsec@hotmail.com

THE OMNIBUS SOCIETY LTD
The Omnibus Society was founded in 1929. Today it is a nationwide organisation with a network of provincial branches, offering a comprehensive range of facilities for those interested in the bus and coach industry. The Society has accumulated a wealth of information on public road transport. Members have the opportunity to receive and exchange data on every aspect of the industry including route developments, operational/traffic matters and fleet changes. Each branch has a full programme of activities and publishes its own Branch Bulletin to give local news of route changes, etc. A scheme exists whereby members subscribe to receive bulletins from branches other than that of which they are a member. A programme of indoor meetings is customary during winter,

including film shows, invited speakers and discussions. In the summer months visits to manufacturers and tours to operators are featured. The Society maintains a comprehensive library and archive which may be visited by members and non-members undertaking research, together with separate photographic and ticket collections.
Address: 100 Sandwell Street, Walsall WS1 3EB
Tel: 01922 629358
E-mail: oslibrary@btconnect.com
Web site: www.omnibus-soc.org.

OFFICERS
President (2014): Ben Colson
President (2015): Sir Brian Souter
Vice-Presidents: F P Groves, A W Mills, G Wedlake, T F McLachlan, K W Swallow, Professor John Hibbs, B LeJeune
Chairman: H L Barker
Secretary: A J Francis, 185 Southlands Road, Bromley BR2 9QZ
Treasurer: R Williams, 191 Station Road, Shotts ML7 4BA
Librarian/Archivist: Alan Mills
Editor, Society's Publications: Cyril McIntyre
Directors: D L Akrigg, K D Barclay, R T Barker, I D Barlex, G A Booth, J Peddle, J D Howie, G Lusher, R Williams
Branch Officers:
Midland Branch: G Lusher, 6 Colling Drive, Lichfield WS13 8FJ
South Wales and West Branch: Mike Walker, Combe Barton, High Street, Dinder, Wells, Somerset BA5 3PL
Northern Branch: Peter Cardno, 22 Welldale Crescent, Fairfield, Stockton-on-Tees TS19 7HU
North Western & Yorkshire Branch: P Wilkinson, 10 Bradley Close, Timperley, Altrincham WA15 6SH
Scottish Branch: R Williams, 191 Station Road, Shotts ML7 4BA
Eastern & Southern Branch: R Barton, 5 Viscount Court, Knights Field, Luton LU2 7LD
Essex & South Suffolk Group: R N Collins, 2 Brickmakers Lane, Turner Rise, Colchester CO4 5WP
East Midland Group: A Oxley, 4 Gordon Close, Attenborough, Nottingham NN4 9UF
Herts & Beds Group: R C Barton, 5 Viscount Court, Knights Field, Luton LU2 7LD
London Historical Research Group: C Holland, 30 Essex Road, Longfield DA3 7QL
Provincial Historical Research Group: A E Jones, 8 Poplar Drive, Church Stretton S76 7BW

POPS – POTTERIES OMNIBUS PRESERVATION SOCIETY
c/o 58 Newcastle Street, Burslem, Stoke-on-Trent ST6 3QF
E-mail: 44lf88@gmail.com
Web site:
www.potteriesomnibus.wordpress.com
The Society was formed in 1977 to preserve former Potteries Motor traction (PMT) buses starting with the purchase of a rare Leyland OPD2/1, the export version of the PD2. The society holds two annual rallies and running days usually in May and late summer/early autumn. A full colour magazine is published quarterly and Society meetings take place monthly to keep its membership informed.
President: John Cooke
Chairman: Adrian Hunt
Hon. Secretary: Lynda Fee
Hon. Treasurer: Dave Roberts

THE PSV CIRCLE
Unit GK, Leroy House, 436 Essex Road, London N1 3QP
E-mail: enquiries@psv-circle.org.uk

Web site: www.psv-circle.org.uk
The aim of the PSV Circle is to be the definitive source of all knowledge on Public Service Vehicles and Operators throughout the United Kingdom. We produce a wide range of Publications including operator fleet histories, chassis lists, body lists, as well as current fleet lists covering Great Britain and Ireland.
HONORARY OFFICERS
Chairman: Chris Elkin
Secretary: John Skilling
Treasurer: Paul Whiteside
Membership & Administration Manager: Steve Fitzgerald
Rally Sales Team & Website Manager: Paul Young
News Sheet Despatch Manager: Adrian Clarke
Publication Manager: Fred Ward

RIBBLE ENTHUSIASTS' CLUB
23 Richmond Road, Hindley Green, Wigan WN2 4ND
Tel: 01942 253497
E-mail: mjyat@msn.com
Founded in 1954 by the late T. B. Collinge for the study of road transport past and present and in particular Ribble Motor Services and associated companies. Meetings are held and a monthly news sheet produced.
Life President: A E Chapman
Life Vice President: M Shires
Vice Presidents: N Winter, L Burton, Ms C Tasker
Committee Chairman: D Bailey MBE
Secretary: M J Yates, 23 Richmond Road, Hindley Green, Wigan WN2 4ND
Treasurer: R A Harpum, 107 New Road, West Parley, Ferndown, Dorset BH22 8EA
Records: S Blake, 23 Fairfield Road, North Shore, Blackpool FY1 2RA
Sales Dept: Mrs T Ashcroft, 11 Regent Road, Walton le Dale, Preston PR5 4QA
Sales Dept: Assistant: Mrs J Yates, 23 Richmond Road, Hindley Green, Wigan WN2 4ND
Archive: B Ashcroft, 11 Regent Road, Walton Le Dale, Preston PR5 4QA
Editor: R Kenyon, 18 Hatfield Road, Accrington BB5 6DF
Membership Sec: B Downham, 203 Brindle Road, Bamber Bridge, Preston PR5 6YL
Publicity Officer/Tours: D Barrow, 25 Birley Street, Bury, Lancashire BL9 5DT

ROADS AND ROAD TRANSPORT HISTORY ASSOCIATION LTD
32 Marina Villas, Swansea SA1 1FZ
Tel: 01792 809095
E-mail: robert.mccloy36@sky.com
Web site: www.rrtha.org.uk
Chairman: Dr Robert McCloy
Co Sec: J D Howie
Registered Address: 100 Sandwell Street, Walsall WS1 3EB
The association's objectives are to promote, encourage and co-ordinate the history of the history of roads and road transport, both passenger and freight. It aims to further understanding of the past to bring wisdom to the present and foresight to the future, whether it is legislation, logistics, urban planning, vehicle design or the environment. The association holds regular meetings, publishes a quarterly journal and books, and maintains a web site. It acts as a clearing house between members, societies, museums and academic bodies.

ROUTEMASTER ASSOCIATION
31 Pooley Avenue, Egham, Surrey TW20 8AD
Web site: www.routemaster.org.uk
The Routemaster Association was formed over 20 years ago in 1988 and is now believed

to be the largest single type bus owners group in the UK, if not the world. In 2014, the Routemaster Association staged the largest ever gathering of Routemasters to commemorate Routemaster 60.
Today, our aims are more valid so than ever before.
- We pool knowledge and operating experience
- We collect and make available technical information
- We look into the past and future developments
- We assist in the procurement and make available spare parts
- We make available information on known Suppliers
- We cater for the historical and preservation interest
- We enable contact with other Routemaster owners
The Routemaster Association exists to help unite Routemaster owners and to assist them in keeping their vehicles running. These days, the remnants of the London fleets are widely distributed across the world, with many now owned by small operators, preservationists or other private owners. Through the economies of scale, together we can commission parts that are now longer available.
Membership is open to all operators and owners of Routemaster type vehicles, as well as to suppliers of parts or services for these vehicles, and also to those with a genuine interest in Routemasters.

All enquiries should be directed to the above address, or via the *contact page* on the website.
Vice Presidents: Andrew Morgan and George Watson

THE SAMUEL LEDGARD SOCIETY
58 Kirklees Drive, Farsley, Pudsey, West Yorkshire LS28 5TE
Tel: 0113 236 3695
E-mail: Rennison@cc-email.co.uk
Web Site: www.samuelledgardsociety.org.uk
The Samuel Ledgard Society was formed in 1998 at the Rose & Crown Inn, Otley, during the second annual reunion of the devotees of this well-known bus company. Reunions are held twice yearly at Armley during April and Otley on or about October 14. A Christmas dinner is also part of the established calendar of events. The quarterly journal of the Society, The Chat, is published in March, June, September and December each year. Founding officers were Barry Rennison, Tony Greaves and Don Bate, all of whom have a wealth of knowledge about the Samuel Ledgard company. Membership is open to all with a subscription of £5 - contact any member of the Committee for details.
Hon President: Mrs Jenny Barron
COMMITTEE
Chairman: Barry Rennison
Vice-Chairman, Magazine Editor & Publicity Officer: Tony Greaves
Treasurer: Bryan Whitham
Secretary: Margaret Rennison

SCOTTISH TRAMWAY & TRANSPORT SOCIETY
87 Holmfauldhead Drive, Glasgow G51 4PZ
Tel: 0141 445 3883
Fax: 0141 440 2955
E-mail: stts.glasgow@virgin.net
Web site: www.scottishtransport.org
The Society aims to study and preserve the history of all aspects of Scottish transport, and to publish the results..
Chairman: Frank Mitchell
Gen Secretary: Hugh McAulay
Hon Treasurer: Alan Ramsay

SOUTH YORKSHIRE TRANSPORT MUSEUM

Waddington Way, Aldwarke, Rotherham
S65 3SH
Tel: 0114 255 3010
E-mail: info@sytm.co.uk
Web site: www.sytm.co.uk
The Sheffield Bus Museum Trust was formed in 1987 with the purpose of co-ordinating the bus preservation movement in Sheffield and to establish a permanent museum. This was initially achieved at the former Sheffield Tramways Company's Tinsley Tram Depot but in 2007 the Trust moved its collection to new premises at Aldwarke, Rotherham. At the same time the museum as re-branded to the name above. The majority of the Trust's collection is local and extremely varied, ranging from a 1919 Sentinel steam lorry to a 1984 Leyland Titan open top bus. In recent years the Museum Trust has benefitted from Heritage Fund Lottery grants. The museum is an educational charity and promotes an ever-expanding schools visits programme. The museum is open to the public on a monthly basis from March to December.
Chairman: Douglas Miller
Membership Secretary: Andrew Nolan (please address enquiries to Andrew at the museum's address)

SOUTHDOWN ENTHUSIASTS' CLUB

Web site:
www.southdownenthusiastsclub.org.uk
The Southdown Enthusiasts' Club (founded 1954) covers the major bus operators in East Sussex, West Sussex, Hampshire and East Kent.
Hon Secretary: Norman Simes, 11 High Cross Fields, Crowborough TN6 2SN (send large SAE for membership details)
Hon Sales Officer: David Chalkley, 6 Valebridge Drive, Burgess Hill RH15 0RW (postal sales only)
Hon Photo Circuit Officer: Michael Cockett, 64 Edinburgh Road, St Leonards-on-Sea TN38 8DB

SWINDON VINTAGE OMNIBUS SOCIETY

10 Fraser Close, Nythe, Swindon SN3 3RP
Tel: 01793 526001
E-mail: davenicol@virginmedia.com
Web site: www.svos112168.webs.com
The Society was formed in 1968. A magazine is published bi-monthly. The Membership Fee is £12 adult, £10 senior citizen and £6 child. Two vehicles are owned, both ex Swindon Corporation, a 1960 Daimler CVG6 and a 1975 Bristol RESL.
Chairman: Michael Naughton
Secretary: David Nicol
Treasurer: Derek Wiggins
Membership Secretary: Nigel Robinson

THE TRANSPORT MUSEUM SOCIETY OF IRELAND

Howth Castle Demesne, Howth,
PO Box 11737, Dublin 13
Tel: 00 353 1 848 0831
E-mail: info@nationaltransportmuseum.org
Web site:
www.nationaltransportmuseum.org
A commercial vehicle collection of trams, buses, fire appliances, military vehicles, lorries and horse-drawn vehicles. Open Sat/Sun/Public Holidays 1400-1700. Groups may attend at other times by appointment.
Hon Chairman: John Kelleher
Hon Secretary: John Molloy

THE TRANSPORT MUSEUM, WYTHALL

Birmingham & Midland Motor Omnibus Trust, The Transport Museum, Chapel Lane, Wythall, Worcestershire B47 6JX
Tel: 01564 826471
E-mail: enquiries@wythall.org.uk
Web site: www.wythall.org.uk
The Trust dates back to 1973, taking its present title in 1977, when it became a registered educational charity to establish and develop a regional transport museum.
The museum comprises an exhibition hall, plus two other halls, housing 100 buses, coaches and battery-electric vehicles, mostly operated and/or built in the Midlands. The Museum is also licensed as a bus operator and some exhibits can be hired for appropriate work.
Trustees: Paul Gray (Treasurer), Kevin Hill, Philip Ireland (Museum Manager), Malcolm Keeley (Collections Manager), James Munro, Peter Murphy, David Potts, Jeremy Price, David Taylor (Chairman).

TRAMWAY & LIGHT RAILWAY SOCIETY

Web site: www.tramwayinfo.co.uk
Founded in 1938, the Tramway & Light Railway Society caters for those interested in all aspects of tramways. Members receive Tramfare, a bi-monthly illustrated magazine. There are regular meetings throughout the country. The Society promotes tramway modelling, drawings, castings, and technical details are available to modellers. There are also comprehensive library facilities. For fuller details of the Society and of membership please write to the Membership Secretary.
HONORARY OFFICERS
President: G B Claydon C.B.
Vice-President: P J Davis
Chairman: J R Prentice, 216 Brentwood Road, Romford RM1 2RP.
Secretary: G R Tribe, 47 Soulbury Road, Linslade, Leighton Buzzard LU7 7RW
Membership Secretary: J T Service, 29 Kennaway Road, Clevedon, Somerset BS21 6JJ

THE TRANSPORT TICKET SOCIETY (TTS)

The TTS is for anyone interested in transport tickets, past and present. Facilities include a monthly illustrated journal, regular meetings, ticket exchange pools, monthly ticket distributions, and postal auctions of scarce tickets.
Membership Secretary: Steve Skeavington, 6 Breckbank, Forest Town, Mansfield NG19 0PZ
Web site: www.transport-ticket.org.uk

THE TRANSPORT TRUST

202 Lambeth Road, London SE1 7JW
Tel: 020 7928 6464
Fax: 020 7928 6565
E-mail: info@transporttrust.com
Web Site: www.transporttrust.com
Patron: HRH Prince Michael of Kent
The Trust is the national charity for the preservation and restoration of Britain's transport heritage.

PASSENGER TRANSPORT MUSEUMS

This list is in addition to those shown in the main Society section above.

ABBEY PUMPING STATION

Corporation Road, Leicester LE4 5PX
Tel: 0116 299 5111
Fax: 0116 299 5125
Web site: www.abbeypumpingstation.org

AMBERLEY MUSEUM & HERITAGE CENTRE

Houghton Bridge, Arundel, West Sussex BN18 9LT
Tel: 01798 831370
Fax: 01798 831831
E-mail: office@amberleymuseum.co.uk
Web site: www.amberleymuseum.co.uk

ASTON MANOR ROAD TRANSPORT MUSEUM

See Societies section

BLACK COUNTRY LIVING MUSEUM TRANSPORT GROUP

Tipton Road, Dudley DY1 4SQ
Tel: 0121 557 9643
E-mail: info@bclm.co.uk
Web site: wwww.bclm.co.uk

BRISTOL ROAD TRANSPORT COLLECTION

E-mail: william.staniforth@virgin.net
Web site: www.bristolbusevents.co.uk

BRITISH COMMERCIAL VEHICLE MUSEUM

King Street, Leyland PR25 2LE
Tel: 01772 451011
Fax: 01772 451015
E-mail: enquiries@bcvm.co.uk
Web site: www.bcvm.co.uk

CARDIFF TRANSPORT PRESERVATION GROUP (BARRY BUS DEPOT)

Secretary: 16 Carter Place, Fairwater, Cardiff CF5 3NP
E-mail: info@ctpg.co.uk
Web site: www.ctpg.co.uk

CASTLE POINT TRANSPORT MUSEUM

105 Point Road, Canvey Island SS8 7TP
Tel: 01268 684272
E-mail: castlepointtransportmuseum@yahoo.co.uk
Web site: www.castlepointtransportmuseum.co.uk

CAVAN AND LEITRIM RAILWAY

Narrow Gauge Station, Station Road, Dromod, Co Leitrim, Ireland
Tel/Fax: 00353 71 963 8599
E-mail: dromod@eircom.net
Web site: www.cavanandleitrim.com

COVENTRY TRANSPORT MUSEUM

Millennium Place, Hales Street, Coventry CV1 1PN
Tel: 024 7623 4270
Fax: 024 7623 4284
E-mail: enquiries@transport-museum.com
Web site: www.transport-museum.com

DOVER TRANSPORT MUSEUM

Willingdon Road, Whitfield, Dover CT16 2HJ
Tel: 01304 822409
E-mail: info@dovertransportmuseum.org.uk
Web site: www.dovertransportmuseum.org.uk
Chairman & General Manager: D Atkins

EAST ANGLIA TRANSPORT MUSEUM

Chapel Road, Carlton Colville, Lowestoft NR33 8BL
Tel: 01502 518459
Fax: 01502 584658
E-mail: eastangliatransportmuseum@live.co.uk
Web site: www.eatm.org.uk

GRAMPIAN TRANSPORT MUSEUM

Alford, Aberdeenshire AB33 8AE
Tel: 01975 562292
Fax: 01975 562180
E-mail: info@gtm.org.uk
Web site: www.gtm.org.uk

IPSWICH TRANSPORT MUSEUM

Cobham Road, Ipswich IP3 9JD
Tel: 01473 715666
E-mail:
enquiries@ipswichtransportmuseum.co.uk
Web site:
www.ipswichtransportmuseum.co.uk
Chair of Trustees: Mark Smith
Secretary: Mike Abbott
A voluntary independent museum with
regular public opening times between Easter
and November. Large exhibits range from
horse drawn carriages through trams and
trolleybuses to motor buses, plus a variety of
other transport and engineering objects. The
museum also has a large archive of documents
and photographs.

ISLE OF WIGHT BUS MUSEUM

Newport Quay, Newport, Isle of Wight
PO30 2EF
Tel: 01983 533352
E-mail: info@iowbusmuseum.org.uk
Web site: www.iowbusmuseum.org.uk

KEIGHLEY BUS MUSEUM TRUST

Contact address: 47 Brantfell Drive, Burnley
BB12 8AW
Tel: 01282 413179
E-mail: shmdboard@aol.com
Web site: www.kbmt.org
Chairman: I S Bonner
Secretary: D A Jones
Treasurer: M J Jessop
The museum's collection comprises some
75 buses, coaches, trolleybuses and ancillary
vehicles, mainly of local origin. The Trust also
operates a small selection of vehicles for hire.

LONDON BUS MUSEUM

See Societies section

LONDON TRANSPORT MUSEUM

Covent Garden Piazza, London WC2E 7BB
Tel: 020 7379 6344; recorded information
020 7565 7299
Fax: 020 7565 7254
E-mail: resourcedesk@ltmuseum.co.uk
Web site: www.ltmuseum.co.uk

MIDLAND ROAD TRANSPORT
GROUP - BUTTERLEY

The Midland Railway, Butterley Hill, Ripley,
Derbyshire DE5 3QZ
Tel: 01773 747674
Fax: 01773 570721
Web site:
www.midlandrailway-butterley.co.uk

MUSEUM OF TRANSPORT, GREATER
MANCHESTER

Boyle Street, Cheetham, Manchester M8 8UW
Tel: 0161 205 2122
Fax: 0161 202 1110

E-mail: email@gmts.co.uk
Web site: www.gmts.co.uk
**Chairman, Greater Manchester
Transport Society:** Dennis Talbot
The museum charts the development of public
transport in Greater Manchester, with exhibits
ranging from a Victorian horse-drawn bus to a
full size prototype Metrolink tram.

SCIENCE MUSEUM GROUP

(Science Museum, National Media Museum,
National Railway Museum)
Exhibition Road, London SW7 2DD
Tel: 0207 942 4000
Web site: www.sciencemuseum.org.uk

THE NORTH OF ENGLAND OPEN
AIR MUSEUM

Beamish, Durham DH9 0RG
Tel: 0191 370 4000
Fax: 0191 370 4001
E-mail: museum@beamish.org.uk
Web site: www.beamish.org.uk

THE NATIONAL TRAMWAY MUSEUM

See Societies Section

NORTH WEST MUSEUM OF ROAD
TRANSPORT

The Old Bus Depot, 51 Hall Street,
St Helens WA10 1DU
Tel: 01744 451681
E-mail: info@nwmort.co.uk
Web site: www.nwmort.co.uk
Chairman: Geoff Nicholson
Secretary: Clive Arnold
The museum is open Saturdays and Sundays
between 1200 and 1600, also at Bank Holidays
(except Christmas and New Year). There are
regular special events – see the web site for
details. Over 70 buses, cars and commercial
vehicles are on display. Free heritage bus
services operate on event days and on the
first Sunday each month.

NOTTINGHAM TRANSPORT
HERITAGE CENTRE

Contact address: Mere Way, Ruddington,
Nottingham NG11 6NX
Tel: 0115 940 5705
Web site:
www.nottinghamtransportheritagecentre.
co.uk

OXFORD BUS MUSEUM

Station Yard, Long Hanborough, Witney
OX29 8LA
Tel: 01993 883617
Web site: www.oxfordbusmuseum.org.uk
The museum has two exhibition halls tracing
the history of local transport. Restoration
can be viewed from the workshop gallery. The
museum is open throughout the year.

RIVERSIDE MUSEUM – SCOTLAND'S
MUSEUM OF TRANSPORT AND
TRAVEL

100 Pointhouse Place, Glasgow G3 8RS
Tel: 0141 287 2720
E-mail: museums@glasgowlife.org.uk
Web site:
www.glasgowlife.org.uk/museums/riverside

SCOTTISH VINTAGE BUS MUSEUM

M90 Commerce Park, Lathalmond,
Dunfermline, Fife KY12 0SJ
Tel: 01383 623380
E-mail: jimc1502@gmail.com
Web site: www.svbm.org.uk

SWANSEA BUS MUSEUM

Langdon Road, Port Tennant, Swansea
SA1 8QY
Tel: 07531 677776
E-mail: info@swtbusgroup.org.uk
Web site: www.swanseabusmuseum.com

THE TRANSPORT MUSEUM,
WYTHALL

Birmingham & Midland Motor Omnibus
Trust
See Societies section

TRANSPORT MUSEUM SOCIETY
OF IRELAND

See Societies section

THE TROLLEYBUS MUSEUM AT
SANDTOFT

Belton Road, Sandtoft, North Lincolnshire
DN8 5SX
Tel: 01724 711391
E-mail: trolleybusmuseum@sandtoft.org
Web site: www.sandtoft.org.uk
Chairman & Engineering Director:
G Bilbe
Managing Director: S Harrison
Company Secretary: C B Lake
Financial & Development Director:
F Whitehead
The museum is home to the world's largest
collection of historic trolleybuses, and is open
selected weekends from April to December.

ULSTER FOLK & TRANSPORT
MUSEUM

Contact address: Cultra, Holywood,
Belfast BT18 0EU
Tel: 028 9042 8428
Web site: www.nmni.com/uftm

WIRRAL TRANSPORT MUSEUM

1 Taylor Street, Birkenhead
CH41 1BG
Tel: 0151 647 2128
Web site: www.wirral.gov.uk

British Operators' Organisations

NOTES

SECTION 4

ARRIVA PLC

1 Admiral Way, Doxford International Business
Park, Sunderland SR3 3XP
Tel: 0191 520 4000
Fax: 0191 520 4001
E-mail: enquiries@arriva.co.uk
Web site: www.arriva.co.uk
Arriva's parent company is Deutsche Bahn

Chief Executive:
David Martin
**Deputy CEO and Managing Director –
Mainland Europe:**
Mike Cooper
Finance Director:
Martin Hibbert
Director – Human Resources:
Alison O'Connor
Director – Business Excellence:
Thomas Oster

Arriva UK Bus
487 Dunstable Road, Luton,
LU4 8DS
Tel: 01582 587000
Fax: 01582 587009

**Operations and Commercial Director
– UK Bus:**
Mark Yexley
Engineering Director – UK Bus:
Ian Tarran
**Finance & Business Development
Director – UK Bus:**
Peter Telford
Human Resources Director – UK Bus:
Rachel Baldwin
**Managing Director, Arriva Transport
Solutions:**
Jonathan May

**Regional Managing Director, Yorkshire &
North East:**
Nigel Featham
**Regional Managing Director, North
West & Wales:**
Phil Stone
Regional Managing Director, Midlands:
Alex Perry
**Regional Managing Director, Southern
Counties & TGM:**
Heath Williams
Regional Managing Director, London:
Bob Scowen

Operating Regions,
Group Companies,
Principal Depots
(UK Bus):

● **Arriva Yorkshire**
(see North Yorkshire, West Yorkshire)
Depots at Castleford, Dewsbury,
Heckmondwike, Selby, Wakefield

● **Arriva North East**
(see Durham, Northumberland, Tyne & Wear)
Depots at Ashington, Blyth, Darlington,
Durham, Newcastle, Redcar, Stockton, Whitby

● **Arriva North West**
(see Cheshire, Greater Manchester, Merseyside)
Depots at Birkenhead, Bolton, Bootle,
Liverpool Green Lane, Liverpool Speke,
Runcorn, St Helens, Southport, Winsford,
Wythenshawe

● **Arriva Buses Wales**
(see Gwynedd)
Depots at Bangor, Chester, Rhyl, Wrexham

● **Arriva Midlands**
*(see Derbyshire, Leicestershire, Shropshire,
Staffordshire, West Midlands)*
Depots at Barwell, Bridgnorth, Burton-

on-Trent, Cannock, Derby, Leicester
(Thurmaston), Oswestry, Shrewsbury, Stafford,
Stoke on Trent (Wardles), Tamworth, Telford,
Wednesfield, Wigston

● **Arriva The Shires**
(see Bedfordshire, Buckinghamshire, Hertfordshire)
Depots at Aylesbury, Hemel Hempstead, High
Wycombe, Luton, Milton Keynes, Stevenage,
Ware, Watford

● **Arriva London**
(see London & Middlesex)
Depots at Barking, Brixton, Clapton, Croydon,
Edmonton, Enfield, Hackney, Norwood,
Palmers Green, Stamford Hill, Thornton Heath,
Tottenham, Wood Green

● **Arriva Southern Counties**
(see Essex, Kent, Surrey)
Depots at Dartford, Gillingham, Grays,
Guildford, Maidstone, Northfleet, Sheerness,
Southend, Tonbridge (New Enterprise
Coaches), Tunbridge Wells

● **T G M Group Ltd**
(see Durham, Essex, London & Middlesex)
Includes Classic Coaches, Network
Colchester, Network Harlow, OFJ
Connections, Tellings Golden Miller Coaches
Depots at Colchester, Gatwick Airport,
Harlow, Heathrow Airport, Stanley, Stansted
Airport

● **Other Operations**
(see West Yorkshire)
Yorkshire Tiger
Depots at Elland, Honley, Huddersfield, Leeds

Overseas Interests:
Arriva has extensive overseas interests in
Croatia (bus), the Czech Republic (bus and
rail), Denmark (bus and rail), Hungary (bus),
Italy (bus), Netherlands (bus and rail), Poland
(bus and rail), Portugal (bus), Serbia (bus),
Slovakia (bus), Slovenia (bus), Spain (bus),
Sweden (bus and rail)

UK Rail Franchises:
Arriva Trains Wales, Chiltern Railways, Cross
Country, Grand Central Railway, London
Overground, Tyne & Wear Metro

Other Interests:
Arriva Bus & Coach *(see Trade Directory)*;
Arriva Transport Solutions

Major Groups

First
transforming travel

FIRSTGROUP PLC
395 King Street, Aberdeen AB24 5RP
Tel: 01224 650100
Fax: 01224 650140
Web Site: www.firstgroupplc.com

Chairman:
John McFarlane
Chief Executive:
Tim O'Toole CBE
Group Finance Director:
Chris Surch
Non-Executive Directors:
Mick Barker, Warwick Brady, Drummond Hall,
Brian Wallace, Imelda Walsh, Jim Winestock

UK Bus
Managing Director UK Bus:
Giles Fearnley
**Business Efficiency & Engineering
Director:**
David Liston
Finance Director:
Stuart Munro
**Regional Managing Director, North and
Scotland:**
Dave Alexander
**Regional Managing Director, Wales &
South of England:**
Neil Barker

**Operating Regions,
Group Companies,
Principal Depots
(UK Bus):**

• **First Aberdeen, First Aberdeen
Coaching Unit**
(Includes Grampian Coaches)
(see City of Aberdeen)
Depot at Aberdeen

• **First Scotland East**
(see Falkirk, Stirling)
Depots at Balfron, Bannockburn, Galashiels,
Larbert, Livingston, Musselburgh, North Berwick

• **First Glasgow**
(see City of Glasgow)
Depots at Blantyre, Dumbarton, Glasgow (3),
Overtown

• **First West Yorkshire**
(see West Yorkshire)
Depots at Bradford, Bramley, Halifax,
Huddersfield, Leeds

• **First South Yorkshire and York**
(see North Yorkshire, South Yorkshire)
Depots at Doncaster, Rotherham, Sheffield,
York

• **First Manchester**
(Includes First Pioneer Bus)
(see Greater Manchester)
Depots at Bolton, Bury, Manchester, Oldham,
Rusholme, Tameside

• **First Midlands**
(Includes First Leicester, First Potteries,
First Wyvern)
*(see Herefordshire, Leicestershire, Staffordshire,
Worcestershire)*

Depots at Hereford, Leicester, Newcastle-
under-Lyme, Stoke-on-Trent, Worcester

• **First Eastern Counties**
(see Norfolk, Suffolk)
Depots at Great Yarmouth, Ipswich, Kings
Lynn, Lowestoft, Norwich

• **First Essex**
(see Essex)
Depots at Basildon, Braintree, Chelmsford,
Clacton, Colchester, Hadleigh, Luton Airport

• **First Hampshire, Dorset and Berkshire**
(see Berkshire, Dorset, Hampshire)
Depots at Bracknell, Bridport, Fareham,
Portsmouth, Slough, Southampton, Weymouth

• **First Bristol, Somerset and the West
of England**
(see Bristol, Somerset)
Depots at Bath, Bristol (3), Weston super
Mare

• **First Devon, Cornwall and Central
Somerset**
(see Cornwall, Devon, Somerset)
Depots at Bridgwater, Camborne, Plymouth,
Taunton

• **First Cymru**
(see City & County of Swansea)
Depots at Bridgend, Cardiff, Carmarthen,
Haverfordwest, Llanelli, Port Talbot, Swansea

Overseas Interests:
First has a bus and coach operation in
Northern Ireland and the Republic of Ireland
– First Aircoach *(See Northern Ireland, Republic
of Ireland)* and extensive bus and coach
operations in the USA

UK Rail Operations:
First Great Western, First Trans Pennine
Express, First ScotRail, First Hull Trains

The Little Red Book 2015

Go-Ahead

GO-AHEAD GROUP PLC
4 Matthew Parker Street, London SW1H 9NP
Tel: 020 799 8999
E-mail: enquiries@go-ahead.com
Web Site: www.go-ahead.com

Chairman:
Andrew Allner
Group Chief Executive:
David Brown
Group Finance Director:
Keith Down
Group Company Secretary:
Carolyn Ferguson
Non-Executive Directors:
Adrian Ewer, Nick Horler, Katherine Innes Ker
Group Corporate Communications Director:
Sarah Boundy
Group Marketing Director:
Gillian Singh
Group Engineering Director:
Phil Margrave
Group HR Director:
Val Proctor

UK Bus
Managing Director, Bus Development:
Martin Dean

Operating Regions
Group Companies
Principal Depots
(UK Bus):

● **Go North East**
(see Durham, Northumberland, Tyne & Wear)

Depots at Chester le Street, Consett, Crook, Gateshead, Hexham, Newcastle, Peterlee, Stanley, Sunderland, Washington

● **Oxford Bus Company**
(see Oxfordshire)
Depot at Oxford

● **Thames Travel**
(see Oxfordshire)
Depot at Wallingford

● **Carousel Buses**
(see Buckinghamshire)
Depot at High Wycombe

● **Konectbus Ltd**
(see Norfolk)
Depot at Dereham

● **Anglian Bus Ltd**
(see Suffolk)
Depots at Beccles, Norwich

● **Hedingham & District Omnibuses Ltd**
(see Essex)
Depots at Clacton, Hedingham, Kelvedon, Tollesbury

● **H C Chambers & Son Ltd**
(see Suffolk)
Depot at Sudbury

● **Go-Ahead London**
(Includes Blue Triangle, Docklands Buses, London Central, London General, Metrobus (London operations)

(see London & Middlesex)
Depots at Belvedere, Bexleyheath, Camberwell, Croydon, Merton, New Cross, Northumberland Park, Orpington, Peckham, Putney, Rainham, Silvertown, Southwark, Stockwell, Sutton, Waterloo, Wimbledon

● **Metrobus**
(see West Sussex)
Depot at Crawley

● **Brighton & Hove Bus & Coach Company**
(see East Sussex)
Depots at Brighton (2), Hove

● **Go South Coast**
(includes Bells Coaches, Bluestar, Damory Coaches, Kingston Coaches, Levers Coaches, Marchwood Motorways, Southern Vectis, Tourist Coaches, Wilts & Dorset)
(see Dorset, Hampshire, Isle of Wight, Wiltshire)
Depots at Blandford, Bournemouth, Carisbrooke IOW, Dorchester, Eastleigh, Figheldean, Henstridge, Lymington, Newport IOW, Poole, Ringwood, Ryde IOW, Salisbury, Swanage, Totton

● **Plymouth Citybus**
(see Devon)
Depot at Plymouth

UK Rail Franchises:
London Midland, South Eastern, Thameslink, Southern & Great Northern

---

national express

NATIONAL EXPRESS GROUP PLC
National Express House, Mill Lane, Digbeth, Birmingham B5 6DD
Tel: 08450 130130
E-mail: info@nationalexpress.com
Web Site: www.nationalexpressgroup.com

Chairman:
Sir John Armitt
Group Chief Executive:
Dean Finch
Group Finance Director:
Jez Maiden
Deputy Chairman:
Jorge Cosmen
Non-Executive Directors:
Joaquin Ayuso, Sir Andrew Foster (retires 2015), Jackie Hunt, Jane Kingston, Chris Muntwyler, Elliott Sander
Company Secretary and Group Legal Director:
Michael Hampson
Trains Director (UK):
Andrew Chivers

Chief Executive, ALSA Group:
Javier Carbajo
Chief Executive Officer, North America:
David Duke

UK Bus and Coach
Managing Director, UK Bus:
Peter Coates
Operations Director, UK Bus:
Paul Thomas
Finance Director, UK Bus:
Matt Ashley

Managing Director, UK Coach:
Tom Stables

Operating Regions
Group Companies
Principal Depots
(UK Bus):

● **Kings Ferry Travel Group**
(see Kent)
Depot at Gillingham

● **National Express Coach**
(See London & Middlesex, West Midlands)
Depots at Gatwick, Luton, Heathrow, Stansted

● **National Express Dundee**
(see Dundee City)
Depot at Dundee

● **Midland Metro**
(see Section 5 – Tram Systems)

● **National Express West Midlands**
(See West Midlands)
Depots at Birmingham, Coventry, Dudley, Walsall, West Bromwich, Wolverhampton

Overseas interests:
National Express has extensive interests in Spain (ALSA), Canada (Stock Transportation), Germany (City2City), Morocco (ALSA) and the USA (Durham School Services, National Express Transit, Petermann)

UK Rail Franchises:
c2c

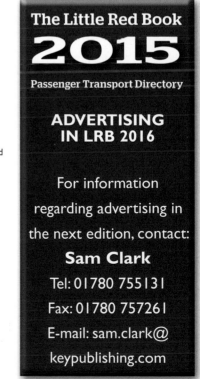
Major Groups

Stagecoach

STAGECOACH GROUP PLC
10 Dunkeld Road, Perth PH1 5TW
Tel: 01738 442111
Fax: 01738 643648
E-mail: info@stagecoachgroup.com
Web Site: www.stagecoach.com

Chairman:
Sir Brian Souter
Deputy Chairman & Senior Independent Director:
Garry Watts MBE
Chief Executive:
Martin Griffiths
Finance Director:
Ross Paterson
Non-Executive Directors:
Gregor Alexander, Sir Ewan Brown CBE, Ann Gloag OBE, Helen Mahy, Phil White CBE, Will Whitehorn
Company Secretary:
Mike Vaux

UK Bus and Coach
Managing Director UK Bus:
Robert Montgomery
Managing Director Coaches & Special Activities:
Elizabeth Esnouf
Finance Director:
Colin Brown
Service Development Director:
Clare Kavanagh
Regional Directors:
Robert Andrew (South)
Sam Greer (Scotland)
Gary Nolan (North)
Mark Threapleton (London)

Operating Regions
Group Companies
Principal Depots
(UK Bus):

● **Stagecoach North Scotland**
(Includes Bluebird Buses, Stagecoach Highland, Stagecoach in Orkney)
(see City of Aberdeen, Aberdeenshire, Highland, Orkney)
Depots at Aberdeen, Aviemore, Elgin, Fort William, Insch, Inverness, Kirkwall, Macduff, Peterhead, Portree, Stonehaven, Tain, Thurso

● **Stagecoach East Scotland**
(Includes Rennies of Dunfermline, Fife Scottish Omnibuses, Stagecoach in Perth, Strathtay Scottish Omnibuses)
(see City of Dundee, Fife, Perth & Kinross)
Depots at Arbroath, Blairgowrie, Cowdenbeath, Dundee, Dunfermline (2), Glenrothes, Leven (Aberhill), Perth, St Andrews

● **Stagecoach West Scotland**
(Includes Stagecoach Glasgow, Western Buses)
(see South Ayrshire)
Depots at Ardrossan, Arran, Ayr, Cumnock, Dumfries, Glasgow, Kilmarnock, Stranraer

● **Scottish Citylink Coaches** (part owned)
(see City of Glasgow)

● **Stagecoach North East**
(Includes Stagecoach Hartlepool, Newcastle, South Shields, Sunderland, Teesside, Transit)
(see Durham, Tyne & Wear)
Depots at Hartlepool, Newcastle (2), South Shields, Stockton, Sunderland

● **Stagecoach Cumbria & North Lancashire**
(see Cheshire, Cumbria, Lancashire, Merseyside)
Depots at Barrow, Carlisle, Kendal, Morecambe, Workington

● **Stagecoach Merseyside & South Lancashire**
(see Cheshire, Lancashire, Merseyside)
Depots at Birkenhead, Chester, Chorley, Liverpool, Preston

● **Stagecoach Manchester**
(see Greater Manchester)
Depots at Manchester (2), Middleton, Stockport, Tameside, Wigan

● **Stagecoach Yorkshire**
(Includes Stagecoach Chesterfield, Stagecoach Sheffield, Stagecoach Yorkshire)
(see Derbyshire, South Yorkshire)
Depots at Barnsley, Chesterfield, Rawmarsh, Sheffield (2)

● **Stagecoach Supertram**
(see Section 5 – Tram Systems)

● **Stagecoach East Midlands**
(Includes Stagecoach East Midlands, Hull, Lincolnshire)
(see East Riding, Lincolnshire, North & North East Lincolnshire, Nottinghamshire)
Depots at Gainsborough, Grimsby, Hull, Lincoln, Mansfield, Scunthorpe, Skegness, Worksop

● **Stagecoach East**
(Includes Stagecoach in Bedford, Cambridgeshire, Peterborough, The Fens, and Norfolk Green)
(see Bedfordshire, Cambridgeshire, Norfolk)
Depots at Bedford, Cambridge, Fenstanton, Kings Lynn, Peterborough

● **Stagecoach Oxfordshire**
(see Oxfordshire)
Depots at Banbury, Oxford, Witney

● **Stagecoach Midlands**
(see Northamptonshire, Warwickshire)
Depots at Corby, Kettering, Leamington Spa, Northampton, Nuneaton, Rugby, Stratford upon Avon

● **Stagecoach London**
(see London & Middlesex)
Depots at Barking, Bow, Bromley, Catford, Leyton, Plumstead, Rainham, Romford, West Ham

● **Stagecoach West**
(Includes Stagecoach Cheltenham, Cotswolds, Gloucester, Swindon, Wye & Dean)
(see Gloucestershire, Wiltshire)
Depots at Cheltenham, Gloucester, Ross-on-Wye, Stroud, Swindon

● **Stagecoach South and South East**
(Includes Stagecoach in East Kent & East Sussex, Hampshire, Hants & Surrey, Stagecoach South, Fleet Buzz)
(see East Sussex, Hampshire, Kent, West Sussex)
Depots at Aldershot, Andover, Ashford, Basingstoke, Chichester, Dover, Eastbourne, Farnham, Folkestone, Hastings, Herne Bay, Portsmouth, Thanet, Winchester, Worthing

● **Stagecoach South West**
(Includes Stagecoach Devon, Stagecoach Somerset)
(see Devon, Somerset)
Depots at Barnstaple, Chard, Exeter, Exmouth, Torquay

● **Stagecoach in South Wales**
(see Torfaen)
Depots at Aberdare, Blackwood, Caerphilly, Cwmbran, Merthyr, Porth

Coaching
● Megabus; Scottish Citylink Coaches (jointly owned with Comfort DelGro)

Overseas Interests:
The group has significant bus and coach operations in North America

Other Interests
National Transport Tokens; Stagecoach Supertram *(see Section 5)*

UK Rail Franchises:
East Midlands Trains, Island Line, South West Trains, Virgin West Coast (joint venture)

Major Groups

ABELLIO

2nd Floor, 1 Ely Place, London EC1N 6RY
Tel: 020 7430 8270
Fax: 020 7430 2239
E-mail: info@abellio.com
Web site: www.abellio.com
Chief Executive: Jeff Hoogesteger
Chief Financial Officer: Chris Smulders
Group HR & Change Director: George Barron
Managing Director, Abellio UK: Dominic Booth
Commercial Director & Deputy Managing Director, UK: Leila Frances
Public Affairs Director, Abellio UK: Cameron Jones

Group Companies (UK Bus):
- **Abellio London & Surrey**
(see London & Middlesex, Surrey)
Depots at Battersea, Beddington, Byfleet, Fulwell, Hayes, Walworth

Overseas Interests
Abellio has bus and rail interests in Germany and a bus operation (Probo Bus) in the Czech Republic
UK Rail Franchises
Greater Anglia, Merseyrail, Northern Rail
Parent Company
Abellio is part of the NedRail Group

CENTREBUS GROUP

102 Cannock Street, Leicester LE4 9HR
Tel: 0116 246 0030
Fax: 0116 246 7221
E-mail: info@centrebus.com
Web site: www.centrebus.info
Directors: Peter Harvey, Julian Peddle, Keith Hayward, David Shelley

Group Operations:
- **Centrebus in Hertfordshire and Bedfordshire**
(see Bedfordshire, Hertfordshire)
Depots at Dunstable, Stevenage
- **Centrebus in Leicestershire and Northamptonshire**
(see Leicestershire, Northamptonshire)
Depots at Corby, Leicester, Melton Mowbray
- **Centrebus in Lincolnshire**
(see Lincolnshire)
Depot at Grantham
- **High Peak Bus Company** (Jointly owned with Wellglade)
(see Derbyshire)
Depot at Dove Holes

COMFORT DELGRO

Comfort DelGro House, 3rd Floor, 329 Edgware Road, London NW2 6JP
Tel: 020 8218 8888
Fax: 020 8218 8899
Web Site: www.comfortdelgro.com
Chief Executive, UK & Ireland: Jaspal Singh

Group Companies (UK Bus):
- **Metroline Travel**
(see London & Middlesex)

Depots at Alperton, Brentford, Cricklewood, Edgware, Greenford, Harrow Weald, Hayes, Holloway, Kings Cross, Potters Bar, Uxbridge, West Perivale, Willesden, Willesden Junction
- **Scottish Citylink Coaches** (part owned)
(see City of Glasgow)
- **Westbus Coach Services**
(see London & Middlesex)
Depot at Hounslow

Other Interests:
Citylink (Ireland)
(see Republic of Ireland)
Also Computer Cab and other taxi interests

Overseas Interests:
The group has extensive interests in Australia, China, Malaysia, Singapore and Vietnam
Parent Company:
Comfort DelGro Corporation

EYMS GROUP LTD

252 Anlaby Road, Hull HU3 2RS
Tel: 01482 327142
Fax: 01482 212040
Web Site: www.eymsgroup.co.uk
Chairman: Peter Shipp
Finance Director: Peter Harrison

Group Companies:
- **East Yorkshire Motor Services**
(Includes Scarborough & District Motor Services)
(see East Riding, North Yorkshire)
Depots at Beverley, Bridlington, Elloughton, Hornsea, Hull, Pocklington, Scarborough, Withernsea
- **Whittle Coach & Bus**
(see Shropshire)
Depot at Kidderminster

RATP DEV UK LTD

Yeomans Way, Bournemouth BH8 0BQ
Tel: 01202 636000
Fax: 01202 636001
E-mail: contact@ratpdev.com
Web site: www.ratpdev.com

Chief Executive Officer, UK & Ireland: Tim Jackson
Group Chief Financial Officer and Executive Chairman, London United & London Sovereign: Richard Casling

Executive Chairman, Bath Bus Company, Bournemouth Transport, Metrolink RATP Dev Ltd: Derek Lott
Northern Regional Director: Steve Whiteway

Group Companies (UK):
- **Bath Bus Company**
(see Somerset)
Depot at Bath
- **Epsom Coaches Group**
(see Surrey)
Depot at Epsom
- **London Sovereign**
(see London & Middlesex)
Depots at Edgware, Harrow
- **London United Busways**
(see London & Middlesex)
Depots at Fulwell, Hounslow, Hounslow Heath, Park Royal, Shepherd's Bush, Stamford Brook, Tolworth, Twickenham
- **Metrolink**
(see Section 5 – Tram Systems)
- **Selwyns Travel Services**
(see Cheshire, Greater Manchester)
Depots at Sharston, Runcorn
- **The Original Tour**
(see London & Middlesex)
Depots at Rainham, Wandsworth
- **Yellow Buses (Bournemouth Transport)**
(see Dorset)
Depot at Bournemouth

Overseas interests:
RATP Dev has bus and rail interests in 12 countries worldwide.

ROTALA PLC

Beacon House, Long Acre, Birmingham B7 5JJ
Tel: 0121 322 2222
Fax: 0121 322 2718
E-Mail: info@rotala.co.uk
Web Site: www.rotalaplc.com
Chairman: John Gunn
Chief Executive: Simon Dunn
Group Finance Director: Kim Taylor
Non-Executive Directors: Robert Dunn, Geoffrey Flight

Group Companies:
- **Diamond Bus (Black Diamond, Blue Diamond, Red Diamond)**
(See West Midlands, Worcestershire)
Depots at Birmingham, Droitwich, Kidderminster, Redditch

Major Groups

- **Flights Hallmark**
(See London & Middlesex, West Midlands)
Depots at Birmingham, Heathrow
- **Preston Bus**
(see Lancashire)
Depot at Preston
- **Wessex Connect, Bath Connect**
(see Bristol, Somerset)
Depots at Avonmouth, Filton, Keynsham

TRANSIT SYSTEMS GROUP

Westbourne Park Garage, Great Western
Road, London W9 3 NW
Tel: 020 7229 7131
Fax: 020 7792 8178
Web site: www.transitsystems.com.au
Chairman: Neil Smith
Chief Executive: Clint Feuerherdt
Chief Executive (London): Adam Leishman

Operating Regions & Group Companies (UK):
- **Tower Transit Operations Ltd**
(see London & Middlesex)
Depots at Harlesden, Leyton,
Westbourne Park

Overseas Interests
Transit Systems has extensive bus and ferry
operations throughout Australia

TRANSDEV UK

3rd Floor, 401 King Street, Hammersmith,
London W6 9NJ
Tel: 020 8600 5650
Fax: 020 8600 5651
E-mail: information@veoliatransdev.com
Web Site: www.transdevplc.co.uk
UK Divisional Director: Nigel Stevens
Finance Director: Peter Brogden
**Light Rail & Corporate Services
Director:** Julia Thomas

Operating Regions & Group Companies (UK):
- **Blazefield Lancashire**
(includes Burnley & Pendle, Lancashire United)
(see Lancashire)
Depots at Blackburn, Burnley
- **Blazefield Yorkshire**
(includes Harrogate & District, Keighley &
District, Transdev York & East Coast)
(see North Yorkshire, West Yorkshire)
Depots at: Harrogate, Keighley, Malton, York
- **Nottingham City Transport**
(part owned)
(see Nottinghamshire)

Overseas interests:
Transdev has extensive bus and rail interests
worldwide.

WELLGLADE LTD

Mansfield Road, Heanor, Derbyshire
DE75 7BG
Tel: 01773 536309
Fax: 01773 536310
Chairman: B R King
Deputy Chairman: R I Morgan
Group Finance Director: G Sutton

Group Companies:
- **Derby Community Transport**
(see Derbyshire)
Depot at Derby
- **High Peak Bus Company**
(Jointly owned with Centrebus)
(see Derbyshire)
Depot at Dove Holes
- **Kinchbus**
(see Leicestershire)
Depot at Loughborough
- **Notts & Derby**
(see Derbyshire)
Depot at Derby
- **TM Travel**
(see South Yorkshire)
Depot at Halfway
- **Trent Barton**
(see Derbyshire)
Depots at Ashfield, Belper, Derby, Langley Mill,
Nottingham
- **Nottingham Express Transit**
(part of operating group)
(see Section 5 – Tram Systems)

• STOP PRESS • STOP PRESS • STOP PRESS • STOP PRESS •

OPERATOR LISTINGS

**Page 112 (Gloucestershire)
Additional Operator:**

BELFITT MINI COACH HIRE
♿ ⛽ ♨ ▨
42 THE KEELINGS, STATION STREET,
CINDERFORD GL14 2NG
Tel: 01594 824713
E-mail: rjbelfitt@btinternet.com
Web site: www.websites.uk-plc.net/Belfitts_
Mini-Coach_Hire
Prop: Richard Belfitt.
Fleet: 19 – 7 single-deck coach, 5 midicoach,
7 minibus.
Chassis: BMC, DAF, Ford Transit, Irisbus,
Iveco, LDV, Mercedes, Volvo.
Ops incl: local bus services, school contracts,
private hire.
Livery: White with Blue/Red.

**Page 149 (Northumberland)
Additional Operator:**

SPIRIT BUSES LTD
♿ ▨
UNIT 3B, ROTHBURY INDUSTRIAL ESTATE,
ROTHBURY NE65 7RZ
Tel: 01669 838349
E-mail: admin@spiritbuses.co.uk
Web site: www.spiritbuses.co.uk
Dir: Steve Hurst
Ops incl: local bus services.

**Page 156 (Somerset)
Additional Operator:**

CROSVILLE MOTOR SERVICES LTD
♿ ⛽ ▨ ▭ ▭
UNIT 2, WESTLAND DISTRIBUTION PARK,
WINTERSTOKE ROAD,
WESTON-SUPER-MARE BS24 9AD

Tel: 01934 635259
Fax: 01934 440031
E-mail:
contact@crosvillemotorservices.co.uk
Web site: www.crosvillemotorservices.co.uk
Dir: Jonathan Pratt.
Fleet: 29 – 4 double-deck bus, 2 open-top
bus, 2 single-deck bus, 9 single-deck coach,
11 midibus, 1 minibus, also 15 heritage
vehicles.
Chassis (main fleet): Bova, Dennis,
Ford Transit, Leyland, Optare, Scania, Volvo.
Chassis (heritage vehicles): AEC, Bristol,
Dennis, Leyland.
Ops incl: local bus services, school contracts,
private hire.
Liveries: Buses: Green & Cream; Coaches:
White with Green lettering.

NOTES

ARRIVA THE SHIRES LTD

487 DUNSTABLE ROAD, LUTON LU4 8DS
Tel: 01582 587000
Fax: 01587 587111
Web site: www.arrivabus.co.uk
Fleet Names: Arriva the Shires & Essex, Green Line, Super Bus.
Area Man Dir: Paul Adcock **Regional Comm Dir:** Kevin Hawkins **Regional Fin Dir:** Beverley Lawson **Eng Dir:** Brian Barraclough.
Fleet: 614 – 123 double-deck bus, 226 single-deck bus, 36 single-deck coach, 171 midibus, 58 minibus.
Chassis: 56 Alexander Dennis, 96 DAF, 89 Dennis, 2 Enterprise, 7 MAN, 25 Mercedes, 72 Optare, 31 Scania, 9 Transbus, 17 Van Hool, 76 VDL, 114 Volvo, 20 Wrightbus.
Ops incl: local bus services, school contracts, excursions & tours, private hire, express.
Liveries: Arriva UK Bus, TfL Red, Green Line, Green Line/Easybus, Local Brands.
Ticket System: Wayfarer 3, TfL Prestige.

BARFORDIAN COACHES LTD

500 GOLDINGTON ROAD, BEDFORD MK41 0DX
Tel: 01234 355440
Fax: 01234 355310
E-mail: holidays@barfordiancoaches.co.uk
Web site: www.barfordcoaches.co.uk
Man Dir: Mrs J M Bullard **Sales Man:** Mrs T Russell **Administrator:** Mr W Sweeting.
Fleet: 13 – 2 double-deck bus, 5 single-deck coach, 2 double-deck coach, 2 midicoach, 2 minicoach.
Chassis: 4 Bova, 1 Dennis, 1 Leyland, 3 Mercedes, 2 Neoplan, 1 Toyota, 1 Volvo.
Ops incl: school contracts, excursions & tours, private hire, continental tours.
Livery: Orange.
A subsidiary of Souls Coaches Ltd (see Buckinghamshire)

BARTON COACH COMPANY

BARTON INDUSTRIAL ESTATE, FALDO LANE, BARTON-LE-CLAY MK45 4RP
Tel: 01582 882881
Web site: www.bartoncoachcompany.com
Prop: K Graniczka
Fleet: 21 – 4 single-deck coach, 3 midicoach, 13 minibus, 1 minicoach.
Chassis: BMC, Bova, Citroen, Ford Transit, Iveco, LDV, Mercedes, Scania, Volkswagen, Volvo.
Ops incl: school contracts, private hire.
Livery: White with Orange/Black.

CEDAR COACHES

ARKWRIGHT ROAD, BEDFORD MK42 0LE
Tel: 01234 354054
Fax: 01234 219210
E-mail: nikki@cedarcoaches.co.uk
Web site:
www.cedarcoaches-bedfordshire.co.uk
Dirs: Nikki Graham, Donna Reid, Kevin Reid.
Fleet: 27 - 15 double-deck bus, 4 single-deck

coach, 1 double-deck coach, 5 midibus, 1 midicoach, 1 minicoach.
Chassis: 2 Ayats, 1 DAF, 5 Dennis, 1 King Long, 5 Leyland, 1 MAN, 1 Mercedes, 4 Optare, 5 Scania, 2 Volvo.
Ops incl: local bus services, school contracts, private hire.
Livery: Red/Yellow.
Business acquired by Herbert's Travel as this LRB goes to press

CENTREBUS LTD

UNIT 34, HUMPHREYS ROAD, WOODSIDE INDUSTRIAL ESTATE, DUNSTABLE, LU5 4TP
Tel: 0844 357 6520
E-mail: info@centrebus.com
Web site: www.centrebus.info
Dirs: Peter Harvey, David Shelley, Julian Peddle, Keith Hayward.
Fleet (Bedfordshire): 44 – 14 single-deck bus, 27 midibus, 3 minibus.
Chassis: 7 Alexander Dennis, 4 DAF, 15 Dennis, 1 MAN, 8 Optare, 7 Scania, 2 Volvo.
Bodies: 3 Alexander, 7 Alexander Dennis, 5 East Lancs, 8 Optare, 17 Plaxton, 1 Reeve Burgess, 3 Wright.
Ops incl: local bus services.
Livery: Blue/Orange/White.
Ticket system: Wayfarer 3.
Part of the Centrebus Group

CHILTERN TRAVEL LTD

THE COACH HOUSE, BARFORD ROAD, BLUNHAM MK44 3NA
Tel: 01767 641400 **Fax:** 01767 641358
E-mail: info@chilterntravel.com
Web site: www.chilterntravel.com
Dir: Trevor Boorman.
Fleet: 25 – 2 double-deck bus, 17 single-deck coach, 2 midibus, 4 minibus.
Chassis: 1 Bova, 1 Ford Transit, 1 LDV, 2 Mercedes, 6 Neoplan, 2 Renault, 1 Scania, 5 Setra, 3 VDL, 3 Volvo.
Ops incl: private hire, continental tours, school contracts.
Livery: White/Blue.
Associated with Enfield Coaches (see Republic of Ireland)

D G (LUTON) LTD

UNIT 4A, PACKHORSE PLACE, WATLING STREET, KENSWORTH LU6 3QL
Tel: 01582 849100
Fax: 01582 842439
E-mail: travel@dg-group.co.uk
Web site: www.dg-group.co.uk
Dir: D Pepper.
Fleet: 13 – 7 single-deck coach, 1 midicoach, 5 minibus.
Chassis: 1 Bova, 2 Ford Transit, 1 Iveco, 2 LDV, 1 MAN, 1 Mercedes, 1 Scania, 4 Volvo.
Ops incl: school contracts, private hire.
Livery: White with Red/Silver.

EXPRESSLINES LTD

FENLAKE ROAD INDUSTRIAL ESTATE,

BEDFORD MK42 0HB
Tel: 01234 268704
Fax: 01234 272212
E-mail: info@expresslinesltd.co.uk
Web site: www.expresslinesltd.co.uk
Dirs: Chris Spriggs, Richard Harris.
Fleet: 17 - 1 midibus, 4 midicoach, 8 minibus, 4 minicoach.
Chassis: 6 Ford Transit, 7 Mercedes, 4 Optare.
Bodies: 2 Autobus, 3 Ferqui, 5 Ford, 1 Marshall, 4 Optare, 1 Unvi, 1 Other.
Ops incl: local bus services, school contracts, private hire.
Livery: Red/White/Silver.

HERBERTS TRAVEL

2 CARDINGTON GATE, ST MARTINS WAY, BEDFORD MK42 0LF
Tel: 01234 342057
Fax: 01234 348936
E-mail: booking@herberts-travel.co.uk
Web site: www.herberts-travel.co.uk
Man Dir: D M Dougall **Ops Dir:** D S Dougall **Fleet Eng:** S Myers.
Fleet: 36 - 19 double-deck bus, 2 single-deck bus, 6 single-deck coach, 4 midibus, 3 midicoach, 2 minibus.
Chassis: 6 Dennis, 5 Leyland, 2 MAN, 2 Mercedes, 21 Volvo.
Ops incl: local bus services, private hire, school contracts.
Livery: White with Blue/Gold.
Ticket system: Wayfarer.

LANDMARK COACHES LTD

UNIT 6, ARLESEY BUSINESS PARK, MILL LANE, ARLESEY SG16 6RF
Tel: 01462 733764
Fax: 01462 835817
E-mail: admin@landmarkhire.com
Web site: www.landmarkhire.com
Fleet: 33 – 8 double-deck bus, 1 single-deck bus, 8 single-deck coach, 2 midibus, 1 midicoach, 13 minibus.
Chassis: 7 Bova, 4 Dennis, 1 Iveco, 11 LDV, 1 Mercedes, 1 Scania, 1 Toyota, 7 Volvo.
Ops incl: local bus services, school contracts, private hire.
Livery: Red/White.

LANES COACHES

96 JEANS WAY, DUNSTABLE LU5 4PP
Tel: 0800 542 4827
Fax: 01582 604331
E-mail: info@lanescoaches.com
Web site: www.uk.lanescoaches.com
Prop: G W Clarke.
Fleet: 8 – 4 single-deck coach, 3 midibus, 1 minibus.
Chassis: 4 Dennis, 1 Renault, 2 Scania, 1 Van Hool.
Bodies: 1 Alexander, 1 EOS, 2 Irizar, 1 Onyx, 2 Plaxton, 1 UVG.
Ops incl: local bus services, school contracts, private hire.
Livery: Yellow/Blue

Symbol	Meaning	Symbol	Meaning	Symbol	Meaning
	Vehicle suitable for disabled		Coach(es) with galley facilities		Vintage Coach(es) available
	Seat belt-fitted Vehicle		Replacement vehicle available		Open top vehicle(s)
R24	24 hour recovery service	R	Recovery service available		Coaches with toilet facilities
T	Toilet-drop facilities available		Air-conditioned vehicle(s)		Hybrid Buses · Gas Buses

Bedford, Central Bedfordshire, Luton

MARSHALLS COACHES

UNIT 4, FIRBANK WAY, LEIGHTON BUZZARD LU7 4YP
Tel: 01525 376077
Fax: 01525 850967
E-mail: info@marshalls-coaches.co.uk
Web site: www.marshalls-coaches.co.uk
Prop: Glen Marshall.
Fleet: 35 - 7 double-deck bus, 1 single-deck bus, 24 single-deck coach, 2 double-deck coach, 1 midicoach.
Chassis: 3 Ayats, 3 Bova, 4 Dennis, 1 Iveco, 1 Leyland, 1 Mercedes, 2 Neoplan, 1 Scania, 19 Volvo.
Bodies: 4 Alexander, 3 Ayats, 1 Beulas, 3 Bova, 1 Caetano, 4 Jonckheere, 2 Neoplan, 13 Plaxton, 1 Scania, 1 Van Hool, 2 Other.
Ops incl: London commuter services, private hire, school contracts.
Livery: Blue/Multicoloured.

GRANT PALMER LTD

UNIT 2C, COMMERCE WAY, FLITWICK INDUSTRIAL ESTATE, FLITWICK MK45 5BP
Tel: 01525 719719
Fax: 01525 718444
E-mail: info@grantpalmer.com
Web site: www.grantpalmer.com
Dirs: Grant Palmer, Peter Morgan, Jeff Wilson.
Fleet: 29 - 4 double-deck bus, 3 single-deck bus, 19 midibus, 3 minibus.
Chassis: 1 AEC, 4 Alexander Dennis, 14 Dennis, 2 Enterprise, 2 Mercedes, 1 Optare, 3 Scania, 2 Volvo.
Bodies: 4 Alexander Dennis, 3 Alexander, 1 East Lancs, 1 Marshall, 1 Optare, 1 Park Royal, 15 Plaxton, 3 Scania.
Ops incl: local bus services, school contracts, private hire.
Livery: Red/White.
Ticket System: Wayfarer 3.

PREMIER CONNECTIONS TRAVEL LTD

THE COACH YARD, EATON GREEN ROAD, LUTON AIRPORT, LU2 9HD
Tel: 01582 424140
Fax: 01582 727093
E-mail: sales@premier.gb.com
Web site: www.premiercoachhire.co.uk
Dirs: J Gardner, R Carville.
Fleet: 16 – 1 double-deck coach, 9 single-deck coach, 1 midibus, 5 minibus.
Chassis: 2 BMC, 1 Dennis, 2 Irisbus, 1 Mercedes, 1 Neoplan, 2 Optare, 2 Renault, 4 Scania, 1 Volvo.
Ops incl: school contracts, private hire.
Livery: Silver/White (coaches), Yellow (school buses).
Incorporating A to B Travel, New City Coaches

RED KITE COMMERCIAL SERVICES LTD

UNIT 2, LEYS YARD, DUNSTABLE ROAD, TILSWORTH, LEIGHTON BUZZARD LU7 9PU
Tel: 01525 211441
Dirs: D Hoar, R H Savage
Fleet: 18 - 14 double-deck bus, 3 single-deck coach, 1 midibus.
Chassis: 1 Bedford, 8 Leyland, 1 Optare, 8 Volvo.
Bodies: 4 Alexander, 2 ECW, 1 Leyland, 7 Northern Counties, 1 Optare, 3 Plaxton.
Ops incl: local bus services, school contracts, excursions and tours, school contracts.
Livery: Red/Blue.

SAFFORD'S COACHES LTD

HIGHBURY FIELDS, ELTISLEY ROAD, GREAT GRANSDEN, SANDY SG19 3AR
Tel: 01767 677395
Fax: 01767 677742
E-mail: saffordcoaches@btconnect.com
Web site: www.saffordscoaches.co.uk
Dirs: Miss T S Gillett, Mrs S I Gillett.
Fleet: 14 – 2 double-deck bus, 9 single-deck coach, 3 minibus.
Chassis: 2 Alexander Dennis, 1 DAF, 3 Iveco, 1 Mercedes, 7 Volvo.
Bodies: 2 Alexander Dennis, 3 Berkhof, 3 Iveco, 2 Jonckheere, 1 Mercedes, 1 Plaxton, 2 Van Hool.
Ops incl: school contracts, excursions & tours, private hire, continental tours.
Livery: White/Blue/Yellow.

SHOREYS TRAVEL

119 CLOPHILL ROAD, MAULDEN MK45 2AE
Tel: 01525 860694
Fax: 01525 861850
E-mail: shoreystravel@talk21.com
Partners: Mrs D Thompson, Ms G Shorey
Ch Eng: D Bunker.
Fleet: 8 - 6 double-deck bus, 2 midibus.
Chassis: 1 Dennis, 3 Leyland, 1 MCW, 1 Optare, 1 Scania, 1 Volvo.
Bodies: 1 Alexander, 1 MCW, 4 Northern Counties, 1 Optare, 1 Plaxton.
Ops incl: school contracts, private hire.
Livery: White/Green.
Ticket System: Wayfarer.

STAGECOACH EAST

23 GREYFRIARS, BEDFORD MK40 1HJ
Tel: 01234 220030   **Fax:** 01234 343534
E-mail: bedford.enquiries@stagecoachbus.com
Web site: www.stagecoachbus.com
Fleet Names: Stagecoach in Bedfordshire, Stagecoach in Cambridge, Stagecoach in the Fens, Stagecoach in Peterborough, Norfolk Green.
Man Dir: Andy Campbell **Comm Dir:** Zoe Paget **Eng Dir:** Bob Dennison.
Fleet: 393 – 174 double-deck bus, 58 single-deck bus, 55 single-deck coach, 89 midibus, 15 minibus.
Chassis: 171 Alexander Dennis, 12 Dennis, 31 MAN, 15 Optare, 27 Scania, 58 Transbus, 78 Volvo.
Fleet excludes Norfolk Green – see separate entry under Norfolk
Ops incl: local bus services, school contracts, private hire, express.
Livery: Stagecoach UK Bus.
Ticket System: ERG.
See also Stagecoach East *(Cambridgeshire)*, Norfolk Green *(Norfolk)*

TATES COACHES LTD

44 HIGH STREET, MARKYATE AL3 8PA
Tel: 01582 840297
Fax: 01582 840014
E-mail: info@tates-coaches.co.uk
Web site: www.tatescoaches.co.uk
Dir & Co Sec: Alan M Tate
Dirs: Anthony J Tate, Stephen W Tate
Fleet: 9 – 1 double-deck bus, 8 single-deck coach
Chassis: 1 Bova, 1 DAF, 1 Dennis, 1 EOS, 1 MAN, 1 Mercedes, 3 Scania.
Bodies: 1 Bova, 1 Caetano, 1 EOS, 1 Hispano, 2 Irizar, 1 Neoplan, 1 Plaxton, 1 Van Hool.
Ops incl: school contracts, excursions & tours, private hire, continental tours.
Livery: Blue/Cream/Orange.

THEOBOLDS COACHES & HOLIDAYS LTD

WATLING STREET, DUNSTABLE LU6 3QP
Tel: 01582 600000
E-mail: sales@theobolds.com
Web site: www.theobolds.com
Fleet: 5 – 4 single-deck coach, 1 minibus.
Chassis: 1 Mercedes, 3 Neoplan, 1 Volvo.
Ops incl: excursions & tours, private hire.
Livery: Maroon/Gold.

THREE STAR (LUTON) LIMITED

UNIT 1, GUARDIAN BUSINESS PARK, DALLOW ROAD, LUTON LU1 1NA
Tel: 01582 722626
Fax: 01582 484034
E-mail: sales@threestarcoaches.com
Web Site: www.threestarcoaches.com
Man Dir: Colin Dudley **Ops Man:** Kevin Green **Ch Eng:** Andrew North
Co Sec: Isabelle Dudley.
Fleet: 15 – 13 single-deck coach, 2 double-deck coach.
Chassis: 2 Dennis, 2 Iveco, 2 MAN, 2 Mercedes, 2 Scania, 5 Volvo.
Bodies: 2 Ayats, 4 Berkhof, 1 Hispano, 1 Irizar, 5 Plaxton, 2 Sunsundegui.
Ops incl: school contracts, excursions & tours, private hire, continental tours.
Livery: Blue.

THE VILLAGER MINIBUS (SHARNBROOK) LTD

SHARNBROOK UPPER SCHOOL, ODELL ROAD, SHARNBROOK MK44 1JL
Tel: 01234 781920
E-mail: villager.sharn@btconnect.com
Man: Stan Jones.
Fleet: 1 minibus.
Chassis: 1 Mercedes.
Ops incl: local bus services, private hire.

ALDERMASTON COACHES

ALDERMASTON, READING RG7 5PP
Tel: 0118 971 3257
Fax: 0118 971 2722
E-mail: info@aldermastoncoaches.co.uk
Web site: www.aldermastoncoaches.co.uk
Prop: Phil Arlott
Fleet: 15 – 6 single-deck coach, 5 midicoach, 4 minibus.
Chassis: 2 LDV, 7 Mercedes, 6 Volvo.
Ops incl: private hire, school contracts.
Livery: Light Blue/Red.

APPLE TRAVEL LTD

STOKE WHARF, STOKE ROAD, SLOUGH SL2 5AU
Tel: 01753 821310
Fax: 01753 693912
E-mail: enquiries@appletravelltd.co.uk
Web site: www.appletravelltd.co.uk
Dirs: J S Sweeney, S J Sweeney.
Fleet: 13 – 9 single-deck coach, 2 midicoach, 2 minibus.
Chassis: 1 Bova, 1 Dennis, 1 LDV, 3 Mercedes, 7 Volvo.
Ops incl: private hire, school contracts.
Livery: White with Red, Green.

BAILEYS COACHES LTD

UNIT E, RED SHUTE HILL, HERMITAGE, THATCHAM RG18 9QL
Tel: 01635 203005
Fax: 01635 203006
E-mail: info@baileyscoaches.co.uk
Web site: www.baileys-of-newbury.co.uk
Fleet: 12 – 7 single-deck coach, 3 midicoach, 2 minibus.
Chassis: 2 Ford Transit, 3 Irisbus, 2 MAN, 2 Mercedes, 3 VDL.
Bodies: 8 Beulas, 1 EVM, 1 Ferqui, 1 Ford Transit, 1 Indcar.
Livery: Grey/Silver/Maroon.

BURGHFIELD MINI COACHES LTD
Ceased trading since LRB 2014 went to press

COURTNEY

22 IVANHOE ROAD, HOGWOOD INDUSTRIAL ESTATE, FINCHAMPSTEAD, WOKINGHAM RG40 4QQ
Tel: 0118 973 3486
Fax: 0118 932 8796
E-mail: info@courtneybuses.com
Web site: www.courtneybuses.com
Prop: William Courtney-Smith **Dir & Co Sec:** Miss Hayley Smith, Mrs Belinda Sheppard.
Fleet: 37 - 8 double-deck bus, 2 single-deck bus, 25 midibus, 2 minibus.
Chassis: 3 Alexander Dennis, 1 Dennis, 29 Optare, 1 Scania, 2 VDL, 1 Volvo.
Bodies: 2 Alexander Dennis, 3 East Lancs, 31 Optare, 1 Plaxton
Ops incl: local bus services, contract hire.
Livery: Orange/White, Local Brands.
Ticket System: Ticketer.

D & P COACHES

3 VULCAN CLOSE, SANDHURST GU47 9DD
Tel: 01252 861250
Fax: 01252 861234
E-mail: enquiries@dp-coaches.co.uk
Web site: www.dp-coaches.co.uk
Partners: B A & G M Thurlby.
Fleet: 12 – 9 single-deck coaches, 3 midicoaches.
Chassis: 1 Bova, 1 Neoplan, 7 Scania, 3 Toyota.
Bodies: 1 Bova, 3 Caetano, 7 Irizar,

1 Neoplan.
Ops incl: private hire, excursions & tours.
Livery: White with Blue.

FARGO COACHES

9 ELLENBOROUGH CLOSE, BRACKNELL RG12 2NB
Tel/Fax: 01344 456561
E-mail: info@fargocoaches.co.uk
Web site: www.fargocoaches.co.uk
Dirs: Lisa Farrugia-Bolt, Christopher Bolt
Fleet: 4 – 3 double-deck bus, 1 midibus.
Chassis: Leyland, Mercedes, Volvo.
Bodies: East Lancs, Leyland, Mercedes, Plaxton.
Ops incl: local bus services, school contracts, private hire.

FERNHILL TRAVEL LTD

UNIT 54, LONGSHOT LANE, BRACKNELL RG12 1RL
Tel: 01344 421423
Fax: 01344 488669
E-mail: office@fernhill.co.uk
Web site: www.fernhill.co.uk
Dirs: R W & M J Holgate.
Fleet: 9 – 1 single-deck bus, 6 single-deck coach, 2 midicoach.
Chassis: 4 Irisbus, 3 MAN, 2 Mercedes.
Ops incl: school contracts, private hire.
Livery: Red/White.

FIRST HAMPSHIRE, DORSET & BERKSHIRE

COLDBOROUGH HOUSE, MARKET STREET, BRACKNELL RG12 1JA
Tel: 01344 782200
Fax: 01344 868332
E-mail: contact.berkshire@firstgroup.com
Web site: www.firstgroup.com
Man Dir: Marc Reddy.
Fleet: 498 - 81 double-deck bus, 3 open-top bus, 218 single-deck bus, 12 single-deck coach, 149 midibus, 35 minibus.
Chassis: 37 Alexander Dennis, 2 Autosan, 8 Bluebird, 13 BMC, 94 Dennis, 33 Mercedes, 32 Optare, 45 Scania, 161 Volvo, 73 Wrightbus.
Ops incl: local bus services, school contracts, private hire.
Livery: FirstGroup UK Bus, Green Line, Local Brands.
See also Dorset, Hampshire

GO RIDE CIC
See Oxfordshire

HAYWARDS COACHES

169 GREENHAM BUSINESS PARK, THATCHAM RG19 6HN
Tel: 0118 947 4561
Fax: 01635 821128
E-mail: info@haywardscoaches.co.uk
Web site: www.haywardscoaches.co.uk
Dirs: Simon Weaver, Michelle Wadsworth.
Fleet: 7 – 5 single-deck coach, 2 double-deck coach.
Chassis: 5 Irisbus, 2 Neoplan.
Bodies: 2 Neoplan, 5 Plaxton.
Ops incl: school contracts, private hire.
Livery: Black or Electric Blue.
A subsidiary of Weavaway Travel

HODGE'S COACHES (SANDHURST) LTD

100 YORKTOWN ROAD, SANDHURST GU47 9BH
Tel: 01252 873131

Fax: 01252 874884
E-mail: enquiries@hodges-coaches.co.uk
Web site: www.hodges-coaches.co.uk
Man Dir: P Hodge **Dirs:** M Hodge, M Hodge
Fleet: 23 - 17 single-deck coach, 3 midicoach, 3 minibus.
Chassis: 1 Dennis, 3 Ford Transit, 3 MAN, 6 Scania, 3 Toyota, 7 Volvo.
Bodies: 7 Berkhof, 7 Caetano, 3 Fast, 2 Ford, 2 Lahden, 1 Plaxton.
Ops incl: excursions & tours, private hire, continental tours, school contracts.
Livery: Blue/Gold.

HORSEMAN COACHES LTD

2 ACRE ROAD, READING RG2 0SU
Tel: 0118 975 3811
Fax: 0118 975 3515
Recovery: 0118 975 3811
E-mail: privatehire@horsemancoaches.co.uk
Web site: www.horsemancoaches.co.uk
Man Dir: Keith Horseman **Ops Dir:** James Horseman **Eng Man:** Derrick Holton.
Fleet: 51 – 36 single-deck coach, 5 midicoach, 10 minicoach.
Chassis: 5 Mercedes, 10 Toyota, 36 Volvo.
Bodies: 5 Berkhof, 10 Caetano, 36 Plaxton.
Ops incl: local bus services, school contracts, excursions & tours, private hire, continental tours, park & ride, commuter express.
Livery: multi-coloured.

KINGFISHER MINI COACHES

357 BASINGSTOKE ROAD, READING RG2 0JA
Tel: 0118 931 3454
Fax: 0118 931 1322
Prop: Kevin Pope.
E-mail: info@kingfisherminicoaches.co.uk
Web site: www.kingfisherminicoaches.co.uk
Fleet: 8 - 5 minibus, 3 minicoach.
Chassis: 1 Ford Transit, 2 LDV, 5 Mercedes.
Ops incl: private hire, school contracts.
Livery: White/Orange.

NEWBURY & DISTRICT LTD

169 GREENHAM BUSINESS PARK, THATCHAM RG19 6HN
Tel: 01635 33855
Fax: 01635 821128
E-mail: info@newburyanddistrict.co.uk
Web site: www.newburyanddistrict.co.uk
Dirs: Simon Weaver, Michelle Wadsworth
Gen Man: Dave Wilder.
Fleet: 26 – 13 double-deck bus, 8 single-deck bus, 5 midibus.
Chassis: 14 Alexander Dennis, 4 Dennis, 8 Optare.
Bodies: 2 Alexander, 14 Alexander Dennis, 2 East Lancs, 8 Optare.
Ops incl: local bus services, school contracts.
Livery: Black.
Ticket System: Wayfarer 3
A subsidiary of Weavaway Travel

NOAH VALE

169 GREENHAM BUSINESS PARK, THATCHAM RG19 6HN
Tel: 01635 820028
Fax: 01635 821128
E-mail: info@weavaway.co.uk
Web site: www.weavaway.co.uk
Dirs: Simon Weaver, Michelle Wadsworth.
Fleet: 8 double-deck bus, 5 single-deck coach.
Chassis: 5 Scania, 8 Volvo.
Bodies: 8 Alexander, 5 Irizar.
Livery: Red/White.
A subsidiary of Weavaway Travel

READING & WOKINGHAM COACHES

c/o ASHRIDGE MANOR GARDEN CENTRE, FOREST ROAD, WOKINGHAM RG40 5QY
Tel: 0118 979 3983
Fax: 0118 979 4330
E-mail: randwcoaches@hotmail.com
Web site: www.coachhireberkshire.com
Props: Mark Way, Sharon Way.
Fleet: 13 - 9 single-deck coach, 4 midicoach.
Chassis: 1 Bova, 1 Dennis, 4 Mercedes, 2 Scania, 1 Toyota, 4 Volvo.
Ops incl: excursions & tours, private hire, school contracts.
Livery: White.

READING HERITAGE TRAVEL

PO BOX 147, READING RG1 6PP
Tel: 07850 220151
Transport Man: M J Russell.
Fleet: 1 double-deck bus.
Chassis: 1 AEC.
Bodies: 1 Park Royal.
Ops incl: private hire.
Livery: Red/Cream.
Ticket System: Almex.

READING BUSES
Reading Transport Ltd t/a

GREAT KNOLLYS STREET, READING RG1 7HH
Tel: 0118 959 4000
Fax: 0118 957 5379
E-mail: info@reading-buses.co.uk.
Web site: www.reading-buses.co.uk
Fleet Name: Reading Buses.
Chairman: David Sutton **Ch Exec Off:** James Freeman (Martijn Gilbert from late 2014) **Dir of Resources:** Tony Pettitt
Perf Dir: Jaqui Gavaghan **HR Dir:** Caroline Anscombe **Ch Eng:** John Bickerton.

Fleet: 154 - 97 double-deck bus, 45 single-deck bus, 12 midibus.
Chassis: 47 Alexander Dennis, 6 Dennis, 93 Scania, 8 Wrightbus.
Bodies: 81 Alexander Dennis, 38 East Lancs/ Darwen, 6 Plaxton, 20 Scania, 9 Wrightbus.
Ops incl: local bus services.
Livery: colour-branded routes.
Ticket System: Ticketer.

STEWARTS OF MORTIMER (PRIVATE HIRE) LTD

HEADLEY PARK 8, HEADLEY ROAD EAST, WOODLEY, READING, RG5 4SA
Tel: 0118 983 1231
Fax: 0118 983 1232
E-mail: info@stewartscoaches.com
Web site: www.stewartscoaches.com
Chairman: Chris Howell **Man Dir:** Andy Cotton **Gen Man:** Matt Taylor.
Fleet: 40 - 8 single-deck bus, 11 single-deck coach, 6 midibus, 10 midicoach, 4 minibus, 1 minicoach.
Chassis: 6 Alexander Dennis, 2 Ford, 8 Irizar, 21 Mercedes, 3 Volvo.
Bodies: 6 Alexander Dennis, 1 EVM, 2 Ford, 8 Irizar, 1 KVC, 8 Mercedes, 9 Plaxton, 5 Unvi.
Ops incl: private hire, contracts.
Liveries: Silver, Gold.
Also controls Woods Coaches Ltd (see Leicestershire)

WEAVAWAY TRAVEL

169 GREENHAM BUSINESS PARK, THATCHAM RG19 6HN
Tel: 01635 820028
Fax: 01635 821128
E-mail: info@weavaway.co.uk
Web site: www.weavaway.co.uk
Dirs: Simon Weaver, Michelle Wadsworth.
Fleet: 15 - 11 single-deck coach, 2 double-

deck coach, 2 midibus.
Chassis: 2 Alexander Dennis, 2 Irisbus, 2 MAN, 9 Neoplan.
Bodies: 2 Alexander Dennis, 9 Neoplan, 2 Plaxton, 2 Van Hool.
Ops incl: school contracts, private hire.
Livery: Black.
Weavaway Group Trading Names and Companies:
Abingdon Coaches (see Oxfordshire)
Countywide Top Travel (see Hampshire)
Haywards Coaches
Noah Vale
Newbury & District Ltd
Tappins Coaches (see Oxfordshire)

WHITE BUS SERVICES (C E JEATT & SONS LTD)

NORTH STREET GARAGE, WINKFIELD, WINDSOR SL4 4TP
Tel: 01344 882612
Fax: 01344 886403
E-mail: enquiries@whitebus.co.uk
Web site: www.whitebus.co.uk
Fleet Name: White Bus Services
Dir: Douglas Jeatt
Ops Supervisor: Geoff Lovejoy.
Fleet: 21 - 12 single-deck bus, 7 single-deck coach, 2 minibus.
Chassis: 3 Alexander Dennis, 3 DAF, 2 Dennis, 6 Optare, 7 Volvo.
Bodies: 3 Alexander Dennis, 9 Optare, 5 Plaxton, 2 Transbus, 2 Wadham Stringer.
Ops incl: local bus services, Windsor park & ride, school contracts, private hire.
Livery: White & Grey.
Ticket System: Wayfarer 3 & Wayfarer Saver.

WINDSORIAN COACHES
Name now owned by London Mini Coaches – see London & Middlesex

---

BRISTOL, SOUTH GLOUCESTERSHIRE

ABUS LTD

104 WINCHESTER ROAD, BRISLINGTON, BRISTOL BS4 3NL
Tel: 0117 971 0251
Fax: 0117 972 3121
E-mail: alan@abus.co.uk
Web site: www.abus.co.uk
Man Dir: Alan Peters.
Fleet: 27 - 20 double-deck bus, 1 single-deck bus, 6 midibus.
Chassis: 12 DAF, 1 Dennis, 4 Leyland, 1 Mercedes, 5 Optare, 2 Scania, 2 Volvo.
Bodies: 4 Alexander, 3 East Lancs, 1 Marshall, 4 Northern Counties, 14 Optare, 1 Plaxton.
Ops incl: local bus services.
Livery: Maroon/White/Cream.
Ticket System: Ticketer.

AZTEC COACH TRAVEL

6/8 EMERY ROAD, BRISLINGTON, BRISTOL BS4 5PF
Tel: 0117 977 0314
Fax: 0117 977 4431
E-mail: info@azteccoaches.co.uk
Man Dir: Iain Fortune
Fleet Eng: D Harvey **Ops Man:** P Rixon
Fleet: 11 - 4 single-deck coach, 7 midicoach.
Chassis: 7 Mercedes, 4 Volvo.
Bodies: 1 Alexander, 2 Berkhof, 2 Jonckheere, 1 Mercedes, 3 Plaxton, 1 Unvi, 1 Other.
Ops incl: excursions & tours, private hire, continental tours, school contracts.
Livery: White with diagonal red/orange stripes.

BERKELEY COACH & TRAVEL

HAM LANE, PAULTON BS39 7PL
Tel: 01761 413196
Fax: 01761 416469
E-mail: mail@berkeleycoachandtravel.co.uk
Web Site: www.berkeleycoachandtravel.co.uk
Proprietor: Tim Pow.
Fleet: 16 - 15 single-deck coach, 1 minicoach.
Chassis: 1 Mercedes, 1 Van Hool, 14 Volvo.
Bodies: 1 Ferqui, 1 Jonckheere, 6 Plaxton, 7 Van Hool, 1 Volvo.
Ops incl: school contracts, private hire.
Livery: Silver with Blue lettering.

BLAGDON LIONESS COACHES LTD
See Somerset

BLUE IRIS COACHES

25 CLEVEDON ROAD, NAILSEA BS48 1EH
Tel: 01275 851121
Fax: 01275 856522
E-mail: enquiry@blueiris.co.uk
Web site: www.blueiris.co.uk
Dirs: Tony Spiller, Avril Spiller, Gina Spiller, Ian Spiller **Transport Man:** Tony Spiller
Ops Man: Clayton Roper.
Fleet: 11 - 6 single-deck coach, 5 midicoach.
Chassis: 6 Scania, 5 Toyota.
Bodies: 5 Caetano, 5 Irizar, 1 Van Hool.
Ops incl: school contracts, excursions & tours, private hire, continental tours.
Livery: Dark Blue/Light Blue/White.

PETER CAROL PRESTIGE COACHING

BAMFIELD HOUSE, WHITCHURCH, BRISTOL BS14 0XD
Tel: 01275 839839
Fax: 01275 835604
E-mail: bookings@petercarol.co.uk
Web site: www.petercarol.co.uk
Dirs: Peter Collis, Carol Collis.
Fleet: 10 - 8 single-deck coach, 1 midicoach, 1 minicoach.
Chassis: 1 BMC, 3 Bova, 1 MAN, 4 Mercedes, 1 Van Hool.
Bodies: 1 BMC, 3 Bova, 1 Caetano, 4 Mercedes, 1 Van Hool.
Ops incl: excursions & tours, private hire.

CT PLUS CIC

UNITS 7/8, BARTON HILL TRADING ESTATE, BARTON HILL, BRISTOL BS5 9RD
Tel: 0117 941 3713
Fax: 0117 955 1368
E-mail: bristol@hctgroup.org
Web site: www.ctplusbristol.org
Senior Manager, Bristol: Donna Dixon.
Fleet: 14 articulated buses.
Chassis: Mercedes
Bodies: Mercedes.
Ops incl: Bristol Park & Ride.
A division of the HCT Group – see also East Riding, London & Middlesex, West Yorkshire and the Channel Islands.

EAGLE COACHES LTD

FIRECLAY HOUSE, NETHAM ROAD,
ST GEORGE, BRISTOL BS5 8HU
Tel: 0117 955 7130
Fax: 0117 941 1107
E-mail: sales@eagle-coaches.co.uk
Dirs: A J Ball, J A Ball.
Fleet: 23 – 21 single-deck coach, 1 midicoach,
1 minibus.
Chassis: 1 Bova, 14 DAF, 1 Iveco, 1 Mercedes,
5 VDL, 1 Volvo.
Bodies: 1 Bova, 1 Excel, 2 Ikarus, 1 Iveco,
1 Jonckheere, 1 Marcopolo, 2 Smit,
13 Van Hool, 1 VDL.
Ops incl: school contracts, excursions &
tours, continental tours.
Livery: Yellow with Red/Orange.

EASTVILLE COACHES LTD

ALBERT CRESCENT, ST PHILLIPS, BRISTOL
BS2 0SU
Tel: 0117 244 7324
E-mail: enquiries@eastvilletravelltd.co.uk
Web site: www.eastvilletravelltd.co.uk
Dirs: W G & N W Phillips.
Fleet: 8 - 3 double-deck bus, 2 double-deck
coach, 3 single-deck coach.
Chassis: 1 Bova, 2 Leyland, 5 Volvo.
Bodies: 1 Alexander, 1 Berkhof, 1 Bova,
1 East Lancs, 1 Jonckheere, 1 Northern
Counties, 2 Van Hool.
Ops incl: school contracts, private hire,
continental tours.
Livery: Myosotis Blue/White.

EUROTAXIS LTD

DEAN ROAD, YATE BS37 5NH
Tel: 0871 250 5555
Fax: 0871 250 4444
Recovery: 0871 250 5555
Web site: www.eurotaxis.com
Fleet Name: Eurocoaches.
Man Dir: Keith Sanzo **Ops Dir:** William
Sanzo **Tran Mans:** Gareth Tanner, Fred Taylor.
Fleet: 75 – 31 single-deck coach, 10
midicoach, 34 minibus.
Chassis: 44 Mercedes, 7 Setra, 24 Volvo.
Bodies: 1 Autobus, 2 Caetano, 1 Excel,
6 Jonckheere, 3 KVC, 2 Mellor, 2 Mercedes,
3 Onyx, 19 Plaxton, 2 Setra, 2 Sunsundegui,
6 UVG, 1 Van Hool, 1 Volvo, 24 Other.
Ops incl: local bus services, school contracts,
private hire, excursions & tours, continental
tours.
Livery: White with Blue Graphics.

FIRST IN BRISTOL, BATH & THE WEST OF ENGLAND

ENTERPRISE HOUSE, EASTON ROAD,
BRISTOL BS5 0DZ
Tel: 0117 955 8211
Fax: 0117 955 1248
Web site: www.firstgroup.com
Man Dir: Paul Matthews (James Freeman
from late 2014)
Fleet: 601 - 243 double-deck bus, 110 single-
deck bus, 9 articulated bus, 214 midibus,
25 minibus.
Chassis: 80 Alexander Dennis, 116 Dennis,
1 Enterprise, 1 Ford Transit, 24 Optare,
1 Transbus, 336 Volvo, 42 Wrightbus.
Ops incl: local bus services, Bath park & ride,
school contracts.
Livery: FirstGroup UK Bus.
Ticket System: Wayfarer.

ARNOLD LIDDELL COACHES

28 HENDRE ROAD, BRISTOL BS3 2LR.
Tel: 0117 953 1782
E-mail: arnoldliddellcoaches@hotmail.co.uk
Web site: www.coachhirebristol.com
Prop: Michael Liddell
Gen Man: Arnold Liddell
Fleet Eng: Robert Liddell.
Fleet: 6 - 1 double-deck bus, 3 single-deck
coach, 1 midicoach, 1 minibus.
Chassis: 1 LDV, 1 Leyland, 2 Mercedes, 2
Volvo.
Ops incl: excursions & tours, school
contracts.
Livery: Blue/White.

MIKE'S TRAVEL

50 CASTLE STREET, THORNBURY
BS35 1HB
Tel/Fax: 01454 281417
E-mail: mikes.travel@blueyonder.co.uk
Web site: www.mikestravel.co.uk
Prop: Beverly Cainey **Gen Man:** Simon
Hewgill.
Fleet: 10 – 2 single-deck bus, 5 single-deck
coach, 1 midibus, 2 midicoach.
Chassis: 1 Bristol, 1 DAF, 2 Leyland, 2 MAN,
4 Mercedes.
Bodies: 1 ECW, 1 Ikarus, 1 Mellor, 2 Neoplan,
1 Optare, 4 Plaxton.
Ops incl: local bus services, school contracts,
excursions & tours, private hire.
Livery: Various.
Ticket System: Wayfarer.

NORTH SOMERSET COACHES

Bus services transferred to Abus (*see Bristol*)
in November 2013; coach operations sold to
Carmel Bristol (*see Somerset*) in January 2014.

SEVERNSIDE TRANSPORT LTD

NORMAN SCOTT PARK, CONISTON
ROAD, PATCHWAY, BRISTOL
BS34 5JR
Tel: 01454 868544
Fax: 01454 868528
E-mail: info_severnside@yahoo.co.uk
Web site: www.severnsidetransport.co.uk
Fleet: 6 – 3 midibus, 2 midicoach, 1 minibus.
Chassis: 5 Mercedes, 1 Toyota.
Ops incl: local bus services, private hire.
Livery: White with Black.

SOUTH GLOUCESTERSHIRE BUS & COACH COMPANY

THE COACH DEPOT, PEGASUS PARK,
GYPSY PATCH LANE, PATCHWAY
BS34 6QD
Tel: 0117 931 4340
Fax: 0117 979 9400
E-mail: info@sgbc-bristol.com
Web site: www.southgloucesterbc.com
Man Dir: Roger Durbin **Gen Man:** Mike
Owen **Workshop Man:** Mark Wood
Route Man: Martyn Edney.
Fleet: 83 – 13 double-deck bus, 3 single-deck
bus, 61 single-deck coach, 2 midibus,
1 midicoach, 3 minibus.
Chassis: 3 DAF, 2 Dennis, 6 Leyland,
4 Mercedes, 18 Scania, 4 VDL, 46 Volvo.
Bodies: 2 Alexander, 36 Caetano, 2 ECW,
2 East Lancs, 1 Irizar, 1 Mercedes, 6 Northern
Counties, 11 Plaxton, 1 Roe, 4 Transbus,
14 Van Hool, 1 Wadham Stringer, 2 Other.
Ops incl: local bus service, school contracts,
excursions & tours, private hire, continental
tours, express.
Livery: Blue/White, National Express.
Ticket system: Wayfarer 2.

SOMERBUS LTD

See Somerset

TURNERS COACHWAYS (BRISTOL) LTD

59 DAYS ROAD, ST PHILIPS BS2 0QS
Tel: 0117 955 9086
Fax: 0117 955 6948
E-mail: admin@turnerscoachways.co.uk
Web site: www.turnerscoachways.co.uk
Man Dir: Tony Turner **Private Hire Man:**
Liz Venn **Traf Man:** Tony Harvey.
Fleet: 54 - 45 single-deck coach, 8 midicoach,
1 minibus.
Chassis: 6 Dennis, 9 Mercedes, 23 Scania,
2 Setra, 2 Temsa, 2 Toyota, 10 Volvo.
Bodies: 2 Caetano, 23 Irizar, 5 Jonckheere,
7 Mercedes, 1 Onyx, 1 Optare, 3 Plaxton,
2 Setra, 2 Temsa, 1 UVG, 2 Van Hool, 5
Wadham Stringer.
Ops incl: school contracts, private hire.
Livery: Silver/Blue.

WESSEX BUS

WESSEX HOUSE, PORT EDWARD CENTRE,
ST ANDREWS ROAD, AVONMOUTH,
BRISTOL BS11 9HS
Tel: 0117 321 3190
Web site: www.wessexbus.com
Fleet Names: Wessex Bristol, Wessex Red.
Man Dir: Simon Dunn **Ops Dir:** Chris Blyth
Gen Man: Stephen Watkins.
Fleet: 129 – 13 double-deck bus, 55 single-
deck bus, 46 midibus, 15 minibus.
Chassis: 17 Alexander Dennis, 21 Dennis,
1 LDV, 1 Mercedes, 20 Optare, 8 Scania,
5 VDL, 43 Volvo, 10 Wrightbus.
Bodies: 11 Alexander, 18 Alexander Dennis,
1 Koch, 1 LDV, 1 MCV, 20 Optare, 29 Plaxton,
8 Scania, 2 Transbus, 38 Wright.
Ops incl: local bus services, Bristol Park and
Ride.
Part of Flights Hallmark, a subsidiary of
Rotala .

Symbol	Meaning	Symbol	Meaning	Symbol	Meaning
♿	Vehicle suitable for disabled	🍴	Coach(es) with galley facilities	🚌	Vintage Coach(es) available
	Seat belt-fitted Vehicle		Replacement vehicle available		Open top vehicle(s)
R24	24 hour recovery service	R	Recovery service available	♦♦	Coaches with toilet facilities
T	Toilet-drop facilities available	❄	Air-conditioned vehicle(s)		Hybrid Buses		Gas Buses

ARRIVA THE SHIRES LTD
487 DUNSTABLE ROAD, LUTON LU4 8DS
Tel: 01582 587000
Fax: 01587 587111
Web site: www.arrivabus.co.uk
Fleet Names: Arriva the Shires & Essex, Green Line, Super Bus.
Area Man Dir: Paul Adcock **Regional Comm Dir:** Kevin Hawkins **Regional Fin Dir:** Beverley Lawson **Eng Dir:** Brian Barraclough.
Fleet: 614 – 123 double-deck bus, 226 single-deck bus, 36 single-deck coach, 171 midibus, 58 minibus.
Chassis: 56 Alexander Dennis, 96 DAF, 89 Dennis, 2 Enterprise, 7 MAN, 25 Mercedes, 72 Optare, 31 Scania, 9 Transbus, 17 Van Hool, 76 VDL, 114 Volvo, 20 Wrightbus.
Ops incl: local bus services, school contracts, excursions & tours, private hire, express.
Liveries: Arriva UK Bus, TfL Red, Green Line, Green Line/Easybus, Local Brands.
Ticket System: Wayfarer 3, TfL Prestige.

BRAZIERS MINI COACHES
17 VICARAGE ROAD, WINSLOW, BUCKINGHAM MK18 3BE
Tel: 01296 712201
E-mail: pbrazier@btconnect.com
Web site: www.brazierswinslow.co.uk
Prop: Peter Brazier
Fleet: 1 minibus, 1 minicoach.
Chassis/Bodies: 2 LDV.
Ops incl: private hire.

CAROUSEL BUSES
UNIT 2, HUGHENDEN AVENUE, HIGH WYCOMBE HP13 5SG
Tel: 01494 533436
E-mail: info@carouselbuses.co.uk
Web site: www.carouselbuses.co.uk
Man Dir: Phil Southall **Eng Dir:** Ray Woodhouse **Fin & Comm Dir:** Luke Marion **Gen Man:** Stefan Soanes.
Fleet: 39 – 13 double-deck bus, 22 single-deck bus, 4 midibus.
Chassis: 2 Alexander Dennis, 10 Dennis, 6 MAN, 5 Mercedes, 13 Optare, 3 Scania.
Bodies: 10 Alexander, 5 Alexander Dennis, 1 East Lancs, 4 MCV, 2 Mercedes, 13 Optare, 2 Plaxton, 2 Scania.
Ops incl: local bus services, school contracts.
Livery: Red.
Ticket system: ERG.
A subsidiary of the Go-Ahead Group

CLIFF'S COACHES LTD
UNIT 6, BINDERS INDUSTRIAL ESTATE, CRYERS HILL, HIGH WYCOMBE HP15 6LJ
Tel: 01494 714878
Fax: 01494 713491
E-mail: info@cliffscoaches.co.uk
Web site: www.cliffscoaches.co.uk
Dir: A Rashid.
Fleet: 10 – 4 single-deck coach, 2 midicoach, 4 minibus.
Ops incl: excursions & tours, private hire.
Livery: Blue/White.

DRP TRAVEL
1 THE MEADWAY, LOUGHTON, MILTON KEYNES MK5 8AN
Tel: 01908 394141
E-mail: drptravel@talktalk.net
Web site: www.drptravel.co.uk
Man: D R Pinnock.
Fleet: 2 minibus.

Chassis: 2 Mercedes.
Ops incl: school contracts, private hire.
Livery: Blue/White.

DRURY TRAVEL
9 WEST FARM WAY, EMBERTON, OLNEY MK46 5QP
Tel: 01234 711318
Fax: 01234 712843
E-mail: mike@drurytravel.co.uk
Web site: www.druryholidays.co.uk
Fleet: 8 single-deck coach.
Chassis: 1 Dennis, 6 Setra, 1 Volvo.
Ops incl: excursions & tours, continental tours.
Livery: Blue

HORSEMAN COACHES LTD
2 ACRE ROAD, READING RG2 0SU
Tel: 0118 975 3811
Fax: 0118 975 3515
Recovery: 0118 975 3811
E-mail: privatehire@horsemancoaches.co.uk
Web site: www.horsemancoaches.co.uk
Man Dir: Keith Horseman **Ops Dir:** James Horseman **Eng Man:** Derrick Holton.
Fleet: 51 – 36 single-deck coach, 5 midicoach, 10 minicoach.
Chassis: 5 Mercedes, 10 Toyota, 36 Volvo.
Bodies: 5 Berkhof, 10 Caetano, 36 Plaxton.
Ops incl: local bus services, school contracts, excursions & tours, private hire, continental tours, park & ride, commuter express.
Livery: multi-coloured.

HOWLETTS COACHES
UNIT 2, STATION ROAD INDUSTRIAL ESTATE, WINSLOW MK18 3DZ
Tel: 01296 713201
Fax: 01296 715879
E-mail: info@howlettscoaches.co.uk
Web site: www.howlettscoaches.co.uk
Prop: R S Durham.
Fleet: 11 – 6 double-deck bus, 5 single-deck coach.
Chassis: 1 Bedford, 3 DAF, 1 EOS, 4 Leyland, 2 MCW.
Ops incl: private hire, continental tours, school contracts.
Livery: Brown/White.

J & L TRAVEL LTD
MOUNT PLEASANT, TAYLORS LANE, ST LEONARDS, TRING HP23 6LU
Tel: 01296 696046
E-mail: coachhire@jlcoaches.com
Web site: www.jlcoaches.com
Fleet: 18 – 4 double-deck bus, 14 single-deck coach.
Chassis: 2 Leyland, 1 MAN, 3 MCW, 9 Scania, 1 Setra, 2 Volvo.
Ops incl: school contracts, excursions & tours, private hire.
Livery: White with Red lettering.

LANGSTON & TASKER
23 QUEEN CATHERINE ROAD, STEEPLE CLAYDON MK18 2PZ
Tel/Fax: 01296 730347
Partners: Mrs J Langston, Mrs M A Fenner
Man: J Langston **Ops Man:** A P Price.
Fleet: 23 – 4 double-deck bus, 10 single-deck coach, 4 midibus, 2 midicoach, 3 minicoach.
Chassis: 7 Dennis, 4 Mercedes, 1 Toyota, 11 Volvo.
Ops incl: local bus services, school contracts, private hire.

Livery: White/Red.
Ticket system: Wayfarer.

MAGPIE TRAVEL LTD
BINDERS INDUSTRIAL ESTATE, CRYERS HILL, HIGH WYCOMBE HP15 6LJ
Tel: 01494 715381
Dir: David Harris.
Fleet: 15 – 2 single-deck bus, 3 single-deck coach, 1 midibus, 4 midicoach, 4 minibus, 1 minicoach
Chassis: 2 Dennis, 1 EOS, 1 Ford Transit, 9 Mercedes, 2 Volvo.
Ops incl: local bus services, school contracts, private hire.
Livery: White/Black.
Ticket System: Almex.

MASONS COACHES
LONG MARSTON AIRFIELD, CHEDDINGTON LANE, LONG MARSTON HP23 4QR
Tel: 01296 661604
Fax: 01296 660341
E-mail: info@masonsminicoachhire.co.uk
Web site: www.masonsminicoachhire.co.uk
Prop: J A Mason.
Fleet: 6 – 5 single-deck coach, 1 midicoach.
Ops incl: excursions & tours, private hire, school contracts, continental tours.
Livery: Grey with Purple Lettering.

MOTTS COACHES (AYLESBURY) LTD
GARSIDE WAY, AYLESBURY HP20 1BH
Tel: 01296 398300
Fax: 01296 398386
E-mail: info@mottstravel.com
Web site: www.mottstravel.com
Fleet Name: Motts Travel
Man Dir: M R Mott **Ops Dir:** C J Mott **Eng Dir:** I Scutt **Tours Dir:** C Joel **Gen Man:** G Messenger **Comm Man:** H Shanks **Training & Devt Man:** R Jones **Senior Traf Man:** S Lane.
Fleet: 65 – 12 double-deck bus, 3 single-deck bus, 43 single-deck coach, 7 midicoach.
Chassis: 2 Leyland, 7 Mercedes, 6 Scania, 12 Setra, 38 Volvo.
Bodies: 15 Alexander, 2 Irizar, 11 Jonckheere, 4 Lahden, 14 Plaxton, 12 Setra, 1 Sunsundegui, 3 Transbus, 2 Unvi.
Ops incl: local bus services, school contracts, excursions & tours, private hire, continental tours.
Livery: White/Yellow/Green.
Ticket System: Wayfarer.
Subsidiary Company: Crusader Holidays (see Essex)

OMEGA TRAVEL LTD
2 MILBURN AVENUE, OLDBROOK, MILTON KEYNES MK6 2WA
Tel: 01908 259988
Web site: www.uk.omegatravel.net
Dirs: H Lu, M L Chen.
Fleet: 27 – 4 double-deck coach, 14 single-deck coach, 2 midicoach, 6 minibus, 1 minicoach.
Chassis: 2 BMC, 4 MAN, 4 Mercedes, 4 Neoplan, 3 Renault, 9 Scania, 1 Volvo.
Ops incl: excursions & tours, private hire.
Livery: White

RED EAGLE BUSES LTD
THE WORKSHOP, COLLEGE ROAD NORTH, ASTON CLINTON HP22 5EZ
Tel: 01296 630402

E-mail: info@redeagle.org.uk
Web site: www.redeagle.org.uk
Prop: S A Khan.
Fleet: 15 – 1 double-deck bus, 14 midibus,
1 minibus.
Chassis: 13 Dennis, 1 Mercedes, 1 Transbus,
1 Volvo.
Bodies: 2 Alexander, 3 Caetano, 1 Marshall,
1 Northern Counties, 9 Plaxton.
Ops incl: local bus services, school contracts.
Livery: Red

REDLINE BUSES LTD

8 GATEHOUSE WAY, AYLESBURY HP19 8DB
Tel: 01296 426786   **Fax:** 01296 431013
E-mail: kwk@redlinebuses.com
Web site: www.redlinebuses.com
Dirs: Khan Wali, Parmeena Begum.
Fleet: 41 - 13 double-deck bus, 1 single-deck
bus, 23 midibus, 4 minibus.
Chassis: 8 Alexander Dennis, 17 Dennis,
4 Leyland, 4 Optare, 2 Transbus, 6 Volvo.
Bodies: 8 Alexander, 8 Alexander Dennis,
1 Leyland, 6 Marshall, 2 Northern Counties,
4 Optare, 6 Plaxton, 2 Transbus, 1 Wrightbus.
Ops incl: local bus services, school contracts,
private hire.
Livery: Red.
Ticket System: Wayfarer TGX.

RED ROSE TRAVEL

OXFORD ROAD, DINTON, AYLESBURY
HP17 8TT
Tel: 01296 747926
Fax: 01296 612196
E-mail: office@redrosetravel.com
Web site: www.redrosetravel.com
Dir: Taj Khan.
Fleet: 32 midibus.
Chassis: 9 Alexander Dennis, 23 Dennis.
Bodies: 3 Alexander, 9 Alexander Dennis,
2 East Lancs, 18 Plaxton.
Ops incl: local bus services, private hire.
Livery: Red/Yellow.
Ticket System: Wayfarer 3.

SOULS COACHES LTD

2 STILEBROOK ROAD, OLNEY MK46 5EA

Tel: 01234 711242   **Fax:** 01234 240130
Recovery: 07739 097775
E-mail: sales@soulscoaches.co.uk
Web site: www.souls-coaches.co.uk
Man Dir: David Soul **Sales Man:** Wendy
Cheshire **Traf Man:** Neil McCormick
Ops Man: Steve Neale **Workshop Man:**
Drew Blunt.
Fleet: 36 - 2 double-deck bus, 1 single-deck
bus, 25 single-deck coach, 1 double-deck
coach, 4 midibus, 2 minibus, 1 minicoach.
Chassis: 8 Dennis, 1 Mercedes,
1 Optare, 1 Renault, 5 Setra, 1 Toyota,
1 Transbus, 14 Volvo.
Bodies: 2 Alexander, 1 Caetano, 2 East Lancs,
6 Jonckheere, 1 LDV, 2 Mercedes, 1 Optare,
14 Plaxton, 5 Setra, 1 Transbus, 1 Other.
Ops incl: local bus services, school contracts,
excursions & tours, private hire, continental
tours.
Livery: Red/Gold.
Ticket System: Wayfarer.
Subsidiary Companies: Barfordian
Coaches (see Bedfordshire), Nightingales of
Beccles Ltd (see Suffolk)

STAR TRAVEL SERVICES

15 OSIER WAY, PARK STREET, AYLESBURY
HP20 1EB
Tel: 01296 435425
E-mail: star-travel@hotmail.co.uk
Web site: www.startravelbuses.co.uk
Fleet: 10 midibus.
Chassis: 2 Mercedes, 8 Optare.
Bodies: 1 Alexander, 8 Optare, 1 Plaxton.
Ops incl: local bus services, private hire.
Livery: Orange.

THREE STAR (LUTON) LIMITED

UNIT 1, GUARDIAN BUSINESS PARK,
DALLOW ROAD, LUTON LU1 1NA
Tel: 01582 722626
Fax: 01582 484034
E-mail: sales@threestarcoaches.com
Web Site: www.threestarcoaches.com
Man Dir: Colin Dudley **Ops Man:** Kevin
Green **Ch Eng:** Andrew North **Co Sec:**
Isabelle Dudley.
Fleet: 15 – 13 single-deck coach, 2 double-

deck coach.
Chassis: 2 Dennis, 2 Iveco, 2 MAN,
2 Mercedes, 2 Scania, 5 Volvo.
Bodies: 2 Ayats, 4 Berkhof, 1 Hispano, 1 Irizar,
5 Plaxton, 2 Sunsundegui.
Ops incl: school contracts, excursions &
tours, private hire, continental tours.
Livery: Blue.

VALE TRAVEL LTD

13 VALE ROAD, AYLESBURY HP20 1JA
Tel: 01296 484348
Fax: 01296 435309
E-mail: info@valetravel.net
Web site: www.valetravel.net
Prop: Wazir Zaman.
Fleet: 21 – 6 double-deck bus, 9 midibus,
6 minibus.
Chassis: 1 Alexander Dennis, 8 Dennis,
2 Mercedes, 4 Optare, 6 Volvo.
Bodies: 5 Alexander, 1 Alexander Dennis,
2 East Lancs, 4 Northern Counties, 4 Optare,
5 Plaxton.
Ops Inc: local bus services, school contracts,
private hire.
Livery: White & Yellow.
Ticket System: Wayfarer.

Z & S INTERNATIONAL

UNITS 5-9, AYLESBURY BUSINESS CENTRE,
CHAMBERLAIN ROAD, AYLESBURY
HP19 8DY
Tel/Fax: 01296 415468
E-mail: info@zands.co.uk
Web site: www.zands.co.uk
Dirs: Umar Zaman, Shah Begum.
Fleet: 52 – 14 double-deck bus, 2 single-deck
bus, 6 single-deck coach, 23 midibus,
1 midicoach, 6 minibus.
Chassis: 8 Alexander Dennis, 20 Dennis,
1 LDV, 5 Leyland, 1 MAN, 4 Mercedes,
4 Optare, 1 Scania, 1 Transbus, 1 VDL, 7 Volvo.
Bodies: 4 Alexander, 7 Alexander Dennis,
1 Excel, 2 Jonckheere, 1 LDV, 2 Leyland,
6 Marshall, 1 MCV, 3 Northern Counties,
5 Optare, 14 Plaxton, 1 Sitcar, 2 Sunsundegui,
1 Transbus, 1 UVG, 2 Van Hool.
Ops incl: local bus services, school contracts,
excursions & tours, private hire.

CAMBRIDGESHIRE, CITY OF PETERBOROUGH

A H SLEEPERS LTD

70-72 AARON ROAD INDUSTRIAL ESTATE,
WHITTLESEY PE7 2EX
Tel: 01733 351694
Fax: 01733 359438
Recovery: 07521 194734
E-mail: anthea@deckerbus.co.uk
Web site: www.deckerbus.co.uk
Prop: Anthea Head.
Fleet: 2 double-deck sleeper coaches
Ops incl: private hire, tours

ANDREWS COACHES

22 CAMBRIDGE ROAD, FOXTON
CB22 6SH
Tel: 01223 873002
Fax: 01223 873036
E-mail: andrewscoaches@aol.com
Web site: www.andrewscoaches.com
Man: Andrew Miller.
Fleet: 7 – 6 single-deck coach, 1 minibus.
Chassis: 1 Dennis, 1 LDV, 1 Scania, 4 Volvo.
Ops incl: school contracts, private hire.
Livery: White.

C & G COACH SERVICES LTD

HONEYSOME LODGE, HONEYSOME

ROAD, CHATTERIS PE16 6SB
Tel: 01354 692200
Fax: 01354 694433
Recovery: 07771 962105
E-mail: info@candgcoaches.co.uk
Web site: www.candgcoaches.co.uk
Partners: Mrs C Mansell, G Ellwood, R Day
Ops Man: C Smith.
Fleet: 17 single-deck coach.
Chassis: 3 Bova, 1 DAF, 1 Iveco, 1 Leyland,
1 Mercedes, 2 Neoplan, 7 Scania, 1 Volvo.
Ops incl: school contracts, excursions &
tours, private hire, continental tours.
Livery: White/Red/Yellow.

CARRIAGEWAYS OF CAMBRIDGE

RECTORY FARM, AKEMAN STREET,
LANDBEACH, CAMBRIDGE CB25 9FQ
Tel: 01223 441100
Fax: 01223 441133
E-mail: bookings@carriageways.co.uk
Web site: www.carriageways.co.uk
Prop: Mrs D Cooper.
Fleet: 3 midicoach.
Chassis: 3 Mercedes.
Bodies: 3 Sitcar.
Ops incl: school contracts, private hire.
Livery: Blue.

COLLINS COACHES

UNIT 4, CAMBRIDGE ROAD INDUSTRIAL
ESTATE, MILTON, CAMBRIDGE
CB4 6AZ
Tel: 01223 658309
Fax: 01223 424739
E-mail: collinscoaches@btconnect.com
Web site: www.collinscoaches-cambridge.
co.uk
Partners: C R Collins, R T Collins **Off Man:**
Jacky Liptrot **Garage Man:** R D Curtis.
Fleet: 17 - 2 single-deck bus, 1 single-deck
coach, 2 midicoach, 10 minibus, 2 minicoach.
Chassis: 1 BMC, 2 Ford Transit, 5 LDV,
3 Iveco, 3 Mercedes, 1 Setra, 2 Volvo.
Ops incl: excursions & tours, school
contracts, private hire.
Livery: White/Orange.

DECKER BUS

70-72 AARON ROAD INDUSTRIAL ESTATE,
WHITTLESEY PE7 2EX
Tel: 01733 351694
Fax: 01733 359438
Recovery: 07521 194734
E-mail: anthea@deckerbus.co.uk
Web site: www.deckerbus.co.uk
Prop: Anthea Head.

Fleet: 21 – 10 double-deck bus, 4 single-deck bus (70 seats), 4 single-deck coach (inc wheelchair access), 1 semi-open top bus, 2 sleeper coaches.
Chassis: 2 DAF, 1 Dennis, 4 Leyland, 2 MAN, 3 Scania, 7 Volvo.
Ops incl: school contracts, excursions & tours, private hire, express.
Livery: Various Colours.

RON W DEW & SONS LTD
CHATTERIS ROAD, SOMERSHAM PE28 3DN
Tel: 01487 740241
Fax: 01487 740341
E-mail: sales@dews-coaches.com
Web site: www.dews-coaches.com
Man Dir: Simon Dew **Gen Man:** Nick Tetley
Maintenance Man: Tom Williams.
Fleet: 41 – 8 double-deck bus, 13 single-deck bus, 12 single-deck coach, 1 midibus, 2 midicoach, 1 minibus, 4 heritage vehicles.
Chassis: 4 Bedford, 1 Dennis, 1 Leyland, 4 Mercedes, 3 Scania, 1 Van Hool, 16 Volvo.
Ops incl: local bus services, excursions & tours, private hire, continental tours, school contracts.
Livery: Green/Grey.

EMBLINGS COACHES LTD
JUDDS TRAVEL LTD
BRIDGE GARAGE, GUYHIRN, WISBECH PE13 4ED
Tel: 01945 450253
Fax: 01945 450770
E-mail: john@emblings.co.uk
Dirs: John Embling, Mark Judd, Stephanie Judd.
Fleet: 41 – 10 double-deck bus, 1 double-deck coach, 1 single-deck bus, 25 single-deck coach, 1 midibus, 3 minibus.
Chassis: 1 BMC, 5 DAF, 3 Dennis, 1 Ford Transit, 2 LDV, 3 Leyland, 6 Scania, 20 Volvo.
Bodies: 7 Alexander, 1 BMC, 2 East Lancs, 1 Ford, 1 Ikarus, 1 Irizar, 1 Jonckheere, 2 LDV, 1 Marcopolo, 2 Northern Counties, 14 Plaxton, 8 Van Hool.
Ops incl: local bus services, school contracts, private hire.
Livery: White with Red/Blue.

FENN HOLIDAYS
WHITTLESEY ROAD, MARCH PE15 0AG
Tel: 01354 653329
Fax: 01354 650647
E-mail: info@fennholidays.co.uk
Web site: www.fennholidays.co.uk
Man Dir: Peter Fenn **Dir:** Margaret Fenn.
Fleet: 3 single-deck coach, 1 minibus.
Chassis: 1 Bova, 1 Mercedes, 2 Van Hool.
Bodies: 1 Bova, 2 Van Hool, 1 Other.
Ops incl: excursions & tours, private hire, continental tours
Livery: Multicoloured.

FREEDOM TRAVEL COACHES (UK) LTD
3A THE MOUNT BUSINESS PARK, CARDINALS GREEN, HORSEHEATH CB21 4QX
Tel: 01223 891783
E-mail: info@freedomtravelcoaches.co.uk
Web site: www.freedomtravelcoaches.co.uk
Dirs: D R Evans, S P Evans.
Fleet: 17 – 9 double-deck bus, 3 single-deck coach, 1 minibus, 3 minibus.
Chassis: 7 Dennis, 2 Leyland, 1 Mercedes, 2 Optare, 1 Volkswagen, 4 Volvo.
Ops incl: local bus services, school contracts, private hire.
Livery: White.

GRETTON'S COACHES
ARNWOOD CENTRE, NEWARK ROAD, PETERBOROUGH PE1 5YH
Tel: 01733 311008
Fax: 01733 319859
E-mail: roger@grettonscoaches.co.uk
Web site: www.grettonscoaches.co.uk
Prop: Roger Gretton.
Fleet: 14 - 12 single-deck coach, 2 midicoach.
Chassis: Iveco, Mercedes, Scania.
Ops incl: school contracts, excursions & tours, private hire.
Livery: Silver/Red/Maroon.

GREYS OF ELY
41 COMMON ROAD, WITCHFORD, ELY CB6 2HY
Tel: 01353 662300
Fax: 01353 662412
E-mail: sales@greysofely.co.uk
Web site: www.greysofely.co.uk
Man Dir: Richard Grey **Dir:** David Grey.
Fleet: 28 – 10 double deck bus, 5 single-deck bus, 12 single-deck coach, 1 midicoach.
Chassis: 10 Dennis, 1 Irizar, 2 Leyland, 3 Mercedes, 12 Volvo.
Ops incl: school contracts, excursions & tours, private hire, continental tours.
Liveries: Grey Metallic.

IMPRESSION COACH TRAVEL
71 LEDBURY ROAD, PETERBOROUGH PE3 9RF
Tel/Fax: 01733 267025
E-mail: enquiries@impressionholidays.com
Web site: www.impressionholidays.com
Man Dir: Aled Evans.
Fleet: 3 - 2 single-deck coach, 1 minicoach.
Chassis: 1 Mercedes, 2 Setra.
Bodies: 1 Optare, 2 Setra.
Ops incl: excursions & tours, school contracts, private hire, continental tours.
Livery: Silver/White.

JANS COACHES
23 TOWNSEND, SOHAM CB7 5DD
Tel: 0845 839 3052
Fax: 01353 721341
E-mail: janscoaches@aol.com
Web site: www.janscoaches.co.uk
Dirs: Roland Edwards, Janet Edwards, Stuart Edwards, Jason Edwards.
Fleet: 12 - 3 double-deck bus, 5 single-deck coach, 3 double-deck coach, 1 midicoach.
Chassis: 1 BMC, 1 DAF, 1 Dennis, 1 MAN, 1 MCW, 2 Mercedes, 5 Neoplan.
Ops incl: excursions & tours, private hire, continental tours, school contracts.
Livery: Maroon.

MIL-KEN TRAVEL LTD
11 LYNN ROAD, LITTLEPORT, ELY CB6 1QG
Tel: 01353 860705
Fax: 01353 863222
E-mail: milken@btconnect.com
Web-site: www.milkentravel.com
Man Dir: Jason Miller
Ops Man: Jon Miller
Fleet Eng: Ian Martin.
Fleet: 40 - 36 single-deck coach, 2 midicoach, 2 minicoach.
Chassis: 2 LDV, 2 Mercedes, 36 Volvo.
Bodies: 7 Jonckheere, 24 Plaxton, 2 Unvi, 3 Van Hool, 2 Volvo, 2 Other.
Ops incl: school contracts, private hire.
Livery: White with Red, Blue, Yellow.

C G MYALL & SON
CHERRY TREE HOUSE, THE CAUSEWAY, BASSINGBOURN, ROYSTON SG8 5JA
Tel: 01763 243225
Fax: 01763 224626
Prop: A Myall.
Fleet: 11 – 1 double-deck bus, 1 double-deck coach, 2 single-deck coach, 4 midibus, 2 midicoach, 1 minibus.
Chassis: 1 Alexander Dennis, 1 Ayats, 3 Dennis, 1 LDV, 4 Mercedes, 1 Optare.
Ops incl: local bus services, school contracts, private hire.
Livery: White.

NEAL'S TRAVEL LTD
102 BECK ROAD, ISLEHAM, ELY CB7 5QP
Tel: 01638 780066
Fax: 01638 780011
E-mail: sales@nealstravel.com
Web site: www.nealstravel.com
Dirs: Bridget Paterson, Graham Neal, Lionel Neal, Nancy Neal.
Fleet: 16 – 9 single-deck coach, 1 midibus, 4 midicoach, 2 minibus.
Chassis: 9 Mercedes, 7 Volvo.
Bodies: 2 Autobus, 5 Jonckheere, 2 Mercedes, 1 Plaxton, 2 Sunsundegui, 4 Other.
Ops incl: school contracts, private hire.
Livery: White/Blue, Silver/Blue.

NENEWAY COACHES
22 GREEN ROAD, EYE GREEN, PETERBOROUGH PE6 7YR
Tel: 01733 223773 **Fax:** 01733 578165
E-mail: robertblunt@nenewaycoaches.freeserve.co.uk
Prop: Robert Blunt.
Fleet: 3 single-deck coaches.
Chassis: 2 Autosan A1012T, 1 Dennis R.
Bodies: 2 Autosan, 1 Plaxton Paragon.
Ops incl: school contracts, private hire.

NORTH STAR TRAVEL LTD
45 ASHTON CLOSE, NEEDINGWORTH, ST IVES PE27 4UA
Tel/Fax: 01480 300222
E-mail: info@north-star-travel.co.uk
Web site: www.north-star-travel.co.uk
Dirs: C Meldrum, D Palmer.
Fleet: 3 single-deck coach.
Chassis: 3 Bova.
Bodies: 3 Bova.
Ops incl: excursions & tours, private hire, continental tours.
Livery: White with Grey/Purple.

D A PAYNE COACH HIRE
STATION LANE, OFFORD CLUNY, ST NEOTS PE19 5ZA
Tel: 01480 811777
Fax: 01480 811799
E-mail: paul@dapaynecoachehire.co.uk
Web site: www.dapaynecoachehire.co.uk
Partners: Mr David Payne, Mrs Sara Hart, Mr Paul Hart.
Fleet: 11 – 3 double-deck bus, 1 single-deck bus, 3 single-deck coach, 1 midibus, 1 midicoach, 2 minibus.
Ops incl: school contracts, excursions & tours, private hire, continental tours.

PLAYBUS LTD
70-72 AARON ROAD INDUSTRIAL ESTATE, WHITTLESEY PE7 2EX
Tel: 01733 303190
Fax: 01733 359438
Recovery: 07521 194734
E-mail: ben@play-bus.co.uk

Web site: www.play-bus.co.uk
Prop: Anthea Head.
Fleet: 2 – 1 double-deck play bus, 1 single-deck play-bus.
Ops incl: private hire.
Livery: Lime Green.

RICHMOND'S COACHES
♿ 🚍 ⏱ ❄ 🔧
THE GARAGE, HIGH STREET, BARLEY, ROYSTON SG8 8JA
Tel: 01763 848226
Fax: 01763 848105
E-mail: postbox@richmonds-coaches.co.uk
Web site: www.richmonds-coaches.co.uk
Dirs: David Richmond, Michael Richmond, Andrew Richmond **Sales & Marketing Man:** Rick Ellis **Asst Ops Man:** Craig Ellis **Ch Eng:** Patrick Granville **Exc & Tours Man:** Natalie Richmond.
Fleet: 23 – 15 single-deck coach, 3 double-deck coach, 2 midibus, 2 midicoach, 1 minibus.
Chassis: 8 Bova, 3 Mercedes, 2 Optare, 7 Van Hool, 3 Volvo.
Bodies: 8 Bova, 2 Optare, 1 Plaxton, 2 Sitcar, 10 Van Hool.
Ops incl: local bus services, school contracts, excursions & tours, private hire, continental tours.
Livery: Cream/Brown.
Ticket System: Wayfarer 3.

ROBINSON KIMBOLTON
⏱ 🚍 ❄
19 THRAPSTON ROAD, KIMBOLTON, HUNTINGDON PE28 0HW
Tel: 01480 860581
Fax: 01480 860801
E-mail: coaches@robinsonkimbolton.co.uk
Web site: www.robinsonkimbolton.co.uk
Man Dir: Charles Robinson **Ops Man:** Jim Darr.
Fleet: 11 single-deck coach, 2 minicoach.
Chassis: Mercedes, Scania, Volvo.
Ops incl: school contracts, excursions & tours, private hire.
Livery: Cream/Red/Brown.

SAFFORD'S COACHES LTD
⏱ 🚍 ❄
HIGHBURY FIELDS, ELTISLEY ROAD, GREAT GRANSDEN, SANDY SG19 3AR
Tel: 01767 677395
Fax: 01767 677742
E-mail: saffordcoaches@btconnect.com
Web site: www.saffordscoaches.co.uk
Dirs: Miss T S Gillett, Mrs S I Gillett.
Fleet: 14 – 2 double-deck bus, 9 single-deck coach, 3 minibus.
Chassis: 2 Alexander Dennis, 1 DAF, 3 Iveco, 1 Mercedes, 7 Volvo.
Bodies: 2 Alexander Dennis, 3 Berkhof, 3 Iveco, 2 Jonckheere, 1 Mercedes, 1 Plaxton, 2 Van Hool.
Ops incl: school contracts, excursions & tours, private hire, continental tours.
Livery: White/Blue/Yellow.

E SHAW & SON
🚍 ⏱ ❄
49 HIGH STREET, MAXEY, PETERBOROUGH PE6 9EF
Tel: 01778 342224
Fax: 01778 380378
E-mail: enquiries@shawscoaches.co.uk
Web site: www.shawscoaches.co.uk
Fleet Name: Shaws of Maxey.
Partners: Jane Duffelen, Richard Shaw, Christopher Shaw.
Fleet: 21 - 2 single-deck bus, 16 single-deck coach, 3 midicoach.
Chassis: 1 Alexander Dennis, 1 Bova, 1 Dennis, 1 Iveco, 2 Mercedes, 1 Scania, 2 Setra, 1 Toyota, 11 Volvo.

Bodies: 1 Alexander Dennis, 1 Berkhof, 1 Bova, 3 Jonckheere, 10 Plaxton, 1 Scania, 2 Sitcar, 2 Setra.
Ops incl: local bus services, school contracts, excursions & tours, private hire, continental tours.
Livery: Blue/White.
Ticket System: Setright.

STAGECOACH EAST
♿ 🚌 🚌
100 COWLEY ROAD, CAMBRIDGE CB4 0DN
Tel: 01223 433250
Fax: 01223 433275
E-mail: cambridge.enquiries@stagecoachbus.com
E-mail: fenland.enquiries@stagecoachbus.com
E-mail: peterborough.enquiries@stagecoachbus.com
Web site: www.stagecoachbus.com
Fleet Names: Stagecoach in Bedfordshire, Stagecoach in Cambridge, Stagecoach in the Fens, Stagecoach in Peterborough, Norfolk Green.
Man Dir: Andy Campbell **Comm Dir:** Zoe Paget **Eng Dir:** Bob Dennison.
Fleet: 393 – 174 double-deck bus, 58 single-deck bus, 55 single-deck coach, 89 midibus, 15 minibus.
Chassis: 171 Alexander Dennis, 12 Dennis, 31 MAN, 15 Optare, 27 Scania, 58 Transbus, 78 Volvo.
Fleet excludes Norfolk Green – see separate entry under Norfolk
Ops incl: local bus services, Cambridge park & ride, Cambridge city sightseeing.
Livery: Stagecoach UK Bus.
Ticket system: Wayfarer 3.
See also Stagecoach East *(Bedfordshire)*, Norfolk Green *(Norfolk)*

SUNFUN LUXURY TRAVEL
♿ ⏱ 🚍 ❄ R R24 🔧
SUN FUN HOUSE, MEADOW DROVE, EARITH PE28 3SA
Tel: 01487 843333
Fax: 01487 843285
E-mail: sales@sunfunholidays.co.uk
Web site: www.sunfuninternational.com
Fleet Names: Sun Fun, Cambridge Coaches.com, ABC Nightliners, Kiddles Coaches.
Dir: D J Collier **Man:** S Fields
Fleet: 43 – 11 double-deck bus, 7 double-deck coach, 6 single-deck bus, 19 single-deck coach.
Chassis: 3 Ayats, 6 Bova, 1 DAF, 6 Irisbus, 7 Neoplan, 1 VDL, 19 Volvo.
Bodies: 6 Alexander, 3 Ayats, 6 Bova, 2 East Lancs, 1 Ikarus, 7 Neoplan, 6 Northern Counties, 10 Plaxton, 1 VDL, 1 Van Hool.
Ops incl: school contracts, excursions & tours, private hire, continental tours.

TOURMASTER COACHES LTD
⏱ 🚍 ⏲ ❄ R R24 🔧
ALDERLANDS, JAMES ROAD, CROWLAND, PETERBOROUGH PE6 0AA
Tel: 01733 211710
Fax: 01733 211378
Recovery: 01733 211639
E-mail: tourmaster@btconnect.com
Web site: www.tourmastercoaches.co.uk
Man Dir: David Dinsey **Dir:** Terri Dinsey
Fleet: 14 - 1 double-deck bus, 12 single-deck coach, 1 minibus.
Chassis: 3 Bova, 2 DAF, 1 LDV, 1 Leyland, 1 Scania, 1 VDL, 5 Volvo.
Bodies: 3 Bova, 1 Irizar, 1 Jonckheere, 1 LDV, 1 Optare, 3 Plaxton, 4 Van Hool.
Ops incl: school contracts, excursions & tours, private hire, continental tours.
Livery: Red/Blue/Turquoise.

TOWLERS COACHES LTD
♿ 🚍 ❄ 🔧
CHURCH ROAD, EMNETH, WISBECH PE14 8AA
Tel: 01945 583645
Fax: 01945 583645
E-mail: towlerscoaches@btconnect.com
Web site: www.towlerscoaches.co.uk
Dirs: Mark Towler, Wendy Shepherd, Anton Towler, Joanne Walton.
Fleet: 10 - 3 double-deck bus, 7 single-deck coach.
Chassis: 2 Iveco, 3 Leyland, 2 Scania, 3 Volvo.
Ops incl: school contracts, tours, private hire.
Livery: White.

UPWELL & DISTRICT COACHES
⏱ 🚍 ⏲ ❄
THE COACH DEPOT, SCHOOL ROAD, UPWELL, WISBECH PE14 9EW
Tel & Fax: 01945 773461
Fleet Name: Hircocks
Partners: Caroline E Parsons, William D Hircock.
Fleet: 2 single-deck coach, 1 midibus.
Chassis: 1 Dennis, 1 Mercedes, 1 Scania.
Bodies: 1 Irizar, 2 Plaxton.
Ops incl: excursions & tours, private hire, school contracts.
Livery: Red/White/Blue.

VEAZEY COACHES LTD
⏱ ❄
WINWICK GARAGE, HAMERTON ROAD, HUNTINGDON PE28 5PX
Tel: 01832 293263
Fax: 01832 293142
Ops incl: school contracts, private hire.

VICEROY OF ESSEX LTD
See Essex

WHIPPET COACHES LTD
♿ 🚍 ⏲ R 🔧
UNIT 1 & 2, ROWLES WAY, BUCKINGWAY BUSINESS PARK, SWAVESEY CB24 4UG
Tel: 01954 230011
Web site: www.go-whippet.co.uk
Dirs: J T Lee, P H Lee, M H Lee.
Fleet: 53 – 28 double-deck bus, 17 single-deck bus, 6 single-deck coach, 2 midibus.
Chassis: 4 DAF, 2 Dennis, 6 Scania, 41 Volvo.
Bodies: 12 Alexander, 12 East Lancs, 3 Jonckheere, 1 MCW, 4 Northern Counties, 10 Plaxton, 3 Van Hool, 9 Wrightbus.
Ops incl: local bus services, school contracts, excursions & tours, private hire, express.
Livery: Blue/Cream with logo.
Ticket System: Almex Eurofare.

W & M TRAVEL
⏱ 🚍 ❄ 🔧
211 MAIN ROAD, CHURCH END, PARSON DROVE, WISBECH PE13 4LF
Tel: 01945 700492
Fax: 01945 700964
E-mail: bill@norman.wanadoo.co.uk
Dir: W Norman.
Fleet: 6 single-deck coach.
Chassis: 4 Dennis, 2 Scania.
Ops incl: local bus services, school contracts, excursions & tours, private hire.

YOUNG'S COACHES
⏱ ❄
42 LODE WAY, HADDENHAM CB6 3UL
Tel: 01353 740991
E-mail: sales@youngscoaches.com
Web site: www.youngscoaches.com
Prop: Brian Young.
Fleet: 3 single-deck coach.
Ops incl: private hire.
Livery: Red & Grey.

ANGEL TRAVEL
& **R24**
108 GORSEY LANE, WARRINGTON
WA2 7RY
Tel: 07930 526132
E-mail: info@angeltravelwarrington.com
Dir: Richard Keane.
Fleet: 3 minibus.
Chassis: Ford, LDV.
Ops incl: school contracts, private hire,
excursions & tours.
Livery: Blue/White.

ANTHONYS TRAVEL
8 CORMORANT DRIVE, RUNCORN
WA7 4UD
Tel: 01928 561460   **Fax:** 01928 561460
Emergency: 07920 154240
E-mail: enquiries@anthonystravel.co.uk
Web site: www.anthonys-travel.co.uk
Partners: Richard Bamber, Anthony Bamber,
Anne Bamber **Ops Mans:** Jodie Waring, Faye
Waring **Ch Eng:** Stephen Knight.
Fleet: 15 – 9 single-deck coach, 1 midibus,
1 midicoach, 4 minibus.
Chassis: 1 Iveco, 2 LDV, 7 MAN, 5 Mercedes,
1 Scania.
Bodies: 3 Beulas, 1 Irizar, 2 Mercedes,
4 Neoplan, 1 Optare, 4 Other.
Ops incl: local bus services, school contracts,
private hire, excursion & tours, wheelchair
accessible executive coaches, corporate team
coaches.
Livery: multi coloured.

ARRIVA NORTH WEST & WALES
Runcorn, Winsford operations – see Arriva
Manchester (Greater Manchester)
Chester operations – see Arriva Buses Wales
(Gwynedd)

ARROWEBROOK COACHES LTD
12 DINGWALL DRIVE, WIRRAL CH49 1SG
Tel: 0800 050 9830
Dirs: A G Parsons, P A Parsons.
E-mail: arrowebrook@fsmail.net
Web site: www.arrowebrookcoaches.com
Fleet: 19 – 4 double-deck bus, 10 single-deck
coach, 2 midibus, 1 midicoach, 1 minibus,
1 minicoach.
Chassis: 1 Alexander Dennis, 1 Bova, 3 DAF,
3 Dennis, 1 Irisbus, 2 Mercedes, 1 Scania,
1 Toyota, 6 Volvo.
Ops incl: local bus services, school contracts,
private hire.
Livery: White/Green.

BARRATT'S COACHES LTD
UNIT 15, MILLBUCK WAY, SPRINGVALE
INDUSTRIAL ESTATE, SANDBACH
CW11 3HZ
Tel: 08450 625096   **Fax:** 08450 627728
E-mail: barrattscoaches@aol.com
Web site: www.barrattscoachessandbach.
co.uk
Man Dir: Gillian Barratt
Fleet: 14 – 1 double-deck bus, 13 single-deck
coaches, 1 minibus.
Chassis: 1 Mercedes, 2 Scania, 11 Volvo.
Bodies: 2 Jonckheere, 1 Leicester, 1
Northern Counties, 2 Plaxton, 8 Van Hool.
Ops incl: local bus services, school contracts,
private hire.
Livery: White & Brown.

BOSTOCK'S COACHES
SPRAGG STREET GARAGE, CONGLETON
CW12 1QH

Tel: 01260 273108
Fax: 01260 276338
E-mail: bostocks@holmeswood.uk.com
Web site: www.holmeswoodcoaches.com
Dirs: J F Aspinall, M Aspinall, C H Aspinall,
D E Aspinall, M F Aspinall, M J Forshaw
Ops Man: M E Bostock **Tours Man:**
J Bostock-Gibson **Ch Eng:** M Boniface.
Fleet: see Holmeswood Coaches.
Ops incl: local bus services, excursions &
tours, private hire, continental tours, school
contracts.
Livery: Green.
A subsidiary of Holmeswood Coaches (see
Lancashire)

CARVERS COACHES
UNIT 10, INDIGO BUSINESS PARK, INDIGO
ROAD, ELLESMERE PORT CH65 4AJ
Tel: 0151 355 8888
Fax: 0151 356 0220
E-mail: carverscoaches@btconnect.com
Web site: www.carverscoaches.co.uk
Prop: M Carver.
Fleet: 28 - 7 double-deck bus, 1 double-deck
coach, 16 single-deck coach, 4 midicoach.
Chassis: Ayats, BMC, Bova, Leyland, MAN,
Mercedes, Scania, Van Hool, Volvo.
Ops incl: school contracts, private hire,
sleeper buses.
Livery: White/Red.

D & G BUS
THE WELLINGTON, 78 HIGH STREET,
UTTOXETER ST14 7JD
Tel: 01270 252970
Fax: 01889 562756
E-mail: info@dgbus.co.uk
Web site: www.dgbus.co.uk
Man Dir: David Reeves **Dir:** Julian Peddle
Gen Man: Heidi Holland **Ops Man:**
Kevin Crawford.
Fleet: 60 – 19 single-deck bus, 30 midibus,
11 minibus.
Chassis: 3 Alexander Dennis, 4 DAF, 6 Dennis,
3 Ford, 1 Iveco, 1 Mercedes, 31 Optare,
3 Scania, 2 VDL, 6 Volkswagen.
Bodies: 3 Alexander Dennis, 1 East Lancs,
2 Marshall, 2 MCV, 11 minibus conversions,
31 Optare, 4 Plaxton, 3 Scania, 4 Wrightbus.
Ops incl: local bus services, school & college
contracts, demand responsive services.
Livery: Red.
Ticket System: Wayfarer TGX150.

FAIRBROTHERS LTD
3 BRATHAY CLOSE, WARRINGTON
WA2 9UY
Tel: 01925 571191
Dir: D Fairbrother.
Fleet: 16 – 9 double-deck bus, 1 single-deck
coach, 6 midibus.
Ops incl: local bus services, school contracts,
private hire.

JOHN FLANAGAN COACH TRAVEL
See Walkers & Flanagan's Coaches (Cheshire)

FREEDOM TRAVEL NORTH LTD, t/a
SMITHS OF MARPLE
72 CROSS LANE, MARPLE SK6 7PZ
Tel: 0161 427 2825
Fax: 0161 449 7731
E-mail: enquiries@smithsofmarple.com
Web site: www.smithsofmarple.com
Dirs: Anthony Vernon, Angie Vernon.
Fleet: 13 - 6 double-deck bus, 2 single-deck
bus, 3 single-deck coach, 2 minibus.

Chassis: Leyland, Mercedes, Setra, Volvo.
Ops incl: local bus services, school contracts,
excursions & tours, private hire.
Livery: White/Orange-Rose.
Ticket System: Wayfarer.

GHA COACHES LTD
See Wrexham

GOLDEN GREEN TRAVEL
COWBROOK LANE, GAWSWORTH,
MACCLESFIELD SK11 0QP
Tel: 01298 83583
E-mail: goldengreentravel@hotmail.co.uk
Web site: www.goldengreentravel.co.uk
Partners: John Worth, Gill Worth,
Derek J Lownds.
Fleet: 11 single-deck coaches.
Chassis: Mercedes.
Ops incl: local bus services, school contracts,
excursions & tours, private hire.

HALTON BOROUGH
TRANSPORT LTD
& **R**
MOOR LANE, WIDNES WA8 7AF
Tel: 0151 423 3333
E-mail: enquiries@haltontransport.co.uk
Web site: www.haltontransport.co.uk
Fleet Name: Halton Transport.
Man Dir & Co Sec: Colin Stafford
Ops Dir: Steve Graham **Fin Dir:**
Adele Cookson.
Fleet: 67 - 57 single-deck bus, 2 midibus,
8 minibus.
Chassis: 12 Alexander Dennis, 25 Dennis,
2 Fiat, 6 Optare, 17 Transbus, 1 VDL.
Bodies: 4 Alexander Dennis, 2 Bluebird,
21 East Lancs, 21 Marshall, 13 MCV, 6 Optare.
Ops incl: local bus services, school contracts.
Livery: Red/Cream.
Ticket System: Wayfarer 200.

HOWARDS TRAVEL GROUP
BELLHOUSE FARM, BELLHOUSE LANE,
HIGHER WALTON, WARRINGTON
WA4 6TR
Tel: 01928 572757
E-mail: info@howards-travel.co.uk
Web site: www.
springfieldsandhowardscoachhire.co.uk
Fleet Names: Howards Travel, Springfield
Bus & Coach.
Prop: Ian Howard.
Fleet: 19 – double-deck bus, single-deck bus,
single-deck coach, midibus.
Ops incl: local bus services, school contracts,
private hire.
Livery: Blue/Cream/Green.

LAMBS
2A BUXTON STREET, HAZEL GROVE,
STOCKPORT SK7 4BB
Tel: 0161 456 1515
Fax: 0161 483 5011
E-mail: lambs139@aol.com
Web site: www.lambscoaches.net
Man Dir: Geoffrey Lamb
Dir: Graham Lamb.
Fleet: 5 – 4 single-deck coach, 1 midicoach.
Chassis: 3 DAF, 1 Mercedes, 1 Setra.
Bodies: 1 Plaxton, 1 Setra, 3 Van Hool.
Ops incl: private hire, school contracts.
Livery: White/Blue.

LE-RAD COACHES & LIMOUSINES
328 HYDE ROAD, WOODLEY SK6 1PF
Tel: 0161 430 2032

Recovery: 07703 145500
Prop: Jean Mycock.
E-mail: le.radtravel@yahoo.co.uk
Fleet: 2 - 1 single-deck coach, 1 minicoach.
Chassis: 1 Ford, 1 LDV.
Ops incl: private hire.

ROY McCARTHY COACHES LTD

THE COACH DEPOT, SNAPE ROAD,
MACCLESFIELD SK10 2NZ
Tel: 01625 425060   **Fax:** 01625 619853
E-mail: sales@roymccarthycoaches.co.uk
Web site: www.roymccarthycoaches.co.uk
Man Dir: Andrew McCarthy
Ops Man: Max McCarthy
Fleet: 11 single-deck coach.
Chassis: 1 Bedford, 1 BMC, 3 Dennis,
6 Volvo.
Bodies: 1 BMC, 10 Plaxton.
Ops incl: school contracts, excursions &
tours, private hire, continental tours.
Livery: Blue/Cream.

MAYNE COACHES LTD

MARSH HOUSE LANE, WARRINGTON
WA1 7ET
Tel: 01925 445588
Fax: 01925 232300
E-mail: coaches@mayne.co.uk
Web site: www.mayne.co.uk
Dirs: D Mayne, C S Mayne **Gen Man:**
Amanda Dykes **Sales Man:** D Williams
Eng Dir: C F Pannell **Eng Man:** E Sutcliffe
Traffic Man: J Drake.
Fleet: 41 - 1 double-deck bus, 40 single-deck
coach.
Chassis: 2 Alexander Dennis, 2 Dennis,
2 Bova, 25 Scania, 10 Volvo.
Bodies: 1 Alexander, 2 Bova, 23 Irizar,
2 Lahden, 11 Plaxton, 2 UVG.
Ops incl: local bus services, school contracts,
excursions & tours, private hire.
Livery: Cream/Red.

MEREDITHS COACHES LTD

LYDGATE, WELL STREET, MALPAS
SK14 8DE
Tel: 01948 860405
Fax: 01948 860162
E-mail: david@meredithscoaches.co.uk
Web site: www.meredithscoaches.co.uk
Dirs: J K Meredith, Mrs M E Meredith,
D J Meredith **Co Sec:** Mrs Kirin Meredith
Ch Eng: C Bellis.
Fleet: 16 single-deck coach.
Chassis: 1 Leyland, 5 Scania, 10 Volvo.
Bodies: 5 Irizar, 1 Jonckheere, 10 Plaxton.
Ops incl: local bus services, school contracts,
private hire.
Livery: Cream with Red/Yellow.

MILLMANS COACHES

STATION YARD, GREEN LANE, PADGATE,
WARRINGTON WA1 4JR
Tel: 01925 822298
Fax: 01925 813181
Prop: Eric Millman.
Fleet: 5 – 2 single-deck bus, 3 single-deck
coach.
Chassis: 2 Leyland, 1 Scania, 2 Volvo.
Bodies: 1 Alexander, 1 Berkhof, 1 East Lancs,
2 Plaxton.
Ops incl: school contracts, excursions &
tours, private hire.
Livery: Blue/White.

MOORE'S COACHES LTD

6 HEREFORD WAY, MIDDLEWICH
CW10 9GS

Tel/Fax: 01606 836733
Dirs: Carol Perez-Garcia, Jose Perez-Garcia.
E-mail: moorestravel@aol.com
Web site: www.moorescoaches.co.uk
Fleet: 4 single-deck coach.
Chassis: 1 Scania, 3 Volvo.
Bodies: 1 Berkhof, 1 Irizar, 1 Jonckheere,
1 Van Hool.
Ops incl: school contracts, private hire.
Livery: White.

SELWYNS TRAVEL SERVICES

CAVENDISH FARM ROAD, WESTON,
RUNCORN WA7 4LU
Tel: 01928 529036
Fax: 01928 591872
Recovery: 01928 572108
E-mail: info@selwyns.co.uk
Web site: www.selwyns.co.uk
Regional Dir: Steve Whiteway
Man Dir: Selwyn A Jones
Gen Man: Alan P Williamson
Co Sec/Acct: Richard E Williams
Fleet Eng: Cledwyn Owen.
Fleet: 83 – 3 double-deck bus, 69 single-deck
coach, 8 midicoach, 1 minibus, 2 minibus.
Chassis: 1 Alexander Dennis, 19 DAF, 3 MAN,
11 Mercedes, 5 Scania, 5 VDL, 39 Volvo.
Bodies: 1 Alexander Dennis, 1 Berkhof,
32 Caetano, 2 East Lancs, 1 EVM, 1 KVC,
1 Marcopolo, 1 Mercedes, 1 Optare,
21 Plaxton, 19 Van Hool.
Ops incl: local bus services, school contracts,
excursions & tours, private hire, express,
continental tours.
Liveries: White/Blue/Orange/Green, National
Express.
Ticket System: Wayfarer.
Incorporating Hardings Tours and Haytons
Travel. A subsidiary of RATP Dev UK Ltd.

SHEARINGS HOLIDAYS

BARLEYCASTLE LANE, APPLETON,
WARRINGTON WA4 4SR
Tel: 01925 214600
Fax: 01925 262606
See Shearings Holidays (Greater Manchester)

STAGECOACH MERSEYSIDE AND SOUTH LANCASHIRE

GILMOSS BUS DEPOT, EAST LANCASHIRE
ROAD, LIVERPOOL L11 0BB
Tel: 0151 330 6200
Fax: 0151 330 6210
E-mail: enquiries.merseyside@
stagecoachbus.com
Web site: www.stagecoachbus.com
Fleet Names: Stagecoach in Merseyside/
Lancashire/Wirral/Chester.
Man Dir: Elisabeth Tasker
Eng Dir: Tony Cockroft **Ops Dir:** Rob Jones
Comm Man: James Mellor.
Fleet: 433 - 117 double-deck bus, 2 open-top
bus, 183 single-deck bus, 90 midibus,
41 minibus.
Chassis: 154 Alexander Dennis, 11 Bluebird,
31 Dennis, 2 Leyland, 50 MAN, 51 Optare,
62 Scania, 26 Transbus, 46 Volvo.
Ops incl: local bus services, school contracts,
excursions & tours, private hire, express.
Livery: Stagecoach UK Bus.
Ticket System: Wayfarer TGX.

JIM STONES COACHES

THE JAYS, LIGHT OAKS ROAD, GLAZEBURY,
WARRINGTON WA3 5LH
Tel/Fax: 01925 766465
E-mail: jimstones@sky.com
Web site: www.jimstonescoaches.com
Partners: J B Stones, Mrs J P Stones
Gen Man: R Dyson **Fleet Eng:** S Mayo.

Fleet: 14 – 2 single-deck bus, 12 midibus.
Chassis: 13 Alexander Dennis, 1 Leyland.
Bodies: 13 Alexander Dennis, 1 DAB.
Ops incl: local bus services, school contracts.
Livery: Blue/White.
Ticket System: Almex, Wayfarer 3.

WALKERS & FLANAGAN'S COACHES

OLD ROAD, ANDERTON, NORTHWICH
CW9 6AG
Tel: 01606 76666
Fax: 01606 781069
E-mail: walkers@holmeswood.uk.com
Web site: www.holmeswoodcoaches.com
Dirs: J F Aspinall, M Aspinall, C H Aspinall,
D E Aspinall, M F Aspinall, M J Forshaw
Ops Man: M E Bostock **Tours Man:**
J Bostock-Gibson **Ch Eng:** M Boniface.
Fleet: see Holmeswood Coaches.
Ops incl: local bus services, excursions &
tours, private hire, continental tours, school
contracts.
Livery: Green.
A subsidiary of Holmeswood Coaches (see
Lancashire)

WARRINGTON BOROUGH TRANSPORT LTD

WILDERSPOOL CAUSEWAY,
WARRINGTON WA4 6PT
Tel: 01925 634296
Fax: 01925 418382
E-mail: mail@networkwarrington.co.uk
Web site: www.networkwarrington.co.uk
Fleet Name: Network Warrington
Chairman: Les Hoyle **Interim Man Dir:**
Damian Graham **Fin Dir:** Ann Marie Slavin
Head of Ops: Richard Mayes
Comm Man: Phil Pearson.
Fleet: 107 – 22 double-deck bus, 31 single-
deck bus, 48 midibus, 6 minibus.
Chassis: 7 Dennis, 1 Leyland, 18 Optare,
48 VDL, 33 Volvo.
Bodies: 17 Alexander, 4 Marshall, 3 MCV,
18 Optare, 65 Wrightbus.
Ops incl: local bus services, school contracts,
private hire.
Livery: Red/Cream.
Ticket System: Wayfarer 3.

WARRINGTON COACHWAYS LTD

ATHLONE ROAD, LONGFORD,
WARRINGTON WA2 8JJ
Tel: 01925 415299
Fax: 01925 652215
Fleet Names: Bennett's Travel, Warrington
Coachways.
Props: B A Bennett, D B Bennett.
Fleet: double-deck bus, single-deck bus,
single-deck coach, midibus, midicoach, minibus.
Ops incl: local bus services, school contracts,
private hire.
Livery: White/Blue.

WHITEGATE TRAVEL LTD

UNIT 38, COSGROVE BUSINESS PARK,
DAISY BANK LANE, ANDERTON
CW9 6AA
Tel: 01606 786833
E-mail: whitegatetravel@btinternet.com
Web site: www.whitegatetravel.com
Dir: K Prince.
Fleet: 10 – 3 midicoach, 6 minibus,
1 minicoach.
Chassis: 2 Ford Transit, 1 Iveco, 2 LDV,
4 Mercedes, 1 Volkswagen.
Ops incl: local bus services, school contracts,
private hire.
Livery: Yellow/White.

A2B NEWQUAY TRAVEL LTD

7 PORTH WAY, NEWQUAY TR7 3LP
Tel: 01637 875555
E-mail: enquiries@newquaytravel.co.uk
Web site: www.a2bnewquay.co.uk
Dirs: D Martin, L Martin.
Fleet: 28 – 5 double-deck bus, 7 single-deck coach, 2 midibus, 2 midicoach, 12 minibus.
Chassis: DAF, Dennis, Ford Transit, Leyland, LDV, MAN, Mercedes, Renault, Scania, Volvo.
Ops incl: local bus services, school contracts, private hire.
Livery: Silver.

A-LINE COACHES

CHAPEL COTTAGE, ST JOHN, TORPOINT PL11 3AW
Tel/Fax: 01752 822740
Prop: D Tweedie.
Fleet: 6 – 1 double-deck bus, 4 midibus, 1 midicoach.
Chassis: 1 Iveco, 4 Mercedes, 1 Volvo.
Ops incl: local bus services, private hire, school contracts.

BAKER'S COACHES

THE GARAGE, DULOE, LISKEARD PL14 4PL
Tel: 01503 262359
Fax: 01503 262422
E-mail: bakersatduloe@aol.com
Fleet Name: KTM Coaches
Fleet: 8 – 4 single-deck coach, 2 midicoach, 2 minibus.
Chassis: 2 DAF, 1 Ford Transit, 1 LDV, 2 Mercedes, 2 Volvo.
Ops incl: school contracts, private hire.
Livery: White with Blue.

CARADON RIVIERA TOURS LTD

THE GARAGE, UPTON CROSS, LISKEARD, PL14 5AX
Tel: 01579 362226
Fleet: single-deck coach, midicoach.
Ops incl: school contracts, private hire, excursions & tours.

CORNWALL BUSWAYS LTD

35 MEADOW RISE, PENWITHICK, ST AUSTELL PL26 8UG
Tel: 01726 71952
Dir: N Siddaway.
Ops incl: local bus services.

DAC COACHES LTD

Ceased trading since LRB 2014 went to press

DARLEY FORD TRAVEL

Ceased trading since LRB 2014 went to press

FIRST DEVON, CORNWALL & CENTRAL SOMERSET

THE RIDE, CHELSON MEADOW, PLYMOUTH PL9 7JT
Tel: 01872 305950
Fax: 01752 495230
E-mail: firstdevonandcornwall@firstgroup.com
Web site: www.firstgroup.com; www.busesofsomerset.co.uk
Man Dir: Alex Carter.
Fleet Names: First, Truronian, The Buses of Somerset.
Fleet: 325 – 113 double-deck bus, 46 single-deck bus, 21 single-deck coach, 7 articulated bus, 108 midibus, 1 midicoach, 29 minibus.
Chassis: 29 Alexander Dennis, 97 Dennis, 1 Ford Transit, 12 Mercedes, 26 Optare,
15 Scania, 16 Transbus, 118 Volvo, 9 Wrightbus.
Bodies: 23 Alexander, 29 Alexander Dennis, 19 East Lancs, 1 Ford, 11 Irizar, 6 Marshall, 9 Mercedes, 42 Northern Counties, 26 Optare, 73 Plaxton, 15 Transbus, 69 Wrightbus.
Ops incl: local bus services, school contracts, private hire.
Livery: FirstGroup UK Bus.
Ticket System: Almex.

GROUP TRAVEL

ENTERPRISE PARK, MIDWAY ROAD, BODMIN PL31 2FQ
Tel/Fax: 01208 77989
E-mail: benneymoon@btinternet.com
Web site: www.grouptravelcoachhire.co.uk
Dirs: Dawn Moon, David Benney
Fleet: 30 – 2 single-deck bus, 12 single-deck coach, 5 midibus, 2 midicoach, 9 minibus.
Chassis: 2 Autosan, 3 Bova, 7 Dennis, 1 King Long, 10 Mercedes, 1 Optare, 5 Volvo.
Ops incl: local bus services, school contracts, excursions & tours, private hire.
Livery: Blue/Silver.
Ticket system: Ticketer.

HILLS SERVICES LTD

See Devon

HOPLEYS COACHES LTD

GOVER FARM, GOVER HILL, MOUNT HAWKE, TRURO TR4 8BH
Tel/Fax: 01872 553786
E-mail: hopleys.coaches@btconnect.com
Web site: www.hopleyscoaches.com
Partners: B Hopley, D R Hopley, N A Hopley.
Fleet: 17 - 1 double-deck bus, 11 single-deck coach, 3 midibus, 2 midicoach.
Chassis: 3 Bova, 3 Mercedes, 2 Optare, 9 Volvo.
Ops incl: local bus services, school contracts, excursions & tours, private hire.
Livery: Red/White/Grey.
Ticket System: Ticketer.

JACKETTS COACHES

KINGSETT HOUSE, ALBASTON, GUNNISLAKE PL18 9AL
Tel: 01752 787797
E-mail: info@jackettscoaches.com
Web site: www.jackettscoaches.co.uk
Prop: T Jackett.
Fleet: 17 – 2 single-deck bus, 3 single-deck coach, 9 midibus, 3 minibus.
Chassis: 2 Alexander Dennis, 5 Dennis, 6 Mercedes, 1 Scania, 1 Transbus, 2 Volvo.
Bodies: 4 Alexander, 1 Autobus, 9 Plaxton, 1 Transbus, 2 Van Hool.
Ops incl: local bus services, school contracts, excursions & tours, private hire.
Liveries: Red (Buses); White (Coaches).

MOUNTS BAY COACHES LTD

4 ALEXANDRA ROAD, PENZANCE TR18 4LY
Tel: 01736 363320
Fax: 01736 366985
E-mail: mountsbaycoaches@btconnect.com
Web site: www.mountsbaycoaches.co.uk
Dir: Jeff Oxenham
Fleet: 9 - 7 single-deck coach, 2 midicoach.
Chassis: 2 Toyota, 7 Volvo.
Bodies: 2 Caetano, 7 Van Hool.
Ops incl: school contracts, excursions & tours, private hire.
Livery: Blue/White.

OATES TRAVEL

1 HIGH STREET, ST IVES
TR26 1RS
Tel: 01736 795343
Fax: 01736 795344
E-mail: margaret@oatestravel.co.uk
Web site: www.oatestravel.co.uk
Prop: D Oates.
Fleet: 6 – 4 single-deck coach, 2 midicoach.
Chassis: 2 Toyota, 4 Volvo.
Bodies: 2 Caetano, 1 Plaxton, 3 Van Hool.
Ops incl: excursions & tours, private hire, continental tours.
Livery: White with Yellow/Orange/Black.

OTS MINIBUS & COACH HIRE

LAMANVA, FALMOUTH
TR10 9BJ
Tel/Fax: 01326 378100
E-mail: office@otsfalmouth.co.uk
Web site: www.otsfalmouth.co.uk
Dirs: Stephen Moore, Ben Moore
Fleet: 6 – 1 single-deck bus, 1 single-deck coach, 1 midicoach, 2 minibus, 1 minicoach.
Chassis: 4 Mercedes, 2 Volvo.
Bodies: 1 Alexander Dennis, 1 Berkhof, 4 Mercedes.
Ops incl: local bus services, school contracts, private hire.
Livery: Brown with Blue Waves.
Ticket system: Ticketer.

PENMERE MINIBUS SERVICES

28 BOSEMEOR ROAD, FALMOUTH
TR11 4PU
Tel: 01326 378100
E-mail: benjamin.moore@tiscali.co.uk
Web site: www.penmereminibus.co.uk
Props: Ben & Sharon Moore.
Fleet: 6 – 1 single-deck coach, 1 midicoach, 4 minicoach.
Chassis: 4 Mercedes, 1 Optare, 1 Volvo.
Ops incl: school contracts, private hire.
Livery: White.

ROSELYN COACHES LTD

MIDDLEWAY GARAGE, ST BLAZEY ROAD, PAR PL24 2JA
Tel: 01726 813737
Fax: 01726 813739
Recovery: 01726 813737
E-mail: info@roselyncoaches.co.uk
Web site: www.roselyncoaches.co.uk
Dir: Jonathan Ede
Ch Eng: Graham Paramor
Ops Man: Brian Allen.
Fleet: 42 - 14 double-deck bus, 2 double-deck executive coach, 6 single-deck bus, 20 single-deck coach.
Chassis: 2 Bova, 4 DAF, 36 Volvo.
Bodies: 14 Alexander, 2 Bova, 4 Northern Counties, 7 Plaxton, 13 Van Hool, 2 Wrightbus.
Ops incl: local bus services, school contracts, excursions & tours, private hire.
Livery: Green/Gold.

ROYAL BUSES

VICTORY HEIGHTS, THE BURROWS, ST IVES TR26 1GD
Tel: 01736 797982
E-mail: info@royalbuses.co.uk
Web site: www.royalbuses.co.uk
Fleet: 6 midibus.
Chassis: Mercedes
Ops incl: local bus services, private hire.
Livery: Red.

Cornwall

SMITHS COACHES (LISKEARD) LTD

SPRINGFIELD VILLA, FIVE LANES,
DOBWALLS, LISKEARD PL14 6JN
Tel: 01579 321607
E-mail: andrew.smith007@yahoo.co.uk
Web site: www.smithscoachesliskeardltd.
co.uk
Fleet: 5 – 4 single-deck coach, 1 minibus.
Chassis: 1 Irisbus, 1 MAN, 1 Renault, 1 Scania,
1 Volvo.
Ops incl: school contracts, private hire.

TAVISTOCK COUNTRY BUS

2 WOODHOLME, WINSOR LANE,
KELLY BRAY PL17 8HE
Tel: 07580 260683
Web site: www.tavistockcountrybus.co.uk
Fleet Name: Tavistock Country Bus
Chairman: K W Potter Sec: A Everitt.
Fleet: 1 minibus.
Chassis: Mercedes.
Ops incl: local bus services, private hire.
Livery: Red/White.
Ticket System: Wayfarer.

TILLEY'S COACHES

THE COACH STATION, WAINHOUSE
CORNER, BUDE EX23 0AZ
Tel: 01840 230244   Fax: 01840 230752
Man Dir: Paul Tilley
Fleet: 7 – 5 single-deck coach, 2 midicoach.
Chassis: 1 DAF, 3 Irisbus, 1 Iveco, 1 Mercedes,
1 Volvo.
Ops incl: school contracts, private hire,
excursions & tours.
Livery: White/Cream/Maroon.

TRAVEL CORNWALL

THE OLD COACH GARAGE, ST AUSTELL
STREET, SUMMERCOURT, NEWQUAY TR8 5DR
Tel: 01726 861108

Fax: 01872 510648
E-mail: enquiries@travelcornwall.uk.com
Web site: www.travelcornwall.uk.com
Dirs: Rob Ryder, Sam Ryder.
Fleet: 19 – 1 single-deck bus, 12 midibus,
6 minibus.
Chassis: 4 Dennis, 1 LDV, 7 Mercedes,
7 Optare.
Bodies: 1 Alexander, 1 Mercedes, 7 Optare,
7 Plaxton, 2 UVG, 1 Other.
Ops incl: local bus services, school contracts,
private hire.
Livery: Red, White & Blue.
Ticket System: Ticketer.

TRELEY COACH HIRE

ST BURYAN GARAGE, ST BURYAN,
PENZANCE TR19 6DZ
Tel: 01736 810322
E-mail: treleycoaches@live.co.uk
Web site: www.treleycoaches.co.uk
Dirs: A J Ley, A D Ley.
Fleet: 5 - 4 single-deck coach, 1 minicoach.
Chassis: 4 Alexander Dennis, 1 Mercedes.
Ops incl: local bus services, school contracts,
private hire.
Livery: White/Orange/Red/Yellow.

TRURONIAN LTD

See First Devon, Cornwall & Somerset.

WESTERN GREYHOUND LTD

WESTERN HOUSE, ST AUSTELL STREET,
SUMMERCOURT, NEWQUAY TR8 5DR
Tel: 01637 871871
Recovery: 01872 510511 Ext *225
E-mail: info@westerngreyhound.com
Web site: www.westerngreyhound.com
Man Dir: Mark Howarth
Dir & Co Sec: Mari Howarth
Dir: Robin Orbell.
Fleet: 74 - 8 double-deck bus, 62 midibus,
4 minibus.
Chassis: 25 Dennis, 21 Mercedes, 28 Optare.

Bodies: 8 Alexander, 28 Optare, 38 Plaxton.
Ops incl: local bus services, school contracts.
Livery: Green & White.
Ticket System: VIX ERG (electronic).

WHEAL BRITON TRAVEL

MOOR COTTAGE, BLACKWATER, TRURO
TR4 8HH
Tel: 01872 560281
Fax: 01872 560691
Web site: www.whealbritontravel.com
Prop: Stephen J Palmer.
Fleet: 27- 22 single-deck coach, 3 midicoach,
2 minibus.
Chassis: 1 LDV, 4 Mercedes, 22 Volvo.
Bodies: 3 Jonckheere, 1 LDV, 1 Mercedes,
1 Onyx, 14 Plaxton, 1 Sitcar, 5 Van Hool,
1 Other.
Ops incl: school contracts, excursions &
tours, private hire, continental tours.
Livery: Cream.

WILLIAMS TRAVEL

DOLCOATH INDUSTRIAL PARK,
DOLCOATH ROAD, CAMBORNE
TR14 8RA
Tel: 01209 717152
Fax: 01209 612511
E-mail: enquiries@williams-travel.co.uk
Web site: www.williams-travel.co.uk
Prop: Fred Williams
Operations Man: Garry Williams
Workshop Man: Shaun Hoskins
Tours Man: Paula Hoskins.
Fleet: 38 – 7 double-deck bus, 13 single-deck
coach, 3 midicoach, 14 minibus, 1 minicoach.
Chassis: 4 Bova, 4 Ford Transit, 7 Iveco,
8 Mercedes, 15 Volvo.
Ops incl: local bus services, school contracts,
excursions & tours, private hire, continental
tours.
Livery: White with Red & Orange.
Ticket System: Wayfarer.

CUMBRIA

ALBA TRAVEL LTD

BECK BANK, GREAT SALKELD, PENRITH
CA11 9LN
Tel: 01768 870219
Fax: 01768 870819
E-mail: enquiries@albatravelcumbria.co.uk
Web site: www.albatravelcumbria.co.uk
Dirs: Allan Holmes, Barbara Holmes.
Fleet: 13 – 2 single-deck coach, 4 midibus, 2
midicoach, 4 minibus, 1 minicoach.
Chassis: 6 Mercedes, 4 Optare, 2 Scania, 1
Volkswagen.
Ops incl: local bus services, excursions &
tours, private hire.
Livery: White with Maroon/Yellow.

FRANK ALLISON LTD

MAIN STREET, BROUGH, KIRKBY STEPHEN
CA17 4AY
Tel: 01768 341328
Fax: 01768 341517
E-mail: julie@grandprixservices.co.uk
Web site: www.grandprixservices.co.uk
Fleet Name: Grand Prix Services.
Dir: Frank Allison.
Fleet: 10 – 2 single-deck bus, 5 single-deck
coach, 1 midibus, 1 midicoach, 1 minibus.
Chassis: 1 Ford Transit, 1 Mercedes, 2
Optare, 6 Volvo.
Bodies: 2 Caetano, 1 Ford, 2 Optare, 3
Plaxton, 1 Van Hool, 1 Wrightbus.
Ops incl: local bus services, school contracts,
excursions & tours, private hire.

Livery: White.
Ticket System: Wayfarer TGX150.

APOLLO 8 TRAVEL

KNOTT HALL FARM, LOWGILL, KENDAL
LA8 9DG
Tel: 01539 824086
Fax: 01539 824239
E-mail: info@apollo8travel.co.uk
Web site: www.coachcumbria.co.uk
Ops incl: local bus services, private hire.
Livery: White.

ROBERT BENSON COACHES LTD

7 MAIN ROAD, SEATON, WORKINGTON
CA14 1ES
Tel: 01900 511245
Fleet incl: single-deck coach, midicoach,
minibus, minicoach.
Chassis: Mercedes, Volkswagen, Volvo.
Ops incl: private hire, school contracts.

BOWMAN'S COACHES

1 GEORGE STREET, NEWCASTLETON
TD9 0QP
Tel/Fax: 01697 473262
Recovery: 07711 280475
E-mail: enquiries@bowmans-coaches.co.uk
Fleet: 3 – 2 single-deck coach, 1 minicoach.
Chassis: 1 Mercedes, 1 Scania, 1 Volvo.
Bodies: 1 Neoplan, 2 Plaxton.
Ops incl: excursions & tours, private hire,

continental tours.
Livery: White with Blue vinyls.
Associated with Telford's Coaches,
Newcastleton (see Scotland, Borders)

S H BROWNRIGG

ENNERDALE MILL, EGREMONT
CA22 2PN
Tel: 01946 820205
Fax: 01946 821919
E-mail: enquiries@shbrownrigg.co.uk
Web site: www.shbrownrigg.co.uk
Dir: R J Cook Ops Man: B Marshall
Senior Officers: Mrs D Marshall,
Mrs L Holliday.
Fleet: 18 - 9 single-deck coach, 2 midicoach,
5 minibus, 2 minicoach.
Chassis: Mercedes, Volvo.
Ops incl: school contracts, private hire.
Livery: White/Purple.

CALDEW COACHES LTD

6 CALDEW DRIVE, DALSTON, CARLISLE
CA5 7NS
Tel/Fax: 01228 711690
E-mail: caldewcoachesltd@aol.com
Dirs: Hugh McKerrell, Ann McKerrell,
Bill Rogers Co Sec: Mandy Rogers.
Fleet: 12 - 1 single-deck coach, 3 midicoach, 5
minibus, 3 minicoach.
Chassis: 1 Bova, 10 Mercedes, 1 Renault.
Ops incl: school contracts, private hire.
Livery: Red/White.

CARR'S COACHES

CONTROL TOWER, SILLOTH INDUSTRIAL ESTATE, SILLOTH CA7 4NS
Tel: 01697 331276
Fax: 01697 333823
Web site: www.carrs-coaches.co.uk
Prop: A J Markley **Tran Man:** P J Markley
Fin Man: Mrs D Markley **Ch Eng:** Paul Allison.
Fleet: 7 - 4 single-deck coach, 1 midicoach, 2 minibus.
Chassis: 1 Dennis, 1 Ford Transit, 2 Mercedes, 2 Scania.
Bodies: 1 Berkhof, 2 Irizar, 2 Van Hool, 2 Other.
Ops incl: school contracts, private hire.
Livery: Blue/White.

CLARKSON'S COACHWAYS

UNIT 2B, ASHBURNER WAY, WALNEY ROAD INDUSTRIAL ESTATE, BARROW IN FURNESS LA14 5UZ
Tel: 01229 828022
Fax: 01229 828067
E-mail: info@clarksoncoachways.co.uk
Web site: www.clarksoncoachways.co.uk
Dirs: Susan Clarkson, Neil Clarkson.
Fleet: 13 - 4 single-deck coach, 1 open-top bus, 5 midicoach, 1 minibus, 1 minicoach.
Chassis: 1 Ford Transit, 3 Irisbus, 1 Iveco, 1 Leyland, 3 MAN, 2 Mercedes, 1 Renault, 1 Temsa.
Ops incl: school contracts, excursions & tours, private hire.
Livery: two-tone Green.

COAST TO COAST PACKHORSE LTD

CHESTNUT HOUSE, CROSBY GARRETT, KIRKBY STEPHEN CA17 4PR
Tel: 01768 371777
Fax: 01768 371777
E-mail: cnquiries@c2cpackhorse.co.uk
Web site: www.c2cpackhorse.co.uk
Props: S & L Jones.
Fleet: 2 minibus.
Chassis: 2 Ford Transit.
Ops incl: local bus services, school contracts, private hire.

CUMBRIA COACHES LTD

A1 GA HOUSE, BRUNEL WAY, DURRANHILL INDUSTRIAL ESTATE, CARLISLE CA1 3NQ
Tel: 01228 404300
Fax: 01228 404309
E-mail: enquiries@cumbriacoaches.co.uk
Web site: www.cumbriacoaches.co.uk
Fleet: 10 - 9 single-deck coach, 1 minibus.
Chassis: 2 Bova, 1 DAF, 1 Ford Transit, 1 VDL, 5 Volvo.
Ops incl: excursions & tours, private hire, express, continental tours, school contracts.

JOHN HOBAN TRAVEL LTD

UNIT 8, KERRY PARK TRADING ESTATE, SOLWAY ROAD, WORKINGTON CA14 3TT
Tel: 01900 603579
Fax: 01900 602741
E-mail: enquiries@johnahoban.co.uk
Web site: www.johnhoban.co.uk
Partners: John Hoban, Allison Hoban.
Fleet: 15 - 8 midicoach, 7 minibus.
Chassis: 1 Fiat, 1 Iveco, 11 Mercedes, 2 Volkswagen.
Ops incl: local bus services, school contracts, private hire.
Livery: White with Blue/Brown.

IRVINGS COACH HIRE LTD

JESMOND STREET, CARLISLE CA1 2DE
Tel: 01228 521666
Fax: 01228 515792
E-mail: office@irvings-coaches.co.uk
Web site: www.irvings-coaches.co.uk
Man Dir: R Irving **Dir:** Mrs A Percival
Tran Man: K Cartner.
Fleet: 10 single-deck coach.
Chassis: 2 DAF, 8 Volvo.
Bodies: 2 Bova, 1 Jonckheere, 2 Plaxton, 5 Van Hool.
Ops incl: school contracts, excursions & tours, private hire, continental tours.
Livery: Orange/White/Black.

K & B TRAVEL LTD

33 KING STREET, PENRITH CA11 7AY
Tel: 01768 868600
Fax: 01768 862715
E-mail: mail@kbtravel.freeserve.co.uk
Web site: www.kbtravel.co.uk
Man Dir: G Lund **Dirs:** B Bainbridge **(Co Sec),** T Lund.
Fleet: 11 - 6 single-deck coach, 2 minibus, 3 minicoach.
Chassis: 5 Mercedes, 4 Neoplan, 2 Volvo.
Ops incl: excursions & tours, private hire, school contracts, continental tours.
Livery: Blue with Green lettering.

LAKES HOTEL & SUPERTOURS

1 HIGH STREET, WINDERMERE LA23 1AF
Tel: 01539 442751
Fax: 01539 446026
E-mail: admin@lakes-supertours.com
Web site: www.lakes-supertours.com
Dirs: R Minford, A Dobson.
Fleet: 3 minibus.
Chassis: 2 Renault, 1 Vauxhall.
Ops incl: excursions & tours.
Livery: White/Purple/Gold.

LECKS TRAVEL INTERNATIONAL

SAUNDERPOT, HAVERTHWAITE, ULVERSTON LA12 8AB
Tel: 01539 531220
Fax: 01539 531225
E-mail: leckstravel@yahoo.co.uk
Web site: www.leckstravel.co.uk
Dir: A Newby.
Fleet: 10 - 2 single-deck coach, 2 midibus, 2 midicoach, 3 minibus, 1 minicoach
Chassis: 2 LDV, 3 Mercedes, 2 Optare, 2 Volvo, 1 Wrightbus.
Ops incl: local bus services, excursions & tours, private hire.

MOUNTAIN GOAT

VICTORIA STREET, WINDERMERE LA23 1AD
Tel: 01539 445161
Fax: 01539 445164
E-mail: tours@mountain-goat.com
Web site: www.mountain-goat.co.uk
Dirs: Peter Nattrass, Stephen Broughton, Norman Stoller **Comm Dir:** Peter Brendling
Fleet Man: John Collens **Office Man:** Sue Todd.
Fleet: 16 minibus.
Chassis: 15 Mercedes, 1 Renault.
Ops incl: local bus services, excursions & tours, private hire.
Livery: White with Green/Red.
Ticket System: Wayfarer.

NBM HIRE LTD

CROMWELL ROAD, PENRITH CA11 7JW
Tel: 01768 892727
Fax: 01768 899680
E-mail: sales@nbmtravel.co.uk
Web site: www.nbmtravel.co.uk
Fleet: 11 – 7 single-deck coach, 2 midicoach, 3 minibus.
Chassis: 1 AEC, 4 DAF, 1 Iveco, 4 Mercedes, 1 Scania.
Ops incl: excursions & tours, private hire, school contracts.
Livery: White/Blue.

REAYS COACHES LTD

STRAWBERRY FIELDS, SYKE PARK, WIGTON CA7 9NE
Tel: 01697 349999
Fax: 01697 349900
E-mail: info@reays.co.uk
Web site: www.reays.co.uk
Fleet Names: Reays, City Hopper, Village Hopper.
Depots at: Wigton, Egremont, Penrith.
Man Dir: Chris Reay **Dir:** Nicola Reay
Ops Man: Chris Bowness.
Fleet: 80 – 1 double-deck bus, 2 open-top bus, 5 single-deck bus, 27 single-deck coach, 13 midibus, 6 midicoach, 26 minibus.
Chassis: 6 Alexander Dennis, 8 Enterprise, 3 Ford Transit, 4 Irisbus, 2 LDV, 14 Mercedes, 3 Optare, 1 Scania, 7 Van Hool, 9 VDL, 21 Volvo, 2 Wrightbus.
Bodies: 15 Alexander, 4 Alexander Dennis, 5 Berkhof, 3 Ford, 1 Koch, 1 LDV, 3 MCV, 1 Mercedes, 1 Northern Counties, 3 Optare, 21 Plaxton, 6 Transbus, 1 Unvi, 9 Van Hool, 2 Wrightbus, 4 Other.
Ops incl: local bus services, school contracts, excursions & tours, private hire, continental tours.
Livery: Reays Blue & White Triangles.
Ticket System: Wayfarer.

ROBINSONS COACHES

STATION ROAD GARAGE, APPLEBY CA16 6TX
Tel: 01768 351424
Prop: S E Graham.
Fleet: 8 – 1 single-deck bus, 4 single-deck coach, 1 midicoach, 1 minibus, 1 minicoach.
Chassis: 1 Bova, 1 DAF, 1 Iveco, 1 Mercedes, 2 Scania, 1 Volkswagen, 1 VDL.
Ops incl: local bus services, school contracts, private hire.
Livery: Green/White.

KEN ROUTLEDGE TRAVEL

ALLERDALE YARD WORKSHOPS, LOW ROAD, BRIGHAM, COCKERMOUTH CA13 0XH
Tel: 01900 822795
Fax: 01900 822593
E-mail: michael@krtravel.co.uk
Web site: www.kenroutledgetravel.co.uk
Fleet: 10 - 5 midicoach, 5 minibus.
Chassis: Mercedes.
Ops incl: local bus services, private hire.
Livery: White with Orange/Brown.

SIMS TRAVEL

HUNHOLME GARAGE, BOOT, HOLMROOK CA19 1TF
Tel: 01946 723227
Fax: 01946 723158
E-mail: info@simstravel.co.uk
Web site: www.simstravel.co.uk
Partners: Andrew Sim, Peter Sim.
Fleet: 12 - 5 single-deck coach, 2 midicoach,

4 minibus, 1 minicoach.
Chassis: 2 Bova, 2 Ford Transit, 1 MAN, 3 Mercedes, 1 Optare, 1 Volkswagen, 2 Volvo.
Ops incl: excursions & tours, private hire, school contracts.
Livery: White/Red/Maroon.

STACEY'S COACHES LTD
♿ ♨ 🍴 ❄
UNIT 7, MILLRACE ROAD, WILLOWHOLME INDUSTRIAL ESTATE, CARLISLE CA2 3RS
Tel: 01228 511127
E-mail: info@staceys-coaches.co.uk
Web site: www.staceys-coaches.co.uk
Dirs: B H Barnes, C Barnes.
Fleet: 19 – 7 single-deck coach, 8 minibus, 4 minicoach.
Chassis: 1 Bova, 1 DAF, 5 LDV, 7 Mercedes, 2 Neoplan, 3 Volvo.
Ops incl: local bus services, excursions & tours, school contracts, private hire
Liveries: White, Silver

STAGECOACH IN CUMBRIA AND NORTH LANCASHIRE
♿ ▭ ☑
BROADACRE HOUSE, 16-20 LOWTHER STREET, CARLISLE CA3 8DA
Tel: 01228 597222
Fax: 01228 597888
E-mail: cumbrianorthlancs.enquiries@ stagecoachbus.com
Web site: www.stagecoachbus.com
Fleet Names: Stagecoach in Cumbria, Stagecoach in Lancaster.
Man Dir: Nigel Winter **Ops Dir:** David Lee-Kong **Chief Eng:** Brian Walkden.
Fleet: 321 - 112 double-deck bus, 91 single-deck bus, 11 single-deck coach, 51 midibus, 56 minibus.

Chassis: 2 AEC, 58 Alexander Dennis, 52 Dennis, 1 Iveco, 53 MAN, 2 Mercedes, 56 Optare, 30 Scania, 8 Transbus, 59 Volvo.
Ops incl: local bus services, school contracts, excursions & tours, private hire, express.
Livery: Stagecoach UK Bus.
Ticket System: Wayfarer TGX.

TITTERINGTON COACHES LTD
♿ ♨ ☑
THE GARAGE, BLENCOW, PENRITH CA11 0DG
Tel: 01768 863594
Fax: 01768 892577
E-mail: enquiries@titteringtonholidays.co.uk
Web site: www.titteringtonholidays.co.uk
Fleet Name: Titterington Holidays.
Dirs: Ian Titterington, Paul Titterington, Colin Titterington.
Fleet: 10 single-deck coach.
Chassis: 2 Mercedes, 3 Setra, 5 Volvo.
Bodies: 4 Jonckheere, 2 Mercedes, 1 Plaxton, 3 Setra.
Ops incl: school contracts, excursions & tours, private hire, continental tours.
Livery: Mustard/White.

THE TRAVELLERS CHOICE
See Lancashire

TUER MOTORS LTD
♨ ☎ R24
BRIDGE HOUSE, MORLAND, PENRITH CA10 3AY
Tel: 01931 714224
Fax: 01931 714236
Fleet: 6 - 3 single-deck coach, 1 midicoach, 2 minibus
Chassis: 1 DAF, 1 Ford Transit, 2 Mercedes, 2 Volvo.

Bodies: 1 Ford, 1 Ikarus, 2 Plaxton, 1 Van Hool, 1 Other.
Ops incl: excursions & tours, private hire, school contracts, continental tours.
Livery: Cream/Red.

WOOFS OF SEDBERGH
♿ ❄
UNIT 2, BUSK LANE, SEDBERGH LA10 5HF
Tel: 01539 620414
E-mail: office@woofs.f9.co.uk
Web site: www.woofsofsedbergh.co.uk
Prop: G Woof.
Fleet: 13 – 3 midibus, 4 midicoach, 6 minibus.
Chassis: 2 Ford Transit, 1 LDV, 10 Mercedes.
Ops incl: local bus services, school contracts, private hire.
Livery: White with Black, Brown.

WRIGHT BROS (COACHES) LTD
♨ ♿ 🍴 ♨ R24 ☎ T ▭
CENTRAL GARAGE, NENTHEAD, ALSTON CA9 3NP
Tel: 01434 381200
Fax: 01434 382089
E-mail: info@wrightbros.co.uk
Web site: www.wrightscoaches.co.uk
Chmn/Man Dir: J G Wright
Dir: C I Wright.
Fleet: 12 - 7 single-deck coach, 2 double-deck sleeper coach, 1 midibus, 2 midicoach.
Chassis: 3 Mercedes, 1 Setra, 8 Volvo.
Bodies: 1 Autobus, 2 Jonckheere, 4 Plaxton, 1 Setra, 1 Unvi, 3 Van Hool.
Ops incl: local bus services, school contracts, private hire, continental tours.
Liveries: Cream/Black/Gold, Yellow (double-deck sleepers).
Ticket System: Almex.

ANDREW'S OF TIDESWELL LTD
♨ ♿ ❄ R24 ☎ T
ANCHOR GARAGE, TIDESWELL SK17 8RB
Tel: 01298 871222
Fax: 01298 872412
E-mail: info@andrews-of-tideswell.co.uk
Web site: www.andrews-of-tideswell.co.uk
Dirs: R B Andrew, P D Andrew.
Fleet: 24 – 3 double-deck bus, 1 double-deck coach, 16 single-deck coach, 3 midicoach, 1 minibus.
Chassis: 1 DAF, 1 MCW, 4 Mercedes, 4 Neoplan, 2 Scania, 12 Volvo.
Bodies: 1 Crest, 2 East Lancs, 4 Neoplan, 11 Plaxton, 6 Van Hool.
Ops incl: excursions & tours, private hire, continental tours, school contracts.
Livery: Cream/Ivory/Red flash.

ARRIVA MIDLANDS LTD
♿ ♨ ♨ ❄ T
4 WESTMORELAND AVENUE, THURMASTON, LEICESTER LE4 8PH
Tel: 0116 264 0400
Fax: 0116 260 8620
E-mail: myattk.midlands@arriva.co.uk
Web site: www.arriva.co.uk
Fleet Name: Arriva serving Derby.
Regional Man Dir: A Perry **Regional Fin Dir:** J Barlow **Regional Eng Dir:** M Evans
Area Director East: S Mathieson
Area Director West: R Cheveaux.
Fleet: 698 - 168 double-deck bus, 267 single-deck bus, 6 articulated bus, 204 midibus, 53 minibus.
Chassis: 24 Alexander Dennis, 173 DAF, 119 Dennis, 26 Mercedes, 121 Optare, 46 Scania, 6 Transbus, 85 VDL, 98 Volvo.
Bodies: 61 Alexander, 24 Alexander Dennis, 4 Caetano, 46 East Lancs, 1 Marshall, 26 Mercedes, 121 Optare, 110 Plaxton,

42 Scania, 6 Transbus, 257 Wrightbus.
Ops incl: local bus services, school contracts, private hire, express.
Liveries: Arriva; Midland (Red); Wardles (Red/White, Red/Cream).
Ticket System: Wayfarer 150 & 200.

BAGNALLS COACHES
♿ ♨ ♨ ❄ T
THE COACH STOP, GEORGE HOLMES WAY, SWADLINCOTE DE11 9DF
Tel: 01283 551964
Fax: 01283 552287
E-mail: info@bagnallscoaches.com
Web site: www.bagnallscoaches.com
Dir/Ops Man: John Bagnall **Dir/Clerk:** Pat Bagnall **Dir/Ch Eng:** Karl Bagnall
Dir/Clerk: Gavin Bagnall.
Fleet: 15 – 1 single-deck bus, 12 single-deck coach, 2 midicoach.
Chassis: 2 Mercedes, 13 Volvo.
Bodies: 1 East Lancs, 1 Jonckheere, 3 Plaxton, 1 Transbus, 9 Van Hool.
Ops incl: local bus services, excursions & tours, private hire, school contracts.
Livery: various.

BAKEWELL COACHES
♨ ♿ ❄
24 MOORHALL ESTATE, BAKEWELL DE45 1FP
Tel: 01629 815827
E-mail: bakewellcoaches@yahoo.com
Web site: www.bakewellcoaches.co.uk
Prop: A Barks.
Fleet: 4 single-deck coach.
Chassis: 1 Bedford, 1 Neoplan, 1 Setra, 1 Volvo.
Bodies: 1 Neoplan, 1 Setra, 2 Van Hool
Ops incl: excursions & tours, private hire.
Livery: White with Yellow/Orange/Blue.

BOWERS COACHES
See High Peak Buses

CLOWES COACHES
❄ ♨ 🍴 ♿ ☎
BARROWMOOR, LONGNOR NEAR BUXTON SK17 0QP
Tel: 01298 83292
Fax: 01298 83838
E-mail: clowescoach@btconnect.com
Web site: www.clowescoaches.co.uk
Prop: George Clowes
Ops incl: excursions & tours, private hire.
Livery: Cream.

COX'S OF BELPER
♿ ♨ ❄ ☎
GOODS ROAD, BELPER DE56 1UU
Tel: 01773 822395
Fax: 01773 821157
E-mail: enquiries@coxsofbelper.co.uk
Web site: www.coxsofbelper.co.uk
Prop: Bernard Bembridge.
Fleet: 6 - 4 single-deck coach, 1 midicoach, 1 minicoach.
Chassis: 1 Dennis, 1 LDV, 2 Mercedes, 2 Volvo.
Bodies: 1 Esker, 2 Jonckheere, 1 LDV, 1 Plaxton, 1 Unvi.
Ops incl: school contracts, private hire.
Livery: White/Blue.

DERBY COMMUNITY TRANSPORT
See Notts & Derby Buses
Part of the Wellglade Group

K & H DOYLE LTD
Ceased trading since LRB 2014 went to press

Cumbria

TIM DRAPER'S GOLDEN HOLIDAYS

♿ ⚙ ✚ ⊞ ⬛

SEVERN SQUARE, ALFRETON DE55 7BQ
Tel: 01773 834401
Fax: 01773 590034
E-mail: tim.draper@btconnect.com
Web site: www.timdrapers.com
Dirs: Tim Draper, Pam Draper, Claire Draper.
Fleet: 5 - 3 single-deck coach, 1 midicoach, 2 minibus.
Chassis: 1 DAF, 1 Dennis, 1 LDV, 1 Mercedes, 2 Volvo.
Ops incl: excursions & tours, school contracts, private hire.
Livery: White/Red/Yellow.

DUNN MOTOR TRACTION LTD

♿ ⚙ ⊞ ⬛

DELVES ROAD, HEANOR GATE INDUSTRIAL ESTATE, HEANOR DE75 7RJ
Tel: 01773 714013
Fax: 01773 713257
Web site: www.catchyourbus.co.uk
Fleet Name: Your Bus.
Depots at: Heanor, Bradford.
Man Dir: Stephen Ward
Fleet: 111 – 4 double-deck bus, 46 single-deck bus, 46 single-deck coach, 12 midibus, 3 minibus.
Chassis: 2 Alexander Dennis, 3 Dennis, 37 Mercedes, 3 Optare, 2 Scania, 52 Volvo, 12 Wrightbus.
Bodies: 2 Alexander Dennis, 46 Caetano, 37 Mercedes, 3 Optare, 4 Plaxton, 19 Wrightbus.
Ops incl: local bus services, school contracts, express.
Liveries: Buses: Magenta; Coaches: National Express.

DW COACHES

♿ ⚙ ⊞ ⬛

147 THANET STREET, CLAY CROSS S45 9JT
Tel: 01246 864039
Prop: D Warden
Fleet: 19 – 7 double-deck bus, 7 single-deck coach, 4 midibus, 1 midicoach.
Chassis: 8 Dennis, 5 Leyland, 1 Scania, 5 Volvo.
Ops incl: local bus services, school contracts, private hire.
Livery: Blue/Cream.

'E' COACHES OF ALFRETON

⚙ ❄ ⬛

1 MANOR COURT, RIDDINGS, ALFRETON DE55 4DG
Tel/Fax: 01773 541222
E-mail: bacon-k@sky.com
Web site: www.ecoachesofalfreton.co.uk
Prop: Keiron Bacon.
Fleet: 8 – 1 single-deck coach, 3 midicoach, 4 minicoach.
Chassis: 2 Iveco, 3 Mercedes, 3 Renault.
Bodies: 1 Beulas, 3 Mercedes, 4 Other.
Ops incl: school contracts, private hire.
Livery: White/Blue.

FLIGHTS HALLMARK

See West Midlands

GLOVERS COACHES LTD

♿ ⚙ ✚ 🍽 ❄

MOOR FARM ROAD EAST, ASHBOURNE DE6 1HD
Tel/Fax: 01335 300043
E-mail: gloverscoaches@btconnect.com
Web site: www.gloverscoaches.co.uk
Dirs: Stephen Mason, Heather Mason.
Fleet: 15 – 1 single-deck bus, 13 single-deck coach, 1 midicoach.
Chassis: 1 Mercedes, 14 Volvo.
Bodies: 1 Mercedes, 14 Plaxton.
Ops incl: School contracts, excursions & tours, private hire, continental tours.
Livery: Blue/Cream.

GOLDEN GREEN LUXURY TRAVEL

See Cheshire

HARPUR'S COACHES LTD

⚙ ✚ ❄ ⬛

WINCANTON CLOSE, DERBY DE24 8NB
Tel: 01332 757677
Fax: 01332 757259
E-mail: harpurscoaches@gmail.com
Web site: www.harpurscoaches.co.uk
Man Dir: Nick Harpur.
Fleet: 24 - double-deck bus, single-deck coach.
Chassis: AEC, Crossley, Ford, Volvo.
Bodies: Alexander, Brush, Northern Counties, Park Royal, Plaxton.
Ops incl: school contracts, excursions & tours, private hire.
Livery: Cream/Brown.

HAWKES TOURS (DERBY) LTD

⚙ ✚ ❄

CENTRAL BUS STATION, DERBY DE1 2AY
Tel: 01332 205400
Fax: 01332 202024
E-mail: david@hawkescoaches.freeserve.co.uk
Web site: www.hawkestours.co.uk
Dirs: D, D, J & C Hawkes.
Fleet: 14 – 2 double-deck bus, 3 single-deck bus, 9 single-deck coach.
Chassis: 1 MCW, 1 Neoplan, 3 Setra, 9 Volvo.
Bodies: 3 Alexander, 1 East Lancs, 1 Jonckheere, 1 MCW, 1 Neoplan, 4 Plaxton, 3 Setra.
Ops incl: school contracts, excursions & tours, private hire.
Livery: Blue.

HENSHAWS COACHES LTD

✚ ⚙ ❄

57 PYE HILL ROAD, JACKSDALE NG16 5LR
Tel: 01773 607909
Prop: Paul Henshaw
E-mail: paul@henshawscoaches.co.uk
Web site: www.henshawscoaches.co.uk
Fleet: 3 single-deck coach.
Chassis: 2 Bova, 1 Mercedes.
Bodies: 2 Bova, 1 Mercedes.
Ops incl: excursions & tours, private hire, school contracts, continental tours.
Livery: White/Orange

HIGH PEAK BUSES

♿ ⚙

HALLSTEADS, DOVE HOLES, HIGH PEAK SK17 8BJ
Tel: 08435 236036
Web site: www.highpeakbuses.com
Man Dir: Peter Harvey **Regional Ops Man:** David Brookes.
Fleet: 47 – 23 single-deck bus, 19 midibus, 5 minibus.
Chassis: 1 DAF, 2 MAN, 26 Optare, 15 Scania, 3 Volvo.
Bodies: 1 Alexander, 4 Northern Counties, 26 Optare, 2 Plaxton, 2 Scania, 12 Wrightbus.
Ops incl: local bus services, school contracts.
Livery: Blue/Orange/White; Brands.
Jointly owned by Centrebus and the Wellglade Group

G & J HOLMES (COACHES) LTD

♿ ⚙ ❄

124A MARKET STREET, CLAY CROSS S45 9LY
Tel/Fax: 01246 863232
E-mail: gj.holmes@tiscali.co.uk
Web site: gandjholmescoachesltd.yellsites.co.uk
Fleet Name: Hallmark
Dirs: N, N & S Holmes.
Fleet: 13 – 2 single-deck coach, 7 midibus, 4 midicoach.
Chassis: 3 Alexander Dennis, 1 DAF, 4 Mercedes, 4 Optare, 1 Volvo.
Bodies: 3 Alexander Dennis, 5 Optare, 4 Plaxton, 1 Van Hool.
Ops incl: local bus services, school contracts, private hire.
Livery: White, or Silver/Blue.

HULLEYS OF BASLOW

♿ ⚙

DERWENT GARAGE, BASLOW, BAKEWELL DE45 1RP
Tel: 01246 582246
Fax: 01246 583161
E-mail: office2008@hulleys-of-baslow.co.uk
Web site: www.hulleys-of-baslow.co.uk
Dir: Richard Eades.
Fleet: 18 – 1 double-deck bus, 12 single-deck bus, 2 single-deck coach, 3 midibus.
Chassis: 6 Alexander Dennis, 1 DAF, 1 Dennis, 4 MAN, 2 Optare, 2 VDL, 2 Volvo.
Bodies: 1 Alexander, 2 Alexander Dennis, 1 Marcopolo, 7 MCV, 3 Optare, 2 Plaxton, 2 Wrightbus.
Ops incl: local bus services, school contracts, private hire.
Livery: Buses: Blue/Cream; Coaches: Blue/White.
Ticket System: Wayfarer 3.

JOHNSON BROS TOURS LTD

♿ ⚙ ✚ 🍽 🚌 ❄ R R24 ⬛ T

PORTLAND HOUSE, DUKERIES INDUSTRIAL ESTATE, CLAYLANDS AVENUE, WORKSOP S81 7BQ
Tel/Recovery: 01909 720337
Fax: 01909 481054
E-mail: lee@johnstonstours.co.uk
Web site: www.johnsonstours.co.uk
Dirs: C A Johnson, S Johnson, A Johnson, L Johnson, C Johnson.

♿	Vehicle suitable for disabled	🍽	Coach(es) with galley facilities	🚌	Vintage Coach(es) available
⚙	Seat belt-fitted Vehicle	⬛	Replacement vehicle available	🚌	Open top vehicle(s)
R24	24 hour recovery service	R	Recovery service available	✚	Coaches with toilet facilities
T	Toilet-drop facilities available	❄	Air-conditioned vehicle(s)	🌿 Hybrid Buses	🔥 Gas Buses

Derby, Derbyshire

Fleet: 103 - 59 double-deck bus, I single-deck bus, 35 single-deck coach, 4 midicoach, I minibus, 3 minicoach.
Chassis: I Autosan, 2 Bova, 9 Bristol, 2 DAF, I Ford Transit, 8 Irisbus, 4 Irizar, 40 Leyland, 5 Mercedes, 6 Neoplan, I Optare, 12 Scania, 2 Van Hool, 9 Volvo.
Bodies: 3 Alexander, I Autosan, 3 Beulas, 2 Bova, 3 Caetano, 30 ECW, I Excel, I Ford, 6 Irizar, 2 Jonckheere, 3 Leyland, 6 Neoplan, 23 Northern Counties, 2 Optare, 8 Plaxton, I Sunsundegui, 3 Transbus, 4 Van Hool.
Ops incl: local bus services, school contracts, excursions & tours, private hire, express, continental tours.
Livery: Blue Fade with Stars.
Ticket System: ITSO.
See also Redfern Travel Ltd.

LITTLE TRANSPORT LTD
&♿♠♨⚙ R24 ✎ T
HALLAM FIELDS ROAD, ILKESTON DE7 4AZ
Tel: 0115 932 8581
Fax: 0115 932 5163
Recovery: 0115 932 8581
E-mail: info@littlestravel.co.uk
Web site: www.littlestravel.co.uk
Fleet Name: Little's Travel.
Dirs: Steve Wells, Paul Wright.
Fleet: 29 – 6 double-deck bus, I double-deck coach, 6 single-deck bus, 10 single-deck coach, I midibus, 3 midicoach, 2 minibus.
Chassis: 3 Alexander Dennis, I DAF, 4 Dennis, I Leyland, 5 Mercedes, I Optare, 8 Scania, I Temsa, I VDL, 4 Volvo.
Bodies: 2 Alexander, 3 Alexander Dennis, 2 Berkhof, I ECW, 3 East Lancs, 4 Irizar, 2 Lahden, I Marcopolo, 2 Optare, 5 Plaxton, I Temsa, I Wrightbus.
Ops incl: local bus services, Derby park & ride, school contracts, excursions & tours, private hire, continental tours.
Livery: White with pink lettering.
Ticket system: Almex.

MACPHERSON COACHES LTD
♿♠♨⚙⚒✎
THE GARAGE, HILL STREET, DONISTHORPE, SWADLINCOTE DE12 7PL
Tel: 01530 270226
Fax: 01530 273669
E-mail: travel@macphersoncoaches.co.uk
Web site: www.macphersoncoaches.co.uk
Man Dir: D C N MacPherson
Co Sec: S MacPherson **Fleet Eng:** C Underwood **Ops Man:** J Bywater.
Fleet: 17 - 6 double-deck bus, I single-deck bus, 8 single-deck coach, I midicoach, I minicoach.
Chassis: I Dennis, 6 Leyland, 4 Mercedes, I Optare, 5 Setra.
Bodies: 3 Alexander Dennis, 2 Caetano, I East Lancs, 2 Mercedes, 3 Northern Counties, I Optare, 5 Setra, I Other.
Ops incl: local bus services, school contracts, excursions & tours, private hire, continental tours.
Livery: Red & Cream.
Ticket System: Wayfarer.

NOTTS & DERBY BUSES
MIDLAND GENERAL
DERBY COMMUNITY TRANSPORT
♿♠
MEADOW ROAD, DERBY DE1 2BH
Tel/Fax: 01332 204568
E-mail: sfrost@nottsderby.co.uk
Web site: www.nottsderby.co.uk
Man Dir: Brian King **Fin Dir:** Graham Sutton
Man: Stuart Frost.
Fleet: 82 - 26 double-deck bus, 20 single-deck bus, 3 single-deck coach, 9 midibus, 24 minibus.
Chassis: I DAF, 2 Dennis, 5 Fiat, 4 Ford,

8 Leyland, II Mercedes, 9 Optare, 3 Scania, 7 VDL, 32 Volvo.
Bodies: 13 Alexander, I East Lancs, I ECW, 4 Ford, 12 Northern Counties, 9 Optare, 23 Plaxton, 5 Rohill, 5 UVG, 3 Wrightbus, 6 Other.
Ops incl: local bus services, school contracts, private hire.
Livery: Green/White/Blue.
Ticket System: Almex.
Part of the Wellglade Group

REDFERN TRAVEL LTD
♿♠♨⚙⛟⚒♨ R R24 ✎ T
THE SIDINGS, DEBDALE LANE, MANSFIELD WOODHOUSE, MANSFIELD NG19 7FE
Tel/Recovery: 01623 627653
Fax: 01909 625787
E-mail: lee@johnsonstours.co.uk
Web site: www.johnsonstours.co.uk
Dirs: C A Johnson, S Johnson, A Johnson, L Johnson, C Johnson.
Fleet: 103 - 59 double-deck bus, I single-deck coach, 35 single-deck coach, 4 midicoach, I minibus, 3 minicoach.
Chassis: I Autosan, 2 Bova, 9 Bristol, 2 DAF, I Ford Transit, 8 Irisbus, 4 Irizar, 40 Leyland, 5 Mercedes, 6 Neoplan, I Optare, 12 Scania, 2 Van Hool, 9 Volvo.
Bodies: 3 Alexander, I Autosan, 3 Beulas, 2 Bova, 3 Caetano, 30 ECW, I Excel, I Ford, 6 Irizar, 2 Jonckheere, 3 Leyland, 6 Neoplan, 23 Northern Counties, 2 Optare, 8 Plaxton, I Sunsundegui, 3 Transbus, 4 Van Hool.
Ops incl: local bus services, school contracts, excursions & tours, private hire, express, continental tours.
Livery: Green Fade/Stars.
Ticket System: ITSO.
A subsidiary of Johnson Bros Tours Ltd

K V & G L SLACK LTD
♿♠♨⚙✎
THE TRAVEL CENTRE, LUMSDALE, MATLOCK DE4 5LB
Tel: 01629 582826
Fax: 01629 580519
E-mail: enquiries@slackscoaches.co.uk
Web site: www.slackscoaches.co.uk
Man Dir: G L Slack **Ch Eng:** R M Slack
Co Sec: D R Slack
Tran Man: J Gough.
Fleet: 26 – I double-deck bus, 19 single-deck coach, 3 midicoach, 3 minibus.
Chassis: 5 DAF, 3 Dennis, I Ford, 3 Ford Transit, I Iveco, 4 MAN, 3 Mercedes, I Neoplan, I Scania, 4 Volvo.
Bodies: I Alexander, 5 Beulas, 3 Ford, I Jonckheere, I Neoplan, 7 Plaxton, 2 Sitcar, 6 Van Hool.
Ops incl: excursions & tours, private hire, continental tours, school contracts.

STAGECOACH YORKSHIRE
♿ T
UNIT 4, ELDON ARCADE, BARNSLEY S70 4PP
Tel: 01246 207103
Fax: 01246 216540
E-mail: chesterfield.enquiries@stagecoachbus.com
Web site: www.stagecoachbus.com
Fleet Names incl: Stagecoach in Chesterfield.
Man Dir: Paul Lynch **Eng Dir:** Joe Gilchrist
Acting Comm Dir: John Young
Ops Dir: Sue Hayes.
Fleet (Chesterfield): 108 - 19 double-deck bus, 18 single-deck bus, 11 single-deck coach, 42 midibus, 18 minibus.
Chassis: 30 Alexander Dennis, 9 Dennis, 18 MAN, 18 Optare, 19 Scania, 3 Transbus, 11 Volvo.

Bodies: 10 Alexander, 61 Alexander Dennis, 8 Caetano, 5 East Lancs, 18 Optare, 3 Plaxton, 3 Transbus.
Ops incl: local bus services, express.
Liveries: Stagecoach UK Bus, National Express.
Ticket System: ERG TP5000.

TM TRAVEL LTD
See South Yorkshire

TRENT BARTON
♿♠
MANSFIELD ROAD, HEANOR DE75 7BG
Tel: 01773 712265
Fax: 01773 536333
E-mail: customer.services@trentbarton.co.uk
Web site: www.trentbarton.co.uk
Chairman: B R King **Deputy Chairman:** R I Morgan **Man Dir:** J Counsell **Group Fin Dir:** G Sutton **Marketing & Comms Dir:** A Hornby.
Fleet: 276 - 260 single-deck bus, 16 single-deck coach.
Chassis: 6 Mercedes, 131 Optare, 85 Scania, 54 Volvo.
Bodies: 13 Irizar, 6 Mercedes, 131 Optare, 3 Plaxton, 123 Wrightbus.
Ops incl: local bus services.
Livery: Various brands.
Ticket System: Init.
Part of the Wellglade Group

VIKING COACHES.COM LTD
♿♠♨⚒♠✎
UNIT 2, RYDER CLOSE, SWADLINCOTE DE11 9EU
Tel: 01283 217012
Fax: 01283 550685
Web Site: www.vikingcoaches.com
Dirs: Andy Garrett, Mark Gadsby, Graham Hopkins.
Fleet: 29 – 23 single-deck coach, I midicoach, 5 minibus.
Chassis: I BMC, I DAF, I Dennis, 2 Ford Transit, 2 LDV, I Leyland, I Scania, I Volkswagen, 19 Volvo.
Ops incl: excursions & tours, private hire, express, continental tours, school contracts.
Livery: Red/White/Grey.
A subsidiary of Solus Coach Travel Ltd (see Staffordshire)

WARRINGTON COACHES LTD
♿♠♨♠
ILAM, ASHBOURNE DE6 2AZ
Tel: 01335 350204
Fax: 01335 350204
E-mail: info@warringtoncoaches.co.uk
Web site: www.warringtoncoaches.co.uk
Dirs: Lynton Boydon, Maureen Boydon, Keith Warrington.
Fleet: 10 - 4 single-deck coach, 3 midicoach, 2 minibus, I minicoach.
Chassis: I Bova, I BMC, 3 Dennis, I Ford Transit, I Iveco, I LDV, 2 Mercedes.
Bodies: I Autobus, I BMC, I Bova, I Indcar, I Marcopolo, I Optare, 2 Plaxton, 2 Other.
Ops incl: local bus services, school contracts, private hire.
Livery: Silver with Red/Gold/Black.

ALBERT WILDE & SON COACHES
♠♠♨✎
121 PARKSIDE, HEAGE, BELPER DE56 2AG
Tel/Fax: 01773 856655
Dirs: Philip J Wilde, Ann Wilde.
Fleet: 3 single-deck coach.
Chassis: 2 DAF, I Scania.
Bodies: 3 Van Hool.
Ops incl: excursions & tours, school contracts.

A B COACHES LTD

WILLS ROAD, TOTNES INDUSTRIAL
ESTATE, TOTNES TQ9 5XN
Tel: 01803 864161
Fax: 01803 864008
E-mail: abcoaches@btconnect.com
Web site: www.abcoachesltd.co.uk
Dirs: Martin Chalk, Rebecca Chalk, Brian
Smith.
Fleet: 15 single-deck coach.
Ops incl: school contracts, private hire.
Livery: Cream & Red/White & Red.

AXE VALLEY MINI TRAVEL

BUS DEPOT, 26 HARBOUR ROAD, SEATON
EX12 2NA
Tel/Fax: 01297 625959
Fleet Name: AVMT
Prop: Mrs F M Searle **Traf Man:** J R Paddon
Fleet: 14 - 5 double-deck bus, 7 midibus,
2 minibus.
Chassis: 10 Dennis, 1 MCW, 1 Mercedes,
2 Optare.
Bodies: 3 Alexander, 2 Caetano, 1 MCW,
2 Optare, 6 Plaxton.
Ops incl: local bus services, school contracts.
Livery: Maroon/White.
Ticket System: Wayfarer.

BEACON BUS & COACH

DOLTON BEACON GARAGE, DOLTON,
WINKLEIGH EX19 8PS
Tel: 01805 804240
Web site: www.beaconbus.co.uk
Props: J Carter, A Carter.
Fleet: single-deck bus, single-deck coach,
midibus, midicoach, minibus, minicoach.
Ops incl: local bus services, school contracts,
private hire.
Livery: White

BLAKES COACHES LTD

EAST ANSTEY, TIVERTON EX16 9JJ
Tel: 01398 341160
Fax: 01398 341594
E-mail: info@blakescoaches.co.uk
Web site: www.blakescoaches.co.uk
Man Dir: David Blake **Dir:** Janet Blake.
Fleet: 11 – 9 single-deck coach, 1 minibus,
1 minicoach.
Chassis: 2 Ford Transit, 1 MAN, 7 Scania,
1 Volvo.
Bodies: 1 Beulas, 1 Ferqui, 1 Ford, 4 Irizar,
4 Van Hool.
Ops incl: school contracts, excursions &
tours, private hire, continental tours.
Livery: Silver/Green/Blue.

CARMEL COACHES LTD

STATION ROAD, NORTHLEW,
OKEHAMPTON EX20 3BN
Tel: 01409 221237
Fax: 01409 221226
E-mail: info@carmelcoaches.co.uk
Web site: www.carmelcoaches.co.uk
Depots at: Northlew, North Tawton,
Okehampton, Exeter, Plymouth.
Dirs: Tony Hazell, Michael Hazell, Carolyn
Alderton.
Fleet: 40 – 6 single-deck bus, 27 single-deck
coach, 4 midicoach, 3 minibus.
Chassis: 5 Bova, 3 DAF, 7 Dennis, 3 Irisbus,
1 King Long, 3 LDV, 7 Mercedes, 2 Optare,
2 Scania, 7 Volvo.
Bodies: 2 Alexander, 2 Berkhof, 2 Beulas, 5
Bova, 1 Caetano, 2 Irizar, 3 Jonckheere,

1 King Long, 1 LDV, 1 Marcopolo, 2 Optare,
12 Plaxton, 1 Sunsundegui, 3 Van Hool,
3 Other.
Ops incl: local bus services, school contracts,
excursions & tours, private hire.
Livery: White.
Ticket System: Ticketer.

CHELSTON LEISURE SERVICES LTD

LONG ROAD, PAIGNTON TQ4 7BL
Tel: 01803 666736
E-mail: info@locallink.it
Web site: www.localbustorbay.com
Fleet Names: Dial-A-Bus, Local-Link.
Dirs: D French, Mrs J French.
Fleet: 18 – 2 midibus, 16 minibus.
Chassis: 1 Dennis, 1 Iveco, 4 Mercedes,
11 Optare, 1 Transbus.
Ops incl: local bus services.
Livery: Blue/White.

COUNTRY BUS

KING CHARLES BUSINESS PARK,
OLD NEWTON ROAD, HEATHFIELD,
NEWTON ABBOT TQ12 6UT
Tel: 01626 833664
Fax: 01626 835648
E-mail: info@countrybusdevon.co.uk
Web site: www.countrybusdevon.co.uk
Man Dir: Ms A Ellison **Dirs:** N Elgar,
N Romig.
Fleet: 45 – 7 double-deck bus, 1 single-deck
bus, 2 single-deck coach, 24 midibus,
11 minibus.
Chassis: 4 Alexander Dennis, 10 Dennis,
2 LDV, 11 Mercedes, 10 Optare, 2 Scania,
2 Transbus, 5 Volvo.
Ops incl: local bus services, school contracts,
private hire.
Livery: White with Blue.
Ticket System: Ticketer.

CRUDGE COACHES LTD

TURBURY FARM, WOLFORD CROSS,
DUNKESWELL, HONITON EX14 4QN
Tel: 01404 841657
Fax: 01404 841668
E-mail: kscrudge@btinternet.com
Dirs: Kevin Crudge, Mrs Susan Crudge.
Fleet: 19 – 10 single deck coach, 5 midicoach,
4 minibus.
Chassis: 3 Bova, 1 DAF, 3 Dennis, 1 Ford
Transit, 3 LDV, 3 MAN, 2 Mercedes, 1 Toyota,
2 Volvo.
Ops incl: school contracts, private hire.

DAISH'S TRAVEL

DEVONSHIRE HOTEL, PARKHILL ROAD,
TORQUAY TQ1 2DY
Tel: 01803 201432
E-mail: info@daishs.com
Web site: www.daishs.com
Fleet: 19 single-deck coach.
Chassis: 19 Volvo.
Bodies: 3 Caetano, 8 Jonckheere, 3 Plaxton,
1 Transbus, 2 Van Hool, 2 Volvo.
Ops incl: excursions & tours, private hire,
continental tours
Livery: White with Blue/Brown.

DARTLINE COACHES

LANGDONS BUSINESS PARK,
CLYST ST MARY, EXETER EX5 1AF
Tel: 01392 872900
Fax: 01392 872909
E-mail: info@dartline-coaches.co.uk

Web site: www.dartline-coaches.co.uk
Dirs: David Dart, Dave Hounslow.
Fleet: 58 – 2 single-deck bus, 27 single-deck
coach, 5 midibus, 2 midicoach, 18 minibus,
4 minicoach.
Chassis: 4 Bova, 2 DAF, 5 Dennis, 1 MAN,
10 Mercedes, 17 Optare, 1 Renault, 8 Scania,
2 VDL, 7 Volvo.
Bodies: 4 Bova, 8 Irizar, 5 Jonckheere,
1 Marcopolo, 1 Mercedes, 1 Onyx, 17 Optare,
11 Plaxton, 1 Renault, 2 UVG, 1 Van Hool,
5 Other.
Ops incl: local bus services, school contracts,
excursions & tours, private hire.
Livery: White/Green.
Ticket System: Ticketer.

DOWN MOTORS & OTTER COACHES

1 MILL STREET, OTTERY ST MARY
EX11 1AB
Tel: 01404 812002
Fax: 01404 811128
Partners: A G Down, C P Down.
Fleet: 7 - 6 single-deck coach, 1 midicoach.
Chassis: 1 Bova, 4 Dennis, 1 Mercedes,
1 Toyota.
Bodies: 1 Bova, 2 Caetano, 1 Mercedes,
3 Plaxton.
Ops incl: school contracts, excursions &
tours, private hire.
Livery: Ivory/Red.

C J DOWN

THE GARAGE, MARY TAVY, TAVISTOCK
PL19 9PA
Tel/Fax: 01822 810242
E-mail: downscoaches@aol.com
Web site: www.cjdowncoachhiretavistock.
co.uk
Proprietors: Mr & Mrs. C J Down
Ops Man: W J Wakem
Chief Eng: W J Lashbrook.
Fleet: 22 - 18 single-deck coach, 4 midicoach.
Chassis: 1 MAN, 3 Mercedes, 18 Volvo.
Bodies: 1 Berkhof, 1 Duple, 8 Jonckheere,
1 Marcopolo, 1 Mercedes, 1 Onyx, 7 Plaxton,
1 Transbus, 1 Van Hool, 1 Other.
Ops incl: school contracts, excursions &
tours, private hire.
Livery: Cream.

FILERS TRAVEL LTD

SLADE LODGE, SLADE ROAD, ILFRACOMBE
EX34 8LB
Tel: 01271 863819
Fax: 01271 867281
E-mail: info@filers.co.uk
Web site: www.filers.co.uk
Dir: Royston J Filer **Office & Tours Man:**
Christina King **Ch Eng:** George Rogers.
Fleet: 23 – 8 single-deck coach, 12 midibus,
2 minibus, 1 minicoach.
Chassis: 7 Alexander Dennis, 4 Bova, 1 Irizar,
1 Irisbus, 1 Iveco, 1 MAN, 2 Mercedes,
4 Optare, 1 Scania, 1 Volkswagen.
Bodies: 6 Alexander Dennis, 4 Bova,
1 Caetano, 1 Irizar, 1 Mercedes, 1 Noge,
4 Optare, 3 Plaxton, 1 Sitcar, 1 Scania.
Ops incl: local bus services, excursions
& tours, private hire, school contracts,
continental tours.
Liveries: White/Blue/Yellow; Red & Cream.
Ticket system: Ticketer.

FIRST DEVON, CORNWALL & CENTRAL SOMERSET

THE RIDE, CHELSON MEADOW,
PLYMOUTH PL9 7JT

Devon, Plymouth, Torbay

Tel: 01752 967800
Fax: 01752 495230
E-mail: firstdevonandcornwall@firstgroup.com
Web site: www.firstgroup.com; www.busesofsomerset.co.uk
Man Dir: Alex Carter.
Fleet Names: First, Truronian, The Buses of Somerset.
Fleet: 325 – 113 double-deck bus, 46 single-deck bus, 21 single-deck coach, 7 articulated bus, 108 midibus, 1 midicoach, 29 minibus.
Chassis: 29 Alexander Dennis, 97 Dennis, 1 Ford Transit, 12 Mercedes, 26 Optare, 15 Scania, 16 Transbus, 118 Volvo, 9 Wrightbus.
Bodies: 23 Alexander, 29 Alexander Dennis, 19 East Lancs, 1 Ford, 11 Irizar, 6 Marshall, 9 Mercedes, 42 Northern Counties, 26 Optare, 73 Plaxton, 15 Transbus, 69 Wrightbus.
Ops incl: local bus services, school contracts, private hire.
Livery: FirstGroup UK Bus.
Ticket System: Almex.

GREY CARS COACHES

6/7 DANEHEATH BUSINESS PARK, HEATHFIELD, NEWTON ABBOT TQ12 6TL
Tel: 01626 833038
Fax: 01626 835920
E-mail: office@greycars.com
Web site: www.greycars.com
Dirs: Duncan Millman, Bruce Millman.
Fleet: 14 – 11 single-deck coach, 3 midicoach.
Chassis: 1 Bova, 3 Mercedes, 1 Toyota, 9 Volvo.
Bodies: 1 Berkhof, 1 Bova, 2 Mercedes, 6 Plaxton, 1 Toyota, 3 Van Hool.
Ops incl: school contracts, excursions & tours, private hire, continental tours.
Livery: Grey/Yellow/Turquoise.

GUSCOTT'S COACHES LTD
Ceased trading since LRB 2014 went to press

HARVEY'S BUS LTD
EXETER COACHES

UNIT 5, STATION ROAD, MORETONHAMPSTEAD TQ13 8SA
Tel: 01647 441221
E-mail: info@harveysbus.com, info@exetercoaches.co.uk
Web sites: www.harveysbus.com, www.exetercoaches.co.uk
Man Dir: Peter Denton.
Fleet: 12 – 1 single-deck coach, 1 midicoach, 10 minibus.
Chassis: 2 Iveco, 3 LDV, 6 Mercedes, 1 Volkswagen.
Ops incl: school contracts, private hire.
Livery: White with Blue.

HEARDS COACHES

FORE STREET, HARTLAND, BIDEFORD EX39 6BD
Tel: 01237 441233
Fax: 01237 441789
E-mail: info@heardscoaches.co.uk
Web Site: www.heardscoaches.co.uk
Fleet Name: Heards Coaches.
Dirs: G Heard, B Heard.
Fleet: 8 single-deck coach.
Chassis: 1 Dennis, 1 MAN, 2 Scania, 4 Volvo.
Ops incl: school contracts, private hire.
Livery: Cream.

HEMMINGS COACHES LTD

POWLERS PIECE GARAGE, EAST PUTFORD, HOLSWORTHY EX22 7XW
Tel: 01237 451282
Fax: 01237 451920
E-mail: enquirehemmings@aol.com
Web site: www.hemmingscoaches.co.uk
Dirs: Ken & Linda Hemmings.
Fleet: 11 – 10 single-deck coach, 1 minicoach.
Chassis: 1 Dennis, 2 Iveco, 4 Mercedes, 1 Scania, 3 Setra.
Bodies: 1 Beulas, 1 Crest, 3 Hispano, 1 Irizar, 1 Mercedes, 1 Plaxton, 3 Setra.
Ops incl: school contracts, excursions & tours, private hire, continental tours.
Livery: Gold & White.

HILLS SERVICES LTD

THE GARAGE, STIBB CROSS, LANGTREE, TORRINGTON EX38 8LH
Tel: 01805 601102
Fax: 01805 601103
E-mail: hills.servicesltd@btinternet.com
Web site: www.hillsholidays.co.uk
Dirs: David J Hearn, Mrs D Hearn, Mrs M E Hearn.
Fleet: 35 – 17 single-deck coach, 6 midicoach, 11 minibus, 1 minicoach.
Chassis: 3 Bova, 3 DAF, 3 Irisbus, 9 LDV, 1 Leyland, 9 Mercedes, 1 Van Hool, 6 Volvo.
Bodies: 2 Autobus, 8 Bova, 3 Bova, 1 Caetano, 1 Ferqui, 2 Ikarus, 2 Jonckheere, 4 LDV, 1 Mercedes, 3 Plaxton, 2 Transbus, 3 Van Hool, 8 Other.
Ops incl: school contracts, excursions & tours, private hire.
Livery: White with Orange, Green.

KINGDOMS TOURS LTD

WESTFIELD GARAGE, EXETER ROAD, TIVERTON EX16 5NZ
Tel: 01884 252646
E-mail: kingdoms-tours@supanet.com
Dirs: Steven Kingdom, Russell Kingdom, Ronald Kingdom.
Fleet: 22 – 11 single-deck coach, 4 midicoach, 6 minibus, 1 minicoach.
Chassis: 1 Bova, 1 DAF, 2 Iveco, 1 LDV, 8 Mercedes, 2 Scania, 5 Volvo.
Ops incl: school contracts, excursions & tours, private hire, express, continental tours.
Livery: White/Red/Orange.

KLS TRAVEL LTD

LAWRENCE HOUSE, DULFORD BUSINESS PARK, BROAD ROAD, DULFORD, CULLOMPTON EX15 2DY
Tel: 01392 308555
Fax: 01392 308556
E-mail: info@klstravel.co.uk
Web site: www.klstravel.co.uk

MID DEVON COACHES

STATION ROAD, BOW, CREDITON EX17 6JD
Tel/Fax: 01363 82200
E-mail: enquiries@mdcoaches.co.uk
Web site: www.middevoncoaches.co.uk
Fleet Names: Mid Devon Coaches, Hamilton Grays.
Depots at: Bow, Dawlish.
Prop: Mrs L A Hamilton.
Fleet: 41 – 2 double-deck bus, 33 single-deck coach, 4 midicoach, 2 minibus.
Chassis: 1 Dennis, 1 Ford, 1 Ford Transit, 1 Leyland, 1 MAN, 4 Mercedes, 6 Scania, 26 Volvo.
Bodies: 2 Alexander, 1 Autobus, 2 Berkhof, 1 Caetano, 1 Crest, 1 Duple, 1 Ford Transit, 5 Irizar, 5 Jonckheere, 17 Plaxton, 2 Sitcar, 1 Sunsundegui, 2 Van Hool.
Ops incl: school contracts, excursions & tours, private hire, continental tours.
Liveries: Green/Cream (Mid Devon Coaches); Grey (Hamilton Grays).

PARAMOUNT COACHES LTD

6 VENN CRESCENT, HARTLEY, PLYMOUTH PL3 5PJ
Tel: 01752 767255
Fax: 01752 767255
Dirs: B M Couch, K Hallett.
Fleet: 6 minibus.
Chassis: 5 LDV, 1 Mercedes.
Ops incl: excursions & tours, private hire, school contracts.

PARKS OF HAMILTON

WALKHAM BUSINESS PARK, BURRINGTON WAY, PLYMOUTH PL5 3LS
Tel: 01752 790565
Fax: 01752 777931
Web site: www.parksofhamilton.co.uk
Chairman: D I Park.
Fleet: single-deck coach, from main fleet.
Chassis: Volvo.
Ops incl: express, continental tours.
Liveries: White with Red and Yellow lining, National Express.
A division of Parks of Hamilton *(see South Lanarkshire)*

PLYMOUTH CITYBUS LTD

1 MILEHOUSE ROAD, MILEHOUSE, PLYMOUTH PL3 4AA
Tel: 0845 077 2223
Fax: 01752 567209
E-mail: hq@plymouthbus.co.uk
Web site: www.plymouthbus.co.uk
Fleet Names: Citybus, Flash, Citycoach.
Man Dir: Richard Stevens.
Fleet: 178 – 65 double-deck bus, 25 single-deck bus, 8 single-deck coach, 79 midibus, 1 minibus.
Ops incl: local bus services, excursions & tours, private hire, school contracts, commercial engineering.
Liveries: Buses: Red; **Coaches:** Two tone Blue.
Ticket system: ITSO Key Card, m-ticketing, Vix ticket machines.
A subsidiary of the Go-Ahead Group

POWELLS COACHES

2 BARRIS VIEW, LAPFORD, CREDITON EX17 6PT
Tel/Fax: 01363 83468
Props: James P Powell, Mrs D M Powell, W R Powell.
Fleet: 5 single-deck coach.
Chassis: 1 DAF, 4 Volvo.
Bodies: 2 Jonckheere, 3 Van Hool.
Ops incl: school contracts, excursions & tours, private hire.

RAYS COACHES

88 KINGS TAMERTON ROAD, ST BUDEAUX PL5 2BW
Tel: 01752 369000
E-mail: wayne@rayscoaches.com
Web site: www.rayscoaches.com
Prop: R Gerry.
Fleet: 5 – 1 midicoach, 4 minibus.
Chassis: 1 Iveco, 2 LDV, 2 Mercedes.
Ops incl: private hire.

REDWOODS TRAVEL

UNIT 3, STATION ROAD, HEMYOCK, CULLOMPTON EX15 3SE
Tel: 01823 680288
Fax: 01823 681096
E-mail: info@redwoodstravel.com
Web site: www.redwoodstravel.co.uk
Dirs: Paul Redwood, Jacquie Redwood,

Michael Redwood.
Fleet: 26 – 2 corporate coaches, 16 single-deck coach, 1 midibus, 2 midicoach, 5 minibus.
Chassis: 1 MAN, 6 Mercedes, 1 Neoplan, 1 Renault, 6 Scania, 11 Volvo.
Bodies: 5 Irizar, 6 Jonckheere, 1 Marshall, 1 Neoplan, 1 Noge, 3 Plaxton, 1 Sitcar, 2 Van Hool, 5 Other.
Ops incl: school contracts, excursions & tours, private hire, continental tours, corporate hospitality.
Livery: Green/Red/White.

RIVER LINK
STATION YARD INDUSTRIAL ESTATE,
5 LOWER STREET, DARTMOUTH
TQ6 9AJ
Tel: 01803 555872
Web site: www.dartmouthrailriver.co.uk
Chairman: Sir William McAlpine
Dirs: David Allan, John Butt, Norman Christy
Co Sec: Philip Smallwood
Group Gen Man: Andrew Pooley
Tran Man: Michael Palmer.
Fleet: 8 - 6 double-deck bus, 1 open-top bus, 1 midibus.
Chassis: 4 Bristol, 1 Dennis, 2 Leyland, 1 Volvo.
Ops incl: local bus services, private hire.
Livery: Dark Blue/Ivory.
Ticket System: Almex.

SEWARDS COACHES
GLENDALE, DALWOOD, AXMINSTER
EX13 7EJ
Tel/Fax: 01404 881343
E-mail: info@sewardscoaches.co.uk
Web site: www.sewardscoaches.co.uk
Partners: Richard M Seward, Ivy A Seward, Catherine E Seward.
Fleet: 18 - 10 single-deck coach, 5 midicoach, 3 minibus.
Chassis: 2 Bova, 1 DAF, 5 Dennis, 1 Irisbus, 1 Iveco, 2 MAN, 4 Mercedes, 1 Temsa, 1 Toyota.
Bodies: 4 Alexander Dennis, 1 Berkhof, 2 Bova, 3 Caetano, 1 Hispano, 1 Marcopolo, 1 Optare, 5 Plaxton.
Ops incl: local bus services, school contracts, private hire.
Livery: Cream with Orange/Green.

STAGECOACH SOUTH WEST
BELGRAVE ROAD, EXETER
EX1 2LB
Tel: 01392 427711
E-mail: southwest.enquiries@stagecoachbus.com
Web site: www.stagecoachbus.com
Man Dir: Michael Watson **Comm Dir:** Robert Williams **Eng Dir:** Michael Bishop.
Fleet: 353- 174 double-deck bus, 1 open-top bus, 16 single-deck bus, 110 midibus, 51 minibus.
Chassis: 1 AEC, 120 Alexander Dennis, 64 Dennis, 12 MAN, 55 Optare, 81 Scania, 20 Transbus.
Bodies: 45 Alexander, 209 Alexander Dennis, 1 Caetano, 1 Marshall, 55 Optare, 1 Park Royal, 1 Plaxton, 40 Transbus.
Ops incl: local bus services, school contracts.
Livery: Stagecoach UK Bus.
Ticket System: ERG EP5000.

STREETS COACHWAYS LTD
UNIT 1, SANDERS YARD, BRYNSWORTHY, BARNSTAPLE EX31 3NS
Tel: 01271 321343
Fax: 01271 321420
E-mail: lin@streetscoachways.co.uk
Web site: www.streetscoachways.co.uk
Dir: Stephen Street.

Fleet: 20 - 5 single-deck coach, 2 midicoach, 10 minibus, 3 taxi.
Chassis: 1 Bova, 1 DAF, 1 Dennis, 1 Ford Transit, 4 LDV, 1 MAN, 5 Mercedes, 2 Volkswagen, 1 Volvo.
Bodies: 1 Berkhof, 1 Bova, 1 Ford Transit, 2 LDV, 1 Mellor, 1 Neoplan, 1 Plaxton, 1 Sitcar, 8 Other.
Ops incl: private hire, school contracts.
Livery: White with Red/Orange.

TALLY HO! COACHES LTD
STATION YARD INDUSTRIAL ESTATE,
KINGSBRIDGE TQ7 1ES
Tel: 01548 853081
Fax: 01548 853602
E-mail: info@tallyhocoaches.com
Web site: www.tallyhocoaches.co.uk
Dir: Don McIntosh
Head of Transport: Mark Drews
Head of Engineering: Steve Pengelly.
Fleet: 50 – double-deck bus, single-deck coach, midibus, midicoach, minibus.
Chassis: 2 DAF, 1 Dennis, 3 Ford Transit, 1 Leyland, 19 Mercedes, 4 Optare, 1 Renault, 6 Scania, 1 Toyota, 3 Volkswagen, 9 Volvo.
Bodies: 6 Alexander/Alexander Dennis, 1 Bova, 1 Caetano, 1 East Lancs, 3 Ford Transit, 4 Irizar, 6 Optare, 10 Plaxton, 1 Sunsundegui, 9 Van Hool, 3 Volkswagen, 5 Other.
Ops incl: local bus services, school contracts, coach holidays, excursions & tours, private hire, HGV/PSV engineering.
Livery: Blue/White.
Ticket system: Ticketer.

TARGET TRAVEL
EAGLE ROAD, LANGAGE BUSINESS PARK,
PLYMOUTH PL7 5BG
Tel: 01752 242000
Fax: 01752 345700
E-mail: admin@targettravel.info
Web site: www.targettravel.co.uk
Dirs: R Risk, L Risk, D Dart, D Hounslow.
Fleet: 70 – 5 double-deck bus, 1 single-deck bus, 25 single-deck coach, 9 midibus, 12 midicoach, 18 minibus.
Chassis: 2 Bova, 10 Dennis, 2 Ford Transit, 6 Irisbus, 2 Iveco, 3 LDV, 6 MAN, 16 Mercedes, 2 Neoplan, 7 Optare, 1 Scania, 13 Volvo.
Ops incl: local bus services, private hire.
Livery: Green/White.

TAVISTOCK COUNTRY BUS
See Cornwall

TAW & TORRIDGE COACHES LTD
GRANGE LANE, MERTON, OKEHAMPTON
EX20 3ED
Tel: 01805 603400
Fax: 01805 603559
Recovery: 01805 603400
E-mail: enquiries@tawandtorridge.co.uk
Web site: www.tawandtorridge.co.uk
Depots at: Merton, Barnstaple, West Down.
Man Dir: Tony Hunt
Dir/Ops Man: Mark Hunt **Dir/Co Sec:** Linda Hunt
Dir: Tracey Laughton
Fleet Eng/Dir: Chris Laughton.
Fleet: 63 - 38 single-deck coach, 12 minibus, 13 midicoach.
Chassis: Various.
Bodies: Various.
Ops incl: school contracts, excursions & tours, private hire, continental tours.
Livery: Blue/Silver.

T.T. COACHES LTD
See Taw & Torridge Coaches Ltd

TURNERS TOURS
BACK LANE INDUSTRIAL ESTATE,
CHULMLEIGH EX18 7DQ
Tel: 01769 580242
Fax: 01769 581281
E-mail: coaches@turnerstours.co.uk
Web site: www.turnerstours.co.uk
Dir: Stephen Gilson.
Fleet: 20 – 9 single-deck coach, 6 midibus, 4 minibus, 1 minicoach.
Chassis: 3 Alexander Dennis, 3 Dennis, 1 LDV, 4 Mercedes, 1 Toyota, 8 Volvo.
Ops incl: local bus services, school contracts, excursions & tours, private hire, continental tours.
Livery: Varied.
Ticket System: Ticketer.

WESTERN GREYHOUND LTD
See Cornwall

WOOD BROTHERS TRAVEL LTD
WHITECLEAVES QUARRY, PLYMOUTH
ROAD, BUCKFASTLEIGH
TQ11 0DQ
Tel: 01364 642666
Fax: 01364 643870
E-mail: woodbrotherstravel@hotmail.co.uk
Dirs: David Wood, Roger Wood, Adrian Carter **Co Sec:** Sue Wood.
Fleet: 9 - 7 single-deck coach, 2 midicoach.
Chassis: 4 Dennis, 1 MAN, 2 Mercedes, 2 Volvo.
Bodies: 1 Autobus, 1 Beulas, 7 Plaxton.
Ops incl: school contracts, private hire.
Livery: Yellow and Black.

Devon, Plymouth, Torbay

BARRY'S COACHES LTD

9 CAMBRIDGE ROAD, GRANBY
INDUSTRIAL ESTATE, WEYMOUTH DT4 9TJ
Tel: 01305 784850
Fax: 01305 782252
E-mail: info@barryscoachesdorset.com
Web site: www.barryscoachesdorset.com
Man Dir: Mrs M Newsam **Fleet Eng:**
Mr G Newsam.
Fleet: 25 – 22 single-deck coach, 1 double-
deck coach, 2 midicoach.
Chassis: 2 MAN, 2 Mercedes, 14 Scania,
7 Volvo.
Ops incl: school contracts, excursions &
tours, private hire, continental tours.
Livery: White/Blue/Yellow.

BLUEBIRD COACHES (WEYMOUTH) LTD

450 CHICKERELL ROAD, WEYMOUTH
DT3 4DH
Tel: 01305 786262
Fax: 01305 766277
Recovery: 01305 786262/07771 561060
E-mail: office@bluebirdcoaches.com
Web site: www.bluebirdcoaches.com
Dirs: Martyn Hoare, Stephen Hoare.
Fleet: 20 - 16 single-deck coach, 2 midicoach,
2 minibus.
Chassis: 1 Citroen, 11 DAF, 1 Mercedes,
1 Toyota, 1 Volkswagen, 5 Volvo.
Bodies: 9 Bova, 1 Caetano, 2 Jonckheere,
3 Plaxton, 1 Sitcar, 1 Van Hool, 3 Other.
Ops incl: school contracts, day excursions &
holiday tours, private hire, continental tours.
Livery: White/Blue/Orange.

CAVENDISH LINER LTD

BANBURY ROAD, NUFFIELD INDUSTRIAL
ESTATE, POOLE BH17 0GA
Tel: 01202 660620
Fax: 01202 660220
E-mail: sales@cavendishliner.com
Web site: www.cavendishliner.com
Fleet: 17 – 5 double-deck bus, 7 single-deck
coach, 2 midicoach, 3 minibus.
Chassis: 1 Bristol, 1 DAF, 1 Dennis, 1 Ford
Transit, 1 Irisbus, 2 LDV, 1 Leyland, 1 Mercedes,
2 Scania, 5 Volvo.
Ops incl: schools contracts, private hire.
Livery: Grey/Black.

DAMORY COACHES
See Go South Coast Ltd

DOLPHIN HOLIDAYS (DORSET) LTD

UNIT 6, STONE LANE INDUSTRIAL ESTATE,
WIMBORNE MINSTER BH21 1HB
Tel: 01202 883134
Fax: 01202 883132
E-mail: enquiries@dolphincoaches.co.uk
Web site: www.dolphincoaches.co.uk
Man Dir: T J Hann **Fin Dir:** Mrs S Hann.
Fleet: 7 single-deck coach.
Chassis: 1 Bova, 1 Dennis, 1 MAN, 4 Scania.
Bodies: 1 Bova, 1 Caetano, 1 Noge, 4 Van
Hool.
Ops incl: school contracts, excursions &
tours, private hire, express, continental tours.
Livery: Cream & Blue.

EXCELSIOR COACHES LTD

CENTRAL BUSINESS PARK,
BOURNEMOUTH BH1 3SJ
Tel: 01202 652222
Fax: 01202 652223
E-mail: coaches@excelsior-coaches.com

Web site: www.excelsior-coaches.com
Man Dir: Kathy Tilbury **Ops Man:** Dave
Bailey.
Fleet: 43 – 40 single-deck coach, 1 minicoach,
2 minibus.
Chassis: 3 Mercedes, 40 Volvo.
Bodies: 19 Caetano, 4 Jonckheere,
3 Mercedes, 9 Plaxton, 4 Sunsundegui, 4 Volvo.
Ops incl: excursions & tours, private hire,
express, continental tours.
Liveries: Cream, National Express.

FIRST HAMPSHIRE, DORSET & BERKSHIRE

EMPRESS ROAD, SOUTHAMPTON
SO14 0JW
Tel: 0333 014 3490
Fax: 023 8071 4891
E-mail: hampshire-dorset.csc@firstgroup.
com
Web site: www.firstgroup.com
Man Dir: Marc Reddy **Gen Man Dorset:**
Simon Newport.
Fleet: 498 - 81 double-deck bus, 3 open-top
bus, 218 single-deck bus, 12 single-deck coach,
149 midibus, 35 minibus.
Chassis: 37 Alexander Dennis, 2 Autosan,
8 Bluebird, 13 BMC, 94 Dennis, 33 Mercedes,
32 Optare, 45 Scania, 161 Volvo, 73 Wrightbus.
Ops incl: local bus services, school contracts,
private hire.
Livery: FirstGroup UK Bus.
See also Berkshire, Hampshire

GARDBUS

1 ALBANY WAREHOUSE, 151
CHRISTCHURCH ROAD, RINGWOOD
BH24 3AL
Tel: 01425 479068
E-mail: info@gardbus.co.uk
Web site: www.gardbus.co.uk
Dir: S A Gard.
Fleet: 3 – 1 single deck bus, 2 midibus.
Chassis: 2 Dennis, 1 Optare.
Ops incl: local bus services, school contracts.
Livery: Green.

GO SOUTH COAST LTD

TOWNGATE HOUSE, 2-8 PARKSTONE
ROAD, POOLE BH15 2PR
Tel: 01202 680888
Fax: 01202 670244
E-mail: enquiries@morebus.co.uk
Web sites: www.morebus.co.uk, www.go-
ahead.com
Fleet Names (Dorset): Damory Coaches,
More.
Chairman: David Brown **Man Dir:** Andrew
Wickham **Eng Dir:** Steve Hamilton
Fin Dir: Nick Woods **Ops Dir:** Ed Wills.
Fleet: 750 - 321 double-deck bus, 134 single-
deck bus, 101 single-deck coach, 10 articulated
bus, 88 midibus, 96 minibus.
Chassis: 118 Alexander Dennis, 2 Bristol,
62 DAF, 14 Dennis, 1 Ford, 4 Iveco, 1 LDV,
20 Leyland, 59 Mercedes, 123 Optare,
127 Scania, 219 Volvo.
Bodies: 121 Alexander Dennis, 1 Autobus,
4 Beulas, 2 Bluebird, 56 East Lancs, 2 ECW,
1 Ford, 2 Ikarus, 11 Irizar, 3 Jonckheere, 1 LDV,
57 Mercedes, 44 Northern Counties,
169 Optare, 86 Plaxton, 73 Scania, 22 Van
Hool, 91 Wrightbus.
Ops incl: local bus services, school contracts.
Liveries: Damory: Blue; **More:** Red/Blue.
Ticket System: Vix ITSO Smart.
Part of the Go-Ahead Group. See also
operations in Hampshire, Isle of Wight,
Wiltshire.

MIKE HALFORD COACHES
Ceased trading since LRB 2014 went to press

HERRINGTON COACHES LTD

MANOR FARM, SANDLEHEATH ROAD,
ALDERHOLT, FORDINGBRIDGE
SP6 3EG
Tel: 01425 652842
E-mail: enquiries@herringtoncoaches.co.uk
Web site: www.herringtoncoaches.co.uk
Props: Alan Herrington, Mrs Janet
Herrington, Kevin Herrington.
Fleet: 5 - 3 single-deck coach, 2 midicoach.
Chassis: 2 Mercedes, 2 Scania, 1 Volvo.
Bodies: 1 Jonckheere, 2 Van Hool, 2 Other.
Ops incl: local bus services, school contracts,
private hire.
Livery: Red/Grey.
Ticket System: Setright.

HIGHCLIFFE COACH HOLIDAYS

312 LYMINGTON ROAD, HIGHCLIFFE,
CHRISTCHURCH BH23 5ET
Tel: 01425 271111
E-mail: info@highcliffecoachholidays.co.uk
Web site: www.highcliffecoachholidays.co.uk
Props: J & S Blackmore.
Fleet: 2 single-deck coach.
Chassis: 1 Volvo, 1 Setra.
Ops incl: excursions & tours, continental
tours.

HOMEWARD BOUND TRAVEL LTD

137 LYNWOOD DRIVE, WIMBORNE
BH21 1UU
Tel: 01202 884491
Fax: 01202 885664
E-mail: enquiries@homewardboundtravel.
co.uk
Web site: www.homewardboundtravel.co.uk
Dir: Mrs Louisa Morgan.
Fleet: 3 minicoach.
Chassis: 3 Volkswagen Crafter.
Ops incl: school contracts, excursions &
tours, private hire, continental tours.
Livery: Silver/Purple/Green.

LAGUNA HOLIDAYS

LAGUNA HOTEL, 6 SUFFOLK ROAD
SOUTH, BOURNEMOUTH
BH2 6AZ
Tel: 01202 767022
Fax: 01202 760561
E-mail: enquiries@lagunaholidays.com
Web site: www.lagunaholidays.com
Fleet: 9 – 1 double-deck coach, 8 single-deck
coach.
Chassis: 8 Scania, 1 Volvo.
Bodies: 1 Berkhof, 8 Irizar.
Ops incl: excursions & tours, private hire.
Livery: White with Red Lettering.

LINKRIDER COACHES LTD

FLOWER MEADOW, HAYCRAFTS LANE,
HARMANS CROSS, SWANAGE
BH19 3EB
Tel: 01929 477344
Fax: 01929 477345
E-mail: enquiries@linkridercoaches.co.uk
Web site: www.linkridercoaches.co.uk
Fleet Names: Cudlipp Coaches, Linkrider
Coaches, South Dorset Coaches.
Dirs: Nick & Anne Hubbard
Ch Eng: Barry Goodwin.
Fleet: 14 – 2 double-deck bus, 1 double-deck
coach, 9 single-deck coach, 2 midicoach..
Chassis: 1 Bova, 3 Dennis, 1 Irisbus,

1 Leyland, 1 Scania, 1 Setra, 2 Toyota, 4 Volvo.
Ops incl: local bus services, school contracts, excursions & tours, private hire, continental tours.
Livery: White with Black lettering.

POWELLS COACHES
Ceased trading since LRB 2014 went to press

SEA VIEW COACHES (POOLE) LTD
10-12 FANCY ROAD, POOLE BH12 4QZ
Tel: 01202 741439
Fax: 01202 740241
E-mail: info@seaviewcoaches.com
Web site: www.seaviewcoaches.co.uk
Man Dir: David Tarr.
Fleet: 23 - 18 single-deck coach, 2 midicoach, 3 minibus.
Chassis: 3 Beulas, 1 King Long, 15 MAN, 1 Mercedes.
Bodies: 3 Beulas, 1 King Long, 1 Mercedes, 15 Neoplan.
Ops incl: school contracts, excursions & tours, private hire.
Livery: Silver with Blue/Red.

SHAFTESBURY & DISTRICT MOTOR SERVICES LTD
UNIT 2, MELBURY WORKSHOPS, CANN COMMON, SHAFTESBURY SP7 0EB
Tel/Fax: 01747 854359
E-mail: info@sdbuses.co.uk
Web site: www.sdbuses.co.uk
Dir: Roger Brown.
Fleet: 9 - 3 double-deck bus, 2 single-deck

bus, 4 single-deck coach.
Chassis: 4 AEC, 1 Leyland, 2 Mercedes, 2 Volvo.
Bodies: 1 Jonckheere, 1 MCW, 1 Optare, 3 Plaxton, 3 Other.
Ops incl: local bus services, school contracts, private hire.
Livery: Red/Cream/Maroon.
Ticket System: Wayfarer.

SOUTH COAST TRAVEL
THROOP BUSINESS PARK, THROOP ROAD, BOURNEMOUTH BH8 0DQ
Tel: 01202 530200
E-mail: sct@southcoasttravel.co.uk
Web site: www.southcoasttravel.co.uk
Fleet: single-deck coach, midicoach, minicoach.
Ops incl: excursions & tours, private hire.
Livery: White.

SOUTH WEST COACHES LTD
UNIT 17, TRADECROFT INDUSTRIAL ESTATE, PORTLAND DT5 2LN
Tel: 01305 823039
See main entry under Somerset

SOVEREIGN COACHES
PINE LODGE, SIDMOUTH ROAD, ROUSDON, LYME REGIS DT7 3RD
Tel: 01297 23000
E-mail: sov_coaches@btinternet.com
Web site: www.sovereigncoaches.co.uk
Partners: Richard C Keech, Mrs Cynthia M Keech.
Fleet: 8 – 1 midibus, 5 midicoach, 1 minibus,

1 minicoach.
Chassis: 5 Mercedes, 1 Optare, 1 Toyota, 1 Volkswagen.
Bodies: 1 Noone, 1 Optare, 1 Onyx, 1 Plaxton, 2 Unvi, 2 Other.
Ops incl: local bus services, school contracts, excursions & tours, private hire.
Livery: White/Red.
Ticket System: Ticketer.

WILTS & DORSET BUS COMPANY LTD
See Go South Coast Ltd

YELLOW BUSES
YEOMANS WAY, BOURNEMOUTH BH8 0BQ
Tel: 01202 636000
Fax: 01202 636001
E-mail: mail@yellowbuses.co.uk
Web site: www.bybus.co.uk
Chairman: D A Lott **Man Dir:** A Smith
Head of Marketing: Mrs J Wilkinson.
Fleet: 171 - 56 double-deck bus, 97 single-deck bus, 18 single-deck coach.
Chassis: 11 Alexander Dennis, 1 DAF, 33 Dennis, 34 Optare, 2 Scania, 2 Transbus, 69 Volvo, 19 Wrightbus.
Bodies: 11 Alexander Dennis, 18 Caetano, 42 East Lancs, 34 Optare, 20 Plaxton, 2 Transbus, 40 Wrightbus, 4 Other.
Ops incl: local bus services, school contracts, express.
Livery: Yellow.
Ticket System: Wayfarer TGX200.
A subsidiary of RATP Dev UK Ltd

DURHAM, HARTLEPOOL, STOCKTON-ON-TEES

ALFA TRAVEL LTD
See Alfa Travel, Lancashire

ARRIVA NORTH EAST
ADMIRAL WAY, DOXFORD INTERNATIONAL BUSINESS PARK, SUNDERLAND SR3 3XP
Tel: 0191 520 4200
Fax: 0191 520 4183
Web site: www.arriva.co.uk
Regional Man Dir: Nigel Featham
Area Man Dir: Nick Knox **Regional Finance Dir:** David Cocker **Eng Dir:** Gavin Peace **Regional Marketing & Comms Man:** Chloe Leach O'Connell
Regional HR Partner: Julie Reynolds.
Fleet: 524 - 112 double-deck bus, 215 single-deck bus, 4 single-deck coach, 116 midibus, 77 minibus.
Chassis: 20 Alexander Dennis, 80 DAF, 80 Dennis, 11 MAN, 77 Optare, 22 Scania, 18 Temsa, 126 VDL, 63 Volvo, 27 Wrightbus.
Bodies: 70 Alexander, 20 Alexander Dennis, 11 Caetano, 13 East Lancs, 79 Optare, 67 Plaxton, 22 Scania, 18 Temsa, 11 Transbus, 221 Wrightbus.
Ops incl: local bus services, school contracts, private hire.
Livery: Arriva UK Bus.
Ticket System: Wayfarer 3.

COCHRANE'S
4 FARADAY ROAD, NORTH EAST INDUSTRIAL ESTATE, PETERLEE SR8 5AP
Tel: 0191 586 2136
Fax: 0191 586 5566
E-mail: cochranes@btconnect.com
Web site: www.cochranescoaches.co.uk
Fleet Name: Cochrane's Kelvin Travel.
Owner: I P Cochrane.

Fleet: 10 - 1 single-deck bus, 8 single-deck coach, 1 midicoach.
Chassis: 1 Bedford, 4 Bova, 2 DAF, 1 Mercedes, 1 VDL, 1 Volvo.
Bodies: 4 Bova, 1 Caetano, 1 Duple, 1 Northern Counties, 1 Unvi, 2 Van Hool.
Ops incl: school contracts.
Livery: Blue.
Ticket System: Setright.

COMPASS ROYSTON TRAVEL LTD
BOWESFIELD LANE INDUSTRIAL ESTATE, STOCKTON-ON-TEES TS18 3EG
Tel: 01642 606644
Fax: 01642 608617
Web site: www.compassroyston.net
Man Dir: G Walton **Trans Man:** M Metcalfe.
Fleet: 81 – 1 single-deck bus, 57 single-deck coach, 12 midibus, 10 minibus.
Chassis: 5 Alexander Dennis, 1 Bova, 2 DAF, 6 Dennis, 2 Ford Transit, 1 Irisbus, 1 Iveco, 1 LDV, 1 MAN, 3 Mercedes, 4 Neoplan, 4 Optare, 49 Volvo.
Bodies: 1 Alexander, 5 Alexander Dennis, 2 Berkhof, 1 Bova, 1 Caetano, 2 Ford Transit, 2 Ikarus, 1 Indcar, 4 Jonckheere, 1 LDV, 4 Neoplan, 1 Noge, 4 Optare, 43 Plaxton, 8 Van Hool, 1 Wrightbus.
Ops incl: local bus services, excursions & tours, private hire, express, continental tours, school contracts.
Livery: White with Blue/Yellow.
Incorporating Leven Valley Coaches Ltd
Associated with Procters Coaches *(see North Yorkshire)*

DURHAM CITY COACHES LTD
BRANDON LANE, BRANDON, DURHAM DH7 8PG
Tel: 0191 378 0540

Fax: 0191 378 1985
E-mail: sales@durhamcitycoaches.co.uk
Web site: www.durhamcitycoaches.co.uk
Man Dir: Michael Lightfoot **Dir:** Christine Lightfoot.
Fleet: 19 – 1 double-deck bus, 13 single-deck coach, 5 midicoach.
Chassis: 3 Bova, 1 DAF, 1 Leyland, 5 Mercedes, 9 Volvo.
Ops incl: excursions & tours, private hire, continental tours, school contracts.
Livery: Black/Red/Gold.

EDEN BUS SERVICES
STAINDROP ROAD, WEST AUCKLAND DL4 9JY
Tel: 0845 051 5201
E-mail: theeden@aol.com
Web site: www.theeden.co.uk
Prop: G Scarlett.
Fleet: 9 – 1 midicoach, 8 minibus.
Chassis: 1 Enterprise, 8 Mercedes.
Ops incl: local bus services, school contracts.
Livery: Red/White.

ENTERPRISE TRAVEL
19 PINE GROVE, DARLINGTON DL3 8JF
Tel: 01325 286924
E-mail: coachhire@aol.com
Web site: www.enterprisecoachhire.co.uk
Dirs: B R Brown, Mrs B M Brown.
Fleet: 5 - 4 single-deck coach, 1 minicoach.
Chassis: 1 Bova, 1 Dennis, 1 Mercedes, 1 Setra, 1 Toyota.
Bodies: 1 Bova, 1 Caetano, 1 Mercedes, 1 Plaxton, 1 Setra.
Ops incl: excursions & tours, private hire, school contracts.
Livery: White with Red/Green reliefs.

GARDINERS NMC TRAVEL
See Northumberland

GARNETT'S COACHES
UNIT E1, ROMAN WAY INDUSTRIAL
ESTATE, TINDALE CRESCENT, BISHOP
AUCKLAND DL14 9AW
Tel: 01388 604419
Fax: 01388 609549
E-mail: info@garnettscoaches.com
Web site: www.garnettscoaches.com
Fleet Ops Man: Paul Garnett.
Fleet: 41 - 16 double-deck bus, 2 single-deck
bus, 18 single-deck coach, 2 double-deck
coach, 3 midicoach.
Chassis: 13 Dennis, 6 Leyland, 1 MAN,
3 Mercedes, 1 Transbus, 17 Volvo.
Ops incl: school contracts, excursions &
tours, private hire, continental tours.
Livery: Yellow/Red/Black.

GO NORTH EAST
117 QUEEN STREET, GATESHEAD
NE8 2UA
Tel: 0191 420 5050
Fax: 0191 420 0225
E-mail: customerservices@gonortheast.
co.uk
Web site: www.simplygo.com
Man Dir: K Carr **Fin Dir:** G C McPherson
Ops Dir: D Curry **Head of Comm:**
A Tyldsley **Ch Eng:** K Trewin.
Fleet: 681 - 192 double-deck bus, 379 single-
deck bus, 28 single-deck coach, 74 midibus,
8 articulated bus.
Chassis: 6 Alexander Dennis, 16 DAF,
34 Dennis, 79 Mercedes, 87 Optare,
137 Scania, 40 Transbus, 13 VDL, 253 Volvo,
16 Wrightbus.
Bodies: 6 Alexander Dennis, 26 Caetano,
45 East Lancs, 79 Mercedes, 16 Northern
Counties, 87 Optare, 45 Plaxton, 41 Scania,
40 Transbus, 296 Wrightbus.
Ops incl: local bus services, school contracts,
express.
Livery: Various route brands, National
Express.
Ticket System: Vix TP5700.

GRIERSONS COACHES
SEDGEFIELD ROAD GARAGE, FISHBURN,
STOCKTON-ON-TEES TS21 4DD
Tel: 01740 620209
Fax: 01740 621243
E-mail: busliberty@aol.com
Web site: www.coachhire-northeast.com
Props: C & D Grierson.
Fleet: 27 - 7 double-deck bus, 15 single-deck
coach, 4 midicoach, 1 minibus.
Chassis: 1 Bristol, 1 Ford Transit, 5 Leyland,
4 Mercedes, 16 Volvo.
Ops incl: excursions & tours, private hire,
express, continental tours.
Livery: Blue/Red.

HODGSONS COACH OPERATORS LTD
16 GALGATE, BARNARD CASTLE DL12
8BG
Tel: 01833 630730
Fax: 01833 630830
E-mail: hodgsonscoach@btconnect.co.uk
Web site: www.hodgsonscoachtravel.co.uk
Man Dir: Keith Hodgson **Ops Man:** Mark
Hodgson.
Fleet: 26 – 15 single-deck coach, 5 midibus,
3 midicoach, 3 minibus.
Chassis: 1 Bova, 1 DAF, 7 Dennis, 2 LDV,
4 Mercedes, 3 Neoplan, 1 Optare,
1 Volkswagen, 6 Volvo.

Ops incl: local bus services, school contracts,
excursions & tours, private hire, continental
tours.
Livery: White/Blue.
Ticket System: Wayfarer Saver.

HUMBLES COACHES
UP YONDER, ROBSON STREET, SHILDON
DL4 1EB
Tel: 01388 772772
Fax: 01388 772211
Dirs: Malcolm Humble, Mrs Pamela West.
Fleet: 2 midicoach.
Chassis: 2 Mercedes.
Ops incl: school contracts, excursions &
tours, private hire.
Livery: White.

HUNTER BROS LTD
THE GARAGE, TANTOBIE, STANLEY
DH9 9TG
Tel: 01207 232392
Fax: 01207 290575
Fleet: 11 – 8 single-deck coach, 2 midibus,
1 midicoach.
Chassis: 3 Mercedes, 1 Optare, 7 Volvo.
Bodies: 1 Jonckheere, 1 Optare, 5 Plaxton.
Ops incl: local bus services, school contracts,
private hire.

J & C COACHES
THE TRAVEL CENTRE, AYCLIFFE
INDUSTRIAL PARK, NEWTON AYCLIFFE
DL5 6HY
Tel: 01325 312705
Fax: 01325 320385
E-mail: nevjandccoaches@fsmail.net
Web site: www.jandccoachesltd.co.uk
Snr Partner: J N Jones
Partners: A Jones, N Jones, D Jones.
Fleet: 9 - 3 single-deck coach, 1 double-deck
coach, 3 minibus, 2 minicoach.
Chassis: 1 DAF, 4 Mercedes, 1 Optare,
1 Scania, 1 Volvo.
Ops incl: school contracts, excursions &
tours, private hire, continental tours.
Livery: various.

JSB TRAVEL
SB TRAVEL
13 HILLSIDE ROAD, COUNDON
DL14 8LS
Tel: 07900 426206
Web site: www.jsbtravel.co.uk
Ops incl: local bus services, private hire.
Fleet: 11 – 3 midibus, 8 minibus.
Chassis: 1 Dennis, 1 Ford Transit, 4 Mercedes,
5 Optare.
Ops incl: local bus services.
Livery: Maroon/White.

JAYLINE BAND SERVICES
1 HACKWORTH ROAD, NORTH WEST
INDUSTRIAL ESTATE, PETERLEE
SR8 2JQ
Tel: 0750 314 2222
E-mail: jaylinetravel@hotmail.com
Web site: jaylinetravel.com
Prop: Jason Rogers **Dir:** Neil Tait.
Fleet: 5- 1 single-deck band coach, 4 double-
deck band coach.
Chassis: 2 Scania, 3 Setra.
Bodies: 1 Berkhof, 3 Setra, 1 Van Hool.
Ops incl: private hire (band buses, film crews)
Livery: Blue.

KINGSLEY COACHES LTD
See Tyne & Wear

LEE'S COACHES LTD
MILL ROAD GARAGE, LITTLEBURN
INDUSTRIAL ESTATE, LANGLEY MOOR
DH7 8HE
Tel: 0191 378 0653
Fax: 0191 378 9086
E-mail: info@leescoaches.co.uk
Web site: www.leescoaches.co.uk
Man Dir: Malcolm Lee **Dir:** Derrick Collin
Eng: David Welch.
Fleet: 21 - 20 single-deck coach, 1 minibus.
Chassis: 1 Bova, 2 DAF, 2 Mercedes,
3 Van Hool, 13 Volvo.
Ops incl: school contracts, excursions &
tours, private hire, continental tours.
Livery: Blue/Silver/White.

MAUDES COACHES
REDWELL GARAGE, HARMIRE ROAD,
BARNARD CASTLE DL12 8QJ
Tel: 01833 637341
Fax: 01833 631888
Prop: Stephen Maude.
Fleet: 8 - 4 single-deck coach, 2 midicoach,
2 minibus.
Chassis: 1 LDV, 3 Mercedes, 4 Volvo.
Bodies: 1 Excel, 1 LDV, 1 Onyx, 5 Plaxton.
Ops incl: local bus services, school contracts,
excursions & tours, private hire.
Livery: Red/White.

METRO COACHES
THE CONIFERS, DARLINGTON ROAD,
LONG NEWTON, STOCKTON-ON-TEES
TS21 1PE
Tel: 01642 219555
E-mail: lewis@metrocoaches.com
Web site: www.metrocoachesuk.co.uk
Fleet: 9 – 1 double-deck bus, 5 single-deck
coach, 1 midibus, 1 midicoach, 1 minibus.
Chassis: 1 Leyland, 3 Mercedes, 5 Volvo.
Ops incl: school contracts, private hire.

NORTON MINI TRAVEL
5 PLUMER DRIVE, NORTON
TS20 1HF
Tel: 01642 555832
E-mail: nortonminitravel@hotmail.co.uk
Web site: www.norton-mini-travel.co.uk
Owner: R Spears.
Fleet: 1 minicoach.
Chassis: Iveco.
Ops incl: private hire, school contracts.
Livery: White/Purple.

RICHARDSONS COACHES
3 OXFORD ROAD, HARTLEPOOL
TS26 0AA
Tel/Fax: 01429 272235
E-mail: richardsonscoaches@btconnect.com
Web site: www.richardsonscoaches.co.uk
Man Dir/Ch Eng: T Richardson
Dir/Co Sec/Traf Man: D Richardson.
Fleet: 9 - 3 single-deck coach, 2 midicoach,
4 minibus.
Chassis: 4 Ford Transit, 2 Mercedes,
2 Scania, 1 Volvo.
Bodies: 4 Ford, 1 Irizar, 4 Plaxton.
Ops incl: excursions & tours, private hire.
Livery: White with Blue/Grey.

ROBERTS TOURS
36 NORTH ROAD WEST, WINGATE
TS28 5AP
Tel: 01429 838268
Fax: 01429 838228
E-mail: robertstours@aol.com
Web site: www.robertstours.co.uk

Dirs: T G Roberts, D Roberts, C A Harper.
Fleet: 12 single-deck coach.
Chassis: 4 Bova, 2 DAF, 2 Leyland, 3 Scania, 1 Volvo.
Bodies: 4 Bova, 1 Ikarus, 1 Jonckheere, 2 Plaxton, 4 Van Hool.
Ops incl: excursions & tours, private hire, express, school contracts.
Livery: Cream/Green.

SCARLET BAND BUS & COACH LTD

WELFARE GARAGE, STATION ROAD, WEST CORNFORTH, FERRYHILL
DL17 9LA
Tel: 01740 654247
Fax: 01740 656068
E-mail: s.band@btconnect.com
Web site: www.scarletbandbuses.co.uk
Fleet Name: Scarlet Band
Dir: Graeme Torrance
Traffic Man: Andrew Dolan
Eng Man: George Lambert.
Fleet: 34 - 1 double-deck bus, 1 single-deck bus, 3 single-deck coach, 18 midibus, 11 minibus.
Chassis: 5 Alexander Dennis, 1 Bova, 1 Dennis, 1 Leyland, 6 Mercedes, 13 Optare, 5 Renault, 2 Volvo.
Bodies: 5 Alexander Dennis, 1 Alexander, 1 Berkhof, 1 Bova, 1 Duple, 5 Koch, 1 MCV, 13 Optare, 1 Plaxton, 6 Other.
Ops incl: local bus services, school contracts, excursions & tours, private hire.
Livery: Red and Cream with Scarlet Band.
Ticket System: Ticketer.

SHERBURN VILLAGE COACHES

FRONT STREET, SHERBURN VILLAGE
DH6 1QY
Tel: 0191 372 1531
Fax: 0191 372 1531
E-mail: sherburncoaches@btconnect.com
Prop: John Cousins.
Fleet: 7 - 2 single-deck coach, 3 midibus, 2 midicoach.
Chassis: 1 MAN, 4 Mercedes, 2 Volvo.
Bodies: 1 Autobus, 1 Berkhof, 1 Caetano, 3 Plaxton, 1 Wadham Stringer.
Ops incl: local bus services, excursions & tours, private hire.
Livery: Red/White
Ticket System: AES.

SIESTA INTERNATIONAL HOLIDAYS LTD

NEWPORT SOUTH BUSINESS PARK, LAMPORT STREET, MIDDLESBROUGH
TS1 5QL
Tel: 01642 257920
Fax: 01642 219153
Recovery: 07739 679957
E-mail: sales@siestaholidays.co.uk
Web site: www.siestaholidays.co.uk
Chairman: Paul R Herbert **Dirs:** C Herbert, J Herbert, J Cofton **Ops Mans:** K Keelan, J Potter.

Fleet: 8 - 2 single-deck coach, 5 double-deck coach, 1 minibus.
Chassis: 1 Ford Transit, 4 Scania, 3 Van Hool.
Bodies: 4 Berkhof, 1 Ford, 3 Van Hool.
Ops incl: excursions & tours, private hire, continental tours.
Livery: Metallic Blue.

SNOWDON'S COACHES

SEASIDE LANE, EASINGTON
SR8 3TW
Tel: 0191 527 0535
Fax: 0191 527 3280
E-mail: info@snowdoncoaches.co.uk
Web site: www.snowdoncoaches.co.uk
Props: Alan Snowdon, Andrew Snowdon.
Fleet: 16 – 3 double-deck coach, 13 single-deck coach.
Chassis: 1 Neoplan, 3 Scania, 12 Volvo.
Bodies: 2 Irizar, 1 Neoplan, 5 Plaxton, 2 Transbus, 6 Van Hool.
Ops incl: private hire, school contracts.
Livery: Grey/White.

STAGECOACH TRANSIT

CHURCH ROAD, STOCKTON ON TEES
TS18 2HW
Tel: 0191 566 0231
Fax: 0191 566 0230
E-mail: northest.enquiries@stagecoachbus.com
Web site: www.stagecoachbus.com
Fleet Names: Stagecoach in Hartlepool, Stagecoach on Teeside.
Man Dir: Phil Medlicott.
Fleet: See Stagecoach North East (Tyne & Wear)
Ops incl: local bus services.
Livery: Stagecoach UK Bus.

STANLEY TRAVEL (NORTH EAST) LTD

EDEN TERRACE, OXHILL, STANLEY
DH9 7LL
Tel: 01207 237424
Fax: 01207 233233
Web site: www.stanley-travel.com
Dirs: Andrew Scott, Ian Scott.
Fleet: 37 - 5 double-deck bus, 15 single-deck coach, 4 midibus, 1 midicoach, 10 minibus, 2 minicoach.
Chassis: 2 Alexander Dennis, 1 Dennis, 4 Ford Transit, 1 Leyland, 8 Mercedes, 2 Optare, 2 Van Hool, 1 VDL, 16 Volvo.
Bodies: 4 Alexander, 2 Alexander Dennis, 1 Crest, 1 Ferqui, 4 Ford, 1 KVC, 1 Northern Counties, 1 Onyx, 3 Optare, 15 Plaxton, 3 Van Hool, 1 Other.
Ops incl: local bus services, school contracts, private hire, excursions & tours.
Livery: White/Orange.

TGM NORTH EAST (CLASSIC COACHES LTD)

CLASSIC HOUSE, MORRISON ROAD,

ANNFIELD PLAIN, STANLEY
DH9 7RX
Tel: 01207 282225
Fax: 01207 281639
E-mail: holidays@tgmgroup.co.uk
Web site: www.classiccoachesholidays.co.uk
Man Dir: Heath Williams
Regional Man Dir: Ian Shipley.
Fleet: 37 - 9 double-deck bus, 2 single-deck bus, 17 single-deck coach, 4 double-deck coach, 5 midibus.
Chassis: 1 Alexander Dennis, 1 Bova, 8 DAF, 2 Dennis, 1 Leyland, 11 Scania, 2 Transbus, 1 Van Hool, 10 Volvo.
Bodies: 8 Alexander, 4 Berkhof, 1 Bova, 8 Caetano, 1 East Lancs, 5 Irizar, 1 Northern Counties, 4 Plaxton, 5 Van Hool.
Ops incl: local bus services, school contracts, excursions & tours, private hire, express, continental tours.
Livery: White with Blue/Yellow.
Part of the TGM Group, a subsidiary of Arriva

PAUL WATSON TRAVEL

BRIDGE HOUSE, MOOR ROAD, STAINDROP, DARLINGTON
DL2 3LF
Tel: 0800 025 7623
E-mail: paul.watson9@btconnect.com
Web site: www.paulwatsontravel.co.uk
Dir: Paul Watson
Co Sec: Joanne Watson.
Fleet: 6 - 3 single-deck coach, 1 midicoach, 2 minibus.
Chassis: 1 Ford Transit, 1 LDV, 1 Mercedes, 1 Setra, 2 Volvo.
Ops incl: school contracts, excursions & tours, private hire, continental tours.
Livery: White.

WEARDALE MOTOR SERVICES LTD

38 EAST END, STANHOPE
DL13 2YQ
Tel: 01388 528235
Fax: 01388 526080
E-mail: enquiries@weardalemotorservices.co.uk
Web site: www.weardale-travel.co.uk
Dirs: A, I, R, S Gibson, A Hewison
Ops Man: C Adams.
Fleet: 60 - 23 double-deck bus, 2 single-deck bus, 19 single-deck coach, 2 midibus, 4 midicoach, 10 minibus.
Chassis: 2 Bova, 7 Dennis, 1 Fiat, 1 LDV, 12 Leyland, 2 MAN, 6 Mercedes, 2 Neoplan, 8 Optare, 2 Scania, 1 Temsa, 5 Van Hool, 1 VDL, 10 Volvo.
Bodies: 9 Alexander, 1 Berkhof, 1 Bluebird, 2 Bova, 5 East Lancs, 1 Koch, 1 KVC, 1 Lahden, 1 LDV, 2 Neoplan, 5 Northern Counties, 8 Optare, 13 Plaxton, 1 Sitcar, 1 Temsa, 6 Van Hool, 2 Wrightbus.
Ops incl: local bus services, excursions & tours, school contracts, private hire, express, continental tours.
Livery: Red/White.
Ticket System: Wayfarer.

♿ Vehicle suitable for disabled	🍴 Coach(es) with galley facilities	🚌 Vintage Coach(es) available
🔔 Seat belt-fitted Vehicle	🔑 Replacement vehicle available	🚌 Open top vehicle(s)
R24 24 hour recovery service	R Recovery service available	🚻 Coaches with toilet facilities
T Toilet-drop facilities available	❄ Air-conditioned vehicle(s)	🔋 Hybrid Buses ⛽ Gas Buses

ABBEY COACHWAYS LTD

MEADOWCROFT GARAGE, LOW STREET,
CARLTON, GOOLE
DN14 9PH
Tel: 01405 860337
Fax: 01405 869433
Dirs: Mrs L E Baker, S J Stockdale.
Fleet: 8 – 2 double-deck bus, 5 single-deck
coach, 1 double-deck coach.
Chassis: 1 MAN, 1 Scania, 6 Volvo.
Bodies: 2 Alexander, 2 Jonckheere, 4 Plaxton.
Ops incl: school contracts, private hire.
Livery: White/Blue.

ACKLAMS COACHES LTD

BARMSTON CLOSE, BEVERLEY
HU17 0LA
Tel: 01482 887666
Fax: 01482 874949
E-mail: sayhello@acklamscoaches.co.uk
Web site: www.acklamscoaches.co.uk
Dir: Paul Acklam.
Fleet: 25 – 5 double-deck bus, 11 single-deck
coach, 1 midicoach, 7 minibus, 1 minicoach.
Chassis: 1 Alexander Dennis, 2 Dennis,
1 Ford Transit, 4 LDV, 2 Mercedes, 2 Optare,
1 Transbus, 12 Volvo.
Bodies: 4 Alexander, 1 Alexander Dennis,
3 Excel, 1 Ford, 1 LDV, 2 Optare, 13 Plaxton.
Ops incl: local bus services, school contracts,
private hire.
Livery: Red/Grey.

BARNETTS FAIRWAY RHODES COACH TRAVEL

308 WINCOLMLEE, HULL
HU2 0QE
Tel: 01482 328473
Fleet: 17 – 7 double-deck bus, 5 single-deck
coach, 1 midicoach, 2 minibus, 2 minicoach.
Chassis: 2 Bova, 1 DAF, 1 Ford Transit,
5 Leyland, 2 Mercedes, 1 Optare, 1 Toyota,
4 Volvo.
Bodies: 4 Alexander, 2 Bova, 1 Caetano,
1 ECW, 1 Ford, 2 Northern Counties,
1 Optare, 4 Plaxton, 1 Other.
Ops incl: school contracts, private hire.

JIM BELL COACHES LTD

27 CROWLE STREET, HEDON ROAD,
HULL HU9 1RH
Tel: 01482 307572
Fax: 01482 307574
E-mail: jim@jimbellcoaches.com
Web site: www.jimbellcoaches.com
Man Dir: Jim Bell
Fleet: 25 – 3 single-deck bus, 6 single-deck
coach, 3 midibus, 3 midicoach, 9 minibus,
1 minicoach.
Chassis: 1 Alexander Dennis, 1 Dennis,
2 Ford Transit, 1 Irisbus, 9 Mercedes, 1 Temsa,
1 Volkswagen, 9 Volvo.
Ops incl: school contracts, private hire.
Livery: White with logos.

CAB EXECUTIVE TRAVEL

21 PARADISE PLACE, GOOLE
DN14 5DL
Tel: 01405 765533
Fax: 01405 765599
E-mail: info@cab-travel.com
Web site: www.cab-travel.com
Prop: C A Bruce.
Fleet: 4 – 3 single-deck coaches, 1 minibus.
Chassis: 1 Mercedes, 3 Setra.
Ops incl: excursions & tours, private hire,
continental tours.

CAIRNGORM COACH TRAVEL LTD

35 AIRE STREET, GOOLE
DN14 5QW
Tel: 01405 761334
Web site: www.cairngorm-travel.co.uk
Dirs: P & D M Southcott.
Fleet: 7 - 6 single-deck coach, 1 minibus.
Chassis: 1 Mercedes, 6 Neoplan.
Bodies: 1 Mercedes, 6 Neoplan.
Ops incl: excursions & tours, continental
tours.
Livery: Blue.

CT PLUS (YORKSHIRE) CIC

GREENS INDUSTRIAL PARK, CALDER VALE
ROAD, WAKEFIELD WF1 5PF
Tel: 01482 226372
Fax: 01482 226350
E-mail: info@hullparkandride.org.uk
Web site: www.hullparkandride.org.uk
Ch Exec: Dai Powell
Dep Ch Exec: Jude Winter
Ch Fin Off: John Smart
Ops Dir: Jane Desmond
Performance Dir: Jon McColl.
Fleet (East Riding): 6 single-deck bus.
Chassis: 6 BMC.
Bodies: 6 BMC.
Ops incl: Hull Park & Ride.
Livery: Park & Ride: Black.
A division of the HCT Group – see also Bristol,
London & Middlesex, West Yorkshire and the
Channel Islands

DRURY COACHES

THE COACH DEPOT, CARTER STREET,
GOOLE DN14 6SL
Tel/Fax: 01405 763440
E-mail: rdrurycoaches@aol.com
Web site: www.drurycoaches.co.uk
Dirs: Roland Drury, Richard Wilson.
Fleet: 6 - 5 single-deck coach, 1 midicoach.
Chassis: 1 Mercedes, 5 Volvo.
Bodies: 6 Plaxton.
Ops incl: school contracts, private hire.
Livery: White/Green.

EAST YORKSHIRE MOTOR SERVICES LTD

252 ANLABY ROAD, HULL
HU3 2RS
Tel: 01482 327142
Fax: 01482 217614
E-mail: enquiries@eyms.co.uk
Web site: www.eyms.co.uk
Chairman: Peter Shipp
Fin Dir: Peter Harrison
Comm Man: Bob Rackley
Ch Eng: Robert Gibson
Co Sec: Peter Harrison
Ops Man: Ray Hill
Marketing Man: Claire Robinson.
Fleet: 335 - 179 double-deck bus, 69 single-
deck bus, 23 single-deck coach, 8 open-top
bus, 49 midibus, 6 minibus, 1 minicoach.
Chassis: 31 Alexander Dennis, 37 Dennis,
6 Enterprise, 12 MAN, 6 Mercedes, 14 Optare,
229 Volvo.
Bodies: 29 Alexander, 28 Alexander Dennis,
16 Caetano, 1 East Lancs, 4 MCV, 20 Northern
Counties, 17 Optare, 115 Plaxton, 2 Volvo,
103 Wrightbus.
Ops incl: local bus services, school contracts,
excursion & tours, private hire, express,
continental tours.
Livery: Burgundy/Cream.
Ticket System: Wayfarer TGX200.

ELLIE ROSE TRAVEL LTD

TOWER HOUSE LANE, SALTEND, HULL
HU12 8EE
Tel: 01482 890616
Fax: 01482 899359
E-mail: jasonreid@ellierosetravel.karoo.co.uk
Dirs: Shane & Sheila Houghton.
Fleet: 33 - 18 double-deck bus, 2 single-deck
bus, 9 single-deck coach, 1 open top bus,
1 midicoach, 2 minibus.
Chassis: 2 DAF, 2 LDV, 3 Leyland, 1 Mercedes,
2 Scania, 23 Volvo.
Ops incl: school contracts, private hire.
Livery: White.
Ticket system: Wayfarer.

LORDS COACHES

YARD 1, WOODHOUSE STREET,
HEDON ROAD, HULL HU9 1RJ
Tel: 01482 321655
E-mail: lordscoaches@hotmail.com
Web site: www.lordscoaches.co.uk
Prop: N Lord.
Fleet: 8 – 3 double-deck bus, 4 single-deck
coach, 1 midibus.
Chassis: 1 Bova, 7 Volvo.
Ops incl: local bus services, school contracts,
excursions & tours, private hire.
Livery: White/Blue.

NATIONAL HOLIDAYS

SPRINGFIELD WAY, ANLABY, HULL
HU10 7LA
Tel: 01482 572572
Fax: 01482 569004
E-mail: info@nationalholidays.com
Web site: www.nationalholidays.com
Man Dir: G Rogers **Ops Man:** A Hutchinson
Transport Man: P Joyce.
Fleet: 130 single-deck coach.
Chassis: 72 Setra, 58 Volvo.
Bodies: 53 Plaxton, 72 Setra, 5 Van Hool.
Ops incl: excursions & tours.
Livery: White & Blue.
A subsidiary company of Shearings Holidays
(see Greater Manchester)

PEARSON COACHES LTD

9 HEADLANDS ROAD, ALDBROUGH,
HU11 4RR
Tel: 01964 527260
Fax: 01964 527774
E-mail: enquiries@pearsonscoaches.co.uk
Web site: www.pearsonscoaches.co.uk
Dir: Mrs V Pearson.
Fleet: 11 - 5 single-deck coach, 1 minibus,
5 minicoach.
Chassis: 6 Mercedes, 5 Volvo.
Bodies: 1 Jonckheere, 2 Mercedes, 3 Plaxton,
1 Sitcar, 1 UVG, 3 Van Hool.
Ops incl: local bus services, school contracts,
excursions & tours, private hire.
Livery: White.
Ticket system: Wayfarer 2.

SHAW'S OF WHITLEY

WHITLEY FARM, SILVER STREET, WHITLEY,
GOOLE DN14 0JG
Tel: 01977 661214
Fax: 01977 662036
Recovery: 07802 249878
E-mail: info@shawsofwhitley.co.uk
Web site: www.shawsofwhitley.co.uk
Prop: Mrs Marjorie Shaw
Ops Man: Philip Shaw.
Fleet: 7 – 1 double-deck bus, 6 single-deck
coach.

Chassis: 1 DAF, 1 Mercedes, 2 Setra,
1 Van Hool, 2 Volvo.
Bodies: 1 East Lancs, 1 Jonckheere,
1 Mercedes, 2 Setra, 2 Van Hool.
Ops incl: excursions & tours, private hire,
continental tours.
Livery: Various.

STAGECOACH EAST MIDLANDS
PO BOX 15, DEACON ROAD, LINCOLN
LN2 4JB
Tel: 01482 222333
Fax: 01522 538229
Fleet Name: Stagecoach in Hull.
E-mail: hull@stagecoachbus.com
Web site: www.stagecoachbus.com

Man Dir: Michelle Hargreaves
Eng Dir: John Taylor
Comm Dir: Dave Skepper
Ops Dir: Richard Kay.
Fleet: 540 - 209 double-deck bus, 122 single-
deck bus, 16 single-deck coach, 165 midibus,
28 minibus.
Chassis: 165 Alexander Dennis, 6 DAF,
109 Dennis, 1 Leyland, 72 MAN, 36 Optare,
26 Scania, 49 Transbus, 76 Volvo.
Bodies: 110 Alexander, 234 Alexander
Dennis, 50 East Lancs, 6 Jonckheere,
5 Northern Counties, 36 Optare, 37 Plaxton,
50 Transbus, 12 Wrightbus.
Ops incl: local bus services.
Livery: Stagecoach UK Bus.
Ticket System: ERG TP5000.

SWEYNE COACHES
LONGSHORE, REEDNESS ROAD,
SWINEFLEET DN14 8ER
Tel: 01405 704263
E-mail: mail@sweyne.co.uk
Web site: www.sweyne.co.uk
Fleet: 16 – 7 double-deck bus, 2 midibus,
7 single-deck coach.
Chassis: 6 DAF, 5 Dennis, 4 Leyland, 1 Setra.
Bodies: 4 Alexander, 4 Ikarus, 5 Plaxton,
1 Setra, 2 Van Hool.
Ops incl: local bus services, school contracts,
private hire.
Livery: Blue/White/Gold.

EAST SUSSEX, BRIGHTON & HOVE

BARCROFT TOURS & EVENTS
247 LONDON ROAD, ST LEONARDS
ON SEA TN37 6LU
Tel: 01424 200201   **Fax:** 01424 200206
Recovery: 07977 004371
E-mail: info@barcrofttours.co.uk
Web site: www.barcrofttours.co.uk
Fleet: 2 single-deck coach.
Chassis: 1 Scania, 1 Volvo.
Bodies: 1 Caetano, 1 Irizar.
Ops incl: excursions & tours, private hire,
London commuter express, continental tours.
Livery: White.

THE BIG LEMON CIC
PROTRAN HOUSE, BOUNDARY ROAD,
BLACK ROCK, BRIGHTON BN2 5TJ
Tel/Fax: 01273 681681
E-mail: lemonbus@thebiglemon.com
Web site: www.thebiglemon.com
Fleet: 12 – 1 open-top bus, 3 single-deck
coach, 2 midibus, 2 midicoach, 4 minibus.
Chassis: 2 Dennis, 1 MCW, 6 Mercedes,
3 Volvo.
Ops incl: local bus services, private hire,
excursions.
Livery: Yellow.

BRIGHTON & HOVE BUS & COACH COMPANY
43 CONWAY STREET, HOVE BN3 3LT
Tel: 01273 886200   **Fax:** 01273 822073
E-mail: info@buses.co.uk
Web site: www.buses.co.uk
Fleet Name: Brighton & Hove
Chairman: David Brown
Man Dir: Martin Harris **Fin Dir:**
Philip Woodgate **Ops Dir:** Mike Best
Eng Dir: Adrian Mitchell
Dir: Keith Down.
Fleet: 272 - 240 double-deck bus, 4 open-top
bus, 7 single-deck bus, 7 single-deck coach,
12 articulated bus, 2 midibus.
Chassis: 1 AEC, 14 Dennis, 12 Mercedes,
151 Scania, 2 Transbus, 92 Volvo.
Bodies: 109 East Lancs, 7 Irizar, 12 Mercedes,
1 Park Royal, 2 Plaxton, 38 Scania, 2 Transbus,
92 Wrightbus.
Ops incl: local bus services, school contracts,
excursions & tours, private hire, continental
tours.
Livery: Red & Cream.
Ticket System: ERG.
A subsidiary of the Go-Ahead Group

BRIGHTONIAN COACHES
3 THE AVENUE, BRIGHTON BN2 4GF
Tel: 01273 696195
E-mail: suewalker3@ntlworld.com
Web site: www.brightoniancoaches.co.uk

Props: Laurence R Walker, Susan M Walker.
Fleet: 2 coach.
Chassis: 2 Volvo.
Bodies: 1 Plaxton, 1 Van Hool.
Ops incl: school contracts, private hire.
Livery: White.

CUCKMERE BUSES
THE OLD RECTORY, LITLINGTON,
POLEGATE BN26 5RB
Tel: 01323 870920
E-mail: info@cuckmerebuses.org.uk
Web site: www.cuckmerebuses.org.uk
Chairman: Mrs B Smith **Man Dir:** P Ayers
Ops Dir: J Bunce **Co Sec:** Mrs S de Angeli
Fin Dir: A Cottingham.
Fleet: 9 minibus.
Chassis: 9 Mercedes.
Bodies: 5 Mellor, 4 Other.
Ops incl: local bus services, private hire.
Livery: Green/Cream.
Ticket system: Wayfarer TGX 150.

L J EDWARDS COACH HIRE
BELLBANKS CORNER, MILL ROAD,
HAILSHAM BN27 2HR
Tel: 01323 440622   **Fax:** 01323 442555
E-mail: info@ljedwards.co.uk
Web site: www.ljedwards.co.uk
Prop: John Edwards **Gen Man:** Antony
Burkill **Co Sec:** David Maynard.
Fleet: 12 - 7 single-deck coach, 3 midicoach,
2 minibus.
Chassis: 5 Bova, 1 DAF, 1 Mercedes, 2 Toyota,
2 Volkswagen, 1 Volvo.
Bodies: 5 Bova, 2 Caetano, 1 Mercedes,
1 Sunsundegui, 1 Van Hool, 2 Other.
Ops incl: school contracts, excursions &
tours, private hire, continental tours.
Workshop services also offered to visiting
operators.
Livery: White with Red detail.

EMPRESS COACHES LTD
10/11 ST MARGARETS ROAD, ST
LEONARDS-ON-SEA TN37 6EH
Tel/Fax: 01424 430621
E-mail: mail@empresscoaches.com
Web site: www.empresscoaches.com
Dir: Stephen Dine **Ch Eng:** Bill Sweetman.
Fleet: 10 - 2 midicoach, 1 minibus,
5 minicoach.
Chassis: 3 Ford Transit, 5 Mercedes.
Ops incl: school contracts, private hire.
Livery: Claret/Cream.

HAMS TRAVEL
THE WHITE HOUSE, LONDON ROAD,
FLIMWELL TN5 7PL
Tel: 01580 879537   **Fax:** 01580 879629

E-mail: info@hamstravel.co.uk
Web site: www.hamstravel.co.uk
Depots at: Flimwell, Benenden.
Partners: D W, P, P & J Ham.
Fleet: 49 – 12 double-deck bus, 1 single-deck
bus, 25 single-deck coach, 4 midibus,
1 midicoach, 6 minibus.
Chassis: 1 Alexander Dennis, 5 Dennis,
2 Ford Transit, 1 Leyland, 3 LDV, 1 Mercedes,
1 Renault, 1 Scania, 1 Toyota, 33 Volvo.
Ops incl: local bus services, excursions &
tours, school contracts, private hire.
Livery: Red/Orange/Brown.

J G COACHES LTD
BUTTONS FARM, MERES LANE, CROSS IN
HAND, HEATHFIELD TN21 0TY
Tel: 01435 862435
Fax: 01435 865735
E-mail: admin@jgcoaches.com
Web site: www.jgcoaches.com
Prop: J Gorwyn.
Fleet: 10 single-deck coach.
Chassis: 9 DAF, 1 Scania.
Ops incl: school contracts, private hire.
Livery: Grey with Red.

OCEAN COACHES
19 STONERY CLOSE, PORTSLADE
BN41 2TD
Tel/Fax: 01273 278385
Recovery: 07887 815798
E-mail: info@oceancoaches.net
Web site: www.oceancoaches.co.uk
Props: Peter & Carol Woodcock.
Fleet: 1 single-deck coach.
Chassis: Volvo.
Body: Ikarus.
Ops incl: private hire, school contracts,
excursions & tours.
Livery: Blue/White.

PAVILION COACHES
144 NEVILL AVENUE, HOVE BN3 7NH
Tel: 01273 732405
E-mail: nicky2168@hotmail.com
Web-site: www.pavilioncoaches.co.uk
Joint owners: Peter Hammer, Nicky Hammer.
Fleet: 2 – 1 single-deck coach, 1 vintage bus.
Chassis: 1 Leyland, 1 Volvo.
Bodies: 1 Park Royal, 1 Plaxton.
Ops incl: excursions & tours, private hire,
continental tours.

RAMBLER COACHES
WESTRIDGE MANOR, WHITWORTH
ROAD, HASTINGS TN37 7PZ
Tel: 01424 752505
Fax: 01424 751815
E-mail: info@ramblercoaches.co.uk

Web site: www.ramblercoaches.co.uk
Partners: Colin Rowland, J Goodwin.
Fleet: 36 – 2 double-deck bus, 3 single-deck bus, 23 single-deck coach, 2 midibus, 5 midicoach, 1 minicoach.
Chassis: 2 Dennis, 10 Mercedes, 24 Volvo.
Ops incl: local bus services, school contracts, excursions & tours, private hire, continental tours.
Livery: White, Green/Black.
Ticket System: Wayfarer.

RDH COACHES
UNIT 27, MOREHOUSE FARM BUSINESS CENTRE, DITCHLING ROAD, WIVELSFIELD RH17 7RE
Tel: 01444 470000
Fax: 01444 470002
E-mail: info@rdhcoaches.co.uk
Web site: www.rdhcoaches.co.uk
Props: T Hawthorne, Mrs G Hawthorne.
Fleet: 30 – 24 single-deck coach, 6 midicoach.
Chassis: 11 DAF, 4 Dennis, 1 Leyland, 2 Mercedes, 2 Scania, 10 Volvo.
Ops incl: school contracts, private hire.
Livery: White with Blue/Orange.

REGENCY COACHES LTD
UPPER STONEHAM FARM, LEWES BN8 5RH
Tel: 01273 477333
E-mail: office@regencycoaches.co.uk
Web site: www.regencycoaches.co.uk

Man Dir: John Durrant.
Fleet: 22 – 1 double-deck bus, 9 single-deck coach, 1 double-deck coach, 8 midicoach, 3 minibus.
Ops incl: school contracts, excursions & tours, private hire.
Livery: White.

RENOWN GROUP
1A BEECHING ROAD, BEXHILL-ON-SEA TN39 3LG
Tel: 01424 210744
Fax: 01424 212651
E-mail: info@renowngroup.co.uk
Web Site: www.renowngroup.co.uk
Man Dir: Christian Harmer
Fleet: 34 – 14 double-deck bus, 5 single-deck coach, 10 midibus, 1 midicoach, 4 minibus.
Chassis: 1 AEC, 4 DAF, 18 Dennis, 1 Mercedes, 4 Optare, 2 Transbus, 4 Volvo.
Bodies: 3 Alexander, 1 Autobus, 1 Berkhof, 1 Caetano, 1 Jonckheere, 2 Marshall, 6 Optare, 1 Park Royal, 13 Plaxton, 1 Transbus, 1 UVG, 3 Van Hool.
Ops incl: local bus services, school contracts, excursions & tours, private hire.
Livery: Green/Cream.

STAGECOACH SOUTH EAST
BUS STATION, ST GEORGE'S LANE, CANTERBURY CT1 2SY
Tel: 01227 812409

Fax: 01227 768963
E-mail: eastsussex.enquiries@stagecoachbus.com
Web site: www.stagecoachbus.com
Fleet Names (East Sussex): Stagecoach in Eastbourne, Stagecoach in Hastings.
Man Dir: Philip Norwell
Ops Dir: Neil Instrall
Eng Dir: Jason Bush
Comm Dir: Jeremy Cooper.
Fleet: 480 - 198 double-deck bus, 78 single-deck bus, 13 single-deck coach, 128 midibus, 63 minibus.
Chassis: 155 Alexander Dennis, 6 DAF, 23 Dennis, 21 MAN, 65 Optare, 90 Scania, 23 Transbus, 97 Volvo.
Ops incl: local bus services, express.
Liveries: Stagecoach UK Bus; National Express.
Ticket System: ERG TP5000.

WISE COACHES LTD
74 HIGH STREET, HAILSHAM BN27 1AU
Tel: 01323 844321
E-mail: info@wisecoaches.co.uk
Web site: www.wisecoaches.co.uk
Dir: J Wise **Ops Man:** W Fortis.
Fleet: 2 single-deck coach.
Chassis: 1 DAF, 1 Volvo.
Bodies: 1 Jonckheere, 1 Ovi.
Ops incl: private hire, school contracts.
Livery: Red/Silver.

ESSEX, SOUTHEND ON SEA, THURROCK

ACME TRANSPORT SERVICES
THE WORKSHOP, WALTHAM HALL FARM, BAMBERS GREEN, TAKELEY CM22 6PF
Tel: 01279 871707
Fax: 01279 870360
E-mail: enquiries@acme-transport.com
Web site: www.acme-transport.com
Prop: R J Sinnott
Fleet: 35 – 2 double-deck bus, 5 single-deck coach, 7 midibus, 10 midicoach, 11 minibus.
Chassis: 1 DAF, 10 Dennis, 1 Ford Transit, 6 Iveco, 2 LDV, 9 Mercedes, 1 Transbus, 2 Volkswagen, 2 Volvo.
Bodies: 2 Alexander, 1 Autobus, 1 Berkhof, 1 Crest, 1 Ferqui, 1 Jonckheere, 1 LDV, 2 Mellor, 1 Marshall, 1 Onyx, 10 Plaxton, 2 Reeve Burgess, 1 Sitcar, 1 Transbus, 1 Wright, 8 Other.
Ops incl: local bus services, school contracts, private hire.
Livery: White

AMBER COACHES LTD
UNIT 4A, RAWRETH INDUSTRIAL ESTATE, RAWRETH LANE, RAYLEIGH SS6 9RL
Tel: 01268 786550
Fax: 01268 786552
E-mail: ambercoachesltd@gmail.com
Web site: www.ambercoachesltd.co.uk
Dirs: G Wilkinson, G Webster.
Fleet: 37 – 8 double-deck bus, 19 single-deck coach, 7 midibus, 1 midicoach, 2 minibus.
Chassis: 2 Autosan, 10 Bova, 1 DAF, 9 Dennis, 1 LDV, 4 Leyland, 2 Mercedes, 1 Scania, 7 Volvo.
Ops incl: local bus services, school contracts, private hire, excursions & tours.
Livery: White/Orange.

ANITA'S COACH & MINIBUS HIRE LTD
15 AIRWAYS HOUSE, FIRST AVENUE, STANSTED AIRPORT CM24 1RY
Tel: 01279 661551
Fax: 01279 661771

E-mail: anitas.coaches@btconnect.com
Web site: www.anitascoaches.com
Dirs: E A S Wheeler, Mrs V A Wyatt.
Fleet: 8 - 6 single-deck coach, 1 minicoach, 1 minibus.
Chassis: 4 Bova, 1 Iveco, 1 Mercedes, 2 Volvo.
Bodies: 4 Bova, 1 Caetano, 1 Ferqui, 1 Volvo, 1 Other.
Ops incl: school contracts, private hire, continental tours.
Livery: Orange/Brown/White.

APT COACHES LTD
UNIT 27, RAWRETH INDUSTRIAL ESTATE, RAWRETH LANE, RAYLEIGH SS6 9RL
Tel: 01268 783878
Fax: 01268 782656
E-mail: admin@aptcoaches.co.uk
Web site: www.aptcoaches.co.uk
Fleet Name: APT Travel.
Man Dir: Peter Thorn.
Fleet: 11 – 10 single-deck coach, 1 midicoach.
Chassis: 1 BMC, 1 Bova, 1 Iveco, 4 Scania, 4 Volvo.
Bodies: 3 Berkhof, 1 Beulas, 1 BMC, 1 Bova, 4 Irizar, 1 Van Hool.
Ops incl: school contracts, private hire.
Livery: White/Pink.

ARRIVA SOUTHEND LTD
20 SHORT STREET, SOUTHEND ON SEA, SS2 5BY
Tel: 01702 442403   **Fax:** 01702 442401
Web site: www.arrivabus.co.uk
Regional Man Dir: Heath Williams
Regional Comm Dir: Kevin Hawkins
Regional Fin Dir: Beverley Lawson
Eng Dir: Tony Ward.
A division of Arriva Southern Counties
(See Kent)

BARKER BUS LTD
POPLAR FARM, HAMLET HILL, ROYDON, HARLOW CM19 5JY

Tel: 01279 793800   **Fax:** 01279 793845
E-mail: info@coachtravel.org
Web site: www.barkerbus.co.uk
Dirs: P J Barker, M P Barker
Fleet: 18 – 4 double-deck coach, 7 single-deck coach, 5 midicoach, 2 minibus.
Chassis: Ayats, Bedford, LDV, Mercedes, Neoplan, Renault, Setra, Van Hool, Volvo.
Ops incl: school contracts, excursions & tours, private hire.

B J S TRAVEL
Now trades as Cheldon Coaches.

BLUE DIAMOND COACHES
37 HOLMES MEADOW, HARLOW CM19 5SG
Tel: 01279 427524
Fax: 01279 427524
E-mail: beau.aukett@ntlworld.com
Prop: J Robilliard **Sec:** A Aukett.
Fleet: 1 minibus.
Chassis: Mercedes.
Body: Plaxton.
Ops incl: school contracts, private hire.
Livery: Blue/White.

BLUE TRIANGLE LTD
See Go-Ahead London *(London & Middlesex)*

BORDACOACH
25B, EASTWOOD ROAD, RAYLEIGH SS6 7JD
Tel: 01268 747608
Prop: David Stubbington
Fleet: 1 single-deck coach.
Chassis: 1 Volvo.
Body: 1 Van Hool.
Ops incl: excursions & tours, private hire.
Livery: White & Blue.

BRENTWOOD COACHES
79 WASH ROAD, HUTTON, BRENTWOOD CM13 1DL

Tel: 01277 233144
Fax: 01277 201386
E-mail: enquiries@brentwoodcoaches.co.uk
Web site: www.brentwoodcoaches.co.uk
Prop: A J Brenson Ch Eng: K Wright
Sec: Mrs P Alexander Traf Man: B Pierce.
Fleet: 11 – 8 single-deck coach, 2 midicoach,
1 minibus.
Chassis: 1 Ford Transit, 2 Irisbus, 2 Mercedes,
6 Volvo.
Bodies: 2 Autobus, 2 Caetano, 1 Ford,
6 Plaxton.
Ops incl: excursions & tours, private hire,
school contracts, continental tours.
Livery: Grey/White.

CHADWELL HEATH COACHES
30 REYNOLDS AVENUE, CHADWELL
HEATH RM6 4NT
Tel: 020 8590 7505
Fax: 020 8597 8883
Prop: John Thompson.
Fleet: 2 single-deck coach.
Chassis: 2 Volvo.
Ops incl: excursions & tours, private hire,
school contracts.
Livery: Country cream.

CHARIOTS OF ESSEX LTD
1 ONE TREE HILL, STANFORD-LE-HOPE
SS17 9NH
Tel: 01268 581444
Fax: 01268 581555
E-mail: enquiries@chariotsofessex.co.uk
Web site: www.chariotsofessex.co.uk
Man Dir: K T Flavin Dir: W J Collier.
Fleet: 9 - 6 single-deck coach, 2 midicoach,
1 minibus.
Chassis: Dennis, LDV, Mercedes, Volvo.
Bodies: Berkhof, LDV, Plaxton, Van Hool.
Ops incl: school contracts, private hire,
express.
Livery: Orange/Yellow.
Ticket system: Wayfarer.

CHELDON COACHES
61A HIGH STREET, GREAT WAKERING
SS3 0EF
Tel: 01702 219403
Prop: Brian Snow.
Fleet: 1 midicoach.
Chassis: Mercedes.
Body: Plaxton.
Ops incl: school contracts, private hire.

CHELMSFORD TAXIBUS
EXCELLENT CONNECTIONS LTD
GROUP TAXIBUS LTD
9 ATHOLL ROAD, DUKES PARK
INDUSTRIAL ESTATE, CHELMSFORD
CM2 6TB
Tel: 01245 350350
E-mail: info@chelmsfordtaxibus.co.uk
Web site: www.chelmsfordtaxibus.co.uk
Dirs: K Knightbridge, R Matthews, M Rogers.
Fleet: 80 – 1 single-deck coach, 78 minibus,
1 minicoach.
Chassis: Fiat, Ford Transit, Iveco, Mercedes,
Vauxhall, Volkswagen, Volvo.
Ops incl: private hire, school contracts.
Livery: Silver with Blue/Red lettering.
Associated with Fargolink.

COACHSTOP
SOUTHERN COUNTIES DEPOT, MAIN
ROAD, RETTENDON COMMON,
CHELMSFORD, ESSEX CM3 8DZ
Tel: 01245 401541
Fax: 01245 401480

Recovery: 07792 627364
E-mail: info@coachstop.co.uk
Web site: www.coachstop.co.uk
Dir: Toby Lyster-Bridge
Ops Man: Christian Lyster-Bridge.
Fleet: 7 single-deck coach.
Chassis: 4 Irisbus, 1 MAN, 2 Setra.
Bodies: 3 Beulas, 1 Noge, 1 Plaxton, 2 Setra.
Ops incl: school contracts, excursions &
tours, private hire, continental tours.
Livery: Black.

COOKS COACHES
607 LONDON ROAD, WESTCLIFF-ON-SEA
SS0 9PE
Tel: 01702 344702
Fax: 01702 436887
E-mail: info@cookscoaches.co.uk
Web site: www.cookscoaches.co.uk
Prop: W E Cook.
Fleet: 14 – 13 single-deck coach, 1 minibus.
Chassis: 13 Bova, 1 Ford Transit.
Bodies: 13 Bova, 1 Ford.
Ops incl: excursions & tours, private hire,
continental tours.
Livery: Red & White.
Ticket System: Distinctive.

COUNTY COACHES
79 WASH ROAD, HUTTON, BRENTWOOD
CM13 1DL
Tel: 01277 201505
Fax: 01277 225918
E-mail: info@countycoaches.com
Web site: www.countycoaches.com
Off Man: C A Jee
Tran Man: R J Pratt.
Fleet: 9 – 7 single-deck coach, 2 midibus.
Chassis: 2 Mercedes, 7 Volvo.
Ops incl: school contracts, private hire.
Livery: Green/White.

CRUSADER HOLIDAYS
CRUSADER BUSINESS PARK, STEPHENSON
ROAD WEST, CLACTON-ON-SEA
CO15 4HP
Tel: 01255 425453
Fax: 01255 222683
Recovery: 01255 431777
E-mail: enquiries@crusader-holidays.co.uk
Web site: www.crusader-holidays.co.uk
CEO: Roger Finch Man Dir: Val Mott.
Ops incl: excursions & tours, continental
tours, private hire.
Livery: White/Blue/Red.
A subsidiary of Motts Coaches (Aylesbury)
Ltd (see Buckinghamshire)

DOCKLANDS BUSES LTD
See Go-Ahead London (London & Middlesex)

DONS COACHES (DUNMOW) LTD
PARSONAGE DOWNS, GREAT DUNMOW
CM6 2AT
Tel: 01371 872644
Fax: 01371 876055
E-mail: info@donscoaches.co.uk
Web: www.donscoaches.co.uk
Dir: S D Harvey
Man: Jamie Bishop.
Fleet: 21 - 6 double-deck bus, 1 single-deck
bus, 11 single-deck coach, 2 midibus,
1 midicoach.
Chassis: 3 Bova, 6 Dennis, 6 Leyland,
1 Neoplan, 1 Scania, 3 Van Hool, 1 Volvo.
Bodies: 7 Alexander, 3 Bova, 1 Jonckheere,
1 Lahden, 1 Marcopolo, 1 Neoplan, 4 Plaxton,
3 Van Hool.
Ops incl: private hire, school contracts.
Livery: Red/Yellow/Blue.

EDS MINIBUS & COACH HIRE
257 PRINCESS MARGARET ROAD, EAST
TILBURY RM18 8SB
Tel/Fax: 01375 858049
Props: E Sammons, Mrs S Sammons.
Fleet: 4 minibus.
Chassis: Iveco, LDV.
Ops incl: private hire, excursions & tours.

ENSIGN BUS COMPANY LTD
JULIETTE CLOSE, PURFLEET INDUSTRIAL
PARK, PURFLEET RM15 4YF
Tel: 01708 865656
Fax: 01708 864340
E-mail: customerservices@ensignbus.com
Web site: www.ensignbus.com
Chairman: Peter Newman
Ops Dir: Ross Newman Comm Dir:
Steve Newman
Eng Dir: Brian Longley Fin Man: Tony Astle
Comm Man: John Lupton Eng Man:
Roger Jackson
Fleet: 111 - 35 double-deck bus, 18 midibus,
2 open-top bus, 2 single-deck coach,
2 articulated coach, 53 heritage vehicles.
Chassis (main fleet): 6 Alexander Dennis,
21 Dennis, 32 Volvo.
Bodies (main fleet): 4 Alexander Dennis,
24 Alexander, 2 Caetano, 4 East Lancs,
2 Jonckheere, 1 MCV, 14 Optare, 2 Plaxton,
6 Wrightbus.
Ops incl: local bus services, private hire
Livery: Blue/Silver.
Ticket System: Ticketer.

EXCALIBUR COACH TRAVEL
44 MOUNTVIEW CRESCENT, ST
LAWRENCE BAY, SOUTHMINSTER
CM0 7NR
Tel: 01621 779980
E-mail: info@excalibur-travel.com
Web site: www.excalibur-travel.com
Prop: Trevor Wynn.
Fleet: 4 minibus.
Chassis: 2 Ford Transit, 2 LDV.
Ops Incl: private hire, school contracts.

FARGOLINK
ALLVIEWS, SCHOOL ROAD, RAYNE,
BRAINTREE CM7 6SS
Tel: 01376 335856
Web site: www.fargolink.co.uk
Prop: L J Smith.
Fleet: 18 minibus.
Ops incl: private hire.
Livery: White.
Associated with Chelmsford Taxibus/Group
Taxibus

FIRST ESSEX BUSES
WESTWAY, CHELMSFORD CM1 3AR
Tel: 0845 602 0121
Fax: 01603 615439
E-mail: contactus.fec@firstgroup.com
Web site: www.firstgroup.com
Man Dir: Adrian Jones Comm Dir: Steve
Wickers Fin Dir: David Marshall
H R Dir: Karen Doores Creative Dir:
Chelsea de Silva.
Fleet: 388 - 81 double-deck bus, 160 single-
deck bus, 4 articulated bus, 8 single-deck
coach, 111 midibus, 24 minibus.
Chassis: 79 Alexander Dennis, 12 BMC,
94 Dennis, 24 Optare, 53 Scania, 126 Volvo.
Ops incl: local bus services, Chelmsford park
& ride, school contracts.
Liveries: FirstGroup UK Bus, National
Express.
Ticket System: Wayfarer.

FLAGFINDERS

267 COGGESHALL ROAD, BRAINTREE
CM7 9EF
Tel: 01376 320501
Fax: 01376 331127
E-mail: enquiries@flagfinders.com
Web site: www.flagfinders.com
Fleet: 22 – double-deck bus, double-deck
coach, single-deck coach, midibus, midicoach,
minibus.
Ops incl: local bus services, private hire,
school contracts, excursions & tours.
Livery: White or Silver.

FLORIDA TAXIS & COACHES LTD

LITTLE STUBLEYS FARM, SUDBURY ROAD,
HALSTEAD CO9 2BB
Tel: 01787 477701
Fax: 01787 475209
E-mail: info@coachcompany.co.uk
Web site: www.coachcompany.co.uk
Man Dir: Patrick Keeble **Ops Man:** Murray
Dean **Office Man:** Lisa Whellem.
Fleet: 5 – 1 double-deck bus, 4 single-deck
coach.
Chassis: 1 MAN, 1 Neoplan, 1 Temsa, 2 Volvo.
Bodies: 1 Caetano, 1 East Lancs, 1 Noge,
1 Temsa.
Ops incl: excursions & tours, private hire,
continental tours.
Livery: Various.

FORDS COACHES

THE GARAGE, FAMBRIDGE ROAD,
ALTHORNE CM3 6BZ
Tel: 01621 740326
Fax: 01621 742781
E-mail: info@fordscoaches.co.uk
Web site: www.fordscoaches.co.uk
Partners: Anthony A W Ford,
Anthony W Ford.
Fleet: 24 – 13 double-deck bus, 1 single-deck
bus, 7 single-deck coach, 2 double-deck coach,
1 midicoach.
Chassis: 1 Ayats, 1 BMC, 5 Dennis, 7 Leyland,
7 Scania, 1 Van Hool, 2 Volvo.
Bodies: 7 Alexander, 1 Ayats, 4 Berkhof,
1 BMC, 1 Caetano, 2 East Lancs, 4 ECW,
1 Lahden, 1 Optare, 2 Van Hool.
Ops incl: local bus services, school contracts,
excursions & tours, private hire.
Livery: White/Multi-colour stripe.
Ticket system: Wayfarer.

FOURWAYS COACHES

POOLS LANE, HIGHWOOD,
CHELMSFORD CM1 3QL
Tel/Fax: 01245 248009
E-mail: 4wayscoaches@btconnect.com
Web site: www.4wayscoaches.com
Fleet: 13 – 9 double-deck bus, 2 single-deck
coach, 2 minibus.
Chassis: 1 DAF, 3 Dennis, 7 Leyland,
2 Mercedes, 1 Volvo.
Ops incl: school contracts, private hire.

GALLEON TRAVEL 2009 LTD

HAILES FARM, LOW HILL ROAD, ROYDON
CM19 5JW
Tel: 0845 894 4747
Fax: 0845 894 4748
E-mail: sales@galleontravel.co.uk
Web site: www.galleontravel.co.uk
Fleet Names: Galleon Travel, Trustybus.
Man Dir: M Bowden-Scott **Dir:** M Baker.
Fleet: 48 – 5 double-deck bus, 1 single-deck
bus, 11 single-deck coach, 1 double-deck
coach, 29 midibus, 1 midicoach.
Chassis: 1 Ayats, 5 Alexander Dennis,

1 BMC, 2 Bova, 17 Dennis, 1 Irizar, 3 MAN,
3 Mercedes, 10 Transbus, 5 Volvo.
Bodies: 3 Alexander, 5 Alexander Dennis,
1 Ayats, 1 Berkhof, 1 BMC, 2 Bova, 1 Caetano,
1 Irizar, 1 Jonckheere, 4 Marcopolo, 4 Marshall,
18 Plaxton, 6 Transbus.
Ops incl: local bus services, school contracts,
private hire.
Liveries: Buses: Red, Blue & Yellow;
Coaches: Maroon, White.

GATWICK FLYER LTD

DANES ROAD, ROMFORD RM7 0HL
Tel: 01708 730555
Fax: 01708 751231
E-mail: enquiries@gatwickflyer.co.uk
Web site: www.gatwickflyer.co.uk
Dirs: G Tovey, C Tovey, R Seboa.
Fleet Names: Gatwick Flyer, Stansted Flyer.
Fleet: 9 – 4 midicoach, 5 minibus.
Chassis: 5 Ford Transit, 4 Mercedes.
Ops incl: airport express.

PETER GODWARD COACHES

UNITS 3&4, MILLS COURT, SWINBOURNE
ROAD, BURNT MILLS INDUSTRIAL ESTATE,
BASILDON SS13 1EH
Tel: 01268 591834
Fax: 01268 591835
E-mail: peter.godward@virgin.net
Web site: www.toursrus.uk.com
Props: P R Godward, J Godward **(Ops)**,
Mrs A M Godward **(Co Sec).**
Fleet: 10 – 9 single-deck coach, 1 minibus.
Chassis: 1 Irisbus, 2 Irizar, 1 LDV, 6 Scania.
Bodies: 1 Beulas, 2 Caetano, 5 Irizar,
1 Lahden, 1 LDV .
Ops incl: school contracts, excursions &
tours, private hire, express, continental tours.
Liveries: White or Yellow with Blue/Orange;
National Express.

GOLDEN BOY COACHES
See Hertfordshire

GO RIDE CIC
See Oxfordshire

GRAHAM'S COACHES LTD

STATION ROAD, KELVEDON CO5 9NP
Tel: 01376 570150
Fax: 01376 570657
E-mail: info@grahamscoaches.ltd.uk
Web site: www.grahamscoaches.com
Prop: G Ellis.
Fleet: 10 – 3 single-deck coach, 3 midicoach,
3 minibus, 1 minicoach.
Chassis: 1 Autosan, 6 Mercedes, 2 Scania,
1 Volkswagen
Livery: White/Blue.

HAILSTONE TRAVEL LTD

82 BRACKLEY CRESCENT, BASILDON
SS13 1RA
Tel: 0845 388 3848
E-mail: info@hailstonetravel.co.uk
Web site: www.hailstonetravel.co.uk
Dirs: Mrs Tina Hailstone, Lawrence Hailstone.
Fleet: 13 – 9 minicoach, 4 minibus.
Chassis: 4 Iveco, 9 Mercedes.
Ops incl: school contracts, excursions &
tours, private hire.
Livery: White.

HEDINGHAM & DISTRICT OMNIBUSES LTD

DUGARD HOUSE, PEARTREE ROAD,
COLCHESTER CO3 0UL
Tel: 01206 769778

E-mail: services@hedingham.co.uk
Web site: www.hedingham.co.uk
Depots at: Clacton, Hedingham, Kelvedon,
Tollesbury.
Fin Dir: Tamara Harris **Gen Man:** Jeff
Clayton
Dep Gen Man: Nick Field.
Fleet: 98 – 48 double-deck bus, 13 single-
deck bus, 7 single-deck coach, 29 midibus,
1 minibus.
Chassis: 15 Alexander Dennis, 29 Dennis,
5 Leyland, 5 Optare, 1 Transbus, 43 Volvo.
Bodies: 24 Alexander, 15 Alexander Dennis,
9 East Lancs, 16 Northern Counties, 5 Optare,
19 Plaxton, 2 Transbus, 8 Wrightbus.
Ops incl: local bus services, school contracts,
excursions & tours, private hire.
Livery: Red/Cream.
Ticket System: Wayfarer TGX150.
A subsidiary of the Go-Ahead Group. Also
manages H C Chambers & Son (see Suffolk).

IMPERIAL BUS CO LTD

COMPOUND 6, MILL FARM ESTATE,
WHALEBONE LANE NORTH, ROMFORD,
RM6 5QT
Tel: 0208 597 7368
Man Dir: M Biddell.
Fleet: 8 - 4 double-deck bus, 4 midibus.
Chassis: 5 AEC, 4 Dennis, 1 Leyland.
Bodies: 1 Marshall, 6 Park Royal, 3 Plaxton.
Ops incl: school contracts, private hire.
Livery: Green.

JACKSONS COACHES

BICKNACRE HOUSE, LEIGHAMS ROAD,
BICKNACRE CM3 4HF
Tel: 01245 320598
Fax: 01245 322988
E-mail: nikki@jacksonscoaches.com
Web site: www.jacksonscoaches.com
Props: A E & M J Jackson.
Fleet: 7 – 5 single-deck coach, 2 midicoach.
Chassis: 3 DAF, 1 MAN, 2 Mercedes, 1 Scania.
Ops incl: school contracts, private hire,
excursions & tours.
Livery: White with Yellow/Mauve.

KB COACHES

AVON, CRANFIELD PARK ROAD,
WICKFORD SS12 9EP
Tel/Fax: 01268 734558
E-mail: raykbcoaches@aol.com
Prop: Ray Bourgein.
Fleet: 6 - 5 single-deck coach, 1 minibus.
Chassis: 1 Ayats, 1 Irisbus, 2 Setra,
1 Volkswagen, 1 Volvo.
Bodies: 1 Ayats, 1 Beulas, 2 Setra, 1 Van Hool,
1 Other.
Ops incl: school contracts, excursions &
tours, private hire.
Livery: Blue.

KELLY'S TRAVEL

58 SHOOTERS DRIVE, NAZEING
EN9 2QD
Tel: 01992 892232
Fax: 01992 892232
E-mail: kellystravel@hotmail.co.uk
Fleet: 6 – 5 single-deck coach, 1 minibus.
Chassis: 1 Mercedes, 5 Setra.
Ops incl: school contracts, private hire,
continental tours.
Livery: White.

KEVENDYS COACHES

13 RIVERSIDE HOUSE, LOWER SOUTHEND
ROAD, WICKFORD SS11 8BB
Tel: 01268 765240

Fax: 01268 570221
E-mail: info@kevendys.co.uk
Web site: www.kevendys.co.uk
Props: K & Mrs W Nash.
Fleet: 7 – 6 single-deck coaches, I minicoach.
Chassis: I Dennis, I Iveco, 2 MAN,
2 Neoplan, I Volvo.
Ops incl: school contracts, private hire,
excursions & tours, continental tours.

KINGS COACHES
♿ 🕴 🧺 🚾
364 LONDON ROAD, STANWAY,
COLCHESTER CO3 8LT
Tel: 01206 210332
Fax: 01206 213861
E-mail: info@kings-coaches.co.uk
Web site: www.kings-coaches.co.uk
Prop: Andrew B Cousins.
Fleet: 7 single-deck coach.
Chassis: 3 Bova, 4 Van Hool.
Bodies: 3 Bova, 4 Van Hool.
Ops incl: excursions & tours, private hire.
Livery: Green/Cream.

KIRBYS COACHES (RAYLEIGH) LTD
🕴 ♿ 🧺 🚾
2 PRINCESS ROAD, RAYLEIGH
SS6 8HR
Tel: 01268 777777
Fax: 01268 777388
E-mail: info@kirbyscoaches.co.uk
Web site: www.kirbyscoaches.co.uk
Dir: Edward Kirby
Co Sec: Elizabeth Kirby.
Fleet: 9 single-deck coach.
Chassis/Bodies: 9 Setra.
Ops incl: excursions & tours, private hire,
continental tours.
Livery: Lilac/Turquoise.

LODGE COACHES
🕴 ♿ 🧺 🚌
THE GARAGE, HIGH EASTER,
CHELMSFORD CM1 4QR
Tel: 01245 231262
Fax: 01245 231825
E-mail: administrator@lodgecoaches.co.uk
Web site: www.lodgecoaches.co.uk
Dirs: R C Lodge, A D Lodge, C J Lodge
Ch Eng: Paul Hartley.
Fleet: 36 – 11 double-deck bus, 3 single-deck
bus, 11 single-deck coach, 1 midicoach,
2 minibus, 2 minicoach, 5 vintage coach.
Chassis: 5 Bedford, 1 BMC, 1 Dennis, 1 Ford
Transit, 1 LDV, 7 Leyland, 1 MAN, 3 Mercedes,
3 Optare, 2 Scania, 7 Setra, 3 Volvo.
Bodies: 3 Alexander, 1 BMC, 5 Duple,
1 East Lancs, 1 Ferqui, 1 Irizar, 1 LDV,
5 Leyland, 2 Mercedes, 2 Northern Counties,
4 Optare, 1 Plaxton, 7 Setra, 1 Van Hool.
Ops incl: local bus services, school contracts,
excursions & tours, private hire, continental
tours.
Livery: Blue/Cream.
Ticket System: Wayfarer.

MILESTONE COACHES
♿ 🧺 🕴 🍴
NORTHWICK ROAD, CANVEY ISLAND
SS8 0PU
Tel: 01268 694483
E-mail: milestonecoaches@btconnect.com
Web site: www.milestonecoaches.co.uk
Prop: G Brailey.
Fleet: 3 single-deck coach.
Chassis: 1 Irisbus, 2 Scania.
Bodies: 1 Beulas, 2 Irizar.
Ops incl: school contracts, private hire.
Livery: Red & White or Cream.

NETWORK COLCHESTER LTD
NETWORK HARLOW
See below under TGM Group

NEW HORIZON TRAVEL LTD
♿ 🕴 🧺
GREAT BENTLEY ROAD, FRATING,
CO7 7HN
Tel: 01206 255255
Fax: 01206 255033
E-mail: nhtltd@aol.com
Web Site: www.horizonbus.co.uk
Man Dir: Ray Connor **Dir:** Deborah
Thirlwell **Ops Mans:** Andy Connor, John
Carter **Ch Eng:** Ed Barteli.
Fleet: 33 – 6 double-deck bus, 11 single-deck
coach, 13 midibus, 2 midicoach, 1 minicoach.
Chassis: 12 Dennis, 1 Leyland, 3 Mercedes,
6 Scania, 11 Volvo.
Ops incl: local bus services, school contracts,
private hire.
Livery: White, with Blue, Red, Yellow.
Ticket System: Wayfarer TGX150.
Incorporating Cedric Coaches

NIBSBUSES LTD
♿ ♿
THE COACH STATION, BRUCE GROVE,
WICKFORD SS11 8BZ
Tel: 01268 767870
Fax: 01268 735307
E-mail: info@nibsbuses.com
Web site: www.nibsbuses.com
Man Dir: Steve Nelson.
Fleet Name: Nelsons Independent Bus
Services.
Fleet: 27 – 23 double-deck bus, 3 midibus,
1 minibus.
Chassis: 6 Dennis, 1 Optare, 18 Scania,
2 Volvo.
Bodies: 7 Alexander, 1 Caetano, 11 East
Lancs, 3 Optare, 2 Plaxton, 3 Scania.
Ops incl: local bus services, school contracts.
Livery: Yellow/Red.

OLYMPUS BUS & COACH LTD
ROADRUNNER COACHES LTD
♿ 🕴 ♿ 🧺
UNIT 17, GREENWAY BUSINESS CENTRE,
HARLOW BUSINESS PARK, HARLOW
CM19 5QE
Tel: 01279 868868
E-mail: enquiries@olympiancoaches.co.uk
Web site: www.olympiancoaches.co.uk
Fleet Name: Olympian.
Fleet: 49 – 1 double-deck bus, 1 single-deck
bus, 16 single-deck coach, 27 midibus,
3 midicoach, 1 minicoach.
Chassis: 1 DAF, 27 Dennis, 3 Irisbus, 9 Iveco,
4 Scania, 5 Volvo.
Ops incl: local bus services, school contracts,
excursions & tours, private hire, express,
continental tours.
Livery: Blue/White.

P & M COACHES
🕴 ♿ 🧺
PIPPS HILL ROAD NORTH, BILLERICAY
CM11 2UJ
Tel: 01268 534454
E-mail: pmcoaches@hotmail.co.uk
Web site: www.pmcoaches.co.uk
Props: M & S Nicholls.
Fleet: 11 – 7 single-deck coach, 3 minibus,
1 minicoach.
Chassis: 4 Mercedes, 7 Volvo.
Livery: White.

PHILLIPS COACHES LTD
🕴 ♿ 🧺
117B HULLBRIDGE ROAD, SOUTH
WOODHAM FERRERS CM3 5LL
Tel: 01245 323039
Fax: 01245 320456
E-mail: info@phillipscoaches.co.uk
Web site: www.phillipscoaches.co.uk
Fleet: 4 – 3 single-deck coach, 1 minicoach.
Chassis: 2 Bova, 1 Mercedes, 1 Volvo.

Ops incl: excursions & tours, private hire,
school contracts.
Liveries: Cream/Maroon, Silver/Maroon.

REGAL BUSWAYS LTD
♿ ♿
LANDVIEW, COOKSMILL GREEN,
CHELMSFORD CM1 3SR
Tel: 01245 249001
Man Dir: Adrian McGarry **Ops Dir:**
Lee Whitehead **Dir:** Mandy McGarry.
Fleet Names: Essex Pullman, Regal Busways.
Fleet: 42 – 8 double-deck bus, 5 single-deck
bus, 2 single-deck coach, 16 midibus,
11 minibus.
Chassis: 19 Dennis, 2 Leyland, 3 MAN,
14 Optare, 2 Transbus, 2 Volvo.
Ops incl: local bus services, private hire,
school contracts.
Livery: Red.
Ticket system: ERG.

RELIANCE LUXURY COACHES
♿ 🕴 🧺 🔧 🍴
54 BROOK ROAD, BENFLEET SS7 5JF
Tel: 01268 758426
E-mail: reliancecoaches@btconnect.com
Web site: www.
relianceluxurycoachesbenfleet.co.uk
Prop: Martyn J Titchen.
Fleet: 4 – 1 double-deck coach, 3 single-deck
coach.
Chassis: 1 MAN, 3 Scania.
Bodies: 1 Jonckheere Monaco, 3 Irizar
Century Club.
Ops incl: school contracts, tours, private hire.
Livery: White/Red/Yellow/Orange.

RICHMOND'S COACHES
♿ 🕴 ♿ 🧺 🚾
THE GARAGE, HIGH STREET, BARLEY,
ROYSTON SG8 8JA
Tel: 01763 848226
Fax: 01763 848105
E-mail: postbox@richmonds-coaches.co.uk
Web site: www.richmonds-coaches.co.uk
Dirs: David Richmond, Michael Richmond,
Andrew Richmond **Sales & Marketing Man:**
Rick Ellis **Asst Ops Man:** Craig Ellis
Ch Eng: Patrick Granville **Exc & Tours
Man:** Natalie Richmond.
Fleet: 23 – 15 single-deck coach, 3 double-
deck coach, 2 midibus, 2 midicoach, 1 minibus.
Chassis: 8 Bova, 3 Mercedes, 2 Optare,
7 Van Hool, 3 Volvo.
Bodies: 8 Bova, 2 Optare, 1 Plaxton, 2 Sitcar,
10 Van Hool.
Ops incl: local bus services, school contracts,
excursions & tours, private hire, continental
tours.
Livery: Cream/Brown.
Ticket System: Wayfarer 3.

SBC LEISURE
🕴 ♿ 🧺 🍴
39 HILLSIDE ROAD, EASTWOOD, LEIGH
ON SEA SS9 5DQ
Tel: 01702 528038
Fax: 01702 528120
E-mail: info@sbcleisure.com
Web site: www.sbcleisure.com
Dir: K Bridge.
Fleet: 11 – 5 double-deck buses, 6 single-deck
coaches.
Chassis: 1 Leyland, 7 Scania, 3 Volvo.
Ops incl: school contracts, excursions &
tours, private hire.
Liveries: Yellow, Blue.

SM COACHES
See Townlink Buses Ltd

SMITH & MAY COACHES
UNIT 30, BRUNEL ROAD, MANOR

TRADING ESTATE, BENFLEET SS7 4PS
Tel: 0844 576 3361
E-mail: linkfast@btconnect.com
Prop: W N May.

STAGECOACH LONDON
See London & Middlesex

STAN'S COACHES
THE COACH HOUSE, BECKINGHAM
ROAD, GREAT TOTHAM, MALDON
CM9 8DY
Tel: 01621 891959   **Fax:** 01621 891365
Web site: www.stans-coaches.co.uk
Props: S J Porter, Mrs J Porter.
Fleet: 5 – 3 single-deck coach, 1 midicoach,
1 minibus.
Chassis: 2 Bova, 2 Dennis, 1 LDV.
Ops incl: excursions & tours, school
contracts, private hire, continental tours.
Livery: White with Blue/Grey stripes.

STEPHENSONS OF ESSEX LTD
RIVERSIDE INDUSTRIAL ESTATE, SOUTH
STREET, ROCHFORD SS4 1BS
Tel: 01702 541511
Fax: 01702 549461
E-mail: lyn@stephensonsofessex.com
Web site: www.stephensonsofessex.com
Man Dir: Bill Hiron **Fin Dir:** Lyn Watson.
Depots at: Rochford, Boreham, Witham,
Haverhill (Suffolk).
Fleet: 95 – 49 double-deck bus, 2 single-deck
bus, 2 single-deck coach, 33 midibus, 7 minibus,
2 heritage vehicles.
Chassis: 15 Alexander Dennis, 15 Dennis,
11 Leyland, 7 Optare, 33 Scania, 14 Volvo.
Ops incl: local bus services, school contracts,
private hire, express.
Livery: Green/White.
Ticket System: Ticketer.
See also Suffolk

SUPREME COACHES
See Coachstop (above)

THE SWALLOW COACH CO LTD
1 BARLOW WAY SOUTH, MARSH WAY,
RAINHAM RM13 8BT
Tel: 01708 630555
Fax: 01708 555135
E-mail: kevin@swallowcoach.co.uk
Web site: www.swallowcoach.co.uk
Chairman: D R Webb **Man Dir:** K I Webb

Sec: Mrs S D Webb.
Fleet: 30 - 22 single-deck coach, 1 double-
deck coach, 2 midibus, 1 midicoach, 1 minibus,
3 minicoach.
Chassis: 2 Dennis, 1 Enterprise, 1 Ford
Transit, 1 King Long, 2 MAN, 1 Mercedes,
3 Neoplan, 3 Scania, 2 Setra, 2 Toyota, 12 Volvo.
Bodies: 2 Berkhof, 5 Caetano, 1 Ford, 3 Irizar,
2 Jonckheere, 1 King Long, 3 Neoplan, 2 Noge,
3 Plaxton, 2 Setra, 1 Unvi, 2 Van Hool, 3 Volvo.
Ops incl: local bus services, private hire,
school contracts.
Livery: White with logos.

TALISMAN COACH LINES
THE COACH STATION, HARWICH ROAD,
GREAT BROMLEY, COLCHESTER CO7 7UL
Tel: 01206 252472
Fax: 01206 251742
E-mail: sales@talismancoachlines.co.uk
Web site: www.talismancoachlines.co.uk
Man Dir: Terry Smith.
Fleet: 19 – 4 double-deck bus, 1 double-deck
coach, 12 single-deck coach, 2 open-top bus.
Chassis: 1 AEC, 1 Bristol, 4 Leyland, 3 Scania,
7 Setra, 2 Van Hool, 1 Volvo.
Ops incl: excursions & tours, private hire,
continental tours.
Livery: Blue/Silver/Yellow.

TGM GROUP LTD
FOURTH AVENUE, HARLOW CM20 1DU
Tel: 0844 800 4411
E-mail: customerservices@arriva-shires.com
Web site: www.networkcolchester.co.uk
Web site: www.harlowbus.com
Web site: www.sxconnect.co.uk
Fleet Names: Network Colchester,
Network Harlow, SX Connect.
Regional Man Dir: Heath Williams
Acting Man Dir: Brian Drury.
Fleet: 99 – 12 double-deck bus, 28 single-
deck bus, 9 single-deck coach, 44 midibus,
6 minibus
Chassis: 2 Alexander Dennis, 21 Dennis,
8 Mercedes, 15 Optare, 10 Scania, 11 Transbus,
32 Volvo.
Ops incl: local bus services, school contracts,
express.
Liveries: Blue (Harlow); Blue/White/Yellow
(Colchester); National Express
Network Harlow, Stansted and Network
Colchester operations form TGM Group East.
A subsidiary of Arriva. For main TGM entry
see London & Middlesex.

TOWNLINK BUSES LTD
9 BURNT MILL, ELIZABETH WAY,
HARLOW CM20 2HT
Tel: 01279 426266
Fax: 01279 431438
Web site: www.townlinkbuses.com
Fleet: 22 midibus.
Chassis: 22 Dennis.
Bodies: 13 Alexander, 9 Plaxton.
Ops incl: local bus services, school contracts,
private hire.
Livery: Blue/White.

TURNERS OF ESSEX
SUDBURY ROAD, LITTLE MAPLESTEAD,
HALSTEAD CO9 2SE
Tel: 01787 479132
Fax: 01787 479147
E-mail: enquiries@turnersofessex.co.uk
Web site: www.turnersofessex.co.uk
Prop: Louise Golding.
Fleet: 22 – 5 double-deck bus, 4 single-deck
bus, 7 single-deck coach, 1 midibus, 5 minibus.
Chassis: 1 Dennis, 5 Leyland, 1 MAN,
3 Mercedes. 1 Peugeot, 1 Renault, 3 Setra,
7 Volvo.
Ops incl: local bus services, school contracts,
excursions & tours, private hire, continental
tours.
Livery: White with multicoloured logos.

TWH BUS & COACH
Ceased trading since LRB 2014 went to press

VICEROY OF ESSEX LTD
12 BRIDGE STREET, SAFFRON WALDEN
CB10 1BU
Tel: 01799 508010
Fax: 01799 510774
E-mail: viceroycoaches@btconnect.com
Web site: www.viceroycoaches.co.uk
Dir: S A Moore
Ops Man: Mrs A L Moore.
Fleet: 11 - 1 single-deck bus, 5 single-deck
coach, 2 midibus, 3 minibus.
Chassis: 1 Bova, 1 Dennis, 1 MAN,
2 Mercedes, 4 Optare, 1 Scania, 1 Volvo.
Bodies: 1 Bova, 1 Mercedes, 1 Neoplan,
4 Optare, 3 Plaxton, 1 Van Hool.
Ops incl: local bus services, school contracts,
excursions & tours, private hire, continental
tours.
Livery: White.
Ticket System: Wayfarer 3.

GLOUCESTERSHIRE

ALEXCARS LTD
11 LOVE LANE, CIRENCESTER
GL7 1YG
Tel: 01285 653985
Fax: 01285 652964
E-mail: info@alexcars.co.uk
Web site: www.alexcars.co.uk
Man Dir: Rod Hibberd **Dirs:** Jenny Jarvis,
Will Jarvis, Ben Jarvis.
Fleet: 25 - 17 single-deck coach, 6 midicoach,
1 minicoach, 1 vintage coach.
Chassis: 2 Bedford (vintage), 1 Dennis,
4 Iveco, 5 Mercedes, 11 Scania, 2 Toyota.
Bodies: 2 Beulas, 2 Caetano, 2 Duple
(vintage), 2 Indcar, 11 Irizar, 1 Marcopolo,
5 Mercedes.
Also operated: 2 vintage Austin wedding
cars.
Ops incl: school contracts, excursions &
tours, private hire, continental tours.
Livery: Dual Blue.

APPLEGATES COACHES
HEATHFIELD GARAGE, NEWPORT,
BERKELEY GL13 9PL
Tel: 01453 810314
Fax: 01453 511184
E-mail: dan@applegates.co.uk
Web site: www.applegates.moonfruit.com
Fleet: 16 – 4 double-deck bus, 1 double-deck
coach, 9 single-deck coach, 2 midicoach.
Chassis: 1 DAF, 1 Irisbus, 1 Leyland, 2 MAN,
1 Mercedes, 3 Neoplan, 2 Scania, 1 Setra, 1
VDL, 3 Volvo.
Bodies: Alexander, Berkhof, East Lancs,
Indcar, Jonckheere, Mellor, Mercedes, Neoplan,
Plaxton, Setra, Van Hool.
Ops incl: school contracts, excursion &
tours, private hire, continental tours.
Livery: Dark Green with Yellow/Red.

BAKERS COACHES
COTSWOLD BUSINESS VILLAGE, LONDON
ROAD, MORETON-IN-THE-MARSH
GL56 0JD
Tel: 01608 652178
Fax: 01608 652693
E-mail: enquiries@bakerscoaches.co.uk
Web site: www.bakerscoaches.co.uk
Dir: Mike Baker **Ops Man:** Dave Goodall.
Fleet: 21 - 15 single-deck coach, 3 midibus,
3 midicoach.
Chassis: 2 Dennis, 2 Irisbus, 6 Mercedes,
1 Scania, 1 Transbus, 9 Volvo.
Ops incl: school contracts, excursions &
tours, private hire.
Livery: White with Red logo.

BENNETT'S COACHES
EASTERN AVENUE, GLOUCESTER GL4 4LP
Tel: 01452 527809

Fax: 01452 384448
E-mail: info@bennettscoaches.co.uk
Web site: www.bennettscoaches.co.uk
Man Dir: Peter Bennett **Ops Man:** Gavin
Bennett **Sales Man:** Chris Lucassi.
Fleet: 35 - 4 double-deck bus, 9 single-deck
bus, 22 single-deck coach.
Chassis: 1 DAF, 21 Mercedes, 13 Volvo.
Bodies: 4 Alexander, 12 Caetano,
19 Mercedes, 1 Van Hool.
Ops incl: local bus services, school contracts,
express, private hire.
Livery: Blue/Orange or Silver; National
Express.

JAMES BEVAN (LYDNEY) LTD
UNIT 1, MEAD LANE INDUSTRIAL ESTATE,
LYDNEY GL15 5DA
Tel: 01594 842859
Fax: 01594 845615
E-mail: enquiries@jamesbevancoaches.co.uk
Web site: www.jamesbevancoaches.com
Chairman: James Bevan **Ops Dir:** J
Zimmerman **Eng Dir:** M Zimmerman.
Fleet: 12 – 2 double-deck bus, 2 single-deck
bus, 5 single-deck coach, 2 midibus, 1 minibus.
Chassis: 2 Alexander Dennis, 2 DAF,
2 Dennis, 1 Optare, 1 Setra, 4 Volvo.
Bodies: 2 Alexander Dennis, 3 Optare,
3 Plaxton, 1 Setra, 1 Sunsundegui, 2 Wadham
Stringer.
Ops incl: local bus services, school contracts,
private hire.
Livery: Silver.
Ticket System: Wayfarer.

CASTLEWAYS LTD
*Ceased trading since LRB 2014 went to press –
owners retired.*

CATHEDRAL COACHES LTD
18 QUAY STREET, GLOUCESTER
GL1 2JS
Tel: 01452 524595
E-mail: info@cathedralcoaches.co.uk
Web site: www.cathedralcoaches.co.uk
Dirs: Irene Chandler, Paul Chandler.
Fleet: 10 - 5 single-deck coach, 5 midicoach.
Chassis: 5 Dennis, 5 Mercedes.
Bodies: 2 Autobus, 2 Berkhof, 4 Plaxton,
2 Sitcar.
Ops incl: school contracts, private hire.
Livery: Blue/Grey/Red/White.

COLEFORDIAN (WILLETTS) LTD
CROWN PARK ESTATE, EDENWALL ROAD,
COALWAY, COLEFORD GL16 7HW
Tel: 01594 810080
Fax: 01594 834480
E-mail: willetts-coaches@live.com
Web site: www.willettsofyorkley.co.uk
Man Dir: Paul Willetts.
Fleet: 10 single-deck coach.
Chassis: 1 Dennis, 1 Scania, 1 Setra, 7 Volvo.
Ops incl: excursions & tours, school
contracts, private hire, continental tours.
Livery: Silver.

COTSWOLD GREEN LTD
UNIT 27A, NAILSWORTH MILLS ESTATE,
AVERNING ROAD, NAILSWORTH GL6 0DS
Tel: 01453 835153
Fleet: single-deck bus, midibus, minibus.
Ops incl: local bus services, school contracts.
Livery: Green/White.

EAGLE LINE TRAVEL
ANDOVERSFORD TRADING ESTATE,
ANDOVERSFORD GL54 4LB

Tel/Fax: 01242 820535
Man Dirs: Brian Davis, Martin Davis, Wayne
Hodges **Ch Eng:** Tony Mezzone.
Fleet: 24 - 7 single-deck coach, 2 double-deck
coach, 4 midibus, 4 midicoach, 7 minibus.
Chassis: 1 Ayats, 1 Bova, 1 Ford Transit,
8 Mercedes, 2 Optare, 1 Scania, 2 Volkswagen,
4 Volvo, 2 Wrightbus.
Ops incl: school contracts, excursions &
tours, private hire, continental tours.
Livery: Dark Blue/Silver/Silver Blue.

EBLEY COACHES LTD
UNIT 27, NAILSWORTH MILLS ESTATE,
AVENING ROAD, NAILSWORTH
GL6 0BS
Tel/Fax: 01453 839333
E-mail: enquiries@ebleyexcursions.co.uk
Web site: www.ebleyexcursions.co.uk
Dirs: C C Levitt, G A Jones.
Fleet: single-deck bus, single-deck coach,
midibus, minibus.
Ops incl: school contracts, excursions &
tours, private hire.
Livery: White.

DAVID FIELD TRAVEL
STONEY ROAD GARAGE, KILCOT,
NEWENT GL18 1PB
Tel: 01531 820979
E-mail: davidfieldcoaches@gmail.com
Web site: www.davidfieldtravel.co.uk
Prop: David Field MSOE, MIRTE.
Fleet: 4 - 2 single-deck coach, 2 midicoach.
Chassis: 1 Dennis, 1 Leyland, 1 Mercedes,
1 Toyota.
Ops incl: school contracts, private hire.
Livery: Black/White.
Ticket System: Setright.

GRINDLES COACHES LTD
4 DOCKHAM ROAD, CINDERFORD
GL14 2AQ
Tel: 01594 822110
Fax: 01594 824575
E-mail: admin@grindlescoaches.co.uk
Web site: www.grindlescoaches.co.uk
Man Dir: P R Grindle
Co Sec: W H R Grindle.
Fleet: 14 – 1 double-deck bus, 11 single-deck
coach, 2 minibus.
Chassis: 1 Bova, 8 DAF, 1 Leyland,
3 Mercedes, 1 Setra.
Ops incl: local bus services, private hire.
Livery: White with Gold.

HENSHAWS EXECUTIVE
TRAVEL LTD
THE RED HOUSE, LONDON ROAD,
MORETON-IN-THE-MARSH GL56 0HH
Tel/Fax: 01608 651414
E-mail: info@henshaws-coaches.co.uk
Web site: www.henshaws-coaches.co.uk
Dirs: D Henshaw, P Drew.
Fleet: 12 – 6 single-deck coach, 3 midibus,
1 midicoach, 1 minibus.
Chassis: 2 Alexander Dennis, 3 Dennis,
2 Mercedes, 1 Optare, 1 Toyota, 3 Volvo.
Ops incl: local bus services, school contracts,
private hire.
Livery: White with Pink/Mauve.

JACKIES COACHES
THE OLD AIRFIELD, MORETON VALENCE,
GLOUCESTER GL2 7NG
Tel/Fax: 01452 720666
E-mail: jackies.coaches@btconnect.com
Web site: www.jackiescoaches.com
Props: D & J Pratt.

Fleet: 12 – 1 double-deck bus, 3 single-deck
coaches, 4 midibus, 4 minibus.
Chassis: DAF, Ford, LDV, MAN, Mercedes,
Volvo.
Ops incl: local bus services, school contracts,
private hire.
Livery: White with Red.

KB COACHES
HILL VIEW GARAGE, CLAYPITS,
EASTINGTON, STONEHOUSE
GL10 3AJ
Tel: 01452 825774
E-mail: kbcoaches@yahoo.co.uk
Web site: www.kbcoaches.co.uk
Prop: A Francis
Fleet: 12 – 9 single-deck coach, 2 midicoach,
1 minibus.
Chassis: 1 King Long, 3 Mercedes, 7 Volvo,
1 Yutong.
Ops incl: school contracts, excursions &
tours, private hire.
Livery: White with Black/Purple Swirls.

MARCHANTS COACHES
61 CLARENCE STREET, CHELTENHAM
GL50 3LB
Tel: 01242 257714
Fax: 01242 251360
E-mail: sales@marchants-coaches.com
Web site: www.marchants-coaches.com
Man Dir: Roger Marchant
Dir/Ops/Tran Man: Richard Marchant
Ch Eng: Russell Marchant
Co Sec: Mrs Jean Ellis.
Fleet: 46 – 8 double-deck bus, 9 single-deck
bus, 18 single-deck coach, 3 double-deck
coach, 1 midibus, 4 minibus, 3 minicoach.
Chassis: 1 Bova, 6 DAF, 1 Leyland,
8 Mercedes, 3 Neoplan, 9 Optare, 2 Scania,
1 Setra, 15 Volvo.
Bodies: 1 Alexander, 1 Berkhof, 1 Bova,
1 East Lancs, 1 Ferqui, 1 Irizar, 4 Jonckheere,
4 Mercedes, 3 Neoplan, 15 Optare, 9 Plaxton,
1 Setra, 1 Transbus, 1 Van Hool, 2 Wrightbus.
Ops incl: local bus services, school contracts,
excursions & tours, private hire, continental
tours.
Livery: Red/Gold.
Ticket System: Wayfarer.

PULHAM & SONS (COACHES) LTD
BOURTON BUSINESS PARK, BOURTON
ON THE WATER, GL54 2HQ
Tel: 01451 820369
Fax: 01451 821721
E-mail: info@pulhamscoaches.com
Web site: www.pulhamscoaches.com
Man Dir: Andrew Pulham.
Fleet: 58 – 5 double-deck bus, 3 single-deck
bus, 36 single-deck coach, 6 midibus,
1 midicoach, 2 minibus, 1 minicoach.
Chassis: 2 Dennis, 2 Leyland, 5 Mercedes,
10 Optare, 1 Toyota, 1 Volkswagen, 37 Volvo.
Bodies: 5 Alexander, 1 Caetano, 4 Jonckheere,
3 MCV, 3 Mercedes, 10 Optare, 26 Plaxton,
4 Van Hool, 1 Volkswagen, 1 Volvo.
Ops incl: local bus services, school contracts,
excursions & tours, private hire.
Livery: Red & Cream.

ROVER EUROPEAN LTD
THE COACH HOUSE, AVENING ROAD,
NAILSWORTH, STROUD
GL6 0BS
Tel: 01453 832121
Fax: 01453 832722
E-mail: info@rovereuropean.co.uk
Web site: www.rovereuropean.co.uk
Man Dir: David Hand

Gloucestershire

Dir: Carole Hand.
Fleet: 18- 14 single-deck coach, 1 midicoach, 3 minibus.
Chassis: 6 Bova, 5 Dennis, 1 Irisbus, 3 Mercedes, 2 Van Hool, 1 Volkswagen.
Ops incl: school contracts, excursions & tours, private hire, continental tours.
Livery: Cream base with Light Blue/Dark Blue/Orange.

STAGECOACH WEST
♿ 🚌 T
3RD FLOOR, 65 LONDON ROAD, GLOUCESTER GL1 3HF
Tel: 01452 418630
Fax: 01452 304857
E-mail: west@stagecoachbus.com
Web site: www.stagecoachbus.com
Man Dir: Rupert Cox **Eng Dir:** Peter Sheldon **Ops Dir:** Rachel Geliamassi
Comm Man: Ben Cole.
Fleet: 235 - 142 double-deck bus, 16 single-

deck bus, 62 midibus, 15 minibus.
Chassis: 131 Alexander Dennis, 16 MAN, 16 Optare, 72 Scania.
Bodies: 215 Alexander Dennis, 16 Optare, 4 Plaxton.
Ops incl: local bus services, school contracts, private hire.
Liveries: Stagecoach UK Bus.
Ticket System: ERG.

SWANBROOK TRANSPORT LTD
♿ 🚌 💺 🚐
GOLDEN VALLEY, STAVERTON, CHELTENHAM GL51 0TE
Tel: 01452 712386   **Fax:** 01452 859217
E-mail: enquiries@swanbrook.co.uk
Web site: www.swanbrook.co.uk
Fleet Name: Swanbrook.
Man Dir: K J Thomas **Eng Dir:** J A Thomas
Ops Dir: Mrs K West **Ops Man:** M Dowle.
Fleet: 24 - 8 double-deck bus, 7 single-deck coach, 4 midibus, 5 minibus.

Chassis: 2 Dennis, 5 Leyland, 1 MCW, 2 Mercedes, 5 Optare, 3 Scania, 4 Volvo, 2 Wrightbus.
Bodies: 7 Alexander, 2 Caetano, 1 Irizar, 1 MCW, 5 Optare, 4 Plaxton, 2 Van Hool, 2 Wrightbus.
Ops incl: local bus services, school contracts, private hire.
Livery: White/Purple/Green.
Ticket System: Wayfarer 2.

GEORGE YOUNG'S COACHES LTD
♿ 💺
HOLME BUNGALOW, GLEBE ROAD, NEWENT GL18 1BJ
Tel: 01989 763889
Dirs: K & Mrs G Young.
Fleet incl: single-deck bus, single-deck coach, midibus, midicoach, minibus
Ops incl: local bus services, school contracts, private hire.
Livery: White with Red/Black.

ARRIVA NORTH WEST & WALES
♿ 🚌 ✎ 🚐 ⛽ ⚫
73 ORMSKIRK ROAD, AINTREE, LIVERPOOL L9 5AE
Tel: 0151 522 2800
Fax: 0151 525 9556
Web site: www.arriva.co.uk
Regional Man Dir: Phil Stone
Reg Fin Dir: Simon Mills **Reg Eng Dir:** Phil Cummins **Area Man Dir (Merseyside):** Howard Farrall **Area Man Dir (Manchester):** John Rimmer
Area Man Dir (Wales): Michael Morton.
Fleet (England): 902 - 209 double-deck bus, 475 single-deck bus, 8 articulated bus, 168 midibus, 42 minibus.
Chassis: 38 Alexander Dennis, 109 DAF, 80 Dennis, 14 MAN, 8 Mercedes, 42 Optare, 483 VDL, 130 Volvo.
Bodies: Alexander, Alexander Dennis, Caetano, East Lancs, Ikarus, Marshall, Mercedes, Optare, Plaxton, Wrightbus.
Ops incl: local bus services, school contracts.
Livery: Arriva UK Bus.
Ticket System: Wayfarer TGX.
See also Arriva Cymru (Gwynedd)

BATTERSBY'S COACHES
♿ 💺 ❄
73 BRIDGEWATER ROAD, WALKDEN M28 3AF
Tel/Fax: 0161 790 2842
E-mail: info@battersbysmanchester.co.uk
Web site: www.battersbysmanchester.co.uk
Dirs: R W Griffiths, S J Griffiths.
Fleet: 1 single-deck coach.
Chassis/Body: Setra.
Ops incl: private hire, school contracts.

BELLE VUE (MANCHESTER) LTD
♿ 💺 🚐 🍴 🚌 ✎ ⚫ ⛽
THE TRAVEL CENTRE, DISCOVERY BUSINESS PARK, CROSSLEY ROAD, HEATON CHAPEL, STOCKPORT SK4 5DZ
Tel: 0161 947 9477
Fax: 0161 947 9479
E-mail: sales@bellevue.mcr.com
Web site: www.bellevue.mcr.com
Man Dir: Philip Hitchen **Transport Dir:** Ian Bragg **Maintenance Dir:** Kenny Walsh.
Fleet: 62 - 6 double-deck bus, 36 single-deck bus, 13 single-deck coach, 1 midibus, 1 midicoach, 3 minibus, 2 minicoach.
Chassis: 1 Bova, 2 DAF, 7 Dennis, 27 Irisbus, 6 Mercedes, 14 Optare, 1 Scania, 2 Setra, 2 Volvo.
Bodies: 4 Alexander, 1 Autobus, 1 Berkhof, 6 Beulas, 1 Bova, 1 Caetano, 1 EVM, 1 Excel, 1 Irizar, 1 Mellor, 1 Northern Counties,

15 Optare, 4 Plaxton, 2 Setra, 1 Unvi, 21 Vehixel.
Ops incl: local bus services, school contracts, private hire, excursions & tours, continental tours.
Livery: Red/White/Black; **School buses:** Yellow.

R BULLOCK & CO (TRANSPORT) LTD
♿ 🏭 💺 ❄ ✎
COMMERCIAL GARAGE, STOCKPORT ROAD, CHEADLE SK8 2AG
Tel: 0161 428 5265
Fax: 0161 428 9074
E-mail: coachinfo@bullockscoaches.com
Web site: www.bullockscoaches.net
Fleet: 49 – 16 double-deck bus, 3 single-deck bus, 24 single-deck coach, 1 midibus, 3 midicoach, 2 minibus.
Chassis: 1 Alexander Dennis, 1 Ford Transit, 3 Leyland, 3 Mercedes, 1 Optare, 15 Scania, 25 Volvo.
Bodies: 5 Alexander, 1 Alexander Dennis, 7 Caetano, 1 East Lancs, 1 Ferqui, 1 Ford, 8 Irizar, 1 Mercedes, 3 Northern Counties, 2 Optare, 9 Plaxton, 3 Scania, 4 Wrightbus.
Ops incl: local bus services, school contracts, excursions & tours, private hire.
Livery: Red/White.

CARSVILLE COACHES
See Elite Services Ltd

CHECKMATE MINI COACHES
♿ 💺
9 SEEL STREET, MOSSLEY OL15 0LW
Tel: 01457 833040
Prop: J Cox.
Fleet: 4 minibus.
Ops incl: local bus services.

COACH OPTIONS
See Options Travel

COURTESY COACHES LTD
See Yelloway Coaches Ltd

CUMFYBUS LTD
See Merseyside

EAVESWAY TRAVEL LTD
♿ 💺 🏭 ❄
BRYN SIDE, BRYN ROAD, ASHTON-IN-MAKERFIELD, WIGAN WN4 8BT
Tel: 01942 727985   **Fax:** 01942 271234
E-mail: sales@eaveswaytravel.com
Web site: www.eaveswaytravel.com
Man Dir: Mike Eaves **Dir:** Phil Rogers
Ops Man: Tim Presley.

Fleet: 35 – 34 double-deck coach, 1 minicoach.
Chassis: 1 Mercedes, 34 Van Hool.
Bodies: 1 EVM, 34 Van Hool.
Ops incl: express, private hire.
Livery: Silver/Green.

ELITE SERVICES LTD
🏭 💺 ❄ R24 ✎
UNITS 3/6, ADSWOOD ROAD INDUSTRIAL ESTATE, ADSWOOD ROAD, STOCKPORT SK3 8LF
Tel: 0161 969 5117   **Fax:** 0161 962 4198
Web site: www.elitecoachessalemoor.co.uk
Dirs: Dave Nickson, Tony Roberts.
Fleet: 16 - 2 double-deck bus, 2 single-deck bus, 10 single-deck coach, 1 midibus, 1 minibus.
Chassis: 1 Ford Transit, 1 Irisbus, 2 Leyland, 6 Scania, 6 Volvo.
Ops incl: local bus service, excursions & tours, private hire, continental tours, school contracts.
Livery: White/Purple/Pink.
Incorporating Carsville Coaches, Hulme Hall Coaches

FINCH COACHES
💺
MOAT HOUSE STREET GARAGE, HIGHER INCE, WIGAN WN2 2EH
Tel: 01942 245820
Prop: B Finch.
Fleet: 13 – 11 double-deck bus, 2 single-deck coach.
Chassis: 2 DAF, 3 Leyland, 8 Volvo.
Ops incl: local bus services, school contracts.
Livery: Orange & Cream.

FINGLANDS COACHWAYS LTD
Bus operations acquired by First in Manchester; coach operations acquired by R Bullock & Co (Transport) Ltd

FIRST IN MANCHESTER
♿ ✎
WALLSHAW STREET, OLDHAM OL1 3TR
Tel: 0161 627 2929
Web site: www.firstgroup.com
Regional Man Dir: Dave Alexander
Man Dir: Teresa Broxton **Regional Strategic Dev Dir:** Richard Soper
Eng Dir: Ian Robinson.
Fleet: 753 - 302 double-deck bus, 301 single-deck bus, 81 midibus, 50 minibus, 19 articulated bus.
Chassis: 128 Alexander Dennis, 29 Dennis, 5 Irisbus, 55 Mercedes, 89 Optare, 19 Scania, 378 Volvo, 50 Wrightbus.
Bodies: Alexander, Alexander Dennis, East

Gloucestershire

Lancs, Mercedes, Northern Counties, Optare, Plaxton, Scania, Vehixel, Wrightbus.
Ops incl: local bus services, school contracts, private hire.
Livery: FirstGroup UK Bus.
Ticket System: ERG TP4004.

GB COACHES LTD
🚹♿🎵⚙
110 DENTON ROAD, AUDENSHAW M34 5BD
Tel: 0161 320 0353   **Fax:** 0161 285 6341
E-mail: gbcoaches@yahoo.co.uk
Web site: www.gbcoaches.co.uk
Dirs: D J Bolton, Mrs M A Bolton.
Fleet: 19 – 4 single-deck bus, 5 single-deck coach, 5 midibus, 1 midicoach, 4 minibus.
Chassis: 1 DAF, 4 Dennis, 1 King Long, 2 LDV, 3 Mercedes, 4 Optare, 1 Scania, 1 Van Hool, 2 Volvo.
Ops incl: local bus services, school contracts, private hire.
Livery: White with Red/Blue; School Buses: Yellow.

GO-GOODWINS COACHES
♿🚹🎵⚙🚌▭
LYNTTON TRADING ESTATE, 186 OLD WELLINGTON ROAD, ECCLES, MANCHESTER M30 9QG
Tel: 0161 789 4545   **Fax:** 0161 789 0939
E-mail: enquiries@gogoodwins.co.uk
Web site: www.gogoodwins.co.uk
Prop: Geoff Goodwin **Co Sec:** Suzanne Goodwin.
Fleet: 41 – 4 double-deck bus, 2 double-deck coach, 7 single-deck bus, 9 single-deck coach, 11 midibus, 1 midicoach, 6 minibus, 1 minicoach.
Chassis: 7 Alexander Dennis, 2 Dennis, 2 Mercedes, 3 Neoplan, 14 Optare, 2 Scania, 3 VDL, 2 Van Hool, 6 Volvo.
Ops incl: local bus services, school contracts, private hire.
Livery: Blue/White/Red.

GPD TRAVEL
🚹♿🎵
27 HARTFORD AVENUE, HEYWOOD OL10 4XH
Tel: 01706 622297   **Fax:** 01706 361494
E-mail: info@gpd-travel.co.uk
Proprietor: Gary Dawson.
Fleet: 4 – 2 single-deck coach, 1 midicoach, 1 minibus.
Chassis: 2 Mercedes, 2 Volvo.
Ops incl: school contracts, excursions & tours, private hire, continental tours.
Livery: White with red lettering.

GRAYWAY COACHES
🚹♿🎵🍴🎵
237 MANCHESTER ROAD, INCE, WIGAN WN2 2AE
Tel: 01942 243165   **Fax:** 01942 824807
E-mail: graywayone@aol.com
Web site: www.grayway.co.uk
Proprietors: Janet Gray, Michael Gray.
Fleet: 30 - 24 single-deck coach, 4 midicoach, 2 minicoach.
Chassis: 2 DAF, 6 Mercedes, 3 VDL, 19 Volvo.
Bodies: 15 Jonckheere, 2 KVC, 1 Mercedes, 2 Plaxton, 8 Van Hool, 1 Other.
Ops incl: school contracts, excursions & tours, private hire, continental tours.
Livery: Cream/Orange/Red.

HEALINGS INTERNATIONAL COACHES
♿🚹🎵
251 HIGGINSHAW LANE, ROYTON, OLDHAM OL2 6HW
Tel: 0161 624 8975   **Fax:** 0161 652 0320
E-mail: healings@healingscoachhire.co.uk

Web site: www.healingscoachhire.co.uk
Partners: Philip Healing, Julie Brooks.
Fleet: 4 – 3 single-deck coach, 1 midicoach.
Chassis: 1 Mercedes, 1 Scania, 1 Volvo, 1 Duple 425.
Ops incl: school contracts, excursions & tours, private hire, continental tours.
Livery: White with coloured decals.

JONES EXECUTIVE COACHES LTD
♿🚹🎵⚙
THE COACH STATION, SHARP STREET, WALKDEN, MANCHESTER M28 3LX
Tel: 0161 790 9495
Fax: 0161 790 9400
E-mail: simon@jonesexecutive.co.uk
Web site: www.jonesexecutive.co.uk
Man Dir: Simon Jones.
Fleet: 8 single-deck coach.
Chassis: 3 DAF, 3 Irisbus, 1 Scania, 1 Volvo.
Bodies: 3 Beulas, 5 Van Hool.
Ops incl: school contracts, private hire.
Livery: White with Blue lettering.

JPT BUSES
Business acquired by Stagecoach Manchester

LAINTON COACHES LTD t/a ASHALL'S COACHES
♿🚹🎵⚙
UNIT 11, FROXMER STREET, GORTON, MANCHESTER M18 8EF
Tel: 0161 231 7777
Fax: 0161 231 7787
E-mail: info@ashallscoaches.co.uk
Web site: www.ashallscoaches.co.uk
Dirs: James A Ashall, Aaron Ashworth.
Fleet: 11 – 5 single-deck bus, 5 single-deck coach, 1 midibus.
Chassis: 1 Bova, 1 Irisbus, 4 MAN, 1 Mercedes, 1 Optare, 1 Scania, 2 Volvo.
Ops incl: school contracts, private hire (UK only).
Livery: White.
Ticket System: Wayfarer 2.

LAMBS
♿🚹🎵🍴🎵
2A BUXTON STREET, HAZEL GROVE, STOCKPORT SK7 4BB
Tel: 0161 456 1515
Fax: 0161 483 5011
E-mail: lambs139@aol.com
Web site: www.lambscoaches.net
Man Dir: Geoffrey Lamb **Dir:** Graham Lamb.
Fleet: 5 – 4 single-deck coach, 1 midicoach.
Chassis: 3 DAF, 1 Mercedes, 1 Setra.
Bodies: 1 Plaxton, 1 Setra, 3 Van Hool.
Ops incl: private hire, school contracts.
Livery: White/Blue.

M TRAVEL MINIBUSES LTD
♿
140 KIRKMANSHULME LANE, LONGSIGHT, MANCHESTER M12 4WB
Tel: 0161 877 0019
Dir: R Butt.
Fleet: 19 – 14 midibus, 5 minibus.
Chassis: 15 Dennis, 2 Ford, 1 Iveco, 2 Mercedes.
Ops incl: local bus services, school contracts.
Livery: Red & White.

MANCHESTER COMMUNITY TRANSPORT
♿♿🎵
CROSSLEY PARK, CROSSLEY ROAD, HEATON CHAPEL, STOCKPORT SK4 5BF
Tel: 0161 946 9255
E-mail: info@manct.org
Web site: www.manct.org
Man Dir: Rob Marshall **Ops Dir:** Gary Young.
Fleet: 59 – 1 double-deck bus, 21 midibus, 37 minibus.

Chassis: 11 Alexander Dennis, 3 Dennis, 16 Mercedes, 5 Optare, 1 Renault, 20 Volkswagen, 3 Wrightbus.
Ops incl: local bus services, private hire.
Livery: White with logos.

MAYNE COACHES LTD
🚹♿🎵⚙🍴🎵
MARSH HOUSE LANE, WARRINGTON WA1 7ET
Tel: 01925 445588
Fax: 01925 232300
E-mail: coaches@mayne.co.uk
Web site: www.mayne.co.uk
Dirs: D Mayne, C S Mayne **Gen Man:** Amanda Dykes **Sales Man:** D Williams
Eng Dir: C F Pannel **Eng Man:** E Sutcliffe
Traffic Man: J Drake.
Fleet: 41 - 1 double-deck bus, 40 single-deck coach.
Chassis: 2 Alexander Dennis, 2 Dennis, 2 Bova, 25 Scania, 10 Volvo.
Bodies: 1 Alexander, 2 Bova, 23 Irizar, 2 Lahden, 11 Plaxton, 2 UVG.
Ops incl: local bus services, school contracts, excursions & tours, private hire.
Livery: Cream/Red.

METROLINK
See Section 5 – Tram and Bus Rapid Transit Systems

OPTIONS TRAVEL
🚹🍴♿🎵🎵
768 MANCHESTER ROAD, CASTLETON, ROCHDALE OL11 3AW
Tel: 0844 855 1844
Fax: 01706 759996
E-mail: options@freeuk.com
Web site: options-travel.co.uk
Dir: Paul Stone.
Fleet: 12 - 7 single-deck coach, 2 midicoach, 2 minibus, 1 minicoach.
Chassis: 1 Bova, 1 Ford Transit, 5 Mercedes, 2 Neoplan, 1 Scania, 1 Van Hool, 1 Other.
Ops incl: school contracts, excursions & tours, private hire, continental tours.
Livery: Blue.

SELWYNS TRAVEL SERVICES
🚹🍴♿🎵🎵R24🎵🎵🎵
CAVENDISH FARM ROAD, WESTON, RUNCORN WA7 4LU
Tel: 01928 529036   **Fax:** 01928 591872
Recovery: 01928 572108
E-mail: info@selwyns.co.uk
Web site: www.selwyns.co.uk
Regional Dir: Steve Whiteway **Man Dir:** Selwyn A Jones **Gen Man:** Alan P Williamson
Co Sec/Acct: Richard E Williams
Fleet Eng: Cledwyn Owen.
Fleet: 83 – 3 double-deck bus, 69 single-deck coach, 8 midicoach, 1 midibus, 2 minibus.
Chassis: 1 Alexander Dennis, 19 DAF, 3 MAN, 11 Mercedes, 3 Scania, 5 VDL, 39 Volvo.
Bodies: 1 Alexander Dennis, 2 Berkhof, 32 Caetano, 2 East Lancs, 1 EVM, 1 KVC, 1 Marcopolo, 2 Mercedes, 1 Optare, 21 Plaxton, 19 Van Hool.
Ops incl: local bus services, school contracts, excursions & tours, private hire, express, continental tours.
Liveries: White/Blue/Orange/Green, National Express.
Ticket System: Wayfarer.
Incorporating Hardings Tours and Haytons Travel
A subsidiary of RATP Dev UK Ltd

SHEARINGS HOLIDAYS
♿🚹🎵🍴🎵R24🎵🎵
MIRY LANE, WIGAN WN3 4AG
Tel: 01942 244246   **Fax:** 01942 242518
Web site: www.shearings.com

Fleet Names: Shearings Holidays, Caledonian Travel, Euro Tourer, Grand Tourer, National Holidays (see East Riding).
Ch Exec: Dennis Wormwell **Man Dir:** Ruth Connor **Man Dir (Hotels)** Vince Flower **Fin Dir:** Gary Speakman **Tran Dir:** Chris Brown **Eng Dir:** Mick Forbes **Group HR Dir:** Jane Burke.
Fleet (Shearings): 139 - 133 single-deck coach, 6 minibus. For National Holidays fleet, see East Riding.
Chassis: 6 Ford, 115 Setra, 18 Volvo.
Bodies: 6 Ford, 2 Jonckheere, 6 Plaxton, 115 Setra, 10 Van Hool.
Ops incl: excursions & tours, private hire, continental tours.
Livery: Blue or Gold.

ELLEN SMITH (TOURS) LTD

STANLEY HOUSE, BROADGATE, OLDHAM
OL9 9XA
Tel: 01706 648126
Fax: 01706 345970
E-mail: enquiries@ellensmith.co.uk
Web site: www.ellensmith.co.uk
Man Dir: Paul Targett.
Fleet: 4 single-deck coach.
Chassis: 3 Bova, 1 Irisbus.
Bodies: 1 Beulas, 3 Bova.
Ops incl: excursions & tours, private hire.
Livery: Black/Orange.

SOUTH LANCS TRAVEL

THE WELLINGTON, 78 HIGH STREET,
UTTOXETER ST14 7JD
Tel: 01942 888893
Fax: 01889 562756
E-mail: enquiries@sltbus.com
Web site: www.sltbus.com
Man Dir: David Reeves **Dir:** Julian Peddle
Gen Man: Heidi Holland
Ops Man: K Crawford.
Fleet: 44 – 2 double-deck bus, 15 single-deck bus, 27 midibus.
Chassis: 16 Dennis, 4 MAN, 15 Optare, 8 Scania, 1 Volvo.
Bodies: 1 East Lancs, 16 Optare, 16 Plaxton, 2 Scania, 9 Wrightbus.
Ops incl: local bus services, school contracts.
Livery: Yellow/Blue/White
Ticket System: Wayfarer TGX150
A subsidiary of D & G Bus (see Cheshire)

STAGECOACH MANCHESTER

HYDE ROAD, MANCHESTER M12 6JS
Tel: 0161 273 3377
Fax: 0161 276 2594
E-mail: manchester.enquiries@ stagecoachbus.com
Web site: www.stagecoachbus.com
Man Dir: Christopher Bowles
Ops Dir: Matthew Davies
Comm Dir: Ray Cossins **Eng Dir:** Peter Sumner.
Fleet: 789 - 496 double-deck bus, 157 single-deck bus, 100 midibus, 36 minibus.
Chassis: 491 Alexander Dennis, 4 BMC, 95 Dennis, 6 Enterprise, 18 Irisbus, 91 MAN,

43 Optare, 4 Transbus, 1 VDL 34 Volvo.
Bodies: Alexander, Alexander Dennis, BMC, East Lancs, MCV, Optare, Plaxton, Transbus, Vehixel, Wrightbus.
Ops incl: local bus services, school contracts.
Livery: Stagecoach UK Bus.
Ticket System: Vix ERG.

STOTT'S TOURS (OLDHAM) LTD

144 LEES ROAD, OLDHAM
OL4 1HT
Tel: 0161 624 4200
Fax: 0161 628 2969
E-mail: admin@stottsbuses.com
Web site: www.stottstours.com
Props: A Stott, G Stott, S Stott.
Fleet: 30 - 19 double-deck bus, 2 single-deck bus, 2 single-deck coach, 7 minibus.
Chassis: 3 Dennis, 1 Leyland, 3 MCW, 7 Optare, 5 Scania, 11 Volvo.
Ops incl: local bus services, school contracts.
Livery: Cream/Red/Black.

STREET CARS

88 WALTHEW LANE, PLATT BRIDGE,
WIGAN WN2 5AL
Tel: 01942 864999
Prop: Ms L Rasburn.
Fleet: 2 minibuses.
Ops incl: local bus services, private hire.
Livery: White with Black.

SWANS TRAVEL LTD

STANLEY HOUSE, BROADWAY BUSINESS PARK, CHADDERTON, OLDHAM
OL9 9XA
Tel: 0800 799 9423
Fax: 0161 681 0777
E-mail: enquiries@swanstravel.com
Web site: www.swanstravel.com
Man Dir: Kieran Swindells **Fin Dir:** Joanne Swindells **Ops Dir:** Reno Peers
Fleet Man: Keith Harrison.
Fleet: 21 – 19 single-deck coach, 1 double-deck coach, 1 minicoach.
Chassis: 2 Alexander Dennis, 1 Irizar, 16 Mercedes, 1 Scania, 1 Volvo.
Bodies: 1 Berkhof, 1 East Lancs, 1 Irizar, 15 Mercedes, 3 Plaxton.
Ops incl: private hire, school contracts.
Livery: White with Blue/Yellow.
Incorporating Freebird, Bury.

VIKING COACHES

DOCTOR FOLD FARM, DOCTOR FOLD LANE, BIRCH, HEYWOOD OL10 2QE
Tel: 01706 368999
Fax: 01706 620011
E-mail: vikingcoaches@btconnect.com
Web site: www.viking-coaches.com
Owners: A Warburton, Ms A Warburton.
Fleet: 2 - 1 single-deck coach, 1 midibus.
Chassis: Dennis, Volvo.
Bodies: Alexander, Jonckheere.
Ops incl: excursions & tours, private hire, continental tours, school contracts.
Livery: White with Blue.

WIGAN BUSES LTD

54B KIRKLESS INDUSTRIAL ESTATE, CALE LANE, NEW SPRINGS, WIGAN
WN2 1HF
Tel: 01942 820343
Dir: Ms E Tresize.
Fleet: 17 - 2 single-deck bus, 12 midibus, 3 minibus.
Chassis: 4 Alexander Dennis, 5 Dennis, 6 Optare, 1 Spartan, 1 Volvo.
Ops incl: local bus services.

WIGAN COACHWAYS

UNIT 2C, CRICKET STREET INDUSTRIAL ESTATE, PRESCOTT STREET, WIGAN
WN6 7TP
Tel: 01942 829068
Fax: 08456 777774
E-mail: wigancoachways@aol.com
Web site: www.wigancoachways.com
Prop: R C Jarvis
Fleet: 13 – 2 double-deck bus, 3 single-deck bus, 4 single-deck coach, 1 midicoach, 3 minibus.
Ops incl: local bus services, school contracts, private hire.
Livery: White with Blue/Orange.

WRIGLEY'S COACHES LTD

4 FIDDLERS LANE, IRLAM
M44 6QE
Tel: 0161 775 2414
Fax: 0161 775 1558
E-mail: sales@wrigleyscoaches.com
Web site: www.wrigleyscoaches.com
Man Dir: Colin Wrigley
Co Sec/Dir: Lesley Wrigley
Ops Man: Alan Grice.
Fleet: 5 - 1 double-deck bus, 3 single-deck coach, 1 midicoach.
Chassis: 2 MAN, 1 Setra, 1 Toyota, 2 Volvo.
Bodies: 1 Alexander, 1 Caetano, 2 Neoplan, 1 Setra.
Ops incl: private hire, school contracts.
Livery: Blue/White.

YELLOWAY COACHES LTD

UNIT 1, PALM BUSINESS CENTRE, STOCK LANE, CHADDERTON, OLDHAM
OL9 9ER
Tel: 0845 045 0344
Fax: 0161 287 3344
E-mail: info@yelloway.co.uk
Web site: www.yelloway.co.uk
Dir: M Brook.
Fleet: 15 – 14 single-deck coach, 1 midicoach.
Chassis: 3 DAF, 1 Leyland, 2 Scania, 1 Temsa, 8 Volvo.
Ops incl: private hire, excursions & tours, continental tours.
Livery: Yellow with logo.
Formerly Courtesy Coaches Ltd.

♿ Vehicle suitable for disabled	🍽 Coach(es) with galley facilities	🚌 Vintage Coach(es) available	
Seat belt-fitted Vehicle	🔧 Replacement vehicle available	Open top vehicle(s)	
R24 24 hour recovery service	**R** Recovery service available	🚻 Coaches with toilet facilities	
T Toilet-drop facilities available	❄ Air-conditioned vehicle(s)	Hybrid Buses	Gas Buses

AIRLYNX EXPRESS LTD

WREN FARM, CASTLE LANE, NORTH
BADDESLEY SO52 9LY
Tel: 02380 736823
Fax: 02380 741736
E-mail: info@airlynxexpress.co.uk
Web site: www.airlynxexpress.co.uk
Man Dir: Ian Harley.
Fleet: 11 – 5 single-deck coach, 6 minicoach.
Chassis: Ford Transit, Irisbus, Mercedes,
Neoplan, Renault, Toyota, Volkswagen.
Ops incl: private hire, school contracts.
Livery: Blue/Yellow

ALTONIAN COACHES LTD

1A WESTBROOK WALK, MARKET SQUARE,
ALTON GU34 1HZ
Tel: 01420 84845
Fax: 01420 541429
Web site: www.wheelerstravel.co.uk
Man Dir: Derek Wheeler **Depot Man:**
David Butcher **Tours Man:** Ian McKee.
Fleet: see Wheelers Travel Ltd
Ops incl: school contracts, excursions &
tours, private hire, continental tours.
Livery: Blue & Orange.
Associated with Wheelers Travel Ltd,
Southampton

AMK CHAUFFEUR DRIVE LTD

MILL LANE, PASSFIELD, LIPHOOK GU30 7RP
Tel: 01428 751675
Fax: 01428 751677
E-mail: info@amkxl.com
Web site: www.amkxl.com
Man Dir: G Fraser **Fin Dir:** M Dummer.
Fleet: 51 – 1 single-deck coach, 49 minibus,
1 minicoach.
Ops incl: local bus services, school contracts,
excursions & tours, private hire.

AMPORT & DISTRICT COACHES LTD

EASTFIELD HOUSE, AMESBURY ROAD,
THRUXTON, ANDOVER SP11 8ED
Tel: 01264 772307
Fax: 01264 773020
E-mail: tedd@onetel.net
Dirs: P J Tedd, A M Tedd, N B Tedd.
Fleet: 13 – 12 single-deck coach, 1 midicoach.
Chassis: 1 Mercedes, 1 Scania, 1 Van Hool,
3 VDL, 7 Volvo.
Bodies: 1 Berkhof, 1 Mercedes, 6 Plaxton,
3 VDL, 2 Van Hool.
Ops incl: private hire, continental tours,
school contracts.
Livery: White/Brown/Orange

ANGELA COACHES LTD

OAKTREE HOUSE, LOWFORD,
BURSLEDON, SOUTHAMPTON SO31 8ES
Tel: 02380 403170
Fax: 02380 406487
E-mail: robert@angelacoaches.com
Web site: www.angelacoaches.com
Man Dir: R J Pressley **Co Sec:**
Mrs H M Pressley **Dir:** R J Pressley
Ch Eng: D Evans **Ops Man:** J Davies.
Fleet: 11 – 5 single-deck coach, 1 midicoach,
5 minicoach.
Chassis: 3 Iveco, 5 MAN, 1 Mercedes,
2 Toyota.
Bodies: 1 Beulas, 2 Caetano, 2 Indcar,
1 Mercedes, 5 Neoplan.
Ops incl: school contracts, excursions &
tours, private hire, continental tours.
Livery: Red/White.

AVENSIS COACH TRAVEL LTD

UNIT 4F & 4F1, CENTRAL CRESCENT,
MARCHWOOD INDUSTRIAL PARK,
MARCHWOOD, SOUTHAMPTON
SO40 4BJ
Tel: 02380 869294   **Fax:** 02380 864956
E-mail: info@avensiscoaches.co.uk
Web site: www.avensiscoaches.co.uk
Dirs: Graham Humby, Simon Humby
Transport Man: Tracey Ralph.
Fleet: 8 single-deck coach.
Chassis: 3 DAF, 1 MAN, 4 Scania.
Bodies: 5 Irizar, 3 Van Hool.
Ops incl: excursions & tours, private hire.
Livery: Yellow & Purple.

BLACK & WHITE MOTORWAYS LTD
KING ALFRED MOTOR SERVICES LTD

31 STONEY LANE, WINCHESTER
SO22 6DP
Tel: 01962 620169
E-mail: info@bwmotorways.co.uk,
kingalfredmotorservices@ntlworld.com
Web site:
www.kingalfredmotorservices.co.uk
Dirs: Peter Bailey, Eve Bailey
Ch Eng: Michael Elliott.
Ops incl: local bus services, school contracts,
excursions & tours, private hire.
Liveries: Black & White; Green & Yellow.
Ticket System: Setright.

BLACK VELVET TRAVEL LTD

BINNING HOUSE, 4A HIGH STREET,
EASTLEIGH SO50 5LA
Tel: 023 8061 2288
Fax: 023 8064 4881
Web site: www.velvetbus.co.uk
Dir: Adam Smith.
Ops incl: local bus services, school contracts,
private hire.
Livery: Purple.

A S BONE & SONS LTD

LONDON ROAD, HOOK RG27 9EQ
Tel: 01256 761388, 762106
Fleet Name: Newnham Coaches
Man Dir: J E Bone **Co Sec:** Mrs M Bone.
Fleet: 6 – 5 double-deck bus, 1 single-deck bus.
Chassis: 2 Leyland, 2 MCW, 1 Scania, 1 Volvo.
Ops incl: private hire.
Livery: Cream/Blue.

BRIJAN TOURS LTD

THE COACH STATION, UNITS 4/5,
BOTTINGS INDUSTRIAL ESTATE,
CURDRIDGE SO30 2DY
Tel: 01489 788138   **Fax:** 01489 789395
Recovery: 07711 435189
E-mail: info@brijantours.com
Web site: www.brijantours.com
Man Dir: Brian Botley **Co Sec:** Janet Botley
Ops Man: Brian Bedford **Fleet Eng:**
Ben Cresswell **Asst Man:** David Thompson.
Fleet: 30 - 10 double-deck bus, 1 single-deck
bus, 8 single-deck coach, 10 midibus, 1 minibus.
Chassis: 12 Dennis, 1 Ford Transit, 1 Iveco,
8 Leyland, 2 MCW, 4 Scania, 2 Volvo.
Bodies: 6 Alexander, 1 Berkhof, 6 ECW,
2 Irizar, 1 Leyland, 2 MCW, 1 Marcopolo,
1 Marshall, 5 Plaxton, 3 Van Hool, 1 Wrightbus,
1 Other.
Ops incl: local bus services, school contracts,
excursions & tours, private hire, continental
tours.
Livery: Cream/Burgundy.
Ticket system: Wayfarer.

CLEGG & BROOKING LTD

WHITE HORSE SERVICE STATION, MIDDLE
WALLOP, STOCKBRIDGE SO20 8DZ
Tel: 01264 781283   **Fax:** 01264 781679
E-mail: cleggandbrooking@btconnect.com
Web site: www.cbcoaches.co.uk
Dirs: Kevin Brooking, Jeanette Cook, John
Cook, Sarah Glasspool.
Fleet: 16 - 13 single-deck coach, 3 midicoach.
Chassis: 1 Bova, 1 DAF, 2 Dennis, 1 Irisbus,
1 King Long, 1 MAN, 1 Mercedes, 2 Neoplan,
3 Scania, 1 Toyota, 2 Volvo.
Bodies: 1 Bova, 2 Caetano, 1 Ikarus, 3 Irizar,
1 King Long, 2 Neoplan, 1 Noge, 2 Plaxton,
1 Sitcar, 1 Sunsundegui.
Ops incl: local bus services, private hire,
school contracts.
Livery: Blue/Grey.

COLISEUM COACHES LTD

BOTLEY ROAD GARAGE, WEST END,
SOUTHAMPTON SO30 3JA
Tel: 02380 472377   **Fax:** 0872 111 4476
E-mail: info@coliseumcoaches.co.uk
Web site: www.coliseumcoaches.co.uk
Gen Man: Mark Pitter.
Fleet: 12 – 10 single-deck coach, 1 minibus,
1 minicoach.
Chassis: 10 MAN, 2 Mercedes.
Bodies: 1 Mercedes, 10 Neoplan, 1 Other.
Ops incl: excursions & tours, private hire.
Livery: Silver.
A subsidiary of Lucketts Travel

COOPERS COACHES

31-35 LAKE ROAD, WOOLSTON SO19 9EB
Tel: 023 8039 3393   **Fax:** 023 8044 4929
E-mail: cooperscoaches@yahoo.co.uk
Props: Stephen & Ellen Cooper.
Fleet: 6 - 4 single-deck coach, 2 minibus.
Chassis: 1 DAF, 1 Dennis, 1 Ford Transit,
2 Scania, 1 Volvo.
Bodies: 1 Berkhof, 1 Caetano, 1 Ikarus,
1 Plaxton, 1 Scania.
Ops incl: local bus services, school contracts,
private hire.

COUNTYWIDE TRAVEL
(BASINGSTOKE)

169 GREENHAM BUSINESS PARK,
THATCHAM RG19 6HN
Tel: 01256 780079
Fax: 01635 821128
E-mail: info@countywidetoptravel.co.uk
Web site: www.countywidetoptravel.co.uk
Dirs: Simon Weaver, Michelle Wadsworth.
Fleet: see Weavaway Travel.
A subsidiary of Weavaway Travel (see Berkshire)

EMSWORTH & DISTRICT MOTOR
SERVICES LTD

UNIT 3, CLOVELLY ROAD, SOUTHBOURNE
PO10 8PE
Tel: 01243 378337
Fax: 01243 374182
E-mail: caren@emsworthanddistrict.co.uk
Web site: www.emsworthanddistrict.co.uk
Man Dir: Paul Lea.
Fleet: 42 - 3 double-deck bus, 10 single-deck
coach, 24 midibus, 1 midicoach, 4 minibus.
Chassis: 3 DAF, 23 Dennis, 2 Ford Transit,
5 Leyland, 3 Mercedes, 6 Van Hool.
Ops incl: local bus services, school contracts,
excursions & tours, private hire, continental
tours
Livery: Green/Silver.
Ticket system: Wayfarer.

FIRST HAMPSHIRE, DORSET & BERKSHIRE

EMPRESS ROAD, SOUTHAMPTON SO14 0JW
Tel: 0333 014 3490
Fax: 023 8071 4891
E-mail: hampshire-dorset.csc@firstgroup.com
Web site: www.firstgroup.com
Man Dir: Marc Reddy.
Fleet: 498 - 81 double-deck bus, 3 open-top bus, 218 single-deck bus, 12 single-deck coach, 149 midibus, 35 minibus.
Chassis: 37 Alexander Dennis, 2 Autosan, 8 Bluebird, 13 BMC, 94 Dennis, 32 Optare, 45 Scania, 161 Volvo, 73 Wrightbus.
Ops incl: local bus services, school contracts, private hire.
Livery: FirstGroup UK Bus.
See also Berkshire, Dorset

FLEET BUZZ LTD

BOWENHURST FARM, CRONDALL FARNHAM, GU10 5RP
Tel: 01252 851009
Fax: 01252 852009
E-mail: info@fleetbuzz.co.uk
Web site: www.fleetbuzz.co.uk
Fleet: 23 – 3 double-deck bus, 4 single-deck bus, 8 midibus, 8 minibus.
Chassis: 4 Dennis, 12 Optare, 4 Transbus, 3 Volvo.
Bodies: 5 Alexander, 2 Caetano, 12 Optare, 4 Transbus.
Ops incl: local bus services.
Livery: Black & Yellow.
Ticket system: Wayfarer III.
A subsidiary of Stagecoach South

GEMINI TRAVEL SOUTHAMPTON LTD

NORTH ROAD, MARCHWOOD INDUSTRIAL PARK, MARCHWOOD, SOUTHAMPTON SO40 4BL
Tel: 02380 660066
Fax: 02380 871308
E-mail: info@travel-gemini.co.uk
Web site: www.travel-gemini.co.uk
Dir: Mark Bennett **Gen Man:** Nigel Smith.
Fleet: 14 - 4 single-deck coach, 4 midicoach, 5 minibus, 1 minicoach.
Chassis: 1 DAF, 2 Ford Transit, 2 LDV, 5 Mercedes, 1 Peugeot, 1 Setra, 2 Volvo.
Ops incl: private hire, school contracts.
Livery: White/Blue.

GO SOUTH COAST LTD

TOWNGATE HOUSE, 2-8 PARKSTONE ROAD, POOLE BH15 2PR
Tel: 01202 680888
Fax: 01202 670244
E-mail: managersmailbox@bluestarbus.co.uk
Web sites: www.bluestarbus.co.uk, www.go-ahead.com
Fleet Names (Hampshire): Bluestar, Unilink.
Chairman: David Brown **Man Dir:** Andrew Wickham **Eng Dir:** Steve Hamilton
Fin Dir: Nick Woods **Ops Dir:** Ed Wills.
Fleet: 750 - 321 double-deck bus, 134 single-deck bus, 101 single-deck coach, 10 articulated bus, 88 midibus, 96 minibus.
Chassis: 118 Alexander Dennis, 2 Bristol, 62 DAF, 14 Dennis, 1 Ford, 4 Iveco, 1 LDV, 20 Leyland, 59 Mercedes, 123 Optare, 127 Scania, 219 Volvo.
Bodies: 121 Alexander Dennis, 1 Autobus, 4 Beulas, 6 Caetano, 56 East Lancs, 2 ECW, 1 Ford, 2 Ikarus, 11 Irizar, 3 Jonckheere, 1 LDV, 57 Mercedes, 44 Northern Counties,

169 Optare, 86 Plaxton, 73 Scania, 22 Van Hool, 91 Wrightbus.
Ops incl: local bus services, school contracts.
Liveries: Bluestar: Blue; **Unilink:** Blue/White.
Ticket System: Vix ITSO Smart.
Part of the Go-Ahead Group. See also operations in Dorset, Isle of Wight, Wiltshire.

HERRINGTON COACHES LTD
See Dorset

HYTHE & WATERSIDE COACHES LTD

1A THE HIGH STREET, HYTHE SO45 6AG
Tel: 02380 844788
Fax: 02380 207284
E-mail: enquiries@watersidetours.co.uk
Web site: www.watersidetours.co.uk
Fleet Name: Waterside Tours.
Man Dir: Roy Barker **Dirs:** Pamela Withey, Jackie Withey.
Fleet: 9 – 6 single-deck coach, 2 midicoach, 1 minibus.
Chassis: 3 Mercedes, 1 Scania, 5 Volvo.
Bodies: 4 Berkhof, 2 Esker, 1 Jonckheere, 1 Lahden, 1 Unvi.
Ops incl: school contracts, excursions & tours, private hire.
Livery: Burgundy & Gold.

LANDTOURER COACHES

96 SCHUBERT ROAD, BRIGHTON HILL, BASINGSTOKE RG22 4JJ
Dirs: P & S Kavanagh
Fleet: 11 single-deck coach.
Chassis: 2 MAN, 2 Scania, 1 Van Hool, 1 VDL, 5 Volvo.
Ops incl: private hire, excursions & tours.
A subsidiary of Bernard Kavanagh & Sons Ltd (see Republic of Ireland)

LUCKETTS TRAVEL

BROADCUT, WALLINGTON, FAREHAM PO16 8TB
Tel: 01329 823755
Fax: 01329 823855
E-mail: sales@lucketts.co.uk
Web site: www.lucketts.co.uk
Chairman: David Luckett MBE **Joint Man Dirs:** Steven Luckett, Ian Luckett **Eng Dir:** Mark Jordan **HR Dir:** Chloe Casey **Group Ops Man:** Ian Macintyre **Group Sales & Marketing Man:** Paul Barringer.
Fleet: 108 – 7 double-deck bus, 1 single-deck bus, 81 single-deck coach, 1 double-deck coach, 5 midicoach, 11 minibus, 3 minicoach.
Chassis: 3 Dennis, 3 Irizar, 14 Mercedes, 1 Neoplan, 4 Optare, 50 Scania, 2 Toyota, 32 Volvo.
Bodies: 5 Alexander, 1 Berkhof, 41 Caetano, 30 Irizar, 8 Lahden, 9 Mercedes, 1 Neoplan, 4 Optare, 9 Plaxton, 1 Sitcar.
Ops incl: school contracts, excursions & tours, private hire, express, continental tours.
Liveries: Grey/White/Orange, National Express.
Lucketts Group Companies:
Coliseum Coaches, Southampton (see Hampshire)
Worthing Coaches, Worthing (see West Sussex)

MARCHWOOD MOTORWAYS
See Go South Coast Ltd

MERVYN'S COACHES

THE NEW COACH HOUSE, INNERSDOWN, MICHELDEVER, WINCHESTER SO21 3BW
Tel/Fax: 01962 774574
E-mail: mervynscoaches@btconnect.com

Web site: www.mervynscoaches.com
Partners: Mervyn Annetts, Carol L Annetts, Linda Porter, James Annetts.
Fleet: 7 - 4 single-deck coach, 2 midicoach, 1 minicoach.
Chassis: 1 AEC, 2 Bedford, 4 Volvo.
Bodies: 1 Duple, 1 Harrington, 4 Plaxton, 1 Van Hool.
Ops incl: local bus services, school contracts, excursions & tours, private hire.
Livery: Brown/Cream.
Ticket System: Setright.

MORTONS TRAVEL LTD

UNIT 11, BERRY COURT BUSINESS PARK, BRAMLEY ROAD, LITTLE LONDON, TADLEY RG26 5AT
Tel: 01256 889082
Fax: 01256 889083
Recovery: 07917 202895
E-mail: enquiries@mortonstravel.com
Web site: www.mortonstravel.com
Man Dir: Adrian Morton
Ops Man: John Simpson.
Fleet: 28 – 1 double-deck bus, 4 single-deck bus, 11 single-deck coach, 8 double-deck coach, 1 articulated coach, 1 open top bus, 1 midicoach, 1 minibus.
Chassis: 5 Bova, 1 Bristol, 2 DAF, 4 Leyland, 1 MAN, 2 Mercedes, 3 Van Hool, 10 Volvo
Bodies: 4 Alexander, 5 Bova, 2 East Lancs, 1 ECW, 1 Leyland, 6 Optare, 2 Plaxton, 6 Van Hool, 1 Other.
Ops incl: school contracts, excursions & tours, private hire, continental tours.
Livery: White or Dark Green.

PIKE'S COACHES LTD

77 SCOTT CLOSE, WALWORTH INDUSTRIAL ESTATE, ANDOVER SP10 5NU
Tel: 01264 312702
Fax: 01264 334329
Props: J S Pike, Jenny Pike, C Pike, R Pike.
Fleet: 16 - 1 double-deck bus, 4 single-deck bus, 7 single-deck coach, 4 minibus.
Chassis: 2 Ford Transit, 2 Mercedes, 12 Volvo.
Ops incl: local bus services, school contracts, excursions & tours, private hire, continental tours.
Livery: White.
Ticket System: Setright.

PRINCESS COACHES LTD

PRINCESS COACH GARAGE, BOTLEY ROAD, WEST END, SOUTHAMPTON SO30 3HA
Tel: 023 8047 2150
Fax: 023 8039 9944
E-mail: admin@princesscoaches.com
Web site: www.princesscoaches.co.uk
Man Dir: Peter Brown **Dirs:** Denise Brown, Yvonne Barfoot **Gen Man:** Jamie Brown.
Fleet: 21 - 18 single-deck coach, 1 midicoach, 2 minibus.
Chassis: 3 Mercedes, 18 Scania.
Bodies: 18 Irizar, 1 Mercedes, 1 Optare, 1 Sitcar.
Ops incl: school contracts, private hire.
Livery: White with multi-coloured flashes.

SOLENT BLUE LINE
See Go South Coast Ltd

SOLENT COACHES LTD

BROOKSIDE GARAGE, CROW LANE, RINGWOOD BH24 3EA
Tel: 01425 473188
Fax: 01425 473669
Recovery: 0784 326 6720/1
E-mail: enquiries@solentcoaches.co.uk

Web site: www.solentcoaches.co.uk
Man Dir/Co Sec: John Skew **Dir/Ch Eng:**
Paul Skew.
Fleet: 11 - 9 single-deck coach, 1 double-deck
coach, 1 minicoach.
Chassis: 4 Neoplan, 1 Scania, 2 Setra,
1 Toyota, 3 Volvo.
Ops incl: excursions & tours, private hire,
continental tours, school contracts.
Livery: White/Blue.

STAGECOACH IN HAMPSHIRE
&

THE BUS STATION, FESTIVAL PLACE,
CHURCHILL WAY, BASINGSTOKE
RG21 7BE
Tel: 0845 121 0190
Fax: 01243 755888
E-mail: south.enquiries@stagecoachbus.com
Web site: www.stagecoachbus.com/
hampshire
Man Dir: Andrew Dyer **Eng Dir:**
Richard Alexander **Fin Dir:** Martin Stoggell
Div Man: Matthew Callow.
Fleet: 153 - 40 double-deck bus, 18 single-
deck bus, 85 midibus, 10 minibus.
Chassis: 108 Alexander Dennis, 9 Dennis,
10 Optare, 3 Scania, 7 Transbus, 15 Volvo.
Bodies: 20 Alexander, 111 Alexander Dennis,
10 Optare, 4 Plaxton, 7 Transbus.
Ops incl: local bus services, school contracts.
Livery: Stagecoach UK Bus.
Ticket System: Wayfarer.

STAGECOACH IN HANTS & SURREY
&

HALIMOTE ROAD, ALDERSHOT GU11 1NJ
Tel: 0845 121 0190
Fax: 01243 755888
E-mail: south.enquiries@stagecoachbus.com
Web site: www.stagecoachbus.com/south
Man Dir: Andrew Dyer **Eng Dir:**
Richard Alexander **Fin Dir:** Martin Stoggell.
Fleet: 100 - 13 double-deck bus, 17 single-
deck bus, 54 midibus, 16 minibus.
Chassis: 31 Alexander Dennis, 7 Dennis,
20 MAN, 16 Optare, 13 Transbus, 13 Volvo.
Bodies: 8 Alexander, 51 Alexander Dennis,
8 Northern Counties, 16 Optare, 4 Plaxton,
13 Transbus.
Ops incl: local bus services, school contracts.
Livery: Stagecoach UK Bus.
Ticket System: Wayfarer.

STAGECOACH SOUTH
& ✿

BUS STATION, SOUTHGATE, CHICHESTER
PO19 8DG
Tel: 0845 121 0190
Fax: 01243 755888
E-mail: south.enquiries@stagecoachbus.com
Web site: www.stagecoachbus.com/south
Fleet Names: Stagecoach in the South
Downs, Stagecoach in Portsmouth.
Man Dir: Andrew Dyer **Eng Dir:** Richard
Alexander **Ops Dir:** Tom Bridge **Comm
Dir:** Mark Turner.
Fleet (Sussex/Portsmouth): 200 – 41
double-deck bus, 91 single-deck bus,
58 midibus, 10 minibus.
Chassis: 130 Alexander Dennis, 16 Dennis,
10 Optare, 20 Transbus, 4 Volvo.
Bodies: 5 Alexander, 150 Alexander Dennis,
10 Optare, 15 Plaxton, 20 Transbus.
Ops incl: local bus services, school contracts,
private hire.
Livery: Stagecoach UK Bus.
Ticket system: Wayfarer.

TGM GROUP LTD
Operations in Hampshire are at Southampton
Airport
See London & Middlesex

TRUEMANS COACHES (FLEET) LTD
& ✚ ❚❚ ✿

TRUEMANS END, LYNCHFORD ROAD,
ASH VALE, GU12 5PQ
Tel: 01252 373303
Fax: 01252 373393
E-mail: sue@truemans.co.uk
Web site: www.truemans.co.uk
Dir: Richard Trueman.
Fleet: 14 single deck coach.
Chassis: 1 Irisbus, 3 Irizar, 4 MAN, 6 Neoplan.
Bodies: 1 Beulas, 3 Irizar, 6 Neoplan,
4 Plaxton.
Ops incl: school contracts, private hire,
excursions & tours, continental tours.
Livery: Electric Blue.

VISION TRAVEL INTERNATIONAL
LTD
& ✚ ✿ ✎ T

COACH YARD, FULFLOOD ROAD,
DUNSBURY BUSINESS PARK, HAVANT
PO9 5AX

Tel: 02392 359168
Fax: 02392 361253
E-mail: visiontravels@aol.com
Web site: www.visiontravel.co.uk
Dir: Peter Sharpe
Ops Man: Paul Donald.
Ops incl: school contracts, excursions &
tours, private hire, continental tours.
Livery: Yellow/Red/White.

WHEELERS TRAVEL LTD
& ✚ ❚❚ ✎ ✿ T

UNIT 9, GROVE FARM, UPPER NORTHAM
DRIVE, HEDGE END, SOUTHAMPTON
SO30 4BG
Tel: 02380 471800
Fax: 02380 470414
E-mail: sales@wheelerstravel.co.uk
Web site: www.wheelerstravel.co.uk
Man Dir: Derek Wheeler
Gen Man: Paul Barker
Traffic Man: Keith Trenchard
Assistant Traffic Man: Nigel Taylor.
Fleet: 53 – 6 double-deck bus, 10 single-deck
bus, 19 single-deck coach, 4 midibus,
7 midicoach, 2 minibus, 5 minicoach.
Chassis: 2 BMC, 1 Bova, 4 DAF, 3 Dennis,
4 Irisbus, 2 Iveco, 3 LDV, 15 MAN, 7 Mercedes,
2 Optare, 2 Scania, 5 Volvo.
Ops incl: local bus services, private hire,
excursions & tours, school contracts,
continental tours.
Liveries: Coaches: Blue Body, Orange
Mirrors; **Buses:** Orange.
Incorporating Altonian Coaches

XELABUS LTD
& ✎ ✿

THE BUS GARAGE, UNIT 10, BARTON
PARK INDUSTRIAL ESTATE, CHICKENHALL
LANE, EASTLEIGH SO50 6RR
Tel: 02380 644715
Web site: www.xelabus.info
Man Dir: Philip Blair
Ops Dir: Gareth Blair
Fleet: 33 – 17 double-deck bus, 1 open-top
bus, 15 midibus.
Chassis: 20 Dennis, 10 Leyland, 3 Volvo.
Bodies: 9 Alexander, 2 East Lancs, 3 Leyland,
1 Marshall, 1 Northern Counties, 17 Plaxton.
Ops incl: local bus services, school contracts,
sightseeing tours, private hire.
Livery: Green.

HEREFORDSHIRE

ABBEY CARS
& ✎

CANNS HILL, ABBEYDORE, HEREFORD
HR2 0AQ
Tel: 01981 570301
E-mail: gillandersabbeycars@yahoo.co.uk
Prop: E C Gillanders.
Fleet: 7 – 1 midibus, 6 minibus.
Chassis: 2 Ford Transit, 1 LDV, 2 Mercedes,
1 Optare, 1 Renault.
Ops incl: local bus services, school contracts,
private hire.

BOWYER'S COACHES
✎

QUARRY GARAGE, PETERCHURCH
HR2 0TF
Tel: 01981 550206
Prop: Fernley C Anning.
Fleet: 4 – 2 midicoach, 2 minibus.
Chassis: 2 Ford Transit, 2 Mercedes.
Ops incl: local bus services, private hire,
school contracts.
Livery: White/Red.

D R M BUS AND CONTRACT
SERVICES
&

THE BUS GARAGE, BROMYARD HR7 4NT
Tel: 01885 483219
E-mail: drm@drmbus.com
Web site: www.drmbus.com
Prop: David R Morris.
Fleet: 12 single-deck bus.
Chassis: 9 Scania, 3 Volvo.
Bodies: 1 Alexander, 2 East Lancs, 9 Scania.
Ops incl: local bus services, school contracts.
Livery: Blue/Silver-White.
Ticket System: Wayfarer 3.

FIRST MIDLANDS
& ✎

HERON LODGE, LONDON ROAD,
WORCESTER WR5 2EU
Tel: 01905 359393
Fax: 01905 351104
Regional Man Dir: Nigel Eggleton
Deputy Man Dir: Mick Branigan
Fin Dir: David Marshall.

Fleet Name: First Wyvern
Fleet (Worcester & Hereford):
104 – 12 double-deck bus, 48 single-deck bus,
2 single-deck coach, 16 midibus, 26 minibus.
Chassis: 41 Alexander Dennis, 2 BMC,
17 Dennis, 26 Optare, 5 Transbus, 13 Volvo.
Bodies: 41 Alexander Dennis, 2 BMC,
11 Caetano, 26 Optare, 8 Plaxton, 5 Transbus,
11 Wrightbus.
Ops incl: local bus services, school contracts.
Livery: FirstGroup UK Bus.
Ticket System: Wayfarer.
See also operations in Leicestershire,
Staffordshire

GOLDEN PIONEER TRAVEL
✚ ❚❚ ✎ ✿

BRANDON, ROSS ROAD, HEREFORD
HR2 8BH
Tel: 01432 274307
E-mail: info@gptgo.com
Web site: www.gptgo.com
Prop: Bryan Crockett **Dir:** J Crockett.
Fleet: 3 single-deck coach.

Chassis: 2 King Long, 1 Van Hool.
Ops incl: excursions & tours, private hire, continental tours.
Livery: White with Red.

H & H COACHES

BROAD MEADOWS, ROSS-ON-WYE
HR9 7AQ
Tel: 01989 566444
Props: M Harris, R Smith.
Fleet: 23 – 11 single-deck coach, 5 midibus, 1 midicoach, 3 minibus, 3 minicoach.
Chassis: DAF, Dennis, Ford Transit, Leyland, LDV, Mercedes, Setra, Toyota, Volvo.
Ops incl: local bus services, school contracts, private hire.

I & S COACHES

10 RED HILL AVENUE, HEREFORD
HR2 7QQ
Tel: 01432 264968
E-mail: iandscoaches@hotmail.co.uk
Prop: I Phillips.
Fleet: 5 – 1 midibus, 2 minibus, 2 minicoach.
Chassis: 1 Dennis, 1 Ford Transit, 1 Irisbus, 2 Renault.
Ops incl: local bus services, school contracts, private hire.

P. W. JONES COACHES

HILBREY GARAGE, BURLEY GATE,
HEREFORD HR1 3QL
Tel: 01432 820214
Fax: 01432 820521
Recovery: 01432 820214
E-mail: holidays@pwjones.com
Web site: www.pwjonesluxurycoachholidays.co.uk
Owner: Philip Jones **Workshop Man:** Richard Edwards.
Fleet: 18 – 14 single-deck coach, 1 midicoach, 3 minibus.
Chassis: 1 Alexander Dennis, 1 Bova, 5 Dennis, 1 Ford Transit, 1 LDV, 1 MAN, 1 Mercedes, 2 Neoplan, 1 Toyota, 4 Volvo.
Bodies: 1 Bova, 2 Caetano, 1 Ford, 1 LDV, 2 Neoplan, 10 Plaxton, 1 Other.
Ops incl: school contracts, excursions & tours, private hire, continental tours.
Livery: Multi Colours.

LUGG VALLEY PRIMROSE TRAVEL LTD

SOUTHERN AVENUE, LEOMINSTER HR6 0QF
Tel: 01432 344341
Fax: 01432 356206
E-mail: sales@luggvalleytravel.co.uk
Man Dir: N D Yeomans **Ops Man:** I Davies
Traffic Man: J Hodges **Fleet Eng:** D W Jones.
Fleet: 26 – 3 single-deck bus, 11 single-deck

coach, 11 midibus, 1 midicoach.
Chassis: 4 Dennis, 1 Mercedes, 14 Optare, 2 Scania, 5 Volvo.
Bodies: 1 Berkhof, 1 Esker, 2 Irizar, 1 Jonckheere, 14 Optare, 7 Plaxton.
Ops incl: local bus services, school contracts, excursions & tours, private hire, continental tours.
Livery: Green/Cream/Orange.
Ticket System: ERG.

M & S COACHES OF HEREFORDSHIRE LTD

UNIT 3, BRIERLEY WAY, SOUTHERN AVENUE, LEOMINSTER HR6 0RW
Tel: 01568 612803
E-mail: maurice@mscoaches.co.uk
Web site: www.mscoaches.co.uk
Dirs: Maurice Peruffo, Mrs Susan Peruffo, Les Allen.
Fleet: 12 – 7 midicoach, 5 minicoach.
Chassis: 1 BMC, 1 Ford Transit, 9 Mercedes, 1 Toyota.
Bodies: 1 BMC, 1 Caetano, 3 Ferqui, 1 KVC, 1 Paramount, 1 Sitcar, 1 Turas, 3 Unvi.
Ops incl: school contracts, private hire, continental tours.
Livery: White with Maroon/Grey lettering.

NICK MADDY COACHES

THE NEVILLE ARMS, ABBEYDORE, HEREFORD HR2 0AA
Tel: 01432 266211
Prop: Nick Maddy.
Fleet: 9 minibus.
Chassis: 2 Ford Transit, 1 Iveco, 5 LDV, 1 Mercedes.
Ops incl: local bus services, school contracts, private hire.

NEWBURY COACHES

LOWER ROAD TRADING ESTATE, LEDBURY HR8 2DJ
Tel: 01531 633483
Fax: 01531 633650
Props: K R, K M, A R & C R Powell.
Fleet: 19 – 12 single-deck coach, 4 midicoach, 3 minibus.
Chassis: 7 Mercedes, 12 Volvo.
Bodies: 1 Mercedes, 2 Onyx, 15 Plaxton, 1 Transbus.
Ops incl: local bus services, school contracts, private hire.
Livery: Blue/White.

SARGEANTS BROS LTD

MILL STREET, KINGTON HR5 3AL
Tel: 01544 230481
Fax: 01544 231892
E-mail: mike@sargeantsbros.com
Web site: www.sargeantsbros.com
Man Dir: Michael Sargeant **Man:** David Lloyd.

Fleet: 25 - 1 double-deck bus, 3 single-deck bus, 4 single-deck coach, 9 midibus, 1 midicoach, 7 minibus.
Chassis: 1 DAF, 3 Ford Transit, 1 LDV, 4 Mercedes, 9 Optare, 2 Renault, 1 Volkswagen, 4 Volvo.
Ops incl: local bus services, school contracts, private hire.
Livery: Red.
Ticket System: ERG.

SMITHS MOTORS (LEDBURY) LTD

COACH GARAGE, HOMEND, LEDBURY HR8 1BA
Tel/Fax: 01531 632953
E-mail: info@smithsmotorsledbury.com
Web site: www.smithsmotorsledbury.com
Dirs: M Sterry, Mrs C Lovering.
Fleet: 5 – 4 single-deck coach, 1 midicoach.
Chassis: 1 BMC, 4 Volvo.
Ops incl: private hire, continental tours.
Livery: White with Blue/Red/Black stripe.

STAGECOACH IN SOUTH WALES

See Torfaen

VILLAGE GREEN MOTOR SERVICES

LYSANDER YARD, CANTERBURY ROAD, SHOBDON, LEOMINSTER HR6 9NN
Tel: 01568 709053
Man Dir: R E Price.
Fleet: 6 – 1 single-deck bus, 4 single-deck coach, 1 minibus.
Chassis: 1 BMC, 1 Ford Transit, 1 Leyland, 1 Scania, 2 Volvo.
Bodies: 1 BMC, 1 Duple, 1 Ford, 1 Jonckheere, 2 Van Hool.
Ops incl: school contracts, private hire.
Livery: Green & Cream.

YEOMANS CANYON TRAVEL LTD

THE TRAVEL CENTRE, OLD SCHOOL LANE, HEREFORD HR1 1EX
Tel: 01432 356201
Fax: 01432 356206
E-mail: sales@yeomanstravel.co.uk
Web site: www.yeomanscoachholidays.com
Man Dir: N D Yeomans **Ops Man:** I Davies
Traffic Man: A Smith **Fleet Eng:** K Hopkins.
Fleet: 40 – 2 single-deck bus, 24 single-deck coach, 13 midibus, 1 midicoach.
Chassis: 2 BMC, 8 Dennis, 13 Optare, 9 Scania, 8 Volvo.
Bodies: 1 Berkhof, 2 BMC, 7 Caetano, 2 Irizar, 2 Marcopolo, 1 Marshall/MCV, 1 Northern Counties, 13 Optare, 10 Plaxton, 2 Van Hool.
Ops incl: local bus services, school contracts, excursions & tours, private hire, express, continental tours.
Liveries: Green/Cream/Orange; National Express.
Ticket System: ERG.

NOTES

A R TRAVEL LTD

34 ROESTOCK LANE, COLNEY HEATH,
ST ALBANS AL4 0PR
Tel: 01727 822404
Fax: 01727 821566
E-mail: info@artravelltd.co.uk
Web site: www.artravelltd.co.uk
Dir: Terry Hill.
Fleet: 5 – 4 midicoach, 1 minibus.
Chassis: 4 Mercedes, 1 Volkswagen.
Ops incl: school contracts, excursions &
tours, private hire.
Livery: White.

ARRIVA THE SHIRES LTD

487 DUNSTABLE ROAD, LUTON LU4 8DS
Tel: 01582 587000
Fax: 01587 587111
Web site: www.arrivabus.co.uk
Fleet Names: Arriva the Shires & Essex,
Green Line, Super Bus.
Area Man Dir: Paul Adcock **Regional
Comm Dir:** Kevin Hawkins **Regional
Fin Dir:** Beverley Lawson **Eng Dir:** Brian
Barraclough.
Fleet: 614 – 123 double-deck bus, 226 single-
deck bus, 36 single-deck coach, 171 midibus,
58 minibus.
Chassis: 56 Alexander Dennis, 96 DAF,
89 Dennis, 2 Enterprise, 7 MAN, 25 Mercedes,
72 Optare, 31 Scania, 9 Transbus, 17 Van Hool,
76 VDL, 114 Volvo, 20 Wrightbus.
Ops incl: local bus services, school contracts,
excursions & tours, private hire, express.
Liveries: Arriva UK Bus, TfL Red, Green Line,
Green Line/Easybus, Local Brands.
Ticket System: Wayfarer 3, TfL Prestige.

CENTREBUS LTD

ALBANY HOUSE, PIN GREEN,
WEDGEWOOD WAY, STEVENAGE
SG1 4PX
Tel: 0844 357 6520
E-mail: info@centrebus.com
Web site: www.centrebus.info
Dirs: Peter Harvey, David Shelley, Julian
Peddle, Keith Hayward.
Fleet (Hertfordshire): 30 – 17 midibus,
13 minibus.
Chassis: 1 Alexander Dennis, 4 DAF,
5 Dennis, 20 Optare.
Bodies: 2 Alexander, 1 Alexander Dennis,
20 Optare, 7 Plaxton.
Ops incl: local bus services.
Livery: Blue/Orange/White.
Ticket System: Wayfarer 3.
Part of the Centrebus Group

CHAMBERS COACHES
(STEVENAGE) LTD

JACKS HILL PARK OFFICE, GREAT NORTH
ROAD, GRAVELEY, HITCHIN SG4 7EG
Tel: 01438 352920
Fax: 01462 486616
E-mail: sales@chamberscoaches.com
Web site: www.chamberscoaches.com
Man Dir: Martin Chambers **Dir & Comp
Sec:** Debra Tidey.
Fleet: 29 - 19 single-deck coach, 2 midicoach,
6 minicoach, 2 minicoach.
Chassis: 1 Alexander Dennis, 1 BMC,
8 Dennis, 1 Ford Transit, 3 Irisbus, 1 LDV,
5 Mercedes, 2 Toyota, 5 Transbus, 5 Volvo.
Bodies: 1 Beulas, 1 BMC, 2 Caetano, 1 Ford,
1 LDV, 2 Marcopolo, 1 Mercedes, 15 Plaxton,
4 UVG, 1 Other.
Ops incl: school contacts, private hire.
Livery: Red/White/Blue.

COZY TRAVEL LTD

AZTEK SITE, WORKS ROAD,
LETCHWORTH SG6 1JZ
Tel: 0345 265 8888
Fax: 01462 673875
E-mail: info@cozys.co.uk
Web site: www.cozys.co.uk
Fleet Name: Cozy's.
Dirs: N Powell, G Powell, B Powell.
Fleet: 22 – 2 single-deck bus, 5 single-deck
bus, 10 single-deck coach, 1 double-deck
coach, 1 midibus, 1 midicoach, 2 minibus.
Chassis: 3 BMC, 5 Dennis, 2 Iveco, 1 MAN,
2 Mercedes, 1 Neoplan, 1 Optare, 2 Scania,
1 Toyota, 5 Volvo.
Ops incl: local bus services, private hire,
school contracts, excursions & tours,
continental tours.
Livery: White/Silver/Multicoloured.

GOLDEN BOY COACHES

JOHN TERENCE HOUSE, GEDDINGS ROAD,
HODDESDON EN11 0NT
Tel: 01992 465747
Fax: 01992 450957
E-mail: sales@goldenboy.co.uk
Web site: www.goldenboy.co.uk
Joint Man Dirs: G A McIntyre, T P McIntyre
Tran Man: G Jaikens
Ch Eng: P Murdoch.
Fleet: 37 – 16 single-deck coach,
10 midicoach, 10 minicoach, 1 MPV (8 seats).
Chassis: 2 Bova, 1 Irizar (DAF), 21 Mercedes,
1 Unvi Touring GTR MAN, 4 Van Hool, 8 Volvo.
Bodies: 2 Bova, 4 EVM, 1 Irizar, 1 Mercedes,
7 Noone Turas, 1 Optare, 3 Paramount,
4 Plaxton, 2 Unvi, 12 Van Hool.
Ops incl: private hire, school contracts,
excursions & tours, continental tours.
Livery: Black/Red/Gold.

GRAVES COACHES & MINIBUSES

134 WINFORD DRIVE, BROXBOURNE
EN10 6PN
Tel/Fax: 01992 445556
E-mail: m.graves@btinternet.com
Prop: Michael Graves.
Fleet: 2 -1 minicoach, 1 minibus.
Chassis: 1 Mercedes, 1 Toyota.
Bodies: 1 Caetano, 1 Mercedes.
Ops incl: private hire, school contracts.

HEMEL MINIBUSES

354 CHAMBERSBURY LANE, HEMEL
HEMPSTEAD HP3 8LW
Tel: 01442 265850
Web site: www.hemelminibuses.co.uk
Dir: Shirley Bunyan.
Fleet: 5 - 1 midibus, 2 midicoach, 2 minicoach.
Chassis: 1 Iveco, 1 LDV, 3 Mercedes.
Bodies: 1 Leicester, 2 Optare, 2 other.
Ops incl: school contracts, private hire.
Livery: Blue/White
Formerly traded as Terry's Coaches

KENZIES COACHES LTD

6 ANGLE LANE, SHEPRETH
SG8 6QH
Tel: 01763 260288
Fax: 01763 262012
Fleet: 20 – 2 single-deck bus, 18 single-deck
coach.
Chassis: 2 Bedford, 18 Volvo.
Bodies: 5 Plaxton, 12 Van Hool, 1 Volvo,
2 Wrightbus.
Ops incl: private hire, school contracts.
Livery: Blue with logos.

LITTLE JIM'S BUSES

5 WILLIAM FISKE HOUSE, CASTLE STREET,
BERKHAMSTED HP4 2HF
Tel: 07736 705520
E-mail: littlejimbuses@aol.com
Web site: www.littlejimsbuses.co.uk
Prop: James H Petty.
Fleet: 3 - 2 single-deck bus, 1 midicoach.
Chassis: 1 Dennis, 1 Mercedes, 1 Optare.
Bodies: 1 Alexander Dennis, 1 Mercedes,
1 Optare.
Ops incl: local bus services, school contracts,
excursions & tours, private hire, continental
tours.
Livery: Red.
Ticket System: Almex.

MARSHALLS COACHES

UNIT 4, FIRBANK WAY, LEIGHTON
BUZZARD LU7 4YP
Tel: 01525 376077
Fax: 01525 850967
E-mail: info@marshalls-coaches.co.uk
Web site: www.marshalls-coaches.co.uk
Prop: Glen Marshall.
Fleet: 35 - 7 double-deck bus, 1 single-deck
bus, 24 single-deck coach, 2 double-deck
coach, 1 midicoach.
Chassis: 3 Ayats, 3 Bova, 4 Dennis, 1 Iveco,
1 Leyland, 1 Mercedes, 2 Neoplan, 1 Scania,
19 Volvo.
Bodies: 4 Alexander, 3 Ayats, 1 Beulas,
3 Bova, 1 Caetano, 4 Jonckheere, 2 Neoplan,
13 Plaxton, 1 Scania, 1 Van Hool, 2 Other.
Ops incl: London commuter services, private
hire, school contracts.
Livery: Blue/Multicoloured.

MASTER TRAVEL COACHES

9-12 PEARTREE FARM, WELWYN GARDEN
CITY AL7 3UW
Tel: 01707 334040
Fax: 01707 334336
E-mail: mastertravel@btclick.com
Partners: R J Goulden, S Goulden.
Fleet: 4 - 1 midicoach, 3 minibus.
Chassis: 1 Iveco, 3 Mercedes.
Bodies: 1 Crest, 1 Mercedes, 1 Optare,
1 Other.
Ops incl: school contracts, private hire.
Livery: White/Blue, White

MBS PREMIER

773 ST ALBANS ROAD, WATFORD
WD25 9LA
Tel: 01923 663432
Fax: 01923 681466
E-mail: minibusservices@btconnect.com
Prop: Russ Crowson.
Fleet: 5 - 2 single-deck coach, 2 midicoach,
1 minibus.
Chassis: 1 Ford Transit, 1 Mercedes, 1 Toyota,
2 Volvo.
Bodies: 1 Caetano, 1 Ford, 1 Optare,
2 Plaxton.
Ops incl: school contracts, private hire.

MINIBUS EXECUTIVE TRAVEL

UNIT 1A, GRAYCAINE ROAD, WATFORD
WD24 7GP
Tel: 0800 037 8081
Fax: 01923 247009
E-mail: info@metcoaches.co.uk
Web site: www.metcoaches.co.uk
Fleet Name: MET Coaches.
Man Dir: P Evans.
Fleet: 23 – 7 single-deck coach, 7 midicoach,

Hertfordshire

4 minibus, 5 minicoach.
Chassis: 3 King Long, 15 Mercedes, 1 Scania, 1 Toyota, 3 Volvo.
Ops incl: school contracts, private hire.
Livery: Silver.

MULLANY'S COACHES LTD
♿ 🅿 ♨ 🏧 🍴
BROOKDELL TRANSPORT YARD, ST ALBANS ROAD, WATFORD WD25 0GB
Tel: 01923 279991
Fax: 01923 682212
E-mail: coachbookings@mullanyscoaches.com
Web site: www.mullanyscoaches.com, www.mullanysbuses.com
Dirs: J & P Kavanagh **Gen Man:** Tim Rampling.
Fleet: 55 – 17 double-deck bus, 3 single-deck bus, 16 single-deck coach, 13 midibus, 1 midicoach, 5 minibus.
Chassis: 6 Alexander Dennis, 12 Dennis, 1 Ford Transit, 2 LDV, 3 Mercedes, 8 Neoplan, 2 Optare, 1 Setra, 20 Volvo.
Bodies: 6 Alexander, 5 Alexander Dennis, 3 East Lancs, 1 Ferqui, 1 Ford, 8 Neoplan, 6 Northern Counties, 2 Optare, 13 Plaxton, 1 Setra, 2 Van Hool, 2 Wrightbus, 3 Other.
Ops incl: local bus services, Warner Studio link, school contracts, private hire.
Livery: Buses: Red and Blue;
Coaches: White with Blue Lettering.
A subsidiary of J J Kavanagh & Sons, Urlingford
(See Republic of Ireland)

PARKSIDE TRAVEL LTD
♿ 🅿
PARADISE WILDLIFE PARK, WHITE STUBBS LANE, BROXBOURNE EN10 7QA
Tel: 01992 444477
Fax: 01992 465441
E-mail: parksidetravel@pwpark.com
Fleet Name: Parkside Travel.
Dirs: P C Sampson, G F Sampson.
Fleet: 7 minibus.
Ops incl: school contracts, private hire.
Livery: Light Blue

PROVENCE PRIVATE HIRE
(P.P.H. COACHES)
♿ 🅿 ♨
HEATH FARM LANE, ST ALBANS AL3 5AE
Tel: 01727 864988
Fax: 01727 855275
E-mail: office@pphcoaches.com
Web site: www.pphcoaches.com
Dirs: A K Hayes, R F Hayes
Ch Eng: D Higgins.
Fleet: 32 – 4 double-deck bus, 21 single-deck coach, 1 double-deck coach, 3 midicoach, 2 minibus, 1 minicoach.
Chassis: 4 Bova, 1 DAF, 4 Dennis, 1 Ford Transit, 1 LDV, 2 Leyland, 3 Mercedes, 10 Scania, 1 Toyota, 1 VDL, 4 Volvo.
Bodies: 3 Autobus, 1 Berkhof, 4 Bova, 2 Caetano, 1 Duple, 4 East Lancs, 1 Ford, 1 Hispano, 6 Irizar, 1 LDV, 6 Plaxton, 2 UVG.
Ops incl: school contracts, excursions & tours, private hire, continental tours.
Livery: Yellow.

REG'S COACHES LTD
🅿 ♨ ♨ 🎫 📞 🚻
113 - 115 CODICOTE ROAD, WELWYN AL6 9TY
Tel: 01483 822000
Fax: 01483 822003
E-mail: regscoaches@btconnect.com
Web site: www.regscoaches.com
Man Dir: Mr T Hunt **Dir:** Mrs B Hunt.
Fleet: 16 – 1 single-deck bus, 12 single-deck coach, 3 midicoach.
Chassis: 5 Dennis, 3 Mercedes, 8 Volvo.
Bodies: 1 Autobus, 1 Berkhof, 1 Mercedes,

1 Northern Counties, 9 Plaxton, 1 Sitcar, 2 Van Hool, 1 Wrightbus.
Ops incl: local bus services, school contracts, excursions & tours, private hire.
Livery: Multi Coloured.
Ticket System: Wayfarer 2/Almex.

REYNOLDS DIPLOMAT COACHES
🅿 🏧 🍴 ♨ 🚻
GROUND HOUSE, GRAHAM CLOSE, ST ALBANS AL1 2QZ
Tel: 01923 213880
Fax: 01923 210020
E-mail: enquiries@reynoldscoaches.com
Web site: www.reynoldscoaches.com
Partners: Richard Reynolds, Mrs Susan Reynolds.
Fleet: 32 – 23 single-deck coach, 4 midicoach, 4 minibus, 1 minicoach.
Chassis: 2 Ford Transit, 1 Irisbus, 1 LDV, 1 MAN, 5 Mercedes, 3 Scania, 1 Setra, 1 Toyota, 17 Volvo.
Bodies: 1 Autobus, 3 Berkhof, 1 Beulas, 1 Caetano, 2 Ford, 14 Jonckheere, 1 Noge, 1 Setra, 4 Unvi, 3 Van Hool, 1 Other.
Ops incl: school contracts, excursions & tours, private hire, continental tours.
Livery: Green/Gold/White.

PETER REYNOLDS COACHES
🅿 ♨
SPRING COTTAGES, ELTON WAY, BUSHEY, WATFORD WD2 8HB
Tel: 01923 841174
Web site: www.peterreynoldscoaches.co.uk
Prop: P J Reynolds.
Fleet: 14 – 1 double-deck bus, 3 single-deck bus, 8 single-deck coach, 2 minicoach.
Chassis: 3 Dennis, 1 Irisbus, 3 Mercedes, 1 Toyota, 6 Volvo.
Ops incl: local bus services, school contracts, private hire.
Livery: White with Black lettering.

RICHMOND'S COACHES
♿ 🏧 🅿 ♨ 🚻
THE GARAGE, HIGH STREET, BARLEY, ROYSTON SG8 8JA
Tel: 01763 848226
Fax: 01763 848105
E-mail: postbox@richmonds-coaches.co.uk
Web site: www.richmonds-coaches.co.uk
Dirs: David Richmond, Michael Richmond, Andrew Richmond **Sales & Marketing Man:** Rick Ellis **Asst Ops Man:** Craig Ellis
Ch Eng: Patrick Granville **Exc & Tours Man:** Natalie Richmond.
Fleet: 23 – 15 single-deck coach, 3 double-deck coach, 3 midibus, 2 midicoach, 1 minibus.
Chassis: 8 Bova, 3 Mercedes, 2 Optare, 7 Van Hool, 3 Volvo.
Bodies: 8 Bova, 2 Optare, 1 Plaxton, 2 Sitcar, 10 Van Hool.
Ops incl: local bus services, school contracts, excursions & tours, private hire, continental tours.
Livery: Cream/Brown.
Ticket System: Wayfarer 3.

ST MARGARETS TRAVEL LTD
🅿 🏧 🍴 ♨ 🚻
99 THE MALTINGS, STANSTEAD ABBOTS, WARE SG12 8HG
Tel: 01920 871280   **Fax:** 01920 872855
E-mail: info@stansted-airport-coach-hire.co.uk
Web site: www.stansted-airport-coach-hire.co.uk
Fleet: 8 – 4 single-deck coach, 2 midicoach, 2 minibus.
Chassis: 1 Bova, 1 LDV, 1 MAN, 5 Mercedes.
Ops incl: excursions & tours, private hire, continental tours.
Livery: Silver, White.

SMITH BUNTINGFORD
♿
CLAREMONT, BALDOCK ROAD, BUNTINGFORD SG9 9DJ
Tel/Fax: 01763 271516
Prop: Graham H Smith **Fleet Eng:** Stewart C Smith.
Fleet: 7 – 1 midibus, 1 midicoach, 4 minibus, 1 minicoach.
Chassis: 7 Mercedes.
Ops incl: private hire, school contracts.
Livery: White/Orange.

SMITHS OF TRING
🅿 ♨ ♨ 🍴
THE GARAGE, WIGGINTON HP23 6EJ
Tel: 01442 823163
Fax: 01442 824799
E-mail: enquiries@smithsoftring.co.uk
Web site: www.smithsoftring.co.uk
Dirs: G A Smith **(Man Dir)**, Mrs S N Smith, J Smith.
Fleet: 8 – 6 single-deck coach, 2 minibus.
Chassis: 2 Ford Transit, 6 Volvo.
Bodies: 2 Ford, 3 Jonckheere, 2 Plaxton, 1 Sunsundegui.
Ops incl: excursions & tours, private hire, continental tours.
Livery: Red/Yellow.

SOUTH MIMMS TRAVEL LTD
🏧 🅿 ♨ 📞
29 EAST BURROWFIELD, WELWYN GARDEN CITY AL7 4SS
Tel: 01707 322555
Fax: 08707 627292
E-mail: office@southmimmstravel.co.uk
Web site: www.southmimmstravel.co.uk
Man Dir: S J Griffiths.
Fleet: 22 – 3 double-deck bus, 11 single-deck coach, 3 midibus, 3 midicoach, 2 minibus.
Chassis: 4 Bova, 3 Dennis, 4 Mercedes, 1 Vauxhall, 9 Volvo.
Bodies: 2 Alexander, 4 Bova, 2 East Lancs, 1 Jonckheere, 1 Marshall, 8 Plaxton, 1 UVG, 2 Van Hool, 1 Vauxhall.
Ops incl: school contracts, excursions & tours, private hire, continental tours.
Livery: Red/Black/Gold.

SULLIVAN BUS & COACH LTD
♿ 🅿 ⬛
FIRST FLOOR, DEARDS HOUSE ST ALBANS ROAD, POTTERS BAR EN6 3NE
Tel: 01707 646803
Fax: 01707 646804
E-mail: admin@sullivanbuses.com
Web site: www.sullivanbuses.co.uk
Man Dir: Dean Sullivan **Co Sec:** Mala Singelee **Eng Man:** Neal Hogg.
Fleet: 63 – 39 double-deck bus, 4 single-deck bus, 20 midibus.
Chassis: 12 Alexander Dennis, 6 AEC, 20 Dennis, 1 Leyland, 1 MCW, 6 Transbus, 17 Volvo.
Bodies: 12 Alexander Dennis, 7 Alexander, 4 Caetano, 1 Duple, 14 East Lancs, 1 MCW, 7 Park Royal, 11 Plaxton, 2 Transbus, 4 Wrightbus.
Ops incl: local bus services, school contracts, private hire, rail replacement
Livery: Red.
Ticket system: Wayfarer TGX; TfL Prestige.

TATES COACHES
🅿 🏧 ♨ 📞
44 HIGH STREET, MARKYATE AL3 8PA
Tel: 01582 840297
Fax: 01582 840014
E-mail: info@tates-coaches.co.uk
Web site: www.tatescoaches.co.uk
Dir & Co Sec: Alan M Tate
Dirs: Anthony J Tate, Stephen W Tate
Fleet: 9 – 1 double-deck bus, 8 single-deck coach

Chassis: I Bova, I DAF, I Dennis, I EOS, I MAN, I Mercedes, 3 Scania.
Bodies: I Bova, I Caetano, I EOS, I Hispano, 2 Irizar, I Neoplan, I Plaxton, I Van Hool.
Ops incl: school contracts, excursions & tours, private hire, continental tours.
Livery: Blue/Cream/Orange.

RICHARD TAYLOR TRAVEL
⚒👫🔛🔧
ST IBBS FARMHOUSE, LONDON ROAD, ST IPPOLYTS, HITCHIN SG4 7NL
Tel: 01462 442409
Fax: 01462 442493
E-mail: rtaylor2004@tiscali.co.uk
Web site: www.richardtaylortravel.co.uk
Props: Mr & Mrs R W J Taylor
Ops Man: R J Lush.
Fleet: 15 – 6 single-deck coach, I midicoach, 8 minibus.
Chassis: I BMC, I Ford Transit, I Iveco, 7 LDV, 4 Scania, I Volvo.
Bodies: I Beulas, I BMC, I Ford Transit, 4 Irizar, I Jonckheere, 6 LDV, I Other.
Ops incl: school contracts, excursions & tours, private hire, continental tours.
Livery: White with Blue/Red.

THREE STAR (LUTON) LIMITED
⚒👫🔛🍴
UNIT 1, GUARDIAN BUSINESS PARK, DALLOW ROAD, LUTON LUI INA
Tel: 01582 722626
Fax: 01582 484034
E-mail: sales@threestarcoaches.com
Web Site: www.threestarcoaches.com
Man Dir: Colin Dudley **Ops Man:** Kevin Green **Ch Eng:** Andrew North **Co Sec:** Isabelle Dudley.
Fleet: 15 – 13 single-deck coach, 2 double-deck coach.
Chassis: 2 Dennis, 2 Iveco, 2 MAN, 2 Mercedes, 2 Scania, 5 Volvo.
Bodies: 2 Ayats, 4 Berkhof, I Hispano, I Irizar, 5 Plaxton, 2 Sunsundegui.
Ops incl: school contracts, excursions & tours, private hire, continental tours.
Livery: Blue.

TIMEBUS TRAVEL
See London

UNICORN COACHES
👫🍴🔛
PO BOX 45, HATFIELD AL9 5LD
Tel: 0845 658 5000
E-mail: unicorncoaches@aol.com
Man Dir: Mrs J E Pleshette **Gen Man:** S T Saltmarsh.
Ops incl: private hire, continental tours.
Livery: White.

UNO (UNIVERSITYBUS LTD)
♿✏️
GYPSY MOTH AVENUE, HATFIELD BUSINESS PARK, HATFIELD AL10 9BS
Tel: 01707 255764
E-mail: unobus@herts.ac.uk
Web site: www.unobus.info
Man Dir: Jim Thorpe **Fin Dir:** Alistair Moffat.
Fleet: 117 - 17 double deck bus, 22 single deck bus, 73 midibus, 5 articulated bus.
Chassis: 12 Alexander Dennis, 6 DAF, 27 Dennis, 23 Mercedes, 13 Optare, 9 Scania, 17 Transbus, 5 Volvo, 5 Wrightbus.
Bodies: 4 Alexander, 4 Alexander Dennis, 11 Caetano, 6 East Lancs, 4 MCV, 23 Mercedes, 14 Optare, 17 Plaxton, 4 Scania, 17 Transbus, 13 Wrightbus.
Ops incl: local bus services, school contracts.
Livery: Pink/Purple.
Ticket System: Wayfarer 3 Inform.
Also operates in Bedfordshire/ Buckinghamshire and Northampton

A L S TRAVEL
👫✏️🔛
SPITHEAD BUSINESS CENTRE, NEWPORT ROAD, LAKE, SANDOWN PO36 9PH
Tel: 01983 401100
E-mail: info@alstravel.co.uk
Web site: www.alstravel.co.uk
Prop: A L Scott.
Fleet: 17 – 16 single-deck coach, I midicoach.
Chassis: I BMC, I DAF, I Dennis, I MAN, I Neoplan, 12 Volvo.
Ops incl: school contracts, excursions & tours, private hire.
Livery: White.

GANGES COACHES
✏️🔛
77 PLACE ROAD, COWES PO31 7AE
Tel/Fax: 01983 296666
E-mail: info@gangescoaches.com
Web site: www.gangescoaches.com
Prop: John Gange.
Fleet: 6 - I single-deck coach, 3 midicoach, 2 minibus.
Chassis: I Leyland, 2 Mercedes, I Renault, I Setra, I Vauxhall.
Bodies: 2 Plaxton, I Setra, 3 Other.
Ops incl: private hire.
Liveries: Red/Cream, Blue/Cream, Silver, White.

GO SOUTH COAST LTD
♿👫🔛✏️🔛
TOWNGATE HOUSE, 2-8 PARKSTONE ROAD, POOLE BH15 2PR
Tel: 01202 680888
Fax: 01202 670244
E-mail: talk2us@southernvectis.com
Web sites: www.islandbuses.info
www.go-ahead.com
Fleet Names (IOW): Southern Vectis, Vectis Blue.
Chairman: David Brown
Man Dir: Andrew Wickham
Eng Dir: Steve Hamilton
Fin Dir: Nick Woods
Ops Dir: Ed Wills.
Fleet: 750 - 321 double-deck bus, 134 single-deck bus, 101 single-deck coach, 10 articulated bus, 88 midibus, 96 minibus.
Chassis: 118 Alexander Dennis, 2 Bristol, 62 DAF, 14 Dennis, I Ford, 4 Iveco, I LDV, 20 Leyland, 59 Mercedes, 123 Optare, 127 Scania, 219 Volvo.
Bodies: 121 Alexander Dennis, I Autobus, 4 Beulas, 6 Caetano, 56 East Lancs, 2 ECW, I Ford, 2 Ikarus, 11 Irizar, 3 Jonckheere, I LDV, 57 Mercedes, 44 Northern Counties, 169 Optare, 86 Plaxton, 73 Scania, 22 Van Hool, 91 Wrightbus.
Ops incl: local bus services, school contracts.
Liveries: Southern Vectis: Green;
Vectis Blue: Blue.
Ticket System: Vix ITSO Smart.
Part of the Go-Ahead Group. See also operations in Dorset, Hampshire, Wiltshire.

KARDAN TRAVEL LTD
👫🍴✏️🔛
1ST FLOOR, 35A ST JAMES STREET, NEWPORT PO30 ILG
Tel: 01983 520995
Fax: 01983 821288
E-mail: info@kardan.co.uk
Web site: www.kardan.co.uk
Dirs: R Hodgson, L Hodgson.
Fleet: 5 single-deck coach.
Chassis: 2 Scania, 3 Setra.
Bodies: 2 Irizar, 3 Setra.
Ops incl: excursions & tours, private hire, continental tours.
Livery: Yellow/White.

A & M A ROBINSON SEAVIEW SERVICES LTD
✏️👫🍴🔛▧🔛R24🔧T
UNIT 10, EAST YAR INDUSTRIAL ESTATE, EAST YAR ROAD, SANDOWN PO36 9AX
Tel: 01983 407070, 400247
Fax: 01983 405647
Recovery: 07753 566826
E-mail: info@seaview-services.co.uk
Web site: www.seaview-services.co.uk
Chairman: Philip Robinson **Ops Mans:** Mairi Robinson, Peter Gray
Eng: D H Price Motors.
Fleet: 7 - 6 single-deck coach, I minibus.
Chassis: I DAF, 2 MAN, I Mercedes, I Setra, 2 Volvo.
Ops incl: school contracts, excursions & tours, private hire, continental tours, express.
Livery: Green/Red.

THE SOUTHERN VECTIS OMNIBUS CO LTD
See Go South Coast Ltd

JOHN WOODHAMS VINTAGE TOURS
🔛
WOODSTOCK, GROVE ROAD, RYDE PO33 3LH
Tel: 01983 812147
E-mail: vintagetours@btconnect.com
Web site: www.vintage-tours.co.uk
Prop: John Woodhams.
Fleet: 3 midicoach.
Chassis: 3 Bedford.
Bodies: 3 Duple.
Ops incl: excursions & tours, private hire.
Livery: Two tone Green.

Isle of Wight

AMB TRAVEL
ASHFORD MINIBUSES
PASSENGER PLUS

45 KINGSNORTH ROAD, ASHFORD TN23 6JB
Tel: 01233 626952
Fax: 01233 620117
E-mail: enquiries@amb-travel.co.uk
Web site: www.ashford-minibuses.co.uk
Depots at: Ashford, Tadworth (Surrey).
Man Dir: Kevin Hughes.
Fleet: single-deck coach, midicoach, minibus.
Chassis: Mercedes, Setra.
Ops incl: private hire.
Livery: Silver.

ARRIVA SOUTHERN COUNTIES

INVICTA HOUSE, ARMSTRONG ROAD,
MAIDSTONE ME15 6TX
Tel: 01622 697000
Fax: 01622 697001
Web site: www.arriva.co.uk
Fleet Names: Arriva Kent & Surrey, Arriva
Kent Thameside, Arriva Southend, New
Enterprise Coaches.
Regional Man Dir: Heath Williams
Regional Comm Dir: Kevin Hawkins
Regional Fin Dir: Beverley Lawson **Eng
Dir:** Tony Ward.
Fleet: 617 – 148 double-deck bus, 116 single-
deck bus, 23 single-deck coach, 313 midibus,
2 midicoach, 14 minibus, 1 open-top bus.
Chassis: 130 Alexander Dennis, 129 DAF,
135 Dennis, 12 Mercedes, 65 Optare, 8 Scania,
1 Transbus, 15 VDL, 110 Volvo, 12 Wrightbus.
Bodies: 129 Alexander Dennis, 74 Alexander,
2 Berkhof, 5 Caetano, 14 East Lancs, 3 Irizar,
9 Mercedes, 4 Northern Counties, 65 Optare,
100 Plaxton, 60 Transbus, 1 Van Hool,
161 Wrightbus.
Ops incl: local bus services, school contracts,
excursions & tours, express, continental tours,
private hire.
Liveries: Arriva UK Bus; TfL Red; White/Red/
Blue (New Enterprise).
Ticket System: Wayfarer 3 & TGX150;
TfL Prestige.

ASM COACHES

15 HAWE FARM ROAD, BROOMFIELD
CT6 7UD
Tel/Fax: 01227 280254
E-mail: info@asmcoaches.co.uk
Web site: www.asmcoaches.co.uk
Prop/Ops Man: Steve Morrish.
Fleet: 3 minicoach (up to 22 seats).
Chassis: 1 Fiat, 1 Iveco, 1 Mercedes.
Ops incl: school contracts, private hire.
Livery: Silver/Purple.

AUTOCAR BUS & COACH SERVICES
LTD

64 WHETSTED ROAD, FIVE OAK GREEN,
TONBRIDGE TN12 6RT
Tel: 01892 833830
Fax: 01892 836977
Dir: Julian Brown **Ops Dir:** Eric Baldock.
Fleet: 22 – 8 double-deck bus, 6 single-deck
bus, 2 single-deck coach, 9 midibus, 3 minibus.
Chassis: 2 AEC, 1 Alexander Dennis, 1 DAF,
8 Dennis, 2 Leyland, 1 MAN, 1 Mercedes,
2 Optare, 1 Scania, 9 Volvo.
Bodies: 8 Alexander, 1 Alexander Dennis, 1
East Lancs, 1 Marshall, 1 MCV, 2 Optare,
2 Park Royal, 10 Plaxton, 2 Wrightbus.
Ops incl: local bus services, private hire.
Livery: White/Purple/Pink.
Ticket System: Wayfarer 2.

BAYLISS EXECUTIVE TRAVEL LTD

UNIT 7, DEAL BUSINESS PARK,
SOUTHWALL ROAD, DEAL CT14 9PZ
Tel: 01304 363600
E-mail: enquiries@baylissexecutivetravel.
co.uk
Web site: www.baylissexecutivetravel.co.uk
Dir: A Bayliss.
Fleet: 12 – 1 double-deck coach, 7 single-
deck coach, 2 midicoach, 2 minibus.
Chassis: 2 Mercedes, 2 Volkswagen, 8 Volvo.
Ops incl: excursions & tours, private hire,
London commuter express.
Livery: White.

BRITANNIA COACHES LTD

HOLLOW WOOD ROAD, DOVER
CT17 0UB
Tel: 01304 228111
Fax: 01304 215350
E-mail: enquiries@britannia-coaches.co.uk
Web site: www.britannia-coaches.co.uk
Partners: Barry Watson, Danny Lawson.
Fleet: 19 minicoach.
Chassis: 1 Ford, 9 Mercedes, 9 Renault.
Ops incl: private hire, school contracts,
excursions & tours.
Livery: White with Blue/Red.

BROOKLINE COACHES LTD

THE STREET, RYARSH, WEST MALLING
ME19 5LQ
Tel: 01732 845656
Fax: 01732 221577
E-mail: info@brooklinecoaches.co.uk
Web site: www.brooklinecoaches.co.uk
Dirs: D Brooks, R Brooks.
Fleet: 11 – 1 double-deck bus, 2 double-deck
coach, 5 single-deck coach, 1 midibus,
1 midicoach, 1 minicoach.
Chassis: 1 Dennis, 1 Temsa, 1 Toyota,
5 Van Hool, 1 VDL, 2 Volvo.
Ops incl: school contracts, private hire,
London commuter express, excursions &
tours, continental tours.
Livery: Green/Cream.

BUZZLINES TRAVEL LTD

LYMPNE DISTRIBUTION PARK, HYTHE
CT21 4LR
Tel: 01303 261870
Fax: 01303 230093
E-mail: info@buzzlinestravel.co.uk
Web site: www.buzzlinestravel.co.uk
Chairman: Lynn Woods **Man Dir:** Adrian
Gilson **Ops Dir:** Nigel Busbridge.
Fleet: 18 – 4 double-deck bus, 9 single-deck
coach, 2 midibus, 3 minibus.
Chassis: 1 Alexander Dennis, 3 Dennis,
2 Irizar, 3 Mercedes, 1 Neoplan, 5 Setra,
1 Transbus, 1 Van Hool, 1 Volvo.
Ops incl: local bus services, school contracts,
excursions & tours, private hire, London
commuter express, continental tours.
Livery: White with Blue.

BZEE BUS & TRAVEL LTD

UNIT 2F, DEACON TRADING ESTATE,
FORSTAL ROAD, AYLESFORD ME20 7SP
Tel: 01622 882288
Fax: 01622 718070
Dirs: D Quick, N Kemp.
Associated with Nu-Venture Coaches Ltd

CAROL PETERS TRAVEL

TIMBERYARD INDUSTRIAL ESTATE,
MANSTON ROAD, RAMSGATE CT12 6HJ

Tel: 01843 591007
Fax: 01843 586466
E-mail: info@carolpeterstravel.com
Web site: www.carolpeterstravel.co.uk
Props: C Howe, P Howe.
Fleet: 20 – 2 double-deck bus, 7 single-deck
coach, 6 midibus, 1 midicoach, 2 minibus,
2 minicoach.
Chassis: 7 Dennis, 1 LDV, 3 Mercedes,
6 Setra, 1 Toyota, 2 Volvo.
Ops incl: private hire, excursions & tours,
continental tours.
Livery: White.

CENTAUR TRAVEL

UNIT 34-35, ACORN INDUSTRIAL PARK,
CRAYFORD DA1 4AL
Tel: 020 8300 3001
Fax: 020 8302 5959
E-mail: info@centaurtravel.co.uk
Web site: www.centaurtravel.co.uk
Man Dir: M. Sims **Dirs:** P Sims, S Durrant.
Fleet: 35 – 2 double-deck bus, 15 single-deck
coach, 4 midicoach, 13 minibus, 1 minicoach.
Chassis: 2 Alexander Dennis, 4 Ford Transit,
4 LDV, 3 MAN, 11 Mercedes, 3 Renault,
4 Scania, 1 Vauxhall, 4 Volvo.
Ops incl: private hire, school contracts,
excursions & tours, London commuter
express.

CENTRAL EXECUTIVE TRAVEL

177 LOWER ROAD, DOVER CT17 1RE
Tel: 01304 204040
Fax: 01304 828922
E-mail: phull4321@aol.com
Web site: www.centralexectravel.co.uk
Prop: P Hull.
Fleet: 2 minibus.
Chassis: 2 Mercedes.
Ops incl: private hire, school contracts.
Livery: White with Blue.

CHALKWELL COACH HIRE & TOURS

195 CHALKWELL ROAD, SITTINGBOURNE
ME10 1BJ
Tel: 01795 423982
Fax: 01795 431855
E-mail: coachhire@chalkwell.co.uk
Web site: www.chalkwell.co.uk
Fleet Name: Chalkwell
Man Dir: Clive Eglinton
Gen Man: Andy Bates.
Fleet: 78 - 5 double-deck bus, 29 single-deck
coach, 24 midibus, 2 midicoach, 18 minibus.
Chassis: 1 DAF, 16 Dennis, 2 Iveco,
9 Mercedes, 11 Optare, 11 Renault, 11 Scania,
1 Volkswagen, 16 Volvo.
Ops incl: local bus services, school contracts,
excursions & tours, private hire, London
commuter services, continental tours.
Livery: White/Red/Black.
Ticket System: Ticketer.

CROSSKEYS COACHES LTD

CROSSKEYS BUSINESS PARK, CAESARS
WAY, FOLKESTONE CT19 4AL
Tel: 01303 272625
Fax: 01303 274085
E-mail: info@crosskeys.uk.com
Web site: www.crosskeys.uk.com
Dir: Alan Johnson.
Fleet: 22 – 1 double-deck bus, 19 single-deck
coach, 2 minibus.
Chassis: 1 Alexander Dennis, 9 Bova,
1 Dennis, 2 Mercedes, 5 Setra, 1 Transbus,
3 Volvo.
Bodies: 1 Autobus, 9 Bova, 1 Northern

Counties, 4 Plaxton, 5 Setra, I Transbus,
I Other.
Ops incl: school contracts, excursions &
tours, private hire, continental tours.
Livery: Orange.

DJ COACHES LTD
♿ ⚌ 🚻 ❄
7 MARK LANE, GRAVESEND DA12 2QB
Tel: 01322 552222
E-mail: enquiries@djcoaches.co.uk
Web site: www.djcoaches.co.uk
Dirs: D W & J C Blanks.
Fleet: 24 – 17 single-deck coach, 4 midicoach,
I minibus, 2 minicoach.
Chassis: I Irisbus, 6 Mercedes, I Scania,
14 Setra, 2 Van Hool.
Ops incl: private hire, excursions & tours.
Livery: White with Orange.

EASTONWAYS LTD
Ceased trading since LRB 2014 went to press

FARLEIGH COACHES
♿ ❄
UNIT E, HOO INDUSTRIAL ESTATE,
VICARAGE LANE, HOO, ROCHESTER
ME3 9LB
Tel: 01634 254000   **Fax:** 01634 254009
E-mail: info@farleighcoaches.com
Web site: www.farleighcoaches.com
Prop: D R Smith.
Fleet: 13 – 5 double-deck bus, I single-deck
bus, 3 single-deck coach, I midicoach,
3 minibus.
Chassis: 5 Mercedes, 8 Volvo.
Ops incl: local bus services, school contracts,
private hire.
Livery: Yellow/Red.

GO-COACH HIRE LTD
♿ ⚌
VESTRY ROAD ESTATE, OTFORD TN14 5EL
Tel: 01732 469800
E-mail: info@go-coach.co.uk
Web site: www.go-coach.co.uk
Man Dir: Austin Blackburn.
Fleet: 37 – 13 double-deck bus, I single-deck
bus, I single-deck coach, 19 midibus, 3 minibus.
Chassis: I AEC, 6 DAF, 13 Dennis, I King
Long, 2 Mercedes, I Optare, I Scania,
2 Transbus, 10 Volvo.
Ops incl: local bus services, school contracts,
private hire.
Livery: Yellow/Purple.

JAY & KAY COACH TOURS
🚻 ⚌ ❄
8 THE PARADE, CRAYFORD WAY,
CRAYFORD DA1 4ja
Tel: 01322 522400
E-mail: lisa@jayandkaycoachtours.co.uk
Web site: www.jayandkaycoachtours.co.uk
Prop: K Brazier.
Fleet: 5 single-deck coach.
Chassis: 2 Bova, 2 Mercedes, I Neoplan.
Ops incl: excursions & tours.
Livery: White with Blue.

JEWELS TOURS
⚌ 🚻 ❄ 🍴
56 NEW ROAD, GRAVESEND DA11 0AD
Tel: 01474 334434
Fax: 01474 322622
E-mail: jeweltours@btconnect.com
Web site: www.jewelstours.co.uk
Man Dir: J Loynes **Dirs:** M Hafner,
P Hafner.
Fleet: 2 single-deck coach.
Chassis: Scania.
Bodies: Irizar.
Ops incl: private hire, excursions & tours,
continental tours.
Livery: Blue

KENT COACH TOURS LTD
♿ ⚌ 🚻 ❄ Ⓡ 🚾 T
THE COACH STATION, MALCOLM
SARGENT ROAD, ASHFORD TN23 6JW
Tel/Recovery: 01233 627330
Fax: 01233 612977
E-mail: sales@kentcoachtours.co.uk
Web site: www.kentcoachtours.co.uk
Dirs: David Farmer, Ann Farmer, Andrew
Farmer **(Co Sec)**, Brian Farmer
(Ch Eng).
Fleet: 13 – I double-deck bus, 8 single-deck
coach, 4 midibus.
Chassis: I Dennis, I Irisbus, 3 Mercedes,
8 Volvo.
Bodies: I East Lancs, 12 Plaxton.
Ops incl: local bus services, school contracts,
excursions & tours, private hire.
Livery: Two Tone Blue.
Ticket System: Wayfarer.

THE KINGS FERRY LTD
♿ ⚌ 🚻 🍴 ❄ T
THE TRAVEL CENTRE, GILLINGHAM
ME8 6HW
Tel: 01634 377577   **Fax:** 01634 370656
E-mail: sales@thekingsferry.co.uk
Web site: www.thekingsferry.co.uk
Ops Dir: Ian Fraser **Comm Dir:** Danny
Elford **Head of Ops:** Nadene Curley
Eng Man: Mick Keohane.
Fleet: 65 – I single-deck bus, 50 single-deck
coach, 6 double-deck coach, 6 midicoach,
2 minicoach.
Chassis: 2 Iveco, 17 Mercedes, 19 Scania,
2 VDL, 25 Volvo.
Bodies: 6 Berkhof, 32 Caetano, I Castrosua,
2 Indcar, 10 Irizar, 4 Mercedes, 2 Plaxton,
4 Sunsundegui, 2 Van Hool.
Ops incl: local bus services, school contracts,
private hire, London commuter express,
Bristol commuter express, continental tours.
Livery: Yellow with Green stripe; Silver.
Part of the National Express Group

KINGSMAN INTERNATIONAL
TRAVEL
♿ 🚻 🍴 ⚌ ❄ 🧳
57 BRAMLEY AVENUE, FAVERSHAM
ME13 8LP
Tel: 01795 531553   **Fax:** 01795 536798
E-mail: jonathanamancini@tiscali.co.uk
Props: J A Mancini, J Mancini.
Fleet: 12 – 4 single-deck coach, 6 midicoach,
2 minibus.
Chassis: I BMC, 5 Mercedes, 3 Neoplan,
I Renault, 2 Setra.
Ops incl: local bus services, excursions &
tours, private hire, continental tours.

LEHANE TRAVEL LTD
🚻 ⚌ ❄
BREDLANDS LANE, STURRY, CANTERBURY
CT2 0HD
Tel: 01227 710493
E-mail: info@lehanetravel.co.uk
Web site: www.lehanetravel.co.uk
Fleet: 17 – 15 single-deck coach, 2 midicoach.
Chassis: I BMC, 2 MAN, I Mercedes,
I Scania, 12 Volvo.
Ops incl: school contracts, private hire.
Livery: Blue/White.

LEO'S PRIDE LTD
⚌ 🚻 ❄
259 CANTERBURY ROAD, HERNE BAY
CT6 7HD
Tel: 01227 363636
E-mail: leospride@lineone.net
Web site: www.leospride.co.uk
Fleet: 6 single-deck coach.
Chassis: I MAN, 2 Neoplan, 3 Scania.
Ops incl: private hire.
Livery: Light Green

LONDON BUS COMPANY LTD
🚌 🚍
UNITS 1-4, NORTHFLEET INDUSTRIAL
ESTATE, LOWER ROAD, NORTHFLEET
DA11 9SN
Tel: 01474 361199
Fax: 01474 361188
E-mail: info@thelondonbuscompany.co.uk
Web site: www.thelondonbuscompany.co.uk
Man Dir: Roger Wright.
Fleet: double-deck bus, single-deck bus,
heritage vehicles.
Ops incl: private hire.
Livery: Red.

MANNS TRAVEL LTD
⚌ 🚻 ❄
ENTERPRISE HOUSE, NORFOLK ROAD,
GRAVESEND DA12 2AX
Tel: 01474 358194
E-mail: gina@mannstravel.co.uk
Web site: www.mannstravel.co.uk
Fleet: 24 - I single-deck bus, 20 single-deck
coach, 2 midicoach, I minibus.
Chassis: I Bova, 2 DAF, I Irisbus, I Iveco,
I MAN, 2 Mercedes, 16 Volvo.
Ops incl: school contracts, excursions &
tours, private hire, continental tours.
Livery: White with Red/Yellow/Blue.

NEW ENTERPRISE COACHES
See Arriva Southern Counties.

NU-VENTURE COACHES LTD
♿ ⚌ 🚻 🍴 ❄
UNIT 2F, DEACON TRADING ESTATE,
FORSTAL ROAD, AYLESFORD ME20 7SP
Tel: 01622 882288
Fax: 01622 718070
E-mail: nuventurecoachesltd@yahoo.co.uk
Web site: www.nu-venture.co.uk
Dir: D Quick **Co Sec:** N Kemp.
Fleet: 59 – 11 double-deck bus, 7 single-deck
bus, 41 midibus.
Chassis: I Alexander Dennis, 30 Dennis,
11 Leyland, 5 Optare, 5 Transbus, 7 Volvo.
Ops incl: local bus services, school contracts,
private hire, excursions & tours.
Livery: Two Tone Green
Ticket System: Wayfarer 3

PLAN IT TRAVEL LTD
See London & Middlesex

POYNTERS COACHES LTD
🚻 ⚌ ❄
WYE BUSINESS PARK, CHURCHFIELD WAY,
WYE TN25 5BX
Tel: 01233 812002
Fax: 01233 813210
Recovery: 07770 874631
E-mail: poyntercoaches@aol.com
Web site: www.poyntersofwyecoaches.co.uk
Man Dir: B Poynter **Ch Eng:** B Poynter.
Fleet: 14 - 2 double-deck bus, 5 single-deck
bus, 7 single-deck coach.
Chassis: I Bova, 2 Dennis, 11 Volvo.
Ops incl: local bus services, school contracts,
excursions & tours, private hire, continental
tours.
Livery: White.
Ticket System: Wayfarer.

PREMIERE TRAVEL
🚻 ⚌ ❄ 🍴
7 ST MARY'S GREEN, BIGGIN HILL
TN16 3RB
Tel: 01959 576519
Web site: www.kentcoaches.co.uk
Prop: C Summerscales.
Fleet: 5 single-deck coach.
Chassis: 2 Scania, 3 Setra.
Ops incl: private hire.
Livery: Blue.

R. K. F. TRAVEL
R24

22 BROMPTON FARM ROAD, ROCHESTER
ME2 3QY
Tel/Fax: 01634 715897
Dir: Ray Fraser.
Fleet: 1 minibus.
Chassis: 1 Mercedes.
Ops incl: private hire.

THE RAINHAM COACH COMPANY LTD

1A SPRINGFIELD ROAD, GILLINGHAM
ME7 1YJ
Tel: 01634 852020
Fax: 01634 582020
Recovery: 07850 657653
E-mail: info@rainhamcoach.co.uk
Web site: www.rainhamcoach.co.uk
Senior Partner: David Graham
Gen Man: Richard Graham.
Fleet: 22 – 1 single-deck coach, 3 midicoach,
18 minicoach.
Chassis: 3 Ford Transit, 19 Mercedes.
Ops incl: school contracts, excursions &
tours, private hire.
Livery: Purple & Grey on White.

REDROUTE BUSES LTD

GRANBY COACHWORKS, GROVE ROAD,
NORTHFLEET DA11 9AX
Tel: 0800 234 6842
Fax: 01424 358475
E-mail: redroutebuses@btconnect.com
Web site: www.redroutebuses.co.uk
Ops Dir: Jason Mee **Eng Dir:** Terry Mee
Tran Man: Peter Brown.
Fleet: 27 – 14 double-deck bus, 1 single-deck
bus, 3 single-deck coach, 5 midibus, 1 open
top bus.
Chassis: 5 AEC Routemaster, 1 DAF,
1 Daimler, 3 Dennis, 3 Leyland, 1 Mercedes,
1 Optare, 1 Scania, 8 Volvo.
Ops incl: local bus services, school contracts,
private hire
Livery: Red/White.
Ticket System: Wayfarer Saver.

REGENT COACHES

UNIT 16, ST AUGUSTINE'S BUSINESS PARK,
SWALECLIFFE CT5 2QJ
Tel: 01227 794345
Fax: 01227 795127
E-mail: info@regentcoaches.com
Web site: www.regentcoaches.com
Partners: Paul Regent, Kerry Regent
Tran Man: Colin MacDonald **Workshop
Man:** Robert Wildish **Office Man:** Sam
Regent **Asst Tran Man:** Nigel Andrews.
Fleet: 38 – 3 single-deck coach, 9 midibus,
8 midicoach, 15 minibus, 3 minicoach.
Chassis: 2 Alexander Dennis, 1 Dennis,
1 Enterprise, 7 Irisbus, 2 Iveco, 2 LDV,
10 Mercedes, 1 Optare, 2 Renault, 4
Volkswagen, 2 Volvo, 2 Wrightbus.
Ops incl: local bus services, school contracts,
excursions & tours, private hire, continental
tours.

Livery: Ivory with Red/Orange lettering.
Ticket system: Ticketer.

RELIANCE TRAVEL

UNIT 8, NORFOLK ROAD, GRAVESEND
DA12 2PS
Tel: 01474 322002
Fax: 01474 536998
E-mail: info@reliance-travel.co.uk
Web site: www.reliance-travel.co.uk
Fleet: 16 single-deck coach.
Chassis: 3 Mercedes, 1 Setra, 12 Scania.
Bodies: 12 Irizar, 3 Mercedes, 1 Setra.
Ops incl: private hire, London commuter
express.
Livery: Red/Cream.

ROUNDABOUT BUSES LTD

25 OLDFIELD ROAD, BEXLEYHEATH
DA7 4DX
Tel: 020 8304 9324
Fax: 07092 131054
Recovery: 07940 771439
E-mail: glyn@roundaboutbuses.co.uk
Man Dir: Glyn Matthews
Ops Man: Ian Evans
Eng Man: Robert Woodruff.
Fleet: 8 – 3 double-deck bus, 5 single-deck
coach.
Chassis: 3 Alexander Dennis, 2 Scania,
3 Volvo.
Bodies: 3 Alexander Dennis, 5 Plaxton.
Ops incl: local bus services, excursions &
tours, private hire, express.
Livery: Green/Cream.
Ticket System: Wayfarer.

SCOTLAND & BATES

HEATH ROAD, APPLEDORE, ASHFORD
TN26 2AJ
Tel: 01233 758325
Fax: 01233 758611
E-mail: info@scotlandandbates.co.uk
Web site: www.scotlandandbatescoaches.
co.uk
Partners: Mr R M Bates, Mrs G A Bates.
Fleet: 18 - 16 single-deck coach, 2 midicoach.
Chassis: 2 Mercedes, 16 Volvo.
Bodies: 1 Plaxton, 2 Sitcar, 15 Van Hool.
Ops incl: school contracts, private hire.
Livery: Cream/Brown/Orange.

SEATH COACHES

THE FIELDINGS, STONEHEAP ROAD,
EAST STUDDAL, DOVER
CT15 5BU
Tel: 01304 374732
Fax: 01304 620825
Prop: Philip J Seath.
Fleet: 4 - single-deck coach, midicoach,
minibus.
Chassis: Ford Transit, MAN, Volvo.
Ops incl: school contracts, private hire.
Livery: White/Blue.

SPOT TRAVEL

STATION APPROACH, BEARSTED STATION,
WARE STREET, MAIDSTONE ME14 4PH
Tel: 01622 738932
E-mail: sales@spottravel.co.uk
Web site: www.spottravel.co.uk
Prop: Ross Young **Tours & Excursions
Man:** Mrs Jodie Young.
Fleet: 9 - 3 single-deck coach, 3 midicoach,
3 minicoach.
Chassis: 1 Ford, 5 Mercedes, 3 Volvo.
Bodies: 3 Esker, 1 Jonckheere, 2 Van Hool,
3 Other.
Ops incl: excursions & tours.
Livery: Cream with three stripes.

STAGECOACH SOUTH EAST

BUS STATION, ST GEORGE'S LANE,
CANTERBURY CT1 2SY
Tel: 01227 812409
Fax: 01227 768963
E-mail: eastkent.enquiries@stagecoachbus.
com
Web site: www.stagecoachbus.com
Fleet Names (Kent): Stagecoach in East
Kent, Unibus.
Man Dir: Philip Norwell
Ops Dir: Neil Instrall **Eng Dir:** Jason Bush
Comm Dir: Jeremy Cooper.
Fleet: 480 - 198 double-deck bus, 78 single-
deck bus, 13 single-deck coach, 128 midibus,
63 minibus.
Chassis: 155 Alexander Dennis, 6 DAF,
23 Dennis, 21 MAN, 65 Optare, 90 Scania,
23 Transbus, 97 Volvo.
Ops incl: local bus services, Canterbury park
& ride, express.
Liveries: Stagecoach UK Bus; National
Express.
Ticket System: ERG TP5000.

STREAMLINE (KENT) LTD

UNIT 8, HEADCORN BUSINESS PARK,
MAIDSTONE ROAD, HEADCORN TN27 9PJ
Tel: 01622 750000
Fax: 01622 752978
E-mail: coaches@streamline.travel
Web site: www.streamline.travel
Man Dir: Ron Parker **Co Sec:** Angela Parker.
Fleet: 8 - 2 midicoach, 6 minibus.
Chassis: Ford, Iveco, Mercedes, Volkswagen.
Ops incl: school contracts, excursions &
tours, private hire, continental tours.
Livery: Silver/Blue.

THOMSETT'S COACHES

50 GOLF ROAD, DEAL CT14 6QB
Tel: 01304 249146
Fax: 01304 374731
E-mail: thomsettscoaches@fsmail.net
Web site: www.thomsetts-coaches.co.uk
Prop: S J Thomsett.
Fleet: 4 - 3 single-deck coach, 1 midicoach.
Chassis: 1 MAN, 3 Scania.
Bodies: 1 Caetano, 3 Van Hool.
Ops incl: school contracts, private hire.
Livery: White & Red.

♿ Vehicle suitable for disabled	🍴 Coach(es) with galley facilities	🚌 Vintage Coach(es) available	
Seat belt-fitted Vehicle	🔧 Replacement vehicle available	Open top vehicle(s)	
R24 24 hour recovery service	**R** Recovery service available	👥 Coaches with toilet facilities	
T Toilet-drop facilities available	❄ Air-conditioned vehicle(s)	Hybrid Buses ⬥ Gas Buses	

TRACKS VEHICLE SERVICES LTD

THE FLOTS, BROOKLAND, ROMNEY MARSH TN29 9TF
Tel: 0845 130 0936
Fax: 01797 344135
E-mail: info@tracks-travel.com
Web site: www.tracks-travel.com
Man Dir: Andrew Toms.
Ops incl: private hire, continental tours.

TRAVELMASTERS

R24 T
DORSET ROAD INDUSTRIAL ESTATE, DORSET ROAD, SHEERNESS ME12 1LT
Tel: 01795 660066   **Fax:** 01795 660033
Recovery: 07850 848008
Dirs: T Lambkin, C Smith.
Fleet: 28 – 10 double-deck bus, 7 single-deck coach, 2 double-deck coach, 6 midibus, 1 midicoach, 1 minibus, 1 minicoach.
Chassis: 1 AEC, 2 Alexander Dennis,

4 Dennis, 5 Mercedes, 16 Volvo.
Ops incl: school contracts, excursions & tours, private hire, continental tours.
Livery: Yellow/Blue.

WESTERHAM COACHES

15 BARROW GREEN ROAD, OXTED RH8 0NJ
Tel: 01883 713633   **Fax:** 01883 730079
E-mail: enquiries@skinners.travel
Web site: www.skinners.travel
Partners: Stephen Skinner, Deborah Skinner.
Fleet: 13 - 10 single-deck coach, 2 midicoach, 1 minicoach.
Chassis: 4 Dennis, 2 Mercedes, 7 Setra.
Bodies: 1 Duple, 1 Mercedes, 3 Neoplan, 1 Optare, 7 Setra.
Ops incl: excursions & tours, private hire, school contracts, continental tours.
Livery: Brown & Cream.
Part of Skinners of Oxted (see Surrey)

WEST KENT BUSES

THE COACH STATION, LONDON ROAD, WEST KINGSDOWN TN15 6AR
Tel: 01474 855444
E-mail: westkentbuses@aol.co.uk
Web site: www.westkentbuses.co.uk
Proprietor: Stuart Gilkes
Fleet Eng: Lloyd Turner
Tran Man: Jason Tilley
Depot Eng Man: Alexandra Pretious
HR Manager: B Pretious.
Fleet: 11 - 9 double-deck bus, 2 single-deck coach.
Chassis: 11 Volvo.
Bodies: 7 Northern Counties, 2 Plaxton, 2 Van Hool.
Ops incl: local bus services, private hire.
Livery: Red/Cream.
Ticket System: Wayfarer.

LANCASHIRE, BLACKBURN & DARWEN, BLACKPOOL

ALFA COACHES LTD

EUXTON LANE, CHORLEY PR7 6AF
Tel: 08451 305666
Fax: 08451 303777
E-mail: req@alfatravel .co.uk
Web site: www.alfatravel.co.uk
Man Dir: Paul Sawbridge **Fin Dir:** Peter Sawbridge **Head of Ops:** Alan Scoles.
Fleet: 48 single-deck coach.
Chassis: 29 Mercedes, 19 Volvo.
Bodies: 29 Mercedes, 19 Plaxton.
Ops incl: excursions & tours, continental tours.
Livery: All over Cream.

ARRIVA NORTH WEST & WALES

See Greater Manchester, Merseyside

ASPDEN'S COACHES

LANCASTER STREET, BLACKBURN BB2 1UA.
Tel: 01254 52020
Fax: 01254 57474
E-mail: aspdens@holmeswood.uk.com
Web site: www.holmeswoodcoaches.com
Dirs: J F Aspinall, M Aspinall, C H Aspinall, D E Aspinall, M F Aspinall, M J Forshaw
Ops Man: M E Bostock **Tours Man:** J Bostock-Gibson **Ch Eng:** M Boniface.
Fleet: see Holmeswood Coaches.
Ops incl: local bus services, excursions & tours, private hire, continental tours, school contracts.
Livery: Green.
A subsidiary of Holmeswood Coaches

AVACAB LTD
AVA TRAVEL

81A BISON PLACE, MOSS SIDE INDUSTRIAL ESTATE, LEYLAND PR26 7QR
Tel: 01772 424242
Fax: 01772 433168
E-mail: enquiries@avacab.net
Web site: www.avacab.net
Dirs: P Burrows, P Tattersall.
Fleet: 47 – 3 double-deck bus, 3 single-deck bus, 7 single-deck coach, 1 midibus, 1 midicoach, 32 minibus.
Ops incl: school contracts, private hire.
Livery: White with Blue/Yellow.

BATTERSBY SILVER GREY COACHES

THE COACH & TRAVEL CENTRE, MIDDLEGATE, WHITE LUND BUSINESS PARK, MORECAMBE LA3 3PE

Tel: 01524 380000   **Fax:** 01524 380800
E-mail: info@battersbys.co.uk
Web site: www.battersbys.co.uk
Chairman & Director: James A Harrison
Director & Co Sec: M F Harrison.
Fleet: 25 – 18 single-deck coach, 3 midibus, 3 midicoach, 1 minibus.
Chassis: 3 Dennis, 1 Fiat, 4 Mercedes, 15 Volvo, 2 Wrightbus.
Bodies: 1 Bluebird, 1 Jonckheere, 18 Plaxton, 1 Van Hool, 2 Wadham Stringer, 2 Wrightbus.
Ops incl: local bus services, excursions & tours, private hire, continental tours, school contracts.
Livery: White.
Ticket system: Wayfarer.

BLACKPOOL TRANSPORT SERVICES LTD

RIGBY ROAD, BLACKPOOL FY1 5DD
Tel: 01253 473001
Fax: 01253 473101
E-mail: enquiries@blackpooltransport.com
Web site: www.blackpooltransport.com
Fleet Name: Metro Coastlines.
Dir of Delivery: Bob Mason **Eng Dir:** Dave Hislop **Fin Dir:** Sue Kennerley
Ops Man: Guy Thornton.
Fleet (Buses): 148 - 75 double-deck bus, 30 single-deck bus, 1 open top bus, 42 midibus.
Chassis: 5 Alexander Dennis, 19 DAF, 30 Dennis, 4 Leyland, 58 Optare, 16 Transbus, 19 Volvo.
Bodies: 1 ECW, 70 East Lancs, 5 Northern Counties, 58 Optare, 9 Plaxton, 5 Wrightbus.
Ops incl: local bus services, tram services.
Livery: Yellow plus route branded route colours.
Ticket System: Wayfarer/Almex A90.
See also Section 5 – Tram and Bus Rapid Transit Systems

BRADSHAWS TRAVEL

46 WESTBOURNE ROAD, KNOTT END ON SEA, POULTON-LE-FYLDE FY6 0BS
Tel/Fax: 01253 810058
Proprietor: Mrs Jill Swift.
Fleet: 10 – 1 double-deck bus, 8 single-deck coach, 1 midicoach.
Chassis: 1 EOS, 1 Iveco, 2 Leyland, 1 Mercedes, 1 Neoplan, 4 Volvo.
Bodies: 1 Alexander, 1 Beulas, 1 EOS, 1 Neoplan, 3 Plaxton, 2 Van Hool, 1 Other.
Ops incl: school contracts, excursions & tours, private hire.
Livery: White/Black/Yellow.
Ticket System: Almex.

COASTAL COACHES

UNIT 2, TOWNSENDS YARD, 148 LYTHAM ROAD, WARTON, PRESTON PR4 1AH
Tel: 01772 635820
E-mail: coastalcoaches@aol.com
Web site: www.coastalcoaches.co.uk
Props: W Holder, Mrs H Holder.
Fleet: 17 – 6 single-deck coach, 5 midibus, 5 midicoach, 1 minicoach
Chassis: 12 Mercedes, 5 Optare.
Bodies: 2 Mercedes, 5 Optare, 10 Unvi.
Ops incl: local bus services, private hire.
Livery: Blue & White.

COLRAY COACHES

14 PRESTBURY AVENUE, BLACKPOOL FY4 1PT
Tel/Fax: 01253 349481
E-mail: colraycoaches@hotmail.co.uk
Dirs: Geoffrey Shaw, V Shaw.
Fleet: 3 – 2 single-deck coach, 1 midicoach.
Chassis: 1 Mercedes, 1 Van Hool, 1 Volvo.
Bodies: 2 Plaxton, 1 Van Hool.
Ops incl: excursions & tours, school contracts, private hire, continental tours.
Livery: White/Blue.

COSGROVE'S COACHES

133 WOODPLUMPTON ROAD, PRESTON PR2 3LF
Tel: 01772 460748
Fax: 01772 722332
E-mail: cosgroves.coaches@googlemail.com
Web site: www.cosgrovestours.co.uk
Props: Mr John R Cosgrove, Mrs Christine Cosgrove, Miss Alyson J Cosgrove.
Fleet: 5 – 4 single-deck coach, 1 midicoach.
Chassis: 3 DAF, 1 Mercedes, 1 VDL.
Bodies: 1 Mercedes, 4 Van Hool.
Ops incl: school contracts, excursions & tours, private hire, continental tours.
Livery: White with logos.

EAVESWAY TRAVEL LTD

BRYN SIDE, BRYN ROAD, ASHTON-IN-MAKERFIELD, WIGAN WN4 8BT
Tel: 01942 727985
Fax: 01942 271234
E-mail: sales@eaveswaytravel.com
Web site: www.eaveswaytravel.com
Man Dir: Mike Eaves **Dir:** Phil Rogers
Ops Man: Tim Presley.
Fleet: 35 – 34 double-deck coach, 1 minicoach.
Chassis: 1 Mercedes, 34 Van Hool.

Bodies: I EVM, 34 Van Hool.
Ops incl: express, private hire.
Livery: Silver/Green.

JOHN FISHWICK & SONS

GOLDEN HILL LANE, LEYLAND PR25 3LE
Tel: 01772 421207
Fax: 01772 622407
E-mail: enquiries@fishwicks.co.uk
Web site: www.fishwicks.co.uk
Dirs: John C Brindle, James F Hustler.
Fleet: 35 - 8 double-deck bus, 26 single-deck bus, I single-deck coach.
Chassis: 9 DAF, 7 Leyland, I Van Hool, 16 VDL, 2 Volvo.
Bodies: 7 Alexander, I ECW, I Leyland, 3 Plaxton, 3 Van Hool, 22 Wrightbus.
Ops incl: local bus services, school contracts, excursions & tours, private hire, continental tours.
Livery: Green.
Ticket System: Wayfarer.

GPD TRAVEL

27 HARTFORD AVENUE, HEYWOOD OL10 4XH
Tel: 01706 622297
Fax: 01706 361494
E-mail: info@gpd-travel.co.uk
Proprietor: Gary Dawson.
Fleet: 4 – 2 single-deck coach, I midicoach, I minibus.
Chassis: 2 Mercedes, 2 Volvo.
Ops incl: school contracts, excursions & tours, private hire, continental tours.
Livery: White with red lettering.

G-LINE HOLIDAYS LTD

54 ST DAVIDS ROAD SOUTH, ST ANNE'S ON SEA FY8 ITS
Tel: 01253 725999
Fax: 01253 781843
E-mail: info@g-lineholidays.co.uk
Web site: www.g-lineholidays.co.uk
Dirs: Mr E W Bradshaw, Mrs P H Jenkinson, Mr A W Bradshaw.
Fleet: 10 single-deck coach.
Chassis: 2 DAF, 4 Van Hool, 4 Volvo.
Bodies: 3 Plaxton, I Sunsundegui, 6 Van Hool.
Ops incl: excursions & tours, private hire, continental tours.
Livery: White, Maroon & Gold.

HEALINGS INTERNATIONAL COACHES

See Greater Manchester

HODDER EXECUTIVE TRAVEL

3 ALDERFORD CLOSE, CLITHEROE BB7 2QP
Tel: 01200 422473
Fax: 01200 422590
E-mail: hoddercoaches@hotmail.co.uk
Dir: Paul Hodgson.
Fleet: 2 single-deck coach.
Chassis: I Mercedes, I Volvo.
Body: I Neoplan, I Van Hool.
Ops incl: private hire, excursions & tours.
Livery: Dark metallic Grey.

HODSONS COACHES

LINK 59 BUSINESS PARK, DEANFIELD WAY, CLITHEROE BB7 1QU
Tel: 01200 429220
E-mail: info@hodsonscoaches.com
Web site: www.hodsonscoaches.com
Prop: M Hodson
Fleet: 30 – 5 double-deck bus, 2 single-deck bus, 9 single-deck coach, 11 midicoach,

3 minibus.
Ops incl: school contracts, private hire, excursions & tours.
Livery: White with Blue.

HOLMESWOOD COACHES LTD

SANDY WAY, HOLMESWOOD, ORMSKIRK L40 IUB
Tel: 01704 821245
Fax: 01704 822090
E-mail: sales@holmeswood.uk.com
Web site: www.holmeswood.uk.com
Dirs: J F Aspinall, M Aspinall, D G Aspinall, C H Aspinall, M F Aspinall, M J Aspinall.
Fleet Names: Aspden's Coaches; Bostock's Coaches; Holmeswood Coaches; John Flanagan Coaches; Tyrer Tours; Walker's Coaches.
Fleet: 194 - 25 double-deck bus, 107 single-deck coach, 4 double-deck coach, 22 midibus, 2 midicoach, 25 minibus, 9 minicoach.
Chassis: I Alexander Dennis, 2 Bova, 5 DAF, 19 Dennis, 7 Enterprise, 24 Irisbus, 14 Iveco, 5 Leyland, 33 MAN, 3 Mercedes, 3 Neoplan, 31 Optare, 13 Scania, I Setra, 3 Transbus, 9 VDL, 18 Volvo, 2 Wrightbus.
Bodies: 9 Alexander, I Alexander Dennis, 6 Berkhof, 33 Beulas, 4 Caetano, 6 East Lancs, I Hispano, I Ikarus, 6 Indcar, 2 Irizar, I Jonckheere, I Leyland, 37 Marcopolo, 4 Neoplan, 3 Noge, 3 Northern Counties, 31 Optare, 27 Plaxton, I Setra, 3 Transbus, 4 Van Hool, 3 Wrightbus, I Other.
Ops incl: local bus services, school contracts, excursions & tours, private hire, continental tours.
Livery: Green
Ticket system: Wayfarer
Holmeswood Group Companies:
Aspden's Coaches, Blackburn (see Lancashire)
Bostock's Coaches, Congleton (see Cheshire)
Tyrer Tours, Nelson (see Lancashire)
Walker's & Flanagan's Coaches (see Cheshire)

JACKSONS COACHES

JACKSON HOUSE, BURTON ROAD, BLACKPOOL FY4 4NW
Tel: 01253 792222
Fax: 01253 692070
E-mail: jacksonscoaches@btconnect.com
Web site: www.jacksonscoachesblackpool.co.uk
Partner: Jon Paul Jackson.
Fleet: 5 – I double-deck bus, 4 single-deck coach.
Chassis: I Irisbus, I Leyland, I MAN, I Scania, I Volvo.
Bodies: I Alexander, I Irizar, 3 Plaxton.
Ops incl: school contracts, private hire, excursions & tours, continental tours.
Livery: White/Blue.

KIRKBY LONSDALE COACH HIRE LTD

OLD STATION YARD, WARTON ROAD, CARNFORTH LA5 9EU
Tel: 01524 733831   **Fax:** 01524 733821
E-mail: office@kirkbylonsdalecoachhire.co.uk
Web site: www.kirkbylonsdalecoachhire.co.uk
Dirs: Stephen Sutton, Matthew Sutton, Tim Sutton, Jane Sutton **Ops Mans:** Matthew Sutton, Richard Blaikie.
Fleet: 20 – 2 single-deck bus, 7 single-deck coach, 8 midibus, 2 midicoach, I minicoach.
Ops incl: local bus services, school contracts, private hire.
Livery: White/Maroon.
Ticket System: Wayfarer TGX.
See also Yellow Rose Coaches

LAKELAND COACHES

SMITHY ROW, HURST GREEN, CLITHEROE BB7 9QA
Tel: 01254 826007
Prop: J R Lakeland.
Fleet: 9 – 7 single-deck coach, 2 midicoach.
Chassis: 2 Mercedes, I Scania, 2 Van Hool, 4 Volvo.
Bodies: I Irizar, I Jonckheere, 3 Plaxton, 4 Van Hool.
Ops incl: excursions & tours, private hire.
Livery: White with Light/Dark Blue.

MOVING PEOPLE LTD

JUNCTION 7 BUSINESS PARK, ACCRINGTON BB5 5JW
Tel: 0845 475 1212
Fax: 0871 714 3115
E-mail: info@movingpeopleltd.co.uk
Web site: www.movingpeopleltd.co.uk
Dirs: S Coates, A Parry.
Fleet: 30 – 15 double-deck bus, 4 single-deck bus, 6 single-deck coach, 3 midibus, I minibus, I minicoach.
Ops incl: local bus services, excursions & tours, School contracts, private hire.

NORTH WEST COACHES & LIMOS

HILLHOUSE INTERNATIONAL BUSINESS PARK, WEST ROAD, THORNTON CLEVELEYS FY5 4DQ
Tel: 01253 855000
Fax: 01253 876177
Recovery: 07850 500015
E-mail: stewart.farrel@tiscali.co.uk
Owner/Operator: Stuart J Farrell
Ops Man: Paul Portisman
Head Fitter: John Keen.
Fleet: 4 - 2 midicoach, 2 minibus.
Chassis: I Ford, 2 Mercedes, I Renault.
Ops incl: local bus services, excursions & tours, school contracts, private hire.

OLYMPIA TRAVEL UK LTD

44 ARGYLE STREET, HINDLEY, WIGAN WN2 3PH
Tel: 01942 522322
Fax: 01942 255845
Recovery: 07736 329133
E-mail: olympia@coach-hire.net
Web site: www.olympiatravel.co.uk
Props: Joseph Lewis, Shaun Lewis.
Fleet: 24 – 4 single-deck bus, 19 single-deck coach, I midicoach.
Chassis: I Iveco, I Mercedes, 3 Optare, 19 Volvo.
Ops incl: local bus services, school contracts, excursions & tours, private hire, continental tours.
Livery: White with blue stripes.
Ticket System: Wayfarer.

OPTIONS TRAVEL

See Greater Manchester

PILKINGTONS

47 ARGYLE STREET, ACCRINGTON BB5 IDQ
Tel: 01254 237083
E-mail: pilkingtonbus@live.co.uk
Web site: www.pilkingtonbus.com
Dir: A Pilkington.
Fleet: double-deck bus, single-deck bus, midibus.
Chassis: Dennis, Leyland, Optare, Volvo.
Ops incl: local bus services, school contracts, private hire.
Livery: Red/Cream.

PRESTON BUS LTD
  R24

221 DEEPDALE ROAD, PRESTON
PR1 6NY
Tel: 01772 253671
Fax: 01772 555840
Recovery: 01772 253671
E-mail: customer.care@prestonbus.co.uk
Web site: www.prestonbus.co.uk
Man Dir: Bob Dunn
Ops Man: John Asquith.
Fleet: 111 – 46 double-deck bus, 24 single-deck bus, 41 midibus
Chassis: 1 DAF, 28 Dennis, 11 Leyland, 1 Mercedes, 48 Optare, 11 Scania, 8 Volvo, 3 Wrightbus.
Bodies: 3 Alexander, 30 East Lancs, 7 Leyland, 1 Mercedes, 4 Northern Counties, 49 Optare, 6 Plaxton, 11 Wrightbus.
Ops incl: local bus services, school contracts.
Livery: Blue/Cream.
Ticket System: Vix TP5700.
A subsidiary of Rotala

REDLINE TRAVEL LTD
  R R24 T

UNIT 5C, CROSSLEY HOUSE INDUSTRIAL
ESTATE, LEYLAND ROAD,
PENWORTHAM, PRESTON
PR1 9QP
Tel: 01772 747877
Fax: 01772 747878
E-mail: enquiries@redlinetravel.co.uk
Web site: www.redlinetravel.co.uk
Dir: Shane Nuttall
Co Sec: Mrs Rowena Nuttall
Fleet: 19 – 9 double-deck bus, 9 single-deck coach, 1 minibus.
Chassis: 1 Ford Transit, 18 Volvo.
Bodies: 2 Alexander, 7 East Lancs, 1 Ford, 3 Jonckheere, 2 Plaxton, 4 Van Hool.
Ops incl: school contracts, private hire, excursions & tours.
Livery: Red, Green & White.

REEVES COACH SERVICES

34 MONKS DRIVE, WITHNELL,
CHORLEY PR6 8SG
Tel/Fax: 01254 830545
E-mail: info@reevescoachholidays.com
Web site: www.reevescoachholidays.com
Prop: John E Reeves.
Fleet: 1 single-deck coach.
Chassis/Body: Setra.
Ops incl: excursions & tours, continental tours.
Livery: Blue.

RIGBY'S EXECUTIVE COACHES LTD

MOORFIELD INDUSTRIAL ESTATE,
MOORFIELD DRIVE, ALTHAM,
ACCRINGTON BB5 5WG
Tel: 01254 388866
Fax: 01254 232505
E-mail: coachcentre@hotmail.co.uk
Web site: www.rigbyscoaches.co.uk
Man Dir: Derek Moorhouse
Eng Dir: Mel Mellor
Dir/Tran Man: Andrew Knowles.
Fleet: 25 – 3 single-deck bus, 14 single-deck coach, 1 midibus, 4 midicoach, 2 minibus, 1 minicoach.
Chassis: 3 Bova, 1 Ford Transit, 7 Mercedes, 1 Scania, 13 Volvo.
Bodies: 3 Alexander, 1 Autobus, 1 Berkhof, 3 Bova, 1 Ford, 1 Irizar, 5 Jonckheere, 5 Plaxton, 4 Van Hool, 1 Other.
Ops incl: school contracts, excursions & tours, private hire.
Livery: Orange.

ROBINSONS HOLIDAYS

PARK GARAGE, GREAT HARWOOD
BB6 7SP
Tel: 01254 889900
Fax: 01254 884708
E-mail: info@robinsons-holidays.co.uk
Web site: www.robinsons-holidays.co.uk
Dirs: D D Lord, J E Bannister
(Sec), J McMillan **Ops Man:** C Skeen
Engineer: P Godwin **Off Man:** B Cooke
Sales Man: G Holdsworth.
Fleet: 23 – 16 single-deck coach, 7 minibus.
Chassis: 4 Neoplan, 7 Volkswagen, 12 Volvo.
Bodies: 4 Jonckheere, 4 Neoplan, 7 Plaxton, 1 Sunsundegui, 7 Volkswagen.
Ops incl: excursions & tours, private hire, continental tours, school contracts.
Livery: Dark Blue.

ROSSENDALE TRANSPORT LTD

KNOWSLEY PARK WAY, HASLINGDEN
BB4 4RS
Tel: 01706 390520
Fax: 01706 390530
E-mail: getintouch@rossobus.co.uk
Web site: www.rossobus.co.uk
Fleet Name: Rosso
Ops Dir: Alastair Nuttall **Comm & Marketing Dir:** Brendan O'Reilly.
Fleet: 109 - 24 double-deck bus, 74 single-deck bus, 11 midibus.
Chassis: 28 Dennis, 3 MAN, 11 Optare, 17 Scania, 50 Volvo.
Bodies: 4 Alexander, 5 Caetano, 17 East Lancs, 4 MCV, 13 Northern Counties, 11 Optare, 13 Plaxton, 43 Wrightbus.
Ops incl: local bus services, school contracts, private hire, express, continental tours.
Livery: White/Red/Cream.
Ticket System: Wayfarer TGX.

STAGECOACH CUMBRIA AND NORTH LANCASHIRE

BROADACRE HOUSE, 16-20 LOWTHER
STREET, CARLISLE CA3 8DA
Tel: 01228 597222
Fax: 01228 597888
E-mail: cumbrianorthlancs.enquiries@stagecoachbus.com
Web site: www.stagecoachbus.com
Fleet Names: Stagecoach in Cumbria, Stagecoach in Lancaster.
Man Dir: Nigel Winter **Ops Dir:** David Lee-Kong **Chief Eng Dir:** Brian Walkden.
Fleet: 321 - 112 double-deck bus, 91 single-deck bus, 11 single-deck coach, 51 midibus, 56 minibus.
Chassis: 2 AEC, 58 Alexander Dennis, 52 Dennis, 1 Iveco, 53 MAN, 2 Mercedes, 56 Optare, 30 Scania, 8 Transbus, 59 Volvo.
Ops incl: local bus services, school contracts, excursions & tours, private hire, express.
Livery: Stagecoach UK Bus.
Ticket System: Wayfarer TGX.

STAGECOACH MERSEYSIDE AND SOUTH LANCASHIRE

GILMOSS BUS DEPOT, EAST LANCASHIRE
ROAD, LIVERPOOL L11 0BB
Tel: 0151 330 6200
Fax: 0151 330 6210
E-mail: enquiries.merseyside@stagecoachbus.com
Web site: www.stagecoachbus.com
Fleet Names: Stagecoach in Merseyside/Lancashire/Wirral/Chester.
Man Dir: Elisabeth Tasker **Eng Dir:** Tony Cockroft **Ops Dir:** Rob Jones
Comm Man: James Mellor
Fleet: 433 - 117 double-deck bus, 2 open-top bus, 183 single-deck bus, 90 midibus, 41 minibus.
Chassis: 154 Alexander Dennis, 11 Bluebird, 31 Dennis, 2 Leyland, 50 MAN, 51 Optare, 62 Scania, 26 Transbus, 46 Volvo.
Ops incl: local bus services, school contracts, excursions & tours, private hire, express.
Livery: Stagecoach UK Bus.
Ticket System: Wayfarer TGX.

TRANSDEV BURNLEY & PENDLE

QUEENSGATE BUS DEPOT, COLNE ROAD,
BURNLEY BB10 1HH
Tel: 0845 604 0110
E-mail: enquire@burnleyandpendle.co.uk
Web site: www.lancashirebus.co.uk
Fleet Names: Mainline, Starship, The Witch Way.
Prop: Blazefield Holdings Ltd.
Man Dir: Russell Revill **Reg Business Development Dir:** John Threlfall.
Fleet: 79 – 23 double-deck bus, 50 single-deck bus, 6 midibus.
Chassis: 1 Dennis, 1 Leyland, 16 Optare, 4 Transbus, 57 Volvo.
Bodies: 4 Alexander, 2 Northern Counties, 16 Optare, 2 Plaxton, 4 Transbus, 51 Wrightbus.
Livery: Red/Cream.
Ticket System: ERG.

TRANSDEV LANCASHIRE UNITED

INTACK GARAGE, WHITEBIRK ROAD,
INTACK, BLACKBURN BB1 3JD
Tel: 0845 272 7272
Fax: 01234 693964
E-mail: info@lancashireunited.co.uk
Web site: www.lancashirebus.co.uk
Fleet Names: Spot On, The Lancashire Way, Hyndburn Connect.
Prop: Blazefield Holdings Ltd
Man Dir: Russell Revill **Reg Business Development Dir:** John Threlfall.
Fleet: 93 – 35 double-deck bus, 53 single-deck bus, 5 midibus.
Chassis: 3 Dennis, 9 Leyland, 16 Optare, 2 Transbus, 63 Volvo.
Bodies: 5 Alexander, 4 ECW, 3 Leyland, 6 Northern Counties, 16 Optare, 4 Plaxton, 2 Transbus, 53 Wrightbus.
Livery: Blue/Cream.
Ticket System: ERG.

TRAVEL OPTIONS
See Greater Manchester

THE TRAVELLERS CHOICE

THE COACH & TRAVEL CENTRE,
SCOTLAND ROAD, CARNFORTH LA5 9RQ
Tel: 01524 720033
Fax: 01524 720044
E-mail: info@travellerschoice.co.uk
Web site: www.travellerschoice.co.uk
Depots at: Carnforth, Dalton in Furness.
Chairman: R Shaw **Man Dir:** J Shaw
Dir: M Shaw **Co Sec:** P Shaw.
Fleet: 101 – 81 single-deck coach, 6 midibus, 6 midicoach, 6 minibus, 2 minicoach.
Chassis: 2 Ford Transit, 1 King Long, 11 Mercedes, 3 Optare, 6 Scania, 1 Volkswagen, 77 Volvo, 2 Wrightbus.
Bodies: 6 Berkhof, 9 Caetano, 2 EVM, 1 Ferqui, 2 Ford, 1 Irizar, 53 Jonckheere, 1 King Long, 1 KVC, 1 Onyx, 3 Optare, 9 Plaxton, 1 Sitcar, 3 Sunsundegui, 1 Transbus, 1 Unvi, 2 Wrightbus, 2 Other.
Ops incl: local bus services, school contracts, excursions & tours, private hire, continental tours, express.
Liveries: White with red/yellow/blue stripe, National Express.

R S TYRER LTD

168 CHORLEY ROAD, ADLINGTON
PR6 9LQ
Tel: 01257 480979
E-mail: sales@tyrerscoaches.co.uk
Web site: www.tyrerscoaches.co.uk
Fleet: 39 – 19 double-deck bus, 12 single-deck bus, 3 double-deck coach, 1 midicoach, 5 minibus.
Chassis: 1 DAF, 8 Dennis, 1 EOS, 1 Leyland, 1 Mercedes, 5 Optare, 3 Scania, 1 Van Hool, 2 VDL, 17 Volvo.
Bodies: 2 Alexander, 9 East Lancs, 1 EOS, 1 Irizar, 2 Northern Counties, 7 Optare, 8 Plaxton, 10 Van Hool.
Ops incl: local bus services, school contracts, excursions & tours, private hire, continental tours.
Livery: Blue & White.

TYRER TOURS LTD

KIRBY ROAD, LOMESHAY INDUSTRIAL ESTATE, NELSON BB9 6RS
Tel: 01282 619141
Fax: 01282 615541
E-mail: tyrers@holmeswood.uk.com
Web site: www.holmeswoodcoaches.com
Dirs: J F Aspinall, M Aspinall, C H Aspinall, D E Aspinall, M F Aspinall, M J Forshaw
Ops Man: M E Bostock **Tours Man:** J Bostock-Gibson **Ch Eng:** M Boniface.
Fleet: see Holmeswood Coaches.
Ops incl: local bus services, excursions & tours, private hire, continental tours, school contracts.
A subsidiary of Holmeswood Coaches

WALTONS COACH HIRE LTD

NAZE LANE EAST, FRECKLETON, PRESTON PR4 1UN
Tel: 01772 634563
Fax: 01772 634680
E-mail: info@waltonscoaches.co.uk
Web site: www.waltonscoaches.co.uk
Man Dir: P Walton **Dir:** Mrs M E Walton.
Fleet: 20 – 5 double-deck bus, 6 single-deck coach, 2 midibus, 4 midicoach, 3 minicoach.
Chassis: 2 Ayats, 1 BMC, 4 DAF, 4 King Long, 3 MAN, 3 Mercedes, 2 Toyota, 1 Volvo.
Ops incl: school contracts, private hire, excursions & tours.
Livery: Blue/Grey/Yellow.

YELLOW ROSE COACHES

OLD STATION YARD, WARTON ROAD, CARNFORTH LA5 9EU
Tel: 01524 735853
Fax: 01524 733821
E-mail: office@yellowrosecoaches.co.uk
Web site: www.yellowrosecoaches.co.uk
Dirs: Matthew Sutton, Tim Sutton, Stephen Sutton.
Fleet: 3 – 2 single-deck coach, 1 midicoach.
Chassis: 1 DAF, 1 Mercedes, 1 Setra.
Bodies: 1 Ferqui, 1 Setra, 1 Van Hool.
Ops incl: local bus services, school contracts, excursions & tours, private hire.
Livery: Yellow/Maroon/White.
A subsidiary of Kirkby Lonsdale Coach Hire Ltd

ABBEY TRAVEL

RMC YARD, THURMASTON FOOTPATH, HUMBERSTONE LANE, LEICESTER LE4 9JU
Tel: 0116 246 1755
Fax: 0116 246 1755
Recovery: 07900 438428
Web site: www.abbeytravel.org.uk
Partners: Bryan A Garratt, Paul Garratt, Diane Sanders **(Co Sec)**, Paul Garratt.
Fleet: 45 – 11 double-deck bus, 1 double-deck coach, 31 single-deck coach, 1 minibus, 1 minicoach.
Chassis: 3 Bova, 1 DAF, 8 Dennis, 3 Irisbus, 3 Leyland, 4 MCW, 4 Mercedes, 1 Neoplan, 3 Scania, 2 Setra, 13 Volvo.
Bodies: Alexander, Berkhof, Beulas, Bova, Caetano, East Lancs, Hispano, Irizar, Jonckheere, Marcopolo, MCW, Mercedes, Neoplan, Noge, Northern Counties, Plaxton, Setra, Van Hool.
Ops incl: local bus services, school contracts, excursions & tours, private hire, continental tours.
Livery: White/Green/Red.

ARRIVA MIDLANDS LTD

4 WESTMORELAND AVENUE, THURMASTON, LEICESTER LE4 8PH
Tel: 0116 264 0400
Fax: 0116 260 8620
E-mail: myattk.midlands@arriva.co.uk
Web site: www.arriva.co.uk
Regional Man Dir: A Perry
Regional Fin Dir: J Barlow
Regional Eng Dir: M Evans
**Area Director
East:** S Mathieson
Area Director West: R Cheveaux.
Fleet: 698 - 168 double-deck bus, 267 single-deck bus, 6 articulated bus, 204 midibus, 53 minibus.
Chassis: 24 Alexander Dennis, 173 DAF, 119 Dennis, 26 Mercedes, 131 Optare, 46 Scania, 6 Transbus, 85 VDL, 98 Volvo.
Bodies: 61 Alexander, 24 Alexander Dennis, 4 Caetano, 46 East Lancs, 1 Marshall, 26 Mercedes, 121 Optare, 110 Plaxton, 42 Scania, 6 Transbus, 257 Wrightbus.
Ops incl: local bus services, school contracts, private hire, express.
Liveries: Arriva; Midland (Red); Wardles (Red/White, Red/Cream).
Ticket System: Wayfarer 150 & 200.

AUSDEN CLARK GROUP

TRANSPORT HOUSE, MURRAYFIELD ROAD, LEICESTER LE3 1UW
Tel: 0116 262 9492
Fax: 0116 251 5551
Recovery: 0116 262 9492
E-mail: info@ausdenclark.co.uk
Web Site: www.ausdenclark.co.uk
Dirs: L Kind, A Jobling
Gen Man: Susan Ward
Ops Man: Adam Frost.
Fleet: 69 – 8 double-deck bus, 14 double-deck coach, 38 single-deck coach, 7 midicoach, 1 minibus, 1 minicoach.
Chassis: 2 MAN, 7 Mercedes, 61 Scania.
Bodies: 1 Alexander, 3 Autobus, 18 Berkhof, 9 East Lancs, 1 Ferqui, 5 Irizar, 1 Noge, 2 Plaxton, 28 Van Hool, 1 Other.
Ops incl: local bus services, school contracts, excursions & tours, private hire, express, continental tours.
Livery: Pink/Black/Purple on Metallic Silver.

BEAVERBUS LTD

UNIT 84, WHITTLE ESTATE, CAMBRIDGE ROAD, WHETSTONE, LEICESTER LE8 6LH
Tel: 0116 284 4877
E-mail: enquiries@beaver-bus.co.uk
Web site: www.beaver-bus.co.uk
Dirs: J McDonald, C McDonald
Fleet: 20 – 18 double-deck bus, 2 single-deck bus.
Chassis: 2 DAF, 3 Dennis, 1 MCW, 1 Optare, 13 Volvo.
Ops incl: local bus services, school contracts, private hire.
Livery: Blue & White.

CENTREBUS LTD

37 WENLOCK WAY, LEICESTER LE4 9HU
Tel: 0844 351 1120
Fax: 0116 276 7221
E-mail: info@centrebus.com
Web Site: www.centrebus.info
Dirs: Peter Harvey, David Shelley, Julian Peddle, Keith Hayward.
Fleet (Leicestershire): 75 – 10 single-deck bus, 60 midibus, 5 minibus.
Chassis: 5 Alexander Dennis, 9 DAF, 19 Dennis, 37 Optare, 2 Scania, 3 VDL.
Bodies: 6 Alexander, 5 Alexander Dennis, 7 MCV, 37 Optare, 16 Plaxton, 2 Scania, 2 Wrightbus.
Ops Inc: local bus services.
Livery: Blue/Orange/White.
Part of the Centrebus Group

CONFIDENCE BUS & COACH LTD

30 SPALDING STREET, LEICESTER LE5 4PH
Tel/Fax: 0116 276 2171
E-mail: confidencebus@btclick.com
Web site: www.confidencebus.co.uk
Dirs: K M Williams, A P Williams, C A Dalby
Sec: Miss Malveena Robinson.
Fleet: 31 - 23 double-deck bus, 8 single-deck coach.
Chassis: 1 AEC, 1 Alexander Dennis, 19 Leyland, 10 Volvo.
Bodies: 5 Alexander, 1 Duple, 12 ECW, 2 Optare, 1 Park Royal, 6 Plaxton, 3 Roe, 1 Van Hool.
Ops incl: school contracts, private hire.
Livery: Black/Grey/Red.
Ticket System: Setright.

COUNTRY HOPPER

Ceased trading since LRB 2014 went to press

FIRST MIDLANDS

PO BOX 8324, LEICESTER LE41 9BF
Tel: 0845 602 0121
Fax: 0116 268 9198
Web site: www.firstgroup.com
Fleet Name: First Leicester.
Man Dir: Nigel Eggleton
Deputy Man Dir: Mick Brannigan
Fin Dir: David Marshall
Gen Man: Steve Zanker.
Fleet (Leicester): 112 – 80 double-deck bus, 32 single-deck bus.
Chassis: 35 Alexander Dennis, 77 Volvo.
Bodies: 35 Alexander Dennis, 43 Alexander, 34 Wrightbus.
Ops incl: local bus services, school contracts, excursions & tours, private hire, express, continental tours.
Livery: FirstGroup UK Bus.
Ticket System: Wayfarer 3.
See also operations in Herefordshire, Staffordshire, Worcestershire

PAUL JAMES HOLIDAYS

⚙♿⑪❄ R24 ✎T

THE LIMES, MIDLAND ROAD,
HUGGLESCOTE LE67 2FX
Tel: 01530 817444
Fax: 01530 817666
Recovery: 07785 572526
E-mail: info@robertscoaches.co.uk
Web site: www.robertstravelgroup.co.uk
Man Dir: Jonathan Hunt **Fin Dir:** Margaret
Bunker **Eng Dir:** Mick Crawford
Sales Man: Helen Jacobs **Compliance Man:**
David Wood **Business Devt & Marketing
Man:** Paul Owen
Coach Holidays Man: Sam Woolley.
Fleet: See Roberts Coaches Ltd
Ops incl: excursions & tours, continental
tours
Livery: Green or Blue/White.
A subsidiary of Roberts Coaches Ltd

KINCHBUS LTD

♿

SULLIVAN WAY, SWINGBRIDGE ROAD,
LOUGHBOROUGH LE11 5QS
Tel: 01509 815637
E-mail: customer.services@kinchbus.co.uk
Web site: www.kinchbus.co.uk
Gen Man: Tom Morgan.
Fleet: 33 - 21 single-deck bus, 5 midibus,
7 minibus.
Chassis: 16 Optare, 10 Scania, 7 Volvo.
Bodies: 16 Optare, 7 Plaxton, 10 Wrightbus.
Ops incl: local bus services.
Livery: Blue/Yellow.
Ticket System: Init.
Part of the Wellglade Group

MACPHERSON COACHES LTD

♿⚙🚂❄✎

THE GARAGE, HILL STREET,
DONISTHORPE, SWADLINCOTE DE12 7PL
Tel: 01530 270226
Fax: 01530 273669
E-mail: travel@macphersoncoaches.co.uk
Web site: www.macphersoncoaches.co.uk
Man Dir: D C N MacPherson
Co Sec: S MacPherson
Fleet Eng: C Underwood
Ops Man: J Bywater
Fleet: 17 - 6 double-deck bus, 1 single-deck
bus, 8 single-deck coach, 1 midicoach,
1 minicoach.
Chassis: 1 Dennis, 6 Leyland, 4 Mercedes,
1 Optare, 5 Setra.
Bodies: 3 Alexander Dennis, 2 Caetano,
1 East Lancs, 2 Mercedes, 3 Northern
Counties, 1 Optare, 5 Setra, 1 Other.
Ops incl: local bus services, school contracts,
excursions & tours, private hire, continental
tours.
Livery: Red & Cream.
Ticket System: Wayfarer.

NESBIT BROS LTD

⚙❄

BURROUGH ROAD GARAGE, SOMERBY,
MELTON MOWBRAY LE14 2PP
Tel: 01664 454284
Fax: 01664 454106
Web site: www.nesbitbros.com
Dirs: I Foster, J H Townsend.
Fleet: 15 single-deck coach.
Chassis: 15 Volvo.
Bodies: 1 Jonckheere, 6 Plaxton, 8 Van Hool.
Ops incl: school contracts, private hire.
Livery: Cream with Red/Blue relief.

NJ TRAVEL SERVICES

⚙♿❄✎

THURMASTON FOOTPATH,
HUMBERSTONE LANE, LEICESTER LE4 9JU
Tel: 0116 276 9456
Fax: 0116 276 1969

E-mail: coaches9@btconnect.com
Web site: www.nigeljacksontravel.co.uk
Prop: Nigel Jackson.
Fleet: 8 - 4 double-deck bus, 2 single-deck
bus, 2 single-deck coach.
Chassis: 1 Bova, 1 MAN, 4 MCW, 1 Toyota.
Bodies: 1 Bova, 4 MCW, 2 Plaxton.
Ops incl: local bus services, school contracts,
private hire.
Livery: Blue/Red.
Ticket System: Wayfarer.

REDFERN TRAVEL LTD

♿⚙♿⑪🚂❄ R24 ✎T

THE SIDINGS, DEBDALE LANE, MANSFIELD
WOODHOUSE, MANSFIELD NG19 7FE
Tel/Recovery: 01623 627653
Fax: 01909 625787
E-mail: lee@johnsonstours.co.uk
Web site: www.johnsonstours.co.uk
Dirs: C A Johnson, S Johnson, A Johnson,
L Johnson, C Johnson.
Fleet: 103 - 59 double-deck bus, 1 single-
deck bus, 35 single-deck coach, 4 midicoach,
1 minibus, 3 minicoach.
Chassis: 1 Autosan, 2 Bova, 9 Bristol, 2 DAF,
1 Ford Transit, 8 Irisbus, 4 Irizar, 40 Leyland,
5 Mercedes, 6 Neoplan, 1 Optare, 12 Scania,
2 Van Hool, 9 Volvo.
Bodies: 3 Alexander, 1 Autosan, 3 Beulas,
2 Bova, 3 Caetano, 30 ECW, 1 Excel, 1 Ford,
6 Irizar, 2 Jonckheere, 3 Leyland, 6 Neoplan,
23 Northern Counties, 2 Optare, 8 Plaxton,
1 Sunsundegui, 3 Transbus, 4 Van Hool.
Ops incl: local bus services, school contracts,
excursions & tours, private hire, express,
continental tours.
Livery: Green Fade/Stars.
Ticket System: ITSO.
A subsidiary of Johnson Bros Tours Ltd

ROBERTS COACHES LTD

♿⚙♿⑪⑪❄ R24 ✎T

THE LIMES, MIDLAND ROAD,
HUGGLESCOTE LE67 2FX
Tel: 01530 817444
Fax: 01530 817666
Recovery: 07785 572526
E-mail: info@robertscoaches.co.uk
Web site: www.robertstravelgroup.co.uk
Man Dir: Jonathan Hunt **Fin Dir:** Margaret
Bunker **Eng Dir:** Mick Crawford
Sales Man: Helen Jacobs
Compliance Man: David Wood **Business
Devt & Marketing Man:** Paul Owen **Coach
Holidays Man:** Sam Woolley.
Fleet: 61 - 20 double-deck bus, 10 single-
deck bus, 15 single-deck coach, 12 midibus,
2 midicoach, 2 minibus.
Chassis: 3 Alexander Dennis, 2 Dennis,
4 Mercedes, 20 MCW, 2 Neoplan, 5 Optare,
1 Setra, 1 Van Hool, 19 Volvo, 4 Wrightbus.
Bodies: 3 Alexander Dennis, 1 Caetano,
2 Ferqui, 5 Jonckheere, 20 MCW, 2 Neoplan,
5 Optare, 12 Plaxton, 1 Setra, 4 Van Hool,
4 Wrightbus.
Ops incl: local bus services, Leicester park
& ride, school contracts, excursions & tours,
private hire, express, continental tours
Livery: Green or Blue/White.
Ticket System: Wayfarer.

TGM GROUP LTD

Operations in Leicestershire are at East
Midlands Airport
See London & Middlesex

PAUL S WINSON COACHES LTD

♿⑪⚙♿✎T

ROYAL WAY, BELTON PARK,
LOUGHBOROUGH LE11 5XR
Tel: 01509 232354
Fax: 01509 265110
Recovery: 01509 237999

E-mail: sales@winsoncoaches.co.uk
Web site: www.winsoncoaches.co.uk
Man Dir: Paul S Winson **Ch Eng:** Paul
B Winson **Ops Man/Co Sec:** Anthony
J Winson.
Fleet: 34 – 9 double-deck bus, 12 single-deck
coach, 11 midibus, 2 midicoach.
Chassis: 8 Alexander Dennis, 4 Bova,
5 Dennis, 2 Leyland, 5 Mercedes, 2 Scania,
6 Volvo, 2 Wrightbus.
Bodies: 2 Alexander, 8 Alexander Dennis,
4 Bova, 5 East Lancs, 1 Irizar, 3 Jonckheere,
3 Mercedes, 1 Northern Counties, 5 Plaxton,
2 Wrightbus.
Ops incl: local bus services, school contracts,
excursions & tours, private hire, continental
tours.
Livery: Red/White/Blue.
Ticket system: Wayfarer.

WOODS COACHES LTD

♿⑪⑪⚙✎T

223 GLOUCESTER CRESCENT, WIGSTON
LE18 4YR
Tel: 0116 278 6374
Fax: 0116 247 7819
E-mail: sales@woods-coaches.co.uk
Web site: www.woodscoaches.com
Gen Man: Bill Tanser **Co Sec:** Jacqui Bates
Ops Man: Peter Skinner.
Fleet: 18- 16 single-deck coach, 1 midicoach,
1 minibus.
Chassis: 2 Irisbus, 1 Irizar, 1 Iveco,
1 Mercedes, 2 Neoplan, 1 Scania, 10 Volvo.
Bodies: 2 Beulas, 2 Irizar, 1 Mercedes,
2 Neoplan, 9 Plaxton, 1 Sunsundegui, 1 Other.
Ops incl: school contracts, excursions &
tours, private hire, continental tours.
Livery: Silver
A subsidiary of Stewarts of Mortimer
(Private Hire) Ltd (see Berkshire)

APPLEBYS COACH TRAVEL
See Radley Coach Travel.

BARNARD COACHES
♿ⓜ✳🍴

STATION ROAD, KIRTON LINDSEY,
GAINSBOROUGH DN21 4BD
Tel: 01652 648381 **Fax:** 01652 640377
E-mail: bookings@barnardcoaches.co.uk
Web site: www.barnardcoaches.co.uk
Fleet: 18 – 17 single-deck coach, 1 midicoach.
Chassis: 1 Bova, 2 DAF, 1 Mercedes, 4 Scania,
3 Temsa, 1 Van Hool, 6 Volvo.
Bodies: 1 Autobus, 1 Bova, 3 Irizar, 5 Plaxton,
3 Temsa, 5 Van Hool.
Ops incl: school contracts, private hire,
excursions & tours.
Livery: White with Red.

MARK BLAND TRAVEL LTD
ⓜ♿✳

ESSENDINE ROAD, RYHALL, STAMFORD
PE9 4JN
Tel: 01780 751671 **Fax:** 01780 763198
E-mail: info@markblandtravel.com
Web site: www.markblandtravel.co.uk
Fleet: 20 - 2 double-deck bus, 1 single-deck
bus, 15 single-deck coach, 2 midibus.
Chassis: 4 DAF, 2 Dennis, 2 Mercedes,
3 Scania, 9 Volvo.
Ops incl: local bus services, school contracts.
Livery: Red/Cream.

BRYLAINE TRAVEL LTD
♿♿

291 LONDON ROAD, BOSTON PE21 7DD
Tel: 01205 364087 **Fax:** 01205 359504
E-mail: enquiries@brylaine.co.uk
Web site: www.brylaine.co.uk
Man Dir: Brian W Gregg **Dir:** Elaine R Gregg
Co Sec: Susan E Bradshaw **Eng Dir:**
Brian P Gregg **Ops Dir:** Malcolm P Wheatley.
Depots at: Boston, Coningsby, Lincoln,
Skegness.
Fleet: 64 - 33 double-deck bus, 14 single-
deck bus, 11 midibus, 6 minibus.
Chassis: 6 BMC, 7 DAF, 20 Dennis, 7 Leyland,
15 Optare, 9 Volvo.
Bodies: 33 Alexander, 6 BMC, 7 Ikarus,
2 Marshall, 1 Northern Counties, 15 Optare.
Ops incl: local bus services, school contracts.
Liveries: Red/Blue/Yellow, Lincolnshire Inter-
Connect.
Ticket system: Wayfarer.

CENTREBUS LTD
♿

TOLLEMARCHE ROAD SOUTH,
SPITALGATE LEVEL, GRANTHAM NG31
7UH
Tel: 0844 351 1120
E-mail: info@centrebus.com
Web site: www.centrebus.info
Dirs: Peter Harvey, David Shelley, Julian
Peddle, Keith Hayward.
Fleet (Lincolnshire): 23 - 11 double-deck bus,
5 single-deck bus, 7 midibus.
Chassis: 2 DAF, 13 Dennis, 7 Optare, 1 Scania.
Bodies: 2 Alexander 7 East Lancs, 1 MCV,
7 Optare, 4 Plaxton, 2 Wrightbus.
Ops incl: local bus services, school contracts.
Livery: Blue/Orange/White.
Part of the Centrebus Group

CROPLEY COACHES
♿ⓜ✳♿🔵🍴

MAIN ROAD, FOSDYKE, BOSTON PE20 2BH
Tel: 01205 260226 **Fax:** 01205 260246
E-mail: enquiries@cropleycoach.co.uk
Web site: www.cropleycoach.co.uk
Man Dir: John Cropley **Co Sec:** Mrs Sandra
Cropley **Ch Eng:** Chris Cropley.

Fleet: 14 - 13 single-deck coach, 1 midicoach.
Chassis: 1 Toyota, 12 Volvo, 1 Yutong.
Bodies: 1 Caetano, 1 Plaxton, 11 Sunsundegui,
1 Yutong.
Ops incl: local bus services, school contracts,
excursions & tours, private hire, continental
tours.
Livery: Turquoise & White.

DELAINE BUSES LTD
♿

8 SPALDING ROAD, BOURNE PE10 9LE
Tel: 01778 422866 **Fax:** 01778 425593
E-mail: enquiries@delainebuses.com
Web site: www.delainebuses.com
Chairman: I Delaine-Smith **Man Dir:**
A Delaine-Smith **Dirs:** M Delaine-Smith,
K Delaine-Smith **Sec:** Miss J A Delaine-Smith.
Fleet: 24 - 18 double-deck bus, 6 single-deck
bus.
Chassis: 22 Volvo.
Bodies: 12 East Lancs, 12 Wrightbus.
Ops incl: local bus services.
Livery: Light/Dark Blue & Cream.
Ticket System: Almex A90.

DICKINSON'S COACHES
♿ⓜ🍴✳

BROADGATE, WRANGLE, BOSTON
PE22 9DY
Tel/Fax: 01205 870633
E-mail: ddickinson@mod-comp.co.uk
Web site: www.dickinsons-coaches.co.uk
Partners: D, J, N & J Dickinson.
Fleet: 12 – 1 double-deck bus, 8 single-deck
coach, 3 midicoach.
Chassis: 3 Dennis, 3 Mercedes, 1 Scania,
5 Volvo.
Bodies: 1 East Lancs, 1 Mercedes, 8 Plaxton,
2 Sitcar.
Ops incl: school contracts, private hire,
excursions & tours.
Livery: White with Orange/Green.

EAGRE COACHES LTD
See Wilfreda Beehive *(South Yorkshire)*

W H FOWLER & SONS
(COACHES) LTD
♿ⓜ🔲✳🔵

155 DOG DROVE SOUTH, HOLBEACH
DROVE, SPALDING PE12 0SD
Tel: 01406 330232 **Fax:** 01406 330923
E-mail: fowlerstravel@btinternet.com
Web site: www.fowlerstravel.co.uk
Fleet Name: Fowlers Travel
Man Dir: John Fowler **Co Sec:** Jackie Fowler
Dir: Andrew Fowler.
Fleet: 20 - 9 double-deck bus, 10 single-deck
coach, 1 midicoach.
Chassis: 4 DAF, 5 Dennis, 1 Leyland, 1 Toyota,
9 Volvo.
Bodies: 2 Alexander, 2 Berkhof, 1 Caetano,
4 East Lancs, 1 Jonckheere, 3 Northern
Counties, 6 Plaxton, 1 Van Hool.
Ops incl: local bus services, school contracts,
excursions & tours, private hire.
Livery: Cream/Orange/Red.
Ticket System: Wayfarer.

GRAYSCROFT BUS SERVICES LTD
♿

15A VICTORIA ROAD, MABLETHORPE
LN12 2AY
Tel: 01507 473236 **Fax:** 01507 477073
E-mail: info@grayscroft.co.uk
Web site: www.grayscroft.co.uk
Dirs: C W Barker, N W Barker, D Birt.
Fleet: 20 - 5 double-deck bus, 10 single-deck
coach, 3 midibus, 1 minibus, 1 minicoach.
Chassis: 1 Dennis, 3 Mercedes, 1 Neoplan,
1 Optare, 1 Toyota, 13 Volvo.

Bodies: 1 Alexander, 2 Caetano, 1 Hispano,
1 Jonckheere, 1 Mellor, 1 Mercedes,
1 Neoplan, 4 Northern Counties, 1 Optare,
3 Plaxton, 3 Van Hool, 1 Wrightbus.
Ops incl: local bus services, school contracts,
excursions & tours, private hire.
Livery: Cream, Blue & Orange.
Ticket system: Wayfarer.

PHIL HAINES COACHES
♿

RALPHS LANE, FRAMPTON WEST, BOSTON
PE20 1QU
Tel: 01205 334738
Web site: www.philhainescoachesboston.
co.uk
Props: N A & S Haines.
Fleet: 16 – 8 single-deck coach, 1 midicoach,
7 minibus.
Chassis: 4 Dennis, 1 Ford Transit, 6 LDV,
1 Leyland, 1 Toyota, 3 Volvo.
Ops incl: local bus services, school contracts,
private hire.
Livery: White.

HODSON COACHES LTD
♿ⓜ✳[R][R24]🔲

SAXILBY ENTERPRISE PARK,
SKELLINGTHORPE ROAD, SAXILBY,
LINCOLN LN1 2LR
Tel: 01522 706030 **Fax:** 01522 706031
E-mail: sales@hodsoncoaches.co.uk
Web Site: www.hodsoncoaches.co.uk
Man Dir: Alistair Gooseman **Ops Dir:** Tim
Gooseman **Fleet Man:** Sue Gooseman.
Fleet: 11 - 5 single-deck coach, 2 midicoach,
4 minibus.
Chassis: 1 LDV, 6 Mercedes, 4 Setra.
Ops incl: school contracts, excursions &
tours, private hire, continental tours.
Livery: Lemon/Purple.
Ticket system: Almex.

HORNSBY TRAVEL SERVICES LTD
♿♿✳🍴

51 ASHBY HIGH STREET, SCUNTHORPE
DN16 2NB
Tel: 01724 282255 **Fax:** 01274 282788
E-mail: office@hornsbytravel.co.uk
Web site: www.hornsbytravel.co.uk
Man Dir: Raymond Hornsby **Gen Man:**
Nicholas Hornsby **Ch Eng:** Rob Andrew.
Fleet: 31 - 3 double-deck bus, 21 single-deck
bus, 3 single-deck coach, 3 executive coaches,
1 minibus.
Chassis: 13 Alexander Dennis, 5 DAF,
2 Leyland, 3 MAN, 2 VDL, 6 Volvo.
Bodies: 3 Alexander, 3 Alexander Dennis,
19 Plaxton, 6 Wrightbus.
Ops incl: local bus services, school contracts,
excursions & tours, private hire.
Livery: Blue/Silver.
Ticket System: ERG.

F HUNT COACH HIRE LTD
♿ⓜ✳🍴

2/3 WEST STREET, ALFORD LN13 9DG
Tel/Fax: 01507 463000
E-mail: travel.office@hunts-coaches.co.uk
Web site: www.hunts-coaches.co.uk
Fleet Name: Hunts Travel.
Dirs: Michael Hunt, Joe Hunt.
Fleet: 24 - 3 double-deck bus, 2 single-deck
bus, 11 single-deck coach, 3 midicoach,
5 minibus.
Chassis: 1 Ford, 1 Iveco, 5 Mercedes,
1 Volkswagen, 16 Volvo.
Ops incl: local bus services, school contracts,
excursions & tours, private hire, express,
continental tours.
Livery: White/Red/Grey.
Ticket System: Almex.

Lincolnshire

KIER GROUP (TRANSLINC)
♿❄✳
JARVIS HOUSE, 157 SADLER ROAD,
LINCOLN LN6 3RS
Tel: 01522 503400
Fax: 01522 503406
Web site: www.kier.co.uk
Man Dir: Paul Wood **Fin Dir & Dir of Southern Operations:** David Foulds
Dir of Midland Ops: Mark Werrell
Dir of Northern Ops: Joe Cleary.
Fleet: 215 – 11 single-deck coach,
9 midicoach, 195 minibus.
Chassis: Citroen, Dennis, Fiat, Ford Transit, Irisbus, Iveco, LDV, Mercedes, Optare, Renault, Scania, Transbus, Vauxhall, Volvo.
Ops incl: local bus services, demand responsive bus services, school contracts, excursions & tours, private hire, express.
Fleet Names: Translinc, Call Connect.
May Gurney, former owners of Translinc, were acquired by Kier in 2013

LAWTON'S EXECUTIVE COACHES
♿✳♿❅✳R
LAST MOORINGS, EAST FEN LANE,
STICKNEY, BOSTON PE22 8DE
Tel: 01205 480462
Fax: 01205 480709
Recovery: 07879 444085
E-mail: info@lawtonscoaches.com
Web site: www.lawtonscoaches.com
Props: Geoff & Liz Lawton.
Fleet: 14 – 7 double-deck bus, 5 single deck coach, 1 midicoach, 1 minibus.
Chassis: 1 Bova, 4 Dennis, 2 Leyland, 1 Mercedes, 2 Scania, 1 Setra, 3 Volvo
Bodies: 1 Alexander, 1 Bova, 2 Duple, 2 East Lancs, 2 Jonckheere, 1 Mercedes, 1 Northern Counties, 3 Plaxton, 1 Setra.
Ops incl: school contracts, excursions & tours, private hire.
Livery: White.

LOVEDEN TRAVEL
✳
16 NORTH ROAD, LEADENHAM LN5 0PG
Tel: 01400 273838
Fax: 01400 272587
E-mail: enquiries@loveden-travel.com
Web site: www.coachhirelincoln.com
Ops incl: school contracts, private hire, excursions & tours.
Livery: White.

MEMORY LANE COACHES
✳
ELM HOUSE, OLD BOLINGBROKE,
SPILSBY PE23 4HF
Tel: 01790 763394
Prop: John B Dorey.
Fleet: 3 - 2 single-deck coach, 1 minibus.
Chassis: 2 Dennis, 1 Mercedes.
Bodies: 2 Plaxton, 1 Other.
Ops incl: school contracts, private hire.
Livery: White/Green/Red.

PC COACHES OF LINCOLN LTD
♿✳♿❅✳R24✆T
17 CROFTON ROAD, LINCOLN LN3 4NL
Tel: 01522 533605
Fax: 01522 560402
E-mail: enquiries@pccoaches.co.uk
Web site: www.pccoaches.co.uk
Man Dir: Peter Smith **Ops Dir:** Miss Sarah Smith **Dir International Ops:** Chris Bristow.
Fleet: 68 - 16 double-deck bus, 3 single-deck bus, 38 single-deck coach, 6 midibus, 1 midicoach, 3 minibus, 1 minicoach.
Chassis: 2 Alexander Dennis, 1 Dennis, 1 Ford Transit, 1 LDV, 3 Mercedes, 3 Optare, 54 Scania, 3 Wrightbus.
Bodies: 2 Alexander Dennis, 1 Berkhof, 14 East Lancs, 1 Ferqui, 29 Irizar, 2 Koch,

6 Lahden, 1 LDV, 3 Optare, 2 Plaxton, 1 Unvi, 2 Van Hool, 4 Wrightbus.
Ops incl: local bus services, school contracts, private hire, continental tours.
Livery: White/Maroon/Red.

ROY PHILLIPS
✳❄✳
69 STATION ROAD, RUSKINGTON
NG34 9DF
Tel: 01526 832279
Prop: R Phillips.
Fleet: 6 single-deck coach.
Chassis: 6 Volvo.
Bodies: 1 Jonckheere, 1 Plaxton, 4 Van Hool.
Ops incl: private hire, school contracts.

PULFREYS COACHES
♿♿✳♿❄✳
1 WILKINSON ROAD, FOSTON,
GRANTHAM NG32 2JX
Tel: 01476 564144
Web site: www.pulfreyscoaches.co.uk
Dir: Andrew Pulfrey.
Fleet: 4 - 2 single-deck coach, 1 midibus, 1 minibus.
Chassis: 1 Dennis, 1 Iveco, 2 Mercedes.
Bodies: 1 Beulas, 2 Plaxton, 1 Other.
Ops incl: school contracts, excursions & tours, private hire, continental tours.
Livery: Blue/White.
Ticket System: Wayfarer.

RADLEY COACH TRAVEL
✳♿❄✳
THE TRAVEL OFFICE, 11 CHAPEL COURT,
BRIGG DN20 8JZ
Tel: 01652 653583   **Fax:** 01652 656020
Fleet Names: Radley Holidays, Applebys Coach Holidays.
E-mail: radleytravel@aol.com
Web site: www.radleytravel.co.uk
Prop: Kevin M Radley.
Fleet: 3 single-deck coach.
Chassis: 3 Scania.
Bodies: 3 Irizar.
Ops incl: excursions & tours, private hire, continental tours.
Livery: Maroon/Gold.
Incorporating Applebys Coach Travel

REDFERN TRAVEL LTD
See Nottinghamshire

SKEGNESS TRAVEL HIRE
♿♿✳
38 ROMAN BANK, SKEGNESS PE25 2SJ
Tel: 01754 763963
E-mail: information@skegnesstravel.com
Web site: www.skegnesstravel.eclipse.co.uk
Owner: John Simpson.
Fleet: 6 – 1 single-deck bus, 2 single-deck coach, 1 midicoach, 2 minibus.
Chassis incl: 2 Scania, 1 Volvo
Ops incl: school contracts, excursions & tours, private hire.

SLEAFORDIAN COACHES
♿✳♿❄✳RT
PRIDE PARKWAY, EAST ROAD, SLEAFORD
NG34 8GL
Tel: 01529 303333/01529 414242
Fax: 01529 303324
E-mail: office@sleafordian.co.uk
Web site: www.sleafordian.co.uk
Dirs: Mark Broughton **(Man Dir)**, Mrs Lisa Broughton **(Co Sec)**, Don Broughton, Mrs Jean Broughton **Chief Eng:** Phillip Kerr.
Fleet: 33 - 16 double-deck bus, 2 single-deck bus, 10 single-deck coach, 2 midibus, 3 midicoach.
Chassis: 12 Alexander Dennis, 1 Dennis, 3 Mercedes, 2 Optare, 15 Volvo.
Bodies: 9 Alexander Dennis, 4 East Lancs,

1 Esker, 2 Northern Counties, 12 Plaxton, 3 Van Hool, 2 Wright.
Ops incl: local bus services, school contracts, excursions & tours, private hire, continental tours.
Livery: White/Orange/Blue.
Ticket System: Wayfarer TGX.

SMITHS COACHES, CORBY GLEN
♿
THE GREEN, CORBY GLEN NG33 4NP
Tel: 01476 550285
Prop: H J Smith.
Ops incl: excursions & tours, private hire, continental tours, school contracts.
Livery: Blue/White.

STAGECOACH EAST MIDLANDS
♿♿◻➖➖
PO BOX 15, DEACON ROAD, LINCOLN
LN2 4JB
Tel: 0345 605 0605
Fax: 01522 538229
Fleet Name: Stagecoach in Lincolnshire.
E-mail: eastmidlands.enquiries@ stagecoachbus.com
Web site: www.stagecoachbus.com
Man Dir: Michelle Hargreaves **Eng Dir:** John Taylor **Comm Dir:** Dave Skepper
Ops Dir: Richard Kay.
Fleet: 540 – 209 double-deck bus, 122 single-deck bus, 16 single-deck coach, 165 midibus, 28 minibus.
Chassis: 165 Alexander Dennis, 6 DAF, 109 Dennis, 1 Leyland, 72 MAN, 36 Optare, 26 Scania, 49 Transbus, 76 Volvo.
Bodies: 110 Alexander Dennis, 234 Alexander Dennis, 50 East Lancs, 6 Jonckheere, 5 Northern Counties, 36 Optare, 37 Plaxton, 50 Transbus, 12 Wrightbus.
Ops incl: local bus services.
Livery: Stagecoach UK Bus.
Ticket System: ERG TP5000.

TOURMASTER COACHES LTD
♿✳♿❄✳RR24✳
ALDERLANDS, JAMES ROAD, CROWLAND,
PETERBOROUGH PE6 0AA
Tel: 01733 211710   **Fax:** 01733 211378
Recovery: 01733 211639
E-mail: tourmaster@btconnect.com
Web site: www.tourmastercoaches.co.uk
Man Dir: David Dinsey **Dir:** Terri Dinsey
Fleet: 14 - 1 double-deck bus, 12 single-deck coach, 1 minibus.
Chassis: 3 Bova, 2 DAF, 1 LDV, 1 Leyland, 1 Scania, 1 VDL, 5 Volvo.
Bodies: 3 Bova, 1 Irizar, 1 Jonckheere, 1 LDV, 1 Optare, 3 Plaxton, 4 Van Hool.
Ops incl: school contracts, excursions & tours, private hire, continental tours.
Livery: Red/Blue/Turquoise.

A C WILLIAMS LTD
♿✳♿♿❄✳RR✳T
1 STATION APPROACH, ANCASTER,
GRANTHAM NG32 3QY
Tel: 01400 230491
Fax: 01400 230296
Recovery: 01400 230491
E-mail: coaches@acwilliams.co.uk
Web site: www.acwcoaches.co.uk
Chairman: Glen Pratt **Fin Dir:** David Pratt
Tran Man: Ian Mansell, Andrew Scotton.
Fleet: 35 – 9 double-deck bus, 18 single-deck coach, 2 double-deck coach, 3 midicoach.
Chassis: 3 Dennis, 1 Leyland, 2 MAN, 7 Scania, 1 Setra, 1 Toyota, 20 Volvo.
Bodies incl: 3 Alexander, 1 Caetano, 7 Irizar, 1 Neoplan, 4 Plaxton, 1 Setra, 7 Van Hool.
Ops incl: school contracts, excursions & tours, private hire, continental tours.
Livery: White.
Incorporating Southern Holidays Ltd

Lincolnshire

This section includes those operators in the London and Middlesex postal areas, as well as operators who have asked to appear under this heading. Other operators within Greater London with a non-London postal address, eg Kingston, Surrey; Bromley, Kent; etc, may be found under their respective postal counties.

ABELLIO LONDON AND SURREY

301 CAMBERWELL NEW ROAD, LONDON SE5 0TF
Tel: 020 7788 8550
Fax: 020 7788 8593
E-mail: customer.care@abellio.co.uk
Web site: www.abellio.co.uk
Man Dir UK Bus: Alan Pilbeam
Man Dir: Tony Wilson **Fin Dir:** Andrew Worboys **Perf Dir:** Mark McGuinness
Ops Dir: Ben Wakerley **Eng Dir:** Phil Pannell
Commercial Man: Alastair Willis
Head of HR: Kerry Smith.
Fleet: 684 - 377 double-deck bus, 307 single-deck bus.
Chassis: 587 Alexander Dennis, 1 Optare, 73 Volvo.
Bodies: 558 Alexander Dennis, 36 Caetano, 16 East Lancs, 1 Optare, 73 Wrightbus.
Ops incl: local bus services, rail replacement, coach parking.
Livery: London: Red; Surrey: White/Red.
Ticket systems: London: TfL Prestige; Surrey: Ticketer.

ABLE COACHES

EURO STORAGE, DEPOT ROAD, LONDON W12 7RZ
Tel: 020 8811 1221
Fax: 020 8951 0964
E-mail: info@ablelondon.com
Web site: www.ablelondon.co.uk
Prop: D Andrews.
Fleet: 8 – 7 single-deck coach, 1 midicoach.
Chassis: 1 Bova, 2 Irizar, 1 Mercedes, 2 Scania, 1 Van Hool, 1 VDL.
Bodies: 1 Berkhof, 1 Bova, 3 Irizar, 1 Unvi, 1 Van Hool, 1 VDL.
Ops incl: school contracts, private hire.
Livery: Black/Silver.

ANDERSON TRAVEL GROUP

178A TOWER BRIDGE ROAD, LONDON SE1 3LS
Tel: 020 7403 8118
Fax: 020 7403 8421
E-mail: sales@andersontravel.co.uk
Web site: www.andersontravel.co.uk
Man Dir: Mark Anderson **Comm Man:** Keith Payne **Ops Man:** Peter Gilbert.
Fleet: 32 – 19 single-deck coach, 5 midicoach, 7 minibus, 1 minicoach.
Chassis: 10 VDL Bova, 8 Mercedes, 5 Volkswagen, 9 Volvo.
Bodies: 10 VDL Bova, 2 EVM, 1 Excel, 1 Ferqui, 8 Plaxton, 5 Sitcar, 1 Sunsundegui, 4 Volkswagen.
Ops incl: school contracts, excursions & tours, private hire, express, continental tours.
Livery: White with Green lettering.

ARRIVA LONDON

16 WATSONS ROAD, LONDON N22 7TZ
Tel: 020 8271 0101
Fax: 020 8271 0120
Web site: www.arrivalondon.com
Man Dir: Bob Scowen
Comm Dir: Peter Batty **Ops Dir:** Jeff Quantrell
Eng Dir: Ian Warr **Fin Dir:** Ravinder Saund.

Fleet: 1687 - 1443 double-deck bus, 244 midibus.
Chassis: 6 AEC, 452 Alexander Dennis, 275 DAF, 20 Dennis, 13 Transbus, 405 VDL, 452 Volvo, 64 Wrightbus NBfL.
Ops incl: local bus services, private hire.
Livery: Red.
Ticket System: TfL Prestige.

ATLAS COACHES LTD

52-68 PALMERSTON ROAD, WEALDSTONE HA3 7RW
Tel: 020 8863 8883
Fax: 020 8863 4443
E-mail: info@atlascoaches.co.uk
Web site: www.atlascoaches.co.uk
Fleet: 11 – 7 single-deck coach, 3 midicoach, 1 minicoach.
Chassis: 1 Irisbus, 4 Mercedes, 6 Volvo.
Bodies: 3 Ferqui, 3 Plaxton, 5 Sunsundegui.
Ops incl: school contracts, private hire, excursions & tours, continental tours.
Livery: White with Pale Blue.

BACK ROADS TOURING CO LTD

LEVEL 1, 107 POWER ROAD, CHISWICK, LONDON W4 5PY
Tel: 020 8987 0990
Fax: 020 8994 0888
E-mail: info@backroadstouring.co.uk
Web site: www.backroadstouring.co.uk
Dirs: Graham Turner, Chris Galanty, James Nathan.
Fleet: 16 minibus.
Chassis: Mercedes.
Ops incl: excursions & tours, private hire, continental tours.
Livery: White.

BEAR BUSES

54 FAGGS ROAD, FELTHAM TW14 0LG
Tel/Fax: 020 8867 0617
E-mail: bearbuses@hotmail.co.uk
Prop: Glenn N Massiah.
Fleet: 14 - 10 double-deck bus, 4 midibus.
Chassis: 4 Dennis, 4 Leyland, 3 MCW, 1 Transbus, 2 Volvo.
Bodies: 2 Alexander, 1 ECW, 2 Leyland, 3 MCW, 1 Northern Counties, 4 Plaxton, 1 Transbus.
Ops incl: local bus services, school contracts, private hire.
Livery: Red with Cream Relief.
Ticket System: Wayfarer Saver; Wayfarer 3.

BEECHES TRAVEL

523 LONDON ROAD, NORTH CHEAM, SURREY SM3 8JR
Tel: 0800 999 6669
E-mail: info@beeches-travel.co.uk
Web site: www.beechestravel.co.uk
Prop: C Miller.
Fleet: 3 minicoach.
Chassis: 1 Ford Transit, 1 Iveco, 1 Mercedes.
Ops incl: school contracts, excursions & tours, private hire.
Livery: White/Yellow.

BESSWAY TRAVEL LTD

COMPOUND 12b, MAGNET ROAD, EAST LANE BUSINESS PARK, WEMBLEY HA9 7RG
Tel: 020 8908 0785
Fax: 020 8904 3124
E-mail: info@besswaytravel.co.uk
Web site: www.besswaytravel.co.uk
Dirs:: Michael Heffernan, Susan Heffernan, Simon Payne.

Fleet: 12 - 5 single-deck coach, 1 midicoach, 2 minicoach, 4 minibus.
Chassis: 3 Alexander Dennis, 2 Iveco, 2 LDV, 4 Mercedes, 1 Scania.
Bodies: 1 Crest, 1 Excel, 2 Ferqui, 1 Lahden, 4 Plaxton, 1 Unvi, 2 Other.
Ops incl: private hire, excursions & tours, school contracts.
Livery: White with Blue/Red.

BIG BUS COMPANY

48 BUCKINGHAM PALACE ROAD, LONDON SW1W 0RN
Tel: 020 7808 6753
Fax: 020 7828 0638
E-mail: info@bigbustours.com
Web site: www.bigbustours.com
Chief Exec: Pat Waterman.
Fleet: 77 open-top bus.
Chassis: 20 Anhui Ankai, 31 Dennis, 26 Volvo.
Bodies: 20 Anhui Ankai, 19 Duple, 22 East Lancs, 16 Optare.
Ops incl: excursions & tours, private hire.
Livery: Burgundy/Cream.
Ticket system: Almex.

BLISS TRAVEL LTD

38-40 VERNEY ROAD, SOUTH BERMONDSEY SE16 3DH
Tel: 020 7394 6358
E-mail: sales@coachcentre.co.uk
Web site: www.coachcentre.co.uk
Dirs: A & A Bliss.
Fleet: 21 – 6 single-deck coach, 7 midicoach, 6 minicoach, 2 minibus.
Chassis: 17 Mercedes, 4 Scania.
Ops include: school contracts, private hire
Livery: White

BLUE TRIANGLE LTD

See Go-Ahead London

BM COACHES & RENTAL LTD

BM HOUSE, SILVERDALE ROAD, HAYES UB3 3BN
Tel: 0845 555 7711
Fax: 0845 555 7722
E-mail: info@bmcoaches.co.uk
Web site: www.bmcoaches.co.uk
Man Dir: B Balasuresh.
Fleet: 29 – 2 double-deck coach, 18 single-deck coach, 3 midicoach, 4 minibus, 2 minicoach.
Chassis: 1 Bova, 1 King Long, 8 Mercedes, 14 Van Hool, 5 Volvo.
Ops incl: excursions & tours, private hire.

BRENTONS OF BLACKHEATH

UNIT 219d, 1 ALDINGTON ROAD, WOOLWICH SE18 5TS
Tel: 020 3260 3430
Fax: 020 8317 8895
E-mail: brentons@brentonsofblackheath.co.uk
Web site: www.brentons-ofblackheath.co.uk
Prop: C Clark **Ch Eng:** I Powell.
Fleet: 12 - 9 single-deck coach, 1 midicoach, 1 minibus, 1 minicoach.
Chassis: 1 DAF, 1 Dennis, 1 Iveco, 1 Leyland, 2 Mercedes, 1 Scania, 5 Volvo.
Ops incl: school contracts, private hire.
Livery: County Cream.

BRYANS OF ENFIELD

19 WETHERBY ROAD, ENFIELD EN2 0NS
Tel: 020 8366 0062
Owner: Brian Nash.

Fleet: 4 double-deck bus.
Chassis: 1 Scania, 3 Volvo.
Bodies: 1 Alexander, 3 Northern Counties.
Ops incl: school contracts, private hire.
Livery: Red.

BUSES EXCETERA
See BETC Ltd, Surrey

CABIN COACHES
1 PARSONAGE CLOSE, HAYES UB3 2LZ
Tel: 020 8573 1100
Fax: 020 8573 8604
E-mail: info@cabincoaches.com
Web site: www.cabincoaches.com
Prop: Peter Martin.
Fleet: 7 - 4 single-deck coach, 2 midicoach, 1 minibus.
Chassis: 2 BMC, 1 Iveco, 4 Scania.
Ops incl: excursions & tours, school contracts, private hire.
Livery: White with Purple/Light Blue signage.

CARAVELLE COACHES
9 CHESTNUT AVENUE, EDGWARE HA8 7RA
Tel/Fax: 020 8952 4025
E-mail: caravelle@aol.com
Prop: Harvey Lawrence.
Fleet: 2 - 1 midibus, 1 minibus.
Chassis: 1 Ford Transit, 1 Mercedes.
Bodies: 1 Mellor, 1 Other.
Ops incl: school contracts, excursions & tours, private hire.

CENTAUR TRAVEL
UNIT 34-35, ACORN INDUSTRIAL PARK, CRAYFORD DA1 4AL
Tel: 020 8300 3001
Fax: 020 8302 5959
E-mail: info@centaurtravel.co.uk
Web site: www.centaurtravel.co.uk
Man Dir: M. Sims **Dirs:** P Sims, S Durrant.
Fleet: 35 – 2 double-deck bus, 15 single-deck coach, 4 midicoach, 13 minibus, 1 minicoach.
Chassis: 2 Alexander Dennis, 4 Ford Transit, 4 LDV, 3 MAN, 11 Mercedes, 3 Renault, 4 Scania, 1 Vauxhall, 4 Volvo.
Ops incl: private hire, school contracts, excursions & tours, London commuter express.

CHALFONT COACHES OF HARROW LTD
200 FEATHERSTONE ROAD, SOUTHALL UB2 5AQ
Tel: 020 8843 2323
Fax: 020 8574 0939
E-mail: chalfontcoaches@btopenworld.com
Web site: www.chalfontcoaches.co.uk
Man Dir: C J Shears **Dirs:** I Shears, M Shears
Ops Man: P Williams **Ch Eng:** M Shears
Co Sec: G Shears.
Fleet: 26 - 25 single-deck coach, 1 minibus.
Chassis: 2 Bova, 1 Mercedes, 23 Volvo.
Bodies: 2 Bova, 9 Caetano, 14 Van Hool, 1 Other.
Ops incl: school contracts, excursions & tours, private hire, express, continental tours.
Liveries: Mauve/White, National Express.
Also operates from Northampton

CHALFONT LINE LTD
4 PROVIDENCE ROAD, WEST DRAYTON UB7 8HJ
Tel: 01895 459540
Fax: 01895 459549
E-mail: info@chalfont-line.co.uk
Web site: www.chalfont-line.co.uk

Chairman: T J Reynolds **Man Dir:** R Chadija
Dir: M Kerr **Tran Man:** Lynn Young.
Fleet: 84 minibus.
Chassis: 64 DAF, 6 Ford Transit, 8 Mercedes, 6 Renault.
Ops incl: school contracts, excursions & tours, private hire, continental tours.
Livery: White/Green.

CITY CIRCLE (UK) LTD – LONDON BRANCH
WEST LONDON COACH CENTRE, NORTH HYDE GARDENS, HAYES UB3 4QT
Tel: 020 8561 2112
Fax: 020 8561 2010
E-mail: go@citycircleuk.com
Web site: www.citycircleuk.com
Man Dir: Neil Pegg **Ops Man:** Nick Morton
Eng Man: Steve Maw.
Fleet: 34 – 28 single-deck coach, 3 midicoach, 3 minicoach.
Chassis: 28 MAN, 3 Mercedes, 3 Scania.
Bodies: 3 Irizar, 28 Neoplan, 3 Plaxton.
Ops incl: excursions & tours, private hire, continental tours, corporate charter.
Livery: White with Silver/Red.
Also operates in Scotland (see *City of Edinburgh, Midlothian*)

E CLARKE & SONS COACHES
KANGLEY BRIDGE ROAD, LOWER SYDENHAM, LONDON SE26 5AT
Tel: 020 8778 6697
Fax: 020 8778 0389
E-mail: info@clarkescoaches.co.uk
Web site: www.clarkescoaches.co.uk
Man Dir: Mrs D Newman **Fin Dir:** S Reeve
Gen Man: A Nixon **Tran Man:** C Stephens
Workshop Man: M Coker.
Fleet: 59 - 55 single-deck coach, 4 minicoach.
Chassis: 12 Irizar, 31 Mercedes, 8 Scania, 6 Setra, 2 Toyota.
Bodies: 7 Berkhof, 2 Caetano, 13 Irizar, 29 Mercedes, 6 Setra, 2 Unvi.
Ops incl: excursions & tours, private hire, Medway-London commuter services, continental tours.
Livery: Turquoise Green & Grey/Silver.

CONISTON COACHES LTD
88 CONISTON ROAD, BROMLEY BR1 4JB
Tel/Fax: 020 8460 3432
E-mail: conistoncoaches31@hotmail.co.uk
Web site: www.conistoncoaches.com
Dir: Richard Smock.
Fleet: 4 single-deck coach.
Chassis: 4 Volvo.
Bodies: 1 Caetano, 3 Plaxton.
Ops incl: private hire, school contracts.
Livery: White/Red.

COUNTY COACHES
See Essex

DAVID CORBEL OF LONDON LTD
RAYS HOUSE, NORTH CIRCULAR ROAD, LONDON NW10 7XP
Tel: 020 8965 0005
Fax: 020 8328 3555
E-mail: corbeloflondon@aol.com
Web site: www.corbel-coaches.co.uk
Dir: Robert Whelan.
Fleet: 14 – 12 single-deck coach, 2 minibus
Chassis: 2 Mercedes, 3 Scania, 3 Setra, 6 Volvo.
Bodies: 3 Irizar, 1 KVC, 6 Plaxton, 3 Setra, 1 Other.
Ops incl: school contracts, private hire.
Livery: Pink/Blue.

CROWN COACHES
DURABLE HOUSE, CRABTREE MANOR WAY SOUTH, BELVEDERE DA17 6AB
Tel: 020 8313 3020
Fleet: 1 minibus.
Chassis: Ford Transit.
Ops incl: school contracts, private hire.

CROYDON COACHES UK LTD
145/147 ST JOHN STREET, LONDON EC1V 4PW
Tel: 020 8665 5561
Fax: 020 8664 8694
E-mail: info@coachesetc.com
Web site: www.coachesetc.com
Fleet Name: Coaches Excetera.
Man Dir: Siri Wong **Tran Man:** Alex Mazza
Comm Man: Paul Fisher.
Fleet: double-deck bus, double-deck coach, single-deck bus, single-deck coach, midibus, midicoach, minibus.
Ops incl: local bus services, school contracts, private hire.
Livery: White with logo.
Incorporates Atbus and Stanley Travel

CRYSTALS COACHES LTD
Ceased trading since LRB 2014 went to press

CT PLUS LTD
1st FLOOR, 141 CURTAIN ROAD, LONDON, EC2 3AR
Tel: 020 7275 2400
Fax: 020 7608 8969
E-mail: info@hctgroup.org
Web site: www.hctgroup.org
Ch Exec: Dai Powell OBE **Dep Ch Exec:** Jude Winter **Ch Fin Off:** John Smart **Ops Dir:** Jane Desmond **Perf Dir:** Jon McColl.
Depots at: Ash Grove, Walthamstow.
Fleet (London): 98 - 29 double-deck bus, 32 midibus, 35 minibus, 1 minicoach.
Chassis: 22 Alexander Dennis, 3 Dennis, 4 Mercedes, 28 Optare, 10 Scania, 27 Transbus, 4 Volkswagen.
Bodies: 15 Alexander Dennis, 3 Bluebird, 9 Caetano, 20 East Lancs, 4 Mercedes, 28 Optare, 3 Plaxton, 10 Scania, 5 Transbus, 1 Volkswagen.
Ops incl: local bus services.
Livery: Red/Yellow.
Ticket System: TfL Prestige.
A division of the HCT Group. See also operations in Bristol, East Riding, West Yorkshire and the Channel Islands.

DANS LUXURY TRAVEL LTD
ROYAL FOREST COACH HOUSE, 109 MAYBANK ROAD, LONDON E18 1EZ
Tel: 020 8505 8833
Fax: 020 8519 1937
E-mail: info@dansluxurytravel.com
Web site: www.dansluxurytravel.com
Man Dir: D J Brown **Dir:** N Brown.
Fleet: 24 – 10 single-deck coach, 4 midicoach, 6 minibus, 4 minicoach.
Chassis: 3 Ford Transit, 2 King Long, 9 Mercedes, 1 Toyota, 1 Volkswagen, 8 Volvo.
Ops incl: school contracts, excursions & tours, private hire, continental tours.
Livery: White with Blue/Red.
See also West's Coaches Ltd

DAVIAN COACHES LTD
1-3 BECKET ROAD, EDMONTON, LONDON N18 3PN
Tel: 020 8807 1515
Fax: 020 8807 2323
E-mail: office@daviancoaches.co.uk

Web site: www.daviancoaches.co.uk
Man Dir: Darren Wardle **Dir & Co Sec:**
Judy Wardle **Man:** David Bee **Transport**
Man: Richard Window.
Fleet: 18 - 10 single-deck coach, 7 minibus,
1 midicoach.
Chassis: 2 Autosan, 1 BMC 1 Irisbus, 2 King
Long, 5 LDV, 2 Mercedes, 4 Scania, 1 Volvo.
Bodies: 2 Autosan, 1 Beulas, 1 BMC, 4 Irizar,
2 King Long, 1 Plaxton, 7 Other.
Ops incl: excursions & tours, school
contracts, private hire, express, continental
tours.
Livery: White with Blue/Orange.

DHILLON OF LONDON

BULLSBRIDGE INDUSTRIAL ESTATE, HAYES
ROAD, SOUTHALL UB2 5NB
Tel: 020 8573 8858
Fax: 020 8573 8843
E-mail: dhillonoflondon@aol.com
Web site: www.dhillonoflondon.com
Dirs: B & R Dhillon
Fleet: 10 -2 double-deck coach, 6 single-deck
coach, 2 midicoach.
Chassis: 2 Mercedes, 2 Van Hool, 6 Volvo.
Bodies: 3 Jonckheere, 2 Mercedes, 1 Plaxton,
4 Van Hool.
Ops incl: private hire.
Livery: Purple.

DOCKLANDS BUSES LTD

See Go-Ahead London

DOCKLANDS COACHES LTD

FACTORY ROAD, SILVERTOWN E16 2EW
Tel: 020 7474 8130
Fax: 020 7474 9580
E-mail: docklandcoaches@aol.com
Dir: F Cheroomi.
Fleet: 4 – 1 midicoach, 1 minibus,
2 minicoach.
Chassis: 1 Iveco, 3 Mercedes.
Ops incl: school contracts, private hire.
Livery: Blue with White/Red.

EASYBUS LTD

EASYBUS HOUSE, NORTH CIRCULAR
ROAD, LONDON NW10 7XP
Web site: www.easybus.co.uk
Chief Exec: Peter Hyde.
Fleet: 74 minibus.
Chassis: 24 Ford Transit, 50 Renault.
Bodies: 24 Ford, 50 Renault.
Operations: Airport Express.
Livery: Orange

P & J ELLIS LTD

22 AINTREE ROAD, PERIVALE, UB6 7LA
Tel: 020 8997 0644
Fax: 020 8810 5898
E-mail: enquiries@pjellis.co.uk
Web site: www.pjellis.co.uk
Dirs: Matthew Ellis, J Ellis.
Fleet: 24 - 22 single-deck coach, 2 midicoach.
Chassis: 2 Mercedes, 22 Volvo.
Bodies: 15 Jonckheere, 1 Noone Turas,
7 Sunsundegui, 1 Unvi.
Ops incl: private hire.
Livery: White with Red lettering.

ELTHAM EXECUTIVE CHARTER LTD

23 CROWN WOODS WAY, LONDON
SE9 2NL
Tel: 020 8850 2011   **Fax:** 020 8850 5210
E-mail: enquiries@eec-minicoaches.co.uk
Web site: www.eec-minicoaches.co.uk
Dirs: Ray Lawrence, Jill Lawrence, Fiona
Lawrence.

Fleet: 5 - 3 midicoach, 1 minibus, 1 minicoach.
Chassis: 1 Ford, 4 Iveco.
Bodies: 3 Indcar, 1 Optare, 1 Other.
Ops incl: private hire.
Livery: White with blue and gold graphics.

EMPRESS OF LONDON

3 CORBRIDGE CRESCENT, LONDON
E2 9DS
Tel: 020 7739 5454
Fax: 020 7729 0237
E-mail: info@empresscoaches.co.uk
Web site: www.empresscoaches.co.uk
Dir: C Clark.
Fleet: 15 – 11 single-deck coach, 1 midicoach,
2 minibus, 1 minicoach.
Chassis: 2 Ford Transit, 1 Mercedes, 1 Toyota,
11 Volvo.
Bodies: 1 Caetano, 1 Ferqui, 10 Plaxton, 1 Van
Hool, 2 Other.
Ops incl: private hire.
Livery: Cream.

EXCALIBUR COACHES

NYES WHARF, FRENSHAM STREET,
LONDON SE1 6TH
Tel: 020 7358 1441
Fax: 020 7358 1661
E-mail: office@excaliburcoaches.com
Web site: www.excaliburcoaches.com
Man Dir: Mark Jewell.
Fleet: 29 single-deck coach.
Chassis: 3 Bova, 5 King Long, 19 Scania,
2 Volvo.
Bodies: 3 Bova, 18 Irizar, 5 King Long,
1 Van Hool, 2 Volvo.
Ops incl: school contracts, excursions &
tours, private hire, express, continental tours.
Livery: Blue.

FALCON COACHES LTD

123 NUTTY LANE, SHEPPERTON TW17
0RQ
Tel: 01932 787752
Fax: 01932 787753
E-mail: sales@falconch.com
Web site: www.falconcoachhire.com
Man Dir: Richard Telling **Ops Dir:** Simon
Telling.
Fleet: single-deck coach, minicoach.
Chassis: Mercedes, Volvo.
Bodies: Mercedes, Sitcar, Van Hool.
Ops incl: private hire, school contracts,
excursions & tours.
Livery: White/Black/Crimson.
Incorporating Hounslow Mini Coaches

FELLSON COACHES

41 STAINFORTH ROAD, ILFORD IG2 7EJ
Tel: 020 8599 7019
Prop: R J Fell.
Fleet: 1 single-deck coach.
Chassis/Body: Neoplan.
Ops incl: private hire.

FLIGHTS HALLMARK

See West Midlands

FORESTDALE COACHES LTD

68 VINEY BANK, COURTWOOD LANE,
FORESTDALE, ADDINGTON CR0 9JT
Tel/Fax: 020 8651 1359
Chairman/Man Dir: V J Holub
Co Sec: Mrs P R Holub.
Fleet: 1 single-deck coach.
Chassis/Body: Bova.
Ops incl: excursions & tours, private hire,
continental tours.
Livery: Red with Gold sign writing.

GO-AHEAD LONDON

18 MERTON HIGH STREET, LONDON
SW19 1DN
Tel: 020 8545 6100
Fax: 020 8545 6101
E-mail: enquiries@goaheadlondon.com
Web site: www.goahead-london.com
Fleet Names: Blue Triangle Buses Ltd,
Docklands Buses Ltd, London Central Bus
Company Ltd, London General Transport
Services Ltd, Metrobus Ltd.
Man Dir: John Trayner **Eng Dir:** Richard
Harrington **Fin Dir:** John Slattery **Ops Dir:**
David Cutts.
Fleet: 2179 - 1417 double-deck bus,
762 single-deck bus, 5 open-top bus.
Chassis: 5 AEC, 962 Alexander Dennis,
2 BYD, 40 DAF, 23 MAN, 50 Mercedes,
2 Optare, 194 Scania, 2 VDL, 837 Volvo,
62 Wrightbus.
Bodies: 714 Alexander Dennis, 2 BYD,
141 East Lancs, 20 Marshall, 44 MCV,
50 Mercedes, 2 Northern Counties,
126 Optare, 5 Park Royal, 300 Plaxton,
48 Scania, 727 Wrightbus.
Ops incl: local bus services, school contracts,
rail replacement, excursions & tours, private
hire.
Livery: Red.
Ticket System: TfL Prestige.
Subsidiaries of the Go-Ahead Group

GOLDENSTAND SOUTHERN

13 WAXLOW ROAD, LONDON
NW10 7NU
Tel: 020 8961 8541
Fax: 020 8961 9949
E-mail: info@goldenstand.co.uk
Web site: www.goldenstand.co.uk
Dir: John Chivrall.
Fleet: 19 – 5 single-deck coach, 14 minibus.
Chassis: 1 Bova, 14 LDV, 4 Scania.
Ops incl: school contracts, private hire.
Livery: Red/White.

GOLDEN TOURS

UNIT 4, FOUNTAIN SQUARE, 123-151
BUCKINGHAM PALACE ROAD,
LONDON SW1W 9SH
Tel: 020 7630 2028
Fax: 020 7233 7039
Web site: www.goldentours.com
Man Dir: Nick Palan.
Fleet: 53 – 43 double-deck/open-top bus,
10 single-deck coach.
Chassis: 19 Dennis, 2 VDL, 32 Volvo.
Bodies: 19 Alexander, 2 Berkhof, 8
Jonckheere, 20 MCV, 3 Optare, 1 Wrightbus.
Ops incl: sightseeing tours, excursions &
tours.
Livery: Multicoloured.

THE GOLD STANDARD

UNIT 38, KINGSPARK BUSINESS CENTRE,
152-178 KINGSTON ROAD, NEW MALDEN
KT3 3ST
Tel: 0845 388 0045
E-mail: paul@luxuryminicoaches.co.uk
Web site: www.mini-coach.co.uk
Prop: Paul Grant.
Fleet: 1 minicoach.
Chassis: Mercedes.
Ops incl: excursions & tours, private hire.

A GREEN COACHES LTD

357A HOE STREET, WALTHAMSTOW,
LONDON E17 9AP
Tel: 020 8520 1138   **Fax:** 020 8520 1139
Recovery: 07563 551679

E-mail: info@agreencoacheslondon.co.uk
Web site: www.agreencoacheslondon.co.uk
Fleet Name: Greens of London.
Dirs: Keith Richards, Ms Janis Grover.
Fleet: 5 – 4 single-deck coach, I minibus.
Chassis: I Renault, I Scania, 3 Volvo.
Ops incl: school contracts, private hire,
continental tours.
Livery: White.

GRIFFIN EXECUTIVE TRAVEL

47 WALLINGFORD ROAD, UXBRIDGE
UB8 2XS
Tel: 0844 7361 465   Fax: 01895 430851
Web site: www.executivecoachhire.net
Dir: G Griffin.
Fleet: I single-deck coach
Chassis/Body: Temsa.
Ops incl: private hire.

GUIDELINE COACHES LONDON LTD

BLUEBELL FARM, HEWITTS ROAD,
CHELSFIELD, ORPINGTON BR6 7QR
Tel: 020 7228 3515
Fax: 020 7228 0290
Web site: www.guidelinecoaches.co.uk
Dirs: Thomas McKechnie.
Fleet: 7 - 4 single-deck coach, 2 midicoach,
I minicoach.
Chassis: 3 Mercedes, 4 Scania.
Bodies: 4 Irizar, 3 Unvi.
Ops incl: excursions & tours, private hire,
continental tours, school contracts.

HAMILTON OF UXBRIDGE

STOCKLEY FARM ROAD, WEST DRAYTON
UB7 9BW
Tel: 01895 232266
E-mail: info@hamiltoncoaches.co.uk
Web site: www.hamiltoncoaches.co.uk
Prop: D L Bennett.
Fleet: II single-deck coach.
Chassis: I Bova, 9 Neoplan, I Yutong.
Bodies: I Bova, 9 Neoplan, I Yutong.
Ops incl: private hire, express, continental
tours.
Livery: White.

HEARNS COACHES

801 KENTON LANE, HARROW WEALD
HA3 6AH
Tel: 020 8954 5444   Fax: 020 8954 5959
E-mail: admin@hearns-coaches.co.uk
Web site: www.hearns-coaches.co.uk
Prop: R J Hearn Ops Man: Ged Newham
Ch Eng: Dave Berry.
Fleet: 46 - 38 single-deck coach, 2 midicoach,
3 minibus.
Chassis: 3 Iveco, 2 MAN, 17 Mercedes,
10 Scania, 14 Setra.
Ops incl: private hire, school contracts,
excursions & tours, continental tours.
Livery: Blue.
Incorporating Venture Transport, Hendon

JOHN HOUGHTON LUXURY MINI
COACHES

2 ELGAR AVENUE, EALING, LONDON W5
3JU
Tel: 020 8567 0056
Fax: 020 8567 5781
E-mail: john@luxuryminicoaches.co.uk
Web site: www.luxuryminicoaches.co.uk
Man Dir: John Houghton
Co Sec: D M Houghton.
Fleet: 2 minicoach.
Chassis: 2 Mercedes.
Ops incl: private hire.
Livery: White.

VIC HUGHES & SON LTD
See Price Global Ltd

IMPACT OF LONDON

7-9 WADSWORTH ROAD, GREENFORD
UB6 7JZ
Tel: 020 8601 3555
Fax: 020 8601 3502
E-mail: info@impactgroup.co.uk
Web site: www.impactgroup.co.uk
Dir: A Hill Gen Man: Joe Hill,
M O'Conner Engs: H Louis, L Singh.
Fleet: 140 – 18 single-deck coach, 4 midibus,
22 midicoach, 82 minibus, 14 minicoach.
Chassis: 2 Alexander Dennis, I Ford Transit,
17 Irisbus, II Iveco, 6 King Long, 16 LDV,
6 MAN, 70 Mercedes, 5 Scania, 4 Volvo,
2 Wrightbus.
Ops incl: excursions & tours, private hire,
express, continental tours, school contracts.
Livery: White.

IMPERIAL COACHES LTD

80 SCOTTS ROAD, SOUTHALL UB2 5DE
Tel: 020 8574 0028
Fax: 020 8574 0061
E-mail: imperialcoaches1@hotmail.com
Web site: www.imperialcoaches.co.uk
Fleet: 29 – 17 double-deck bus, 6 single-deck
coach, 2 midicoach, 2 minibus, 2 minicoach.
Chassis: 9 Dennis, 2 Ford Transit, 4 Mercedes,
3 Scania, II Volvo.
Bodies: 10 Alexander, 3 East Lancs, 2 Ford,
3 Irizar, I KVC, I Mercedes, 4 Optare, 2
Plaxton, 3 Van Hool.
Ops incl: school contracts, excursions &
tours, private hire.
Livery: White/Silver.

INTERNATIONAL COACH LINES

19 NURSERY ROAD, THORNTON HEATH
CR7 8RE
Tel: 020 8684 8308
Fax: 020 8689 3483
Recovery: 07738 282840
E-mail: louise@internationalcoachlines.co.uk
Web site: www.internationalcoaches.co.uk
Fleet Name: I.C.L.
Dirs: Sue Wood, Louise Gaynor.
Fleet: 27 - 4 double-deck bus, 7 single-deck
coach, I double-deck coach, 15 minibus.
Chassis: I AEC, 3 Dennis, 4 Ford Transit,
2 Iveco, 9 LDV, 3 Scania, 2 Setra, 3 Volvo.
Ops incl: school contracts, private hire,
continental tours.
Livery: Blue/White.

J & D EUROTRAVEL

58 WEALD LANE, HARROW WEALD
HA3 5EX
Tel: 020 8861 1829   Fax: 020 8424 2585
E-mail: jdetravel1@aol.co.uk
Web site: www.jandd-eurotravel.co.uk
Man Dir: J T Thomas.
Fleet: II - 6 single-deck coach, 3 midicoach,
2 minibus.
Chassis: I LDV, 6 Mercedes, 4 Volvo.
Ops incl: school contracts, excursions &
tours, private hire, express, continental tours.
Livery: White.

THE KINGS FERRY
See Kent

LEOLINE TRAVEL

UPPER SUNBURY ROAD, HAMPTON
TW12 2DW
Tel: 020 8941 3370
Fax: 020 8941 3372

E-mail: leolinecoaches@aol.com
Web site: www.leolinetravel.co.uk
Prop: David Baker Ops Man: Judy Dale.
Fleet: 6 - 5 single-deck coach, I midicoach.
Chassis: 4 Iveco, I Toyota, I Volvo.
Bodies: 4 Beulas, I Caetano, I Van Hool.
Ops incl: excursions & tours, school
contracts, private hire.
Liveries: White/Orange, Blue/Orange.

LEWIS TRAVEL

145 NATHAN WAY, THAMESMEAD SE28
0AB
Tel: 020 8858 0031
Fax: 020 8858 7631
E-mail: info@lewistravel.co.uk
Web site: www.lewiscoaches.co.uk
Fleet: 12 – 11 single-deck coach, I midicoach.
Chassis: DAF, Mercedes, Volvo.
Ops incl: school contracts, excursions &
tours, private hire, continental tours.
Livery: Red/White/Blue.

THE LITTLE BUS COMPANY

HOME FARM, ALDENHAM ROAD, ELSTREE
WD6 3AZ
Tel: 020 8953 0202
Fax: 020 8953 9553
E-mail: enquiry@littlebus.co.uk
Web site: www.littlebus.co.uk
Prop: Jeremy Reese.
Fleet: 10 – I single-deck coach, 6 midicoach,
10 minibus, I minicoach.
Chassis: I BMC, I Ford Transit, I Iveco,
I MAN, II Mercedes, 2 Renault, I Volvo.
Ops incl: school contracts, private hire.
Livery: White with Blue.

LONDON CENTRAL BUS CO LTD
LONDON GENERAL TRANSPORT
SERVICES LTD
See Go-Ahead London

LONDON DIAL-A-RIDE LTD

PROGRESS HOUSE, 5 MANDELA WAY,
LONDON SE1 5SS
Tel: 020 7446 0251
Fax: 020 7394 5218
E-mail: DAR@tfl.gov.uk
Web site: www.tfl.gov.uk
Gen Man: Paul Blackwell
Ops Man: John Daley Head of Passenger
Services: Joyce Mamode
Eng Dir: Gary Filbey
Fleet: minibus.
Chassis: Mercedes, Volkswagen.
Bodies: Bluebird, Caetano, Mellor.
Ops incl: demand responsive dial-a-ride
service.
Livery: Red.
A subsidiary of Transport for London

LONDON MINI COACHES LTD

UNITS 17-18, AIRLINKS INDUSTRIAL
ESTATE, SPITFIRE WAY, HESTON
TW5 9NR
Tel: 020 8589 0795
Fax: 020 8589 0796
E-mail: info@lmcoaches.co.uk
Web site: www.lmcoaches.co.uk
Fleet Names: London Mini Coaches,
Windsorian.
Dir: David Phillips.
Fleet: 17 – 5 single-deck coach, 8 midicoach,
2 minicoach, 2 minibus.
Chassis: 12 Mercedes, I VDL, 4 Volvo.
Bodies: 4 Plaxton, 8 Sitcar, 2 Unvi, I VDL.
Ops incl: school contracts, private hire,
excursions & tours, continental tours.
Liveries: Silver/Maroon, Blue/White.

LONDON SOVEREIGN

APPROACH ROAD, EDGWARE, MIDDLESEX
HA8 7AN
Tel: 020 8238 5505
Fax: 020 8238 5519
E-mail: customerservices@londonsovereign.
co.uk
Exec Chairman: Richard Casling **Man Dir:**
Richard Hall
Fleet: 151 – 82 double-deck bus, 69 midibus.
Chassis: 57 Alexander Dennis, 36 Scania,
12 Transbus, 46 Volvo.
Bodies: 1 Alexander, 57 Alexander Dennis,
29 East Lancs, 9 Plaxton, 20 Scania,
13 Transbus, 23 Wright.
Ops Incl: local bus services, private hire.
Livery: Red.
Ticket System: TfL Prestige.
A subsidiary of RATP Dev UK Ltd

LONDON TRAMLINK

See Section 5 – Tram and Bus Rapid Transit
Systems.

LONDON UNITED BUSWAYS LTD

BUSWAYS HOUSE, WELLINGTON ROAD,
TWICKENHAM TW2 5NX
Tel: 020 8400 6665
Fax: 020 8943 2688
E-mail: customer@lonutd.co.uk
Web site: www.londonutd.co.uk
Exec Chairman: Richard Casling **Man Dir:**
Richard Hall **Human Res Dir:** Karen Fuller
Eng Dir: Les Birchley **Ops Dir:** Maurice
Bulmer.
Fleet: 884 - 570 double-deck bus, 59 single-
deck bus, 2 single-deck coach, 253 midibus.
Chassis: 1 AEC, 326 Alexander Dennis,
33 Dennis, 7 Mercedes, 56 Optare, 207 Scania,
118 Transbus, 66 Volvo, 80 Wrightbus NBfL.
Ops Incl: local bus services, private hire.
Livery: Red.
Ticket system: TfL Prestige.
A subsidiary of RATP Dev UK Ltd

M C H MINIBUSES LTD

47 WALLINGFORD ROAD, UXBRIDGE
UB8 2XS
Tel: 01895 230643
Fax: 01895 234891
E-mail: info@mch-coaches.co.uk
Web site: www.mch-coaches.co.uk
Dirs: P Webber, E Gavin.
Fleet: 31 – 9 single-deck coach, 12 midicoach,
6 minibus, 4 minicoach.
Chassis: 1 King Long, 22 Mercedes,
7 Neoplan, 1 Volkswagen.
Bodies: 1 Excel, 5 EVM, 2 Ferqui, 1 King Long,
1 KVC, 2 Mercedes, 7 Neoplan, 6 Noone
Turas, 6 Unvi.
Ops incl: excursions & tours, private hire,
continental tours.
Livery: White with Blue.

MAYDAY TRAVEL LTD

See Surrey

METROBUS LTD

See Go-Ahead London

METROLINE TRAVEL LTD

COMFORT DELGRO HOUSE, 3rd FLOOR,
329 EDGWARE ROAD, CRICKLEWOOD,
LONDON NW2 6JP
Tel: 020 8218 8888
Fax: 020 8218 8899
E-mail: info@metroline.co.uk
Web site: www.metroline.co.uk
Chief Exec Off: Jaspal Singh **Ch Op
Officer:** Sean O'Shea **Fin Dir:** Damian

Rowbotham **Eng Dir:** Ian Foster.
Fleet: 1680 - 1156 double-deck bus,
41 single-deck bus, 483 midibus.
Chassis: 2 AEC, 829 Alexander Dennis,
6 Dennis, 38 MAN, 3 Optare, 72 Scania,
130 Transbus, 568 Volvo, 32 Wrightbus NBfL.
Ops incl: local bus services, school contracts,
private hire.
Livery: Red.
Ticket System: TfL Prestige.
A subsidiary of the Comfort Delgro Group

NATIONAL EXPRESS LTD

MILL LANE, DIGBETH, BIRMINGHAM
B5 6DD
Tel: 08717 818178
E-mail: help@nationalexpress.com
Web site: www.nationalexpress.com
Fleet Names: National Express, Airlinks.
Man Dir: Tom Stables **Service Delivery
Dir:** Kevin Gale **HR Dir:** Jennifer Richmond.
Fleet: 190 – 7 single-deck bus, 122 single-
deck coach, 16 articulated bus, 41 midibus,
4 minibus.
Chassis: 37 Alexander Dennis, 1 Ford Transit,
29 Mercedes, 37 Scania, 1 Volkswagen,
85 Volvo.
Bodies: 37 Alexander Dennis, 113 Caetano,
4 East Lancs, 1 Ford, 1 Hispano, 26 Mercedes,
1 Plaxton, 5 Transbus, 1 Wrightbus, 1 Other.
Ops incl: express coach services, airport
operations.
Livery: Red/White/Blue.
Ticket System: Pre-sale, Wayfarer.

NEW BHARAT COACHES LTD

1A PRIORY WAY, SOUTHALL UB2 5EB
Tel: 020 8574 6817
Fax: 020 8813 9555
E-mail: info@newbharat.co.uk
Web site: www.newbharat.co.uk
Dirs: H K, T S & R S Dhaliwal
Ch Eng: Alan Littlemore.
Fleet: 11 – 3 double-deck coach, 6 single-
deck coach, 2 midicoach.
Chassis: 2 Mercedes, 4 Van Hool, 5 Volvo.
Bodies: 1 Ferqui, 1 Mercedes, 9 Van Hool.
Ops incl: school contracts, excursions &
tours, private hire, express, continental tours.
Livery: Red/Yellow/Blue on white base.

NEWBOURNE COACHES

FIRBANK WAY, LEIGHTON BUZZARD
LU7 4YP
Tel: 01525 376077
Fax: 01525 850967
E-mail: info@marshalls-coaches.co.uk
Web site: www.marshalls-coaches.co.uk
Prop: Glen Marshall.
Fleet: See Marshalls Coaches.
Ops incl: private hire, school contracts, local
bus services.
Livery: Blue/Multicoloured.
A subsidiary of Marshalls Coaches
(See Bedfordshire)

OFJ CONNECTIONS LTD

See TGM Group Ltd.

THE ORIGINAL LONDON TOUR

JEWS ROW, LONDON SW18 1TB
Tel: 020 8877 1722
Fax: 020 8877 1968
E-mail: info@theoriginaltour.com
Web site: www.theoriginaltour.com
Man Dir: Colin Atkins **Ops Dir:** Alistair
Fraser.
Fleet: 104 open-top bus.
Chassis: 44 DAF, 16 Leyland, 8 MCW,
36 Volvo.

Bodies: 16 Alexander, 10 Ayats, 10 East Lancs,
8 MCW, 16 Optare, 44 Plaxton.
Ops incl: London Sightseeing Tours.
Livery: Red/Cream.
A subsidiary of RATP Dev Uk Ltd

PLAN-IT TRAVEL LTD

BLUEBELL FARM, HEWITTS ROAD,
CHELSFIELD, ORPINGTON BR6 7QR
Tel: 01959 535076
Fax: 01959 535068
E-mail: sales@plan-ittravel.co.uk
Web site: www.plan-ittravel.co.uk
Dir: T Bowser.
Fleet: 7 – 6 single-deck coach, 1 minicoach.
Chassis: 3 Setra, 1 Toyota, 3 Volvo.
Bodies: 1 Caetano, 3 Setra, 3 Volvo.
Ops incl: school contracts, excursions &
tours, private hire.
Livery: Silver with Blue.

PREMIERE TRAVEL

See Kent

PREMIUM COACHES LTD

86-88 GRESHAM ROAD, BRIXTON
SW9 7NP
Tel: 020 7713 1311
Web site: www.premiumcoaches.co.uk
Man Dir: Neil Wootton **Gen Man:** Paul
Frankland **Traffic Man:** John Jamieson.
Fleet: 25 – 2 double-deck bus, 4 open-top
bus, 1 double-deck coach, 15 single-deck
coach, 1 midicoach, 2 minibus.
Chassis: 6 AEC Routemaster, 1 Ford Transit,
2 Mercedes, 6 Neoplan, 2 VDL, 8 Volvo.
Bodies: 1 Berkhof, 1 Ford, 6 Jonckheere,
6 Neoplan, 6 Park Royal, 3 Plaxton, 1 Unvi,
1 VDL.
Ops incl: excursions & tours, private hire.
Liveries: Coaches: White with Purple/Grey;
Routemasters: Red, Harrods Green.

PRICE GLOBAL LTD
V B HUGHES & SON LTD

APTIGA, GATE 5, STAINES ROAD EAST,
SUNBURY-ON-THAMES
TW16 5AX
Tel: 020 8831 0770
Fax: 020 8831 0660
E-mail: vbhughes_and_son_ltd@yahoo.co.uk
Web site: www.vbhughesandson.com
Dirs: P M Diamond, D Diamond.
Fleet: 7 – 6 midicoach, 1 minibus.
Chassis: Mercedes.
Ops incl: school contracts, excursions &
tours, private hire.
Livery: White/Black.

REDWING COACHES

10 DYLAN ROAD, LONDON
SE24 0HL
Tel: 020 7733 1124
Fax: 020 7733 5194
E-mail: redwingsales@redwing-coaches.
co.uk.
Web site: www.redwing-coaches.co.uk.
Joint Man Dirs: Paul Hockley, Nigel Taylor
Fin Dir: Matt Evans
Gen Man: Colin Miller **Ch Eng:** Robbie
Hodgekiss.
Fleet: 47 - 44 single-deck coach, 3 minicoach.
Chassis: 38 Mercedes, 2 Neoplan, 4 Scania,
3 Setra.
Bodies: 1 Ferqui, 4 Irizar, 35 Mercedes,
2 Neoplan, 3 Setra, 2 Unvi.
Ops incl: excursions & tours, private hire,
continental tours.
Livery: Red/Cream.

ROUNDABOUT BUSES LTD
See Kent

ROYALE EUROPEAN COACHES
LAND C, PHOENIX DISTRIBUTION PARK, PHOENIX WAY, HESTON
TW5 9NB
Tel: 020 8754 0322　　**Fax:** 020 8897 9583
E-mail: enquiries@royaleeuropean.co.uk
Web site: www.royaleeuropean.co.uk
Prop: Jack Kent, **Gen Man:** Mike Kenny.
Fleet: 7 – 3 single-deck coach, 1 double-deck coach, 1 midicoach, 2 minibus.
Chassis: 3 Mercedes, 3 Neoplan, 1 Van Hool.
Bodies: 1 Ferqui, 1 KVC, 3 Neoplan, 1 Noone Turas, 1 Van Hool.
Ops incl: excursions & tours, private hire, continental tours.
Livery: Red/Grey/White.

SEAWARD TRAVEL LTD
WILLESDEN FREIGHT DEPOT, CHANNEL GATE ROAD, LONDON
NW10 6UQ
Tel: 0844 800 1239
Fax: 01305 835215
E-mail: seaminigroup@aol.com
Web site: www.seaward-travel.co.uk
Man Dir: Philip Seaward
Gen Man: Richard Cassell.
Fleet: 11 – 8 single-deck coach, 2 midicoach, 1 minicoach.
Chassis: 2 Irisbus, 3 Mercedes, 1 VDL, 5 Volvo.
Bodies: 2 Jonckheere, 1 Marcopolo, 5 Plaxton, 3 Unvi, 1 Other.
Ops incl: private hire
Livery: White with Blue.

SILVERDALE LONDON LTD
A subsidiary of Silverdale Tours
(See Nottinghamshire)

SOUTHGATE & FINCHLEY COACHES LTD
231A COLNEY HATCH LANE, FRIERN BARNET, LONDON N11 3DG
Tel: 020 8368 0040/3190
Fax: 020 8361 1934
E-mail: office@southgate-finchley-coaches.co.uk
Web site: www.southgate-finchley-coaches.co.uk
Jt Man Dirs: Mr P M Rice, Mrs E B Scrivens
Dirs: Mrs V M Rice, Mr M Rice.
Fleet: 27 - 25 single-deck coach, 1 midibus, 1 minibus.
Chassis: 1 Iveco, 1 Mercedes, 25 Volvo.
Bodies: 6 Jonckheere, 19 Plaxton, 2 Other.
Ops incl: school contracts, excursions and tours, private hire, continental tours.
Livery: Yellow.

SPEEDICARS LTD
ILDERTON WHARF, ROLLINS STREET, LONDON SE15 1EP
Tel: 020 8694 2244　　**Fax:** 020 7732 1102
E-mail: info@speedicars.co.uk
Web site: www.speedicars.co.uk
Man Dir: Ian Ferguson
Ops Man: Paul Buckley
Travel Hire Consultant: Mike Luther.
Fleet: 9 – 3 single-deck coach, 3 midicoach, 3 minicoach.
Chassis: 2 MAN, 5 Mercedes, 1 Setra, 1 Volkswagen.
Bodies: 1 Optare, 1 Sitcar, 1 Setra, 1 Unvi, 1 Van Hool, 1 VDL, 3 other.
Ops incl: school contracts, excursions & tours, private hire, continental tours.
Livery: White.

STAGECOACH LONDON
WEST HAM GARAGE, STEPHENSON STREET, CANNING TOWN, LONDON E16 4SA
Tel: 020 7055 9600　　**Fax:** 020 7055 9601
E-mail: PR.London@stagecoachbus.com
Web site: www.stagecoachbus.com
Man Dir: Mark Threapleton.
Fleet: 1329 – 1084 double-deck bus, 32 single-deck bus, 213 midibus.
Chassis: 11 AEC, 493 Alexander Dennis, 59 Dennis, 13 Mercedes, 19 Optare, 174 Scania, 414 Transbus, 23 Volvo, 34 Wrightbus NBfL.
Bodies: 59 Alexander, 588 Alexander Dennis, 13 Mercedes, 19 Optare, 11 Park Royal, 174 Scania, 410 Transbus, 57 Wrightbus.
Operations: local bus services.
Livery: Red.
Ticket System: TfL Prestige.

SUNBURY COACHES LTD
Ceased trading since LRB 2014 went to press

THE SWALLOW COACH CO LTD
See Essex

SYMPHONY COACHES
UNIT 11, HEATHROW INTERNATIONAL TRADING ESTATE, GREEN LANE, HOUNSLOW TW4 6HB
Tel: 020 8756 0004　　**Fax:** 0208789 0804
E-mail: info@s-coaches.com
Web site: www.s-coaches.com
Dirs: A Jeyakumar, A Ramakrishnan.
Fleet: single-deck coach, midicoach, minicoach.
Ops incl: excursions & tours, private hire.
Livery: White.

TGM GROUP LTD
BUILDING 16300 MT2, ELECTRA AVENUE, HEATHROW AIRPORT, HOUNSLOW TW6 2DN
Tel: 020 8757 4700　　**Fax:** 020 8757 4719
E-mail: info@tgmgroup.co.uk
Web site: www.tellingsgoldenmiller.co.uk
Fleet Names: Tellings Golden Miller, OFJ Connections, Hotel by Bus.
Regional Man Dir: Heath Williams **Acting Man Dir:** Brian Drury **Regional Director (North East):** Ian Shipley.
Fleet: double-deck bus, single-deck bus, single-deck coach, midibus, midicoach, minibus, minicoach.
Additional vehicles work airside at London Airports. Car park services operate at East Midlands and Southampton airports.
Ops incl: local bus services, school contracts, excursions & tours, private hire, express, continental tours.
Liveries: White/Blue/Yellow;
TfL Bus Services: Red.
A subsidiary of Arriva
See also TGM Group *(Essex)*; TGM North East *(Durham)*

TIMEBUS TRAVEL
7 BOLEYN DRIVE, ST ALBANS AL1 2BP
Tel: 01727 866248
Web site: www.timebus.co.uk
Fleet Name: Timebus.
Prop: David Pring.
Fleet: 16 – 13 double-deck bus, 1 single-deck bus, 2 open-top bus.
Chassis: 16 AEC.
Bodies: 1 Metro-Cammell, 12 Park Royal, 3 Weymann.
Ops incl: private hire.
Livery: Red with grey lining.

TOWER TRANSIT OPERATIONS LTD
WESTBOURNE PARK GARAGE, GREAT WESTERN ROAD, LONDON W9 3NW
Tel: 020 7229 7131
Fax: 020 7792 8178
Web site: www.tower-transit.co.uk
Chairman: Neil Smith **Man Dir:** Adam Leishman **Fin Dir:** Paul Cox
Ops Dir: Andrew Edwards
Dev Dir: Charlie Beaumont
Eng Dir: Alan Coney.
Fleet: 417 – 316 double-deck bus, 8 single-deck bus, 95 midibus.
Chassis: 10 AEC, 172 Alexander Dennis, 4 Dennis, 14 Transbus, 8 VDL, 207 Volvo, 4 Wrightbus.
Bodies: 172 Alexander Dennis, 4 Caetano, 2 Marshall, 2 Plaxton, 10 Park Royal, 10 Transbus, 219 Wrightbus.
Operations: local bus services.
Livery: Red.
Ticket System: TfL Prestige.

TRINA COACHES LTD
80 GLOUCESTER PLACE, LONDON W1U 6HL
Tel: 020 7486 1432
Fleet: 5 – 4 single-deck coach, 1 minicoach.
Chassis: 1 Toyota, 4 Volvo.
Bodies: 1 Caetano, 4 Van Hool.
Ops incl: excursions & tours.
Livery: Silver/Blue.

VENTURE TRANSPORT (HENDON) (1965) LTD
307 PINNER ROAD, HARROW HA1 4HG
Tel: 020 8427 0101
Fax: 020 8427 1707
Ops incl: private hire.
A subsidiary of Hearns Coaches, Harrow Weald

WESTBUS COACH SERVICES LTD
27A SPRING GROVE ROAD, HOUNSLOW TW3 4BE
Tel: 020 8572 6348
Fax: 020 8570 2234
Recovery: 020 8572 6348
E-mail: reservations@westbus.co.uk
Web site: www.westbus.co.uk
Gen Man: Tim Miles **Ops Man:** Chris Shaw
Ch Eng: Graham Bessant.
Fleet: 37 – 4 double-deck bus, 26 single-deck coach, 4 double-deck coach, 3 midicoach.
Chassis: 7 Mercedes, 1 Scania, 17 Van Hool, 6 VDL, 6 Volvo.
Bodies: 4 Alexander, 1 Berkhof, 1 Irizar, 1 Jonckheere, 4 Mercedes, 3 Sitcar, 23 Van Hool.
Ops incl: private hire, continental tours, excursions & tours, school contracts.
Livery: Red/Beige.
Part of the Comfort Delgro Corporation

WEST'S COACHES LTD
ROYAL FOREST COACH HOUSE, 109 MAYBANK ROAD, LONDON E18 1EZ
Tel: 020 8505 8833
Fax: 020 8519 1937
Man Dir: D J Brown **Dir:** N Brown.
Fleet: 13 single-deck coach.
Chassis: 6 Dennis, 1 Irisbus, 1 Transbus, 5 Volvo.
Bodies: 1 Caetano, 2 Marcopolo, 9 Plaxton, 1 Transbus.
Ops incl: school contracts, private hire, excursions & tours.
Livery: Red/White/Blue.
A subsidiary of Dan's Luxury Travel Ltd

London & Middlesex

WESTWAY COACH SERVICES LTD

7A RAINBOW INDUSTRIAL ESTATE,
STATION APPROACH, RAYNES PARK,
LONDON SW20 0JY
Tel: 020 8944 1277
Fax: 020 8947 5339
E-mail: info@westway-coaches.co.uk
Web site: www.westwaycoaches.co.uk
Dir: David West **Gen Man:** Kevin Pates
Eng Man: James Lloyd.
Fleet: 34 - 14 single-deck coach, 14 double-deck coach, 5 midicoach, 1 minibus.

Chassis: 1 DAF, 1 EOS, 1 LDV, 5 Mercedes, 7 Van Hool, 19 Volvo.
Bodies: 1 Berkhof, 1 EOS, 3 Jonckheere, 1 LDV, 1 Plaxton, 4 Sitcar, 23 Van Hool.
Ops incl: school contracts, excursions & tours, private hire, continental tours.
Livery: Blue/Orange.

WINGS LUXURY TRAVEL LTD

47 WALLINGFORD ROAD, UXBRIDGE
UB8 2XS
Tel: 01895 239999

Fax: 01895 270022
E-mail: info@wingstravel.co.uk
Web site: www.wings-luxury-coach-hire.co.uk
Chairman: F L Gritt
Gen Man: W Gritt **Ops Man:** S Hughes.
Fleet: 16 - 10 midicoach, 2 minicoach, 4 minibus.
Chassis: 16 Mercedes.
Ops Incl: school contracts, excursions and tours, private hire.
Liveries: White with Red; Silver with Red.

A1A LTD

373 CLEVELAND STREET, BIRKENHEAD
CH41 4JW
Tel: 0151 650 1616
Fax: 0151 650 0007
Prop: Barbara Ashworth.
Fleet: 10 minibus.
Chassis: 1 Ford Transit, 8 LDV, 1 Mercedes.
Ops incl: school contracts, private hire.
Livery: White/Blue.

A2B TRAVEL UK LTD

PRENTON WAY, NORTH CHESHIRE
TRADING ESTATE, PRENTON CH43 3DU
Tel: 0151 609 0600
Fax: 0151 609 0601
E-mail: info@a2b-travel.com
Web site: www.a2b-travel.com
Dirs: G Evans, D Evans.
Fleet: 26 - 7 midibus, 2 midicoach, 17 minibus
Chassis: 4 Alexander Dennis, 9 LDV, 5 Mercedes, 8 Optare.
Ops incl: school contracts, private hire, excursions & tours.
Livery: White/Blue.

ACE TRAVEL NORTH WEST LTD

BARCLAY TRADING ESTATE, WAREING
ROAD, AINTREE L9 7AU
Tel: 0151 203 3920
Fax: 0151 530 4948
E-mail: acetravelnorthwest@btconnect.com
Web site: www.citysightseeingliverpool.com
Dirs: A Denson, S Stubbs.
Fleet: 33 - 5 double-deck bus, 6 open-top bus, 21 midibus, 1 minibus.
Chassis: 15 Alexander Dennis, 6 Dennis, 1 MCW, 2 Optare, 2 Transbus, 7 Volvo.
Ops incl: local bus services, Liverpool sightseeing tours.
Liveries: Maroon/Cream, City Sightseeing.

AINTREE COACHLINE

UNIT 10, SEFTON INDUSTRIAL ESTATE,
SEFTON LANE, MAGHULL L31 8BX
Tel: 0151 922 8630
Fax: 0151 933 6994
E-mail: aintreecoachline1@gmail.co.uk
Web site: www.aintreecoachline.co.uk
Prop: J Cherry.
Fleet: 43 – 19 double-deck bus, 1 single-deck bus, 2 single-deck coach, 19 midibus, 2 minibus.
Chassis: 1 AEC, 3 Alexander Dennis, 15 Dennis, 1 Leyland, 3 Optare, 2 Scania, 1 Transbus, 1 VDL, 16 Volvo.
Ops incl: local bus services, school contracts, private hire.
Livery: Red/Cream.
Incorporating Helms of Eastham.

ALS COACHES LTD

400 CELEVLAND STREET, BIRKENHEAD
CH41 8EQ

Tel: 0151 653 0053
Fax: 0151 670 0509
Fleet Name: Happy Al's.
Man Dir: T A Cullinan **Gen Man:** M Cullinan
Tran Man: C Cullinan.
Fleet: 76 - 47 double-deck bus, 10 single-deck bus, 18 single-deck coach, 1 minibus.
Chassis: 1 BMC, 1 Bova, 8 DAF, 1 Leyland, 1 Volkswagen, 64 Volvo.
Ops incl: school contracts, private hire, excursions & tours.
Ticket System: Wayfarer.
Livery: Red/Gold.

ARRIVA NORTH WEST & WALES

73 ORMSKIRK ROAD, AINTREE, LIVERPOOL
L9 5AE
Tel: 0151 522 2800
Fax: 0151 525 9556
Web site: www.arriva.co.uk
Regional Man Dir: Phil Stone
Reg Fin Dir: Simon Mills **Reg Eng Dir:** Phil Cummins **Area Man Dir (Merseyside):** Howard Farrall **Area Man Dir (Manchester):** John Rimmer
Area Man Dir (Wales): Michael Morton.
Fleet (England): 902 - 209 double-deck bus, 475 single-deck bus, 8 articulated bus, 168 midibus, 42 minibus.
Chassis: 38 Alexander Dennis, 109 DAF, 80 Dennis, 14 MAN, 8 Mercedes, 42 Optare, 483 VDL, 130 Volvo.
Bodies: Alexander, Alexander Dennis, Caetano, East Lancs, Ikarus, Marshall, Mercedes, Optare, Plaxton, Wrightbus.
Ops incl: local bus services, school contracts.
Livery: Arriva UK Bus.
Ticket System: Wayfarer TGX.

G. ASHTON COACHES

WATERY LANE, ST HELENS WA9 3JA
Tel: 01744 733275
Fax: 01744 454122
E-mail: enquiries@gashtoncoachholidays.co.uk
Web site: www.gashtoncoachholidays.co.uk
Prop: Simon Ashton.
Fleet: 6 – 4 single-deck coach, 1 double-deck coach, 1 minicoach, 1 minibus.
Chassis: 1 Ford Transit, 1 Scania, 1 Toyota, 3 Van Hool, 1 VDL.
Bodies: 1 Berkhof, 1 Caetano, 1 Ford, 1 Irizar, 3 Van Hool.
Ops incl: excursions & tours, private hire, continental tours.
Livery: Multicoloured.

AVON BUSES LTD

10 BROOKWAY, NORTH CHESHIRE
TRADING ESTATE, PRENTON CH43 3DT
Tel: 0151 608 8000
Fax: 0151 608 9955
E-mail: enquiries@avonbuses.com
Fleet: 38 single-deck bus.
Chassis: 20 Alexander Dennis, 14 Dennis,

4 Transbus.
Bodies: 6 Alexander Dennis, 5 East Lancs, 12 Marshall/MCV, 9 Plaxton, 6 Transbus.
Ops incl: local bus services.
Livery: Blue & Cream.
Ticket System: Parkeon Wayfarer 200.

BLUELINE TRAVEL

54-56 STATION ROAD, MAGHULL L31 3DB
Tel: 0151 526 5050
Fax: 0151 526 2727
E-mail: blueline5050@hotmail.com
Web site: www.bluelineuk.com
Prop: C P Carr.
Fleet: 12 – 3 double-deck bus, 3 single-deck coach, 1 midicoach, 4 minibus, 1 minicoach.
Chassis: 6 Mercedes, 3 Scania, 3 Volvo.
Ops incl: private hire, school contracts.
Livery: White.

CUMFYBUS LTD

178 CAMBRIDGE ROAD, SOUTHPORT
PR9 7LW
Tel: 01704 227321
Fax: 01704 505781
E-mail: info@cumfybus.co.uk
Web site: www.cumfybus.co.uk
Depots at: Southport, Bootle, Aintree, Bolton, Wirral.
Man Dir: M R Vickers **Admin:** Mrs P Lyon.
Fleet: 121 – 4 double-deck bus, 11 single-deck bus, 9 midibus, 97 minibus.
Chassis: 4 DAF, 8 Dennis, 2 Fiat, 104 Optare, 3 Renault.
Bodies: 2 Bluebird, 4 Caetano, 8 East Lancs, 104 Optare, 3 Renault.
Ops incl: local bus services, school contracts.
Livery: Yellow.

ELLISONS TRAVEL LTD

QUEENS GARAGE, 61 BOUNDARY ROAD,
ST HELENS WA10 2LX
Tel: 0800 917 4917
Fax: 01744 24402
E-mail: info@ellisonstravel.com
Web site: www.ellisonstravel.com
Dirs: A Magowan, M Magowan.
Fleet: 30 single-deck coach.
Chassis: 23 Neoplan, 6 Van Hool, 1 Volvo.
Bodies: 1 Jonckheere, 23 Neoplan, 6 Van Hool.
Ops incl: private hire.
Livery: Silver.

FIVE STAR TRAVEL

SNAPE GATE, FOX'S BANK LANE,
WHISTON, PRESCOT L35 3SS
Tel: 0151 481 0000
Fax: 0151 493 9999
E-mail: admin@fivestar.co.uk
Web site: www.fivestartravel.co.uk
Prop: Phil Riley.
Fleet: 3 single-deck coach.
Chassis: 3 DAF.

Bodies: 3 Bova.
Ops incl: excursions & tours, private hire, continental tours.
Livery: White with Blue.

HARDINGS TOURS LTD
A subsidiary of Selwyn's Travel *(See Cheshire)*

HATTON'S TRAVEL
🚻♿❄
WALKERS LANE, ST HELENS WA9 4AF
Tel: 0845 291 5631
E-mail: enquiries@hattonstravel.co.uk
Web site: www.hattonstravel.co.uk
Fleet: 31 – 2 single-deck bus, 7 single-deck coach, 20 midibus, 1 midicoach, 1 minibus.
Chassis: 3 Alexander Dennis, 2 Bova, 11 Dennis, 3 King Long, 2 Leyland, 1 MAN, 2 Mercedes, 2 Optare, 1 Setra, 1 Transbus, 2 VDL, 1 Volvo.
Ops incl: local bus services, school contracts, private hire, excursions & tours, continental tours.
Livery: White with Blue/Red.

HUYTON TRAVEL LTD
♿❄
37 WILSON ROAD, LIVERPOOL L36 6AN
Tel: 0151 449 3868
Fax: 0151 480 0087
E-mail: info@huytontravel.co.uk
Web site: www.huytontravel.co.uk
Fleet Name: HTL Buses.
Dirs: P Yates, J Yates Jnr **Ops Man:** D Stewart.
Fleet: 60 – 17 midibus, 43 minibus.
Chassis: 8 Alexander Dennis, 1 Dennis, 6 Mercedes, 37 Optare, 1 Renault, 1 Transbus, 6 Volkswagen.
Bodies: 8 Alexander Dennis, 1 Mellor, 1 Marshall, 1 Mercedes, 37 Optare, 1 Renault, 1 Transbus, 10 Other.
Ops incl: local bus services, school contracts.
Livery: Green.

IMPERA BUS & COACH LTD
Ceased trading since LRB 2014 went to press

MAGHULL COACHES LTD
🚻♿❄
1 CANAL STREET, BOOTLE L20 8AE
Tel: 0151 922 4284
Fax: 0151 922 7521
E-mail: bookings@maghullcoaches.co.uk
Web site: www.maghullcoaches.co.uk
Dirs: B Reilly, Mrs C Reilly, J Reilly, Mrs A Meek **Fleet Eng:** P Bucknall.
Fleet: 44 – 17 double-deck bus, 8 single-deck coach, 7 open-top bus, 5 midicoach, 6 minibus, 1 minicoach.
Chassis: 3 DAF, 10 Dennis, 4 LDV, 3 Leyland, 2 MAN, 1 MCW, 8 Mercedes, 9 Scania, 1 Setra, 3 Volvo.
Ops incl: school contracts, private hire, sightseeing tours.
Livery: Red/Orange/White.

DAVID OGDEN COACHES
🚻♿🚻❄⛟T
BAXTERS LANE, SUTTON, ST HELENS WA9 3DH
Tel: 01744 606176
Fax: 01744 822146
E-mail: reservations@davidogdenholidays.co.uk
Web site: www.davidogdenholidays.co.uk
Prop: John David Ogden **Co Sec:** Carol Ogden.
Fleet: 20 - 5 single-deck bus, 12 single-deck coach, 2 minibus.
Chassis: 1 Bova, 4 DAF, 1 Dennis, 1 EOS, 1 Ford Transit, 2 Leyland, 2 Mercedes, 2 Optare, 1 Scania, 2 Temsa, 2 Van Hool.
Ops incl: school contracts, excursions & tours, private hire, continental tours.
Livery: Red/White/Blue.

PEOPLESBUS LIMITED
♿❄🚻❄⛟
CUSTOMER SERVICE CENTRE, PO BOX 57, LIVERPOOL L9 8YX
Tel: 0151 523 4010
Fax: 0151 523 4010
E-mail: enquiries@peoplesbus.com

Web site: www.peoplesbus.com
Man Dir: Andrew Cawley
Co Sec: Hilda Cawley
Office Man: Joanne Ashcroft **Eng Man:** James Myers.
Ops incl: local bus services, school contracts, private hire.
Fleet: 35 – 24 double-deck bus, 5 single-deck bus, 1 double-deck coach, 1 single-deck coach, 1 articulated bus, 3 midibus.
Chassis: 17 Alexander Dennis, 1 BMC, 2 Dennis, 1 Leyland, 1 MCW, 2 Optare, 1 Scania, 1 VDL, 9 Volvo.
Bodies: 20 Alexander Dennis, 1 BMC, 1 Irizar, 1 MCW, 5 Northern Counties, 2 Optare, 2 Plaxton, 3 Wrightbus.
Ops incl: local bus services, school contracts, private hire.
Livery: Blue/Pink.
Ticket System: Wayfarer TGX200.

STAGECOACH MERSEYSIDE AND SOUTH LANCASHIRE
♿🚌♿
GILMOSS BUS DEPOT, EAST LANCASHIRE ROAD, LIVERPOOL L11 0BB
Tel: 0151 330 6200
Fax: 0151 330 6210
E-mail: enquiries.merseyside@stagecoachbus.com
Web site: www.stagecoachbus.com
Fleet Names: Stagecoach in Merseyside/Lancashire/Wirral/Chester.
Man Dir: Elisabeth Tasker **Eng Dir:** Tony Cockroft **Ops Dir:** Rob Jones
Comm Man: James Mellor.
Fleet: 433 - 117 double-deck bus, 2 open-top bus, 183 single-deck bus, 90 midibus, 41 minibus.
Chassis: 154 Alexander Dennis, 11 Bluebird, 31 Dennis, 2 Leyland, 50 MAN, 51 Optare, 62 Scania, 26 Transbus, 46 Volvo.
Ops incl: local bus services, school contracts, excursions & tours, private hire, express.
Livery: Stagecoach UK Bus.
Ticket System: Wayfarer TGX.

NORFOLK

AMBASSADOR TRAVEL (ANGLIA) LTD
♿❄🚻❄R R24 ⛟T
JAMES WATT CLOSE, GAPTON HALL INDUSTRIAL ESTATE, GREAT YARMOUTH NR31 0NX
Tel/Recovery: 01493 440350
Fax: 01493 440367
E-mail: ambassador.travelmail@gmail.com
Fleet Name: Ambassador Travel
Chairman: R H Green **Man Dir:** M C Green **Ops Man:** B Picton **Dep Ops Man:** M Pleasants.
Fleet: 41 - 1 single-deck bus, 36 single-deck coach, 4 midibus.
Chassis: 7 Scania, 30 Volvo, 4 Other.
Bodies: 6 Caetano, 2 Irizar, 4 Jonckheere, 4 Optare, 22 Plaxton, 4 Sunsundegui.
Ops incl: local bus services, school contracts, private hire, National Express, UK tours.
Liveries: White, National Express.
Ticket System: Various.

ANGLIAN BUS LTD
See Suffolk

CARTERS COACHES
🚻♿❄
TITTLESHALL ROAD, LITCHAM PE32 2PB
Tel: 01328 701210
E-mail: graham@carterscoaches.com
Web site: www.carterscoaches.com
Partners: G Carter, K Carter.
Fleet: 11 – 8 single-deck coach, 2 midicoach, 1 minibus.

Chassis: 1 Ford, 2 Mercedes, 8 Volvo.
Bodies: 1 Ford, 3 Jonckheere, 3 Plaxton, 2 Unvi, 2 Van Hool.
Ops incl: school contracts, excursions & tours, private hire.
Livery: Green.

CHENERY TRAVEL
♿🚻❄⛟
THE GARAGE, DICKLEBURGH, DISS IP21 4NJ
Tel: 01379 741221
Fax: 01379 740728
Recovery: 01379 741656
Web site: www.chenerytravel.co.uk
Dir: Mrs P G Garnham
Gen Man: Mrs J M McGraffin.
Fleet: 19 single-deck coach.
Chassis: 14 Setra, 5 Volvo.
Bodies: 3 Caetano, 2 Jonckheere, 14 Setra.
Ops incl: school contracts, excursions & tours, private hire, express, continental tours.
Liveries: Blue/Green; National Express.

COACH SERVICES LTD
♿❄🚻🚌❄⛟T
1A HOWLETT WAY, THETFORD IP24 1HZ
Tel: 01842 821509
Fax: 01842 766581
E-mail: info@coachservicesltd.co.uk
Web site: www.coachservicesltd.com
Man Dir: Allen Crawford **Tran Man:** Robert Crawford **Ops Man:** Thomas Crawford
Gen Man: Rick Martin.
Fleet: 45 - 5 double-deck bus, 15 single-deck

bus, 22 single-deck coach, 3 minibus.
Chassis: 4 Alexander Dennis, 2 AEC Routemaster, 2 Ford Transit, 7 Mercedes, 9 Scania, 21 Volvo.
Ops incl: local bus services, school contracts, excursions & tours, private hire, continental tours.
Livery: White.
Ticket System: Wayfarer.

CRASKE COACHES
🚻♿❄
39 LAXFIELD ROAD, SUTTON, NORWICH NR12 9QP
Tel: 01692 582093
Fax: 01692 580587
E-mail: christophercraske@keme.co.uk
Web site: www.craskecoaches.co.uk
Prop: C Craske, Mrs B Craske.
Fleet: 5 single-deck coach.
Chassis: 1 DAF, 4 Scania.
Bodies: 2 Berkhof, 2 Irizar, 1 Plaxton.
Ops incl: school contracts, private hire.
Livery: White.

CRUSADER HOLIDAYS
See Essex

D-WAY TRAVEL
See Suffolk

DEREHAM COACHWAYS LTD
♿🚻❄
RASH'S GREEN INDUSTRIAL ESTATE, DEREHAM NR19 1JG
Tel: 01362 692202

Fax: 01362 697785
Dirs: V T, L J & S V Rollins.
Fleet: 10 single-deck coach.
Chassis: 10 Volvo.
Bodies: 2 Jonckheere, 1 Plaxton, 7 Van Hool.
Ops incl: school contracts, private hire.
Livery: White with Blue.

DOLPHIN AUTOS (NORWICH) LTD
🚍🚌❄️

2 SWANTON ROAD, NORWICH NR2 4LR
Tel: 01603 400400
Fax: 01603 400220
E-mail: quotes@dolphincoachhire.co.uk
Web site: www.dolphincoachhire.co.uk
Dirs: C, M & D Cooke.
Fleet: 34 – 12 single-deck coach,
10 midicoach, 11 minibus, 1 minicoach.
Chassis: 5 Bova, 1 DAF, 1 Dennis, 7 Ford
Transit, 16 Mercedes, 1 Scania, 1 Setra, 2 Volvo.
Ops incl: school contracts, private hire.
Livery: White with Blue.

EAGLES COACHES
🚍🚌❄️

EAGLES COACH YARD, PRIORY ROAD,
CASTLE ACRE, KINGS LYNN PE32 2AA
Tel: 01760 755641
Fax: 01760 755108
Web site: www.eaglescoaches.co.uk
Prop: M J Eagle.
Fleet: 15 – 13 single-deck coach, 1 midicoach,
1 minibus
Chassis: 2 Mercedes, 13 Volvo.
Ops incl: school contracts, private hire.

EASTONS COACHES
🚍🚌🅿️🚐❄️🚽🇹

THE OLD COACH HOUSE, PARISH ROAD,
STRATTON STRAWLESS, NORWICH
NR10 5LR
Tel: 01603 754155
Fax: 01603 754133
E-mail: admin@eastonsholidays.co.uk
Web site: www.eastonsholidays.co.uk
Dirs: Robert Easton, Derek Easton.
Fleet: 18- 14 single-deck coach, 2 minibus,
2 vintage coaches.
Chassis: 1 Albion, 1 Bedford, 4 Bova, 1 DAF,
1 Mercedes, 6 Setra, 1 VDL, 1 Volkswagen,
1 Volvo.
Ops incl: excursions & tours, private hire,
continental tours.
Livery: Purple.

EUROVIEW COACHING LTD
🚌🚍❄️

13 BERTIE WARD WAY, RASH'S GREEN,
DEREHAM NR19 1TE
Tel: 01362 698667
Fax: 01362 692554
E-mail: euroview@btconnect.com
Web site: www.euroview-travel.co.uk
Fleet: 5 – 3 single-deck coach, 2 minibus.
Chassis: 1 Ford Transit, 1 Mercedes,
2 Scania, 1 Volvo.
Ops incl: school contracts, excursions &
tours, private hire.
Livery: White with logos.
A subsidiary of Coach Services Ltd

FARELINE COACH SERVICES
See Suffolk

FIRST EASTERN COUNTIES
🚍🚌🚐❄️

ROUEN HOUSE, ROUEN ROAD, NORWICH
NR1 1RB
Tel: 0845 602 0121
Fax: 01603 615439
E-mail: contactus.fec@firstgroup.com
Web site: www.firstgroup.com
Man Dir: David Squire **Comm Dir:**
Steve Wickers **Fin Dir:** David Marshall

HR Director: Karen Doores
Creative Dir: Chelsea de Silva
Ch Eng: Mark Reynolds **Business Man:**
Chris Speed.
Fleet: 257 - 151 double-deck bus, 73 single-
deck bus, 2 single-deck coach, 25 midibus,
6 minibus.
Chassis: 33 Alexander Dennis, 61 Dennis,
6 Optare, 16 Scania, 141 Volvo.
Bodies: 36 Alexander Dennis, 11 Alexander,
12 Caetano, 2 Northern Counties, 6 Optare,
75 Plaxton, 10 Transbus, 105 Wright.
Ops incl: local bus services, school contract,
private hire.
Livery: FirstGroup UK Bus.
Ticket System: Wayfarer 3.

FREESTONES COACHES LTD
🚐🚍🚌❄️🖊️

GREEN LANE, BEETLEY, DEREHAM
NR20 4DL
Tel: 01362 860236
Fax: 01362 860276
E-mail: enquiries@freestonescoaches.co.uk
Web site: www.freestonescoaches.co.uk
Dir: Mrs Gloria Feeke **Ops Man:** Robert
Tibbles **Co Sec:** Gary Feeke.
Fleet: 18 - 16 single-deck coach, 2 minibus.
Chassis: 1 Ford Transit, 1 Iveco, 1 Mercedes,
5 Scania 1 Setra, 2 Van Hool, 1 Volkswagen,
6 Volvo.
Ops incl: excursions & tours, express
(Megabus), school contracts, private hire,
continental tours.
Liveries: White/Red; Silver/Red; Megabus.

D&H HARROD (COACHES) LTD
🚍🚌❄️🇹🚐🚽

BEXWELL AERODROME, DOWNHAM
MARKET PE38 9LU
Tel: 01366 381111
Fax: 01366 382010
E-mail: info@harrodscoaches.co.uk
Web site: www.harrodscoaches.co.uk
Prop: Derek Harrod **Ops Man:** Paul Harrod.
Fleet: 15 – 13 single-deck coach, 2 midicoach.
Chassis: 1 Bedford, 1 Dennis, 1 Irisbus,
1 Mercedes, 1 Volvo.
Bodies: 1 Duple, 3 Jonckheere, 1 Mercedes,
5 Plaxton, 1 UVG, 4 Van Hool.
Ops incl: school contracts, excursions &
tours, private hire, continental tours.
Liveries: Gold/Cream & Blue.

KONECTBUS LTD
🚍🚐🚽

JOHN GOSHAWK ROAD, RASH'S GREEN
INDUSTRIAL ESTATE, DEREHAM
NR19 1SY
Tel: 01362 851210
E-mail: feedback@konectbus.co.uk
Web site: www.konectbus.co.uk
Fleet: 62 - 27 double-deck bus, 1 open-top
bus, 23 single-deck bus, 5 articulated bus,
6 midibus.
Chassis: 15 Alexander Dennis, 2 Dennis,
5 Mercedes, 29 Optare, 5 VDL, 6 Volvo.
Bodies: 15 Alexander Dennis, 2 East Lancs,
5 Mercedes, 1 Northern Counties, 29 Optare,
10 Wrightbus.
Ops incl: local bus services.
Livery: Blue/Yellow/Grey.
Ticket System: Wayfarer TGX
A subsidiary of the Go-Ahead Group

MARETT'S CHARIOTS
🚌🚍❄️

THE OLD SCHOOL, AYLMERTON
NR11 8RA
Tel: 01263 837900
Fax: 01263 838046
E-mail: info@marettschariots.co.uk
Web site: www.marettschariots.co.uk
Depots at: Cromer, North Walsham.

Fleet Names: Marett's Chariots, Bluebird
Coaches.
Fleet: 18 – 9 single-deck coach, 6 midicoach,
3 minibus.
Chassis: 1 Ford Transit, 8 Mercedes, 9 Volvo.
Ops incl: school contract, excursions &
tours, private hire.
Livery: Bronze/White.

MATTHEWS COACHES
🚍🚌❄️

50 WESTGATE STREET, SHOULDHAM,
KING'S LYNN PE33 0BN
Tel: 01366 347220
Fax: 01366 347293
E-mail: john@matthewscoaches.co.uk
Web site: www.matthewscoaches-norfolk.
co.uk
Man Dir: John P Lloyd.
Fleet: 3 – 2 single-deck coach, 1 minibus.
Chassis: 1 Iveco, 1 LDV, 1 Volvo.
Bodies: 1 Jonckheere, 1 Plaxton, 1 Other.
Ops incl: school contracts, excursions &
tours, private hire.
Livery: White.

NEAVES COACHES
Business acquired by Sanders Coaches Ltd

NORFOLK GREEN
🚍🚐

HAMLIN WAY, KINGS LYNN PE30 4NG
Tel: 01553 776980
Fax: 01553 770891
E-mail: enquiries@norfolkgreen.co.uk
Web site: www.norfolkgreen.co.uk
Man Dir: Andrew Dyer.
Fleet: 77 – 17 double-deck bus, 25 single-
deck bus, 35 midibus.
Chassis: 4 Alexander Dennis, 9 DAF,
7 Dennis, 8 Irisbus, 49 Optare.
Bodies: 4 Alexander Dennis, 2 Alexander,
2 East Lancs, 8 Irisbus, 58 Optare, 3 Plaxton.
Ops incl: local bus services.
Livery: two-tone Green.
Ticket System: Wayfarer TGX.
A subsidiary of Stagecoach

NORSE
🚍🚐❄️

280 FIFERS LANE, NORWICH
NR6 6EQ
Tel: 01603 894100
E-mail: info@ncsgrp.co.uk
Web site: www.ncsgrp.co.uk
Comm Dir: Paul Bonham **Tran Man
(Passenger Services):** Andrew Quinsee.
Fleet (Norfolk): 47 – 13 double-deck bus,
21 single-deck bus, 10 single-deck coach,
3 midibus.
Chassis: 35 Dennis, 2 Irisbus, 2 Mercedes,
1 Optare, 7 Volvo.
Bodies: 20 Caetano, 1 Irisbus, 1 Marcopolo,
1 Optare, 24 Plaxton
Ops incl: local bus services, Norwich park &
ride, school contracts.

PEELINGS COACHES
🚍🚌❄️🚽🖊️

THE GARAGE, CLAY HILL, TITTLESHALL,
KING'S LYNN PE32 2RQ
Tel/Fax: 01328 701531
E-mail: info@peelings-coaches.co.uk
Web site: www.peelings-coaches.co.uk
Prop: Jonathan Joplin **Comp Sec:** Ruth
Joplin **Ch Eng:** Jonathan Sayer.
Fleet: 8 single-deck coach.
Chassis: 2 Dennis, 6 Volvo.
Bodies: 1 Caetano, 1 Jonckheere, 2 Plaxton,
1 Transbus, 3 Van Hool.
Ops incl: local bus services, school contracts,
excursions & tours, private hire, express.
Livery: White/Blue/Silver.
Ticket System: Setright.

REYNOLDS COACHES LTD

THE GARAGE, ORMESBY ROAD, CAISTER-ON-SEA, GREAT YARMOUTH NR30 5QJ
Tel: 01493 720312
Fax: 01493 721512
E-mail: info@reynolds-coaches.co.uk
Web site: www.reynolds-coaches.com
Man Dir: Charles Reynolds
Tours Dir:
Mrs Julie Reynolds **Co Sec:** Mrs Grace Reynolds **Ch Eng:** Jeffrey Buckle.
Fleet: 21 – 15 single-deck coach, 3 midicoach, 1 minibus, 2 minicoach.
Chassis: 1 Ford Transit, 8 Dennis, 1 MAN, 4 Mercedes, 2 Toyota, 5 Volvo.
Ops incl: school contracts, excursions & tours, private hire, continental tours.
Livery: Silver.

RICHARDS COACHES LTD

NORWICH ROAD, GUIST, DEREHAM NR20 5LU
Tel: 01362 683831
E-mail: enquiries@richardscoachesltd.co.uk
Web site: www.richardscoachesltd.co.uk
Dir: Mrs R Morant.
Fleet: 13 – 8 single-deck coach, 2 double-deck coach, 2 midicoach, 1 minibus.
Chassis: 1 MAN, 2 Mercedes, 2 Scania, 8 Volvo.
Ops incl: school contracts, private hire, excursions & tours.
Livery: White/Purple.

SANDERS COACHES LTD

HEATH DRIVE, HEMPSTEAD ROAD INDUSTRIAL ESTATE, HOLT NR25 6ER
Tel: 01263 712800
Fax: 01263 710920
E-mail: info@sanderscoaches.com
Web site: www.sanderscoaches.com
Man Dir: Charles Sanders
Ops Dir: Paul Sanders
Head of Tours & Finance: Carole Willimott
Fleet Eng: Andrew Sanders.
Fleet: 100 – 10 double-deck bus, 29 single-deck bus, 33 single-deck coach, 12 midibus, 9 midicoach, 7 minibus.
Chassis: 1 Bova, 19 DAF, 13 Dennis, 14 Mercedes, 6 Optare, 24 Scania, 11 VDL, 13 Volvo.
Bodies: 2 Alexander, 1 Bova, 1 Crest, 12 East Lancs, 1 Ikarus, 2 Jonckheere, 1 Mercedes, 6 Optare, 35 Plaxton, 14 Scania, 10 Van Hool, 13 Wrightbus, 1 Other.
Ops incl: local bus services, school contracts, excursions & tours, private hire, continental tours.

Livery: Orange/Yellow/Blue.
Ticket System: Wayfarer.

H SEMMENCE & CO LTD

34 NORWICH ROAD, WYMONDHAM NR18 0NS
Tel: 01953 602135
Fax: 01953 605867
E-mail: sales@semmence.co.uk
Web site: www.semmence.co.uk
Man Dir: Sean Green.
Fleet: 25 – 20 single-deck coach, 4 midicoach, 1 minibus.
Chassis: 5 Dennis, 5 Mercedes, 5 Scania, 1 Transbus, 9 Volvo.
Bodies: 2 Caetano, 1 Duple, 14 Plaxton, 3 Transbus, 4 Van Hool, 1 Other.
Ops incl: local bus services, school contracts, excursions & tours, express, private hire.
Livery: White.
Ticket System: Wayfarer.
Associated with Ambassador Travel

SIMONDS COACH & TRAVEL

ROSWALD HOUSE, OAK DRIVE, DISS IP22 4GX
Tel/Recovery: 01379 647300
Fax: 01379 647350
E-mail: info@simonds.co.uk
Web site: www.simonds.co.uk
Chairman: D O Simonds
Man Dir: M S Simonds
Dir: R S Simonds
Eng Dir: A P Tant.
Fleet: 50 – 1 double-deck bus, 12 single-deck bus, 27 single-deck coach, 5 midibus, 3 midicoach, 1 minibus, 1 minicoach.
Chassis: 1 Dennis, 4 Enterprise, 9 MAN, 4 Mercedes, 1 Neoplan, 3 Optare, 1 Van Hool, 27 Volvo.
Bodies: 1 Alexander, 1 East Lancs, 1 Ferqui, 1 Jonckheere, 10 MCV, 1 Mercedes, 1 Neoplan, 3 Optare, 8 Plaxton, 1 Sitcar, 21 Van Hool.
Ops incl: local bus services, school contracts, excursions & tours, private hire, continental tours.
Livery: White base with Red/Gold leaves.
Ticket system: Wayfarer TGX/Paycell.

SMITHS COACHES

WOLFORD HOUSE, DYES ROAD, BLOFIELD, NORWICH NR13 4DQ
Tel: 01603 720628
Fax: 01603 722134
E-mail: smithscoaches@email.com
Web site: www.smithscoaches.com
Prop: D J Smith.

Fleet: 11 – 9 single-deck coach, 2 midicoach.
Chassis: 1 Bedford, 4 Dennis, 1 Iveco, 2 Toyota, 3 Volvo.
Ops incl: school contracts, private hire.
Livery: White with Blue.

SPRATTS COACHES (EAST ANGLIAN & CONTINENTAL) LTD

THE GARAGE, WRENINGHAM, NORWICH NR16 1AZ
Tel: 01508 489262
Fax: 01508 489404
E-mail: sprattscoaches@btconnect.com
Web site: www.sprattscoaches.co.uk
Dirs: Richard Spratt, Christine Bilham.
Fleet: 15 - 9 single-deck coach, 4 midibus, 1 vintage coach, 1 minibus.
Chassis: Bedford, Ford Transit, Iveco, MAN, Mercedes, Scania.
Bodies: Berkhof, Caetano, Duple, Mercedes, Van Hool.
Ops incl: school contracts, excursions & tours, private hire.
Livery: White.

SUNBEAM COACHES LTD

WESTGATE STREET, HEVINGHAM, NORWICH NR10 5NH
Tel/Fax: 01603 754211
E-mail: sunbeamcoaches@aol.com
Web site: www.sunbeamcoaches.co.uk
Dirs: G M Coldham, G J Coldham.
Fleet: 7 - 3 single-deck coach, 2 midicoach, 1 minibus, 1 minicoach.
Chassis: 2 MAN, 3 Mercedes, 1 Toyota, 1 Volvo.
Bodies: 1 Autobus, 1 Caetano, 2 Neoplan, 1 Plaxton, 1 Van Hool.
Ops incl: school contracts, private hire, excursions & tours.
Livery: White with Orange/Blue/Yellow.

UPWELL & DISTRICT COACHES

THE COACH DEPOT, SCHOOL ROAD, UPWELL, WISBECH PE14 9EW
Tel & Fax: 01945 773461
Fleet Name: Hircocks
Partners: Caroline E Parsons, William D Hircock.
Fleet: 2 single-deck coach, 1 midibus.
Chassis: 1 Dennis, 1 Mercedes, 1 Scania.
Bodies: 1 Irizar, 2 Plaxton.
Ops incl: excursions & tours, private hire, school contracts.
Livery: Red/White/Blue.

NORTH & NORTH EAST LINCOLNSHIRE

AMVALE LTD

7 SOUTH HUMBERSIDE INDUSTRIAL ESTATE, GRIMSBY DN31 2TP
Tel: 01472 355600
E-mail: coaches@amvale.com
Web site: www.home2.btconnect.com/Amvale
Dir: M J Godfrey.
Fleet: 56 – 1 single-deck bus, 22 single-deck coach, 1 midicoach, 30 minibus, 2 minicoach.
Chassis: Ford Transit, LDV, Mercedes, Peugeot, Volkswagen, Volvo.
Ops incl: local bus services, school contracts, private hire.

APPLEBYS COACH TRAVEL

See Radley Coach Travel

BLACK & WHITE COACHES

22B HEBDEN ROAD, SCUNTHORPE DN15 8DT
Tel: 01724 843355 **Fax:** 01724 853749
E-mail: blackwhite.coaches@btconnect.com
Web site: www.bwcoaches.com
Props: P & T Anelay.
Fleet: 8 – 5 single-deck coach, 3 midicoach.
Chassis: 3 Mercedes, 4 Scania, 1 Setra.
Bodies: 1 Irizar, 1 Onyx, 2 Plaxton, 1 Setra, 2 Van Hool, 1 Other.
Ops incl: school contracts, private hire.
Livery: Black/White.

BEN GEORGE TRAVEL LTD

39 ESTATE AVENUE, BROUGHTON, BRIGG DN20 0JZ

Tel: 01652 654681   **Fax:** 01652 650396
E-mail: s.p.easton@btinternet.com
Dirs: Stephen & John Easton.
Fleet: 2 single-deck coach, 1 minicoach.
Chassis: 1 Dennis, 1 Toyota, 1 Volvo.
Bodies: 1 Caetano, 1 Plaxton, 1 Van Hool.
Ops incl: school contracts, private hire.
Livery: Red/White/Blue

HOLLOWAYS COACHES LTD

COTTAGE BECK ROAD, SCUNTHORPE DN16 1TP
Tel: 01724 282277, 281177
Fax: 01724 289945
Dirs: P A & K Holloway.
Fleet: 34 - 12 double-deck bus, 12 single-deck bus, 8 single-deck coach, 1 midibus, 1 minibus.

Chassis: 2 DAF, 1 Dennis, 1 Ford Transit, 2 Leyland, 1 Optare, 27 Volvo.
Bodies: 8 Alexander, 1 Caetano, 1 Ford, 4 Northern Counties, 1 Optare, 14 Plaxton, 5 Wrightbus.
Ops incl: local bus services, school contracts, excursions & tours, express.
Liveries: Red/White/Blue, Yellow (school buses).

HORNSBY TRAVEL SERVICES LTD
♿ 🚌 🚐 🏫 🚂 🅣
51 ASHBY HIGH STREET, SCUNTHORPE DN16 2NB
Tel: 01724 282255
Fax: 01274 282788
E-mail: office@hornsbytravel.co.uk
Web site: www.hornsbytravel.co.uk
Man Dir: Raymond Hornsby
Gen Man: Nicholas Hornsby **Ch Eng:** Rob Andrew.
Fleet: 31 - 3 double-deck bus, 21 single-deck bus, 3 single-deck coach, 3 executive coaches, 1 minibus.
Chassis: 13 Alexander Dennis, 5 DAF, 2 Leyland, 3 MAN, 2 VDL, 6 Volvo.
Bodies: 3 Alexander, 3 Alexander Dennis, 19 Plaxton, 6 Wrightbus.
Ops incl: local bus services, school contracts, excursions & tours, private hire.
Livery: Blue/Silver.
Ticket System: ERG.

JOHNSONS COACHES
🚐
THORNTON ROAD, GOXHILL DN19 7HN
Tel: 01469 530267
Props: M Gregory, D Wilson.
Fleet: 7 – 5 single-deck coach, 2 midibus.
Chassis: 2 Mercedes, 5 Volvo.
Ops incl: local bus services, school contracts, private hire.

MILLMAN COACHES
🏫 🚐 🚌
17 WILTON ROAD, HUMBERSTON, GRIMSBY DN36 4AW
Tel: 01472 210297   **Fax:** 01472 595915
E-mail: enquiries@millmancoaches.co.uk
Web site: www.millmancoaches.co.uk
Partners: David Millman, Amanda J Millman.
Fleet: 9 - 6 single-deck coach, 3 midicoach.
Chassis: 1 Dennis, 1 MAN, 2 Mercedes, 5 Volvo.
Bodies: 1 Caetano, 1 Excel, 4 Jonckheere, 2 Plaxton, 1 Sitcar.
Ops incl: private hire, school contracts.
Livery: White/Blue/Yellow.

RADLEY COACH TRAVEL
🚐 🏫 🚌
THE TRAVEL OFFICE, 11 CHAPEL COURT, BRIGG DN20 8JZ
Tel: 01652 653583   **Fax:** 01652 656020
Fleet Names: Radley Holidays, Applebys Coach Holidays.
E-mail: radleytravel@aol.com
Web site: www.radleytravel.co.uk
Prop: Kevin M Radley.
Fleet: 3 single-deck coach.
Chassis: 3 Scania.
Bodies: 3 Irizar.
Ops incl: excursions & tours, private hire, continental tours.
Livery: Maroon/Gold.
Incorporating Applebys Coach Travel

SELWYN MOTORS
🚐
WESTGATE, SANDTOFT ROAD, BELTON DN9 1QA
Tel: 01427 872334
Prop: B S Dodd.
Fleet: 3 – 1 double-deck bus, 2 single-deck coach.
Ops incl: local bus service, school contracts.
Livery: Red/Grey.

SHERWOOD TRAVEL
🚐 🏫 🚌
19 QUEENS ROAD, IMMINGHAM DN40 1QR
Tel: 01469 571140
Fax: 01469 574937
E-mail: enquiries@sherwoodtravel.co.uk
Web site: www.sherwoodtravel.co.uk
Dirs: Stuart Oakland, Jane Oakland.
Fleet: 9 - 5 single-deck coach, 3 midicoach, 2 minicoach.
Chassis: 5 Mercedes, 2 Scania, 3 Volvo.
Ops incl: school contracts, excursions & tours, private hire.
Livery: Black/Silver/White.

STAGECOACH EAST MIDLANDS
♿ 🏫 🖃
PO BOX 15, DEACON ROAD, LINCOLN LN2 4JB
Tel: 0345 605 0605
Fax: 01522 538229
E-mail: eastmidlands.enquiries@stagecoachbus.com
Web site: www.stagecoachbus.com
Fleet Names: Stagecoach in Grimsby-Cleethorpes, Stagecoach in Lincolnshire.
Man Dir: Michelle Hargreaves
Eng Dir: John Taylor **Comm Dir:** Dave Skepper **Ops Dir:** Richard Kay.
Fleet: 540 - 209 double-deck bus, 122 single-deck bus, 16 single-deck coach, 165 midibus, 28 minibus.
Chassis: 165 Alexander Dennis, 6 DAF, 109 Dennis, 1 Leyland, 72 MAN, 36 Optare, 26 Scania, 49 Transbus, 76 Volvo.
Bodies: 110 Alexander, 234 Alexander Dennis, 50 East Lancs, 6 Jonckheere, 5 Northern Counties, 36 Optare, 37 Plaxton, 50 Transbus, 12 Wrightbus.
Ops incl: local bus services.
Livery: Stagecoach UK Bus.
Ticket System: ERG TP5000.

NORTH YORKSHIRE, DARLINGTON, MIDDLESBROUGH, REDCAR & CLEVELAND, YORK

ABBEY COACHWAYS LTD
🚐 🚌
MEADOWCROFT GARAGE, LOW STREET, CARLTON, GOOLE DN14 9PH
Tel: 01405 860337
Fax: 01405 869433
Dirs: Mrs L E Baker, S J Stockdale.
Fleet: 8 – 2 double-deck bus, 5 single-deck coach, 1 double-deck coach.
Chassis: 1 MAN, 1 Scania, 6 Volvo.
Bodies: 2 Alexander, 2 Jonckheere, 4 Plaxton.
Ops incl: school contracts, private hire.
Livery: White/Blue.

G. ABBOTT & SONS
♿ 🚐 🚌 🏫 R24 🚂
AUMANS HOUSE, LEEMING, NORTHALLERTON DL7 9RZ
Tel: 01677 424987
Fax: 01677 427435
E-mail: quotes@abbottscoaches.co.uk
Web site: www.abbottscoaches.co.uk
Fleet Name: Abbotts of Leeming.
Partners: David C Abbott, Clifford G Abbot.
Fleet: 74 - 49 single-deck coach, 4 midicoach, 21 minibus.
Chassis: 5 DAF, 1 Fiat, 4 Ford Transit, 2 Irisbus, 5 LDV, 3 Leyland, 9 Mercedes, 6 Optare, 21 Scania, 18 Volvo.
Bodies: 6 Beulas, 1 Caetano, 4 Duple, 1 Ford, 1 Hispano, 2 Ikarus, 13 Irizar, 2 Lahden, 5 LDV, 2 Mercedes, 6 Optare, 17 Plaxton, 7 Sunsundegui, 7 Van Hool, 5 Other.
Ops incl: local bus services, school contracts, excursions & tours, private hire, express, continental tours.
Livery: Orange/Cream/Red.

ARRIVA YORKSHIRE LTD
♿ 🖊
24 BARNSLEY ROAD, WAKEFIELD WF1 5JX
Tel: 01924 231300   **Fax:** 01924 200106
Web site: www.arrivabus.co.uk
Regional Man Dir: Nigel Featham **Regional Fin Dir:** David Cocker **Eng Dir:** Neil Craig **Ops Dir:** Colin Newbury **Regional HR Business Partner:** Julie Reynolds **Regional Marketing & Comms Man:** Chloe Leach O'Connell.
Fleet: 344 - 163 double-deck bus, 91 single-deck bus, 82 midibus, 8 minibus.
Chassis: 65 Alexander Dennis, 28 DAF, 31 Dennis, 21 Optare, 118 VDL, 81 Volvo.
Bodies: 23 Alexander, 65 Alexander Dennis, 30 East Lancs, 2 Ikarus, 47 Optare, 48 Plaxton, 129 Wrightbus.
Ops incl: local bus services, school contracts.
Livery: Arriva UK Bus.

H ATKINSON & SONS (INGLEBY) LTD
🏫 🚐 🚌 🚂 🅣
NORWOOD GARAGE, INGLEBY ARNCLIFFE, NORTHALLERTON DL6 3LN
Tel: 01609 882222
Fax: 01609 882476
E-mail: office@atkinsoncoaches.co.uk
Web site: www.atkinsoncoaches.co.uk
Dirs: M T Atkinson, D Atkinson, R Atkinson.
Fleet: 11 - 10 single-deck coach, 1 midicoach.
Chassis: 1 DAF, 1 Iveco, 1 MAN, 2 Neoplan, 2 Scania, 1 Setra, 2 Temsa, 1 Van Hool.
Bodies: 1 Beulas, 1 Indcar, 2 Neoplan, 1 Setra, 2 Temsa, 4 Van Hool.
Ops Incl: schools contracts, excursions & tours, private hire, continental tours.
Livery: Yellow with Maroon/Gold.

BALDRY'S COACHES
🚐 🖃 🚌 🏫
LEYLANDII, SELBY ROAD, HOLME-ON-SPALDING-MOOR YO43 4HB
Tel: 01430 860992
E-mail: baldryscoaches@live.co.uk
Web site: www.baldryscoaches.co.uk
Prop: A Baldry.
Fleet: 5 single-deck coach.
Chassis: 1 Bedford, 2 Iveco, 1 Mercedes, 1 Volvo.
Bodies: 2 Beulas, 1 Hispano, 1 Jonckheere, 1 Plaxton.
Ops incl: school contracts, excursions & tours, private hire.
Livery: White & Blue.

BEECROFT COACHES
🏫 🚐 🅣
POST OFFICE, FEWSTON HG3 1SG
Tel/Fax: 01943 880206
Prop: D Beecroft.
Fleet: 1 single-deck coach.
Chassis: 1 Dennis.
Bodies: 1 Caetano.
Ops incl: school contracts, excursions & tours, private hire, continental tours.
Livery: Green/Orange/White.

BIBBY'S OF INGLETON LTD
🚐 🏫 🚌 🚂 🅣
INGLETON INDUSTRIAL ESTATE, NEW ROAD, INGLETON LA6 3NU
Tel: 01524 241330
Fax: 01524 242216
E-mail: enquiries@bibbys.co.uk
Web site: www.bibbys.co.uk
Man Dir: P Bibby **Co Sec:** Mrs S Holcroft

Ch Eng: M Stephenson.
Fleet: 37 - 25 single-deck coach, 4 midicoach, 4 minibus, 3 minicoach, 1 vintage.
Chassis: 1 Bedford, 17 DAF, 2 Ford Transit, 9 Mercedes, 2 Temsa, 2 Van Hool, 4 VDL.
Bodies: 1 Crest, 1 Duple, 2 Ford, 7 Ikarus, 1 KVC, 1 Onyx, 2 Plaxton, 2 Temsa, 3 Unvi, 16 Van Hool, 1 Other.
Ops incl: school contracts, excursions & tours, private hire, continental tours.
Livery: Blue/Grey/Red with white stripes.

BOTTERILLS MINIBUSES

HIGH STREET GARAGE, THORNTON LE DALE, PICKERING YO18 7QW
Tel: 01751 469117
E-mail: botterills@hotmail.com
Web site: www.botterills.org.uk
Fleet: 4 minibus.
Chassis/Bodies: 4 Mercedes.
Ops incl: local bus services, school contracts, private hire.
Livery: White.

EDDIE BROWN TOURS LTD

UNIT 370, THORP ARCH TRADING ESTATE, WETHERBY, YORK LS23 7EG
Tel: 01423 321248
Fax: 01423 326213
Recovery: 07736 692702
E-mail: sales@eddiebrowntours.com
Web site: www.eddiebrowntours.com
Man Dir: Gary Priest **Fleet Eng:** Ian Laking
Ops Man: Andy Knowles.
Fleet: 52 - 6 single-deck bus, 33 single-deck coach, 3 midibus, 8 midicoach, 2 minibus.
Chassis: 2 King Long, 1 MAN, 9 Mercedes, 1 Neoplan, 7 Scania, 32 Volvo.
Bodies: 1 Autobus, 2 King Long, 1 KVC, 1 Neoplan, 3 Optare, 33 Plaxton, 6 Van Hool, 5 Wrightbus.
Ops incl: local bus services, school contracts, excursions & tours, private hire, continental tours.
Livery: White/Red/Orange.

BURRELLS (BARNARD CASTLE COACHES)

SOUTH VIEW GARAGE, NEWSHAM, RICHMOND DL11 7RA
Tel: 01833 621302
Fax: 01833 621431
E-mail: alburrell@hotmail.com
Dirs: Alan Burrell, Mrs Sandra Burrell.
Fleet: 5 single-deck coach.
Chassis: 1 Leyland, 4 Volvo.
Bodies: 1 Duple, 4 Van Hool.
Ops incl: school contracts, excursions & tours, private hire, express, continental tours.
Livery: Yellow/White.

COASTAL AND COUNTRY COACHES LTD

THE GARAGE, FAIRFIELD WAY, WHITBY BUSINESS PARK, WHITBY YO22 4PU
Tel: 01947 602922
Fax: 01947 600830
E-mail: enquiries@coastalandcountry.co.uk
Web site: www.coastalandcountry.co.uk

Man Dir: C Vasey **Dir:** J Vasey
Ch Eng: A Caley.
Fleet: 22 - 14 single-deck coach, 3 open-top bus, 2 midibus, 2 midicoach, 1 minicoach.
Chassis: 1 Alexander Dennis, 2 Bedford, 2 Leyland, 3 Mercedes, 1 Volkswagen, 13 Volvo.
Bodies: 1 Alexander, 1 Alexander Dennis, 2 Berkhof, 2 Duple, 1 Optare, 12 Plaxton, 2 Van Hool, 1 Volkswagen.
Ops incl: local bus services, school contracts, excursions & tours, private hire.
Livery: White/Blue.
Ticket system: Wayfarer.

COATHAM COACHES

MARGROVE PARK VILLAGE, SALTBURN-BY-THE-SEA
Tel: 01287 652222
E-mail: admin@coathamcoaches.com
Web site: www.coathamcoaches.co.uk
Props: M J & B Hodgson.
Fleet: 16 - 7 single-deck coach, 3 midicoach, 4 minibus, 2 minicoach.
Chassis: 2 Bova, 3 Iveco, 1 LDV, 5 Mercedes, 5 Volvo.
Ops incl: school contracts, excursions & tours, private hire.
Livery: White with Black/Grey.

COLLINS COACHES

CLIFFE SERVICE STATION, YORK ROAD, CLIFFE, SELBY YO8 6NN
Tel: 01757 210111
Fax: 01757 630196
E-mail: collins.coaches@hotmail.co.uk
Prop: Alan Collins.
Fleet: 4 - 3 single-deck coach, 1 midicoach.
Chassis: 1 Mercedes, 3 Volvo.
Bodies: 1 Plaxton, 3 Van Hool.
Ops incl: local bus service, school contracts, private hire.
Livery: White.

CONNEXIONS BUSES

6 ST THOMAS'S WAY, GREEN HAMMERTON, YORK YO26 8BE
Tel: 01423 339600
Fax: 01423 339785
E-mail: harrogatecoach@aol.com
Web site: www.harrogatecoachtravel.com
Man Dir: Craig Temple **Fin Dir:** Julie Temple.
Fleet: 26 - 3 double-deck bus, 23 single-deck bus.
Chassis: 1 Alexander Dennis, 1 Leyland, 7 Optare, 14 Scania, 3 Volvo.
Bodies: 5 Alexander Dennis, 1 East Lancs, 1 Northern Counties, 7 Optare, 3 Scania, 9 Wrightbus.
Ops incl: local bus services, school contracts, private hire.
Livery: Green/White.
Ticket System: Ticketer.

JOHN DODSWORTH (COACHES) LTD

WETHERBY ROAD, BOROUGHBRIDGE YO5 9HS
Tel: 01423 322236
Fax: 01423 324682
Dir: John Dodsworth.

Fleet: 6 - 1 single-deck coach, 1 midicoach, 1 minibus.
Chassis: 1 Bova, 1 LDV, 1 Mercedes, 1 Setra, 2 Volvo.
Bodies: 1 Bova, 1 LDV, 3 Plaxton, 1 Setra.
Ops incl: excursions & tours, private hire, continental tours, school contracts.
Livery: Cream/Orange.

FIRST YORK

45 TANNER ROW, YORK YO1 6JP
Tel: 01904 883000
Fax: 01904 883057
Web site: www.firstgroup.com
Regional Man Dir: Dave Alexander
Man Dir: Ben Gilligan **Eng Dir:** Andy Foster.
Fleet: 106 - 17 double-deck bus, 63 single-deck bus, 11 midibus, 15 articulated bus.
Chassis: 15 Mercedes, 6 Optare, 80 Volvo, 5 Wrightbus.
Bodies: 15 Mercedes, 6 Optare, 85 Wrightbus.
Ops incl: local bus services, York park & ride, school contracts.
Livery: FirstGroup UK Bus.
Ticket System: Wayfarer.

HANDLEY'S COACHES

NORTH ROAD, MIDDLEHAM, LEYBURN DL8 4PJ
Tel: 01969 623216 **Fax:** 01969 624546
Dirs: Mr M Anderson, Mrs J Anderson, Mr E Bowes, Mrs L Cooke.
Fleet: 9 - 3 single-deck coach, 5 midicoach, 1 minicoach.
Chassis: 1 Iveco, 5 Mercedes, 1 Scania, 2 Volvo.
Bodies: 1 Autobus, 1 Caetano, 1 Ferqui, 1 Irizar, 1 Jonckheere, 1 Mellor, 1 Onyx, 2 Plaxton.
Ops incl: private hire, school contracts.
Livery: White.

HARGREAVES COACHES

BRIDGE HOUSE, HEBDEN, SKIPTON BD23 5DE
Tel: 01756 752567
Fax: 01756 753768
E-mail: info@hargreavescoaches.co.uk
Web site: www.hargreavescoaches.co.uk
Prop: Andrew C Howick.
Fleet: 8 - 3 single-deck coach, 1 double-deck coach, 3 minicoach, 1 minibus.
Chassis: DAF, MAN, Neoplan, Van Hool.
Bodies: 1 Ayats, 1 LDV, 1 MAN, 3 Mercedes, 1 Neoplan, 1 Van Hool.
Ops incl: School contracts, excursions & tours, private hire, continental tours.
Livery: Silver Grey/Pink/White.

P & D A HOPWOOD

22 MAIN STREET, ASKHAM BRYAN, YORK YO23 3QU
Tel: 01904 707394
Dirs: P Hopwood, D A Hopwood, R C Baker, A J Baker.
Fleet: 2 single-deck coach.
Chassis: 2 Dennis.
Bodies: 1 Duple, 1 Plaxton.
Ops incl: school contracts, private hire.

Vehicle suitable for disabled	Coach(es) with galley facilities	Vintage Coach(es) available
Seat belt-fitted Vehicle	Replacement vehicle available	Open top vehicle(s)
R24 24 hour recovery service	R Recovery service available	Coaches with toilet facilities
T Toilet-drop facilities available	Air-conditioned vehicle(s)	Hybrid Buses Gas Buses

W P & M HUTCHINSON

ROXBY HOUSE, YORK ROAD, EASINGWOLD YO61 3EF
Tel: 01347 821853
Fleet: 6 – 1 single-deck coach, 2 midicoach, 3 minibus.
Chassis: 5 Mercedes, 1 Volvo.
Ops incl: local bus services, school contracts, private hire.
Livery: White with Blue/Yellow.

INDEPENDENT COACHWAYS LTD
See combined entry under Thornes Independent Ltd

INGLEBY'S LUXURY COACHES LTD

24 HOSPITAL FIELDS ROAD, FULFORD ROAD, YORK YO10 4DZ
Tel: 01904 637620
Fax: 01904 612944
E-mail: sales@inglebyscoaches.co.uk
Web site: www.inglebyscoaches.co.uk
Dir: C Ingleby **Fleet Eng:** R Atkinson
Ops: A Evans.
Fleet: 16 - 8 single-deck coach, 4 midicoach, 4 minibus.
Chassis: 1 Bova, 1 Ford Transit, 7 Mercedes, 1 Van Hool, 2 VDL, 4 Volvo.
Bodies: 1 Bova, 1 Crest, 1 Ford, 2 KVC, 1 Plaxton, 3 Sitcar, 7 Van Hool, 3 Other.
Ops incl: school contracts, private hire.
Livery: Blue/Cream.

JUST TRAVEL YORK LTD

BROCKETTS PARK, ACASTER AIRFIELD, YORK YO23 2PT
Tel: 01904 702020
E-mail: info@coachhireyork.co.uk
Web site: www.coachhireyork.co.uk
Fleet Names: Just Travel, Venue Mini Coaches.
Fleet: 20 – 2 single-deck bus, 7 single-deck coach, 6 midicoach, 5 minibus.
Chassis: 1 DAF, 1 Dennis, 10 Mercedes, 1 Optare, 2 Scania, 5 Volvo.
Ops incl: local bus services, school contracts, private hire.
Livery: White with Orange or Red/Yellow.

KINGS LUXURY COACHES
Operator retired since LRB 2014 went to press

LEVEN VALLEY COACHES
Business acquired by Compass Royston Travel Ltd *(see Durham)*

OLYMPIC MINI COACHES

3 ROWAN CLOSE, SCARBOROUGH YO12 6NH
Tel: 01723 503172
E-mail: olympicminicoaches@yahoo.com
Web site: www.olympic-coaches.org,
Ops incl: local bus services.
Livery: White.

PENNINE MOTOR SERVICES
Ceased trading since LRB 2014 went to press

PERRY'S COACHES

RICCAL DRIVE, YORK ROAD INDUSTRIAL PARK, MALTON YO17 6YE
Tel: 01653 690500
Fax: 01653 690800
E-mail: info@perrystravel.com
Web site: www.perrystravel.com
Partners: D J Perry **(Gen Man/Ch Eng)**, Mrs A Holtby **(Co Sec).**
Fleet: 14 - 6 single-deck coach, 6 midicoach, 2 minicoach.

Chassis: 8 Mercedes, 4 VDL, 2 Volvo.
Bodies: 1 Jonckheere, 2 Onyx, 6 Plaxton, 5 Van Hool.
Ops incl: school contracts, excursions & tours, private hire, continental tours.
Livery: Red/Yellow/White.

PRIDE OF THE DALES

STATION ROAD, GRASSINGTON BD23 5NQ
Tel: 01756 753123
E-mail: info@prideofthedales.co.uk
Web site: www.prideofthedales.co.uk
Prop: M Stewart-Clarke.
Fleet: 7 midibus.
Chassis: 1 Mercedes, 6 Optare.
Ops incl: local bus services.

PROCTERS COACHES (NORTH YORKSHIRE) LTD

TUTIN ROAD, LEEMING BAR INDUSTRIAL ESTATE, LEEMING BAR, NORTHALLERTON DL7 9UJ
Tel: 01677 425203
Fax: 01677 426550
Recovery: 07817 422371
E-mail: kevin@procterscoaches.co.uk
Web site: www.procterscoaches.com
Fleet Names: Procters Coaches, Dales & District.
Man Dir: Kevin Procter **Co Sec:** Claire Alenius **Fleet Eng:** Philip Kenyon
Gen Man: Andrew Fryatt.
Fleet: 82 – 1 double-deck bus, 1 single-deck bus, 37 single-deck coach, 1 double-deck coach, 15 midibus, 1 midicoach, 26 minibus.
Chassis: 5 Alexander Dennis, 2 Bova, 1 DAF, 2 Dennis, 2 Enterprise, 2 Ford Transit, 1 Irisbus, 2 Iveco, 3 LDV, 4 MAN, 6 Mercedes, 3 Neoplan, 14 Optare, 1 Scania, 1 Temsa, 2 Van Hool, 2 VDL, 26 Volvo, 3 Wrightbus.
Bodies: 2 Alexander, 5 Alexander Dennis, 3 Berkhof, 1 Beulas, 1 Bluebird, 2 Bova, 3 Caetano, 3 Crest, 1 Excel, 1 Fast, 1 Ford, 1 Irizar, 9 Jonckheere, 1 LDV, 1 MCV, 1 Mellor, 1 Mercedes, 3 Neoplan, 2 Noge, 14 Optare, 13 Plaxton, 1 Sunsundegui, 1 Temsa, 5 Van Hool, 5 Wrightbus, 1 Other.
Ops incl: local bus services, school contracts, private hire.
Livery: White.
Ticket System: Wayfarer.

RELIANCE MOTOR SERVICES

RELIANCE GARAGE, YORK ROAD, SUTTON-ON-THE-FOREST, YORK YO61 1ES
Tel/Fax: 01904 768262
E-mail: reliance.motors@btconnnect.com
Web site: www.reliancebuses.co.uk
Prop: John H Duff.
Fleet: 12 - 3 double-deck bus, 9 single-deck bus.
Chassis: 12 Volvo.
Bodies: 2 Alexander, 10 Wrightbus.
Ops incl: local bus services, school contracts.
Livery: Cream/Green.
Ticket System: Wayfarer TGX 150.

SCARBOROUGH & DISTRICT

BARRY'S LANE, SCARBOROUGH YO12 4HA
Tel: 01723 500064   **Fax:** 01723 370064
E-mail: sd@eyms.co.uk
Web site: www.eyms.co.uk
Ops incl: local bus services, school contracts, excursions & tours, private hire, express, continental tours.
Livery: Burgundy/Cream
Ticket system: Wayfarer TGX200
A division of East Yorkshire Motor Services Ltd *(see East Riding)*

SHAW'S OF WHITLEY

WHITLEY FARM, SILVER STREET, WHITLEY, GOOLE DN14 0JG
Tel: 01977 661214
Fax: 01977 662036
Recovery: 07802 249878
E-mail: info@shawsofwhitley.co.uk
Web site: www.shawsofwhitley.co.uk
Prop: Mrs Marjorie Shaw
Ops Man: Philip Shaw.
Fleet: 7 – 1 double-deck bus, 6 single-deck coach.
Chassis: 1 DAF, 1 Mercedes, 2 Setra, 1 Van Hool, 2 Volvo.
Bodies: 1 East Lancs, 1 Jonckheere, 1 Mercedes, 2 Setra, 2 Van Hool.
Ops incl: excursions & tours, private hire, continental tours.
Livery: Various.

SHORELINE SUNCRUISERS

6 STEPNEY RISE, SCARBOROUGH YO12 5BP
Tel: 01723 360969
E-mail: info@shorelinesuncruisers.co.uk
Web site: www.shorelinesuncruisers.co.uk
Props: J, R & T Stephenson.
Ops incl: local bus services, school contracts, private hire, open top tours.
Fleet: 16 – 7 double-deck bus, 5 open-top bus, 1 single-deck bus, 3 single-deck coach.
Liveries: Blue & Yellow; White with Blue & Yellow.

SIESTA INTERNATIONAL HOLIDAYS LTD

NEWPORT SOUTH BUSINESS PARK, LAMPORT STREET, MIDDLESBROUGH TS1 5QL
Tel: 01642 257920
Fax: 01642 219153
Recovery: 07739 679957
E-mail: sales@siestaholidays.co.uk
Web site: www.siestaholidays.co.uk
Chairman: Paul R Herbert
Dirs: C Herbert, J Herbert, J Cofton
Ops Mans: K Keelan, J Potter.
Fleet: 8 - 2 single-deck coach, 5 double-deck coach, 1 minibus.
Chassis: 1 Ford Transit, 4 Scania, 3 Van Hool.
Bodies: 4 Berkhof, 1 Ford, 3 Van Hool.
Ops incl: excursions & tours, private hire, continental tours.
Livery: Metallic Blue.

JOHN SMITH & SONS LTD

THE AIRFIELD, DALTON, THIRSK YO7 3HE
Tel/Recovery: 01845 577250
Fax: 01845 577752
E-mail: admin@johnsmithandsons.net
Web site: www.johnsmithandsons.net
Man Dir: Neville Smith
Ops Man: John Smith
Ch Eng: Ivan Smith
Co Sec: Sarah Smith.
Fleet: 22 - 1 double-deck coach, 1 single-deck bus, 13 single-deck coach, 2 midicoach, 3 minibus, 1 minicoach, 1 vintage coach.
Chassis: 1 Bedford, 4 DAF, 3 Dennis, 1 Ford, 2 Ford transit, 1 Iveco, 1 Leyland, 3 Mercedes, 3 Neoplan, 1 Setra, 2 Volvo.
Ops incl: local bus services, school contracts, excursions & tours, private hire, continental tours.
Livery: Green/Cream/Gold.
Ticket system: Wayfarer.

STAGECARRIAGE LTD

LEE ROAD, GRANGETOWN,
MIDDLESBROUGH TS6 7AR
Tel: 01642 440809
Fax: 01642 467288
E-mail: wayne@stagecarriage.co.uk
Web site: www.satgecarriage.co.uk
Props: W Brown, S Brown.
Fleet: 16 - 8 double-deck bus, 3 single-deck
bus, 2 single-deck coach, 1 midicoach,
2 minibus.
Chassis: 2 DAF, 3 Dennis, 2 Leyland,
3 Mercedes, 1 Scania, 5 Volvo.
Ops incl: local bus services, school contracts,
excursions & tours, private hire.
Livery: Red.

STEPHENSONS OF EASINGWOLD LTD

MOOR LANE INDUSTRIAL ESTATE,
THOLTHORPE, YORK YO61 1SR
Tel: 01347 838990
Fax: 01347 830189
E-mail: sales@stephensonsofeasingwold.
co.uk
Web site: www.stephensonsofeasingwold.
co.uk
Depots at: Tholthorpe, Kirkbymoorside.
Chairman: Harry J Stephenson
Man Dir/Co Sec: David A Stephenson.
Fleet: 66 - 7 double-deck bus, 14 single-deck
bus, 31 single-deck coach, 1 midibus,
5 midicoach, 7 minibus, 1 minicoach.
Chassis: 8 Alexander Dennis, 3 DAF,
3 Dennis, 1 Ford Transit, 1 Irisbus, 2 Leyland,
12 Mercedes, 8 Scania, 1 VDL, 27 Volvo.
Bodies: 6 Alexander, 6 Alexander Dennis,
1 Caetano, 1 Crest, 1 East Lancs, 1 Ford,
2 Ikarus, 1 Irizar, 1 Jonckheere, 2 Koch,
1 Marcopolo, 2 Northern Counties,
27 Plaxton, 3 Scania, 1 Transbus, 1 Unvi,
4 Van Hool, 6 Wrightbus.
Ops incl: local bus services, school contracts,
private hire.
Livery: Red/Orange/Cream/Gold.
Ticket system: Wayfarer.

STEVE STOCKDALE COACHES

(Validford Ltd t/a)

14 GREEN LANE, SELBY YO8 9AW
Tel: 01757 703549
Fax: 01757 210956
Dirs: S Stockdale, J Stockdale, Julie O'Neill
(Co Sec).
Fleet: 5 - 2 double-deck bus, 3 single-deck
coach
Chassis: 1 Leyland, 1 Scania, 3 Volvo.
Bodies: 1 East Lancs, 1 ECW, 2 Jonckheere,
1 Van Hool.
Ops incl: school contracts, private hire.
Livery: Red/White.

THORNES INDEPENDENT LTD
INDEPENDENT COACHWAYS LTD

THE COACH STATION, HULL ROAD,
HEMINGBROUGH, SELBY YO8 6QG
Tel: 01757 630777
Fax: 01757 630666
E-mail: coaches@thornes.info
Web site: www.thornes.info
Man Dir: Philip Thornes **Co Sec:** Christine
Thornes **Ops Dir:** Jane Thornes
Ch Eng: Steven Cotton.
Fleet: 26 - 2 double-deck bus, 2 single-deck
bus, 15 single-deck coach, 2 midibus,
4 midicoach, 1 minibus, 1 minicoach.
Chassis: 3 AEC, 1 Alexander Dennis,
1 Beadle, 1 Bedford, 3 Bristol, 1 DAF, 1 Dennis,
1 Ford Transit, 1 Leyland, 2 Mercedes,
1 Seddon, 1 Setra, 9 Volvo .

Ops incl: school contracts, excursions &
tours, private hire, continental tours.
Livery: Blue/Grey.
Ticket System: Wayfarer.

TRANSDEV HARROGATE & DISTRICT

PROSPECT PARK, BROUGHTON WAY,
STARBECK, HARROGATE HG2 7NY
Tel: 01423 566061
Fax: 01423 885670
E-mail: enquire@harrogateanddistrict.co.uk
Web site: www.harrogatebus.co.uk
Fleet Names: Harrogate & District, The 36.
Ch Exec: Martin Gilbert **Man Dir:** Russell
Revill **Fin Dir:** Jim Wallace
Reg Business Development Dir: John
Threlfall.
Fleet: 67 - 26 double-deck bus, 38 single-
deck bus, 1 single-deck coach, 1 midibus,
1 minibus.
Chassis: 5 Dennis, 10 Leyland, 9 Optare,
43 Volvo.
Bodies: 2 Alexander, 1 ECW, 6 Leyland,
2 Northern Counties, 9 Optare, 7 Plaxton,
40 Wrightbus.
Ops incl: local bus services, school contracts.
Livery: Red/Cream.
Ticket System: Wayfarer 3.

TRANSDEV YORK & EAST COAST

11-12 STONEBOW HOUSE, STONEBOW,
YORK YO1 7NP
Tel: 01904 633990
Fax: 01904 655587
E-mail: info@transdevyork.co.uk; enquire@
coastliner.co.uk
Web site: www.yorkbus.co.uk
Fleet Names: Coastliner, Transdev York,
Unibus, York City Sightseeing.
Chief Exec: Martin Gilbert **Fin Dir:** Jim
Wallace **Reg Business Development Dir:**
John Threlfall.
Fleet: 54 - 23 double-deck bus, 15 single-
deck bus, 9 open-top bus, 4 midibus, 4 minibus.
Chassis: 4 Dennis, 6 Leyland, 2 MAN,
8 Optare, 1 Transbus, 33 Volvo.
Bodies: 6 Alexander, 2 Alexander Dennis,
3 East Lancs, 8 Optare, 6 Plaxton, 1 Transbus,
28 Wrightbus.
Ops incl: local bus services, city sightseeing
tours, school contracts.
Liveries: Red, Blue/Cream (Coastliner).
Ticket System: Almex A90/Wayfarer
TGX150.

UTOPIA COACHES

UNIT 4, THE MALTINGS, FENTON LANE,
SHERBURN IN ELMET, LEEDS LS25 6EZ
Tel/Fax: 01977 680044
E-mail: utopiacoaches@clara.co.uk
Web site: www.utopiacoaches.co.uk
Ops incl: local bus services, school contracts,
excursions & tours, private hire.
Livery: White with Blue.

WINN BROS

8 MILL HILL CLOSE, BROMPTON,
NORTHALLERTON DL6 2QP
Tel: 01609 773520
Fax: 01609 775234
E-mail: garrywinn@hotmail.co.uk
Web site: www.websites.uk-plc.net/
winn_bros
Fleet: 12 – 7 single-deck coach, 2 midicoach,
3 minibus.
Chassis: 4 Bova, 1 Ford Transit, 1 LDV,
1 Mercedes, 1 Scania, 1 Toyota, 1 Van Hool,
2 Volvo.
Ops incl: school contracts, private hire.

WISTONIAN COACHES

PLANTATION GARAGE, CAWOOD ROAD,
WISTOW, SELBY YO8 0XB
Tel/Fax: 01757 269303
Prop: John Firth.
Fleet: 4 single-deck coach.
Chassis: 4 Volvo.
Bodies: 4 Plaxton.
Ops incl: school contracts, private hire.
Livery: Cream with Red/Orange/Yellow
stripes.

YORK PULLMAN BUS CO LTD

WETHERBY ROAD, RUFFORTH,
YORK YO23 3QA
Tel: 01904 622992
Fax: 01904 622993
Recovery: 07753 670742
E-mail: sales@yorkpullmanbus.co.uk
Web site: www.yorkpullmanbus.co.uk
Man Dir: Tom James **Co Sec:** Maxine James
Coaching Man: Kevin Walker
Comm Man: Richard Startup
Chief Eng: Paul Hirst
Sales Man: Chloe Fenton.
Fleet: 106 – 25 double-deck bus, 1 open-top
bus, 8 single-deck bus, 55 single-deck coach,
3 midibus, 8 midicoach, 6 minibus.
Chassis: 3 AEC, 1 Bristol, 7 DAF, 3 Dennis,
2 Ford, 2 Irisbus, 1 Iveco, 18 Leyland, 2 LDV,
16 Mercedes, 3 Scania, 2 Temsa, 1 Transbus,
2 Van Hool, 1 VDL, 42 Volvo.
Bodies: 20 Alexander, 1 Autobus, 1 Berkhof,
1 Beulas, 1 Caetano, 2 Crest, 2 Duple, 2 ECW,
4 East Lancs, 1 Hispano, 1 Indcar, 1 Irizar,
1 Jonckheere, 1 LDV, 3 Leyland, 1 Marshall,
7 Mercedes, 2 Northern Counties, 2 Onyx,
2 Park Royal, 25 Plaxton, 1 Reeve Burgess,
1 Roe, 2 Temsa, 1 UVG, 18 Van Hool, 1
Wrightbus, 1 Other.
Ops incl: school contracts, excursions &
tours, private hire, express, continental tours.
Livery: Maroon, Cream & Yellow.

CENTREBUS LTD

UNIT 5, SOUTH FOLDS ROAD, CORBY
NN18 9EU
Tel: 0844 351 1120
E-mail: info@centrebus.com
Web site: www.centrebus.info
Dirs: Peter Harvey, David Shelley, Julian
Peddle, Keith Hayward.
Fleet (Northants): 29 – 1 single-deck bus,
8 midibus, 20 minibus.
Chassis: 2 Alexander Dennis, 1 DAF,
5 Dennis, 3 Fiat, 18 Optare.
Bodies: 3 Alexander, 2 Alexander Dennis,
3 Fiat, 18 Optare, 2 Plaxton, 1 Wrightbus.
Ops incl: local bus services, school contracts.
Livery: Blue/Orange.

COUNTRY LION (NORTHAMPTON) LTD

87-89 ST JAMES MILL ROAD,
NORTHAMPTON NN5 5JP
Tel: 01604 754566   **Fax:** 01604 664062
Web site: www.countrylion.co.uk
Dirs: A J Bull, J S F Bull.
Fleet: 53 – 9 double-deck bus, 30 single-deck
coach, 12 midicoach, 2 minibus.
Chassis: 4 Alexander Dennis, 4 Dennis,
4 Irisbus, 1 Iveco, 4 Leyland, 11 Mercedes,
1 Neoplan, 2 Optare, 2 Setra, 20 Volvo.
Bodies: 3 Alexander, 3 Beulas, 1 Caetano,
1 Duple, 4 East Lancs, 1 ECW, 2 Mercedes,
1 Neoplan, 2 Optare, 32 Plaxton, 2 Setra,
1 Transbus.
Ops incl: local bus services, school contracts,
excursions & tours, continental tours, private
hire.

GOODE COACHES

47 BURFORD AVENUE, NORTHAMPTON
NN3 6AF
Tel: 01604 862700
Prop: David W L Goode.
Fleet: 4 single-deck coach.
Chassis: 1 DAF, 3 Leyland
Bodies: 1 Ikarus, 3 Van Hool
Ops incl: local bus services, school contracts,
private hire.
Livery: Cream/Maroon.

HAMILTON'S AND BUCKBY'S COACHES

3 FOX STREET, ROTHWELL, KETTERING
NN14 6AN
Tel: 01536 710344   **Fax:** 01536 712244
Recovery: 07887 945564
E-mail: hamiltoncoaches@googlemail.com
Web site: www.buckbyscoaches.co.uk
Prop: Minesh Uka.
Fleet: 33 - 15 double-deck bus,
17 single-deck coach, 1 double-deck coach.

Chassis: 10 MCW, 23 Volvo.
Ops incl: local bus services, school contracts,
excursions & tours, private hire, continental
tours.
Livery: White with Yellow, Orange & Red
stripes.

J & M B TRAVEL

15 BERWICK ROAD, STANION, KETTERING
NN14 1BT
Tel: 0500 321700
E-mail: info@jambtravel.co.uk
Web site: www.jambtravel.co.uk
Props: Jackie Burton, Michael Burton.
Fleet: 6 - 4 single-deck coach, 2 midicoach.
Chassis: 1 Bova, 3 DAF, 2 Mercedes.
Bodies: 1 Bova, 1 Caetano, 1 Ikarus,
1 Marshall, 1 Plaxton, 1 Van Hool.
Ops incl: school contracts, excursions &
tours, private hire.
Livery: Silver.

JEFFS TRAVEL LTD

1 STATION ROAD, HELMDON, BRACKLEY
NN13 5QT
Tel: 01295 768292   **Fax:** 01295 760365
E-mail: admin@jeffscoaches.com
Web site: www.jeffscoaches.com
Man Dir: Sarah Bayliss **Ops Man:** Darren
Wootton **Traffic Man:** Richard Yates
Ch Eng: Graham Ayres.
Fleet: 26 - 3 double-deck bus, 20 single-deck
coach, 3 midicoach.
Chassis: 1 Dennis, 2 Iveco, 3 King Long,
3 Leyland, 17 Volvo.
Bodies: 1 Beulas, 12 Caetano, 3 ECW,
1 Indcar, 6 Jonckheere, 3 King Long, 1 Plaxton.
Ops incl: school contracts, excursions &
tours.
Livery: White /Red/Green/Silver.

R S LAWMAN COACHES LTD

7 ROBINSON WAY, KETTERING NN16 8PT
Tel: 01536 517664   **Fax:** 01536 513474
E-mail: sales@lawmanscoaches.co.uk
Web site: www.lawmanscoaches.co.uk
Fleet: 15 – 11 single-deck coach, 1 midicoach,
3 minibus.
Chassis: 1 Bova, 3 LDV, 2 Mercedes, 1 Scania,
8 Volvo.
Ops incl: school contracts, excursions &
tours.
Livery: White with Green/Orange.

MERIDIAN BUS

23 MILLBROOK CLOSE, ST JAMES,
NORTHAMPTON NN5 5JF
Tel: 0844 500 0131
E-mail: info@meridianbus.co.uk
Web site: www.meridianbus.co.uk

Fleet: 10 – 3 single-deck bus, 6 midibus,
1 minibus.
Chassis: 6 Dennis, 1 Mercedes, 3 Optare.
Ops incl: local bus services.
Livery: Red/Blue/White.

R B TRAVEL

ISHAM ROAD, PYTCHLEY NN14 1EW
Tel: 01536 791066   **Fax:** 01536 791490
E-mail: enquiries@rbtravel.co.uk
Web site: www.rbtravel.co.uk
Prop: Roger Bull.
Fleet: 12 single-deck coach.
Chassis: 1 Bova, 3 DAF, 1 Leyland, 1 MAN,
4 Scania, 1 Van Hool, 1 VDL.
Bodies: 1 Beulas, 1 Berkhof, 1 Bova, 1 Lahden,
1 Plaxton, 7 Van Hool.
Ops incl: school contracts, excursions &
tours, private hire, continental tours.

RODGER'S COACHES LTD

102 KETTERING ROAD, WELDON
NN17 3JG
Tel: 01536 200500   **Fax:** 01536 407407
Recovery: 01536 200500
E-mail: enquiries@rodgerscoaches.co.uk
Web site: www.rodgerscoaches.co.uk
Props: James Rodger, Linda Rodger.
Fleet: 27 - 15 double-deck bus, 10 single-deck
coach, 1 midicoach, 1 minibus.
Chassis: 1 Bova, 2 Dennis, 1 LDV, 6 Leyland,
1 Mercedes, 16 Volvo.
Ops incl: school contracts, private hire,
excursions & tours.
Livery: White/Red.

SOUL BROTHERS

See Buckinghamshire

STAGECOACH MIDLANDS

UNIT 7/8, MAIN ROAD, FAR COTTON,
NORTHAMPTON NN4 8ES
Tel: 01604 676060
Fax: 01604 662286
E-mail: midlands.enquiries@stagecoachbus.com
Web site: www.stagecoachbus.com
Man Dir: Steve Burd
Eng Dir: David Heptinstall.
Fleet (Northants): 191 - 68 double-deck
bus, 29 single-deck bus, 60 midibus, 34 minibus.
Chassis: 67 Alexander Dennis, 2 Dennis,
17 MAN, 34 Optare, 55 Scania, 4 Transbus,
12 Volvo.
Ops incl: local bus services, school contracts,
private hire, express.
Livery: Stagecoach UK Bus.
Ticket System: ERG.
See also operations in Warwickshire

UNO BUSES (NORTHAMPTON) LTD

A subsidiary of Universitybus *(see Hertfordshire)*

ADAMSON'S COACHES

8 PORLOCK COURT, NORTHBURN CHASE,
CRAMLINGTON NE23 3TT
Tel/Fax: 01670 734050
Recovery: 07721 633351
E-mail: adamsonscoaches@btconnect.com
Web site: www.adamsonscoaches.co.uk
Prop: Allen Mullen **Ch Eng:** Paul Mullen
Co Sec: Mrs Wendy Mullen.
Fleet: 4 single-deck coach.
Chassis: 3 DAF, 1 Van Hool.
Bodies: 4 Van Hool.
Ops incl: excursions & tours, private hire.
Livery: White.

ARRIVA NORTH EAST

ADMIRAL WAY, DOXFORD
INTERNATIONAL BUSINESS PARK,
SUNDERLAND SR3 3XP
Tel: 0191 520 4200
Fax: 0191 520 4183
Web site: www.arriva.co.uk
Regional Man Dir: Nigel Featham
Area Man Dir: Nick Knox
Regional Finance Dir: David Cocker
Eng Dir: Gavin Peace
Regional Marketing & Comms Man:
Chloe Leach O'Connell
Regional HR Partner: Julie Reynolds.

Fleet: 524 - 112 double-deck bus, 215 single-
deck bus, 4 single-deck coach, 116 midibus,
77 minibus.
Chassis: 20 Alexander Dennis, 80 DAF,
80 Dennis, 11 MAN, 77 Optare, 22 Scania,
18 Temsa, 126 VDL, 63 Volvo, 27 Wrightbus.
Bodies: 70 Alexander, 20 Alexander Dennis,
11 Caetano, 13 East Lancs, 79 Optare,
67 Plaxton, 22 Scania, 18 Temsa, 11 Transbus,
221 Wrightbus.
Ops incl: local bus services, school contracts,
private hire.
Livery: Arriva UK Bus.
Ticket System: Wayfarer 3.

Northamptonshire

BELL'S COACHES

BURNSIDE GARAGE, STAMFORDHAM
NE18 0PN
Tel: 01661 886207
Fax: 01661 886807
E-mail: enquiries@bellscoaches.com
Web site: www.bellscoaches.com
Man Dir: M Bell.
Fleet: 9 – 7 single-deck coach, 1 midicoach,
minibus.
Chassis: 1 Ford Transit, 1 MAN, 1 Temsa,
6 Volvo.
Ops incl: school contracts, private hire.
Livery: White with Black.

HENRY COOPER COACHES
See Tyne & Wear

JAMES COOPER & SON
See Tyne & Wear

COOPER'S TOURMASTER LTD

RIVERSIDE, KITTYBREWSTER BRIDGE,
BEDLINGTON NE22 7BS
Tel: 01670 824900
Fax: 01670 824800
E-mail: john@cooperstourmaster.co.uk
Web site: www.cooperstourmaster.co.uk
Dirs: D M & J Cooper.
Fleet: 21 - 1 single-deck bus, 17 single-deck
coach, 1 midibus, 2 minibus.
Chassis: 2 Dennis, 1 Ford Transit, 1 Mercedes,
12 Scania, 5 Volvo.
Ops incl: school contracts, private hire,
excursions & tours.
Livery: Blue & Orange.

CRAIGGS TRAVEL EUROPEAN

1 CENTRAL AVENUE, AMBLE, MORPETH
NE65 0NQ
Tel/Fax: 01665 710614
E-mail: classicalholiday@tiscali.co.uk
Partners: Joan Craiggs, Ian Craiggs.
Man: Lawrence Craiggs.
Fleet: 2 single-deck coach.
Chassis: 1 DAF, 1 Setra.
Bodies: 1 Setra, 1 Van Hool.
Ops incl: excursions & tours, private hire,
continental tours.
Livery: Silver.

DREADNOUGHT COACHES
Owner retired since LRB 2014 went to press

GARDINERS NMC TRAVEL

18 COOPIES HAUGH, COOPIES LANE
INDUSTRIAL ESTATE, MORPETH NE61 6JN
Tel: 01388 818235, 01670 519952
Fax: 01670 512126
E-mail: info@nmctours.co.uk
Web site: www.nmctours.co.uk
Dirs: G & A Smith.
Fleet: 18 – 16 single-deck coach, 1 double-
deck coach, 1 minibus.
Chassis: 6 DAF, 3 Mercedes, 2 Scania, 2 Setra,
5 Volvo.
Ops incl: excursions & tours, private hire,
continental tours.
Livery: White with Orange/Black.

GARFIELD EXECUTIVE TRAVEL LTD

FERGUSON'S BUSINESS PARK WEST, WEST
SLEEKBURN, BEDLINGTON NE22 7DH
Tel: 0191 250 2066
Fax: 01670 811172
E-mail: info@garfieldtravel.co.uk
Web site: www.garfieldtravel.co.uk
Dir: G Irving.
Fleet: 7 – 6 single-deck coach, 1 minibus.

Chassis: 5 Van Hool, 1 Volkswagen, 1 Volvo.
Bodies: 1 Sunsundegui, 5 Van Hool, 1 Other.
Ops incl: private hire.

GLEN VALLEY TOURS LTD

STATION ROAD, WOOLER NE71 6SP
Tel: 01668 281578
Fax: 01668 281169
E-mail: enquiries@glenvalley.co.uk
Web site: www.glenvalley.co.uk
Fleet: 15 – 8 single-deck coach, 1 midibus,
1 midicoach, 3 minibus, 1 minicoach.
Chassis: 4 Mercedes, 4 Optare, 7 Volvo.
Bodies: 1 Berkhof, 3 Jonckheere, 2 Mercedes,
4 Optare, 1 Plaxton, 1 Unvi, 2 Van Hool,
1 Volvo.
Ops incl: local bus services, school contracts,
private hire, excursions & tours.
Livery: Green & White.

GO NORTH EAST

117 QUEEN STREET, GATESHEAD NE8 2UA
Tel: 0191 420 5050
Fax: 0191 420 0225
E-mail: customerservices@gonortheast.
co.uk
Web site: www.simplygo.com
Man Dir: K Carr **Fin Dir:** G C McPherson
Ops Dir: D Curry **Head of Comm:**
A Tyldsley **Ch Eng:** K Trewin.
Fleet: 681 - 192 double-deck bus, 379 single-
deck bus, 28 single-deck coach, 74 midibus,
8 articulated bus.
Chassis: 6 Alexander Dennis, 16 DAF,
34 Dennis, 79 Mercedes, 87 Optare,
137 Scania, 40 Transbus, 13 VDL, 253 Volvo,
16 Wrightbus.
Bodies: 6 Alexander Dennis, 26 Caetano,
45 East Lancs, 79 Mercedes, 16 Northern
Counties, 87 Optare, 45 Plaxton, 41 Scania,
40 Transbus, 296 Wrightbus.
Ops incl: local bus services, school contracts,
express.
Livery: Various route brands, National
Express.
Ticket System: Vix TP5700.

HILLARYS COACHES

20 CASTLE VIEW, PRUDHOE NE42 6NG
Tel/Fax: 01661 832560
Props: Lawrence Hillary.
Fleet: 5 - 3 midicoach, 2 minibus.
Chassis: 1 Ford Transit, 1 King Long,
2 Mercedes, 1 Toyota.
Ops incl: school contracts, excursions &
tours, private hire.

JEWITTS COACHES

CHOLLERFORD BUNGALOW,
CHOLLERFORD, HEXHAM NE46 4EW
Tel: 01434 681325
Fax: 01434 681517
E-mail: shaun.jewitt@jewittscoaches.co.uk
Web site: www.jewittscoaches.co.uk
Fleet: 12 – 6 single-deck coach, 4 midicoach,
2 minibus.
Chassis: 1 Dennis, 1 Ford Transit, 5 Mercedes,
3 Neoplan, 1 Van Hool, 1 VDL.
Ops incl: school contracts, excursions &
tours, private hire, continental tours.
Livery: White with Blue/Red.

LONGSTAFF'S TRAVEL LTD

UNIT 107, COQUET ENTERPRISE PARK,
AMBLE, MORPETH NE65 0PE
Tel: 01665 713300
Fax: 01665 710987
Dir: Glyn Griffiths.
Fleet: 5 – 4 single-deck coach, 1 midicoach.

Chassis: 1 Mercedes, 1 Neoplan, 3 Volvo.
Bodies: 1 Neoplan, 3 Plaxton, 1 Sitcar.
Ops incl: school contracts, excursions &
tours, private hire, continental tours.
Livery: White.

PERRYMAN'S BUSES LTD

RAMPARTS BUSINESS PARK, NORTH ROAD,
BERWICK UPON TWEED TD15 1TX
Tel: 01289 308719
Fax: 01289 309970
E-mail: enquiries@perrymansbuses.com
Web site: www.perrymansbuses.com
Depots at: Berwick, St Boswells.
Dirs: R J Perryman L M Perryman.
Fleet: 43 - 16 single deck bus, 6 single-deck
coach, 13 midibus, 5 midicoach, 2 minibus,
1 minicoach.
Chassis: 1 Ford Transit, 1 Iveco, 8 Mercedes,
1 Neoplan, 25 Optare, 7 Volvo.
Bodies: 3 MCV, 1 Onyx, 25 Optare,
10 Plaxton, 1 Wrightbus, 3 Other.
Ops incl: local bus services, school contracts,
private hire.
Livery: White with Red/Blue.
Ticket System: Wayfarer TGX.

PHOENIX TAXIS & COACHES

NORTHUMBERLAND TAXI & COACH
CENTRE, SOUTH ALBION RETAIL PARK,
BLYTH NE21 5BW
Tel: 01670 540222
E-mail: contact@phoenixtaxis.net
Web site: www.phoenixtaxis.net
Fleet: 17 – 1 single-deck coach, 5 midibus,
3 midicoach, 8 minibus.
Chassis: 1 Alexander Dennis, 1 Citroen,
2 Ford Transit, 3 Iveco, 1 LDV, 5 Mercedes,
3 Optare, 1 Volvo.
Ops incl: local bus services, private hire.
Livery: White.

PREMIER BUS & COACH LTD

RSL BUILDING, BLYTH RIVERSIDE
BUSINESS PARK, BLYTH NE24 4RN
Tel: 01670 540770
E-mail: premierbus@yahoo.co.uk
Web site: www.premierbus.yolasite.com
Dirs: J Brown, P Donaldson, S Elliott.
Fleet: 10 – 9 single-deck coach, 1 midibus.
Chassis: 4 Autosan, 1 Leyland, 1 Optare,
2 Scania, 2 Volvo.
Ops incl: local bus services, school contracts,
private hire.
Livery: White.

ROTHBURY MOTORS LTD

HAWTHORN CLOSE, LIONHEART
ENTERPRISE PARK, ALNWICK NE66 2HT
Tel: 01665 606616
Fax: 01665 606611
E-mail: info@rothburymotors.co.uk
Web site: www.rothburymotors.co.uk
Dirs: J Gutherson, M Manzoor.
Fleet: 21 – 1 single-deck bus, 8 single-deck
coach, 1 midibus, 1 midicoach, 8 minibus,
2 minicoach.
Chassis: 1 BMC, 4 Bova, 4 DAF, 2 Ford Transit,
1 LDV, 9 Mercedes.
Ops incl: local bus services, school contracts,
private hire, excursions & tours.
Livery: White with Blue Lettering.

ROWELL COACHES

CROSSBANK GARAGE, ACOMB, HEXHAM
NE46 4NY
Tel: 01661 832316
E-mail: sales@rowellcoaches.co.uk
Web site: www.rowellcoaches.co.uk

Northumberland

Dir: I D Plumley.
Fleet: 3 single-deck coach.
Chassis: 2 Bova, I Leyland.
Ops incl: school contracts, excursions & tours, private hire.
Livery: White

HOWARD SNAITH COACHES
THE COACH HOUSE, BRIERLEY GARDENS, OTTERBURN NE19 1HB
Tel: 01830 520609   **Fax:** 01830 520462
E-mail: howardsnaith@btconnect.com
Web site: www.howardsnaith.co.uk
Fleet: 85 – 54 single-deck coach, 4 midibus, 11 midicoach, 14 minibus, 2 minicoach.
Chassis: 2 Alexander Dennis, I DAF, 8 Ford Transit, 5 LDV, 16 Mercedes, 53 Volvo.
Bodies: 2 Alexander Dennis, 7 Ford, 5 LDV, 2 Optare, 64 Plaxton, 2 Reeve Burgess, 2 Transbus, I Other.
Ops incl: local bus services, school contracts, private hire, excursions & tours, continental tours.
Livery: White with Blue/Pink.

STAGECOACH NORTH EAST
See Tyne & Wear

TRAVELSURE COACHES LTD
STATION ROAD, BELFORD NE70 7DT
Tel: 01665 720955
E-mail: travelsure@travelsure.co.uk
Web site: www.travelsure.co.uk
Dirs: Barrie Patterson, Karen Patterson.
Fleet: 26 - I single-deck bus, 11 single-deck coach, 9 midibus, 3 midicoach, I minibus, I minicoach.
Chassis: I Alexander Dennis, I BMC, 3 Dennis, 2 Enterprise, 4 Irisbus, 2 Iveco, I LDV, 5 Mercedes, I Optare, I Scania, 4 Setra, I Transbus.
Bodies: I Alexander Dennis, 6 Beulas, I BMC, I Caetano, I Irizar, I Mellor, 2 Optare, 6 Plaxton, 4 Setra, I Sitcar, 2 Other.
Ops incl: local bus services, school contracts, excursions & tours, private hire, continental tours.
Livery: Blue.
Ticket System: Wayfarer.

TYNEDALE GROUP TRAVEL
TOWNFOOT GARAGE, HALTWHISTLE NE49 0EJ
Tel: 01434 322944   **Fax:** 01434 322955
E-mail: admin@tynedalegrouptravel.co.uk
Web site: www.tynedalegrouptravel.co.uk
Partner: Andy Sinclair.
Fleet: 8 - 4 single-deck coach, 3 minibus, I minicoach.
Chassis: I Mercedes, 4 Neoplan, 3 Volkswagen.
Bodies: 4 Neoplan, 3 Volkswagen, I Other.
Ops incl: school contracts, excursions & tours, private hire, continental tours.
Livery: Grey.

TYNE VALLEY COACHES LTD
ACOMB, HEXHAM NE46 4QT
Tel: 01434 602217   **Fax:** 01434 604150
E-mail: alistair@tynevalleycoaches.co.uk
Web site: www.tynevalleycoaches.co.uk
Man Dir: Alistair Weir.
Fleet: 22 - 2 single-deck bus, 17 single-deck coach, 2 midibus, I minibus.
Chassis: I Bova, 2 DAF, I Iveco, 7 Leyland, I Optare, 11 Volvo.
Ops incl: local bus services, school contracts, private hire.
Livery: Blue/Silver.
Ticket System: AES.

AOT COACHES NOTTINGHAM LLP
THE AERODROME, WATNALL ROAD, HUCKNALL NG15 6EN
Tel: 08450 170 747
E-mail: office@aotcoaches.com
Web site: www.aotcoaches.com
Dirs: M N Rogers, N Rogers.
Fleet: 18 – 6 double-deck bus, I single-deck bus, 5 single-deck coach, 6 midibus.
Chassis: 6 Dennis, I MCW, 2 Optare, 5 Scania, 4 Volvo.
Ops incl: local bus services, school contracts, private hire.
Livery: Blue & White.

TREVOR BAILEY TRAVEL LTD
Ceased trading since LRB 2014 went to press

BUTLER BROTHERS COACHES
60 VERNON ROAD, KIRKBY IN ASHFIELD NG17 8ED
Tel: 01623 753260
Fax: 01623 754581
E-mail: butlerscoaches@btconnect.com
Web site: www.butlerscoaches.co.uk
Dirs: Robert Butler, Anita Butler, James Butler.
Fleet: 11 - 2 double-deck bus, 7 single-deck coach, 2 midicoach.
Chassis: I DAF, I Dennis, I EOS, 2 MAN, I Mercedes, I Scania, 4 Volvo.
Bodies: I Berkhof, 2 Caetano, I EOS, I Ikarus, I Jonckheere, 2 Northern Counties, I Onyx, I Plaxton, I Van Hool.
Ops incl: school contracts, excursions & tours, private hire, continental tours.
Livery: Dual Blue.

DUNN MOTOR TRACTION (YOUR BUS)
See Derbyshire

GILL'S TRAVEL
Ceased trading since LRB 2014 went to press

HAMMONDS COACHES LTD
14 BOURNE DRIVE, LANGLEY MILL NG16 4BJ
Tel: 0845 838 1518
E-mail: info@hammondscoaches.com
Web site: www.hammondscoaches.com
Prop: N Hammond.
Fleet: 3 single-deck coaches.
Chassis: I Neoplan, 2 Setra.
Ops incl: private hire, excursions & tours.
Livery: Blue & White.

HENSHAWS COACHES LTD
57 PYE HILL ROAD, JACKSDALE NG16 5LR
Tel: 01773 607909
Prop: Paul Henshaw
E-mail: paul@henshawscoaches.co.uk
Web site: www.henshawscoaches.co.uk
Fleet: 3 single-deck coach.
Chassis: 2 Bova, I Mercedes.
Bodies: 2 Bova, I Mercedes.
Ops incl: excursions & tours, private hire, school contracts, continental tours.
Livery: White/Orange.

JB TOURS (WATNALL) LTD
EEL HOLE FARM, LONG LANE, WATNALL NG16 1HY
Tel: 0115 822 5698
E-mail: jbtours@btconnect.com
Web site: www.jbtourswatnallnottingham.co.uk
Fleet: 6 – I double-deck bus, I single-deck bus, 3 single-deck coach, I midicoach.

Chassis: 2 Dennis, I Duple 425, I Mercedes, I Scania, I Volvo.
Ops incl: schools contracts, excursions & tours, private hire.
Livery: White with Grey/Purple.

JOHNSON BROS TOURS LTD
PORTLAND HOUSE, DUKERIES INDUSTRIAL ESTATE, CLAYLANDS AVENUE, WORKSOP S81 7BQ
Tel/Recovery: 01909 720337
Fax: 01909 481054
E-mail: lee@johnsonstours.co.uk
Web site: www.johnsonstours.co.uk
Dirs: C A Johnson, S Johnson, A Johnson, L Johnson, C Johnson.
Fleet: 103 - 59 double-deck bus, I single-deck bus, 35 single-deck coach, 4 midicoach, I minibus, 3 minicoach.
Chassis: I Autosan, 2 Bova, 9 Bristol, 2 DAF, I Ford Transit, 8 Irisbus, 4 Leyland, 5 Mercedes, 6 Neoplan, I Optare, 12 Scania, 2 Van Hool, 9 Volvo.
Bodies: 3 Alexander, I Autosan, 3 Beulas, 2 Bova, 3 Caetano, 30 ECW, I Excel, I Ford, 6 Irizar, 2 Jonckheere, 3 Leyland, 6 Neoplan, 23 Northern Counties, 2 Optare, 8 Plaxton, I Sunsundegui, 3 Transbus, 4 Van Hool.
Ops incl: local bus services, school contracts, excursions & tours, private hire, express, continental tours.
Livery: Blue Fade with Stars.
Ticket System: ITSO.
See also Redfern Travel Ltd.

K & S COACHES
21 CLIFTON GROVE, MANSFIELD NG18 4HY
Tel/Fax: 01623 656768
Web site: www.kandscoaches.com
Prop: K & Sue Burnside.
Fleet: 2 - I midicoach, I minicoach.
Chassis: Ford Transit, Mercedes.
Ops incl: school contracts, excursions & tours, private hire.
Livery: White/Red/Grey.

KETTLEWELL (RETFORD) LTD
GROVE STREET, RETFORD DN22 6LA
Tel: 01777 860360
Fax: 01777 710351
E-mail: info@kettlewellscoaches.co.uk
Web site: www.kettlewellscoaches.co.uk
Man Dir: Paul Kettlewell **Chairman:** Aubrey Kettlewell **Tours Dir:** Christine Kettlewell
PA to Man Dir: Margaret Burton
PA to Tours Dir: Jane Bushby
Ops Man: Tony Bradley.
Fleet: 13 - I double-deck coach, 10 single-deck coach, 2 minicoach.
Chassis: I LDV, I Leyland, I MAN, I Mercedes, 9 Scania.
Bodies: I Ajoki, I East Lancs, 7 Irizar, I Jonckheere, I LDV, I Mercedes, I Neoplan.
Ops incl: local bus services, school contracts, excursions & tours, private hire, continental tours.
Livery: White with Yellow.
Ticket System: Wayfarer.

LOWES COACHES
THE AERODROME, WATNALL ROAD, HUCKNALL NG15 6EN
Tel: 0115 955 0104
E-mail: lowes.coaches1@gmail.com
Web site: www.lowescoaches.co.uk
Prop: A Lowe.
Fleet: 15 – 2 double-deck bus, 11 single-deck

Northumberland

coach, 1 midibus, 1 midicoach.
Chassis: 1 Mercedes, 1 Optare, 3 Scania, 10 Volvo.
Ops incl: local bus services, school contracts, excursions & tours, private hire.
Liveries: White with Red, Blue with Red.

McEWENS COACHES
♿👥🚦R R24 T

MILLENNIUM BUSINESS PARK, CHESTERFIELD ROAD, MANSFIELD NG19 7JX
Tel: 01623 646733
Fax: 01623 621366
E-mail: info@mcewenscoaches.com
Web site: www.mcewenscoaches.com
Chairman: Nigel Skill **Ops Dir:** Peter Hallam **Fin Dir:** Simon Skill
Gen Man: John McEwen
Ops Man: Andy Poyser.
Fleet: 14 – 5 double-deck bus, 1 double-deck coach, 5 single-deck coach, 3 minibus, 1 minicoach.
Chassis: 1 Irisbus, 3 Leyland, 1 Neoplan, 2 Optare, 1 Toyota, 1 Transbus, 6 Volvo.
Bodies: 3 Alexander, 4 Caetano, 1 East Lancs, 1 Neoplan, 2 Optare, 1 Plaxton, 1 Transbus, 1 Van Hool, 1 Other.
Ops incl: school contracts, excursions & tours, private hire, continental tours.
Livery: White with Grey relief.
A subsidiary of Skills Motor Coaches Ltd

MARSHALLS OF SUTTON-ON-TRENT LTD
♿♿👥🚦⚙T

11 MAIN STREET, SUTTON-ON-TRENT NG23 6PF
Tel: 01636 821138
Fax: 01636 822227
E-mail: office@marshallscoaches.co.uk
Web site: www.marshallscoaches.co.uk
Man Dir: John Marshall **Eng Dir:** Paul Marshall **Financial Dir:** Sally Sloan
Ops Dir: Kenneth Tagg.
Fleet: 30 - 10 double-deck bus, 4 single-deck bus, 6 single-deck coach, 7 midibus, 3 midicoach.
Chassis: 1 Bova, 6 Dennis/Alexander Dennis, 1 Irisbus, 1 Leyland, 2 Mercedes, 8 Optare, 1 VDL, 10 Volvo.
Bodies: 5 Alexander, 2 Alexander Dennis, 1 Bova, 4 East Lancs, 1 Indcar, 2 Mercedes, 8 Optare, 4 Plaxton, 1 Transbus, 1 VDL, 1 Wrightbus.
Ops incl: local bus services, school contracts, excursions & tours, private hire, continental tours.
Livery: Blue/Cream.
Ticket System: Wayfarer TGX.

C W MOXON LTD
♿♿⚙

16 MALTBY ROAD, OLDCOTES, WORKSOP S81 8JN
Tel: 01909 730345
Fax: 01909 733670
E-mail: enquiries@moxons-tours.co.uk
Web site: www.moxons-tours.co.uk
Fleet Name: Moxons Coaches.
Dirs: Mrs L Marlow, Mrs M Moxon
Co Sec: Mrs J Holder
Ch Eng: M Marlow.
Fleet: 20 - 11 double-deck bus, 1 double-deck coach, 7 single-deck coach, 1 midicoach.
Chassis: 3 Bova, 8 Leyland, 1 Mercedes, 1 Neoplan, 1 Van Hool, 6 Volvo.
Bodies: 8 Alexander, 3 Bova, 1 ECW, 1 Jonckheere, 1 Northern Counties, 1 Neoplan, 1 Optare, 1 Plaxton, 1 Sitcar, 2 Van Hool.
Ops incl: excursions & tours, private hire, continental tours, school contracts.
Livery: Cream/Red.

NOTTINGHAM CITY TRANSPORT LTD
♿

LOWER PARLIAMENT STREET, NOTTINGHAM NG1 1GG
Tel: 0115 950 5745
Fax: 0115 950 4425
E-mail: travelcentre@nctx.co.uk, info@nctx.co.uk
Web site: www.nctx.co.uk
Chairman: Brian Parbutt **Man Dir:** Mark Fowles **Eng Dir:** Gary Mason
Fin Dir/Co Sec: Rob Hicklin **Marketing & Communications Dir:** Nicola Tidy
HR Dir: Mick Leafe **Comm Man:** Barrie Burch **Fleet Eng:** Farrell Smith
Fleet: 374 - 223 double-deck bus, 56 single-deck bus, 6 articulated bus, 89 midibus.
Chassis: 33 Alexander Dennis, 10 Dennis, 56 Optare, 275 Scania.
Bodies: 73 Alexander Dennis, 115 East Lancs, 125 Optare, 6 Plaxton, 50 Scania, 5 Wrightbus.
Ops incl: local bus services.
Livery: Multi-Branded.
Ticket system: Almex.

NOTTINGHAM EXPRESS TRANSIT
See Section 5 – Tram & Bus Rapid Transit Systems

REDFERN TRAVEL LTD
♿♿👥🍴🚌⚙R R24 🔧T

THE SIDINGS, DEBDALE LANE, MANSFIELD WOODHOUSE, MANSFIELD NG19 7FE
Tel/Recovery: 01623 627653
Fax: 01909 625787
E-mail: lee@johnsonstours.co.uk
Web site: www.johnsonstours.co.uk
Dirs: C A Johnson, S Johnson, A Johnson, L Johnson, C Johnson.
Fleet: 103 - 59 double-deck bus, 1 single-deck bus, 35 single-deck coach, 4 midicoach, 1 minibus, 3 minicoach.
Chassis: 1 Autosan, 2 Bova, 9 Bristol, 2 DAF, 1 Ford Transit, 8 Irisbus, 4 Irizar, 40 Leyland, 5 Mercedes, 6 Neoplan, 1 Optare, 12 Scania, 2 Van Hool, 9 Volvo.
Bodies: 3 Alexander, 1 Autosan, 3 Beulas, 2 Bova, 3 Caetano, 30 ECW, 1 Excel, 1 Ford, 6 Irizar, 2 Jonckheere, 3 Leyland, 6 Neoplan, 23 Northern Counties, 2 Optare, 8 Plaxton, 1 Sunsundegui, 3 Transbus, 4 Van Hool.
Ops incl: local bus services, school contracts, excursions & tours, private hire, express, continental tours.
Livery: Green Fade/Stars.
Ticket System: ITSO.
A subsidiary of Johnson Bros Tours Ltd

SHARPE & SONS (NOTTINGHAM) LTD
♿♿👥🍴⚙🚌🔧T

UNIT 10, CANALSIDE INDUSTRIAL PARK, CROPWELL BISHOP, NOTTINGHAM NG12 3BE
Tel/Recovery: 0115 989 4466
Fax: 0115 989 4666
E-mail: enquiries@sharpesofnottingham.com
Web site: www.sharpesofnottingham.com
Fleet Name: Sharpes of Nottingham
Man Dir: Trevor Sharpe **Ops Dir:** James Sharpe **Dirs:** Russell Sharpe, Neil Sharpe
Fin Dir: Simon Sharpe.
Fleet: 37 - 11 double-deck bus, 3 single-deck coach, 16 single-deck coach, 2 double-deck coach, 2 minibus.
Chassis: 2 Ford Transit, 4 MAN, 2 MCW, 1 VDL, 4 Van Hool, 28 Volvo.
Bodies: 14 Alexander, 2 Ford, 2 MCW, 1 Plaxton, 18 Van Hool.
Ops incl: local bus services, school contracts, excursions & tours, UK and continental private hire.

Livery: Silver with Two Tone Blue relief.
Ticket System: Wayfarer.

SILVERDALE TOURS LTD
♿♿👥⚙

LITTLE TENNIS STREET SOUTH, NOTTINGHAM NG2 4EU
Tel: 0115 912 1000 **Fax:** 0115 912 1558
E-mail: info@silverdaletours.co.uk
Web site: www.silverdaletours.co.uk
Dirs: Shaun Doherty, John Doherty.
Fleet: 53 - 7 double-deck bus, 2 single-deck bus, 43 single-deck coach, 1 midicoach.
Chassis: 1 DAF, 3 Irisbus, 2 MAN, 3 Mercedes, 13 Neoplan, 7 Scania, 1 Transbus, 1 VDL, 22 Volvo.
Bodies: 3 Alexander, 5 Beulas, 16 Caetano, 4 East Lancs, 1 Irizar, 2 Jonckheere, 2 Mercedes, 13 Neoplan, 4 Plaxton, 1 Sunsundegui, 1 Transbus, 1 VDL.
Ops incl: local bus services, private hire, express, school contracts, continental tours.
Livery: Yellow/Red/Black; National Express.

SKILLS MOTOR COACHES LTD
♿👥🍴⚙🔧T

BELGRAVE ROAD, BULWELL, NOTTINGHAM NG6 8LY
Tel: 0115 977 0080
Fax: 0115 977 7439
E-mail: enquiry@skills.co.uk
Web site: www.skills.co.uk
Fleet Names: Skills, Motorvation Passenger Logistics, Nottingham City Coaches.
Chairman: Nigel Skill **Fin Dir:** Simon Skill
Ops Dir: Peter Hallam **Gen Man Holidays:** Martin Laver **Groups Man:** Michele Else
Eng Man: Sean Stevenson **Traffic Man:** Stewart Ryalls.
Fleet: 74 - 25 double-deck bus, 1 single-deck bus, 37 single-deck coach, 1 midibus, 5 midicoach, 4 minibus, 1 minicoach.
Chassis: 1 Bova, 1 Ford Transit, 4 Irisbus, 2 Iveco, 3 MAN, 6 Mercedes, 12 Neoplan, 1 Optare, 15 Scania, 1 Setra, 2 VDL, 21 Volvo.
Bodies: 13 Alexander, 4 Berkhof, 4 Beulas, 1 Bova, 1 Carlyle, 10 East Lancs, 1 Ford, 8 Lahden, 3 Noge, 12 Neoplan, 1 Onyx, 1 Optare, 7 Plaxton, 1 Setra, 1 Transbus, 2 VDL, 1 Volvo, 1 Wadham Stringer, 2 Other.
Ops incl: school contracts, excursions & tours, private hire, continental tours.
Livery: Green.
Also controls McEwens Coaches

STAGECOACH EAST MIDLANDS
♿👥🚌

PO BOX 15, DEACON ROAD, LINCOLN LN2 4JB
Tel: 0345 605 0605
Fax: 01522 538229
E-mail: eastmidlands.enquiries@stagecoachbus.com
Web site: www.stagecoachbus.com
Fleet Name: Stagecoach in Bassetlaw; Stagecoach in Mansfield; Stagecoach in Newark.
Man Dir: Michelle Hargreaves **Eng Dir:** John Taylor **Comm Dir:** Dave Skepper
ps Dir: Richard Kay.
Fleet: 540 - 209 double-deck bus, 122 single-deck bus, 16 single-deck coach, 165 midibus, 28 minibus.
Chassis: 165 Alexander Dennis, 6 DAF, 109 Dennis, 1 Leyland, 72 MAN, 36 Optare, 26 Scania, 49 Transbus, 76 Volvo.
Bodies: 110 Alexander, 234 Alexander Dennis, 50 East Lancs, 6 Jonckheere, 5 Northern Counties, 36 Optare, 37 Plaxton, 50 Transbus, 12 Wrightbus.
Ops incl: local bus services.
Livery: Stagecoach UK Bus.
Ticket System: ERG TP5000.

TIGER EUROPEAN (UK) LTD

UNIT E PRIVATE ROAD, NO.4 COLWICK
INDUSTRIAL ESTATE, NOTTINGHAM
NG2 2JT
Tel: 01159 404040
Fax: 01159 404030
E-mail: info@tiger-european.com
Web site: www.tiger-european.com
Dirs: Mr G Golar, Mrs B Golar.
Fleet: 28 - 7 double-deck bus, 1 double-deck
coach, 2 single-deck bus, 4 single-deck coach,
3 midicoach, 9 minibus, 2 minicoach.
Chassis: 5 Ford Transit, 1 Iveco, 3 Leyland,
2 LDV, 1 MCW, 6 Mercedes.
Bodies: 4 Alexander, 1 Berkhof, 2 Caetano,
1 Duple, 2 Ferqui, 5 Ford, 1 Jonckheere,
2 LDV, 1 Leyland, 1 MCW, 1 Mellor, 1
Northern Counties, 4 Plaxton, 1 Other.
Ops incl: School contracts, private hire.

TRAVEL WRIGHT LTD

BRUNEL BUSINESS PARK, JESSOP CLOSE,
NEWARK NG24 2AG
Tel: 01636 703813
Fax: 01636 674641
E-mail: info@travelwright.fsnet.co.uk
Web site: www.travelwright.co.uk.
Dirs: D C Wright, C A Wright, T D Wright
Dir/Co Sec: Mrs P J Allen **Ch Eng:** D Walker.
Fleet: 36 — 4 double-deck bus, 17 single-deck
coach, 14 midibus, 1 midicoach.
Chassis: 16 Dennis, 5 MAN, 4 Mercedes,
4 Optare, 1 Scania, 2 Setra, 4 Volvo.
Bodies: 3 Alexander, 1 Alexander Dennis,
2 Berkhof, 10 Caetano, 1 Marshall, 2 Mercedes,
1 Neoplan, 2 Noge, 1 Northern Counties,
4 Optare, 5 Plaxton, 2 Setra, 1 Transbus,
1 UVG.
Ops incl: local bus services, school contracts,
excursions & tours, private hire, continental
tours.
Livery: Cream/Red/Black.
Ticket System: Wayfarer.

UNITY COACHES

BECK GARAGE, CLAYWORTH DN22 9AG
Tel: 07777 817556
E-mail: info@unity-coaches.com
Web site: www.unity-coaches.com
Partners: F Marriott, Mrs J Marriott.
Fleet: 11 — 5 single-deck coach, 2 midibus,
1 midicoach, 1 minibus, 1 minicoach.
Chassis: 7 Mercedes, 3 Scania, 1 Setra.
Livery: White with Orange.

VALLANCES COACHES LTD

13 GLEBE STREET, ANNESLEY
WOODHOUSE NG17 9HP
Tel: 01623 752423
E-mail: vallancescoaches@btconnect.com
Web site: www.vallancescoachesltd.com
Dir: G & S Vallance.
Fleet: 7 — 4 single-deck coach, 2 midicoach,
1 minibus.
Chassis: 1 MAN, 3 Mercedes, 2 Scania,
1 Volvo.
Ops incl: school contracts, private hire,
excursions & tours.
Livery: Cream.

WALLIS COACHWAYS

100 KIRKLINGTON ROAD, BILSTHORPE
NG22 8SP
Tel: 01623 870655   **Fax:** 01623 870655
Prop: Stephen Wallis.
Fleet: 3 - 2 midicoach, 1 minibus.
Chassis: 2 Mercedes, 1 Toyota.
Ops incl: school contracts, private hire.
Livery: White.

ABINGDON COACHES

169, GREENHAM BUSINESS PARK,
THATCHAM RG19 6HN
Tel: 01235 420520
Fax: 01635 821128
E-mail: info@abingdoncoaches.co.uk
Web site: www.abingdoncoaches.co.uk
Dirs: Simon Weaver, Michelle Wadsworth.
Fleet: 5 - 3 single-deck coach, 2 midicoach.
Chassis: 3 Irisbus, 2 Mercedes.
Bodies: 5 Plaxton.
Ops incl: school contracts, private hire.
Livery: Black
A subsidiary of Weavaway Travel *(See Berkshire)*

BAKERS COACHES

COTSWOLD BUSINESS VILLAGE, LONDON
ROAD, MORETON-IN-THE-MARSH
GL56 0JD
Tel: 01608 652178
Fax: 01608 652693
E-mail: enquiries@bakerscoaches.co.uk
Web site: www.bakerscoaches.co.uk
Dir: Mike Baker **Ops Man:** Dave Goodall.
Fleet: 21 - 15 single-deck coach, 3 midibus,
3 midicoach.
Chassis: 2 Dennis, 2 Irisbus, 6 Mercedes,
1 Scania, 1 Transbus, 9 Volvo.
Ops incl: school contracts, excursions &
tours, private hire.
Livery: White with Red logo.

BLUNSDON'S COACH TRAVEL

13 HAMBLESIDE, BICESTER OX26 2GA
Tel: 01993 811320
E-mail: blunsdonsct@talktalk.net
Prop: Michael Blunsdon **Ops Man:** Stanley
Hunt.
Fleet: 6 single-deck coach.
Chassis: 1 Dennis, 1 King Long, 1 Mercedes,
1 Scania, 2 Volvo.
Bodies: 1 Irizar, 1 Jonckheere, 1 King Long,
2 Neoplan, 1 Plaxton.
Ops incl: school contracts, private hire.
Livery: Mixed Colour Schemes.

CHARLTON SERVICES

THE GARAGE, CHARLTON-ON-OTMOOR
OX5 2UQ
Tel: 01865 331249
Fax: 01865 331080
Web site: www.charltonservices.co.uk
Partners: N G J Holder, P D Holder.
Fleet: 20 - 1 double-deck bus, 3 single-deck
bus, 11 single-deck coach, 1 midibus,
3 midicoach, 1 minibus.
Chassis: 3 Leyland, 5 Mercedes, 12 Volvo.
Ops incl: local bus services, school contracts,
private hire.
Livery: Blue.

CHENEY COACHES LTD

THORPE MEAD, BANBURY OX16 4RZ
Tel: 01295 254254
Fax: 01295 271990
E-mail: travel@cheneycoaches.co.uk
Web site: www.cheneycoaches.co.uk
Chairman: Graham Peace **Man Dir:** Mark
Peace **Dir:** Andrew Peace **Fleet Eng:** Tony
Piotrowski **Ops Man:** Ian Brown **Admin
Man:** Michael Murray.
Fleet: 33 – 3 double-deck bus, 1 single-deck
bus, 23 single-deck coach, 1 midicoach,
5 minibus.
Chassis: 1 Dennis, 2 Ford Transit, 3 Leyland, 1
Leyland National, 4 Mercedes, 1 Neoplan,
8 Scania, 13 Volvo.

Bodies: 1 Berkhof, 2 Ford, 5 Jonckheere,
1 Leyland National, 1 Neoplan, 2 Plaxton,
1 Sitcar, 4 Transbus, 10 Van Hool, 3 Other.
Ops incl: school contracts, private hire.
Livery: White/Blue/Red vinyls.

GO RIDE CIC

12 ELWES CLOSE, ABINGDON OX14 3UY
Tel: 0330 330 8489
E-mail: hello@goridebus.co.uk
Web site: www.goridebus.co.uk
Dirs: D Harrison, D Douglas.
Fleet: 15 minibus.
Ops incl: local bus services.
Also operates in Berkshire, Cambridgeshire
and Essex.

GRAYLINE COACHES

STATION APPROACH, BICESTER OX26 6HU
Tel: 01869 246461
Fax: 01869 240087
Recovery: 07980 796028
E-mail: sales@grayline.co.uk
Web site: www.grayline.co.uk
Dir/Co Sec: Alan Gray **Dir:** Brian Gray
Ops Man: Paul Gray
Traffic Man: Stuart Gray.
Fleet: 20 –1 double-deck coach, 3 single-
deck bus, 13 single-deck coach, 1 midicoach,
2 minibus.
Chassis: 4 Irisbus, 3 Iveco, 3 MAN, 2
Mercedes, 2 Optare, 4 Volvo, 3 Wrightbus.
Bodies: 6 Beulas, 1 Caetano, 2 Jonckheere,
1 Mercedes, 2 Optare, 6 Plaxton, 3 Wright.
Ops incl: local bus services, school contracts,
excursions & tours, private hire, continental
tours.
Livery: White/Red/Blue.
Ticket System: Wayfarer 3.

HEYFORDIAN TRAVEL LTD

MURDOCK ROAD, BICESTER OX26 4PP
Tel: 01869 241500   **Fax:** 01869 360011
E-mail: info@heyfordian.co.uk
Web site: www.heyfordian.travel
Depots at: Bicester, Aylesbury, High
Wycombe.
Dir: Graham Smith.
Fleet: 98 – 14 double-deck bus, 1 single-deck
bus, 56 single-deck coach, 4 double-deck
coach, 19 midibus, 3 midicoach, 1 minicoach.
Chassis: 1 Alexander Dennis, 2 Ayats, 2 DAF,
5 Dennis, 1 Enterprise, 9 Leyland, 1 MAN,
4 Mercedes, 1 Neoplan, 12 Optare, 9 Scania,
2 Toyota, 49 Volvo.
Bodies: 5 Alexander, 1 Alexander Dennis,
2 Ayats, 1 Berkhof, 3 Caetano, 5 ECW, 2 East
Lancs, 2 Irizar, 35 Jonckheere, 1 Mercedes,
1 Neoplan, 1 Northern Counties, 14 Optare,
10 Plaxton, 3 Sunsundegui, 10 Van Hool,
1 Volvo, 1 Other.
Ops incl: local bus services, school contracts,
excursions & tours, private hire, continental
tours.
Livery: White/Red/Orange/Black.
Ticket System: Wayfarer.

HORSEMAN COACHES LTD

2 ACRE ROAD, READING RG2 0SU
Tel: 0118 975 3811
Fax: 0118 975 3515
Recovery: 0118 975 3811
E-mail: privatehire@horsemancoaches.co.uk
Web site: www.horsemancoaches.co.uk
Man Dir: Keith Horseman **Ops Dir:** James
Horseman **Eng Man:** Derrick Holton.
Fleet: 51 – 36 single-deck coach, 5 midicoach,
10 minicoach.

Chassis: 5 Mercedes, 10 Toyota, 36 Volvo.
Bodies: 5 Berkhof, 10 Caetano, 36 Plaxton.
Ops incl: local bus services, school contracts, excursions & tours, private hire, continental tours, park & ride, commuter express.
Livery: multi-coloured.

OXFORD BUS COMPANY

COWLEY HOUSE, WATLINGTON ROAD, OXFORD OX4 6GA
Tel: 01865 785400
E-mail: info@oxfordbus.co.uk
Web site: www.oxfordbus.co.uk
Fleet Names: City, Park & Ride, The Airline, X90, Brookes Bus.
Man Dir: Phil Southall **Eng Dir:** Ray Woodhouse **Fin & Comm Dir:** Luke Marion.
Fleet: 154 – 82 double-deck bus, 35 single-deck bus, 37 single-deck coach.
Chassis: 36 Alexander Dennis, 1 Dennis, 35 Mercedes, 44 Scania, 38 Volvo.
Bodies: 62 Alexander Dennis, 1 Alexander, 35 Mercedes, 37 Plaxton, 19 Wrightbus.
Ops incl: local bus services, express.
Liveries: Red (City) Green (Park & Ride) Blue (The Airline, Brookes Bus) Grey/Silver (X90).
Ticket System: ERG.
A subsidiary of the Go-Ahead Group

PEARCES PRIVATE HIRE LTD

TOWER ROAD INDUSTRIAL ESTATE, BERINSFIELD, WALLINGFORD OX10 7LN
Tel: 01865 340560
Fax: 01865 341582
E-mail: enquiries@pearcescoaches.co.uk
Web site: www.pearcescoaches.co.uk
Props: Clive Pearce, Martin Pearce.
Fleet: 13 - 9 single-deck coach, 3 midicoach, 1 minibus.
Chassis: 2 Alexander Dennis, 6 Irisbus, 1 MAN, 3 Mercedes, 1 Volkswagen.
Bodies: 1 Caetano, 11 Plaxton, 1 Volkswagen.
Ops incl: school contracts, excursions and tours, private hire.
Livery: White with Yellow/Brown.

PLASTOWS COACHES

134 LONDON ROAD, WHEATLEY OX33 1JH
Tel: 01865 872270
Fax: 01865 875066
E-mail: plastowscoaches@btconnect.com
Web site: www.plastows.co.uk
Fleet: 9 single-deck coach.
Chassis: 9 Volvo.
Bodies: 9 Jonckheere.
Ops incl: private hire, school contracts.
Livery: White with Yellow/Orange.

STAGECOACH IN OXFORDSHIRE

HORSPATH ROAD, COWLEY, OXFORD OX4 2RY
Tel: 01865 772250
Fax: 01865 405500
E-mail: oxford.enquiries@stagecoachbus.com
Web site: www.stagecoachbus.com/oxfordshire
Man Dir: Martin Sutton **Service Delivery Dir:** Paul O'Callaghan **Ops Man:** Carole Stevens **Comm Man:** Ross Hitchcock **Business Development Man:** Karen Coventry.
Fleet: 174 – 76 double-deck bus, 11 single-deck bus, 26 double-deck coach, 41 midibus, 20 minibus.
Chassis: 72 Alexander Dennis, 11 MAN, 20 Optare, 45 Scania, 26 Van Hool.

Bodies: 128 Alexander Dennis, 20 Optare, 26 Van Hool.
Ops incl: local bus services, express, school contracts.
Livery: Stagecoach UK Bus, Oxford Tube.
Ticket system: Vix.

TAPPINS COACHES

COLLETT ROAD, SOUTHMEAD PARK, DIDCOT OX11 7ET
Tel: 01865 772778
Fax: 0844 247 6768
E-mail: coaches@tappins.co.uk
Web site: www.tappins.co.uk
Fleet Names: Tappins, South Midland, Southern Railroad Company.
Dirs: Simon Weaver, Michelle Wadsworth **Gen Man:** D Walker.
Fleet: 29 – 3 single-deck bus, 16 single-deck coach, 7 midibus, 3 midicoach.
Chassis: 10 Alexander Dennis, 2 Bova, 3 Mercedes, 2 Neoplan, 12 Volvo.
Bodies: 10 Alexander Dennis, 2 Bova, 1 Jonckheere, 2 Neoplan, 4 Plaxton, 10 Van Hool.
Ops incl: local bus services, school contracts, excursions & tours, private hire, express.
Livery: Orange/Black
Ticket System: Wayfarer.
A subsidiary of Weavaway Travel *(see Berkshire)*

TOM TAPPIN LTD

No 1 SHOP, OXFORD RAILWAY STATION, PARK END STREET, OXFORD OX1 1HS
Tel: 01865 790522
Fax: 01865 202154
E-mail: info@citysightseeingoxford.com
Web site: www.citysightseeingoxford.com
Fleet Names: Guide Friday, City Sightseeing Oxford.
Chairman: Bill Allen **Gen Man:** Jane Marshall **Ops Man & Transport Man:** Darren Birch **Consultant:** Thomas Knowles.
Fleet: 11 open top bus.
Chassis: 8 Dennis, 3 Volvo.
Bodies: 4 Alexander, 6 East Lancs, 1 Transbus.
Ops incl: open top city sightseeing tours, private hire.
Livery: 7 City Sightseeing Red with pictorial vinyls; 4 Guide Friday Green with pictorial vinyls.
Ticket System: Casio.

TEX COACHES

UNIT 5, POWER PARK, STATION APPROACH, BANBURY OX16 5AB
Tel: 01295 251579
Fax: 01295 673800
E-mail: sales@texcoaches.co.uk
Web site: www.texcoaches.co.uk
Dirs: Graham Harris, Alicia Harris, Danielle Harris, Gemma Harris, Kyle Harris, Geoff Coles.
Fleet: 21 – 2 double-deck bus, 1 single-deck bus, 10 single-deck coach, 1 midibus, 1 midicoach, 6 minibus.
Chassis: 1 Bluebird, 4 Dennis, 2 Ford Transit, 2 Iveco, 2 Leyland, 2 MAN, 2 Mercedes, 1 Volkswagen, 5 Volvo.
Ops incl: local bus services, school contracts, private hire.
Livery: White & Burgundy.
Ticket System: Almex.

THAMES TRAVEL

WYNDHAM HOUSE, LESTER WAY, WALLINGFORD OX10 9TD
Tel: 01491 837988
Fax: 01491 838562
E-mail: office@thames-travel.co.uk

Web site: www.thames-travel.co.uk
Man Dir: Phil Southall **Eng Dir:** Ray Woodhouse **Fin & Comm Dir:** Luke Marion **Gen Man:** Stephan Soanes.
Fleet: 45 - 7 double-deck bus, 22 single-deck bus, 16 midibus.
Chassis: 8 Alexander Dennis, 2 Dennis, 1 MAN, 13 Mercedes, 16 Optare, 5 Scania.
Bodies: 2 Alexander, 4 Alexander Dennis, 3 MCV, 13 Mercedes, 16 Optare, 6 Plaxton, 1 Scania.
Ops incl: local bus services, school contracts.
Livery: Green/Blue.
Ticket system: ERG.
A subsidiary of the Go-Ahead Group

WHITES COACHES

90 COLWELL ROAD, BERINSFIELD, WALLINGFORD OX10 7NU
Tel: 01865 340516
E-mail: sue@whitescoaches.com
Web site: www.whitescoaches.com
Props: David Bainbridge, Nick Bland.
Fleet: 16 - 4 single-deck coach, 9 midibus, 3 midicoach.
Chassis: 4 Alexander Dennis, 3 Mercedes, 9 Optare.
Ops incl: local bus services, school contracts, excursions & tours, private hire.
Liveries: Buses – Yellow; Coaches: White with Red/Blue.

WORTHS MOTOR SERVICES LTD

ENSTONE, CHIPPING NORTON OX7 4LQ
Tel: 01608 677322
Fax: 01608 677298
E-mail: enquiries@worthscoaches.co.uk
Web site: www.worthscoaches.co.uk
Dirs: Richard Worth, Paul Worth.
Fleet: 16 – 14 single-deck coach, 1 midibus, 1 midicoach.
Chassis: 1 Dennis, 1 Mercedes, 14 Volvo.
Bodies: 1 Caetano, 1 Ferqui, 2 Jonckheere, 11 Plaxton.
Ops incl: school contracts, continental tours, private hire.
Livery: Silver/Blue.

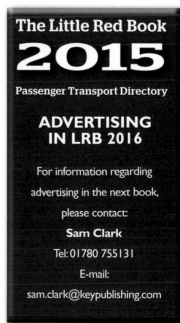
Oxfordshire

Shropshire, Telford & Wrekin

ARRIVA MIDLANDS LTD

4 WESTMORELAND AVENUE, THURMASTON, LEICESTER LE4 8PH
Tel: 0116 264 0400
Fax: 0116 260 8620
E-mail: myattk.midlands@arriva.co.uk
Web site: www.arriva.co.uk
Regional Man Dir: A Perry **Regional Fin Dir:** J Barlow **Regional Eng Dir:** M Evans
Area Director East: S Mathieson
Area Director West: R Cheveaux.
Fleet: 698 - 168 double-deck bus, 267 single-deck bus, 6 articulated bus, 204 midibus, 53 minibus.
Chassis: 24 Alexander Dennis, 173 DAF, 119 Dennis, 26 Mercedes, 121 Optare, 46 Scania, 6 Transbus, 85 VDL, 98 Volvo.
Bodies: 61 Alexander, 24 Alexander Dennis, 4 Caetano, 46 East Lancs, 1 Marshall, 26 Mercedes, 121 Optare, 110 Plaxton, 42 Scania, 6 Transbus, 257 Wrightbus.
Ops incl: local bus services, school contracts, private hire, express.
Liveries: Arriva; Midland (Red); Wardles (Red/White, Red/Cream).
Ticket System: Wayfarer 150 & 200.

BOULTONS OF SHROPSHIRE LTD

SUNNYSIDE, CARDINGTON, CHURCH STRETTON SY6 7JZ
Tel: 01694 771226
Fax: 01694 771296
Dir: Mick Boulton.
E-mail: info@boultonsofshropshire.co.uk
Web site: www.boultonsofshropshire.co.uk
Fleet: 20 - 8 single-deck bus, 7 single-deck coach, 4 midicoach, 1 minibus.
Chassis: Alexander Dennis, Autosan, BMC, Mercedes, Optare, VDL.
Bodies: Alexander Dennis, BMC, Bova, Mercedes, Optare.
Ops incl: local bus services, school contracts, private hire, continental tours.
Livery: Cream/Brown/Orange.
Ticket System: Microfare.

A T BROWN (COACHES) LTD

FREEMAIN HOUSE, HORTON ENTERPRISE PARK, HORTON WOOD 50, TELFORD TF1 7GZ
Tel: 01952 605331
Fax: 01952 608011
Recovery: 07983 562340
E-mail: enquiries@atbrowncoaches.co.uk
Web site: www.atbrowncoaches.co.uk
Dir: Ewen MacLeod.
Fleet: 26 - 23 single-deck coach, 1 midicoach, 1 minibus, 1 minicoach.
Chassis: 4 Bova, 7 DAF, 1 Dennis, 1 Irisbus, 5 Iveco, 4 MAN, 3 Mercedes, 1 Temsa.
Ops incl: school contracts, private hire.
Livery: Sky Blue/Navy.

CARADOC COACHES LTD

2 NURSERY FIELDS, RUSHBURY ROAD, RUSHBURY, CHURCH STRETTON SY6 7DY
Tel: 01694 724522
Fax: 01694 771632
E-mail: enquiries@caradoccoaches.co.uk
Web site: www.caradoccoaches.co.uk
Prop: Mr & Mrs Graham Gough.
Fleet: 12 - 6 single-deck coach, 1 midicoach, 4 minibus, 1 minicoach.
Chassis: 3 LDV, 3 Mercedes, 1 Neoplan, 1 Scania, 1 Toyota, 3 Volvo.
Ops incl: local bus services, school contracts, excursions & tours, private hire, continental tours.
Livery: White with Orange lettering.

M H ELCOCK & SON LTD

THE MADDOCKS, MADELEY, TELFORD TF7 5HA
Tel: 01952 585712
Fax: 01952 582577
E-mail: enquiries@elcockreisen.co.uk
Web site: www.elcockreisen.co.uk
Fleet Name: Elcock Reisen.
Dirs: J H Prince, P Taylor, J Elcock, N J Prince.
Fleet: 30 - 21 single-deck coach, 4 midicoach, 1 minibus, 2 minicoach.
Chassis: 7 Mercedes, 23 Volvo.
Bodies: 1 Autobus, 1 Esker, 10 Plaxton, 3 Unvi, 15 Van Hool.
Ops incl: school contracts, excursions & tours, private hire, continental tours.
Livery: Silver/Red.

HAPPY DAYS COACHES
See Staffordshire

HORROCKS BUS LTD

IVY HOUSE, BROCKTON, LYDBURY NORTH SY7 8BA
Tel: 01588 680364
Prop: A P Horrocks.
Fleet: 12 – 2 single-deck bus, 1 single-deck coach, 2 midibus, 8 minibus.
Chassis: 2 Dennis, 7 Mercedes, 2 Volvo.
Ops incl: school contracts, private hire
Livery: White/Blue.

LAKESIDE COACHES LTD

THE COACH CENTRE, ELLESMERE BUSINESS PARK, ELLESMERE SY12 0EW
Tel: 01691 622761
Fax: 01691 623694
E-mail: mailbox@lakesidecoaches.co.uk
Web site: www.lakesidecoaches.co.uk
Man Dir: John Davies **Dirs:** Dorothy Davies, Gareth Davies, Neal Hall **Ops Man:** Carole Sykes **Fleet Eng:** Simon Tomkins.
Fleet: 30 – 19 single-deck coach, 1 midibus, 5 midicoach, 1 minibus, 4 minicoach.
Chassis: 1 Dennis, 1 LDV, 10 Mercedes, 1 Optare, 1 Setra, 2 Toyota, 14 Volvo.
Bodies: 3 Caetano, 1 Excel, 1 Ferqui, 1 LDV, 6 Mercedes, 1 Optare, 11 Plaxton, 1 Setra, 1 Sitcar, 4 Sunsundegui.
Ops incl: local bus services, excursions & tours, private hire, school contracts.
Livery: Green/White.

LONGMYND TRAVEL LTD

THE COACH DEPOT, LEA CROSS, SHREWSBURY SY5 8HX
Tel: 01743 861999
Fax: 01743 861901
E-mail: info@longmyndtravel.co.uk
Web Site: www.longmyndtravel.co.uk
Dirs: T G Evans, F J Evans, V M Sheppard-Evans, D M Sheppard.
Fleet: 24 - 19 single-deck coach, 2 midicoach, 2 minibus, 1 minicoach.
Chassis: 3 Bova, 1 Iveco, 3 Mercedes, 1 Toyota, 16 Volvo.
Bodies: 3 Bova, 1 Caetano, 1 Jonckheere, 1 Mercedes, 1 Onyx, 15 Plaxton, 1 Sunsundegui, 1 Unvi.
Ops incl: school contracts, private hire.
Livery: White/Red.

M & J TRAVEL

COACH GARAGE, NEWCASTLE, CRAVEN ARMS SY7 8QL
Tel: 01588 640273
Prop: J E & J M Price.

Fleet: 9 - 5 single-deck coach, 1 midicoach, 3 minibus.
Chassis: 1 DAF, 1 LDV, 3 Mercedes, 1 Scania, 3 Volvo.
Ops incl: local bus services, school contracts, excursions & tours, private hire, continental tours.
Livery: White/Black/Gold.

M P MINICOACHES LTD

14 REDBURN CLOSE, KETLEY GRANGE, TELFORD TF2 0EE
Tel: 01952 415607 **Fax:** 01952 619188
E-mail: mpminicoaches@hotmail.co.uk
Web site: www.mpmcoaches.co.uk
Fleet Name: MPM of Telford.
Prop: M Perkins.
Fleet: 1 minicoach.
Chassis: Iveco.
Bodies: Crest.
Ops incl: school contracts, private hire.
Livery: Two-tone Blue.

MINSTERLEY MOTORS LTD

STIPERSTONES, MINSTERLEY, SHREWSBURY SY5 0LZ
Tel: 01743 791208 **Fax:** 01743 790101
E-mail: bookings@minsterleymotors.co.uk
Web site: www.minsterleymotors.com
Dirs: John B Jones, Carl Evans.
Fleet: 26 - 7 single-deck bus, 14 single-deck coach, 3 midicoach, 2 minibus.
Chassis: 4 Mercedes, 2 Optare, 3 Scania, 2 VDL, 15 Volvo.
Bodies: 2 Berkhof, 1 Jonckheere, 2 Optare, 11 Plaxton, 1 Transbus, 2 VDL, 7 Wrightbus.
Ops incl: local bus services, school contracts, excursions & tours, private hire, continental tours.
Livery: Two Tone Blue with Red & White.
Ticket system: Wayfarer.

N.C.B. MOTORS LTD

EDSTASTON GARAGE, WEM, SHREWSBURY SY4 5RF
Tel: 01939 232379 **Fax:** 01939 234892
E-mail: mail@ncb-motors.co.uk
Web site: www.ncb-motors.co.uk
Dirs: Paul R Brown, Derek N Brown.
Fleet: 13 single-deck coach.
Chassis: 13 Volvo.
Bodies: 8 Jonckheere, 5 Plaxton.
Ops incl: private hire, school contracts.
Livery: Brown/Cream.

OWENS COACHES LTD

36 BEATRICE STREET, OSWESTRY SY11 1QG
Tel: 01691 652126
Fax: 01691 670047
E-mail: info@owenstravel.co.uk
Web site: www.travelmasterholidays.com
Fleet Name: Owen's Travelmaster.
Dir: Michael Owen **Ops Man:** Peter Worthy.
Fleet: 29 - 1 single-deck bus, 17 single-deck coach, 3 midibus, 4 midicoach, 4 minibus.
Chassis: 4 BMC, 4 Dennis, 1 Ford Transit, 2 Irisbus, 1 MAN, 7 Mercedes, 1 Neoplan, 2 Optare, 1 Setra, 5 Volvo.
Bodies: 2 Beulas, 2 Berkhof, 4 BMC, 1 Ferqui, 1 Ford, 1 Marshall, 1 Mellor, 4 Mercedes, 1 Neoplan, 2 Optare, 8 Plaxton, 1 Setra, 1 Sitcar.
Ops incl: local bus services, excursions & tours, private hire, continental tours, school contracts.
Livery: White with Blue/Red stripes.
Ticket System: Wayfarer.

R & B TRAVEL

PLEASANT VIEW, KNOWLE, CLEE HILL, LUDLOW SY8 3NL
Tel/Fax: 01584 890770
E-mail: admin@randbtravel.org
Prop: A Radnor.
Fleet: 11 – 1 single-deck bus, 2 single-deck coach, 6 minibus, 2 minicoach.
Chassis: 1 DAF, 1 Dennis, 2 LDV, 1 MAN, 2 Mercedes, 3 Optare, 1 Toyota.

Ops incl: local bus services, school contracts, private hire, excursions & tours.
Livery: Grey or White.

WORTHEN MOTORS/TRAVEL

BENTHALL STONE FARM BUILDINGS, ALDERBURY ROAD, FORD, SHREWSBURY SY5 9NA
Tel: 01686 668443
E-mail: jackie@worthentravel.freeserve.co.uk

Prop: D A Pye **Sec:** J Davies.
Fleet: 10 – 8 single-deck coach, 2 midicoach.
Chassis: 4 DAF, 3 Dennis, 2 Mercedes, 1 Scania.
Bodies: 1 Caetano, 1 Duple, 1 Irizar, 4 Plaxton, 1 Reeve Burgess, 2 Van Hool.
Ops incl: school contracts, excursions & tours, private hire.
Livery: White/Blue.

SOMERSET, BATH & N E SOMERSET, N SOMERSET

ANDREWS COACHES

UNIT 3, GYPSY LANE, FROME BA11 2NA
Tel: 01373 836303
E-mail: amy@andrewscoachesfrome.co.uk
Web site: www.andrewscoachesfrome.co.uk
Props: L J Andrews, P D Andrews.
Ops incl: school contracts, private hire.

ARLEEN COACH HIRE & SERVICES LTD

14 BATH ROAD, PEASEDOWN ST JOHN, BATH BA2 8DH
Tel: 01761 434625
Fax: 01761 436578
E-mail: arleen.coach-hire@virgin.net
Web site: www.arleen.co.uk
Chairman: Alan Spiller **Co Sec:** Mrs Mary Spiller **Dir/Office Man:** Mrs Carol Spiller **Dir/Ops Man:** Justin Spiller **Dir/Ch Eng:** Kristian Spiller.
Fleet: 20 - 14 single-deck coach, 3 midicoach, 3 minibus.
Chassis: 2 DAF, 1 Dennis, 1 LDV, 1 Leyland, 5 Mercedes, 1 Neoplan, 1 Van Hool, 8 Volvo.
Ops incl: school contracts, excursions & tours, private hire.
Livery: Red/White/Blue.

AVALON COACHES LTD

PARK FARM TRADING ESTATE, PARK FARM ROAD, GLASTONBURY BA6 9NN
Tel: 01458 832293
E-mail: avaloncoaches@btconnect.com
Web site: www.avaloncoaches.co.uk
Man Dir: Geoff Rouse.
Fleet: 23 – 19 single-deck coach, 2 midicoach, 2 minibus.
Chassis: 1 Bova, 1 Ford Transit, LDV, 3 MAN, 2 Mercedes, 2 Scania, 13 Volvo.
Ops incl: school contracts, excursions & tours.
Livery: Red & Yellow.

AXE VALE COACHES LTD

BIDDISHAM, AXBRIDGE BS26 2RD
Tel: 01934 750321
Fax: 01934 751949
E-mail: enquiries@axevale.com
Web site: www.axevale.com
Partners: C P Bailey, J I Bailey, J Bailey.
Fleet: 15 – 1 double-deck bus, 13 single-deck coach, 1 midicoach.
Chassis: 1 Autosan, 6 Bova, 1 DAF, 1 Dennis, 1 Leyland, 1 Mercedes, 4 Volvo.
Bodies: 1 Alexander, 1 Autosan, 6 Bova, 1 Jonckheere, 4 Plaxton, 1 UVG, 1 Van Hool.
Ops incl: local bus services, school contracts, excursions & tours, private hire, continental tours.
Livery: White with Blue/Grey.
Ticket system: Setright.

BAKERS COACHES YEOVIL

8 BUCKLAND ROAD, PEN MILL TRADING ESTATE, YEOVIL BA21 5EA

Tel: 01935 312316
Fax: 01935 410423
Recovery: 01935 428401
E-mail: enquiries@bakerscoaches-somerset.co.uk
Web site: www.bakerscoaches-somerset.co.uk
Dir: S Baker.
Fleet: 10 - 7 single-deck coach, 1 midicoach, 2 minicoach.
Chassis: 1 Bova, 1 DAF, 2 Ford Transit, 2 Irisbus, 1 Iveco, 1 Van Hool, 2 Volvo.
Bodies: 1 Berkhof, 2 Beulas, 1 Bova, 1 Indcar, 3 Van Hool, 2 Other.
Ops incl: school contracts, excursions & tours, private hire, continental tours.
Livery: White.

BAKERS DOLPHIN COACH TRAVEL

48 LOCKING ROAD, WESTON-SUPER-MARE BS23 3DN
Tel: 01934 415000
Fax: 01934 641162
E-mail: info.coaches@bakersdolphin.com
Web site: www.bakersdolphin.com
Chairman: John Baker **Man Dir:** Max Fletcher **Ch Eng:** Mark Vearncombe **Marketing Dir:** Amanda Harrington **Fin Dir:** Steve Hunt **Ops Man:** Chris Rubery.
Fleet: 76 – 19 single-deck bus, 44 single-deck coach, 1 double-deck coach, 6 midibus, 6 minibus.
Chassis: 1 Dennis, 1 Iveco, 11 Leyland, 12 Mercedes, 6 Optare, 6 Scania, 24 Volvo, 2 Wrightbus.
Bodies: 1 Beulas, 6 Irizar, 13 Mercedes, 6 Optare, 21 Plaxton, 20 Van Hool, 1 Volkswagen, 2 Wrightbus.
Ops incl: local bus services, excursions & tours, private hire, express, continental tours, school contracts.
Livery: Blue/White/Green/Yellow.
Ticket System: Ticketer.

BATH BUS COMPANY

6 NORTH PARADE, BATH BA1 1LF
Tel: 01225 330444
Fax: 01225 330727
E-mail: hq@bathbuscompany.com
Web site: www.bathbuscompany.com
Chairman: Derek Lott **Man Dir:** Martin Curtis **Eng Man:** Collin Brougham-Field **Ops Man:** Darren Mather **Tourism Man:** Lena Cook.
Fleet: 34 - 8 double-deck bus, 1 single-deck bus, 25 open-top bus.
Chassis: 2 AEC, 3 Dennis, 1 Scania, 28 Volvo.
Ops incl: local bus services, sightseeing services, private hire.
Liveries: Green; Red.
Ticket Systems: Almex; Ticketer.
Also operates at Cardiff, Eastbourne, Windsor
A subsidiary of RATP Dev UK Ltd

BERKELEY COACH & TRAVEL

HAM LANE, PAULTON BS39 7PL
Tel: 01761 413196

Fax: 01761 416469
E-mail: mail@berkeleycoachandtravel.co.uk
Web Site: www.berkeleycoachandtravel.co.uk
Proprietor: Tim Pow.
Fleet: 16 - 15 single-deck coach, 1 minicoach.
Chassis: 1 Mercedes, 1 Van Hool, 14 Volvo.
Bodies: 1 Ferqui, 1 Jonckheere, 6 Plaxton, 7 Van Hool, 1 Volvo.
Ops incl: school contracts, private hire.
Livery: Silver with Blue lettering.

BERRY'S COACHES (TAUNTON) LTD

CORNISHWAY WEST, NEW WELLINGTON ROAD, TAUNTON TA1 5NA
New address for 2015: PETER-CLIFFORD HOUSE, GREAT WESTERN WAY, TAUNTON TA2 6BX
Tel: 01823 331356
Fax: 01823 322347
E-mail: info@berryscoaches.co.uk
Web site: www.berryscoaches.co.uk
Dir: S A Berry.
Fleet: 44 - 39 single-deck coach, 5 double-deck coach.
Chassis: 3 MAN, 2 Mercedes, 39 Volvo.
Bodies: 1 Caetano, 2 Jonckheere, 1 Mercedes, 4 Plaxton, 3 Van Hool, 5 Volvo 9700.
Ops incl: local bus services, school contracts, excursions & tours, private hire, express, continental tours.
Livery: White/Red/Orange.
Ticket system: Manual.

BLAGDON LIONESS COACHES LTD

MENDIP GARAGE, BLAGDON BS40 7TL
Tel: 01761 462250 **Fax:** 01761 463237
Recovery: 01761 462250
Dir: T M Lyons **Gen Man:** M A Lyons.
Fleet: 3 - 2 single-deck coach, 1 minibus.
Chassis: 1 Bova, 1 Leyland, 1 Mercedes.
Bodies: 1 Bova, 2 Plaxton.
Ops incl: local bus services, excursions & tours, private hire, school contracts.
Livery: White.
Ticket System: Wayfarer.

BLUE IRIS COACHES

25 CLEVEDON ROAD, NAILSEA BS48 1EH
Tel: 01275 851121 **Fax:** 01275 856522
E-mail: enquiry@blueiris.co.uk
Web site: www.blueiris.co.uk
Dirs: Tony Spiller, Avril Spiller, Gina Spiller, Ian Spiller **Transport Man:** Tony Spiller **Ops Man:** Clayton Roper.
Fleet: 11 - 6 single-deck coach, 5 midicoach.
Chassis: 6 Scania, 5 Toyota.
Bodies: 5 Caetano, 5 Irizar, 1 Van Hool.
Ops incl: school contracts, excursions & tours, continental tours.
Livery: Dark Blue/Light Blue/White.

BUGLERS COACHES LTD

TYNE DEPOT, STOWEY ROAD, CLUTTON, BRISTOL BS39 5TG
Tel: 01225 444422 **Fax:** 01225 466665

E-mail: info@buglercoaches.co.uk
Web site: www.buglercoaches.co.uk
Prop: Computer Village Group.
Fleet: 21 – 4 single-deck bus, 8 single-deck coach, 7 midibus, 2 midicoach.
Chassis: 7 Dennis, 3 Mercedes, 11 Volvo.
Ops Incl: local bus services, private hire, excursions & tours, school contracts.
Livery: Red/White/Yellow.

CARMEL BRISTOL
COATES INDUSTRIAL ESTATE,
SOUTHFIELD ROAD, NAILSEA BS48 1JN
Tel: 0117 303 5214
Prop: Carolyn Alderton
Ops incl: private hire, express.

CENTURION TRAVEL LTD
WEST ROAD GARAGE, WELTON,
MIDSOMER NORTON, RADSTOCK
BA3 2TP
Tel: 01761 417392   **Fax:** 01761 417369
E-mail: coach-hire@centuriontravel.co.uk
Web site: www.centuriontravel.co.uk
Man Dir: Martin Spiller.
Fleet: 24 - 18 single-deck coach, 4 midicoach, 2 minicoach.
Chassis: 3 Bova, 2 DAF, 4 Dennis, 1 Leyland, 7 Mercedes, 4 Scania, 1 Temsa, 2 Volvo.
Bodies: 1 Berkhof, 3 Bova, 1 Caetano, 2 Duple, 1 EVM, 1 Irizar, 2 Jonckheere, 2 Marcopolo, 1 Onyx, 2 Optare, 2 Plaxton, 1 Temsa, 1 Unvi, 1 Van Hool.
Ops incl: school contracts, private hire, continental tours.
Livery: Red/Cream/Burgundy.

COOMBS TRAVEL
COOMBS HOUSE, SEARLE CRESCENT,
WESTON-SUPER-MARE BS23 3YX
Tel: 01934 428555   **Fax:** 01934 428559
E-mail: coombscoaches@aol.com
Dirs: Brian F Coombs, Ruth A Coombs
Ops Man: Mrs June Carroll
Admin: Mrs M Lillie.
Fleet: 22 - 1 double-deck bus, 1 single-deck bus, 9 single-deck coach, 4 midicoach, 6 minibus, 1 minicoach.
Chassis: 2 Dennis, 2 LDV, 8 Mercedes, 9 Scania, 1 Toyota.
Ops incl: local bus services, school contracts, excursions & tours, private hire.
Livery: Yellow/White.
Ticket system: Wayfarer.

FIRST IN BRISTOL, BATH & THE WEST OF ENGLAND
ENTERPRISE HOUSE, EASTON ROAD,
BRISTOL BS5 0DZ
Tel: 0117 955 8211   **Fax:** 0117 955 1248
Web site: www.firstgroup.com
Man Dir: Paul Matthews (James Freeman from late 2014)
Fleet: 601 - 243 double-deck bus, 110 single-deck bus, 9 articulated bus, 214 midibus, 25 minibus.
Chassis: 80 Alexander Dennis, 116 Dennis, 1 Enterprise, 1 Ford Transit, 24 Optare, 1 Transbus, 336 Volvo, 42 Wrightbus.
Ops incl: local bus services, Bath park & ride, school contracts.
Livery: FirstGroup UK Bus.
Ticket System: Wayfarer.

FIRST DEVON, CORNWALL & CENTRAL SOMERSET
THE RIDE, CHELSON MEADOW,
PLYMOUTH PL9 7JT
Tel: 01823 211180   **Fax:** 01752 495230
E-mail:

firstdevonandcornwall@firstgroup.com
Web site: www.firstgroup.com; www.busesofsomerset.co.uk
Man Dir: Alex Carter.
Fleet Names: First, Truronian, The Buses of Somerset.
Fleet: 325 – 113 double-deck bus, 46 single-deck bus, 21 single-deck coach, 7 articulated bus, 108 midibus, 1 midicoach, 29 minibus.
Chassis: 29 Alexander Dennis, 97 Dennis, 1 Ford Transit, 12 Mercedes, 26 Optare, 15 Scania, 16 Transbus, 118 Volvo, 9 Wrightbus.
Bodies: 23 Alexander, 29 Alexander Dennis, 19 East Lancs, 1 Ford, 11 Irizar, 6 Marshall, 9 Mercedes, 42 Northern Counties, 26 Optare, 73 Plaxton, 15 Transbus, 69 Wrightbus.
Ops incl: local bus services, school contracts, private hire.
Livery: FirstGroup UK Bus.
Ticket System: Almex.

FROME MINIBUSES LTD
GEORGES GROUND, FROME BA11 4RP
Tel: 01373 471474
Fax: 01373 455294
Web site: s101282612.websitehome.co.uk/frome
Man Dir: Andrew Young.
Fleet: 16 – 3 midibus, 1 midicoach, 10 minibus, 2 minicoach.
Chassis: 7 Mercedes, 9 Optare.
Ops incl: local bus services.
Livery: White.

HATCH GREEN COACHES
HATCH GREEN GARAGE, HATCH
BEAUCHAMP, TAUNTON TA3 6TN
Tel: 01823 480338
Fax: 01823 480500
E-mail: info@hatchgreencoaches.com
Web site: www.hatchgreencoaches.co.uk
Fleet: 37 – 8 midibus, 2 midicoach, 25 minibus, 2 minicoach.
Chassis: 1 Enterprise, 1 Ford Transit, 9 LDV, 14 Mercedes, 7 Optare.
Ops incl: local bus services, school contracts, private hire.
Livery: White/Grey/Black.

HUTTON COACH HIRE
95 MOORLAND ROAD, WESTON-SUPER-MARE BS23 4HS
Tel: 01934 618292
Fax: 01934 641362
E-mail: jnjlawrence@onetel.com
Owner: John Lawrence **Man:** Wendy Dover.
Fleet: 5 - 3 single-deck coach, 2 midibus.
Chassis: 1 Alexander Dennis, 1 DAF, 1 MAN, 1 Mercedes, 1 Volvo.
Bodies: 1 Autobus, 1 Caetano, 1 UVG, 2 Van Hool.
Ops incl: school contracts, excursions & tours, private hire.
Livery: White with orange/green logo.

NORTH SOMERSET COACHES
Bus services transferred to Abus (see Bristol) in November 2013; coach operations sold to Carmel Bristol (see Somerset) in January 2014.

QUANTOCK HERITAGE
THE OLD COAL YARD, BROADGAUGE
BUSINESS PARK, BISHOPS LYDEARD,
TAUNTON TA4 3BU
Tel: 01823 431578
E-mail: sales@quantockheritage.com
Web site: www.quantockheritage.com
Man Dir: Steve Morris.
Fleet: 15 heritage vehicles.
Ops incl: local bus services, private hire.

Non-heritage fleet and operations sold to Berry's Coaches (Taunton) Ltd

RIDLERS LTD
JURY ROAD GARAGE, DULVERTON
TA22 9EJ
Tel: 01398 323398
Fax: 01398 324398
E-mail: info@ridlers.co.uk
Web site: www.ridlers.co.uk
Man Dir: Gary Ridler **Dir:** Sarah Ridler
Ops Dir: Mark Jamieson.
Fleet: 23 - 19 single-deck coach, 4 midicoach.
Chassis: 6 Dennis, 1 Ford Transit, 1 Iveco, 2 Leyland, 1 Mercedes, 6 Scania, 2 Toyota, 2 Van Hool, 2 Volvo.
Bodies: 1 Berkhof, 2 Caetano, 4 Duple, 1 Ford Transit, 1 Irizar, 1 Jonckheere, 7 Plaxton, 6 Van Hool.
Ops incl: local bus services, school contracts, excursions & tours, private hire, continental tours.
Livery: Red/White/Silver.
Ticket system: Almex.

SMITH'S COACHES (B E & G W SMITH)
BYFIELDS, PYLLE BA4 6TA
Tel: 01749 830126   **Fax:** 01749 830888
E-mail: smithscoachespylle@yahoo.co.uk
Web site: websites.uk-plc.net/smiths_coaches
Prop: Graham Smith.
Fleet: 11 single-deck coach.
Chassis: 2 Bedford, 3 Leyland, 6 Volvo.
Bodies: 11 Plaxton.
Ops incl: school contracts, private hire.
Livery: Maroon/Cream.

SOMERBUS LIMITED
42 NIGHTINGALE WAY, MIDSOMER
NORTON, RADSTOCK BA3 4GD
Tel/Fax: 01761 490760
E-mail: somerbus@tinyworld.co.uk
Web site: www.somerbus.co.uk
Dir: Tim Jennings.
Fleet: 5 - 2 single-deck bus, 3 midibus.
Chassis: 1 Mercedes, 4 Optare.
Bodies: 1 MCV, 4 Optare.
Ops incl: local bus services, school contracts.
Livery: White/Orange.
Ticket system: Ticketer.

SOUTH WEST COACHES LTD
SOUTHGATE ROAD, WINCANTON
BA9 9EB
Tel: 01963 33124   **Fax:** 01963 31599
E-mail: info@southwestcoaches.co.uk
Web site: www.southwestcoaches.co.uk
Depots at: Wincanton, Portland, Yeovil.
Man Dir: A M Graham **Co Sec:** Mrs S Graham **Comm Dir:** S Caine
Ops Dir: P Fairey **Eng Man:** K Jeffrey.
Fleet: 101 - 5 single-deck bus, 48 single-deck coach, 17 midibus, 3 midicoach, 26 minibus, 2 minicoach.
Chassis: 1 BMC, 2 DAF, 13 Dennis, 1 Ford, 1 Irisbus, 5 LDV, 5 Leyland, 3 MAN, 21 Mercedes, 8 Optare, 3 Scania, 8 Setra, 1 Toyota, 1 Transbus, 2 Volkswagen, 24 Volvo.
Bodies: 6 Alexander, 6 Berkhof, 1 BMC, 8 Caetano, 1 Excel, 2 Ford, 2 Irizar, 5 Jonckheere, 3 LDV, 5 Marshall, 1 MCV, 2 Mercedes, 1 Onyx, 8 Optare, 22 Plaxton, 8 Setra, 1 Transbus, 1 UVG, 4 Van Hool, 1 Volkswagen, 1 Wadham Stringer, 5 Wrightbus, 7 Other.
Ops incl: local bus services, school contracts, excursions & tours, private hire, continental tours.

Livery: Red, White & Blue.
Ticket Systems: Wayfarer, Almex.

STAGECOACH SOUTH WEST
(formerly COOKS COACHES)
♿ ❄
BELGRAVE ROAD, EXETER EX1 2LB
Tel: 01392 427711
Fax: 01392 889727
E-mail: southwest.enquiries@stagecoachbus.com
Web site: www.stagecoachbus.com
Officers: See Stagecoach South West (Devon)
Fleet: See Stagecoach South West (Devon)
Ops incl: local bus services, school contracts.
Livery: Stagecoach UK Bus.

STONES OF BATH
A subsidiary of Hatts Coaches (ceased trading) (See Wiltshire)

TAYLORS COACH TRAVEL LTD
♿ ✏ ♿ ❄ R R24 ✎
BOUNDARY WAY, LUFTON TRADING ESTATE, YEOVIL BA22 8HZ
Tel: 01935 423177   **Fax:** 01935 427775
E-mail: info@taylorscoachtravel.co.uk
Web site: www.taylorscoachtravel.co.uk
Man Dir: Adam Elliott **Dirs:** Dennis Elliott, Chris Elliott **Ops Dir:** Mike Kirkland.
Fleet: 40 – 4 single-deck bus, 25 single-deck coach, 1 double-deck coach, 3 midicoach, 6 minibus, 1 minicoach.
Chassis: 2 Alexander Dennis, 2 Autosan, 2 Bova, 1 BMC, 1 DAF, 8 Dennis, 2 Irisbus, 1 Irizar, 2 Iveco, 2 LDV, 2 Leyland, 1 MAN, 4 Mercedes, 1 Neoplan, 7 Volvo.
Bodies: 1 Alexander, 1 Autobus, 2 Autosan, 1 BMC, 2 Bova, 2 Ford, 2 Indcar, 1 Irizar, 1 Jonckheere, 2 LDV, 2 Mercedes, 1 Noge, 11 Plaxton, 3 Van Hool, 2 Vehixel, 1 Wadham Stringer, 1 Other.
Ops incl: local bus services, school contracts, excursions & tours, private hire, continental tours.
Liveries: White, Burgundy & Gold; Yellow (School Buses).
Ticket system: Wayfarer.

UNICONNECT
See Wessex Bath

WEBBER BUS
♿ ✏ ♿ ❄ ❄ ✎
UNIT 8C, BEECH BUSINESS PARK, BRISTOL ROAD, BRIDGWATER TA6 4FF
Tel: 0800 096 3039
Fax: 01278 455250
E-mail: sales@webberbus.com
Web site: www.webberbus.com
Fleet Names: Easy Link, Village Link.
Man Dir: Tim Gardner **Eng & Ops Dir:** David Webber.
Fleet: 78 – 8 double-deck bus, 31 single-deck bus, 18 single-deck coach, 2 midibus, 2 midicoach, 17 minibus.
Chassis: 1 Alexander Dennis, 13 Dennis, 1 Ford Transit, 5 Irisbus, 1 Leyland, 2 MAN, 5 Mercedes, 27 Optare, 1 Scania, 18 Volvo, 4 Wrightbus.
Ops incl: local bus services, Taunton Park & Ride, school contracts, excursions & tours, private hire.
Ticket system: Wayfarer.

WESSEX BATH
♿ ✏
UNIT 53, BURNETT BUSINESS PARK, GYPSY LANE, KEYNSHAM BS31 2ED
Tel: 0117 986 9953
Web site: www.wessexbus.com
Fleet Names: Wessex Bath, Uniconnect.
A division of Wessex Bus – see main entry under Bristol.

ANDERSON COACHES LTD
✏ ❄
36 BONET LANE, BRINSWORTH, ROTHERHAM S60 5NE
Tel: 01709 364750
E-mail: andersoncoaches@btconnect.com
Web site: www.andersoncoaches.com
Dir: Mrs P Carpendale.
Fleet: 4 - 3 single-deck coach, 1 minibus.
Chassis: 1 Dennis, 1 LDV, 1 MAN, 1 Neoplan.
Ops incl: excursions & tours, private hire.

ASHLEY TRAVEL LTD
♿ ✏ ❄
42 BRIDGE STREET, KILLAMARSH S21 1AH
Tel: 0114 251 1234
Fax: 0114 251 1900
E-mail: ashley-travel@btconnect.com
Web site: www.ashleytravel.co.uk
Dirs: A Powell, D W Burdett.
Fleet: 9 single-deck coach.
Chassis: 9 Volvo.
Bodies: 1 Berkhof, 1 Jonckheere, 2 Plaxton, 5 Van Hool.
Ops incl: excursions & tours, private hire.
Livery: Turquoise/Blue/White.

BUCKLEYS TOURS LTD
♿ ✏ ❄
THORNE ROAD, BLAXTON, DONCASTER DN9 3AX
Tel: 01302 770379
E-mail: info@buckleysholidays.co.uk
Web site: www.buckleysholidays.co.uk
Man Dir: Richard Buckley.
Fleet: 7 single-deck coach.
Chassis: 1 DAF, 5 Neoplan, 1 Scania.
Ops incl: private hire, excursions & tours.
Livery: Orange.

BURDETTS COACHES LTD
♿ ✏ ✎
8 STATION ROAD, MOSBOROUGH, SHEFFIELD S20 5AD
Tel: 0114 248 2341
Fax: 0114 247 5733
Dirs: F, K J & D W Burdett.
Fleet: 2 single-deck coach.
Chassis: 2 Volvo.
Bodies: 2 Van Hool.
Ops incl: school contracts, excursions & tours, private hire.

CENTRAL TRAVEL
♿ ✏ ♿ ❄ ❄ R R24 ✎ T
313 COLEFORD ROAD, DARNALL, SHEFFIELD S9 5NF
Tel: 0114 243 2223
Web site: www.centralcoachhiresheffield.co.uk
Props: Paul Harrison, Joy Harrison.
Fleet: 27 – 13 single-deck coach, 2 midicoach, 12 minibus.
Chassis: 1 Bova, 1 DAF, 3 Dennis, 4 Ford Transit, 1 Iveco, 3 LDV, 1 MAN, 5 Mercedes, 1 Renault, 2 Scania, 4 Volvo.
Ops incl: school contracts, excursions & tours, private hire, continental tours.
Livery: White with Blue/Yellow.

CLARKSONS HOLIDAYS
See Wilfreda Beehive.

COOPERS TOURS LTD
♿ ✏ ♿ ❄ ❄ R24 ✎ T
14 BRIDGE STREET, KILLAMARSH S21 1AH
Tel: 0114 248 2859
Fax: 0114 248 3867
Web site: www.cooperstours.co.uk
Depots at: Killamarsh, Grimsby.
Dirs: Alan Cooper, Graham Cooper.
Fleet: 30 - 2 double-deck bus, 2 single-deck

bus, 26 single-deck coach, 1 midibus, 1 minibus.
Chassis: 1 AEC, 1 Autosan, 3 Dennis, 3 Irisbus, 1 LDV, 6 Leyland, 3 Scania, 1 Van Hool, 13 Volvo.
Ops incl: excursions & tours, private hire, continental tours.
Livery: Yellow/White.

ELLENDERS COACHES
♿ ✏ ❄ ✎ ✎
71 HURLFIELD AVENUE, SHEFFIELD S12 2TL
Tel: 0114 264 1837
Partners: P J D. Ellender, C S Ellender.
Fleet: 1 single-deck coach.
Chassis: Volvo.
Bodies: Jonckheere.
Ops incl: excursions & tours, private hire, continental tours, school contracts.

EXPRESSWAY COACHES
♿ ♿ ✏ ❄ ❄ T
DERWENT WAY, WATH WEST INDUSTRIAL ESTATE, WATH ON DEARNE, ROTHERHAM S63 6EX
Tel: 01709 877797
E-mail: expresswaycoaches@btconnect.com
Web site: www.expressway-coaches.co.uk
Dirs: Peter Regan.
Fleet: 22 - 9 single-deck coach, 1 midibus, 4 midicoach, 7 minibus, 1 minicoach.
Chassis: 2 MAN, 13 Mercedes, 1 Neoplan, 1 Scania, 1 Van Hool, 2 VDL, 2 Volvo.
Ops incl: private hire, continental tours, school contracts, excursions & tours.
Livery: Orange/Yellow/White.

FIRST SOUTH YORKSHIRE
♿ 🚌
MIDLAND ROAD, ROTHERHAM S61 1TF
Tel: 01709 566000
Fax: 01709 566063
E-mail: enquiries@firstgroup.com
Web site: www.firstgroup.com
Regional Man Dir: Dave Alexander
Man Dir: Ben Gilligan **Eng Dir:** Brian Wilkinson.
Fleet: 483 - 236 double-deck bus, 235 single-deck bus, 12 midibus.
Chassis: 3 Alexander Dennis, 31 Dennis, 4 Transbus, 377 Volvo, 68 Wrightbus.
Bodies: 68 Alexander, 3 Alexander Dennis, 41 Plaxton, 20 Transbus, 352 Wrightbus.
Ops incl: local bus services, school contracts.
Livery: FirstGroup UK Bus.
Ticket System: Wayfarer 3.

GEE-VEE TRAVEL
✏ ♿ ❄ ✎ T
7 KENDRAY STREET, BARNSLEY S70 1DB
Tel: 01226 287403
Fax: 01226 284783
E-mail: info@geeveetravel.co.uk
Web site: www.geeveetravel.co.uk
Prop: Gordon Clark.
Fleet: 21 - 19 single-deck coach, 2 minibus.
Chassis: 19 DAF, 2 Ford Transit.
Bodies: 19 Bova, 1 Ford, 1 Other.
Ops incl: excursions & tours, private hire, continental tours.
Livery: Blue/White/Yellow.

GLOBE COACHES
Business acquired by Tate's Travel Group (see below)

W GORDON & SONS
♿ ✏ ♿ ❄ ❄ ✎ T
CHESTERTON ROAD, EASTWOOD TRADING ESTATE, ROTHERHAM S65 1SU
Tel: 01709 363913
Fax: 01709 830570
E-mail: gordonscoaches@live.co.uk

South Yorkshire

Dir: David Gordon.
Fleet: 7 single-deck coach.
Chassis: I EOS, 3 Van Hool, 3 Volvo.
Bodies: I EOS, 3 Plaxton, 3 Van Hool.
Ops incl: school contracts, excursions & tours, private hire.
Livery: Red.

GRAYS TRAVEL GROUP

30-32 SHEFFIELD ROAD, HOYLAND COMMON S74 0DQ
Tel: 01226 743109
Fax: 01226 749430
E-mail: chris@graystravel.co.uk
Web site: www.graystravelgroup. co.uk
Man Dir: S Gray **Ch Eng:** P Winter.
Fleet: 8 - 7 single-deck coach, I midicoach.
Chassis: I DAF, I Dennis, 2 EOS, I Mercedes, 3 Volvo.
Ops incl: excursions & tours, private hire, school contracts.
Livery: White/Blue/Yellow.

HEATON'S OF SHEFFIELD LTD

66 POLLARD AVENUE, SHEFFIELD S5 8QA
Tel: 0114 233 1333
E-mail: enquiries@heatonscoaches-sheffield. co.uk
Web site: www.heatonscoaches-sheffield. co.uk
Prop: Angela Hancock.
Fleet: 7 - 5 single-deck coach, I midicoach, I minibus.
Chassis: 2 Dennis, I Iveco, I Mercedes, I Volkswagen, 2 Volvo.
Ops incl: school contracts, excursions & tours.
Livery: White with Red/Black.

ISLE COACHES

97 HIGH STREET, OWSTON FERRY DN9 IRL
Tel: 01427 728227
Props: J & C Bannister
Ch Eng: E Scotford **Sec:** Jill Bannister.
Fleet: 17 - 9 double-deck bus, 8 single-deck bus.
Chassis: 2 DAF, 4 Dennis, I Leyland, I Optare, 10 Volvo.
Bodies: 5 Alexander, 5 East Lancs, 3 Northern Counties, 2 Optare, I Wrightbus.
Ops incl: local bus services, school contracts.
Livery: Blue/Cream.
Ticket System: Almex.

JOHNSON BROS TOURS LTD

PORTLAND HOUSE, DUKERIES INDUSTRIAL ESTATE, CLAYLANDS AVENUE, WORKSOP S81 7BQ
Tel/Recovery: 01909 720337
Fax: 01909 481054
E-mail: lee@johnsonstours.co.uk
Web site: www.johnsonstours.co.uk
Dirs: C A Johnson, S Johnson, A Johnson, L Johnson, C Johnson.
Fleet: 103 - 59 double-deck bus, I single-deck bus, 35 single-deck coach, 4 midicoach, I minibus, 3 minicoach.
Chassis: I Autosan, 2 Bova, 9 Bristol, 2 DAF, I Ford Transit, 8 Irisbus, 4 Irizar, 40 Leyland, 5 Mercedes, 6 Neoplan, I Optare, 12 Scania, 2 Van Hool, 9 Volvo.
Bodies: 3 Alexander, I Autosan, 3 Beulas, 2 Bova, 3 Caetano, 30 ECW, I Excel, I Ford, 6 Irizar, 2 Jonckheere, 3 Leyland, 6 Neoplan, 23 Northern Counties, 2 Optare, 8 Plaxton, I Sunsundegui, 3 Transbus, 4 Van Hool.
Ops incl: local bus services, school contracts, excursions & tours, private hire, express,

continental tours.
Livery: Blue Fade with Stars.
Ticket System: ITSO.
See also Redfern Travel Ltd.

JOURNEYS-DESTINATION

42-45 WILSON STREET, NEEPSEND, SHEFFIELD S3 8DD
Tel: 0800 298 1938
Fax: 0114 242 0885
E-mail: info@journeys-destination.com
Web site: www.journeys-destination.com
Prop: Mrs Patricia R Russell.
Fleet: 3 minibus.
Chassis: 2 Iveco, I LDV.
Ops incl: school contracts, excursions & tours, private hire.

K. M. MOTORS LTD

WILSON GROVE, LUNDWOOD, BARNSLEY S71 5JS
Tel: 01226 245564
Fax: 01226 213004
E-mail: info@kmtravelbarnsley.co.uk
Web site: www.kmtravelbarnsley.co.uk
Man Dir: Keith Meynell.
Fleet: 9 - 7 single-deck coach, 2 minibus.
Chassis: 4 Bova, I Ford Transit, 2 Irizar, I Mercedes, I VDL.
Ops incl: excursions & tours, continental tours, private hire.
Livery: Gold/Maroon/White.

LADYLINE
Ceased trading since LRB 2014 went to press - operator retired.

LINBURG BUS & COACH

UNIT 7, 35 CATLEY ROAD, DARNALL, SHEFFIELD S9 5JF
Tel: 0114 261 9172
Fax: 0114 256 1159
E-mail: info@linburg.co.uk
Web site: www.linburg.co.uk
Dirs: John Hadaway, Gill Dawson
Ops Man: Paul Major **Fleet Eng:** Mark Toon.
Fleet: 26 - 7 double-deck bus, I double-deck coach, 15 single-deck coach, 2 midibus, I minibus.
Chassis: 7 DAF, 2 Dennis, I Ford Transit, 9 Leyland, 3 VDL, 4 Volvo.
Ops incl: school contracts, excursions & tours, private hire, express.
Livery: White/Multi Colour.
Ticket System: Wayfarer 2.

LL TRAVEL

20 MELTON STREET, MEXBOROUGH S64 0EZ
Tel: 01709 585359
Prop: J L Law.
Fleet: 10 - 4 single-deck coach, 4 midicoach, 2 minibus.
Chassis: I Ford Transit, I LDV, I MAN, 4 Mercedes, 3 Volvo.
Ops incl: excursions & tours, private hire.

WALTER MARTIN COACHES

57 OLD PARK AVENUE, GREENHILL, SHEFFIELD S8 7DQ
Tel: 0114 274 5004
E-mail: info@waltermartincoaches.co.uk
Web site: www.waltermartincoaches.co.uk
Prop: John Martin, June Martin.
Fleet: 3 single-deck coach.
Chassis: I Bova, I Scania, I Volvo.
Ops incl: excursions & tours, private hire.

MAS BRIGHT BUS

HOUGHTON ROAD, ANSTON, SHEFFIELD S25 4JJ
Tel: 01909 550480
Fax: 01909 550486
Recovery: 01909 550480
E-mail: info@bright-bus.co.uk
Web site: www.bright-bus.co.uk
Fleet Name: Brightbus.
Man Dir: Mick Strafford
Co Sec: Carol Morton
Eng Man:
Richard Harrison.
Fleet: 63 - 62 double-deck bus, I minibus.
Chassis: 6 DAF, 13 Dennis, 23 Leyland, 3 MCW, I Optare, 8 Scania, 9 Volvo.
Bodies: 22 Alexander, 13 Duple, 9 East Lancs, I Leyland, 3 MCW, 8 Northern Counties, 7 Optare.
Ops incl: local bus services, school contracts.
Livery: Green.

J A MAXFIELD & SONS LTD

172 AUGHTON ROAD, AUGHTON, SHEFFIELD S26 3XE
Tel: 0114 287 2622
Fax: 0114 287 5003
E-mail: info@maxfieldstravel.co.uk
Web site: www.maxfieldstravel.co.uk
Fleet: 16 - 12 single-deck coach, I midicoach, 3 minibus.
Chassis: I DAF, 2 EOS, I Ford Transit, I Irisbus, 2 LDV, I MAN, 2 Mercedes, 2 Scania, 4 Volvo.
Ops incl: excursions & tours, private hire.
Livery: Yellow with Orange/Green.

OAKLEAF COACHES

CARLTON INDUSTRIAL ESTATE, CARLTON, BARNSLEY S71 IHS
Tel: 01226 723361
Web site: www.oakleafcoaches.com
Prop: D Nichols.
Fleet: 12 - 10 single-deck coach, 2 midicoach.
Chassis: I MAN, 2 Mercedes, 3 Scania, 6 Volvo.
Ops incl: school contracts, excursions & tours, private hire.
Livery: White with Orange/Logo.

JOHN POWELL TRAVEL LTD

UNIT 2, 6 HELLABY LANE, HELLABY, ROTHERHAM S66 8HA
Tel: 01709 700900
Fax: 01709 701521
E-mail: info@johnpowelltravel.co.uk
Web site: www.powellsbus.co.uk
Dir: Ian Powell **Co Sec:** Jane Powell
Chief Eng: Ian Slater
Office Man: Lynn Oliver.
Fleet: 31 - 5 double-deck bus, 4 single-deck bus, 8 single-deck coach, 13 midibus, I midicoach.
Chassis: I BMC, 12 Dennis, 2 Iveco, I Leyland, I Optare, 14 Volvo.
Ops incl: local bus services, school contracts, private hire.
Livery: Blue/Yellow/Orange.
Ticket system: Wayfarer III.

RED LINE BUSES
Ceased trading since LRB 2014 went to press

ROYLES TRAVEL

114 TUNWELL AVENUE, SHEFFIELD S5 9FG
Tel: 0114 245 4519
Fax: 0114 257 8585
E-mail: enquire@roylestravel.co.uk
Web site: www.roylestravel.co.uk

Partners: Ricky Eales, Roy Eales.
Fleet: 2 single-deck coach.
Chassis: 1 Iveco, 1 MAN.
Bodies: 2 Beulas.
Ops incl: excursions & tours, private hire.
Livery: Maroon/Gold.

SAXON TRAVEL LTD
♿👬❄

EAST LANE, STAINFORTH, DONCASTER
DN7 5HF
Tel: 01302 849999
E-mail: saxon_travel@hotmail.co.uk
Web site: www.saxontravel.co.uk
Fleet: 9 – 6 single-deck coach, 2 midicoach,
1 minibus.
Chassis: 1 DAF, 3 Mercedes, 2 Scania, 3 Volvo.
Ops incl: school contracts, excursions &
tours, private hire.

STAGECOACH YORKSHIRE
♿🚌♿👬🚌❄T♿

UNIT 4, ELDON ARCADE, BARNSLEY
S70 4PP
Tel: 01226 202555
Fax: 01226 346715
E-mail: yorkshire.enquiries@stagecoach.com
Web site: www.stagecoachbus.com
Man Dir: Paul Lynch **Eng Dir:** Joe Gilchrist
Ops Dir: Sue Hayes **Acting Comm Dir:**
John Young.
Fleet: 321 – 80 double-deck bus, 112 single-
deck bus, 105 midibus, 24 minibus
Chassis: 127 Alexander Dennis, 14 Dennis,
122 MAN, 30 Optare, 23 Scania, 2 Transbus,
1 VDL, 2 Volvo.
Bodies: 23 Alexander, 231 Alexander Dennis,
18 East Lancs, 8 MCV, 30 Optare, 8 Plaxton,
2 Transbus, 1 Wrightbus.
Fleet excludes Chesterfield – see separate
entry *(Derbyshire)*.
Ops incl: local bus services, school contracts,
private hire.
Livery: Stagecoach UK Bus.
Ticket system: Wayfarer.

STAGECOACH SUPERTRAM
See Section 5 – Trams and Bus Rapid Transit
Systems.

SWIFTS HAPPY DAYS TRAVEL
♿👬♿T

THORNE ROAD, BLAXTON, DONCASTER
DN9 3AX
Tel/Fax: 01302 770999
A subsidiary of Buckley's Tours (see above)

TATE'S TRAVEL GROUP
♿♿

WHALEY ROAD, BARUGH GREEN,
BARNSLEY S75 1HT
Tel: 01226 205800
Fax: 01226 390048
E-mail: info@tates-travel.com
Web site: www.tates-travel.com
Fleet Names: Tate's Travel, Globe Coaches,
Globe Holidays.
Props: Graham Mallinson, Scott Woolley.
Fleet: 75 – 3 single-deck bus, 13 single-deck
coach, 46 midicoach, 2 midicoach, 9 minibus,
2 minicoach.

Chassis: 12 Alexander Dennis, 1 Bova,
18 Dennis, 1 Ford Transit, 8 King Long, 2 MAN,
6 Mercedes, 13 Optare, 1 Setra, 4 Transbus,
5 Volvo, 4 Wrightbus.
Bodies: 4 Alexander, 12 Alexander Dennis,
2 Berkhof, 1 Bova, 1 Ford, 8 King Long, 2 Koch,
3 Marshall, 2 Mercedes, 2 Noge, 13 Optare,
11 Plaxton, 1 Setra, 4 Transbus, 1 Wadham
Stringer, 4 Wrightbus, 2 Other.
Ops incl: local bus services, school contracts,
private hire.
Liveries: Buses: Blue/White; **Coaches:**
Multicoloured.
Incorporating Globe Coaches

TM TRAVEL LTD
♿♿❄

HALFWAY BUS GARAGE, STATION ROAD,
HALFWAY S20 3GZ
Tel: 0114 263 3890
Fax: 0114 563 3899
E-mail: info@tmtravel.co.uk
Web site: www.tmtravel.co.uk
Man: Phil Stockley **Deputy Man:** Paul
Hopkinson **Chief Eng:** Mark Clare.
Fleet: 67 - 13 double-deck bus, 3 single-deck
bus, 4 single-deck coach, 2 midibus, 45 minibus.
Chassis: 1 Alexander Dennis, 4 DAF,
1 Dennis, 6 Leyland, 47 Optare, 2 VDL, 6 Volvo.
Bodies: 10 Alexander, 3 East Lancs, 1 Ikarus,
2 Northern Counties, 47 Optare, 4 Plaxton.
Ops incl: local bus services, school contracts,
private hire.
Livery: Red, Cream & Maroon.
Ticket system: Ticketer.
Part of the Wellglade Group

TRAVELGREEN COACHES LTD
♿🚌❄R R24 ♿

CANDA LODGE, HAMPOLE BALK LANE,
SKELLOW, DONCASTER DN6 8LF
Tel/Recovery: 01302 722227
Fax: 01302 727999
E-mail: travelgreen@btconnect.com
Web site: www.travelgreen.co.uk
Dir: David Green.
Fleet: 4 – 1 double-deck bus, 1 midicoach,
2 minicoach.
Chassis: 1 AEC, 1 Ford Transit, 2 Mercedes.
Bodies: 1 Ford, 1 Park Royal, 1 Plaxton,
1 Other.
Ops incl: excursions & tours, private hire,
continental tours.
Livery: Maroon/White.

WILFREDA BEEHIVE
👬🍴♿❄🚌♿T♿

APEX HOUSE, CHURCH LANE, ADWICK-
LE-STREET, DONCASTER DN6 7AY
Tel: 01302 330330　**Fax:** 01302 330204
E-mail: sales@wilfreda.co.uk
Web site: www.wilfreda.co.uk
Man Dir: Mrs S M Scholey DL **Dirs:** P G
Haxby, N G Haxby, P A Scholey **Ops Dept:**
A Woolams, C Slater **Ch Eng:** P Whitaker.
Fleet: 37 - 3 double-deck bus, 2 single-deck
bus, 20 single-deck coach, 3 midibus,
4 midicoach, 5 minibus.
Chassis: 2 Alexander Dennis, 4 BMC, 1 DAF,
5 Ford Transit, 1 Leyland, 4 MAN, 4 Mercedes,
3 Optare, 13 Scania.

Bodies: 2 Alexander, 3 Beulas, 4 BMC,
2 East Lancs, 4 Ferqui, 5 Ford Transit, 7 Irizar,
4 Lahden, 3 Optare, 1 Park Royal, 2 Van Hool.
Ops incl: school contracts, excursions &
tours, private hire, continental tours.
Livery: Blue & Silver.
Ticket System: Wayfarer TGX150.
Incorporating Clarksons Holidays, Eagre
Coaches

WILKINSONS TRAVEL
👬♿♿

2 REDSCOPE CRESCENT, KIMBERWORTH
PARK, ROTHERHAM S61 3LX
Tel: 01709 553403
Fax: 01709 550550
Owner: M D Wilkinson.
Fleet: 9 - 5 single-deck coach, 2 midicoach,
2 minibus.
Chassis: Ford Transit, Iveco, LDV, MAN,
Mercedes, Scania, Setra, Volvo.
Ops incl: excursions & tours, private hire,
continental tours, school contracts.

WILSON'S COACHES
👬♿🍴❄♿

PLOT 5, BANKWOOD LANE INDUSTRIAL
ESTATE, ROSSINGTON, DONCASTER
DN11 0PS
Tel: 01302 866193
E-mail: info@wilson-tours.co.uk
Web site: www.wilson-tours.co.uk
Prop: E Wilson.
Fleet: 5 – 4 single-deck coach, 1 minibus.
Chassis: 1 EOS, 1 LDV, 3 Volvo.
Bodies: 1 Berkhof, 1 EOS, 1 LDV, 2 Van Hool.
Ops incl: excursions & tours, private hire,
continental tours.

WOMBWELL COACH HIRE LTD
Ceased trading since LRB 2014 went to press

WOODS COACHES
👬♿❄

NEW LODGE, WAKEFIELD ROAD,
BARNSLEY S71 1PA
Tel: 01226 286830
E-mail: contact@woodscoachesbarnsley.
co.uk
Fleet: 3 single-deck coach.
Chassis: 1 Van Hool, 2 VDL.
Bodies: 3 Van Hool.
Ops incl: excursions & tours, private hire.
Livery: White with Blue/Yellow.

YORKSHIRE ROSE COACHES
👬♿❄

20 RACECOMMON ROAD, BARNSLEY
S70 1BH
Tel: 01226 241843
E-mail:
yorkshirerosecoaches@blueyonder.co.uk
Web site: www.yorkshireroseholidays.co.uk
Props: S R & S Mills.
Fleet: 8 single-deck coaches.
Chassis: 2 Bova, 1 Mercedes, 4 Van Hool,
1 Volvo.
Bodies: 2 Bova, 1 Mercedes, 1 Sunsundegui,
4 Van Hool.
Ops incl: private hire, excursions & tours.
Livery: White with Blue/Red.

South Yorkshire

♿	Vehicle suitable for disabled	🍴	Coach(es) with galley facilities
♿	Seat belt-fitted Vehicle	♿	Replacement vehicle available
R24	24 hour recovery service	R	Recovery service available
T	Toilet-drop facilities available	❄	Air-conditioned vehicle(s)

🚌	Vintage Coach(es) available
🚌	Open top vehicle(s)
👬	Coaches with toilet facilities
♿ Hybrid Buses	🔥 Gas Buses

ACE TRAVEL

10 BIDDULPH PARK, IRONSTONE ROAD,
BURNTWOOD WS7 1LG
Tel: 01543 279068
Prop: G E Elson.
Fleet: 3 – 1 single-deck coach, 2 midicoach.
Chassis: 1 Dennis, 2 Toyota.
Bodies: 2 Caetano, 1 Plaxton.
Ops incl: excursions & tours, private hire,
continental tours, school contracts.

ACORN COACH & BUS GROUP

LICHFIELD ROAD INDUSTRIAL ESTATE,
TAMWORTH B79 7XE
Tel: 01827 311744   **Fax:** 01827 271327
E-mail: info@invinciblecoaches.com
Web site: www.invinciblecoaches.com
Fleet Names: Heartlands Travel, Invincible
Travel, Vals Coach & Bus.
Fleet: double-deck bus, single-deck bus,
single-deck coach, midibus, minibus..
Chassis: Dennis, Iveco, Leyland, MCW,
Mercedes, Optare, Scania, Volvo.
Ops incl: local bus services, school contracts,
private hire.
Livery: Blue/White.

AIMEES COACHES

UNIT 1, BARNFIELD INDUSTRIAL ESTATE,
SUNNY HILLS ROAD, LEEK ST13 5RJ
Tel: 01538 385050
Fax: 01538 385151
E-mail: garage@aimeestravel.com
Web site: www.aimeestravel.com
Prop: G Goldstraw.
Fleet: 13 - 3 single-deck bus, 3 single-deck
coach, 3 midibus, 2 midicoach, 2 minibus.
Chassis: 2 Alexander Dennis, 3 BMC,
3 Dennis, 3 Mercedes, 2 Volvo.
Ops incl: school contracts, private hire.
Livery: Buses: Yellow; Coaches: White with
Pink.

ARRIVA MIDLANDS LTD

4 WESTMORELAND AVENUE,
THURMASTON, LEICESTER LE4 8PH
Tel: 0116 264 0400
Fax: 0116 260 8620
E-mail: myattk.midlands@arriva.co.uk
Web site: www.arriva.co.uk
Regional Man Dir: A Perry
Regional Fin Dir: J Barlow
Regional Eng Dir: M Evans **Area Director
East:** S Mathieson **Area Director West:**
R Cheveaux.
Fleet: 698 - 168 double-deck bus, 267 single-
deck bus, 6 articulated bus, 204 midibus,
53 minibus.
Chassis: 24 Alexander Dennis, 173 DAF,
119 Dennis, 26 Mercedes, 121 Optare,
46 Scania, 6 Transbus, 85 VDL, 98 Volvo.
Bodies: 61 Alexander, 24 Alexander Dennis,
4 Caetano, 46 East Lancs, 1 Marshall,
26 Mercedes, 121 Optare, 110 Plaxton,
42 Scania, 6 Transbus, 257 Wrightbus.
Ops incl: local bus services, school contracts,
private hire, express.
Liveries: Arriva; Midland (Red); Wardles
(Red/White, Red/Cream).
Ticket System: Wayfarer 150 & 200.

BAKERS COACHES

THE COACH TRAVEL CENTRE, PROSPECT
WAY, VICTORIA BUSINESS PARK,
BIDDULPH ST8 7PL
Tel: 01782 522101
Fax: 01782 522363

E-mail: sales@bakerscoaches.com
Web sites: www.bakerscoaches.com; www.
bakerbus.com
Dir: Mark Ready **Ops Man:** Andy Fish
Sales & Marketing Man: Stephanie Dean.
Fleet: 63 – 7 double-deck bus, 2 single-deck
bus, 27 single-deck coach, 18 midibus,
4 midicoach, 5 minibus.
Chassis: 4 Alexander Dennis, 2 DAF,
4 Dennis, 4 Enterprise, 1 Ford Transit,
10 King Long, 2 Mercedes, 1 Neoplan,
2 Optare, 7 Scania, 1 Van Hool, 1 VDL,
22 Volvo, 2 Wrightbus.
Bodies: 4 Alexander, 4 Alexander Dennis,
3 Berkhof, 2 Caetano, 1 Ford, 3 Irizar,
2 Jonckheere, 10 King Long, 1 Neoplan,
2 Optare, 17 Plaxton, 3 Van Hool,
11 Wrightbus.
Ops incl: local bus services, school contracts,
excursions & tours, private hire, continental
tours.
Livery: Coach – Green/White;
Bus – Yellow/Blue.
Ticket System: Wayfarer TGX150.

BENNETTS TRAVEL (CRANBERRY) LTD

THE GARAGE, CRANBERRY, COTES HEATH,
STAFFORD ST21 6SQ
Tel: 01782 791468
Fax: 01782 791480
Web site:
www.bennettstravelcranberryltd.co.uk
Prop/Gen Man: M McCormick, P M Keeling.
Fleet: 34 – 4 single-deck bus, 14 single-deck
coach, 10 midibus, 5 midicoach, 1 minibus.
Chassis: 1 Alexander Dennis, 1 Ayats, 3 Bova,
1 DAF, 5 Dennis, 2 Leyland, 9 Mercedes,
1 Optare, 3 Scania, 8 Volvo.
Ops incl: local bus services, excursions &
tours, private hire.
Livery: Blue/White.

TERRY BUSHELL TRAVEL

14 DERBY STREET, BURTON-UPON-TRENT
DE14 2LA
Tel/Fax: 01283 538242
E-mail: info@terrybushelltravel.co.uk
Web site: www.terrybushelltravel.co.uk
Prop: Terry Bushell.
Fleet: 3 - 2 single-deck coach, 1 minicoach.
Chassis: 2 Mercedes, 1 Volvo.
Bodies: 1 Mercedes, 1 Neoplan, 1 Van Hool.
Ops incl: excursions & tours, private hire,
continental tours.
Livery: Red/Poppy/Gold.

CLOWES COACHES
See Derbyshire

COPELAND TOURS (STOKE-ON-TRENT) LTD

1005 UTTOXETER ROAD, MEIR,
STOKE ON TRENT, ST3 6HE
Tel: 01782 324466
Fax: 01782 319401
Recovery: 01782 324466
E-mail: enquiry@copelandstours.co.uk
Web site: www.copelandstours.co.uk
Chairman/Man Dir: J E M Burn **Dir:** Mrs P
Burn **Ch Eng:** J C Burn **Co Sec:** J E M Burn.
Fleet: 26 – 23 single-deck coach, 3 midibus.
Chassis: 3 Bova, 12 DAF, 3 Dennis, 1 Duple
425, 3 Leyland, 1 Van Hool, 3 Volvo.
Ops incl: local bus services, school contracts,
excursions & tours, private hire, express,
continental tours.
Livery: Blue-Blue/Orange.
Ticket System: Wayfarer.

CRUSADE TRAVEL LTD

THE COACHYARD, BUXTON ESTATES,
PENKRIDGE ST19 5RP
Tel: 01785 714124   **Fax:** 01543 579678
E-mail: office@crusade-travel.co.uk
Web site: www.crusade-travel.co.uk
Dir: J P McDonnell **Ops Man:** Gavin Pardoe.
Fleet: 8 - 4 single-deck coach, 2 midicoach,
2 minibus.
Chassis: 4 Mercedes, 3 Scania, 1 Setra.
Ops incl: school contracts, excursions &
tours, private hire.
Livery: White.

D & G COACH AND BUS LTD
See Cheshire

ELIZABETHAN & MAJESTIC TRAVEL

HILTON LANE, SHARESHILL,
WOLVERHAMPTON WV10 7HU
Tel: 01922 401338   **Fax:** 01922 710783
E-mail: info@elizabethantravel.co.uk
Web site: www.elizabethantravel.co.uk
Dirs: K Horton, R S Lavender.
Fleet: 13 – 11 single-deck coach, 2 midicoach.
Chassis: 1 Bova, 3 Irisbus, 2 King Long,
2 MAN, 1 Mercedes, 2 Scania, 1 Setra, 1 Volvo.
Ops incl: excursions & tours, private hire.

FIRST MIDLANDS

ADDERLEY GREEN GARAGE, DIVIDY
ROAD, STOKE-ON-TRENT ST3 0AJ
Tel: 08456 020121   **Fax:** 01782 592541
Fleet Name: First Potteries.
Man Dir: Nigel Eggleton
Deputy Man Dir: Mick Brannigan
Fin Dir: David Marshall.
Fleet (Potteries): 195 – 23 double-deck bus,
99 single-deck bus, 44 midibus, 29 minibus.
Chassis: 6 Alexander Dennis, 21 Dennis,
3 Leyland, 29 Optare, 87 Scania, 17 Transbus,
32 Volvo.
Bodies: 16 Alexander, 6 Alexander Dennis,
18 Caetano, 2 Leyland, 2 Marshall, 2 Northern
Counties, 29 Optare, 11 Plaxton, 17 Scania,
92 Wright.
Ops incl: local bus services, school contracts.
Livery: FirstGroup UK Bus.
See also operations in Herefordshire,
Leicestershire, Worcestershire

GOLDEN GREEN TRAVEL

COWBROOK LANE, GAWSWORTH,
MACCLESFIELD SK11 0QP
Tel: 01298 83583
E-mail: goldengreentravel@hotmail.co.uk
Web site: www.goldengreentravel.co.uk
Partners: John Worth, Gill Worth,
Derek J Lownds.
Fleet: 11 single-deck coaches.
Chassis: Mercedes.
Ops incl: local bus services, school contracts,
excursions & tours, private hire.

HAPPY DAYS COACHES

PATON DRIVE, TOLLGATE PARK,
BEACONSIDE, STAFFORD ST16 3EF
Tel/Recovery: 01785 229797
Fax: 01785 229790
E-mail: info@happydayscoaches.co.uk
Web site: www.happydayscoaches.co.uk
Fleet: 27 - 20 single-deck coach, 1 midibus,
2 midicoach, 4 minibus.
Chassis: 1 DAF, 3 Ford Transit, 4 Mercedes,
1 Neoplan, 4 Scania, 1 Van Hool, 13 Volvo.
Bodies: 3 Ford, 2 Irizar, 2 Jonckheere, 2
Lahden, 1 Neoplan, 11 Plaxton, 6 Van Hool.

Ops incl: excursions & tours, private hire, express, school contracts, continental tours.
Livery: Rising Sun.
Also at Bronington, Shropshire
A subsidiary of Leons Coach Travel (Stafford) Ltd (see below)

HOLLINSHEAD COACHES LTD
WHARF ROAD, BIDDULPH ST8 6AG
Tel: 01782 512209
E-mail: hollinsheadcoach@btconnect.com
Web site: www.hollinsheadcoach.com
Fleet: 10 - 7 single-deck coach, 2 midicoach, 1 minibus.
Chassis: 1 LDV, 2 Mercedes, 7 Volvo.
Bodies: 1 Jonckheere, 1 LDV, 2 Sitcar, 5 Van Hool, 1 Volvo.
Ops incl: school contracts, excursions & tours, private hire.
Livery: Red/Cream.

JOSEPHS MINI COACHES
171 CRACKLEY BANK, CHESTERTON, NEWCASTLE-UNDER-LYME ST5 7AB
Tel: 01782 564944
Prop: Joseph Windsor.
Fleet: 2 - 1 minibus.
Chassis: Mercedes.
Ops incl: private hire.
Livery: Red/White.

LEONS COACH TRAVEL (STAFFORD) LTD
PATON DRIVE, TOLLGATE PARK, BEACONSIDE, STAFFORD ST16 3EF
Tel: 01785 241319
Fax: 01785 258444
E-mail: info@leons.co.uk
Web site: www.leonsholidays.co.uk
Dirs: A Douglas, R L Douglas, L H Douglas
Co Sec: S Douglas.
Fleet: 26 - 19 single-deck coach, 1 midibus, 1 midicoach, 4 minibus, 1 minicoach.
Chassis: 2 Iveco, 2 LDV, 3 Mercedes, 2 Neoplan, 2 Scania, 13 Van Hool, 2 Volvo.
Bodies: 1 Carlyle, 1 Irizar, 2 LDV, 1 Mercedes, 3 Plaxton, 14 Van Hool, 2 Other.
Ops incl: school contracts, excursions & tours, private hire, continental tours.
Livery: Burgundy.

MIDLAND CLASSIC LTD
UNIT 5, 290 STANTON ROAD, BURTON-ON-TRENT DE15 9SQ
Tel/Fax: 01283 500228
E-mail: info@midlandclassic.com
Web site: www.midlandclassic.com
Dirs: James Boddice, Julian H Peddle, John Mitcheson.
Fleet: 23 - 6 double-deck bus, 1 open-top bus, 13 single-deck bus, 4 midibus.
Chassis: 1 AEC, 6 Dennis, 1 Leyland, 3 Optare, 13 Scania.
Bodies: 5 Alexander, 1 ECW, 3 Optare, 1 Park Royal, 1 Plaxton, 13 Wrightbus.
Ops incl: local bus services, private hire.
Livery: LT Red/Stevensons Yellow.
Ticket System: Ticketer.

PARRYS INTERNATIONAL TOURS LTD
LANDYWOOD GREEN, CHESLYN HAY WS6 7QX
Tel: 01922 414576
Fax: 01922 413416
E-mail: info@parrys-international.co.uk
Web site: www.parrys-international.co.uk
Man Dir: David Parry.
Fleet: 15 - 11 single-deck coach, 4 minicoach.

Chassis: 3 Mercedes, 4 Neoplan, 7 Van Hool, 1 Renault.
Bodies: 1 Mellor, 3 Mercedes, 1 Neoplan, 7 Van Hool.
Ops incl: excursions & tours.
Livery: Red/Gold.

PLANTS LUXURY TRAVEL LTD
167 TEAN ROAD, CHEADLE ST10 1LS
Tel: 01538 753561
Fax: 01538 757025
E-mail: julie.plant@plantsluxurytravel.co.uk
Web site: www.plantsluxurytravel.co.uk
Partners: T J Plant, M P Plant.
Fleet: 9 - 2 midicoach, 7 minicoach.
Chassis: 1 Fiat, 2 Ford Transit, 6 Mercedes.
Ops incl: private hire, school contracts.
Livery: Silver with Burgundy/Gold/Mustard stripes.

ROBIN HOOD TRAVEL LTD
HIGHWAY GARAGE, MACCLESFIELD ROAD, LEEK ST13 8PS
Tel: 01538 306618
Fax: 01538 306079
E-mail: info@robinhoodtravel.co.uk
Web site: www.robinhoodtravel.co.uk
Fleet: 14 - 10 single-deck coach, 3 minibus, 1 minicoach.
Chassis: 6 Bova, 1 DAF, 2 Dennis, 1 LDV, 3 Mercedes, 1 VDL.
Ops incl: school contracts, excursions & tours, private hire, continental tours.
Livery: Green/Gold stars.

SCRAGGS COACHES
PARKHALL ROAD, ADDERLEY GREEN, STOKE-ON-TRENT ST3 5AT
Tel: 01782 336677
Fax: 01782 284631
E-mail: info@scraggs.co.uk
Web site: www.scraggs.co.uk
Fleet Names: Scraggs Coaches, Blue Buses.
Fleet: 30 - 1 double-deck bus, 5 single-deck coach, 1 midicoach, 17 minibus, 6 minicoach.
Chassis: 2 DAF, 2 Dennis, 5 Enterprise, 1 Ford Transit, 1 Leyland, 15 Mercedes, 1 Optare, 2 Toyota, 1 Volvo.
Ops incl: local bus services, school contracts, private hire.
Liveries: Blue (Buses); Cream/Brown/Yellow (Coaches).

SELECT BUS SERVICES
2 NAGINGTON DRIVE, PENKRIDGE ST19 5TA
Dirs: B Brown, W Parry.
Fleet: single-deck coach, midibus.
Chassis: Dennis, Leyland, Volvo.
Ops incl: local bus services, school contracts.
Livery: Red/Yellow.

SHIRE TRAVEL INTERNATIONAL LTD
CANNOCK WOOD INDUSTRIAL ESTATE, CANNOCK WOOD STREET, CANNOCK WS12 0PL
Tel: 01543 469777
E-mail: hire@shiretravel.co.uk
Web site: www.shiretravel.co.uk
Dir: Robert Garrington
Comp Sec: Michelle Wassell.
Fleet: 9 - 3 single-deck coach, 1 midibus, 5 minibus.
Chassis incl: 1 Scania, 2 Setra, 5 Mercedes.
Bodies: 1 Irizar, 6 Mercedes, 2 Setra.
Ops incl: private hire, school contracts, excursions & tours, continental tours.
Livery: White/Red + end three lions flag.

SOLUS COACHES
R24 T
LOVELL, Off APPOLLO, LICHFIELD ROAD INDUSTRIAL ESTATE, TAMWORTH B79 7TA
Tel: 01827 51736
Fax: 0871 900 4124
Recovery: 07773 785143
E-mail: enquiries@soluscoaches.co.uk
Web site: www.soluscoaches.co.uk
Man Dir: A Garratt Tran Man: L Richardson
Eng Dir: G Hopkins.
Fleet: 38 - 26 single-deck coach, 1 midibus, 1 midicoach, 7 minibus, 3 minicoach.
Chassis: 1 Alexander Dennis, 6 Ford Transit, 2 Irisbus, 1 Leyland, 1 MAN, 4 Mercedes, 2 Neoplan, 11 Scania, 1 Setra, 1 Transbus, 6 Volvo.
Ops incl: local bus services, school contracts, excursions & tours, private hire, continental tours.
Livery: White/Red/Black.
Also controls Viking Coaches.com Ltd (see Derbyshire)

STANWAYS COACHES
ODLUMS GARAGE, KNUTSFORD ROAD, RODE HEATH, STOKE-ON-TRENT ST7 3QT
Tel: 01270 884242
Fax: 01270 884262
E-mail: stanwayscoaches@yahoo.co.uk
Web site: www.stanwayscoaches.co.uk
Partners: David Elliot, Paul Richman.
Fleet: 16 - 1 single-deck bus, 9 single-deck coach, 2 midibus, 3 minibus, 1 minicoach.
Chassis: 5 Dennis, 1 Ford Transit, 1 LDV, 4 Leyland, 2 Mercedes, 1 Scania, 2 Volvo.
Ops incl: local bus services, school contracts, private hire.
Livery: Red/Orange/Cream.
Ticket System: Wayfarer.

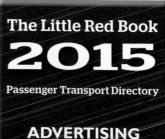
Staffordshire, City of Stoke On Trent

STODDARDS COACHES

GREENHILL GARAGE, LEEK ROAD,
CHEADLE ST10 1JF
Tel: 01538 754420
E-mail: info@stoddards.co.uk
Web site: www.stoddards.co.uk
Man Dir: Judith Stoddard
Workshop/Service: Paul Stoddard
HSE/Environmental: Peter Stoddard.
Fleet: 4 single-deck coach.
Chassis: 4 DAF.
Bodies: 4 Bova.
Ops incl: excursions & tours, private hire,
school contracts.
Livery: Silver/Blue.

SWIFTSURE TRAVEL (BURTON UPON TRENT) LTD

UNIT 6, 290 STANTON ROAD, BURTON-
UPON-TRENT DE15 9SQ
Tel: 01283 512974   **Fax:** 01283 516728
E-mail: info@swiftsure-travel.co.uk
Web site: www.swiftsure-travel.co.uk
Man Dir: Richard Hackett
Dirs: Julian Peddle, Brian Kershaw
Co Sec: Kathleen Hackett.
Fleet: 7 - 5 single-deck coah, 2 midicoach.
Chassis: 2 Bova, 2 Mercedes, 2 Scania,
1 Toyota.
Bodies: 1 Autobus, 2 Bova, 1 Caetano, 1 Irizar,
2 Other.
Ops incl: excursions & tours, private hire.
Livery: White/Blue/Green.

WARDLE TRANSPORT

See Arriva Midlands

WARRINGTON COACHES

See Derbyshire

WINTS COACHES

MONTANA, WETTON ROAD, BUTTERTON
ST13 7ST
Tel: 01538 304370
E-mail:
enquiries@wintscoachesstaffordshire.co.uk
Props: Andrew Wint, Maxine Wint.
Fleet: 6 - 5 single-deck coach, 1 midicoach.
Chassis: 1 DAF, 4 Mercedes, 1 Scania.
Bodies: 1 Irizar, 3 Mercedes, 1 Plaxton,
1 Van Hool.
Ops incl: school contracts, excursions &
tours, private hire, continental tours.
Livery: White/Blue.

ANGLIAN BUS LTD

BECCLES BUSINESS PARK, BECCLES
NR34 7TH
Tel: 01502 711109
Fax: 01502 711161
E-mail: office@anglianbus.co.uk
Web site: www.anglianbus.co.uk
Fin Dir: Tamara Harris **Ops Man:** Philip
Eden.
Fleet: 57 – 5 double-deck bus, 37 single-deck
bus, 15 midibus.
Chassis: 4 Dennis, 13 MAN, 18 Optare,
17 Scania, 4 Wrightbus.
Bodies: 13 Caetano, 5 East Lancs, 18 Optare,
17 Scania, 4 Wrightbus.
Ops incl: local bus services, school contracts.
Livery: Yellow with blue.
Ticket System: Wayfarer 3.
A subsidiary of the Go-Ahead Group

BEESTONS (HADLEIGH) LIMITED

THE COACH DEPOT, IPSWICH ROAD,
HADLEIGH IP7 6BG
Tel: 01473 823243
Fax: 01473 823608
Recovery: 07789 534857
E-mail: info@beestons.co.uk
Web site: www.beestons.co.uk
Man Dir: Philip Munson
Fin Dir: Mrs Sharon Munson
Ops Dir: Tom Munson.
Fleet: 41 - 15 double-deck bus, 3 single-deck
bus, 9 single-deck coach, 5 double-deck coach,
7 midibus, 2 minibus.
Chassis: 1 Ford Transit, 1 LDV, 5 Mercedes,
4 Optare, 14 Scania, 1 Van Hool, 15 Volvo.
Bodies: 2 Alexander, 10 East Lancs, 1 Ford,
1 LDV, 2 Mercedes, 1 Northern Counties, 5
Optare, 3 Plaxton, 12 Van Hool, 2 Wrightbus.
Ops incl: local bus services, school contracts,
excursions & tours, private hire, continental
tours.
Liveries: Buses: Blue; **Coaches:** Black/Gold.
Ticket System: Wayfarer 3.

BORDERBUS LTD

UNIT 3, MOOR BUSINESS PARK, ELLOUGH
ROAD, BECCLES NR34 7TQ
Tel: 01502 714565
E-mail: office@border-bus.co.uk
Web site: www.border-bus.co.uk
Dir: Andrew Pursey

Fleet: 9 – 4 double-deck bus, 5 midibus.
Chassis: 5 Alexander Dennis, 4 Volvo
Bodies: 5 Alexander Dennis, 4 Plaxton.
Livery: Blue/White/Yellow.
Ops incl: local bus services, school contracts,
private hire.

BUCKLAND OMNIBUS COMPANY

IVY COTTAGE, MARLESFORD ROAD,
HATCHESTON, WOODBRIDGE
IP13 0DP
Tel: 01728 747093
E-mail: bucklandcoaches@yahoo.co.uk
Web site: www.bucklandbuses.co.uk
Props: A J & G A Buckland.
Fleet: 6 – 4 single-deck coach, 2 vintage
vehicles.
Chassis: 1 Bristol, 1 Dennis, 4 Volvo.
Ops incl: school contracts, private hire.
Livery: White with Blue.

CARTERS COACH SERVICES LTD

LONDON ROAD, CAPEL ST MARY,
IPSWICH IP9 2JT
Tel: 01473 313188
E-mail: enquiries@cartersbusdepot.demon.
co.uk
Web site: www.carterscoachservices.co.uk
Dirs: L V Carter, S E Wythe.
Fleet: 14 - 9 double-deck bus, 1 midibus,
4 heritage.
Chassis (main fleet): 7 Dennis, 1 Leyland,
1 VDL, 1 Volvo.
Bodies (main fleet): 7 Alexander, 1 Leyland,
1 MCV, 1 Plaxton.
Ops incl: local bus services, school contracts,
private hire.
Livery: Red/Yellow/Black.

H C CHAMBERS & SON LTD

MEEKINGS ROAD, CHILTON INDUSTRIAL
ESTATE, SUDBURY CO10 2XE
Tel: 01787 375360
Fax: 01787 371451
E-mail: info@chamberscoaches.co.uk
Web site: www.chambersbus.co.uk
Fin Dir: Tamara Harris
Gen Man: Jeff Clayton
Dep Gen Man: Nick Field.
Fleet: 28 - 23 double-deck bus, 3 single-deck
coach, 2 midibus.
Chassis: 2 Mercedes, 2 Optare, 24 Volvo.

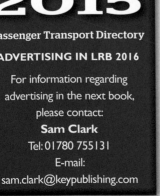

The Little Red Book
2015
Passenger Transport Directory

ADVERTISING IN LRB 2016

For information regarding
advertising in the next book,
please contact:

Sam Clark
Tel: 01780 755131
E-mail:
sam.clark@keypublishing.com

Bodies: 2 Mercedes, 2 Northern Counties, 2 Optare, 21 Plaxton, 1 Van Hool.
Ops incl: local bus services, excursions & tours, private hire.
Livery: Red.
Ticket System: Wayfarer.
A subsidiary of the Go-Ahead Group, jointly managed with Hedingham & District Omnibuses Ltd (see Essex).

D-WAY TRAVEL

GREENWAYS, THE STREET, EARSHAM, BUNGAY NR35 2TZ
Tel: 01986 895375
Fax: 05600 751425
E-mail: david@dwaytravel.com
Web site: www.dwaytravel.com
Prop: David Thompson
Ops Man: Dale Jermy.
Fleet: 10 - 7 single-deck coach, 1 minibus, 1 minicoach, 1 midicoach.
Chassis incl: 1 Ford Transit, 5 MAN, 2 Mercedes, 1 Peugeot, 1 Volvo.
Ops incl: school contracts, excursions & tours, private hire, continental tours.
Livery: White/Multi Colours.

EUROSUN COACHES

25 REGENT ROAD, LOWESTOFT NR32 1PA
Tel: 01520 501015
Fax: 01502 589382
E-mail: eurosuncoaches@hotmail.com
Web site: www.eurosuncoaches.co.uk
Dirs: Phil Overy, Jack Overy.
Fleet: 9 - 7 single-deck coach, 2 minibus.
Chassis: 1 DAF, 1 Dennis, 1 King Long, 1 Leyland, 2 MAN, 2 Mercedes, 1 Scania.
Bodies: 2 Duple, 2 Jonckheere, 1 King Long, 1 Marcopolo, 1 Marshall, 1 Plaxton, 1 Other.
Ops incl: local bus services, school contracts, excursions & tours, private hire, continental tours.
Livery: Red and Gold.

FARELINE BUS & COACH SERVICES

OLD ROSES, SYLEHAM ROAD, WINGFIELD, EYE IP21 5RF
Tel: 01379 668151
Prop: Jeff Morss.
Fleet: 1 single-deck coach.
Chassis: Volvo.
Body: Jonckheere.
Ops incl: local bus services, school contracts, excursions & tours, private hire.
Livery: Blue/White.
Ticket System: Setright Mk 3.

FELIX OF LONG MELFORD

8 WINDMILL HILL, LONG MELFORD, SUDBURY CO10 9AD
Tel: 01787 310574, 372125
Fax: 01787 310584
Web site: www.felixcoaches.co.uk
Fleet: 20 – 2 midibus, 4 midicoach, 7 minibus, 2 minicoach, 5 heritage.
Chassis (main fleet): 1 BMC, 1 Leyland DAF, 1 MAN, 11 Mercedes, 1 Optare.
Ops incl: local bus services, school contracts, excursions & tours, private hire
Livery: White with Red/Black.

FIRST EAST OF ENGLAND
(formerly **FIRST EASTERN COUNTIES**)

ROUEN HOUSE, ROUEN ROAD, NORWICH NR1 1RB
Tel: 0845 602 0121
Fax: 01603 615439
E-mail: contactus.fec@firstgroup.com

Web site: www.firstgroup.com
Man Dir: David Squire **Comm Dir:** Steve Wickers **Fin Dir:** David Marshall
HR Director: Karen Doores **Creative Dir:** Chelsea de Silva **Ch Eng:** Mark Reynolds
Business Man: Chris Speed.
Fleet (Norfolk & Suffolk): 257 - 151 double-deck bus, 73 single-deck bus, 2 single-deck coach, 25 midibus, 6 minibus.
Chassis: 33 Alexander Dennis, 61 Dennis, 6 Optare, 16 Scania, 141 Volvo.
Bodies: 36 Alexander Dennis, 11 Alexander, 12 Caetano, 2 Northern Counties, 6 Optare, 75 Plaxton, 10 Transbus, 105 Wright.
Ops incl: local bus services, school contract, private hire.
Livery: FirstGroup UK Bus.
Ticket System: Wayfarer 3.

FORGET-ME-NOT (TRAVEL) LTD

CHAPEL ROAD, OTLEY, IPSWICH IP6 9NT
Tel: 01473 558334
E-mail: sales@forgetmenot-travel.co.uk
Web site: www.forgetmenottravel.co.uk
Fleet Name: Soames
Dirs: A F Soames, Mrs M A Soames **(Co Sec),** A M Soames **(Ch Eng).**
Fleet: 17 - 16 single-deck coach, 1 midicoach.
Chassis: 1 Mercedes, 16 Volvo.
Bodies: 1 Ferqui, 1 Jonckheere, 13 Plaxton, 2 Van Hool.
Ops incl: private hire, school contracts.
Livery: Three tone Blue.

PAUL FROST TRAVEL

24 GROVE ROAD, WOODBRIDGE IP12 4LH
Tel: 01394 388333
Fleet: 7 – 1 midibus, 3 midicoach, 3 minibus.
Chassis: 6 Mercedes, 1 Optare.
Ops incl: local bus services, school contracts, private hire.

GALLOWAY TRAVEL GROUP

DENTERS HILL, MENDLESHAM, STOWMARKET IP14 5RR
Tel: 01449 766323
Fax: 01449 766241
E-mail: david@gallowayeuropean.co.uk
Web: www.gallowayeuropean.com
Man Dir: David Cattermole **Comm Dir:** John Miles **Fin Dir:** Roger Stedman **Group Ops:** Richard Smith **Fleet Man:** Andy Kemp **Ops Man:** Andy Cook **Comm Man:** Liz Palfrey **Training Man:** Ian Brain.
Fleet: 49 - 2 double-deck bus, 17 single-deck bus, 28 single-deck coach, 2 midicoach.
Chassis: 20 DAF/VDL, 2 Dennis, 1 Leyland, 14 Mercedes, 1 Scania, 1 Temsa, 10 Volvo.
Bodies: 8 Caetano, 2 Ikarus, 2 MCV, 2 Mercedes, 6 Optare, 10 Plaxton, 3 Setra, 1 UVG, 8 Van Hool, 2 Volvo, 4 Wrightbus, 1 Other.
Ops incl: local bus services, school contracts, excursions & tours, private hire, express, continental tours.
Livery: Multi Globe & Star based; National Express.
Ticket System: Ticketer.

GOLDLINE TRAVEL

UNIT 5A, MOOR BUSINESS PARK, ELLOUGH ROAD, BECCLES NR34 7TQ
Tel: 01502 711611
E-mail: info@goldlinecoachessuffolk.co.uk
Props: I J & K J Trussler.
Fleet: 9 – 2 single-deck coach, 7 minibus.
Chassis: 6 Ford Transit, 2 Setra, 1 Volkswagen.
Ops incl: school contracts, private hire.
Livery: White.

HARLEQUIN TRAVEL

77 LANERCOST WAY, IPSWICH IP2 9DP
Tel: 01473 407408
Fax: 01473 407409
E-mail: paul.lewis80@ntlworld.com
Web site: www.harlequintravel-ipswich.co.uk
Dirs: P D Lewis, Mrs L M Lewis.
Fleet: 4 – 1 midibus, 2 midicoach, 1 minibus.
Chassis: 1 Ford Transit, 3 Mercedes.
Ops incl: school contracts, private hire.
Livery: Maroon/White.

IPSWICH BUSES LTD

7 CONSTANTINE ROAD, IPSWICH IP1 2DL
Tel: 01473 344800
Fax: 01473 232062
E-mail: info@ipswichbuses.co.uk
Web site: www.ipswichbuses.co.uk
Chair: Peter Matthews **Man Dir:** Malcolm Robson **Fin Dir:** Julie Dyson
Ops Man: Dean Robbie
Fleet: 86 - 31 double-deck bus, 1 open-top bus, 50 single-deck bus, 4 minibus.
Chassis: 46 Alexander Dennis, 11 DAF, 1 Leyland, 16 Optare, 11 Scania, 1 Volvo.
Bodies: 24 Alexander Dennis, 32 East Lancs, 22 Optare, 1 Plaxton, 1 Roe, 6 Scania.
Ops incl: local bus services, school contracts, excursions & tours, private hire, park & ride.
Livery: Green/Purple.
Ticket System: Ticketer.

LAMBERT'S COACHES (BECCLES) LTD

UNIT 4A, MOOR BUSINESS PARK, BENACRE ROAD, BECCLES NR34 7TQ
Tel: 01502 717579
Fax: 01502 711209
E-mail: lorraine@lambertscoaches.co.uk
Web site: www.lambertscoaches.co.uk
Dirs: Beryl Reade, Lorraine Reade.
Fleet: 9 single-deck coach.
Chassis: 5 DAF, 4 Volvo.
Bodies: 9 Van Hool.
Ops incl: private hire, school contracts.
Livery: White with Blue Signwriting.

LEWIS COACHES

LONDON ROAD INDUSTRIAL ESTATE, BRANDON IP27 0NZ
Tel: 01842 815566
Fax: 01842 815656
E-mail: info@lewiscoaches.co.uk
Web site: www.lewiscoaches.co.uk
Prop: A M Lewis.
Fleet: 17 – 14 single-deck coach, 1 midicoach, 2 minicoach.
Chassis: 1 BMC, 1 Dennis, 4 MAN, 5 Mercedes, 1 Setra, 3 Scania, 2 Volvo.
Ops incl: local bus services, school contracts, excursions & tours, private hire.

MIL-KEN TRAVEL LTD

UNIT 5, KENTFORD SERVICE STATION, BURY ROAD, KENTFORD CB8 7PZ
Tel: 01353 860705
Fax: 01353 863222
E-mail: milken@btconnect.com
Web-site: www.milkentravel.com
Man Dir: Jason Miller
Ops Dir: Jon Miller
Fleet Eng: Ian Martin.
Fleet: 40 - 36 single-deck coach, 2 midicoach, 2 minicoach.
Chassis: 2 LDV, 2 Mercedes, 36 Volvo.
Bodies: 7 Jonckheere, 24 Plaxton, 2 Unvi, 3 Van Hool, 2 Volvo, 2 Other.
Ops incl: school contracts, private hire.
Livery: White with Red, Blue, Yellow.

Suffolk

MULLEYS MOTORWAYS LTD

STOW ROAD, IXWORTH,
BURY ST EDMUNDS IP31 2JB.
Tel: 01359 230234
Fax: 01359 232451
E-mail: enquiries@mulleys.co.uk
Web site: www.mulleys.co.uk
Dir/Co Sec: Jayne D Munson
Man Dir: David J Munson
Ops Man: Daniel Munson.
Fleet: 40 - 6 double-deck bus, 10 single-deck
bus, 15 single-deck coach, 1 double-deck
coach, 1 midicoach, 6 midibus, 1 minibus.
Chassis: 3 BMC, 2 Dennis, 2 Iveco, 6 Leyland,
1 Mercedes, 5 Optare, 9 Scania, 1 Setra, 11 Volvo.
Bodies: 6 Alexander, 3 BMC, 1 Berkhof,
1 Beulas, 3 East Lancs, 1 Indcar, 1 Irizar,
8 Jonckheere, 1 Northern Counties, 5 Optare,
2 Plaxton, 1 Setra, 4 Van Hool, 3 Wrightbus.
Ops incl: local bus services, school contracts,
excursions & tours, private hire, continental
tours.
Livery: Orange/Silver.
Ticket System: Wayfarer.

NIGHTINGALES OF BECCLES LTD

BENACRE ROAD, ELLOUGH, BECCLES
NR34 7TD
Tel: 01502 476048
Web site: www.nightingales-of-beccles.co.uk
Fleet: double-deck bus, midibus, minibus.
Ops incl: school contracts.
A subsidiary of Souls Coaches Ltd *(see Buckinghamshire)*

PERRY'S

OAKTREE LODGE, WARREN LANE,
THE HEATH, WOOLPIT IP30 9RT
Tel: 01359 240291
Prop: M J Perry.
Fleet: 5 midicoach.
Chassis: 1 BMC, 4 Toyota.
Ops incl: school contracts, private hire.
Livery: White with Black lettering.

ROUTESPEK COACH HIRE LTD

3 ELMS CLOSE, EARSHAM, NR BUNGAY
NR35 2TD
Tel/Fax: 01968 893035
Dirs: Mr K Reeve, Mrs R Reeve.
Fleet: 7 single-deck coach.
Chassis: 5 Dennis, 1 Scania, 1 Volvo.
Bodies: 5 Plaxton, 1 UVG, 1 Van Hool.

Ops incl: local bus service, school contracts,
private hire.
Livery: Fawn.

B R SHREEVE & SONS LTD

HADENHAM ROAD, LOWESTOFT
NR33 7NF
Tel: 01502 574669   **Fax:** 01502 532009
E-mail: info@bellecoaches.co.uk
Web site: www.bellecoaches.co.uk
Fleet Name: Belle Coaches.
Dirs: Ken J Shreeve, Robert B Shreeve.
Co Sec: Susan Speed.
Fleet: 43 - 35 single-deck coach, 2 midicoach,
3 minibus, 1 minicoach.
Chassis: 1 DAF, 2 Ford Transit, 5 Mercedes,
10 Scania, 18 Setra, 1 Toyota, 1 Volkswagen,
3 Volvo.
Bodies: 1 Caetano, 1 Duple, 1 Euro, 2 Ford,
3 Lahden, 3 Mercedes, 2 Plaxton, 18 Setra,
9 Van Hool, 1 Other.
Ops incl: local bus services, school contracts,
excursions & tours, private hire, continental
tours.
Livery: Blue.

SQUIRRELL'S COACHES LTD

THE COACH HOUSE, THE CAUSEWAY,
HITCHAM, IPSWICH IP7 7NF
Tel/Fax: 01449 740582
E-mail: info@squirrellscoaches.co.uk
Web site: www.squirrellscoaches.co.uk
Dirs: R J Squirrell, J A Squirrell.
Fleet: 11 - 6 single-deck coach, 2 midibus,
2 midicoach, 1 minicoach.
Chassis: 8 Mercedes, 3 Volvo.
Ops incl: school contracts, private hire.
Livery: Silver/Black/Orange.

STEPHENSONS OF ESSEX LTD

DUDDERY HILL, HAVERHILL
CB9 8DR
Tel: 01440 704583
Fax: 01702 549461
E-mail:
haverhilltraffic@stephensonsofessex.com
Web site: www.stephensonsofessex.com
Man Dir: Bill Hiron
Fin Dir: Lyn Watson.
Fleet: 95 - 49 double-deck bus, 2 single-deck
bus, 2 single-deck coach, 33 midibus, 7 minibus,
2 heritage vehicles.
Chassis: 15 Alexander Dennis, 15 Dennis,
11 Leyland, 7 Optare, 33 Scania, 14 Volvo.
Ops incl: local bus services, school contracts,

private hire, express.
Livery: Green/White.
Ticket System: Ticketer.
See also Essex for main entry

STOWMARKET MINIBUS & COACH HIRE LTD

LINGS FARM, BLACKSMITHS LANE,
FORWARD GREEN, EARL STONHAM
IP14 5ET.
Tel: 01449 711117
Fax: 01449 711977
Dirs: Mrs L J Eustace, S Eustace.
Fleet: 7 minibus.
Chassis: 4 Ford Transit, 2 Iveco, 1 LDV.
Ops incl: local bus services, school contracts,
excursions & tours, private hire.

SUFFOLK NORSE LTD

PHOENIX HOUSE, 3 GODDARD ROAD,
IPSWICH IP1 5NP
Tel: 01473 341500
Web site: www.ncsgrp.co.uk
Fleet Name: Travel Services.
Man Dir: Trevor Whiting.
Fleet: 60 – 3 double-deck bus, 10 single-deck
bus, 21 single-deck coach, 26 minibus.
Chassis: Alexander Dennis, Dennis, Ford
Transit, Iveco, MAN, Mercedes, Renault, Volvo.
Ops incl: local bus services, school contracts.
Livery: White.
Jointly owned by Norse Commercial Services
Group and Suffolk County Council

VENTURER COACHWAYS

UNIT 2, CLOPTON COMMERCIAL PARK,
WOODBRIDGE IP13 6QT
Tel: 01473 737733
Fleet: 14 – 7 double-deck bus, 2 single-deck
bus, 5 single-deck coach.
Ops incl: school contracts, private hire.

WHINCOP'S COACHES

THE GARAGE, PEASENHALL,
SAXMUNDHAM IP17 2HJ
Tel: 01728 660233
Fax: 01728 660156
E-mail: whincop4coaches@btconnect.com
Owner: Paul S Whincop.
Fleet: 8 – 7 single-deck coach, 1 midicoach.
Chassis: 1 Mercedes, 7 Volvo.
Bodies: 2 Jonckheere, 4 Plaxton, 2 Van Hool.
Ops incl: school contracts, excursions &
tours, private hire.

SURREY

ABELLIO LONDON AND SURREY

301 CAMBERWELL NEW ROAD, LONDON
SE5 0TF
Tel: 020 7788 8550
Fax: 020 7788 8593
E-mail: customer.care@abellio.co.uk
Web site: www.abellio.co.uk
Man Dir UK Bus: Alan Pilbeam **Man Dir:**
Tony Wilson **Fin Dir:** Andrew Worboys
Perf Dir: Mark McGuinness **Ops Dir:** Ben
Wakerley **Eng Dir:** Phil Pannell **Commercial
Man:** Alastair Willis **Head of HR:** Kerry
Smith.
Fleet: 684 - 377 double-deck bus, 307 single-
deck bus.
Chassis: 587 Alexander Dennis, 1 Optare,
73 Volvo.
Bodies: 558 Alexander Dennis, 36 Caetano,
16 East Lancs, 1 Optare, 73 Wrightbus.
Ops incl: local bus services, rail replacement,
coach parking.
Livery: London: Red; Surrey: White/Red.

Ticket systems: London: TfL Prestige;
Surrey: Ticketer.

ALLENBY COACH HIRE LTD

415 LIMPSFIELD ROAD, WARLINGHAM
CR6 9HA
Tel: 01883 330095   **Fax:** 01883 818546
E-mail: enquiries@allenbycoachhire.co.uk
Web site: www.allenbycoachhire.co.uk
Fleet: 8 – 5 midicoach, 3 minicoach.
Chassis: 1 Ford Transit, 1 King Long,
5 Mercedes, 1 Toyota.
Ops incl: school contracts, private hire.
Livery: Silver/Maroon.

ARRIVA SOUTHERN COUNTIES

INVICTA HOUSE, ARMSTRONG ROAD,
MAIDSTONE ME15 6TX
Tel: 01622 697000   **Fax:** 01622 697001
Web site: www.arriva.co.uk
Fleet Names: Arriva Kent & Surrey, Arriva

Kent Thameside, Arriva Southend, New
Enterprise Coaches.
Regional Man Dir: Heath Williams
Regional Comm Dir: Kevin Hawkins
Regional Fin Dir: Beverley Lawson
Eng Dir: Tony Ward.
Fleet: 617 – 148 double-deck bus, 116 single-
deck bus, 23 single-deck coach, 313 midibus,
2 midicoach, 14 minibus, 1 open-top bus.
Chassis: 130 Alexander Dennis, 129 DAF,
135 Dennis, 12 Mercedes, 65 Optare, 8 Scania,
1 Transbus, 15 VDL, 110 Volvo, 12 Wrightbus.
Bodies: 129 Alexander Dennis, 74 Alexander,
2 Berkhof, 5 Caetano, 14 East Lancs, 3 Irizar,
9 Mercedes, 4 Northern Counties, 65 Optare,
100 Plaxton, 60 Transbus, 1 Van Hool,
161 Wrightbus.
Ops incl: local bus services, school contracts,
excursions & tours, express, continental tours,
private hire.
Liveries: Arriva UK Bus; TfL Red; White/Red/
Blue (New Enterprise).
Ticket System: Wayfarer 3 & TGX150; TfL
Prestige.

BANSTEAD COACHES LTD

1 SHRUBLAND ROAD, BANSTEAD
SM7 2ES
Tel: 01737 354322
Fax: 01737 371090
E-mail: sales@bansteadcoaches.co.uk
Web site: www.bansteadcoaches.co.uk
Dirs: D C Haynes, C J Haynes, M C Haynes.
Fleet: 19 - 17 single-deck coach, 2 midicoach.
Chassis: 1 Bedford, 2 DAF, 5 Dennis, 2 MAN,
5 Mercedes, 2 Toyota, 2 Volvo.
Bodies: 2 Berkhof, 2 Beulas, 2 Caetano,
5 Mercedes, 6 Plaxton, 2 Van Hool.
Ops incl: school contracts, private hire.
Livery: Pink/White.

BETC LTD

MERSTHAM BUS GARAGE, STATION ROAD
NORTH, MERSTHAM RH1 3ED
Tel: 0844 414 5410
E-mail: info@busesetc.com
Web site: www.busesetc.com
Fleet Name: Buses Excetera.
Dir: Richard Hill **Group Ops Man:** Adam
Smith **Bus Ops Man:** Nigel Thomas
Fleet: 25 – single-deck bus, single-deck bus,
single-deck coach, midibus.
Ops incl: local bus services, school contracts,
private hire.
Livery: Blue/White/Black.

BUSES4U

EAST SURREY RURAL TRANSPORT
PARTNERSHIP, TANDRIDGE DISTRICT
COUNCIL, STATION ROAD EAST, OXTED
RH8 0BT
Tel: 01883 732791
E-mail: rtp@tandridge.gov.uk
Web site: www.buses4u.org.uk
Ops incl: local bus services.

CALL-A-COACH

CAPRI HOUSE, WALTON-ON-THAMES
KT12 2LY
Tel: 01932 223838
Fax: 01932 269109
E-mail: callacoach@aol.com
Owner: Arthur Freakes.
Fleet: 8 – 2 single-deck coach, 2 midicoach,
2 minibus, 2 minicoach.
Chassis: 1 Bova, 1 DAF, 2 LDV, 2Mercedes,
1 Van Hool.
Bodies: 1 Bova, 2 LDV, 2 Mercedes, 1 Onyx,
1 Van Hool.
Ops incl: school contracts, excursions &
tours, private hire.
Livery: White with Lettering.

CHIVERS COACHES LTD

40 LEIGHTON GARDENS, SANDERSTEAD,
SOUTH CROYDON CR2 9DY
Tel: 020 8647 6648
E-mail: enquiries@chiverscoaches.co.uk
Web site: www.chiverscoaches.co.uk
Dirs: Lynne Lucas, Melanie Chivers.
Fleet: 3 - 2 single-deck coach, 1 midicoach
Chassis: 1 Mercedes, 2 Volvo.
Bodies: 2 Van Hool, 1 Other.
Ops Incl: private hire, school contracts.
Livery: White with blue graphics.

CROYDON COACHES UK LTD

120 BEDDINGTON LANE, CROYDON
CR9 4ND
Tel: 020 8665 5561
Fax: 020 8664 8694
E-mail: info@coachesetc.com
Web sites: www.coachesetc.com

Fleet Names: Atbus, Coaches Excetera.
Man Dir: Siri Wong **Tran Man:** Alex Mazza
Comm Man: Paul Fisher
Fleet: double-deck bus, single-deck coach,
midibus, midicoach, minibus.
Ops incl: local bus services, school contracts,
private hire.
Livery: White with logo.
Incorporates Atbus and Stanley Travel

CRUISERS LIMITED

UNIT M, KINGSFIELD BUSINESS CENTRE,
REDHILL RH1 4DP
Tel: 01737 770036   **Fax:** 01737 770046
E-mail: enq@cruisersltd.co.uk
Web site: www.cruisersltd.co.uk
Dir: M J Walter.
Fleet: 39 – 3 single-deck bus, 4 single-deck
coach, 10 midicoach, 22 minibus.
Chassis: Alexander Dennis, Ford Transit,
Iveco, LDV, Mercedes, Peugeot, Renault, Volvo.
Bodies incl: Mercedes, Plaxton.
Ops incl: local bus services, school contracts,
private hire.
Livery: Multi Metallic.
Ticket System: Wayfarer.

EPSOM COACHES GROUP (H R RICHMOND LTD)

ROY RICHMOND WAY, EPSOM KT19 9AF
Tel: 01372 731700
Fax: 01372 731740
E-mail: sales@epsomcoaches.com
Web site: www.epsomcoaches.com
Fleet Names: Epsom Buses, Epsom Coaches,
Quality Line.
Man Dir: S Whiteway **Fin Dir:** N Mandvia
Performance & Planning Dir:
H Barrington **Ch Eng:** S Appleby **Gen Man:**
J Ball **Coach Services Man:** J Fowler **Bus
Services Man:** J Cracknell **Sales Man:**
M Cox **Training Man:** T Torch.
Fleet: 134 - 18 double-deck bus, 24 single-
deck bus, 16 single-deck coach, 26 midibus,
47 minibus, 3 minicoach.
Chassis: 31 Alexander Dennis, 20 Mercedes,
66 Optare, 12 Setra, 1 Transbus, 4 Volvo.
Bodies: 31 Alexander Dennis, 4 Caetano,
16 Mercedes, 66 Optare, 2 Plaxton, 12 Setra,
1 Transbus, 2 Other.
Ops incl: local bus services, excursions &
tours, private hire, express, continental tours.
Livery: Buses: Red (TfL), Silver
(Commercial); **Coaches:** Maroon/Cream,
National Express.
Ticket system: TfL Prestige.
A subsidiary of RATP Dev UK Ltd

FARNHAM COACHES

See Safeguard Coaches

HARDINGS COACHES

WELLWOOD, WELLHOUSE LANE,
BETCHWORTH RH3 7HH
Tel: 01737 842103   **Fax:** 01737 842831
E-mail: sales@bookhardings.com
Web site: www.minibushiresurrey.com
Fleet: 12 - 6 single-deck coach, 5 midicoach,
1 minibus.
Chassis: 4 Mercedes, 1 Optare, 2 Scania,
1 Toyota, 4 Volvo.
Ops incl: private hire.
Livery: Grey.

HARWOOD'S COACHES

51 ELLESMERE ROAD, WEYBRIDGE
KT13 0HW
Tel: 01932 227272
E-mail: gillian.harwood@btinternet.com
Prop: Gillian Harwood.

Fleet: 3 single-deck coach.
Chassis: 3 Volvo.
Bodies: 3 Van Hool.
Ops incl: school contracts, private hire.
Livery: Red/Beige/Brown.

HILLS COACHES OF HERSHAM

155 STATION ROAD, ADDLESTONE
KT15 2AT
Tel: 01932 254795   **Fax:** 01932 222671
E-mail: info@hillscoachesofhersham.com
Web site: www.hillscoachesofhersham.com
Dir: Danny Hill
Fleet: 10 – 8 single-deck coach, 2 midicoach
Chassis: 3 Iveco, 2 Mercedes, 2 Scania,
3 Volvo.
Bodies: 3 Beulas, 2 Mercedes, 2 Scania,
1 Van Hool, 2 Volvo.
Ops incl: school contracts, excursions &
tours, private hire, continental tours.
Livery: Red/White.

JEAKINS LTD

EVERSLEY WAY, THORPE TW20 8RL
Tel: 0845 833 8818
Web site: www.jeakins.com
Dirs: D C & M E Jeakins.
Fleet: 8 – 3 single-deck coach, 2 midicoach,
3 minibus.
Chassis: 2 Ford Transit, 3 Mercedes, 1 Scania,
2 Volvo.
Ops incl: local bus services, private hire.

MAYDAY TRAVEL LTD

ANCHOR BUSINESS PARK, 102
BEDDINGTON LANE, CROYDON CR0 4YX
Tel: 020 8680 5111
Fax: 020 8680 8624
E-mail: info@maydaytravel.co.uk
Web site: www.coachhirelondon.co.uk
Man Dir: K D'Souza.
Fleet: 17 – 1 double-deck bus, 8 single-deck
coach, 1 midicoach, 2 minibus, 5 minicoach.
Chassis: 1 DAF, 1 Dennis, 1 Ford Transit,
1 Iveco, 2 Mercedes, 3 Neoplan, 2 Setra,
6 Toyota.
Ops incl: private hire, excursions & tours,
continental tours.
Livery: Silver/White/Blue.

M&E COACHES

10 MEADOW WAY, ADDLESTONE
KT15 1UF
Tel: 01932 244664
Prop/Gen Man: M W Oram
Sec: Mrs A E Oram.
Fleet: 5 – 3 midicoach, 2 minibus.
Chassis: 1 Ford Transit, 2 Mercedes, 2 Toyota.
Ops incl: school contracts, excursions &
tours, private hire.
Livery: Blue/White.

MERTON COMMUNITY TRANSPORT

WANDLE VALLEY RESOURCE CENTRE,
CHURCH ROAD, MITCHAM CR4 3BE
Tel: 020 8648 1001   **Fax:** 020 8648 9767
E-mail: info@mct.uk.com
Web site: www.mct.uk.com

METROBUS LTD

See West Sussex

PICKERING COACHES

12 HAYSBRIDGE COTTAGES, WHITE
WOOD LANE, SOUTH GODSTONE
RHG 8JN
Tel: 01342 843731   **Fax:** 01342 841535
E-mail: pickeringcoaches@aol.com

Props: R Pickering, Ms D Pickering.
Fleet: 5 single-deck coach.
Chassis: 5 Volvo.
Bodies: 1 Jonckheere, 4 Van Hool.
Ops incl: private hire, school contracts.

REPTON'S COACHES

GUILDFORD ROAD, LITTLE BOOKHAM
KT23 4HB
Tel: 01372 452330
Fax: 01372 456302
E-mail: info@reptonscoaches.com
Web site: www.reptonscoaches.com
Fleet: 8 – 6 single-deck coach, 2 midibus.
Chassis: 1 Alexander Dennis, 1 DAF,
1 Dennis, 1 Van Hool, 4 Volvo.
Ops incl: local bus services, school contracts,
private hire, excursions & tours.
Livery: Blue/Cream.

SAFEGUARD COACHES LTD

GUILDFORD PARK ROAD, GUILDFORD
GU2 7TH
Tel: 01483 561103
Fax: 01483 455865
E-mail: enquiries@safeguardcoaches.co.uk
Web site: www.safeguardcoaches.co.uk
Man Dir: Andrew Halliday
Eng Man: Brett Lambley.
Fleet: 38 - 9 single-deck bus, 27 single-deck
coach, 1 minibus, 1 heritage bus.
Chassis: 1 AEC, 3 Dennis, 3 Mercedes,
8 Optare, 23 Volvo.
Bodies: 1 Burlingham, 1 EVM, 1 Mercedes,
9 Optare, 14 Plaxton, 12 Van Hool.
Ops incl: local bus services, school contracts,
private hire.
Livery: Red/Cream (except minibus: Graphite
Grey).
Ticket System: Wayfarer TGX 150
Incorporating Farnham Coaches

SKINNERS OF OXTED

15 BARROW GREEN ROAD, OXTED
RH8 0NJ
Tel: 01883 713633
Fax: 01883 730079
E-mail: enquiries@skinners.travel
Web site: www.skinners.travel
Partners: Stephen Skinner, Deborah Skinner.
Fleet: 13 - 10 single-deck coach, 2 midicoach,
1 minicoach.
Chassis: 4 Dennis, 2 Mercedes, 7 Setra.
Bodies: 1 Duple, 1 Mercedes, 3 Neoplan,
1 Optare, 7 Setra.
Ops incl: excursions & tours, private hire,
school contracts, continental tours.
Livery: Brown & Cream.
Incorporating Westerham Coaches

STAGECOACH
IN HANTS & SURREY
See Hampshire

SUNRAY TRAVEL LTD
Ceased trading since LRB 2014 went to press.

SUTTON COMMUNITY TRANSPORT

UNIT 3, BROOKMEAD, JESSOPS WAY,
CROYDON CR0 4TS
Tel: 020 8665 1147
Web site: www.suttonct.co.uk
Ch Exec: Vacant **Admin Man:** Sharon Sadler
Dirs: Bob Harris **(Chair)**, Andrew Theobald,
Brian Wilson, Pam Wilson, Tony Pattison
Co Sec: David Mason.
Fleet: 13 minibus.
Chassis: 2 LDV, 10 Mercedes, 1 Volkswagen.
Bodies: 3 LDV, 2 Plaxton, 8 Other.
Ops incl: school contracts, excursions &
tours, private hire.
Livery: White with purple logo.

TGM GROUP LTD
See London & Middlesex

EDWARD THOMAS & SON

442 CHESSINGTON ROAD, EPSOM, SURREY
KT19 9EJ
Tel: 020 8397 4276
Fax: 020 8397 5276
E-mail: edwardthomasandson@btconnect.
com
Web site: www.edwardthomasandson.co.uk
Owner: Ivan Thomas **Ch Eng:** Manny Seager
Ops Man: Neil Seager.
Fleet: 42 - 1 double-deck bus, 9 single-deck
bus, 32 single-deck coach.
Chassis: 5 Leyland, 37 Volvo.
Bodies: 5 Alexander, 4 Jonckheere,
32 Plaxton, 1 Van Hool.
Ops incl: local bus services, school contracts,
private hire.
Livery: Green/Cream.

W H MOTORS
See West Sussex

WESTERHAM COACHES
See Skinners of Oxted

WOKING COMMUNITY TRANSPORT

MOORCROFT, OLD SCHOOL PLACE,
WESTFIELD, WOKING GU22 9LY
Tel: 01483 744800
Fax: 01483 757115
E-mail: enquiries@wokingbustler.co.uk
Web site: www.wokingbustler.org.uk
Fleet Name: Woking Bustler
Dir: Clive Wood **Sec:** Sheila Rapley.
Fleet: 28 minibus.
Ops incl: local bus services, private hire.
Livery: Yellow.

TYNE & WEAR

A & J COACHES OF WASHINGTON

6 SKIRLAW CLOSE, GLEBE VILLAGE,
WASHINGTON NE38 7RE
Tel: 0191 417 2564   **Fax:** 0191 415 4672
E-mail: info@ajcoaches.co.uk
Man Dir: Ian Ashman **Co Sec:** Jean Ashman.
Fleet: 1 single-deck coach.
Chassis: Volvo.
Bodies: Plaxton.
Ops incl: school contracts, private hire.
Livery: White/Blue.

A LINE COACHES

UNIT 1, GREEN LANE INDUSTRIAL ESTATE,
PELAW, GATESHEAD NE10 0UW
Tel/Fax: 0191 495 2424
E-mail: enquiries@a-linecoaches.co.uk
Web site: www.a-linecoaches.co.uk
Partners: David C Annis, Leslie B Annis
Sec: Sheila Reay **Tours Man:** Tony Clark.
Fleet: 9 – 5 single-deck bus, 2 single-deck
coach, 2 midibus.
Chassis: 1 Alexander Dennis, 1 DAF, 1 Dennis,
2 MAN, 3 Optare, 1 Volvo.
Bodies: 1 Alexander Dennis, 1 Caetano,
1 Marshall, 3 Optare, 2 Plaxton, 1 Van Hool.
Ops incl: local bus services, school contracts,
excursions & tours, private hire, continental
tours.
Livery: Red/White.
Ticket System: AES 2000 Datafare.

ALTONA COACH SERVICES LTD

LIDDELL TERRACE, KIBBLESWORTH,
GATESHEAD NE11 0XJ
Tel: 0191 469 2193   **Fax:** 0191 469 3025
Fleet Name: Altona Travel
Dirs: A I Hunter, M Hunter
Ops Man: A I Hunter
Office Man: R Dudding.
Fleet: 6 - 5 single-deck coach, 1 minibus.
Chassis: 1 LDV, 1 Leyland, 2 Scania, 2 Volvo.
Bodies: 1 Jonckheere, 3 Plaxton, 1 Van Hool,
1 Other.
Ops incl: excursions & tours, private hire,
continental tours.
Livery: Two tone Blue and Orange.

ARRIVA NORTH EAST

ADMIRAL WAY, DOXFORD
INTERNATIONAL BUSINESS PARK,
SUNDERLAND SR3 3XP
Tel: 0191 520 4200
Fax: 0191 520 4183
Web site: www.arriva.co.uk
Regional Man Dir: Nigel Featham
Area Man Dir: Nick Knox
Regional Finance Dir: David Cocker
Eng Dir: Gavin Peace **Regional Marketing
& Comms Man:** Chloe Leach O'Connell
Regional HR Partner: Julie Reynolds.
Fleet: 524 - 112 double-deck bus, 215 single-
deck bus, 4 single-deck coach, 116 midibus,
77 minibus.
Chassis: 20 Alexander Dennis, 80 DAF,
80 Dennis, 11 MAN, 77 Optare, 22 Scania,
18 Temsa, 126 VDL, 63 Volvo, 27 Wrightbus.
Bodies: 70 Alexander, 20 Alexander Dennis,
11 Caetano, 13 East Lancs, 79 Optare,
67 Plaxton, 22 Scania, 18 Temsa, 11 Transbus,
221 Wrightbus.
Ops incl: local bus services, school contracts,
private hire.

Livery: Arriva UK Bus.
Ticket System: Wayfarer 3.

ASHLEY COACHES
ROWLANDS GILL COACHES & TAXIS

1 THORNEY VIEW, ROWLANDS GILL,
TYNE & WEAR NE39 1QL
Tel: 01207 543118
E-mail: ashleycoaches@aol.com
Prop: David Murphy.

COACHLINERS OF TYNESIDE

16 BRANDLING COURT, SOUTH SHIELDS
NE34 8PA
Tel/Fax: 0191 427 1515
E-mail: coachliners@yahoo.co.uk
Prop: John Dorothy.
Fleet: 2 midicoach.
Chassis: 2 Mercedes.
Bodies: 2 Plaxton.
Ops incl: school contracts, excursions &
tours, private hire.
Livery: White with red stripes.

HENRY COOPER COACHES

LANE END GARAGE, ANNITSFORD
NE23 7BD
Tel: 0191 250 0260
Fax: 0191 250 1820
E-mail: graham@henrycoopercoaches.com
Web site: www.henrycoopercoaches.com
Partners: Graham, Lily & Pamela Greaves.
Fleet: 9 – 1 double-deck bus, 1 single-deck
bus, 7 single-deck coach.
Chassis: 1 AEC, 1 Leyland, 7 Volvo.
Bodies: 1 Park Royal, 8 Plaxton.

Ops incl: school contracts, private hire.
Livery: Orange/Cream.

JAMES COOPER & SON (TYNESIDE) LTD

BURNSIDE GARAGE, BURRADON ROAD, ANNITSFORD NE23 7BD
Tel: 0191 250 1680
Dirs: J & Mrs M D Cooper.
Fleet: 10 – 1 double-deck bus, 8 single-deck coach, 1 minibus.
Chassis: 1 Ford Transit, 1 Irizar, 5 Scania, 3 Volvo.
Ops incl: school contracts, private hire.

GO NORTH EAST

117 QUEEN STREET, GATESHEAD NE8 2UA
Tel: 0191 420 5050
Fax: 0191 420 0225
E-mail: customerservices@gonortheast.co.uk
Web site: www.simplygo.com
Man Dir: K Carr **Fin Dir:** G C McPherson
Ops Dir: D Curry **Head of Comm:** A Tyldsley **Ch Eng:** K Trewin.
Fleet: 681 - 192 double-deck bus, 379 single-deck bus, 28 single-deck coach, 74 midibus, 8 articulated bus.
Chassis: 6 Alexander Dennis, 16 DAF, 34 Dennis, 79 Mercedes, 87 Optare, 137 Scania, 40 Transbus, 13 VDL, 253 Volvo, 16 Wrightbus.
Bodies: 6 Alexander Dennis, 26 Caetano, 45 East Lancs, 79 Mercedes, 16 Northern Counties, 87 Optare, 45 Plaxton, 41 Scania, 40 Transbus, 296 Wrightbus.
Ops incl: local bus services, school contracts, express.
Livery: Various route brands, National Express.
Ticket System: Vix TP5700.

JIM HUGHES COACHES LTD

WEAR STREET, LOW SOUTHWICK, SUNDERLAND SR5 2BH
Tel: 0191 548 9600
Fax: 0191 549 3728
E-mail: john@jhcoaches.com; sales@jhcoaches.com
Web site: www.jhcoaches.com
Man Dir: John Shipley **Private Hire Man:** Jonathan Brown **Eng:** Trevor Todd.
Fleet: 14 single-deck coach.
Chassis: 8 Mercedes, 6 Volvo.
Bodies: 6 Mercedes, 6 Plaxton, 2 Setra.
Ops incl: school contracts, excursions & tours, private hire, express, continental tours.
Livery: Gold.

KEITH'S COACHES LTD

THE COACH HOUSE, HEXHAM ROAD, BLUCHER, NEWCASTLE-UPON-TYNE NE15 9SN
Tel: 0191 229 0202
Fax: 0191 267 2758
E-mail: sales@keithscoaches.com
Web site: www.keithscoaches.com
Dirs: K Grimes, D Grimes.
Fleet: 14 – 7 single-deck coach, 5 midicoach, 2 minibus.
Chassis: 2 Bova, 1 Dennis, 2 Irisbus, 1 Irizar, 7 Mercedes, 1 Volvo.
Ops incl: school contracts, excursions & tours, private hire.
Livery: White with Blue.

KINGSLEY COACHES LTD

UNIT 20, PENSHAW WAY, PORTOBELLO INDUSTRIAL ESTATE, BIRTLEY DH3 2SA
Tel: 0191 492 1299
Fax: 0191 410 9281
E-mail: accounts@kingsleycoaches.co.uk
Dir: David Kingsley (senior)
Ch Eng: David Kingsley (junior)
Co Sec: Mrs Eileen Kingsley.
Fleet: 27 - 14 double-deck bus, 3 single-deck bus, 1 double-deck coach, 6 single-deck coach, 1 midibus, 2 minibus.
Chassis: 16 Dennis, 1 Iveco, 2 LDV, 2 MAN, 1 Scania, 2 Setra, 3 Volvo.
Ops incl: local bus services, school contracts, excursions & tours, private hire.
Livery: Blue/White.
Ticket System: Wayfarer.

NATIONAL HOLIDAYS

SPRINGFIELD WAY, ANLABY, HULL HU10 7LA
Tel: 01482 572572   **Fax:** 01482 569004
E-mail: info@nationalholidays.com
Web site: www.nationalholidays.com
Man Dir: G Rogers **Ops Man:** A Hutchinson
Transport Man: P Joyce.
Fleet: 130 single-deck coach.
Chassis: 72 Setra, 58 Volvo.
Bodies: 53 Plaxton, 72 Setra, 5 Van Hool.
Ops incl: excursions & tours.
Livery: White & Blue.
A subsidiary company of Shearings Holidays (see Greater Manchester)

PRIORY COACH & BUS LTD

59 CHURCH WAY, NORTH SHIELDS NE29 0AD
Tel/Fax: 0191 257 0283
E-mail: info@priorycoaches.com
Web site: www.priorycoaches.com
Dirs: S Kirkpatrick, P Harris, I Fenwick, L Stewart.
Fleet: 9 - 6 single-deck coach, 1 minibus.
Chassis: 1 DAF, 1 LDV, 1 Mercedes, 6 Volvo.
Bodies: 1 Autobus, 1 Berkhof, 1 Caetano, 1 LDV, 5 Van Hool.
Ops incl: excursions & tours, private hire, school contracts.
Livery: White/Blue vinyls.

STAGECOACH NORTH EAST

WHEATSHEAF, NORTH BRIDGE STREET, SUNDERLAND SR5 1AQ
Tel: 0191 566 0231
Fax: 0191 566 0230
E-mail: northeast.enquiries@stagecoachbus.com
Web site: www.stagecoachbus.com
Fleet Names: Stagecoach in Newcastle, Stagecoach in South Shields, Stagecoach in Sunderland.
Man Dir: Philip Medlicott
Ops Dir: Matthew Cranwell
Eng Dir: Gary Chisholm
Comm Dir: Robin Knight.
Fleet: 473 – 132 double-deck bus, 195 single-deck bus, 146 midibus.
Chassis: 194 Alexander Dennis, 47 Dennis, 5 Leyland, 206 MAN, 17 Scania CNG, 4 Volvo.
Bodies: 79, Alexander, 277 Alexander Dennis, 5 Northern Counties, 112 Transbus.
Ops incl: local bus services, school contracts.
Livery: Stagecoach UK Bus.
Ticket System: ERG TP5000.

THIRLWELL'S COACHES

MILLERS BRIDGE, WHICKHAM BANK, SWALWELL, NEWCASTLE NE16 3BP
Tel: 0191 488 2430
Fax: 0191 488 4940
E-mail: thirlwellcoaches@aol.com
Web site: www.thirlwellcoaches.co.uk
Man Dir: Susan Searl
Dirs: John Thirlwell, Ian Thirlwell **Fleet Engineer:** Ian Thirlwell.
Fleet: 7 – 6 single-deck coach, 1 minibus.
Chassis: 1 Mercedes, 6 Volvo.
Bodies: 1 Mercedes, 6 Plaxton.
Ops incl: excursions & tours, private hire, continental tours.
Livery: Red & Grey.

YOURBUS (DURHAM) LTD

Durham depot closed since LRB 2014 went to press. See Derbyshire for main operation.

Tyne & Wear

Warwickshire

A-LINE COACHES

BRANDON ROAD, BINLEY, COVENTRY
CV3 2JD
Tel: 024 7645 0808
Fax: 024 7645 6434
E-mail: office@a-linecoaches.com
Web site: www.a-linecoaches.com
Dirs: B Haywood, K Prosser.
Fleet: 14 - 2 single-deck bus, 10 single-deck coach, 2 minicoach.
Chassis: 6 Bova, 3 Mercedes, 2 Scania, 3 Volvo.
Ops incl: local bus services, private hire, school contracts.
Livery: White.

CATTERALLS COACHES

74 COVENTRY STREET, SOUTHAM
CV47 0EA
Tel: 01926 813192
Fax: 01926 813915
Recovery: 01926 813192
E-mail: info@travelcatteralls.co.uk
Web site: www.travelcatteralls.co.uk
Dir: Paul Catterall.
Fleet: 25 – 3 double-deck bus, 21 single-deck coach, 1 double-deck coach.
Chassis: 1 Ayats, 1 Irisbus, 4 MAN, 4 Neoplan, 1 Setra, 2 Scania, 12 Volvo.
Ops incl: local bus services, school contracts, excursions & tours, private hire, continental tours.
Livery: Blue, Yellow and White.

CHAPEL END COACHES

WILSON HOUSE, 3 OASTON ROAD,
NUNEATON CV11 6JX
Tel: 024 7635 4588
Fax: 024 7635 6406
E-mail: chapelendcoaches@btconnect.com
Web site: www.chapelendcoaches.co.uk
Man Dir/Trans Man: Ian Wilson
Dir/Sec: Mrs Tracey Wilson.

Fleet: 6 single-deck coaches.
Chassis: 1 Dennis, 1 Mercedes, 4 Volvo.
Ops incl: local bus services, excursions & tours, private hire, continental tours, school contracts.
Livery: White/Red/Black.

CHAUFFEURS OF BIRMINGHAM

CEDAR HOUSE, KINGSBURY ROAD,
MARSTON, SUTTON COLDFIELD B76 0DS
Tel: 01675 475999
Fax: 01675 475909
E-mail: enquiries@c-o-b.co.uk
Web site: www.c-o-b.co.uk
Fleet: 5 – 2 single-deck coach, 1 minibus, 2 minicoach.
Chassis: 1 Mercedes, 2 Setra, 2 Toyota.
Ops incl: excursions & tours, private hire.
Livery: Blue/White.

COACHLEASING

UNIT 4, POOL ROAD, CAMP HILL
INDUSTRIAL ESTATE, NUNEATON
CV10 9AE
Tel: 02476 325515   **Fax:** 02476 373439
E-mail: info@coachleasing.com
Web site: www.coachleasing.com
Fleet: 15 – 1 double-deck bus, 1 single-deck bus, 9 single-deck coach, 1 minibus, 3 minicoach.
Chassis: 2 DAF, 1 LDV, 1 Leyland, 1 MCW, 7 Mercedes, 3 Setra.
Ops incl: school contracts, private hire, excursions & tours.
Livery: Black.

MIKE DE COURCEY TRAVEL LTD
See West Midlands.

MARTIN'S OF TYSOE

20 OXHILL ROAD, MIDDLE TYSOE
CV35 0SX

Tel: 01295 680642
Prop: Martin Thomas.
Fleet: 1 single-deck coach.
Chassis: Scania.
Body: Irizar.

MIDLAND RED COACHES/WHEELS HERITAGE

POSTAL OFFICE, 23 BROAD STREET,
BRINKLOW CV23 0LS
Tel: 07582 532133   **Fax:** 02476 354900
E-mail: buses@wheels.co.uk
Web site: www.wheels.co.uk
Props: Ashley Wakelin, Rob Paramour.
Fleet: vintage vehicles.
Ops incl: private hire, excursions & tours, bus driver experiences.
Livery: Midland Red.

STAGECOACH MIDLANDS

UNIT 7/8, MAIN ROAD, FAR COTTON,
NORTHAMPTON NN4 8ES
Tel: 01604 476060
Fax: 01604 662286
E-mail:
midlands.enquiries@stagecoachbus.com
Web site: www.stagecoachbus.com/
warwickshire
Man Dir: Steve Burd **Eng Dir:** David
Heptinstall **Comm Mgr:** Clive Jones
Marketing Man: Adam Rideout.
Fleet (Warwickshire): 246 - 56 double-deck bus, 9 single-deck bus, 10 double-deck coach, 30 single-deck coach, 109 midibus, 32 minibus.
Chassis: 93 Alexander Dennis, 6 Dennis, 16 MAN, 32 Optare, 9 Scania, 18 Transbus, 10 Van Hool, 46 Volvo.
Ops incl: local bus services, school contracts, private hire, express.
Livery: Stagecoach UK Bus.
Ticket System: ERG.
See also operations in Northamptonshire.

ADAMS TOURS

75 SAND BANK, BLOXWICH, WALSALL
WS3 2HL
Tel: 01922 406469
Fax: 01922 406469
E-mail: enquiries@adamstours.co.uk
Web site: www.adamstours.co.uk
Partners: David Adams, Robert Adams.
Fleet: 6 - 3 single-deck coach, 3 midicoach.
Chassis: 3 DAF, 3 Mercedes.
Bodies: 1 Autobus, 1 Onyx, 1 Plaxton, 4 Van Hool.
Ops incl: private hire, school contracts.
Livery: Cream/Green.

AIRPARKS SERVICES LTD

100 MACKADOWN LANE, BIRMINGHAM
B33 0JD
Tel: 0800 747 777
Fax: 0121 788 0778
E-mail: enquiries@airparks.co.uk
Web site: www.airparks.co.uk
Chief Exec: Howard Dove
Ops Dir: Paul Humphrey
Group Fleet Man: David Rowe
Trans Man: Matt Lawton
Co Sec: Elisabeth Hirlemann.
Fleet: 15 single-deck bus.
Chassis: 3 King Long, 12 MAN.
Bodies: 3 King Long, 9 MCV, 3 Plaxton.
Ops incl: car park to airport shuttles.
Airparks operate at a number of UK airports.

ARRIVA MIDLANDS LTD

4 WESTMORELAND AVENUE,
THURMASTON, LEICESTER LE4 8PH
Tel: 0116 264 0400
Fax: 0116 260 8620
E-mail: myattk.midlands@arriva.co.uk
Web site: www.arriva.co.uk
Regional Man Dir: A Perry **Regional Fin Dir:** J Barlow **Regional Eng Dir:** M Evans
Area Director East: S Mathieson
Area Director West: R Cheveaux.
Fleet: 698 - 168 double-deck bus, 267 single-deck bus, 6 articulated bus, 204 midibus, 53 minibus.
Chassis: 24 Alexander Dennis, 173 DAF, 119 Dennis, 26 Mercedes, 121 Optare, 46 Scania, 6 Transbus, 85 VDL, 98 Volvo.
Bodies: 61 Alexander, 24 Alexander Dennis, 4 Caetano, 46 East Lancs, 1 Marshall, 26 Mercedes, 121 Optare, 110 Plaxton, 42 Scania, 6 Transbus, 257 Wrightbus.
Ops incl: local bus services, school contracts, private hire, express.
Liveries: Arriva; Midland (Red); Wardles (Red/White, Red/Cream).
Ticket System: Wayfarer 150 & 200.

ASTON MANOR COACHES

137 WAINWRIGHT STREET, ASTON,
BIRMINGHAM B6 5TG
Tel: 0121 327 9111
Fax: 0121 328 7222

E-mail: info@astonmanorcoaches.com
Web site: www.astonmanorcoaches.com
Prop: N Ali.
Fleet: 8 – 7 single-deck coach, 1 midicoach.
Chassis: 3 Bova, 1 DAF, 2 King Long, 1 Scania, 1 VDL.
Bodies: 3 Bova, 1 Irizar, 2 King Long, 1 Van Hool, 1 VDL.
Ops incl: school contracts, excursions & tours, private hire.
Livery: Blue.

ATTAIN TRAVEL LTD

ATLAS TRADING ESTATE, BROOKVALE
ROAD, BIRMINGHAM B6 7EX
Tel: 0800 047 6983
Fax: 0121 356 9513
Web site: www.attaintravel.com
Dirs: D Costello, Ms J Mauremoottoo, Ms S Bollard.
Fleet: 30 – 11 single-deck coach, 1 midibus, 1 midicoach, 17 minibus.
Chassis: 1 BMC, 8 Ford, 2 Iveco, 1 LDV, 4 Mercedes, Renault, 11 Scania, 1 Vauxhall, 2 Volkswagen.
Ops incl: private hire.
Livery: Coaches: Red; **Minibuses:** White with Red.

AZIZ COACH SERVICE

9-13 WOODFIELD ROAD, SPARKBROOK,
BIRMINGHAM B12 8TD

Tel: 0121 440 2015
E-mail: aziz_coach_service@hotmail.co.uk
Web site: www.azizcoachhire-birmingham.co.uk
Prop: A Aziz.
Fleet: 14 – 8 single-deck coach, 6 midicoach.
Chassis: 6 Mercedes, 6 Scania, 2 Volvo.
Ops incl: school contracts, private hire, excursions & tours.
Livery: White.

BIRMINGHAM INTERNATIONAL COACHES LTD

10 FORTNUM CLOSE, TILE CROSS, BIRMINGHAM B33 0JT
Tel: 0121 783 4004
Fax: 0121 785 0967
E-mail: info@birminghaminternationalcoaches.co.uk
Web site: www.birminghaminternationalcoaches.co.uk
Dirs: M Watkiss, A Watkiss, N Watkiss.
Fleet: 15 single-deck coach.
Chassis: 7 Bova, 2 Van Hool, 3 VDL, 3 Volvo.
Bodies: 7 Bova, 3 Jonckheere, 2 Van Hool, 3 VDL.
Ops incl: school contracts, excursions & tours, private hire, continental tours.
Livery: Grey.

DEN CANEY COACHES LTD

THE COACH STATION, STONEHOUSE LANE, BARTLEY GREEN, BIRMINGHAM B32 3AH
Tel: 0121 427 2078
Fax: 0121 427 8905
E-mail: enquiry@dencaneycoaches.co.uk
Web site: www.dencaneycoaches.co.uk
Man Dir: D Stevens **Dir:** M Stevens
Ch Eng: A Doggett **Ops Man:** J Clarke
Administrator: Mrs D Johnston.
Fleet: 8 – 6 single-deck coach, 2 midicoach.
Chassis: 2 Toyota, 6 Volvo.
Ops incl: private hire, school contracts.

CENTRAL BUSES

UNIT 14A, TAMEBRIDGE INDUSTRIAL ESTATE, ALDRIDGE ROAD, BIRMINGHAM B42 2TX
Tel: 0121 356 3487
Fax: 0870 199 2923
E-mail: email@centralbuses.com
Web site: www.centralbuses.com
Man Dir: Geoff Cross.
Fleet: 24 – 4 double-deck bus, 20 single-deck bus.
Chassis: 2 AEC Routemaster, 18 Alexander Dennis, 4 Optare.
Ops incl: local bus services, school contracts, rail replacement.
Livery: Red/Grey.
Ticket System: Wayfarer TGX250.

CHAUFFEURS OF BIRMINGHAM
See Warwickshire

CLARIBEL COACHES LTD

10 FORTNUM CLOSE, TILE CROSS, BIRMINGHAM B33 0JT
Tel: 0121 789 7878
Fax: 0121 785 0967
Dirs: M J Watkiss, M Watkiss, A Watkiss, N Watkiss.
Fleet: 27 – 1 double-deck bus, 26 single-deck bus.
Chassis: 1 Alexander Dennis, 3 DAF, 3 Optare, 20 VDL.
Bodies: 1 Alexander Dennis, 1 East Lancs, 3 Optare, 1 Plaxton, 21 Wrightbus.
Ops incl: local bus services, school contracts, private hire.

Livery: Blue/White.
Ticket System: Wayfarer TGX.

COACH CHOICE LTD

HUDLEY HOUSE, 22 HICKMAN ROAD, BILSTON, WOLVERHAMPTON WV14 0QW
Tel: 0845 230 1577
Fax: 0845 230 1579
E-mail: info@coachchoice.co.uk
Web site: www.coachchoice.net
Man Dir: Christopher Evitt.
Fleet: 11 – 1 double-deck coach, 9 single-deck coach, 1 minibus.
Chassis: 1 Irizar, 1 MAN, 2 Neoplan, 2 Scania, 1 Vauxhall, 4 Volvo.
Ops incl: school contracts, excursions & tours, continental tours.
Livery: White with logos.

N N CRESSWELL COACH HIRE LTD
See Worcestershire

MIKE DE COURCEY TRAVEL LTD

ROWLEY DRIVE, COVENTRY CV3 4FG
Tel: 024 7630 2656
Fax: 024 7663 9276
E-mail: buses@decourceytravel.com, coaches@decourceytravel.com
Web site: www.decourceytravel.com
Fleet Name: Travel De Courcey.
Depots at: Coventry, Birmingham.
Man Dir: Mike de Courcey
Co Sec: Adrian de Courcey
Fleet Eng: Neville Collins
Bus Man: Mick Rossiter
Coach Man: John Bowns.
Fleet: 120 - 24 double-deck bus, 48 single-deck bus, 42 single-deck coach, 1 midibus, 5 minibus.
Chassis: 17 Dennis, 1 LDV, 2 Leyland, 29 MAN, 24 Mercedes, 8 Optare, 6 Scania, 33 Volvo.
Bodies: 18 Alexander, 28 Caetano, 4 East Lancs, 3 EVM, 1 Jonckheere, 1 LDV, 4 Marcopolo, 1 Marshall, 27 MCV, 18 Mercedes, 10 Optare, 4 Plaxton, 1 Other.
Ops incl: local bus services, school contracts, excursions & tours, private hire, express.
Livery: White/Blue/Orange; National Express.
Ticket System: Parkeon Wayfarer TGX

DIAMOND BUS LTD

HALLBRIDGE WAY, TIPTON ROAD, TIVIDALE B39 3HW
Tel: 0121 322 2222
E-mail: comments@diamondbuses.com
Web site: www.diamondbuses.com
Fleet Names: Black Diamond, Blue Diamond, Central Connect, Flights Hallmark, Red Diamond.
Depots at: Birmingham, Kidderminster, Redditch, Tividale.
Ops Dir: Chris Blyth
Gen Man: Martin Evans.
Fleet: 257 – 5 double-deck bus, 73 single-deck bus, 11 single-deck coach, 160 midibus, 2 midicoach, 6 minibus.
Chassis: 4 Alexander Dennis, 14 DAF, 116 Dennis, 3 Enterprise, 8 MAN, 5 Mercedes, 44 Optare, 1 Transbus, 2 Volkswagen, 55 Volvo, 5 Wrightbus.
Bodies: 35 Alexander, 4 Alexander Dennis, 1 Bova, 2 Caetano, 4 Mercedes, 44 Optare, 113 Plaxton, 4 Transbus, 1 Volkswagen, 48 Wrightbus, 1 Other.
Ops incl: local bus services.
Liveries: Black, Blue, Red.
Part of Rotala PLC.

ELIZABETHAN & MAJESTIC TRAVEL

HILTON LANE, SHARESHILL, WOLVERHAMPTON WV10 7HU
Tel: 01922 401338
Fax: 01922 710783
E-mail: info@elizabethantravel.co.uk
Web site: www.elizabethantravel.co.uk
Dirs: K Horton, R S Lavender.
Fleet: 13 – 11 single-deck coach, 2 midicoach.
Chassis: 1 Bova, 3 Irisbus, 2 King Long, 2 MAN, 1 Mercedes, 2 Scania, 1 Setra, 1 Volvo.
Ops incl: excursions & tours, private hire.

ENDEAVOUR COACHES LTD

30 PLUME STREET, ASTON, BIRMINGHAM B6 7RT
Tel: 0121 326 4994
Fax: 0121 326 4999
E-mail: enquiries@endeavourcoaches.co.uk
Web site: www.endeavourcoaches.co.uk
Dirs: J Mitchell, G Mitchell, D Mitchell.
Fleet: 17 – 9 single-deck coach, 8 minibus.
Chassis: 1 Bova, 1 DAF, 6 Ford Transit, 2 LDV, 1 MAN, 1 Scania, 2 Van Hool, 3 Volvo.
Ops incl: school contracts, excursions & tours, private hire, continental tours.
Livery: Silver with Mauve/Green.

EUROLINERS
See Worcestershire

EVERGREEN COACHES LTD
THANDI EXPRESS
BOWENS HOLIDAYS

THE COACH STATION, ALMA STREET, SMETHWICK B66 2RL
Tel: 0121 559 1237, 0121 420 2929
Fax: 0121 555 7405
E-mail (Bowens): info@bowensholidays.com
E-mail (Evergreen): sales@evergreencoaches.com
E-mail (Thandi): sales@thandicoaches.com
Web site (Bowens): www.bowensholidays.com
Web site (Evergreen): www.evergreencoaches.co.uk
Web site (Thandi): www.thandiexpress.com
Dir: Ravi Soomal **Gen Man:** Barry Cobb.
Fleet: 39 – 17 double-deck bus, 6 double-deck coach, 11 single-deck coach, 4 midicoach, 1 minibus.
Chassis: 5 DAF, 1 King Long, 6 Mercedes, 2 Neoplan, 5 Scania, 1 Setra, 20 Volvo.
Ops incl: school contracts, private hire, express.
Liveries: Green (Evergreen); Maroon (Thandi).

FLIGHTS HALLMARK LTD
West Midlands operations included in Diamond Bus (see above)
See Bristol and Somerset for Wessex Connect operations in Bristol and Bath
See London & Middlesex for Flights Hallmark operations in London
Part of Rotala PLC

THE GREEN BUS

386 PARK ROAD, HOCKLEY, BIRMINGHAM B18 5ST
Tel: 0845 234 2222 **Fax:** 0845 234 3333
E-mail: hello@thegreenbus.co.uk
Web site: www.thegreenbus.co.uk
Chairman: John Handley **Man Dir:** Ian Mack
Ops Dir: Mick Burkitt **Sales Dir:** Adam Brookes **Head of Finance:** Phil Young.
Fleet: 40 – 38 double-deck bus, 1 single-deck bus, 1 midibus.

West Midlands

Chassis: 5 DAF, 25 Dennis, 10 Volvo.
Bodies: 15 Alexander, 10 Northern Counties, 5 Optare, 10 Plaxton.
Ops incl: local bus services, school contracts, private hire.
Livery: Green.
Services are also operated in Berkshire in conjunction with Reading Buses, and in Surrey with Abellio Surrey

HANSONS BUSES
[icon]
60A HAYES LANE, LYE, STOURBRIDGE
DY9 8RD
Tel: 01384 894020
Fax: 01384 894030
E-mail: info@hansonslocalbus.co.uk
Web site: www.hansonslocalbus.co.uk
Props: M & L Hanson.
Fleet: 26 midibus.
Chassis: 7 Alexander Dennis, 19 Dennis.
Bodies: 3 Alexander, 7 Alexander Dennis, 16 Plaxton.
Ops incl: local bus services.
Livery: Blue/White.

HILLS COACHES LTD
[icons]
CANAL SIDE, HORDERN ROAD,
WOLVERHAMPTON WV6 0HS
Tel: 01902 753770
Fax: 01902 756628
E-mail: enquirydesk@hillscoaches.co.uk
Web site: www.hillscoaches.co.uk
Fleet: 20 – 18 single-deck coach, 2 midicoach.
Chassis: 2 Mercedes, 4 Scania, 2 Setra, 12 Volvo.
Bodies: 1 Autobus, 4 Irizar, 4 Plaxton, 2 Setra, 5 Sunsundegui, 3 Van Hool, 1 Volvo.
Ops incl: private hire, excursions & tours.
Livery: White with Grey.

J R HOLYHEAD INTERNATIONAL
[icons]
32 CROSS STREET, WILLENHALL WV13 1PG
Tel: 01902 607364
Fax: 01902 609772
E-mail: contact@jrholyhead.co.uk
Web site: www.jrholyhead.co.uk
Prop: J R Holyhead.
Fleet: 6 single-deck coach.
Chassis: 1 Bova, 5 Volvo.
Bodies: 1 Bova, 5 Van Hool.
Ops incl: excursions & tours, private hire, express, continental tours.
Livery: White.

JOHNSONS COACH & BUS TRAVEL
[icons]
LIVERIDGE HOUSE, LIVERIDGE HILL,
HENLEY-IN-ARDEN, SOLIHULL B95 5QS
Tel: 01564 797000
Fax: 01564 797050
E-mail: info@johnsonscoaches.co.uk
Web site: www.johnsonscoaches.co.uk
Fleet Names: Countylinks, Excelbus.
Comm Dir: John Johnson
Ops Dir: John Johnson
Dir/Co Sec: Joan Johnson
Ops Man: Steph Payne **Eng Man:** Neville Collins.
Fleet: 81 – 4 double-deck bus, 24 single-deck bus, 37 single-deck coach, 9 midibus, 4 minibus, 3 minicoach.
Chassis: 29 Bova, 1 DAF, 3 Mercedes, 29 Optare, 14 Scania, 4 VDL, 1 Volvo.
Bodies: 1 Alexander, 29 Bova, 1 East Lancs, 1 Ferqui, 3 Irizar, 1 Lahden, 32 Optare, 1 Plaxton, 7 Scania, 1 Unvi, 4 VDL.
Ops incl: local bus services, school contracts, excursions & tours, private hire, express, continental tours.
Livery: Yellow/Blue/White.
Ticket system: Wayfarer TGX150.

JOSEPHS MINI COACHES
See Staffordshire

KEN MILLER TRAVEL
[icons] R24 [icon]
10 CHURCHILL ROAD, SHENSTONE
WS14 0LP
Tel: 01827 60494
Fax: 01827 60494
Recovery: 07976 303951
Web site: www.kenmillertravel.co.uk
Prop: Ken Miller.
Fleet: 4 – 3 single-deck coach, 1 minibus.
Chassis: 3 MAN, 1 Renault.
Ops incl: school contracts, excursions & tours, private hire.
Livery: White with Orange lettering.

KINGSNORTON COACHES
[icons]
COOMBES WHARF, CHANCEL WAY,
HALESOWEN B62 8RP
Tel: 0121 550 8519
Fax: 0121 501 6554
E-mail: info@kingsnortoncoaches.co.uk
Web site: www.kingsnortoncoaches.co.uk
Partners: Richard Egan, Malcolm Stanley.
Fleet: 25 – 1 open top bus, 3 single-deck coach, 2 midicoach, 19 minibus.
Chassis: 2 Iveco, 16 LDV, 1 Leyland, 1 MAN, 2 Mercedes, 3 Volvo.
Ops incl: school contracts, excursions & tours, private hire.
Livery: Red/White.

KINGSWINFORD COACHWAYS LTD
[icons] R24 [icon]
HIGH STREET, PENSNETT, BRIERLEY HILL
DY6 8XB
Tel: 01384 401626
Fax: 01384 401580
Recovery: 07831 148626
Web site: www.kingswinfordcoachways.co.uk
Dir: David Edmunds
Ch Eng: Robert Lamesdale
Sec: Robert Morgan
Advisor: David Moor.
Fleet: 8 - 6 single-deck coach, 1 midicoach, 1 minibus.
Chassis: 1 Ford Transit, 1 Mercedes, 6 Volvo.
Body: 1 Ford, 1 Jonckheere, 5 Plaxton, 1 Van Hool.
Ops incl: school contracts, private hire.
Livery: White/Yellow/Red.

LAKESIDE COACHES LTD
See Shropshire

MAJOR COACHWAYS LTD
[icons]
10 MILFORD CROFT, ROWLEY REGIS
B65 8QD
Tel: 01384 230191
Web site: www.majorcoachways.com
Dir: S Bahia.
Fleet: 9 – 8 single-deck coach, 1 minibus.
Chassis: 1 Mercedes, 5 Scania, 3 Volvo.
Bodies: 1 Crest, 5 Irizar, 3 Plaxton.
Ops incl: school contracts, private hire.
Livery: White with Pink relief.

MEADWAY PRIVATE HIRE LTD
[icons]
28-32 BERKELEY ROAD, HAY MILLS,
BIRMINGHAM B25 8NG
Tel: 0121 773 8389, 8380
Fax: 0121 693 7171
E-mail: meadwaycoaches@btconnect.com
Fleet Name: Meadway Coaches.
Fleet: 7 – 6 single-deck coach, 1 midicoach.
Chassis: 2 Dennis, 2 Mercedes, 2 VDL, 1 Volvo.
Ops incl: private hire, school contracts.
Livery: White/Green.

MIDLAND METRO
See Section 5 – Tram and Bus Rapid Transit Systems.

NASH'S COACHES LTD
[icons]
83 RAGLAN ROAD, SMETHWICK B66 3TT
Tel: 0121 558 0024
Fax: 0121 558 0907
E-mail: info@nashcoaches.co.uk
Web site: www.nashcoaches.co.uk
Dirs: Ian Powell, Miss Linda Powell.
Fleet: 7 – 6 single-deck coach, 1 midicoach.
Chassis: 1 Mercedes, 1 Neoplan, 3 Setra, 1 Volvo.
Bodies: 1 Berkhof, 1 Neoplan, 1 Plaxton, 3 Setra, 1 Van Hool.
Ops incl: school contracts, excursions & tours, private hire, continental tours.
Livery: White/Red/Grey Multi coloured.

NATIONAL EXPRESS LTD
[icons]
MILL LANE, DIGBETH, BIRMINGHAM
B5 6DD
Tel: 08717 818178
E-mail: help@nationalexpress.com
Web site: www.nationalexpress.com
Fleet Names: National Express, Airlinks.
Man Dir: Tom Stables **Service Delivery Dir:** Kevin Gale **HR Dir:** Jennifer Richmond.
Fleet: 190 – 7 single-deck bus, 122 single-deck coach, 16 articulated bus, 41 midibus, 4 minibus.
Chassis: 37 Alexander Dennis, 1 Ford Transit, 29 Mercedes, 37 Scania, 1 Volkswagen, 85 Volvo.
Bodies: 37 Alexander Dennis, 113 Caetano, 4 East Lancs, 1 Ford, 1 Hispano, 26 Mercedes, 1 Plaxton, 5 Transbus, 1 Wrightbus, 1 Other.
Ops incl: express coach services, airport operations.
Livery: Red/White/Blue.
Ticket System: Pre-sale, Wayfarer.

NATIONAL EXPRESS WEST MIDLANDS
[icons]
51 BORDESLEY GREEN, BIRMINGHAM
B9 4BZ
Tel: 0121 254 7200
Fax: 0121 254 7207
E-mail: travelcare@nationalexpress.com
Web site: www.nxbus.co.uk/west-midlands
Man Dir UK Bus: Peter Coates **Fin Dir UK Bus:** Matt Ashley **Comm Dir:** David Bradford **HR Dir:** Madi Pilgrim.
Man Dir National Express Coventry: Peter Power.
Fleet: 1616 – 963 double-deck bus, 21 articulated bus, 544 single-deck bus, 84 midibus, 4 minibus.
Chassis: 286 Alexander Dennis, 20 DAF, 242 Dennis, 118 Mercedes, 3 Optare, 196 Scania, 125 Transbus, 636 Volvo.
Ops incl: local bus services, school contracts, private hire.
Livery: Red/White/Blue.

NEWBURY TRAVEL LTD
[icons]
NEWBURY LANE, OLDBURY B69 1HF
Tel: 0121 552 3262
Fax: 0121 552 0230
E-mail: newburytravel@aol.com
Web site: www.newburytravel.co.uk
Man Dir: David Greenhouse
Ch Eng: Chris Phillips.
Fleet: 11 - 3 single-deck coach, 2 midicoach, 6 minibus.
Chassis: 1 Ford Transit, 1 Iveco, 1 LDV, 5 Mercedes, 3 Volvo.
Ops incl: school contracts, private hire.
Livery: White.

PROSPECT COACHES (WEST) LTD
♿ ⚕ ♨ ❄
81 HIGH STREET, LYE, STOURBRIDGE
DY9 8NG
Tel: 01384 895436
Fax: 01384 898654
E-mail: enquiries@prospectcoaches.co.uk
Web site: www.prospectcoaches.co.uk
Man Dirs: Geoffrey Watts, Roslynd A D
Hadley **Tran Man:** Nathan Hadley
Ops Man: David Price
Garage Man: Martin Hadley.
Fleet: 44 single-deck coach.
Chassis: 32 Alexander Dennis, 2 DAF,
4 King Long, 6 Volvo.
Bodies: 4 King Long, 1 Marcopolo, 39 Plaxton.
Ops incl: school contracts, private hire,
international travel, corporate travel, event
project management.
Livery: Silver with Red/Blue/White stripes.

HARRY SHAW TRAVEL
⚕ ♨ ❄ ✎
MILL HOUSE, MILL LANE, BINLEY,
COVENTRY CV3 2DU
Tel: 024 7645 5544   **Fax:** 024 7663 5684
E-mail: changes@harryshaw.co.uk
Web site: www.harryshaw.co.uk
Fleet: 23 - 22 single-deck coach, 1 midicoach.
Chassis: 5 Bova, 1 MAN, 2 Mercedes,
10 Scania, 1 Van Hool, 3 VDL, 1 Volvo.
Bodies: 5 Bova, 1 Hispano, 8 Irizar,
1 Jonckheere, 2 Lahden, 1 Mercedes, 1 Sitcar,
1 Van Hool, 3 VDL.
Ops incl: excursions & tours, school
contracts, private hire, continental tours.
Livery: Orange.

SILVERLINE LANDFLIGHT LTD
♨ ⚓ ♨ ✎
ARGENT HOUSE, VULCAN ROAD,
SOLIHULL B91 2JY
Tel: 0121 705 5555   **Fax:** 0121 709 0556
E-mail: silverline@landflight.co.uk
Web site: www.landflight.co.uk
Man Dir: M E Breakwell
Ops Dir: R G Knott
Bus Dev Dir: W J Matthews
Eng Man: R J Nowlan.
Fleet: 21 - 5 single-deck coach, 12 midibus,
2 midicoach, 2 minicoach.
Chassis: 5 Alexander Dennis, 2 Mercedes,
3 Optare, 5 Scania, 2 Toyota, 4 Wrightbus.
Bodies: 5 Alexander Dennis, 2 Caetano,
5 Irizar, 5 Optare, 2 Unvi, 4 Wrightbus.
Ops incl: local bus services, private hire,
continental tours.
Livery: Silver/Blue.
Ticket System: Parkeon/ITSO.

SOLUS COACH TRAVEL LTD
See Staffordshire

STAGECOACH MIDLANDS
See Warwickshire

T. N. C. COACHES
Ceased trading since LRB 2014 went to press

TERRYS COACH HIRE
♨ ⚕ ⚓ ❄ R R24 ✎
16 COLLIERY LANE, EXHALL, COVENTRY
CV7 9NW

Tel/Fax/Recovery: 024 7636 2975
E-mail: enquiries@terrys-coaches.co.uk
Web site: www.terrys-coaches.co.uk
Prop: T C Hall **Ops Man:** L Hall
Chief Engs: D Harris, J Hall **Co Sec:** S Hall
Finance: A Hall.
Fleet: 9 – 1 double-deck coach, 8 single-deck
coach.
Chassis: 4 MAN, 3 Neoplan, 2 Volvo.
Bodies: 1 Berkhof, 3 Neoplan, 3 Noge,
2 Plaxton.
Ops incl: school contracts, excursions &
tours, private hire, continental tours.
Livery: Gold/Green Motif.

THANDI EXECUTIVE
♨ ⚓ ❄
LONDON STREET, SMETHWICK B66 2SH
Tel: 0121 565 2002   **Fax:** 0121 558 4703
E-mail: contact@thandicoachesuk.com
Web site: www.thandicoachesuk.com
Fleet: 39 – 2 double-deck bus, 3 double-deck
coach, 25 single-deck coach, 7 midibus,
1 midicoach, 1 minibus.
Chassis: 9 Dennis, 2 Mercedes, 3 Neoplan,
25 Volvo.
Livery: Blue & Yellow.

TRAVEL EXPRESS LTD
30 COTON ROAD, PENN,
WOLVERHAMPTON WV41 5AT
Tel/Fax: 01902 330653
E-mail: kishan.chumber@sky.com
Props: Kishan Chumber, Nirmal Chumber.
Fleet: 18 midibus.
Chassis: 18 Dennis.
Bodies: 9 Alexander, 2 Carlyle, 7 Plaxton.
Ops incl: local bus services.
Ticket System: Wayfarer.

TRAVELSTAR EUROPEAN LTD
♿ ♨ ⚓ ❄
MARLOW STREET, WALSALL WS2 8AQ
Tel: 01922 64/100
Fax: 01922 644402
E-mail: info@travelstareuropean.com
Web site: www.travelstareuropean.com
Fleet: 13 - 12 single-deck coach, 1 minibus.
Chassis: 4 Bova, 1 Volkswagen, 1 VDL, 7 Volvo.
Bodies: 4 Bova, 6 Caetano, 1 VDL, 1 Volvo,
1 Other.
Ops incl: excursions & tours, express, private
hire, continental tours.
Liveries: Silver; National Express.

WEST MIDLANDS SPECIAL NEEDS
TRANSPORT
♿ ⚓
80 PARK ROAD, ASTON, BIRMINGHAM
B6 5PL
Tel: 0121 327 8128   **Fax:** 0121327 9559
E-mail: enquiries@wmsnt.org
Web sites: www.ringandride.org, www.
busservices.wmsnt.org
Fleet Name: Ring and Ride.
Chief Executive: Peter Maggs
Ops Man: Des Rogers.
Fleet: 308 - 41 minibus, 267 minibus.
Chassis: Alexander Dennis, Dennis,
Enterprise, Fiat, Ford Transit, Iveco, LDV,
Optare, Mercedes, Renault, Volkswagen.
Ops incl: local bus services, demand
responsive transport, private hire.

WHITTLE COACH & BUS LTD
See Worcestershire

WICKSONS TRAVEL
♿ ⚓ ♨ ❄ ✎ T
COPPICE ROAD, BROWNHILLS, WALSALL
WS8 7DG
Tel: 01543 372247
Fax: 01543 374271
E-mail: enquiries@wicksons.co.uk
Web site: www.wicksons.co.uk
Dirs: Martin Wickson, Ann Wickson
(Co Sec).
Fleet: 10 – 9 single-deck coach, 1 midicoach.
Chassis: 2 Bova, 1 Mercedes, 1 Temsa, 4 VDL,
2 Van Hool.
Bodies: 1 Berkhof, 2 Bova, 1 Plaxton, 1 Temsa,
2 VDL, 3 Van Hool.
Ops incl: school contracts, excursions &
tours, private hire, continental tours.
Livery: White/Blue/Orange.

WINDSOR-GRAY TRAVEL
♿ ⚓ ❄
WATERY LANE, WEDNESFIELD,
WOLVERHAMPTON WV13 3SU
Tel: 01902 722392
Fax: 01902 722339
E-mail: grahamwgt@hotmail.co.uk
Web site: www.minibushirewolverhampton.
com
Owner: Graham Williams.
Fleet: 2 – 1 midicoach, 1 minicoach.
Chassis: 1 Dennis, 1 Iveco.
Bodies: 1 Duple, 1 Elite.
Ops incl: private hire, excursions & tours.
Livery: Cream/Brown/Orange.

YARDLEY TRAVEL LTD
♨ ⚓ ❄ ✎
68 BERKELEY ROAD EAST, HAY MILLS,
BIRMINGHAM B25 8NP
Tel: 0121 772 3700
Fax: 0121 773 8649
E-mail: info@yardleytravel.co.uk
Web site: www.yardleytravel.co.uk
Dirs: Mr Mohammed Saleem, Mrs Tasneem
Saleem.
Fleet: 1 single-deck coach.
Chassis: Volvo.
Body: Plaxton.
Ops incl: local bus services, school contracts,
excursions & tours, excursions & tours,
private hire.
Livery: White/Yellow/Black.
Business acquired by Aziz Coach Service as
this LRB goes to press.

P & D YORK TRAVEL LLP
⚓ ♨ ⚕ ❄
BROOKDALE HOIUSE, LATHERFORD
CLOSE, FOUR ASHES, WOLVERHAMPTON
WV10 7DY
Tel: 01902 416197
E-mail: info@pd-york-travel.co.uk
Web site: www.pd-yorktravel.com
Props: P J York, D J York.
Fleet: 14 – 11 single-deck coach, 1 midicoach,
2 minibus.
Chassis: 2 Ford Transit, 1 Mercedes, 6 Scania,
3 VDL, 2 Volvo.
Ops incl: excursions & tours, private hire.
Livery: White with Red.

♿	Vehicle suitable for disabled	⚕	Coach(es) with galley facilities	🚌	Vintage Coach(es) available
⚓	Seat belt-fitted Vehicle	✎	Replacement vehicle available	🚐	Open top vehicle(s)
R24	24 hour recovery service	R	Recovery service available	♨	Coaches with toilet facilities
T	Toilet-drop facilities available	❄	Air-conditioned vehicle(s)	🍃 Hybrid Buses	🔥 Gas Buses

ARUN COACHES

71 CURZON AVENUE, HORSHAM
RH12 2LA
Tel: 01403 272999
Fax: 01403 272777
E-mail: hugo@aruncoaches.co.uk
Web site: www.aruncoaches.co.uk
Prop/Ch Eng: H. Miller.
Fleet: 2 single-deck coach.
Chassis: 2 Hestair/Duple.
Bodies: 2 Duple.
Ops incl: private hire.
Livery: Red/Gold.

COMPASS TRAVEL

FARADAY CLOSE, WORTHING BN13 3RB
Tel: 01903 690025
Fax: 01903 690015
E-mail: office@compass-travel.co.uk
Web site: www.compass-travel.co.uk
Man Dir: Chris Chatfield **Eng Dir:**
Malcolm Gallichan **Co Sec:** Roger Cotterell
Ops Man: Andrew McKinnon.
Fleet: 74 – 2 double-deck buses, 15 single-deck bus, 8 single-deck coach, 47 midibus, 2 midicoach.
Chassis: 48 Alexander Dennis, 3 DAF, I Ford Transit, I Mercedes, 13 Optare, 4 Scania, I Volvo, 3 Wrightbus.
Bodies: 48 Alexander Dennis/Plaxton, I Ford, 3 Irizar, 13 Optare, I Sitcar, 4 Van Hool, 3 Wrightbus.
Ops incl: local bus services, school contracts, private hire.
Livery: White/Burgundy.
Ticket System: Wayfarer.

CRAWLEY LUXURY

STEPHENSON WAY, THREE BRIDGES
RH10 1TN
Tel: 01293 521007
Fax: 01293 522450
E-mail: crawleylux@aol.com
Fleet Name: Crawley Luxury Coaches.
Dirs: David Brown, Darren Brown, Gavin Brown **Ops Man:** Stephen Burse.
Fleet: 68 – I single-deck bus, 62 single-deck coach, 4 minibus, I minicoach.
Chassis: I Bedford, 2 Ford Transit, I LDV, 5 Mercedes, 2 Setra, 57 Volvo.
Bodies: I Alexander, 5 Berkhof, 3 Caetano, I Duple, 2 Ford, I LDV, I Mellor, 3 Mercedes, 46 Plaxton, 2 Setra, I Transbus, I Van Hool, I Other.
Ops incl: private hire, school contracts.
Livery: Cream/Green/Grey.

HERITAGE TRAVEL

STAR ROAD, PARTRIDGE GREEN RH13 8RD
Tel: 0800 652 5251
E-mail: info@heritagecoaches.com
Web site: www.heritage-coaches.com
Fleet: 30 - double-deck bus, single-deck bus, single-deck coach, double-deck coach.
Ops incl: school contracts, excursions & tours, private hire.
Livery: Pink/Maroon.
Associated with The Sussex Bus.com

METROBUS LTD

WHEATSTONE CLOSE, CRAWLEY
RH10 9UA
Tel: 01293 449192
Fax: 01293 404281
E-mail: info@metrobus.co.uk
Web site: www.metrobus.co.uk
Chief Operating Officer: Kevin Carey

Fin Dir: Kevin Lavender **Ch Eng:** Les Bishop.
Fleet: 134 - 30 double-deck bus, 50 single-deck bus, 54 midibus.
Chassis: 22 Alexander Dennis, 18 Dennis, 62 Scania, 14 Transbus, 18 Volvo.
Bodies: 22 Alexander Dennis, 12 Caetano, 28 East Lancs, 6 Plaxton, 34 Scania, 14 Transbus, 18 Wrightbus.
Note: London operations and fleet transferred to Go-Ahead London (see London & Middlesex)
Ops incl: local bus services.
Livery: Two Tone Blue.
Ticket Systems: Vix, Wayfarer.
Part of the Go-Ahead Group

PAVILION COACHES
See East Sussex

RICHARDSON TRAVEL LTD

THE COACH DEPOT, PITSHAM LANE,
MIDHURST GU29 9RA
Tel: 01730 813304
Fax: 01730 815985
E-mail: sales@richardson-travel.co.uk
Web site: www.richardson-travel.co.uk
Dir: C Richardson.
Fleet: 14 - 5 double-deck bus, 2 single-deck bus, 6 single-deck coach, I midicoach.
Chassis: I Alexander Dennis, I Dennis, I Mercedes, 11 Volvo.
Bodies: I Alexander Dennis, I Alexander, 3 East Lancs, I Northern Counties, 7 Plaxton, I Wrightbus.
Ops incl: local bus services, school contracts, excursions & tours, private hire, continental tours.
Livery: Blue; **School Buses:** Yellow.

ROADMARK TRAVEL LTD

STOCKBURY HOUSE, CHURCH STREET,
STORRINGTON, PULBOROUGH RH20 4LD
Tel: 01903 741233
Fax: 01903 741232
E-mail: coaches@roadmarktravel.co.uk
Web site: www.roadmarktravel.co.uk
Man Dir: David Coster **Co Sec:** Leslie Anderson.
Fleet: 2 single-deck coach.
Chassis: I DAF Irizar, I Mercedes.
Bodies: I Irizar, I Mercedes.
Ops incl: excursions & tours, continental tours.
Livery: White/Blue.

RUTHERFORDS TRAVEL

BRAMFIELD HOUSE, CHURCH LANE,
EASTERGATE, CHICHESTER PO20 3UZ
Tel: 01243 543673
E-mail: rutherfordstravel@hotmail.co.uk
Web site: www.rutherfordstravel.webeden.co.uk
Owner: George Bell.
Fleet: 12 single-deck coach.
Chassis: 2 Dennis, 8 Leyland, I MAN, I Scania.
Bodies: I Duple, I Noge, 8 Plaxton, 2 Wadham Stringer.
Ops incl: private hire, school contracts.
Livery: White.

SOUTHDOWN PSV LTD

SILVERWOOD, SNOW HILL, COPTHORNE
RH10 3EN
Tel: 01342 719619
Fax: 01342 719617
E-mail: info@southdownpsv.co.uk
Web site: www.southdownpsv.co.uk

Man Dir: Steve Swain **Fin Dir:** Peter Larking
Ops Dir: Gary Wood **Fleet Eng:** Francis Reed.
Fleet: 31 - 7 double-deck bus, 24 single-deck bus.
Chassis: 9 Alexander Dennis, 2 DAF, 12 Dennis, 3 Transbus, 5 Volvo.
Bodies: I Alexander, 5 Alexander Dennis, 5 East Lancs, 17 Plaxton, 3 Transbus.
Ops incl: local bus services, school contracts, private hire.
Livery: Blue/White/Light Green.
Ticket System: Wayfarer TGX.

SOUTHERN TRANSIT

THE OLD CEMENT WORKS, SHOREHAM
ROAD, BEEDING BN44 3TX
Tel/Fax: 01273 464754
E-mail: info@southerntransit.co.uk
Web site: www.southerntransit.co.uk
Prop: N Bird.
Ops incl: private hire, rail replacement.
Fleet: 11 – 5 double-deck bus, I open-top bus, 2 single-deck bus, 2 single-deck coach, I minibus.
Chassis: DAF, Dennis, Leyland, Mercedes, Scania, Volvo.
Ops incl: local bus services, private hire, school contracts, rail replacement, vehicle engineering.
Livery: Red/Cream.

STAGECOACH SOUTH

BUS STATION, SOUTHGATE,
CHICHESTER PO19 8DG
Tel: 0845 121 0190
Fax: 01243 755888
E-mail: south.enquiries@stagecoachbus.com
Web site: www.stagecoach.com/south
Fleet Names: Stagecoach in the South Downs, Stagecoach in Portsmouth.
Man Dir: Andrew Dyer **Eng Dir:** Richard Alexander **Ops Dir:** Tom Bridge
Comm Dir: Mark Turner.
Fleet (Sussex/Portsmouth):
200 – 41 double-deck bus, 91 single-deck bus, 58 midibus, 10 minibus.
Chassis: 130 Alexander Dennis, 16 Dennis, 10 Optare, 20 Scania, 20 Transbus, 4 Volvo.
Bodies: 5 Alexander, 150 Alexander Dennis, 10 Optare, 15 Plaxton, 20 Transbus.
Ops incl: local bus services, school contracts, private hire.
Livery: Stagecoach UK Bus.
Ticket system: Wayfarer.

THE SUSSEX BUS.COM

STAR ROAD, PARTRIDGE GREEN
RH13 8RD
Tel: 01444 246693
E-mail: enquiries@thesussexbus.com
Web site: www.thesussexbus.com
Fleet: 22 – 3 double-deck bus, 3 single-deck bus, 15 midibus.
Chassis: 14 Dennis, 3 VDL, 5 Volvo.
Bodies: 2 Alexander, I East Lancs, 4 Optare, 12 Plaxton, 3 Wright.
Ops incl: local bus services.
Livery: Red.
Associated with Heritage Travel

SUSSEX COACHES

SAILORS CROSS, GREEN STREET, SHIPLEY,
HORSHAM RH13 8PB
Tel: 01403 741976
Fax: 01403 780605
E-mail: info@sussex-coaches.co.uk
Web site: www.sussex-coaches.co.uk

Dir: Samuel Ayling.
Fleet: 18 – 5 double-deck bus, 2 single-deck bus, 8 single-deck coach, 2 double-deck coach, 1 midicoach.
Chassis: DAF, Leyland, Mercedes, Neoplan, Scania, Volvo.
Bodies: Alexander Dennis, Berkhof, Irizar, MCW, Neoplan, Optare, Plaxton, Van Hool.
Ops incl: local bus services, school contracts, private hire.
Livery: Red & Gold.

TGM GROUP LTD
See London & Middlesex

TRAVELSTAR GATWICK
⚿🅰❌
LAKELAND BUSINESS PARK, PARISH LANE, PEASE POTTAGE, CRAWLEY RH10 5NY
Tel: 01293 612583
E-mail: info@travelstargatwick.co.uk
Web site: www.travelstargatwick.co.uk
Dirs: A Grace, Ms M Daubney.
Fleet: 9   5 single-deck coach, 3 midicoach, 1 minibus.
Chassis: 3 Mercedes, 1 Renault, 5 Scania.
Bodies: 2 Irizar, 3 Lahden, 1 Renault, 3 Unvi.
Ops incl: excursions & tours, private hire.
Livery: White with Blue.

TURBOSTYLE COACHES LTD
🅰❌🅰❌
WALLAGE LANE, ROWFANT RH10 4NF
Tel: 01342 719900
Fax: 01342 719901
E-mail: info@turbostylecoaches.co.uk
Web site: www.turbostylecoaches.co.uk
Dirs: P James, Mrs L James.
Fleet: 15 – 11 single-deck coaches, 4 midicoach.
Chassis: 2 Dennis, 4 Mercedes, 6 Scania, 3 Volvo.

Bodies: 6 Irizar, 4 Plaxton, 1 Sitcar, 3 Sunsundegui, 1 Unvi.
Ops incl: school contracts, excursions & tours, private hire.
Liveries: White with Red; Yellow.

VISION TRAVEL INTERNATIONAL LTD
🅰❌🅰❌🅰T
COACH YARD, FULFLOOD ROAD, DUNSBURY BUSINESS PARK, HAVANT PO9 5AX
Tel: 02392 359168
Fax: 02392 361253
E-mail: visiontravels@aol.com
Web site: www.visiontravel.co.uk
Dir: Peter Sharpe **Ops Man:** Paul Donald.
Ops incl: school contracts, excursions & tours, private hire, continental tours.
Livery: Yellow/Red/White.

W H MOTORS LTD
🅰❌🅰❌R24T🅰
KELVIN WAY, CRAWLEY RH10 9SF
Tel: 01293 510220
Fax: 01293 513263
Recovery: 01293 548111
E-mail: sales@wandhgroup.co.uk
Web site: www.wandhgroup.co.uk
Man Dir: G M Heron.
Fleet: 14 – 11 single deck coach, 2 double-deck coach, 1 midicoach.
Chassis: 4 MAN, 1 Toyota, 9 Volvo.
Ops incl: excursions and tours, private hire, continental tours.
Livery: White.

WESTRINGS COACHES LTD
🅰❌🅰❌
46 GRAYDON AVENUE, CHICHESTER PO19 8RG
Tel: 01243 672411

E-mail: westringstravel@hotmail.co.uk
Web site: www.westringscoaches.co.uk
Dir: W J Buckland **Co Sec:** T S West.
Ops incl: school contracts, excursions & tours, private hire.
Livery: Silver/Pink.

WOODS TRAVEL LTD
🅰❌🅰❌🅰
PARK ROAD, BOGNOR REGIS PO21 2PX
Tel: 01243 868080
Fax: 01243 871669
E-mail: info@woodstravel.co.uk
Web site: www.woodstravel.co.uk
Man Dir: R Elsmere **Transport Man:** P Dobson **Excursions:** M Wiseman
Tours: K Elsmere **Co Sec:** T Shaw-Morton.
Fleet: 16 - 14 single-deck coach, 1 midicoach, 1 minibus.
Chassis: 14 DAF, 1 Mercedes, 1 Volkswagen.
Bodies: 14 Bova, 1 Crafter, 1 Sitcar.
Ops incl: school contracts, excursions & tours, private hire, continental tours.
Livery: Red/White/Blue.

WORTHING COACHES
🅰❌🅰❌
117 GEORGE V AVENUE, WORTHING BN11 5SA.
Tel: 01903 505805
Fax: 01903 507285
E-mail: contact@worthing-coaches.co.uk
Web site: www.worthing-coaches.co.uk
Dirs: David Luckett MBE, Steven Luckett, Ian Luckett.
Fleet: See Lucketts Travel.
Ops incl: excursions & tours, express, private hire, continental tours.
Liveries: Red/White/Yellow, National Express. A subsidiary of Lucketts Travel
(See Hampshire)

ANDERSON'S COACHES
🅰❌🅰❌
HOLMFIELD HOUSE, STRANGLANDS LANE, FERRYBRIDGE WF11 8SD
Tel: 01977 552980
Fax: 01977 557823
E-mail: andersonscoaches@yahoo.co.uk
Web site: www.amdersonscoaches.co.uk
Partners: Paul Anderson, Gillian Anderson.
Fleet: 1 single-deck coach.
Chassis: 1 Setra.
Bodies: 1 Setra.
Ops incl: excursions & tours, private hire, continental tours.
Livery: Silver & Salmon.

ARRIVA YORKSHIRE LTD
🅰❌
24 BARNSLEY ROAD, WAKEFIELD WF1 5JX
Tel: 01924 231300
Fax: 01924 200106
Web site: www.arrivabus.co.uk
Regional Man Dir: Nigel Featham
Regional Fin Dir: David Cocker
Eng Dir: Neil Craig
Ops Dir: Colin Newbury **Regional HR Business Partner:** Julie Reynolds
Regional Marketing & Comms Man: Chloe Leach O'Connell.
Fleet: 344 - 163 double-deck bus, 91 single-deck bus, 82 midibus, 8 minibus.
Chassis: 65 Alexander Dennis, 28 DAF, 31 Dennis, 21 Optare, 118 VDL, 81 Volvo.
Bodies: 23 Alexander Dennis, 65 Alexander Dennis, 30 East Lancs, 2 Ikarus, 47 Optare, 48 Plaxton, 129 Wrightbus.
Ops incl: local bus services, school contracts.
Livery: Arriva UK Bus.

B L TRAVEL (YORKSHIRE) LTD
🅰❌🅰❌
3 ACRES, HOYLE MILL ROAD, KINSLEY, PONTEFRACT WF9 5JB
Tel: 01977 610313
Fax: 01977 613999
E-mail: bookings@bltravel.co.uk
Web site: www.bltravelpontefract.co.uk
Dir: Paul Lockwood.
Fleet: 17 - 8 single-deck bus, 3 single-deck coach, 6 minibus.
Chassis: 1 Ford, 3 Mercedes, 5 Optare, 2 VDL, 6 Volvo.
Bodies: 1 Crest, 1 Ford, 1 Mellor, 5 Optare, 1 Plaxton, 1 UVG, 2 Van Hool, 6 Wrightbus.
Ops incl: local bus services, school contracts, excursions & tours, private hire, express.
Livery: Blue/Yellow.

BAILDON MOTORS LTD
See Dalesman Coaches

BRITANNIA TRAVEL
🅰❌🅰❌🅰
BRITANNIA HOUSE, 113 WESTON LANE, OTLEY LS21 2DX
Tel/Fax: 01943 465591
E-mail: Britannia-Travel@tinyworld.co.uk
Web site: www.britannia-travel.com
Props: Antony Broome, Mrs Susan Eastwood.
Fleet: 1 single-deck coach.
Chassis: Setra.
Body: Setra.
Ops incl: private hire.
Livery: Silver.

BROWNS COACHES (SK) LTD
🅰❌🅰❌🅰
OLD FORGE GARAGE, WHITE APRON

STREET, SOUTH KIRKBY, PONTEFRACT WF9 3HQ
Tel: 01977 644777
Fax: 01977 643210
E-mail: sales@brownscoaches.com
Web site: www.brownscoaches.com
Fleet Name: Browns.
Man Dir: Mrs J M Brown
Co Sec: Mrs M Stoppard
Gen Man: A Griffith **Eng Man:** D Brown
Traffic Man: S Covell.
Fleet: 13 - 5 single-deck coach, 4 midicoach, 4 minicoach.
Chassis: 1 Iveco, 1 MAN, 7 Mercedes, 3 Scania, 1 Temsa.
Bodies: 1 Beulas, 1 Indcar, 1 Irizar, 2 Onyx, 2 Scania, 1 Temsa, 4 Unvi, 1 Other.
Ops incl: private hire, school contracts, continental tours.
Livery: White.

CENTRAL GARAGE
🅰
STANSFIELD ROAD, TODMORDEN OL14 5DL
Tel/Fax: 01706 813909
E-mail: centralgaragetod@outlook.com
Web site: ww.central-garage-tod.co.uk
Man Dir: David P Guest **Man:** A J Gledhill.
Fleet: 3 - 1 midibus, 1 minibus, 1 minicoach.
Chassis/bodies: 3 Mercedes.
Ops incl: school contracts, private hire.

CITY TRAVEL (YORKSHIRE) LTD
🅰❌🅰❌
UNIT 1, BOCKING FARM CROSSROADS, KEIGHLEY BD22 9BG
Tel: 01535 275522   **Fax:** 01533 274400
E-mail: enquires@citytraveluk.com

Web site: www.citytraveluk.com
Dir: Graham Town
Fleet: 6 - 4 single-deck coach, 1 midicoach,
1 minibus.
Chassis: 1 DAF, 1 Ford Transit, 2 Irisbus,
1 Mercedes, 1 Volvo.
Ops incl: school contracts, private hire,
excursions & tours.
Livery: Multicoloured.

CLARKSONS HOLIDAYS
See Wilfreda Beehive *(South Yorkshire)*

CT PLUS (YORKSHIRE) CIC
GREENS INDUSTRIAL PARK, CALDER VALE
ROAD, WAKEFIELD WF1 5PF
Tel: 01924 377084
Fax: 01924 365324
E-mail: info@hctgroup.org
Web site: www.hctgroup.org
Ch Exec: Dai Powell **Dep Ch Exec:** Jude
Winter **Ch Fin Off:** John Smart
Ops Dir: Jane Desmond **Performance**
Dir: Jon McColl **Senior Man (Leeds &**
Wakefield): Shirley Wilkinson.
Depots at: Hull, Leeds, Wakefield.
Fleet (West Yorkshire): 89 – 2 double-deck
bus, 69 single-deck bus, 18 minibus.
Chassis: 69 BMC, 1 LDV, 2 Mercedes,
15 Optare, 2 Volvo.
Bodies: 2 Alexander, 69 BMC, 1 LDV,
2 Mellor, 15 Optare.
Ops incl: local bus services, school contracts,
park & ride (Hull).
Liveries: School Buses: Yellow; **Park &**
Ride: Black; **Local Buses:** WYPTE.
A subsidiary of the HCT Group – see also
CT Plus operations in *Bristol, East Riding,*
London & Middlesex and the *Channel Islands.*

DALESMAN COACHES
VICTORIA ROAD, GUISELEY, LEEDS
LS20 8DG
Tel: 01943 870228
E-mail: info@dalesmancoaches.co.uk
Web site: www.dalesmancoaches.co.uk
Dirs: K Hartshorne, Mrs P J Hartshorne
Fleet: 7 – 4 single-deck coach, 3 midicoach.
Chassis: 3 Mercedes, 4 VDL.
Bodies: 3 Unvi, 4 Van Hool.
Ops incl: private hire, excursions & tours,
group travel.
Livery: White/Blue.

DEWHIRST COACHES LTD
TRAVEL TECH HOUSE, THORNCLIFFE
ROAD, BRADFORD BD8 7DD
Tel/Fax: 01274 481208
E-mail: dewhirstcoaches@hotmail.co.uk
Web site: www.dewhirstcoaches.co.uk
Man Dir: S R Dewhirst
Co Sec: Mrs L Dewhirst.
Fleet: 7 - 4 double-deck bus, 3 single-deck
coach.
Chassis: 4 DAF, 1 Scania, 2 Volvo.
Bodies: 1 Alexander, 3 East Lancs, 3 Van Hool.
Ops incl: school contracts, excursions &
tours, private hire.
Livery: Blue/White.

DUNN MOTOR TRACTION LTD
(YOUR BUS)
NEVILLE ROAD, BRADFORD BD4 8TU
Ops incl: express.
See main entry under Derbyshire.

FIRST WEST YORKSHIRE
HUNSLET PARK, DONISTHORPE STREET,
LEEDS LS10 1PL
Tel: 0845 604 5460

Fax: 0113 242 9721
E-mail: contact.us@firstgroup.com
Web site: www.firstgroup.com
Regional Man Dir: Dave Alexander
Man Dir: Paul Matthews (from late 2014).
Fleet: 919 – 504 double-deck bus,
343 single-deck bus, 18 midibus, 20 minibus,
34 articulated bus.
Chassis: 86 BMC, 8 Dennis, 23 Optare,
42 Scania, 760 Volvo.
Bodies: 120 Alexander, 86 BMC, 8 Marshall,
4 Northern Counties, 23 Optare,
678 Wrightbus.
Ops incl: local bus services, school contracts.
Liveries: FirstGroup UK Bus, Metro School
Bus Yellow.
Ticket System: Wayfarer 3.

FOUR SQUARE COACH COMPANY
HOYLE MILL ROAD, KINSLEY,
PONTEFRACT WF9 5JB
Tel: 01977 616398
Fax: 01977 616344
E-mail: foursquarecoachco@btinternet.com
Web site: www.four-square.co.uk
Fleet: 6 – 5 single-deck coach, 1 minibus.
Chassis: 1 DAF, 2 Scania, 3 Volvo.
Bodies: 2 Irizar, 3 Sunsundegui, 1 Other.
Ops incl: private hire, excursion & tours.
Livery: White with Blue/Yellow.

FOURWAY COACHES
FOURWAY'S GARAGE, LOW MILLS, GHYLL
ROYD, GUISELEY, LEEDS LS20 9LT
Tel: 0113 250 5800
Fax: 0113 250 2727
E-mail: fourway@freezone.co.uk
Web site: www.fourwaycoaches.co.uk
Fleet: 31 – 13 single-deck coach, 7 midicoach,
11 minibus.
Chassis: 1 DAF, 1 Ford Transit, 2 Irisbus,
4 Iveco, 8 Mercedes, 1 Optare, 1 Scania,
4 Volkswagen, 9 Volvo.
Ops incl: private hire, excursions & tours.
Livery: White/Multicoloured.

GELDARD'S COACHES LTD
16B ASHFIELD WAY, WHITEHALL ESTATE,
WHITEHALL ROAD, LEEDS
LS12 5JB
Tel: 0113 263 9491
Fax: 0113 231 1447
E-mail: info@geldardscoaches.co.uk
Web site: www.geldardscoaches.co.uk
Fleet: 63 - 54 double-deck bus, 1 single-deck
bus, 8 single-deck coach.
Chassis: 1 AEC, 11 DAF, 32 Dennis, 1 MCW,
7 Scania, 1 VDL, 10 Volvo.
Bodies: 33 Alexander, 1 East Lancs, 1 Ikarus,
2 Irizar, 1 MCW, 7 Northern Counties,
2 Optare, 1 Park Royal, 9 Plaxton, 6 Van Hool.
Ops incl: local bus services, school contracts,
private hire.

J D GODSON
65 STATION ROAD, CROSSGATES
LS15 8DT
Tel: 0113 264 6166
Fax: 0113 390 9669
E-mail: enquiries@godsonscoaches.co.uk
Web site: www.godsonscoaches.co.uk
Man Dir: David Godson.
Fleet: 15 – 2 double-deck bus, 4 single-deck
bus, 8 single-deck coach, 1 midicoach.
Chassis: 1 Bova, 1 DAF, 4 Irisbus, 4 Leyland,
1 Mercedes, 4 Volvo.
Ops incl: local bus services, school contracts,
private hire.
Livery: Red/Beige.

B & J GOULDING LTD
64 THE RIDGEWAY, KNOTTINGLEY
WF11 0JS
Tel: 01977 672265
E-mail: bjgoulding@live.co.uk
Web site: www.bjgoulding.co.uk
Prop: G W Goulding
Fleet: 3 - 1 minicoach, 2 minibus.
Chassis: 1 Ford, 2 Mercedes.
Ops incl: excursions & tours, private hire,
continental tours.
Livery: White with Red/Yellow/Blue.

HALIFAX BUS COMPANY LTD
17A SOUTH PARADE, HALIFAX
HX1 2LY
Tel: 01422 363600
Web site: www.tjwalsh.co.uk
Dirs: N Walsh, V Walsh.
Fleet: 43 minibus.
Chassis: 16 Enterprise, 2 Ford Transit,
14 Iveco, 10 Mercedes, 1 Optare.
Ops incl: local bus services.
Livery: Red.

HALIFAX JOINT COMMITTEE
UNIT 10, THRUM HALL INDUSTRIAL PARK,
ALBERT ROAD, HALIFAX HX2 0DB
Tel: 01422 353330
Prop: A R Blackman.
Fleet: double-deck bus, midibus, heritage
vehicles.
Ops incl: school contracts, private hire.
Livery: Green/Orange.

HUDDERSFIELD BUS COMPANY
See Yorkshire Tiger

HUNTERS COACHES LTD
30 TYNWALD ROAD, MOORTOWN,
LEEDS LS17 5ED
Tel: 0113 239 0034
Fax: 0113 239 0101
E-mail: sales@huntercoaches.co.uk
Web site: www.huntercoaches.co.uk
Dirs: P Hunter, F Healey.
Fleet: 14 – 3 double-deck bus, 1 double-deck
coach, 6 single-deck coach, 2 midicoach,
2 minicoach.
Chassis: 7 King Long, 1 MAN, 2 Mercedes,
4 Scania.
Bodies: 1 Autobus, 3 East Lancs, 1 Irizar,
1 Jonckheere, 7 King Long, 1 Other.
Ops incl: school contracts, private hire,
excursions & tours.
Livery: White/Blue.

INDEPENDENT COACHWAYS LTD
See North Yorkshire

J & B TRAVEL LTD
PICKUP BUSINESS PARK, GRANGEFIELD
ROAD, STANNINGLEY, LEEDS
LS28 6JP
Tel: 0113 258 6870
Fax: 0113 239 0075
E-mail: gill@jandbtravel.co.uk
Web site: www.jandbtravel.co.uk
Fleet: 11 – 5 double-deck bus, 5 single-deck
coach, 1 midicoach.
Chassis: 2 King Long, 1 Irisbus, 1 MCW,
1 Solbus, 6 Volvo.
Bodies: 3 Alexander, 2 King Long, 1 MCW,
1 Northern Counties, 2 Plaxton, 1 Solbus,
1 Sunsundegui.
Ops incl: school contracts, private hire.
Liveries: School Buses: Yellow;
Coaches: White with Blue/Orange.

JACKSONS OF SILSDEN

UNIT 8, RYEFIELD WAY, BELTON ROAD,
SILSDEN, KEIGHLEY BD20 0EF
Tel: 01535 652376   **Fax:** 01535 653300
E-mail: enquiries@jacksonsofsilsden.com
Web site: www.jacksonsofsilsden.com
Fleet: 11 – 3 midibus, 1 midicoach, 7 minibus.
Chassis: 5 LDV, 4 Mercedes, 2 Optare.
Ops incl: local bus services, excursions &
tours, private hire.
Livery: White with Blue.

JAK TRAVEL LTD

368 BRADFORD ROAD, SANDBEDS,
KEIGHLEY BD20 5LY
Tel: 01274 566200
Fax: 01274 566803
E-mail: office@jaktravel.co.uk
Web site: www.jaktravel.co.uk
Dirs: A Bonson, Mrs K Bonson.
Fleet: 5 – 4 single-deck coach, 1 midicoach.
Chassis: 1 Temsa, 4 Volvo.
Bodies: 4 Plaxton, 1 Temsa.
Ops incl: excursions & tours, private hire.
Livery: Blue with Red/White.

K-LINE TRAVEL
See Yorkshire Tiger

A. LYLES & SON

63 COMMONSIDE, BATLEY WF17 6LA
Tel: 01924 464771
Fax: 01924 469267
E-mail: alyles&son@aol.com
Web site: www.alyles-coaches.co.uk
Fleet Names: A Lyles & Son, Longstaff of
Mirfield.
Senior Partner: Terence Lyles
Partner: Howard Lyles.
Fleet: 11 - 1 single-deck bus, 7 single-deck
coach.
Chassis: 3 Bova, 1 DAF, 1 Optare, 4 Van Hool,
2 Volvo.
Bodies: 3 Bova, 1 Northern Counties,
1 Optare, 4 Van Hool, 2 Wrightbus.
Ops incl: local bus services, school contracts,
excursions & tours, private hire, continental
tours.
Liveries: Beige/Brown/Red; Blue (Longstaff).

M TRAVEL LTD

VANGUARD YARD, CARR WOOD ROAD,
CASTLEFORD WF10 4SB
Tel: 01977 553353
Dirs: D Mayes, M Brown.
Fleet: 33 – 24 double-deck bus, 2 single-deck
bus, 2 single-deck coach, 5 midibus.
Chassis: 1 DAF, 18 Dennis, 2 Irisbus,
3 Leyland, 1 MAN, 4 Optare, 1 Scania, 3 Volvo.
Bodies: 14 Alexander, 8 East Lancs, 2 Irisbus,
1 Noge, 1 Northern Counties, 5 Optare,
1 Plaxton, 1 Van Hool.
Ops incl: local bus services, school contracts.
Livery: Green/Yellow/Red/White.

DAVID PALMER COACHES LTD

THE TRAVEL OFFICE, WAKEFIELD ROAD,
NORMANTON WF6 2BT
Tel: 01924 895849   **Fax:** 01924 897750
E-mail: enquiries@glentonpalmer.com
Web site: www.davidpalmercoaches.co.uk
Fleet Name: Glenton Palmer.
A subsidiary of Glenton Holidays

JOHN RIGBY TRAVEL

231 BRADFORD ROAD, BATLEY WF17 6JL
Tel: 01924 669733
Fax: 01924 485151

E-mail: rigbytransport@hotmail.co.uk
Web site: www.johnrigbytravel.co.uk
Prop: John Rigby.
Fleet: 7 - 5 single-deck coach, 1 midicoach,
1 minicoach.
Chassis: 1 DAF, 1 Dennis, 2 MAN,
1 Mercedes, 1 Van Hool, 1 Volvo.
Bodies: 2 Caetano, 1 Marcopolo, 1 Mercedes,
1 Plaxton, 1 Van Hool, 1 Volvo.
Ops incl: private hire, school contracts.
Livery: White.

ROLLINSON SAFEWAY LTD

RSL HOUSE, 65 HALL LANE, LEEDS
LS12 1PQ
Tel: 0113 228 2222
Fax: 0113 228 2230
E-mail: info@doortoplane.com
Web site: www.rollinson.co.uk
Fleet Name: Air-Line Connections.
Man Dir: Paul Rollinson **Dir:** Peter Rollinson
Contracts Man: M J Joyce.
Fleet: 72 minibus
Ops incl: private hire, school contracts.
Liveries: Brown/Gold, White with Blue/Red.

ROSS TRAVEL GROUP

THE GARAGE, ALLISON STREET,
FEATHERSTONE WF7 5BL
Tel: 01977 791738   **Fax:** 01977 690109
E-mail: info@rosstravelgroup.co.uk
Web Site: www.rosstravelgroup.co.uk
Partners: Peter Ross, Mary Ross **Ops Man:**
Andrew Stirling **Ch Eng:** Stephen Ross.
Fleet: 18 - 10 single-deck bus, 5 single-deck
coach, 3 midicoach.
Chassis: 2 Alexander Dennis, 2 Bova,
5 Mercedes, 5 Optare, 2 Scania, 2 Volvo.
Bodies: 3 Alexander Dennis, 2 Bova,
5 Optare, 3 Plaxton, 2 Sitcar, 2 Van Hool,
1 Volvo.
Ops incl: local bus services, school contracts,
excursions & tours, private hire, continental
tours.
Livery: Buses: Blue/White; **Coaches:** Red/
White/Silver.
Ticket System: Ticketer.

SAFEWAY COACHES LTD

ALEXANDRA ROAD, BATLEY WF17 6JA
Tel: 01924 472521
Web site: www.safewaycoaches.com
Fleet: 16 – 7 single-deck coach, 4 midicoach,
4 minibus, 1 minicoach.
Chassis: 1 DAF, 2 LDV, 6 Mercedes, 1 Setra,
6 Volvo.
Ops incl: school contracts, excursions &
tours, private hire.
Liveries: White with Grey; Yellow.

SANDLA TRANSPORT SERVICES
Ceased trading since LRB 2014 went to press

SHEARINGS HOLIDAYS
MILL LANE, NORMANTON WF6 1RF
Tel: 01977 603088   **Fax:** 01977 603114
Ops Man: Martin Guy.
See Shearings Holidays *(Greater Manchester)*

STAR COACHES

25 TALBOT STREET, BATLEY WF17 5AW
Tel: 01924 477111
E-mail: info@star-coaches.com
Web site: www.star-coaches.com
Fleet: 12 – 3 single-deck coach, 5 midicoach,
4 minibus.
Chassis: 9 Mercedes, 3 Volvo.
Ops incl: school contracts, excursions &
tours, private hire.
Livery: Blue.

STAR TRAVEL COACH HOLIDAYS

29 QUEEN STREET, HORBURY, WAKEFIELD
WF4 6LP
Tel: 01924 261166
Fax: 01924 277194
E-mail: info@startravelcoachholidays.co.uk
Web site: www.startravelcoachholidays.co.uk
Dirs: K Thorpe, Mrs D Thorpe.
Fleet: 7 – 3 single-deck coach, 2 midibus,
1 minibus, 1 minicoach.
Chassis: 2 Mercedes, 1 Neoplan, 1 Optare,
1 Setra, 2 Volvo.
Ops incl: local bus services, excursions &
tours, private hire.
Liveries: Buses: Red & White; **Coaches:**
Maroon.

STEELS LUXURY COACHES LTD

61A MAIN STREET, ADDINGHAM LS29 0PD
Tel: 01943 830206
Fax: 01943 831499
E-mail: info@steelscoaches.co.uk
Web site: www.steelscoaches.co.uk
Dir: T Steel **Transport Man:** M Steel
Co Sec: Mrs J Steel.
Fleet: 4 - 1 single-deck coach, 1 midicoach,
1 minibus, 1 minicoach.
Chassis: 3 Mercedes, 1 Volvo.
Bodies: 2 EVM, 1 Plaxton, 1 Unvi.
Ops incl: excursions & tours, private hire,
school contracts.
Livery: White/Red/Black.

STEVENSONS TRAVEL

THE WILLOWS, LIDGATE CRESCENT,
SOUTH KIRKBY, PONTEFRACT WF9 3NR
Tel: 01977 645060
E-mail: stevensonstravel@hotmail.co.uk
Prop: Ricky Stevenson.
Fleet: 7 minibus.
Chassis: 2 Ford, 4 Ford Transit, 1 LDV.
Ops incl: school contracts, excursions &
tours, private hire.

E STOTT & SONS LTD

COLNE VALE GARAGE, OFF SAVILE STREET,
MILNSBRIDGE, HUDDERSFIELD HD3 4PG
Tel: 01484 460463
Fax: 01484 461463
E-mail: info@stottscoaches.co.uk
Web site: www.stottscoaches.co.uk
Dirs: Mark Stott, Carl Stott
Fleet: 39 - 15 single-deck coach, 6 midibus,
1 midicoach, 17 minibus.
Chassis: 6 Dennis, 5 Mercedes, 13 Optare,
15 Volvo.
Bodies: 1 Alexander, 4 Caetano, 1 Ferqui,
13 Optare, 16 Plaxton, 1 Reeve Burgess,
1 Sunsundegui, 1 Van Hool, 1 Other.
Ops incl: local bus services, school contracts,
private hire, express.
Liveries: White with Red/Black/Silver; Yellow
(School Buses); National Express.
Ticket System: Wayfarer 3.

STRINGERS PONTEFRACT MOTORWAYS

102 SOUTHGATE, PONTEFRACT WF8 1PN
Tel: 01977 600205
Fax: 01977 704178
E-mail: enquires@stringerscoaches.co.uk
Web: www.stringerscoaches.co.uk
Prop: Mark G Stringer
Ops Man: Mark E Stringer **Co Sec:** Sonia
Stringer **Ch Eng:** Chris Palmer.
Fleet: 9 – 5 single-deck bus, 3 single-deck
coach, 1 midicoach.
Chassis: 5 Alexander Dennis, 1 Bova,
1 Mercedes, 2 Volvo.

Bodies: 5 Alexander Dennis, I Bova,
2 Jonckheere, I Mercedes.
Ops incl: local bus service, school contracts,
excursions & tours, private hire.
Livery: Black/White/Red.
Ticket system: Ticketer.

TETLEYS MOTOR SERVICES LTD
76 GOODMAN STREET, LEEDS
LS10 INY
Tel: 0113 276 2276
Fax: 0113 276 2277
E-mail: sales@tetleyscoaches.co.uk
Web site: www.tetleyscoaches.co.uk
Dir: Ian Tetley **Co Sec:** Angela Tetley
Ch Eng: David Leach
Gen Man: David Venner.
Fleet: 35 – 5 double-deck bus, 7 single-deck
bus, 19 single-deck coach, 3 midicoach,
I minibus.
Chassis: 6 BMC, I DAF, I Dennis, 2 Irisbus,
3 Mercedes, I Optare, I Renault, I Scania,
19 Volvo.
Ops incl: school contracts, private hire,
express.
Liveries: Blue lettering on White; Yellow
(School Buses).

TLC TRAVEL LTD
7 LINTON STREET, BRADFORD
BD4 7EZ
Tel: 01274 727811
Fax: 01274 723640
E-mail: enquiries@tlctravelltd.co.uk
Web site: www.tlctravelltd.co.uk
Man Dir: P Lambert.
Fleet: 52 - 12 midibus, 40 minibus.
Chassis: 12 Alexander Dennis, I Mercedes,
39 Optare.
Ops incl: local bus services.
Livery: Blue/White.

TRANSDEV KEIGHLEY & DISTRICT
CAVENDISH HOUSE, 91-3 CAVENDISH
STREET, KEIGHLEY BD21 3DG
Tel: 01535 603284   **Fax:** 01535 610065
E-mail: info@keighleyanddistrict.co.uk
Web site: www.keighleybus.co.uk
Fleet Names: Mainline, The Shuttle,
The Zone.
Man Dir: Russell Revill **Reg Business
Development Dir:** John Threlfall.
Fleet: 113 - 20 double-deck bus, 84 single-
deck bus, 9 midibus.
Chassis: 19 BMC, I Dennis, 8 Leyland,
8 Transbus, 77 Volvo.
Bodies: 16 BMC, 12 Northern Counties,
9 Plaxton, 8 Transbus, 65 Wrightbus.
Ops incl: local bus services, school contracts.
Liveries: Buses: Blue/White, Blue/Red;
School Buses: Yellow.

TRAVEL EUROPE
15 PARKINSON CLOSE, EASTMOOR,
WAKEFIELD WF1 4NR
Tel: 07901 914899
Prop: G R Evans.
Fleet: 3 single-deck coach.
Chassis/Bodies: 3 Setra.

TWIN VALLEY COACHES
INDUSTRIAL ROAD, SOWERBY BRIDGE
HX6 2RA
Tel/Fax: 01422 833358
E-mail: twinvalleycoaches@talktalkbusiness.
net
Web site: www.halifaxcoachhire.co.uk
Dirs: D Pilling, E Pilling.
Fleet: 5 - 2 single-deck coach, I midicoach,
2 minibus.
Chassis: 2 LDV, 2 Mercedes, I Volvo.
Ops incl: private hire, school contracts.
Livery: Green/White.

WELSH'S COACHES LTD
FIELD LANE, UPTON, PONTEFRACT
WF9 IBH
Tel: 01977 643873
Fax: 01977 648143
E-mail: info@welshscoaches.com
Web site: www.welshscoaches.co.uk
Man Dir: John Welsh **Co Sec:** Judy Welsh.
Fleet: 8 – 5 single-deck coach, I midicoach,
2 minicoach.
Chassis: I BMC, 2 Mercedes, 5 Setra.
Bodies: I Autobus, I BMC, I Mercedes,
5 Setra.
Ops incl: excursions & tours, private hire,
continental tours.
Livery: Green/White/Red.

YORKSHIRE TIGER LTD
UNIT G10, LOWFIELDS BUSINESS PARK,
ELLAND HX5 9HD
Tel: 0843 289 5135
E-mail: help@yorkshiretiger.co.uk
Web site: www.yorkshiretiger.co.uk
Man Dir: Nigel Featham
Fin Dir: David Cocker
Gen Man: Steve Ottley
Comm Man: Michael Moore.
Fleet: 131 – 11 double-deck bus, 44 single-
deck bus, 29 midibus, 47 minibus.
Chassis: 3 Alexander Dennis, 12 DAF,
17 Dennis, 2 Leyland, 5 MAN, 57 Optare,
15 Scania, 2 VDL.
Bodies: 9 Alexander, I Caetano, 10 East
Lancs, I Ikarus, I Leyland, 13 MCV, 4 Marshall,
I Northern Counties, 57 Optare, 9 Plaxton,
13 Scania, 13 Wrightbus.
Ops incl: local bus services, school contracts.
Livery: Orange.
Incorporates Huddersfield Bus Company,
K-Line Travel, White Rose Bus Company
A subsidiary of Arriva.

WILTSHIRE, SWINDON

AD-RAINS OF BRINKWORTH
THE COACH YARD, THE COMMON,
BRINKWORTH SN15 5DX
Tel: 01666 510874
Recovery: 07831 303295
E-mail: enquiries@adrainscoaches.co.uk
Web site: www.adrainscoaches.com
Prop: Adrian Griffiths **Ops Man:** Colin Minchin.
Fleet: 25 – I single-deck bus, 8 single-deck
coach, 7 midibus, 4 midicoach, 5 minibus.
Chassis: 3 Bedford, 5 Dennis, 2 LDV,
I Leyland, 6 Mercedes, 2 Optare, 3 Scania,
3 Volvo.
Ops incl: local bus services, school contracts,
private hire.
Livery: White/Blue/Yellow.
Ticket system: Wayfarer.

ANDREW JAMES QUALITY TRAVEL
(ANDYBUS AND COACH LTD)
UNIT 6, WHITEWALLS, EASTON GREY,
MALMESBURY SN16 0RD
Tel: 01666 817364   **Fax:** 01666 825651
Recovery: 07740 88710
E-mail: ajcoaches@andrew-james.co.uk
Web site: www.andrew-james.co.uk
Dir: Andrew James.
Fleet: 21 – 9 single-deck coach, 2 single-deck
bus, 4 midibus, I heritage vehicle.
Chassis: I Alexander Dennis, I Bedford,
3 Bova, 4 Dennis, I MAN, I Mercedes,
4 Optare, 2 VDL, I Volkswagen.
Bodies: 3 Bova, I Duple, I Excel, I Ikarus,
2 Jonckheere, I Marshall, 5 Optare, 3 Plaxton,
2 VDL, I Volkswagen.

Ops incl: school contracts, private hire.
Liveries: Bus - Cream/Orange; **Coach** -
Yellow/Black.
Ticket System: Wayfarer.

APL TRAVEL LTD
PEAR TREE COTTAGE, CRUDWELL
SN16 9ES
Tel: 01666 577774
E-mail: info@apltravelltd.co.uk
Web site: www.apltravelltd.co.uk
Dirs: Alan Legg, Shane Legg, Elizabeth Legg.
Fleet: 21 - 3 single-deck bus, 7 single-deck
coach, 6 midibus, I midicoach, 4 minibus.
Chassis: I Bova, 6 Dennis, I Leyland, 2 MAN,
4 Mercedes, 5 Optare, 2 Volvo.
Bodies: I Autobus, 2 Berkhof, I Bova,
I Duple, 2 Ikarus, 2 Jonckheere, I Marshall,
5 Optare, 6 Plaxton.
Ops incl: local bus services, school contracts,
excursions & tours, private hire.
Livery: White with logos.
Ticket System: Wayfarer.

ASSISI TRAVEL LTD
I OLD SARUM COTTAGES, THE PORTWAY,
OLD SARUM, SALISBURY SP4 6BY
Tel: 01722 415181
Fax: 01722 341724
E-mail: assisi@hotmail.co.uk
Web site: www.salisburycoaches.co.uk
Dir: Kevin Tedd.
Fleet: 16 – 8 single-deck coach, 5 midicoach,
2 minibus, I minicoach.
Chassis: I Dennis, 2 LDV, 6 Mercedes,

I Temsa, 6 Volvo.
Livery: White with Red/Blue.

BARNES COACHES
WOODSIDE ROAD, SOUTH MARSTON
BUSINESS PARK, SWINDON SN3 4AQ
Tel: 01793 821303
Fax: 01793 828486
E-mail: travel@barnescoaches.co.uk
Web site: www.barnescoaches.co.uk
Dirs: L T Barnes, M T Barnes, L E Barnes.
Fleet: 31 – 2 double-deck coach, 27 single-
deck coach, 2 minicoach.
Chassis: 11 Bova, I Ford Transit, I Mercedes,
2 Van Hool, 2 VDL, 12 Volvo.
Bodies: 11 Bova, I East Lancs, I Ford,
3 Jonckheere, I Mercedes, I Optare,
9 Van Hool, 2 VDL.
Ops incl: local bus services, excursions
& tours, school contracts, private hire,
continental tours
Livery: Mint Green.

BEELINE (R & R) COACHES LTD
WARMINSTER BUSINESS PARK, FURNAX
LANE, WARMINSTER BA12 8PE
Tel: 01985 213503   **Fax:** 01985 213922
E-mail: markhayball@beelinecoaches.co.uk
Web site: www.beelinecoaches.co.uk
Dirs: Mark Hayball, Andrew Hayball
Gen Man: Noel Ennis.
Fleet: 36 – 16 single-deck coach, 7 midibus,
6 midicoach, 7 minibus.
Chassis: 6 LDV, 13 Mercedes, I Renault,
16 Volvo.

Bodies: 1 Autobus, 1 Berkhof, 4 Caetano, 1 Jonckheere, 6 LDV, 1 Mellor, 2 Noone Turas, 11 Plaxton, 1 Transbus, 8 Van Hool.
Ops incl: local bus services, school contracts, excursions & tours, private hire.
Livery: White.
Ticket system: Setright.

BETTER MOTORING SERVICES
♿ ❋
104a SWINDON ROAD, STRATTON
ST MARGARET, SWINDON SN3 4PT
Tel: 01793 823747
Fax: 01793 831898
E-mail: bmscoaches@btconnect.com
Web site: www.bmscoaches.co.uk
Fleet Name: BMS Coaches.
Prop: D G Miles **Fleet Eng:** M J Hopkins
Sec: Mrs M Mulhern.
Fleet: 10 - 8 midicoach, 2 minicoach.
Chassis: 2 Ford, 8 Mercedes.
Bodies: 2 Autobus, 2 Esker, 2 Mellor, 2 Optare, 2 Other.
Ops incl: school contracts, excursions & tours, private hire, continental tours.
Livery: Coffee/Cream.

BODMAN COACHES/WILTSHIRE BUSES
Ceased trading since LRB 2014 went to press

CALNE TRAVEL
♿ 🚌 ❋
11 WESSINGTON AVENUE, CALNE
SN11 9RR
Tel: 01249 821821
Fax: 01249 821222
E-mail: customercare@calnetravel.co.uk
Web site: www.calnetravel.co.uk
Prop: K Witte.
Fleet: 15 – 12 single-deck coach, 2 midibus, 1 midicoach.
Chassis: 2 Ayats, 6 Dennis, 1 Leyland, 1 Mercedes, 1 Scania, 1 Transbus, 3 Volvo.
Ops incl: local bus services, school contracts, private hire.
Livery: White with Red/Blue lettering.

CHANDLERS COACH TRAVEL
♿ 🚌 🍴 ❋ 🅃
158 CHEMICAL ROAD, WEST WILTS
TRADING ESTATE, WESTBURY BA13 4JN
Tel: 01373 824500
Fax: 01373 824300
E-mail: info@chandlerscoach.co.uk
Web site: www.chandlerscoach.co.uk
Prop: Margaret l'Anson **Operations:** Christopher l'Anson **Tours:** Andy Stevens.
Fleet: 11 single-deck coach.
Chassis: 1 Alexander Dennis, 4 Bova, 3 MAN, 3 Volvo.
Bodies: 4 Bova, 2 Caetano, 2 Jonckheere, 2 Van Hool, 1 Volvo.
Ops incl: school contracts, excursions & tours, private hire, continental tours.
Livery: Burgundy & Gold.

COACHSTYLE LTD
♿ 🚌 ❋ ❋ ⚒
HORSDOWN GARAGE, NETTLETON,
CHIPPENHAM SN14 7LN
Tel/Fax: 01249 782224
E-mail: mail@coachstyle.ltd.uk
Web site: www.coachstyle.ltd.uk
Owners: Andrew Jones, Mrs A L Jones.
Fleet: 19 - 9 single-deck coach, 10 midibus.
Chassis: 2 Dennis, 1 Mercedes, 7 Optare, 9 Volvo.
Bodies: 1 Berkhof, 5 Jonckheere, 1 Marshall, 7 Optare, 5 Plaxton.
Ops incl: local bus services, school contracts, excursions & tours, private hire, continental tours.
Livery: White with Purple.

DANGERFIELDS TRAVEL LTD
♿ ❋
CENTRAL TRADING ESTATE, SIGNAL WAY,
SWINDON SN3 1PD
Tel: 01793 534445
Fax: 01793 531648
E-mail: danger3303@aol.com
Web site: www.dangerfields.co.uk
Fleet: 5 minibus.
Chassis: 2 LDV, 3 Mercedes.
Ops incl: private hire.
Livery: Gold/Black.

ELLISON'S COACHES LLP
♿ 🚌 ❋ ❋
THE GARAGE, HIGH ROAD, ASHTON
KEYNES, SWINDON SN6 6NX
Tel: 01285 861224
Fax: 01285 862115
E-mail: sales@ellisonscoaches.co.uk
Web site: www.ellisonscoaches.co.uk
Dirs: Alan Ellison, David Ellison, Trevor Ellison, Barry Ellison.
Fleet: 20 single-deck coach.
Chassis: 1 Autosan, 1 BMC, 4 Dennis, 2 Mercedes, 12 Neoplan.
Ops incl: school contracts, private hire.
Livery: White/Green/Red.

FARESAVER BUSES
♿ ♿ ❋
THE COACH YARD, VINCIENTS ROAD,
BUMPERS FARM INDUSTRIAL ESTATE,
CHIPPENHAM SN14 6QA
Tel: 01249 444444
Fax: 01249 448844
E-mail: enquiries@faresaver.co.uk
Web site: www.faresaver.co.uk
Prop: J V Pickford **Ops Man:** D J Pickford
Tran Man: D Beard **Ch Eng:** J M Pickford.
Fleet: 76 - 18 single-deck bus, 53 midibus, 2 midicoach, 3 minibus.
Chassis: 1 Alexander Dennis, 13 Dennis, 18 MAN, 29 Mercedes, 13 Optare.
Bodies: 2 Alexander, 1 Alexander Dennis, 3 Caetano, 8 Marshall, 17 MCV, 14 Optare, 27 Plaxton, 1 Reeve Burgess, 1 Transbus, 1 Wrightbus, 1 Other.
Ops incl: local bus services, school contracts.
Liveries: Purple/Silver.
Ticket System: Ticketer.

GO SOUTH COAST LTD
♿ 🚌 ▭ ♿ ❋
TOWNGATE HOUSE, 2-8 PARKSTONE
ROAD, POOLE BH15 2PR
Tel: 01202 680888
Fax: 01202 670244
E-mail: talk2us@salisburyreds.co.uk
Web sites: www.salisburyreds.co.uk, www.touristcoaches.co.uk, www.go-ahead.com
Fleet Names (Wiltshire): Salisbury Reds, Bell's Coaches, Kingston Coaches, Lever's Coaches, Tourist Coaches.
Chairman: David Brown **Man Dir:** Andrew Wickham **Eng Dir:** Steve Hamilton
Fin Dir: Nick Woods **Ops Dir:** Ed Wills.
Fleet: 750 - 321 double-deck bus, 134 single-deck bus, 101 single-deck coach, 10 articulated bus, 88 midibus, 96 minibus.
Chassis: 118 Alexander Dennis, 2 Bristol, 62 DAF, 14 Dennis, 1 Ford, 4 Iveco, 1 LDV, 20 Leyland, 59 Mercedes, 123 Optare, 127 Scania, 219 Volvo.
Bodies: 121 Alexander Dennis, 1 Autobus, 4 Beulas, 6 Caetano, 56 East Lancs, 2 ECW, 1 Ford, 2 Ikarus, 1 Irizar, 3 Jonckheere, 1 LDV, 57 Mercedes, 44 Northern Counties, 169 Optare, 86 Plaxton, 73 Scania, 22 Van Hool, 91 Wrightbus.
Ops incl: local bus services, school contracts, private hire.
Liveries: Buses: Red; **Coaches:** Blue.
Ticket System: Vix ITSO Smart.

Part of the Go-Ahead Group. See also operations in Dorset, Hampshire, Isle of Wight.

HATTS TRAVEL
Ceased trading since LRB 2014 went to press

KINCH COACHES LTD
♿ 🚌 ❋ ❋
HORNBURY HILL FARM, MINETY,
MALMESBURY SN16 9QH
Tel: 01666 860339
E-mail: info@kinchcoaches.co.uk
Web site: www.wiltshirecoachhire.co.uk
Man Dir: Anthony D Kinch.
Fleet: 13 – 9 single-deck coach, 3 midicoach, 1 minibus.
Chassis: 4 Mercedes, 9 Volvo.
Bodies: 1 Alexander, 1 Autobus, 1 Duple, 1 Jonckheere, 1 Marshall, 1 Mercedes, 6 Plaxton, 1 Van Hool.
Ops incl: school contracts, excursions & tours, private hire.
Livery: Cream & Purple.

MANSFIELD'S COACHES
♿ ❋
27 FINCHDALE, COVINGHAM, SWINDON
SN3 5AL
Tel/Fax: 01793 525375
Prop: R E Mansfield **Man:** A Mansfield
Tran Man: P Mansfield
Sec: Mrs M S Mansfield.
Fleet: 3 – 2 midicoach, 1 minibus.
Chassis: 3 Mercedes.
Ops incl: excursions & tours, private hire, express, school contracts.
Livery: Yellow/Green/Red.

PARNHAM COACHES LTD
♿ 🚌 ❋ 🍴
31 ANDOVER ROAD, LUDGERSHALL
SP11 9LU
Tel: 01264 790606   **Fax:** 01264 791891
Web site: www.parnhams.com
Dir: Ray Parnham
Fleet: 15 – 14 single-deck coach, 1 minibus.
Chassis: 7 Bova, 1 Mercedes, 4 VDL, 3 Volvo.
Bodies: 7 Bova, 1 Plaxton, 2 Van Hool, 4 VDL, 1 Other.
Ops incl: excursions & tours, private hire.
Livery: White.

PEWSEY VALE COACHES LTD
♿ 🚌 ♿ ❋
HOLLYBUSH LANE, PEWSEY SN9 5BB
Tel: 01672 562238
Fax: 01672 502238
E-mail: sales@pewseyvalecoaches.co.uk
Web site: www.pewseyvalecoaches.co.uk
Dirs: Andrew Thorne, Anne Thorne, Joanna Bottoms.
Fleet: 14 – 1 single-deck bus, 13 single-deck coach.
Chassis: 4 Bova, 1 Dennis, 2 MAN, 2 Van Hool, 5 Volvo.
Bodies: 1 Berkhof, 1 Beulas, 4 Bova, 1 MCV, 3 Plaxton, 4 Van Hool.
Ops incl: local bus services, school contracts, excursions & tours, private hire, continental tours.
Livery: White/Blue/Red.
Ticket system: Ticketer.

STAGECOACH WEST
See Gloucestershire

THAMESDOWN TRANSPORT
♿ 🅁
BARNFIELD ROAD, SWINDON SN2 2DJ
Tel: 01793 428400
Recovery: 01793 428432
E-mail: customerservices@thamesdown-transport.co.uk

Web site: www.thamesdownbus.com
Man Dir: Paul Jenkins
Head of Eng: David Spencer
Exec Director/Fin Controller:
Cliff Connor **Ops Dir:** Gordon Frost.
Fleet: 81 - 11 double-deck bus, 70 single-deck bus.
Chassis: 1 Daimler, 21 Dennis, 8 Optare,
37 Scania, 8 Transbus, 6 Wrightbus.
Bodies: 1 Alexander Dennis, 9 East Lancs,
1 Northern Counties, 8 Optare, 20 Plaxton,
8 Transbus, 34 Wrightbus.
Ops incl: local bus services, school contracts.
Livery: Blue/Green.
Ticket System: Wayfarer 200.

TOURIST COACHES LTD
**(Incorporating Bells Coaches Ltd,
Kingston Coaches, Levers Coaches Ltd)**
See Go South Coast Ltd.

**WILTS & DORSET BUS
COMPANY LTD**
See Go South Coast Ltd.

Worcestershire

ASTONS COACHES
♿ 📶 🏍 🚻 ❄ R R 24 🔌 T
CLERKENLEAP, BROOMHALL,
WORCESTER WR5 3HR
Tel: 01905 820201   **Fax:** 01905 829249
E-mail: info@astons-coaches.co.uk
Web site: www.astons-coaches.co.uk
Gen Man: Richard Conway **Tran Man:**
Matthew Wells **Ops Man:** Jon Elsdon
Sales & Marketing Man: Becki Muir.
Fleet: 66 - 8 double-deck bus, 7 single-deck
bus, 27 single-deck coach, 12 midibus,
3 midicoach, 7 minibus, 2 minicoach.
Chassis: 6 Alexander Dennis, 6 DAF,
4 Dennis, 1 EOS, 1 Iveco, 6 Mercedes,
14 Optare, 1 Renault, 16 Scania, 2 Setra,
7 Volvo, 2 Wrightbus.
Bodies: 4 Alexander, 4 Alexander Dennis,
2 Berkhof, 6 East Lancs, 1 EOS, 1 Ferqui,
1 Indcar, 7 Irizar, 15 Optare, 7 Plaxton, 2 Setra,
1 Unvi, 8 Van Hool, 3 Wrightbus, 4 Other.
Ops incl: local bus services, school contracts,
excursions & tours, private hire, continental tours.
Livery: White with Purple logo.
Ticket system: ERG.

COMMANDERY COACHES
♿ 🏍 🔌
4 OLD TOLLADINE ROAD, WORCESTER
WR4 9NW
Tel: 01905 458529
E-mail: enquiries@commandery-coaches.co.uk
Web site: www.commandery-coaches.co.uk
Fleet: 11 – 5 single-deck coach, 6 midicoach.
Chassis: 5 Mercedes, 5 Scania, 1 Toyota.
Ops incl: school contracts, excursions &
tours, private hire.
Livery: White with Blue/Red/Yellow.

N N CRESSWELL COACH HIRE LTD
♿ 🔌
WORCESTER ROAD, EVESHAM WR11 4RA
Tel/Recovery: 01386 48655
Fax: 01386 48656
E-mail: nncresswell@btinternet.com
Web site: www.nncresswell.co.uk
Dirs: Mrs Mary Everatt, Mrs Elizabeth Everatt.
Fleet: 20 - 14 single-deck coach, 4 midicoach,
2 minibus.
Chassis: 1 Bedford, 1 BMC, 13 Dennis,
5 Mercedes.
Bodies: 1 BMC, 1 Optare, 18 Plaxton.
Ops incl: local bus services, school contracts,
excursions & tours, private hire.
Livery: Blue/White.
Ticket System: Wayfarer.

DIAMOND BUS LTD
See West Midlands

DUDLEY'S COACHES
♿ 📶 🏍 🔌 ❄ 🚻 T
POPLAR GARAGE, ALCESTER ROAD,
RADFORD, WORCESTER WR7 4LS
Tel: 01386 792206
Fax: 01386 793373
E-mail: info@dudleys-coaches.co.uk
Web site: www.dudleys-coaches.co.uk
Dir: C E Dudley
Fleet: 17 - 15 single-deck coach, 2 minicoach.
Chassis: 2 Toyota, 15 Volvo.
Bodies: 2 Caetano, 1 Jonckheere, 9 Plaxton,
1 Sunsundegui, 1 Transbus, 2 Van Hool, 1 Volvo.
Ops incl: local bus services, school contracts,
excursions & tours, private hire.
Livery: Green/Cream.

EUROLINERS
♿ 🔌 ❄
1631 BRISTOL ROAD SOUTH, REDNAL,
BIRMINGHAM BH45 9UA
Tel: 0121 453 5151   **Fax:** 0121 453 5504
E-mail: info@euroliners.co.uk
Web site: www.euroliners.co.uk
Prop: Anthony Armstrong.
Fleet: 15 - 2 single-deck coach, 5 midicoach,
8 minicoach.
Chassis: 5 LDV, 10 Mercedes.
Bodies: 6 Mercedes, 4 Optare, 5 Plaxton.
Ops incl: local bus services, school contracts,
private hire.
Livery: White with Blue/Yellow.

FIRST MIDLANDS
♿ 🔌
HERON LODGE, LONDON ROAD,
WORCESTER WR5 2EU
Tel: 08456 020121   **Fax:** 01905 351104
Regional Man Dir: Nigel Eggleton
Deputy Man Dir: Mick Branigan
Fin Dir: David Marshall.
Fleet Name: First Wyvern
Fleet (Worcester & Hereford):
104 – 12 double-deck bus, 48 single-deck bus,
2 single-deck coach, 16 midibus, 26 minibus.
Chassis: 41 Alexander Dennis, 2 BMC,
17 Dennis, 26 Optare, 5 Transbus, 13 Volvo.
Bodies: 41 Alexander Dennis, 2 BMC,
11 Caetano, 26 Optare, 8 Plaxton, 5 Transbus,
11 Wrightbus.
Ops incl: local bus services, school contracts.
Livery: FirstGroup UK Bus.
Ticket System: Wayfarer.
See also operations in Herefordshire,
Leicestershire, Staffordshire.

HARDINGS TRAVEL LTD
🔌 🏍 🚻 ❄
PETERSON HOUSE, NORTH BANK, BERRY
HILL INDUSTRIAL ESTATE, DROITWICH
WR9 0AU
Tel: 01905 777119   **Fax:** 01905 777105
E-mail: sales@hardingscoaches.com
Web site: www.hardingscoaches.co.uk
Man Dir: John Dyson **Gen Man:** Rob Lyng.
Fleet: 20 single-deck coach.
Chassis: 3 Bova, 2 Irizar, 3 Mercedes,
8 Scania, 4 VDL.
Bodies: 3 Bova, 6 Irizar, 4 Lahden,
3 Mercedes, 1 VDL, 3 Van Hool.
Ops incl: school contracts, excursions &
tours, private hire.
Livery: Silver with Red/Blue.

HARRIS EXECUTIVE TRAVEL
🏍 🚻 ❄ 🔌 T
58 MEADOW ROAD, CATSHILL,
BROMSGROVE B61 0JL
Tel: 01527 872857   **Fax:** 01527 872708
E-mail: info@harriscoaches.com
Web site: www.harriscoaches.com
Joint Man Dirs: J G Harris, S W Harris.
Fleet: 7 - 6 single-deck coach, 1 minicoach.
Chassis: 7 Mercedes.
Bodies: 6 Neoplan, 1 Other.
Ops incl: excursions & tours, private hire,
continental tours.
Livery: White/Red/Yellow/Orange.

LMS TRAVEL
♿ 📶 🔌 ❄
TOLLADINE ROAD, WORCESTER WR4 9NB
Tel: 01905 25252   **Fax:** 01905 729986
E-mail: info@lmstravel.co.uk
Web site: www.lmstravel.co.uk
Fleet: 29 – 2 single-deck coach, 10 midibus,
2 midicoach, 10 minibus, 5 minicoach.
Chassis: Dennis, Iveco, LDV, Mercedes,
Optare, Setra, Toyota, Volkswagen.
Ops incl: local bus services, school contracts,
private hire.

WHITTLE COACH & BUS LTD
♿ 🔌 📶 🚻 ❄ 🚌 T
FOLEY BUSINESS PARK, STOURPORT
ROAD, KIDDERMINSTER DY11 7QL
Tel: 01562 820002   **Fax:** 01562 820027
E-mail: webenquiries@whittlecoach.co.uk
Web site: www.whittlecoach.co.uk
Fleet Name: Whittles
Chairman: Peter Shipp **Fin Dir:** Peter
Harrison **Gen Man:** Andrew McKinnon
Ops Man: Paul McLellan.
Fleet: 39 – 5 single-deck bus, 17 single-deck
coach, 17 midibus.
Chassis: 7 Alexander Dennis, 8 Dennis,
2 Transbus, 22 Volvo.
Bodies: 5 Alexander, 6 Alexander Dennis,
8 Caetano, 2 Transbus, 17 Plaxton, 1 Volvo.
Ops incl: local bus services, school contracts,
excursions & tours, private hire, express,
continental tours.
Livery: Bus: Green/White; **Coach:** White with
Blue/Green/Yellow Relief; National Express.
Ticket system: Wayfarer III.
A subsidiary of the EYMS Group

WOODSTONES COACHES LTD
♿ 🔌
ARTHUR DRIVE, HOO FARM
INDUSTRIAL ESTATE, WORCESTER ROAD,
KIDDERMINSTER DY11 7RA
Tel: 01562 823073   **Fax:** 01562 827277
E-mail: enquiries@woodstones.org.uk
Web site: www.woodstones.org.uk
Man Dir: Ivan Meredith **Dir:** Richard Meredith.
Fleet: 6 single-deck coach.
Chassis: 6 Volvo.
Bodies: 6 Plaxton.
Ops incl: school contracts, excursions &
tours, private hire.
Livery: White/Yellow/Orange/Red.

YARRANTON BROS LTD
♿ 🔌 ❄ 🚻 T
EARDISTON GARAGE, TENBURY WELLS
WR15 8JL
Tel: 01584 881229
E-mail: info@yarrantons.co.uk
Web site: www.yarrantons.co.uk
Dirs: A L Yarranton **(Gen Man)**,
M L Yarranton, D A Yarranton.
Fleet: 12 – 2 single-deck bus, 8 single-deck
coach, 1 minibus, 1 minicoach.
Chassis: 4 Dennis, 1 LDV, 1 Mercedes,
1 Scania, 1 Setra, 1 Toyota, 1 Transbus, 2 Volvo.
Bodies: 1 Berkhof, 1 Caetano, 1 LDV,
1 Mercedes, 2 Plaxton, 1 Scania, 1 Setra,
1 Transbus, 1 Van Hool, 2 Wadham Stringer.
Ops incl: local bus services, school contracts,
excursions & tours, private hire, continental
tours.
Livery: Green/White/Orange.

ALDERNEY

RIDUNA BUSES

ALLEE ES FEES, ALDERNEY
GY9 3XD
Tel: 01481 823700
Fax: 01481 823030
Prop: A J Curtis.
Ops incl: local bus services, excursions & tours, private hire.

GUERNSEY

CT PLUS GUERNSEY LTD

LES BANQUES, PETER PORT
GY1 2HZ
Tel: 01481 700456
E-mail: guernsey@hctgroup.org
Web site: www.buses.gg
Fleet Name: Buses.gg
Ops Man (Interim): Lee Murphy
Asst Ops Man: Rick de Garis.
Fleet: 41 single-deck bus.
Chassis: 41 Dennis.
Bodies: 8 Caetano, 33 East Lancs.
Ops incl: local bus services, school contracts.
Livery: Green/Yellow.
CT Plus is part of the HCT Group. See also operations in *Bristol, East Riding, London & Middlesex,* and *West Yorkshire.*

ISLAND COACHWAYS LTD

THE TRAMSHEDS, LES BANQUES,
ST PETER PORT GY1 2HZ
Tel: 01481 720210
Fax: 01481 710109
E-mail: admin@icw.gg
Web site: www.icw.gg
Man Dir: Hannah Beacom
Dir: Ben Boucher **Ops Man:** Tom Whyte
Strategic Planning Man: Rob Branigan
Fleet Man: Tom Wilson
Sales Man: Isabel de Menezes.
Fleet: 15 - 6 single-deck coach, 6 midicoach, 1 minibus, 2 minicoach.
Chassis: 1 Ford Transit, 3 Iveco, 6 Mercedes, 4 Renault, 1 Other.
Bodies: 1 Leicester, 6 Plaxton, 8 Other.
Ops incl: excursions & tours, private hire.
Livery: Green/Cream.

JERSEY

LIBERTY BUS

LA COLLETTE BUS DEPOT,
ST HELIER JE2 3NX
Tel: 01534 828555
E-mail: info@libertybus.je
Web site: www.libertybus.je

Fleet: 84 – 6 double-deck bus, 74 midibus, 4 minibus.
Chassis: 6 Alexander Dennis, 36 Dennis, 4 Fiat, 33 Optare, 5 Transbus
Bodies: 6 Alexander Dennis, 4 Bluebird, 26 Caetano, 33 Optare, 10 Plaxton, 5 Transbus
Ops incl: local bus services, school contracts.
Livery: White with multi-colours.
A subsidiary of CT Plus, part of the HCT Group. See also operations in *Bristol, East Riding, London & Middlesex,* and *West Yorkshire.*

TANTIVY BLUE COACH TOURS

ALBERT QUAY, ST HELIER
JE2 3NE
Tel: 01534 706706
Fax: 01534 706705
E-mail: info@jerseycoaches.com
Web site: www.tantivybluecoach.com
Man Dir: Chris Lewis
Gen Man: Carl Pickering
Eng Man: Tony Donahue
Fleet: 43 - 24 single-deck coach, 6 midibus, 1 heritage coach, 12 midibus.
Chassis: Bedford, Cannon, Dennis, Ford, Leyland, Renault, Volkswagen.
Ops incl: excursions & tours, private hire.
Livery: Blue.

WAVERLEY COACHES LTD

UNIT 3, LA COLLETTE, ST HELIER JE2 3NX
Tel: 01534 758360
Fax: 01534 732627
E-mail: tours@waverleycoaches.co.uk
Web site: www.waverleycoaches.co.uk
Dir/Gen Man: S E Pedersen
Ch Eng: Peter Evans.
Fleet: 18 - 12 single-deck coach, 1 midibus, 5 minibus.
Chassis: 1 Bedford, 3 Ford Transit, 6 Cannon, 1 Iveco, 5 Leyland, 2 LDV.
Bodies: 1 Bedwas, 1 Duple, 3 Ford, 6 Leicester, 2 LDV, 5 Wadham Stringer.
Ops incl: excursions & tours, private hire.
Livery: Yellow/White.

ISLE of MAN

DOUGLAS CORPORATION TRAMWAY

See Section 5 – Tram and Bus Rapid Transit Systems.

ISLE OF MAN TRANSPORT

TRANSPORT HEADQUARTERS, BANKS CIRCUS, DOUGLAS IM1 5PT
Tel: 01624 663366
Fax: 01624 663637
E-mail: info@busandrail.dtl.gov.im
Web site: www.gov.im/publictransport,

Director of Public Transport: Ian Longworth.
Fleet Name: Bus Vannin.
Depots at: Douglas, Port Erin, Ramsey.
Fleet: 103 - 34 double-deck bus, 42 single-deck bus, 2 minibus, 25 trams.
Chassis: 8 Alexander Dennis, 8 DAF, 1 Dennis, 32 Mercedes, 17 Volvo, 12 Wrightbus.
Bodies: 17 East Lancs, 32 Mercedes, 29 Wrightbus.
7 heritage vehicles are also retained.
Ops incl: local bus/tram services, private hire.
Livery: Red/Cream.
Ticket System: Wayfarer.

TOURS ISLE OF MAN LTD

BALLASALLA, ISLE OF MAN
Tel: 01624 822611
E-mail: info@tours.co.im
Web site: www.toursisleofman.co.uk
Chairman: John Guilford
Dir: Roy Lightfoot
Man Dir: David Midghall.
Fleet: 15 - 9 single-deck coach, 1 midicoach, 3 minibus, 2 vintage coach.
Chassis: 2 Bedford, 1 BMC, 1 Bova, 2 DAF, 2 Iveco, 1 Mercedes, 2 Scania, 4 Volvo.
Bodies: 1 BMC, 1 Bova, 2 Duple, 2 Irizar, 2 Jonckheere, 1 Mercedes, 3 Plaxton, 1 Van Hool, 2 Other.
Ops incl: school contracts, excursions & tours, private hire, corporate travel, coach holiday programme.
Livery: White/Blue.

ISLES OF SCILLY

HERITAGE TOUR

SANTAMANA, 9 RAMS VALLEY,
ST MARY'S TR21 0JX
Tel: 01720 422387
Props: G Twynham, Mrs P Twynham.
Fleet: 1 single-deck bus (1948 vehicle).
Chassis: Austin K2.
Body: Barnard.
Ops incl: excursions & tours, private hire.
Livery: Blue/Cream.

ISLAND ROVER

THE NOOK, CHURCH STREET,
ST MARYS TR21 0JT
Tel/Fax: 01720 422131
E-mail: island.rover@btinternet.com
Web site: www.islandrover.co.uk
Prop: Glynne Lucas.
Fleet: 3 - 1 single-deck coach, 2 midibus.
Chassis: 1 Austin, 1 Optare, 1 Volvo.
Bodies: 1 Optare, 1 Plaxton, 1 Other.
Livery: Blue/White.

♿	Vehicle suitable for disabled	🍴	Coach(es) with galley facilities	🚌 Vintage Coach(es) available
	Seat belt-fitted Vehicle	🔧	Replacement vehicle available	Open top vehicle(s)
R24	24 hour recovery service	**R**	Recovery service available	Coaches with toilet facilities
T	Toilet-drop facilities available	❄	Air-conditioned vehicle(s)	Hybrid Buses Gas Buses

Scottish Operators

ABERDEEN, CITY OF

BLUEBIRD BUSES LTD
♿♲👥🅿✕
UNION SQUARE BUS STATION,
GUILD STREET, ABERDEEN AB11 6NA
Tel: 01224 591381   **Fax:** 01224 584202
E-mail: bluebird.enquiries@stagecoachbus.com
Web site: www.stagecoachbus.com
Fleet Name: Stagecoach Bluebird.
Man Dir: Steve Walker **Ops Dir:** Stephie
Barber **Eng Dir:** Russell Henderson.
Fleet: 237 - 23 double-deck bus, 81 single-deck
bus, 86 single-deck coach, 21 midibus, 26 minibus.
Chassis: 83 Alexander Dennis, 7 Dennis,
13 MAN, 32 Optare, 13 Van Hool, 1 Volkswagen,
88 Volvo.
Bodies: 26 Alexander, 83 Alexander Dennis,
1 East Lancs, 1 Jonckheere, 7 Northern
Counties, 32 Optare, 73 Plaxton, 13 Van Hool,
1 Volkswagen.
Ops incl: local bus services, school contracts,
express.
Livery: Stagecoach UK Bus/Megabus/Citylink.
Ticket System: ERG TP5000.

CENTRAL COACHES
♿♲👥🍴✕
DEREK SMITH HOUSE, HARENESS ROAD,
ALTENS, ABERDEEN AB12 3LE
Tel: 01224 890089   **Fax:** 01224 899434
E-mail: central898989@yahoo.co.uk
Web site: www.centralaberdeen.co.uk
Fleet: 50 – 14 single-deck coach, 1 double-deck
coach, 9 midicoach, 1 midibus, 21 minibus,
4 minicoach.
Chassis: 1 Bova, 13 Ford Transit, 1 Irisbus,
3 Iveco, 1 LDV, 17 Mercedes, 1 Neoplan,
1 Optare, 5 Scania, 7 Volvo.
Ops incl: local bus services, school contracts,
excursions & tours, continental tours.
Livery: White.

FIRST IN ABERDEEN
♿📠♲🖥R24✕
395 KING STREET, ABERDEEN AB24 5RP
Tel: 01224 650000
Fax: 01224 650099
Web site: www.firstgroup.com
Dir & Gen Man: Duncan Cameron
Eng Dir: Iain Ferguson.
Fleet: 162 - 26 double-deck bus, 103 single-
deck bus, 33 articulated bus.
Chassis: 23 Alexander Dennis, 14 Dennis,
125 Volvo.
Bodies: 6 Alexander, 23 Alexander Dennis,
14 Plaxton, 119 Wrightbus.
Ops incl: local bus services, school contracts,
private hire.
Livery: FirstGroup UK Bus.

FIRST ABERDEEN LTD, COACHING UNIT
👥🍴♲✕✕
FIRST ABERDEEN LTD, 395 KING STREET,
ABERDEEN AB24 5RP
Tel: 01224 219225
Fax: 01224 650123
Recovery: 01224 650151
E-mail: coachhire.aberdeen@firstgroup.com
Web site: www.firstgroup.com
Dir & Gen Man: Duncan Cameron
Eng Dir: Iain Ferguson **Coaching Ops Man:**
Tom Gordon.
Fleet: 33 – 23 single-deck coach, 3 single-deck
bus, 7 midicoach.
Chassis: 1 Bluebird, 2 BMC, 7 Mercedes,
6 Scania, 4 Temsa, 13 Volvo.
Bodies: 1 Bluebird, 2 BMC, 1 Ferqui, 6 Irizar,
2 Jonckheere, 17 Plaxton, 4 Temsa.
Ops incl: school contracts, excursions & tours,
private hire, continental tours.
Livery: First Group Magenta/Blue/Grey.
A division of First Aberdeen

FOUNTAIN EXECUTIVE
♿♲🍴✕✕T
HILL OF GOVAL, DYCE, ABERDEEN
AB21 7NX
Tel: 01224 729090
Fax: 01224 729898
E-mail: info@fountainexecutive.co.uk
Web site: www.fountainexecutive.co.uk
Prop: Michael Ewen.
Fleet: 11 - 6 single-deck coach, 1 midicoach,
2 minibus, 1 minicoach.
Chassis: 5 Mercedes, 6 Scania.
Bodies: 2 Concept, 6 Irizar, 3 Unvi.
Ops incl: private hire, continental tours.
Livery: Gold.

MAIR'S THISTLE COACHES
Ceased trading since LRB 2014 went to press

WHYTES COACHES LTD
👥♲♿✕T
SCOTSTOWN ROAD, NEWMACHAR,
ABERDEEN AB21 7PP
Tel: 01651 862211
Fax: 01651 862918
E-mail: sales@whytes.co.uk
Web Site: www.whytescoaches.co.uk
Man Dir: Steven W Whyte.
Fleet: 18 – 5 single-deck coach, 9 midicoach,
4 minibus.
Chassis: 1 Ford Transit, 1 King Long,
11 Mercedes, 5 VDL.
Bodies: 1 Ford, 1 King Long, 2 KVC, 1 Onyx,
8 Unvi, 5 VDL.
Ops incl: school contracts, excursions & tours,
private hire, express, continental tours.
Livery: Light Green.

ABERDEENSHIRE

ALLAN & BLACK
♲🍴✕R
DRUMDUAN DEPOT, DESS, ABOYNE
AB34 5BN
Tel: 01339 886326   **Fax:** 01336 886008
E-mail: info-enq@allanandblackcoaches.co.uk
Web site: www.allanandblackcoaches.co.uk
Props: Andrew C Brown, Murray W Brown,
Jane W Brown, Cameron W Brown.
Fleet: 14 – 1 double-deck bus, 10 single-deck
coach, 3 minibus.
Chassis: 1 Iveco, 2 Mercedes, 1 Neoplan,
1 Peugeot, 4 Scania, 4 Setra, 1 Volvo.
Ops incl: local bus services, school contracts,
excursions & tours, private hire.
Livery: White & Purple.
Ticket System: Almex.

BAIN'S COACHES
♿♲👥✕
STATION GARAGE, STATION ROAD,
OLDMELDRUM AB51 0EZ
Tel: 01651 872365
E-mail: enquiries@bainscoaches.co.uk
Web site: www.bainscoaches.co.uk
Props: D Bain, Mrs W Bain.
Fleet: 40 – 1 double-deck coach, 10 single-deck
bus, 9 single-deck coach, 3 midibus, 4 midicoach,
10 minibus, 3 minicoach.
Chassis: 10 BMC, 2 DAF, 2 Dennis, 2 Ford
Transit, 3 King Long, 1 LDV, 3 MAN, 5 Mercedes,
1 Neoplan, 1 Optare, 2 Scania, 2 Toyota,
1 Vauxhall, 2 Volkswagen, 3 Volvo.
Ops incl: local bus services, school contracts,
private hire.
Liveries: Silver with Blue lettering; **School
Buses:** Yellow.

J & M BURNS
♲👥🍴✕
DINNESWOOD, TARVES, ELLON AB41 7LR
Tel: 01651 851279   **Fax:** 01651 851844
E-mail: info@burnscoaches.co.uk
Web site: www.burnscoaches.co.uk

Props: J Burns, Mrs M Burns.
Fleet: 13 – 4 single-deck coach, 1 midicoach,
6 minibus, 2 minicoach.
Chassis: 2 DAF, 9 Mercedes, 1 VDL, 1 Volvo.
Ops incl: school contracts, private hire,
excursions & tours.
Livery: Purple.

CHEYNE OF INVERURIE
♲♿
ALLANDALE, DAVIOT, INVERURIE AB51 0EJ
Tel: 01467 671400
Fax: 01467 671479
E-mail: lesley@cheynescoaches.co.uk
Partners: W A Cheyne, R Cheyne, L A Cheyne,
M F Cheyne.
Fleet: 8 - 3 single-deck coach, 3 midicoach,
2 minibus.
Chassis: 1 Bova, 2 Ford Transit, 3 Mercedes,
2 Volvo.
Bodies: 2 Autobus, 1 Bova, 2 Ford Transit,
1 Plaxton, 2 Van Hool.
Ops incl: school contracts, excursions & tours,
private hire.
Livery: Silver/Pink/Purple.

DEVERON COACHES LTD
♿♲
6 UNION ROAD, MACDUFF AB44 1UJ
Tel: 01261 833555
E-mail: gary@deveroncoaches.com
Web site: www.deveroncoaches.com
Dirs: M Milne, E Milne, P Bruce.
Depots at: Macduff, Buckie, Huntly, Keith.
Fleet: 73 - 1 single-deck bus, 40 single-deck
coach, 9 midibus, 7 midicoach, 11 minibus,
5 minicoach.
Chassis: 1 Bova, 8 Ford Transit, 2 Leyland,
14 Mercedes, 7 Optare, 2 Scania, 2 Transbus,
37 Volvo.
Ops incl: local bus services, school contracts,
private hire, excursions & tours.
Livery: Red/White.

JOUN C KEIR COACHES
♲✕
HAUGH OF EDINGLASSIE, GLASS AB54 4YB
Tel: 01466 700283
Partners: I D Keir, G A Keir, J Keir.
Fleet: 6 – 3 single-deck coach, 2 midicoach,
1 minibus.
Chassis: 1 Dennis, 1 LDV, 2 Mercedes, 2 Volvo.
Bodies: 4 Plaxton, 1 Sitcar, 1 Other.
Ops incl: school contracts, private hire.
Livery: Yellow/White/Orange.

KINEIL COACHES LTD
♿👥♲✕
ANDERSON PLACE, WEST SHORE
INDUSTRIAL ESTATE, FRASERBURGH
AB43 9LG
Tel: 01346 510200
Fax: 01346 516266
E-mail: kineilcoaches@btconnect.com
Web site: www.kineilcoachesltd.co.uk
Man Dir: Ian Neilson.
Depots at: Fraserburgh, Elgin, Inverurie.
Fleet: 51 – 25 single-deck coach, 5 midibus,
9 midicoach, 5 minibus, 7 minicoach.
Chassis: 1 Alexander Dennis, 4 Bova,
21 Mercedes, 5 Optare, 1 Scania, 1 VDL, 18 Volvo.
Bodies: 1 Autobus, 4 Bova, 1 EVM, 1 KVC,
4 Onyx, 5 Optare, 10 Plaxton, 2 Sitcar, 3 Unvi,
1 VDL, 18 Van Hool.
Ops incl: local bus services, school contracts,
private hire.
Livery: White/Red/Blue.
Ticket System: Almex.

MAYNES COACHES LTD
♲👥✕R R24✕T
CLUNY GARAGE, 4 MARCH ROAD WEST,
BUCKIE AB56 4BU
Tel: 01542 831219

Fax: 01542 833572
E-mail: info@maynes.co.uk
Web site: www.maynes.co.uk
Dirs: Gordon Mayne, David Mayne, Kevin Mayne.
Fleet (Buckie): 18 –14 single-deck coach,
3 midicoach, I minicoach.
Chassis: I King Long, 3 Mercedes, 7 Neoplan,
7 Van Hool.
Bodies: I EVM, I King Long, 7 Neoplan,
2 Plaxton, 7 Van Hool.
Ops incl: local bus services, school contracts,
excursions & tours, private hire, continental
tours.
Livery: Silver.
Ticket System: Setright.
Additional operations at Elgin and St Margaret's
Hope (see Moray, Orkney)

ALEX MILNE COACHES

THE GARAGE, 4 MAIN STREET,
NEW BYTH AB53 5XD
Tel: 01888 544340
Fax: 01888 544154
E-mail: info@alexmilnecoaches.co.uk
Partners: Alex Milne Brian Milne.
Fleet: 14 - 4 single-deck coach, 6 midicoach,
4 minibus.
Chassis: I BMC, I Dennis, 3 Ford Transit,
6 Mercedes, 3 Volvo.
Ops incl: local bus services, school contracts,
private hire, excursions & tours.
Livery: Blue/White.
Ticket system: Wayfarer.

M W NICOLL'S COACH HIRE

THE BUSINESS PARK, ABERDEEN ROAD,
LAURENCEKIRK AB30 IEY
Tel: 01561 377262
Fax: 01561 378822
E-mail: mwnicollscoaches@btconnect.com
Web site: www.nicoll-coaches.co.uk
Dirs: J Petrie, C A McConnell.
Fleet: 41 - 10 single-deck coach, 8 midibus,
5 minicoach, 10 minibus, 8 minicoach.
Chassis: 5 Alexander Dennis, 4 Bova, 3 Ford
Transit, 20 Mercedes, 2 Optare, I Toyota, 6 Volvo.
Ops incl: local bus services, school contracts,
private hire.
Livery: White.
Ticket System: Almex.
Associated with JP Minicoaches Ltd (see Angus)

J D PEACE CO ABDN LTD

FARE PARK, ECHT, WESTHILL
AB32 7AL
Tel: 01330 860542
Fax: 01330 860543
E-mail: info@peacescoaches.co.uk
Web: www.peacescoches.co.uk
Dirs: David J Collie, Kathleen Collie.
Fleet: 15 - 8 single-deck coach, 3 midicoach,
3 minibus, I minicoach.
Chassis: 8 Bova, I Ford Transit, 6 Mercedes.
Bodies: 8 Bova, I Ford, 2 KVC, I Plaxton,
3 Unvi.
Ops incl: school contracts, private hire.
Livery: White with Red & Stripes.

PREMIER COACHES LTD

HILL OF COTTOWN, KINTORE
AB51 0YA
Tel: 01467 642409
E-mail: premiercoacheskintore@btconnect.
com
Web site: www.premiercoaches.co.uk
Dir: Alan Findlater
Fleet: 12 – single-deck coach, midicoach,
minibus, minicoach.
Ops incl: school contracts, private hire.
Livery: White with Light/Dark Green.

RS TAXIS & MINICOACH HIRE

BLACKSTOCK, SAUCHEN, INVERURIE
AB51 7RD
Tel: 01330 833314
Prop: R Bain.
Fleet: 17 – I double-deck bus, I double-deck
coach, 2 single-deck coach, I midibus,
4 midicoach, 8 minibus.
Chassis: I Bova, 2 LDV, 2 MAN, 5 Mercedes,
I Neoplan, 4 Renault, 2 Volvo.
Ops incl: local bus services, private hire.

REIDS OF RHYNIE

22 MAIN STREET, RHYNIE, BY HUNTLY
AB54 4HB
Tel/Fax: 01464 861212
Recovery: 07831 173681
Owner: Colin Reid.
Fleet: 3 minibus.
Chassis: Ford Transit.
Ops incl: school contracts, private hire.
Livery: White/Blue/Water Green.
Ticket system: Wayfarer 3.

SHEARER OF HUNTLY LTD

OLD TOLL ROAD, HUNTLY
AB54 6JA
Tel: 01466 792410
Fax: 01466 793926
E-mail: shearerofhuntly@btconnect.com
Dirs: Mr James Shearer, Mrs Irene Shearer.
Fleet: 13 - I single-deck coach, 10 minibus,
2 minicoach.
Chassis: I Dennis, 8 Ford Transit, 2 LDV,
2 Mercedes.
Ops incl: local bus services, school contracts,
private hire.

SIMPSON'S COACHES

21 UNION STREET, ROSEHEARTY,
FRASERBURGH AB43 7JQ
Tel: 01346 571610
Fax: 01346 571070
E-mail: info@simpsonscoaches.co.uk
Web site: www.simpsonscoaches.co.uk
Prop: Ron Simpson, Pat Simpson.
Fleet: 11 - 8 single-deck coach, 3 midicoach.
Chassis: I Bova, 3 MAN, 3 Mercedes,
I Neoplan, 3 Volvo.
Ops incl: excursions & tours, private hire,
continental tours.
Livery: Silver/Blue.

STABLES OF KEITH

64 MAIN STREET, NEWMILL, KEITH
AB55 6TS
Tel: 01542 882482
Prop: R E Stables.
Fleet: 9 – 6 single-deck coach, 3 midicoach.
Chassis: 2 Dennis, 4 Mercedes, 3 Volvo.
Ops incl: school contracts, private hire.
Livery: White with Blue.

VICTORIA COACHES

BRAIKLAW, BLACKHILLS, PETERHEAD
AB42 3LA
Tel: 01779 480480
Fax: 01779 474850
E-mail: info@victoriacoaches.co.uk
Web site: www.victoriacoaches.co.uk
Props: Mr & Mrs Ewan Mowat & Son.
Fleet: 16 – 8 single-deck coach, 4 midicoach,
4 minibus.
Chassis: I Bova, I Ford Transit, 7 Mercedes,
I Scania, 6 Volvo.
Ops incl: school contracts, excursions & tours,
private hire.
Livery: White with Green.

WATERMILL COACHES LTD

88 COLLEGE BOUNDS, FRASERBURGH
AB43 9QS
Tel/Fax: 01346 513050
E-mail: info@watermillcoaches.co.uk
Web site: www.watermillcoachesltd.co.uk
Depots at: Ellon, Fraserburgh, Peterhead.
Dirs: B Smith, A J Clark.
Fleet: 51 – 2 double-deck bus, 11 single-deck
bus, 17 single-deck coach, 2 midibus, 8 midicoach,
5 minibus, 5 minicoach.
Chassis: 8 Bova, 13 Dennis, I Ford Transit,
2 Leyland, 18 Mercedes, I Optare, 7 Volvo.
Bodies: 2 Alexander, 8 Bova, 2 Caetano, I Ford,
3 KVC, 4 Onyx, I Optare, 12 Plaxton, 2 Sitcar,
I Van Hool, 13 Wadham Stringer, I Other.
Ops incl: local bus services, school contracts,
private hire, excursions & tours.
Livery: White with Purple.

ANGUS

BLACK'S OF BRECHIN

UNIT 9, BRECHIN BUSINESS PARK, WEST
ROAD, BRECHIN DD9 6RJ
Tel: 01356 622119   **Fax:** 01356 623053
E-mail: coachhire@blacksofbrechin.com
Web site: www.blackscoaches.co.uk
Props: Robert P W Black, Ann-Marie Black.
Fleet: 5 – 2 single-deck coach, I midicoach.
Chassis: I BMC, I Dennis, I Irizar, I King Long,
I Scania.
Bodies: I BMC, 2 Irizar, I King Long, I Plaxton.
Ops incl: private hire.
Livery: White with Red.

GLENESK TRAVEL CO LTD

5 MANSE ROAD, EDZELL DD9 7TJ
Tel: 01356 648666
Ops incl: local bus services, private hire.
Web site: www.glenesktravel.co.uk
Dirs: A Gray, R Gray.
Fleet: 10 - 5 midicoach, 5 minibus.
Chassis: 9 Mercedes, I Renault.
Ops incl: local bus services, school contracts,
private hire.
Livery: White with Blue.

JP MINICOACHES LTD

UNIT 3, ORCHARDBANK INDUSTRIAL
ESTATE, FORFAR DD8 1TD
Tel: 01307 461431
Fax: 01307 467028
E-mail: jpminicoaches@btconnect.com
Web site: www.jpcoaches.co.uk
Man Dir: J Petrie.
Fleet: 48 – I single-deck bus, 13 single-deck
coach, 3 midibus, 10 midicoach, 16 minibus,
5 minicoach.
Chassis: I Alexander Dennis, 6 Dennis, I Ford
Transit, 2 LDV, 24 Mercedes, 4 Optare, 7 Volvo.
Ops incl: local bus services, private hire.
Livery: White with Black/Orange.
Also controls M W Nicoll's Coach Hire (see
Aberdeenshire)

RIDDLER'S COACHES LIMITED
Owner retired since LRB 2014 went to press.

SIDLAW EXECUTIVE TRAVEL
(SCOTLAND) LTD

UNIT 5, ARDYLE INDUSTRIAL ESTATE,
PERRIE STREET, DUNDEE DD2 2RD
Tel: 01382 610410
Fax: 01382 624333
E-mail: travel@sidlaw.co.uk
Web site: www.sidlaw.co.uk
Dir: Bob Costello **Fleet Eng:** Jamie Costello.
Fleet: 10 - I double-deck bus, 3 single-deck

coach, 3 midicoach, 3 minibus.
Chassis: I Dennis, I LDV, 5 Mercedes, I Neoplan, I Scania, I Setra.
Ops incl: school contracts, excursions & tours, private hire.
Livery: White/Silver.

STRATHTAY SCOTTISH OMNIBUSES LTD
See Dundee City

TEEJAY TRAVEL LTD
ELLIOT BUSINESS PARK, ELLIOT INDUSTRIAL ESTATE, ARBROATH DD11 2NJ
Tel: 01241 854717
E-mail: tomjordan@teejaytravel.co.uk
Fleet: 5 minibus.
Chassis: 3 Mercedes, 2 Optare.
Ops incl: local bus services, private hire.
Livery: White with Blue lettering.

WISHARTS (FRIOCKHEIM) LTD
STATION ROAD, FRIOCKHEIM, ARBROATH DD11 4SF
Tel: 01241 828747
Dirs: G & Mrs S Kinnear.
Fleet: 19 – I single-deck bus, 10 single-deck coach, 4 midicoach, 4 minibus.
Chassis: 4 Mercedes, 3 Optare, I Volkswagen, II Volvo.
Ops incl: local bus services, school contracts, private hire.

ARGYLL & BUTE

CRAIG OF CAMPBELTOWN LTD
BENMHOR, CAMPBELTOWN PA28 6DN
Tel: 01586 552319
Fax: 01586 552344
E-mail: enquiries@westcoastmotors.co.uk
Web site: www.westcoastmotors.co.uk
Fleet Name: West Coast Motors.
Depots at: Ardrishaig, Campbeltown, Dunoon, Mull, Oban, Rothesay.
Chairman/Man Dir: W G Craig
Dir: C R Craig **Co Sec:** J M Craig **Tran Man:** D M Halliday **Fleet Eng:** D Martin.
Fleet: 131 - 5 double-deck bus, 2 open-top bus, 12 single-deck bus, 47 single-deck coach, 38 midicoach, 20 minibus, 3 minicoach.
Chassis: 7 Alexander Dennis, 3 Bova, 33 DAF, 22 Dennis, 2 Enterprise, I Ford Transit, I LDV, 5 Leyland, 2 MAN, 17 Mercedes, 13 Optare, 13 Scania, 4 VDL, 8 Volvo.
Bodies: 17 Alexander, 7 Alexander Dennis, 3 Bova, I Caetano, I Fast, 2 Ferqui, 3 Ikarus, 10 Irizar, I KVC, I Leyland, 4 Mercedes, 2 Onyx, 14 Optare, 25 Plaxton, 29 Van Hool, 7 Wrightbus, 2 Other.
Ops incl: local bus services, school contracts, excursions & tours, private hire, express.
Liveries: Red/Blue/Honeysuckle, Scottish Citylink.
Ticket System: Wayfarer.
West Coast Motors Group Companies:
Fairline Coaches (see *City of Glasgow*)
Glasgow Citybus (see *City of Glasgow*)
Glasgow Sightseeing (see *City of Glasgow*)

GARELOCHHEAD MINIBUSES & COACHES LTD
WOODLEA GARAGE, MAIN ROAD, GARELOCHHEAD PA65 6BA
Tel: 01436 810200
Fax: 01436 810050
E-mail: enquiries@garelochheadcoaches.co.uk
Web site: www.garelochheadcoaches.co.uk
Depots: Garelochhead, Isle of Jura.
Prop: Stuart McQueen.
Fleet: 18 – 2 double-deck bus, I single-deck

bus, 2 single-deck coach, 3 midibus, I midicoach, 9 minibus.
Chassis: 7 Ford Transit, 2 Mercedes, 3 Optare, 6 Volvo.
Ops incl: local bus services, school contracts, private hire.
Livery: Silver Blue.
Also operates on the Isle of Jura

HIGHLAND HERITAGE COACH TOURS
CENTRAL ADMINISTRATION OFFICE, DALMALLY PA33 IAY
Tel: 01838 200444
E-mail: info@highlandheritage.co.uk
Web site: www.highlandheritage.co.uk
Man Dir: Ian Cleaver **Gen Man:** Sheena Thompson.
Fleet: 16 single-deck coach.
Chassis: 16 Volvo.
Bodies: 16 Van Hool.
Ops incl: excursions & tours.
Livery: Gold.

HIGHLAND ROVER COACHES
AWE SERVICE STATION, TAYNUILT, OBAN PA35 IHT
Tel/Fax: 0845 291 7369
E-mail: info@highlandrovercoachesoban.co.uk
Web site: www.highlandrovercoachesoban.co.uk
Prop: Angus Douglas.
Fleet: 2 - I single-deck coach, I minibus.
Chassis: 2 Mercedes.
Ops incl: local bus services, school contracts, private hire.
Livery: White/Brown/Orange.
Ticket system: Almex.

ISLAY COACHES
BARDARAVINE, TARBERT PA29 6YF
Tel: 01496 840273
E-mail: info@bmundell.co.uk
Web site: www.bmundell.co.uk/islay-coaches
Prop: B Mundell Ltd
Ops incl: local bus services (Isle of Islay).
Fleet: 4 single-deck coach, I midibus.
Chassis: 2 Dennis, I Optare, I Scania, I Volvo.
Bodies: I Ikarus, I Optare, I Plaxton, I UVG, I Wadham Stringer.
Livery: Green/White.

WILSON'S OF RHU
RHU GARAGE, MANSE BRAE, RHU G84 8RE
Tel: 01436 820300
Fax: 01436 820337
E-mail: info@wilsonsofrhu.co.uk
Web site: www.wilsonsofrhu.co.uk
Fleet: 14 – I double-deck bus, 4 single-deck coach, 6 midibus, 2 midicoach, I minibus.
Chassis: I Dennis, 4 Mercedes, 5 Optare, I Temsa, I Van Hool, 2 Volvo.
Ops incl: local bus services, private hire.
Livery: Grey/White/Red.

BORDERS

AUSTIN TRAVEL GROUP
STATION ROAD, EARLSTON TD4 6BZ
Tel: 01896 849360
Fax: 01896 849623
E-mail: info@scotlinetours.co.uk
Web site: www.scotlinetours.co.uk
Fleet Names: Capital Coaches, Scotline Tours.
Partners: Douglas Austin, Barry Austin.
Fleet: 9 – 8 single-deck coach, I minibus.
Chassis: 2 Bova, I Mercedes, 6 Van Hool.
Bodies: 2 Bova, I Unvi, 6 Van Hool.
Ops incl: school contracts, excursions & tours, private hire, continental tours.
Livery: Pearlescent white.

BARC COACH HIRE
52 EDDERSTON RIDGE, PEEBLES EH45 9NA
Tel: 01721 722222
Props: T Hughes, K Gibb.
Fleet: 14 – 6 single-deck coach, 2 midibus, 6 minibus.
Chassis: Alexander Dennis, DAF, Ford, Iveco, Mercedes, Optare, Scania, Volvo.
Ops incl: local bus services, school contracts, private hire.
Livery: White.

BUSKERS LTD
NORTHCOTE, BARR ROAD, GALASHIELS TD1 3HX
Tel: 0800 050 9454
E-mail: brucemethven@btopenworld.com
Web site: www.buskerscoachhire.co.uk
Prop: Bruce Methven.
Fleet: 6 – 3 single-deck coach, 2 midibus, I midicoach.
Chassis: I Iveco, 4 Mercedes, I Scania.
Ops incl: local bus services, private hire.

FIRST SCOTLAND EAST LTD
See Falkirk/Stirling

PETER HOGG COACHES
BANKEND SOUTH, JEDBURGH TD8 6ED
Tel/Fax: 01835 833755
Web Site: www.roadhoggs.net
Props: Mrs E Hogg, P M A Hogg.
Fleet: 15 – 3 single-deck coach, 12 minibus.
Chassis: 3 DAF, I EOS, 2 Ford Transit, I Iveco, 4 LDV, 2 Mercedes, I Volkswagen, I Volvo.
Ops incl: local bus services, school contracts, private hire.

PERRYMAN'S BUSES LTD
RAMPARTS BUSINESS PARK, NORTH ROAD, BERWICK UPON TWEED TD15 ITX
Tel: 01289 308719
Fax: 01289 309970
E-mail: enquiries@perrymansbuses.com
Web site: www.perrymansbuses.com
Depots at: Berwick, St Boswells.
Dirs: R J Perryman L M Perryman.
Fleet: 43 - 16 single deck bus, 6 single-deck coach, 13 midibus, 5 midicoach, 2 minibus, I minicoach.
Chassis: I Ford Transit, I Iveco, 8 Mercedes, I Neoplan, 25 Optare, 7 Volvo.
Bodies: 3 MCV, I Onyx, 25 Optare, 10 Plaxton, I Wrightbus, 3 Other.
Ops incl: local bus services, school contracts, private hire.
Livery: White with Red/Blue.
Ticket System: Wayfarer TGX.

E & A J ROBERTSON
ERAN, SUNNYSIDE, DUNS TD11 3QG
Tel: 01361 882340
Fleet: 4 – 2 single-deck coach, I midicoach, I minibus.
Chassis: I LDV, I Mercedes, 2 Volvo.
Ops incl: local bus services, school contracts, private hire.

TELFORD'S COACHES
I GEORGE STREET, NEWCASTLETON TD9 0QP
Tel/Fax: 01387 375677
Recovery: 07711 280475
E-mail: alistair@telfordscoaches.com
Web site: www.telfordscoaches.com
Man Dir: Alistair Telford **Ch Eng:** Rod Swan
Ops Man: Sarah Little.
Fleet: 24 - 12 single-deck coach, 3 midibus,

4 midicoach, 2 minibus, 3 minicoach.
Chassis: I Bova, I I Mercedes, I Optare, I VDL, 10 Volvo.
Bodies: I Berkhof, I Bova, 3 Jonckheere, I Optare, 13 Plaxton, I Sitcar, I Van Hool, I VDL, 2 Other.
Ops incl: local bus services, school contracts, excursions & tours, private hire, continental tours.
Livery: White with Blue vinyls.
Ticket System: Almex.
Also controls Bowman's Coaches (see *Cumbria*)

A WAIT & SON
⚑♿❄
WEST END GARAGE, CHIRNSIDE, DUNS TD11 3UJ
Tel/Fax: 01890 818216
Props: J A & I A Cockburn.
Fleet: 6 – 2 single-deck coach, I midicoach, 3 minibus.
Chassis: I Ford Transit, I Irisbus, I Iveco, I Mercedes, 2 Volvo.
Ops incl: local bus services, school contracts, private hire.

CLACKMANNANSHIRE

FIRST SCOTLAND EAST LTD
See Falkirk/Stirling.

HUNTER'S EXECUTIVE COACHES LTD
♿⚑⚑❄
THE GARAGE, LOCHIES ROAD, CLACKMANNAN FK10 4ENH
Tel: 01259 215560   **Fax:** 01259 723638
E-mail: hunterscoaches@btconnect.com
Web site: www.huntersexecutivecoaches.co.uk
Prop: John Hunter.
Fleet: 18 – I double-deck bus, I single-deck bus, 13 single-deck coach, 2 midibus, 2 midicoach, 3 minibus, I minicoach.
Chassis: I Bova, 3 Dennis, I MAN, 6 Mercedes, I Optare, 4 Scania, 7 Volvo.
Ops incl: local bus services, school contracts, private hire, excursions & tours.
Livery: Bluc.

M LINE
⚑⚑❄🔧
RIVERBANK INDUSTRIAL ESTATE, ALLOA FK10 1NT
Tel: 01259 212802
E-mail: info@m-line.co.uk.
Web Site: www.m-line.co.uk.
Ops Man: Tom Matchett, Andy McLellan
Eng: Dave Craig.
Fleet: 23 – 9 double-deck bus, I double-deck coach, I I single-deck coach, I midicoach, 2 minibus.
Chassis: I DAF, I Ford Transit, I Irisbus, I Iveco, I Leyland, 2 Mercedes, I Neoplan, 5 Scania, 2 Setra, 9 Volvo.
Ops incl: local bus services, school contracts, excursions & tours, continental tours.
Livery: Cream/Beige.

MACKIE'S COACHES
♿⚑⚑❄
32 GLASSHOUSE LOAN, ALLOA FK10 1PE
Tel: 01259 216180
Fax: 01259 217508
E-mail: enquiries@mackiescoaches.com
Web site: www.mackiescoaches.com
Fleet: 18 – 7 single-deck bus, I I single-deck coach
Chassis: 7 Bova, I DAF, 10 Volvo.
Ops incl: local bus services, school contracts, excursions & tours, private hire.
Liveries: Buses: White/Red; **Coaches:** White/Brown/Beige.
Ticket System: Wayfarer.

WOODS COACHES
♿⚑❚❄🔧T❄R24
2 GOLFVIEW, TILLICOULTRY FK13 6DH
Tel: 01259 751753
Fax: 01259 751824
E-mail: jwcoaches@btinternet.com
Web site: www.woodscoaches.net
Owner: James Woods **Ops Man:** John Woods.
Fleet: 13 – 3 single-deck coach, 2 midicoach, 4 minibus, 4 minicoach
Chassis: I Ford Transit, 9 Mercedes, 2 Van Hool, I Volvo.
Ops incl: school contracts, excursions & tours, private hire.
Livery: Grey.

DUMFRIES & GALLOWAY

ANDERSON'S COACHES
♿⚑
UNIT 1, WHITSHIELS INDUSTRIAL ESTATE, LANGHOLM DG13 0HX
Tel: 01387 201057   **Fax:** 01387 380553
Partners: I R Anderson, K Irving
Ch Eng: C Anderson.
Fleet: 15 – 7 single-deck coach, 3 midibus, I midicoach, 4 minibus.
Chassis: I AEC, 3 Ford Transit, I Iveco, 2 Leyland, 4 Mercedes, 4 Volvo.
Ops incl: local bus services, school contracts, private hire.
Livery: Red/Orange/Yellow stripe.
Ticket System: Almex.

WILLIAM BROWNRIGG
⚑⚑
THE GARAGE, THORNHILL DG3 5LZ
Tel/Fax: 01848 330203
E-mail: info@brownriggsthornhill.co.uk
Web site: www.brownriggsthornhill.co.uk
Dir: William Brownrigg.
Fleet: I I – 6 single-deck coach, 2 midicoach, 2 minibus.
Chassis: I Bova, I Irisbus, I Leyland, 4 Mercedes, I Scania, 2 Volvo.
Ops incl: school contracts, excursions & tours, private hire.
Livery: Orange/White.
Ticket System: Almex.

DGC BUSES
♿⚑
DUMFRIES & GALLOWAY COUNCIL, COUNCIL OFFICES, ENGLISH STREET, DUMFRIES DG1 2HR
Tel: 01387 260124
Prop: Dumfries & Galloway Council.
Fleet: 66 – 5 single-deck bus, I single-deck coach, 39 midibus, 3 midicoach, 18 minibus.
Chassis: 3 Alexander Dennis, 3 BMC, I DAF, 10 Dennis, 2 Ford Transit, 2 Iveco, 6 LDV, 23 Mercedes, 8 Optare, 4 Renault, I Van Hool, 3 VDL.
Ops incl: local bus services, school contracts.
Livery: Red/Yellow.
Ticket System: Almex.

HOUSTON'S COACHES
♿⚑⚑❄
61-63 BRIDGE STREET, LOCKERBIE DG11 2HS
Tel: 01576 203874
E-mail: info@houstonscoaches.co.uk
Web site: www.houstonscoaches.co.uk
Depots at: Lockerbie, Dumfries.
Props: W J & H J Houston
Fleet: 41 - 2 single-deck bus, 5 single-deck coach, 7 midibus, 4 midicoach, 21 minibus.
Chassis: I Alexander Dennis, 2 BMC, 2 Dennis, 2 Fiat, I Ford Transit, 5 Iveco, 9 Mercedes, 13 Optare, 2 Renault, 4 Volvo.
Ops incl: local bus services, school contracts, private hire, excursions & tours.
Livery: Blue/White.

A & F IRVINE & SON
Ceased trading since LRB 2014 went to press

JAMES KING COACHES/ABC TRAVEL
Ceased trading since LRB 2014 went to press

MacEWAN'S COACH SERVICES
⚑⚑❄
UNIT 4, CATHERINE FIELD INDUSTRIAL ESTATE, DUMFRIES DG1 3PQ
Tel: 01387 266528
Prop: John Mac Ewan
Ch Eng: Peter Maxwell.
Fleet: 38 – 4 double-deck bus, 8 single-deck bus, 5 single-deck coach, 10 midibus, I midicoach, 10 minibus.
Chassis: 2 BMC, I Fiat, 3 Ford Transit, I Leyland, I LDV, 4 MCW, 15 Mercedes, I Optare, 6 Scania, 4 Volvo.
Ops incl: local bus services, school contracts.
Livery: White/Red/Blue.
Ticket system: ERG Transit 400.

McCALL'S COACHES LTD
♿⚑⚑❄
4 LAMMONBIE COTTAGE, LOCKERBIE DG11 2RN
Tel: 01576 204309
E-mail: enquiries@mccallscoaches.com
Web site: www.mccallscoaches.com
Fleet: 20 – 14 single-deck coach, 3 midibus, I midicoach, I minibus, I minicoach.
Chassis: I DAF, 3 Dennis, 2 Leyland, I Marshall, 2 Mercedes, 2 Optare, 4 Scania, 5 Volvo.
Ops incl: local bus services, school contracts, private hire.

Mc CULLOCH AND SON
♿⚑⚑❄🔧
MAIN ROAD, STONEYKIRK, STRANRAER DG9 9DH
Tel/Fax: 01776 830236
E-mail: info@coachhirestranraer.co.uk
Web site: www.coachhirestranraer.co.uk
Fleet Name: McCulloch Coaches.
Partners: D F McCulloch, E A McCulloch.
Fleet: 6 – 4 single-deck coach, 2 midicoach.
Chassis: I Bedford, 2 Mercedes, 3 Volvo.
Bodies: I Caetano, I Duple, I Euro, 2 Plaxton, I Sitcar.
Ops incl: local bus services, excursions & tours, school contracts, private hire.
Livery: White/Blue lettering.

OOR COACHES LTD
⚑⚑
SWORDWELL COTTAGE, ANNAN DG12 6QZ
Tel: 01461 202159
E-mail: info@oorcoaches.co.uk
Web site: www.oorcoaches.co.uk
Fleet: 12 – 5 single-deck coach, 2 midibus, 2 midicoach, 3 minibus.
Chassis: I Bova, I Dennis, I Ford Transit, 5 Mercedes, I Renault, 3 Volvo.
Ops incl: local bus services, private hire.
Livery: White with Multicolours.

STAGECOACH WEST SCOTLAND
See South Ayrshire

DUNDEE CITY

FISHERS TOURS
⚑⚑❄🔧T
16 WEST PORT, DUNDEE DD1 5EP
Tel/Fax: 01382 455177
E-mail: enquiries@fisherstours.co.uk
Web site: www.fisherstours.co.uk
Partners: James Cosgrove, Catherine Cosgrove
Transport Mans: James Cosgrove, David Kidd.
Fleet: 24 – 23 single-deck coach, I midicoach.
Chassis: 2 DAF, 2 Dennis, 2 Iveco, I Mercedes, 17 Volvo.

Bodies: I Caetano, I Hispano, I Indcar, I Jonckheere, I Marcopolo, 4 Plaxton, I Sunsundegui, 13 Van Hool, I Wadham Stringer.
Ops incl: local bus services, school contracts, private hire, express.
Livery: White.

NATIONAL EXPRESS DUNDEE

44-48 EAST DOCK STREET, DUNDEE DD1 3JS
Tel: 01382 340006
Fax: 01382 201997
Web site: www.nxdundee.co.uk
Man Dir: Phil Smith Ops Man: Paul Clark
Ch Eng: Frank Sheach Business Man: Elsie Turbyne.
Fleet: 113 - 37 double-deck bus, 63 single-deck bus, 4 midibus, 9 minibus.
Chassis: 13 Alexander Dennis, 9 Optare, 3 Scania, 88 Volvo.
Bodies: 13 Alexander Dennis, 9 Optare, 10 Plaxton, 3 Scania, 78 Wrightbus.
Ops incl: local bus services, school contracts, excursions & tours, private hire.
Livery: Red/White.
Part of the National Express Group

SIDLAW EXECUTIVE TRAVEL (SCOTLAND) LTD

UNIT 5, ARDYLE INDUSTRIAL ESTATE, PERRIE STREET, DUNDEE DD2 2RD
Tel: 01382 610410
Fax: 01382 624333
E-mail: travel@sidlaw.co.uk
Web site: www.sidlaw.co.uk
Dir: Bob Costello Fleet Eng: Jamie Costello.
Fleet: 10 – I double-deck bus, 3 single-deck coach, 3 midicoach, 3 minibus.
Chassis: I Dennis, I LDV, 5 Mercedes, I Neoplan, I Scania, I Setra.
Ops incl: school contracts, excursions & tours, private hire.
Livery: White/Silver.

STAGECOACH EAST SCOTLAND

OFFICES 47-51, EVANS BUSINESS CENTRE, JOHN SMITH BUSINESS PARK, KIRKCALDY KY2 6HD
Tel: 01592 645680
Fax: 01592 645677
E-mail: eastscotland.enquiries@stagecoachbus.com
Web site: www.stagecoachbus.com
Fleet Names: Stagecoach in Fife, Stagecoach in Perth, Strathtay Scottish.
Man Dir: Andrew Jarvis Ops Dir: Mark Whitelocks Eng Dir: John Harper.
Fleet: 526 - 196 double-deck bus, 142 single-deck bus, 87 single deck coach, 39 midibus 62 minibus.
Chassis: 126 Alexander Dennis, 49 Dennis, 2 Leyland, 89 MAN, 62 Optare, 20 Scania, 146 Volvo.
Bodies: 195 Alexander Dennis, 93 Alexander, 22 East Lancs, I Northern Counties, 62 Optare, 95 Plaxton, 9 Scania, 34 Transbus, 17 Wrightbus.
Fleet excludes Rennies – see separate entry.
Ops incl: local bus services, school contracts, excursions & tours, private hire, express.
Livery: Stagecoach UK Bus/Citylink/Megabus.
Ticket System: ERG.
Part of the Stagecoach Group

EAST AYRSHIRE

LIDDELL'S COACHES

I MAUCHLINE ROAD, AUCHINLECK KA18 2BJ
Tel: 01290 424300/420717
Fax: 01290 425637

Prop: J Liddell Ch Eng: J Quinn
Co Sec: Ms J Samson Ops Man: Ms M Milroy.
Fleet: 75 - 14 double-deck bus, 10 single-deck bus, 23 single-deck coach, I midibus, 8 midicoach, 17 minibus, 2 minicoach.
Chassis: I Bedford, 3 DAF, 3 Dennis, 5 Ford Transit, 12 LDV, 2 Leyland, 2 MCW, 8 Mercedes, 2 Scania, I Setra, 36 Volvo.
Ops incl: local bus services, school contracts, excursions & tours, private hire, express.
Livery: White with Brown/Orange/Lemon stripes.

MILLIGAN'S COACH TRAVEL LTD

LOAN GARAGE, 20 THE LOAN, MAUCHLINE, KA5 6AN
Tel/Recovery: 01290 550365
Fax: 01290 553291
E-mail: enquiries@milliganscoachtravel.co.uk
Web site: www.milliganscoachtravel.co.uk
Dir: William J Milligan.
Fleet: 18 single -deck coach.
Chassis: I Bova, 12 Scania, 5 Volvo.
Bodies: I Bova, 11 Irizar, 6 Van Hool
Ops incl: school contracts, excursions & tours, private hire.
Livery: Black and Silver.

ROWE & TUDHOPE

UNIT 2, PALMERMOUNT INDUSTRIAL PARK, KILMARNOCK ROAD, DUNDONALD KA2 9BL
Tel: 01563 851349
E-mail: info@roweandtudhope.com
Web site: www.roweandtudhope.com
Prop: George Rowe.
Fleet: 18 – 6 double-deck bus, 3 single-deck bus, 7 single-deck coach, 2 minicoach.
Chassis: I Bova, 4 Dennis, I Leyland, 2 Mercedes, I Scania, 9 Volvo.
Ops incl: school contracts, private hire.
Livery: White with Blue vinyls.

STAGECOACH WEST SCOTLAND
See South Ayrshire

EAST LOTHIAN

EAST LOTHIAN BUSES
See Lothian Buses PLC (City of Edinburgh)

EVE CARS & COACHES

SPOTT ROAD, DUNBAR EH42 1RR
Tel: 01368 865500
Fax: 01368 865400
E-mail: admin@eveinfo.co.uk
Web site: www.eveinfo.co.uk
Partners: Gary Scougall, Vona Scougall.
Fleet: 23 – 2 double-deck bus, I double-deck coach, 7 single-deck coach, 4 midibus, 2 midicoach, 6 minibus, I minicoach.
Chassis: I Ford Transit, 2 MAN, 3 Mercedes, 8 Optare, 2 Scania, I Toyota, I VDL, 5 Volvo.
Bodies: 2 Alexander, I Beulas, I Caetano, I EVM, I Hispano, 2 Irizar, 9 Optare, 5 Plaxton, I Other.
Ops incl: local bus services, school contracts, private hire.
Livery: Brown/Cream.

FIRST SCOTLAND EAST LTD
See Falkirk/Stirling.

PRENTICE COACHES LTD

STATION GARAGE, HOSPITAL ROAD, HADDINGTON EH41 3BH
Tel: 01620 822620
Fax: 01620 823544
E-mail: mail@prentice.info
Web site: www.prenticeofhaddington.info

Dirs: L Prentice, R Prentice.
Fleet: 18 – I single-deck bus, 7 single-deck coach, 4 midibus, 5 midicoach, I minicoach.
Chassis: 3 Alexander Dennis, 2 Dennis, I Irisbus, 6 Mercedes, I VDL, 5 Volvo.
Bodies: 3 Alexander Dennis, I KVC, 12 Plaxton, I Tawe, I Wrightbus.
Ops incl: local bus services, school contracts, excursions & tours, private hire.
Livery: Silver/Blue.
Ticket System: Wayfarer.

EAST RENFREWSHIRE

HENRY CRAWFORD COACHES LTD

SHILFORD MILL, NEILSTON G78 3BA
Tel: 01505 850456
Fax: 01505 850479
E-mail: henrycrawford@talk21.com
Web site: www.henrycrawfordcoaches.co.uk
Dirs: James Crawford (Ops), John Crawford (Eng), Isobel Crawford (Co Sec).
Fleet: 22 - 17 single-deck coach, 5 minicoach.
Chassis: 10 Bova, 5 Mercedes, I Van Hool, 2 VDL, 4 Volvo.
Bodies: 10 Bova, I Indcar, I Plaxton, 3 Sitcar, I Unvi, 6 Van Hool.
Ops incl: private hire, school contracts.
Livery: White/Red.

McGILLS BUS SERVICE LTD

99, EARNHILL ROAD, LARKFIELD INDUSTRIAL ESTATE, GREENOCK PA16 0EQ
Tel: 08000 515651
Fax: 01475 711133
E-mail: enquiries@mcgillsbuses.co.uk
Web Site: www.mcgillsbuses.co.uk
Chairman: J Easdale Man Dir: R Roberts
Fin Dir: G Davidson Gen Man: B Hendry
Eng Dir: B Smith Head of Service Delivery: C Napier Marketing & Comms Man: I Murray Comm Man: L McColl.
Depots at: Barrhead, Greenock, Inchinnan, Johnstone.
Fleet: 326 – 41 double-deck bus, 74 single-deck bus, 8 single-deck coach, 16 articulated bus, 175 midibus, 12 minibus.
Chassis: 19 Alexander Dennis, 3 Bova, 44 DAF, 140 Dennis, I Fiat, I MAN, 44 Mercedes, 13 Optare, 8 Scania, 5 Transbus, 10 VDL, 2 Volkswagen, 37 Volvo.
Bodies: 98 Alexander, 20 Alexander Dennis, 3 Bluebird, 3 Bova, 8 Caetano, 3 East Lancs, I Fast, I Jonckheere, 9 Marshall, 33 Mercedes, 13 Optare, 37 Plaxton, 6 Scania, 86 Wrightbus.
Ops incl: local bus services, express.
Livery: Blue/White.

SOUTHERN COACHES (NM) LTD

LOCHIBO ROAD, BARRHEAD G78 1LF
Tel: 0800 298 1655
Fax: 0141 881 1148
E-mail: reservations@southerncoaches.co.uk.
Web site: www.glasgowcoaches.co.uk
Dirs: R Wallace, D Wallace, Mary Wallace.
Fleet: 14 - 12 single-deck coach, 2 minicoach.
Chassis: I Bova, I Mercedes, I Toyota, 11 Volvo.
Bodies: I Bova, I Caetano, 6 Plaxton, 6 Van Hool.
Ops incl: school contracts, excursions & tours, private hire, express.
Livery: Cream/Blue/Orange.

EDINBURGH, CITY OF

AAA COACHES

UNIT 7, RAW CAMPS INDUSTRIAL ESTATE, KIRKNEWTON EH27 8DF
Tel: 01506 883000   Fax: 01506 884000

E-mail: info@aaacoaches.co.uk
Web site: www.aaacoaches.co.uk
Man Dir: Mr J T Renton **Dir:** Mrs A Renton.
Fleet: 32 - 22 single-deck coach, 4 midicoach,
6 minibus.
Chassis: 6 Bova, 4 Ford Transit, 1 LDV, 3 MAN,
6 Mercedes, 1 Renault, 1 Setra, 5 VDL, 5 Volvo.
Livery: White with Blue lettering.

ALLAN'S COACHES EDINBURGH
🚌🎫♿✎✏🅃

THE COACH YARD, NEWTONLOAN
GARAGE, GOREBRIDGE EH23 4LZ
Tel/Recovery: 01875 820377
Fax: 01875 822468
E-mail: allanscoaches@aol.com
Web Site: www.allanscoaches.co.uk
Prop: David W Allan **Ops Man:** John Blair
Ch Eng: Neil Mitchell **Mechanic:** Warren Allan
Office Man: Mrs Dawn Allan.
Fleet: 10 - 7 single-deck coach, 2 midicoach,
1 minibus.
Chassis: DAF, Mercedes, Scania, Volvo.
Bodies: Irizar, Plaxton, Unvi, VDL.
Ops incl: school contracts, excursions & tours,
private hire, corporate & VIP, express.
Livery: Allan's Blue.

CITY CIRCLE UK LTD (EDINBURGH
BRANCH)
🎫🚌🎫♿

14 QUEEN ANNE DRIVE, NEWBRIDGE,
EDINBURGH EH28 5LD
Tel: 0131 333 2700
Fax: 0131 335 7929
E-mail: go@citycircleuk.com
Web site: www.citycircleuk.com
Man Dir: Neil Pegg **Gen Man:** John Docherty
Ops Man: Jennifer Gibson.
Fleet: 22 – 18 single-deck coach, 3 midicoach,
1 minicoach.
Chassis: 2 DAF, 14 MAN, 1 Mercedes, 3 Scania,
2 Volvo.
Bodies: 3 Irizar, 2 Jonckheere, 14 Neoplan,
1 Plaxton, 2 Van Hool.
Ops incl: excursions & tours, private hire,
continental tours, corporate charter.
Livery: White with Silver, Red.
Associated with City Circle UK Ltd, London
(see London & Middlesex)

EAST LOTHIAN BUSES
See Lothian Buses PLC

EDINBURGH BUS TOURS LTD
♿🚌📠♿

WAVERLEY BRIDGE, EDINBURGH EH1 1BQ
Tel: 0131 554 4494
E-mail: info@edinburghtour.com
Web site: www.edinburghtour.com
Fleet Names: City Sightseeing Edinburgh,
Edinburgh Tour, Mac Tours, Majestic Tours.
Chief Exec Officer: W Ian G Craig
Fin Dir: Norman J Strachan **Ops Dir:** William
W Campbell **Eng Dir:** William Devlin
Head of Operations (Buses): Sarah Boyd.
Fleet: 48 – 2 double-deck bus, 46 open-top bus.
Chassis: 12 AEC, 35 Dennis, 1 Volvo.
Bodies: 6 Alexander, 30 Plaxton, 12 Park Royal.
Ops incl: local bus services, private hire.
Livery: Various.
Ticket system: Casio.
A subsidiary of Lothian Buses Ltd

EDINBURGH COACH LINES LTD
🎫🚌📠♿✎🅃

81 SALAMANDER STREET, LEITH,
EDINBURGH EH6 7JZ
Tel: 0131 554 5413
Fax: 0131 553 3721
E-mail: enquiries@edinburghcoachlines.com.
Web site: www.edinburghcoachlines.com.
Dir: Patrick Kavanagh **Gen Man:** Peter Fyvie
Traffic Man: Gary Forbes-Burns.

Fleet: 36 – 1 single-deck bus, 25 single-deck
coach, 6 midibus, 2 midicoach, 2 minibus.
Chassis: 1 Dennis, 1 MAN, 4 Mercedes,
14 Scania, 8 VDL, 8 Volvo.
Bodies: 1 Berkhof, 1 Caetano, 1 Euro, 9 Irizar,
5 MCV, 6 Plaxton, 3 Unvi, 7 Van Hool, 3 Volvo.
Ops incl: local bus services, school contracts,
excursions & tours, private hire, continental
tours.
Liveries: Pink/Purple/White, Megabus Blue/
Yellow.
Ticket System: Wayfarer TGX.
A subsidiary of Bernard Kavanagh & Sons
(See Republic of Ireland)

EDINBURGH GROUP TRAVEL
♿🎫🚌📠♿Ⓡ R24✎🅃

UNIT 1, LADY VICTORIA BUSINESS PARK,
NEWTONGRANGE EH22 4QN
Tel: 0131 440 4400
Fax: 0131 454 0308
E-mail: info@edinburghgrouptravel.co.uk
Web site: www.edinburghgrouptravel.co.uk
Dirs: Robbie Prentice, David Cowen
Tran Man: David Reid
Fleet: 16 – 14 single-deck coach, 2 midicoach.
Chassis: 4 Bova, 1 MAN, 2 Mercedes, 9 Volvo.
Bodies: 1 Berkhof, 4 Bova, 1 Caetano, 1 Esker,
8 Plaxton, 1 Van Hool.
Ops Incl: school contracts, excursions & tours,
private hire, continental tours.
Livery: White with two Blues and Red stripes.
A subsidiary of Prentice Westwood Ltd *(see
West Lothian)*

FIRST SCOTLAND EAST LTD
See Falkirk/Stirling.

CHARLIE IRONS COACHES LTD
🚌♿♿

44 BABERTON CRESCENT, EDINBURGH
EH14 5BP
Tel: 0131 441 2222
Fax: 01506 880099
E-mail: charlie@ironscoaches.co.uk
Web site: www.ironscoaches.co.uk
Fleet: 8 – 6 single-deck coach, 2 minibus.
Chassis: 1 Ford Transit, 1 Irisbus, 2 MAN,
1 Mercedes, 1 Neoplan, 1 Setra, 1 Volvo.
Ops incl: private hire.

LOTHIAN BUSES LTD
♿🚽

ANNANDALE STREET, EDINBURGH
EH7 4AZ
Tel: 0131 554 4494
Fax: 0131 554 3942
E-mail: mail@lothianbuses.com
Web site: www.lothianbuses.com
Fleet Names: Lothian Buses, East Lothian
Buses.
Chief Exec Officer: W Ian G Craig
Fin Dir: Norman J Strachan **Ops Dir:** William
W Campbell **Eng Dir:** William Devlin
HR Director: Guy Hughes **Head of
Operations (Buses):** Sarah Boyd **Chair:**
Ann Faulds **Non Exec Dirs:** Owen Boyle,
Dr Steve Cassidy, Tony Depledge, Donald
Macleod, Marjory Rodger, John Martin.
Lothian Buses Fleet: 653 – 498 double-deck
bus, 102 single-deck bus, 47 midibus, 6 minibus.
Chassis: 15 Alexander Dennis, 110 Dennis,
6 Optare, 15 Scania, 45 Transbus, 462 Volvo.
Bodies: 15 Alexander Dennis, 6 Optare,
95 Plaxton, 15 Scania, 60 Transbus, 10 Volvo,
452 Wrightbus.
East Lothian Buses Fleet: 7 – 2 double-deck
bus, 5 single-deck bus.
Chassis: 2 Dennis, 5 Volvo
Bodies: 2 Plaxton, 5 Wrightbus.
Ops incl: local bus services.
Livery: Maroon/White; **East Lothian Buses:**
Green/Cream.
Ticket system: Wayfarer TGX200.

JAMES E McNEE COACH HIRE LTD
♿♿

76 STATION ROAD, RATHO STATION
EH28 8QT
Tel: 0131 333 4044
Fax: 0131 333 4341
E-mail: james@mcneecoaches.co.uk
Web site: www.mcneecoaches.co.uk
Fleet: 9 – 4 single-deck coach, 3 midicoach,
2 minibus.
Chassis: 5 Mercedes, 1 Van Hool, 3 Volvo.
Ops incl: excursions & tours, private hire.
Livery: White.

RABBIES TRAIL BURNERS LTD
♿♿

207 HIGH STREET, EDINBURGH EH1 1PE
Tel: 0131 226 3133
Fax: 0131 225 7028
E-mail: info@rabbies.com
Web site: www.rabbies.com
Dir: R Worsnop.
Fleet: 32 minicoach.
Chassis: Mercedes
Bodies: EVM, KVC.
Ops incl: tours.

RADICAL TRAVEL GROUP
♿♿

7-11 BLACKFRIARS STREET, EDINBURGH
EH1 1NB
Tel: 0131 557 9393
Web site: www.radicaltravel.com
Fleet name: Haggis Adventures.
Fleet: 9 – 6 midicoaches, 1 minibus, 2 minicoach.
Chassis: 9 Mercedes.
Bodies: 1 Ferqui, 7 Unvi, 1 Mercedes.
Ops incl: tours.
Livery: Yellow.

RATHO COACHES LTD
🚌♿♿

NEWBRIDGE INDUSTRIAL ESTATE,
NEWBRIDGE EH28 8PJ
Tel: 0131 333 2635
Fax: 0131 333 5426
E-mail: info@rathocoaches.com
Web site: www.rathocoaches.co.uk
Man Dir: A Cowan.
Fleet: 16 – 7 single-deck coach, 2 midibus,
2 minicoach, 5 minibus.
Chassis: 2 Ford Transit, 1 Iveco, 2 LDV,
2 Mercedes, 1 Neoplan, 2 Optare, 1 Scania,
5 Volvo.
Bodies: 1 Bluebird, 2 Ford Transit, 1 Irizar,
2 LDV, 1 Neoplan, 2 Optare, 1 Sunsundegui,
1 Unvi, 4 Volvo.
Ops incl: private hire, excursions & tours.
Livery: White with Blue.

FALKIRK

COLES COACHES
♿♿

113 EASTBURN DRIVE, FALKIRK FK1 1TX
Tel: 01324 679561
Fleet: 6 – 1 single-deck bus, 5 midibus.
Chassis: 3 Dennis, 2 Optare, 1 Volvo.
Ops incl: local bus services, school contracts,
private hire.

DEWAR COACHES
🚌♿♿

24 PARKHEAD ROAD, GLEN VILLAGE,
FALKIRK FK1 2AR
Tel: 01324 629275 **Fax:** 01324 613303
E-mail: info@dewarcoaches.co.uk
Web site: www.dewarcoaches.co.uk
Fleet: 6 – 5 single-deck coach, 1 midicoach.
Chassis: 1 Mercedes, 5 Volvo.
Bodies: 1 Plaxton, 5 Van Hool.
Ops incl: private hire, excursions & tours,
continental tours.
Livery: White.

FIRST SCOTLAND EAST LTD

CARMUIRS HOUSE, 300 STIRLING ROAD, LARBERT FK5 3NJ
Tel: 01324 602200
Fax: 01324 611287
E-mail: contact.scotlandeast@firstgroup.com
Web site: www.firstgroup.com/scotlandeast
Fleet Names: First Scotland East, Midland Bluebird.
Man Dir: Paul McGowan **Ops Dir:** John Gorman.
Fleet: 396 – 152 double-deck bus, 191 single-deck bus, 23 single-deck coach, 16 midibus, 3 midicoach, 11 minibus.
Chassis: 12 Alexander Dennis, 7 BMC, 56 Dennis, 2 Enterprise, 9 Mercedes, 9 Optare, 127 Scania, 4 Transbus, 170 Volvo.
Bodies: 57 Alexander, 12 Alexander Dennis, 7 BMC, 6 East Lancs, 9 Marshall, 6 Mercedes, 9 Optare, 82 Plaxton, 18 Scania, 2 Transbus, 184 Wrightbus.
Ops incl: local bus services, school contracts, private hire, express.
Livery: FirstGroup UK Bus.
Ticket System: Almex.

FIFE

BAY TRAVEL

GUTHRIE HOUSE, 3 GLENFIELD INDUSTRIAL ESTATE, COWDENBEATH KY4 9HT
Tel: 01383 516161
Fax: 01383 511647
E-mail: enquiries@bay-travel.co.uk
Web site: www.bay-travel.co.uk
Props: I Robertson, V Derighetti.
Fleet: 22 – 3 double-deck bus, 8 single-deck coach, 5 midicoach, 5 minibus, 1 minicoach.
Chassis: 2 BMC, 1 Bova, 3 Dennis, 1 Iveco, 7 Mercedes, 2 Optare, 6 Volvo.
Ops incl: local bus services, school contract, private hire.
Livery: White with Blue.

HAMISH GORDON COACHES

BANK PLACE GARAGE, LESLIE KY6 3LD
Tel/Fax: 01592 620202
E-mail: hamish_gordon@btconnect.com
Web site: www.hamishgordoncoaches.co.uk
Prop: Hamish Gordon.
Fleet: 14 – 10 single-deck coach, 2 midicoach, 2 minibus.
Chassis: 7 Bova, 1 DAF, 1 Duple 425, 4 Mercedes, 1 VDL.
Ops incl: school contracts, private hire.
Livery: White.

MOFFAT & WILLIAMSON LTD

OLD RAILWAY YARD, ST FORT, NEWPORT-ON-TAY DD6 8RG
Tel: 01382 541159   **Fax:** 01382 541169
E-mail: enquiries@moffat-williamson.co.uk
Web site: www.moffat-williamson.co.uk
Dirs: G Devine, L A Devine.
Depots at: St Fort, Glenrothes.
Fleet: 60 - 2 single-deck bus, 42 single-deck coach, 12 midibus, 1 midicoach, 3 minibus.
Chassis: 5 Alexander Dennis, 8 Dennis, 2 Ford, 4 Mercedes, 9 Optare, 1 VDL, 31 Volvo.
Bodies: 1 Alexander Dennis, 1 East Lancs, 1 Ford, 9 Optare, 44 Plaxton, 1 Sunsundegui, 3 Transbus.
Ops incl: local bus services, school contracts, excursions & tours, private hire, express.
Livery: Brown/Cream/Orange.

RENNIES OF DUNFERMLINE LTD

WELLWOOD, DUNFERMLINE KY12 0PY
Tel: 01383 620600   **Fax:** 01383 620624

E-mail: gordon@rennies.co.uk
Web site: www.rennies.co.uk
Man Dir: Andrew Jarvis **Gen Man:** Gordon Menzies **Tran Man:** Iain Robertson
Ch Eng: George Clark.
Fleet: 50 - 18 double-deck bus, 4 single-deck bus, 23 single-deck coach, 2 midicoach, 1 minibus, 2 minicoach.
Chassis: 4 Autosan, 2 BMC, 18 Dennis, 4 Mercedes, 1 Optare, 21 Volvo.
Bodies: 18 Alexander, 4 Autosan, 2 BMC, 1 Excel, 4 Jonckheere, 2 Mercedes, 1 Optare, 16 Plaxton, 1 Onyx, 1 Sunsundegui.
Ops incl: local bus services, school contracts, excursions & tours, private hire, express, continental tours.
Liveries: Blue/White, Citylink.
Ticket system: Almex.
A subsidiary of the Stagecoach Group

ST ANDREWS EXECUTIVE TRAVEL LTD

BROWNHILLS GARAGE, ST ANDREWS KY16 8PL
Tel: 01334 470080   **Fax:** 01334 470081
E-mail: orders@saxtravel.co.uk
Web Site: www.saxtravel.co.uk
Dir: Gordon Donaldson.
Fleet: 20 - 10 midicoach, 10 minicoach.
Chassis: 20 Mercedes.
Bodies: 1 Beulas, 19 Unvi.
Ops incl: excursions & tours, private hire.
Livery: White.

STAGECOACH EAST SCOTLAND

OFFICES 47-51, EVANS BUSINESS CENTRE, JOHN SMITH BUSINESS PARK, KIRKCALDY KY2 6HD
Tel: 01592 645680   **Fax:** 01592 645677
E-mail: eastscotland.enquiries@stagecoachbus.com
Web site: www.stagecoachbus.com
Fleet Names: Stagecoach in Fife, Stagecoach in Perth, Strathtay Scottish.
Man Dir: Andrew Jarvis **Ops Dir:** Mark Whitelocks **Eng Dir:** John Harper.
Fleet: 526 - 196 double-deck bus, 142 single-deck bus, 87 single deck coach, 39 midibus, 62 minibus.
Chassis: 126 Alexander Dennis, 49 Dennis, 2 Leyland, 89 MAN, 62 Optare, 20 Scania, 146 Volvo.
Bodies: 195 Alexander Dennis, 93 Alexander, 22 East Lancs, 1 Northern Counties, 62 Optare, 95 Plaxton, 9 Scania, 34 Transbus, 17 Wrightbus.
Fleet excludes Rennies – see separate entry.
Ops incl: local bus services, school contracts, excursions & tours, private hire, express.
Livery: Stagecoach UK Bus/Citylink/Megabus.
Ticket System: ERG.
Part of the Stagecoach Group

GLASGOW, CITY OF

ALLANDER COACHES LTD

UNIT 19, CLOBERFIELD INDUSTRIAL ESTATE, MILNGAVIE, GLASGOW G62 7LN
Tel: 0141 956 5678
Fax: 0141 956 6669
E-mail: enquiries@allandercoaches.co.uk
Web site: www.allandertravel.co.uk
Man Dir: James Fulton Wilson **Dir:** Mrs Elizabeth E Wilson **Tran Man:** Gary Wilson
Ch Eng: Graham Wilson **Co Sec:** Miss Margaret Brown.
Fleet: 26 - 5 single-deck bus, 19 single-deck coach, 2 midicoach.
Chassis: 17 Bova, 2 Mercedes, 1 VDL, 6 Volvo.
Ops incl: local bus services, school contracts, private hire.
Livery: Black/Orange/Gold.

CITY SIGHTSEEING GLASGOW

ST GEORGE'S BUILDING, 153 QUEEN STREET, GLASGOW G1 3BJ
Tel: 0141 204 0444
Fax: 0141 248 6582
E-mail: info@citysightseeingglasgow.co.uk
Web site: www.citysightseeingglasgow.co.uk
Man Dir: Colin Craig **Ops Man:** Donald Booth.
Fleet: 16 – 2 double-deck bus, 14 open top bus.
Chassis: 1 Leyland, 2 MCW, 6 Scania, 8 Volvo.
Bodies: 8 Alexander, 3 East Lancs, 2 MCW, 2 Optare, 1 Roe.
Ops incl: excursions & tours, private hire.
Livery: City Sightseeing Red.
Ticket system: Wayfarer 3.
A subsidiary of West Coast Motors
(see Argyll & Bute)

DOIGS OF GLASGOW LTD

TRANSPORT HOUSE, SUMMER STREET, GLASGOW G40 3TB
Tel: 0141 554 5555   **Fax:** 0141 551 9000
E-mail: info@doigs.com
Web site: www.doigs.com
Chairman/Man Dir: Andrew Forsyth
Co Sec: Iain Forsyth.
Fleet: 22 - 1 double-deck bus, 1 articulated bus, 16 single-deck coach, 4 minicoach.
Chassis: 3 Irizar, 4 Mercedes, 7 Scania, 8 Volvo.
Bodies: 2 Ferqui, 8 Irizar, 1 Lahden, 1 Mercedes, 1 Optare, 7 Sunsundegui, 1 Unvi, 1 Wrightbus.
Ops incl: school contracts, excursions & tours, private hire, continental tours.
Livery: Silver/Red lettering.

FAIRLINE COACHES LTD

331 CHARLES STREET, GLASGOW G21 3QA
Tel: 0141 553 1313
E-mail: info@fairlinecoaches.co.uk
Web site: www.fairlinecoaches.co.uk
Fleet: 19 – 8 single-deck coach, 5 midicoach, 3 minibus, 3 minicoach.
Chassis: 7 Bova, 1 Ford Transit, 9 Mercedes, 1 Volkswagen, 1 Volvo.
Ops incl: excursions & tours, private hire.
Livery: Silver with Red/Grey.
A subsidiary of West Coast Motors
(see Argyll & Bute)

FIRST GLASGOW

197 VICTORIA ROAD, GLASGOW G42 7AD
Tel: 0141 423 6600   **Fax:** 0141 636 3228
Web Site: www.firstgroup.com
Regional Man Dir: Neil Barker **Regional Comm Dir:** Kevin Belfield **Man Dir:** Fiona Kerr **Eng Dir:** Kenny Dickson.
Fleet: 913 – 365 double-deck bus, 463 single-deck bus, 65 midibus, 20 minibus.
Chassis: 223 Alexander Dennis, 129 Dennis, 7 Fiat, 10 Optare, 56 Scania, 37 Transbus, 3 Volkswagen, 420 Volvo, 28 Wrightbus.
Ops incl: local bus services, express.
Livery: FirstGroup UK Bus.

GLASGOW CITYBUS LTD

739 SOUTH STREET, GLASGOW G14 0BX
Tel: 0141 954 2255
E-mail: mail@glasgowcitybus.co.uk
Web site: www.glasgowcitybus.co.uk
Man Dir: Colin Craig.
Fleet: 53 – 1 open-top bus, 4 single-deck bus, 4 single-deck coach, 37 midibus, 7 minibus.
Chassis: 26 Alexander Dennis, 5 DAF, 5 Dennis, 2 Fiat, 5 Optare, 5 Renault, 5 VDL.
Bodies: 26 Alexander Dennis, 2 Bluebird, 1 East Lancs, 4 Irizar, 2 MCV, 5 Optare, 8 Plaxton, 5 Wrightbus.
Ops incl: local bus services.

Livery: Red/White/Blue/Yellow.
A subsidiary of West Coast Motors
(see Argyll & Bute)

McGILLS BUS SERTVICE LTD
See Inverclyde

MEARNS EXCLUSIVE TRAVEL LTD
BLOCK 19, SOUTH AVENUE, BLANTYRE,
GLASGOW G72 0XB
Tel: 01698 538638
E-mail: brian@mearnsexclusivetravel.co.uk
Web site: www.mearnsexclusivetravel.co.uk
Dir: Brian Murray **Tran Man:** Andy Shaw.
Fleet: 26 – 23 single-deck coach, 1 midicoach,
2 minibus.
Chassis: 1 Bova, 1 Irizar, 3 Mercedes,
11 Neoplan, 9 Scania, 1 VDL.
Bodies: 1 Bova, 10 Irizar, 1 KVC, 1 Mercedes,
11 Neoplan, 1 Unvi, 1 VDL.
Ops incl: excursions & tours, private hire.
Liveries: White, Brands.

MEGABUS
BUCHANAN BUS STATION, KILLERMONT
STREET, GLASGOW G2 3NW
Tel: 0141 332 9644
E-mail: enquiries@megabus.com
Web site: www.uk.megabus.com
Man Dir: Elizabeth Esnouf **Gen Man:** Ian Laing.
Ops incl: express.
Livery: Stagecoach UK Bus/Megabus Blue/
Yellow.
A division of the Stagecoach Group
Megabus Contractors: Edinburgh Coach
Lines *(see City of Edinburgh)*, Freestones Coaches
(see Norfolk), Rennies of Dunfermline *(see Fife)*,
Stagecoach Bluebird, Stagecoach East Midlands,
Stagecoach Glasgow, Stagecoach Midlands,
Stagecoach East Scotland, Stagecoach South
Wales.

SCOTTISH CITYLINK COACHES LTD
BUCHANAN BUS STATION, KILLERMONT
STREET, GLASGOW G2 3NW
Tel: 0871 266 3333
Fax: 0141 332 4488
E-mail: info@citylink.co.uk.
Web site: www.citylink.co.uk
Man Dir: Edward Hodgson.
Ops incl: private hire, express.
Livery: Blue/yellow.
Ticket system: Wayfarer.
Jointly owned by Comfort DelGro and the
Stagecoach Group
Scottish Citylink Contractors: Bruce
Coaches *(see North Lanarkshire)*, Glasgow
Citybus *(see Glasgow)*, Park's of Hamilton
(see South Lanarkshire), Rennies of Dunfermline
(see Fife), Shiel Buses *(see Highland)*, Stagecoach
Glasgow, Stagecoach Highland, West Coast
Motors Group *(see Argyll & Bute)*

SELVEY'S COACHES
1/7 NEW ROAD, CAMBUSLANG
G72 7PU
Tel: 0141 641 1080
Fax: 0141 641 0586
E-mail: enquiries@selveyscoaches.co.uk
Web site: www.selveyscoaches.co.uk
Owner: Tom Selvey.
Fleet: 8 – 5 single-deck coach, 2 midicoach,
1 minicoach.
Chassis: 3 Bedford, 2 Leyland, 1 Mercedes,
2 Volvo.
Bodies: 1 Duple, 1 Jonckheere, 1 Mercedes,
3 Plaxton.
Ops incl: excursions & tours, private hire,
school contracts.
Livery: White with Red.

STAGECOACH GLASGOW
See Stagecoach West Scotland *(South Ayrshire)*

HIGHLAND

BREMNER'S OF AVIEMORE
39 MILTON PARK, AVIEMORE PH22 1RS
Tel: 01479 812322
E-mail: bremnersofaviemore@gmail.com
Web Site: www.bremnersaviemore.co.uk
Prop: K Bremner.
Fleet: 4 – 2 single-deck coach, 1 midicoach,
1 minibus.
Chassis: 1 Bova, 2 Mercedes, 1 Scania.
Ops incl: local bus services, school contracts,
private hire.
Livery: White.

D&E COACHES LTD
39 HENDERSON DRIVE, INVERNESS IV1 1TR
Tel: 01463 222444   **Fax:** 01463 226700
Recovery: 07770 222612
E-mail: info@decoaches.co.uk
Web site: www.decoaches.co.uk
Man Dir: Donald Mathieson **Dir:** Elizabeth
Mathieson **Co Acct:** Gayle Kennedy **Ops
Man:** Willie Bell **Ch Eng:** Calum McGregor
Workshop Foreman: Bryan Fiddy.
Fleet: 49 – 7 double-deck bus, 10 single-deck
bus, 20 single-deck coach, 3 midibus, 3 midicoach,
6 minibus.
Chassis: 12 Bova, 1 DAF, 1 Dennis,
11 Mercedes, 2 Temsa, 1 Volkswagen, 21 Volvo.
Bodies: 16 Alexander, 1 Berkhof, 12 Bova,
1 KVC, 3 Mercedes, 8 Plaxton, 2 Temsa, 1 UVG,
4 Van Hool, 1 Volkswagen.
Ops incl: local bus services, school contracts,
private hire.
Livery: Coaches: White; **Buses:** Red/Silver.
Ticket system: Almex.

FRASER'S COACHES
THE GARAGE, MUNLOCHY IV8 8NE
Tel: 01463 811219   **Fax:** 01463 811619
E-mail: fraserscoaches@yahoo.co.uk
Web site: www.fraserscoaches.co.uk
Prop: Charles Fraser.
Fleet: 11 – 1 double-deck bus, 7 single-deck
coach, 1 midicoach, 1 minibus.
Chassis: 1 Dennis, 1 Ford Transit, 2 Leyland,
2 Mercedes, 5 Volvo.
Ops incl: school contracts, excursions & tours,
private hire.
Livery: Silver/White & Blue.

HIGHLAND TRANSLINK LTD
8 LONGMAN DRIVE, INVERNESS IV1 1SU
Tel: 01463 214410
E-mail: info@scotbus.co.uk
Web site: www.scotbus.co.uk
Dirs: M Smillie, R MacLeod.
Fleet: 4 – 3 single-deck coach, 1 midibus.
Chassis: 1 Bova, 1 Scania, 1 VDL, 1 Wrightbus.
Ops incl: local bus services, private hire.
Livery: Green & White.
Also controls Scotbus

MacLEAN COACHES LTD
LOCHALSH BUSINESS PARK, AUCHTERTYRE,
KYLE OF LOCHALSH IV40 8EG
Tel: 01599 566766
E-mail: info@maclean-coaches.co.uk
Web Site: www.maclean-coaches.co.uk
Prop: R MacLean.
Fleet: 6 – 3 single-deck coach, 1 midicoach, 1
minibus, 1 minicoach.
Ops incl: local bus services, school contracts,
private hire.
Livery: Blue.

MacLEOD'S COACHES
TIGH AN ALT, ACHEILIDH, ROGART
IV28 3UD
Tel/Fax: 01408 641354
Web site: www.macleodscoaches.co.uk
Prop: J MacLeod.
Fleet: 11 – 6 single-deck coach, 2 midibus,
1 midicoach, 2 minibus.
Chassis: 1 DAF, 2 Mercedes, 2 Optare, 1 Temsa,
5 Volvo.
Ops incl: local bus services, school contracts,
private hire.
Livery: White/Blue.

SCOTBUS LTD
8 LONGMAN DRIVE, INVERNESS
IV2 3HY
Tel: 01463 214410
Fax: 01463 224558
E-mail: info@scotbus.co.uk
Web site: www.scotbus.co.uk
Fleet Name: Highland Scotbus.
Dirs: M Smillie, R MacLeod.
Fleet: 31 - 13 double-deck bus, 2 single-deck
bus, 4 single-deck coach, 2 midicoach,
9 minibus, 1 minibus.
Chassis: 2 Ford Transit, 1 Iveco, 10 Leyland,
9 Mercedes, 1 Renault, 8 Volvo.
Ops incl: local bus services, school contracts,
private hire.
Liveries: Blue/White; Green/Orange.
Controlled by Highland Translink

SHIEL BUSES LTD
BLAIN GARAGE, ACHARACLE
PH36 4JY
Tel/Fax: 01967 431272
E-mail: info@shielbuses.co.uk
Web site: www.shielbuses.co.uk
Dir: Donnie MacGillivray.
Depots at: Acharacle, Fort William.
Fleet: 27 - 7 single-deck coach, 2 midibus,
11 midicoach, 5 minibus, 2 minicoach.
Chassis: 1 Ford Transit, 16 Mercedes, 1 Optare,
1 Toyota, 1 Van Hool, 7 Volvo.
Ops incl: local bus services, express, school
contracts, private hire.
Livery: Blue/Silver.
Ticket system: Almex.
Incorporates White Heather Travel

SKYEWAYS
TOWER HOUSE, DORNIE, KYLE OF
LOCHALSH IV40 8DA
Tel: 01599 555477
Web Site: www.skyeways.co.uk
Props: A & Mrs M MacRae.
Fleet: 5 – 3 single-deck coach, 1 midicoach,
1 minibus.
Chassis: 1 Mercedes, 1 Toyota, 3 Volvo.
Ops incl: school contracts, private hire.
Livery: Blue.

SPA COACHES
KINETTAS, STRATHPEFFER
IV14 9BH
Tel: 01997 421311
Fax: 01997 421983
E-mail: info@spacoaches.co.uk
Web site: www.spacoaches.com
Prop: N MacArthur.
Fleet: 21 – 14 single-deck coach, 4 midicoach,
1 minibus, 2 minicoach.
Chassis: 6 Mercedes, 2 Toyota, 13 Volvo.
Bodies: 1 Caetano, 1 Dormobile, 1 Jonckheere,
1 Mercedes, 1 Onyx, 4 Plaxton, 2 Van Hool.
Ops incl: school contracts, excursions & tours,
private hire, continental tours.
Livery: Orange/White.

STAGECOACH HIGHLAND

&♿🅿♨🚻📶📱

INVERNESS BUS STATION, FARRALINE PARK, INVERNESS IV1 1LT
Tel: 01463 233371
Fax: 01463 251360
Recovery: 01463 239292
E-mail: highland.enquiries@stagecoachbus.com
Web site: www.stagecoachbus.com
Fleet Name: Stagecoach in the Highlands.
Man Dir: Steve Walker **Ops Dir:** Stephie Barber **Eng Dir:** Russell Henderson.
Fleet: 143 - 19 double-deck bus, 56 single-deck bus, 34 single-deck coach, 14 midibus, 20 minibus
Chassis: 45 Alexander Dennis, 8 Dennis, 20 Optare, 13 Scania, 57 Volvo.
Bodies: 58 Alexander Dennis, 16 Alexander, 2 East Lancs, 3 Jonckheere, 1 Northern Counties, 20 Optare, 38 Plaxton, 5 Wrightbus. Fleet excludes Orkney – see separate entry.
Ops incl: local bus services, school contracts, excursions & tours, private hire, express.
Livery: Stagecoach UK Bus/Citylink/Megabus.
Ticket System: Wayfarer/ERG.

GRAHAM URQUHART TRAVEL LTD

🅿♨🚻📶📱🔧

28 MIDMILLS ROAD, INVERNESS IV2 3NY
Tel: 01463 222292
Fax: 01463 238880
E-mail: enquiries@grahamurquharttravel-inverness.co.uk
Web site: www.grahamurquharttravel.co.uk
Dir: John G Urquhart **Sec:** John G Prant.
Fleet: 5 - 3 single-deck coach, 1 midicoach, 1 minibus.
Chassis: 2 Mercedes, 1 Scania, 2 Volvo.
Bodies: 1 Irizar, 1 KVC, 1 Unvi, 2 Volvo.
Ops incl: excursions & tours, private hire.

WESTERBUS

🅿♨🚻📶

THE GARAGE, GAIRLOCH IV21 2BH
Tel: 01445 712255
Props: M MacKenzie, I MacLennan.
Fleet: 8 –6 single-deck coach, 2 midicoach.
Chassis: 1 Bova, 1 MAN, 1 Mercedes, 1 Scania, 4 Volvo.
Ops incl: local bus services, school contracts, private hire.
Livery: White with Two Tone Blue.

INVERCLYDE

C & M DUNN

🅿♨🚻

194 INVERKIP ROAD, GREENOCK PA16 9EX
Tel: 01475 785988
Fleet Names: C & M Coaches, Dunns Coaches.
Fleet: 42 – 6 single-deck coach, 3 midicoach, 30 minibus, 3 minicoach.
Chassis: DAF, Leyland, Mercedes, Optare, Volvo.
Ops incl: local bus services, school contracts, private hire.

FIRTH COACHES LTD

&♿🅿♨🚻

11 DELLINGBURN STREET, GREENOCK PA15 4RN
Tel: 01475 888388
Dirs: S McPherson, G Findlay.
Fleet: 11 – 5 single-deck bus, 2 single-deck coach, 2 midicoach, 2 minibus.
Chassis: 5 BMC, 1 Ford Transit, 3 Mercedes, 2 Volvo.
Ops incl: school contracts, private hire.

GILLEN'S COACHES LTD

🅿♨🚻

11 DELLINGBURN STREET, GREENOCK PA15 4RN
Tel/Fax: 01475 888000
Dirs: S McPherson, G Findlay.

Fleet: 13 – 1 single-deck bus, 3 single-deck coach, 1 midicoach, 8 minibus.
Chassis: 1 BMC, 1 Bova, 1 Dennis, 2 Fiat, 1 Ford, 1 LDV, 2 Mercedes, 2 Optare, 1 Scania, 1 Volkswagen.
Ops incl: local bus services, excursions & tours, private hire.
Livery: White.
Ticket system: Wayfarer.

McGILLS BUS SERVICE LTD

&♿

99, EARNHILL ROAD, LARKFIELD INDUSTRIAL ESTATE, GREENOCK PA16 0EQ
Tel: 08000 515651
Fax: 01475 711133
E-mail: enquiries@mcgillsbuses.co.uk
Web Site: www.mcgillsbuses.co.uk
Chairman: J Easdale **Man Dir:** R Roberts
Fin Dir: G Davidson **Gen Man:** B Hendry
Eng Dir: B Smith **Head of Service Delivery:** C Napier **Marketing & Comms Man:** I Murray **Comm Man:** L McColl.
Depots at: Barrhead, Greenock, Inchinnan, Johnstone.
Fleet: 326 – 41 double-deck bus, 74 single-deck bus, 8 single-deck coach, 16 articulated bus, 175 midibus, 12 minibus.
Chassis: 19 Alexander Dennis, 3 Bova, 44 DAF, 140 Dennis, 1 Fiat, 1 MAN, 44 Mercedes, 13 Optare, 8 Scania, 5 Transbus, 10 VDL, 2 Volkswagen, 37 Volvo.
Bodies: 98 Alexander, 20 Alexander Dennis, 3 Bluebird, 3 Bova, 8 Caetano, 3 East Lancs, 1 Fast, 1 Jonckheere, 9 Marshall, 33 Mercedes, 13 Optare, 37 Plaxton, 6 Scania, 86 Wrightbus.
Ops incl: local bus services, express.
Livery: Blue/White.

PRIDE OF THE CLYDE COACHES LTD

🅿♨🚻

11 DELLINGBURN STREET, GREENOCK PA15 4RN
Tel: 01475 888000
Fax: 01475 888333
E-mail: info@prideoftheclyde.net
Web Site: www.prideoftheclyde.net
Dirs: S McPherson, S McPherson, G Findlay.
Fleet: 35 – 1 double-deck bus, 4 single-deck bus, 23 single-deck coach, 3 midicoach, 3 minibus, 1 minicoach.
Chassis: BMC, Bova, DAF, LDV, Leyland, Mercedes, Scania, Temsa, Volvo.
Ops incl: private hire.
Livery: White with Blue.

SLAEMUIR COACHES LTD

&♿🅿♨🚻

11 DELLINGBURN STREET, GREENOCK PA15 4RN
Tel: 01475 731216
Fax: 01475 797175
Dirs: S McPherson, S McPherson, G Findlay.
Fleet: 29 – 1 double-deck bus, 1 single-deck bus, 7 single-deck coach, 20 minibus.
Chassis: BMC, Dennis, Fiat, LDV, MAN, Mercedes, Optare, Volkswagen, Volvo.
Ops incl: local bus services, school contracts, private hire.

MIDLOTHIAN

ABBOT TRAVEL

&♿🅿♨🚻

7-1 EDGEFIELD ROAD INDUSTRIAL ESTATE, LOANHEAD EH20 9TB
Tel: 0131 202 7606
E-mail: abbottravel@btconnect.com
Web site: www.abbottravel-loanhead.co.uk
Fleet: 11 – 10 single-deck coach, 1 minicoach.
Chassis: 1 Mercedes, 10 Volvo.
Bodies: 8 Jonckheere, 1 Plaxton, 1 Van Hool, 1 Other.
Livery: White with Blue/Brown.

ALLAN'S COACHES EDINBURGH

🅿♨🚻📶🔧📱

THE COACH YARD, NEWTONLOAN GARAGE, GOREBRIDGE EH23 4LZ
Tel/Recovery: 01875 820377
Fax: 01875 822468
E-mail: allanscoaches@aol.com
Web Site: www.allanscoaches.co.uk
Prop: David W Allan **Ops Man:** John Blair
Ch Eng: Neil Mitchell **Mechanic:** Warren Allan
Office Man: Mrs Dawn Allan.
Fleet: 10 - 7 single-deck coach, 2 midicoach, 1 minibus.
Chassis: DAF, Mercedes, Scania, Volvo.
Bodies: Irizar, Plaxton, Unvi, VDL.
Ops incl: school contracts, excursions & tours, private hire, corporate & VIP, express.
Livery: Allan's Blue.

CITY CIRCLE UK LTD (EDINBURGH BRANCH)

🅿♨🚻📶📱

14 QUEEN ANNE DRIVE, NEWBRIDGE, EDINBURGH EH28 5LD
Tel: 0131 333 2700   **Fax:** 0131 335 7929
E-mail: go@citycircleuk.com
Web site: www.citycircleuk.com
Man Dir: Neil Pegg **Gen Man:** John Docherty
Ops Man: Jennifer Gibson.
Fleet: 22 – 18 single-deck coach, 3 midicoach, 1 minicoach.
Chassis: 2 DAF, 14 MAN, 1 Mercedes, 3 Scania, 2 Volvo.
Bodies: 3 Irizar, 2 Jonckheere, 14 Neoplan, 1 Plaxton, 2 Van Hool.
Ops incl: excursions & tours, private hire, continental tours, corporate charter.
Livery: White with Silver, Red.
Associated with City Circle UK Ltd, London *(see London & Middlesex)*

EDINBURGH GROUP TRAVEL

&♿🅿♨🚻📶R R24📱T

UNIT 1, LADY VICTORIA BUSINESS PARK, NEWTONGRANGE EH22 4QN
Tel: 0131 440 4400
Fax: 0131 454 0308
E-mail: info@edinburghgrouptravel.co.uk
Web site: www.edinburghgrouptravel.co.uk
Dirs: Robbie Prentice, David Cowen
Tran Man: David Reid
Fleet: 16 – 14 single-deck coach, 2 midicoach.
Chassis: 4 Bova, 1 MAN, 2 Mercedes, 9 Volvo.
Bodies: 1 Berkhof, 4 Bova, 1 Caetano, 1 Esker, 8 Plaxton, 1 Van Hool.
Ops incl: school contracts, excursions & tours, private hire, continental tours.
Livery: White with two Blues and Red stripes.
A subsidiary of Prentice Westwood Ltd *(see West Lothian)*

FIRST SCOTLAND EAST LTD

See Falkirk/Stirling.

WILLIAM HUNTER

🅿♨🚻📶🔧📱

OAKFIELD GARAGE, THE LOAN, LOANHEAD EH20 9AE
Tel: 0131 440 0704
Fax: 0131 448 2184
E-mail: sales@hunterscoaches.co.uk
Web Site: www.hunterscoaches.co.uk
Props: G I Hunter, W R Hunter.
Fleet: 13 – single-deck coach, 1 minicoach.
Chassis: 2 Toyota, 11 Volvo.
Bodies: 2 Caetano, 11 Van Hool.
Ops incl: school contracts, private hire.
Livery: Brown/Cream.

McKENDRY TRAVEL

🅿♨🚻

100 STRAITON ROAD, LOANHEAD EH20 9NP
Tel: 0131 440 1013   **Fax:** 0131 448 2160

E-mail: info@mckendrycoachhire.co.uk
Web site: www.mckendrycoachhire.co.uk
Dir: Ann McKendry **Tran Man:** Stuart McCaw.
Fleet: 18 – 14 single-deck coach, 2 minibus,
2 minicoach.
Chassis: DAF, Dennis, Ford transit, Mercedes,
Scania, Volvo
Ops incl: excursions & tours, private hire,
school contracts.
Livery: White/Blue/Purple/Red vinyls.

MORAY

BLUEBIRD BUSES LTD
See Aberdeenshire.

KINEIL COACHES LTD
♿🚍♿❄
ANDERSON PLACE, WEST SHORE
INDUSTRIAL ESTATE, FRASERBURGH
AB43 9LG
Tel: 01346 510200
Fax: 01346 516266
E-mail: kineilcoaches@btconnect.com
Web site: www.kineilcoachesltd.co.uk
Man Dir: Ian Neilson.
Depots at: Fraserburgh, Elgin, Inverurie.
Fleet: 51 – 25 single-deck coach, 5 midibus,
9 midicoach, 5 minibus, 7 minicoach.
Chassis: 1 Alexander Dennis, 4 Bova,
21 Mercedes, 5 Optare, 1 Scania, 1 VDL, 18 Volvo.
Bodies: 1 Autobus, 4 Bova, 1 EVM, 1 KVC,
4 Onyx, 5 Optare, 10 Plaxton, 2 Sitcar, 3 Unvi,
1 VDL, 18 Van Hool.
Ops incl: local bus services, school contracts,
private hire.
Livery: White/Red/Blue.
Ticket System: Almex.

MAYNES COACHES LTD
♿🚍❄R R24✎T
LINKWOOD WAY, ELGIN IV30 1XS
Tel: 01343 555227
Fax: 01542 833572
E-mail: info@maynes.co.uk
Web site: www.maynes.co.uk
Dirs: Gordon Mayne, David Mayne, Kevin
Mayne.
Fleet (Elgin): 6 – 4 single-deck coach,
2 minicoach.
Chassis: 1 BMC, 1 King Long, 3 MAN,
1 Mercedes.
Bodies: 1 BMC, 1 King Long, 3 Marcopolo,
1 Plaxton.
Ops incl: local bus services, school contracts,
excursions & tours, private hire.
Livery: Silver.
Ticket System: Setright.
Additional operations at Buckie and St
Margaret's Hope (see Aberdeenshire, Orkney)

NORTH AYRSHIRE

CUMBRAE COACHES
♿
14 MARINE PARADE, MILLPORT,
ISLE OF CUMBRAE KA28 0ED
Tel: 01475 530692
Fax: 01475 530314
Web site: www.cumbraecoaches.co.uk
Prop: A G Wright.
Fleet: 2 single-deck bus.
Chassis: 2 Alexander Dennis.
Bodies: 2 Alexander Dennis.
Ops incl: local bus services, private hire.
Livery: Red/White.

MARBILL COACHES LTD
♿🚍❄❄
HIGH MAINS GARAGE, MAINS ROAD,
BEITH KA15 2AP
Tel: 01505 503367
Fax: 01505 504736
E-mail: enquiries@marbillcoaches.com

Web site: www.marbillcoaches.co.uk
Man Dir: Margaret Whiteman **Eng Dir:** David
Barr **Ops Dir:** Connie Barr.
Fleet: 63 - 11 double-deck bus, 34 single-deck
bus, 14 single-deck coach, 3 midicoach, 1 minibus.
Chassis: 9 Bova, 1 Ford Transit, 4 Leyland,
3 Mercedes, 2 VDL, 44 Volvo.
Bodies: 38 Alexander, 9 Bova, 1 ECW, 1 Ford,
6 Plaxton, 3 Sitcar, 3 Van Hool, 2 VDL.
Ops incl: school contracts, excursions & tours,
private hire.

McGILLS BUS SERVICE LTD
See North Ayrshire

MILLPORT MOTORS LTD
♿
16 BUTE TERRACE, MILLPORT, ISLE OF
CUMBRAE KA28 0BA
Tel: 01475 530954
Fleet: 3 single-deck bus.
Chassis: 1 BMC, 1 Dennis, 1 Volvo.
Bodies: 1 BMC, 1 Caetano, 1 Wrightbus.
Ops incl: local bus services, private hire.
Livery: Blue/White.
Ticket System: Almex.

SHUTTLE BUSES LTD
♿♿🚍❄
CALEDONIA HOUSE, LONGFORD AVENUE,
KILWINNING KA13 6EX
Tel: 0800 072 0373
Fax: 01294 558822
E-mail: enquiries@shuttlebuses.co.uk
Web site: www.shuttlebuses.co.uk
Man Dir: David Granger.
Fleet: 41 - 11 single-deck coach, 5 midibus,
3 midicoach, 20 minibus, 2 minicoach.
Chassis: 1 AEC, 2 Dennis, 2 Fiat, 3 Leyland,
1 MAN, 10 Mercedes, 13 Optare, 5 Volkswagen,
4 Volvo.
Bodies: 4 Alexander, 1 Beulas, 7 Bluebird,
6 Caetano, 1 Noone Turas, 2 Mercedes, 1 Onyx,
13 Optare, 5 Plaxton, 1 Other.
Ops incl: local bus services, school contracts,
private hire.
Livery: Yellow/White.
Ticket System: Wayfarer TGX.

STAGECOACH WEST SCOTLAND
See South Ayrshire.

STEELE'S OF STEVENSTON
🚍♿❄
1 PORTLAND PLACE, STEVENSTON
KA20 3NN
Tel: 01294 463268
Fax: 01294 462007
E-mail: info@rbsteeles.co.uk
Web site: www.rbsteeles.co.uk
Fleet: 6 – 4 single-deck coach, 2 midicoach.
Chassis: 2 Mercedes, 4 Volvo.
Bodies: 4 Plaxton, 2 Van Hool.
Ops incl: private hire, excursions & tours.
Liveries: Silver/Pink, White.

NORTH LANARKSHIRE

A&C LUXURY COACHES
♿♿🚍❄✎
3 FINDLAY COURT, MOTHERWELL
ML1 1LA
Tel: 01698 252652
Fax: 01698 259898
E-mail: enquiries@acluxurycoaches.co.uk
Web site: www.acluxurycoaches.co.uk
Prop: Alex Grenfell.
Fleet: 10 - 1 single-deck coach, 2 midicoach,
5 minibus, 2 minicoach.
Chassis: 1 Ford Transit, 1 LDV, 7 Mercedes,
1 Volvo.
Ops incl: school contracts, private hire,
excursions & tours.
Livery: White with Blue.

A TRIP IN TIME LTD
Ceased trading since LRB 2014 went to press

BLUE BUS LTD
♿🚍❄
34 BURNBRAE ROAD, SHOTTS ML7 5DW
Tel: 01501 820598
Web site: www.bluebuslimited.com
Dirs: D & D Law.
Fleet: 24 – 1 single-deck coach, 6 midibus,
1 midicoach, 16 minibus.
Chassis: Alexander Dennis, Irisbus, Mercedes,
Optare, Volvo.
Ops incl: local bus services, school contracts,
private hire.
Livery: Blue & White.

BRUCE COACHES LTD
♿🚍🚍❄
40 MAIN STREET, SALSBURGH ML7 4LW
Tel: 01698 870909
Web site: www.brucecoaches.com
Prop: J Bruce.
Fleet: 16 single-deck coach.
Chassis: 1 Bova, 15 Scania.
Bodies: 1 Bova, 15 Caetano.
Ops incl: private hire, express.
Liveries: Blue/White, National Express, Scottish
Citylink.

CANAVAN'S COACHES
♿
4 ARCHES, AUCHINSTARRY ROAD,
KILSYTH G65 9SG
Tel: 01236 822600
Prop: G & J Canavan.
Fleet: 22 – 2 single-deck bus, 20 midibus.
Chassis: 20 Dennis, 2 Volvo.
Bodies: 6 Alexander, 4 Alexander Dennis,
5 Marshall, 7 Plaxton.
Ops incl: local bus services.

CLAN TRAVEL
🚍♿❄
115 JERVISTON STREET, NEW STEVENSTON,
MOTHERWELL ML1 4HT
Tel: 01698 833299
Prop: M Docherty.
Fleet: 9 – 3 single-deck bus, 5 minibus,
1 minicoach.
Chassis: 1 Bova, 6 Mercedes, 2 Volvo.
Ops incl: local bus services, school contracts,
private hire.

DUNN'S COACHES LTD
♿🚍🍴♿❄
560 STIRLING ROAD, AIRDRIE
ML6 7SS
Tel: 01236 722385
Fax: 01236 722385 E-mail: fraser@
dunnscoaches.com
Web site: www.dunnscoaches.com
Prop: Craig Dunn.
Fleet: 16 – 1 double-deck bus, 2 single-deck
bus, 7 single-deck coach, 6 midibus.
Chassis: 1 DAF, 3 Dennis, 1 Leyland,
2 Mercedes, 9 Volvo.
Ops incl: local bus services, school contracts,
excursions & tours, private hire, express.
Livery: White.
Ticket System: Wayfarer TGX.

ESSBEE COACHES (HIGHLANDS &
ISLANDS) LTD
♿🚍🍴♿❄
7 HOLLANDHURST ROAD, GARTSHERRIE
ML5 2EG
Tel: 01236 423621
Fax: 01236 433677
E-mail: info@essbeecoaches.com
Web site: www.essbeecoaches.com
Man Dir: B Smith **Gen Man:** J Kinnaird
Ops Man: S Stewart.
Fleet: 35 – 16 single-deck bus, 11 single-deck

coach, 4 midicoach, 1 minibus, 3 minicoach.
Chassis: 1 DAF, 14 Leyland, 8 Mercedes, 12 Volvo.
Ops incl: school contracts, excursions & tours, private hire.
Livery: Red/Silver.

FIRST GLASGOW
See Glasgow, City of

GOLDEN EAGLE COACHES
MUIRHALL GARAGE, 197 MAIN STREET, SALSBURGH, BY SHOTTS
ML7 4LS
Tel: 01698 870207
Fax: 01698 870217
E-mail: info@goldeneaglecoaches.com
Web site: www.goldeneaglecoaches.com
Dirs: Peter Irvine, Robert Irvine, Ishbel Irvine.
Fleet: 33 - 17 double-deck bus, 5 single-deck bus, 11 single-deck coach.
Chassis: 6 Dennis, 8 Leyland, 19 Volvo.
Ops incl: school contracts, excursions & tours, private hire.
Livery: White, Gold & Maroon.

JMB TRAVEL LTD
UNIT 1, 101 MAIN STREET, NEWMAINS
ML2 9BG
Tel: 01698 386030
E-mail: mail@jmbtravel.co.uk
Web site: www.jmbtravel.co.uk
Dir: M Bell.
Fleet: 50 – 13 double-deck bus, 6 single-deck bus, 2 single-deck coach, 29 midibus.
Chassis: 29 Dennis, 5 Leyland, 1 Scania, 15 Volvo.
Ops incl: local bus services, school contracts, private hire.
Livery: Purple/Green/Cream.

MACPHAILS COACHES
40 MAIN STREET, SALSBURGH, BY SHOTTS
ML7 4LW
Tel: 01698 870768
Fax: 01698 870826
E-mail: macphail7@aol.com
Web site: www.macphailscoaches.co.uk
Dir: Martin MacPhail.
Fleet: 11 – 10 single-deck coach, 1 minibus.
Chassis: 5 Bova, 1 MAN, 4 Volvo.
Ops incl: school contracts, excursions & tours, private hire, continental tours.
Livery: White with Red lettering.

McCREADIE COACHES
53 MOTHERWELL STREET, AIRDRIE
ML6 7HU
Tel: 01236 769666
E-mail: enquiries@mccreadiescoaches.co.uk
Web site: www.mccreadiescoaches.co.uk
Prop: LT McCreadie.
Fleet: 15 – 8 single-deck coach, 1 midibus, 5 minibus, 1 midicoach.
Chassis: Bova, Dennis, Iveco, MAN, Mercedes, Optare, Volvo.
Ops incl: local bus services, school contracts, private hire.

McNAIRN'S COACHES
30 NORTHBURN ROAD, COATBRIDGE
ML5 2HY
Tel: 01236 441188
Fax: 01236 422083
Prop: J McNairn.
Fleet: double-deck bus, single-deck coach, midibus.
Ops incl: local bus services, school contracts, private hire.
Livery: Cream.

M.C.T. GROUP TRAVEL LTD
NETHAN STREET DEPOT, NETHAN STREET, MOTHERWELL ML1 3TF
Tel: 01698 253091
Fax: 01698 259208
E-mail: enquiries@mctgrouptravel.com
Web site: www.mctgrouptravel.com
Man Dir: Desmond Heenan.
Fleet: 14 - 1 single-deck bus, 8 single-deck coach, 1 minibus, 4 minicoach.
Chassis: 1 Iveco, 2 MAN, 1 Renault, 3 Toyota, 7 Volvo.
Ops incl: school contracts, excursions & tours, private hire, continental tours.
Livery: Turquoise/Silver.

MILLER'S COACHES SCOTLAND LTD
FASKINE BRAE, SYKESIDE ROAD, AIRDRIE
ML6 9RQ
Tel: 01236 763671
Man Dir: Tom Miller.
Web site: www.millerscoachesairdrieltd.co.uk
Fleet: 15 - 7 single-deck coach, 3 midicoach, 2 minibus, 3 midicoach.
Chassis: 8 Mercedes, 7 Volvo.
Ops incl: local bus services, school contracts, private hire.
Livery: White/Yellow/Orange.

SILVERDALE COACHES
UNIT 4, FLOWERHILL INDUSTRIAL ESTATE, AIRDRIE ML6 6BH
Tel: 01236 765656
E-mail: info@silverdalecoaches.co.uk
Web site: www.silverdalecoaches.co.uk
Prop: J Chapman.
Fleet: 18 – 4 single-deck coach, 6 midibus, 1 midicoach, 5 minibus, 2 minicoach.
Chassis: BMC, Enterprise, Iveco, King Long, MAN, Mercedes, Optare, Volvo.
Ops incl: local bus services, school contracts, private hire.
Livery: Red/White.

TRAMONTANA TRAVEL
CHAPELKNOWE ROAD, CARFIN, MOTHERWELL ML1 5LE
Tel: 01698 861790
Fax: 01698 860778
E-mail: info@tramontanacoach.co.uk
Web site: www.tramontanacoach.co.uk
Prop: Douglas Telfer.
Fleet: 5 – 4 single-deck coach, 1 minicoach.
Chassis: 1 Mercedes, 4 Volvo.
Bodies: 1 Berkhof, 2 Caetano, 1 Jonckheere, 1 Unvi.
Ops incl: private hire.
Livery: White.

ORKNEY

M & J HARCUS
MEADOWBANK, PIEROWALL, ISLE OF WESTRAY KW17 2BZ
Tel: 01857 677758
Web site: www.westraybusservice.com
Props: J Harcus, K J Harcus.
Fleet: 3 minibuses.
Chassis: 2 Iveco, 1 Mercedes.
Ops incl: local bus service.

J & V COACHES
VART TUN, STROMNESS KW16 3LL
Tel: 01856 851425
Web site: www.jandvcoaches.co.uk
Props: C J Poke, Mrs V Poke.
Fleet: 16 – 12 single-deck coach, 1 midicoach, 2 minibus, 1 minicoach.

Chassis: 2 Bova, 2 Ford, 1 Irisbus, 1 MAN, 2 Mercedes, 8 Volvo.
Ops incl: excursions & tours, private hire.

MAYNES COACHES LTD
ST MARGARETS HOPE KW17 2TG
Tel: 01856 831333
Fax: 01542 833572
Recovery: 07836 322200
E-mail: info@maynes.co.uk
Web site: www.maynes.co.uk
Dirs: Gordon Mayne, David Mayne, Kevin Mayne.
Fleet (Orkney): 5 – 3 single-deck coach, 2 minicoach.
Chassis: 1 Iveco, 2 MAN, 2 Mercedes.
Bodies: 2 Marcopolo, 2 Plaxton, 1 Tata.
Ops incl: school contracts, excursions & tours, private hire.
Livery: Silver.
Ticket System: Setright.
Additional operations at Buckie and Elgin *(see Aberdeenshire, Moray)*

STAGECOACH IN ORKNEY
INVERNESS BUS STATION, FARRALINE PARK, INVERNESS IV1 1LT
Tel: 01463 233371
Fax: 01463 251360
E-mail: highland.enquiries@stagecoachbus.com
Web site: www.stagecoachbus.com
Man Dir: Steve Walker **Ops Dir:** Stephie Barber **Eng Dir:** Russell Henderson.
Fleet (Orkney): 30 – 1 open-top bus, 6 single-deck bus, 15 single-deck coach, 8 midibus.
Chassis: 6 MAN, 8 Optare, 16 Volvo.
Bodies: 6 Alexander, 2 Jonckheere, 1 Northern Counties, 8 Optare, 3 Plaxton.
Ops incl: local bus services, school contracts, excursions & tours, private hire.
Livery: Stagecoach UK Bus.

PERTH & KINROSS

ABERFELDY MOTOR SERVICES
BURNSIDE GARAGE, ABERFELDY PH15 2DD
Tel: 01887 820433   **Fax:** 01887 829534
E-mail: aberfeldymotors@btconnect.com
Web site: www.aberfeldycoaches.com
Prop: John Stewart **Co Sec:** Lynda Stewart
Ch Eng: David Matthew.
Fleet: 6 - 5 single-deck coach, 1 midicoach.
Chassis: 2 Bova, 1 Mercedes, 1 Van Hool, 2 Volvo.
Bodies: 2 Bova, 1 Plaxton, 1 Sitcar, 2 Van Hool.
Ops incl: excursions & tours, private hire, continental tours, school contracts.
Livery: Blue.

CABER COACHES LTD
CHAPEL STREET GARAGE, ABERFELDY
PH15 2AS
Tel: 01887 820090
Fax: 01887 829352
E-mail: cabercoaches@btinternet.com
Fleet: 9 - 1 single-deck coach, 1 midibus, 1 midicoach, 6 minibus.
Chassis: 4 Ford Transit, 2 LDV, 2 Mercedes, 1 Scania.
Ops incl: local bus services, school contracts, private hire.
Livery: White.
Ticket system: Almex.

DOCHERTY'S MIDLAND COACHES
PRIORY PARK, AUCHTERARDER PH3 1GB
Tel: 01764 662218
Fax: 01764 664228
E-mail: info@dochertysmidlandcoaches.co.uk

Web site:
www.dochertysmidlandcoaches.co.uk
Props: Jim & Edith Docherty, Colin Docherty,
Neil Docherty, William Docherty.
Fleet: 35 - 8 single-deck bus, 12 single-deck
coach, 5 midibus, 5 midicoach, 5 minibus.
Chassis: 1 Bova, 2 Dennis, 10 Mercedes,
1 Optare, 1 Van Hool, 18 Volvo, 2 Wrightbus.
Bodies: 3 Alexander, 1 Bova, 1 EVM,
2 Jonckheere, 1 KVC, 1 Optare, 10 Plaxton,
3 Sitcar, 4 Van Hool, 2 Volvo, 7 Wrightbus.
Ops incl: local bus services, school contracts,
private hire.
Livery: White/Black.
Ticket System: Almex.

EARNSIDE COACHES
♿ 🚻 ♿ ❄
GREENBANK ROAD, GLENFARG,
PERTH PH2 9NW
Tel: 01577 830360   **Fax:** 01577 830599
E-mail: info@earnside.com.
Web site: www.earnside.com
Dirs: David Rutherford, Fiona Rutherford,
Gary Rutherford.
Fleet: 10 - 9 single-deck coach, 1 minibus.
Chassis: 1 Ford Transit, 1 Irizar, 5 Neoplan,
1 Scania, 2 Volvo.
Bodies: 1 Ford, 2 Irizar, 5 Neoplan, 2 Plaxton.
Ops incl: school contracts, excursions & tours,
private hire, continental tours.
Livery: White with Yellow/Maroon.

KINGSHOUSE TRAVEL LTD
♿ ♿ ❄
BALQUHIDDER, LOCHEARNHEAD
FK19 8NY
Tel: 01877 384768
E-mail: bookings@kingshousetravel.com
Web site: www.kingshousetravel.com
Dirs: W G, C & W J Courtney.
Fleet: 6 – 2 single-deck coach, 1 midibus,
1 midicoach, 2 minibus.
Chassis: 2 Iveco, 3 Mercedes, 1 Volvo.
Ops incl: local bus services, school contracts,
private hire, excursions & tours.

MEGABUS
See Glasgow, City of

SMITH & SONS COACHES
♿ ♿ ❄ R24 T
THE COACH DEPOT, WOODSIDE, COUPAR
ANGUS, BLAIRGOWRIE PH13 9LW
Tel: 01828 626262
Fax: 01828 628518
Recovery: 01828 626262
E-mail: info@smithandsonscoaches.co.uk
Web site: www.smithandsonscoaches.co.uk
Partners: Ian F Smith, Gordon Smith, Kenneth
F Smith.
Fleet: 25 – 2 single-deck bus, 12 single-deck
coach, 1 midibus, 1 midicoach, 9 minibus.
Chassis: 2 Bova, 1 DAF, 1 Dennis, 2 LDV,
6 Mercedes, 3 Optare, 10 Volvo.
Bodies: 1 Alexander, 2 Bova, 1 Caetano,
3 Jonckheere, 1 LDV, 3 Optare, 4 Plaxton,
1 Sitcar, 6 Van Hool, 3 Other.
Ops incl: local bus services, school contracts,
private hire.
Livery: White with Orange.
Ticket System: Almex.

STAGECOACH EAST SCOTLAND
♿ ♿ ♿ T
OFFICES 47-51, EVANS BUSINESS CENTRE,
JOHN SMITH BUSINESS PARK, KIRKCALDY
KY2 6HD
Tel: 01592 645680   **Fax:** 01592 645677
E-mail:
eastscotland.enquiries@stagecoachbus.com
Web site: www.stagecoachbus.com
Fleet Names: Stagecoach in Fife, Stagecoach in
Perth, Strathtay Scottish.

Man Dir: Andrew Jarvis **Ops Dir:** Mark
Whitelocks **Eng Dir:** John Harper.
Fleet: 526 - 196 double-deck bus, 142 single-
deck bus, 87 single deck coach, 39 midibus,
62 minibus.
Chassis: 126 Alexander Dennis, 49 Dennis,
2 Leyland, 89 MAN, 62 Optare, 20 Scania,
146 Volvo.
Bodies: 195 Alexander Dennis, 93 Alexander,
22 East Lancs, 1 Northern Counties, 62 Optare,
95 Plaxton, 9 Scania, 34 Transbus, 17 Wrightbus.
Fleet excludes Rennies – see separate entry.
Ops incl: local bus services, school contracts,
excursions & tours, private hire, express.
Livery: Stagecoach UK Bus/Citylink/Megabus.
Ticket System: ERG.
Part of the Stagecoach Group

ELIZABETH YULE
♿ ♿ ♿ ❄
STATION GARAGE, STATION ROAD,
PITLOCHRY PH16 5AN
Tel: 01796 472290
Fax: 01796 474214
E-mail: sandra.elizabeth-yule@btconnect.com
Web site: www.elizabethyulecoaches.co.uk
Partners: Elizabeth Yule, Sandra Bridges.
Fleet: 8 - 3 single-deck coach, 2 midibus,
1 midicoach, 2 minibus.
Chassis: 1 Ford Transit, 2 Mercedes, 2 Optare,
3 Volvo.
Ops incl: local bus services, school contracts,
excursions & tours, private hire.
Livery: White.
Ticket System: Almex.

RENFREWSHIRE

CITY SPRINTER LTD
♿
131 WOODHEAD ROAD, NITSHILL
G53 7NN
Tel: 0141 881 2999
Fax: 0141 886 2897
E-mail: info@citysprinter.com
Web site: www.citysprinter.com
Dirs: I Cunningham, J Healy
Fleet: 36 – 3 single-deck bus, 25 midibus,
8 minibus.
Chassis: 2 Alexander Dennis, 23 Dennis,
8 Mercedes, 3 Volvo.
Ops incl: local bus services.
A subsidiary of Enfield Coaches Ltd
(see Republic of Ireland)

COLCHRI LTD
♿ ♿ ♿
WESTWAYS BUSINESS PARK, PORTERFIELD
ROAD, RENFREW PA4 8DJ
Tel: 0141 886 4307
E-mail: info@colchri.com
Web site: www.colchri.com
Prop: Anthony Morrin.
Fleet: 47 – 4 single-deck bus, 3 single-deck
coach, 21 midibus, 18 minibus, 1 minicoach.
Chassis: 4 Alexander Dennis, 14 Dennis,
2 Enterprise, 1 Fiat, 3 LDV, 2 MAN, 12 Mercedes,
2 Volkswagen, 5 Volvo.
Ops incl: local bus services, school contracts.

FIRST GLASGOW
See Glasgow, City of

GIBSON DIRECT LTD
♿ ♿ ♿ ❄
6 NEIL STREET, RENFREW PA4 8TA
Tel: 0141 886 7772
Fax: 0141 886 7776
E-mail: enquiries@gibsondirectltd.com
Web site: www.gibsondirectltd.co.uk
Dir: R Gibson **Ops Man:** A Todd.
Fleet: 43 – 5 double-deck bus, 1 double-deck
coach, 3 single-deck bus, 18 single-deck coach,
3 midibus, 2 midicoach, 10 minibus, 1 minicoach.

Chassis: 1 DAF, 2 Dennis, 2 Ford Transit, 1 Irizar,
1 LDV, 6 Leyland, 9 Mercedes, 2 Neoplan,
3 Optare, 2 VDL, 14 Volvo.
Operations: local bus services, private hire,
school contracts.
Livery: Blue/White.

McGILLS BUS SERVICE LTD
♿ ♿
99, EARNHILL ROAD, LARKFIELD
INDUSTRIAL ESTATE, GREENOCK PA16 0EQ
Tel: 08000 515651
Fax: 01475 711133
E-mail: enquiries@mcgillsbuses.co.uk
Web Site: www.mcgillsbuses.co.uk
Chairman: J Easdale **Man Dir:** R Roberts
Fin Dir: G Davidson **Gen Man:** B Hendry
Eng Dir: B Smith **Head of Service Delivery:**
C Napier **Marketing & Comms Man:**
I Murray **Comm Man:** L McColl.
Depots at: Barrhead, Greenock, Inchinnan,
Johnstone.
Fleet: 326 – 41 double-deck bus, 74 single-deck
bus, 8 single-deck coach, 16 articulated bus,
175 midibus, 12 minibus.
Chassis: 19 Alexander Dennis, 3 Bova,
44 DAF, 140 Dennis, 1 Fiat, 1 MAN, 44 Mercedes,
13 Optare, 8 Scania, 5 Transbus, 10 VDL,
2 Volkswagen, 37 Volvo.
Bodies: 98 Alexander, 20 Alexander Dennis,
3 Bluebird, 3 Bova, 8 Caetano, 3 East Lancs,
1 Fast, 1 Jonckheere, 9 Marshall, 33 Mercedes,
13 Optare, 37 Plaxton, 6 Scania, 86 Wrightbus.
Ops incl: local bus services, express.
Livery: Blue/White.

SHETLAND

ANDREW'S (SHETLAND) LTD
♿ ♿ ♿ 🚻 ♿ 🔧 T
THE DYKES, WORMADALE, WHITENESS
ZE2 9LJ
Tel: 01595 840292
Fax: 01595 840252
E-mail: andrews.adventures@virgin.net
Man Dir: Morris H S Morrison
Dir: Andrew G S Morrison.
Fleet: single-deck coach, midicoach, minicoach.
Chassis: Mercedes, Volvo.
Ops incl: local bus services, school contracts,
private hire, continental tours.
Livery: Red/White.
Ticket system: ERG.

R G JAMIESON & SON
♿ ♿ ❄
MOARFIELD GARAGE, CULLIVOE,
YELL ZE2 9DD
Tel: 01957 744214
Fax: 01957 744270
E-mail: info@rgjamieson.com
Web site: www.rgjamieson.com
Partners: Robert H, Lee & Julie Jamieson.
Fleet: 8 - 4 single-deck coach, 4 minibus.
Ops incl: local bus services, school contracts,
excursions & tours, private hire, continental
tours.
Livery: White/Blue (three shades).

JOHNSON TRANSPORT
♿ ♿ ❄
WESTVALE, BRAE
ZE2 9QG
Tel: 01806 522443
Fax: 01806 522644
E-mail: enquiries@johnsontransport.co.uk
Web site: www.johnsontransport.co.uk
Prop: G Johnson.
Fleet: 16 - 5 single-deck coach, 1 midibus,
3 midicoach, 5 minibus, 2 minicoach.
Chassis: 1 Alexander Dennis, 1 Dennis, 3 Ford
Transit, 1 Iveco, 6 Mercedes, 4 Volvo.
Ops incl: local bus services, school contracts,
Livery: Blue/White/Orange.

JOHN LEASK & SON
♿🚍✈

ESPLANADE, LERWICK ZE1 0LL
Tel: 01595 693162 **Fax:** 01595 693171
E-mail: info@leaskstravel.co.uk
Web site: www.leaskstravel.co.uk
Partners: Peter R Leask, Andrew J N Leask.
Fleet: 22 - 7 single-deck bus, 7 single-deck coach, 3 midibus, 2 midicoach, 1 minibus, 1 minicoach.
Chassis: 1 Alexander Dennis, 6 DAF, 4 Mercedes, 1 Optare, 2 Temsa, 2 VDL, 6 Volvo.
Ops incl: local bus services, school contracts, private hire.
Livery: Ivory/Blue.
Ticket system: ERG.

WHITES COACHES
♿🖊

ENGAMOOR, WEST BURRAFIRTH, BRIDGE OF WALLS, ZE2 9NT
Tel: 01595 809433
E-mail: john@engamoo-shetland.co.uk
Partner: John White.
Fleet: 5 - 1 single-deck bus, 2 midibus, 1 midicoach, 1 minibus.
Chassis: 1 Ford Transit, 3 Mercedes, 1 Scania.
Bodies: 1 Ford Transit, 3 Plaxton, 1 Scania.
Ops incl: local bus services, school contracts, private hire.
Livery: White/Yellow/Black.

SOUTH AYRSHIRE

DODDS OF TROON LTD
🖊👥🍴❄T

4 EAST ROAD, AYR KA8 9BA
Tel: 01292 288100
Fax: 01292 287700
E-mail: info@doddsoftroon.com
Web site: www.doddsoftroon.com
Man Dir: James Dodds
Ops Dir: Douglas Dodds **Admin Dir:** Norma Dodds.
Fleet: 31 – 10 single-deck bus, 18 single-deck coach, 1 minibus, 2 minicoach.
Chassis: 7 Leyland, 1 Mercedes, 2 Toyota, 20 Volvo.
Ops incl: school contracts, excursions & tours, private hire.
Livery: Green/Cream.

KEENAN OF AYR COACH TRAVEL
🖊👥🍴❄🔧

DARWIN GARAGE, COALHALL, BY AYR KA6 6ND
Tel: 01292 591252
Fax: 01292 590980
E-mail: mail@keenancoaches.co.uk
Web site: www.keenancoaches.co.uk
Dirs: Tony Keenan, Jamie Keenan.
Fleet: 28 – 4 double-deck bus, 11 single-deck bus, 11 single-deck coach, 1 midicoach, 1 minibus.
Chassis: 1 Bova, 9 Leyland, 2 Mercedes, 16 Volvo.
Ops incl: school contracts, excursions & tours, private hire.
Livery: Red/Yellow/Orange/White.

MILLIGAN'S COACH TRAVEL LTD
🖊👥🍴R❄🔧T

LOAN GARAGE, 20 THE LOAN, MAUCHLINE, KA5 6AN
Tel/Recovery: 01290 550365
Fax: 01290 553291
E-mail: enquiries@milliganscoachtravel.co.uk
Web site: www.milliganscoachtravel.co.uk
Dir: William J Milligan.
Fleet: 18 single -deck coach.
Chassis: 1 Bova, 12 Scania, 5 Volvo.
Bodies: 1 Bova, 11 Irizar, 6 Van Hool
Ops incl: school contracts, excursions & tours, private hire.
Livery: Black and Silver.

STAGECOACH WEST SCOTLAND
♿🖊🚍🍴🚍🚍❄T

SANDGATE, AYR KA7 1DD
Tel: 01292 613500
Fax: 01292 613502
E-mail: westscotland.enquiries@stagecoachbus.com
Web site: www.stagecoachbus.com
Man Dir: Edward Hodgson **Ops Dir:** Alison McCluskie.
Fleet: 404 - 59 double-deck bus, 123 single-deck bus, 28 double-deck coach, 77 single-deck coach, 63 midibus, 54 minibus.
Chassis: 79 Alexander Dennis, 2 Dennis, 2 Fiat, 8 Leyland, 75 MAN, 4 Mercedes, 18 Neoplan, 56 Optare, 52 Scania, 7 Transbus, 10 Van Hool, 93 Volvo.
Ops incl: local bus services, school contracts, private hire, express.
Liveries: Stagecoach UK Bus, Citylink, Megabus, Megabus Gold.
Ticket System: ERG.

SOUTH LANARKSHIRE

FIRST GLASGOW
See Glasgow, City of.

HENDERSON TRAVEL LTD
♿🖊

UNIT 4, WHISTLEBERRY PARK, HAMILTON ML3 0ED
Tel: 01698 713007
Fax: 0141 626 4205
E-mail: admin@htbuses.com
Web site: www.htbuses.com
Dirs: John Henderson, Mark Ready.
Fleet: 57 – 2 single-deck bus, 17 midibus, 38 minibus.
Chassis: 6 Alexander Dennis, 1 Dennis, 18 Fiat, 29 Optare, 3 Volkswagen.
Bodies: 6 Alexander Dennis, 21 Bluebird, 1 Caetano, 29 Optare.
Ops incl: local bus services, school contracts.
Liveries: Blue/White, SPT.

McDADE TRAVEL LTD
♿👥🖊❄🍴

JOHN HENDRY ROAD, UDDINGSTON G71 7EJ
Tel: 01698 818509
Web site: www.mcdades.co.uk
Dirs: A & M McDade.
Fleet: 36 – 14 double-deck bus, 8 single-deck coach, 2 midibus, 3 midicoach, 7 minibus, 2 minicoach.
Chassis: 1 Bova, 1 Irisbus, 8 Leyland, 13 Mercedes, 13 Volvo.
Ops incl: school contracts, private hire.

MEARNS EXCLUSIVE TRAVEL LTD
👥🖊❄🍴

BLOCK 19, SOUTH AVENUE, BLANTYRE, GLASGOW G72 0XB
Tel: 01698 538638
E-mail: brian@mearnsexclusivetravel.co.uk
Web site: www.mearnsexclusivetravel.co.uk
Dir: Brian Murray
Tran Man: Andy Shaw.
Fleet: 26 – 23 single-deck coach, 1 midicoach, 2 minibus.
Chassis: 1 Bova, 1 Irizar, 3 Mercedes, 11 Neoplan, 9 Scania, 1 VDL.
Bodies: 1 Bova, 10 Irizar, 1 KVC, 1 Mercedes, 11 Neoplan, 1 Unvi, 1 VDL.
Ops incl: excursions & tours, private hire.
Liveries: White, Brands.

PARK'S OF HAMILTON
♿👥🍴❄R24🔧T

78 FORREST STREET, BLANTYRE G72 0JL
Tel: 01698 281222
Fax: 01698 303731
E-mail: coachhire@parks.uk.com

Web site: www.parksofhamilton.co.uk
Chairman: Douglas Park **Ch Eng:** Malcolm Fisher **Co Sec/Dir:** Gerry Donnachie
Dir: Michael Andrews **Ops Man:** Graeme Hoggan.
Fleet: 95 single-deck coach.
Chassis: 95 Volvo.
Bodies: 30 Jonckheere, 65 Plaxton
Ops incl: school contracts, excursions & tours, private hire, express, continental tours.
Liveries: Black/Gold, Citylink, National Express.
Ticket System: Wayfarer.
Also operates at Plymouth (see Devon)

SILVER CHOICE COACHES
👥🖊❄R R24🔧T

1 MILTON ROAD, EAST KILBRIDE G74 5BU
Tel: 01355 249499
Fax: 01355 265111
Recovery: 01355 249499
E-mail: enquiries@silverchoice.co.uk
Web site: www.silverchoice.co.uk
Dir: David W Gardiner **Ch Eng:** Jim Beaton.
Fleet: 12 single-deck coach.
Chassis: 5 Bova, 1 Iveco, 1 Scania, 5 Volvo.
Bodies: 1 Beulas, 5 Bova, 1 Caetano, 3 Plaxton, 2 Van Hool.
Ops incl: school contracts, excursions & tours, private hire, continental tours.
Livery: Silver.

STUART'S COACHES LTD
♿🖊👥🍴🍴❄

CASTLEHILL GARAGE, AIRDRIE ROAD, CARLUKE ML8 5UF
Tel: 01555 773533
Fax: 01555 752220
E-mail: stuartscarluke@btconnect.com
Web site: www.stuarts-coaches.com.
Prop: Stuart A Shevill.
Fleet: 66 - 10 double-deck bus, 5 single-deck bus, 28 single-deck coach, 8 midibus, 3 midicoach, 12 minibus.
Chassis: 2 Alexander Dennis, 1 Ayats, 5 Bova, 1 Dennis, 1 Fiat, 1 Leyland, 3 Mercedes, 17 Optare, 1 Renault, 1 Scania, 33 Volvo.
Bodies: 7 Alexander, 2 Alexander Dennis, 1 Autobus, 1 Ayats, 2 Bluebird, 5 Bova, 3 Caetano, 3 East Lancs, 1 Irizar, 6 Jonckheere, 17 Optare, 9 Plaxton, 1 Transbus, 8 Van Hool.
Ops incl: local bus services, school contracts, private hire, express.
Liveries: Silver/Blue, National Express.
Ticket system: Almex.

THE RURAL DEVELOPMENT TRUST
♿🖊

1 POWELL STREET, DOUGLAS WATER ML11 9PP
Tel: 01555 880551
E-mail: gordon@ruraldevtrust.co.uk.
Web site: www.ruraldevtrust.co.uk
Man Dir: Gordon Muir.
Fleet: 10 - 1 midibus, 3 midicoach, 6 minicoach.
Chassis: 7 Mercedes, 1 Optare, 1 Toyota, 1 Other.
Bodies: 1 Caetano, 6 Mercedes, 1 Optare, 1 Plaxton, 1 Other.
Ops incl: local bus services, school contracts, private hire.
Livery: Blue with Yellow.

WHITELAWS COACHES
♿👥🖊❄🔧

LOCHPARK INDUSTRIAL ESTATE, STONEHOUSE ML9 3LR
Tel: 01698 792800 **Fax:** 01698 793309
E-mail: enquiries@whitelaws.co.uk
Web site: www.whitelaws.co.uk
Man Dir/Co Sec: Sandra Whitelaw Ginestri
Dir: George Whitelaw **Ops Dir:** Janet Whitelaw **Eng Dir:** George A Whitelaw.
Fleet: 41 - 9 single-deck bus, 13 single-deck coach, 19 midibus.

Chassis: 14 Alexander Dennis, 1 Iveco, 4 Leyland, 5 MAN, 17 Volvo.
Bodies: 14 Alexander Dennis, 1 Marshall, 5 MCV, 6 Plaxton, 6 Van Hool, 5 Volvo, 4 Wright.
Ops incl: local bus services, school contracts, excursions & tours, private hire, continental tours.
Livery: Silver with Red/White/Blue.
Ticket System: Wayfarer TGX 150.

STIRLING

BILLY DAVIES EXECUTIVE COACHES
Ceased trading since LRB 2014 went to press

BRYANS COACHES LTD
♿👥♿❄
WHITEHILL FARM, DENNY FK6 5NA
Tel: 01324 824146
E-mail: info@bryanscoaches.com
Web site: www.bryanscoaches.com
Fleet: 11 – 1 double-deck bus, 6 single-deck coach, 3 midibus, 1 midicoach.
Chassis: 1 Alexander Dennis, 1 Bova, 2 Mercedes, 1 Optare, 1 Temsa, 1 VDL, 4 Volvo.
Ops incl: local bus services, school contracts, private hire, excursions & tours.
Livery: White

FERGUSON MINIBUS HIRE
♿♿
33 SPEY COURT, BRAEHEAD, STIRLING FK7 7QZ
Tel/Fax: 01786 461538
E-mail: john.ferguson2@virgin.net
Fleet: 4 – 2 midibus, 1 midicoach, 1 minibus.
Chassis: 1 Ford Transit, 2 Mercedes, 1 Optare.
Ops incl: local bus services, private hire, excursions & tours.
Livery: White/Blue.

FIRST SCOTLAND EAST LTD
♿♿❄♿
CARMUIRS HOUSE, 300 STIRLING ROAD, LARBERT FK5 3NJ
Tel: 01324 602200
Fax: 01324 611287
E-mail: contact.scotlandeast@firstgroup.com
Web site: www.firstgroup.com/scotlandeast
Fleet Names: First Scotland East Midland Bluebird.
Man Dir: Paul McGowan
Ops Dir: John Gorman.
Fleet: 396 – 152 double-deck bus, 191 single-deck bus, 23 single-deck coach, 16 midibus, 3 midicoach, 1 minibus.
Chassis: 12 Alexander Dennis, 7 BMC, 56 Dennis, 2 Enterprise, 9 Mercedes, 9 Optare, 127 Scania, 4 Transbus, 170 Volvo.
Bodies: 57 Alexander, 12 Alexander Dennis, 7 BMC, 6 East Lancs, 9 Marshall, 6 Mercedes, 9 Optare, 82 Plaxton, 18 Scania, 2 Transbus, 184 Wrightbus.
Ops incl: local bus services, school contracts, private hire, express.
Livery: FirstGroup UK Bus.
Ticket System: Almex.

FITZCHARLES COACHES LTD
♿👥🍴❄♿
87 NEWHOUSE ROAD, GRANGEMOUTH FK3 8NJ
Tel: 01324 482093
Fax: 01324 665411
E-mail: info@fitzcharles.co.uk
Web site: www.fitzcharles.co.uk
Man Dir: George Fitzcharles
Dir/Sec: Olive King **Accts & Training:** David Fitzcharles **Transport Man:** Allan Dick
Fleet Eng: Stewart McArthur.
Fleet: 17 - 16 single-deck coach, 1 minicoach.
Chassis: 2 Ayats, 1 Mercedes, 5 Neoplan, 9 Volvo.
Bodies: 2 Ayats, 3 Caetano, 5 Neoplan,

5 Plaxton, 2 Sunsundegui.
Ops incl: school contracts, excursions & tours, private hire, express, continental tours.
Livery: Red/Cream.
Ticket System: ERG TP5000.

MITCHELL'S COACHES
♿👥❄
PRESIDENT KENNEDY DRIVE, PLEAN FK7 8AY
Tel: 01786 814319
Fax: 01786 814165
E-mail: mitchellscoaches@btconnect.com
Fleet: 8– 1 double-deck bus, 4 single-deck coach, 1 midibus, 2 midicoach.
Chassis: 2 Dennis, 3 Mercedes, 1 Irisbus, 2 Volvo.
Ops incl: local bus services, school contracts, private hire.
Livery: White.

MYLES COACHES
♿👥❄
PLEAN INDUSTRIAL ESTATE, PLEAN FK7 8BJ
Tel: 01786 816664
Fax: 01786 827128
E-mail: enquiries@mylescoaches.com
Fleet: 4 – 1 single-deck coach, 1 midicoach, 2 minibus.
Chassis: 1 Ford Transit, 2 Mercedes, 1 Volvo.
Ops incl: local bus services, private hire.
Livery: White.

ORDER OF MALTA
DIAL-A-JOURNEY LTD
♿♿
17 MUNRO ROAD, STIRLING FK7 7UU
Tel: 01786 465355
Web site: www.dial-a-journey.org
Fleet: 36 – 7 single-deck bus, 11 midibus, 18 minibus.
Ops incl: local bus services, demand responsive services.

WEST DUNBARTONSHIRE

AVONDALE COACHES LTD
♿♿
9 DOCK STREET, CLYDEBANK G81 1LX
Tel: 0141 952 2727
Fax: 0141 941 0070
E-mail: info@avondalecoaches.co.uk
Web site: www.avondalecoaches.co.uk
Dirs: C A Irving, D Gold.
Fleet: 55 – 32 midibus, 1 midicoach, 22 minibus.
Chassis: 20 Dennis, 24 Mercedes, 11 Optare.
Ops incl: local bus services, school contracts, private hire.
Livery: Red with Yellow lettering.

FIRST GLASGOW
See Glasgow, City of.

LOCHS AND GLENS HOLIDAYS
♿👥❄
SCHOOL ROAD, GARTOCHARN G83 8RW
Tel: 01389 713713
Fax: 01389 713700
E-mail: enquiries@lochsandglens.com
Web site: www.lochsandglens.com
Chairman: Michael Wells **Man Dir:** Neil Wells
Dir: Ian Wells **Tran Man:** Steve Nicols.
Fleet: 16 single-deck coach.
Chassis: 16 Volvo.
Bodies: 11 Jonckheere, 5 Van Hool.
Ops incl: excursions & tours,
Livery: White with blue lettering.

McCOLL'S COACHES LTD
♿♿🍴❄R♿
BLOCK 4C, VALE OF LEVEN INDUSTRIAL ESTATE, DUMBARTON G82 3PD
Tel: 01389 754321
Fax: 01389 755354
E-mail: customer.services@mccolls.org.uk

Web site: www.mccolls.org.uk
Man Dir: William McColl
Dirs: Thomas McColl, Janet McColl
Co Sec: Ann McKinlay
Ops Man: Liam McColl **Head Mechanic:** Eddie McKinley.
Fleet: 89 – 25 double-deck bus, 2 single-deck bus, 22 single-deck coach, 25 midibus, 2 midicoach, 12 minibus, 1 minicoach.
Chassis: 4 Dennis, 3 Fiat, 2 LDV, 1 Leyland, 1 MAN, 6 Mercedes, 5 Optare, 1 Scania, 66 Volvo.
Ops incl: local bus services, school contracts, excursions & tours, private hire.

McGILLS BUS SERVICE LTD
♿♿
99, EARNHILL ROAD, LARKFIELD INDUSTRIAL ESTATE, GREENOCK PA16 0EQ
Tel: 08000 515651
Fax: 01475 711133
E-mail: enquiries@mcgillsbuses.co.uk
Web Site: www.mcgillsbuses.co.uk
Chairman: J Easdale **Man Dir:** R Roberts
Fin Dir: G Davidson **Gen Man:** B Hendry
Eng Dir: B Smith **Head of Service Delivery:** C Napier **Marketing & Comms Man:** I Murray **Comm Man:** L McColl.
Depots at: Barrhead, Greenock, Inchinnan, Johnstone.
Fleet: 326 – 41 double-deck bus, 74 single-deck bus, 8 single-deck coach, 16 articulated bus, 175 midibus, 12 minibus.
Chassis: 19 Alexander Dennis, 3 Bova, 44 DAF, 140 Dennis, 1 Fiat, 1 MAN, 44 Mercedes, 13 Optare, 8 Scania, 5 Transbus, 10 VDL, 2 Volkswagen, 37 Volvo.
Bodies: 98 Alexander, 20 Alexander Dennis, 3 Bluebird, 3 Bova, 8 Caetano, 3 East Lancs, 1 Fast, 1 Jonckheere, 9 Marshall, 33 Mercedes, 13 Optare, 37 Plaxton, 6 Scania, 86 Wrightbus.
Ops incl: local bus services, express.
Livery: Blue/White.

WEST LOTHIAN

LES BROWN TRAVEL
♿♿
UNIT 3, BLOCK 12, WHITESIDE INDUSTRIAL ESTATE, BATHGATE EH10 2RX
Tel: 01506 656129
Fax: 01506 656129
E-mail: les-brown@btconnect.com
Props: Les Brown, Colin Brown,
Fleet: 10 - 1 single-deck coach, 9 minibus.
Chassis: 1 EOS, 5 Ford Transit, 1 Iveco, 3 Mercedes.
Ops incl: school contracts, excursions & tours, private hire.
Livery: White with Blue, Red.

FIRST SCOTLAND EAST LTD
See Falkirk/Stirling.

E & M HORSBURGH LTD
♿♿👥❄
180 UPHALL STATION ROAD, PUMPHERSTON EH53 0PD
Tel: 01506 432251
Fax: 01506 438066
E-mail: horsburgh@btconnect.com
Web site: www.horsburghcoaches.com
Dirs: Eric Horsburgh, Mark Horsburgh **Tran Man:** Marshall Nisbet **Ch Eng:** Brian Martin.
Fleet: 107 - 34 double-deck bus, 5 single-deck bus, 9 single-deck coach, 36 midibus, 1 midicoach, 22 minibus.
Chassis: 9 Dennis, 2 Ford Transit, 13 LDV, 12 Leyland, 10 Mercedes, 25 Optare, 5 Scania, 31 Volvo.
Ops incl: local bus services, school contracts, excursions & tours, private hire.
Livery: White/Yellow.
Ticket System: Almex.

PRENTICE WESTWOOD LTD

WESTWOOD, WEST CALDER EH55 8PW
Tel/Recovery: 01506 871231
Fax: 01506 871734
E-mail: sales@prenticewestwoodcoaches.co.uk
Web site:
www.prenticewestwoodcoaches.com
Dirs: Robbie Prentice, David Cowen
Ops Mans: John Grant, David Reid.
Fleet: 47 - 2 double-deck bus, 36 single-deck
coach, I double-deck coach, 5 midibus,
3 midicoach.
Chassis: 5 Bova, I DAF, 2 Dennis, I EOS,
2 Leyland, I MAN, 3 Mercedes, 4 Optare,
I Scania, I Setra, I Van Hool, 3 VDL, 22 Volvo.
Bodies: 2 Alexander, 3 Berkhof, I Beulas,
5 Bova, I Caetano, I EOS, I Irizar, 5 Jonckheere,
4 Optare, 12 Plaxton, I Setra, I Unvi, 5 Van Hool,
3 VDL, I Volvo 9700, I Wadham Stringer.
Ops incl: local bus services, school contracts,
excursions & tours, private hire, continental tours.
Livery: Red/White/Blue.
Ticket System: Almex.
Group Company: Edinburgh Group Travel
(see City of Edinburgh, Midlothian)

SD TRAVEL

53 GLEBE ROAD, WHITBURN EH47 0AZ
Tel: 01501 743333
Fleet Name: SD Travel.
Prop: S Douglas.
Fleet: 15 – I double-deck bus, 5 midibus,
I midicoach, 8 minibus.
Chassis: I Alexander Dennis, 3 Dennis,
I Ford Transit, I Iveco, I Marshall, 5 Mercedes,
2 Optare, I Scania.
Ops incl: local bus services.

WAVERLEY TRAVEL

5 LIGGET SYKE PLACE, EAST MAINS
INDUSTRIAL ESTATE, BROXBURN EH52 5NA
Tel: 0131 317 7695
Prop: R Jack.
Fleet: 5 – 4 midibus, I midicoach.
Chassis: 4 Alexander Dennis, I BMC.
Ops incl: local bus services, private hire.
Livery: White.

WESTERN ISLES

COMHAIRLE NAN EILEAN SIAR

BUS COMHAIRLE, SANDWICK ROAD,
STORNOWAY, ISLE OF LEWIS HS1 2BW
Tel: 01851 822661   **Fax:** 01851 709750
Head of Service: Donald Stuart
Fleet Man: Donald Stewart
Fleet Eng: Neil McLeod.
E-mail: bus@cne-siar.gov.uk
Web site: www.cne-siar.gov.uk
Fleet Name: Bus Na Comhairle
Ops incl: local bus services, school contracts,
private hire.
Livery: White/Yellow stripe.
Ticket System: ERG.

DA TRAVEL LTD

10A KILDONAN, LOCHBOISDALE,
SOUTH UIST HS8 5RZ
Tel: 01878 710266
E-mail: info@datravel.co.uk
Web site: www.datravel.co.uk
Dir: Duncan Aitken.
Fleet: 8 – 2 single-deck coach, 2 midibus,
2 midicoach, 2 minibus.
Chassis: I DAF, I Dennis, 2 LDV, 4 Mercedes.
Ops incl: local bus services, school contracts,
excursions & tours, private hire.
Livery: White.
Ticket System: ERG.

GALSON-STORNOWAY MOTOR SERVICES LTD

I LOWER BARVAS, ISLE OF LEWIS
HS2 0QZ
Tel: 01851 840269
Fax: 01851 840445
E-mail: galson@sol.co.uk
Dir: I Morrison **Ops Man:** I Morrison.
Fleet: 13 - 7 single-deck coach, 2 midicoach,
4 minibus.
Chassis: 4 Ford Transit, 2 Mercedes, 7 Volvo.
Bodies: 4 Ford, 5 Plaxton, 4 Van Hool.
Ops incl: local bus services, school contracts,
excursions & tours, private hire.
Livery: White/Yellow/Brown.
Ticket System: ERG.

GRENITOTE TRAVEL

20 GRENITOTE, NORTH UIST
HS6 5BP
Tel/Fax: 01876 560244
E-mail: mike@grenitotetravel.co.uk
Web site: www.grenitotetravel.co.uk
Prop: M Bull.
Fleet: 6 minibus.
Chassis: 3 Ford, 3 Renault.
Ops incl: local bus services, school contracts,
excursions & tours.
Ticket System: ERG.

HEBRIDEAN COACHES

HOWMORE, SOUTH UIST HS8 5SH
Tel: 01870 620345
Fax: 01870 620301
Recovery: 01870 620345
E-mail: admin@hebco.co.uk
Web site: www.hebrideancoaches.co.uk
Prop: D A MacDonald.
Fleet: 17 - 8 single-deck coach, 4 midicoach,
5 minibus.
Chassis: 2 Bedford, 6 Dennis, 3 Ford Transit,
I Ford, 2 LDV, 3 Mercedes.
Ops incl: local bus services, school contracts,
excursions & tours, private hire.
Livery: Cream/Green.
Ticket System: ERG.

HEBRIDEAN TRANSPORT

PARKHEAD INDUSTRIAL ESTATE,
STORNOWAY HS2 0AN
Tel: 01851 709886
Props: I A MacIver, C MacIver.
Fleet: 11 – 7 single-deck coach, 4 minibus.
Chassis: 4 Dennis, 3 Ford Transit, I Mercedes,
3 Volvo.
Bodies: 3 Ford, I Mercedes, 7 Plaxton.
Ops incl: local bus services, school contracts.
Livery: Maroon/Cream.
Ticket System: ERG.

LOCHS MOTOR TRANSPORT LTD

CAMERON TERRACE, LEURBOST, LOCHS,
ISLE OF LEWIS HS2 9PE

Tel: 01851 860288
Fax: 01851 860247
E-mail: lochsmotors@btconnect.com
Web site: www.lochsmotortransport.co.uk
Dirs: C MacDonald, R MacDonald,
S MacDonald, A MacDonald
Ch Eng: I MacKinnon.
Fleet: 7 – I single-deck bus, 6 single-deck coach.
Chassis: I Alexander Dennis, 6 Volvo.
Bodies: I Alexander Dennis, 5 Plaxton,
I Van Hool.
Ops incl: local bus services, school contracts,
express, private hire.
Livery: White with Blue.
Ticket System: ERG.

A MacDONALD

4 BALALLAN, LOCHS, ISLE OF LEWIS
HS2 9PT
Tel: 01851 830327
Fleet: 3 - 2 single-deck coach, I minibus.
Chassis: I Ford, 2 Volvo.
Ops incl: local bus services, school contracts.
Livery: White with logos.
Ticket System: ERG.

MacLENNAN COACHES

INACLETE ROAD, STORNOWAY
HS1 2RN
Tel: 01851 702114
Fax: 01851 700889
E-mail: maclennan.coaches@stornoway.co.uk
Prop: A I MacLennan
Fleet: 11 – 9 single-deck coach, I midicoach,
I minibus.
Chassis: 2 Dennis, I LDV, I Mercedes, 2 Scania,
I Transbus, 4 Volvo.
Ops incl: local bus services, school contracts,
excursions & tours, private hire.
Livery: Blue/Silver.
Ticket System: ERG.

K MacLENNAN

6 GROSEBAY, ISLE OF HARRIS
HS3 3EF
Tel: 01859 511253
Fax: 01859 511230
E-mail: kennycarrier@btinternet.com
Fleet: 10 – 2 single-deck coach, 2 midicoach,
6 minibus.
Ops incl: local bus services, school contracts.
Livery: White with Blue lettering.
Ticket System: ERG.

PETER MacLENNAN (MINIBUSES) LTD

24 LAXAY LOCHS, ISLE OF LEWIS
HS2 9PJ
Tel: 01851 830403
Fleet: 6 – I single-deck coach, 5 minibus.
Chassis: I Dennis, 2 Ford Transit, 3 Mercedes.
Ops incl: local bus services, school contracts.
Livery: White with Purple.
Ticket System: ERG.

H MacNEIL

68, TANGASDALE, ISLE OF BARRA
HS9 5XW
Tel/Fax: 01871 810262
E-mail: hectormacneil@aol.com
Prop: Hector MacNeil.
Fleet: minibus, minicoach.
Ops incl: local bus services, private hire.
Livery: White.
Ticket System: ERG.

ANGLESEY

ARRIVA BUSES WALES
See Gwynedd

CARREGLEFN COACHES
♿🅰🚹♨
CARREGLEFN GARAGE, AMLWCH
LL68 0PR
Tel/Fax: 01407 710217
Prop: Alun Lewis.
Fleet: 14 - 10 single-deck coach, 1 minibus,
3 minicoach.
Chassis: 1 Ford Transit, 1 MAN, 3 Toyota,
9 Volvo.
Bodies: 7 Caetano, 1 Ford, 5 Plaxton,
1 Van Hool.
Ops incl: local bus services, school contracts,
excursions & tours, private hire.
Livery: Blue/Cream.

EIFION'S COACHES LTD
♿🅰
MONA INDUSTRIAL PARK,
GWALCHMAI LL65 4RJ
Tel: 01407 721111
Fax: 01407 721122
E-mail: mail@eifionscoaches.co.uk
Web site: www.eifionscoaches.co.uk
Prop: H Humphreys
Fleet: 13 - 4 single-deck coach, 4 midibus,
1 midicoach, 3 minibus, 1 minicoach.
Chassis: 3 Alexander Dennis, 1 Ford Transit,
1 MAN, 6 Mercedes, 2 Volvo.
Bodies: 4 Alexander Dennis, 1 Caetano,
1 EVM, 1 Ford Transit, 1 Koch, 1 KVC, 1 Mellor,
3 Mercedes.
Ops incl: local bus services, school contracts,
private hire, excursions & tours.
Livery: White with Red/Green/Yellow logos.

GOODSIR COACHES
♿🅰
VICTORIA ROAD, HOLYHEAD LL65 1UD
Tel: 01407 764340
Web site:
www.goodsircoachdepotholyhead.co.uk
Partners: G Goodsir, T Hughes.
Fleet: 18 - 1 double-deck bus, 8 single-deck
coach, 3 midibus, 1 midicoach, 4 minibus,
1 minicoach.
Chassis: 3 Dennis, 1 Ford Transit, 1 MCW,
3 Mercedes, 3 Optare, 1 Setra, 6 Volvo.
Ops incl: local bus services, school contracts,
private hire.
Livery: White.

GWYNFOR COACHES
♿🅰♨🚹
1 GREENFIELD AVENUE, LLANGEFNI
LL77 7NU
Tel/Fax: 01248 722694
E-mail: mail@gwynforcoaches.co.uk
Web site: www.gwynforcoaches.co.uk
Prop: G Hughes.
Fleet: 11 - 1 single-deck bus, 3 single-deck
coach, 4 midibus, 2 midicoach, 1 minibus.
Chassis: 2 DAF, 2 Dennis, 2 Enterprise,
1 Mercedes, 1 Optare, 1 Toyota, 2 Volvo.
Bodies: 1 Alexander, 1 Caetano, 2 Optare,
6 Plaxton, 1 Van Hool.
Ops incl: local bus services, school contracts,
private hire.
Livery: White with Blue.

HDA TRAVEL LTD
♿
GILFACH, LON GOES, GAERWEN
LL60 6DE
Tel: 01248 421476
Prop: H D Ashton.
Fleet: 1 midibus.
Chassis: Optare.
Ops incl: local bus services.

O R JONES & SONS LTD
♿🅰🚹📻🔲🔲**R24**🔲
THE BUS & COACH DEPOT, LLANFAETHLU,
HOLYHEAD LL65 4NW
Tel: 01407 730204   **Fax:** 01407 730083
Recovery: 01407 730759
E-Mail: orjonescoaches@hotmail.co.uk
Web site: www.orjones.co.uk
Ops Man: Iolo O Jones **Tran Man:** Maldwyn
O Jones.
Fleet: 22 - 8 single-deck bus, 8 single-deck
coach, 2 midicoach, 4 minibus.
Chassis: 1 Alexander Dennis, 1 Bova, 9 DAF,
2 Dennis, 1 Leyland, 1 MAN, 4 Mercedes,
2 Optare, 2 Volvo.
Bodies: 1 Alexander Dennis, 1 Bova, 1 Caetano,
2 Ikarus, 1 Koch, 2 Marcopolo, 6 Optare,
2 Plaxton, 1 Unvi, 2 Van Hool, 1 Wadham
Stringer.
Ops incl: local bus services, school contracts,
excursions & tours, private hire, Holyhead port
operations.
Livery: Silver.
Ticket system: Wayfarer.

W E JONES & SON
♿🅰♨🔲🔲
THE GARAGE, LLANERCHYMEDD LL71 8EB
Tel: 01248 470228   **Fax:** 01248 852893
Props: Gwilym Evans Jones, Wyn Evans Jones.
Fleet: 16 – 1 double-deck bus, 6 single-deck
bus, 5 single-deck coach, 1 midibus, 1 midicoach,
2 minibus.
Chassis: 3 DAF, 6 Dennis, 2 Mercedes,
2 Optare, 3 Volvo.
Bodies: 1 Autobus, 1 Caetano, 1 Duple,
1 Northern Counties, 5 Optare, 6 Plaxton,
1 UVG.
Ops incl: local bus services, school contracts,
private hire.
Livery: Red/White.

LEWIS-Y-LLAN
♿🅰
MADYN INDUSTRIAL ESTATE, AMLWCH
LL68 9DL
Tel: 01407 832181
Fax: 0140/ 830112
Props: A H Lewis, R M Lewis, D A Lewis.
Fleet: 8 - 2 single-deck coach, 2 midibus,
4 minibus.
Chassis: 2 Alexander Dennis, 2 Dennis,
2 Mercedes, 2 Optare.
Bodies: 2 Alexander Dennis, 2 Optare,
4 Plaxton.
Livery: White/Blue.

BLAENAU GWENT

GARY'S COACHES OF TREDEGAR
🅰🅰♨**R24**
42 COMMERCIAL STREET, TREDEGAR
NP22 3DJ
Tel: 01495 726500
Fax: 01495 726400
Recovery: 01495 723264
E-mail: sales@garys-coaches.co.uk
Web site: www.garys-coaches.co.uk
Props: Mr & Mrs G A Lane **Ops Man:**
D Williams **Ch Eng:** G Cresswell.
Fleet: 12 – 10 single-deck coach, 2 midibus.
Chassis: 2 Dennis, 1 Duple 425, 2 Mercedes,
7 Volvo.
Ops incl: excursions & tours, private hire,
school contracts, continental tours.
Livery: White/Blue.

HENLEYS BUS SERVICES LTD
🅰🅰♨
HENLEYS COACH GARAGE, VICTOR ROAD,
ABERTILLERY NP13 1HU
Tel: 01495 212288   **Fax:** 01495 320720
E-mail: admin@henleys.org.uk
Web site: www.henleysbusservicesltd.co.uk
Dir: Martin Henley **Head Mech:** Michael

Henley **Sec:** Daphne Henley.
Fleet: 12 – 5 single-deck coach, 2 midicoach,
5 minibus.
Chassis: 1 Leyland, 4 Mercedes, 3 Optare,
2 Setra, 2 Volvo.
Bodies: 1 Alexander, 2 Jonckheere, 3 Optare,
2 Plaxton, 2 Setra, 1 Sitcar, 1 Unvi.
Ops incl: local bus services, school contracts,
excursions & tours, private hire.
Livery: White/Orange/Green.
Ticket system: Wayfarer.

STAGECOACH IN SOUTH WALES
See Torfaen

BRIDGEND

CRESTA COACHES
🅰🅰♨
UNIT 6, LITCHARD INDUSTRIAL ESTATE,
BRIDGEND CF31 2AL
Tel: 01656 660366
Fax: 01656 660566
E-mail: bookings@crestacoaches.co.uk
Web site: www.crestacoaches.co.uk
Dirs: I A & D Williams **Ops Man:** H Watson
Head of Vehicle Eng: D Miller.
Fleet: 14 – 9 single-deck coach, 4 midicoach,
1 minicoach.
Chassis: 1 MAN, 5 Mercedes, 8 Volvo.
Bodies: 1 Excel, 1 Ferqui, 1 Jonckheere, 1 Noge,
2 Noone Turas, 5 Plaxton, 1 Sitcar, 2 Van Hool.
Ops incl: school contracts, excursions & tours,
private hire.
Livery: White with Red/Yellow/Blue.

EASYWAY MINI COACH HIRE LTD
♿🅰
KENT ROAD, BRIDGEND INDUSTRIAL
ESTATE, BRIDGEND CF31 3TU
Tel: 01656 655655
E-mail: easywayminibus@aol.com
Web site: www.easywayminicoachhire.co.uk
Dir: R A Morris.
Fleet: 22 – 2 single-deck coach, 1 midibus,
2 midicoach, 14 minibus, 3 minicoach.
Chassis: 1 Alexander Dennis, 1 Ford Transit,
1 Iveco, 10 Mercedes, 6 Optare, 2 Volkswagen,
1 Volvo.
Ops incl: local bus services, school contracts,
private hire.
Livery: White with Red lettering.

EXPRESS MOTORS
🅰🅰♨
37 COMMERCIAL STREET, KENFIG HILL
CF33 6DH
Tel: 01656 740323
Prop: D V Evans.
Fleet: 9 single-deck coach.
Chassis: 8 Volvo.
Bodies: 3 Jonckheere, 5 Plaxton, 1 Van Hool.

FIRST CYMRU BUSES LTD
See City & County of Swansea

GWYN JONES & SON LTD
🅰♨🅰🔲
WHITECROFT GARAGE, BRYNCETHIN
CF32 9YR
Tel: 01656 720300
Recovery: 01656 720182
E-mail: enquiries@gwynjonescoaches.co.uk
Web site: www.gwynjonescoaches.co.uk
Chair: John Gwyn Jones **Dir:** Miriam J Jones.
Fleet: 30 – 29 single-deck coach, 1 minibus.
Chassis: 1 DAF, 1 Dennis, 1 Ford Transit,
2 MAN, 1 Neoplan, 10 Scania, 6 Setra, 1 Transbus,
7 Volvo.
Bodies: 6 Berkhof, 1 Ford Transit, 3 Irizar,
5 Jonckheere, 2 Marcopolo, 1 Neoplan, 6 Setra,
Transbus, 5 Van Hool.
Ops incl: excursions & tours, private hire,
continental tours, school contracts.
Livery: White/Gold/Maroon.

KEITH JONES COACHES (TRAVEL FINAL LTD)

2 BRIDGE STREET, BLAENGARW CF32 8AY
Tel: 01656 871933
E-mail: info@keithjonescoaches.com
Web site: www.keithjonescoaches.com
Prop: K Jones.
Fleet: 14 – 5 single-deck coach, 2 midibus,
4 midicoach, 3 minibus.
Chassis: 3 Dennis, 2 Ford Transit, 1 LDV,
4 Mercedes, 3 Scania, 1 Volvo.
Bodies: 2 Alexander, 1 Autobus, 1 Berkhof,
1 Ferqui, 1 Ford Transit, 2 Irizar, 1 LDV, 2 Plaxton,
3 Other.
Ops incl: local bus services, school contracts,
private hire.
Livery: White with Red.

LLYNFI COACHES

UNIT 7-9, HEOL TY GWYN INDUSTRIAL
ESTATE, MAESTEG CF34 0BQ
Tel: 01656 739928   **Fax:** 01656 727858
Props: David Stolzenberg, Liam Morgan.
Fleet: 15 – 1 single-deck bus, 12 single-deck
coach, 1 midicoach, 1 minibus.
Chassis: 4 Autosan, 2 Ayats, 1 Dennis, 1 Ford
Transit, 1 Irisbus, 3 King Long, 1 MAN,
1 Mercedes, 1 Scania.
Bodies: 4 Autosan, 2 Ayats, 1 Ford Transit,
1 Irizar, 3 King Long, 1 Noge, 1 Plaxton.
Ops incl: local bus services, school contracts,
excursions & tours, private hire.
Livery: Yellow or White.

PENCOED TRAVEL LTD

18 CAER BERLLAN, PENCOED CF35 6RR
Tel: 01656 860200   **Fax:** 01656 864793
E-mail: info@pencoedtravel.co.uk
Web site: www.pencoedtravel.co.uk
Man Dir: Denise Cook **Dir:** Andrea Talbot
Ops: David Morris **Ch Eng:** Neil Cook.
Fleet: 10 – 1 double-deck bus, 8 single-deck
coach, 1 minibus.
Chassis: 4 Bova, 3 DAF, 1 LDV, 1 VDL, 1 Volvo.
Bodies: 4 Bova, 1 Excel, 1 Northern Counties,
4 Van Hool.
Ops incl: school contracts, excursions & tours,
private hire, continental tours.
Livery: White/Blue.

PEYTON TRAVEL LTD

DUNRAVEN BUSINESS PARK, COYCHURCH
ROAD, BRIDGEND CF31 3AP
Tel: 01656 661221
E-mail: info@peytontravel.co.uk
Web site: www.peytontravel.co.uk
Dirs: P Brain, A Spallek.
Fleet: 40 – 9 single-deck coach, 5 midicoach,
26 minibus.
Ops incl: school contracts, private hire.
Livery: White.

STAGECOACH IN SOUTH WALES

See Torfaen

CAERPHILLY

CAERPHILLY CONTRACT SERVICES

UNIT 9, TRECENYDD BUSINESS PARK,
TRECENYDD, CAERPHILLY CF83 2RZ
Tel: 029 2086 1863   **Fax:** 029 2086 1864
E-mail: sales@castellcoaches.co.uk
Web site: www.castellcoaches.co.uk
Fleet Name: Castell Coaches
Props: Brian Kerslake, Alan Morris.
Fleet: 16 single-deck coach.
Chassis: 6 Dennis, 1 Leyland, 9 Volvo.
Bodies: 2 Berkhof, 1 Jonckheere, 2 Marcopolo,
5 Plaxton, 1 UVG, 1 Van Hool, 4 Wadham
Stringer.

Ops incl: excursions & tours, private hire,
school contracts.
Livery: Silver & White.

HARRIS COACHES

BRYN GWYN STREET, FLEUR-DE-LIS NP12 3RZ
Tel: 01443 832290   **Fax:** 01443 830455
Man Dir: John Harris **Dir:** G Harris.
Fleet Name: Shuttle.
Fleet: 26 – 5 single-deck bus, 2 single-deck
coach, 6 midibus, 1 midicoach, 12 minibus.
Chassis: 1 DAF, 6 Dennis, 1 Mercedes,
12 Optare, 6 Volvo.
Bodies: 4 Alexander, 2 Berkhof, 2 Marshall,
13 Optare, 5 Plaxton.
Ops incl: local bus services, school contracts,
private hire.
Liveries: Cream/Maroon/Red; Yellow
(School Buses).

HOWELLS COACHES LTD

UNIT 6-8, PENALLTA INDUSTRIAL ESTATE,
HENGOED CF82 7SU
Tel: 01443 816581
Dirs: R E Howells, P Howells, D E Howells,
D R Howells.
Fleet: 26 – 24 single-deck coach, 2 minibus.
Chassis: 7 Bova, 1 DAF, 3 Dennis, 11 Duple 425,
1 Ford Transit, 1 LDV, 2 Plaxton 425.
Bodies: 1 Berkhof, 7 Bova, 11 Duple, 1 LDV,
2 Lorraine, 1 Neoplan, 1 Plaxton, 1 UVG, 1 Other.
Ops incl: school contracts, private hire.
Livery: White.

STAGECOACH IN SOUTH WALES

See Torfaen

CARDIFF

CARDIFF BUS

SLOPER ROAD, LECKWITH, CARDIFF
CF11 8TB
Tel: 029 2078 7710
E-mail: talktous@cardiffbus.com
Web site: www.cardiffbus.com
Chairman: Cllr Ben Thomas **Man
Dir:** Cynthia Ogbonna **Operations &
Commercial Dir:** Peter Heath **Engineering
Dir:** Gareth Mole.
Fleet: 213 - 13 double-deck bus, 122 single-
deck bus, 59 midibus, 19 articulated bus.
Chassis: 22 Alexander Dennis, 64 Dennis,
20 Mercedes, 63 Scania, 44 Transbus.
Bodies: 22 Alexander Dennis, 33 East Lancs,
20 Mercedes, 33 Plaxton, 43 Scania, 75 Transbus,
7 Wright.
Ops incl: local bus services, school contracts,
park and ride.
Livery: Blue-Green/Orange.
Ticket Systems: Parkeon TGX 150, Corethree
Mobile app.

CREIGIAU TRAVEL LTD

THE OLD STATION YARD, STATION ROAD,
CREIGIAU, CARDIFF CF15 9NT
Tel: 02920 890220   **Fax:** 02920 892212
E-mail: info@creigiautravel.co.uk
Web site: www.creigiautravel.co.uk
Dirs: R M Matthews, L Matthews **Transport
Man:** J E Elson **Fleet Eng:** D Hawkins.
Fleet: 35 - 22 single-deck coach, 1 double-deck
coach, 5 midicoach, 5 minibus, 1 VIP coach,
1 VIP minibus.
Chassis: 1 Bova, 5 Dennis, 9 Mercedes,
1 Neoplan, 1 Scania, 14 Volvo.
Bodies: 6 Berkhof, 1 Bova, 1 Crafter,
3 Jonckheere, 1 Mellor, 1 Neoplan, 1 Optare,
12 Plaxton, 1 Sitcar, 3 Van Hool.
Ops incl: school contracts, excursions & tours,
private hire, continental tours.
Livery: Glasurit Blue.

NEW ADVENTURE TRAVEL LTD

COASTER PLACE, CARDIFF CF10 4XZ
Tel: 02920 442040
E-mail: sales@natgroup.co.uk
Web site: www.natgroup.co.uk
Depots at: Cardiff, Sully, Abercrave, Pontypridd.
Dir: Kevyn Jones **Fleet Eng:** Jason Campfield.
Fleet: 121 – 9 double-deck bus, 35 single-deck
bus, 2 double-deck coach, 48 single-deck coach,
12 midibus, 3 midicoach, 12 minibus, 1 minicoach.
Chassis: 8 Alexander Dennis, 2 Bova, 1 Bristol,
8 DAF, 19 Dennis, 2 Enterprise, 1 Ford Transit,
1 Irisbus, 1 King Long, 1 Leyland, 25 MAN,
2 Mercedes, 4 Neoplan, 5 Optare, 11 Scania,
1 Toyota, 2 Transbus, 5 VDL, 5 Volkswagen,
20 Volvo.
Bodies: 10 Alexander, 8 Alexander Dennis,
1 Autobus, 1 Berkhof, 1 Beulas, 2 Bova,
2 Caetano, 1 ECW, 2 East Lancs, 1 Ford, 3 Ikarus,
4 Irizar, 4 Jonckheere, 1 King Long, 1 KVC,
4 Lahden, 22 MCV, 4 Neoplan, 1 Noge,
1 Northern Counties, 5 Optare, 23 Plaxton,
2 Scania, 1 Transbus, 2 UVG, 5 Van Hool, 3
Wadham Stringer, 2 Wrightbus, 5 Other.
Ops incl: local bus services, private hire.
Livery: White with Blue.
Also trades as Humphreys Coaches

STAGECOACH IN SOUTH WALES

See Torfaen

WALTONS COACHES

VIKING PLACE, ROATH DOCK, CARDIFF
CF10 4TS
Tel: 02920 489955
E-mail: waltonscoaches@btconnect.com
Web site: www.waltonscoaches.com
Dir: R J Walton.
Fleet: 4 - 1 single-deck coach, 3 midicoach.
Chassis: 1 DAF, 3 Mercedes.
Ops incl: private hire, school contracts.
Livery: Blue/White/Red.

WATTS COACHES LTD

OLD POST GARAGE, BONVILSTON
CF5 6TQ
Tel: 01446 781277   **Fax:** 01446 781450
E-mail: enquiries@wattscoaches.co.uk
Web site: www.wattscoaches-cardiff.co.uk
Dirs: Clive P Watts, Carol Watts, James Watts.
Fleet: 38 - 3 double-deck bus, 23 single-deck
coach, 2 double-deck coach, 7 midibus,
2 midicoach, 1 minibus.
Chassis: 2 Alexander Dennis, 2 Bova, 3 DAF,
1 Dennis, 1 Iveco, 3 Leyland, 1 MAN, 4 Mercedes,
4 Scania, 3 Setra, 3 Transbus, 2 Van Hool, 3 VDL,
6 Volvo.
Bodies: 2 Alexander, 2 Alexander Dennis,
1 Beulas, 3 Berkhof, 2 Bova, 1 Caetano, 1 Duple,
1 East Lancs, 1 Irizar, 1 Jonckheere, 1 Noge,
8 Plaxton, 2 Setra, 3 Transbus, 1 Unvi, 4 Van Hool,
3 VDL.
Ops incl: local bus services, school contracts,
excursions & tours, private hire, continental
tours.
Livery: Buses: White/Green; **Coaches:**
Cream/Red/Gold.

WHEADONS GROUP TRAVEL LTD

STATION TERRACE, ELY BRIDGE,
COWBRIDGE ROAD WEST, CARDIFF
CF5 4AA
Tel: 02920 575333   **Fax:** 02920 575384
E-mail: enquiries@wheadons-group.co.uk
Web site: www.wheadons-group.co.uk
Chairman: E K Wheadon **Man:** R Tucker
Ch Eng: S Osling.
Fleet: 20 – 4 single-deck bus, 10 single-deck
coach, 4 midicoach, 2 minibus.
Chassis: 1 Irisbus, 3 Iveco, 2 LDV, 3 Mercedes,
1 Setra, 1 Toyota, 9 Volvo.

Bodies: I Caetano, I Jonckheere, 2 LDV,
2 Mellor, 5 Plaxton, I Setra, 4 Van Hool, 4 Vehixel.
Ops incl: private hire, school contracts,
excursions & tours.
Livery: Blue/Yellow/Silver over White.

CARMARTHENSHIRE

1ST CHOICE TRANSPORT LTD
SANDY ROAD, LLANELLI SA15 4DP
Tel: 01554 706316   **Fax:** 01554 750978
E-mail: info@1stchoiceltd.co.uk
Web site: www.1stchoiceltdcoachhire.co.uk
Dir: A Phillips.
Fleet: 32 – 2 single-deck bus, 29 single-deck
coach, I midicoach.
Chassis: 2 Bluebird, 12 Dennis, 2 Irisbus,
I Mercedes, 15 Volvo.
Bodies: 2 Berkhof, 2 Beulas, 2 Bluebird,
I Caetano, I Jonckheere, 22 Plaxton, I Other.
Ops incl: school contracts, private hire.
Livery: White with Plum.

BRODYR WILLIAMS LTD
BRYNEGLUR GARAGE, UPPER TUMBLE
SA14 6BW
Tel: 01269 841338   **Fax:** 01269 832338
E-mail: susanpugh@btconnect.com
Web site: www.brodyrwilliams.co.uk
Dirs: T Thomas, A Thomas, S Pugh.
Fleet: 12 – 11 single-deck coach, I midicoach.
Chassis: 3 DAF, I EOS, I Mercedes, I VDL,
6 Volvo.
Bodies: I EOS, I Ikarus, 6 Plaxton, I Sitcar,
I Transbus, 2 Van Hool.
Ops incl: school contracts, private hire.
Livery: White with Blue.

BYSIAU CWM TAF/TAF VALLEY COACHES LTD
PENRHEOL, WHITLAND SA34 0NH
Tel: 01994 240908
Fax: 01994 241264
E-mail: tafvalley@btconnect.com
Web site: www.tafvalleycoaches.co.uk
Dirs: Clive Edwards, Heather Edwards.
Fleet Name: Taf Valley Coaches.
Fleet: 23 - 15 single-deck coach, 4 midibus,
3 midicoach, I minicoach.
Chassis: I Bova, 3 Alexander Dennis, 3 Dennis,
2 Irisbus, 5 Mercedes, I Setra, I VDL, 7 Volvo.
Ops incl: local bus services, excursions & tours,
school contracts, private hire, continental tours.
Livery: White/Silver/Blue.

CASTLE GARAGE LTD
BROAD STREET, LLANDOVERY SA20 0AA
Tel: 01550 720335
E-mail: enquiries@castle-garage.com
Web site: www.castle-garage.com
Man Dir: Derek Jones.
Fleet: 7 - 2 midibus, 5 minibus.
Chassis: 4 LDV, 3 Mercedes.
Ops incl: local bus services, school contracts,
private hire.

DAVIES COACHES LTD
65 STEPNEY STREET, LLANELLI SA15 3YA
Tel: 01554 773378
Fax: 01554 752691
E-mail: sales@daviescoachesonline.co.uk
Web site: www.daviescoachesonline.co.uk
Dir: K Davies.
Fleet: 39 – 29 single-deck coach, 7 midicoach,
3 minibus.
Chassis: 4 Dennis, I Ford Transit, 4 Leyland,
6 Mercedes, 24 Volvo.
Ops incl: school contracts, excursions & tours,
private hire.
Livery: White/Green.

GARETH EVANS COACHES
80 GLYN ROAD, BRYNAMMAN SA18 1SS
Tel: 01269 823127
Fax: 01269 824533
Props: K Davies, Mrs S Davies.
Fleet: 11 – 3 single-deck bus, 5 single-deck
coach, I midicoach, 2 minibus.
Chassis: 2 Autosan, I Ford Transit, I Leyland,
2 Mercedes, 3 Scania, I Setra, I Volvo.
Ops incl: school contracts, private hire.

FFOSHELIG COACHES LTD
MAES Y PRIOR, ST PETERS, CARMARTHEN
SA33 5DS
Tel: 01267 237584   **Fax:** 01267 236059
E-mail: ffoshelig@btconnect.com
Web site: www.ffoshelig.co.uk
Dirs: Rhodri Evans, Debbie Evans.
Fleet: 14 – 2 single-deck bus, 7 single-deck
coach, I midicoach, 4 minibus.
Chassis: I Alexander Dennis, I Autosan,
2 Dennis, 3 Mercedes, 2 Optare, I Setra, 4 Volvo.
Bodies: I Autosan, I Jonckheere, 2 Optare,
8 Plaxton, I Setra, I Van Hool.
Ops incl: local bus services, school contracts,
private hire, excursions and tours.
Livery: Cream with Red vinyls.
Incorporating Lewis Coaches, Whitland

FIRST CYMRU BUSES LTD
See City & County of Swansea

JONES INTERNATIONAL
STATION ROAD, LLANDEILO SA19 6NG
Tel: 01558 822985   **Fax:** 01558 822984
Recovery: 01267 235467
Prop: Myrddin Jones **Traffic Man:** Neil Jones
Co Sec: Carole Thompson
Ch Eng: M Hayward.
Fleet: 2 single-deck coach.
Chassis: I DAF, I Leyland.
Bodies: I Plaxton, I Van Hool.
Ops incl: excursions & tours, private hire.
Livery: Yellow/Blue.

JONES LOGIN – TEITHIAU OSAFON/ QUALITY COACH TRAVEL
LOGIN, WHITLAND SA34 0UX
Tel: 01437 563277   **Fax:** 01437 563393
E-mail: info@joneslogin.co.uk
Web Site: www.joneslogin.co.uk
Dirs: Endaf Jones, Arwel Jones, Ann Jones,
Hannah Jones.
Fleet: 12 – 1 single-deck bus, 7 single-deck
coach, I midicoach, 3 minibus.
Chassis: 2 Alexander Dennis, I Ford Transit,
2 LDV, I Mercedes, I Optare, 5 Volvo.
Bodies: I East Lancs, I Ford Transit, 2 LDV,
I Optare, 7 Plaxton.
Ops incl: local bus services, school contracts,
excursions & tours, private hire, continental
tours.
Livery: Turquoise/Midnight Blue/White.
Ticket System: ERG.

MORRIS TRAVEL
ALLT Y CNAP ROAD, JOHNSTOWN,
CARMARTHEN SA31 3QY
Tel: 01267 235090
E-mail: morristravel2000@yahoo.co.uk
Web site: www.morristravel.co.uk
Man Dir: T J Freeman **Ops Dir:** C J Freeman
Ops Man: V R Shambrook **Workshop Man:**
A Jones **Fleet Man:** L Davies.
Fleet: 32 - 13 single-deck coach, 11 midibus,
8 minibus.
Chassis: 3 Autosan, 10 Dennis, I Leyland,
3 Mercedes, 8 Optare, 2 Renault, 5 Volvo.
Bodies: I Alexander, 3 Autosan, I Jonckheere,
2 Marshall, 2 Mellor, 8 Optare, 9 Plaxton,

I Transbus, 3 UVG, 2 Wadham Stringer.
Ops incl: local bus services, school contracts,
private hire.
Livery: Blue/Navy/White.
Ticket System: Wayfarer.

GWYNNE PRICE TRANSPORT LTD
38 HEOL LLANELLI, TRIMSARAN SA17 4AA
Tel: 01554 810217
E-mail: coachhire@gwynneprice.co.uk
Web site: www.gwynneprice.co.uk
Dir: C Price.
Fleet: 20 – 14 single-deck coach, 2 midicoach,
4 minibus.
Chassis: I Autosan, I Citroen, 4 Dennis, I Ford
Transit, I LDV, 2 Leyland, 3 MAN, 4 Mercedes,
I Volkswagen, 2 Volvo.
Ops incl: school contracts, private hire.
Livery: Yellow/Orange.

THOMAS BROS
TOWY GARAGE, LLANGADOG SA19 9LU
Tel: 01550 777438   **Fax:** 01550 777807
Prop: Gareth Thomas.
Depots at: Llangadog, Llandeilo.
Fleet: 14 – 6 single-deck coach, 5 midicoach,
3 minibus.
Chassis: I Ford Transit, I LDV, 6 Mercedes,
I Setra, 5 Volvo.
Ops incl: school contracts, excursions & tours,
private hire.
Livery: Cream/Green.

GWYN WILLIAMS & SONS LTD
Ceased trading since LRB 2014 went to press

WINDY CORNER COACHES
WINDY CORNER GARAGE, PENCADER
SA39 9HP
Tel: 01559 384779   **Fax:** 01559 384928
E-mail: windycornercoaches@hotmail.co.uk
Prop: W D Thomas **Ops Man:** R Thomas.
Fleet: 16 - 14 single-deck coach, 2 minibus.
Chassis: I Alexander Dennis, I Bova, I DAF,
8 Dennis, I Ford Transit, I MAN, 2 Mercedes,
I Volvo.
Ops incl: school contracts, private hire.

CEREDIGION

ARRIVA BUSES WALES
See Gwynedd

CERBYDAU CENARTH COACHES
FALLS GARAGE, CENARTH SA38 9JP
Tel: 01239 710463   **Fax:** 01239 710073
Props: D C R James, W G E James.
Fleet: 25 – 1 single-deck bus, 16 single-deck
coach, 2 midibus, 3 midicoach, 3 minibus.
Chassis: I BMC, 2 DAF, 14 Dennis, I Iveco,
I King Long, I LDV, 2 Mercedes, 2 Renault,
I Van Hool.
Ops incl: school contracts, private hire.

VINCENT DAVIES & SON
BRYNMEDDYG, 4 VICTORIA TERRACE,
LAMPETER SA48 7DF
Tel: 01570 422493   **Fax:** 01570 422490
Prop: Huw Davies.
Fleet: 18 – 1 single-deck bus, 4 single-deck
coach, 4 midicoach, 9 minibus.
Chassis: I BMC, I Citroen, I Dennis,
11 Mercedes, I Volkswagen, 3 Volvo.
Ops incl: school contracts, private hire.

EVANS COACHES TREGARON LTD
OLD STATION YARD, TREGARON SY25 6HX
Tel: 01974 298546
Man Dir: J A Evans.

Fleet: 13 - 6 single-deck coach, 2 midibus, 2 midicoach, 3 minibus.
Chassis: I Bedford, I Bova, 2 Dennis, I LDV, 3 Mercedes, 2 Optare, 3 Volvo.
Bodies: I Autobus, I Bova, I Caetano, 2 Optare, 4 Plaxton, I Van Hool, 3 Other.
Ops incl: local bus services, school contracts, private hire.

BRODYR JAMES
GLANYRAFON, LLANGEITHO, TREGARON SY25 6TT
Tel: 0800 084 3596   **Fax:** 01974 251618
Web site: www.brodyrjamestregaron.co.uk
Dirs: D E James, T M G James.
Fleet: 16 - 8 single-deck coach, 2 midicoach, 5 minibus, I minicoach.
Chassis: 2 Alexander Dennis, 2 Dennis, I Ford Transit, I LDV, I MAN, 4 Mercedes, I Toyota, 4 Volvo.
Bodies: 2 Alexander, 3 Caetano, I Excel, I Ford Transit, I Jonckheere, 6 Plaxton, I Sitcar, I Other.
Ops incl: local bus services, school contracts, private hire.
Livery: White/Red/Gold.
Ticket System: ERG TP5000.

G & M COACHES
PONTFAEN GARAGE, PONTFAEN ROAD, LAMPETER SA48 7JL
Tel: 01570 423772
Props: D G Isaac, M W Morgan.
Fleet: 10 — 4 single-deck coach, 4 midicoach, 2 minibus.
Chassis: I Ford Transit, 2 Irisbus, 4 Mercedes, I Renault, I Scania, I Setra.
Bodies: I Ferqui, I Ford Transit, I Irizar, I Noone Turas, 3 Plaxton, I Setra, 2 Other.
Ops incl: school contracts, private hire.

R J JONES TRAVEL
TYNYGRAIG, TY NANT, YSTRAD MEURIG, ABERYSTWYTH SY25 6AE
Tel: 01974 261474
Prop: R J Jones.
Fleet: 4 — 3 single-deck coach, I midicoach.
Chassis: I BMC, I Mercedes, 2 Setra.
Ops incl: school contracts, private hire.
Livery: Red & White.

LEWIS COACHES
BRYNEITHIN YARD, LLANRHYSTUD SY23 5DN
Tel: 01974 202495
Fax: 01974 202481
E-mail: enquiries@lewis-coaches.co.uk
Web site: www.lewis-coaches.co.uk
Prop: Gwyn R Lewis.
Fleet: 29 — 4 single-deck bus, 14 single-deck coach, 3 midibus, I midicoach, 7 minibus.
Chassis: I Alexander Dennis, 4 Autosan, I Citroen, 2 DAF, 5 Dennis, 2 Irisbus, 3 Mercedes, 3 Optare, I Renault, 3 Scania, 3 Van Hool, I Wadham Stringer, 2 Volvo.
Ops incl: local bus services, private hire, excursions & tours.
Liveries: White/Blue; **School Buses:** Yellow.
Ticket System: Wayfarer.

LEWIS-RHYDLEWIS CYF
PENRHIW-PAL GARAGE, RHYDLEWIS, LLANDYSUL SA44 5QG
Tel: 01239 851386
Fax: 01239 858899
E-mail: post@lewis-rhydlewis.co.uk
Web site: www.lewis-rhydlewis.co.uk
Dirs: Maldwyn Lewis, Rhiannon Williams, Gwenda Savins, Meirion Lewis.
Fleet: 22 - 15 single-deck coach, 3 midibus, 4 minibus.

Chassis: I Bedford, I BMC, 3 Dennis, 4 Ford Transit, I Iveco, I Leyland, 2 Setra, 9 Volvo.
Ops incl: local bus services, school contracts, private hire, excursions & tours, continental tours.
Livery: Cream/Maroon/Orange/Red.

MID WALES TRAVEL
BRYNHYFRYD GARAGE, PENRHYNCOCH, ABERYSTWYTH SY23 3EH
Tel: 01970 828288   **Fax:** 01970 828940
E-mail: enquires@midwalestravel.co.uk
Web site: www.midwalestravel.co.uk
Dir: J M Evans **Co Sec:** J H Morgan.
Fleet: 23 — 13 single-deck coach, 9 midibus, I midicoach.
Chassis: 8 Alexander Dennis, 4 Dennis, I Mercedes, I Van Hool, 3 VDL, 6 Volvo.
Bodies: 6 Alexander Dennis, 9 Plaxton, 3 Transbus, I UVG, 4 Van Hool.
Ops incl: local bus services, school contracts, excursions & tours, private hire.
Livery: White with Blue.

RICHARDS BROS
MOYLGROVE GARAGE, PENTOOD INDUSTRIAL ESTATE, CARDIGAN SA43 3AG
Tel: 01239 613756   **Fax:** 01239 615193
E-mail: enquiries@richardsbros.co.uk
Web site: www.richardsbros.co.uk
Gen Man: W J M Richards **Ch Eng:** D N Richards **Traf Man:** R M Richards
Ops Man: S M Richards.
Fleet: 84 - 38 single-deck bus, 29 single-deck coach, 10 midibus, 7 minibus.
Chassis: Alexander Dennis, DAF, LDV, Mercedes, Optare, Transbus, VDL, Volvo.
Bodies: Alexander, Alexander Dennis, Autobus, Caetano, Carlyle, Ikarus, Jonckheere, LDV, Marshall, MCV, Northern Counties, Optare, Plaxton, Transbus, Van Hool, Wrightbus.
Ops incl: local bus services, school contracts, excursions & tours, private hire, continental tours.
Livery: Blue/White/Maroon.
Ticket System: ERG.

CONWY

ALPINE TRAVEL
CENTRAL COACH GARAGE, BUILDER STREET WEST, LLANDUDNO LL30 1HH
Tel: 01492 879133   **Fax:** 01492 876055
E-mail: info@alpine-travel.co.uk
Web site: www.alpine-travel.co.uk
Depots at: Llandudno, Llanrwst, Rhyl.
Dirs: Bryan Owens, Patricia Owens, Christopher Owens, Christopher Bryan Owens
Gen Man: Jason Beattie.
Fleet: 68 - 27 double-deck bus, I open-top bus, 35 single-deck coach, 2 midibus, 2 midicoach, I minibus.
Chassis: I Bristol, 4 Dennis, 3 Duple 425, 27 Leyland, 7 Mercedes, 25 Volvo.
Bodies: 11 Alexander, I Caetano, 4 Duple, 13 ECW, I Harrington, I Marshall, I Marcopolo, 2 Mercedes, 32 Plaxton, I Roe, I Sunsundegui.
Ops incl: local bus services, school contracts, excursions & tours, private hire, Llandudno sightseeing tours, continental tours.
Livery: Red/White/Green.
Ticket System: Setright.
Also owns Silver Star North Wales (see Gwynedd)

ARRIVA BUSES WALES
See Gwynedd

LLEW JONES INTERNATIONAL
STATION YARD, LLANRWST LL26 0EH
Tel: 01492 640320   **Fax:** 01492 642040

Recovery: 07795 347476
E-mail: info@llewjonesinternational.co.uk
Web site: www.llewjonesinternational.co.uk
Man Dir: Stephen Jones **Fin Dir:** Eirlys Jones
Ops Man: Kevin Williams **Workshop Man:** Erfyl Roberts **HR & Compliance Man:** Julie Jones.
Fleet: 43 — 30 single-deck coach, 4 midicoach, 7 minibus, 2 minicoach.
Chassis: 3 DAF, 3 Dennis, 2 Duple 425, I Ford Transit, 2 Irisbus, 3 MAN, 8 Mercedes, 3 Neoplan, 5 Optare, 4 Scania, I Setra, I VDL, 6 Volvo.
Bodies: 2 Ayats, 2 Berkhof, 2 Beulas, 3 Caetano, 3 Duple, 2 Ferqui, I Hispano, 3 Irizar, I Koch, 3 Mercedes, 2 Neoplan, 3 Noge, 5 Optare, 5 Plaxton, I Setra, I Sitcar, I Unvi, I Van Hool, I Volvo, I Other.
Ops incl: local bus services, school contracts, express, private hire.
Liveries: White/Blue/Magenta Flashes; National Express.
Ticket system: Wayfarer TGX 1000.

ROBERTS MINI COACHES
RHANDIR GARAGE, RHANDIR LL22 8BW
Tel: 01492 650449
Prop: W T Roberts.
Fleet: 3 - 2 midicoach, I minibus.
Chassis: 2 Mercedes, I Vauxhall.
Ops Inc: schools contracts, private hire.

DENBIGHSHIRE

ARRIVA BUSES WALES
See Gwynedd

GHA COACHES LTD
MILL GARAGE, BETWS GWERFIL GOCH, CORWEN LL21 9PU
See main entry under Wrexham.

M & H COACHES LTD
UNIT 2, BRICKWORK GARAGE, BODFARI ROAD, TREFNANT, DENBIGH LL16 4UH
Tel: 01745 730700   **Fax:** 01745 730777
E-mail: info@mandhcoaches.co.uk
Web site: www.mandhcoaches.co.uk
Prop: Mrs M Owen.
Fleet: 15 — 8 single-deck coach, 2 midibus, 2 midicoach, 3 minibus.
Chassis: I BMC, 3 Mercedes, 5 Optare, I Setra, 5 Volvo.
Bodies: 2 Berkhof, I BMC, 2 Jonckheere, 3 Mercedes, 5 Optare, I Setra, I Van Hool.
Livery: Blue/White.
Ops incl: local bus services, school contracts, private hire.

VOEL COACHES LTD
PENISA FILLING STATION, FFORD TALARGOCH, DYSERTH LL18 6BP
Tel: 01745 570154
Fax: 01745 570307
E-mail: sales@voelcoaches.com
Web site: www.voelholidays.com
Man Dir: W M Kerfoot-Davies **Dir:** M Kerfoot-Davies **Comm Man:** Michelle Kerfoot Higginson.
Fleet: 35 - 9 double-deck bus, 22 single-deck coach, 2 midibus, 2 minibus.
Chassis: I DAF, 6 Leyland, I Mercedes, I MCV, I Neoplan, I Optare, I Renault, 5 Scania, I Volkswagen, 17 Volvo.
Bodies: 2 Alexander, 4 Caetano, I ECW, I Excel, I Ikarus, 2 Jonckheere, 2 Lahden, I MCV, I Neoplan, 5 Northern Counties, I Optare, 5 Plaxton, 6 Van Hool, I Volkswagen, 2 Volvo.
Ops incl: local bus services, school contracts, excursions & tours, private hire, continental tours.
Livery: Orange.

A N ANDREW COACHES

♿ ♻

RHEWL ROAD, MOSTYN, HOLYWELL
CH8 9HW
Tel: 01745 560853
Fleet: 3 – 2 single-deck coach, 1 midicoach.
Chassis: 1 Mercedes, 2 Volvo.
Bodies: 2 Plaxton, 1 Van Hool.
Ops incl: school contracts, private hire.

ARRIVA BUSES WALES
See Gwynedd

EAGLES AND CRAWFORD

♿ ♻ ♻ ♻

RUTHIN ROAD, GWERNYMYNYDD, MOLD
CH7 5LG
Tel: 01352 700217/8   **Fax:** 01352 750211
E-mail: eaglesandcrawford@supanet.com
Partners: J F, J K & W P Eagles.
Fleet: 8 – 1 single-deck bus, 5 single-deck coach,
2 minibus.
Chassis: 1 Autosan, 3 Dennis, 1 LDV, 1 MAN,
1 Mercedes, 1 Volvo.
Bodies: 1 Autosan, 1 Marcopolo, 4 Plaxton,
2 Other.
Ops incl: excursions & tours, private hire,
continental tours.
Livery: White/Blue/Orange.

FOUR GIRLS COACHES

♻ ♻

THE OLD POST OFFICE YARD, CORWEN
ROAD, PONTYBODKIN, MOLD CH7 4TG
Tel: 01352 770438   **Fax:** 01352 770253
E-mail: carolyn_fg@hotmail.com
Web site: www.fourgirlscoaches.co.uk
Partners: Carolyn Thomas, Elaine Williams.
Fleet: 7 - 6 single-deck coach, 1 minibus.
Chassis: 1 Mercedes, 6 Volvo.
Bodies: 1 Onyx, 5 Plaxton, 1 Van Hool.
Ops incl: school contracts, private hire.
Livery: Turquoise/Red/Yellow.

H D HUTCHINSON & SON

♿ ♻

NEWLYN, PADESWOOD ROAD, BUCKLEY
CH7 2JW
Tel: 01244 543907
Fleet: 9 – 2 midicoach, 6 minibus, 1 minicoach.
Chassis: 1 Dennis, 2 Iveco, 2 LDV, 3 Optare,
1 Toyota.
Ops incl: local bus services, school contracts,
private hire.

JONES MOTOR SERVICES

♻ ♻ ♻ ♻ T

CHESTER ROAD, OAKENHOLT, FLINT
CH6 5DZ
Tel: 01352 733292   **Fax:** 01352 763353
E-mail: tours@jonescoaches.co.uk
Web site: www.jonesholidays.co.uk
Prop: A W Jones.
Fleet: 9 - 4 single-deck coach, 5 minibus.
Chassis: 1 Citroen, 3 DAF, 1 Ford Transit,
1 Iveco, 1 Mercedes, 1 Optare, 1 VDL.
Bodies: 1 Optare, 4 Van Hool, 4 Other.
Ops incl: excursions & tours, private hire,
school contracts.
Livery: Blue.

P. & O. LLOYD LTD

♿ ♻ ♻ ♻

RHYDWEN GARAGE, BAGILLT CH6 6JJ
Tel: 01352 710682   **Fax:** 01352 710093
E-mail: info@polloydcoaches.co.uk
Web site: www.polloydcoaches.co.uk
Man Dir: David Lloyd.
Fleet: 44 - 6 double-deck bus, 8 single-deck bus,
15 single-deck coach, 8 midibus, 7 minibus.
Chassis: 1 Alexander Dennis, 3 Autosan,
4 BMC, 3 Leyland, 2 MAN, 2 Mercedes,

15 Optare, 14 Volvo.
Bodies: 5 Alexander, 1 Alexander Dennis,
3 Autosan, 4 BMC, 1 ECW, 2 Mercedes,
3 Northern Counties, 15 Optare, 9 Plaxton,
1 Transbus.
Ops incl: local bus services, private hire, school
contracts.
Liveries: Cream/Red or Cream/Maroon/Gold;
Yellow (school buses).
Ticket System: Almex.

OARE'S COACHES

♿ ♻

TY DRAW, BRYNFORD, HOLYWELL CH8 8LP
Tel: 01352 713339   **Fax:** 01352 714871
Web site: www.oarescoachesholywell.co.uk
Prop: G A Oare.
Fleet: 12– 8 single-deck coach, 1 midicoach,
3 minibus.
Chassis: 1 Ford Transit, 1 Leyland, 1 Mercedes,
1 Optare, 3 Scania, 1 Vauxhall, 4 Volvo.
Bodies: 1 Irizar, 1 Optare, 2 Plaxton,
1 Sunsundegui, 4 Van Hool, 1 Wadham Stringer,
2 Other.
Livery: White/Red/Silver.
Ops incl: local bus services, school contracts,
private hire.

PHILLIPS MOTOR SERVICES
Ceased trading since LRB 2014 went to press

TOWNLYNX LTD

♿ ♻ ♻ ♻

CAETIA LLWYD, NORTHOP ROAD,
HOLYWELL CH8 8AE
Tel: 01352 715757
Dirs: S A Lee, C Lee.
Fleet: 26 – 3 double-deck bus, 1 single-deck bus,
6 single-deck coach, 13 midibus, 3 minibus.
Chassis: 1 BMC, 4 Dennis, 2 Iveco, 1 Irisbus,
2 Leyland, 1 Mercedes, 1 Optare, 1 Transbus,
13 Volvo.
Bodies: 3 Alexander, 1 Beulas, 1 BMC,
1 Marcopolo, 2 Mellor, 1 Optare, 3 Plaxton,
2 Transbus, 12 Wrightbus.
Ops incl: local bus services, school contracts.
Livery: White/Yellow/Blue.

ARRIVA BUSES WALES

♿ 🚌 ♻ ♻ ♻ T

HEAD OFFICE, LLANDYGAI INDUSTRIAL
ESTATE, BANGOR LL57 4YH
Tel: 01248 360530   **Fax:** 01248 360531
Web site: www.arrivabus.co.uk/wales
Regional Man Dir: Phil Stone **Regional Eng
Dir:** Phil Cummins **Regional Finance Dir:**
Simon Mills **Area Man Dir:** Michael Morton
Head of Service Delivery: Simon Finnie
Head of Eng: Nigel Cross.
Fleet: 224 - 51 double-deck bus, 5 open-top
bus, 58 single-deck bus, 2 single-deck coach,
86 midibus, 22 minibus.
Chassis: 31 Alexander Dennis, 22 DAF,
69 Dennis, 1 Leyland, 25 Optare, 48 VDL,
13 Volvo, 10 Wrightbus.
Bodies: 12 Alexander, 31 Alexander Dennis,
5 Northern Counties, 25 Optare, 68 Plaxton,
2 Van Hool, 76 Wrightbus.
Ops incl: local bus services, school contracts,
private hire, express.
Livery: Arriva UK Bus.
Ticket System: Wayfarer TGX200.

ARVONIA COACHES LTD

♻ ♻ ♻ T

THE SQUARE, LLANRUG LL55 4AA
Tel: 01286 675175   **Fax:** 01286 671126
E-mail: info@arvonia.co.uk
Web site: www.arvonia.co.uk
Props: R Stokes, M Stokes.
Fleet: 5 single-deck coach.
Chassis: 2 Mercedes, 2 Neoplan, 1 Setra.
Bodies: 2 Mercedes, 2 Neoplan, 1 Setra.

Ops incl: excursions & tours, private hire,
continental tours.
Livery: White/Orange/Red.

CERBYDAU BERWYN COACHES

♿ ♻ ♻ R R24

TREFOR WORKSHOPS, TREFOR,
CAERNARVON LL54 5LH
Tel: 01286 660315   **Fax:** 01286 660110
Recovery: 01286 660315
E-mail: berwyncoaches@aol.com
Props: Brian Japheth, Mrs Marina Japheth.
Fleet: 30 – 3 double-deck bus, 13 single-deck
coach, 8 midibus, 4 midicoach, 2 minicoach.
Chassis: 1 Bova, 8 Mercedes, 6 Optare, 15 Volvo.
Ops incl: local bus services, school contracts,
private hire.
Livery: White/Yellow/Brown.

CAELLOI MOTORS
(T. H. JONES & SON)

♿ ♻ ♻ ♻

UNIT 17, GLAN Y DON INDUSTRIAL ESTATE,
PWLLHELI LL53 5YT
Tel: 01758 612719   **Fax:** 01758 612335
E-mail: tours@caelloi.co.uk
Web site: www.caelloi.co.uk
Props: Eryl B Jones, Thomas H Jones.
Fleet: 9 – 2 single-deck bus, 6 single-deck coach,
1 midibus.
Chassis: 1 Bova, 1 DAF, 1 Optare, 6 Volvo.
Bodies: 1 Alexander, 1 Bova, 1 Optare,
1 Plaxton, 4 Van Hool, 1 Wrightbus.
Ops incl: local bus services, school contracts,
excursions & tours, private hire, continental
tours.
Livery: Multi.
Ticket System: Almex.

CLYNNOG & TREFOR

♿ ♻ ♻ R R24

THE GARAGE, TREFOR, CAERNARFON
LL54 5HP
Tel: 01286 660208   **Fax:** 01286 660538
E-mail: info@clynnogandtrefor.com
Web site: www.clynnogandtrefor.com
Dirs: D C Jones, E W Griffiths
Co Sec: I Williams.
Fleet: 46 - 5 double-deck bus, 8 single-deck bus,
14 single-deck coach, 9 midibus, 4 midicoach,
6 minibus.
Chassis: 1 Alexander Dennis, 6 Dennis, 3 Ford
Transit, 2 Leyland, 1 LDV, 6 Mercedes, 1 Optare,
26 Volvo.
Bodies: 12 Alexander, 1 Alexander Dennis,
1 ECW, 3 Ford Transit, 8 Jonckheere, 1 LDV,
3 Northern Counties, 1 Optare, 9 Plaxton,
6 Van Hool, 1 Wrightbus.
Ops incl: local bus services, school contracts,
private hire.
Livery: White.
Ticket system: Wayfarer TGX.

EMMAS COACHES
INTERNATIONAL LTD

♿ ♻

GARTH YARD, PENMAENPOOL, DOLGELLAU
LL40 1YF
Tel/Recovery: 01341 423934
Fax: 01341 423321
E-mail: info@emmascoaches.co.uk
Dir: Barrie Thomas.
Fleet: 5 - 1 single-deck coach, 1 midibus,
1 midicoach, 2 minibus.
Chassis: 1 Ford Transit, 1 Leyland, 1 Mercedes,
1 Renault, 1 Scania.
Ops incl: private hire.
Livery: White/Blue, Green/Gold.

EXPRESS MOTORS

♿ 🚌 ♻ ♻ 🚌 R R24 ♻ T

THE GARAGE, LLYNFI ROAD, PENYGROES,
CAERNARFON LL54 6ND
Tel: 01286 881108   **Fax:** 01286 882331
E-mail: post@expressmotors.co.uk

Web site: www.expressmotors.co.uk
Props: Eric Wyn Jones, Jean A Jones
Ops Man: Kevin Wyn Jones **Ch Eng:** Ian Wyn Jones **Service Man:** Keith Jones.
Fleet: 60 - 2 double-deck bus, 1 open-top bus, 15 single-deck bus, 7 single-deck coach, 1 double-deck coach, 25 midibus, 6 minibus, 3 vintage.
Chassis: 4 Alexander Dennis, 1 Bedford OB, 2 Bristol, 1 DAF, 5 Dennis, 9 MAN, 5 Mercedes, 2 Neoplan, 14 Optare, 4 Scania, 1 Transbus, 1 Van Hool, 1 VDL, 9 Volvo.
Ops incl: local bus services, school contracts, private hire.
Livery: Yellow/White.
Ticket System: Wayfarer 3.

JOHN'S COACHES

81 MANOD ROAD, BLAENAU FFESTINIOG LL41 4AF
Tel: 01766 831781　**Fax:** 01766 831781
E-mail: info@johns-taxis.co.uk
Web site: www.johns-taxis.co.uk
Prop: J R Edwards.
Fleet: 3 – 2 midibus, 1 minibus.
Chassis: 1 Ford Transit, 2 Mercedes.
Bodies: 1 Ford Transit, 2 Plaxton.
Ops incl: local bus service, school contracts, private hire.
Livery: White/Red.
Ticket System: Wayfarer.

NEFYN COACHES LTD

WEST END GARAGE, ST DAVIDS ROAD, NEFYN LL53 6HE
Tel: 01758 720904
Fax: 01758 720331
Dirs: B G Owen, M A Owen, A. G Owen.
Fleet: 17 - 2 single-deck coach, 1 midicoach, 6 midibus, 8 minibus.
Chassis: 2 BMC, 10 Mercedes, 3 Optare, 2 Volvo.
Bodies: 1 Alexander, 2 BMC, 3 Optare, 10 Plaxton, 1 Van Hool.
Ops incl: local bus services, school contracts, excursions & tours, private hire.
Livery: Silver/Red/Yellow.

PADARN BUS LTD
Ceased trading since LRB 2014 went to press

SILVER STAR NORTH WALES LTD

11 CASTLE SQUARE, CAERNARFON LL55 2NF
Tel: 01286 672333
Fax: 01286 678118
E-mail: enquiries@silverstarholidays.com
Web site: www.silverstarholidays.com
Gen Man: Gavin Owen **Ops Man:** Graeme Tilley.
Fleet: 3 single-deck coach.
Chassis: 3 Volvo.
Bodies: 3 Plaxton..
Ops incl: excursions & tours, private hire, continental tours.
Livery: Green.
A subsidiary of Alpine Travel *(see Conwy)*

WILLIAMS OF BALA

BODOLWYN GARAGE, ARENIG STREET, BALA LL23 7AH
Tel: 01678 520777
E-mail: williamsofbala@btconnect.com
Partners: Geoffrey Williams, Alan Williams.
Fleet: 8 – 5 single-deck coach, 2 midicoach, 1 minibus.
Chassis: 1 DAF, 1 Ford, 2 Mercedes, 4 Volvo.
Ops incl: school contracts, excursions & tours, private hire.
Livery: White.

MERTHYR TYDFIL

1ST CALL TRAVEL LTD

UNIT 48, PANT INDUSTRIAL ESTATE, MERTHYR TYDFIL CF48 2SR
Tel: 01685 371012
E-mail: enquiries@firstcalltravelltd.co.uk
Web site: www.firstcalltravelltd.co.uk
Dirs: S Mahoney, P Rajani.
Fleet: 31 – 1 single-deck bus, 20 single-deck coach, 6 midibus, 2 midicoach, 4 minibus.
Chassis: 2 Bova, 1 DAF, 15 Dennis, 3 EOS, 1 Ford Transit, 2 Leyland, 4 Mercedes, 3 Scania, 1 Volkswagen, 1 Volvo.
Ops incl: local bus services, school contracts, private hire, excursions & tours.
Livery: White with Blue.

GIBBONS COACHES

17 UPPER HIGH STREET, BEDLINOG CF46 6RY
Tel: 01443 710604
Web Site: www.gibbonscoaches.co.uk
Prop: Adrian Gibbons
Fleet: 8 – 5 single-deck coach, 1 midicoach, 2 minibus.
Chassis: 2 Ford Transit, 1 king Long, 4 Setra, 1 Van Hool.
Bodies: 2 Ford Transit, 1 King Long, 4 Setra, 1 Van Hool.
Ops incl: excursions & tours, private hire.

JOHN'S TRAVEL

19 SIX BELLS ESTATE, HEOLGERRIG, MERTHYR TYDFIL CF48 1TU
Tel: 01685 373765
Prop: Mrs E Davies.
Fleet: 8 – 6 midibus, 2 minibus.
Chassis: 1 LDV, 6 Mercedes, 1 Optare.
Ops incl: local bus service, school contracts.
Livery: Blue/White.

MINTAX MINICOACHES

3 RIVERSIDE CLOSE, ABERFAN CF48 4RN
Tel: 01443 690608
E-mail: info@mintax.net
Web site: www.mintax.net
Prop: C Minard.
Fleet: 4 – 3 midibus, 1 minibus.
Chassis: 1 Ford Transit, 3 Iveco.
Ops incl: local bus service, private hire.
Livery: Green.

SIXTY SIXTY COACHES

THE COACH DEPOT, MERTHYR INDUSTRIAL PARK, PENTREBACH CF48 4DR
Tel: 01443 692060
Fax: 01443 699061
E-mail: enquiries@sixsixty.co.uk
Web site: www.sixtysixty.co.uk
Props: G Handy, C T Handy.
Fleet: 17 - 9 single-deck coach, 2 midicoach, 6 minibus.
Chassis: 1 DAF, 3 EOS, 1 Ford Transit, 1 Iveco, 1 LDV, 2 Mercedes, 3 Renault, 2 Scania, 1 Van Hool, 2 Volvo.
Ops incl: school contracts, excursions & tours, private hire.
Livery: Silver.

STAGECOACH IN SOUTH WALES
See Torfaen

VR TRAVEL
Business acquired by New Adventure Travel Ltd *(see Cardiff)*

MONMOUTHSHIRE

CHEPSTOW CLASSIC BUSES

UNIT 6, BULWARK INDUSTRIAL ESTATE, BULWARK, CHEPSTOW NP16 5QZ
Tel/Fax: 01291 625449
E-mail: chepstowclassic@btconnect.com
Web site: www.chepstow-classic-buses.co.uk
Prop: D L Hoare.
Fleet: double-deck bus, single-deck bus, midibus, minibus, also heritage vehicles.
Chassis: Bristol, Dennis, Leyland, Mercedes, Scania, Volvo.
Bodies: Alexander, East Lancs, ECW, Leyland, Northern Counties, Plaxton.
Ops incl: local bus services, private hire.
Livery: Blue.

REES MOTOR TRAVEL

WAUNLAPRA, LLANELLY HILL, ABERGAVENNY NP7 0PW
Tel: 01873 830210　**Fax:** 01873 832167
Web site: reestravel@yahoo.co.uk
Partners: Nigel A Rees, Mrs Margo E Rees.
Fleet: 10 - 8 single-deck coach, 2 midicoach.
Chassis: 1 Bedford, 1 Dennis, 3 Duple 425, 1 Mercedes, 1 Plaxton 425, Scania, 2 Setra.
Ops incl: local bus services, school contracts, excursions & tours, private hire, continental tours.
Livery: Green/White.

STAGECOACH IN SOUTH WALES
See Torfaen

NEATH & PORT TALBOT

BLUEBIRD OF NEATH/ PONTARDAWE

9-10 LONDON ROAD, NEATH SA11 1HB
Tel/Fax: 01639 643849
E-mail: bluebird-coaches@btconnect.com
Web site: www.bluebirdcoachesneath.com
Fleet Name: Bluebird Coaches (Neath).
Props: E G & Ian S Warren.
Fleet: 15 - 12 single-deck coach, 2 midibus, 1 minibus.
Chassis: 4 Bova, 1 DAF, 1 Dennis, 3 Mercedes, 1 Scania, 1 Temsa, 4 Volvo.
Bodies: 1 Berkhof, 4 Bova, 1 Irizar, 2 Jonckheere, 4 Plaxton, 1 Temsa, 1 Van Hool, 1 Other.
Ops incl: school contracts, excursions & tours, private hire.
Livery: White/Blue/Red.

DANSA COMMUNITY TRANSPORT

CRYNANT BUSINESS CENTRE, CRYNANT BUSINESS PARK, CRYNANT, NEATH SA10 8PX
Tel: 01639 751067　**Fax:** 01639 750805
E-mail: mail@dansa.org.uk
Web site: www.dansa.org.uk
Fleet: 9 minibus.
Ops incl: local bus services, community transport services.

FIRST CYMRU BUSES LTD
See City & County of Swansea

NELSON & SON (GLYNNEATH) LTD

74A HIGH STREET, GLYNNEATH SA11 5AW
Tel: 01639 720308
Fax: 01639 721949
E-mail: nelsoncoaches@aol.com
Web site: www.nelsonscoaches.co.uk
Fleet Name: Nelson's Travel.
Man Dir: J L R Nelson **Co Sec:** Mrs J Nelson
Fleet Eng: P Watkins **Tran Man:** G Powell.
Fleet: 18 - 15 single-deck coach, 3 midicoach.

Chassis: 2 Bova, 4 DAF, 5 Dennis, 3 Mercedes, 1 Temsa, 3 Volvo.
Bodies: 1 Autobus, 1 Berkhof, 2 Bova, 2 Caetano, 6 Plaxton, 1 Temsa, 1 UVG, 4 Van Hool.
Ops incl: school contracts, excursions & tours, private hire.
Livery: White with Orange reliefs.

RIDGWAYS COACHES LTD
UNIT 22, ENDEAVOUR CLOSE, PURCELL AVENUE INDUSTRIAL ESTATE, PORT TALBOT SA12 7PT
Tel: 01639 883374
E-mail: info@ridgwayscoaches.co.uk
Web site: www.ridgwayscoaches.co.uk
Prop: D Ridgway.
Fleet: 15 – 1 double-deck bus, 4 single-deck bus, 5 single-deck coach, 2 midibus, 2 midicoach, 1 minibus.
Chassis: 4 DAF, 5 Dennis, 2 Mercedes, 1 Renault, 1 Setra, 2 Volvo.
Ops incl: local bus services, school contracts, private hire, excursions & tours.
Livery: White with Orange.

SELECT BUS & COACH
UNIT 3, WINIFRED ROAD, SKEWEN SA10 6HP
Tel: 07980 618419
Props: H R Hoskins, J Hoskins.
Fleet: 14 – 5 single-deck bus, 7 midibus, 2 minibus.
Chassis: 12 Dennis, 2 Mercedes.
Bodies: 2 Caetano, 2 Koch, 5 Marshall, 5 Plaxton.
Ops incl: local bus services.
Livery: White/Blue/Grey.

SOUTH WALES TRANSPORT (NEATH) LTD
UNIT 19, MILLAND ROAD INDUSTRIAL ESTATE, NEATH SA11 1NJ
Tel: 01639 643311
Fax: 01639 644963
E-mail: info@southwalestransport.com
Web site: www.southwalestransport.com
Fleet Names: South Wales Transport, Neath & District.
Dirs: B Fowles, P Fowles **Eng Man:** C Jones
Fleet: 30 – 1 single-deck bus, 10 single-deck coach, 15 midibus, 2 midicoach, 2 minibus.
Chassis: 7 Alexander Dennis, 2 Mercedes, 3 Optare, 10 Volvo, 8 Wrightbus.
Bodies: 5 Alexander Dennis, 1 Autobus, 9 Jonckheere, 2 MCV, 3 Optare, 2 Plaxton, 8 Wrightbus.
Ops incl: local bus services, school contracts, private hire.
Livery: Green & White.

D J THOMAS COACHES LTD
MILLAND ROAD INDUSTRIAL ESTATE, NEATH SA11 1NJ
Tel/Fax: 01639 635502
E-mail: contact@djthomascoaches.com
Web site: www.djthomascoaches.com
Man Dir/Co Sec: Mrs Andrea Gibson
Man Dir: Richard Thomas
Ch Eng: Lee Gibson.
Fleet: 26 – 5 double-deck bus, 15 single-deck coach, 1 midibus, 4 midicoach, 1 minibus.
Chassis: 1 Bova, 1 Dennis, 4 Mercedes, 1 Renault, 19 Volvo.
Bodies: 1 Alexander, 3 Berkhof, 1 Bova, 2 Jonckheere, 1 Mercedes, 13 Plaxton, 2 Van Hool, 1 Other.
Ops incl: local bus services, excursions & tours, private hire, school contracts.
Ticket system: Wayfarer.

TONNA LUXURY COACHES LTD
TENNIS VIEW GARAGE, HEOL-Y-GLO, TONNA SA11 3NJ
Tel: 01639 642727   **Fax:** 01639 646052
Fleet Name: Ken Hopkins.
Dirs: K M Hopkins, A Hopkins.
Fleet: 11 - 8 single-deck coach, 3 midicoach.
Chassis: 3 Mercedes, 1 Setra, 7 Volvo.
Bodies: 1 Caetano, 1 Jonckheere, 8 Plaxton, 1 Setra.
Ops incl: school contracts, private hire.
Livery: White/Blue.

WILKINS BROS (CYMMER) LTD
UNIT 1, EASTERN AVENUE, CYMMER, PORT TALBOT SA13 3PB
Tel: 01639 852600   **Fax:** 01639 646350
Dirs: C D & G Wilkins.
Fleet: 17 – 1 single-deck bus, 12 single-deck coach, 4 midicoach.
Chassis: 1 BMC, 4 DAF, 6 Dennis, 1 MAN, 2 Mercedes, 1 Temsa, 1 VDL, 1 Volvo.
Bodies: 1 Autobus, 1 BMC, 1 Ikarus, 2 Marcopolo, 1 Optare, 5 Plaxton, 1 Smit, 1 Temsa, 1 UVG, 2 Wadham Stringer, 1 Other.
Ops incl: school contracts, private hire.

NEWPORT

NEWPORT TRANSPORT LTD
160 CORPORATION ROAD, NEWPORT NP19 0WF
Tel: 01633 670563   **Fax:** 01633 242589
Web site: www.newporttransport.co.uk
E-mail: enquiries@newporttransport.co.uk
Fleet Name: Newport Bus.
Chairman: H Thomas **Man Dir:** S Pearson
Fin Dir: D Jenkins **Eng Dir:** C Yeaman
Ops Man: M Stevens.
Fleet: 91 – 16 double-deck bus, 45 single-deck bus, 2 single-deck coach, 26 midibus, 1 minicoach, 1 heritage double-deck bus.
Chassis: 26 Alexander Dennis, 16 Dennis, 1 Leyland, 6 MAN, 1 Mercedes, 39 Scania, 2 Volvo.
Bodies: 11 Alexander, 26 Alexander Dennis, 1 Ferqui, 1 Longwell Green, 8 Plaxton, 31 Scania, 13 Wrightbus.
Ops incl: local bus services, school contracts, excursions & tours, private hire.
Livery: Green/Cream.
Ticket System: Wayfarer TGX150.

STAGECOACH IN SOUTH WALES
See Torfaen

PEMBROKESHIRE

W. H. COLLINS & CO LTD
CUFFERN GARAGE, ROCH, HAVERFORDWEST SA62 6HB
Tel: 01437 710337
Fleet Name: Collins Coaches.
Dirs: P N Collins, L Beattie, R Beattie.
Fleet: 11 – 1 single-deck coach, 10 minibus.
Ops incl: local bus services, school contracts, private hire.
Livery: Blue/Grey/White.

EDWARDS BROS (TIERS CROSS) LTD
THE GARAGE, BROAD HAVEN ROAD, TIERS CROSS, HAVERFORDWEST SA62 3BZ
Tel: 01437 890230   **Fax:** 01437 890337
E-mail: enquiries@edwards-tiers-cross.co.uk
Web site: www.edwards-tiers-cross.co.uk
Dirs: Robert Edwards, Jayne Edwards.
Fleet: 23 – 9 single-deck coach, 6 midibus, 2 midicoach, 5 minibus, 1 minicoach.
Chassis: 1 Bova, 2 Dennis, 1 Fiat, 1 Ford Transit, 1 LDV, 8 Mercedes, 1 Optare, 7 Volvo, 1 Wrightbus.

Ops incl: local bus services, school contracts, excursions & tours, private hire.
Livery: Coaches: Gold; **Buses:** White with Orange.
Ticket System: ERG.

FIRST CYMRU BUSES LTD
See City & County of Swansea

MIDWAY MOTORS (CRYMYCH) LTD
MIDWAY GARAGE, CRYMYCH SA41 3QU
Tel: 01239 831267   **Fax:** 01239 831279
E-mail: reesmidway@hotmail.com
Dirs: Elan Rees, Iwan Rees.
Fleet: 10 - 6 single-deck coach, 1 midibus, 2 midicoach, 1 minibus.
Chassis: 3 Dennis, 1 Mercedes, 1 Renault, 1 Setra, 1 Toyota, 3 Volvo.
Ops incl: local bus services, school contracts, excursions & tours, private hire, continental tours.
Livery: Silver/Blue.
Ticket system: Electronic.

RICHARDS BROS
MOYLGROVE GARAGE, PENTOOD INDUSTRIAL ESTATE, CARDIGAN SA43 3AG
Tel: 01239 613756   **Fax:** 01239 615193
E-mail: enquiries@richardsbros.co.uk
Web site: www.richardsbros.co.uk
Gen Man: W J M Richards **Ch Eng:** D N Richards **Traf Man:** R M Richards
Ops Man: S M Richards.
Fleet: 84 - 38 single-deck bus, 29 single-deck coach, 10 midibus, 7 minibus.
Chassis: Alexander Dennis, DAF, LDV, Mercedes, Optare, Transbus, VDL, Volvo.
Bodies: Alexander, Alexander Dennis, Autobus, Caetano, Carlyle, Ikarus, Jonckheere, LDV, Marshall, MCV, Northern Counties, Optare, Plaxton, Transbus, Van Hool, Wrightbus.
Ops incl: local bus services, school contracts, excursions & tours, private hire, continental tours.
Livery: Blue/White/Maroon.
Ticket System: ERG.

SILCOX MOTOR COACH COMPANY LTD
WATERLOO GARAGE, PEMBROKE DOCK SA72 4RR
Tel: 01646 683143   **Fax:** 01646 621787
E-mail: travel@silcoxcoaches.co.uk
Web site: www.silcoxcoaches.co.uk
Man Dir: K W Silcox **Dirs:** R M Silcox, D E Miller, T E Miller.
Fleet: 85 - 20 single-deck bus, 33 single-deck coach, 17 midibus, 2 midicoach, 13 minibus.
Chassis: 3 Alexander Dennis, 3 Bova, 30 Dennis, 2 King Long, 19 Leyland, 1 MAN, 11 Mercedes, 8 Optare, 1 Renault, 1 Scania, 1 Transbus, 6 Volvo.
Bodies: 1 Alexander, 2 Alexander Dennis, 4 Berkhof, 3 Bova, 9 Caetano, 2 Ferqui, 1 Irizar, 2 King Long, 2 Marcopolo, 2 Marshall, 1 MCV, 3 Mellor, 8 Optare, 37 Plaxton, 1 Transbus, 3 UVG, 1 Van Hool, 1 Wadham Stringer, 3 Other.
Ops incl: local bus services, school contracts, excursions & tours, private hire, continental tours.
Livery: Red/Cream.
Ticket System: ERG.

SUMMERDALE COACHES
SUMMERDALE GARAGE, HAVERFORDWEST ROAD, LETTERSTON SA62 5UB
Tel: 01348 840270
Props: D G Davies, G R Jones, M A Jones.
Fleet: 12 – 7 single-deck coach, 2 midicoach, 3 minibus.
Chassis: 1 LDV, 4 Mercedes, 7 Volvo.
Bodies: 1 Autobus, 1 LDV, 9 Plaxton, 1 Other.
Livery: Yellow/Blue.

Welsh Operators

ARWYN's
HENIARTH, LLANGYNIEW, WELSHPOOL SY21 0JR
Tel: 01938 810518
Dir: Arwyn P Davies.
Fleet: 1 minibus.
Chassis/Body: Ford Transit.
Ops incl: school contracts, private hire.

A W COACHES LTD
BODAWEL GARAGE, WESLEY STREET, LLANFAIR CAEREINION SY21 0RX
Tel/Fax: 01938 810452
E-mail: enquiries@awcoaches-welshpool.co.uk
Web site: www.awcoaches-welshpool.co.uk
Dirs: T A Watkin, Mrs S E Watkin.
Fleet: 9– 7 single-deck coach, 2 midicoach.
Chassis: 1 Dennis, 1 Iveco, 1 Leyland, 1 Mercedes, 4 Scania, 1 Volvo.
Bodies: 1 Indcar, 1 KVC, 1 Neoplan, 6 Van Hool.
Livery: Cream/Orange/Brown.

ROY BROWNS COACHES
R24
15 HIGH STREET, BUILTH WELLS LD2 3DN
Tel: 01982 552597   **Fax:** 01982 552286
E-mail: neil@rbci.fsnet.co.uk
Prop: N W Brown **Ops Man:** P H Davies.
Fleet: 32 – 1 single-deck bus, 11 single-deck coach, 3 midibus, 4 midicoach, 13 minibus.
Chassis: 1 Alexander Dennis, 3 Bedford, 2 DAF, 7 Dennis, 1 Iveco, 4 LDV, 1 MAN, 3 Mercedes, 8 Optare, 1 Toyota, 1 Volvo.
Bodies: 1 Alexander Dennis, 2 Berkhof, 1 Beulas, 4 Caetano, 2 Duple, 1 Koch, 4 LDV, 8 Optare, 4 Plaxton, 1 Smit, 1 Transbus, 1 Wadham Stringer, 1 Other.
Ops incl: local bus services, school contracts, excursions & tours, private hire.

CELTIC TRAVEL (LLANIDLOES) LTD
NEW STREET, LLANIDLOES SY18 6EH
Tel/Fax: 01686 412231
E-mail: info@celtic-travel.co.uk
Web site: www.celtic-travel.co.uk
Props: W P L Davies, Mrs J Davies
Ops Man: P Davies.
Fleet: 33 – 1 open-top bus, 5 single-deck bus, 12 single-deck coach, 3 midibus, 2 midicoach, 10 minibus.
Chassis: 1 Alexander Dennis, 3 Dennis, 5 Ford Transit, 1 LDV, 1 Leyland, 5 Mercedes, 1 Renault, 1 Scania, 1 Vauxhall, 13 Volvo, 2 Wrightbus.
Bodies: 2 Alexander, 1 Alexander Dennis, 5 Ford Transit, 1 Irizar, 1 LDV, 1 Mercedes, 1 Park Royal, 7 Plaxton, 4 Van Hool, 1 Vauxhall, 3 Wadham Stringer, 5 Wrightbus, 1 Other.
Ops incl: local bus services, school contracts, excursions & tours, private hire, continental tours.
Livery: Green/White.

CENTRAL TRAVEL
53 CHURCHILL DRIVE, NEWTOWN SY16 2LH
Tel: 01686 627901
Prop: R W Bowen.
Fleet: 2 – 1 single-deck coach, 1 minibus.
Chassis: 1 Mercedes, 1 Scania.
Livery: White.

COOKSON TRAVEL LTD
HOPE LANE, HOPE, WELSHPOOL SY21 8HF
Tel: 01938 553465
Dirs: M G & C E Cookson.
Fleet: 21 – 17 single-deck coach, 2 midicoach, 2 minibus.
Chassis: 2 DAF, 2 Ford Transit, 4 Leyland,

3 MAN, 1 Toyota, 9 Volvo.
Bodies: 2 Caetano, 2 Ford Transit, 2 Jonckheere, 15 Van Hool
Livery: Grey with Black Lettering.

R G GITTINS – COACHES
THE GARAGE, DOLANOG, WELSHPOOL SY21 0LQ
Tel/Fax: 01938 810439
E-mail: ggittins@aol.co.uk
Prop: Richard G Gittins.
Fleet: 2 midicoach.
Chassis: 1 MAN, 1 Mercedes.
Bodies: 1 Autobus, 1 Caetano.
Ops incl: school contracts, private hire.
Livery: White.

GOLDSTAR SERVICES
71 CLEDAN, TREOWEN, NEWTOWN SY16 1NB
Tel/Fax: 01686 628895
Web site: www.coachhirenewtown.com
Prop: H B Williams.
Fleet: 9 – 4 single-deck coach, 2 midicoach, 3 minibus.
Livery: White with Gold & Blue Lettering.

HERDMAN COACHES
HOM GARAGE, CLYRO, HAY-ON-WYE HR3 5JL
Tel: 01497 847100
Props: P & G M Herdman.
Fleet: 30 – 1 single-deck bus, 15 single-deck coach, 1 midicoach, 12 minibus, 1 minicoach.
Chassis: 1 Bedford, 4 DAF, 6 Dennis, 1 Ford Transit, 1 Irisbus, 9 LDV, 2 Mercedes, 2 Optare, 2 Scania, 1 Setra, 1 Transbus.
Bodies: 1 Beulas, 1 Caetano, 1 Ferqui, 4 Ikarus, 2 Irizar, 8 LDV, 2 Optare, 6 Plaxton, 1 Setra, 1 Transbus, 1 UVG, 1 Wrightbus, 1 Other.
Livery: Pale Blue & White.

LAKELINE OF POWYS
EBRAN-DDU, FELINDRE, KNIGHTON LD7 1YN
Tel: 01547 510234
Dir: S J Reynolds.
Fleet: 3 - 2 single-deck coach, 1 minibus.
Chassis: 1 LDV, 2 Volvo.
Ops incl: school contracts, private hire.
Livery: Pale Blue/Dark Blue.

LLOYDS COACHES LTD
R24
OLD CROSVILLE GARAGE, DOLL STREET, MACHYNLLETH SY20 8BH
Tel: 01654 702100   **Fax:** 01654 703900
E-mail: info@lloydscoaches.com
Web site: www.lloydscoaches.com
Dirs: D W Lloyd, S K Lloyd.
Fleet: 44 – 3 double-deck bus, 5 single-deck bus, 13 single-deck coach, 16 midibus, 2 midicoach, 5 minibus.
Chassis: 7 Alexander Dennis, 1 Bova, 6 Dennis, 2 Ford Transit, 10 Mercedes, 7 Optare, 1 Transbus, 1 VDL, 9 Volvo.
Bodies: 4 Alexander, 5 Alexander Dennis, 1 Bova, 1 Ford, 2 Mercedes, 1 Northern Counties, 7 Optare, 18 Plaxton, 1 Transbus, 1 VDL, 2 Wadham Stringer, 1 Other.
Ops incl: local bus services, school contracts, private hire.
Livery: Silver.
Ticket system: Wayfarer.

OWEN's MOTORS LTD
TEMESIDE HOUSE, STATION ROAD, KNIGHTON LD7 1DT
Tel: 01547 528303   **Fax:** 01547 520512
Ops Man: D Owen **Ch Eng:** T Owen
Sec/Dir: J Owen.
Fleet: 8 - 7 single-deck coach, 1 minibus.

Chassis: 2 Dennis, 1 LDV, 5 Volvo.
Ops incl: local bus services, school contracts, excursions & tours, private hire, continental tours.
Livery: Blue/Grey.

RHIEW VALLEY MOTORS LTD
HENFAES GARAGE, BERRIEW, WELSHPOOL SY21 8BJ
Tel: 01686 640554
E-mail: enquiries@rhiewvalleymotors.co.uk
Web site: www.rhiewvalleymotors.co.uk
Dirs: D G & S M Haycock.
Fleet: 10 – 5 single-deck coach, 1 midicoach, 4 minibus.
Chassis: 1 DAF, 2 Dennis, 4 Ford, 1 Mercedes, 1 Scania, 1 Volvo.
Livery: White with Blue Relief.

STAGECOACH IN SOUTH WALES
See Torfaen

STOCKHAMS COACH & TAXIS
19 PLAS DERWEN, LLANGATTOCK, CRICKHOWELL NP8 1HY
Tel: 01873 810343
Prop: Mrs Nancy Stockham.
Fleet: 5 - 3 single-deck coach, 2 minibus, also 4 taxis.
Chassis: 2 Iveco, 3 Volvo.
Bodies: 2 Plaxton, 1 Van Hool, 2 Other.
Ops incl: school contracts, private hire.
Livery: Green/Cream.

TANAT VALLEY COACHES
THE GARAGE, LLANRHAEDR YM MOCHNANT, OSWESTRY SY10 0AD
Tel: 01691 780212   **Fax:** 01691 780634
E-mail: info@tanat.co.uk
Web site: www.tanat.co.uk
Depots at: Llanrhaedr, Kerry (Newtown).
Dirs: Michael Morris, Peter Morris
Ops Man: Nick Culliford.
Fleet: 34 – 4 double-deck bus, 9 single-deck bus, 11 single-deck coach, 7 midibus, 1 midicoach, 1 minibus, 1 classic bus.
Chassis: 3 Bova, 1 DAF, 4 Dennis, 1 Irisbus, 3 Leyland, 4 Mercedes, 10 Optare, 8 Volvo.
Bodies: 5 Alexander, 1 Berkhof, 1 Beulas, 3 Bova, 1 Frank Guy, 2 Jonckheere, 2 Northern Counties, 10 Optare, 3 Plaxton, 1 Sitcar, 1 UVG, 2 Wrightbus.
Ops incl: local bus services, school contracts, excursions & tours, private hire.
Livery: Burgundy/Cream.
Ticket System: ERG.

WEALES WHEELS
THE GRADING STATION, LLANDEWI, LLANDRINDOD WELLS, LD1 6SE
Tel: 01597 851141   **Fax:** 01597 850007
Prop: M J Weale.
Fleet: 14 – 7 single-deck coach, 1 midicoach, 6 minibus.
Chassis: 6 Dennis, 3 Ford Transit, 2 LDV, 1 MAN, 1 Mercedes, 1 Toyota.
Livery: White & Yellow.

WILLIAMS COACHES
R24
CAMBRIAN WAY, BRECON LD3 7BE
Tel: 01874 622223   **Fax:** 01874 625218
Recovery: 01874 611534
E-mail: office@williams-coaches.co.uk
Web site: www.williams-coaches.co.uk
Fleet: 31 – 23 single-deck coach, 4 midicoach, 4 minibus.
Chassis: 2 DAF, 2 Dennis, 1 Irisbus, 2 Iveco, 1 MAN, 7 Mercedes, 3 Neoplan, 5 Scania, 6 Setra, 1 Temsa.
Bodies: 1 Caetano, 2 Indcar, 5 Irizar, 2 Mercedes,

3 Neoplan, 6 Plaxton, 6 Setra, 2 Sitcar, I Temsa,
I Transbus, I Van Hool, I Other.
Ops incl: school contracts, private hire,
excursions & tours, continental tours.
Livery: Cream with Orange & Brown Reliefs.

RHONDDA CYNON TAF

CAVENDISH COACHES &
LIMOUSINES LTD
LLANWONNO ROAD, PORTH CF39 0HU
Tel: 0800 542 1652   **Fax:** 01443 381813
E-mail: sales@cavendishcoaches.co.uk
Web site: www.cavendishcoaches.co.uk
Dir: Stephen Hollister.
Fleet: 12 – 8 single-deck coach, I midicoach,
2 minibus, I minicoach.
Chassis: I Bova, I Dennis, I Irisbus, 2 Irizar,
3 Mercedes, 3 Scania, I Volvo.
Bodies: I Beulas, 2 Berkhof, I Bova, I Crest,
4 Irizar, I Mellor, I Onyx, I Plaxton.
Ops incl: school contracts, excursions & tours,
private hire, continental tours.
Livery: White with multi-colours.

CHAPMANS TRAVEL LTD
Ceased trading since LRB 2014 went to press

T R COLE
7 HIGH STREET, TREORCHY CF42 6AE
Tel: 01443 774773
Prop: Ralph Cole.
Fleet: 13 – 5 double-deck bus, 7 single-deck
coach, I minibus.
Chassis: 2 Bristol, I DAF, 3 Dennis, I Leyland,
I MAN, 2 Mercedes, 2 Scania, I Volvo.
Bodies: 5 Alexander, I Berkhof, I ECW, I
Ikarus, I Noge, 2 Plaxton, I Van Hool, I Wadham
Stringer.
Ops incl: school contracts, excursions & tours,
private hire.
Livery: Red.

EDWARDS COACHES LTD
NEWTOWN INDUSTRIAL ESTATE,
LLANTWIT FADRE CF38 2EE
Tel: 01443 202048   **Fax:** 01443 217583
Recovery: (Day) 01443 217123;
(Night) 07747 694047.
E-mail: jason@edwardscoaches.co.uk
Web site: www.edwardscoaches.co.uk
Man Dir: Mike Edwards **Dirs:** Jason Edwards,
Shaun Edwards, Kelly Edwards, Jessica Edwards
Fleet Eng: Paul Bluett **Workshop Man:**
Brandon Lewis.
Fleet: 277 – 9 double-deck bus, 25 single-deck
bus, 221 single-deck coach, 6 midicoach,
4 midicoach, 12 minibus.
Chassis: 9 Ailsa, 10 Alexander Dennis,
I Bedford, 5 Bluebird, 16 Bova, 6 DAF, 8 Dennis,
16 Ford Transit, I Iveco, I LDV, 8 MAN, 8 MCW,
8 Mercedes, 5 Neoplan, I Optare, 10 Scania,
15 Setra, 5 Van Hool, 141 Volvo.
Ops incl: local bus services, school contracts,
excursions & tours, private hire, express,
continental tours.
Liveries: Blue, National Express.

FERRIS COACH HOLIDAYS
THE COACH HOUSE, CARDIFF ROAD,
NANTGARW CF15 7SR
Tel: 01443 844222
E-mail: sales@ferriscoachholidays.co.uk
Web site: www.ferriscoachholidays.co.uk
Dirs: J Ferris, L Ferris.
Fleet: 32 – 20 single-deck coach, 10 double-
deck coach, I midicoach, I minibus.
Chassis: 4 Bova, I Mercedes, 2 Neoplan,
3 Temsa, 4 Van Hool, I Volkswagen, 3 VDL,
14 Volvo.
Ops incl: excursions & tours, continental tours.

GLOBE COACHES
BROOKLANDS, FFORCHNEOL ROW,
GODREAMAN, ABERDARE CF44 6HD
Tel: 01685 873622   **Fax:** 01685 876526
E-mail: wayne@globecoaches.entadsl.com
Web site: www.globecoaches.co.uk
Prop: Stephen Wayne Jarvis.
Fleet: 24 - 15 single-deck coach, I midicoach,
7 minibus, I minicoach.
Chassis: 8 Mercedes, 2 Optare, 14 Volvo.
Ops incl: local bus services, school contracts,
excursions & tours, private hire, continental
tours.
Livery: White/Blue.
Ticket System: Wayfarer.

V G JARVIS COACHES
CASA MIA, LLWYDCOED ROAD, ABERDARE
CF44 0UL
Tel: 01685 882222
Props: B & M Jenkins.
Fleet: 17 – 8 single-deck coach, 2 midicoach,
7 minibus.
Chassis: 8 Dennis, 2 Ford Transit, 2 Iveco,
5 Mercedes.
Ops incl: school contracts, private hire.

KEEPINGS COACHES
RHEOLA HOUSE, PENRHIWCEIBER,
MOUNTAIN ASH CF45 3TE
Tel: 01443 474849
Fleet: 23 – 9 single-deck coach, I midicoach,
13 minibus.
Chassis: Bova, DAF, Dennis, Ford Transit,
Mercedes, Scania, Volvo.
Ops incl: school contracts, private hire.
Livery: White with Blue.

LASER MINICOACHES & MINITRAVEL
UNIT 4, FOUNDRY ROAD, TONYPANDY
CF40 2XD
Tel: 01443 431133   **Fax:** 01433 431433
E-mail: laser251@aol.com
Web site: www.lasertravel.co.uk
Fleet: 30 – 9 single-deck coach, 21 minibus.
Chassis: I Bova, 6 Ford Transit, I Irizar, 2 Iveco,
6 LDV, 6 Mercedes, I Volkswagen, 5 Volvo.
Ops incl: school contracts, excursions & tours,
private hire.
Livery: White

MAINLINE COACHES LTD
KINGS HEAD GARAGE, GLANNANT ROAD,
EVANSTOWN CF38 8RL
Tel: 01443 670095   **Fax:** 01443 676695
E-mail: info@mainlinecoaches.co.uk
Web site: www.mainlinetravel.co.uk
Fleet: 43 – 37 single-deck coach, 2 midicoach,
3 minibus, I minicoach.
Chassis: 6 Bova, 2 Ford Transit, 2 King Long,
2 MAN, 2 Mercedes, 18 Scania, 4 VDL, 7 Volvo.
Bodies: 6 Berkhof, 6 Bova, I EVM, 2 Ford,
12 Irizar, 2 King Long, I KVC, I Marcopolo,
6 Plaxton, 2 Van Hool, 4 VDL.
Ops incl: school contracts, excursions & tours,
private hire, continental tours.
Livery: Green/Yellow.

STAGECOACH IN SOUTH WALES
See Torfaen

THOMAS OF RHONDDA
BUS DEPOT, ABERRHONDDA ROAD,
PORTH CF39 0AG
Tel: 01443 433714   **Fax:** 01443 436542
E-mail: enquiries@thomasofrhondda.co.uk
Web site: www.thomasofrhondda.co.uk
Props: W A Thomas, I G Thomas, J E Thomas,
D Thomas, T D Thomas, A A Thomas.

Fleet: 49 – 7 single-deck bus, 29 single-deck
coach, 2 double-deck coach, 3 midibus, 8 minibus.
Chassis: 10 Bova, 3 Dennis, 4 Enterprise, 2 Ford
Transit, 2 LDV, 5 Leyland, 6 MAN, 5 Mercedes,
I Optare, 2 Scania, 3 Transbus, 2 Van Hool,
4 Volvo.
Bodies: 3 Alexander, 6 Berkhof, 10 Bova,
5 Caetano, I Duple, 2 Ford, I LDV, 5 Marcopolo,
I Optare, 8 Plaxton, 2 Van Hool, I Wadham
Stringer, 3 Wrightbus, I Other.
Ops incl: local bus services, excursions & tours,
school contracts, private hire, continental tours.
Livery: Gold.
Ticket System: Almex.

BRENT THOMAS COACHES LTD
FOUNDRY ROAD INDUSTRIAL ESTATE,
TONYPANDY CF40 2XD
Tel: 01443 431240
Fax: 01443 441586
E-mail: info@brentthomascoaches.com
Web site: www.brentthomascoaches.com
Fleet: 12 – 9 single-deck coach, I midicoach,
2 minibus.
Chassis: I Dennis, I Ford Transit, 2 Mercedes,
8 Volvo.
Bodies: I Ford, 7 Jonckheere, 2 Plaxton,
I Van Hool, I Other.
Ops incl: excursions & tours, private hire.
Livery: Green/Grey/Cream

CITY & COUNTY OF SWANSEA

BRIGGS COACHES LTD
ELBA CRESCENT, SWANSEA SA1 8QQ
Tel: 01792 462979
Web site: www.briggscoaches.co.uk
Prop: W G Briggs.
Fleet: 11 – 2 midibus, 4 midicoach, 2 minibus,
3 minicoach.
Chassis: 2 BMC, I Irisbus, 4 Iveco, 4 Mercedes.
Ops incl: school contracts, private hire,
excursions & tours.
Livery: White with Blue/Yellow/Red.

CYMRU COACHES LTD
PICTON HOUSE, BAILEY COURT, FELINFACH,
SWANSEA WEST BUSINESS PARK, SWANSEA
SA5 4DE
Tel: 01792 583610
E-mail: cymrucoaches@btconnect.com
Web site: www.cymrucoaches.co.uk
Fleet: 23 – I double-deck bus, 16 single-deck
coach, I midibus, 3 midicoach, 2 minibus.
Chassis: 2 Ford Transit, I Irisbus, 2 Mercedes,
8 Scania, 2 Setra, 8 Volvo.
Ops incl: school contracts, private hire.

FIRST CYMRU BUSES LIMITED
HEOL GWYROSYDD, PENLAN
SA5 7BN
Tel: 01792 572255
Fax: 01792 561356
Web site: www.firstgroup.com
Fleet Names: First, Greyhound.
Man Dir: Justin Davies.
Fleet: 336 - 4 double-deck bus, 88 single-deck
bus, 9 articulated bus, 16 single-deck coach,
210 midibus, 9 minibus.
Chassis: 104 Alexander Dennis, 3 BMC,
77 Dennis, I Leyland, I Mercedes, 32 Optare,
12 Scania, 39 Transbus, 50 Volvo, 17 Wrightbus.
Bodies: 24 Alexander, 103 Alexander Dennis,
3 BMC, 12 Irizar, 25 Marshall, 3 Northern
Counties, 32 Optare, 34 Plaxton, I Roe,
39 Transbus, 60 Wrightbus.
Ops incl: local bus services, school contracts,
excursions & tours, private hire, express.
Livery: FirstGroup UK Bus.
Ticket System: Wayfarer III.

LETS GO TRAVEL WALES

AZTEC CENTRE, QUEENSWAY,
FFORESTFACH, SWANSEA SA5 4DJ
Tel: 01792 586605
Web site: www.letsgotravelwales.com
Fleet Names: Lets Go Travel, Swansea Bus &
Coach.
Fleet: 29 – 23 single-deck coach, 6 minibus.
Chassis: 3 DAF, 23 Dennis, 2 Ford Transit,
1 Mercedes.
Ops incl: school contracts, private hire,
excursions & tours.

TORFAEN

PHIL ANSLOW COACHES

UNIT 1, VARTEG INDUSTRIAL ESTATE,
VARTEG HILL, PONTYPOOL NP4 7PZ
Tel: 01495 775599
Fax: 01495 774000
E-mail: susan_anslow@hotmail.com
Web site: www.philanslowcoaches.co.uk
Dir: Philip Anslow
Co Sec: Susan Anslow
Ops Man: Terry Wyburn.
Fleet: 25 – 4 single-deck coach, 18 midibus,
3 midicoach.
Chassis: 1 Dennis, 13 Mercedes, 8 Optare,
1 Setra, 2 Volvo.
Ops incl: local bus services, school contracts,
private hire.
Livery: White, Purple & Grey.
Ticket System: Wayfarer.

B'S TRAVEL

13 EAST VIEW, GRIFFITHSTOWN
NP4 5DW
Tel/Fax: 01495 756889
E-mail: kay@bstravel.fsnet.co.uk
Partners: James Benning, Kay Benning.
Fleet: 2 minicoach.
Chassis: 1 Iveco, 1 Mercedes.
Ops incl: private hire, school contracts.
Livery: White.

JENSON TRAVEL

UNIT 10, PONTNEWYNDD INDUSTRIAL
ESTATE, PONTNEWYNDD, PONTYPOOL
NP4 6YW
Tel/Fax: 01495 760539
E-mail: enquiries@jensontravel.co.uk
Web site: www.jensontravel.co.uk
Props: Gwyn Jenkins, Miss Nicola Jenkins
Tran Man: Nicola Jenkins.
Fleet: 17 – 11 single-deck coach, 5 midicoach,
1 minibus.
Chassis: 2 Alexander Dennis, 6 Mercedes,
9 Volvo.
Bodies: 1 Excel, 1 Ferqui, 2 Jonckheere,
1 Optare, 7 Plaxton, 3 Sunsundegui, 1 Van Hool,
1 Other.
Ops incl: school contracts, excursions & tours,
private hire.
Livery: Blue/White.

PEAKES COACHES LTD

REAR OF UNIT 10, PONTNEWYNYDD
INDUSTRIAL ESTATE, PONTNEWYNYDD,
PONTYPOOL NP4 6YW
Tel: 01495 740184
E-mail: info@peakescoachesltd.co.uk
Web site: www.peakescoaches.com
Fleet: 29 – 3 single-deck bus, 16 single-deck
coach, 5 midibus, 5 minibus.
Chassis: 1 DAF, 12 Dennis, 1 Irizar,
2 Mercedes, 3 Optare, 6 Scania, 4 Volvo.
Ops incl: local bus services, private hire,
school contracts, excursions & tours.
Incorporating Town & Country Bus

STAGECOACH IN SOUTH WALES

1 ST DAVID'S ROAD, CWMBRAN
NP44 1PD
Tel: 01633 838856
Fax: 01633 865299
E-mail: south.wales@stagecoachbus.com
Web site: www.stagecoachbus.com
Man Dir: John Gould
Comm Dir: Richard Davies
Eng Dir: David Howe.
Fleet: 379 - 1 double-deck bus, 60 single-deck
bus, 15 single-deck coach, 11 double-deck
coach, 165 midibus, 127 minibus.
Chassis: 158 Alexander Dennis, 23 MAN,
140 Optare, 7 Scania, 14 Transbus,
11 Van Hool, 30 Volvo, 10 Wrightbus.
Bodies: 162 Alexander Dennis, 4 East Lancs,
5 Jonckheere, 1 Northern Counties,
140 Optare, 39 Plaxton, 14 Transbus,
11 Van Hool, 7 Wrightbus.
Ops incl: local bus services, school contracts,
express, Megabus.
Liveries: Stagecoach UK Bus, Megabus.
Ticket System: ERG.

VALE OF GLAMORGAN

HAWTHORN TRAVEL & CARING COACHES

UNIT 10, TY VERLON TRADING ESTATE,
CARDIFF ROAD, BARRY
CF63 2BE
Tel: 01446 421117
E-mail: caringcoaches@hotmail.co.uk
Web site: www.caringcoaches-barry.co.uk
Prop: N P Martlew.
Fleet: 7 – 1 double-deck bus, 6 single-deck
coach.
Chassis: 1 Bedford, 1 Bova, 1 Leyland, 4 Volvo.
Bodies: 1 Bova, 1 Duple, 1 ECW, 3
Jonckheere, 1 Plaxton.
Ops incl: school contracts, private hire.

WATTS COACHES LTD

OLD POST GARAGE, BONVILSTON
CF5 6TQ
Tel: 01446 781277
Fax: 01446 781450
E-mail: enquiries@wattscoaches.co.uk
Web site: www.wattscoaches-cardiff.co.uk
Dirs: Clive P Watts, Carol Watts, James Watts.
Fleet: 38 – 3 double-deck bus, 23 single-deck
coach, 2 double-deck coach, 7 midibus,
2 midicoach, 1 minibus.
Chassis: 2 Alexander Dennis, 2 Bova, 3 DAF,
1 Dennis, 1 Iveco, 3 Leyland, 1 MAN,
4 Mercedes, 4 Scania, 3 Setra, 3 Transbus,
2 Van Hool, 3 VDL, 6 Volvo.
Bodies: 2 Alexander, 2 Alexander Dennis,
1 Beulas, 3 Berkhof, 2 Bova, 1 Caetano,
1 Duple, 1 East Lancs, 1 Irizar, 1 Jonckheere,
1 Noge,
8 Plaxton, 2 Setra, 3 Transbus, 1 Unvi,
4 Van Hool, 3 VDL.
Ops incl: local bus services, school contracts,
excursions & tours, private hire, continental
tours.
Livery: Buses: White/Green; **Coaches:**
Cream/Red/Gold.

WREXHAM

ACTON COACHES

DERWYN HOUSE, SOUTHSEA ROAD,
SOUTHSEA, WREXHAM
LL11 6PP
Tel/Fax: 01978 352470
Prop: D B Evans.
Fleet: 1 midicoach.
Chassis: 1 Mercedes.
Bodies: 1 Plaxton.

Livery: Blue/White.
Ops incl: school contracts, private hire.

ARRIVA BUSES WALES

See Gwynedd

GEORGE EDWARDS & SON LTD

BERWYN, BWLCHGWYN
LL11 5UE
Tel/Fax: 01978 757281
Web site: www.georgeedwardsandson.co.uk
Dirs: G F, G & C Edwards.
Fleet: 5 single-deck coaches.
Chassis: 1 Bova, 2 DAF, 1 Dennis, 1 VDL.
Bodies: 1 Bova, 1 Plaxton, 3 Van Hool.
Ops incl: school contracts, excursions &
tours, private hire, continental tours.
Livery: Red/Ivory/Maroon.

GHA COACHES LTD

UNIT 11, VAUXHALL INDUSTRIAL ESTATE,
RUABON, WREXHAM LL14 6UY
Tel: 01978 820820
E-mail: info@ghacoaches.co.uk
Web site: www.ghacoaches.co.uk
Props: E G & A Lloyd Davies.
Gen Man: Stephen Bryce.
Depots at: Ruthin, Tarvin, Macclesfield,
Winsford.
Fleet: 267 – 31 double deck bus, 49 single
deck bus, 65 single-deck coach, 58 midibus,
9 midicoach, 53 minibus, 3 minicoach.
Chassis: 2 Alexander Dennis, 5 BMC, 4 Bova,
12 DAF, 37 Dennis, 1 Ford Transit, 1 Irisbus,
1 LDV, 17 Leyland, 2 MAN, 29 Mercedes,
56 Optare, 8 Scania, 5 Transbus, 9 VDL,
79 Volvo.
Bodies: 26 Alexander, 6 Autobus, 4 Berkhof,
1 Beulas, 4 Bova, 5 BMC, 5 Caetano, 1 Duple,
10 East Lancs, 1 Ford, 2 Ikarus, 3 Irizar,
7 Jonckheere, 1 LDV, 8 Marshall, 1 Mellor,
2 Neoplan, 15 Northern Counties, 1 Onyx,
57 Optare, 61 Plaxton, 1 Reeve Burgess,
1 Scania, 7 Transbus, 1 UVG, 9 Van Hool,
22 Wrightbus, 4 Other.
Ops incl: local bus services, private hire,
school contracts.
Livery: Grey/Red/Maroon, Route Brands.
Includes Bryn Melyn Motor Services,
Chaloner's, Dobson's Buses, Hanmer's
Coaches, Vale Travel

D. JONES & SON

CENTRAL GARAGE, KING STREET,
ACREFAIR LL14 3RH
Tel: 01978 824666
Mobile: 07739 206623
E-mail: info@djonesandson.co.uk
Web site: www.djonesandson.co.uk
Dir: David Jones
Ops Man: Gary Jones.
Fleet: 12 - 4 single-deck bus, 8 midibus.
Chassis: 1 Alexander Dennis, 2 Dennis,
1 Mercedes, 8 Optare.
Bodies: 1 Alexander Dennis, 2 Caetano,
8 Optare, 1 Plaxton.
Ops incl: local bus services, school contracts.
Livery: Blue/White.
Ticket system: Wayfarer TGX.

E JONES & SONS

MOUNTAIN VIEW, BANK STREET,
PONCIAU LL14 1EN
Tel: 01978 841613
Props: J B & G Jones.
Fleet: 9 – 6 single-deck coach, 3 midicoach.
Chassis: 4 Mercedes, 4 Scania, 1 Volvo.
Bodies: 1 Hispano, 4 Irizar, 1 Jonckheere,
2 Plaxton, 1 Unvi.
Ops incl: school contracts, private hire.
Livery: Blue/White/Orange.

PAT'S COACHES LTD

DERWEN HOUSE, SOUTHSEA ROAD,
SOUTHSEA, WREXHAM,
LL11 6PP
Tel: 01978 720171
Fax: 01978 758459
E-mail: enquiry@patscoaches.co.uk
Web site: www.patscoaches.co.uk
Partners: P C Davies, J M Davies, D K Davies.
Fleet: 16 – 12 single-deck coach, 1 midibus,
2 midicoach, 1 minibus.
Chassis: 1 Dennis, 1 Ford Transit, 2 Mercedes,
1 Neoplan, 8 Scania, 3 Volvo.
Bodies: 1 Autobus, 2 Berkhof, 1 Ford, 1 Irizar,
2 Lahden, 1 Neoplan, 4 Plaxton, 1 Unvi, 3 Van
Hool.

PRICES COACHES

THE HAVEN, BERSHAM ROAD,
SOUTHSEA LL11 6TF
Tel/Fax: 01978 756834
Props: David Price, Terence Price.
Fleet: 5 - 1 double-deck bus, 3 single-deck
coach, 1 midicoach.
Chassis: 1 Mercedes, 4 Volvo.
Bodies: 1 Autobus, 1 Jonckheere, 1 Northern
Counties, 1 Plaxton, 1 Van Hool.
Ops incl: school contracts, private hire.
Livery: Primrose/Green/Orange.

Ops incl: school contracts, excursions &
tours, Private hire, continental tours.
Livery: White/Red/Gold.

STRAFFORDS COACHES

UNITS 7/8, FIVE CROSSES INDUSTRIAL
ESTATE, MINERA, WREXHAM
LL11 3RD
Tel: 01978 756106 **Fax:** 01978 722705
E-mail: info@straffordscoaches.co.uk
Web site: www.straffordscoaches.co.uk
Props: Mr & Mrs G A Strafford.
Fleet: 11 - 8 single-deck coach, 8 midicoach.
Chassis: 1 Dennis, 1 Iveco, 2 Mercedes,
7 Scania.
Bodies: 1 Berkhof, 1 Indcar, 7 Irizar, 1 Plaxton,
1 Unvi.
Ops incl: school contracts, private hire,
excursions & tours, continental tours.
Liveries: White, Silver.

NORTHERN IRELAND

A1 COACH TRAVEL LTD

21 WHITEHOUSE ROAD, LONDONDERRY
BT48 0NE
Tel/Fax: 028 7130 9323
Web site: www.a1coachtravellondonderry.co.uk
Dir: J Bradshaw.
Fleet: 8 – 1 single-deck coach, 7 midicoach.
Chassis: 7 Mercedes, 1 VDL.
Ops incl: private hire, continental tours, school
contracts.

AGNEW TRAVEL

15 TANNAGHMORE NORTH ROAD,
LURGAN, Co ARMAGH BT67 9JA
Tel: 028 3832 6755
E-mail: info@agnewcoachhire.co.uk
Web site: www.agnewcoachhire.co.uk
Prop: A Agnew.
Fleet: 8 – 2 single-deck bus, 3 single-deck coach,
1 midicoach, 2 minibus.
Chassis: 2 Dennis, 3 Mercedes, 2 Setra, 1 Volvo.
Ops incl: private hire, continental tours, school
contracts.

AIRPORTER

1 BAY ROAD, CULMORE ROAD,
LONDONDERRY BT48 7SH
Tel: 028 7126 9996
E-mail: info@airporter.co.uk
Web site: www.airporter.co.uk
Man Dir: Niall McKeever **Dirs:** Janet McKeever,
Norma Smyth.
Fleet: 16 minicoach.
Chassis: Mercedes.
Bodies: EVM.
Ops incl: airport express, private hire.
Livery: White with Blue/Red logos.

ALLEN'S TOURS

29 DONEGAL ROAD, BELFAST BT12 5JJ
Tel: 028 9091 5613
E-mail: info@allenstours.co.uk
Web site: www.allensbelfastbustours.com
Prop: Benn Allen.
Fleet: 9 – 1 double-deck bus, 2 single-deck bus,
2 single-deck coach, 1 midibus, 3 minibus.
Chassis: AEC, Dennis, LDV, Leyland, Mercedes,
Volkswagen, Volvo.
Ops incl: private hire, excursions & tours,
sightseeing tours.

SANDY ARTHUR COACH HIRE LTD

AGHANLOO INDUSTRIAL ESTATE,
LIMAVADY Co LONDONDERRY BT49 0HE
Tel: 028 7772 2221
E-mail: enquiries@coachhireni.com
Web site: www.coachhireni.com
Dir: S Arthur.
Fleet: 25 – 7 single-deck bus, 8 single-deck
coach, 2 midibus, 4 midicoach, 3 minibus,

1 minicoach
Chassis: Bova, Dennis, Iveco, Leyland, MAN,
Mercedes, Solbus, Toyota, Volvo.
Ops incl: private hire, school contracts,
excursions & tours.
Livery: White with Blue lettering.

BELFAST BUS COMPANY

UNIT 1 BAYVIEW INDUSTRIAL ESTATE,
DARGEN CRESCENT, BELFAST BT3 9JP
Tel: 028 9074 2444 **Fax:** 028 9074 2555
E-mail: info@belfastbuscompany.com
Web site: www.belfastbuscompany.com
Man Dir: E Moore **Dirs:** E-T Moore,
T A Moore **Tran Man:** R Thompson
Fleet Eng: W Kane.
Fleet: 44 – 13 single-deck coach, 16 midicoach,
8 minibus, / minicoach.
Chassis: 1 Iveco, 1 LDV, 28 Mercedes, 1 Optare,
13 Volvo.
Ops incl: school contracts, private hire.
Livery: White with Pink lettering.

BELFAST CITY SIGHTSEEING LTD

MOSCOW ROAD, BELFAST BT3 9ED
Tel: 028 9032 1321
E-mail: info@belfastcitytour.com
Web site: www.belfastcitysightseeing.com
Fleet: 9 - 8 double-deck and open-top bus,
1 minibus.
Chassis: 2 Leyland, 1 Mercedes, 6 Volvo.
Ops incl: Belfast sightseeing tours.
Livery: Red & Yellow.

BRITTONS COACH TOURS

Ceased trading

R J G BULLICK COACH HIRE

71 NEWRY STREET, RATHFRILAND,
Co DOWN BT34 5PZ
Tel: 028 4063 8006
E-mail: ronnie@rjgbullick.co.uk
Web site: www.rjgbullick.co.uk
Prop: Ronnie Bullick.
Fleet: 4 – 2 single-deck coach, 2 midicoach.
Chassis: 2 Mercedes, 2 Volvo.
Ops incl: private hire.
Livery: White with Pale Blue.

CHAMBERS COACH HIRE

Cease trading since LRB 2014 went to press

CROSS COUNTRY COACHES LTD

31 BALLYLINTAGH ROAD,
COLERAINE BT51 3SP
Tel: 028 7086 8989 **Fax:** 028 7086 9191
E-mail: sales@crosscountrycoaches.com
Web site: www.crosscountrycoaches.net
Dirs: J R Telford, B Telford.
Fleet: 3 - 2 single-deck coach, 1 vintage.
Chassis: 1 Bedford, 2 DAF.

Bodies: 1 Duple, 2 Van Hool.
Ops incl: school contracts, excursions & tours,
private hire, continental tours.
Livery: White with Yellow/Green/Blue/Red logo.

DARRAGH COACHES

22 LISHEEGHAN ROAD, BALLYMONEY,
Co ANTRIM BT53 7JY
Tel: 028 2954 0684 **Fax:** 028 2954 0785
Recovery: 07736 485999
E-mail: rdarragh@hotmail.co.uk
Prop: Robert Darragh.
Fleet: 19 – 6 single-deck coach, 1 midicoach,
11 minibus, 1 minicoach.
Ops incl: school contracts, excursions & tours,
private hire.

DIAL A BUS LTD

90-92 GROSVENOR ROAD, BELFAST BT12 4GL
Tel: 028 9031 4151
E-mail: dialabus@btconnect.com
Web site: www.dialabusltd.co.uk
Dir: D Monaghan.
Fleet: 16 – 1 single-deck coach, 1 midibus,
9 midicoach, 2 minibus, 3 minicoach.
Chassis: 14 Mercedes, 1 Optare, 1 Volvo.
Ops incl: local bus services, school contracts,
private hire, excursions & tours.

EUROCOACH

CORNWALLIS HOUSE, 47 MULLAGHTEIGE
ROAD, BUSH, DUNGANNON, Co TYRONE
BT71 6QU
Tel: 028 8772 3031
E-mail: eurocoach@btconnect.com
Web site: www.eurocoachni.co.uk
Props: Sam Sinnamon, Lorna Sinnamon,
Nigel Sinnamon.
Fleet: 33 – 8 single-deck coach, 3 midibus,
2 midicoach, 18 minibus, 2 minicoach.
Chassis: DAF, Iveco, LDV, Mercedes, Volkswagen,
Volvo.
Ops incl: school contracts, private hire,
excursions & tours.
Livery: Red/Orange, White.

FIRST AIRCOACH/FIRST NORTHERN IRELAND LTD

AIRPORT BUSINESS PARK, DUBLIN AIRPORT,
Co DUBLIN
Tel (Dublin): 00 353 1 844 7118
Tel (Belfast): 028 9023 0655
Fax: 00 353 1 844 7119
E-mail: info@aircoach.ie
Web site: www.aircoach.ie
Man Dir: Allen Parker **Customer Services
Man:** Brendan Gallagher.
Fleet: 57 – 1 single-deck bus, 45 single-deck
coach, 11 articulated bus.
Chassis: 12 Mercedes, 4 Scania, 12 Setra,
29 Volvo.

Bodies: 4 Caetano, 19 Jonckheere, 12 Mercedes, 10 Plaxton, 12 Setra.
Ops incl: airport operations, express.
Livery: Blue.
A subsidiary of First Group Plc

GILES TOURS

63 ABBEYDALE AVENUE, NEWTOWNARDS
BT23 8RT
Tel/Fax: 028 9181 1099
E-mail: enquiries@gilestours.co.uk
Web site: www.gilestours.co.uk
Dirs: Neil Giles, Patricia Giles.
Fleet: 5 – 3 single-deck coach, 1 midicoach, 1 minibus.
Chassis: 3 Bova, 2 Mercedes.
Ops incl: excursions & tours, private hire, continental tours.
Livery: Blue/Yellow.

J & K COACHES

4 COLTRIM ROAD, MONEYMORE,
Co LONDONDERRY BT45 7QG
Tel: 028 8673 7776
Web site: www.jandkcoaches.co.uk
Prop: J Quinn.
Fleet: 12 – 6 single-deck coach, 1 midicoach, 2 minibus, 3 minicoach.
Chassis: 5 Mercedes, 5 Scania, 1 Volkswagen, 1 Volvo.
Ops incl: school contracts, private hire, excursions & tours.
Livery: White with Blue/Black lettering.

LAKELAND TOURS

ENNISKILLEN AIRPORT, TRORY, ENNISKILLEN,
Co FERMANAGH BT94 2FP
Tel: 028 6632 9900   **Fax:** 028 6634 2979
Recovery: 07779 026597
E-mail: info@lakelandtours.co.uk
Web site: www.lakelandtours.co.uk
Prop: Ian McCutcheon.
Fleet: 4 - 1 single-deck coach, 3 midicoach.
Chassis: 3 Mercedes, 1 Volvo.
Ops incl: excursions & tours, private hire.
Livery: White with Blue/Yellow.

LOGAN'S EXECUTIVE TRAVEL LTD

58 GALDANAGH ROAD, DUNLOY,
BALLYMENA BT44 9DB
Tel: 028 2765 7203   **Fax:** 028 2765 7559
E-mail: coaches@loganstravel.com
Web site: www.loganstravel.com
Fleet Names: Corporate Coaching, Logan's Executive Travel.
Man Dir: Sean Logan **Man:** Jarlath O'Donnell.
Fleet: 53 –34 single-deck coach, 2 midibus, 1 midicoach, 11 minibus, 5 minicoach.
Chassis: 3 LDV, 11 Mercedes, 2 Optare, 3 Volkswagen, 34 Volvo.
Ops incl: local bus services, school contracts, excursions & tours, private hire.

LYNCH COACH HIRE

8A JOHN STREET, CASTLEDERG, Co TYRONE
BT81 7AN
Tel: 028 8167 1344   **Fax:** 028 8167 1578
E-mail: info@lynchcoachhire.com
Web site: www.lynchcoachhire.com
Prop: Paul Lynch.
Fleet: 12 – 3 single-deck coach, 2 midibus, 3 midicoach, 4 minibus.
Chassis: 2 Ford Transit, 7 Mercedes, 1 Scania, 2 Van Hool.
Ops incl: school contracts, excursions & tours, private hire.
Livery: White.

McAVOY COACH TRAVEL

29B CARROWDORE ROAD, GREYABBEY,
Co DOWN BT22 2LU
Tel: 028 4278 8589
E-mail: enquiries@mcavoycoachtravel.com
Web site: www.mcavoycoachtravel.com
Fleet: 2 – 1 single-deck coach, 1 midicoach.
Chassis: 1 BMC, 1 Volvo.
Bodies: 1 BMC, 1 Plaxton.
Ops incl: excursions & tours, private hire.
Livery: White with swirls/logos.

McCOMB'S COACHES

2 LYNDA MEADOWS, NEWTOWNABBEY,
Co ANTRIM BT37 0AT
Tel: 028 9086 6162
E-mail: info@mccombscoaches.com
Web site: www.minicoachni.co.uk
Prop: Rodney McComb.
Fleet: 11 – 1 double-deck bus, 6 single-deck coach, 1 midicoach, 1 minibus, 2 minicoach.
Chassis: 4 King Long, 5 Mercedes, 1 VDL, 1 Volvo.
Ops incl: school contracts, excursions & tours, private hire.
Livery: White with Blue lettering.

McDERMOTT COACH HIRE

20B CLOUGHEY ROAD, PORTAFERRY,
Co DOWN BT22 1ND
Tel: 028 4272 8482
E-mail: info@mcdcoaches.co.uk
Prop: A McDermott.
Fleet: 10 – 6 single-deck coach, 4 midicoach.
Chassis: 4 Mercedes, 1 Scania, 5 Volvo.
Ops incl: excursions & tours, private hire.
Livery: White

McGREAD 'S COACHES

110A TATTYREAGH ROAD, FINTONA,
Co ARMAGH BT78 2HU
Tel: 028 8284 1731   **Fax:** 028 8284 1916
E-mail: enquiries@mcgreadomagh.com
Web site: www.mcgreadomagh.com
Props: Bill Dunne, Isabella Dunne.
Fleet: 26 – 3 single-deck coach, 6 midicoach, 15 minibus, 1 minicoach.
Ops incl: excursions & tours, private hire.
Livery: White.

ORCHARD COUNTY TRAVEL

22 ALTATURK ROAD, RICHHILL, COLLONE,
Co ARMAGH BT61 9SG
Tel: 028 3887 9917   **Fax:** 028 3887 9919
E-mail: orchardcountytravel@btconnect.com
Web site: www.orchardcountytravel.co.uk
Prop: W Browne.
Fleet: 12 – 8 single-deck coach, 1 midibus, 1 midicoach, 2 minibus.
Ops incl: school contracts, private hire, excursions & tours.

RICHMOND COACHES LTD

39b BALLINDERRY ROAD, LISBURN,
Co ANTRIM BT28 2QT
Tel: 028 9262 2888
Fax: 028 9262 2777
E-mail: info@richmondcoaches.com
Web site: www.richmondcoaches.com
Dirs: H McKenna, B McKenna.
Fleet: 8 – 1 double-deck coach, 5 single-deck coach, 1 midicoach, 1 minibus.
Chassis: 1 DAF, 1 MAN, 1 Mercedes, 2 Scania, 2 Van Hool, 1 Volvo.
Ops incl: school contracts, excursions & tours, private hire.
Livery: White with Blue.

O. ROONEY COACH HIRE LTD

4 DANA PLACE, HILLTOWN, NEWRY,

Co DOWN BT34 5UE
Tel: 028 4063 0825   **Fax:** 028 4063 8028
Recovery: 077721 510955
E-mail: office@orcoachireland.com
Web site: www.orcoachireland.com
Man Dir: Oliver Rooney.
Ops incl: local bus services, excursions & tours, school contracts, private hire.
Livery: White with Red/Yellow stripe.

ROONEY INTERNATIONAL COACH HIRE LTD

30 NEWRY ROAD, HILLTOWN,
Co DOWN BT34 5TG
Tel/Fax: 028 4063 8922
E-mail: eamonnrooney@btinternet.com
Web site: www.rooneycoachhire.com
Prop: Eamonn Rooney.
Fleet: 24 – 2 single-deck bus, 10 single-deck coach, 5 midibus, 7 midicoach.
Chassis: 3 King Long, 12 Mercedes, 3 Scania, 6 Volvo.
Ops incl: local bus services, express, school contracts, private hire, excursions & tours.
Livery: White with Blue.

SLANE'S COACH & TAXI HIRE

60 DUNDALK STREET,
NEWTOWNHAMILTON, Co ARMAGH
BT35 0PB
Tel: 028 8308 8715
Fleet: 10 – 3 single-deck coach, 5 midicoach, 2 minibus.
Chassis: 7 Mercedes, 3 Volvo.
Ops incl: private hire.

SWILLY BUS SERVICE

Ceased trading since LRB 2014 went to press

TITANIC & CITY BUS TOURS

UNIT 1, 143 NORTHUMBERLAND STREET,
BELFAST BT13 2JF
Tel: 028 9032 1912
E-mail: info@citytoursbelfast.com
Web site: www.citytoursbelfast.com
Prop: Diamond Leisure Transport Ltd.
Fleet: 14 – 12 open-top bus, 1 minibus, 1 minicoach.
Chassis: Leyland, Mercedes, Volvo.
Ops incl: Belfast sightseeing tours.
Livery: Black.

TRANSLINK

MILEWATER ROAD, BELFAST BT3 9BG
Tel: 028 9066 6630
E-mail: feedback@translink.co.uk
Web site: www.translink.co.uk
Fleet Names: Ulsterbus, Citybus, Goldline, Metro, Ulsterbus Tours, Northern Ireland Railways
Chairman: John Trethowan **Group Chief Exec:** David Strahan **Board Members:** James Brown, Angela Coffey, Tony Depledge, Bernard Mitchell, Frank Hewitt **Chief Op Officer:** Philip O'Neill **HR & Organisational Development Dir:** Gordon Milligan **Dir of Finance:** Stephen Armstrong **Gen Man (Bus Services):** Ciaran Doherty **Gen Man (Rail Services):** Malachy McGreevy **Op Planning & Perf Man:** Frank Clegg **Marketing Exec:** Ciaran Rogan **Infrastructure Exec:** Clive Bradberry.
Fleet: 1,406 – 283 double-deck bus, 727 single-deck bus, 277 single-deck coach, 24 double-deck coach, 4 articulated bus, 1 minicoach, 90 minibus.
Chassis: 2 Enterprise, 7 Leyland, 24 MAN, 11 Mercedes, 88 Optare, 576 Scania, 698 Volvo.
Bodies: 44 Alexander, 140 Alexander Dennis, 24 Ayats, 2 Caetano, 227 Irizar, 10 Mercedes, 88 Optare, 30 Plaxton, 20 Sunsundegui, 21 Transbus, 1 Ulsterbus, 799 Wright.
Ops incl: local bus services, excursions &

tours, school contracts, private hire, express, continental tours.
Liveries incl: Pale Blue/White (Ulsterbus), Pink/White (Citybus, Metro), Blue/Gold/White (Goldline).

TRAVELWISE COACHES
🚹♿✈❄
9A VICTORIA ROAD, LARNE Co ANTRIM BT40 1RY
Tel: 028 2827 8600
E-mail: alex.travelwise@btconnect.com
Web site: www.travelwisecoaches.co.uk
Prop: A Cairns.
Fleet: 7 – 6 single-deck coach, 1 midicoach.
Chassis: 2 MAN, 5 Scania.
Ops incl: private hire, school contracts.
Livery: White with Maroon/Grey.

32 COUNTIES COACH GROUP
♿❄✦R24✦
ULSTER BANK CHAMBERS, 2-4 LOWER O'CONNELL STREET, DUBLIN 1,
Tel: 00 353 1 878 8898
Fax: 00 353 1 878 8916
E-mail: info@32ccgroup.ie
Web site: www.32ccgroup.ie
Exec Chairman: Donal Hughes **Exec Dir:** Sandra Curtin **Dirs:** Dermot Cronin, Mary Fitzpatrick, Mike Healy, Martin Leydon, James McGinley, Patrick Slevin.
Fleet: provided by affiliated members.
Ops incl: excursions & tours, private hire, continental tours.

ALLIED COACHES
🚹♿✈❄
113 GRANGE WAY, BALDOYLE INDUSTRIAL ESTATE, BALDOYLE, DUBLIN 13
Tel: 00 353 1 832 4415
E-mail: info@alliedcoaches.ie
Web site: www.alliedcoaches.ie
Man Dir: Jim Nolan **Man:** Seamus Nolan.
Fleet: 5 – 2 single-deck coach, 2 midicoach, 1 minicoach.
Chassis: 1 DAF, 3 Mercedes, 1 VDL.
Bodies: 1 Berkhof, 1 Marcopolo, 2 Noone Turas, 1 Unvi.
Ops incl: excursions & tours, private hire.
Livery: Silver.

ALPINE COACH HIRE LTD
♿❄
CHARVEY LANE, RATHNEW, Co WICKLOW
Tel: 00 353 404 62547 **Fax:** 00 353 404 32742
E-mail: info@alpinecoachhire.ie
Web site: www.alpinecoachhire.ie
Prop: Kevin Mulvey
Fleet: 12 – 1 single-deck bus, 5 single-deck coach, 2 midicoach, 3 minibus, 1 minicoach.
Ops incl: excursions & tours, private hire.
Livery: White or Cream.

ARAN TOURS LTD
♿❄
14 LOWER ALBERT ROAD, SANDYCOVE, Co DUBLIN
Tel: 00 353 1 280 1899
Fax: 00 353 1 280 1799
E-mail: info@wildwicklow.ie
Web site: www.wildwicklow.ie
Fleet Name: Wild Wicklow Tours.
Fleet: 2 single-deck coach.
Chassis: 2 Mercedes.
Bodies: 2 Unvi.
Ops incl: excursions & tours.

ARDCAVAN COACH TOURS LTD
🚹♿❄🍴
ARDCAVAN, CASTLEBRIDGE, Co WEXFORD
Tel: 00 353 53 912 2561
Fax: 00 353 53 912 4073
E-mail: info@ardcavan.com

Web site: www.ardcavan.com
Dirs: Philip O'Leary, George O'Leary.
Fleet: 13 – 2 single-deck bus, 7 single-deck coach, 2 midicoach, 1 minibus, 1 minicoach.
Chassis: 1 MAN, 4 Mercedes, 2 Setra, 2 Van Hool, 4 Volvo.
Bodies: 2 Alexander, 2 Jonckheere, 1 Noone Turas, 1 Onyx, 1 Paramount, 2 Setra, 2 Unvi, 2 Van Hool.
Ops incl: private hire, express.
Livery: White with Blue, Beige swirls.

BARRY'S COACHES LTD
🚹♿✈❄
THE GLEN, MAYFIELD, CORK CITY
Tel: 00 353 21 450 5390, 86 600 8825 (emergencies only)
Fax: 00 353 21 450 9628
E-mail: info@barryscoaches.com
Web site: www.barryscoaches.com
Fleet: 19 – 11 single-deck coach, 6 midicoach, 2 minibus.
Chassis: 2 Ford Transit, 2 MAN, 4 Mercedes, 2 Scania, 9 Volvo.
Bodies: 4 Euro, 2 Ford, 2 Indcar, 2 Irizar, 1 Plaxton, 1 Sunsundegui, 2 Van Hool, 5 Volvo.
Livery: White or Silver.
Ops incl: local bus service, private hire.
A subsidiary of Bernard Kavanagh & Sons, Urlingford

BARTON TRANSPORT
♿♿❄
STRAFFAN ROAD, MAYNOOTH, Co KILDARE
Tel: 00 353 1 628 6338
Fax: 00 353 1 628 6722
E-mail: info@bartons.ie
Web site: www.bartons.ie
Man Dir: Patrick Barton **Man:** Feargal Barton
Chief Eng: Brendan Barton.
Fleet: 50 - 9 double-deck bus, 7 single-deck bus, 19 single-deck coach, 4 midibus, 5 midicoach, 3 minibus, 3 minicoach.
Chassis: 1 Autosan, 1 BMC, 19 DAF/VDL, 1 Leyland, 5 MAN, 14 Mercedes, 1 Temsa, 8 Volvo.
Bodies: 9 Alexander, 1 Autosan, 3 Beulas, 1 BMC, 13 Berkhof, 1 Camo, 1 Euro, 3 Ikarus, 4 Marcopolo, 2 Noone Turas, 7 Plaxton, 1 Temsa, 1 Unvi, 2 Wadham Stringer.
Ops incl: local bus services, private hire, school contracts.
Livery: Cream with Red/Blue.

BLUEBIRD COACHES LTD
🚹♿❄
72 KILBARRON DRIVE, COOLOCK, DUBLIN 5
Tel/Fax: 00 353 1 847 7896
Dirs: Ronnie Bruen, Lisa Bruen.
Fleet: 7 – 1 double-deck bus, 1 double-deck coach, 5 single-deck coach.
Chassis: Irisbus, Leyland, Scania, VDL.
Bodies: Alexander, East Lancs, Hispano, Irizar.
Ops incl: private hire, express, school contracts.
Livery: Cream/Red.

BOYCE COACH TRAVEL LTD
🚹♿❄
MOOREFIELD, RAMELTON, LETTERKENNY, Co DONEGAL
Tel: 00 353 74 915 1043
Fax: 00 353 74 915 1736
E-mail: info@boycetravel.com
Web site: www.boycetravel.com
Fleet: 9 – 5 single-deck coach, 2 midibus, 1 midicoach, 1 minicoach.
Chassis: 1 MAN, 4 Mercedes, 1 Scania, 2 Van Hool, 1 Volvo.
Ops incl: excursions & tours, private hire.
Livery: White with multicoloured swirls.

BURKE BROS (COACHES) LTD
🚹♿✦
CLARETUAM, TUAM, Co GALWAY
Tel: 00 353 93 55416

Fax: 00 353 93 55356
E-mail: info@burkesbus.com
Web site: www.burkesbus.com
Dirs: P Burke, Ms M Burke **Ops Man:** P Steede.
Fleet: 15 - 12 single-deck coach, 3 midicoach.
Chassis: 1 DAF, 3 Irisbus, 3 Mercedes, 8 VDL.
Bodies: 5 Berkhof, 5 Plaxton, 1 Unvi, 4 Van Hool.
Ops incl: local bus services, private hire, express, continental tours.
Livery: White.

BUS EIREANN
♿♿❄
BROADSTONE, PHIBSBOROUGH, DUBLIN 7
Tel: 00 353 1 703 3447
Fax: 00 353 1 830 3486
E-mail: info@buseireann.ie
Web site: www.buseireann.ie
Chairman: Aidan Murphy **Ch Exec:** Martin Nolan **Board Members:** Bill McCamley, John Moloney, Henry Minogue, Kieran Fay, Gerard Ryan, Deirdre Ashe, Dennis Mackin **Co Sec:** Andrea Keane **Ch Mech Eng:** Joe Neiland **Man HR:** Des Tallon **Man Sales & Marketing:** Barry Doyle.
Fleet: 1177 – 41 double-deck bus, 189 single-deck bus, 876 single-deck coach, 40 double deck coach, 23 midibus, 8 minibus, 1 open-top bus.
Chassis: 35 Alexander Dennis, 12 BMC, 31 DAF, 12 Irisbus, 49 Mercedes, 17 Optare, 427 Scania, 89 VDL, 505 Volvo.
Bodies: 35 Alexander Dennis, 12 BMC, 89 Berkhof, 179 Caetano, 21 East Lancs, 13 Eurocoach, 28 Hispano, 12 Irisbus, 437 Irizar, 8 Leicester, 17 Optare, 182 Plaxton, 20 Sunsundegui, 12 Van Hool, 124 Wrightbus.
Ops incl: local bus services, school contracts, excursions & tours, private hire, express, continental tours.
Livery: Green/Orange/Red/White.
Ticket System: Wayfarer.

BUS FEDA (FEDA O'DONAILL COACHES)
♿❄
RANAFAST, ANNAGRY, Co DONEGAL
Tel/Fax: 00 353 74 954 8114
E-mail: info@feda.ie
Web site: www.feda.ie
Fleet: 9 – 6 single-deck coach, 2 minibus, 1 minicoach.
Chassis: 2 Ford Transit, 1 Toyota, 6 Volvo.
Bodies: Caetano, Ford, Jonckheere, Plaxton.
Ops incl: express, Donegal – Scotland express, private hire.
Livery: White.

BUTLERS BUSES LTD
♿❄
17 BROOKVALE, COBH, Co CORK
Tel: 00 353 21 481 1660
Fax: 00 353 21 238 0242
E-mail: ian@butlers-buses.com
Web site: www.butlers-buses.com
Prop: Ian Butler.
Fleet: 9 – 2 single-deck coach, 2 midicoach, 3 minibus, 2 minicoach.
Chassis: 7 Mercedes, 2 Volvo.
Ops incl: excursions & tours, private hire, continental tours.
Livery: White with Blue/Red lettering.

CAHALANE COACHES
♿❄
UNIT 6, KILBARRY ENTERPRISE CENTRE, DUBLIN HILL, CORK
Tel: 00 353 21 430 4606
Fax: 00 353 21 430 1200
E-mail: info@cahalanecoaches.ie
Web site: www.cahalanecoaches.ie
Fleet: 6 – 1 minicoach, 3 midicoach, 2 minibus.
Chassis: Ford Transit, Mercedes.
Ops incl: excursions & tours, private hire, continental tours.
Livery: Silver, White.

CALLINAN COACHES LTD

🚍 👥 ♿ Ⓡ

KINISKA, GLAREGALWAY, Co GALWAY
Tel: 00 353 91 798324 **Fax:** 00 353 91 798962
Recovery: 00 353 87 241 3691
E-mail: info@callinancoaches.ie
Web site: www.callinancoaches.ie
Man Dir: T Callinan.
Fleet: 46 – 10 double-deck bus, 27 single-deck coach, 1 double-deck coach, 8 articulated bus.
Chassis: 8 Mercedes, 19 Van Hool, 19 Volvo.
Bodies: 10 Alexander, 2 Jonckheere, 8 Mercedes, 19 Van Hool, 7 Volvo.
Ops incl: excursions & tours, private hire, continental tours.
Livery: White, Irish Citylink Coaches (Blue/Yellow).

CAROLAN COACH HIRE

👥 ♿ ❄

SPIDDAL LODGE, SPIDDAL, NOBBER,
Co MEATH
Tel: 00 353 46 905 2336
Fax: 00 353 46 905 2552
E-mail: info@carolancoachhire.ie
Web site: www.carolancoachhire.ie
Prop: James Carolan.
Fleet: 22 – 1 double-deck bus, 1 single-deck bus, 7 single-deck coach, 1 midicoach, 8 minibus, 4 minicoach.
Chassis: 1 Dennis, 4 Ford Transit, 2 Iveco, 2 LDV, 1 Leyland, 1 MAN, 4 Mercedes, 3 Scania, 4 Volvo.
Ops incl: excursions & tours, private hire, continental tours.
Livery: White with Green.

GERRY CARROLL COACH HIRE

♿ ❄ ❄

BALLYMAKENNY ROAD, DROGHEDA,
Co LOUTH
Tel: 00 353 41 98 36074
Prop: Gerry Carroll **Dir:** Patrick Carroll
Sec: Betty Carroll.
Fleet: 4 – 3 single-deck coach, 1 midicoach.
Chassis: Bedford, Mercedes, Volvo.
Bodies: Plaxton.
Ops incl: local bus services, excursions & tours, private hire.
Livery: White/Blue.

CITYLINK

♿ ❄

17 FORSTER STREET, GALWAY
Tel: 00 353 91 564164
E-mail: info@citylink.ie
Web site: www.citylink.ie
Fleet Names: Citylink, Eireagle.com
Man Dir: Cathy Cullen **Business Ops Man:** David Conway.
Ops incl: express and commuter services.
Liveries: Blue/Yellow (Citylink); Blue/Silver (Eireagle).
Citylink is a division of Metroline, part of Comfort DelGro. Service operations and fleet outsourced to Callinan Coaches Ltd.

COLLINS COACHES

♿ 👥 ❄ 🍴

DRUMCONRATH ROAD, CARRICKMACROSS,
Co MONAGHAN
Tel: 00 353 42 966 1631
Fax: 00 353 42 969 0760
E-mail: info@collinscoaches.ie
Web site: www.collinscoaches.ie
Man Dir: D Collins.
Fleet: 9 single-deck coach.
Chassis: 1 EOS, 3 Scania, 5 Van Hool.
Ops incl: excursions & tours, private hire, Dublin commuter express.
Livery: White with Blue.

CONWAY COACHES & CHUFFEUR DRIVE LTD

♿ ❄

RAHEEN, LIMERICK

Tel: 00 353 61 303030 **Fax:** 00 353 61 303202
Prop: A Conway.
Fleet: 2 minicoach.
Livery: White/Red.

CORCORAN'S EXECUTIVE TRAVEL

♿ ❄

8 COLLEGE STREET, KILLARNEY, Co KERRY
Tel: 00 353 64 663 6666
Fax: 00 353 64 663 5666
E-mail: corcorantours@eircom.net
Web site: www.corcorantours.com
Fleet: 4 – 1 single-deck coach, 3 midicoach.
Chassis: 3 Iveco, 1 MAN.
Ops incl: excursions & tours, private hire.
Livery: White.

CORDUFF TRAVEL

♿ 👥 ❄

ROSSPORT, BALLINA, Co MAYO
Tel: 00 353 97 88949 **Fax:** 00 353 97 88055
E-mail: info@cordufftravel.ie
Web site: www.cordufftravel.ie
Prop: M Corduff.
Fleet: 32 – 21 single deck coach, 6 midicoach, 4 minibus, 1 minicoach.
Chassis: 2 Bova, 1 Dennis, 1 Ford Transit, 1 Irisbus, 2 Iveco, 2 MAN, 8 Mercedes, 3 Scania, 4 VDL, 8 Volvo.
Ops incl: excursions & tours, private hire, express.
Livery: White.
Incorporating Walsh's Coaches, Westport

COYLES COACHES

♿ ❄

GLASSAGH, GWEEDORE, LETTERKENNY,
Co DONEGAL
Tel: 00 353 75 31208 **Fax:** 00 353 75 31718
E-mail: coylescoaches@eircom.net
Transport Man: Martin Coyle.
Fleet: 2 single-deck coach, 1 midicoach.
Chassis: 1 Mercedes, 2 Volvo.

CREMIN COACHES

♿ 👥 ❄ 🍴

GEARAGH, KILKEEL, Co CORK
Tel: 00 353 86 238 5611 **Fax:** 00 353 27 66906
E-mail: info@cremincoaches.com
Web site: www.cremincoaches.com
Fleet incl: 13 – 3 single-deck coach, 7 midicoach, 3 minibus.
Chassis incl: Ford, Iveco, Mercedes, Setra, Volvo
Ops incl: excursions & tours, private hire.
Livery: White with logos.

CRONIN'S COACHES LTD

♿ 👥 ❄

SHANNON BUILDINGS, MALLOW ROAD,
CORK CITY
Tel: 00 353 21 430 9090
Fax: 00 353 21 430 5508
E-mail: anne.cronin@croninscoaches.com.
Web Site: www.croninscoaches.com.
Dirs: D. & Joan Cronin **Ch Eng:** Niall Cronin
Gen Man: Nora Cronin.
Fleet: 40 – 4 double-deck bus, 29 single-deck coach, 1 midicoach, 1 minibus, 1 minicoach, 4 open top bus.
Chassis: 2 EOS, 3 Leyland, 1 MAN, 2 Mercedes, 1 Setra, 1 Temsa, 1 Toyota, 22 Van Hool, 1 VDL, 6 Volvo.
Bodies: 8 Alexander, 1 Berkhof, 2 EOS, 1 KVC, 1 Noge, 1 Plaxton, 1 Setra, 1 Temsa, 1 Toyota, 1 Unvi, 22 Van Hool.
Ops incl: school contracts, private hire, sightseeing tours.
Livery: Silver, White with red flash.

MARTIN CROWLEY COACHES/PARADISE COACHES LTD

👥 ♿ ❄

CLANCOOLBEG, BANDON, Co CORK
Tel/Fax: 00 353 87 205 9226
E-mail: bookings@martincrowleycoaches.ie

Web site: www.martincrowleycoaches.ie
Web site: www.paradisecoaches.com
Prop: Martin Crowley.
Fleet incl: single-deck coach, midibus, minibus, minicoach, midicoach
Ops incl: school contracts, private hire
Livery: White.

CUMMER COACHES LTD

👥 ♿ ❄

TAVANAGH, CUMMER, TUAM, Co GALWAY
Tel: 00 353 91 564600
E-mail: info@gobus.ie
Web site: www.gobus.ie
Fleet Name: gobus.ie
Man Dir: Jim Burke.
Fleet: 10 – 9 single-deck coach, 1 double-deck coach.
Chassis: 1 Ayats, 3 Neoplan, 6 Volvo
Bodies: 1 Ayats, 3 Neoplan, 6 Volvo.
Ops incl: Dublin Express.
Livery: White with Red/Blue.

DERO'S COACH TOURS LTD

👥 ❄ ♿ Ⓡ 24

22 MAIN STREET, KILLARNEY, Co KERRY
Tel: 00 353 64 663 1251
Fax: 00 353 64 663 4077
E-mail: info@derostours.com
Web site: www.derostours.com
Dirs: Ms E O'Sullivan Quille, Ms C O'Sullivan (Sales Dir), D O'Sullivan.
Fleet: 14 – 10 single-deck coach, 2 midicoach, 2 minicoach.
Chassis: 2 Iveco, 1 MAN, 2 Mercedes, 1 Van Hool, 3 VDL, 5 Volvo.
Ops incl: excursions & tours, private hire.
Livery: White with multi Red/Silver/Orange.
Also provides relief drivers and guide agency.

P J DIGAN COACHES

👥 ♿ ❄

LEINSTER HOUSE, ATHY, Co KILDARE
Tel: 00 353 59 863 1177
Fax: 00 353 59 863 2881
E-mail: digancoaches@eircom.net
Prop: P J Digan.
Fleet: 14 – 1 single-deck bus, 5 single-deck coach, 4 midicoach, 4 minibus.
Chassis: DAF, Ford Transit, Mercedes, VDL, Volvo.
Ops incl: school contracts, private hire.

DOHERTY'S COACHES

♿ 👥 🍴 ❄

14 MAIN STREET, DUNGLOE, Co DONEGAL
Tel: 00 353 74 952 1105
Fax: 00 353 74 952 1867
E-mail: enquiries@dohertyscoaches.com
Web site: www.dohertyscoaches.com
Prop: Seamus Doherty.
Fleet: 8 – 3 single-deck coach, 2 midicoach, 3 minibus.
Chassis: Mercedes, Setra.
Ops incl: local bus services, excursions & tours, private hire, Donegal – Scotland express.
Livery: White, Gold.

DONNELLY COACHES

♿ ❄

46 IRISH STREET, ENNISCORTHY,
Co WEXFORD
Tel: 00 353 53 923 3956
Ptnrs: James Donnelly, Mary Donnelly, Keith Donnelly.
Fleet: 3 minibus.
Chassis: Mercedes.
Ops incl: school contracts, excursions & tours, private hire.
Livery: White/Orange.

DONNELLYS COACHES

👥 ♿ ❄

BARRACK STREET, GRANARD,
Co LONGFORD
Tel: 00 353 43 86540

E-mail: donnellyscoaches@gmail.com
Fleet: 9 – 5 single-deck coach, 2 midibus, 2 midicoach.
Chassis: DAF, Mercedes, VDL.
Ops incl: school contracts, private hire.

DONOGHUE'S COACHES

CLOUGHBALLY UPPER, MULLAGH, Co CAVAN
Tel: 00 353 46 924 2091
Fax: 00 353 46 924 2011
Web site: www.donoghuescoaches.ie
Prop: N Donoghue
Fleet: 3 single-deck coach.
Chassis: 1 DAF, 2 Volvo.
Ops incl: local bus services, school contracts, excursions & tours, private hire.
Livery: White.

DONOGHUES OF GALWAY

TARAMUID, CLARENBRIDGE, Co GALWAY
Tel: 00 353 86 259 6347
Fax: 00 353 91 776434
E-mail: info@donoghuesofgalway.com
Web site: www.donoghuesofgalway.com
Man Dir: Joe Donoghue.
Fleet incl: single-deck coach, midibus, midicoach, minicoach.
Livery: Silver.

DONOVAN'S COACHES LTD

HEADFORD, KILLARNEY, Co KERRY
Tel: 00 353 64 775 4041
Fax: 00 353 64 775 4041
Dirs: Joe & Maureen Donovan **Ch Eng:** Joseph Donovan.
Fleet: 5 – 4 single-deck coach, 1 midicoach.
Chassis: 1 Mercedes, 4 Volvo.
Bodies: 2 Caetano, 2 Jonckheere, 1 KVC.
Ops incl: local bus services, school contracts, excursions & tours, private hire.

P. DOYLE LTD

ROUNDWOOD, Co WICKLOW
Tel: 00 353 1 281 8119
E-mail: info@glendaloughbus.com
Web site: www.glendaloughbus.com
Fleet Name: St Kevins Bus Service.
Prop/Traf Man: P Doyle **Gen Man/Ch Eng:** J Doyle **Sec:** John Doyle.
Fleet: 4 single-deck coach.
Chassis: 2 DAF, 1 Scania, 1 VDL.
Bodies: 1 Plaxton, 1 Irizar, 2 Van Hool.
Ops incl: local bus service.
Livery: Blue/Cream.
Ticket System: Setright.

TONY DOYLE COACHES LTD

BROMLEY, KILPEDDER, Co WICKLOW
Tel: 00 353 1 488 0043 **Fax:** 00 353 1 687 4878
E-mail: info@tonydoyle.com
Web site: www.tonydoyle.com
Dir: Tony Doyle.
Fleet: 19 – 13 single-deck coach, 5 midicoach, 1 minicoach.
Chassis: 3 Irisbus, 1 Iveco, 5 MAN, 4 Mercedes, 2 Neoplan, 2 Scania, 1 VDL, 1 Volvo.
Bodies: 5 Beulas, 1 Euro, 3 Indcar, 2 Irizar, 4 Marcopolo, 2 Neoplan, 1 Sunsundegui, 1 Unvi.
Ops incl: local bus services, excursions & tours, school contracts, private hire, continental tours.
Livery: White with Blue/Red logo, Silver.

THE DUALWAY GROUP

KEATINGS PARK, RATHCOOLE, Co DUBLIN
Tel: 00 353 1 458 0054
Fax: 00 353 1 458 0808
E-mail: info@dualway.com
Web site: www.dualway.com

Fleet Names: Dualway, City Sightseeing, Gray Line, Airport Hopper.
Man Dir: Anthony McConn **Gen Man:** David McConn **Fin Controller:** Trish McConn **Admin Man:** Dawn Nolan.
Fleet: 62 - 22 double-deck bus, 8 single-deck coach, 21 open-top bus, 2 midibus, 5 midicoach, 2 minibus, 2 minicoach.
Chassis: 2 AEC, 3 Leyland, 1 MCW, 9 Mercedes, 2 Scania, 6 VDL, 39 Volvo.
Bodies: 29 Alexander, 2 Berkhof, 1 Beulas, 5 East Lancs, 5 Euro, 2 Irizar, 1 Jonckheere, 3 Marcopolo, 1 MCW, 3 Noone Turas, 2 Optare, 2 Park Royal, 2 Plaxton, 4 Transbus, 3 Unvi, 1 Wrightbus.
Ops incl: local bus services, sightseeing buses, excursions & tours, school contracts, private hire.
Liveries: White; Red; Orange/White (Airport Hopper).

DUBLIN BUS (BUS ATHA CLIATH)

59 UPPER O'CONNELL STREET, DUBLIN 1.
Tel: 00 353 1 873 4222 **Fax:** 00 353 1 873 1195
E-mail: info@dublinbus.ie
Web site: www.dublinbus.ie
Chairman: Kevin Bonner **Ch Exec:** Paddy Doherty **Dirs:** Dr Patricia Barker, Kathleen Barrington, Ms Gary Joyce, Bill McCamley, Dr Kevin Rafter **Co Sec:** R O'Farrell **Head of Finance:** Paul O'Neill **Ch Eng:** Shane Doyle **Human Resources Man:** Gerry Maguire **Ops Man:** Mick Matthews.
Fleet: 970 - 951 double-deck bus, 15 open-top bus, 4 midibus.
Chassis: 7 Leyland, 10 Transbus, 953 Volvo.
Bodies: 291 Alexander, 420 Alexander Dennis, 46 Transbus, 213 Wright.
Ops incl: local bus services.
Livery: Blue/Yellow with Dublin Blue/White/Darker Blue swoosh.

DUBLIN COACH

UNIT 20, WESTERN INDUSTRIAL ESTATE, NAAS ROAD, DUBLIN 12
Tel: 00 353 1 465 9972
E-mail: info@dublincoach.ie
Web site: www.dublincoach.ie
Fleet Names: Dublin Coach, Quickpark.
Prop: Last Bus Ltd.
Fleet: 48 – 1 open-top bus, 18 single-deck coach, 7 single-deck bus, 8 articulated bus, 13 double-deck coach, 1 minibus.
Chassis: 1 AEC, 1 King Long, 16 Mercedes, 13 Neoplan, 17 Setra.
Ops incl: Dublin Airport parking, Dublin express, private hire.
Livery: Lime Green.

DUBLIN MINI COACHES & CHAUFEUR DRIVE

MILLAR TRAVEL & TRANSPORT LTD, WASDALE HOUSE, UNIT 14, CAMAC PARK, BLUEBELL INDUSTRIAL ESTATE, OLD NAAS ROAD, DUBLIN 12
Tel: 00 353 86 178 0049 **Fax:** 00 353 1 901 0377
E-mail: info@dublinminicoaches.com
Web site: www.dublinminicoaches.com
Man Dir: Stephen Millar **Dir:** Brenda Mackin **Gen Man:** Melissa Pau.
Fleet: 12 – 1 double-deck bus, 1 single-deck bus, 1 single-deck coach, 1 midibus, 4 midicoach, 4 minibus.
Chassis: Dennis, MAN, Mercedes, Renault, Volvo.
Ops incl: excursions & tours, private hire.
Livery: Blue.

EIREBUS LTD

CORDUFF ROAD, BLANCHARDSTOWN, DUBLIN 15
Tel: 00 353 1 824 2626
Fax: 00 353 1 824 2627
E-mail: info@eirebus.ie

Web site: www.eirebus.ie
Man Dir: Patrick Kavanagh **Marketing Dir:** Sinead Kavanagh **Gen Tran Man:** Derek Graham **Garage Man:** Paul Curtis **Transport Supervisor:** Jeff Clarke
Fleet Names: Budget Bus, Eirebus, Swords Express.
Fleet: 46 - 40 single-deck coach, 4 midicoach, 1 minibus, 1 minicoach.
Chassis: 2 MAN, 2 Marbus, 4 Mercedes, 24 Scania, 3 Van Hool, 6 Volvo.
Bodies: 2 Euro, 2 Farebus, 14 Irizar, 4 Jonckheere, 2 Marbus, 1 Noone Turas, 2 Plaxton, 11 Van Hool, 4 Volvo.
Ops incl: local bus services, excursions & tours, airport express, private hire.
Livery: White.
A division of Bernard Kavanagh & Sons, Urlingford

ENFIELD COACHES LTD

ROCHFORDBRIDGE, Co WESTMEATH
Tel: 00 353 46 922 2666
Fax: 00 353 46 922 2777
E-mail: info@enfieldcoaches.ie
Web site: www.enfieldcoaches.ie
Man Dir: J Healy **Tran Man:** Ms L Healy.
Fleet: 12 – 2 open-top bus, 4 single-deck coach, 2 midicoach, 1 minibus, 3 minicoach.
Chassis: 1 Irisbus, 2 Leyland, 7 Mercedes, 1 Neoplan, 1 Volvo.
Ops incl: excursions & tours, private hire.
Livery: Silver.
Associated with Chiltern Travel Ltd (see Bedfordshire) and City Sprinter Ltd (see Renfrewshire)

EXPRESS BUS LTD/ALAN MARTIN COACHES

BYRMANE HOUSE, MULHUDDART, DUBLIN 15
Tel: 00 353 1 822 1122
Fax: 00 353 1 820 9364
E-mail: helpdesk@amconline.ie
Web site: www.amconline.ie
Web site: www.expressbus.ie
Dirs: A Martin, B C Martin
Ch Eng: M Reilly **Traf Man:** M Clarke.
Fleet Name: AMC Coaches, Express Bus.
Fleet: 12 – 7 double-deck bus, 1 single-deck bus, 2 single-deck coach, 2 midicoach.
Chassis: DAF, Leyland, Mercedes, Volvo.
Ops incl: local bus services, school contracts, excursions & tours, private hire, express.
Livery: White with Red logos.

FAHERTY'S COACH HIRE

DRUMAVEG, MOYCULLEN, Co GALWAY
Tel: 00 353 87 251 5508
Fax: 00 353 91 555505
Prop: P Faherty.
Fleet: 6 – 5 single-deck coach, 1 midicoach.
Chassis: MAN, Scania, Volvo.
Ops incl: excursions & tours, private hire.

FARRELLY'S COACHES LTD

THE OLD PRESBYTERY, KENAGH, Co LONGFORD
Tel: 00 353 43 332 2222
Fax: 00 353 43 332 2233
E-mail: info@farrellyscoaches.com
Web site: www.farrellyscoaches.com
Fleet Names: Farrelly's Coaches, Athlone Coaches
Fleet: 24 – 10 single-deck coach, 5 midibus, 7 midicoach, 2 minibus.
Chassis: 3 DAF, 2 Fiat, 13 Mercedes, 1 Van Hool, 2 VDL, 3 Volvo
Bodies: Euro, Indcar, Plaxton, Van Hool.
Ops incl: local bus services, excursions & tours, school contracts, private hire.
Livery: White with Pink lettering.

ROBBIE FINEGAN COACH HIRE

CARRICKMACROSS, Co MONAGHAN
Tel: 00 353 87 259 5730
Web site: www.robbiefinegancoaches.
goldenpages.ie
Prop: F Finegan.
Fleet: 9 - 6 single-deck coach, 3 midicoach.
Chassis: 3 Mercedes, 4 Scania, 2 Volvo.
Ops incl: private hire.

FINLAY'S COACH HIRE

IRISH STREET, ARDEE, Co LOUTH
Tel: 00 353 41 685 6505
Fax: 00 353 41 685 7656
E-mail: info@finlaycoaches.com
Web site: www.finlaycoaches.com
Fleet: 8 - 1 double-deck bus, 6 single-deck coach,
1 midicoach.
Chassis: 1 Mercedes, 2 Scania, 5 Volvo.
Ops incl: local bus services, school contracts,
excursions & tours, private hire.
Livery: White with Blue relief.

FINNEGAN – BRAY COACH & BUS

OLDCOURT INDUSTRIAL ESTATE, BOGHALL
ROAD, BRAY, Co WICKLOW
Tel: 00 353 1 286 0061
Fax: 00 353 1 286 8121
E-mail: buses@finnegan-bray.ie
Web site: www.finnegan-bray.ie
Dir: Eugene Finnegan.
Fleet: 19 - 1 double-deck bus, 5 single-deck
coach, 4 midicoach, 8 midibus, 1 minibus.
Chassis: DAF, Dennis, LDV, Mercedes, Optare,
VDL, Volvo.
Bodies: Alexander, Ikarus, Indcar, LDV, Marcopolo,
Optare, Plaxton, Van Hool.
Ops incl: local bus services, excursions & tours,
school contracts, private hire.
Livery: Red.

DECLAN FINNEGAN

KENMARE COACH & CAB, KENMARE,
Co KERRY
Tel: 00 353 87 248 0800
E-mail: info@kenmarecoachandcab.com
Web site: www.kenmarecoachandcab.com
Fleet: 8 - 1 single-deck coach, 1 midibus,
2 midicoach, 4 minibus.
Ops incl: excursions & tours, private hire.

FIRST AIRCOACH/FIRST NORTHERN IRELAND LTD

AIRPORT BUSINESS PARK, DUBLIN AIRPORT,
Co DUBLIN
Tel (Dublin): 00 353 1 844 7118
Tel (Belfast): 028 9023 0655
Fax: 00 353 1 844 7119
E-mail: info@aircoach.ie
Web site: www.aircoach.ie
Man Dir: Allen Parker **Customer Services
Man:** Brendan Gallagher.
Fleet: 57 - 1 single-deck bus, 45 single-deck
coach, 11 articulated bus.
Chassis: 12 Mercedes, 4 Scania, 12 Setra,
29 Volvo.
Bodies: 4 Caetano, 19 Jonckheere, 12 Mercedes,
10 Plaxton, 12 Setra.
Ops incl: airport operations, express.
Livery: Blue.
A subsidiary of First Group Plc

FOXHOUND TRAVEL LTD

MONAGHAN ROAD, ROCKCORRY, Co
MONAGHAN
Tel: 00 353 42 974 2284
Fax: 00 353 42 974 2544
E-mail: info@foxhoundtravel.com
Web site: www.foxhoundtravel.com

Fleet: 6 - 1 single-deck coach, 2 midicoach,
1 minibus, 2 minicoach.
Chassis: 5 Mercedes, 1 Scania.
Livery: White.

FOYLE COACHES
NORTH WEST BUSWAYS

CLAR, REDCASTLE, Co DONEGAL
Tel: 00 353 74 938 2116
Fax: 00 353 74 938 2619
E-mail: foylecoaches@eircom.net
Web site: www.foylecoaches.com
Fleet Names: Foyle Coaches, North West
Busways.
Props: J Mc Gonagle Snr, J McGonagle Jnr.
Fleet: 21 - 10 single-deck coach, 6 midibus,
5 midicoach.
Chassis: 1 Iveco, 1 King Long, 2 MAN,
12 Mercedes, 5 Volvo.
Ops incl: local bus services, private hire,
excursions & tours.
Liveries: Coaches: White with Red/Orange/
Yellow; **Buses:** Red.

MARTIN FUREY COACHES LTD

MILLTOWN, DRUMCLIFFE, Co SLIGO
Tel: 00 353 71 916 3092
Fax: 00 353 71 916 3092
E-mail: info@fureysofsligo.com
Web sites: www.fureysofsligo.com, www.
thebus.ie
Fleet: 9 - 4 single-deck coach, 3 midicoach,
2 minibus.
Chassis: 2 DAF, 5 Mercedes, 1 VDL, 1 Volvo.
Ops incl: excursions & tours, private hire,
express.
Livery: White, Silver.

FURLONG'S BUS & COACH

95 SANDYFORD ROAD, SANDYFORD,
DUBLIN
Tel: 00 353 1 295 6254 **Fax:** 00 353 1 294 1260
E-mail: eec@indigo.ie
Web site: www.executiveexpress.ie
Fleet Names: Central Park Express, Executive
Express.
Dirs: Adrian Furlong, Mrs Grainne Furlong.
Fleet: 7 - 3 double-deck bus, 1 single-deck bus,
1 single-deck coach, 1 midibus, 1 midicoach.
Chassis: 1 BMC, 1 Mercedes, 5 Volvo.
Ops incl: local bus services, private hire.
Liveries: Red (double decks), White.

PATRICK GALLAGHER COACHES

BRINALACK, GWEEDORE, Co DONEGAL
Tel: 00 353 74 953 1107
Fax: 00 353 74 953 2873
E-mail: info@gallagherscoaches.com
Web site: www.gallagherscoaches.com
Prop: P Gallagher.
Fleet: 6 - 5 single-deck coach, 1 minicoach.
Chassis: 1 Toyota, 5 Volvo.
Bodies: 1 Caetano, 2 Jonckheere, 3 Plaxton.
Ops incl: school contracts, private hire, Donegal
– Belfast express.
Livery: White with Red lettering.

GALVINS COACHES

R24
MAIN STREET, DUNMANWAY, Co CORK
Tel: 00 353 23 884 5125
Fax: 00 353 23 884 5407
E-mail: info@galvinscoaches.com
Web site: www.galvinscoaches.com
Dir: R E Galvin.
Fleet: 22 - 14 single-deck coach, 5 midicoach,
2 minibus, 1 minicoach.
Chassis: 1 Ford Transit, 7 Mercedes, 11 Scania,
2 Setra, 1 Volvo.
Bodies: 3 Euro, 1 Ford, 1 Irizar, 1 KVC, 1 Setra,
3 Unvi, 11 Van Hool.

Ops incl: school contracts, excursions & tours,
private hire.
Livery: White.

GALWAY CITY DIRECT LTD

MINCLOON, RAHOON ROAD, GALWAY CITY
Tel: 00 353 91 86 0814
Fax: 00 353 91 86 0815
E-mail: info@citydirect.ie
Web site: www.citydirectgalway.ie
Fleet Name: City Direct.
Fleet: 13 - 1 double-deck bus, 1 single-deck bus,
1 single-deck coach, 10 midibus.
Chassis: 1 Alexander Dennis, 9 Dennis, 1 MAN,
1 Transbus, 1 Volvo.
Ops incl: local bus services, private hire.
Livery: Red.

GLYNNS COACHES.COM

KNOCKADERRY, TULLA ROAD, ENNIS,
Co CLARE
Tel: 00 353 65 682 8234
Fax: 00 353 65 684 0678
E-mail: info@glynnscoaches.com
Web site: www.glynnscoaches.com
Dirs: Niamh Cronin, Jackie Cronin.
Fleet: 9 - 1 single-deck bus, 5 single-deck coach,
2 midicoach, 1 minibus.
Chassis: 1 BMC, 1 Irisbus, 1 Iveco, 2 MAN,
3 Mercedes, 1 Setra.
Bodies: Beulas, BMC, Indcar, Setra, Unvi.
Ops incl: school contracts, excursions & tours,
private hire.
Livery: White with Purple logo.

NOEL GLYNN

GRAIGUE NA SPIDOGUE (POST
GRAIGUECULLEN), NURNEY, Co CARLOW
Tel: 00 353 503 46616
Prop/Gen Man/Traf Man: J Glynn **Prop/Ch
Eng:** A Glynn **Prop/Sec:** Mrs J Glynn.
Fleet: 7 - 2 single-deck bus, 2 single-deck coach,
3 midicoach.
Chassis: 1 Dennis, 3 Mercedes, 1 Scania, 3 Volvo.
Livery: Cream/Blue.

HALPENNY TRAVEL

ASHVILLE, THE SQUARE, BLACKROCK,
DUNDALK, Co LOUTH
Tel: 00 353 42 932 2023
Fax: 00 353 42 932 2023
E-mail: info@halpennytravel.com
Web site: www.halpennytravel.com
Fleet Name: Halpenny Transport.
Man Dir: John Halpenny.
Fleet: 10 - 2 double-deck bus, 2 single-deck bus,
3 single-deck coach, 1 midibus, 1 midicoach, 1
minicoach.
Chassis: 1 Dennis, 2 Mercedes, 1 Scania, 6 Volvo.
Ops incl: local bus services, private hire,
continental tours.
Livery: Blue/Yellow/Red.

HEALY COACHES

CASTLEGAR, GALWAY
Tel: 00 353 91 770066 **Fax:** 00 353 91 753335
E-mail: healybus@iol.ie
Web site: www.healytours.ie
Prop: Michael Healy, Paul Healy.
Fleet: 18 - 2 open-top bus, 2 single-deck bus,
10 single-deck coach, 3 midicoach, 2 midibus,
1 minibus.
Chassis: 1 DAF, 3 Dennis, 1 Leyland, 5 MAN,
3 Mercedes, 7 Volvo.
Ops incl: local bus services, excursions & tours,
Galway sightseeing tours, private hire.
Livery: White with Blue lettering.

IRISH COACHES

See 32 Counties Coach Group

BERNARD KAVANAGH & SONS LTD

BRIDGE GARAGE, URLINGFORD, Co
KILKENNY
Tel: 00 353 56 883 1189
Fax: 00 353 56 883 1314
E-mail: info@bkavcoaches.com
Web site: www.bkavcoaches.com
Fleet: 64 – 1 single-deck bus, 49 single-deck
coach, 7 midicoach, 3 midibus, 1 minibus,
3 minicoach.
Chassis: 4 MAN, 9 Mercedes, 1 Optare 13
Scania, 2 Setra, 1 Temsa, 1 Toyota, 2 Van Hool,
31 Volvo.
Bodies: 1 Berkhof, 1 Caetano, 3 Euro, 4 Indcar,
9 Irizar, 12 Jonckheere, 1 Noone Turas, 1 Onyx,
1 Optare, 3 Plaxton, 2 Setra, 1 Sunsundegui,
1 Temsa, 1 Transbus, 10 Van Hool, 12 Volvo,
1 Other.
Ops incl: local bus services, excursions & tours,
private hire, express, continental tours.
Livery: White/Multi.
Group Companies:
Barry's Coaches, Eirebus, Matt Kavanagh Coaches
(see Republic of Ireland)
Edinburgh Coach Lines Ltd *(see City of Edinburgh,
Scotland)*
Landtourer Coaches *(see Hampshire).*

J J KAVANAGH & SONS LTD

MAIN STREET, URLINGFORD, Co KILKENNY
Tel: 00 353 81 833 3222
Fax: 00 353 56 883 1172
E-mail: info@jjkavanagh.ie
Web site: www.jjkavanagh.ie
Joint Man Dir/Fin Cont: J J Kavanagh
Joint Man Dir/Ops Man: Paul Kavanagh
Maintenance Man: Edward Scully.
Fleet: 82 – 4 single-deck bus, 75 single-deck
coach, 2 midibus, 1 midicoach.
Chassis: 7 Mercedes, 5 Neoplan, 2 Optare,
68 Setra.
Bodies: 1 Indcar, 6 Mercedes, 5 Neoplan,
2 Optare, 68 Setra.
Ops incl: local bus services, private hire,
excursions & tours, Dublin and Shannon Airport
express, continental tours.
Livery: White with Blue/Green.
Group Companies:
Kenneally's Bus Service, Waterford
Mullany's Coaches Ltd *(see Hertfordshire)*

MATT KAVANAGH COACHES

ROSANNA ROAD, TIPPERARY
Tel: 00 353 62 51563
Fax: 00 353 62 80808
E-mail: mattkavanagh3@aol.net
Web site: www.mattkavanagh.com
Fleet: 10 – 5 single-deck coach, 2 midibus,
3 midicoach.
Chassis: 2 Dodge, 3 MAN, 5 Scania.
Bodies: 1 Ikarus, 3 Indcar, 2 Irizar, 2 Van Hool,
2 Wadham Stringer.
Ops incl: private hire, excursions & tours.
Livery: White with Blue/Yellow logo.
Associated with Bernard Kavanagh & Sons Ltd

PIERCE KAVANAGH COACHES

CHURCHVIEW, URLINGFORD, Co KILKENNY
Tel: 00 353 56 883 1213
Fax: 00 353 56 883 1599
E-mail: info@kavanaghcoaches.com
Web site: www.kavanaghcoaches.com
Dirs: Pierce Kavanagh Jnr, John Kavanagh.
Fleet: 32 – 20 single-deck coach, 2 midibus,
2 midicoach, 4 minibus, 4 minicoach.
Chassis: 1 DAF, 1 Dennis, 1 EOS, 1 Ford Transit,
1 Iveco, 1 MAN, 9 Mercedes, 1 Neoplan, 2 Scania,
14 Volvo.
Bodies: 1 Caetano, 1 Duple, 1 EOS, 1 Ford,
1 Hispano, 1 Indcar, 2 Irizar, 3 Jonckheere, 1 KVC,
1 Neoplan, 4 Nu-Track, 8 Plaxton, 1 Sunsundegui,

1 Unvi, 2 Volvo, 1 Wadham Stringer, 2 Other.
Ops incl: private hire, excursions & tours.
Liveries: White, Red.

KEALY'S COACHES LTD

LISLEHANE, CULLEN, Co CORK
Tel: 00 353 29 79016
E-mail: info@kealyscoaches.com
Web site: www.kealyscoaches.com
Dirs: D Kealy, Mrs M Kealy
Fleet: 8 – 6 single-deck coach, 1 midicoach,
1 minibus.
Chassis: 1 Bova, 1 DAF, 1 Irisbus, 1 Iveco,
1 Mercedes, 2 Setra, 1 Van Hool.
Ops incl: school contracts, excursions & tours,
private hire.

KEARNEY COACHES
GLENFERRY COACHES LTD
MALLOW COACHES LTD

UNIT 3 & 4, WATERFRONT BUSINESS PARK,
LITTLE ISLAND, Co CORK
Tel: 00 353 21 423 2252
Fax: 00 353 21 423 2257
E-mail: kearneysofcork@eircom.net
Web site: www.kearneysofcork.com
Fleet Names: Glenferry Coaches, Kearney
Coaches, Mallow Coaches.
Fleet: 48 – double-deck bus, double-deck coach,
single-deck bus, single-deck coach, midicoach,
minibus.
Chassis: BMC, DAF, EOS, Irisbus, Iveco, King Long,
Leyland, MAN, Mercedes, Neoplan, Scania, Volvo.
Ops incl: school contracts, private hire.
Livery: White.

KEENAN COMMERCIALS LTD t/a
ANCHOR TOURS

BELLURGAN POINT, DUNDALK, Co LOUTH
Tel: 00 353 42 937 1405
Fax: 00 353 42 937 1893
E-mail: bookings@anchortours.ie
Web site: www.anchortours.ie
Fleet Name: Anchor Tours.
Man Dir: Seamus Keenan.
Fleet: 22 – 19 single-deck coach, 3 midicoach.
Chassis: 1 Marbus, 2 Mercedes, 8 Scania, 10 Volvo.
Ops incl: private hire, excursions & tours,
continental tours.
Livery: White with Blue relief.

KELLY TRAVEL

KILDUFF, PALLASGREEN, Co LIMERICK
Tel: 00 353 61 384422
Fax: 00 353 61 384307
E-mail: info@kellytravel.ie
Web site: www.kellytravel.ie
Prop: M Kelly
Fleet: 11 – 3 single-deck coach, 6 midicoach,
2 minibus.
Ops incl: local bus services, express, excursions
& tours, private hire.
Livery: White.

KENNEDY COACHES LTD

MAIN STREET, ANNASCAUL, TRALEE,
Co KERRY
Tel: 00 353 66 91 57106
Fax: 00 353 66 91 57427
E-mail: info@kennedycoaches.com
Web site: www.kennedycoaches.com
Dirs: Paddy Kennedy, Patrick Kennedy.
Fleet: 12 – 4 single-deck coach, 4 midicoach,
3 minibus, 1 minicoach.
Chassis: 8 Mercedes, 1 Scania, 1 VDL, 2 Volvo.
Bodies: 1 Berkhof, 1 Irizar, 2 Jonckheere, 3 KVC,
1 Noone Turas, 4 Unvi.
Ops incl: private hire, excursions & tours,
express.
Livery: Lilac.

P. J. KEOGH/P K EXECUTIVE TRAVEL

See PK Travel Co Ltd

KERRY COACHES LTD

WOODLANDS INDUSTRIAL PARK,
KILLARNEY, Co KERRY
Tel: 00 353 64 663 1945
Fax: 00 353 64 663 1903
E-mail: info@kerrycoaches.com
Web site: www.kerrycoaches.com
Man Dir: Mike Buckley **Ops Man:** Alan
O'Connor.
Fleet: 40 – 20 single-deck coaches, 8 midicoach,
12 minicoach.
Chassis: 1 EOS, 1 Iveco, 10 Mercedes,
5 Neoplan, 2 Setra, 9 Van Hool, 3 Volvo.
Bodies: 1 EOS, 11 Indcar, 5 Neoplan, 2 Noone
Turas, 2 Setra, 7 Unvi, 10 Van Hool, 2 Volvo.
Ops incl: excursions & tours, private hire,
continental tours.
Livery: White.

KINGDOM COACHES LTD
NORTH WEST KERRY TRANSPORT LTD

2 OAKPARK DRIVE, TRALEE, Co KERRY
Tel: 00 353 64 32496
Fax: 00 353 66 718 0123
E-mail: loch@eircom.net
Web site: www.kingdomcoaches.ie
Fleet Names: Kingdom Coaches, O'Shea's of
Kerry.
Fleet: 15 – 8 single-deck coach, 6 midicoach,
1 minibus.
Chassis: 7 Bova, 2 Iveco, 4 Mercedes, 2 VDL.
Bodies: 7 Bova, 1 EVM, 2 Indcar, 3 Sitcar, 2 VDL.
Ops incl: excursions & tours, private hire.
Liveries: Gold, Silver.

LALLY COACHES

4 FORSTER STREET, GALWAY CITY
Tel: 00 353 91 562905
Fax: 00 353 91 564995
E-mail: info@lallytours.com
Web site: www.lallytours.com
Fleet: 11 – 2 double-deck bus, 1 open top bus,
5 single-deck coach, 1 double-deck coach,
2 midicoach.
Chassis: 1 Leyland, 2 MAN, 1 Mercedes, 1 VDL,
6 Volvo.
Ops incl: local bus services, excursions & tours,
Galway City Tours, private hire.
Livery: Metallic Green.

DAVE LONG COACH TRAVEL LTD

CURRAGH, SKIBBEREEN, Co CORK
Tel: 00 353 282 1138
Fax: 00 353 282 3653
E-mail: davelongcoachtravel@eircom.net
Fleet: 10 – 4 single-deck coach, 1 double-deck
coach, 5 midicoach.
Chassis: 1 MAN, 4 Mercedes, 3 Scania, 1 Volvo.

LUAS

See Section 5 – Tram and Bus Rapid Transit
Systems.

McELLIGOTT COACHES

CLARINA CROSS, CLARINA, Co LIMERICK
Tel: 00 353 61 353477
Fax: 00 353 61 353035
E-mail: McElligotts@eircom.net
Web site: www.mcelligottcoaches.com
Prop: Kevin McElligott **Transport Man:** Maura
Moore.
Fleet: 6 – 2 single-deck coach, 4 midicoach.
Chassis: 2 Irisbus, 1 Iveco, 3 Mercedes.
Bodies: 1 Ferqui, 1 Indcar, 3 Beulas, 1 Unvi.
Ops incl: school contracts, excursions & tours,
private hire.
Livery: Silver with Red logos.

JAMES McGEE BUS HIRE

BALLINA MAIN ROAD, FALCARRAGH, LETTERKENNY, Co DONEGAL
Tel: 00 353 74 913 5174
Prop: M McGee.
Fleet: 4 – 1 midicoach, 3 minibus.
Chassis: 3 Ford Transit, 1 Mercedes.
Livery: White.

McGEEHAN COACHES

FINTOWN, Co DONEGAL
Tel: 00 353 74 954 6150
E-mail: coaches@iol.ie
Web site: www.mcgeehancoaches.com
Fleet: 4 – 1 single-deck coach, 1 midicoach, 2 minibus.
Chassis: 3 Mercedes, 1 Volvo.
Ops incl: local bus services, private hire, Dublin express.
Livery: White with Black logos.

JOHN McGINLEY COACH TRAVEL

MAGHEROARTY, GORTAHORK, LETTERKENNY, Co DONEGAL
Tel: 00 353 74 913 5201
Fax: 00 353 74 913 5960
E-mail: info@johnmcginley.com
Web site: www.johnmcginley.com
Prop: James McGinley.
Fleet: 18 – single-deck coach, midibus, midicoach, minibus.
Chassis: Ford Transit, Mercedes, Volvo.
Bodies: Jonckheere, Plaxton, Sitcar, Van Hool.
Ops incl: local bus services, excursions & tours, school contracts, private hire, Dublin express, Donegal to Glasgow express, continental tours.
Liveries: White with Blue/Orange; Black/Yellow.

MALAHIDE COACHES LTD

ST JOSEPHS, COAST ROAD, MALAHIDE, Co DUBLIN
Tel: 00 353 1 845 3809 **Fax:** 00 353 1 845 3099
E-mail: info@malahidecoaches.com
Web site: www.malahide-coaches.com
Fleet: 18 – double-deck bus, double-deck coach, single-deck bus, single-deck coach, midibus, midicoach.
Chassis: 1 Leyland, 1 MAN, 1 MCW, 2 Mercedes, 6 Scania, 7 Volvo.
Ops incl: private hire, excursions & tours, school contracts.
Livery: Blue with multicoloured relief.

MANNING'S COACHES

CASTLE ROAD, CROOM, LIMERICK
Tel: 00 353 61 397311 **Fax:** 00 353 61 397931
E-mail: info@manningscoaches.com
Web site: www.manningscoaches.com
Fleet: 18 – single-deck bus, single-deck coach, midibus, midicoach, minibus.
Chassis: 1 Irisbus, 1 MAN, 6 Mercedes, 1 Optare, 9 Volvo.
Ops incl: excursions & tours, private hire, continental tours.
Livery: White with logos.

MARTIN'S COACHES (CAVAN) LTD

CORRATILLION, CORLOUGH, BELTURBET, Co CAVAN
Tel: 00 353 49 952 6222
Fax: 00 353 49 952 3116
E-mail: jimmartin@eircom.net
Dirs: James G Martin Snr, James G Martin Jnr, Derek Martin, Alan Martin.
Fleet: 15 - 4 single-deck bus, 5 midicoach, 6 minibus.
Chassis: 4 DAF, 6 Ford Transit, 5 Mercedes.
Ops incl: local bus services, school contracts, private hire.

MARTINS OF LIMERICK

UNIT 7, ANNACOTTY BUSINESS PARK, BIDDYFORD, ANNACOTTY, Co LIMERICK
Tel: 00 353 61 333100   **Fax:** 00 353 61 333102
E-mail: martinscoach@eircom.net
Web site: www.martinscoaches.ie
Props: R Martin, Mrs E Martin, P Martin, W Martin.
Fleet: 15 – 12 single-deck coach, 3 midicoach.
Ops incl: private hire.
Livery: White.

MATTHEWS COACH HIRE LTD

CALLENBERG, INNISKEEN, Co MONAGHAN
Tel: 00 353 42 937 8188
Fax: 00 353 42 937 8709
E-mail: info@matthews.ie
Web site: www.matthews.ie
Dirs: P Matthews, Mrs M Matthews.
Fleet: 35 – 2 double-deck coach, 30 single-deck coach, 2 midicoach, 1 minibus.
Chassis: 3 Mercedes, 4 Scania, 7 VDL, 21 Volvo.
Bodies: 2 Berkhof, 1 Hispano, 1 Irizar, 4 Marcopolo, 1 Noone Turas, 21 Plaxton, 1 Unvi, 3 Van Hool, 1 Other.
Ops incl: local bus services, private hire, excursions & tours, Dublin express, continental tours.
Livery: White.

MICHAEL MEERE COACH HIRE

33 CHURCH DRIVE, CLARE CASTLE, Co CLARE
Tel: 00 353 65 682 4833
Fax: 00 353 65 684 4544
E-mail: info@michaelmeere.com
Web site: www.michaelmeere.com
Prop: Michael Meere.
Fleet: 1 minibus.
Chassis: Mercedes.
Ops incl: private hire.
Livery: White with multicoloured relief.

MIDLAND BUS CO LTD

BLYRY INDUSTRIAL ESTATE, ATHLONE, Co WESTMEATH
Tel: 00 353 90 647 2427
Fax: 00 353 90 647 8420
E-mail: info@midlandbus.com
Dirs: N. Henry, A Henry, B Henry.
Fleet: 5 – 4 single-deck coach, 1 midicoach.
Chassis: 1 MAN, 4 Volvo.
Ops incl: local bus services, private hire, school contracts, excursions & tours, express.

JOE MORONEY

OLD COURT INDUSTRIAL ESTATE, BRAY, Co WICKLOW
Tel: 00 353 1 276 1466
E-mail: info@joemoroney.com
Web site: www.joemoroney.com
Fleet: 6 – 1 double-deck bus, 4 single-deck coach, 1 midicoach.
Chassis: 1 MAN, 1 Van Hool, 4 Volvo.
Bodies: 1 Alexander, 1 Indcar, 3 Van Hool, 1 Volvo.
Ops incl: private hire, excursions & tours, express, continental tours.
Livery: White.

MORTON'S COACHES DUBLIN LTD

TAYLOR'S LANE, BALLYBODEN, RATHFARNHAM, DUBLIN 16
Tel: 00 353 1 494 4927
Fax: 00 353 1 494 4694
E-mail: info@mortonscoaches.ie
Web site: www.mortonscoaches.ie
Prop: Paul Morton.
Fleet: 14 – 1 double-deck bus, 1 double-deck coach, 1 single-deck bus, 7 single-deck coach,

3 midicoach, 1 minicoach.
Chassis: MAN, Mercedes, Scania, VDL, Volvo.
Bodies: Berkhof, East Lancs, Irizar, Marcopolo, Plaxton, Wright.
Ops incl: school contracts, excursions & tours, private hire, continental tours.
Livery: White with red lettering & logo.

NAUGHTON COACH TOURS LTD

SHANAGURRANE, SPIDDAL, Co GALWAY
Tel: 00 353 91 553188 **Fax:** 00 353 91 553302
E-mail: naugtour@iol.ie
Web site: www.ontours.biz
Fleet Name: O'Neachtain Tours.
Dir: Steve Naughton **Dir/Sec:** Maureen Naughton.
Fleet: 13 – 12 single-deck coach, 1 minibus.
Ops incl: excursions & tours, Galway sightseeing tours, private hire
Livery: Red.

NOLAN COACHES

19 CLONSHAUGH LAWN, COOLOCK, DUBLIN 17
Tel: 00 353 1 847 3487 **Fax:** 00 353 1 867 8855
Mobile: 0862 592000
E-mail: info@nolancoaches.ie
Web site: www.nolancoaches.ie
Prop: David Nolan.
Fleet: 4 – 1 double-deck bus, 2 single-deck coach, 1 minibus.
Chassis: 1 EOS, 1 Mercedes, 2 Volvo.
Ops incl: school contracts, private hire.

J O'CALLAGHAN & SONS

ROCKFIELD, TRALEE ROAD, KILLARNEY, Co KERRY
Tel: 00 353 64 663 1095
Fax: 00 353 64 663 6397
E-mail: sales@jocgroup.com
Web site: www.jocgroup.com
Partners: E, P & C O'Callaghan.
Fleet: 27 – 2 single-deck bus, 6 single-deck coach, 4 midicoach, 8 minicoach, 7 minibus.
Chassis: 1 Ford Transit, 2 MAN, 20 Mercedes, 1 Van Hool, 2 VDL, 1 Volvo.
Ops incl: excursions & tours, private hire.
Livery: Black/White.

O'CONNOR AUTOTOURS LTD

ARD ROSS, ROSS ROAD, KILLARNEY, Co KERRY
Tel: 00 353 64 663 1052
Fax: 00 353 64 663 1703
E-mail: oconnorautotours@eircom.net
Web site: www.oconnorautotours.ie
Fleet Name: Wild Kerry Day Tours
Dir/Gen Man: B O'Connor **Ch Eng:** R Downing **Sec:** C Enright **Traf Man:** D Fenton.
Fleet: 10 – 1 single-deck coach, 3 midicoach, 6 minicoach.
Chassis: 9 Mercedes, 1 Volvo.
Ops incl: excursions & tours, private hire.
Livery: Maroon/Yellow.

LARRY O'HARA MINI COACHES

13 SKIBBEREEN LAWN, LISMORE HEIGHTS, WATERFORD CITY
Tel: 00 353 51 372232   **Fax:** 00 353 51 357566
E-mail: larryohara@eircom.net
Fleetname: O'Hara Autotours.
Props: Larry O'Hara, Helen O'Hara.
Fleet: 4 - 3 midicoach, 1 minibus.
Chassis: Mercedes.

O'MALLEY COACHES

FOILDARRIG, NEWPORT, Co TIPPERARY
Tel: 00 353 61 378119   **Fax:** 00 353 61 378002
E-mail: eomalleycoaches@eircom.net

Web site: www.omalleycoaches.com
Owner: E O'Malley.
Fleet: 18 – single-deck bus, single-deck coach, midibus, midicoach, minibus.
Ops incl: local bus services, school contracts, excursions & tours, private hire, express.
Livery: Blue/White.

O'SULLIVANS COACHES
FARRAHY ROAD, KILDORRERY, MALLOW, Co CORK
Tel: 00 353 22 25185
Fax: 00 353 22 25731
Prop: Gerard O'Sullivan.
E-mail: gosull@gofree.indigo.ie
Web site: www.osullivanscoaches.com
Fleet: 14 – 7 single-deck coach, 7 midicoach.
Chassis: 7 Mercedes, 7 Volvo.
Ops incl: school contracts, excursions & tours, private hire, continental tours.

PK TRAVEL CO LTD
SUITE 3, BUILDING 4100, ATLANTIC AVENUE, WEST PARK BUSINESS CAMPUS, SHANNON AIRPORT, Co CLARE
Tel: 00 353 61 365365
E-mail: info@pkexectravel.com
Web site: www.pkexectravel.com
Fleet Name: PK Travel.
Man Dir: P J Keogh **Tran Man:** Mike Lawlor.
Fleet: 12 – 5 single-deck coach, 6 midicoach, 1 minibus.
Ops incl: local bus services, private hire, excursions & tours, express.
Livery: White.

JACKY POWER TOURS
2 LOWER ROCK STREET, TRALEE, Co KERRY
Tel: 00 353 66 713 6300
Fax: 00 353 66 713 6509
E-mail: jackiepowertours@eircom.net
Web site: www.discoverkerry.com/jackiepowertours
Fleet: 2 midicoach.

PROBUS & CAR
KENMARE, Co KERRY
Tel: 00 353 64 664 2500
E-mail: info@probusandcar.com
Web site: www.probusandcar.com
Props: B & S Schmidt.
Fleet: 2 minibus.
Chassis: Mercedes.
Ops incl: private hire.

ROVER COACHES
LYNN ROAD, MULLINGAR, Co WESTMEATH
Tel: 00 353 44 934 2449
Fax: 00 353 44 938 5020
E-mail: info@rovercoaches.ie
Web site: www.rovercoaches.ie
Prop: Patrick O'Brien.
Fleet: 11 - 3 single-deck coach, 8 minibus.
Chassis: Mercedes, Renault, Volvo.
Ops incl: private hire, excursions & tours.
Livery: White.

SEALANDAIR COACHING (IRELAND) LTD
53 MIDDLE ABBEY STREET, DUBLIN 1
Tel: 00 353 1 871 9819
Fax: 00 353 1 873 2639
E-mail: sales@pabtours.com
Web site: www.pabtours.com
Fleet Name: PAB Tours.
Man Dir: Anthony Kelly.
Fleet: 7 single-deck coach.
Chassis: Volvo.
Bodies: Plaxton.

SILLAN TOURS LTD
KINGSCOURT ROAD, SHERCOCK, Co CAVAN
Tel: 00 353 42 966 9130
Fax: 00 353 42 966 9666
E-mail: info@sillan.ie
Web site: www.sillan.ie
Fleet: 4 single-deck coach.
Chassis: VDL.
Bodies: Marcopolo.
Ops incl: Dublin commuter express, private hire.
Livery: White with red relief.

SLIEVE BLOOM COACH TOURS LTD
FOREST VIEW, KILLEEN, MOUNTMELLICK, Co LAOIS
Tel: 00 353 5786 24416
Fax: 00 353 5786 24692
E-mail: slievebloomcoaches@hotmail.com
Web site: www.slievebloomcoaches.ie
Fleet Names: Slieve Bloom Coaches, Townlink Express
Fleet: 16 – 9 single-deck coach, 3 midibus, 1 midicoach, 3 minibus.
Ops incl: local bus services, excursions & tours, private hire.
Livery: White.

ST KEVIN'S BUS SERVICE
See P Doyle Ltd, above.

SUIRWAY BUS & COACH SERVICES LTD
PASSAGE EAST, Co WATERFORD
Tel: 00 353 51 382209
Fax: 00 353 51 382676
E-mail: info@suirway.com
Web site: www.suirway.com
Fleet Name: www.suirway.com
Dir: Brian Lynch.
Fleet: 6 - 2 single-deck bus, 3 single-deck coach, 1 midicoach.
Chassis: 1 Dennis, 1 Mercedes, 4 Volvo.
Bodies: 1 Plaxton, 1 Sunsundegui, 1 Unvi, 1 Van Hool, 1 Volvo, 1 Wright.
Ops incl: local bus services, school contracts, excursions & tours, private hire.
Livery: White & Blue.

SWILLY BUS SERVICE
Ceased trading since LRB 2014 went to press

TRAVEL DIRECT LTD
SEEFIN, CRAUGHWELL, Co GALWAY
Tel: 00 353 91 876876
Fax: 00 353 91 876555
E-mail: info@traveldirectireland.com
Web site: www.traveldirectireland.com
Man Dir: John Gavin.
Fleet: 1 minicoach.
Chassis: Mercedes.
Ops incl: excursions & tours.
Livery: White/Red.

TREACY COACHES
ERRIGAL, KILLALA ROAD, BALLINA, Co MAYO
Tel: 00 353 96 22563
Fax: 00 353 96 70968
E-mail: treacycoaches@eircom.net
Dirs: A Treacy (Gen Man), M Treacy (Sec).
Fleet: 6 – 4 single-deck coach, 2 midicoach.
Ops incl: excursions & tours, private hire, express.
Livery: White/Blue.

WEXFORD BUS
RATHASPECK, WEXFORD
Tel: 00 353 914 2742
E-mail: info@wexfordbus.com
Web site: www.wexfordbus.com
Props: B & L Crowley.
Fleet: 11 – 5 single-deck coach, 3 midibus, 3 midicoach.
Chassis: Alexander Dennis, MAN, Mercedes, Scania.
Ops incl: local bus services, Dublin express, private hire.
Livery: White with Blue/Orange.

WHARTONS TRAVEL LTD
CROSSDONEY, Co CAVAN
Tel: 00 353 49 433 7000
Fax: 00 353 49 433 7634
E-mail: info@whartonstravel.com
Web site: www.whartonstravel.com
Fleet: 5 – 3 single-deck coach, 2 midicoach.
Chassis: 2 Mercedes, 2 Neoplan, 1 Volvo.
Bodies: Neoplan, Plaxton, Unvi, Van Hool.
Ops incl: private hire, excursions & tours, continental tours.
Livery: Red with multi-colours.

NOTES

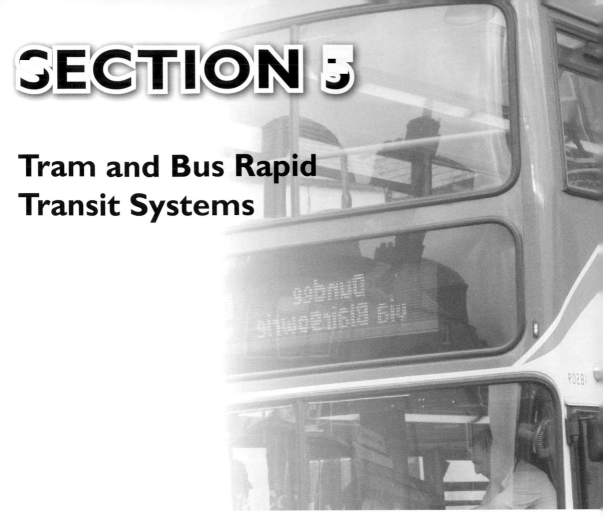

SECTION 5

Tram and Bus Rapid Transit Systems

This section of LRB brings all of the tram systems together in one place, and also provides a brief profile of each of the principal Bus Rapid Transit systems.

TRAM SYSTEMS

BLACKPOOL TRANSPORT SERVICES LTD

RIGBY ROAD, BLACKPOOL FY1 5DD
Tel: 01253 473001
Fax: 01253 473101
E-mail: enquiries@blackpooltransport.com
Web site: www.blackpooltransport.com
Dir of Delivery: Bob Mason **Eng Dir:** Dave Hislop **Fin Dir:** Sue Kennerley **Ops Man:** Guy Thornton.
Fleet: 41 trams.
Chassis/Bodies: Blackpool Transport, Bombardier, Brush, East Lancs, English Electric.
Livery: Green/Cream and special liveries.
Ticket System: Wayfarer/Almex A90.
See also main Blackpool Transport Services entry (Lancashire).

DOUGLAS CORPORATION TRAMWAY

STRATHALLAN CRESCENT, DOUGLAS, ISLE OF MAN IM2 4NR
Tel: 01624 696420
E-mail: pcannon@douglas.gov.im

Web site: www.douglas.gov.im
Transport Ops Supervisor: P Cannon.
Fleet: 21 horse drawn tramcars.
Builders: Metropolitan, Milnes, United Electric.
Ops incl: tram services, private hire.

EDINBURGH TRAMS

EDINBURGH TRAMS CUSTOMER SERVICES, 55 ANNANDALE STREET, EDINBURGH EH7 4AZ
Tel: 0131 475 0177
E-mail: customer@edinburghtrams.com
Web site: www.edinburghtrams.com
Fleet: 27 trams.
Chassis/Bodies: CAF.
Livery: Grey/Madder/White.
The system opened on 31 May 2014.

LONDON TRAMLINK

Part of TfL London Rail
COOMBER WAY, CROYDON CR0 4TQ
Tel: 020 8665 9695
Web site: www.tfl.gov.uk

Man Dir, London Rail: Mike Brown.
Fleet: 30 trams.
Chassis/Bodies: 24 Bombardier, 6 Stadler.
Livery: Lime Green/Blue/White.

LUAS

LUAS DEPOT, RED COW ROUNDABOUT, CLONDALKIN, DUBLIN 22
Tel: 00 353 1 461 4910
Fax: 00 353 1 461 4992
E-mail: info@luas.ie
Web site: www.luas.ie
Man Dir: Richard Dujardin **Gen Man:** Brian Brennan.
Fleet: 66 trams.
Chassis/Bodies: Alstom Citadis.
Operated by Transdev Ireland for the Irish Railway Procurement Agency

MANCHESTER METROLINK

METROLINK RATP DEV UK, TRAFFORD DEPOT, WARWICK ROAD SOUTH, STRETFORD, MANCHESTER M16 0GZ
Tel: 0161 205 2000

Fax: 0161 205 8699
E-mail: customerservices@metrolink.co.uk
Web site: www.metrolink.co.uk
Chairman: Derek Lott **Man Dir:** Chris Coleman.
Depots at: Queens Road, Trafford.
Fleet: 82 trams.
Chassis/Bodies: Bombardier.
Livery: Silver/Yellow.
The East Manchester line opened in October 2013 and the Oldham and Rochdale line in January 2014. Further lines are under construction.
Operated by Metrolink RATP Dev UK Ltd for Transport for Greater Manchester

MIDLAND METRO

METRO CENTRE, POTTERS LANE, WEDNESBURY WS10 0AR
Tel: 0121 502 2006
Fax: 0121 556 6299
Web site: www.nxbus.co.uk/the-metro
General Manager: Dean Watkins.
Fleet: 28 trams.
Chassis/Bodies: 16 Ansaldo, 12 CAF.
Liveries: Silver/Magenta (Network West Midlands) or Blue/Green/Grey/Red/Yellow.
The service is to be extended through Birmingham City Centre. 8 further CAF trams are on order.
Operated by National Express West Midlands for Centro

NOTTINGHAM EXPRESS TRANSIT

NET DEPOT, WILKINSON STREET, NOTTINGHAM NG7 7NW
Tel: 0115 942 7777
E-mail: info@thetram.net
Web site: www.thetram.net
Commercial Manager: Colin Lea.
Fleet: 31 trams.
Chassis/bodies: 16 Alsthom, 15 Bombardier.
Liveries: Green/Black/Silver or advertising liveries.
6 further new Alstom trams are on order for the Phase 2 extensions to the network.
NET is operated by Tramlink Nottingham (Alstom, Keolis UK, Meridiam Infrastructure, OFI InfraVia, Vinci, Wellglade). The promoters are Nottingham City Council and Nottinghamshire County Council.

STAGECOACH SUPERTRAM

NUNNERY DEPOT, WOODBOURN ROAD, SHEFFIELD S9 3LS
Tel: 0114 272 8282   **Fax:** 0114 279 8120
E-mail: enquiries@supertram.com
Web site: www.supertram.com
Man Dir: Margaret Kay **Head of Finance & Commercial:** Tom Bilby **Head of Eng:** Chris Elliott.
Fleet: 25 tramcars.
Chassis/Bodies: Siemens Duewag.
Livery: Blue/Orange/Red.
Operated by Stagecoach for South Yorkshire PTE.

BUS RAPID TRANSIT SYSTEMS

CAMBRIDGESHIRE BUSWAY

Route: Between St Ives and Cambridge, opened 2011.
Promoter: Cambridgeshire County Council, Passenger Transport Services, Shire Hall, Cambridge CB3 0AP.
Tel: 0345 045 0675
E-mail: passenger.transport@cambridgeshire.gov.uk
Web sites: www.cambridgeshire.gov.uk and www.thebusway.info
Operators: Stagecoach East, Whippet Coaches (see Cambridgeshire).

CENTRELINK

Route: Between Gateshead and the Metro Centre Shopping Centre.
Promoter: Nexus (Tyne & Wear PTE).
Web site: www.nexus.org.uk
Operator: Go North East (Go-Ahead Group) (see Tyne & Wear).

EAST LONDON TRANSIT

Route: Between Ilford, Barking and Dagenham Dock, opened 2010.
Promoters: Transport for London, London Boroughs of Barking and Dagenham, Redbridge.
Web site: www.tfl.gov.uk/corporate/projectsandschemes
Operator: Go-Ahead London (see London & Middlesex).
The first bus only section, between Thames View and Dagenham, is now open, used by TfL services EL1, EL2. The second section will link Barking Town Centre with Barking Riverside.

ECLIPSE (SOUTH EAST HAMPSHIRE) BUS RAPID TRANSIT

Route: Between Fareham and Gosport, opened 2012.

Promoter: Hampshire County Council, Environment Department.
Tel: 0845 603 5633
E-mail: eclipse@hants.gov.uk
Web site: www3.hants.gov.uk/eclipse
Operator: First Hampshire, Dorset & Berkshire (see Hampshire).

FASTRACK

Route: Between Dartford and Gravesend, opened 2006.
Promoter: Kent Thameside Regeneration Partnership.
E-mail: info@go-fastrack.co.uk
Web site: www.go-fastrack.co.uk
Operator: Arriva Southern Counties (see Kent).
The system was extended to Ingress Park in 2012. Additional sections of route are planned.

FASTWAY

Route: Between Crawley, Gatwick Airport and Horley, opened 2003.
Promoters: Surrey and West Sussex County Councils; Crawley and Reigate & Banstead Borough Councils; BAA Gatwick; Go-Ahead Group.
Web site: www.fastway.info
Operator: Metrobus (Go-Ahead Group) (see West Sussex).

IPSWICH RAPID TRANSIT

Route: Between Kesgrave and Grange Farm, opened 1995.
Promoter: Suffolk County Council.
Operator: First Eastern Counties (see Suffolk).

LEEDS SUPERBUS

Route: Sections of the A61, A63 and A64 in Leeds, opened 1995.

Promoter: West Yorkshire PTE.
Operator: First West Yorkshire (see West Yorkshire).

LEIGH-SALFORD-MANCHESTER BRT

Route: Leigh to Manchester via Salford.
Promoter: Transport for Greater Manchester.
Web site: www.tfgm.com
The system is currently planned to open in 2015.

LUTON TO DUNSTABLE BUSWAY

Route: Houghton Regis to Luton via Dunstable, opened 2013.
Promoter: Luton Borough Council, Busway Team, Town Hall, George Street, Luton LU1 2BQ
Tel: 0800 028 1755
E-mail: info@travelluton.org.uk
Web site: www.busway.net
Operators: Arriva The Shires, Centrebus, Grant Palmer (see Bedfordshire).

RUNCORN BUSWAY

Route: Through Runcorn New Town (22 km), opened 1977.
Operators: Halton Borough Transport (see Cheshire), Arriva North West & Wales (see Merseyside).

SWANSEA METRO

Route: Sections between Morriston, Swansea City Centre and Singleton Hospital, opened 2009.
Promoter: City & County of Swansea Council.
Web site: www.swansea.gov.uk
Operator: First Cymru (see City & County of Swansea).

SECTION 6

Indices

Several of the traders listed in this index will have more than one entry; only the first is shown here in each case.

Index - Trade

Index - Operator

C

Index - Operator

Index - Operator

Index - Operator

Index - Operator

Index - Operator

Index - Operator